THE JERUSALEM TALMUD
FIRST ORDER: ZERAÏM
TRACTATES *KILAIM* AND *ŠEVIÏT*

STUDIA JUDAICA

FORSCHUNGEN ZUR WISSENSCHAFT
DES JUDENTUMS

HERAUSGEGEBEN VON
E. L. EHRLICH

BAND XX

WALTER DE GRUYTER · BERLIN · NEW YORK
2001

THE JERUSALEM TALMUD

תלמוד ירושלמי

FIRST ORDER: ZERAÏM
סדר זרעים
TRACTATES *KILAIM* AND *ŠEVIÏT*
מסכות כלאים ושביעית

EDITION, TRANSLATION, AND COMMENTARY

BY

HEINRICH W. GUGGENHEIMER

WALTER DE GRUYTER · BERLIN · NEW YORK
2001

ISBN 978-3-11-068131-4
e-ISBN (PDF) 978-3-11-084919-6

This volume is text- and page-identical with the hardback published in 2001.

Library of Congress Control Number: 2020942829

Bibliographic information published by the Deutsche Nationalbibliothek
The Deutsche Nationalbibliothek lists this publication in the
Deutsche Nationalbibliografie;
detailed bibliographic data are available on the Internet at http://dnb.dnb.de.

Printing and Binding: LSC Communications, United States

www.degruyter.com

Preface

The present volume is the third in a projected series of five volumes covering the entire first order of the Jerusalem Talmud. The principles of the edition regarding text, vocalization and commentary have been spelled out in detail in the Introduction to the first volume. The text is based on the *editio princeps* and, where that text is manifestly corrupt, on manuscript readings. There are no emendations. For ease of study, the text in the present edition has been subdivided into paragraphs and vocalized following the rules of Sephardic rabbinic Hebrew. In contrast to the Babylonian Talmud whose language is Aramaic with Hebrew quotes, the Jerusalem Talmud is composed in Aramaized Hebrew with Aramaic inserts.

The extensive commentary is not based on emendations. Biographical notes have been attached to the names of those personalities not already mentioned in the previous volumes.

Again I wish to thank my wife, Dr. Eva Guggenheimer, who acted as critic, style editor, proof reader, and expert on the Latin and Greek vocabulary. Her own notes on some possible Latin and Greek etymologies are identified by (E. G.).

Contents

Introduction to Tractate Kilaim

The Tractate deals with the rules implied by three Biblical verses. (*Lev.* 19:19) "You should not breed your animals *kilaim*; you should not sow your field *kilaim*; and *kilaim* cloth, שעטנז, should not be worn by you." (*Deut.* 22:9-10) "Do not sow *kilaim* in your vineyard, lest the fullness of the seed you are sowing become sanctified, the yield of your vineyard. Do not plough with an ox and a donkey together."

The word כלאים has no cognate in Hebrew but occurs in other Semitic languages. In Arabic, كلاء ,كلان (כִּלָא, פְּלָאן) means "two; two kinds". The same holds for Amharic ከለአ (כִּלָא). It is one of the restrictions put on fields in the Holy Land that different crops may not be planted on one field without recognizable separation. This includes the prohibition to graft unrelated trees on one another. In addition, produce that grows in a vineyard is "sanctified"; *any* use of it is forbidden. This Biblical use of "sanctified" parallels Rabbinic Hebrew "sacrifice" (קָרְבָּן, κορβᾶν) for an object that may not be used at all (Mishnah *Nedarim* 1:2, *Matthew* 15:5); cf. *Demay* Chapter 5, Note 141.

The other two rules do not depend on the Land and have to be obeyed worldwide. They are the prohibition of actively breeding two different animal species together and to wear *ša'aṭnez* cloth. The unexplained word שעטנז is defined in *Deut.* 22:11: "Do not wear שעטנז, wool and linen together." Other mixtures of textiles are permitted.

The first three chapters deal with *kilaim* relating to all plants except vines. Chapter One defines related and unrelated varieties; Chapter Two classifies fields by size and shape and their rules; Chapter Three deals similarly with garden plots. Chapters Four to Seven contain the stricter rules for vineyards. Since good viticultural practice demands that vineyards be kept clean of weeds and other growths, many of these rules seem to be purely theoretical. Chapter Eight gives the rules for permitted and forbidden cross breeding of animals and the final Chapter Nine deals with *ša'aṭnez*. Since shrouds for burials are permitted to contain *kilaim*, the chapter contains a long digression on death and burial, important for Jewish burial customs.

A number of Halakhot in the early chapters are more interesting for their mathematics, mainly combinatorial geometry, than their practical value.

The determination of plant names uses Gaonic sources, Maimonides and the *Arukh* whenever possible. Modern attempts to identify the plants are in E. Ben Yehudah's *Thesaurus* and in the books by I. Felix (בלאים, Dvir: Tel Aviv, 1967, and *The Plant World of the Bible*, Massadah: Jerusalem, 1953).

For the interpretation, the main guides are Maimonides and R. Simson of Sens. Of the Eighteenth Century commentators, the most useful is R. Eliahu Fulda; the least useful are R. Moses Margalit (פני משה), R. Eliahu Wilna and R. H. Kanievski who tend to emend away the difficult portions. Similarly, the preliminary translation and explanation by Irving J. Mandelbaum (Chicago 1991) heavily depends on emendations and readings by R. S. Cirillo. The manuscript evidence, while meager, definitely excludes most emendations. Of modern commentaries, those by R. Saul Lieberman (*Tosefta ki-fshuṭah*, New York, 1955) and R. Y.

Qafeḥ's commented edition of Maimonides's Commentary are most useful.
Other sources are quoted by name where used.

A useful survey of the controversies surrounding the practical
applications of the rules of *kilaim*, based mostly on the short treatment of
the subject in the Babli, is in: הרב שאול ישראלי, ספר ארץ חמדה בהלכות
ארץ־ישראל[4], Jerusalem, 1998.

מַשְׁנָה א: (fol. 26d) הַחִטִּים וְהַזּוּנִין אֵינָן כִּלְאַיִם זֶה בָּזֶה. הַשְּׂעוֹרִים וְשִׁבּוֹלֶת שׁוּעָל הַכּוּסְמִין וְהַשִּׁיפוֹן הַפּוֹל וְהַסְּפִיר וְהַפּוּרְקְדָן וְהַטּוֹפֵחַ וּפוֹל הַלָּבָן וְהַשְּׁעוּעִית אֵינָן כִּלְאַיִם זֶה בָּזֶה.

Mishnah 1: Wheat and *zĕwānin*[1] are not *kilaim* one with the other. Barley and fox tail[2], spelt and oats[3], beans[4] and Indian peas[5] and grass peas[6] and chick peas[7] and fava beans and green beans[8] are not *kilaim* one with the other[9].

1 Arabic זَוַאן, זَוَאן, זَוַאן defined in the dictionaries as "*Lolium temulentum L.*, tare, darnel grass." E. and H. Hareubeni, in a memoir dedicated to זונין (*Tarbiz* 10, 1939, 172-189), indicate that the same name is also used in many places for *Cephalaria Syriaca L.*; the common denominator of the two very different plants is that they are weeds and their seeds spoil the flour if they are ground with it. The grains produced by *Lolium* are light gray; if infected by a fungus they become dark and poisonous. *Lolium* belongs to the same family as most grains. It is used as fodder for chickens. *Cephalaria* is a grass from the family of dipsaceas. Its grains are almost black, about the size of a wheat kernel, and are poisonous to humans but eagerly eaten by pigeons. One has to wonder whether the word could also designate grain blight, whose poison is generated by a fungus just as that of *Lolium*.

Maimonides defines זונין as a kind of inedible wheat; this could indicate blight. *Arukh* explains by Italian *niella*, "black kernels." This translation would fit both *Cephalaria* and grain blight. The Hareubenis report that in the Arabic of Galilee and Syria, the same word שִׁילָם denotes *Lolium*, *Cephalaria*, and blight.

2 Maimonides defines this as

"prairie barley," R. Asher and R. Obadia from Bertinoro as (Spanish and Italian) *avena* "oats."

3   R. Asher defines as French *seigle*, "rye," following Rashi and Rabbenu Gershom to Babli *Pesaḥim* 35a.   Maimonides: "prairie wheat." Arukh: *espelda* (modern Italian *spelta*) "spelt." The Babli *Menaḥot* 70b defines שיפון by Aramaic דישרא which can be compared either to Syriac/Arabic دوسر "*aegilops*, barley darnel" (which would parallel זונין for wheat) or to Accadic *dišarru* "a kind of grain, oats, or rye."

4   In Hebrew and Arabic used only for beans not eaten with their pods,

mostly *vicia faba*.

5   Maimonides: Arabic מאש *Phaseolus maximus L.* (in the opinion of H. L. Fleischer, *Phaseolus mungo*), Arukh: *cicercula*, chick-pea.

6   Maimonides: Arabic גלבָּאן *Lathyrus sativus* or *Lathyrus cicera*, Arukh: Italian *piso* "pea."

7   Maimonides: A kind of peas that are spherical and hard, resembling oat grains.   Arukh: Arabic גלבָּאן *Lathyrus sativus*.

8   Eaten for their pods. Maimonides: Arabic לוּבִיָא "beans."

9   This refers separately to each group of two plants connected by "and".

הלכה א: כְּתִיב שָׂדְךָ לֹא תִזְרַע כִּלְאָיִם. הָיִּיתִי אוֹמֵר אֲפִילוּ שְׁנֵי מִינֵי חִטִּים וַאֲפִילוּ שְׁנֵי מִינֵי שְׂעוֹרִים. בְּהֶמְתְּךָ לֹא תַרְבִּיעַ כִּלְאָיִם. הָיִּיתִי אוֹמֵר אֲפִילוּ שׁוֹר שָׁחוֹר עַל גַּבֵּי שׁוֹר לָבָן אוֹ שׁוֹר לָבָן עַל גַּבֵּי שָׁחוֹר. וּבֶגֶד כִּלְאַיִם שַׁעַטְנֵז לֹא יַעֲלֶה עָלֶיךָ. הָיִּיתִי אוֹמֵר שְׁנֵי מִינֵי צֶמֶר וַאֲפִילוּ שְׁנֵי מִינֵי פִּשְׁתִּים. פֵּירַשׁ בִּבְגָדִים לֹא תִלְבַּשׁ שַׁעַטְנֵז צֶמֶר וּפִשְׁתִּים יַחְדָּיו. מַה כִּלְאֵי בְגָדִים שֶׁאָסַרְתִּי לָךְ שְׁנֵי מִינִין לֹא זֶה מִמִּין זֶה וְלֹא זֶה מִמִּין זֶה. אַף כִּלְאַיִם שֶׁאָסַרְתִּי לָךְ בְּכָל־מָקוֹם10 לֹא זֶה מִמִּין זֶה וְלֹא זֶה מִמִּין זֶה.

Halakhah 1: It is written: (*Lev.* 19:19) "you should not sow your field *kilaim*;" I could think, even two kinds of wheat or two kinds of barley. "You should not breed your animals *kilaim*;" I could think, even black on white cattle, or white on black cattle. "And *kilaim* cloth, שעטנז, should not be worn by you;" I could think, even two kinds of wool or two kinds of linen. It was made explicit about garments, (*Deut.* 22:11) "do not wear

שעטנז, wool and linen together." Just as for garments where I forbade you two kinds, neither one is of the genus of the other, so *kilaim* that I forbade you at any place, neither one is of the genus of the other.

10   The Rome ms. has בכל מקום שני   previous sentence. This probably is the
מינין for a full parallel with the   better text.

הַחִטִּים וְהַזּוּנִין אֵינָן כִּלְאַיִם זֶה בְּזֶה. הָא עִם הַשְּׂעוֹרִים כִּלְאַיִם. וְהַחִטִּים וְהַזּוּנִין אֵינָן כִּלְאַיִם זֶה בְּזֶה דָּבָר שֶׁאֵינוֹ אוֹכֶל חַיִּינָן מַטְעֵי וּמַתְנֵי כִּלְאַיִם. אָמַר רְבִּי בָּא בַּר זַבְדָּא שֶׁכֵּן מְקוֹמוֹת מְקַיְּימִין אוֹתָן לְיוֹנִים. אָמַר רְבִּי בָּא בַּר זַבְדָּא כְּרְבִּי לִיעֶזֶר דְּתַנִּינָן תַּמָּן הַמְקַיֵּים קוֹצִים בַּכֶּרֶם רְבִּי לִיעֶזֶר אוֹמֵר קִידֵּשׁ. וַחֲכָמִים אוֹמְרִים לֹא קִידֵּשׁ. אָמַר רְבִּי אַבָּהוּ טַעֲמָא דְּרְבִּי לִיעֶזֶר שֶׁכֵּן מְקוֹמוֹת מְקַיְּימִין אוֹתָן לִגְמַלִּים בַּעֲרַבְיָא. מַה דְּרַבָּנִין סָבְרִין מֵימַר אֵין מְקוֹמוֹת מְקַיְּימִין אוֹתָן לִגְמַלִּים בַּעֲרַבְיָא וְיִבְדְּקוּ. רַבָּנִין אָמְרִין מָקוֹם שֶׁמְּקַיְּימִין אוֹתָן אֲסוּרִין. וּמָקוֹם שֶׁאֵין מְקַיְּימִין אוֹתָן מוּתָּרִין. מַה טַעֲמָא דְּרְבִּי לִיעֶזֶר מִכֵּיוָן שֶׁמְּקַיְּימִין אוֹתָן בְּמָקוֹם אֶחָד נֶאֱסוֹר מִינָן בְּכָל־מָקוֹם שֶׁהוּא. וְלֹא רְבִּי בָּא בַּר זַבְדָּא כְּרְבִּי לִיעֶזֶר. תַּמָּן אֵין דֶּרֶךְ בְּנֵי אָדָם לְהָבִיא קַרְנַיִם מִמָּקוֹם לְמָקוֹם. בְּרַם הָכָא דֶּרֶךְ בְּנֵי אָדָם לְהָבִיא זוּנִין מִמָּקוֹם לְמָקוֹם.

"Wheat and *zĕwānîn* are not *kilaim* one with the other." Hence, with barley they would constitute *kilaim*[11]. "Wheat and *zĕwānîn* are not *kilaim* one with the other;" could anybody err about something that is not food and state it as *kilaim*[12]? Rebbi Abba bar Zavda said, because there are places where they are collected as food for pigeons[13]. Rebbi Abba bar Zavda said, this follows Rebbi Eliezer, as we have stated there[14]: "If somebody lets thorns grow in his vineyard, they become 'sanctified', the words of Rebbi Eliezer. But the Sages say, they do not become 'sanctified'." Rabbi Abbahu said, the reason of Rebbi Eliezer is that at some places in Arabia one stores them for camels[15]. Does this imply that the Sages think that there are no places in Arabia where one stores them for the camels? Let them check it out! The Sages say, where one stores them they are forbidden, but at places where one does not store them they are permitted. But Rebbi Abba bar Zavda cannot follow Rebbi Eliezer[16]! There, people do not transport horns[17] from place to place. But here, people do transport *zewānin* from place to place[18].

11 The Hareubenis note that neither *Cephalaria* nor *Lolium* grow in barley fields since the larger leaves of the barley obstruct the sunlight they need for growth. Hence, the question is theoretical.

12 Since one may not sow one's field *kilaim*, the prohibition refers only to crops that are raised by the farmer and excludes weeds.

13 This applies only to *Cephalaria*, not to *Lolium*. It might apply to blighted wheat.

14 Mishnah 5:8. That text reads: "But the Sages say, nothing becomes forbidden unless it is allowed to grow."

15 There, thorns may represent a cash crop. (One might wonder why Arabia, not a place where *kilaim* are forbidden, should be of interest here.

But since practice does not follow R. Eliezer, a discussion is not necessary.) The statement is quoted in Babli *Šabbat* 134b, in the name of R. Ḥanina.

16 Since practice does not follow Rebbi Eliezer in his disputes with the Sages, and our Mishnah is anonymous, the Mishnah cannot be explained as being R. Eliezer's.

17 R. Simson reads קוֹצִים "thorns;" this is appropriate here. The two manuscripts of the Yerushalmi read קרנים "horns," which is difficult but not impossible since most points of thorns are horn-shaped.

18 At places in the Holy Land, *zĕwānin* are an object of trade and, hence, a cash crop subject to the rules of *kilaim*. This was still found true by the Hareubenis in the early 1930's.

מֵעַתָּה יְהוּ כִלְאַיִם עִם הַחִטִּים. אָמַר רִבִּי יוֹנָה מִין חִטִּין הֵן אֶלָּא שֶׁהַפֵּירוֹת מְזַנִּין. כְּהָדָא דְתַנֵּי וְלֹא תִזְנֶה הָאָרֶץ מִיכָּן שֶׁהַפֵּירוֹת מְזַנִּין.

If so[19], should they not be *kilaim* with wheat? Rebbi Jonah said, they are a kind of wheat but the fruits went astray[20]. As it was stated: (*Lev.* 19:29) "The Land should not go whoring," from here that produce may go astray.

19　If *zĕwānîn* can be a cash crop, they should be *kilaim* with anything that is not their own kind.

20　This certainly fits blight, but *Lolium* also belongs to the same family (*gramineae*) as wheat and rye.

רבִּי יַעֲקֹב בַּר זַבְדִּי בָּעָא קוֹמֵי רבִּי יִרְמְיָה מַתְנִיתִין דְּרִבִּי יִשְׁמָעֵאל בֵּי רבִּי יוֹסֵי. דְּתַנֵּי רבִּי יִשְׁמָעֵאל בֵּי רבִּי יוֹסֵי אוֹמֵר מִשׁוּם אָבִיו תּוֹרְמִין מִן הַיַּיִן עַל הַחוֹמֶץ אֲבָל לֹא מִן הַחוֹמֶץ עַל הַיַּיִן. עָבַר וְתָרַם תְּרוּמָתוֹ תְּרוּמָה. רבִּי אוֹמֵר הַיַּיִן וְהַחוֹמֶץ שְׁנֵי מִינִין הֵן אֵין תּוֹרְמִין וְלֹא מְעַשְּׂרִין מִזֶּה עַל זֶה. וַהֲוָה מִסְתַּכֵּל בֵּיהּ. אָמַר לֵיהּ מַה אַתְּ מִסְתַּכֵּל בִּי. הֲבָא לָךְ רְצוּעָה בְּכָאן. תַּמָּן לְמַעְשְׂרוֹת וְכָאן לְכִלְאַיִם. אָמַר רבִּי יוֹנָה הָא כֵן הֲוָה צָרִיךְ מִסְתַּכֵּל בֵּיהּ כַּד הֲווֹן רַבָּנִין קַדְמָאֵיי בְּעַיִן מְקַיְּימָא הָדָא מִילְתָא הֲווֹן מְקַיְּימִין לָהּ תַּמָּן לְמַעְשְׂרוֹת וְכָאן לְכִלְאַיִם.

Rebbi Jacob bar Zavdi asked before Rebbi Jeremiah: Is our Mishnah from Rebbi Ismael ben Rebbi Yose? As it was stated[21]: "Rebbi Ismael ben Rebbi Yose says in the name of his father that one may take heave from wine on vinegar but not from vinegar on wine. If somebody transgressed, his heave is heave. Rebbi says that wine and vinegar are two distinct kinds and one does not give heave nor does one tithe from one on the other." He[22] was looking at him. He said to him, what are you staring at me? Bring a lash for yourself[23]; there it is for tithing[24], here it is for *kilaim*[25]. Rebbi Jonah said, he should not have stared at him since the earlier rabbis wanted to understand this matter and understood that there it refers to tithing but here to *kilaim*.

21   In Tosephta *Terumot* 4:6,7, this appears in a different formulation: "Rebbi Ismael ben Rebbi Yose says in the name of his father that one may take heave from wine on vinegar but not from vinegar on wine. Even if one gives heave, one gives only in proportion. (That means, one gives enough vinegar that it would equal in value the wine which should have been given.) If somebody gives an amphora of wine as heave and it turns out to be vinegar, when it was known that it was vinegar before he gave the heave, it is not heave. But if it turned into vinegar after it was given, it is heave. In case of doubt it is heave and he should give

heave a second time, the words of Rebbi, who says that wine and vinegar are two distinct kinds, but the Sages say, it is one kind."

22   Rebbi Jeremiah looked at R. Jacob to indicate that he found the question stupid and a waste of time.

23   That you can be whipped for asking such a stupid question.

24   An obligation on the finished product.

25   An obligation on the fruit growing on the field. It was implied in the first paragraph that wine grapes and grapes used for producing vinegar should not be treated as two separate kinds.

רִבִּי יוֹסָה בְּשֵׁם רִבִּי יוֹחָנָן כּוּלְהוֹן זוּגוֹת זוּגוֹת. מַה עַל כָּל־פִּירְקָא אִתְאַמֲרַת אוֹ עַל הָדָא הִילְכְתָא. מִן מַה (fol. 27a) דְּאָמַר רַב חֲמִשָּׁה יְרָקוֹת שֶׁאָדָם יוֹצֵא בּוֹ יְדֵי חוֹבָתוֹ בַּפֶּסַח כּוּלָם מוּתָּרִין לִיזָּרַע בַּעֲרוּגָה. וְאָמַר הָדָא דְּרַב פְּלִיגָא עַל רִבִּי יוֹחָנָן. הָדָא אֲמְרָה עַל כָּל־פִּירְקָא אִתְאַמְּרָא. רָבָא בְּשֵׁם רַב כּוּלְהוֹן זוּגוֹת זוּגוֹת. מִחְלְפָה שִׁיטָתֵיהּ דְּרַב תַּמָּן הוּא אָמַר כּוּלָן מִין אֶחָד. וְהָכָא הוּא אָמַר הָכֵין. לֹא דְּרַב אָמַר כּוּלָן מִין אֶחָד לֹא אָמַר אֶלָּא מִינֵי יְרָקוֹת הֵן וְכוּלָּן מוּתָּרִין לִיזָּרַע בַּעֲרוּגָה.

Rebbi Yosa in the name of Rebbi Joḥanan: All of these form pairs. Has that been said for the entire Chapter, or only for this Halakhah? From what Rav said, that the five vegetables with which one may satisfy one's obligation at Passover time can all be sown in one vegetable bed[26], and one says that the statement of Rav disagrees with Rebbi Joḥanan[27], it follows that it has been said for the entire Chapter. Rav Abba in the name of Rav: All[28] have been stated in pairs. The reasoning of Rav is inverted; there he says that they all constitute one kind, and here, he says so? No, Rav did not say that they all constitute one kind, but rather that they all are kinds of vegetables that may be sown in one vegetable bed[29].

26   The five vegetables which may be used for bitter herbs on Passover are enumerated in Mishnah *Pesaḥim* 2:5; cf. the author's *The Scholar's Haggadah*, pp. 332-333. The parallel discussion to the one given here is in Babli *Pesaḥim* 39a, also in the name of Rav. The statement of Rav was understood to mean that the five kinds may be sown *together*.

27   Since some of the bitter herbs are mentioned in Mishnah 2, dividing them into groups seems to contradict the opinion of Rav.

28   Referring to the Chapter here, identical with the previous statement of R. Joḥanan that only pairs of plants

enumerated with a connecting ו may be planted together.

29   In Mishnah 3:1 it will be stated that in planting vegetable beds one may not mix vegetables but one may plant different kinds so that they almost touch at corners, whereas grain and legume fields need much greater distances between different crops. All Rav wanted to state was that they can be sown under the lenient rules for vegetable beds, for intensive cultivation, in contrast to produce that can only be sown in fields, for extensive cultivation. Rav did not mean to say that they all were one kind.

רְבִּי יוֹסֵי בְּשֵׁם רְבִּי חִייָא בַּר וָוא אַשְׁכְּחוֹן כְּתִיב עַל פִּינְקָסֵיהּ דְּרְבִּי הֶלֵל בֵּי רְבִּי אָלֵס רְבִּי יוֹנָה בְּשֵׁם רְבִּי חִייָא בַּר וָוא אַשְׁכְּחוֹן כְּתִיב עַל כּוֹתְלָא דְּרְבִּי הֶלֵל בֵּי רְבִּי אָלֵס. פּוּלָא פּוּשׁוֹנָה גִּילְבּוֹנָה מִילוּתא כרפוונה פְּתִילָתָא.

Rebbi Yose in the name of Rebbi Ḥiyya bar Abba, they found written in the notebook of Rebbi Hillel ben Rebbi Vales[30]; Rebbi Jonah in the name of Rebbi Ḥiyya bar Abba, they found written on the wall of Rebbi

Hillel ben Rebbi Vales: Beans, πίσον[31], chick peas[32], *mlwt'*[33], *krpwnh*[34], climbing beans[35].

30   A companion of Rebbi Jehudah Nesia, the grandson of Rebbi, reputed to have been very rich.

31   Reading of R. Simson: פייסונא, of Rome ms. פרשונה . These are all explanations in the vernacular of the different kinds of beans and peas mentioned in the Mishnah. Here, the Greek for "peas" is the explanation of ספיר.

32   The Aramaic word is identical with the Arabic גלובאן mentioned in Note 6. Readings of R. Simson: גולבינא, of Rome ms.: גיבלונה

33   An unexplained word for the Mishnah word טופח . R. Simson reads as

our text, Rome ms. מלוחא (which in Syriac would be a plural, "pitchers.") The attempt by Jastrow to explain the word as describing peas grown by hydroponics is impossible, since acquatic plants are not subject to the laws of *kilaim*. Arukh reads מיליתא I. Löw proves that all proposed identifications are impossible (*Flora der Juden* 2, p. 437.)

34   Another unexplained word. R. Simson reads מרשיא, the Rome ms. שרפוה.

35   R. Simson reads פסילתא, Greek φάσηλος, Latin *phaselus* "bean".

כִּינִי מַתְנִיתָא הַלָּבָן וְהַשְּׁעוּעִית. אָמַר רִבִּי יוֹנָה לָמָּה נִקְרָא שְׁמָהּ שְׁעוּעִית שֶׁהִיא מְשַׁעֲשָׁעַת אֶת הַלֵּב וּמְהַלֶּכֶת אֶת בְּנֵי מֵעַיִם.

So is the Mishnah: Fava beans and string beans[36]. Rebbi Jonah said, why is it called שעועית? Because if makes the heart happy and the intestines going.

36   These are two different kinds and not one long name. In the Rome ms., פול והשעונית .

מִשְׁנָה ב: הַקִּישׁוּת וְהַמְּלָפְפוֹן אֵינָן כִּלְאַיִם זֶה בָזֶה. רַבִּי יְהוּדָה אוֹמֵר (fol. 26d)
כִּלְאַיִם. חֲזֶרֶת וַחֲזֶרֶת גַּלִּין³⁷. עוּלְשִׁין וְעוּלְשֵׁי שָׂדֶה. כְּרֵישִׁין וְכָרֵישֵׁי שָׂדֶה.
כּוּסְבָּר וְכוּסְבַּר שָׂדֶה. חַרְדָּל וְהַרְדָּל מִצְרִי. וּדְלַעַת מִצְרִית וְהָרוּמְצָא. וּפוֹל
הַמִּצְרִי וְחָרוּב אֵינָן כִּלְאַיִם זֶה בָזֶה.

Mishnah 2: Green melon[38] and sweet melon[39] are not *kilaim* one with the other. Rebbi Jehudah says, they are *kilaim*. Lettuce and garden lettuce[40], endives and field endives[41], leeks[42] and field leeks, coriander and field coriander, mustard and Egyptian mustard[43], Egyptian pumpkin and ash-gourd[44], Egyptian beans[45] and carob beans are not *kilaim* one with the other.

37   Vocalization by מלאכת שלמה from ms. In one manuscript of the text, and in the ms. of a Gaonic commentary, גנים

38   The word is etymologically equivalent with Arabic قِثّا qittā "cucumber, *cucumis sativus L.*" This is Maimonides's definition, in Yemenite mss., for all three occurrences of the word in Mishnah *Zeraïm*. However, in Mishnah *Uqezin* 2:1 and apparently in the *Zera'im* ms. before Alharizi, he defines it as Arabic فُقّوس *fuqūs*, in classical Arabic "green melon" (possibly water melon?). In modern Hebrew, קישות means "zucchini."

39   In the Halakhah, the word is explained as Greek μηλοπέπων "apple melon," composite of μῆλον "apple," πέπων "sun ripened." Pliny [*Hist. nat.*

XIX (23)] defines *melopepon* as "golden melon, *cucumis melo L.*" The Yerushalmi *Targum* to *Num.* 11:5 translates Hebrew אבטיח as מלפפון (in contrast to modern Hebrew where אבטיח means "water melon.") Maimonides translates מלפפון as Arabic כיאר خِيَار *kiyār* "cucumber." This is the meaning of the word in Modern Hebrew, vocalized מְלָפְפוֹן.

40   The wild form of Romaine lettuce and its cultivated variety. [In Modern Hebrew, following Ashkenazic Medieval usage, the word is used for horseradish.]

41   Here, the cultivated form is mentioned first and the wild one second; one might conclude that in the days of the Mishnah, wild Romaine lettuce was still collected for sale but

endives were mostly produced in the vegetable garden.

42　　Also ברחי, Arabic كُرّاث‎ *kurrāṭ*.

43　　The difference between these two plants can no longer be determined.

44　　Maimonides defines Egyptian gourd as دلاع *dalā'*, which in Moroccan means "watermelon". He defines ash-gourd as a naturally bitter pumpkin which becomes edible only when roasted for some time in hot ashes (רמץ). In the Babli, *Nedarim* 51a, Samuel defines the fruit as "Caucasian gourd."

45　　Arabic also فول *fūl* "large flat greenish beans," the main ingredient of *falafel*. חרוב means "carob, carob tree," but here it means elongated black beans that imitate the looks and shape of carob.

(fol. 27a) **הלכה ב**: אָמַר רִבִּי יוּדָן בַּר מְנַשֶּׁה דִּבְרֵי חֲכָמִים אָדָם נוֹטֵל מָעָה אַחַת מִפִּיטְמָהּ שֶׁל קִישׁוּת וְנוֹטְעָהּ וְהִיא נַעֲשֵׂית אֲבַטִּיחַ. אָדָם נוֹטֵל מָעָה אַחַת מִפִּיטְמָהּ שֶׁל אֲבַטִּיחַ וְנוֹטְעָהּ וְהִיא נַעֲשֵׂית מֶלָפְפוֹן. רִבִּי יוּדָה אוֹמֵר עִיקְרוֹ כִּלְאַיִם. אָדָם נוֹטֵל מָעָה אַחַת מִפִּיטְמָהּ שֶׁל אֲבַטִּיחַ וּמָעָה אַחַת מִפִּיטְמָהּ שֶׁל תַּפּוּחַ וְנוֹתְנָן בְּתוֹךְ גּוּמָא אַחַת וְהֵן נִתְאַחוֹן וְנַעֲשִׂין כִּלְאַיִם. לְפוּם כָּךְ צְוָוחִין לֵיהּ בְּלִישְׁנָא יְוָנָא מֵילָפְפוֹן.

Halakhah 2: Rebbi Yudan bar Menasheh[46] said: The opinion of the Sages is that one takes a small piece from the pericarp[47] of a green melon and plants it and it grows to a water melon. One takes a small piece from the pericarp of a water melon and plants it and it grows to a sweet melon. Rebbi Jehudah says, it in itself is *kilaim*. One takes a small piece from the pericarp of a water melon and a small piece from the pericarp of an apple and puts them into one cavity where they unite and become *kilaim*. Therefore it is called "apple melon" in the Greek language.

46　　A third generation Galilean Amora; his surviving statements are all aggadic.

47　　Some fertilized seeds with the carpic tissue surrounding it.

הַקִּישׁוּת וְהָאֲבַטִּיחַ מַה אָמַר בָּהּ רִבִּי יוּדָה. נִשְׁמְעִינָהּ מִן הָדָא הַקִּישׁוּאִין
וְהָאֲבַטִּיחִין וְהַמֶּלָפְפוֹנוֹת אֵינָן כִּלְאַיִם זֶה בָּזֶה רִבִּי יְהוּדָא אוֹמֵר כִּלְאַיִם. נֶאֱמַר
הַקִּישׁוּאִין וְהַמֶּלָפְפוֹן אֵינָן כִּלְאַיִם זֶה בָּזֶה. הָאֲבַטִּיחַ וְהַמֶּלָפְפוֹן אֵינָן כִּלְאַיִם זֶה
בָּזֶה רִבִּי יוּדָה אוֹמֵר כִּלְאַיִם. הַקִּישׁוּת וְהָאֲבַטִּיחַ צְרִיכָא.

What does Rebbi Jehudah say about green melon and water melon?
Let us hear from the following[48]: "Green melon, water melon, and sweet
melon are not *kilaim* [if combined] one with the other; Rebbi Jehudah
says, they are *kilaim*." It has been said that green melon and water melon
are not *kilaim* one with the other, and water melon and sweet melon are
not *kilaim* one with the other; Rebbi Jehudah says they are *kilaim*. Green
melon and water melon are questionable[49].

48   Tosephta *Kilaim* 1:1: "Green
melon and squash, water melon and
melopepon, are not *kilaim* one with the
other, and one may tithe from one on
the other; these are the words of R.
Meïr. R. Jehudah and R. Simeon say,
they are *kilaim* one with the other, and
one may not tithe from one on the
other."

49   Since in the entire chapter we
are dealing with comparisons of pairs,
it is assumed that the teacher of the
baraita only compares pairs. Hence, it
is questionable whether the *baraita*
teaches anything new. We know from

the Mishnah about the comparison of
green melon and sweet melon, also
from the Tosephta about water melon
and sweet melon (cf. Notes 39, 48).
Since Rebbi Jehudah is only quoted as
reacting to the statements of the first
teacher, nothing can be inferred about
his opinion if the reference to sweet
melon is omitted. In any case, the
argument teaches that the absence of
kilaim is not a transitive notion: If A is
not *kilaim* with B, and B not with C, it
does not follow that A is not *kilaim*
with C.

חֲזֶרֶת וַחֲזֶרֶת גַּלִּים רִבִּי חֲנַנְיָה אָמַר חַסָּא דִיגְרִין⁵⁰. שִׁמְעוֹן בְּרֵיהּ דְּרִבִּי אָבִי
אָמַר אַנְטוֹכִין. רִבִּי יוֹסֵי בֵּי רִבִּי בּוּן אָמַר יַסֵּי חַלְיִי⁵¹. עוּלְשִׁין טְרוֹקְסִימוֹן.
עוּלְשֵׁי הַשָּׂדֶה עוּלְתִין. כְּרֵיתִין. כָּרָתֵי שָׂדֶה קֶפַלוֹטוֹן.

"Lettuce and garden lettuce." Rebbi Ḥananiah said, roof lettuce.
Simeon, the son of Rebbi Avi, said, Antiochian (lettuce⁵².) Rebbi Yose ben
Rebbi Abun said, sweet *yase*⁵³. Endives may be eaten raw⁵⁴, field endives
are '*ulthin*⁵⁵. Leeks. Fields leeks are κεφαλωτόν⁵⁶.

50   Reading of R. Simson. In the
Rome ms. conflated חסדיגרון, in the
Leyden ms. הסדיגרון.

51   Reading of the Rome ms.
Leyden: יסיח לי, but in *Pesaḥim* 2:5, fol.
29c, the reading is also יסי חלי as
explanation of חרחבינה, one of the bitter
herbs used for the Passover *seder*.

52   Musaphia, in his additions to
Arukh, reads אינטובין ἔντυβον
"endives."

53   An unidentified plant. Kohut's

identification as *jacea* is unconvincing.
The identifications in *Kilaim* and
Pesaḥim 5:2 refer to different plants.

54   Τρώξιμα, τά "what is eaten raw,
vegetable", from τρώγω "to nibble, eat
raw"; in Jewish sources only used for
endives.

55   Arabic غَلَثَ עללה "bitter
vegetable".

56   Meaning "with big head" (*allium
capitatum*), found also in Syriac and
Arabic.

דְּלַעַת מִצְרִית. מַתְנִיתִין דְּלָא⁵⁷ כְּרִבִּי נְחֶמְיָה. ⁵⁸בְּשֵׁם רִבִּי נְחֶמְיָה דְּלַעַת אֲרָמִית
הִיא דְּלַעַת מִצְרִית כִּלְאַיִם עִם הַיְּוָנִית כִּלְאַיִם עִם הָרַמּוּצָה.

"Egyptian gourd.⁵⁹" Our Mishnah does not follow Rebbi Neḥemiah. In
the name of Rebbi Neḥemiah⁶⁰: Aramean gourd is Egyptian gourd; it is
kilaim with Greek gourd, *kilaim* with ash-gourd.

57   Reading of Rome ms. Leyden:
אלא

58   Reading of R. Simson: תני תנא רבי

נחמיה .

59   This and the following items are
quoted from the Mishnah.

60   In Tosephta 1:5: "Rebbi Neḥemiah said, Aramean and Egyptian gourds are *kilaim* with ash-gourd." In that Tosephta, the identification of Aramean with Egyptian gourds is missing. The Yerushalmi text is quoted in Babli *Nedarim* 51a. See also below, Mishnah 5.

וְהָרמוּצָה. אָמַר רבּי חִינְנָה כְּמִין דְּלַעַת מָרָה הִיא וְהֶם מְמַתְּקִין אוֹתָהּ בְּרֶמֶץ.

"Ash gourd." Rebbi Ḥinenah said, it is a kind of bitter gourd and they sweeten it in hot ashes.

וְהָחָרוּב. אָמַר רבּי יוֹנָה כְּמִין פוּל מִצְרִי פַּרְסִי הוּא וקִצְצוֹי דּוֹמִין לָחָרוּבָה.

"And carob beans." Rebbi Jonah said, they are a kind of Egyptian - Persian beans and their pods look like carob[61].

61   From all these explanations one may infer that many of the kinds mentioned in the Mishnah either were no longer known in the Fourth Century or were known under different names.

(fol. 26d) **משנה ג:** הַלֶּפֶת וְהַנַּפוּס וְהַכְּרוּב וְהַתְּרוֹבְתּוֹר הַתְּרָדִים וְהַלְּעוֹנִים אֵינָן כְּלָאִים זֶה בָזֶה. הוֹסִיף רבּי עֲקִיבָה הַשׁוּם וְהַשּׁוּמָנִית וְהַבָּצָל וְהַבְּצַלְצוֹל וְהַתּוּרְמוֹס וְהַפְּלוֹסְלוֹס אֵינָן כְּלָאִים זֶה בָזֶה.

Mishnah 3: Turnips and naphew[62], cabbage and cauliflower[63], beets[64] and orach[65], are not *kilaim* one with the other. Rebbi Aqiba added that garlic and dwarf garlic[66], onion and dwarf onion, lupine and wild lupine[67] are not *kilaim* one with the other.

62   Latin *napus*. In most Mishnah manuscripts, the word is נפוץ with emphatic ṣ. [Maimonides defines as radish (*raphanus*) of the Holy Land.]

63   Definition of *Arukh*, Arabic قرنبيط *qarnabīṭ*. [Jellinek wants to

derive the Hebrew word from Arabic תַּרְבָּה, name of a plant, from תרב "to be dusty". This might be combined with תַּאר "fat", as a fat plant whose surface looks as if dusty.]

64   Defined by Maimonides as Arabic سلق silq, modern Hebrew סֶלֶק (from Babylonian Aramaic, Babli *Berakhot* 35b.)

65   Definition of Maimonides, Arabic قَطَف qaṭaf.

66   According to Maimonides, this is a medicinal variety of garlic whose root is not separated into cloves as is kitchen garlic.

67   R. Isaac Simponti refers to Greek δενδροφάσηλος, a kind not recorded in Byzantine Greek botanical lists. In the opinion of J. Löw, the word is a Semitic diminutive and designates probably *Lupinus luteus L.* The Gaonic commentary to the Mishnah published by S. Asaph (תשובות הגאונים, מקיצי נרדמים ירושלים תשׁׁג) explains the word as Arabic قُرّاص qurrāṣ "stinging nettle, *urtica.*"

הלכה ג: הַלֶּפֶת וְהַנַּפוּס הַכְּרוּב וְהַתְּרוֹבְתוֹר. כְּרוּב דַּקִּיק. הַתְּרָדִין וְהַלְּעוּנִין הַמְּעוּיִין. הוֹסִיף רִבִּי עֲקִיבָה הַשּׁוּם וְהַשּׁוּמָנִית תּוּמָנִיתָא. הַבָּצֶל וְהַבְּצַלְצַל פַּגְלְגוּלָה[68]. הַתּוּרְמוֹס וְהַפְּלוֹסְלוֹס פדמועה וְאֵין כִּלְאַיִם זֶה בָּזֶה.

Halakhah 3: "Turnips and naphew, cabbage and cauliflower," thin cabbage. "Beets and orach," orach[69]. "Rebbi Aqibah added garlic and dwarf garlic," little garlic. "Onion and dwarf onion," little "radish." "Lupine and wild lupine," *pdmw'h*[70], are not *kilaim* one with the other[71].

68   Reading of Rome ms. and *Arukh.* A diminutive of Aramaic פּוּגְלָא, "radish," applied to some kind of small radish.

69   This is the same word as in the Mishnah, except for a dialectal change *l – m* of liquids. In ms. Rome: חמועיין, an otherwise undocumented form.

70   This word is unexplained. R.

Saul Lieberman is correct in rejecting all explanations based on emendations since the text is corroborated by the Rome ms.

71   This seems to be the statement of the Talmud, not of the Mishnah, deciding practice following R. Aqiba, against the opinion of Maimonides.

(fol. 26d) **מִשְׁנָה ד:** וּבָאִילָן הָאֲנָסִין וְהַקְּרוּסְטָמֵלִין וְהַפְּרִישִׁים וְהָעֲזָרְדִים אֵינָן כִּלְאַיִם זֶה בָזֶה. הַתַּפּוּחַ וְהַחֲזָרֵר[72] הַפָּרְסְקִין וְהַשְּׁקֵדִין הַשִּׁיזְפִין וְהָרִמִּין אַף עַל פִּי שֶׁדּוֹמִין זֶה לַזֶּה כִּלְאַיִם זֶה בָזֶה.

Mishnah 4: Among trees, pears and golden apples[73], quince and sorbs[74] are not *kilaim* one with the other. Apple and *hizrar*[75], peaches[76] and almonds, jujubes[77] and lotus fruit, even though they resemble one another, they are *kilaim* one with the other.

72   In Mishnah manuscrips also עזרד, עוזרד, חזרד.

73   Χρυσόμηλον, *chrysomelum*, "a kind of quince also known as κυδώνιον μῆλον." Maimonides defines קרוסטמלין as "pears" and אגסין by an Arabic word مُرَقّش having many meanings depending on local dialects (including apricots and prunes.) R. Y. Qafeh notes that in Yemen, the standard Arabic word for pear means apricot and that for apricot pear.

74   Definition of Alharizi on basis of Maimonides's Arabic זערור. R. Y. Qafeh translates by *crataegus* "hawthorn". Quince, sorb tree, and hawthorn all belong to the same botanical family.

75   Maimonides gives the Arabic equivalent אל עזרן; עֻזר means in classical literary Arabic anything (plant, flock, earth) yielding abundantly. R. Isaac ben Malkizedeq Simponti translates by Italian *mele forcaroli* "fork apples" [possibly apple trees with forked support (espaliers)? (E. G.)]

76   *Prunus persicus*, "Persian plum."

77   *Zizyphus vulgaris L*. The Greek form exists also as ζίζυφος; in I. Löw's opinion, the word is originally Semitic. (In modern Hebrew, the word means "plum.")

(fol. 27a) **הֲלָכָה ד:** פְּרִישִׁין אָמַר רִבִּי יוֹנָה אַסְפַּרְלְגִין וְלָמָּה נִקְרָא שְׁמָן פְּרִישִׁין שֶׁאֵין לָךְ אִילָן פְּרִישׁ לְקְדֵירָה אֶלָּא מִין זֶה בִלְבָד.

Halakhah 4: "Quince." Rebbi Jonah said, quince[78]. Why are they called "prepared", because there is no tree only producing for the pot except that kind[79].

78 In Syriac אספרגלל, in Arabic سَفَرجَل safarjal.	79 No other edible fruit requires cooking under all circumstances.

שַׁלְמוֹן בַּר לֵוִי אַחוֹי דְּזַבְדִּי בַּר לֵוִי בְּשֵׁם רְבִּי יְהוֹשֻׁעַ בֶּן לֵוִי כּוּלְּהוֹן זוּגוֹת זוּגוֹת. רַב אָמַר כּוּלְּהוֹן מִן אֶחָד. מַתְנִיתָא פְּלִיגָא עַל רַב דְּתַנֵּי אַף הַבְּכָיִים. הָתִיב רְבִּי יוֹסֵי בֵּי רְבִּי בּוּן וְהָתַנֵּי אַף הָרוֹגִיְינִין.

Salman the Levite, the brother of Zavdi the Levite, in the name of Rebbi Joshua ben Levi: All statements are pair by pair[80]. Rav said, all are one kind[81]. A *baraitha* disagrees with Rav, for we have stated: also the baka-bush[82]. Rebbi Yose ben Rebbi Abun objected, did we not also state oregano[83]?

80 This applies only to the positive first part of the Mishnah. The opinion of R. Joshua ben Levi parallels that of R. Johanan in Halakhah 1. 81 All four trees mentioned as not being *kilaim*. This statement can draw support from the fact that the names of all trees mentioned are connected by ו	82 A bush of the balsam family, not really a tree. Hence, such a plant cannot be in one family with pears etc., and not all are one kind. 83 Oregano is a small bush, much less of a tree than the baka-bush. Since no answer is given, Rav's position is rejected.

בְּשׁוּקֵי שֶׁל צִיפּוֹרִין הָיוּ מַרְכִּיבִין קְרוּסְטָמֵלִין עַל גַּבֵּי אֱנָס. רָאֶם תַּלְמִיד אֶחָד אָמַר לָהֶן אֲסוּרִים אַתֶּם הָלְכוּ וּקְצָצוּם וּבָאוּ וְשָׁאֲלוּ בְּיַבְנֶה אָמַר לָהֶן מִי שֶׁפָּגַע בָּכֶם מִתַּלְמִידֵי בֵית שַׁמַּאי הָיוּ. לֹא אָמַר אֶלָּא קְרוּסְטָמֵיל עַל גַּבֵּי אֱנָס. הָא אֱנָס עַל גַּבֵּי חִיזְרָר לֹא.

"[84]They used to graft quince onto pears in the markets of Sepphoris. A student saw them and said to them, you are forbidden [to do so.] They went and cut them down. Then they went and asked at Jabneh. They said to them, the one who hit you was from the students of the House of Shammai[85]." It says only, quince on a pear tree. Hence, not a pear tree on a *ḥizrar*[86].

84   Tosephta 1:4, with slight ·changes in spelling and better attention to number; on the other hand, the spelling of endings here fits the period of Jabneh better than the Tosephta. The Court sat at Jabneh only from 70-

138 C. E.

85   The practice to be followed is that of the House of Hillel, not that of the House of Shammai.

86   Which is a kind of wild apple, not of the family of pears.

בִּתְחוּם אָרִיחַ הָיוּ מַרְכִּיבִין תַּפּוּחַ עַל גַּבֵּי חִיזְרָר וּבָא תַּלְמִיד אֶחָד אָמַר לָהֶן אֲסוּרִין אַתֶּם קָלְכוּ קְצָצוּם וּבָאוּ וְשָׁאֲלוּ בְיַבְנֶה אָמַר לָהֶן יָפֶה אָמַר הַתַּלְמִיד. לֹא אָמַר אֶלָּא הַתַּפּוּחַ עַל גַּבֵּי חִיזְרָר. הָא חִיזְרָר עַל גַּבֵּי אֲנָס לֹא. מַה דַהֲוָה עוּבְדָא הֲוָה עוּבְדָא.

"[87]In the region of Ariaḥ they grafted apple on *ḥizrar*. A student came and told them, this is forbidden to you. They went, cut them down, and came to ask at Jabneh. They said to them, that student said correctly[88]." He[89] said only, apple on *ḥizrar*. Hence, not about *ḥizrar* on pear? What the occasions were, they were[90].

87   Tosephta 1:3. Ariaḥ was a town of priests of the family Ma'aziyah, in the neighborhood of Tiberias. In the Kalirian *qinnah* איכה ישבה חבצלת השרון the place is called "the hot springs of Ariaḥ."

88   Since apple and *ḥizrar* are declared *kilaim* in the Mishnah.

89   That student mentioned only the prohibition of grafting *ḥizrar* on an apple tree. Does it follow that grafting *ḥizrar* on a pear tree would be

permitted? In that case, this Tosephta would contradict the conclusions we had drawn from the preceding Tosephta.

90 Neither Tosephta can be used for logical inferences; they report only what happened. They are not theoretical statements.

תַּנֵּי גּוֹי שֶׁהִרְכִּיב אֱגוֹז עַל גַּבֵּי פֶּרְסֵק אַף עַל פִּי שֶׁאֵין יִשְׂרָאֵל רַשַּׁאי לַעֲשׂוֹת כֵּן נוֹטֵל מִמֶּנּוּ יִיחוּר וְהוֹלֵךְ וְנוֹטֵעַ בְּמָקוֹם אַחֵר. מַה נָּפַק מִינְהוֹן קדריה פֶּרְסְקִיָּה. הִרְכִּיב תְּרִיד עַל גַּבֵּי יַרְבּוּן[91] אַף עַל פִּי שֶׁאֵין יִשְׂרָאֵל רַשַּׁאי לַעֲשׂוֹת כֵּן נוֹטֵל הֵימֶנּוּ זֶרַע וְהוֹלֵךְ וְזוֹרֵעַ בְּמָקוֹם אַחֵר. מַה נָּפַק מִינְהוֹן כְּרוּסְלַבְּיָנִין[92]. זַרְגּוּן וְלֶפֶת מַה נָּפַק מִינְהוֹן פֵּיטְרָא סוֹלִינוֹן. לוּזִין וּבוֹטְמִין מַה נָּפַק מִבֵּינֵיהוֹן פִּיסְטַקִין. זֵיתִין וְרמּוֹן מַה נָּפַק מִבֵּינֵיהוֹן שִׁיזְפִין.

It was stated: If a Gentile grafted walnut on a peach stump, a Jew, even though he is not permitted to do this, may take a shoot and go and plant it at another location. What results from them? Persian *qdryh*[93]. If he crosses beet and purslain[94], a Jew, even though he is not permitted to do this[95], may take a seed and go and plant it at another location. What results from them? Groundsel[96]. *Zargun*[97] and turnips, what results from them? Parsley[98]. Almonds and terebinths, what results from them? Pistachios. Olive trees and pomegranate trees, what results from them? *Zizyphus.*

91 Reading of R. Simson. Yerushalmi mss: דרכון, *Arukh* דרקון ("dragon"!).

92 Reading of Rome ms. *Kaphtor waperaḥ* reads בורסילבנון. Leyden has כיירבי לבנון "Lebanese cabbage," which is impossible; R. Simson reads קירבו לבנין "white innards."

93 R. Simson reads קירדו. Musaphia (*Arukh*, s. v. שזף) reads קריא and explains καρύα περσική "Persian nut." This probably is an arbitrary emendation.

94 *Albersia Blitum.* For the identification of the plant from dialectal Arabic, see H. L. Fleischer in

Levy's dictionary, II, p. 445. The explanations of Arukh, Italian *asparago* "asparagus" or *fenicoli* "fennel", do not fit.

95   As spelled out in Tosephta *Kilaim* 1:11. There, the spelling of the second plant is ירבוז, in accordance with the Arabic.

96   Reading with Löw ברוסלכינין, χρυσολάχανον, *atriplex agrestis*. In Syrian Arabic, the plant is identified with قطف, "orach."

97   From Persian زرگون *zargūn* "gold colored." In Arabic, this is a common name for shoots of the vine. The identification does not fit here at all. It is much better to derive the word from Persian زرچوبه *zarčūbeh* "turmeric." (The problem is the pronunciation of ג, ڗ which may represent g, غ *gh* as in Syrian Judeo-Arabic, or g, ج *j* as in Yemenite Judeo-Arabic.)

98   Πετροσέλινον. The Venice text has dittography פטר פיטרה סוליינון. R. Simson: אסטפלינון, σταφυλῖνος, "carrot," *daucus carota*. This seems to be the better reading by far.

(fol. 26d) **משנה ה**: הַצְּנוֹן וְהַנַּפּוּס וְהַחַרְדָּל וְהַלַּפְסָן וּדְלַעַת יְוָנִית עִם הַמִּצְרִית וְהָרְמוּצָה אַף עַל פִּי שֶׁדּוֹמִין זֶה לָזֶה כִּלְאַיִם זֶה בְזֶה.

Mishnah 5: Radish and naphew, mustard and hoar-hound[99]; Greek gourd with the Egyptian and ash ones, even though they look similar, are *kilaim* one with the other.

99   Greek λαψάνη (also λαμψάνη, "charlock", *brassica arvensis*), defined by *Arukh* as Italian *marrobio*, "white hoar-hound."

(fol. 27a) **הלכה ה**: אָמַר רִבִּי יוֹנָתָן יֵשׁ מֵהֶן שֶׁהִילְכוּ אַחַר הַפְּרִי וְיֵשׁ מֵהֶן שֶׁהִילְכוּ אַחַר הֶעָלִין. הַלֶּפֶת וְהַצְּנוֹן הִילְכוּ בָהֶן אַחַר הַפְּרִי. הַלֶּפֶת וְהַנַּפּוּס הִילְכוּ בָהֶן אַחַר הֶעָלִין. הָתִיבוּן הֲרֵי צְנוֹן וְנַפּוּס הֲרֵי פְּרִי דוֹמֶה וְהֶעָלִין דּוֹמִין וְתֵימַר כִּלְאַיִם. אָמַר רִבִּי יוֹנָה בְּזֶה הִילְכוּ בָהֶן אַחַר טַעַם הַפְּרִי.

Halakhah 5: Rebbi Jonathan said, there are some where they considered the fruit[100], and there are some where they considered the leaves. Turnips and radish[101], they went in their regard after the fruit. Turnips and naphew, they considered after the leaves. They objected: But radish and naphew have similar fruits and similar leaves, and you say, they are *kilaim*? Rebbi Jonah said, in that case, they considered the taste of the produce.

100   "Considering" means establishing a criterion for close relationship which excludes *kilaim*. "Fruit", as with the benedictions over vegetables, does not mean the fruit in the botanical sense but the edible part. In the examples here, "fruit" is always the root.

101   Any radish mentioned here has a large white root, quite similar to turnips, not small and red. It is exemplified by the German *Bierrettich*, and the Chinese radish sold in New York.

(fol. 26d) **מִשְׁנָה וּ**: הַזְּאֵב וְהַכֶּלֶב כָּלֶב הַכּוּפְרִי וְהַשּׁוּעָל וְהָעִזִּים וְהַצְּבָאִים הַיְּעֵילִים וְהָרְחֵלִים הַסּוּס וְהַפֶּרֶד הַפֶּרֶד וְהַחֲמוֹר הַחֲמוֹר וְהָעָרוֹד אַף עַל פִּי שֶׁדּוֹמִין זֶה לְזֶה כִּלְאַיִם זֶה בָזֶה.

Mishnah 6: Wolf and dog, rural dog[102] and fox, goat and deer, mountain goats and sheep, horse and mule, mule and donkey, donkey and wild donkey, even though they look similar, they are *kilaim* one with the other.

102   According to *Arukh* these are small dogs barking at night in the deserted places surrounding villages; according to Maimonides and a Gaonic source they are hunting dogs. The Halakhah is only intelligible through the definition of *Arukh*.

(fol. 27a) **הלכה ו**: הָא כֶּלֶב עִם כֶּלֶב כּוּפְרִין אֵינוֹ כִלְאַיִם. וּדְלֹא כְרָבִּי מֵאִיר
דְּרָבִּי מֵאִיר אוֹמֵר כִּלְאַיִם. אַף עַל גַּב דְּרָבִּי מֵאִיר אָמַר כֶּלֶב מִין בְּהֵמָה מוֹדֶה
בְּכֶלֶב כּוּפְרִי שֶׁהוּא מִין חַיָה. הָא כֶּלֶב עִם כֶּלֶב כּוּפְרִי עַל דַּעְתֵּיהּ דְּרָבִּי מֵאִיר
כִּלְאַיִם.

Halakhah 6: Hence, dog and rural dog are not *kilaim*[103]. This is not
following Rebbi Meïr, since Rebbi Meïr says that they are *kilaim*. Even
though Rebbi Meïr says that the dog is a domesticated animal, he agrees
that the rural dog is a wild animal[104]. Hence, according to Rebbi Meïr,
dog and rural dog are *kilaim*.

103   Since they are not mentioned as
a pair that cannot be mated. An
anonymous Mishnah is supposed to
follow R. Meïr's opinion unless the
opposite is proven.

104   Domesticated and wild animals,
even though they might belong to the
same family, cannot be treated as

kindred since the fat of domesticated
kasher animals is forbidden (*Lev.* 3:17)
but the fat of *kasher* wild animals is
permitted; the blood of *kasher* wild
animals has to be spilled, the blood of
kasher domesticated animals may be
used for industrial purposes.

עוֹף לֹא תַנִּיתָהּ. אָמַר רִבִּי יוֹחָנָן אַיְיתִיתֵיהּ מִן דְּבַר דְּלָיָה תַּרְנְגוֹל עִם הַפּוֹסְיוֹנִי
תַּרְנְגוֹל עִם הַטַּווָס אַף עַל פִּי שֶׁדּוֹמִין זֶה לְזֶה כִּלְאַיִם זֶה בָזֶה. רִבִּי שִׁמְעוֹן בֶּן
לָקִישׁ אָמַר מִשְׁנָה שְׁלֵימָה שָׁנָה לָנוּ רִבִּי וְכֵן חַיָה וְעוֹף כַּיּוֹצֵא בָהֶן. אָמַר רִבִּי
יוֹנָה[105] צְרִיכָה לְהָדָא דְּרִבִּי יוֹחָנָן תַּנִּינָן הָכָא חַיָה וּפֵרַשְׁתָּנָה תַּמָּן. תַּנִּינָן בְּהֵמָה
הָכָא וּפֵרַשְׁתָּנָה תַּמָּן. עוֹף תַּנִּיתָהּ תַּמָּן אָתָא וּפֵרַשְׁתָּנָה הָכָא. אָמַר רִבִּי יוֹסֵי
וְיֵאוּת. בָּא לְהוֹדִיעָךְ שֶׁהָעוֹף אָסוּר בְּכִלְאַיִם.

Birds are not mentioned in the Mishnah. Rebbi Joḥanan said, it is
inferred from [the statement of] Bar Dalaiah[106]: "Chicken with pheasant,
chicken with peacock, even though they look similar, are *kilaim* one with

the other." Rebbi Simeon ben Laqish said that Rebbi stated for us a complete Mishnah: "The same applies to wild animals and birds[107]." Rebbi Jonah said, we need that of Rebbi Joḥanan, we state here "wild animal" and explain it there[108]. We state here "domesticated animal" and explain it there. Birds, we stated there and explain it here[109]. Rebbi Jose said, is that correct? It comes to tell you that birds are forbidden in *kilaim*[110]!

105   Reading of Rome ms. and R. Simson. Leyden: ר' יוחנן. The latter reading is impossible since in talmudic theory an author cannot himself declare that his statement is necessary.

106   His statement parallels a Tosephta (1:7). In the parallel in Babli *Baba Qama* 55a, R. Simeon ben Laqish is quoted to the effect that in the Mishnah, Rebbi taught that chicken, pheasant, and peacock are *kilaim* one with the other. The language of the Babli is close to that of the Tosephta. R. Simeon ben Laqish's position in the Babli is that of R. Yose (the Amora, colleague of R. Jonah) later in the present paragraph.

107   Mishnah *Baba Qama* 5:7. The Mishnah notes that the Biblical precept regarding the responsibility of somebody who digs a hole in the public domain and "an ox or a donkey" falls into it (*Ex.* 21:33) extends to all domesticated animals, to damages assessed

on a thief, to the requirement of returning stray animals to their owners, to unload animals in distress, to the prohibition of muzzling an animal used for threshing, to *kilaim*, and to Sabbath rest. Then the Mishnah adds, "The same applies to wild animals and birds." Hence, the applicability of all rules of *kilaim* to birds is spelled out there.

108   We give here cases involving domesticated and wild animals but the underlying principle is given there, in *Baba Qama*.

109   We really do not explain anything here but the statements of the Tosephta and Bar Dalaiah show that the detailed rules imply that birds from the same family are *kilaim* one with the other if one is domesticated (chicken) and the other is wild (pheasant) or semi-wild (peacock).

110   Since the Mishnah states that "the same applies," it is implied that all

rules apply uniformly. Hence, the
examples of birds are unnecessary as

proclaimed rules.

רְבִּי יִרְמְיָה אָמַר כַּהֲנָא שָׁאַל לְרֵישׁ לָקִישׁ הַמַּרְבִּיעַ בְּחַיּוֹת הַיָּם מַהוּ. אָמַר לֵיהּ
עוֹד הֵן כְּתִיב בָּהֶן לְמִינֵיהֶן. רִבִּי אָחָא לֹא אָמַר כֵּן אֶלָּא הֲוָה אָמַר רִבִּי אָחָא
בְּשֵׁם רֵישׁ לָקִישׁ כָּל־שֶׁכָּתוּב בּוֹ לְמִינֵיהוּ כִּלְאַיִם נוֹהֵג בּוֹ. הָתִיב רִבִּי כַּהֲנָא הֲרֵי
חַיַּית הַיָּם הֲרֵי כְתִיב בָּהֶן לְמִינֵיהֶן מֵעַתָּה כִּלְאַיִם נוֹהֵג בָּהֶן. אָמַר רִבִּי יוֹסֵי בֵּי
רִבִּי בּוֹן הָכָא פָּרַס כַּהֲנָא מְצוּדָתֵיהּ עַל רֵישׁ לָקִישׁ וְצַיְידֵיהּ. אָמַר רִבִּי יוֹנָה יָכִיל
אֲנָא פָּתַר לָהּ מִשּׁוּם מַנְהִיג. מַיְיתִי חוּט וְקָטַר בְּעוּדְגֵיהּ דְּלָכִיסָא וּבְעוּדְגֵנֵיהּ
דְּירוֹקָא וְאִינּוּן שַׁיְיפִין דֵּין עִם דֵּין וּמַזְרְעִין.

Rebbi Jeremiah said, Cahana asked R. Simeon ben Laqish[111]: What is
the rule for someone who mates sea animals[112]? He said to him, it is
written about them (*Gen.* 1:21): "By their kinds[113]." Rebbi Aḥa did not say
so, but Rebbi Aḥa used to say in the name of Rebbi Simeon ben Laqish,
wherever "by their kinds" is written, *kilaim* applies to it. Rebbi Cahana
objected, it is written about the animals of the sea[114] "by their kinds;"
kilaim should apply to them! Rebbi Yose ben Rebbi Abun said, here did
Cahana spread his net over Rebbi Simeon ben Laqish and caught him[115].
Rebbi Jonah said, I can explain it, because of one who leads[116]. He brings
a string and binds it to the gills of a white fish[117] and a green fish; they
rub one another and spawn[118].

111   The abbreviation ריש לקיש is
Babylonian. The entire paragraph has
a parallel in *Gen. rabba* 7(6); it is
mentioned in Babli *Baba Qama* 55a.

112   In this version, one speaks about
aquatic mammals who do copulate.

113   As explained in the next

version, "by their kinds" is written to
forbid cross-mating.

114   In *Gen. rabba*, one reads "fish."
The verse speaks of all sea creatures,
including fish, sea reptiles, and sea
mammals. It is difficult to see how
copulation could apply to fish.

115   Since R. Simeon had no answer to his objection.

116   Mishnah *Kilaim* 8:2 states that any two kinds of animals that are *kilaim* with one another may not be driven or led when harnessed together and may not be used for plowing together.

117   Greek λεῦκος, name of a fish;

cf. also λευκός "white".

118   Hence, while copulation is a notion not applicable to fish, any actions to induce cross-breeding are still forbidden. (The Babli, *Baba Qama* 55a, does not consider the crossing of fish species, only that of marine mammals.)

(fol. 26d) **משנה ז:** אֵין מְבִיאִין אִילָן בְּאִילָן יָרָק בְּיָרֶק וְלֹא אִילָן בְּיָרֶק וְלֹא יָרָק בְּאִילָן. רִבִּי יְהוּדָה מַתִּיר יָרָק בְּאִילָן.

Mishnah 7: One does not bring[119] a tree on a tree, a vegetable on a vegetable, and neither a tree on a vegetable nor a vegetable on a tree. Rebbi Jehudah permits vegetable on tree[120].

119   This general expression covers an array of agricultural techniques, not just grafting. The details are explained

in the following Halakhot.

120   Because the tree stump is only a kind of soil for the vegetable.

(fol. 27a) **הלכה ז:** מֵחְלְפָה שִׁיטָתֵיהּ דְּרִבִּי יוּדָה. תַּמָּן הוּא אוֹמֵר נוֹטֵל הוּא אָדָם מָעָה אַחַת מִפִּיטְמוֹ שֶׁל אֲבַטִּיחַ וּמָעָה אַחַת מִפִּיטְמוֹ שֶׁל תַּפּוּחַ וְנוֹתְנָן בְּתוֹךְ גּוּמָא אַחַת (fol. 27b) וְהֵן מִתְאָחִין וְנַעֲשִׂין כִּלְאַיִם. וְכָא הוּא אָמַר הָכֵין. תַּמָּן עַל יְדֵי שֶׁהוּא נוֹתֵן זֶה בְּצַד זֶה הֵן מִתְאָחִין וְנַעֲשִׂין כִּלְאַיִם. בְּרַם הָכָא יָרָק בְּאִילָן הוּא.

Halakhah 7: The opinion of Rebbi Jehudah seems inverted. There[121], he says that a man takes a small piece from the pericarp of a water melon and a small piece from the pericarp of an apple, places them into one cavity where they unite and become *kilaim*, and here he says so? There, because he places them so that they touch one another, unite and become *kilaim*, but here it is vegetable on tree.

121   Halakhah 2.

תַּנֵּי מְנַיִּין שֶׁאֵין מַרְכִּיבִין עֵץ סְרָק עַל גַּבֵּי עֵץ מַאֲכָל וְלֹא עֵץ מַאֲכָל עַל גַּבֵּי עֵץ מַאֲכָל מִין בְּשֶׁאֵינוֹ מִינוֹ מְנַיִּין תַּלְמוּד לוֹמַר אֶת חוּקוֹתַי תִּשְׁמוֹרוּ. רְבִּי יוֹנָה רְבִּי לָעֵזָר בְּשֵׁם כַּהֲנָא דְּרְבִּי לָעֵזָר הִיא מְשׁוּם חוּקִים שֶׁחָקַקְתִּי בְּעוֹלָמִי. מֵאַתָּה אָסוּר לְאָדָם הָרִאשׁוֹן. רְבִּי יוֹסֵי בְּשֵׁם רְבִּי הִילָא דִּבְרֵי הַכֹּל הִיא מְשׁוּם חוּקִים שֶׁחָקַקְתִּי בְּעוֹלָמִי. מֵעַתָּה אָסוּר לְהַרְכִּיב תְּאֵינָה שְׁחוֹרָה עַל גַּבֵּי תְּאֵינָה לְבָנָה. אָמַר רְבִּי אָבִין וְלֹא מִכְּלְאֵי הַבְּגָדִים לָמַדְתָּ. מַה כִּלְאֵי בְגָדִים שֶׁאָסַרְתִּי לָךְ שְׁנֵי מִינִין לֹא זֶה מִמִּין זֶה וְלֹא זֶה מִמִּין זֶה אַף כִּלְאַיִם שֶׁאָסַרְתִּי לָךְ בְּכָל־מָקוֹם לֹא זֶה מִמִּין זֶה וְלֹא זֶה מִמִּין זֶה.

It was stated: From where that one may not graft a tree bearing no edible fruit onto a fruit-bearing tree, or a fruit-bearing tree onto another fruit-bearing tree of a kind that is not his own kind, from where? The verse says (*Lev.* 19:19): "You must keep My basic Laws[122]." Rebbi Jonah, Rebbi Eleazar[123], in the name of Cahana: This is Rebbi Eleazar's, "because of the basic Laws I gave."[124] If this is so, it was forbidden to Adam, the first man[125]! Rebbi Yose in the name of Rebbi La, it is the opinion of everybody, because of the basic Laws that I gave to My world[126]. If it is so, is should be forbidden to graft a black fig tree on a white[127] fig tree. Rebbi Avin said, did you not infer the rules from *kilaim* of textiles? Just as for *kilaim* of textiles two kinds, not one from this kind and the other from the other kind[128], also any other *kilaim* that I forbade you, not one from this kind and the other from the other kind.

122   The verse reads: "You must keep My basic Laws, your animals you shall not breed *kilaim*, your field you shall not sow *kilaim*, and *kilaim* cloth, *š'ṭnz*, shall not come onto you." It is concluded (*Sifra Qedošim* 4:13-18) that the rules of all three cases are parallel to one another.

123   The Amora. R. Eleazar mentioned next is R. Eleazar ben Shamua, the Tanna.

124   The Tanna R. Eleazar states in Tosephta *Avodah Zarah* 8:8 and Babli *Sanhedrin* 56b that mating two different kinds or grafting two different kinds are activities forbidden in the Law of Nature given to Adam and Noah. He holds that the reference to חוק, "basic law," here is to the Law of Creation, where all living things were created "in their kinds." In the Tosephta and the Babli, he is alone in his opinion.

125   This is the opinion of R. Eleazar; why is he alone in that opinion? The Sages hold that the laws of *kilaim* were given at Sinai only to the Jewish people. It is not sinful for a Gentile to cross-breed species.

126   This is the position of the anonymous Tanna in *Sifra Qedošim*(4:14): "Not only your animals with your animals, your animals with the animals of a Gentile, the animals of a Gentile with your animals, Gentile animals with Gentile animals; the verse reads: You must keep my basic Laws." If Gentiles were exempt, their animals could not be included in the prohibition. R. Eleazar will agree that sowing a field with two different kinds, and wearing clothing made from wool and linen together are prohibitions addressed only to Jews. Only *kilaim* connected to the story of Creation are obligations of Gentiles.

127   Not really white, but rather light green.

128   But yarns of different color, or from different strains of flax, may be made into one garment. Similarly, different varieties of the same species may be mated or grafted.

תַּנֵּי בְּשֵׁם רִבִּי לְעָזָר מוּתָּר הוּא גּוֹי לִזְרוֹעַ וְלִלְבּוֹשׁ כִּלְאַיִם אֲבָל לֹא לְהַרְבִּיעַ בְּהֶמְתּוֹ כִּלְאַיִם וְלֹא לְהַרְכִּיב אִילָנוֹ כִּלְאַיִם. לָמָּה מִפְּנֵי שֶׁכָּתוּב בָּהֶן לְמִינֵיהֶן. וַחֲרֵי דְשָׁאֵין כְּתִיב בָּהֶן לְמִינֵיהֶן. אֵין כְּתִיב בְּצִיצֵי אֶלָּא בְהוֹצָאָה. וְאִם כֵּן לָמָּה נִתְקַלְלָה הָאָרֶץ. רִבִּי יוּדָן בַּר שָׁלוֹם אָמַר עַל יְדֵי שֶׁעָבְרָה עַל גְּזֵירוֹתָיו שֶׁל

הַקָּדוֹשׁ בָּרוּךְ הוּא. תַּדְשֵׁה הָאָרֶץ דֶּשֶׁא עֵשֶׂב מַזְרִיעַ זֶרַע וְהִיא לֹא עָשְׂתָה אֶלָּא
וַתּוֹצֵא הָאָרֶץ דֶּשֶׁא עֵשֶׂב מַזְרִיעַ זֶרַע לְמִינֵהוּ. רִבִּי פִּינְחָס אָמַר שָׂמְחָה בְצִיוּוּיֶהָ
וְהוֹסִיפָה אִילָנֵי סְרָק. עַל דַּעְתֵּיהּ דְּרִבִּי יוּדָן בַּר שָׁלוֹם יָפֶה נִתְקַלְלָה הָאָרֶץ. עַל
דַּעְתֵּיהּ דְּרִבִּי פִּינְחָס לָמָּה נִתְקַלְלָה הָאָרֶץ. כְּאִינָשׁ דַּאֲמַר לִיט בִּיזָא דְּכֵן
אַייְנִיק. וְאָתְיָא כַּיי רִבִּי נָתָן שְׁלֹשָׁה נִכְנְסוּ לְדִין וְאַרְבָּעָה יָצְאוּ מְקוּלָלִין.
אֲרוּרָה הָאֲדָמָה בַּעֲבוּרֶךָ.

It was stated in the name of Rebbi Eleazar[129]: "The Gentile may sow
and wear *kilaim,* but he may not mate his animals as *kilaim* or graft his
tree *kilaim*." Why? Because about these, it is written "by their kinds."
But is it not also written for grasses "by their kinds?[130]" It is not written
for the commandment, only at the realization. If this is so, why was Earth
cursed[131]? Rebbi Judan bar Shalom said, because it transgressed the
orders of the Holy One, praise to Him! (*Gen.* 1:11) "The earth should produce lawns, grasses producing seed," but it produced only (*Gen.* 1:12)
"lawns, grasses producing seed by their kinds.[132]" Rebbi Phineas said, it
enjoyed the commandment and added shade trees. In the opinion of
Rebbi Yudan bar Shalom, Earth was justly cursed. In the opinion of Rebbi
Phineas, why was Earth cursed? Like a man who said: The breastnipples
should be cursed that this one[133] suckled from. This follows Rebbi
Nathan: Three stood in judgment and four went out cursed, (*Gen.* 3:17)
"Earth is cursed because of you."

129　Tosephta *Avodah Zarah* 8:8.

130　Why may one graft grasses; they
are never mentioned in the Mishnah.

131　From here on, an expanded
version is in *Gen. rabba* 5(9).

132　As explained in *Gen. rabba*, the

difference is about trees, for which
Earth was commanded to produce "fruit
trees" but bore "trees producing fruit."
In the opinion of R. Yudan bar Shalom,
this is disobedience since the entire
tree should have been edible, not only

the fruit. In the opinion of R. Phineas, Earth produced more than it was commanded, since all trees, even those which today do not grow edible fruit, did produce edible fruit before Adam's sin.

In all cases, only the first words of the verse are quoted, as is customary in both Talmudim. The inference is from the other parts of the verses.

133   A criminal; in that case, Adam.

עַד כְּדוֹן לֵית כְּתִיב אֶלָא בְּהֶמְתְּךָ לֹא תַרְבִּיעַ כִּלְאַיִם. עוֹף מְנַיִן. אִית תַּנָּיֵי תַּנֵּי מֵאֵת חוּקוֹתַי תִּשְׁמוֹרוּ וְאִית תַּנֵּי מִבְּהֶמְתְּךָ לֹא תַרְבִּיעַ כִּלְאַיִם. הִרְכִּיב אִילָן וְהִרְבִּיעַ עוֹף מָאן דַּאֲמַר מֵחוּקוֹתַי תִּשְׁמוֹרוּ חַיָּיב שְׁתַּיִם. מָאן דְּאָמַר מִבְּהֶמְתְּךָ לֹא תַרְבִּיעַ כִּלְאַיִם אֵינוֹ חַיָּיב אֶלָא אַחַת. כְּשֶׁהִרְבִּיעַ בְּהֵמָה וְהִרְבִּיעַ עוֹף מָאן דְּאָמַר מֵחוּקוֹתַי תִּשְׁמוֹרוּ אֵינוֹ חַיָּיב אֶלָא אַחַת. מָאן דְּאָמַר מִבְּהֶמְתְּךָ לֹא תַרְבִּיעַ כִּלְאַיִם חַיָּיב שְׁתַּיִם.

So far it only is written, "do not mate your animals *kilaim*." Birds from where[134]? Some Tannaim state from (*Lev.* 19:19): "You must keep My basic Laws[135]," some state from: "your animals[136] you shall not mate *kilaim*." If somebody grafted a tree and mated birds[137], following him who says "you must keep My basic Laws," he is guilty of two offenses[138], according to him who says, "your animals you shall not mate *kilaim*," he is guilty only of one offense. When he mated animals and birds, following him who says "you must keep My basic Laws," he is guilty only of one offense[139]; according to him who says, "your animals you shall not mate *kilaim*," he is guilty of two offenses[140].

134   How do we know that they fall under the prohibition of *kilaim*?

135   As explained above, birds were also created למיניהם and hence may not be artificially crossed with other kinds.

136   It was established earlier (Note 107) that for the Sabbath, *kilaim*, etc., "animal" includes wildlife and birds.

137   Simultaneously. Sins committed at different times are certainly

punishable separately. It is always
understood that breeding of birds and
grafting of trees, etc., refer to
forbidden acts and not to legitimate
breeding or grafting.

138   In this paragraph, "him" refers
to one of the Tannaïm just quoted.

All commentators emend the text
and switch "one offense" and "two
offenses" between the two cases in
order to make sense of the statement.
However, since the Rome ms. confirms
the text, such an emendation is unacceptable.

The verse, "you must keep My basic
Laws; your animals you shall not mate
kilaim, your field you shall not sow
kilaim, and *kilaim* cloth, *ša'aṭnez*, shall
not come onto you," contains three
separate prohibitions (mating, sowing,
cloth) and one general one. The
introductory clause is a general
statement which expresses a general
prohibition, but since it expresses a
general principle (לאו שבכלות) it does
not define a prosecutable criminal

offense. The count of offenses in our
text does not refer to morality or to the
view of Heaven unknown to us, but to
human jurisdiction. If birds are
included because of the legal
importance of the story of Creation,
the perpetrator committed two crimes
simultaneously, transgressing the first
two of the prohibitions, and has to be
punished accordingly. If birds are
included only because of an extensive
interpretation of בהמה, the prohibition
is not explicitly Biblical and not
punishable in court. Hence, for the
second position, while two sins were
committed, only one of them is subject
to sanction by the court.

139   Since he simultaneously transgressed the same prohibition in two
instances.

140   An original one, mating domestic animals in a forbidden way, and a
secondary one for birds. Since he
transgressed the Biblical commandment, the secondary transgression is
also punishable.

תְּנֵי אֵין מַרְכִּיבִין זֵתִים בְּרֶכֶב שֶׁל תְּמָרָה מִפְּנֵי שֶׁהוּא אִילָן בְּאִילָן. רַבִּי יוּדָן
בָּעֵי וְלֵית הָדָא פְלִיגָא עַל רַבִּי לֵוִי. אֶשְׁתְּךָ כְּגֶפֶן פּוֹרִיָּה בְּיַרְכְּתֵי בֵיתֶךָ בָּנֶיךָ
כִּשְׁתִילֵי זֵתִים סָבִיב לְשׁוּלְחָנֶךָ. מַה זֵיתִים אֵין בָּהֶן הַרְכָּבָה אַף בָּנֶיךָ לֹא יְהֵא
בָּהֶן פְּסוֹלֶת. הָא מִכְּלָל שֶׁיֵּשׁ בָּהֶן פְּסוֹלֶת. שַׁנְיָיא הִיא הָכָא שֶׁהוּא עָתִיד
לְמָתְקָה. כְּהָדָא רַבִּי שִׁמְעוֹן בְּרַבִּי הֲוָא מַשְׁקֵה פֶּרְסְתְּקֵיהּ יַיִן מְבוּשָּׁל בִּשְׁבִיל
לְמָתְקָה.

It was stated[141]: "One does not graft olives on the stem[142] of a date palm because that would be tree on tree." Rebbi Yudan asked, does that not disagree with Rebbi Levi[143]? "(*Ps.* 128:3) 'Your wife be like a fruitful vine on the sides of your house, your sons like saplings of olive trees around your table.' Just as olive trees are not subject to grafting[144], thus in your sons shall not be found any flaws[145]." But here it follows that there are flaws in them[146]. There is a difference here, because in the end it[147] will sweeten its fruit. Similar to that, Rebbi Simeon, the son of Rebbi[148], used to water his peach tree with cooked wine[149] in order to sweeten its fruit.

141   Tosephta *Kilaim* 1:10.

142   Explanation of Rashbam to Babli *Baba Batra* 62b. Explanations of the Mayence commentary, "a row of date palms," and of R. Saul Lieberman, "branch of a date palm." Literally: "One does not make an olive tree ride on the vehicle of a date palm."

143   The sermon is brought in *Midrash Tehillim* 128(4), in the name of R. Joshua ben Levi. Since R. Levi was a professional preacher, the attribution to him is more convincing. The objection here is not to the sermon but to its underlying hypothesis; one cannot object to sermons.

144   Meaning that one does not graft olive trees since nothing could be gained by it.

145   Neither should your sons be of uncertain paternity, or from an unlawful wife, nor should they have such problems in their families.

146   If olive trees can be grafted onto something else, your sons could be grafted on you.

147   The sap from the date palm stump.

148   The second son of Rebbi, colleague of R. Ḥiyya. In his will, Rebbi appointed his older son, Gamliel, as political head, and his younger son as *ḥakham*, the final halakhic authority.

149   Pasteurized grape juice without alcohol.

(fol. 26d) **מִשְׁנָה ח**: אֵין נוֹטְעִין יֶרֶק בְּתוֹךְ סַדָּן שֶׁל שִׁיקְמָא אֵין מַרְכִּיבִין פֵּיגָם
עַל גַּבֵּי קִידָה לְבָנָה מִפְּנֵי שֶׁהוּא יֶרֶק בָּאִילָן. אֵין נוֹטְעִין יִיחוּר שֶׁל תְּאֵינָה לְתוֹךְ
הֶחָצוּב שֶׁיִּהְיֶה מַקוּרוֹ. אֵין תּוֹחְבִין זְמוֹרָה שֶׁל גֶּפֶן לְתוֹךְ הָאֲבַטִּיחַ שֶׁתְּהֵא זוֹרֶקֶת
מֵימֶיהָ לְתוֹכוֹ מִפְּנֵי שֶׁהוּא אִילָן בְּיֶרֶק. אֵין נוֹתְנִין זֶרַע דְּלַעַת לְתוֹךְ הֶחָלָמוּת
שֶׁתְּהֵא מְשַׁמְּרָתוֹ מִפְּנֵי שֶׁהוּא יֶרֶק בְּיֶרֶק.

Mishnah 8: One does not plant vegetables in the stump[150] of a Sycamore tree, one does not graft rue on white cassia, because that would be vegetable on tree. One does not plant a fig tree shoot into rue[151] so that the latter should cool it[152]; one does not put a shoot of a vine into a watermelon so that it should supply the shoot with its fluid, because that would be tree on vegetable. One does not put a pumpkin seed into a mallow[153] so that it should protect it, because that would be vegetable on vegetable[154].

150   "Anvil." Sycamores were mainly planted for their wood and cut down regularly. Their stumps do regenerate.

151   For the determination of חצוב, cf. *Peah* 2:1, Note 26.

152   Interpretation of Maimonides and R. Isaac Simponti. R. Simson suggests either this translation or "that it serve as a wall around it."

153   Identification of *Arukh* and R. Isaac Simponti. The Italian *malva* given by these authors means either mallow or marshmallow. I. Löw identifies the plant as bugloss (*Anchusa officinalis L.*).

154   One has to assume that all combinations forbidden here were taken from contemporary agricultural practice.

(fol. 27b) **הֲלָכָה ח**: רִבִּי זְכַרְיָה חַתְנֵיהּ דְּרִבִּי לֵוִי בָּעֵי כָּךְ אֵינוֹ אָסוּר מִשּׁוּם
זְרָעִים תַּחַת הַגֶּפֶן. אָמַר רִבִּי יוֹסֵי תִּיפְתָּר בְּמַעֲמִיק שׁוֹרֶשׁ לְמַטָּה מִשְּׁלוֹשָׁה
טְפָחִים חוּץ לְשִׁשָּׁה. כְּהָדָא דְּתַנֵּי שָׁרְשֵׁי פִיאָה הַנִּכְנָסִין לְתוֹךְ אַרְבַּע אַמּוֹת
שֶׁבְּכֶרֶם. לְמַטָּה מִשְּׁלוֹשָׁה טְפָחִים הֲרֵי אֵלּוּ מוּתָּרִין.

Halakhah 8: Rebbi Zachariah, son-in-law of Rebbi Levy, asked: Apart from that, is it not forbidden because of seeds under a vine[155]? Rebbi Yose said, explain it if he sets its root[156] down more than three hand-breadths[157], distant more than six hand-breadths [from the vine], following what was stated[158]: "roots of madder[159] that enter within four cubits of a vineyard are permitted below three hand-breadths."

155　As indicated in the Introduction, vineyards have particularly strict rules, based on *Deut.* 22:9. These rules are spelled out in later Chapters of the Tractate. The questioner is of the opinion that planting a shoot of vine in a water melon would be forbidden even if in general trees on vegetables were permitted.

156　Meaning the watermelon, that the root of the new vine will grow down there, not that the shoot is set into a watermelon.

157　A hand-breadth is one sixth of a cubit.

158　Tosephta *Kilaim* 4:11.

159　Following the reading of R. Solomon Adani in מלאכת שלמה from his manuscripts: פוּאָה *Rubia tinctorum L.*, an industrial plant whose roots were used to produce dye. Hence, the roots of the plant are more important for כלאים than the parts above ground. This is the reading of R. Saul Lieberman; it is offered for ease of translation.

However, the few manuscript sources at our disposal all read פִּיאָה, and one must explain the text with this reading. (As Lieberman correctly notes, the attempt by R. Moses Margalit is incomprehensible.) In Tractates *Kilaim* and *Eruvin*, the word פִּיאָה does not have the meaning "corner" as in Tractate *Peah*, but means a wire or string strung as a symbolic fence around a field to separate it from the next one, or around a town to make it a "walled" town for the rules of Sabbath. Now, it is stated in Mishnah and Tosephta of Chapter 4 that a solid wall permits one to plant vegetables on one side and vines on the other. This clearly is inadmissible for a *peah*-fence; one may not plant vines within four cubits of such a symbolic fence. Then the Tosephta states that even in this case the roots that enter from the outside do not cause *kilaim* if they are at a depth of at least half a cubit.

(fol. 26d) **משנה ט:** הַטּוֹמֵן לֶפֶת וּצְנוֹנוֹת תַּחַת הַגֶּפֶן אִם הָיוּ מִקְצַת הֶעָלִין מְגוּלִין אֵינוֹ חוֹשֵׁשׁ לֹא מִשּׁוּם כִּלְאַיִם וְלֹא מִשּׁוּם שְׁבִיעִית וְלֹא מִשּׁוּם מַעְשְׂרוֹת וְנִיטָּלִין בַּשַּׁבָּת. הַזּוֹרֵעַ חִיטָּה וּשְׂעוֹרָה כְּאַחַת הֲרֵי זֶה כִּלְאַיִם. רַבִּי יוּדָה אוֹמֵר אֵינוֹ כִּלְאַיִם עַד שֶׁיְּהוּ שְׁתֵּי חִטִּים וּשְׂעוֹרָה אוֹ חִיטָּה וּשְׁתֵּי שְׂעוֹרִים אוֹ חִטָּה וּשְׂעוֹרָה וְכוּסֶּמֶת.

Mishnah 9: If someone hides turnips and radishes under a vine[160] and some of the leaves were showing he does not have to worry either because of *kilaim*[161], or because of the Sabbatical year, or because of tithes, and they may be removed on the Sabbath[162]. If someone sows wheat and barley together, that is *kilaim*[163]. Rebbi Jehudah says, it is not *kilaim* unless there are two wheat kernels and a barley kernel, or a wheat kernel and two barley kernels, or one each of wheat, barley, and spelt.

160   These turnips and radishes have been harvested and tithed; now they are put into a hole dug in the earth and covered with earth in order to be preserved over the summer. Since the plants were taken out of the gound, they have lost the capillary roots that fed them in the ground, and if put again into a hole, they will not grow again. In the opinion of R. Simson and R. Abraham ben David of Posquières, it is necessary that some leaves are showing only if one desires to take them out on the Sabbath, since on that day one may neither dig nor harvest. For the other rules, turnips or radishes may be completely covered. In the interpretation of Maimonides and R. Joseph Caro, the leniencies of the Mishnah apply only if some leaves are uncovered (Maimonides, *Hilkhot Kilaim* 2:11, 3:6). The Babli (*Eruvin* 77b, *Sabbath* 50b, 113a) supports the interpretation of R. Simson since it forbids the taking on the Sabbath only if the turnips cannot be pulled by hand. The scenario is difficult to understand since the leaves of harvested plants will soon wilt or rot.

161   Since the produce will not grow, there is no planting and no hint of *kilaim*. Similarly, if the turnips were put into the ground before the start of the Sabbatical year, they do not

become Sabbatical produce while in the ground. If they were tithed, they need not be tithed again when taken out.

162   In this case, the radishes have to be pulled out by their leaves. Since radishes are eaten raw, they are permitted food on the Sabbath and may be taken. Earth by itself may not be moved, but if earth falls by the side when the food is moved, its motion is unintentional and not forbidden.

163   Obviously, the minimum number of different kinds for *kilaim* is 2. Rebbi Jehudah requires uniform rules for all kinds of *kilaim* and, since *Deut.* 22:9 states that one may not sow *kilaim* in one's vineyard, the minimum is the vine plus *kilaim*, i. e., three components. [The Babli does not accept the Mishnah as practice but requires at least one seed each from three different species.}

(fol. 27b) **הלכה ט**: חִזְקִיָּה אָמַר לֹא שָׁנוּ אֶלָּא לֶפֶת וּצְנוֹנוֹת הָא שְׁאָר דְּבָרִים לֹא. רִבִּי יוֹחָנָן אָמַר לֹא שַׁנְיָא הִיא לֶפֶת הִיא צְנוֹנוֹת הִיא שְׁאָר כָּל־דְּבָרִים. מַה נָן קַייְמִין אִי מִשּׁוּם זְרָעִים בְּאִילָן לָמָּה לִי גֶּפֶן וּצְנוֹנוֹת אֲפִילוּ שְׁאָר כָּל־דְּבָרִים הָאֵילוּ. אִי מִשּׁוּם שֶׁאֵינוֹ רוֹצֶה בְּהַשְׁרָשָׁתָן לָמָּה לִי לֶפֶת וּצְנוֹנוֹת אֲפִילוּ שְׁאָר כָּל־דְּבָרִים. מִן מַה דְּתַנֵּי רִבִּי חִייָא כְּגוֹן אֲגוּדָה שֶׁל לֶפֶת וַאֲגוּדָה שֶׁל צְנוֹנוֹת. הֲוֵי לֵית טַעֲמָא דְּלֹא מִשּׁוּם שֶׁאֵינוֹ רוֹצֶה בְּהַשְׁרָשָׁתָן.

Halakhah 9: Hizqiah said, they stated only turnips and radishes, nothing else. Rebbi Johanan said, there is no difference whether turnips, radishes, or any other plants. What are we talking about[164]? If because of the rules of vegetables and trees, why do I need vine and radishes, even any other plants[165]? If because he does not want them to take root, why turnips and radishes, even any other species also? From what Rebbi Hiyya stated, "for example bunches of turnips and bunches of radishes," it follows that the reason is only because he does not want them to take root[166].

164 According to R. Johanan, why does the Mishnah give only one example and not establish a principle, as in Mishnah 7?

165 If the reason is to say that in such a situation the prohibition to sow vegetables too close to a tree does not apply, then the particular example is irrelevant. The same question is asked for the alternative reason in the next sentence.

166 If we accept R. Ḥiyya as authoritative, then all our questions are resolved. First, since he says "for example," it is clear that he is of R. Johanan's opinion and opposes his own son, Ḥizqiah. Second, the Mishnah mentions turnips and radishes, because they are bound in bunches after the harvest. Hence, not all produce may be so stored but only produce one can store in such a way that the formation of new roots is prevented (e. g., storing cabbage after the roots have been cut away.) This means, in the end we accept neither Ḥizqiah nor R. Johanan, but we allow only produce which certainly will not grow new roots, similar to turnips and radishes. (For the requirement that the leaves be uncovered, see Note 160.) Vines are mentioned because they follow the most restrictive rules; what is permissible for vines is *a fortiori* permissible for all other fruit trees.

תַּנֵּי פַּגָּה שֶׁטְּמָנָהּ בְּטֶבֶל וַחֲרָרָה שֶׁטְּמָנָהּ בְּגֶחָלִים אִם הָיוּ מִקְצָתָן מְגוּלִין נִיטְּלִין בְּשַׁבָּת וְאִם לָאו אֵין נִיטְּלִין בְּשַׁבָּת. רַבִּי לָעֶזֶר בֶּן תַּדַּאי אָמַר בֵּין כָּךְ וּבֵין כָּךְ תּוֹחֵב בְּשִׁפּוּד אוֹ בְּסַכִּין וְנוֹטְלָן. אַתְיָא דְּרַבִּי לָעֶזֶר בֶּן תַּדַּאי כְּרַבִּי שִׁמְעוֹן דְּתַנֵּי לֹא יָגוּר אָדָם אֶת הַכִּיסֵא וְאֶת הַמִּיטָּה וְאֶת הַקַּתֵּידְרָה מִפְּנֵי שֶׁהוּא עוֹשֶׂה חָרִיץ. רַבִּי שִׁמְעוֹן מַתִּיר. רַבָּא בְּשֵׁם רַב הוּנָא רַבִּי חַנָּיי בְּשֵׁם רַבִּי זְעִירָא רַבִּי יוֹסֵי בְּשֵׁם רַבִּי הִילָא מוֹדִין חֲכָמִים לְרַבִּי שִׁמְעוֹן בְּכִסֵּא שֶׁרַגְלָיו מְשׁוּקָּעוֹת בְּטִיט שֶׁמּוּתָּר לְטַלְטְלוֹ. וּכְמָה דְּתֵימַר מוּתָּר לְטַלְטְלוֹ. וְדִכְוָונָתָהּ מוּתָּר לְהַחֲזִירוֹ. אָמַר רַבִּי יוֹסֵי אוּף אֲנָן תַּנִּינָן נִיטְּלִין בְּשַׁבָּת. אָמַר רַבִּי יוֹסֵי בֵּי רַבִּי בּוּן דְּרַבִּי שִׁמְעוֹן הִיא. וְהָא תַּנִּינָן שְׁבִיעִית. אִית לָךְ מֵימַר שְׁבִיעִית דְּרַבִּי שִׁמְעוֹן. פָּתַר לָהּ שְׁבִיעִית דְּרַבִּי שִׁמְעוֹן מַתִּיר בִּסְפִיחֵי שְׁבִיעִית וְהָכָא אָמַר הָכֵן. אַף עַל גַּב דְּרַבִּי שִׁמְעוֹן מַתִּיר בִּסְפִיחֵי שְׁבִיעִית אִית לֵיהּ מִשּׁוּם קְדוּשַׁת שְׁבִיעִית. אוּף הָכָא אֵינוֹ חוֹשֵׁשׁ לֹא מִשּׁוּם שְׁבִיעִית וְלֹא מִשּׁוּם קְדוּשַׁת שְׁבִיעִית.

It was stated[167]: "If unripe figs that one hid in *ṭevel*[168] or a flat pita that one hid in glowing charcoal[169] were partially uncovered they may be taken on the Sabbath, otherwise they may not be taken on the Sabbath[170]. Rebbi Eleazar ben Taddeus[171] said, in either case he pushes in a spear or a knife and lifts them out[172]." The statement of Rebbi Eleazar ben Taddeus turns out following Rebbi Simeon, as we have stated[173]: "One should not drag[174] a chair, or a bed, or an easy chair because one makes a groove, but Rebbi Simeon permits it." Rebbi Abba in the name of Rav Huna, Rebbi Haggai in the name of Rebbi Zeïra, Rebbi Yose in the name of Rebbi Illaï: The Sages admit to Rebbi Simeon that a chair whose legs are stuck in mud one is permitted to move[175]. And just as you say that one is permitted to move it, so one is permitted to bring it back. Rebbi Yose said, we also have stated[176]: "They may be taken on the Sabbath." Rebbi Yose ben Rebbi Abun said, that is from Rebbi Simeon. But we have stated[177]: "The Sabbatical year!" Can you say that "the Sabbatical year" follows Rebbi Simeon? Explain "the Sabbatical year!" For Rebbi Simeon permits the aftergrowth of the Sabbatical year, and here he says so? Even though Rebbi Simeon permits aftergrowth of the Sabbatical year, he still holds it subject to the holiness of the Sabbatical year[178]. Here also, he worries neither about the Sabbatical year nor about the holiness of the Sabbatical year!

167   Also quoted in Babli *Eruvin* 77a, *Sabbath* 123a. The opinion of R. Eleazar ben Taddeus is not found in *Eruvin*.

168   Since *ṭevel*, produce from which no heave was taken, may not be consumed on the Sabbath, it may not be moved on the Sabbath. (Cf. *Peah*, Chapter 1, Note 303. The Babli reads תבן, "straw"; cf. יפה ענים on *Šabbat* 123a.) The figs are covered by grain to hasten the ripening process.

169   As Rashi points out in the Babli, the charcoal was glowing Friday evening at the start of the Sabbath but now it is cold. Otherwise, moving the coals would increase the flow of oxygen to the coals and stir the fire; this would be a transgression of a Biblical commandment and R. Simeon could not permit it. Since the coals could not be moved when Sabbath started, they cannot be moved during the entire Sabbath.

170   If the desired piece is not visible, one must intentionally move the material serving as cover, and this is forbidden. But if some pieces are uncovered, they may be taken; *ṭevel* or coals fall into the void by gravity, not by intentional moving.

171   A Tanna of whom only this *baraita* is known.

172   If one uses a knife, he has the intention only to move what is permitted; in contrast, if one has to remove the cover to get to the figs, he would have to move things which he is forbidden to move. Rebbi Simeon always holds that unintended side effects of an action are not forbidden on the Sabbath since only מלאכת מחשבת "deliberate action" (*Ex.* 35:33) is forbidden.

173   A slightly different version appears in Babli *Šabbat* 22a (and 5 other places); a shorter version is in Tosephta *Yom Ṭov* 2:18.

174   On a dirt floor or outside. In the Babli, the meaning is made clearer: "One may drag ... if he does not intend to make a groove." In practical terms, this means that one may not drag the chair on the ground if the resulting groove is of any use.

175   In this case, the groove will disappear by itself in the soft mud; it was not "made" since it has no permanence.

176   In our Mishnah. (The language is slightly different from that of the Mishnah; it is influenced by Mishnah *Šabbat* 17:1: "All vessels may be taken on the Sabbath.")

177   Again in the Mishnah. The problem is that R. Simeon declares in Mishnah *Ševiït* 9:1 that "all aftergrowth of the Sabbatical year is permitted except for that of cabbage," because the aftergrowth is not usually harvested. This means that aftergrowth may be traded and unlike food harvested in the Sabbatical year, it does not have to be disposed of once there is no more food for the wild animals on the fields. Since any growth of the hidden turnips and radishes can be compared to aftergrowth, there is

no way one could possibly worry about the growth in the Sabbatical year, according to R. Simeon. If one cannot worry, then it would be superfluous for R. Simeon to mention that one does not have to worry and he cannot be the author of the Mishnah.

Babli *Pesaḥim* 51b and a few Mishnah sources have R. Simeon stating that "all aftergrowth of the Sabbatical year is forbidden except for that of cabbage." This reading contradicts the

position of the Yerushalmi and will be discussed in Mishnah *Ševiït* 9:1.

178   The Biblical precept is that the produce of the Sabbatical year is to be eaten by man or animal (*Lev.* 25.6) but may not be used for industrial purposes, nor may it be left to decay. Holdover turnips and radishes from the previous year may be used for industrial purposes in the Sabbatical year.

זָרַע שְׁנֵי מִינִין בְּבִקְעָה שְׁנֵי מִינִין בְּחוֹרָבָה שְׁנֵי מִינִין וְחִלְּקָן גָּדֵר. רִבִּי יוֹחָנָן אָמַר פָּטוּר. רִבִּי שִׁמְעוֹן בֶּן לָקִישׁ אָמַר חַיָּב. מוֹדֶה רִבִּי שִׁמְעוֹן בֶּן לָקִישׁ בְּזוֹרֵעַ עַל גַּבֵּי הַיָּם עַל גַּבֵּי פִּיטְרָא עַל גַּבֵּי סְלָעִים עַל גַּבֵּי טְרָשִׁים שֶׁהוּא פָטוּר. מוֹדֶה רִבִּי שִׁמְעוֹן בֶּן לָקִישׁ בְּזוֹרֵעַ עַל מְנָת לְהַתְקִין גָּדֵר שֶׁהוּא פָטוּר. אָמַר רִבִּי בָּא קַרְתָּגִינָיָא מוֹדֶה רִבִּי שִׁמְעוֹן בֶּן לָקִישׁ לְעִנְיַין שַׁבָּת עַד שֶׁתָּנוּחַ. מַתְנִיתִין פְּלִיגָא עַל רִבִּי יוֹחָנָן הַזּוֹרֵעַ חִיטָה וּשְׂעוֹרָה כְּאַחַת הֲרֵי זֶה כִּלְאַיִם. פָּתַר לָהּ בִּנְתוּנִים בְּתוֹךְ שִׁשָּׁה עַל שִׁשָּׁה. דְּאָמַר רִבִּי יוֹחָנָן אֵינוֹ חַיָּב עַד שֶׁיְּהוּ שִׁשָּׁה עַל שִׁשָּׁה מוּקְרָחִין בְּתוֹךְ שְׂדֵה תְבוּאָה אוֹ מוּקָפִּין גָּדֵר.

One sowed two kinds in a valley[179], two kinds in a dry spot[180], or two kinds that he separated[181] by a fence. Rebbi Joḥanan said, he is free from sanction[182], Rebbi Simeon ben Laqish said, he is guilty[183]. Rebbi Simeon ben Laqish agrees that one who sows on the sea[184], on a stone[185], on a rock, on hard stones cannot be sanctioned[186]. Rebbi Simeon ben Laqish agrees that one who sows with the intention of erecting a fence[187] cannot be sanctioned. Rebbi Abba from Carthage said, Rebbi Simeon ben Laqish agrees that on the Sabbath it must come to rest[188]. Our Mishnah disagrees

with Rebbi Johanan: "If someone sows wheat and barley together, that is
kilaim[189]." He explains it, if they are put inside a six[190] [hand-breadths] by
six [hand-breadths] spot, since Rebbi Johanan said, he is not guilty unless
there is a bare spot of six by six inside a grain field[191] or enclosed by a
fence[192].

179   "Valley" is a technical term for an agricultural area not accessible by a public road.

180   In the context of agriculture, חורבה is derivate of חָרֵב I "to be dry, unfit for agriculture," not from חָרֵב II "to be ruined."

181   Only after they started growing.

182   פטור denotes an action that, while forbidden, is not punishable.

183   He can be found guilty in court for violating the prohibition of *kilaim*.

184   The "sea" is a stone tub in the building of the olive press in which the harvested olives are stored before pressing, cf. Mishnah *Baba Batra* 4:5. However, it is possible that "sea" here really means "lake" (since Hebrew ים means both sea and lake, as in ים כנרת "Lake Genezareth,") and one excludes hydroponics from the rules of *kilaim*. This is the meaning of Tosephta *Kilaim* 1:14: "If one sows seeds that grow on swamps, on dunes, he is guilty. But on rocks and on a water canal, he cannot be sanctioned."

185   Greek πέτρα "rock by the sea, rocky peak". "On a *petra* or on a rock" expresses the same thing in two languages.

186   One has to assume that there is a thin layer of earth on the stone, otherwise nothing would grow. But if the layer is thin, roots cannot spread and the kinds cannot mix.

187   Before he started sowing, even if he erected the fence only afterwards. Since sowing vegetables on either side of a fence is permitted, sowing with the intention of putting up a fence is forbidden but not sanctionable. This contrasts with the next statement about R. Simeon ben Laqish's position.

188   On the Sabbath, moving something from a private to the public domain or vice versa is a desecration. Moving is defined as 1) taking up, 2) changing its place, and 3) putting down. R. Johanan is quoted in Tractate *Šabbat* 1:1 (fol. 2b) that this is punishable only if all three actions have been completed. (This means that if one

takes up something in the house, carries it outside and delivers it running to a relay of runners who never stop before the end of the Sabbath, he it is not punishable.) R. Simeon ben Laqish agrees that, even if one had the intention of putting the object down on the Sabbath, a punishable action did not occur as long as the piece had not been put down and come to rest.

189   There are no qualifications in the Mishnah.

190   Since the measure is given by a number in the masculine, it must refer to hand-breadths (טפחים). A square of six by six cubits would be noted as שש על שש.

191   The minimal distances required for two adjacent fields of different crops are detailed in Mishnah 2:11; they are different for grains and vegetables. Rebbi Johanan asserts that infringing on these minimal distances is sinful but not punishable unless the grain field contains at least a surface area of one square cubit bare of the main crop. Then anything sown there is a punishable transgression, but an unavoidable occasional strange seed among the seed grain does not cause a punishable offense.

192   If inside a grain field one separates any area, even less that a square cubit, by erecting a fence, sowing any two kinds there is punishable since the minimal distances have not been observed.

בְּהָדָא רִבִּי יוּדָה אוֹמֵר אֵינוֹ כִּלְאַיִם. אָמַר רִבִּי זְעִירָא רִבִּי יוּדָה כְּדַעְתֵּיהּ. דְּרִבִּי יוּדָה אָמַר בְּשָׂדֶה יָרֶק טְפַח. אָמַר רִבִּי יוֹסֵי מָאן דְּבָעֵי מַקְשְׁיָה עַל הָדָא דְּרִבִּי זְעִירָא יְלִיף הָדָא דְּרִבִּי יוּדָה מִן דְּרַבָּנִין. כְּמָה דְּרַבָּנִין אָמְרִין בְּאִיסּוּר בֵּית רוֹבַע לִלְקוֹת שִׁשָּׁה עַל שִׁשָּׁה. כֵּן רִבִּי יוּדָה אָמַר בְּאִיסּוּר שִׁשָּׁה עַל שִׁשָּׁה לִלְקוֹת טֶפַח. וְהָתַנֵּי רִבִּי יוּדָה מַתִּיר. וְקַשְׁיָיא מָה טַעֲמָא דְּרִבִּי שִׁמְעוֹן בֶּן לָקִישׁ. מִכֵּיוָן שֶׁהוֹצִיא מִתּוֹךְ יָדוֹ לְזֶרַע חַיָּיב. וְהָא תַנִּינָן רִבִּי יוּדָה אוֹמֵר אֵינוֹ כִּלְאַיִם. פָּתַר לָהּ עַד שָׁעָה שֶׁתָּנוּחַ. וְהָתַנֵּי רִבִּי יוּדָה מַתִּיר לֹא אֲפִילוּ נָחָה רִבִּי יוּדָה מַתִּיר. אָמַר רִבִּי הִילָא רִבִּי שִׁמְעוֹן בֶּן לָקִישׁ כְּדַעְתֵּיהּ. דְּאָמַר רִבִּי שִׁמְעוֹן בֶּן לָקִישׁ בְּשֵׁם חִזְקִיָּה רֹאשׁ תּוֹר מְחוֹרְבָּה מוּתָּר. מֵעַתָּה אֲפִילוּ שְׁנֵי חִטִּין וּשְׂעוֹרָה. וְכֵן הִיא וְהָתַנִּינָן עַד שֶׁיִּהְיוּ שְׁנֵי חִטִּין וּשְׂעוֹרָה אוֹ חִטָּה אַחַת וּשְׁנֵי שְׂעוֹרִין אוֹ חִטָּה

אַחַת וּשְׂעוֹרָה וְכוּסֶּמֶת. פְּתָרֵי לָהּ חִיטָה מִכָּן וְחִיטָה מִכָּן (fol. 27c) מִכָּן גֶּדֶר מִכָּן
וְגֶדֶר מִכָּן וּשְׂעוֹרָה חֲבוּשָׁה בָאֶמְצַע. אָמַר רִבִּי מַתַּנְיָה הָדָא דְּתֵימַר שֶׁאֵין שָׁם
חוֹרְבָה אֲבָל יֵשׁ שָׁם חוֹרְבָה מוּתָּר.

Does Rebbi Judah say that in this case[193] it is not *kilaim*? Rebbi Zeïra
said, Rebbi Jehudah follows his own opinion, since Rebbi Jehudah said, in
the case of a vegetable field one hand-breadth[194]. Rebbi Yose said, he
who wants to question this statement of Rebbi Zeïra might deduce the
opinion of Rebbi Jehudah from that of the rabbis. Just as the rabbis say,
in the case of the prohibition of *bet rova'*[195] one needs six-by-six to whip,
so Rebbi Judah said in the case of the prohibition of six-by-six[196] that one
needs a hand-breadth to whip. But did we not state, Rebbi Judah permits
it[197]? Then it is difficult: what is the reason of Rebbi Simeon ben
Laqish[198]? Since he threw it out from his hand as seed, he is guilty[199].
But did we not state that "Rebbi Jehudah says, it is not *kilaim*?" Explain it,
until the moment that it comes to rest[200]. But was it not stated that Rebbi
Judah permits it? Even if it came to rest, Rebbi Jehudah permits it[201].
Rebbi Illaï said, Rebbi Simeon ben Laqish follows his own opinion, since
Rebbi Simeon ben Laqish said in the name of Hizqiah: A vertex[202] from
a dry spot is permitted. Then it also should be thus in the case of two
wheat grains and one of barley[203]? That is correct. But did we not state,
"unless there are two wheat kernels and one barley kernel, or one wheat
kernel and two barley kernels, or one each of wheat, barley, and spelt?"
Explain it if there is a grain of wheat on each side, a fence on each side,
and the grain of barley caught in the middle[204]. Rebbi Mattaniah said,
that is only if there is no dry spot, but if there is a dry spot there, it is
permitted[205].

193 The case indicated by R. Johanan, that there was a bald spot of six-by-six in a field, and another kind was planted there. Does R. Jehudah accept this as *kilaim* or not?

194 In Mishnah 3:3. If one has vegetables planted in orderly rows and he desires to plant different vegetables in different rows, R. Jehudah requires that the rows be separated by "a foot width," which is the same as a hand-breadth.

195 The area in which a quarter *kab*, or one twenty-fourth of a *seah*, can be sown. Since the *bet seah* is standardized as 2500 square cubits, the *bet rova‘* is 104.1$\bar{6}$ square cubits. A square of area of a *bet rova‘* has edge length 10.20621 cubits. It is explained in Mishnah 2:11 that two fields of different kinds of grain have to be separated by a fallow *bet rova‘*. However, an infringement of this rule is not necessarily punishable in court by whipping since more narrow criteria apply in criminal cases where the rule of R. Johanan holds as explained in the previous paragraph.

196 In the same Mishnah 2:11 it is explained that the required space between two beds of different vegetables is only 36 square cubits. This is the criterion of what is permitted outright but R. Jehudah holds that a criminal infraction only occurs if the linear distance between two rows of vegetables is less than a hand-breadth.

197 A *baraita* which parallels the Mishnah states flatly that R. Jehudah permits this kind of sowing outright, not, as assumed here, forbidden but not punishable.

198 He declares any illegal sowing punishable.

199 Since the verse reads, "do not sow your field *kilaim*," the act of sowing is forbidden, not its consequence in the soil. This explains why one had to state earlier that in respect of the laws of Sabbath, even R. Simeon ben Laqish requires that the seed come to rest on the ground.

200 R. Simeon ben Laqish states his rule according to the rabbis. He will agree that R. Jehudah requires that the seeds actually fall to the ground, since it says "do not sow *your field kilaim*;" even if he had the intention of sowing *kilaim* but the wind carried the seeds away, there is no criminal act committed. Hence, in this interpretation intent alone cannot be the determining factor.

201 The previous interpretation is contradicted; R. Simeon ben Laqish

only expresses his opinion according to the rules of the rabbis, not at all following R. Jehudah.

202 ראש תור "ox head, trapezoid, vertex" describes the configuration in which two fields are not parallel but are at an angle to each other, so that a vertex of one field touches the other field in the middle of a side. (Musaphia wants to derive the expression from the Greek adjective τορός, ά, όν "sharp, piercing," but probably it means ראש תור, "head of the line.") It is spelled out in Mishnah 3:3 that in this case, no minimal distance has to be observed since the fields appear distinct by their neat geometrical form. Ḥizqiah adds that even if one of the fields does not have a regular shape, e. g., if it ends in a dry spot, if in the neighborhood of the other field it forms a triangle with a vertex touching the other field the leniency of ראש תור applies.

Cf. the discussion of ראש תור in Chapter 2, Note 101.

203 The one barley grain should be ראש תור between the row of two wheat grains!

204 In this case, the configuration of ראש תור is excluded since the field represented by the barley grain enters the field represented by the wheat grains, and the minimal distances of separation will have to be observed. If the three grains are sown together in a straight line, the separation requirements are certainly violated.

205 Since Ḥizqiah admitted a ראש תור pointing to a dry spot, if the three kernels were sown in the neighborhood of a dry spot, R. Jehudah will recognize the barley grain as ראש תור But in other circumstances, ראש תור is only admitted for rectangular fields. In the absence of a dry spot, the barley grain cannot possibly count as ראש תור and is forbidden.

כל סאה פרק שני

משנה א: (fol. 27c) כָּל־סְאָה שֶׁיֵּשׁ בָּהּ רוֹבַע זֶרַע מִמִּין אַחֵר יְמָעֵט. רְבִּי יוֹסֵי אוֹמֵר יָבוֹר בֵּין מִמִּין אֶחָד בֵּין מִשְּׁנֵי מִינִין. רְבִּי שִׁמְעוֹן אוֹמֵר לֹא אָמְרוּ אֶלָּא מִמִּין אֶחָד. וַחֲכָמִים אוֹמְרִים כָּל־שֶׁהוּא כִלְאַיִם בִּסְאָה מִצְטָרֵף לְרוֹבַע.

Mishnah 1: Every *seah* that contains a quarter[1] of seeds from another kind should be diminished[2]; Rebbi Yose says, he must pick it out, whether it be from one kind or from two kinds[3]. Rebbi Simeon said, they said it only for one kind, but the Sages say, everything that is *kilaim* with the *seah* counts together for a quarter.

1 A quarter *qab* which is $1/24$ *seah*. Here one speaks about seeds. Since seeds usually come mixed with weeds and other seeds, some sowing of different kinds together is unavoidable. In *Baba Batra*, Mishnah 6:2, up to a quarter *qab* of foreign material in a *seah* of grain is established as the standard accepted in any trading contract unless otherwise specified. From the Biblical requirement, it is only necessary that the farmer have no intention of sowing the undesirable seeds with his crop. But in order to avoid the appearance of intentional *kilaim*, the rabbis gave an upper limit

also of one *qab* in 24 before requiring action.

2 Some of the foreign seeds have to be taken out, so that the entire contamination is brought below the limit. R. Yose requires that once one has started cleaning up the seeds, all foreign seeds should be eliminated.

3 Kinds of weeds and contamination with other crops. Rebbi Simeon says that each kind of contamination has its own limit, Rebbi Yose says that all those are counted together which are *kilaim* in any way; the Sages say that everything which is *kilaim* with the main crop is added together. So if

wheat seed is contaminated with barley, *zewanin*, and peas, and together they are more than one in 24 but any two of them together are less than that amount, then for the Sages one does not have to act since *zewanin* are not *kilaim* with wheat, but R. Yose would require that the entire seed grain be sifted since *zewanin* are *kilaim* with peas.

הלכה א: אֲנָן תַּנִּינָן שֶׁיֵּשׁ בָּהּ. אִית תַּנָּיֵי תַּנֵּי שֶׁנָּפַל לְתוֹכָהּ. אָמַר רבִּי מָנָא מָאן דְּאָמַר שֶׁיֵּשׁ בָּהּ אֶחָד מֵעֶשְׂרִים וְאַרְבָּעָה. מָאן דְּאָמַר שֶׁנָּפַל לְתוֹכָהּ אֶחָד מֵעֶשְׂרִים וַחֲמִשָּׁה. אָמַר רבִּי יוֹסֵי בֵּי רבִּי בּוּן בֵּין כְּמָאן דְּאָמַר שֶׁיֵּשׁ בָּהּ בֵּין כְּמָאן דְּאָמַר שֶׁנָּפַל לְתוֹכָהּ אֶחָד מֵעֶשְׂרִים וְאַרְבָּעָה. מִי כְדוֹן מָאן דְּאָמַר שֶׁיֵּשׁ בָּהּ בִּתְלוּשׁ. מָאן דְּאָמַר שֶׁנָּפַל לְתוֹכָהּ בִּמְחוּבָּר.

Halakhah 1: We have stated, "which contains." Some Tannaïm state[5], "into which fell." Rebbi Mana said, he who says "which contains" means one in 24[6], he who says "into which fell" means one in 25[7]. Rebbi Yose ben Rebbi Abun said, both for him who says "which contains" and for him who says "into which fell," it means one in 24[8]. How is that? "Which contains," if it is cut, "into which fell," if it is standing[9].

5   In a parallel *baraita*. The Tosephta (*Kilaim* 1:16) has the same language as the Mishnah.

6   If 24 quarters contain 1 quarter of foreign material, that is 1 in 24 of the total, 1 in 23 of useful grain.

7   Since a *seah* is 24 quarters, if an additional quarter fell in, then the total adds up to 25 quarters, and we have 1 quarter of rejects in 24 good ones.

8   Since this is the commercial standard, there is no reason to change the standard here. This is also the position of the Babli, *Baba Batra* 94a.

9   The first case deals with grain bought as grain. In the second case, the contamination of the seed grain is detected after sowing, when the grain already is growing. This proves that the standard applies also to growing produce, not only to seed grain, supporting the position of Tosaphot (*Baba Batra* 94a, *s. v.* סאה) against R. Samuel ben Meïr.

מַה נָן קַיָּימִין. אִם בְּמִתְכַּוֵּין לְזֶרַע אֲפִילוּ חִטָּה אַחַת אָסוּר. אִם לְעָרֵב אֲפִילוּ
כָּל־שֶׁהוּא אָסוּר לְעָרֵב. רִבִּי יַעֲקֹב בַּר אָחָא אַבָּא בַּר חִייָא בְשֵׁם רַב הַבּוֹרֵר
צְרוֹרוֹת מִתּוֹךְ כֵּירִיוֹ שֶׁל חֲבֵירוֹ חַייָב לְהַעֲמִיד לוֹ חִיטִּין יָפוֹת תַּחְתֵּיהֶן. אָמַר
רִבִּי יוֹסֵי זֹאת אוֹמֶרֶת שֶׁהוּא אָסוּר לְעָרֵב. אִם אָמַר אַתְּ שֶׁמּוּתָּר לְעָרֵב לָמָּה לִי
חִיטִּין יָפוֹת תַּחְתֵּיהֶן.

What are we talking about[10]? If he intended it for seed[11] then even one grain of wheat is forbidden. If to mix in[12], it is forbidden to mix. Rebbi Jacob bar Aḥa, Abba bar Ḥiyya[13] in the name of Rav: He who takes out impurities from his neighbor's heap has to give him good grain in their stead[14]. Rebbi Yose said, this implies that one is forbidden to mix in; if you say that one is permitted to mix them back in, why require good grain instead?

10   How can the case of the Mishnah appear legitimate?

11   If he recognizes the impurities in the seeds and intends to grow them for themselves, then it is *kilaim* and the standards of Mishnah 1:9 apply. The implication is that the yield from these impurities may not be selected out after harvest and sold separately, because that would make the entire harvest *kilaim* and forbidden.

12   Since no farmer may sell grain with more than the permitted impurities, at harvest time he and the grain wholesalers will see to it that the impurities are not more than 1 in 24. In order to get illegitimate seed, he would have to mix in impurities; this is forbidden and we are not concerned here with intentional lawbreakers.

13   In the parallel in the Babli (*Baba Batra* 93b), the name is Rav Abba bar Ḥiyya from Ktesiphon (on the Tigris) in the name of Rabba (Rav Abba bar Naḥmani, of the third generation after Rav.) In any case, it is clear that the author here is Babylonian and not identical with Rebbi Abba bar Rebbi Ḥiyya bar Abba.

14   Since the neighbor could have sold his grain with the impurities under a standard contract, the one who sifts the grain causes him to lose the value of the volume of the impurities he

removes. [The word צרור translated
here as "impurity" is not the biblical
word (I. money pouch, II. flintstone),
but is connected with Hebrew צרר II (to

be hostile), more directly with the corresponding Arabic صَرّ (to be noxious,
pernicious).]

מָכַר לוֹ חִיטִין יָפוֹת וְנִמְצְאוּ בְּרוּרוֹת. מַהוּ שֶׁיְּנַכֶּה לוֹ דְּמֵי אוֹתוֹ הָרוֹבַע.
מִילֵּיהוֹן דְּרַבָּנִין אָמְרִין אֵינוֹ מְנַכֶּה לוֹ דְּמֵי אוֹתוֹ הָרוֹבַע. דְּאָמַר רִבִּי יַעֲקֹב בַּר
אָחָא אַבָּא בַּר חִייָא בְּשֵׁם רַב הַבּוֹרֵר צְרוֹרוֹת מִתּוֹךְ חִיטִין שֶׁל חֲבֵירוֹ חַיָּיב
לְהַעֲמִיד לוֹ חִיטִין יָפוֹת תַּחְתֵּיהֶן. בֵּירֵר רוֹבַע אֶחָד וּמֶחֱצָה מַהוּ שֶׁיְּנַכֶּה לוֹ דְּמֵי
אוֹתוֹ הָרוֹבַע. רִבִּי חִינְנָא וְרִבִּי מָנָא. רִבִּי חִינְנָא אָמַר מְנַכֶּה לוֹ. רִבִּי מָנָא אָמַר
אֵינוֹ מְנַכֶּה לוֹ. דְּהוּא אָמַר לֵיהּ אִילּוּ יְהַבְתּוּן לִי הֲוֵינָא צְרַר לוֹן בְּסִירְקִי מַה
דַּהֲוָה זְבוּנָה חֲמֵי הוּא זְבָן.

If one sold wheat as [standard] good quality and it turned out to be
sifted, may he take out the value of that quarter[15]? The words of the
rabbis say that he cannot take out the value of that quarter, for Rebbi
Jacob bar Aḥa, Abba bar Ḥiyya said in the name of Rav: He who takes
out impurities from his neighbor's grain has to give him good grain in
their stead. If he[16] removed one and one half quarters, may he take out
the value of that quarter? Rebbi Ḥinena and Rebbi Mana. Rebbi Ḥinena
said, he takes it out[17]. Rebbi Mana said, he does not take it out, because
he can say to him, if you had returned it to me, I would have bundled it
for the Saracens who would have bought it; what that buyer sees is what
he buys[18].

15   Since the standard contract
allows for impurities, may the seller
deliver only the $^{23}/_{24}$ seah of seeds
guaranteed by the standard contract or
does the buyer have to pay extra for

the good grain he receives instead of
the standard impurities? This problem
belongs to *Baba Batra*; it is treated
here because the problem comes up
naturally from the statement of Rav

which belongs to *Baba Batra.*

16   The buyer noticed that the grain he bought contained more impurities than those allowed by the standard contract. He has the right to return the merchandise for a full refund (Mishnah *Baba Batra* 6:2). He chose instead to clean up the grain. Everybody agrees that he does not have to pay for the volume of the half quarter which exceeds the standard. The question is, since he started cleaning and took all impurities out, does he pay only for the

remaining grain or may the seller insist to be paid also for the quarter of impurities which would have been legal and is reflected in the price charged for a unit of volume?

17   He pays only for the sifted grain, at the rate of standard grain.

18   Saracens, Arab traders without fixed residence, buy and sell "as is", without warranties. The buyer would have inspected the grain before buying and offered a price based on his inspection.

אֶלָּא כְשֶׁנִּתְעָרְבוּ דֶּרֶךְ מַכְנֵס. וְהָא תַנִּינָן בֶּאֱמֶת אָמְרוּ זֵירְעוֹנֵי גִינָּה שֶׁאֵינָן
נֶאֱכָלִין מִצְטָרְפִין אֶחָד מֵעֶשְׂרִים וְאַרְבָּעָה. בְּנוֹפֵל לְבֵית סְאָה. וְתַנֵּי עֲלָהּ בְּגִין[19]
קַב וַחֲצִי קַב. וְאֶחָד מֵעֶשְׂרִים וְאַרְבָּעָה לַחֲצִי קַב טָב הוּא כְּלוּם. עַד כָּאן חָשׁוּ
לְמַרְאִית הָעַיִן. מִיכָּן וְאֵילַךְ לֹא חָשׁוּ לְמַרְאִית הָעַיִן.

But when they were mixed up during transport[20]. But did we not state[21]: "In truth, they said that garden seeds which are not eaten add up together for one in 24 when they fall on a *bet seah.*" And we stated on that, this is a *qab* or half a *qab*[22]. What could one do with the twenty-fourth part of half a *qab*[23]? For that, they are worried because of the bad impression[24]. They were not worried because of the bad impression from a lesser amount.

19   In Halakhah 2, בְּגִין

20   After the interruption by the theme from *Baba Batra*, one returns to the original question and answers that

more than one in 24 may contaminate the harvest by accidents during transport from the field to the storage facility. From here on to the end of the Halakhah one deals exclusively with seed grain.

21 Next Mishnah, dealing with the details of the rule of Mishnah 1. "Garden seeds which are not eaten" are seeds of kitchen greens which in themselves are not food. They are usually very small and the resulting contamination will be more than 1 in 24 at harvest time. Any statement introduced by "in truth" is unquestioned practice.

22 The standard of maximal contamination for seeds of kitchen greens is a *qab* for the larger seeds and half a *qab* for the smaller seeds. Since these seeds are so much smaller than seed grain, they cannot be 1 in 24 of the full *seah* since that would overwhelm all the grain, but only 1 in 144 or 1 in 288, depending on the size of the seeds. The standard is a contamination of 1 in 24 of the harvest, not the seeds.

23 About 0.09 liter.

24 The entire rule is rabbinical so people should not think the contamination was intentional. One forbids only accidental weeds or strange admixtures which exceed the commercial standard.

יְמָעֵט. בְּאֵי זֶה צַד הוּא מְמָעֵט אוֹ פּוֹחֵת מִן הָרוֹבַע אוֹ מוֹסִיף עַל הַסְּאָה. לֹא כֵן אָמַר רִבִּי יוֹחָנָן רִבִּי אַבָּהוּ בְּשֵׁם רִבִּי יוֹחָנָן כָּל־הָאִיסּוּרִין שֶׁרִיבָּה עֲלֵיהֶן שׁוֹגֵג מוּתָּר מֵזִיד אָסוּר. תַּמָּן אַתְּ מַרְבֶּה לְבַטֵּל אִיסּוּר תּוֹרָה. בְּרַם הָכָא אַתְּ מַרְבֶּה לְבַטֵּל מִפְּנֵי מַרְאִית עַיִן.

"Should be diminished[25]." How does he diminish? Either he removes from the quarter or he adds to the *seah*. But did not Rebbi Joḥanan say (Rebbi Abbahu in the name of Rebbi Joḥanan), for all prohibitions, if one added in error, it is permitted, if intentionally, it is forbidden[26]. There you add to annul a Torah prohibition, but here you add because of the bad impression.

25 Quote from the Mishnah.

26 For example, if some dairy product fell into a meat dish, if the meat dish by volume is more than 60 times that of the dairy product, the contamination is declared minimal and the dish is permitted to be eaten. (This is the rabbinical standard.) If the ratio

was less at the time of the accident but later some more of the meat dish was added inadvertently or unknowingly, the measure at the end is determining. But if the addition was made in the knowledge of the prior prohibited contamination, then the measure at the time of the accident is determining and the later addition must be disregarded. How can the Mishnah here permit intentionally adding to legalize the prohibited mixture?

רְבִּי יוֹסֵי (fol. 27d) אוֹמֵר יְבָרֵר. מַה טַעְמָא דְּרְבִּי יוֹסֵי. מִכֵּיוָן שֶׁהִתְחִיל בְּרוֹבַע צָרִיךְ לְהַשְׁלִים אֶת כָּל־הָרוֹבַע. מוֹדֵי רִבִּי יוֹסֵי שֶׁאִם שָׁם הָיָה שָׁם פָּחוֹת מִן הָרוֹבַע מִשָּׁעָה רִאשׁוֹנָה אֵינוֹ זָקוּק לוֹ. הֵיךְ עֲבִידָה. הָיָה שָׁם אֶחָד מִשְּׁנֵי מִינִין בּוֹרֵר מִין אֶחָד וְדַיוֹ אוֹ צָרִיךְ לָבוּר אֶת כּוּלוֹ.

"Rebbi Yose says, he must pick it out." What is the reason of Rebbi Yose? Because he started with the quarter, he must finish the entire quarter. Rebbi Yose agrees that if there was less than a quarter when he started, he does not need to attend to it[27]. How is that done? If there was a quarter composed of two kinds, does he pick out one kind and that is sufficient, or does he have to pick out everything[28]?

27   If he started to remove the foreign seeds when he did not have to he may stop in the middle, before removing all of it. We do not say that the fact of his removing impurities shows that he is bothered by their presence and, therefore, any sowing would be intentional sowing of *kilaim* and forbidden.

28   The question is not answered since practice does not follow R. Yose.

רִבִּי שִׁמְעוֹן אוֹמֵר לֹא אָמְרוּ אֶלָּא מִין אֶחָד מִין שְׁנֵי מִינִין לֹא. עַד הֵיכָן. עַד רוּבָּה שֶׁל סְאָה. חָזַר וְהוֹסִיף חֶזְרָה הַתְּבוּאָה לְהֵיתֵירָהּ. כְּמָה דְּרִבִּי שִׁמְעוֹן אָמַר אֵין שְׁנֵי מִינִין מִצְטָרְפִין לְאִסוּר. כֵּן הוּא אָמַר הָכָא אֵין שְׁנֵי מִינִין מִצְטָרְפִין לְהֵיתֵר. הֵיךְ עֲבִידָה. הָיָה שָׁם עֶשְׂרִים וּשְׁנַיִם רְבָעִים וּמֶחֱצָה שֶׁל חִיטִים וַחֲצִי

רוֹבַע שְׂעוֹרִין וְנָפַל לְתוֹכוֹ פָּחוֹת מֵרוֹבַע עֲדָשִׁים אֲפִילוּ כֵּן אֵין שְׁנֵי מִינִין מִצְטָרְפִין לְהֶתֵּיר.

"Rebbi Simeon said, they said it only for one kind," not two kinds. How far? Up to the greater part of the *seah*[29]. If he added afterwards, the grain returned to its permitted status[30]. Just as Rebbi Simeon said, two kinds do not combine for prohibition, so he says that they do not combine for permission. How is that done? If there were twenty-three and one half quarters of wheat and half a quarter of barley, and into that fell less than a quarter of lentils[31], even so the two kinds would not combine for permission.

29   As long as the total of foreign seeds is less than 50% and each single contamination is less than 1 in 24, the seeds remain permitted. (Up to 12 contaminants of maximum volume are possible.)

30   R. Simeon accepts the earlier interpretation that adding of the main seedstock makes everything permitted again.

31   It is supposed here that the

volume of the lentils is at least $^{23.5}/_{24}$ = 0.9792 quarters but less than one quarter. In that case, if the lentils were judged against the combined volume into which they fell, it would be less than 1 in 24. But since the barley is not counted at all, the contamination is at least a full twenty-fourth of the volume of wheat grain and the mixture is forbidden.

(fol. 27c) **מִשְׁנָה ב:** בְּמֶה דְּבָרִים אֲמוּרִים תְּבוּאָה בִּתְבוּאָה וְקִטְנִית בְּקִטְנִית תְּבוּאָה בְּקִטְנִית וְקִטְנִית בִּתְבוּאָה. בָּאֱמֶת אָמְרוּ זֵירְעוֹנֵי גִינָּה שֶׁאֵינָן נֶאֱכָלִין מִצְטָרְפִין אֶחָד מֵעֶשְׂרִים וְאַרְבָּעָה בְּנוֹפֵל לְבֵית סְאָה. אָמַר רִבִּי שִׁמְעוֹן כְּשֵׁם

שֶׁאָמְרוּ לְהַחֲמִיר אַף לְהָקֵל. הַפִּשְׁתָּן בִּתְבוּאָה מִצְטָרֶפֶת אֶחָד מֵעֶשְׂרִים וְאַרְבָּעָה בְּנוֹפֵל לְבֵית סְאָה.

Mishnah 2: When is this said[32]? Grain with grain, legumes with legumes, grain with legumes, legumes with grain[33]. In truth, they said that garden seeds which are not eaten add up together for one in 24 when they fall on a *bet seah*. Rebbi Simeon said, that which they said to restrict, they also said for leniency. Flax seeds[34] in grain add up together for one in 24 when they fall on a *bet seah*.

32   That a quarter *kab* of foreign seeds makes a *seah* of seeds unusable.

33   All these need approximately one *seah* for a field of 2500 square cubits (a *bet seah*). But if seeds need appreciably less than that, the amount which makes seed grain unusable is 1 in 24 of the amount used for the contaminant. It was already explained in Halakhah 1, Note 22, that for kitchen greens whose seeds are not edible, the amount of seed used for one *bet seah* is only one sixth or one twelfth of a *seah*. The amount of these seeds sufficient to make a *seah* of seed grain unusable is $1/24$ of either a *qab* or half a *qab*.

34   This is explained in the Halakhah, text following Note 44.

(fol. 27d) **הלכה ב**: וְתַנֵּי עֲלָהּ כְּגוֹן שְׁלֹשָׁה קַבִּין וְאַרְבָּעַת קַבִּין הָא קַבַּיִים אֶחָד מֵעֶשְׂרִים וְאַרְבַּע. בֶּאֱמֶת אָמַר רִבִּי לָעֶזָר כָּל־מָקוֹם שֶׁשָּׁנוּ בֶּאֱמֶת הֲלָכָה לְמֹשֶׁה מִסִּינַי. וְתַנֵּי עֲלָהּ כְּגוֹן קַב וַחֲצִי קַב. הָא קַבַּיִים בְּרוֹבַע. הָכָא אַתְּ אָמַר קַבַּיִים בְּרוֹבַע. וְהָכָא אַתְּ אָמַר קַבַּיִים אֶחָד מֵעֶשְׂרִים וְאַרְבָּעָה. רִבִּי זְעִירָא וְרִבִּי אָבוּנָא בְשֵׁם רַב הוּנָא. חַד אָמַר תִּשְׁעָה קַבִּין וְחָרָנָה אָמַר עַד שְׁמוֹנָה.

Halakhah 2: We have stated about this, "three or four *qab*," hence two *qab* go by one in 24[35]. "In truth;" Rebbi Eleazar said that every place where they stated "in truth," it is practice going back to Moses on Mount Sinai.[36] And we stated about this, for example a *qab* or half a *qab*[37].

Hence, two *qab* go by a quarter. Here you say, two *qab* by a quarter, and there you say, two *qab* by one in 24. Rebbi Zeïra and Rebbi Abun in the name of Rav Huna; one says, nine *qab*, the other says, eight *qab*[38].

35   The rule of the first Mishnah covers all seeds which need between four and three *qab*, i. e., between $\frac{2}{3}$ and $1/2$ *seah* per *bet seah*. Hence, seeds that need less volume are considered kitchen vegetables and go by $1/24$. In slightly different language, this is explicitly stated in Tosephta *Kilaim* 1:16.

36   This principle is also accepted in the Babli, *Baba Meẓia'* 60a.

37   Halakhah 1, Notes 22–24..

38   If one only needs 2 *qab*, $1/3$ *seah*, for seeding, then the contamination is by a quarter, as expressed in the Tosephta, not for 1 *seah* but for $1^1/3$ to $1^1/2$ *seah* (8 to 9 *qab*). For smaller quantities, one goes by the $1/24$ rule; the two statements are complementary, not contradictory.

תִּשְׁעָה וַעֲשָׂרָה מַהוּ שֶׁיִּצְטָרְפוּ. אִיתָא חֲמֵי תִּשְׁעָה וּשְׁלֹשָׁה מִצְטָרְפִין. תִּשְׁעָה וַעֲשָׂרָה לֹא כָּל־שֶׁכֵּן.

Do nine and ten join together[39]? Come and see, nine and three come together, so much more nine and ten!

39   It was stated that seeds which need 8 or 9 *qab* are contaminated by a quarter of seeds which need two *qab*. Does this rule extend to seeds that need 10 *qab*? The answer is, since 3 *qab* go by the quarter rule, and 9 *qab* go by the same rule, the difference between 9 and 10, a mere 10% from above, is not large enough to change the rules.

Hence, if seeds which need 9 or 10 *qab* contaminate seeds which need one *seah*, they are measured by $9/24 = 3/8$ *qab* per *seah* of the main seed. In the opinion of R. Simson, if half of the contamination is by seeds which need 9 *qab*, this half is measured by $9/24$, the other half by $10/24$. (Maimonides does not mention these rules in his Code.)

רְבִּי אָבִין וְרְבִּי חֲנִינָה תַּרְוֵיהוֹן אָמְרִין סְאָה חוֹלֶקֶת בֵּינֵיהוֹן וְרוֹבַע סְאָה אָסוּר
בִּשְׁלֹשֶׁת קַבִּין וְרוֹבַע שְׁלוֹשֶׁת קַבִּין אָסוּר בִּסְאָה. רוֹבַע סְעָה אָסוּר בְּתִשְׁעָה
קַבִּין וְרוֹבַע תִּשְׁעַת קַבִּין אֲסוּרִין בִּסְאָה. שְׁלוֹשֶׁת רְבָעִים שֶׁל פִּשְׁתָּן אוֹסְרִין
בִּסְאָה. הֵיךְ עֲבִידָא. אֲתַר דְּזְרַע רוֹבַע דְּחִיטִּין זְרַע תְּלָתָא רוֹבְעִין דְּכִיתָּן.

Rebbi Abin and Rebbi Ḥanina both say that a split *seah* is between
them[40]. A quarter *seah* may prohibit three *qab*[41], and a quarter of three
qab may prohibit a *seah*[42]. A quarter *seah* may prohibit nine *qab*[43], and a
quarter of nine *qab* may prohibit a *seah*[44]. Three quarters of flax seed
prohibit a *seah*. How is this? On a plot on which one sows one quarter of
wheat, one sows three quarters of flax seed.

40   The difference between the
Sages and Rebbi Simeon is whether
wheat grain is the standard by which
everything is measured or whether
every kind has its own standard. The
examples given all go by the rule of R.
Simeon.

41   A quarter *seah* is half of three
qab, not 1 in 24. The explanation is
that if some plants need 6 *seah* of seeds
for a *bet seah*, then they contaminate in
$6 \div 24 = .25$ *seah*, even if the main seed

is one that needs only half a *seah* to
cover a *bet seah*. All other examples
follow the same pattern and are really
superfluous.

42   Here the contaminating seed
needs 18 *qab* = 3 *seah* per *bet seah*.

43   The contaminating seed needs 4
seah per *bet seah*, the contaminated
seed is standard.

44   The contaminating seed needs 6
seah per *bet seah*.

(fol. 27c) **מִשְׁנָה ג:** קָיְתָה שָׂדֵהוּ זְרוּעָה חִטִּים וְנִמְלַךְ לְזוֹרְעָהּ שְׂעוֹרִים יַמְתִּין לָהּ
עַד שֶׁיַּתְלִיעַ וְיוֹפֶךְ וְאַחַר כָּךְ יִזְרַע. אִם צָמְחָה לֹא יֹאמַר אֶזְרַע וְאַחַר כָּךְ אוֹפֵךְ.

אֶלָּא הוֹפֵךְ וְאַחַר כָּךְ זוֹרֵעַ. כַּמָּה יְהִי חָרוּשׁ כְּתַלְמֵי הָרְבִיעָה. אַבָּא שָׁאוּל אוֹמֵר
כְּדֵי שֶׁלֹּא יְשַׁיֵּיר רוֹבַע לְבֵית סְאָה.

Mishnah 3: If his field was sown with wheat and he changes his mind to sow it with barley, he should wait until it gets wormy[45], then[46] he turns it over[46] and after that he may sow. If it is sprouting, he should not say, I am going to sow and then turn it over, but he turns it over and then he sows. How deep does he have to plough? Like furrows for the rainy season[48]. Abba Shaul says, so that there should not remain a quarter for a *bet seah*[49].

---

45   The seeds, or the grain fallen to the ground, are seen to attract worms. If the grains are from the harvest in the dry season, one has to wait longer. Maimonides (*Kilaim* 2:13) applies the Mishnah only to freshly sown grain, but the mention of dry fields in the Halakhah does not seem to support that position.

46   R. Abraham ben David (Maimonides, *Kilaim* 2:13) interprets ויופך to mean "or he turns it over." His argument seems to be that waiting until the worms eat the grain is not mentioned in the later parts of the Mishnah.

47   I. e., he ploughs the seeds or the sprouting wheat under.

48   Coarse furrows made so that the autumn rains should penetrate the soil, not the second ploughing of straight and parallel furrows for sowing.

49   He may leave $1/_{24}$ of the surface area unploughed, following the rule established in the first two Mishnaiot.

(fol. 27d) **הלכה ג**: עַד כַּמָּה הִיא מַזְרַעַת עַד כְּדֵי שֶׁתְּהֵא בָּאָרֶץ שְׁלֹשָׁה יָמִים
בִּמְקוֹם הַטִּינָא אֲבָל לֹא בִּמְקוֹם הַגָּרִיד בְּעָנְיָא הִיא יוֹתֵר. וְתַגֵּי כֵּן מִקְצָת הַיּוֹם
כְּכוּלּוֹ בִּמְקוֹם הַטִּינָא וְאִם צָמְחָה וְהוֹרִיד בְּהֶמְתּוֹ לְתוֹכָהּ וְקִירְטְמָתָהּ הֲרֵי זוּ
מוּתֶּרֶת.

"[50]How long can it remain sprouting? That it should remain in the
ground three days in a muddy place, but in a dry place it needs more
[time]." We have stated on that: Part of the day is like an entire day[51] in
a muddy place, and if it started growing but he brought his animals and
they browsed it clean[52] it is permitted.

50   Tosephta *Kilaim* 1:16.

51   In the Babli, that is an accepted
principle in most cases, not only in this

particular case.

52   Biblical Hebrew ברסם, Arabic
قرصم , قرصم .

מַה טַעְמָא דְּרַבָּנִין. מִכֵּיוָן שֶׁנָּתַן דַּעְתּוֹ לַחֲרוֹשׁ אֲפִילוּ לֹא רָצָף. אַבָּא שָׁאוּל
אוֹמֵר אֵין מְחַיְּיבִין אוֹתוֹ לִהְיוֹת חוֹרֵשׁ דַּק אֶלָּא כְּתַלְמֵי הָרְבִיעָה. רַבָּן שִׁמְעוֹן
בֶּן גַּמְלִיאֵל אוֹמֵר זָנָב הַסּוּס הָיְתָה נִקְרֵאת כְּדֵי שֶׁיְּהֵא סוֹף עֲפָרָהּ שֶׁל זוֹ נוֹגֵעַ
בְּזוֹ וְסוֹף עֲפָרָהּ שֶׁל זוֹ נוֹגֵעַ בְּזוֹ. מַה טַעְמָא דְּאַבָּא שָׁאוּל מִכֵּיוָן שֶׁהִתְחִיל בְּרוֹבַע
דַּיּוֹ. מַה אַבָּא שָׁאוּל כְּרִבִּי יוֹסֵי כְּרַבָּנִין הוּא דְּרַבָּנִין אָמְרֵי מִכֵּיוָן שֶׁנָּתַן דַּעְתּוֹ
לַחֲרוֹשׁ אֲפִילוּ לֹא רָצָף. אַבָּא שָׁאוּל אוֹמֵר מִכֵּיוָן שֶׁהִתְחִיל דַּעְתּוֹ בְּרוֹבַע דַּיּוֹ.
רִבִּי יוֹסֵי אוֹמֵר צָרִיךְ לְהַשְׁלִים אֶת כָּל־הָרוֹבַע.

What is the reason of the rabbis? Because he intended to plough, even
if it is not covering[53].   Abba Shaul said, "one does not oblige him to
plough finely, only like the furrows of the rainy season. Rabban Simeon
ben Gamliel says, it used to be called 'horse tail,' so that the end of dust of
any one furrow touch that of the next one."[54] What is the reason of Abba
Shaul? Since he started, it is enough up to a quarter[55]. Does Abba Shaul
hold with Rebbi Yose? He is with the rabbis, for the rabbis said, because
he intended to plough, even if it is not covering. Abba Shaul says, because
he started intentionally to plough, it is enough up to a quarter. Rebbi
Yose said, he must finish that entire quarter[57].

53   In modern Hebrew, one would translate "not continuous." However, the image here is that of a floor tiling that does not cover the entire floor (a stone-covered floor is רצפה, "tiled.")

54   Tosephta *Kilaim* 1:17. The position of Abba Shaul here is that of the anonymous Tanna there. Rabban Gamliel notes that one has to plough only half the ground; the other half then is covered by the earth thrown up in ploughing.

55   A quarter *qab* of contamination is acceptable by Mishnah 1.

56   Since R. Yose held in Mishnah 1

that once you start to sift, you have to finish sifting, here he must hold that once you start ploughing you have to finish ploughing. Abba Shaul only objects to Rabban Gamliel's interpretation of the position of the rabbis, that one may leave half of the field unploughed as long as the rest is covered by overturned ground. He holds that less than a quarter *bet kab* (104.167 square cubits) per *bet seah* (2500 square cubits) may remain unploughed but, in principle, his position is that of the rabbis.

(fol. 27c) **משנה ד**: זְרוּעָה וְנִמְלַךְ לִיטְעָהּ לֹא יֹאמַר אֶטַּע וְאַחַר כָּךְ אוֹפֵךְ. אֶלָּא הוֹפֵךְ וְאַחַר כָּךְ נוֹטֵעַ. נְטוּעָה וְנִמְלַךְ לְזוֹרְעָהּ לֹא יֹאמַר אֶזְרַע וְאַחַר כָּךְ אַשָּׁרֵשׁ. אֶלָּא מְשָׁרֵשׁ וְאַחַר כָּךְ זוֹרֵעַ. אִם רָצָה גוֹמֵם עַד פָּחוֹת מִטֶּפַח וְזוֹרֵעַ וְאַחַר כָּךְ מְשָׁרֵשׁ.

Mishnah 4: [If the field was] sown and he decided to plant, he should not say, I shall plant and then I shall turn over, but he shall turn over and then plant. [If it was] planted and he decided to sow, he should not say, I shall sow and then I shall uproot, but he should uproot and then sow. If he wishes, he cuts down to less than a hand–breadth, plants, and then takes out the roots.

(fol. 27d) **הלכה ד**: תַּנֵּי סוֹמְכִין עוֹמְרִין בְּצַד גְּפָנִים. אָמַר רבִּי יוֹסֵי הָדָא אֲמְרָה שֶׁאָסוּר לִיטַע בְּצַד קָמָה יְבֵישָׁה גֶּפֶן יָבֵשׁ. מַהוּ לִזְרַע בְּצַד גְּפָנִים יְבֵשׁוֹת. נִשְׁמְעִינָהּ מִן הָדָא גֶּפֶן שֶׁיָּבְשָׁה אֲסוּרָה וְאֵינָהּ מְקַדֶּשֶׁת. וְאָמַר רבִּי לַעְזָר דְּרבִּי מֵאִיר הִיא דְּרבִּי מֵאִיר אָמַר אֲפִילוּ גֶּפֶן הַצֶּמֶר אָסוּר וְאֵינוֹ מְקַדֵּשׁ.

Halakhah 4: It was stated: One may put sheaves next[57] to dried-up vines. Rabbi Yose said, that means that one may not plant a dry vine next to dry standing grain[58]. May one sow next to dry vines? Let us hear from the following[59]: "A dried-up vine is forbidden but does not sanctify[60]." Rabbi Eleazar said, this is the opinion of Rabbi Meïr, since Rabbi Meïr said[59], even cotton[61] is forbidden but does not sanctify.

57   The meaning of סומך "to lean on" was studied by J. N. Epstein, מבוא לנוסח המשנה, 2nd ed. (Jerusalem/Tel Aviv 1964) p. 446.

58   Since only sheaves, bundles of cut grain, may lean on dry vines, it follows that dry, standing grain must be separated even from dried-up vines.

59   Mishnah 7:2.

60   *Deut.* 22:9 declares that grain growing in a vineyard sanctifies both the grain and the vines. This means that it acquires a status similar to sacrifices; all profane use of it is forbidden. But since it is not a sacrifice, it has to be burned. In tractate *Kilaim*, "sanctified" means "it must be destroyed by burning." *Kilaim* not involving vines are sinful but not sanctified.

61   Determination of Maimonides and R. Simson, see Mishnah 7:2. Cotton is not food but cottonseed is.

הָדָא אֲמְרָה שֶׁמוּתָּר לִזְרַע בְּצַד גְּפָנִים יְבֵשׁוֹת וְאִם צָמְחוּ מוּתָּרוֹת לְשֶׁעָבַר וַאֲסוּרוֹת לְעָתִיד לָבוֹא. כְּהָדָא רבִּי שִׁמְעוֹן בֶּן יְהוּדָה גַּם כְּרָמַיָּיא אֲמַר לְאָרִיסֵיהּ פּוּק זְרַע. מִן דִּזְרַע צָמְחִין. אֲמַר לֵיהּ פּוּק חֲצוֹד. מִן דַּחֲצַד אַרְטְבוּן אֲמַר לֵיהּ פּוּק סְמַךְ. רבִּי זְעִירָא בָּעֵי עַד כְּדוֹן כְּרבִּי שִׁמְעוֹן בֶּן יְהוּדָה שֶׁהוּא אָמַר לְדַעַת גְּמוּרָה. שְׁאָר בְּנֵי אָדָם שֶׁאֵינָן אוֹמְרִין לְדַעַת גְּמוּרָה. חָזַר וְאָמַר אֲפִילוּ רבִּי שִׁמְעוֹן בֶּן יְהוּדָה אֵינוֹ אוֹסֵר אֶלָּא מִפְּנֵי מַרְאִית הָעַיִן.

That[62] means that one may sow next to dry vines and "when they produce leaves again, the past is permitted and the future prohibited.[63]" Like that of Rebbi Simeon ben Jehudah[64] who cut down his vines and told his sharecropper, go and sow! After he had sown, they[65] started to grow leaves. He said to him, go and cut[66]! After he had cut, they rotted; he said to him, go and sow close up[67]. Rebbi Zeïra asked: Is that only for Rebbi Simeon ben Jehudah, for he said it in full knowledge; what about common people who do not have full knowledge? He returned and said, even Rebbi Simeon ben Jehudah said it only because of the bad appearance[68].

62   The last sentence of the Mishnah, that one may cut down, plant, and only then uproot.

63   Tosephta *Kilaim* 1:18. There is added: "If he reduced the stumps to less than a hand-breadth in height, but when he returned he found new vine leaves over the growing grain, the past is permitted but the future forbidden. He removes any kind he chooses and keeps the other kind."

64   A Tanna of the Fifth generation, student of R. Simeon ben Iohai, from Kefar Akko.

65   The stumps of the vines.

66   Harvest the unripe grain for fodder.

67   Rotting vine stumps are certain not to produce fruit; they can be disregarded.

68   As long as the vine stumps do not produce blossoms, the prohibition is purely rabbinical and not universally accepted.

(fol. 27c) **משנה ח:** הָיְתָה שָׂדֵהוּ זְרוּעָה קַנְּבֹס אוֹ לוּף לֹא יְהֵא זוֹרֵעַ וּבָא עַל גַּבֵּיהֶן שֶׁאֵינָן עוֹשִׂין אֶלָּא לִשְׁלֹשׁ שָׁנִים.

תְּבוּאָה שֶׁעָלוּ בָהּ סְפִיחֵי אַסְטִיס וְכֵן מְקוֹם הַגְּרָנוֹת שֶׁעָלוּ בָּהֶן מִינִין הַרְבֵּה
וְכֵן תִּלְתָּן שֶׁהֶעֱלָת מִינֵי עֲשָׂבִים אֵין מְחַיְּבִין אוֹתוֹ לְנַכֵּשׁ. וְאִם נִיכֵּשׁ אוֹ כִיסֵּחַ
אוֹמֵר לוֹ עֲקוֹר אֶת הַכֹּל חוּץ מִמִּין אֶחָד.

Mishnah 5: If his field was sown with hemp or arum[69], one should not
sow on it because they produce all of three years[70].

One is not required to weed grain in which there appeared aftergrowth
of indigo, or the threshing floor on which many kinds are appearing[71], or
fenugreek in which grasses appeared[72]. But if he weeded or cut, one says
to him, uproot everything except one kind.

69   See *Peah*, Mishnah 6:9.
70   The next paragraph (next Mishnah in the Mishnah part of the
Yerushalmi) will explain that, in
general, aftergrowth may be disregarded. But if a kind is known to
produce commercially valuable aftergrowth, even if no new seeds were
provided, then this is to be considered
as a continued crop and any other kind
on that field is *kilaim*. A field of hemp
cannot be used for another crop the

next year unless all hemp roots are
taken out.
71   They never were sown; this is
growth from the grains which remained from the different kinds that
were threshed at that floor.
72   Fenugreek is an expensive spice
and medicinal plant with tiny seeds
which is cultivated only on plots the
size of a garden bed. Since the plants
are of such high value, weeding has to
be done with the utmost care.

(fol. 27d) **הלכה ח:** תַּנֵּי יְהוֹשֻׁעַ הָיוּ מְלַקְּטִין עֲשָׂבִים מִכָּל־מָקוֹם חוּץ מִשָּׂדֵה
תִּלְתָּן. רְבִּי יַעֲקֹב בַּר אָחָא בְּשֵׁם רְבִּי יִצְחָק בַּר נַחְמָן כְּשֶׁזְרָעָהּ לְעָמִיר הִיא
מַתְנִיתָא. וְהָא תַנִּינָן וְכֵן תִּלְתָּן שֶׁהֶעֱלָת מִינֵי עֲשָׂבִים אֵין מְחַיְּבִין אוֹתוֹ לְנַכֵּשׁ.
רְבִּי יַעֲקֹב בַּר אָחָא בְּשֵׁם גַּרְמֵיהּ כְּשֶׁהֶעֱלָת לְזֶרַע. אָמַר רְבִּי יוֹסֵי וְכִי לֹא בָא
יְהוֹשֻׁעַ לְפָרֵשׁ אֶלָּא לְעוֹבְרֵי עֲבֵירָה. עָבַר עֲבֵירָה אָסוּר מִשּׁוּם גֵּזֶל. לֹא עָבַר
עֲבֵירָה מוּתָּר מִשּׁוּם גֵּזֶל הֲוֵי לֹא שַׁנְיָא הִיא שֶׁזְּרָעָהּ לְזֶרַע הִיא שֶׁזְּרָעָהּ לְעָמִיר.

וְהָתַנִינָן וְכֵן תִּלְתָּן שֶׁהֶעֱלָה מִינֵי עֲשָׂבִים אֵין מְחַיְּיבִין אוֹתוֹ לְנַכֵּשׁ. אִם אֶת

שֶׁדַּעְתּוֹ עֲלֵיהֶן יְחַיְּיבוּ אוֹתוֹ לְנַכֵּשׁ. רִבִּי אָחָא בְּשֵׁם רִבִּי מֵיָשָׁא רוֹצֶה הֵן בָּהֶן

כְּאִלּוּ עֲקוּרִין וּמוּנָחִין לְפָנָיו. מֵעַתָּה מָצָא כִלְאַיִם בְּכֶרֶם יְהוּ אֲסוּרִין מִשּׁוּם גֵּזֶל

שֶׁהוּא רוֹצֶה בָּהֶן כְּאִלּוּ עֲקוּרִין וּמוּנָחִין לְפָנָיו. רִבִּי יוֹסֵי לֹא אָמַר כֵּן אֶלָּא

שֶׁבְּסוֹף הוּא רוֹצֶה בָּהֶן כְּאִלּוּ עֲקוּרִין וּמוּנָחִין לְפָנָיו. מֵעַתָּה מָצָא כִלְאַיִם בְּכֶרֶם

יְהוּ אֲסוּרִין מִשּׁוּם גֵּזֶל שֶׁבְּסוֹף הוּא רוֹצֶה בָּהֶם כְּאִלּוּ עֲקוּרִין וּמוּנָחִין לְפָנָיו. כָּאן

יֵשׁ לוֹ עִם מִי לְהִכָּנֵס. וְכָאן אֵין לוֹ עִם מִי לְהִכָּנֵס. רַב נַחְמָן אָמַר רִבִּי מָנָא בָּעֵי

הַגַּע עַצְמָךְ שֶׁהָיְתָה שָׁם שָׂדֶה אַחֶרֶת שֶׁל תִּלְתָּן סְמוּכָה לוֹ הֲרֵי יֵשׁ לוֹ עִם מִי

לְהִכָּנֵס. מִילֵּיהוֹן דְּרַבָּנִין פְּלִיגִין. דְּאָמַר רִבִּי זְרִיקָן בְּשֵׁם דְּבֵית רִבִּי יַנַּאי

כָּל־הַסְּפִיחִין מוּתָּרִין חוּץ מִן הָעֲלִין בִּשְׂדֵה בוּר בִּשְׂדֵה נִיר בִּשְׂדֵה כֶרֶם וְאָמַר

חוּץ מִשְׂדֵה תִלְתָּן שֶׁזְּרָעָן לְזֶרַע. אָמַר רִבִּי יוֹסֵי מִילְתָא דְּרִבִּי יוֹחָנָן מְסַיְּיעָא לִי.

מַעֲשֶׂה בְּאֶחָד שֶׁלָּקַח יְרָקָה שֶׁל גִּינָה מִן הַגּוֹי. אָתָא וְשָׁאַל לְרִבִּי יוֹחָנָן. אָמַר

לֵיהּ צֵא וּלְקוֹט וּלְפִי הַשּׁוּק מְכוֹר. הוֹתִיב רִבִּי אַבָּהוּ קוֹמֵי רִבִּי יוֹחָנָן וְהָא תַנִינָן

וְכֵן מָקוֹם הַגְּרָנוֹת שֶׁעָלוּ בָהֶן מִינִין הַרְבֵּה. אָמַר לֵיהּ מְקוֹמוֹ מוֹכִיחַ עֲלֵיהּ שֶׁאֵינוֹ

רוֹצֶא בְקִיּוּמוֹ. וְיִתְבֵּינָא כָּאן אָסוּר מִשּׁוּם גֵּזֶל וְכָאן מוּתָּר מִשּׁוּם גֵּזֶל. הֵיךְ אַתְּ

מְשִׁיבֵּנִי דָּבָר שֶׁהוּא אָסוּר מִשּׁוּם גֵּזֶל עִם דָּבָר שֶׁהוּא מוּתָּר מִשּׁוּם גֵּזֶל. כְּהַהִיא

דְּאָמַר רִבִּי אִימִי עֲשִׁירִים הָיוּ בִתְשׁוּבוֹת. אוֹ יִיבָּא כְּהַהִיא דְּאָמַר רִבִּי נְסָא

כְּאִינַשׁ דְּאִית בֵּיהּ תְּרֵין טַעֲמִין וְהוּא מֵתִיב חַד מִינְהוֹן.

Halakhah 5: It is a condition of Joshua[73] that one may collect grasses everywhere except in a field of fenugreek. Rebbi Jacob bar Aḥa in the name of Rebbi Isaac bar Naḥman: The Mishnah deals with him who sowed for sheaves[74]. But did we not state: "One is not required to weed ... fenugreek in which grasses appeared?[75]" Rebbi Jacob bar Aḥa in his own name: "When it grew for seeds[76]." Rebbi Yose said, did Joshua come only to help sinners[77]? If he committed a sin, it is forbidden as robbery[78], if he did not commit a sin it is permitted in respect to robbery. Hence, there is no difference whether he sowed for seeds or for sheaves[79]. But did we not state: "One is not required to weed . . . fenugreek in which grasses appeared?" If he intends to use the grasses, one should oblige him to weed! Rebbi Aḥa in the name of Rebbi Miasha: He would be happy if they were torn out and lying before him[80]. Rebbi Yose did not say so, but in the end he approves that they should be torn out and lying before him[81]. But then, if somebody found *kilaim* in a vineyard, they should be forbidden as robbery since in the end he desires that they should be torn out and lie before him[82]! There[83], he has the means to bring it in, here he does not have the means to bring it in. Rav Naḥman said that Rebbi Mana asked: Think about it, if he had another field of fenugreek close by, then he has the means to bring it in[84]! The words of the rabbis disagree, since Rebbi Zeriqan said in the name of the House of Yannai: All aftergrowth is forbidden except for that which appears[85] on a fallow field, a field ready to be ploughed under, and a vineyard. He should have added, except for a field of fenugreek sown for the production of seeds! Rebbi Yose said, the words of Rebbi Johanan support me. It happened that somebody bought a garden plot of vegetables from a Gentile. He came and asked Rebbi Johanan[86], who said to him, go, harvest and sell at the going rate. Rebbi Abbahu objected before Rebbi Johanan: Did we not state: "or the threshing place on which many kinds are appearing?[87]" He said to him, that place proves that he does not want them to exist. Could he not have answered, the one is like robbery, the other is permitted with respect to robbery[88]? How can you object based on a scenario where it is forbidden as robbery to a decision in a case which is permitted with respect to robbery? It is as Rebbi Immi said, they were rich in answers[89]. Or it is as Rebbi Nasa said, like a person who has two reasons but he answers only with one of them.

73   Ten categories of public use of private property are attributed to Biblical Joshua, attached as liens to the original distribution of land. The detailed discussion is in Babli *Baba Qama* 80b-82a, Yerushalmi *Baba Batra* 5:1 (fol. 15a). Since tractate *Neziqin* in the Yerushalmi was edited differently from the rest of the Yerushalmi, the text in Yerushalmi *Baba Batra* is similar to but not identical with the text here.

74   He wants to sell fenugreek in retail bundles. The buyer can take the seeds as spices anytime he wants and in the meantime store the plants so they will not be lost.

75   If he grows fenugreek for sheaves, he can use the grasses to bind the "sheaves" that in reality are thin bundles. The grasses represent a value for him, he wants them there, and the entire crop should be forbidden because of *kilaim*! How can the Mishnah exempt fenugreek from an obligation of weeding?

76   In that case, the grasses are really weeds; they have to be removed before the fenugreek seeds can be taken from the stems.

77   Why should one be prohibited to take grasses which should have been weeded and whose existence is proof of a sin?

78   Since then the owner is deprived of his material to bind the bundles.

79   The Mishnah applies to both cases.

80   The entire previous argument is untenable; even if the farmer wants to sell fenugreek in small bundles, the loss because of weeds is much larger than the money or work saved in having the grasses ready as material for tying the bundles.

81   Even if he wants to sell fenugreek in bundles, he would first have to remove the grasses from the field before harvesting, in order to have a commercially usable crop. However, he wants to preserve them in order to use them to tie the bundles; he does not want to have them treated as ownerless.

82   There will be some use for weeds, probably as animal feed, even though without the religious obligation

of *kilaim* the vineyard must be weeded to ensure the growth of the grapes.

83 The grape harvest is transported in vessels; fenugreek bundles are tied on the "field," i. e., the garden plot.

84 The grasses growing on one plot could also be used for the other.

85 Vocalization and translation follows the parallel in *Baba Batra*, עולין instead of העלין "the leaves." There, the three cases are explained. The farmer does not care what grows on a fallow field in crop rotation since everything will be ploughed under. If a field is being prepared for ploughing, after-growth will be removed as a matter of priority. In a vineyard, the owner will take out everything that could make his vineyard forbidden.

86 What to do with the various garden vegetables growing together on the plot in violation of the laws of *kilaim*. R. Johanan told him that only the future growth is forbidden. Any possible profit from plants growing as *kilaim* is forbidden, but in this case, the buyer could sell the undesirable produce for the full market value.

87 The objection is not really from this sentence but from the following, that if one starts to remove some of the growth, everything has to be treated as *kilaim* except for one (main) crop. How could R. Johanan declare all kinds of produce equally acceptable?

88 This is R. Yose's argument, that R. Johanan would support his position. If taking grasses from the field of fenugreek were not a case of robbery, the situation here would be totally different since the garden plot certainly is protected by the laws of robbery against taking from it (not grasses, but valuable produce!)

89 The argument of R. Yose is invalid; if there are several possible explanations, one is never required to give an exhaustive list of all possibilities; one satisfactory answer is enough.

(fol. 27c) **משנה ו:** הָרוֹצֶה לַעֲשׂוֹת שָׂדֵהוּ מֵשַׁר מֵשַׁר מִכָּל מִין בֵּית שַׁמַּאי אוֹמְרִים שְׁלֹשָׁה תְלָמִין שֶׁל פָּתִיחַ. וּבֵית הִלֵּל אוֹמְרִים מְלוֹא הָעוֹל הַשָּׁרוֹנִי. וּקְרוֹבִים דִּבְרֵי אֵלּוּ לִהְיוֹת כְּדִבְרֵי אֵלּוּ.

Mishnah 6: If someone wants to make his field into separate garden beds[90] of different kinds, the House of Shammai say, three furrows of the ploughshare, and the House of Hillel say, the width of a Sharon yoke. Both criteria are close to one another[91].

90   Borrowed from Aramaic מישרא, parallel Arabic شَارَة "plant life". According to Maimonides in his Code (*Kilaim* 3:8), משר applies only to a rectangular garden bed that is not square. A square garden bed is called ערוגה if it is isolated and קרחת if it is part of a field. The latter assertion is difficult to accept, cf. Note 150. One might accept that קרחת applies to congruent rectangular patches but משר

to rectangular patches of differing sizes. This seems to be the position of R. Abraham ben David of Posquières.

91   According to Maimonides, the criterion is that of the minimal distance between beds. According to R. Isaac Simponti, the criterion is that of the minimal size of a garden bed, with only a minimal but orderly separation. The Halakhah can be interpreted both ways; this is the position of R. Simson.

(fol. 27d) **הלכה ו**: רְבִּי זְעִירָא רְבִּי לָעֶזֶר בְּשֵׁם רְבִּי חִיָּיה רוֹבָא עוֹשֶׂה שְׁתֵּי אַמּוֹת עַל שְׁתֵּי אַמּוֹת וּמֵיצַר וְהוֹלֵךְ אֲפִילוּ כָּל־שֶׁהוּא. אָמַר רְבִּי יוֹנָה הָדָא דְּתֵימַר בַּעֲשׂוּיָה מֵשָׁרִין מֵשָׁרִין אֲבָל בַּעֲשׂוּיָה מֵשָׁר אֶחָד לֹא בְדָא. וְאָתְיָא כַּיי דְּאָמַר רְבִּי יַנַּאי יָכִיל אֲנָא זָרַע חַקְלִי חַמְשִׁין מִינִין עֶשְׂרִין וַחֲמִשָּׁה מִיכָּא וְעֶשְׂרִין וַחֲמִשָּׁה מִיכָּא. אַף בִּשְׁתֵּי שׁוּרוֹת כֵּן. מֵעַתָּה אֲפִילוּ בֵּינוֹ לְבֵין חֲבֵירוֹ מוּתָּר. אַף בְּחוֹרְבָה (fol. 28a) כֵּן. אוֹ יַיבָּה כַּיי דְּאָמַר רֵישׁ לָקִישׁ בְּשֵׁם חִזְקִיָּה רֹאשׁ תּוֹר הַבָּא מֵחוֹרְבָה מוּתָּר. רְבִּי אוֹמֵר מַתְחִיל בֵּית רוֹבַע וּמֵיצַר וְהוֹלֵךְ עַד שְׁלֹשָׁה תְלָמִין שֶׁל פָּתִיחַ. וְלֵית לֵיהּ לְרְבִּי תְּבוּאָה בִתְבוּאָה בֵּית רוֹבַע. תַּמָּן בִּמְרוּבָּע וְכָאן בְּמֵישָׁר. וְלֵית לְרַבָּנִין מֵישָׁר. אָמַר רְבִּי יוּדָן סוֹף מֵישָׁר לְרְבִּי תְּחִילַת מֵשָׁר לְרַבָּנִין.

Halakhah 6: Rebbi Zeïra, Rebbi Eleazar, in the name of Rebbi Ḥiyya the Elder: He makes it two by two cubits, but decreases continuously to an arbitrarily small distance[92]. Rebbi Jonah said, that is, if it is subdivided into garden beds, but if all is one bed, it does not apply. This parallels what Rebbi Yannai said: I may sow my field[93] with fifty kinds, twenty-five here and twenty-five there; this is in two rows. If that is so, would it be permitted even between himself and his neighbor[94]? Or in a dry spot[95]? Then it parallels what Rebbi Simeon ben Laqish said in the name of Ḥizqiah: A vertex from a dry spot is permitted! Rebbi said, he starts with an area of *bet rova'* and narrows it down to three furrows of the ploughshare. Does Rebbi not accept that between grains one needs a *bet rova'*[96]? That is for a square field[97], here for a garden bed. Do the rabbis not recognize garden beds? Rebbi Yudan said, the minimal distance for Rebbi is the maximal distance for the rabbis[98].

92   The total area must be four square cubits, but the division into strips is left to the farmer. This interpretation seems required by the question of R. Eleazar in the next paragraph.

R. Simson thinks that somewhere there must be an empty space of two by two cubits, otherwise the border strips can be as narrow as one desires. Maimonides in his Commentary and *Hilkhot Kilaim* 4:6 explains: "He makes it two by two cubits, but the border can be minimal;" i. e., if the field is subdivided into garden beds, inside between any two beds must be 4 square cubits of fallow land. At the border of

the entire field, a border strip must be left empty. That strip has no minimal size (but presumably it must be wide enough to allow the farmer to walk there on his own property.) This interpretation takes מצר as a noun, "border strip," a word otherwise documented only in the Babli. The translation and R. Simson take the word as a verb, "to narrow," a usage that is required later in the statement of Rebbi. In addition, the phrase והולך עד "doing something continuously," is only used in conjunction with transitive verbs.

93   The standard field understood in all these Mishnaiot, a *bet seah* of 50

by 50 cubits. Rebbi Yannay splits the field into two strips, each of length 50 and width 25-ε cubits (ε being a small positive quantity) and reserving two cubits in length for each crop and its border.

94   This is the case of Mishnah 6.

95   This was discussed in Chapter 1, Halakhah 9 (Note 203), as a matter of dispute between Rebbi Johanan and R. Simeon ben Laqish.

96   Stated in Rebbi's own Mishnah 2:9; it is extremely rare to find Rebbi

accepting into the Mishnah anonymous opinions conflicting with his own basic positions.

97   Of a minimum size of 2500 square cubits.

98   For Rebbi, the width of three furrows is the lower limit of what is acceptable; for the rabbis, the width of three furrows is the upper limit of what is required. So everybody agrees that the separation by three furrows is acceptable under all circumstances.

רְבִּי לְעָזָר שָׁאַל הָיְתָה שָׂדֶה קְטַנָּה מַהוּ. נִשְׁמְעִינָהּ מִן הָדָא רְבִּי לְעָזָר בַּר שִׁמְעוֹן
אַבָּא יוֹסֵי בֶּן יוֹחָנָן אִישׁ יָנוֹחַ אָמַר בִּגְדוֹלָה חֲמִשִּׁים אַמּוֹת. וּבְקְטַנָּה עַל פִּי
רוּבָּהּ. מַה אִם אֵלּוּ שֶׁנָּתְנוּ שִׁיעוּר לִגְדוֹלָה לֹא נָתְנוּ שִׁיעוּר לִקְטַנָּה. חֲכָמִים
שֶׁלֹּא נָתְנוּ שִׁיעוּר לִגְדוֹלָה לֹא כָל־שֶׁכֵּן שֶׁלֹּא יִתְּנוּ שִׁיעוּר לִקְטַנָּה.

Rebbi Eleazar asked: What are the rules for a small field[99]? Let us hear from the following: "[100]Rebbi Eleazar ben Simeon: Abba Yose ben Johanan from Yanoah said for a large field 50 cubits, for a small field along most of it." Since those who specified a measure for a large field did not do so for a small one, the Sages who did not specify a measure for a large field certainly would not specify a measure for a small field.

99   Since for a standard field (50 by 50 cubits), the total area of the strips between the garden beds must be four square cubits, what is the required minimum for a field that does not contain the required 2500 square

cubits?

100   Parallel statements appear in Tosephta *Kilaim* 2:1, 2:4, about the border strips, or furrows, that are required between two fields, either in the situation of the preceding or the

present Mishnah. For fields longer than 50 cubits, they do not require that the separation of the fields, by empty strip or by planted flax, be longer than 50 cubits. (Probably, this means that in designating the border by one row of flax, one may not use a furrow longer than 50 cubits, in order to avoid commercially usable flax that would be

kilaim and make the field forbidden.) The statement about a small field is not in the Tosephta concerned only with fields having at least the standard size.

Abba Yose bar Joḥanan (Ḥanan) from Yanoaḥ in Upper Galilee, a Tanna of the fifth generation, was a student of R. Meïr and Abba Cohen Bar Dalaiah.

(fol. 27c) **משנה ז:** הָיָה רֹאשׁ תּוֹר חִטִּים וְנִכְנַס בְּתוֹךְ שֶׁל שְׂעוֹרִים מוּתָּר מִפְּנֵי שֶׁהוּא נִרְאֶה כְּסוֹף שָׂדֵהוּ. שֶׁלוֹ חִטִּים וְשֶׁל חֲבֵירוֹ מִין אַחֵר מוּתָּר לִסְמוֹךְ לוֹ מֵאוֹתוֹ הַמִּין. שֶׁלוֹ חִטִּים וְשֶׁל חֲבֵירוֹ חִטִּים מוּתָּר לִסְמוֹךְ לוֹ תֶּלֶם שֶׁל פִּשְׁתָּן וְלֹא תֶלֶם שֶׁל מִין אַחֵר. רַבִּי שִׁמְעוֹן אוֹמֵר אֶחָד זֶרַע פִּשְׁתָּן וְאֶחָד כָּל־הַמִּינִין. רַבִּי יוֹסֵי אוֹמֵר אַף בְּאֶמְצַע שָׂדֵהוּ מוּתָּר לִבְדּוֹק בְּתֶלֶם שֶׁל פִּשְׁתָּן.

Mishnah 7: A vertex of wheat[101] coming close[102] to a field of barley is permitted since it visibly is the end of its field. If someone's field was sown with wheat and that of his neighbor with another kind, he may have of that kind adjacent to it[103]. If both his and his neighbor's fields were growing wheat, it is permitted that he have one row of flax adjacent to his, but no other kind[104]. Rebbi Simeon says, either flax or any other kind[105]. Rebbi Yose says, even in the middle of his field he may test a row for flax[106].

101 See Chapter 1, Note 202. "Vertex" is the interpretation of

Maimonides, who translates תורי זהב (*Cant.* 1:11) not by "golden chains" but "golden triangular earrings," and ראש חור by "vertex of a triangle." R. Simson and R. Isaac Simponti explain that ראש חור really is a Hebrew/Aramaic hybrid and means "ox head", "trapezoid" as schematical approximation to the shape of an ox head. In the technical sense, ראש חור is applied to any trapezoidal or pentagonal field in which the furrows are not parallel, in particular if the last furrow in a field is not parallel to the other furrows and certainly not to the furrows in the adjacent field. The two explanations are probably identical; usually ראש חור is created if the outermost furrow of a field is not straight but approximately forms the legs of an obtuse triangle, with its vertex touching the other field. (In *Targum Yerushalmi* to *Ex.* 39:10, a direction is called טריגון τρίγωνον "triangle," meaning an arrowhead pointing in a direction. The identification of directions with triangular features is traditional.)

102   On the basis of both the usage of the Babli and Modern Hebrew, it would seem that one has to translate נכנס by: "enters into." This cannot be the meaning of the expression here because, at the end of the first paragraph of the Halakhah, a furrow

entering into another field is characterized by מובלעת "absorbed into." Hence, נכנס must mean: "coming closer than permitted by the separation rules but not actually entering the row of growing barley."

103   He may sow in his own field of the kind his neighbor grows and not separate it from his neighbor's crop by the distance required by the Mishnaiot of this Chapter but only by a minimal strip that would designate the border between two fields of separate owners.

104   Instead of having an empty strip as boundary marker, he may plant one row of flax to indicate the border. Since one row is much too little to serve as commercial crop, nobody will think that he is raising *kilaim*; everybody will know that this is a boundary marker.

105   Probably, this applies only to kinds routinely sown on fields, not garden beds, since for the latter one row may yield worthwhile produce.

106   While the grain is growing, he may test in a short row whether flax will grow there. Since everybody knows that such a small quantity can only be a test, not production for use, it never will look like *kilaim*.

(fol. 28a) **הלכה ז**: רֵישׁ לָקִישׁ בְּשֵׁם חִזְקִיָּה רֹאשׁ תּוֹר הַבָּא מֵחוֹרֶבָה מוּתָּר. אָמַר רִבִּי יוֹחָנָן לֹא שָׁנוּ אֶלָּא תּוֹר הָא רֹאשׁ תּוֹר הַבָּא מֵחוֹרֶבָה אָסוּר.

Halakhah 7: Rebbi Simeon ben Laqish in the name of Ḥizqiah: A vertex from a dry spot is permitted! Rebbi Joḥanan said, they stated only: "A vertex of wheat[107];" hence, a vertex that comes from a dry spot is forbidden.

107   Meaning the case of a well defined field, not an irregularly shaped plot resulting from sowing near a dry spot. (This paragraph may be used to support the interpretation by R. Simson and R. Isaac Simponti of ראש תור).

חִזְקִיָּה אָמַר מִי שֶׁיֶּשׁ לוֹ בֵּית רוֹבַע וְכָל־שֶׁהוּא. אוֹתוֹ כָּל־שֶׁהוּא זוֹרֵעַ לְתוֹכוֹ כָּל־מִין שֶׁיִּרְצֶה. אָמַר רִבִּי יוֹחָנָן אֵינוֹ זוֹרֵעַ לְתוֹכוֹ אֶלָּא מִין אֶחָד בִּלְבָד. אָמַר רִבִּי זְעִירָא מוֹדֶה רִבִּי יוֹחָנָן שֶׁאִם הִיא בֵּית רוֹבַע וּמֶחֱצָה שֶׁהוּא זוֹרֵעַ חֲצִי רוֹבַע מִכָּן וַחֲצִי רוֹבַע מִכָּן אוֹתוֹ חֲצִי רוֹבַע נִידוֹן לְכָאן וּלְכָאן. מַתְנִיתָא פְּלִיגָא עַל רִבִּי יוֹחָנָן הָיוּ לוֹ שָׂדוֹת אַחַת זְרוּעָה חִיטִּין וְאַחַת זְרוּעָה שְׂעוֹרִין מוּתָּר לְהָבִיא תֶּבֶן בֵּינְתַיִם וְלִזְרוֹעַ אַחַת חִיטָה וְאַחַת שְׂעוֹרָה מִפְּנֵי שֶׁהַחִיטִּין נִרְאוֹת בְּסוֹף שָׂדֵהוּ שֶׁל חִיטִּין וּשְׂעוֹרִין בְּסוֹף שָׂדֵהוּ שֶׁל שְׂעוֹרִין. מַה עָבַד לָהּ רִבִּי יוֹחָנָן. פָּתַר לָהּ כְּרִבִּי לִיעֶזֶר בֶּן יַעֲקֹב. דְרִבִּי אֱלִיעֶזֶר בֶּן יַעֲקֹב אָמַר אֲפִילוּ חִיטָה אַחַר חִיטָה נִכְנֶסֶת לְתוֹךְ שֶׁל שְׂעוֹרִין וּשְׂעוֹרָה אַחַר שְׂעוֹרָה נִכְנֶסֶת לְתוֹךְ חִיטִּין מוּתָּר. מִפְּנֵי שֶׁהַחִיטָה אַחַר חִיטָה נִכְנַס לְתוֹךְ שֶׁל שְׂעוֹרִין חִיטִים וּשְׂעוֹרָה אַחַר שְׂעוֹרָה נִכְנֶסֶת לְתוֹךְ שֶׁל שעורין. אֲבָל אִם הָיְתָה חִיטָה אַחַת מוּבְלַעַת לְתוֹךְ שֶׁל שְׂעוֹרָה אוֹ שְׂעוֹרָה אַחַת מוּבְלַעַת בְּשֶׁל חִיטִּין הֲרֵי זֶה אָסוּר.

Ḥizqiah said, if somebody has slightly more than a *bet rova'*, then in that excess he may sow anything he likes[108]. Rebbi Joḥanan said, he may sow in it only one kind. Rebbi Zeïra said, Rebbi Joḥanan agrees that if he had a *bet rova'* and a half, he may sow half a *bet rova'* from either side and the last half *bet rova'* is valid for both sides[109]. A *baraita* disagrees with Rebbi Joḥanan: "[110]If he had fields, one sown with wheat and the other sown with barley, he may bring straw[111] in between and sow one side[112] with wheat and the other with barley because the wheat looks like the end of the wheat field, and the barley like the end of the barley field." What does Rebbi Joḥanan do with that? He explains it[113] following Rebbi Eliezer ben Jacob, for Rebbi Eliezer ben Jacob said[114]: "Even if wheat after wheat comes close to barley[115], barley after barley comes close to wheat, it is permitted." For wheat after wheat only comes close to barley (wheat), barley after barley comes close to (barley) [wheat][116], but if only one wheat stalk is absorbed into the barley, or one stalk of barley is absorbed into the wheat, then that is forbidden.

108   Assuming one has a small strip along which the kinds can be sown in linear order, each kind being separated from the other. The discussion here follows the previous disagreement between Ḥizqiah and R. Joḥanan.

109   The middle half is enough of a separation; one does need a full *bet rova'* of separation only for a standard field.

110   A similar text is found in Tosephta *Kilaim* 2:1.

111   All commentators replace תבן "straw" by תלם "a furrow." But that substitution is not supported by any manuscript. It is induced by a mis-

reading of the Tosephta, where one reads: "He ploughs and brings wheat into the barley field, or barley into the wheat field; this is permitted since the wheat looks like part of the wheat field, the barley like part of the barley field." Similarly, the statements of R. Eliezer ben Jacob are close to the quote here but not identical. "Ploughing" here certainly means ploughing at least two furrows; so the substitution is not supported.

112   Of the straw-covered middle strip. One certainly cannot permit sowing the two slopes of one and the same furrow with two different kinds;

that would constitute *kilaim* according to all definitions.

113   The *baraita* and the corresponding Tosephta follow R. Eliezer ben Jacob; he follows the Sages of the Mishnah.

114   Tosephta *Kilaim* 2:2-3, language close to the quote here.

115   If the second field is not triangular in shape but trapezoidal (or, maybe, even rectangular) there still is no *kilaim* as long as the visual impression of the two fields is one of separation.

116   This now is the explanation of the interpretation of R. Johanan. The words in parentheses are in the text and do not make sense, even though they appear in both manuscripts. The word in brackets is inserted as conjecture. The main point is the difference in meaning between "coming close to" and "being absorbed in." The way Ḥizqiah lets one sow a narrow strip would be classified as one kind being absorbed in the other, at least if the excess area forms a thin strip all around the *bet rova'* square.

מַה נָן קַיָּמִין. אִם בְּמִתְכַּוֵּין לִבְדּוֹק אֲפִילוּ בָּאֶמְצַע שָׂדֵהוּ מוּתָּר. אִם בְּשֶׁאֵינוּ
מִתְכַּוֵּין לִבְדּוֹק לוֹ לָמָה לִי זֶרַע פִּשְׁתָּן אֲפִילוּ שְׁאָר כָּל־הַמִּינִין. מִתְכַּוֵּין לִבְדּוֹק
אָנָן קַיָּמִין. רְבִּי יוֹסֵי לֹא חוֹשֵׁשׁ לְמַרְאִית הָעַיִן וְרַבָּנִין חֲשָׁשׁוּ לְמַרְאִית הָעַיִן.

What are we dealing with[117]? If he wants only to test, even in the middle of his field it should be permitted. If he does not intend only to test, why just linseed, and not any other kinds? We deal with the case he wants to test. Rebbi Yose does not worry about bad appearances[118]; the rabbis worry about bad appearances.

117   This refers to the last sentence in the Mishnah, the statement of Rebbi Yose. If somebody plants with the intention of not harvesting, but only to test the soil, why should the rabbis disagree (on condition that the test plot be clearly delineated)? The answer is that the rabbis are afraid that the neighbors either will suspect the farmer of sowing *kilaim*, or they might conclude from his action that one may sow flax in a grain field even as a commercial crop.

118   Nevertheless, he will never

allow testing for another kind of food crop in a field growing food, only an industrial crop.

רִבִּי שְׁמוּאֵל בְּשֵׁם רִבִּי זְעִירָא דְּרִבִּי שִׁמְעוֹן הִיא דְּרִבִּי שִׁמְעוֹן אָמַר אֵין אָדָם מַקְדִּישׁ דָּבָר שֶׁאֵינוֹ שֶׁלוֹ. רַב אָמַר אֵין אָדָם חוֹבֵשׁ דָּבָר שֶׁאֵינוֹ שֶׁלוֹ. אָמַר רִבִּי יוֹנָה אַתְיָא דְּרַב כְּרִבִּי שִׁמְעוֹן. כְּמָה דְּרִבִּי שִׁמְעוֹן אָמַר אֵין אָדָם מַקְדִּישׁ דָּבָר שֶׁאֵינוֹ שֶׁלוֹ כֵּן רַב אָמַר אֵין אָדָם חוֹבֵשׁ דָּבָר שֶׁאֵינוֹ שֶׁלוֹ. בְּרַם כְּרַבָּנִין לֹא אַתְיָא.

Rebbi Samuel said in the name of Rebbi Zeïra, it is Rebbi Simeon's, for Rebbi Simeon said, nobody can sanctify property that is not his own[119]. Rav said, nobody can jail property that is not his own[120]. Rebbi Jonah said, Rav comes out like Rebbi Simeon; just as Rebbi Simeon said, nobody can sanctify property that is not his own; so Rav said, nobody can jail property that is not his own. But it cannot be explained following the Sages.

119   R. Simeon's (and R. Yose's) statement is in Mishnah 7:4: "Somebody who draws his vine over another person's grain, sanctifies the latter and has to pay for it. R. Simeon and R. Yose say, nobody can sanctify property that is not his own." Similarly, any action of a farmer in his field cannot implicate his neighbor in a sin. Hence, the Mishnah itself must be R. Simeon's: if no crop of the active farmer A has any influence on that of the passive farmer B, then farmer A's crop itself cannot be forbidden. R. Simeon's statement is an explanation of the Mishnah, not a disagreement. But the anonymous rabbis of 7:4 will not agree.

120   I. e., make it forbidden to be used. Here and in the following, "to jail" means to have it enclosed from all sides by other produce.

(fol. 27c) **מִשְׁנָה ח:** אֵין סוֹמְכִין לִשְׂדֵה תְבוּאָה חַרְדָּל וַחֲרִיעַ אֲבָל סוֹמְכִין לִשְׂדֵה יְרָקוֹת חַרְדָּל וַחֲרִיעַ. סוֹמֵךְ לְבוּר וּלְנִיר וּלְגָפָה וּלְדֶרֶךְ וּלְגָדֵר שֶׁהוּא גָבוֹהַּ עֲשָׂרָה טְפָחִים וּלְחָרִיץ שֶׁהוּא עָמוֹק עֲשָׂרָה וְרָחָב אַרְבָּעָה וּלְאִילָן שֶׁהוּא מֵיסַךְ עַל הָאָרֶץ וּלְסֶלַע שֶׁהוּא גָבוֹהַּ עֲשָׂרָה וְרָחָב אַרְבָּעָה.

Mishnah 8: One does not sow mustard or saffron close[121] to a grain field, but one may sow mustard or saffron close to a vegetable field. One does sow close to a fallow field, a ploughed[122] field, a closure, a foot path, a fence ten hand-breadths high, a ditch ten[123] deep and four wide, a tree giving shade on the ground[124], and a rock ten high and four wide.

121 Without any bare strip between one crop and the other. As R. Simson notes, the reason for this Mishnah is not explained. The explanation of Maimonides in his Mishnah Commentary is contradicted by the Halakhah. Probably the correct explanation is given by Maimonides in his Code, *Kilaim* 2:18, that a crop of mustard or saffron surrounding a field of fifty by fifty (i. e., from a single furrow 200 cubits in length) is enough for a domestic crop (a commercial crop of mustard seed is defined in the next Mishnah as needing three *bate rova'*).

The translation of חריע as saffron (*crocus sativus*) follows Targum *Cant.*, *Arukh* (*s. v.* חריע) and Rashi. The Gaonic Commentary to *Ṭahorot* and

Maimonides define it as safflower (*carthamus tinctorius*), a red dye. In the Halakhah, חריע is defined as "yellow dye."

122 A field on which the stubs of the previous harvest have been ploughed under but which has not been sown with a new crop.

123 All measurements given in the masculine are hand-breadths.

124 The place under the tree free of superficial roots is not the tree's domain; hence, it may be used. This excludes vines which go under specially stringent rules because they cause *kilaim* to become sanctified and forbidden. For any other crop, it is only necessary that fields or garden beds be clearly distinguished.

(fol. 28a) **הלכה ח:** מַהוּ חֲרִיעַ מוֹרִיקָא.

Halakhah 8: What is חריע? Yellow dye.

כֵּינֵי מַתְנִיתָא אֵין מַקִּיפִין הָא לִסְמוֹךְ סוֹמְכִין. מַתְנִיתָן דְּרִבִּי יוּדָה. דְּתַנֵּי אֵין
מַקִּיפִין חַרְדָּל וַחֲרִיעַ אֶלָּא לַחֲסִיּוֹת בִּלְבַד דִּבְרֵי רִבִּי מֵאִיר. רִבִּי יוּדָה אָמַר לַכֹּל
מַקִּיפִין חַרְדָּל וַחֲרִיעַ חוּץ מִן הַתְּבוּאָה. רִבִּי שִׁמְעוֹן אָמַר לַכֹּל מַקִּיפִין חַרְדָּל
וַחֲרִיעַ. רַבָּן שִׁמְעוֹן בֶּן גַּמְלִיאֵל אוֹמֵר עֲרוּגוֹת קְטַנּוֹת שֶׁל יָרָק מַקִּיפִין אוֹתָן
חַרְדָּל וַחֲרִיעַ.

So is the Mishnah: "One does not surround," hence one may sow close up[125]. Our Mishnah is Rebbi Jehudah's, as it was stated: "One may surround by mustard or saffron only bulbous vegetables[126], the words of Rebbi Meïr. Rebbi Jehudah said, any field one may surround by mustard or saffron except a grain field. Rebbi Simeon said, any field one may surround by mustard or saffron[127]. Rabban Simeon ben Gamliel said, one may surround small vegetable beds by mustard or saffron."

125   For the meaning of סומך "to sow close to another crop", cf. Note 57. The language of the Mishnah is corrected by a text close to Tosephta *Kilaim* 2:5, quoted in the following. On the basis of that correction, J. N. Epstein, and S. Lieberman who follows him, want to explain מקיף by "coming really close, closer than leaning to." However, since they have to admit that in the statement of Rabban Simeon ben Gamliel מקיף means "surround," it is irrational to accept any other meaning for the other parts of the Tosephta.

126   So defined in Tosephta *Terumot* 9:5. Etymologically, חוסית or חסית is related to Syriac חסוסא "bulbous."

127   This sentence is not in the Tosephta.

תַּנֵּי מוּתָּר הוּא אָדָם לִזְרֹעַ בְּתוֹךְ שָׂדֵהוּ שׁוּרָה שֶׁל חַרְדָּל וַחֲרִיעַ וּבִלְבַד שֶׁיַּעֲשֶׂה
אוֹרֶךְ שׁוּרָה אוֹרֶךְ עֶשֶׂר אַמּוֹת וּמֶחֱצָה עַל רֹחַב מְלוֹאוֹ. אָמַר רִבִּי לֶעְזָר לֹא שָׁנוּ

אֶלָּא שָׂדֶה קְטַנָּה. הָא בִגְדוֹלָה לֹא. אֵי זוֹ הִיא גְדוֹלָה וְאֵי זוֹ הִיא קְטַנָּה. אִם
יֵשׁ בֵּין בַּד לְבַד בֵּית רוֹבַע זוֹ הִיא גְדוֹלָה. וְאִם לָאו זוֹ הִיא קְטַנָּה. לֵית הָדָא
פְּלִיגָא עַל רִבִּי יוֹחָנָן. רִבִּי יוֹחָנָן אָמַר רֹאשׁ תּוֹר הַבָּא בְּחוֹרְבָה אָסוּר. תַּמָּן
לִזְרָעִין וְכָאן לִירָקוֹת. אַף עַל גַּב דְּרִבִּי יוֹחָנָן פְּלִיג בִּזְרָעִים מוֹדֶה הוּא הָכָא
בִּירָקוֹת.

It was stated[128]: "One may sow a row of mustard or saffron in the
middle of one's field on condition to make the row long, a length of 10.5
cubits the entire width." Rebbi Eleazar said, that applies only to a small
field, not to a large one. What is large and what is small? If there is
between the two ends a *bet rova'*, that is large, otherwise it is small. Does
this not disagree with Rebbi Johanan, for Rebbi Johanan said that a vertex
that comes from a dry spot is forbidden[129]? There it is for grain, here for
vegetables[130]. Even though Rebbi Johanan disagrees for grain, he will
agree here with respect to vegetables.

128   A similar text, but without the
condition, is in Tosephta *Kilaim* 2:4 in
the name of R. Yose.

129   Hence, in the middle of a field

it certainly will be forbidden.

130   Whose plants are much larger
than the grasses grown for grain.

גָּרִיד מוּתָּר לִיזְרַע בּוֹ כָּל־מִין שֶׁיִּרְצֶה. אָמַר רִבִּי יוֹחָנָן וּבִלְבַד שֶׁיַּעֲשֶׂה שְׁלוֹשָׁה
בְתוֹךְ שִׁשָּׁה וּשְׁלוֹשָׁה שֶׁהֵן סְמוּכִין לַגָּדֵר כִּגְרִיד. הָיוּ שְׁלוֹשָׁה בְתוֹךְ שִׁשָּׁה וְאֶחָד
חוּץ לְשִׁשָּׁה מֵאַחַר שֶׁהוֹצִיאֲלוּ אֵלּוּ אַף זֶה הוּצַל. הָיוּ שְׁנַיִם בְּתוֹךְ שִׁשָּׁה וְאֶחָד חוּץ
לְשִׁשָּׁה. מֵאַחַר שֶׁלֹּא הוֹצִּאֲלוּ אֵלּוּ אַף זֶה לֹא הוּצַל. הָיָה שָׁם גָּרִיד שׁוּרָה וְשׁוּרָה
גָדֵר וְשׁוּרָה חוֹבְשִׁין אֶת הַשּׁוּרָה גַּבֵּי שֶׁל גָּדֵר בְּשָׂדוֹת. שְׁתֵּי שָׂדוֹת זוֹ עַל גַּבֵּי זוֹ.
הָעֶלְיוֹנָה סְמוּכָה לֶחָרִיץ. וְהַתַּחְתּוֹנָה סְמוּכָה לַגָּדֵר.

On dry soil[131] one may sow any kind he desires. Rebbi Johanan said,
only if he uses three of six [hand-breadths][132]. Three that are close to a

fence are like dry land[133]. If there were three inside six and one outside six[134], since the former ones were saved, that one also is saved. If only two were inside six and one outside six[135], since the first ones were not saved, neither is that one. If there was one row dry, one row fence, and another row, one jails the row[136] by the fence on fields[137]. Two fields[138], one above the other, the upper one is close to a ditch, the lower one close to a fence.

131   Hard soil which cannot be ploughed to the depth required for grain and vegetables. Only a few adapted species grow there. Since the ground is different from the surrounding agricultural soil, a different crop is not *kilaim* but visibly forms another field.

132   To make the other crop stand out, a minimal width of the cultivated area is required.

133   The three hand-breadths close to a fence are not usable in a regular way. If they can be added to another three hand-breadths of irregular soil, the conditions for their use for other crops are given.

134   Adjacent to the dry spot but outside it. Then the special crop introduced on the dry soil does not have to stop exactly at the border of the dry spot but can exceed it, up to a hand-breadth, presumably to give a more regular shape to the plot sown or planted with the dry crop.

135   If the dry soil itself is not used for at least 50%, it cannot be used at all for crops differing from the surrounding one. Hence, even good adjacent soil cannot be used to make up for the deficiency on the dry soil.

136   If there was a narrow strip of good soil between the less usable strip along the fence and the less usable strip of dry soil, the good soil is caught in between ("jailed", cf. Note 120) and cannot be sown with the regular crop but must be used for the same crop planted on the dry strip and along the fence. In addition, the three hand-breadths each along the fence and of dry soil add up to the required minimum of six hand-breadths for separate use, even though they are separated by three hand-breadths of good soil. The good soil is added to

the strip along the fence.

137   The language is very difficult. Ms. Rome is completely different: גגו של גדר כשרות "the roof of a fence is permitted," meaning that on the soil forming the top of a stone fence one may plant anything, irrespective of what is growing below. In the Leyden version of the Yerushalmi, the rule is restricted to fields, i. e., to plots that measure at least 50 by 50 cubits.

138   The fields are terraced, the upper one bounded at the upside by a ditch, either an irrigation ditch or one to catch rain water, the lower field is bounded below by a stone fence. In that case, both the upper and the lower borders have the status of fences.

דְּבֵי רִבִּי יַנַּאי אָמְרֵי גָּדֵר מוּתָּר לִזְרוֹעַ בּוֹ כָּל־מִין תּוֹרְבְּכִינָה. וְגָדֵר יֶשׁ בּוֹ לְהָקֵל וְיֶשׁ בּוֹ לְהַחֲמִיר. הֵיךְ עֲבִידָא פָּחוֹת מִבֵּית רוֹבַע מוּקְרָח בְּתוֹךְ שָׂדֶה תְבוּאָה אָסוּר לִזְרוֹעַ בּוֹ. הִקִּיפוֹ גָּדֵר מוּתָּר. בֵּית רוֹבַע בְּבִקְעָא מוּתָּר לִזְרוֹעַ בּוֹ שְׁנֵי מִינִין. הִקִּיפוֹ גָּדֵר אָסוּר.

The House of Yannai said, on the fence one may sow all kinds of mixtures[139]. A fence implies leniencies and stringencies. How is this? Less than a *bet rova'* shaven[140] in a grain field may not be sown[141]; if surrounded with a fence it may be sown. A *bet rova'* in open country may be sown with two kinds[142]; if surrounded with a fence this is forbidden.

139   Root רבך "to mix" (also in Accadic and Arabic.) The statement seems to mean that on top of a stone fence one may sow anything he wants, irrespective of the crops on either side of the fence.

140   Not empty, but shaven of the surrounding crop. The next Mishnaiot will elaborate this notion. Cf. also Note 150.

141   Sown with a kind different from the one growing around it.

142   If the clear separation rules established earlier are followed. If the *bet rova'* is enclosed, it does not qualify as a field and must follow the rules of משר.

גֶּדֶר מַהוּ שֶׁיַּצִּיל אֶת הַזְּרָעִים. גְּרִיד זְרוּעַ מַהוּ שֶׁיַּצִּיל אֶת הַיֶּרֶק. רבי שְׁמוּאֵל
בְּשֵׁם רְבִּי זְעִירָא שָׁמַע לָהּ מִן הָדָא. וְסוֹמֵךְ לְשָׁרְשֵׁי אִילָן שֶׁיָּבְשׁוּ. לֹא אָמַר
אֶלָּא יָבְשׁוּ הָא לַח אָסוּר. רְבִּי יוֹסֵי שָׁמַע לֵיהּ מִן הָדָא סוֹמֵךְ לְבוּר וּלְנִיר וּלְגָפָה
לְדָרֶךְ וּלְגָדֵר שֶׁהוּא גָבוֹהַּ עֲשָׂרָה טְפָחִים. הָדָא אֲמָרָה שֶׁגָּדֵר זְרוּעַ מַצִּיל אֶת
הַזְּרָעִים. אֲפִילוּ תֵימָא וּלְגָדֵר שֶׁהוּא גָבוֹהַּ עֲשָׂרָה טְפָחִים אֵין גָּדֵר זְרוּעַ מַצִּיל
אֶת הַזְּרָעִים. שַׁנְיָיא הִיא הָכָא שֶׁהוּא גָּדֵר זְרוּעַ וְאֵין גָּדֵר זְרוּעַ מַצִּיל אֶת
הַזְּרָעִים.

Does a fence save grains[143]? Does sown dry land save vegetables? Rebbi Samuel in the name of Rebbi Zeïra understood it from the following[144]: "One sows close to dried-up tree roots." This mentions only dry ones; hence, if they are moist, it is forbidden. Rebbi Yose understood it from the following[145]: "One does sow close to a fallow field, a ploughed field, a closure, a foot path, a fence ten hand-breadths high." That implies that a sown fence saves grains! Even if you accept "fence ten hand-breadths high," a sown fence does not have to save grains. There is a difference here because the fence is sown and no sown fence saves grains[146].

143 The question as it stands makes no sense since the Mishnah states clearly that a fence absolutely separates crops. One has to say that one does not speak of a (wooden) fence but of a stone wall and the question is whether the stone wall loses its status if it is used as a field in itself. (R. Moses Margalit wants to emend the following גריד to גדר and take the next sentence as explaining the meaning of the present one. This is impossible since the text is also supported by the Rome ms. and, as R. Eliahu Fulda notes, dry land is only mentioned to separate vegetables, whose rules are not as strict as those for grains.) One has to take the text here parallel to the following one and interpret "fence" as "stone wall topped by soil on which produce is growing."

144 Tosephta *Kilaim* 2:5. There it is

added that the roots have to be 10 hand-breadths high, corresponding to the minimal size of a separating stone wall. Hence, living roots are not different from a stone wall on which some crop was planted.

145 Quote from the current Mishnah. Here, "fence" (and also, "closure") is used without qualification and includes stone walls on which produce is grown.

146 Since the stone wall carries produce, all separation rules for fields apply; there is no longer any wall in the legal sense once it became a field.

רְבִּי יוּדָן בָּעֵי גְרִיד וּמְשָׁךְ מַהוּ שֶׁיִּצְטָרְפוּ. הֵיךְ עֲבִידָא הָיָה שָׁם מָקוֹם אוֹרֶךְ עֶשֶׂר אַמּוֹת וּמֶחֱצָה עַל רוֹחַב שִׁשָּׁה אֵינוֹ צָרִיךְ גְּרִיד. עָשָׂה גְרִיד מִיכָּן מוּתָּר לִסְמוֹךְ שְׁתֵּי רוּחוֹתָיו.

Rebbi Judan asked: Do dry land and length add together? How is that? If there was space ten and a half cubits long and six hand-breadths wide[147], one does not have to have dry land[148]. If dry land was added on both sides, one may sow close on both sides.

147 On separate ground in a grain field one may sow a row of vegetables since, as was just stated, dry land only helps for vegetables.

148 In order to permit the planting. But if dry land is added, one can sow grain close to it. Since the row of vegetables also takes up space, without the dry strip there would not be the required separation of at least three hand-breadths from the grain.

תַּנֵּי רִבִּי יוֹנָתָן בַּר יוֹסֵי אוֹמֵר הָיָה שָׁם סֶלַע אֲרוּכָה עֲשָׂרָה וְרָחַב אַרְבָּעָה מוּתָּר לִסְמוֹךְ לוֹ מִשְׁתֵּי רוּחוֹתֶיהָ. קִיְתָה עֲשָׂרָה עַל עֲשָׂרָה מוּתָּר לָהּ מֵאַרְבַּע רוּחוֹתֶיהָ.

It was stated: Rebbi Jonathan ben Yose[149] said, one may sow close to a rock ten hand-breadths long and four hand-breadths wide on both of its sides. If it was ten by ten hand-breadths, one may sow close to it on all four sides.

149   A Tanna of the fourth generation, student of R. Aqiba, and perhaps also of R. Ismael. He is mentioned only in Tosephta and *baraitot*. His statement here refers to the Mishnah, that one may plant different crops at the sides of a rock outcropping that is at least ten hand-breadths high (about a yard). He states that any side of the outcropping at least one yard long forms an absolute barrier for *kilaim*.

(fol. 27c) **משנה ט**: הָרוֹצֶה לַעֲשׂוֹת שָׂדֵהוּ קָרַחַת קָרַחַת מִכָּל־מִין עוֹשֶׂה עֶשְׂרִים וְאַרְבַּע קְרָחוֹת לְבֵית סְאָה מְקָרַחַת בֵּית רוֹבַע וְזוֹרֵעַ בְּתוֹכָהּ כָּל־מִין שֶׁיִּרְצֶה. הָיְתָה קָרַחַת אַחַת אוֹ שְׁתַּיִם זוֹרְעָן חַרְדָּל. שָׁלֹשׁ לֹא יִזְרָעֵם חַרְדָּל מִפְּנֵי שֶׁהִיא נִרְאֵית כִּשְׂדֵה חַרְדָּל דִּבְרֵי רִבִּי מֵאִיר. וַחֲכָמִים אוֹמְרִין תֵּשַׁע קְרָחוֹת מוּתָּרוֹת וְעֶשֶׂר אֲסוּרוֹת. רִבִּי אֱלִיעֶזֶר בֶּן יַעֲקֹב אוֹמֵר אֲפִילוּ כָּל־שָׂדֵהוּ בֵּית כּוֹר לֹא יַעֲשֶׂה בְּתוֹכָהּ חוּץ מִקָּרַחַת אַחַת.

Mishnah 9: He who wants to turn his field into patches[150] for all different kinds makes 24 patches per *bet seah*, each patch one *bet rova'*, and sows in each one any kind that he desires. If there were one or two patches[151], he may sow them with mustard; three he should not sow because that would look like a mustard field, the words of Rebbi Meïr[152]. But the Sages say, nine patches are permitted, ten are forbidden[153]. Rebbi Eliezer ben Jacob says, even if its field is a *bet kor*[154], he should not make in it more than one patch.

150   Arabic קַרְאָה "terrain appropriate for being sown," used here for equal patches all sown or planted with different kinds. Clearly, R. Meïr cannot require the patches all to be square and equal, since 24 is not a square number. Since a *seah* contains 24 *rova'*, each plot will have just the minimal size that allows different seeds to be sown. Since the patches have to be rectangular and equal in shape, on a field of 50 by 50 cubits the sides of the rectangles are 50/4=12.5 by 50/6=8.$\bar{3}$ cubits (or 50/3=16.$\bar{6}$ by 50/8=6.25 cubits.)

151   A new statement. If an otherwise continuous field has two square excisions of a *bet rova'* each, separated from one another, he may sow both of them with mustard because that is still less than a commercial crop. Three he may not sow because the yield would be enough for a commercial crop and would make the remainder *kilaim*.

152   The entire Mishnah up to here is R. Meïr's.

153   This is explained in the Halakhah. Maimonides, who insists that a קְרָחַת must be square, takes as model of the 50 by 50 cubits field a five-by-five square checkerboard. All white fields in the first, third, and fifth rows are squares of a *bet rova'* each (squares of $\sqrt{2500}/24 = 10.207$ cubits edge length) while the black fields in these rows are rectangles of edge lengths 10.207 and 9.69 cubits. In rows 2 and 4, the black fields are squares of a *bet rova'*, the white fields are rectangles of edge lengths 9.69 and 10.207 cubits. Together, they fill the large square, but only the nine fields selected first may be sown and all others must lie fallow.

According to Maimonides, the number 9 as maximum of patches is a mathematical fact. In the interpretation of R. Simson who admits rectangular patches, 10 patches would be possible but are forbidden. In a 4-by-6 checkerbord, a valid centrally symmetric configuration of 10 patches might contain (1,1) (1,4) (2,2) (3,1) (3,3) (4,2) (4,4) (5,3) (6,1) (6,4). The expression "ten are forbidden" supports R. Simson.

154   1 *kor* = 30 *seah*. 1 *bet kor* = 75'000 square cubits, larger than the *bet kor* appearing in cuneiform documents.

(fol. 28a) **הלכה ט:** רִבִּי חִזְקִיָּה רִבִּי יָסָא בְּשֵׁם רִבִּי יוֹחָנָן עַל רֹאשָׁהּ רִבִּי מֵאִיר
אוֹמֵר אֲפִילוּ חֲבוּשׁוֹת אֲפִילוּ סְמוּכוֹת. וְרַבָּנִין אָמְרִין וּבִלְבַד שֶׁלֹּא יְהוּ לֹא
חֲבוּשׁוֹת וְלֹא סְמוּכוֹת. הֵיךְ עֲבִידָא תְּלַת וְתַרְתֵּי וְחָדָא וְתַרְתֵּי וְחָדָא.

Halakhah 9: Rebbi Ḥizqiah, Rebbi Yasa, in the name of Rebbi
Johanan: For the first part, Rebbi Meïr says, even jailed, even adjacent,
but the rabbis say, on condition that they were neither jailed nor
adjacent[155]. How is that done? 3,2,1,2,1[156].

155 Two rectangular fields may
meet one another at a vertex, since
each one is ראש חור for the other.
"Jailed" means here that a rectangular
field forms ראש חור at all four of its
vertices. Rebbi Meïr permits to sow
rectangular fields, each of the
minimum size of *bet rova'*, even if they
are adjacent, i. e., they are joined at an
edge, and even if they are jailed at all
corners, which means that he permits
to use the entire field. The Sages do
not disagree that a קרחת must have a
minimum size of *bet rova'*. If the field
is divided into equal rectangles, one
may imagine that the different
rectangles are alternately black and
white in checkerboard fashion. Since
the rabbis do not permit adjacent
rectangles to be sown, the first
condition is that only rectangles of the
same color are chosen. The second
condition is that no chosen rectangle

can be surrounded by 4 chosen
rectangles. The opinion of Maimonides
about the position of the rabbis was
explained in the Mishnah. His opinion
is difficult to accept, since he does not
permit any two fields to touch at all, so
the mention of "jailing" is totally
redundant. It is therefore better to
look for a partition of the 50 by 50
field into 24 equal parts. The rabbis
cannot speak about division of the field
into squares since their number would
have to be either 16 (with 7 chosen
squares) or 25 (where 12 chosen
squares are possible.) Also, the squares
in the second case would be smaller
than a *bet rova'*. If the Sages would
follow the division of R. Meïr and
cover the field by a 4-by-6
checkerboard, they could accomodate
10 chosen rectangles (fields 1,3,5 in the
first row, 2,4,6 in the second, 1,5 in the
third, 2,4 in the fourth.) Hence, it

seems that the rabbis insist that the area for קרחת should be strictly larger than a *bet rova'*, and on a 5-by-4 board one may select at most nine (e. g., fields 1,3,5 in row 1; 2,4 in row 2; 1,5 in row 3; 2,4 in row 4.) The area of each plot is then 125 sq. cubits. (Explanation of R. Eliahu Fulda.)

156 This statement fails in two respects. First, the underlying checkerboard is 5-by-5, allowing only 100 sq. cubits per plot, and second, on such a checkerboard that has 13 white and 12 black fields, one may choose all white fields with the exception of the central one (#3 in row 3), for a total of 12 admissible fields. Hence, this sentence (choosing 3 plots in the first row, 2 in the second, 1 in the third, 2 in the fourth, 1 in the fifth) must be a later addition. Even if one chooses the central element in row three, one still could accomodate 10 plots (1,3,5 in the first row, 2,4 in the second, 3 in the third, 1,5,in the fourth, 2,4 in the fifth).

The argument is not part of R. Joḥanan's statement since it is in Aramaic. R. I. J. Kanievski proposes to read תְּלַת תַּרְתֵּי וְחָדָא תַּרְתֵּיי וְחָדָא eliminating two conjunctions and translating "three [times] two and one each." The syntax is very unusual.

(fol. 27c) **משנה י**: כָּל־שָׁהוּא בְּתוֹךְ בֵּית רוֹבַע עוֹלֶה בְּמִידַּת בֵּית רוֹבַע. אֲכִלַת הַגֶּפֶן וְהַקֶּבֶר וְהַסֶּלַע עוֹלִין בְּמִידַּת בֵּית רוֹבַע. תְּבוּאָה בִּתְבוּאָה בֵּית רוֹבַע יָרָק בְּיָרָק שִׁשָּׁה טְפָחִים. תְּבוּאָה בְּיָרָק וְיָרָק בִּתְבוּאָה בֵּית רוֹבַע. רִבִּי אֶלִיעֶזֶר אוֹמֵר יָרָק בִּתְבוּאָה שִׁשָּׁה טְפָחִים.

Mishnah 10: Anything that is inside the *bet rova'* counts for the measurement of *bet rova'*[157]. The surroundings of a vine[158], a grave, or a rock[159] count for the measurement of *bet rova'*. Grain and grain need a *bet rova'*[160], vegetable and vegetable six hand-breadths. Grain and vegetables, vegetables and grain[161] need a *bet rova'*. Rebbi Eliezer says, vegetable and grain six hand-breadths.

157   The *bet rova'* which must be left uncultivated between two fields. The separating space need not be fallow agricultural land; land which cannot be used for agriculture may be counted since all that is needed is a separation.

158   The space around a vine that must be left free for tending it. This space must also be kept free of weeds.

159   A rock outcropping less than 10 hand-breadths high; otherwise it would separate by itself. The same will hold for the space of a fence which does not have the required height.

160   Between two grain fields, the empty space is determined by a surface area of one *bet rova'*. Between two vegetable fields, the space is 1 cubit in linear distance. This adds up to a *bet rova'* only if the fields are longer than 100 cubits.

161   Irrespective of which field was there first. These rules apply only to distances between fields; as noted earlier, for a single row of vegetables even the rabbis only ask for a distance of six hand-breadths.

(fol. 28a) **הלכה י**: רבִּי בּוּן בַּר חִיָּיה בְּשֵׁם רבִּי זְעִירָא לֹא שָׁנוּ אֶלָּא אוֹכֶלֶת הַגֶּפֶן הָא גֶּפֶן עַצְמָהּ לֹא. לָמָּה מִפְּנֵי שֶׁהִיא אֲסוּרָה בַּהֲנָיָיה. וַהֲרֵי הַקֶּבֶר אָסוּר בַּהֲנָיָיה. קֶבֶר אֵין אִסּוּרוֹ נִיכָּר. וַעֲבוֹדַת הַגֶּפֶן אֵין אֲסוּרָה בַּהֲנָיָיה אֶלָּא כְּרבִּי יִשְׁמָעֵאל דְּרבִּי יִשְׁמָעֵאל אָמַר אֵין עֲבוֹדָה לְגֶפֶן יְחִידִית. וַהֲרֵי הַקֶּבֶר (fol. 28b) אָסוּר בַּהֲנָיָיה. קֶבֶר אֵין אִסּוּרוֹ נִיכָּר.

Halakhah 10: Rebbi Abun bar Ḥiyya in the name of Rebbi Zeïra: They taught only the surroundings of the vine, hence, not the vine itself[162]. Why? Because it is forbidden for usufruct. But is not the grave also forbidden for usufruct? A grave is not recognizable as forbidden[163]. And is the working space of a vine forbidden for usufruct? This follows Rebbi Ismael, since Rebbi Ismael said that a single vine does not have working space[164]. But is not the grave forbidden for usufruct? A grave is not recognizable as forbidden.

162   This must be a dried-up vine; a fruit-bearing vine certainly makes *kilaim* forbidden.

163   While the remains of the dead are forbidden for any use, the status of the surrounding grave as forbidden is only rabbinical, and if the grave is covered only by a flat stone, as is usual in the Middle East, it is not directly recognizable.

164   One does not have to give a single vine six hand-breadths outside of the area shadowed by its branches and leaves, in which any *kilaim* would be "sanctified" and forbidden by Biblical decree. This goes against Mishnah 3:8. It follows that for a vineyard the surrounding working area cannot count as separation, since that would allow planting grain in the neighborhood of the vineyard.

תְּבוּאָה בִתְבוּאָה בֵּית רוֹבַע וּבִלְבַד שֶׁלֹא תְהֵא חֲבוּשָׁה מֵאַרְבַּע רוּחוֹתֶיהָ. רִבִּי זְעִירָא בָּעָא קוֹמֵי רִבִּי יָסָא כִּי נָן אָמְרִין הָדָא בְּקַעַת סִימוֹנְיָא אֵין זוֹרְעִין לְתוֹכָהּ אֶלָּא מִין אֶחָד בִּלְבַד.

"Grain and grain need a *bet rova'*." But only if it is not jailed on all four sides[165]. Rebbi Zeïra asked before Rebbi Yasa: Does this mean that we say that in the ravine of Simonia[166] one may sow only one kind?

165   A wheat field may not be surrounded by four other grain fields, none of them wheat.

166   The Biblical Shimron, Semunieh, West of Nazareth. Since in a narrow ravine, the field is surrounded ("jailed") from all sides, do the walls of the ravine play the role of fields in flat country? The question is not answered.

מָתִיב לְרִבִּי אֱלִיעֶזֶר לְרַבָּנִין כְּמָה דְאִית לְכוֹן קַל בְּשׁוּרָה וְחוֹמֶר בִּמְרוּבָּע. כֵּן אַשְׁכְּחָן דְּאִית לְרַבָּנִין[167] קַל בְּשׁוּרָה וְחוֹמֶר בִּמְרוּבָּע. כְּהָדָא דְּתַנֵּי הָרוֹצֶה לַעֲשׂוֹת שׁוּרָה שֶׁל יֶרֶק לְתוֹךְ שְׂדֵה תְבוּאָה. הֲרֵי זֶה עוֹשֶׂה אוֹרֶךְ שׁוּרָה אוֹרֶךְ עֶשֶׂר אַמּוֹת וּמֶחֱצָה עַל רוֹחַב שִׁשָּׁה. אָמַר רִבִּי יוֹחָנָן אֵינוֹ זוֹרֵעַ לְתוֹכָהּ אֶלָּא מִין אֶחָד בִּלְבַד. אָמַר רִבִּי זְעִירָא מוֹדֶה רִבִּי יוֹחָנָן כְּשֶׁהָיוּ שִׁבְעָה שֶׁהוּא זוֹרֵעַ טֶפַח

מִכָּן וְטֶפַח מִכָּן אוֹתָן חֲמִשָּׁה נִידוֹנִין לְכָאן וּלְכָאן. מִן מַה דְּרִבִּי זְעִירָא מָתִיב
עַל דְּרִבִּי יוֹחָנָן תַּמָּן.

Rebbi Eliezer objected to the rabbis: Are you not lenient for one row and restrictive for rectangles[168]? It is so, we find that the rabbis are lenient for one row and restrictive for rectangles, as it was stated: He who wants to make one row of vegetables in a grain field makes a row $10^1/_2$ cubits long and six hand-breadths wide[169]. Rebbi Joḥanan said, therein he sows only one kind. Rebbi Zeïra said, Rebbi Joḥanan agrees that if it is seven wide he sows one hand-breadth on one side, one on the other side, and the remaining five count for both sides[170], just as Rebbi Zeïra had explained Rebbi Joḥanan's opinion there[171].

167　　The Rome ms. here has quite a different reading, . . . כן אנא יהיב קל that כן אנא יהיב קל seems to be based on a misunderstanding of the text.

168　　To require a *bet rova'* for rectangles when you require only three or six hand-breadths for rows, as above in Halakhah 7?

169　　He sows in the middle and has half a cubit distance from the field in both directions. The value 10.5 is a practical upper estimate of the edge length of a square containing a *bet rova'* (Note 153). R. Simson wants to take the 10 cubits as standard cubits of 6 hand-breadths each and .5 cubits as half a small cubit of 5 hand-breadths only, in order to get a better approximation. But such an exactness is illusory in agriculture; it is better to err a little on the upside.

170　　So that each row of vegetables has six hand-breadths for itself.

171　　Halakhah 7, in which R. Zeïra asserted that R. Joḥanan permits the sowing of two rectangles in 1.5 *bet rova'*.

נָטַע חֲצִי שׁוּרָה וְעָמַד לוֹ וּבִקֵּשׁ לְהַתְחִיל בְּשׁוּרָה אַחֶרֶת. רַב חִסְדָּא אָמַר אָסוּר
אָמַר לוֹ עֲקוֹר אֶת הַשּׁוּרָה אוֹ מַלֵּא אֶת הַשּׁוּרָה.

Somebody planted half a row, stopped, and wanted to start a second row. Rav Ḥisda said, this is forbidden. One tells him, either tear out that row or finish it.

רְבִּי יוּדָן אָמַר אִיתְפַּלְגוּן רִבִּי חִיָּיא בַּר בָּא וְרְבִּי שְׁמוּאֵל בַּר רַב יִצְחָק. חַד אָמַר אֲפִילוּ שְׁלֹשָׁה לְתוֹךְ שִׁשָּׁה. וְחָרָנָה אָמַר אֲפִילוּ אֶחָד מִכָּן וְאֶחָד מִכָּן וְאֶחָד בָּאֶמְצַע. [172] וְלָא יָדְעִין מָאן דְּאָמַר דָּא וּמָאן אָמַר דָּא. מִן מַה דְּאָמַר רִבִּי יוֹסֵי רִבִּי חִיָּיא בְּשֵׁם רִבִּי יוֹחָנָן וּבִלְבַד שֶׁלֹּא יְהֵא שָׁם חָרֵבָה. הֲוֵי רִבִּי שְׁמוּאֵל בַּר רַב יִצְחָק הוּא דְּאָמַר אֲפִילוּ אֶחָד מִכָּן וְאֶחָד מִכָּן וְאֶחָד בָּאֶמְצַע. אִם הָיוּ צְדָדִין רָבִין עַל הֶחָרֵבָה מוּתָּר.

Rebbi Judan said: Rebbi Ḥiyya bar Abba and Rebbi Samuel bar Rav Isaac disagree. One says, even three in a width of six[173], the other said, one on one side, the other on the other side, and the third in the middle. We do not know who said what. Since Rebbi Yose said, Rebbi Ḥiyya[174] in the name of Rebbi Joḥanan, only if there is no dry patch, that means that Rebbi Samuel bar Rav Isaac said: One on one side, the other on the other side, and the third in the middle. If the sides were more than the dry patch, it is permitted[175].

172   Missing in the Venice print, but appearing in the quote a few lines later and in mss.

173   One may not sow anything that does not belong to the field unless one carves out a patch 10.5 by 1 cubits, but once one has that size, and the minimal width of 6 hand-breadths, one may plant there three rows of vegetables, if only one has orderly rows. The other opinion is that the rows must be equally spaced and there must be three hand-breadths between any two rows.

174   R. Ḥiyya bar Abba. Since he has to say that the rule does not apply if there is a dry patch in the rectangle, he cannot otherwise require that the rows be equally spaced since then the statement would be superfluous. Since he puts the distances between the rows at the discretion of the farmer, he has to add that one may not plan close-up

rows in order to avoid a dry patch.

175   If the strip is wider than six
hand-breadths, so that there are six
hand-breadths of good soil on any

perpendicular to the length of the rows
of vegetables, the dry patch is no
obstacle.

(fol. 27c) **משנה יא**: תְּבוּאָה נוֹטָה עַל גַּבֵּי תְבוּאָה וְיָרֶק עַל גַּבֵּי יָרֶק. תְּבוּאָה עַל גַּבֵּי יָרֶק וְיָרֶק עַל גַּבֵּי תְבוּאָה. הַכֹּל מוּתָּר חוּץ מִדְּלַעַת יְוָנִית. רְבִּי אוֹמֵר אַף הַקִּישׁוּת וּפוֹל הַמִּצְרִי וְרוֹאֶה אֲנִי אֶת דִּבְרֵיהֶם מִדְּבָרַי.

Mishnah 11: Grain leaning over grain[176], vegetable over vegetable, grain over vegetable, vegetable over grain, all is permitted except Greek gourd. Rebbi says, also green melon and Egyptian beans, but I prefer their words over my words[177].

176   If oats with their soft stalks lean over straight wheat at the border between two fields, that is not bad, as long as the sowing was done correctly. The same is true for all other annual plants grown from seeds, except for Greek gourd having wide leaves and long, crawling stems which enter

neighboring fields and appear as *kilaim* even if sown strictly separately. These must be confined to their own field.

177   The Halakhah will explain Rebbi's argument. One must assume that his statement expresses a family tradition.

(fol. 28b) **הלכה יא**: תַּנֵּי חֲמִשָּׁה דְּבָרִים נֶאֶמְרוּ בִּדְלַעַת יְוָנִית אֵין מְסַכְּכִין אוֹתָהּ עַל גַּבֵּי זְרָעִים. וּמְבִיאִין אֶת הַטּוּמְאָה וְחוֹצֶצֶת אֶת הַטּוּמְאָה וְעוּקְצָהּ טֶפַח וְאוֹסֶרֶת כָּל־שֶׁהוּא. וְהַנּוֹדֵר מִן הַדִּילוּעִין אֵינוֹ אָסוּר אֶלָּא בִדְלַעַת יְוָנִית בִּלְבַד. רְבִּי יוֹנָה בָּעֵי וְלָמָּה לֵית אֲנַן אֱמְרִין מְבִיאָה אֶת הַטּוּמְאָה וְחוֹצֶצֶת אֶת

הַטּוּמְאָה תִּרְתֵּי. תַּנֵּי בַּר קַפָּרָא שֶׁבַע. אֵין מְסַכְּכִין אוֹתָהּ עַל גַּבֵּי זְרָעִים

וּמְבִיאָה אֶת הַטּוּמְאָה וְחוֹצֶצֶת אֶת הַטּוּמְאָה וְיָדָהּ טֶפַח וְנוֹתְנִין לָהּ עֲבוֹדָתָהּ

וְכִלְאַיִם עִם אֲרָמִית וְכִלְאַיִם עִם הַרְמוּצָה וְלֹא תָנָא אוֹסֶרֶת וְלֹא תָנָא נְדָרִים.

Halakhah 11: It was stated[178]: "Five things were said about Greek
gourd: One may not allow it to cover grains[179], it brings impurity and
stops impurity[180], its stalk is one hand-breadth[181], the tiniest amount of it
makes forbidden[182], and to him who makes a vow not to use pumpkins,
only Greek gourd is forbidden." Rebbi Jonah asked, why do we not count
"it brings impurity and stops impurity" as two? Bar Qappara stated seven:
"One may not allow it to cover grains, it brings impurity, it stops impurity,
its stalk is one hand-breadth, one gives it its working space[183], it is *kilaim*
with Aramean [pumpkin], and *kilaim* with ash pumpkin[184]." He did not
state that it makes forbidden or anything about making a vow[185].

---

178   Tosephta *Kilaim* 1:5.

179   As explained in the previous
Halakhah, its leaves cannot be allowed
to grow over other plants because it
would look like *kilaim.*

180   If the leaves of Greek gourd are
growing on a trellis, they act as roof.
A human corpse in a house ("a tent,"
Num. 19:14) brings impurity on
everything in the house. On the other
hand, the roof of the house and anything above it are free from impurity.
If the corpse is not in a house, anybody
who would step over it would create a
temporary tent and hence would
become impure. The leaves of the

pumpkin act as roof, so that a dead
body under part of it would bring
impurity to all vessels or people found
under any other leaves extending from
the same vine. Consequently, a person
being above these leaves would not
become impure because the roof under
him protects him from impurity.

181   Food can become impure, the
plant on which it grows cannot. The
connection of the fruit to the stem is
the stalk; this can still become impure.
This rule is found in Mishnah *'Uqezin*
1:6.

182   If the pumpkin is forbidden for
any reason, then even the smallest

amount mixed with other food makes all the food forbidden because of its importance. The complete list of vegetables with this property is given in Mishnah *'Orlah* 3:7.

183   In this respect it is like vines,

since the working space around it is not counted as empty for the minimum separation of different species.

184   See Mishnah 1:5.

185   He disagreed with the statements about these topics.

אָמַר רִבִּי יוֹסֵי רִבִּי גַמְלִיאֵל בְּרִבִּי נְפַק לְשׁוּקָא. אָתוּן שָׁאֲלוּן לֵיהּ סִיכּוּךְ שֶׁאָמְרוּ בְּנוֹגֵעַ. אֲתָא שָׁאַל לְאָבוֹי אֲמַר לֵיהּ סִיכּוּךְ שֶׁאָמְרוּ בְּנוֹגֵעַ. אָמַר רִבִּי יוֹנָה רִבִּי הֵלֵּל בֵּי רִבִּי וַלֶּס נְפַק לְשׁוּקָא. אֲתוּן וְשָׁאֲלוּן לֵיהּ סִיכּוּךְ שֶׁאָמְרוּ בְּנוֹגֵעַ. אֲתָא שָׁאַל לְאָבוֹי אֲמַר לֵיהּ סִיכּוּךְ שֶׁאָמְרוּ בְּנוֹגֵעַ.

Rebbi Yose said, Rebbi Gamliel, the son of Rebbi, went to the market[186]. They came and asked him whether the roofing they mentioned[187] referred to touching. He went and asked his father, who told him that the roofing they mentioned referred to touching. Rebbi Jonah said, Rebbi Hillel ben Rebbi Vales went to the market. They came and asked him whether the roofing they mentioned referred to touching. He went and asked his father, who told him that the roofing they mentioned referred to touching.

186   This paragraph is partially in Aramaic since it involves the unlearned.

187   For Greek gourd, whether it forms *kilaim* only if the leaves actually

touch the other produce, or whether it is also *kilaim* if the plant stretches out on a high trellis. The answer is, *kilaim* only applies in the first case.

מַהוּ רוֹאֶה אֲנִי אֶת דִּבְרֵיהֶם מִדִּבְרָי. אָמַר רִבִּי חִינְנָא אִם דְּלַעַת מִצְרִית שֶׁהִיא מְסַכֶּכֶת אָמַר מוּתָּר. קִישׁוּת וּפוֹל הַמִּצְרִי לֹא כָּל־שֶׁכֵּן. אָמַר רִבִּי אַבָּא מָרִי לֹא כֵן הֲוָה רִבִּי מָנָא אוֹמֵר. רִבִּי אָמַר כָּל־הֵן דְּתַנִּינָן קִישׁוּת וּפוֹל הַמִּצְרִי אַף דְּלַעַת

מִצְרִית בִּכְלָל. מַהוּ רוֹאֶה אֲנִי אֶת דִּבְרֵיהֶם מִדְּבָרַיי. שֶׁאֵין כּוּלָּן מְסַכְּכִין כִּדְלַעַת יְוָנִית.

What means "but I prefer their words over my words?" Rebbi Ḥinena said, if Egyptian pumpkin whose leaves form roofs is permitted, green melon and Egyptian beans so much more. Rebbi Abba Mari said, Rebbi Mana did not say so. Rebbi said, all those about which we did state "green melon and Egyptian beans," also include Egyptian pumpkin. What means "but I prefer their words over my words?" That none of these form roofs like Greek gourd[188].

188   Their leaves are not as large as those of Greek gourd.

ערוגה פרק שלישי

(fol. 28b) **משנה א:** עֲרוּגָה שֶׁהִיא שִׁשָּׁה עַל שִׁשָּׁה טְפָחִים זוֹרְעִין בְּתוֹכָהּ חֲמִשָּׁה זְרעוֹנִין אַרְבָּעָה בְּאַרְבַּע רוּחוֹת עֲרוּגָה וְאֶחָד בָּאֶמְצַע. הָיָה לָהּ גְּבוּל גָּבוֹהַּ טֶפַח זוֹרְעִין בְּתוֹכָהּ שְׁלֹשָׁה עֶשְׂרֵה שְׁלֹשָׁה עַל כָּל־גּוֹבֶל וְגוֹבֶל וְאֶחָד בָּאֶמְצַע. לֹא יִטַּע רֹאשׁ הַלֶּפֶת בְּתוֹךְ הַגּוֹבֶל מִפְּנֵי שֶׁהוּא מְמַלֵּיהוּ. רַבִּי יְהוּדָה אוֹמֵר שִׁשָּׁה בָּאֶמְצַע.

Mishnah 1: In a garden bed that is six by six hand-breadths[1] one may sow five kinds of seeds, four at its four sides and one in the middle[2]. If it has a wall around it at least one hand-breadth high, one may sow in it thirteen kinds: three on each of the three sides of the wall, and one in the middle[3]. One should not plant a head of turnip in that wall because it fills it[4]. Rebbi Jehudah says, six kinds may be in the middle[5].

1 This is the minimal size (about 0.3 m²) of a plot that can be planted with different kinds. The rules for garden beds are different from those of fields. If no trees are involved, then the only requirements are that the different kinds not be sown together and that they form distinct smaller beds (with straight boundaries), so that they should not appear continuous. It will be stated in later Mishnaiot that two different patches either may come together as the vertex of a triangle, ראש חור, touching a straight side, or that the two patches meet in a pair of vertical angles, or that the patch boundaries are parallel and separated, either by a ditch one hand-breadth deep and wide and six long, or by an earthwall one hand-breadth high and one wide, or by a strip of flat empty ground 1¹/₂ hand-breadths wide. The Halakhah will explain that under most circumstances, one must leave the corners of the ערוגה-square empty. The problem of interpretation of the

Mishnah is to find a way that gives the farmer maximum use of his soil. The maximum problem was solved by Maimonides, whose interpretation we follow here. A similar explanation is given by Rashi, Babli *Šabbat* 84b; Rashi's explanation is identical with one by an unnamed Gaon, *Oẓar Hageonim Šabbat* p. 83-86. [In all these discussions, "six hand-breadths" is used, not "one cubit," since there is an opinion (Tosephta *Kelim Baba Meẓia'* 6:13) that in all that concerns *kilaim*, a cubit is only five hand-breadths. For the metric equivalents of these measurements, cf. Chapter 4, Note 2.]

2   Divide the 6×6 plot into 36 squares of one hand-breadth edge length each. Along the four edges, the corner squares are left fallow. Then on each edge, a rectangle, 4 long and 1 wide, can be planted. These 4 rectangles can be planted with 4 different kinds since they meet only at a pair of vertical angles. Together, they contain 16 of the 1-by-1 squares. The interior edges of the rectangles enclose a 4×4 square. In this square, a square can be planted in the shape of a diamond, having its vertices at the midpoints of the inner edges of the rectangles. This is permitted as ראש חור since the rules of "jailing" do not apply

to flower beds. The diagonals of the diamond have length 4; it covers exactly half of the internal square of 16 square hand-breadths. Hence, the entire cultivated area is 8 + 4×4 = 24 hand-breadths square.

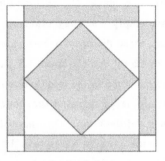

fig. 3-1

[If we assume that the fallow squares at the corners have edge length a, then the total cultivated area, in square hand-breadths, is

$$f(a) = 4a(6 - 2a) + 0.5(6 - 2a)^2.$$

A simple computation then shows that the maximum is attained for $a = 1$, $f(1) = 24$. R. Obadiah of Bertinoro objects to the use of diamonds in farming; his optimal solution has 4 1.5-by-3 rectangles along the sides and a single plant in the center of the square, total area 18+ε. A different approach by R. Ḥananel, based on the Halakhah here, leads only to a cultivated area of 13, and a more detailed analysis of the Halakhah by R. Simson to 15.04. R. Simson's explanation is given in the

Halakhah; the statement it refers to proves the existence of an arrangement of five different kinds, not the optimal arrangement.]

3   Since now the entire plot is 8-by-8 hand-breadths, if on the elevated border one leaves the corner 1-by-1 square empty, one may plant on the border three different 1-by-1 patches separated by the required 1.5 hand-breadths. Then in the middle one may plant one large diamond that touches the sides of the ערוגה at their midpoints. The total area is 64 square hand-breadths, the cultivated area is

$$4×3 + 18 = 30.$$

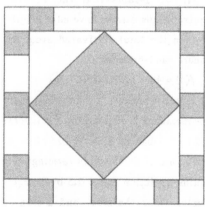

fig. 3-2

4   The leaves of the turnip will grow into the empty spaces between the different kinds and no separation will be visible.

5   If 12 little patches are sown on the border wall, the internal 6-by-6 bed

may be planted in two rows of three rhombs each. Each rhomb is three high and two wide. (The edge length of each rhomb is $l = \sqrt{3.25}$, half the acute vertex angle is given by $\sin \alpha = 2/3$. Hence, the distance between two parallel edges of two parallel rhombs is $d = l \sin 2\alpha = 1.792 > 1.5$, and the arrangement is legitimate. If the inner ערוגה would be filled by 9 1-by-1 diamonds, the distance between parallel patches would be only 1; this is too small. Hence, for regular patterns, 6 is the maximum number.)

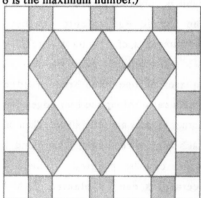

fig. 3-3

This arrangement increases the number of kinds that can be sown but it does not change the total cultivated area. (According to R. Obadiah of Bertinoro, R. Jehudah refers only to the ערוגה that is surrounded by an earth wall, so that the corners can also be sown. His configuration is of six 2.25-

by-1 rectangles separated by strips 1.5   the square.)
wide, sitting on two parallel edges of

הלכה א: זְרָעֶיהָ מִיעוּט זְרָעִים שְׁנָיִם. אָמַר רִבִּי שְׁמוּאֵל בַּר סִיסַרְטָא (fol. 26c)
מִשְּׁנַיִם אַתְּ לָמֵד אַרְבָּעָה. מַה שְּׁנַיִם אַתְּ נוֹתֵן בִּתְחִילַת שִׁשָּׁה וּמֵיצַר וְהוֹלֵךְ. אַף
אַרְבָּעָה אַתְּ נוֹתֵן בִּתְחִילַת שִׁשָּׁה וּמֵיצַר וְהוֹלֵךְ. אִי אֶיפְשָׁר שֶׁלֹא יְהֵא שָׁם נֶקֶב
אֶחָד פָּנוּי לִיטַּע בּוֹ אֶת הָאֶמְצָעִית. אָמַר רִבִּי יוֹנָה עֲבוֹדָה פּוֹגֵע בַּעֲבוֹדָה וְאֵין
מִין פּוֹגֵע בַּחֲבֵירוֹ לְחוֹבְשׁוֹ. רִבִּי יְהוֹשֻׁעַ בֶּן לֵוִי זַרְעָהּ זְרָעָהּ זְרָעֶיהָ זְרוּעֶיהָ. וּכְרִבִּי יוּדָה
דְּרִבִּי יוּדָה אָמַר שִׁשָּׁה זָרַע זַרְעָהּ זְרָעֶיהָ[6] זְרָעֶיהָ. רִבִּי חַגַּיי אָמַר זְרָעֶיהָ חֲמֵשָׁה
כָּל־הֵן דַּאֲנָה מַשְׁכַּח לָהּ וי אֲנָא[7] מְחַק לָהּ. אִישְׁתָּאִילַת לְרַב הוּנָא סַפְרָא
דְּסִידְרָא וַאֲמַר זֵירוּעֶיהָ מָלְיָא. רִבִּי יוֹחָנָן בְּשֵׁם רִבִּי יַנַּיי כּוֹלְהוֹן בְּתוֹךְ שִׁשָּׁה.
כַּהֲנָא בְּשֵׁם רִבִּי שִׁמְעוֹן בֶּן לָקִישׁ כּוֹלְהוֹן חוּץ לְשִׁשָּׁה. אִם כּוֹלְהוֹן חוּץ לְשִׁשָּׁה
נִיתְנֵי תִשְׁעָה. אָמַר רִבִּי תַּנְחוּם בּוֹצַרְיָיא וְכֵן הִיא בַּעֲרוּגָה שֶׁבָּעֲרוּגוֹת הִיא
מַתְנִיתָא.

Halakhah 1: (*Is.* 61:11) "Its sown seeds," the minimum of seeds are
two[8]. Rebbi Samuel bar Sisarṭa[9] said, from two you infer four. Just as for
two you start at the beginning of six and reduce continuously, so for four
you start at the beginning of six and reduce continuously. It is impossible
that there should not be a free space to plant in the middle[10]. Rebbi Jonah
said, working space joins working space but a kind does not meet another
kind to jail it[11]. Rebbi Joshua ben Levi: "Its seed, its seeds, its sown
seeds.[12]" That follows Rebbi Jehudah, since Rebbi Jehudah said six, "seed,
its seed, its seeds, its sown seeds." Rebbi Ḥaggai said, זרעיה has five letters;
everywhere I find ו,י I delete them[13]. This was asked of Rav Huna, the
scribe of the assembly, and he said, זרועיה is written *plene*[14]. Rebbi
Joḥanan in the name of Rebbi Yannai: All inside of six[15]. Cahana in the
name of Rebbi Simeon ben Laqish: All at the outside of six[16]. Then we

should state "nine!" Rebbi Tanḥum from Bostra[17] said, that is true. But our Mishnah speaks of a garden bed in the middle of garden beds[18].

6   Reading of the parallel in *Šabbat* 9:2, which has better readings. The word is missing in the Leyden/Venice texts here.

7   Reading of the text in *Šabbat*. Here וראינא

8   The entire paragraph appears in *Šabbat* 9:2 as commentary on the Mishnah: "(R. Aqiba said,) from where do we know that one may sow five different kinds in a garden bed that is six-by-six hand-breadths, four at the four edges and one in the middle? For it is said: For as earth will produce its plants, and as a garden will make its seedlings germinate . . . It does not say, 'it will make germinate its seedling' but 'its seedlings.'" The verse uses a plural for the seedlings in a garden (interpreted as one garden bed); this proves only that it is possible to sow more than one kind.

9   He appears elsewhere as R. Samuel bar Sosarṭa, bar Sotar (*Berakhot* p. 63).

10   The argument as explained by R. Simson: At the end of the paragraph, it is stated that one deals with a vegetable bed surrounded by other vegetable beds. The rules of "jailing" require that at the corners squares of one hand-breadth each must be empty. In order to grow two kinds of plants, one may sow two strips, each 4 hand-breadths long, along parallel edges, each one 2.25 hand-breadths wide, so that the required separation of 1.5 hand-breadths be observed in the middle. But then the argument may be used also for the other two edges. That means that one sows four triangular patches; each one has a base of 4 hand-breadths on an edge of the garden bed, with base angles of 45°. These triangles must be separated by strips 1.5 hand-breadths wide. This means that at the edges, we must leave a square of edge length a empty, whose diagonal is $1.5 = a\sqrt{2}$. Hence, $a = 1.061$; the bases of the triangle can only be 3.878 hand-breadths. In that case, the distance of the third vertex of the triangle from its base is equal to half the base on the edge, or 1.939 hand-breadths. The distance from the center is $a = 1.061 < 1.5$. In order to plant a single seed in the middle, it is therefore necessary to cut off the

triangles at distance 1.5 from center and edge, creating four congruent trapezoids. The height of a trapezoid is $h=1.5$, its base $2b=3.878$. By similar triangles, the length t of its top is given by $2b/b = t/(b-h)$ or $t = 0.878$. That makes it possible to plant a single fifth kind in a small space in the middle. The total area planted amounts to four times the area of the trapezoids, 15.044 square hand-breadths, plus the area of the small space in the middle.

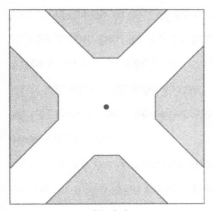

fig. 3-4

11   Each separate kind needs a working space around it, given by the strip of width 1.5 hand-breadths, but the same strip does serve two different kinds without problem. Also, the rules of "jailing" only apply to fields, not to garden beds.

12   Here starts a new approach, that the verse itself implies more than 2 kinds. The word זרוע appears only twice in the Bible, *Is.* 61:11 and in a description of grain (*Lev.* 11:37): "seeds of seedlings that may be sown." In contrast to modern dictionaries which take זרוע as a word different from זרע, the authors here take it as expansion of זרע "seed." The root is expanded three times, by taking the plural, adding a possessive suffix, and adding the letter ו Each change is taken as a plural, hence three plurals are added for a total of six.

13   R. Ḥaggai assumes that originally all Hebrew spelling was what is called defective. Hence, any ו or י that is neither part of the root nor required by grammatical rules is considered an addition by later scribes and therefore is disregarded. That eliminates the ו but leaves the י which is required as sign of plural. One ends up with five letters, following the anonymous opinion in the Mishnah.

14   The spelling זירועיה in the text is certainly wrong since the expression of ִ by י is standard only in Mishnaic and later texts, not in Biblical ones. Hence, the *plene* writing refers to the masoretic spelling of the word; one has six letters supporting Rebbi Jehudah.

15   All seeds are sown in the interior of the bed, away from the

corners.

16   The corners at the boundary, which are at the outside, are sown. Then one may sow four 1-by-1 corner patches, four 1-by-1 patches at the center of each edge, and a center diamond, for a total of nine patches.

17   A student of R. Jeremiah and teacher of R. Eliezer ben R. Yose, from the town of Bostra, at the Southern border of the province of Trachonitis, on the road from Damascus to Edrei.

18   Since the rules of "jailing" apply to garden beds as a whole, not to smaller patches, the corners cannot be sown. This is the opinion of Samuel in the Babli (Šabbat 86b). Otherwise, it really is possible to sow 9 kinds, as the Babli puts it (Šabbat 86a), in the case of a garden bed planted on land otherwise dry, with no other beds nearby. Rav in the Babli still admits only five kinds even on dry land.

רִבִּי יִצְחָק וְרִבִּי אִימִי הֲווֹן יָתְבִין מַקְשֵׁיי תַּנִּינָן הָיָה לוֹ גּוֹבֶל גָּבוֹהַּ טֶפַח זוֹרְעִין בְּתוֹכָהּ שְׁלֹשָׁה עָשָׂר שְׁלֹשָׁה עַל כָּל־גּוֹבֶל וְגוֹבֶל וְאֶחָד בָּאֶמְצַע. נִיתְנֵי שִׁשָּׁה בָּאֶמְצַע. תִּיפְתָּר שֶׁהַגּוֹבְלִין מְמַעֲטִין שִׁשָּׁה. אִם בְּשֶׁהַגּוֹבְלִין מְמַעֲטִין שִׁשָּׁה בְּדָה תַּנִּינָן רִבִּי יוּדָה אוֹמֵר שִׁשָּׁה בָּאֶמְצַע. וְקִייַמְנוּהָ וְלָא יָדְעִין אִי חַבְרַייָא קִייַמְנוּהָ אִי רִבִּי אִימִי קִייְמָהּ: עַל רֹאשָׁהּ. וְאֵין עַל רֹאשָׁהּ בְּדָה תַּנֵּי רִבִּי חִייָא רִבִּי יוּדָה אוֹמֵר שְׁמוֹנָה עָשָׂר.

Rebbi Isaac and Rebbi Immi were sitting and asking, did we not state: "If it had a wall around it at least one hand-breadth high, one may sow in it thirteen kinds: three at each of the three sides of the wall, and one in the middle." Should we not state, 'six in the middle?'[19] Explain it if the walls diminish six[20]. If the walls diminish six, is it that about which we stated: "Rebbi Jehudah says, six kinds may be in the middle?" We upheld it, but we do not know whether the colleagues upheld it or Rebbi Immi did; it refers to the beginning[21]. And if it refers to the beginning, it is that about which Rebbi Ḥiyya stated: Rebbi Jehudah says, 18[22].

19   As was shown in the Mishnah, a six-by-six plot may be sown in six rhombs.

20   The leaves of the three patches on the border wall hang down and leave less than a 6-by-6 plot in the middle.

21   Rebbi Jehudah disagrees with the anonymous Tanna of the first statement in the Mishnah and asserts that one may sow 6 distinct kinds in a garden bed.

22   This can only refer to the case of the garden bed with 12 little patches on the surrounding elevated wall and 6 rhombs in the middle, for a total of 18. This is possible since the outer patches are a hand-breadth higher than the planted rhombs which, therefore, do not have to be 1.5 hand-breadths distant from the border patches (the actual horizontal distance is only

$$1.5/\sqrt{3.25} = .832.)$$

מַהוּ לְהַקְרִיחַ בֵּית רוֹבַע וְלִזְרֹעַ בְּתוֹכוֹ חֲמִשָּׁה מִינֵי תְבוּאָה. מַה אִם שִׁשָּׁה עַל שִׁשָּׁה שֶׁלוֹקִין עָלָיו דְּבַר תּוֹרָה אַתְּ אָמַר מוּתָּר. כָּאן שֶׁאֵין לוֹקִין עָלָיו דְּבַר תּוֹרָה לֹא כָל־שֶׁכֵּן. מַהוּ לְהַקְרִיחַ בִּתְחִילַת שִׁשָּׁה לִהְיוֹת מֵיצַר וְהוֹלֵךְ. מַה אִם בְּשָׁעָה (שֶׁאֵין) עֲבוֹדָה פוֹגַעַת בַּעֲבוֹדָה אַתְּ אָמַר מוּתָּר. כָּאן שֶׁאֵין עֲבוֹדָה פוֹגַעַת בַּעֲבוֹדָה לֹא כָל־שֶׁכֵּן. לֹא צוּרְכָא דִי לָא.²³ מַהוּ לְהַקְרִיחַ בִּתְחִילַת בֵּית רוֹבַע לִהְיוֹת מֵיצַר וְהוֹלֵךְ. מַה אִם שִׁשָּׁה עַל שִׁשָּׁה שֶׁלוֹקִין עָלָיו דְּבַר תּוֹרָה אַתְּ אָמַר מוּתָּר. כָּאן שֶׁאֵין לוֹקִין עָלָיו דְּבַר תּוֹרָה לֹא כָל־שֶׁכֵּן.

May one raze a *bet rova'* and sow in it five different kinds of grain[24]? If about a six-by-six, for whose infringement one is whipped by Biblical decree[25], you say it is permitted, then so much more here where you are not whipped by Biblical decree. May one raze at the corners of a six-by-six to make a continously narrowing patch[26]? If in a case where working space does meet working space[27], you say that it is permitted, then so much more in this case where working space does not meet working space. That[28] was unnecessary. May one raze at the corners of a *bet rova'* to make a continously narrowing patch? If about a six-by-six, for whose infringement one is whipped by Biblical decree, you say it is permitted, then so much more here where you are not whipped by Biblical decree[29].

23   The usual technical term is לא צורכא דלא.

24   In one of the patterns established for a garden bed, homothetically amplified. The side of a square containing a *bet rova'* is 10.206 cubits (*Peah*, Chapter 2, Note 78).

The Arabic verb קרח has many disparate meanings. One of them in the first conjugation is: "to dig a well", another one in the eighth, "to improvise". As noted in Chapter 2, Note 150, the derived noun קראח means "plot prepared for sowing". Since Arabic terms for agriculture are mostly taken from the languages of sedentary people living near Arabia, it might be that הקריח is an unrecognized Hebrew verb meaning "to prepare for agricultural use".

25   As given in Mishnah 2:10, a violation of the requirement of a six-by-six empty space is punishable, but the six-by-six plot itself may be sown in different patches. Hence, the *bet rova'*, which for separation is only a rabbinical requirement, cannot have more stringent rules.

26   Is the construction of the trapezoids described in the first paragraph of the Halakhah legitimate?

27   In the case of the arrangement described in the Mishnah (following Maimonides and Rashi) there is no space reserved for working the patches; they cannot be shared. In the case of the trapezoids there is space reserved and the spaces are shared.

Translation and explanation follow the Rome ms. in which the word שאין is missing. If the word is read, with the Leyden ms. and the Venice print, the argument following has no basis.

28   The entire question, since the triangular-trapezoidal configuration described in the Halakhah is far from optimal as far as utilization of the soil is concerned.

29   For a *bet rova'* one proposes to make trapezoids with sides inclined 45°, starting out at a distance of 1.061 from the vertex and narrowing to a distance of 1.5 from the center; see Note 10, fig. 3-4. In that case, the base is 8.084 cubits, the vertex of the isosceles triangle of angle 45° is again

at distance $a = 1.061$ from the center and the length of the top of the trapezoid is again $t = 0.878$. Since in the trapezoidal configuration the plots do not touch, there is no question of "jailing", which is permitted for garden beds and forbidden for larger fields; hence, what is permitted for garden beds in this case is also permitted for a *bet rova'*. (The configuration of Maimonides cannot be carried over to larger fields.)

רִבִּי נַסָא שָׁאַל לֹא מִסְתַּבְּרָא בְּנַגּוֹ שֶׁל גּוֹבֶל שֶׁל שְׁנֵי טְפָחִים מוּתָּר לִזְרוֹעַ בּוֹ שְׁנֵי מִינִין. רִבִּי נָסָה שָׁאַל עָשָׂה פֵּיאָה בְּאֶמְצַע זָרַע בְּנוּ מֵסִין מְשָׁכוֹ בְּכַמָּה. מִן מָה דְּאָמַר רִבִּי יִצְחָק וְרִבִּי אִימִי תִּיפְתָּר שֶׁהַגּוֹבְלִין מְמַעֲטִין שִׁשָּׁה. הָדָא אֶמְרָה אֲפִילוּ פֵּרָה מִיכָן. עַד הֵיכָן. נִישְׁמְעִינָהּ מִן הָדָא גוּמְמִיּוֹת שֶׁהֵן עֲמוּקוֹת טֶפַח זוֹרְעִין לְתוֹכָהּ שְׁלֹשָׁה זֵירְעוֹנִין אֶחָד מִיכָן וְאֶחָד מִיכָן וְאֶחָד בְּאֶמְצַע. הָדָא אֶמְרָה עַד טֶפַח. רִבִּי בָּא בַּר כַּהֲנָא שִׁמְעוֹן בַּר נְרָשִׁיָּה בְּשֵׁם רִבִּי שִׁמְעוֹן בֶּן לָקִישׁ בְּנוֹטִים לְחוֹרְבָה שָׁנוּ.

Rebbi Nassa asked: Is it not reasonable that, if the top of the surrounding wall is two hand-breadths wide, one is permitted to sow on it two kinds[30]? Rebbi Nassa asked: If he drew a string[31] in the middle[32], sowed in half of it, how far can he draw it? From what Rebbi Isaac and Rebbi Immi said[33], "explain it if the walls diminish six," that means that it may be even less[34] than that. Let us hear from the following[35]: "In depressions that are one hand-breadth deep one may sow three seeds, one on each side and one in the middle." That means, down to one hand-breadth[36]. Rebbi Abba bar Cahana, Simeon from Nerash[37] in the name of Rebbi Simeon ben Laqish: They taught "leaning towards a dry spot"[38].

30   Leave the outermost one hand-breadth square at the outer edge empty, then plant one hand-breadth square at the inner part of the 2-by-2 corner and then four times 1-by-1.5 of different kinds alternatingly on both

sides of the wall along an edge, and so on all around the bed.

31   For this meaning of פיאה cf. Chapter 1, Note 159. Since in the absence of vines all that is demanded to avoid *kilaim* is that the patches in which different kinds are sown be divided by clear dividing lines and, as a rabbinic requirement, that the kinds be visibly separated, the erection of a symbolic wall satisfies the rabbinic requirement. The question is, how narrow is the minimum domain cordoned off by the פיאה?

32   Greek μέσος, η, ov "middle-, in the middle". (Rome ms: גימוס)

33   Earlier in this Halakhah.

34   Latin *parum*, cf. *Demai*, p. 521.

35   Tosephta *Kilaim* 2:9, with slightly changed language, תלמיות "little furrows," instead of גוממיות "little holes."

36   Any strip one hand-breadth wide may be cordoned off and sown in its entire length, irrespective of anything surrounding it.

37   Nothing is known about him. Nerash is a town on the Euphrates (in the Babli its reputation is bad.) The word בר is missing in the Rome ms.

38   The main point of this remark is in Halakhah 5. R. Simeon ben Laqish rejects the Tosephta quoted earlier which asserts that "a man may make little furrows in his field," and asserts that seeds of three different species, planted along the diagonal of a unit square, are permitted only if the surroundings are dry spots, nothing is planted there, and one will be able to turn the leaves of the plants growing in the corners to the outside in opposite directions and the leaves of the plant growing in the middle in the direction of the other (perpendicular) diagonal. (This is the position of Rav in the Babli, *Šabbat* 85a. It is rejected there by Samuel, *loc. cit.* 85b.)

אָמַר רִבִּי זְעִירָא כָּל־טֶפַח וְטֶפַח שֶׁל גוֹבֶל עָשׂוּ אוֹתוֹ מָקוֹם בִּפְנֵי עַצְמוֹ. וְיִהְיוּ
עֶשְׂרִים וַחֲמִשָּׁה שִׁשָּׁה עַל כָּל־גוֹבֶל וְגוֹבֶל וְאֶחָד בָּאֶמְצַע. וְכֵן הוּא הָתִיב רִבִּי בּוּן
בַּר חִייָה בְּשֵׁם רִבִּי שְׁמוּאֵל בַּר רַב יִצְחָק. וְהָתַנִּינָן הַתֶּלֶם וְאַמַּת הַמַּיִם שֶׁהֵן
עֲמוּקִין טֶפַח זוֹרְעִין לְתוֹכָן שְׁנֵי זֵירְעוֹנִין אֶחָד מִיכָּן וְאֶחָד מִיכָּן וְאֶחָד בָּאֶמְצַע.
וְנִיתְנֵי חֲמִשָּׁה שְׁנַיִם מִיכָּן וּשְׁנַיִם מִיכָּן וְאֶחָד בָּאֶמְצַע. לֵית יָכִיל צַד שֶׁכָּאן וְצַד
שֶׁכָּאן חוֹבֵשׁ אֶת הָאֶמְצָעִי.

Rebbi Zeïra said, they made every single hand-breadth[39] on the border
wall a domain for itself. Then there should be 25, six on each side of the
border wall and one in the middle! Is that so? Rebbi Abun bar Ḥiyya in
the name of Rebbi Samuel bar Rav Isaac objected: Did we not state[40] that
"in a furrow or a water canal one hand-breadth deep one may sow (two)[41]
kinds of seeds, one on each side and one in the middle." Should one not
state five, two on each side[42] and one in the middle? That is impossible;
the two sides jail the middle one.

39   Each 1-by-1 square on the elevated wall.

40   Mishnah 3:2.

41   Obviously, it should read "three"
as in the Mishnah, but the same
mistake "two" is found in both mss.

42   One at the bottom and one at

the top, separated by a vertical distance of at least one hand-breadth.
This arrangement does not have the
exemption from the rules of jailing but
is considered a regular field. Hence,
the arrangement is impossible.

רְבִּי בּוּן בַּר חִיָּה בְּשֵׁם רְבִּי שְׁמוּאֵל בַּר רַב יִצְחָק בָּעֵי גּוֹבֶל מַהוּ שֶׁיַּצִּיל אֶת
הַיֶּרֶק מִיַּד מוּקְשָׁה. מַה אִם זְרָעִים בְּזָרְעִים שֶׁהֵן נִיצוֹלִין בְּעֶשֶׂר אַמּוֹת וּמֶחֱצָה
אֵין הַגּוֹבֶל מַצִּיל מִיָּדָם. מוּקְשָׁה שֶׁהוּא נִיצוֹל בִּשְׁתֵּים עֶשְׂרֵה לֹא כָּל־שֶׁכֵּן.
מוּקְשָׁה עַצְמוֹ מַהוּ שֶׁיַּצִּיל בְּרֹאשׁ הַגּוֹבֶל. מַה אִם זְרָעִים בְּזָרְעִים שֶׁהֵן נִיצוֹלִין
בְּעֶשֶׂר אַמּוֹת וּמֶחֱצָה אֵינָן נִיצוֹלִין בְּרֹאשׁ הַגּוֹבֶל. מוּקְשָׁה שֶׁהוּא נִיצוֹל בִּשְׁמוֹנֶה
אַמּוֹת לֹא כָּל־שֶׁכֵּן. אָמַר רְבִּי יוּדָן אָבוֹיי דְּרְבִּי מַתַּנְיָא[43] וְהֵן הוּא כָּל־שֶׁכֵּן.
אֶלָּא הָכֵן הוּא. וּמַה אִם זְרָעִים בְּזָרְעִים שֶׁנִּיצוֹלִין בִּשְׁנַיִם עָשָׂר אַמָּה וּמֶחֱצָה
אֵינָן נִיצוֹלִין בְּרֹאשׁ הַגּוֹבֶל. מוּקְשָׁה שֶׁהוּא נִיצוֹל בִּשְׁתֵּים עֶשְׂרֵה לֹא כָּל־שֶׁכֵּן.

Rebbi Abun bar Ḥiyya in the name of Rebbi Samuel bar Rav Isaac
asked: Does the border wall save vegetables from melons[44]? If the
border wall does not save different kinds of grains that are saved by 10.5

cubits[45], does this not apply *a fortiori* to melons that are saved only by twelve cubits? Does planting melon save on top of the border wall[46]? If different kinds of grains that are saved by 10.5 cubits are not saved on top of the border wall, does this not apply *a fortiori* to melons that are saved by eight cubits[47]? Rebbi Judan, the father of Rebbi Mattaniah, said, is that a reasoning *a fortiori*? It must be as follows: If different kinds of grains that are saved by 12.5[48] cubits are not saved on top of the border wall, does this not apply *a fortiori* to melons that are saved only by twelve cubits?

43   Reading of the Rome ms. Venice has מחליא by a change of liquids *l - n*. Everywhere else the authority quoted is the father of Rebbi Mattaniah.

44   Melons and squash whose stems grow meandering over large areas and whose leaves are broad are subject to special rules expressed in Mishnaiot 3:3 ff. Since they also can be counted as vegetables, do the leniencies of the border wall extend to these plants?

45   Grains sown in fields must be separated by a *bet rova'*, 10.21 cubits square (here rounded upwards to 10.5), and no border wall is ever mentioned in the rules that govern these fields.

Squash and melon for whom we require a separation of 12 cubits along the entire length of the field cannot possibly have more lenient rules.

46   If a melon or squash is planted on top of the wall, may one sow other vegetables in the garden bed, immediately adjacent to that melon but one hand-breadth lower?

47   Opinion of R. Aqiba in Mishnah 6, opposed by the Sages. If this is chosen, the argument goes the wrong way!

48   This is clearly a scribal error; it must be 10.5 as above. The error must be an old one since it appears in both manuscripts.

(fol. 28b) **מֹשׁנֹה ב:** כָּל־מִין זְרָעִים אֵין זוֹרְעִין בַּעֲרוּגָה וְכָל־מִין יְרָקוֹת זוֹרְעִין בַּעֲרוּגָה. חַרְדָּל וַאֲפוּנִין הַשּׁוּפִין מִין זְרְעוֹנִין. אֲפוּנִין הַגַּמְלוֹנִין מִן יָרָק. גּוֹבֵל שֶׁהָיָה גָבוֹהַּ טְפַח וְנִתְמָעֵט כָּשֵׁר. שֶׁהָיָה כָּשֵׁר מִתְּחִילָתוֹ. הַתֶּלֶם וְאַמַּת הַמַּיִם שֶׁהֵן עֲמוּקִין טֶפַח זוֹרְעִין לְתוֹכָן שְׁלֹשָׁה זֵירְעוֹנִין אֶחָד מִיכָּן וְאֶחָד מִיכָּן וְאֶחָד בָּאֶמְצַע.

Mishnah 2: One does not sow any kind of seed-plants in a garden bed[49]; but one may sow any kind of vegetables in a garden bed. Mustard and smooth peas are counted as seed-plants, large peas are vegetables. A border wall that was one hand-breadth high and shrank is in order because it was in order at the start[50]. In a furrow or a water canal one hand-breadth deep one may sow three kinds of seeds, one on each side and one in the middle.

49   "Seed-plants" are plants whose seeds are used as food, such as grains and legumes. [Sometimes, זרעים denotes only grains.] "Vegetables" are plants whose edible parts are leaves and/or roots (e. g. cabbage or turnips) or the fruit is distinct from the seeds (e. g. cucumbers or melons.) Since it is not customary to sow such little quantities of seeds, one may not sow grains and similar produce in garden beds that contain multiple kinds of plants since it would look like *kilaim*. What one does with a small plot planted only with one kind is not regulated here.

50   The "start" is planting or sowing time when the full height is required.

הֲלָכָה ב: כָּל־מִין זְרָעִים וכו'. חַרְדָּל וְהָאֲפוּנִין הַשּׁוּפִין מִין זְרָעִים שֶׁזַּרְעָן לְיָרָק אֵין נוֹתְנִין אוֹתָן עַל גַּבֵּי עֲרוּגָה. הָאֲפוּנִין הַגַּמְלוֹנִין וּפוֹל הַמִּצְרִי שֶׁזַּרְעָן לְזֶרַע אֵין נוֹתְנִין אוֹתָן עַל גַּבֵּי עֲרוּגָה. זַרְעָן לְיָרָק נוֹתְנִין אוֹתָן עַל גַּבֵּי עֲרוּגָה. וּשְׁאָר זֵירְעוֹנֵי גִינָה שֶׁאֵין נֶאֱכָלִין. אַף עַל פִּי שֶׁזַּרְעָן לְזֶרַע נוֹתְנִין אוֹתוֹ עַל גַּבֵּי עֲרוּגָה.

Halakhah 2: "Any kind of seeds, etc." Mustard and smooth peas are counted as seed-plants; if one sowed them for use as vegetables he may not put them in a garden bed. Large peas and Egyptian beans sown to produce seeds one may not put in a garden bed. If one sowed them for use as vegetables he may put them in a garden bed. All other garden seeds that are not eaten, even though one sowed to produce seeds, he may put them in a garden bed[51].

51   A similar text, likewise not free from corruption, is in Tosephta *Kilaim* 2:8: "Mustard, beans, and oats, even if sown for use as vegetables, may be put in a garden bed. Large peas and Egyptian beans sown to produce seeds may be put in a garden bed; if one sowed them for use as vegetables he may not put them in a garden bed. All field or garden vegetables, even though one sowed to produce seeds, he may not put in one garden bed." R. S. Lieberman prefers to read instead of שופין "oats" שיפון "smooth ones," referring to beans, parallel to "peas" of the Mishnah. But the manuscripts of the Tosephta are too corrupt here to be of any value.

נִתְמָעֵט כָּשֵׁר. אָמַר רִבִּי אִימִּי הָדָא דְּאַתְּ אָמַר לִזְרָעִים שֶׁבּוֹ הָא לִזְרַע בּוֹ בַּתְּחִילָּה אָסוּר. עָבַר וְזָרַע מֵאַחַר שֶׁאֵלּוּ מוּתָּרִין אַף אֵלּוּ מוּתָּרִין. רִבִּי יִרְמְיָה בָּעֵי נִיחָא נֶעֶקְרוּ הַשְּׁנִייִם הָרִאשׁוֹנִים מוּתָּרִין. נֶעֶקְרוּ הָרִאשׁוֹנִים הַשְּׁנִייִם מַה הֵן. נִישְׁמְעִינָהּ מִן הָדָא. הַמִּיטָה שֶׁנִּיטְּלוּ שְׁתֵּי אֲרוּבוֹת שֶׁלָּהּ וְעָשָׂה לָהּ אֶת הַחֲדָשׁוֹת וְלֹא שִׁינָה אֶת הַנְּקָבִים. נִשְׁתַּבְּרוּ חֲדָשׁוֹת טְמֵיאָה וִישָׁנוֹת טְהוֹרָה שֶׁהַכֹּל הוֹלֵךְ אַחַר הַיְשָׁנוֹת. הָדָא אָמְרָה נֶעֶקְרוּ הַשְּׁנִייִם הָרִאשׁוֹנִים מוּתָּרִין. נֶעֶקְרוּ הָרִאשׁוֹנִים הַשְּׁנִייִם אֲסוּרִין.

"If it shrank it is in order." Rebbi Immi said, that means for the seeds that were already on it; hence, it is forbidden to sow anew. If one transgressed and sowed, since the earlier ones are permitted, so are the new ones. Rebbi Jeremiah asked: It is acceptable that if the later ones

were uprooted, the earlier ones are permitted. If the earlier ones were
uprooted, what is the status of the later ones? Let us hear from the
following[52]: "If the two long boards of a bed were removed and one
made two new ones in their stead but did not change the holes, if the new
boards were broken, it is impure, if the old ones, it is pure, since all goes
after the prior status." That means, if the later ones were uprooted, the
earlier ones are permitted. If the earlier ones were uprooted, the later
ones are forbidden.

52   Mishnah *Kelim* 19:6. One has to
read ארוכות instead of ארובות   One
speaks of a bed that has a wooden
frame, consisting of two short (head-
and foot-) boards and two long ones on
the sides. The mattress lies on strings
that are strung from one long board to
the opposite one. The bed has become
impure. It is a utensil, and any utensil
can become pure either by immersion
in a ritual bath (which is a problem for

a large bed) or by becoming unusable.
The Mishnah states that if the two long
boards are broken we no longer have a
bed and the remainder becomes pure,
even if the boards are later replaced
by new ones. But if the long boards
are simply removed and replaced by
new ones, the impurity is not removed,
even if the replacement boards break,
since the old ones could be returned to
their place.

רִבִּי יוֹנָה אָמַר רִבִּי זְעִירָא וְרִבִּי אִימִי תְּרַוֵּיהוֹן בְּשֵׁם רִבִּי יוֹחָנָן חַד אָמַר סוֹמְכִין
לְגֶדֶר וְאֵין סוֹמְכִין לְגוֹבֵל. וְחָרָנָה אָמַר גוֹבֵל שֶׁנִּתְמָעֵט כָּשֵׁר. הָא גֶדֶר שֶׁנִּתְמָעֵט
פָּסוּל. וְלֹא יֵדְעִין מָאן אָמַר דָּא וּמָאן אָמַר דָּא. מִן דְּאָמַר רִבִּי יוֹסֵי רִבִּי
זְעִירָא בְּשֵׁם רִבִּי יוֹחָנָן סוֹמְכִין לְגֶדֶר וְאֵין סוֹמְכִין לְגוֹבֵל. הֲוֵי רִבִּי אִימִי דוּ
אָמַר גוֹבֵל שֶׁנִּתְמָעֵט כָּשֵׁר הָא גֶדֶר שֶׁנִּתְמָעֵט פָּסוּל. אָמַר רִבִּי יוֹסֵי אוּף אֲנָן
תַּנִּינָן תַּרְתֵּיהוֹן גוֹבֵל שֶׁנִּתְמָעֵט כָּשֵׁר. הָא גֶדֶר שֶׁנִּתְמָעֵט פָּסוּל. (fol. 28d) סוֹמְכִין
לְגֶדֶר. דְּתַנִּינָן הַסּוֹמֵךְ לַבּוּר וּלְנִיר וּלְנָפָה וּלְדֶרֶךְ וּלְגֶדֶר שֶׁהוּא גָּבוֹהַּ עֲשָׂרָה
טְפָחִים. אֵין סוֹמְכִין לְגוֹבֵל. דְּתַנִּינָן הַתֶּלֶם וְאַמַּת הַמַּיִם שֶׁהֵן עֲמוּקִין טֶפַח

זוֹרְעִין לְתוֹכָן שְׁלֹשָׁה[53] מִינֵי זֵירְעוֹנִין אֶחָד מִיכָן וְאֶחָד מִיכָן וְאֶחָד בָּאֶמְצַע. אִם
אוֹמֵר אַתְּ שֶׁסוֹמְכִין לְגוֹבֵל. יִזְרַע לְמַטָּן כַּמָּה שׁוּרוֹת. אָמְרִין חַבְרַיָּא קוֹמֵי רִבִּי
שְׁמוּאֵל בַּר אָבִין תִּיפְתָּר שֶׁהָיָה זוֹרֵעַ בְּרֹאשׁ הַגּוֹבֵל. אָמַר לוֹ אִין כֵּינִי יַעֲקוֹר
אוֹתוֹ הַקֶּלַח וְיִזְרַע לְמַטָּן כַּמָּה שׁוּרוֹת. לֹא מוּטָב לַעֲקוֹר קֶלַח אֶחָד וְלִזְרֹעַ
לְמַטָּן כַּמָּה שׁוּרוֹת.

Rebbi Jonah said, Rebbi Zeïra and Rebbi Immi, both in the name of
Rebbi Johanan, one said one plants near a fence but not near a border
wall[54], and the other said, a border wall which lost height is in order,
hence a fence which lost height is invalid. But we do not know who said
what. Since Rebbi Yose said, Rebbi Zeïra in the name of Rebbi Johanan:
One plants near a fence but not near a border wall, this means Rebbi
Immi is the one who said that a border wall that lost height is in order,
hence a fence which lost height is invalid. Rebbi Yose said, we also did
make both statements, that a border wall that lost height is in order, hence
a fence that lost height[55] is invalid. One plants near a fence, as we have
stated (Mishnah 2:8): "One does sow close to a fallow field, a plowed field,
a stone wall, a foot path, a fence ten hand-breadths high." One does not
plant near a border wall, as we have stated (Mishnah 3:2): "In a furrow or
a water canal that are one hand-breadth deep one may sow three kinds of
seeds, one on each side and one in the middle." If you say that one may
sow close to a border wall, he should sow several rows down in the ditch.
The colleagues said before Rebbi Samuel bar Abin: Explain it if the top of
the border wall was sown[56]. He said to them, if it is so, let him uproot
that stem and sow several rows down in the ditch. Is it not better to
uproot one stem and sow several rows down in the ditch?

53   Reading of the Rome ms., parallel to the Mishnah. Venice: ששה .

54   However, everybody agrees that one may sow ראש חור under all circumstances. This shows that the explanation of Maimonides in Mishnah 3:1, using a diamond-shaped field in the center ערוגה, is consistent with the Halakhah here, while R. Obadiah of Bertinoro's explanation of the position of R. Jehudah is not.

The statement means that one may sow close to the fence on both sides of the fence, even if the thickness of the fence is less than 1.5 hand-breadths, but sowing near a border wall that is 1 hand-breadth high requires one to leave half a hand-breadth empty in the ערוגה or on top of the wall adjacent to the ערוגה, for a total separation of 1.5 hand-breadths.

55   To less than 10 hand-breadths, unless the fence itself was 1.5 hand-breadths wide.

56   One may not sow parallel to it in the ditch unless the total distance was 1.5 hand-breadths. But a single seed acts as ראש חור and is permitted.

(fol. 28b) **משנה ג:** הָיָה רֹאשׁ תּוֹר יָרָק וְנִכְנַס לְתוֹךְ שָׂדֶה יָרָק אַחֵר מוּתָּר מִפְּנֵי שֶׁהוּא נִרְאָה כְּסוֹף שָׂדֵהוּ. הָיְתָה שָׂדֵהוּ זְרוּעָה יָרָק וְהוּא מְבַקֵּשׁ לִיטַּע בְּתוֹכָהּ שׁוּרָה שֶׁל יָרָק אַחֵר. רִבִּי יִשְׁמָעֵאל אוֹמֵר עַד שֶׁיְּהֵא הַתֶּלֶם מְפוּלָּשׁ מֵרֹאשׁ הַשָּׂדֶה וְעַד רֹאשׁוֹ. וְרִבִּי עֲקִיבָה אוֹמֵר אוֹרֶךְ שִׁשָּׁה טְפָחִים וְרוֹחַב מְלוֹאוֹ. רִבִּי יוּדָה אוֹמֵר רוֹחַב כִּמְלוֹא רוֹחַב הַפַּרְסָה.

Mishnah 3: It is permitted that a vertex of vegetables enter[57] a field of other vegetables, since it is visibly the end of its field[58]. If one's field was sown with vegetables and he wants to plant in it a row of a different vegetable, Rebbi Ismael says, not unless he has an open furrow from one end of the field to the other[59]. Rebbi Aqiba says, a length of six hand-breadths for a full width[60]. Rebbi Jehudah says, the width must be the width of the sole of a foot[61].

57   As before, "enter" means that it touches the last row of vegetables, not that there should be a straight line on which the last plant of the ראש חור is bordered on both sides by plants of the field.

58   Visual separation is all that is needed.

59   If the new vegetable is inside the field, there must be an empty open furrow on each side of the new vegetable. The six hand-breadths given as minimum separating distance in Mishnah 2:10 apply only to the distance between two vegetable fields, not to one row inside a field.

60   "Full width" according to R. Simson means six hand-breadths; according to Maimonides it means the full depth of the furrow. Both explanations conllide with parts of the Halakhah.

61   Exactly one hand-breadth. The language of R. Jehudah refers to the verse *Deut.* 11:10: "You did irrigate it with your foot like a vegetable garden."

(fol. 28d) **הלכה ג**: הָיָה רֹאשׁ תּוֹר כו'. תַּנֵּי בַּר קַפָּרָא אֵינוֹ זוֹרֵעַ לְתוֹכָהּ אֶלָּא מִין אֶחָד בִּלְבָד.

Halakhah 3: "A vertex[62], etc." Bar Qappara stated: He sows in it only one kind.

62   A quote from the Mishnah. However, the discussion is not about that sentence at all. In the opinion of R. Moses Margalit, the statement of Bar Qappara is out of place here and belongs to the Mishnah quoted last in the preceding Halakhah, about the ditch that is one hand-breadth deep. According to the more likely opinion of R. Eliahu Fulda, the statement refers to the one row of vegetables that one plants in a field of other vegetables.

מַה אָמַר רְבִּי יִשְׁמָעֵאל בְּרוֹחַב. מַה אֵין רְבִּי עֲקִיבָה חוֹבֵשׁ בְּשָׁלֹשׁ שׁוּרוֹת. אִית לֵיהּ רוֹחַב מְלוֹאוֹ. רְבִּי יִשְׁמָעֵאל שֶׁהוּא חוֹבֵשׁ בִּשְׁתֵּי רוּחוֹת לֹא כָל־שֶׁכֵּן. מַה אָמַר רְבִּי יִשְׁמָעֵאל בְּשׁוּרָה שֶׁיֶּרֶק בִּשְׂדֵה תְבוּאָה. מַה אֵין רְבִּי עֲקִיבָה דְּהוּא מֵיקֵל הָכָא הוּא מַחְמִיר תַּמָּן. רְבִּי יִשְׁמָעֵאל דְּהוּא מַחְמִיר הָכָא לֹא כָל־שֶׁכֵּן

דְּיַחְמִיר תַּמָּן. לֹא צוּרְכָא דְּלָא מָה דְּאָמַר רְבִּי יִשְׁמָעֵאל תַּמָּן בְּרוֹחַב. כְּמָה
דְּאַתְּ אָמַר תַּמָּן לֹא שַׁנְיָיא הִיא רְבִּי עֲקִיבָה הִיא רְבִּי יִשְׁמָעֵאל בְּרוֹחַב.

What did Rebbi Ismael say about the width? Now if Rebbi Aqiba, who
encloses it from three sides, requires a full width, Rebbi Ismael who
encloses it by two rows[63], not so much more[64]? What does Rebbi Ismael
say about a row of vegetables in a grain field[65]? Now if Rebbi Aqiba,
who is more lenient here, is restrictive there, Rebbi Ismael, who is more
restrictive here, certainly will be restrictive there! No, this is not
necessarily so. What does Rebbi Ismael say there about width? As we say
there, there is no difference between Rebbi Aqiba and Rebbi Ismael in
matters of width[66].

63   In the Rome ms: חובש משתי שורות,
"encloses by two rows." R. Aqiba
permits the insert to be enclosed even
from three sides. R. Ismael insists that
strictly only two sides are permitted;
therefore, he must require that the
dividing empty furrow extend from one
end of the field to the other.

64   For an argument *a fortiori*, R.
Aqiba must be less restrictive than R.
Ismael. This is the case since R. Aqiba
requires only a separation along six
hand-breadths. But then, in order for
the argument to make sense, "a full
width" must mean the maximum
separation mentioned in the Mishnah, i.

e., six hand-breadths. Otherwise, R.
Ismael could be more restrictive than
R. Aqiba even in regard to width.
Hence, the explanation of Maimonides
of the Mishnah cannot be accepted.

65   This is the topic of Mishnah 7;
there a separation of six hand-breadths
is quoted as universally accepted
opinion.

66   Since the relevant statement is
anonymous. The corresponding
statement of the Tosephta, *Kilaim* 2:13,
reads: "Whether there be a row of
melon or a row of any other vegetable
in a grain field, a length of 10.5 cubits
by a width of six hand-breadths."

שְׁמוּאֵל אָמַר לֹא שָׁנוּ אֶלָּא שׁוּרָה אַחַת הָא שְׁתַּיִם אָסוּר. רְבִּי יוֹחָנָן וְרְבִּי
שִׁמְעוֹן בֶּן לָקִישׁ תְּרֵוֵיהוֹן אָמְרֵי לֹא שַׁנְיָא הִיא אַחַת הִיא שְׁתַּיִם.

Samuel said, they taught only one row[67], hence two are forbidden.
Rebbi Joḥanan and Rebbi Simeon ben Laqish both say that there is no
difference between one and two rows.

67   "A row" mentioned in the Mish-   opinion, two rows form a field and are
nah may mean "one row." In Samuel's   subject to the rules of Mishnah 2:10.

רְבִּי שִׁמְעוֹן בֶּן לָקִישׁ אָמַר מוּתָּר לְהַבְקִיעַ אַרְבַּע שׁוּרוֹת בְּבִקְעָה.   אָמַר רְבִּי
יוֹחָנָן וּבִלְבַד שֶׁיִּהוּ[68] שְׁתֵּי שׁוּרוֹת הַחִיצוֹנוֹת נִידוֹנוֹת כַּעֲרוּגָה.   אָמַר רְבִּי זְעִירָא
וּבִלְבַד שְׁלֹשָׁה בְּתוֹךְ שִׁשָּׁה.

Rebbi Simeon ben Laqish said, it is permitted to split four rows in an
open field[69]. Rebbi Joḥanan said, only if the two outer rows be[70] treated
as garden beds. Rebbi Zeïra said, only if three are within six[71].

68   Rome ms.: שֶׁלֹּא יְהוּ.

69   בקעה (Arabic בְּקְעָה) everywhere
is agricultural land accessible only by
footpaths, not by public road. At such
a place not visited by non-farmers, R.
Simeon ben Laqish permits an insert of
up to four rows in a field growing
other kinds.

70   Version of the Rome ms: "That
they cannot be treated." This reading
seems to be the original one. Four
rows are permitted only if those adjacent to the other crops are single
rows, not garden beds, since otherwise
no clean separation of the vegetable
rows and the rest of the crop is
possible.

71   The rows must be compact, not
more than two hand-breadths allotted
to each row. Together with a separation of six hand-breadths from the
rest of the crop, this makes for a neat
insert.

אָמַר רבִּי הוּנָא טַעֲמָא דְּרבִּי יוּדָה וְהִשְׁקִיתָ בְרַגְלְךָ כְּגַן הַיָּרָק. וְכַמָּא הִיא
שִׁעוּרָהּ שֶׁל פַּרְסָה טֶפַח.

Rebbi Ḥuna said, what is the reason of Rebbi Jehudah[72]? (*Deut.* 11:10)
"That you irrigated with your feet as in a vegetable garden." What is the
measure of a foot sole? A hand-breadth.

72   In the Babli (*Šabbat* 85a), this is
the opinion of R. Zeïra (Zera). It
would appear that the author here is
not the Galilean Rebbi Huna but the
Babylonian Rav Huna, teacher of R.

Zeïra. This paragraph can be added to
the list of parallels given in the Yerushalmi in the name of a Babylonian and
in the Babli in the name of a Galilean.

תַּנִּינָן הָכָא דְּרבִּי יוּדָה וְתַנִּינָן תַּמָּן. אִילוּ תַנִּיתָהּ הָכָא וְלֹא תַנִּיתָהּ תַּמָּן הֲוֵינָן
אָמְרִין מַה אִין רבִּי יְהוּדָה דְּהוּא מַחְמִיר הָכָא מֵיקַל תַּמָּן. רַבָּנָן דְּאִילֵּין מֵקִילִין
הָכָא לֹא כָּל־שֶׁכֵּן יָקִילוּן תַּמָּן. הֲוֵי צוּרְכָא מַתְנֵי תַּמָּן. אוֹ אִילוּ תַנִּיתָהּ תַּמָּן
וְלֹא תַנִּיתָהּ הָכָא. הֲוֵינָן אָמְרִין מַה אִין רַבָּנָן דְּאִינוּן מַחְמְרִין תַּמָּן אִינּוּן
מֵיקִילִין הָכָא. רבִּי יְהוּדָה דְּהוּא מֵיקַל תַּמָּן לֹא כָּל־שֶׁכֵּן דְּיָקִיל הָכָא. הֲוֵי
צוּרְכָא מַתְנֵי הָכָא וְצוּרְכָה מַתְנֵי תַּמָּן.

We have stated the opinion of Rebbi Jehudah here, and we have stated
it there[73]. If it had been stated here but not there, we would have said
that just as Rebbi Jehudah who is restrictive here[74] is permissive there, the
rabbis who are permissive here certainly will be permissive there. Hence,
it is necessary to state there. Or if it was stated there but not here, we
would have said that just as the rabbis who are restrictive there are
permissive here, Rebbi Jehudah who is permissive there certainly will be
permissive here. Hence, it is necessary to state both here and there.

73   In Mishnah 3:1, where the rabbis
permit only five kinds in a garden bed

but Rebbi Jehudah permits six.
74   Rebbi Jehudah requires a full

hand-breadth of empty space as walk-
way between the two parts of the field.
The rabbis require less, according to
the argument here. The problem is
that the rabbis are not mentioned here,
nor are they in any parallel Tosephta.
By the rules of decision accepted in the
Babli, practice follows R. Aqiba against
any one of his colleagues. If we accept
this here, then the explanation of R.
Aqiba's statement in the Mishnah must
follow Maimonides and the opinion of

R. Simson becomes unacceptable!
There is no indication that the Yerushalmi accepts that rule; in addition, R.
Aqiba here disagrees with two of his
colleagues, so that there is a two to one
majority which rejects his position.
We must assume that in the opinion of
the Yerushalmi, the rabbis will be
ready to accept any furrow as
separation, without prescribing any
minimal width.

(fol. 28b) **משנה ד**: הַנּוֹטֵעַ שְׁתֵּי שׁוּרוֹת שֶׁל קִישׁוּאִין שְׁתֵּי שׁוּרוֹת שֶׁל דִּילוּעִין
שְׁתֵּי שׁוּרוֹת שֶׁל פּוֹל הַמִּצְרִי מוּתָּר.   שׁוּרָה שֶׁל קִישׁוּאִין שׁוּרָה שֶׁל דִּילוּעִין שׁוּרָה
שֶׁל פּוֹל הַמִּצְרִי אָסוּר.   שׁוּרָה שֶׁל קִישׁוּאִין שֶׁל דִּילוּעִין שֶׁל פּוֹל הַמִּצְרִי וְשׁוּרָה
שֶׁל קִישׁוּאִין רְבִּי לִיעֶזֶר מַתִּיר וַחֲכָמִים אוֹסְרִין.

Mishnah 4: If someone plants two rows of green melons, two rows of
pumpkin, two rows of Egyptian beans, this is permitted[75]. One row of
melons, one row of pumpkin, one row of Egyptian beans is forbidden.
One row each of melons, pumpkin, Egyptian beans, and one row of
melons, Rebbi Eliezer permits but the Sages forbid.

75   We are now talking about one
field on which several kinds of
vegetables are planted. If there are
two rows, each of them appears as a

separate planting if a certain amount of
separation is kept between rows of
different kinds; this is permitted. The
plants enumerated here are those with

meandering stems and very broad leaves; in that case, single rows are not easily kept apart and the field looks like *kilaim*. The restrictions apply only to these kinds of vegetables.

(fol. 28d) **הלכה ד**: הַנּוֹטֵעַ שְׁתֵּי שׁוּרוֹת כו'. חִזְקִיָּה אָמַר בְּמַחְלוֹקֶת. מָאן דְּאָמַר תַּמָּן שְׁתֵּים עֶשְׂרֵה. אוּף הָכָא שְׁתֵּים עֶשְׂרֵה. מָאן דְּאָמַר תַּמָּן בִּשְׁמוֹנֶה אוּף הָכָא בִּשְׁמוֹנֶה. אָמַר רִבִּי יוֹחָנָן דִּבְרֵי הַכֹּל הִיא. יָפֶה כֹּחַ מוּקְשָׁה בֵּין[76] הַמּוּקְשִׁיּוֹת לְהַצִּיל בִּשְׁמוֹנֶה.

Halakhah 4: "If one plants two rows", etc. Hizqiah said, there is disagreement. He who says there 12 [cubits], here also 12 [cubits][77]. He who says there eight, here also eight. Rebbi Johanan said, this Mishnah is according to everybody. A strip of melon is good enough among strips of melons to be saved by eight[78].

76   Reading of Rome ms. Venice and Leyden: גין "protection". In the next paragraph, all sources read בין.

77   The reference is to the next Mishnah, where planting onions (with no spreading leaves at all) and melons (with very large, spreading leaves) in one field is discussed. It is established there that one row of melons or pumpkins needs a strip four cubits wide. Hence, two rows create a strip eight cubits wide. The distance between the two adjacent kinds, melon on one side and Egyptian beans on the other, therefore is eight cubits (plus two hand-breadths for an empty furrow on each side.) This corresponds to the opinion of R. Aqiba in the next Mishnah. However, the Sages in the next Mishnah require a swath 12 cubits wide between the two outer kinds, that is three rows of each kind. Hence, Hizqiah is of the opinion that the Mishnah here follows R. Aqiba and not the anonymous Sages, even though it is formulated as an anonymous statement.

78   In R. Johanan's opinion, the sages require 12 cubits only between squash and onion, completely different plants. But melon and pumpkin grow in the same fashion (and, it seems, also Egyptian beans, which might not be beans in the botanical sense). In that case, the Sages also will require only

strips 8 cubits wide and the Mishnah   R. Aqiba.

does not indicate that practice follows

אוֹרְכוֹ בְּכַמָּה חוֹבֵשׁ. אָמַר רִבִּי זְעִירָא וְלַמְדִינָהּ מִן הַכָּרֶם. כְּמָה דְּתֵימַר גַּבֵּי

כָּרֶם לֹא שַׁנְיָיא הִיא אָרְכוֹ הִיא הֶפְלֵיגוֹ. אַף הָכָא לֹא שַׁנְיָיא הִיא אָרְכוֹ הִיא

הֶפְלֵיגוֹ. עַל דַּעְתֵּיהּ דְּחִזְקִיָּה נִיחָא. מָאן דְּאָמַר תַּמָּן בִּשְׁמוֹנֶה אוֹף הָכָא

בִּשְׁמוֹנֶה. עַל דַּעְתֵּיהּ דְּרִבִּי יוֹחָנָן אוֹרְכוֹ בְּכַמָּה חוֹבֵשׁ. אִין תֵּימַר בִּשְׁמוֹנֶה קַל

וָחוֹמֶר לְמוּקְשָׁה בֵּין הַבְּצָלִים שֶׁלֹּא יַחְבִּישׁ אֶלָּא שְׁתֵּים עֶשְׂרֵה. מַה אִם מוּקְשָׁה

בֵּין הַמּוּקְשִׁיּוֹת שֶׁיַּפִּיתָהּ כּוֹחוֹ לְהַצִּיל בִּשְׁמוֹנָה נֶחֱבַשׁ בִּשְׁמוֹנָה. מוּקְשָׁה בֵּין

הַבְּצָלִים שֶׁהוֹרַעְתָּ כּוֹחוֹ לְהַצִּיל בִּשְׁתֵּים עֶשְׂרֵה לֹא כָל־שֶׁכֵּן שֶׁלֹּא יַחְבֵּשׁ אֶלָּא

בִּשְׁמוֹנָה. אִין תֵּימַר מוּקְשָׁה בֵּין הַבְּצָלִים אֵין נֶחֱבַשׁ אֶלָּא בִשְׁתֵּים עֶשְׂרֵה. קַל

וָחוֹמֶר לְמוּקְשָׁה בֵּין הַמּוּקְשִׁיּוֹת שֶׁלֹּא יַחְבֵּשׁ אֶלָּא בִשְׁתֵּים עֶשְׂרֵה.

How long does it have to be to jail[79]? Rebbi Zeïra said, let us infer it
from a vineyard. Just as you say in regard to a vineyard that there is no
difference between length and separation[80], so here also there is no
difference between length and separation. That is fine according to the
opinion of Ḥizqiah; there eight[81] and here also eight[82]. According to
Rebbi Joḥanan, with how much will it jail? If you say with eight, is there
an argument *a fortiori*[83] that a strip of melons among onions will jail only
with twelve? But a melon strip, which you empowered among melon
strips to save by a mere eight, will be jailed by eight, melon strips among
onions, which you weakened to save only by twelve, certainly will be
jailed only by eight. If you say that a melon strip among onions will be
jailed only by twelve, then an argument *a fortiori* shows that a melon
strip among melons should be jailed only by twelve.

79   How long do the rows of   "jailing" do apply, that one kind cannot
vegetables have to be that the rules of   be surrounded on all four sides by

other kinds of vegetables.

80   Width is called here "separation" since all assertions about separations are formulated by the number of rows, i. e., by width. For vineyards, the main rule precribes the same separation in all directions, i. e., in a circle centered in the offending growth (Mishnah 5:5).

81   Eight cubits of separation are indicated both in Mishnah 3:6 for the planting of broad-leaved vegetables with other vegetables, as also in Mishnah 4:8 for the vineyard. (For single plantings in a vineyard, one needs a separation of 16 cubits, Mishnah 5:5).

82   Eight cubits length of the planted row.

83   Given two predicate functions $A(x,y,z, \ldots)$, $B(x,y,z, \ldots)$ and a partial ordering < by severity. I. e., if $A(x)$ expresses an action that is legal and $B(x)$ one that is illegal, we note $A(x) < B(x)$. Similarly, if both actions are illegal but the punishment for $A(x)$ is less than that for $B(x)$, then $A(x) < B(x)$. The rule now is: if it is known that $A(x_1, \ldots, x_n) < B(x_1, \ldots, x_n)$, but nothing is known about $A(x_1, \ldots, x_n, u)$ and $B(x_1, \ldots, x_n, u)$, then the consistency of the logical system requires the assertion $A(x_1, \ldots x_n, u) \leq B(x_1, \ldots x_n, u)$ meaning that $B(x_1, \ldots x_n, u)$ cannot be strictly less severe than $A(x_1, \ldots x_n, u)$; but if in all other respects B is strictly more severe than A, it cannot be asserted that with respect to u B must be more severe than A. (Cf. H. Guggenheimer, Logical Problems in Jewish Tradition, in: *Confrontations with Judaism*, ed. Ph. Longworth, London, 1967, pp. 171-196.)

עַד כְּדוֹן בְּרוֹצֵף. בְּעוֹשֶׂה קְלָחִים יְחִידִים. כְּמָה דְּתֵימַר גַּבֵּי כֶּרֶם לֹא שַׁנְיָיא הוּא רוֹצֵף הוּא עוֹשֶׂה. אַף הָכָא לֹא שַׁנְיָיא הוּא רוֹצֵף הוּא עוֹשֶׂה קְלָחִים יְחִידִים.

So far if [the planting] is covering [the entire area]. What about producing single stalks? Just as you say of a vineyard that there is no difference between covering or producing [single stalks], so here also there is no difference between continuous planting or producing single stalks.

רִבִּי יַנַּאי אָמַר בְּמַחְלוֹקֶת שְׁנֵי מִינִין מִצְטָרְפִין לְהַצִּיל וְאֵין שְׁנֵי מִינִין מִצְטָרְפִין
לֵיאָסֵר. רַב אָמַר דִּבְרֵי הַכֹּל הִיא כְּשֵׁם שֶׁשְּׁנֵי מִינִין מִצְטָרְפִין לְהַצִּיל כָּךְ שְׁנֵי
מִינִין מִצְטָרְפִין לֵיאָסֵר. מַתְנִיתִין מְסַיְּיעָא לְרִבִּי יַנַּאי דְּתַנִּינָן רִבִּי לִיעֶזֶר מַתִּיר.
מַתְנִיתִין פְּלִיגָא עַל רַב שׁוּרָה שֶׁל קִישּׁוּאִין שׁוּרָה שֶׁל דִּילוּעִין שׁוּרָה שֶׁל פּוֹל
הַמִּצְרִי וְשׁוּרָה שֶׁל קִישּׁוּאִין. עַד שֶׁלֹּא נָטַע אֶת הָרְבִיעִית לֹא כְבָר נָאֱסְרוּ.
תִּיפְתָּר שֶׁנָּטַע אַרְבַּעְתָּן כְּאַחַת.

Rebbi Yannai said, it is a controversy whether two kinds join together
to save but do not join together to prohibit[84]. Rav said, it is everybody's
opinion that just as two kinds join together to save so they do join
together to prohibit. Our Mishnah supports Rebbi Yannai, as we have
stated: "Rebbi Eliezer permits it." Our Mishnah differs with Rav: "One
row of melons, one row of pumpkin, one row of Egyptian beans, and one
row of melons." Before he started the fourth one, was it not already
forbidden? Explain it that he planted the four rows simultaneously[85].

84   According to R. Yannai, when R.
Eliezer permits four rows with the two
middle ones of different kinds, he
cannot forbid three rows of different
kinds, and the previous statement about
three single rows follows the Sages but
not R. Eliezer, as noted later in this
paragraph, since otherwise three are
already forbidden and the fourth row,
which makes matters worse, could not
make the first three permitted again.
According to Rav, everybody agrees
that if between two rows of the same
kind there are at least eight cubits
distance, then R. Eliezer permits the
planting, but in the case of only three
rows he will join his colleagues in
forbidding it.

85   This tortured explanation is
needed only for Rav.

(fol. 28b) **מַשְׁנָה ה**: נוֹטֵעַ אָדָם קִישׁוּת וּדְלַעַת לְתוֹךְ גּוּמָא אַחַת וּבִלְבַד שֶׁתְּהֵא זוֹ
נוֹטָה לְצַד זוֹ וְזוֹ נוֹטָה לְצַד זוֹ. (וְנוֹטֵעַ שֵׂעָר שֶׁל זוֹ לְכָאן וְשֶׁל זוֹ לְכָאן. שֶׁכֵּן מַה
שֶׁאָסְרוּ חֲכָמִים לֹא גָּזְרוּ אֶלָּא מִפְּנֵי מַרְאִית הָעַיִן.)

Mishnah 5: One may plant melon and pumpkin in the same hole on
condition that one of them points to one side, the other to the other side[86].
(One plants so that the hair of one be here, the hair of the other one there,
for what the Sages forbade is only because of the misleading
impression.)[87]

86   They have to grow out of their
common hole in two opposite
directions. The hole presumably is
square and the two plants are planted
in opposite corners.

87   In the Leyden ms., the text in
parentheses is written on the margin.
In many Mishnah mss., the text is
missing. It must be an old gloss that

entered the text; cf. *Mishnah with
Variant Readings*, Institute of the
Complete Israeli Talmud, Jerusalem
1972. If the text were original, the
Halakhah would discuss it. In addition,
the verb גזר in the acceptation "to
decree" is Babylonian only (cf. *Demay*
Chapter 1, Note 89).

(fol. 28d) **הֲלָכָה ה**: נוֹטֵעַ אָדָם קִישׁוּת כו'. תַּנֵּי מוּתָּר הוּא אָדָם לַעֲשׂוֹת בְּתוֹךְ
שָׂדֵהוּ גּוּמָא קְטַנָּה עֲמוּקָה טָפַח וְלִזְרֹע בְּתוֹכוֹ אַרְבַּע זֵירְעוֹנִין וּלְהַפְכָּן לְאַרְבַּע
רוּחוֹתֶיהָ. רִבִּי אַבָּא בַּר כַּהֲנָא שִׁמְעוֹן נָרְשִׁיָּיה בְּשֵׁם רִבִּי שִׁמְעוֹן בֶּן לָקִישׁ בְּנוֹטִין
לְחוֹרְבָה שָׁנוּ. רִבִּי מָנָא בָּעֵי אִם בְּנוֹטִין לְחוֹרְבָה נִיתְנֵי שְׁמוֹנָה שָׁנַיִם מִכָּן וּשְׁנַיִם
מִכָּן וּשְׁנַיִם מִכָּן וּשְׁנַיִם מִכָּן.

Halakhah 5: "One may plant melon", etc. It was stated[88]: "One may
make a small hole in one's field, one hand-breadth deep, sow in it four
seeds, and turn them to the four directions of the compass." Rebbi Abba
bar Cahana, Simeon of Nerash in the name of Rebbi Simeon ben Laqish:
That was taught regarding those which lean towards a dry spot[89]. Rebbi

Mana asked, if we deal with those that lean towards a dry spot, should we not state "eight," two on each of the edges[90]?

88   Tosephta *Kilaim* 2:9. There, the text reads "four kinds," somewhat more explicit and less restrictive than the wording given here.

89   See above, Halakhah 1. One can turn each growing plant away from the others only if outside there is space, not in a field. Hence, the Mishnah, if interpreted according to this statement, disagrees with the Tosephta.

90   The hole is square. An "edge" of the square is a semi-open interval which contains one of its endpoints but not the other. Then one may plant one seed at the endpoint and one at the midpoint of the edge, let the seed in the corner grow in the opposite direction of the diagonal, and the one planted in the middle of the edge perpendicular to the edge towards the outside. The question is not answered, but for broad-leaved plants the scenario is impossible.

(fol. 28b) **משנה ו:** הָיְתָה שָׂדֵהוּ זְרוּעָה בְּצָלִים וּבִיקֵשׁ לִיטַּע בְּתוֹכָהּ שׁוּרוֹת שֶׁל דִּילוּעִין. רְבִּי יִשְׁמָעֵאל אוֹמֵר עוֹקֵר שְׁתֵּי שׁוּרוֹת וְנוֹטֵעַ שׁוּרָה אַחַת וּמַנִּיחַ קָמַת בְּצָלִים בִּמְקוֹם שְׁתֵּי שׁוּרוֹת. וְעוֹקֵר שְׁתֵּי שׁוּרוֹת וְנוֹטֵעַ שׁוּרָה אַחַת. רְבִּי עֲקִיבָה אוֹמֵר עוֹקֵר שְׁתֵּי שׁוּרוֹת וְנוֹטֵעַ שְׁתֵּי שׁוּרוֹת וּמַנִּיחַ קָמַת בְּצָלִים בִּמְקוֹם שְׁתֵּי שׁוּרוֹת וְעוֹקֵר שְׁתֵּי שׁוּרוֹת וְנוֹטֵעַ שְׁתֵּי שׁוּרוֹת. וַחֲכָמִים אוֹמְרִים אִם אֵין בֵּין שׁוּרָה לַחֲבֵירְתָהּ שְׁתֵּים עֶשְׂרֵה לֹא יְקַיֵּים זֶרַע שֶׁל בֵּנְתַּיִם.

Mishnah 6: If one's field was sown with onions and he desired to plant there rows of pumpkin, Rebbi Ismael says, he uproots two rows, plants one row, and leaves two rows of onion standing, uproots two rows, plants one row[91]. Rebbi Aqiba says, he uproots two rows, plants two rows, and leaves two rows of onion standing, uproots two rows, plants two rows[92]. But the Sages say, if between one row and the next is less than twelve [cubits], he should not keep the seeds in between[93].

91   A row of vegetables together with its surroundings is four cubits wide. In the interpretation of Maimonides, R. Ismael requires that a swath eight cubits wide be cleared, in which a row of pumpkin four cubits wide is planted. Hence, in the interpretation given in the Halakhah, he envisages a field with a regular pattern: Eight cubits wide onions, two cubits fallow, four cubits pumpkins, two cubits fallow, eight cubits onions, etc. (R. Simson takes the Mishnah to mean that eight cubits have to be fallow between any two beds of onion.)

Since onions usually are planted, not sown, either the language of the Mishnah is imprecise or one speaks of a field in which onions were sown and then thinned to produce straight rows.

92   R. Aqiba requires only one furrow between different kinds. He has parallel strips of equal width, alternatingly pumpkins and onions. Then the farmer has to watch closely lest the pumpkins expand into the domain of the onions. (R. Simson holds also in this case that eight cubits have to be fallow between any two beds of onions; R. Aqiba holds that four of these eight are for tending the onions, four for tending pumpkins, and that for a single row of pumpkins one does not have to provide space around them. He holds that for a single row of pumpkins, R. Aqiba requires only four cubits to be fallow between any two beds of onions.)

93   In the interpretation of Maimonides, the Sages require only that between any two strips of pumpkin there be 12 cubits distance, but they do not require any fallow land between pumpkins and onions, except for the obligatory single furrow. In the interpretation of R. Simson, the total fallow land between two such rows must be 12 cubits, or six cubits between any two strips of differing kinds.

(fol. 28d) **הלכה ו**: הנוטע את כרמו כו׳. כַּהֲנָא אָמַר דִּבְרֵי רִבִּי יִשְׁמָעֵאל פְּעָמִים שֵׁשׁ עֶשְׂרֵה פְּעָמִים שְׁתֵּים עֶשְׂרֵה פְּעָמִים שְׁמוֹנֶה. בְּשָׁעָה שֶׁהוּא נוֹתֵן כָּל־הָעֲבוֹדָה

מִבְּפָנִים שֵׁשׁ עֶשְׂרֵה. מִקְצָתָהּ בִּפְנִים וּמִקְצָתָהּ בַּחוּץ שְׁתֵּים עֶשְׂרֵה. כּוּלָהּ מִבַּחוּץ
שְׁמוֹנֶה. שְׁמוּאֵל אָמַר לְעוֹלָם שְׁתֵּים עֶשְׂרֵה. וְתַנֵּי כֵּן קוֹצֵב עַל דִּבְרֵי שְׁנֵיהֶן. רִבִּי
יִשְׁמָעֵאל אָמַר שְׁתֵּים עֶשְׂרֵה. רִבִּי עֲקִיבָה אָמַר שְׁמוֹנֶה. הָא רִבִּי יִשְׁמָעֵאל אָמַר
שְׁתֵּים עֶשְׂרֵה. וְרַבָּנִין אֱמְרִין שְׁתֵּים עֶשְׂרֵה. מַה בֵּינֵיהוֹן סְמִיכָה. עַל דַּעְתֵּיהּ
דְּרִבִּי יִשְׁמָעֵאל אָסוּר לִסְמוֹךְ. וְרַבָּנִין אֱמְרִין מוּתָּר לִסְמוֹךְ.

Halakhah 6: (He who plants his vineyard, etc.)94. Cahana said, according to the words of Rebbi Ismael sometimes there are 16, sometimes 12, sometimes 895. When he gives all the working space in the interior, 16. Part interior and part exterior, 12. All exterior, 8. Samuel says, it always must be 1296. We have stated thus: "It is determined according to the statements of both of them: Rebbi Ismael says 12, Rebbi Aqiba says 8." Now, Rebbi Ismael says 12, and the rabbis say 12; in what do they disagree? Closing up! In the opinion of Rebbi Ismael one may not close up, but the rabbis say he may97.

94 This should be a quote from the Mishnah but is from Mishnah 4:9 and should be disregarded.

95 According to Rav Cahana, all R. Ismael requires is an empty swath four cubits wide, but its placement is arbitrary. Hence, if the pattern is 4 cubits pumpkin, 4 cubits empty, 8 cubits onions, 4 cubits empty, 4 cubits pumpkin, the distance from the last row of the first set of pumpkins to the first row of the second set of pumpkins is 4+8+4 = 16 cubits. If the pattern is regular, as explained in the Mishnah, the distance is 2+8+2 = 12. If the

empty spaces are all at the far side of the pumpkins, away from the onions, then the space is only 8 cubits (+ the space of the required furrows, half of which can be accounted for by the rows of pumpkins, leaving one handbreadth empty from the space of the onions.)

96 This is the pattern explained in Note 92, regular empty spaces two cubits wide between any two different species. This interpretation is accepted because it is supported by the following baraita.

97 R. Ismael requires empty strips

two cubits wide but the rabbis would accept an onion patch 12 cubits wide, separated from the pumpkins only by an empty furrow.

(fol. 28b) **משנה ז**: דְּלַעַת בְּיֶרֶק יָרֶק. בִּתְבוּאָה נוֹתְנִין לָהּ בֵּית רוֹבַע. הָיְתָה שָׂדֵהוּ זְרוּעָה תְבוּאָה וּבִיקֵשׁ לִיטַּע בְּתוֹכָהּ שׁוּרָה שֶׁל דִּילוּעִין נוֹתְנִין לַעֲבוֹדָתָהּ שִׁשָּׁה טְפָחִים. וְאִם הִגְדִּילָה יַעֲקוֹר מִלְּפָנֶיהָ. רַבִּי יוֹסֵי אוֹמֵר נוֹתְנִין לָהּ לַעֲבוֹדָתָהּ אַרְבַּע אַמּוֹת.

Mishnah 7: Pumpkin in the middle of vegetables goes by the rules of vegetables[98], in the middle of grain it needs a *bet rova'*. If one's field was sown with grain and he desired to plant there one row of pumpkin[99], he must allow six hand-breadths to tend it.[100] If it grows, he has to uproot before it. Rebbi Yose said, he allows four cubits to tend it.

98   In this last Mishnah dealing with *kilaim* on fields, we are back to considering fields, not garden plots. The rule referred to is Mishnah 2:10 which prescribes an empty space of six by six hand-breadths square.

99   Adhering to the minimal length of a row as given in Chapter 2.

100   Even though pumpkin plants spread widely, to start out one needs only a separating strip six hand-breadths wide for access. However, if the pumpkin should spread to the fallow strip, one must remove additional grain to maintain an access strip to the pumpkins that is one cubit wide. [This is the interpretation of Maimonides in his Commentary; in his Code (*Kilaim* 3:13), following the Gaonim, he requires only that grain be removed if the leaves of the pumpkin grow over the entire strip. R. Abraham ben David also adheres to the Gaonic interpretation. R. Simson is silent in the matter.]

חלכה ז: אָמַר רְבִּי יוֹחָנָן דִּבְרֵי רְבִּי יִשְׁמָעֵאל אֲפִילוּ שׁוּרָה יְחִידִית(fol. 28d) נוֹתְנִין לָהּ עֲבוֹדָה.

Halakhah 7: Rebbi Joḥanan said: The words of Rebbi Ismael imply that one allows space for tending even for a single row.[101]

101　This sentence seems to indicate that the Mishnah follows R. Ismael. This is convincing, as R. Aqiba in the previous Mishnah requires only one furrow of separation. (Commentary by R. Eliahu Fulda.)

מַהוּ לִיתֵּן עֲבוֹדָה לָרִאשׁוֹן. כְּמָה דְּתֵימַר גַּבֵּי כֶרֶם נוֹתְנִין עֲבוֹדָה לָרִאשׁוֹן. אוּף הָכָא נוֹתְנִין עֲבוֹדָה לָרִאשׁוֹן. מַהוּ לִזְרוֹעַ בֵּין הַגּוּמוֹת. כְּמָה דְּתֵימַר גַּבֵּי כֶרֶם אָסוּר לִזְרוֹעַ בֵּין הַגְּפָנִים. אַף הָכָא אָסוּר לִזְרוֹעַ בֵּין הַגּוּמוֹת.

Does one allow space for tending the first plant? Just as you say in regard of a vineyard that one gives space for tending the first plant, so here also one allows space for tending the first plant[102]. May one sow between the holes[103]? Just as you say in regard of a vineyard that one may not sow between the vines, so here also one may not sow between the holes.

102　This is an explicit Tosephta, *Kilaim* 2:13. Since it is formulated as an Amoraic argument, that Tosephta was not known to the editors of the Yerushalmi.

103　This refers to pumpkins that are not sown but planted, transferred as saplings from another plot where many seeds were grown. The saplings are put into separate depressions, very widely spaced. Does one have the right to sow plants between these depressions as long as the pumpkin has not spread into the cubit adjacent to the seeds? (If the pumpkin spreads, then the Mishnah has stated that one must clear the ground before it.)

(fol. 28b) **משנה ח**: אָמְרוּ לוֹ הֲתַחְמוּר זוֹ מִן הַגֶּפֶן. אָמַר לָהֶן מָצִינוּ שֶׁזוֹ חֲמוּרָה מִן הַגֶּפֶן. שֶׁל גֶּפֶן יְחִידִית נוֹתְנִין לָהּ עֲבוֹדָתָהּ שִׁשָׁה טְפָחִים. וְלִדְלַעַת יְחִידִית בֵּית רוֹבַע. רִבִּי מֵאִיר אוֹמֵר מְשׁוּם רִבִּי יִשְׁמָעֵאל (fol. 28c) כָּל־שְׁלשָׁה דִּילוּעִין לְבֵית סָאָה לֹא יָבִיא זֶרַע לְתוֹךְ בֵּית סָאָה. רִבִּי יוֹסֵי בֶּן הַחוֹטֵף אֶפְרָתִי מְשׁוּם רִבִּי יִשְׁמָעֵאל כָּל־שְׁלשָׁה דִּילוּעִין לְבֵית כּוֹר לֹא יָבִיא זֶרַע לְתוֹךְ בֵּית כּוֹר.

Mishnah 8: They[104] said to him, are you making this more restrictive than for a vine? He said to them, we find that this case is more restrictive than that of a vine. For a single vine[105] one allows six hand-breadths to tend it, but for a single pumpkin a *bet rova'*. Rebbi Meïr says in the name of Rebbi Ismael, if there are three pumpkin plants in a *bet seah* one should not sow[106] in that *bet seah*. Rebbi Yose, the son of the Snatcher from Efrat[107], says in the name of Rebbi Ismael, if there are three pumpkin plants in a *bet kor* one should not sow in that *bet kor*[108].

104   The anonymous Sages to R. Yose. This Mishnah is the continuation of the previous one.

105   Not only a single vine, but up to five vines in a single row; cf. Mishnah 4:5 according to the House of Hillel.

106   Sowing grain, the topic discussed in the Mishnah. R. Ismael, in

this version, expects a single pumpkin plant to spread over $2500/3 = 833.\overline{3}$ square cubits.

107   This personage is mentioned only here; nothing is known about him.

108   In this version, a single pumpkin occupies 10 *bet seah* = 25'000 square cubits.

(fol. 28d) **הלכה ח**: רִבִּי יוֹנָה בָּעֵי נָטַע חֲמִשָׁה דִּילוּעִין וּסְמָכָן לְגָדֵר מַהוּ לָתֵת לָהֶן הוֹלָכַת עָרִיס.

Rebbi Jonah asked: If somebody planted five pumpkins and trained them to grow on a fence, does one give it the rules of a trellis[109]?

109   It is explained in Mishnah 6:1 that five vines in a row growing on a trellis form a vineyard and, therefore, require the full space of four cubits for tending.   The question is whether pumpkins climbing a fence as trellis also are considered a full row and need separation on both sides. The question is not answered.

מַהוּ בְּכָל־הַדִּילוּעִין מְשַׁעֲרִין אוֹ לֹא.   כָּל־מָקוֹם שֶׁעָשִׂיתָ קִישׁוּת וּפוֹל הַמִּצְרִי כִּדְלַעַת יְוָנִית אַתְּ עוֹשֶׂה דְּלַעַת מִצְרִית כִּדְלַעַת יְוָנִית.   וְכָאן שֶׁלֹּא עָשִׂיתָ קִישׁוּת וּפוֹל הַמִּצְרִי כִּדְלַעַת יְוָנִית.   אֵין אַתְּ עוֹשֶׂה דְּלַעַת מִצְרִית כִּדְלַעַת יְוָנִית.

Does one estimate so for all kinds of pumpkins[110]?   Every place at which you made green melon and Egyptian beans equal to Greek gourd, you make Egyptian pumpkin equal to Greek gourd. Here, where you did not make melon and Egyptian beans equal to Greek gourd, you do not make Egyptian pumpkin equal to Greek gourd.

110   Is "pumpkin" in the Mishnah a generic name, or does it apply only to Greek gourd that has the most expansive leaves? The Mishnah applies only to Greek gourd. Melon and Egytian beans are treated in parallel with pumpkin in Halakhah 2:11.

וְתָיבִינֵיהּ הֲרֵי הַמְּקַיֵּם קְלָחִים לַחִים לְזֶרַע יְחִידִים צָרִיךְ לְהַפְנוֹת לָהֶם בֵּית רוֹבַע אוֹ לַעֲשׂוֹת לָהֶם מְחִיצָה גְּבוֹהָה עֲשָׂרָה טְפָחִים.   קַל הוּא בְּשׁוּרָה. (fol. 29a) מִן מַה דְּלָא מְתִיב לֵיהּ.   הֲוֵו כֵן רִבִּי יוֹסֵי סָבַר מֵימַר הִיא שׁוּרָה הִיא מְרוּבַּע. דְּאָמַר רִבִּי יוֹנָה וְרִבִּי יוֹסֵי גְּלִילָאָה בְּשֵׁם רִבִּי יוֹסֵי בֵּי רִבִּי חֲנִינָה הַמְּקַיֵּים קֶלַח אֶחָד בְּתוֹךְ שֶׁלּוֹ לְזֶרַע צָרִיךְ לְהַפְנוֹת לוֹ בֵּית רוֹבַע אוֹ לַעֲשׂוֹת לוֹ מְחִיצָה גְּבוֹהָה עֲשָׂרָה טְפָחִים.   אֲפִילוּ מִין בְּמִינוֹ.   הָתִיב רִבִּי בּוּן בַּר חִיָּיה קוֹמֵי רִבִּי זְעִירָא. וְהָתַנִינָן כּוּסְבָּר שֶׁזְּרָעָהּ לְזֶרַע יַרְקָהּ פָּטוּר.   אָמַר לֵיהּ שַׁנְיָיא הִיא כּוּסְבָּר שֶׁהִיא וְזַרְעָהּ נֶאֱכָלִין.

Why did they not object to him[111]: If someone keeps single fresh stalks growing to produce seeds, must he not clear around them a *bet rova'* or fence them in by a fence of ten hand-breadths? For a row one is more lenient[112]. Since they did not object to him, it follows that Rebbi Yose thinks that row and square[113] are the same. For Rebbi Jonah and Rebbi Yose the Galilean[114] said in the name of Rebbi Yose ben Rebbi Ḥanina: He who keeps a single fresh stalk growing to produce seeds must clear around it a *bet rova'* or fence it in by a fence of ten hand-breadths, even if it is the same kind[115]. Rebbi Abun bar Ḥiyya objected before Rebbi Zeïra, did we not state[116]: "If coriander was sown for its seeds, its greens are exempt?" He answered him, coriander is a special case since both the plant and its seeds are eaten.

111   Why did the Sages not find an answer to the argument of R. Yose in the Mishnah?

112   If a plant is grown for its greens and the seeds are not edible, then, as will be stated, plants grown for seeds are considered a kind different from those grown for food and, on a field, are subject to all rules of separation for *kilaim*. Nevertheless, if the plants raised for seeds form a row, they are under the general rules for rows. This is all according to the anonymous majority opinion in the Mishnah. Hence, for them, the argument of R. Yose is totally irrelevant, since his argument is about single plants!

113   One plant in the middle of a square as in Mishnah 5:5.

114   The third generation Amora, not the third generation Tanna whose title is always given in Hebrew.

115   If a vegetable is grown for its edible parts then the same vegetable grown to produce seeds has the status of a different crop.

116   Mishnah *Ma'serot* 4:5: "If coriander was sown for its seeds, the greens of it are exempt; if it is sown for greens, both greens and seeds must be tithed." The question is really about the second part of the sentence, not quoted in the text: If it is sown for greens, the seeds also must be tithed.

Hence, the seeds cannot be considered a different crop. Why should plants grown for seeds have to be fenced off from the rest of the field? The answer is that they do not have to be fenced off but that the rule of R. Yose ben R. Hanina refers only to plants whose seeds are not eaten with the rest of the plant.

אָמַר רִבִּי יוֹסֵי בֵּי רִבִּי בּוּן בֹּא וּרְאֵה מַה בֵּין תְּחִילַת רִבִּי יִשְׁמָעֵאל לְסוֹפוֹ. שֶׁתְּחִילָתוֹ בְּבֵית כּוֹר וְסוֹפוֹ בְּבֵית סְאָה.

Rebbi Yose ben Rebbi Abun said, come and see the difference between the early and the late statements of Rebbi Ismael! He started out with a *bet kor* and ended up with a *bet seah*[117]!

117 Since it is known that Rebbi Meïr went to study with R. Ismael after the death of R. Aqiba, the opinion first quoted in the Mishnah in the name of R. Ismael is in fact the opinion of R. Ismael in his old age. It follows that the second opinion in the Mishnah is earlier in time; it may be ascribed to R. Ismael in his earlier years. (This is the explanation of R. Moses Margalit, supported by the mss. R. Simson switches *bet kor* and *bet seah* in the statement to adapt them to the order of the Mishnah.)

(fol. 29a) **משנה א**: קָרַחַת הַכֶּרֶם בֵּית שַׁמַּאי אוֹמְרִים עֶשְׂרִים וְאַרְבַּע אַמּוֹת. וּבֵית הֶלֵּל אוֹמְרִים שֵׁשׁ עֶשְׂרֵה אַמָּה. מָחוֹל הַכֶּרֶם בֵּית שַׁמַּאי אוֹמְרִים שֵׁשׁ עֶשְׂרֵה אַמָּה וּבֵית הֶלֵּל אוֹמְרִים שְׁתֵּים עֶשְׂרֵה אַמָּה. וְאֵי זוֹ הִיא קָרַחַת הַכֶּרֶם כֶּרֶם שֶׁחָרַב מֵאֶמְצָעוֹ אִם אֵין שָׁם שֵׁשׁ עֶשְׂרֵה אַמָּה לֹא יָבִיא זֶרַע לְשָׁם. הָיוּ שָׁם שֵׁשׁ עֶשְׂרֵה אַמָּה נוֹתְנִין לָהּ עֲבוֹדָתָהּ וְזוֹרֵעַ אֶת הַמּוֹתָר.

Mishnah 1: A bald spot in a vineyard[1]: the House of Shammai say 24 cubits[2] but the House of Hillel say 16 cubits. The circumference[3] of a vineyard: the House of Shammai say 16 cubits but the House of Hillel say 12 cubits. What is a bald spot in a vineyard? A vineyard that dried up in the middle; if there are less than 16 cubits one should not bring seeds there[4]. If there are 16 cubits, one allows it space to be tended[5] and the rest one may sow.

1 Here start the rules for *kilaim* in a vineyard, where the rules have to be more strict than for fields since other crops in a vineyard make everything "sanctified". For a biblical basis of the treatment of a partially dead vineyard, cf. Chapter 7, Note 44.

A dried-up vineyard cannot be successfully replanted unless lupines and other nitrogen-enriching plants grow there for a few years. The

vintner will want to sow these plants as soon as possible.

Instead of interpreting קרחת הכרם as "bald spot in a vineyard" one might think of "agricultural area in a vineyard", cf. Chapter 2, Note 150.

2 The cubit used to measure vessels can be determined from Mishnah *Kelim* 17:11 which states that some authorities define liquid measures as Roman. The Roman *quartarius*,

equivalent to the Jewish *reviït*, is 133 cm³. The Yerushalmi states in *Pesaḥim* 10:1 (fol. 37c) that the *reviït is* $7^1/_3$ cubic digits [the Babli (*Pesaḥim* 109a) defines it as 10.8 cubic digits.] The Yerushalmi digit is therefore the cube root of $(133/7.3333)$cm³ or 2.63 cm. Then the cubit of 24 digits is 63 cm. (The corresponding Babylonian cubit would be only 55.5 cm.) On the other hand, Rashi (*Erubin* 60b) defines the cubit used for measuring terrain as half a pace, 2000 cubits being 1000 paces or one mile. If one uses the Roman mile (1000 *passus*) of 1473 m, one obtains 73.7 cm for the cubit. If Rashi would define the half-step as two Parisian feet, one would obtain 65 cm, in reasonable correspondence with the Yerushalmi cubit derived earlier, but if he would refer to half an *aune*, his cubit would be 59 cm, closer to the Babylonian standard.

In Tosephta *Kelim Baba Meẓi'a* 6:13, R. Meïr states that all cubits referred to in the laws of a vineyard are cubits of five hand-breadths. This makes the Palestinian vineyard cubit 20 digits or 52.6 cm, close to the standard Babylonian cubit.

3　　From the root חול "to turn in a circle," from which also the Biblical homonym מחול "fife." The rules of bald spots at the outer edge of a vineyard are given in Mishnah 2.

4　　The rules given here apply if the bald spot contains a circle of 16 cubits diameter (for the House of Hillel), i. e., if there is a point in the bald spot from which the minimal distance to any living vine is at least 8 cubits.

5　　The space needed to tend a vineyard is a path 4 cubits wide so that the ox-drawn cart of the vintner may move there. Even though the House of Hillel forbid sowing if the minimal width is less than eight cubits, if somebody sowed illegally on a smaller patch neither the seeds nor the vines become "sanctified" as long as a minimal distance of 4 cubits is observed everywhere (Mishnah 7:3).

הלכה א: קָרַחַת הַכֶּרֶם. אָמַר רִבִּי יוֹחָנָן קָרַחַת הַכֶּרֶם הוּא כֶּרֶם שֶׁחָרֵב. קָרַחַת הַכֶּרֶם מַקְרִיחִין אוֹתוֹ מֵאֶמְצָעוֹ. כֶּרֶם שֶׁחָרֵב מַקְרִיחִין אוֹתוֹ מִכָּל־צְדָדָיו. אָמַר רִבִּי יוֹסֵי וְהוּא שֶׁבָּא מִמַּטָּע כֶּרֶם גָּדוֹל. אֲבָל אִם בָּא מִמַּטָּע כֶּרֶם קָטוֹן אֵין זֶה קָרַחַת הַכֶּרֶם. וְתַנִּינָן אֵי זֶהוּ קָרַחַת הַכֶּרֶם כֶּרֶם שֶׁחָרֵב מֵאֶמְצָעוֹ וְנִשְׁתַּיֵּיר בּוֹ כְּדֵי כֶרֶם. בֵּין מֵאַרְבַּע רוּחוֹת בֵּין מִשְּׁלֹשׁ בֵּין מִשְׁתַּיִם זוֹ כְנֶגֶד זוֹ. הֵיךְ עֲבִידָא

חָמֵשׁ שׁוּרִין מִן שׁוּבַע שׁוּבַע נְסַב חַד כַּרְמוֹן. כְּיⁱ⁵ אִית אַרְבָּעָה כְּרָמִין וּתְלָתָא
בֵּינַיִין נְסַב חַד חוֹרָן אִית תַּמָּן תְּלָתָא כְּרָמִין וּתְרֵין בֵּינַיִין. נְסַב חַד חוֹרָן אִית
תַּמָּן תְּרֵין כְּרָמִין וְחַד⁶ בֵּינַיִין.

Halakhah 1: "A bald spot in a vineyard." Rebbi Joḥanan said that the rules for a bald spot in a vineyard and a dried-up vineyard[7] are the same. A bald spot is cleared in its middle, a dried-up vineyard is cleared on all four sides[8]. Rebbi Yose said, this applies to a large vineyard but if it comes from the plants of a small vineyard[9], the rules of a bald spot in a vineyard do not apply. Also, we have stated[10]: "What is a bald spot in a vineyard? A vineyard that dried up in its middle but enough for a vineyard remained, whether it be from all four sides, or from three, or from two opposite sides." How is that? Five rows of seven each[11], one took out one row of vineyard[12], that leaves four vineyards and three intervals. One takes out another one, that leaves three vineyards and two intervals. One takes out another one, that leaves two vineyards and one interval.

5   R. Eliahu Fulda and R. S. Lieberman want to read כמין כי "in the form of a χ" instead of כי. ברמון. R. Eliahu Wilna deletes כרמון and also takes כי as the name of the Greek letter χ. However, if one continues to take out χ-shaped groups of vines, one will not diminish the number of intervals. It will be seen later that vines planted in the shape of a χ never form a vineyard.

6   Reading of the Rome ms. Most older commentators emend the text to this reading since two parallel rows generate only one space between them.

Venice and Leyden: תרין

7   The rules of the dried spot are explained in Mishnah 5:1.

8   The dry spot reaches the border of the vineyard at 1, 2, 3, or 4 sides.

9   As explained in Mishnah 4:6, a minimal vineyard is formed by two rows, one with two, the other one with three vines in two parallel rows. A small vineyard here is one of which a circle of 16 cubits diameter has been cleared and no two minimal vineyards are still standing.

10   A similar statement is Tosephta

Kilaim 3:1: "What is a bald spot in a vineyard? A vineyard that dried up in its middle but four or five vines remained, whether it be from all four sides, or from three, or from two opposite sides." [R. Saul Lieberman has an ingenious explanation to harmonize Mishnah, Tosephta, and Yerushalmi, (תוספתא כפשוטה, p. 621) which, however, contradicts both the definition of קרחת הכרם (*loc. cit.*, a few lines earlier) and the fact that in all sources of the Tosephta the numerals are spelled out and not abbreviated. Similarly, R. Moses Margalit presents an extremely elegant solution but it seems contradicted by Rebbi Joḥanan in the next paragraph.]

11   The commentators want to change "7" into "5" but this is not warranted. The large vineyard of five rows of seven vines each contains 35 vines. A minimal vineyard has five vines. If three minimal vineyards are removed, 20 vines remain along the edges.

12   כרם is a vineyard, כרמון (a word

not recognized by the dictionaries) is not quite a vineyard. It is a row of five vines which according to the Mishnah do not form a vineyard for the House of Hillel, but will form one if the vines are drawn on a trellis as explained in Mishnah 6:1 and at the end of the Halakhah, Note 22. In our case, one takes out one row, given in the figure as o. Then one takes out two more minimal vineyards (see Note 9), indicated by c and e. The vines left standing are indicated by x. One cannot do a similar construction with less than a 5-by-7 vineyard. The distance between two vines usually is four cubits; then between first and last row the empty space is a required 16 cubits.

```
x  x  x  x  x  x  x
x  c  c  e  e  e  x
x  c  c  c  e  e  x
x  o  o  o  o  o  x
x  x  x  x  x  x  x
```

fig. 4-1

כַּהֲנָא אָמַר כִּתְחִילַת מַטָּעֲתוֹ עוֹשִׂין אוֹתוֹ. בֵּית שַׁמַּאי אוֹמְרִים תְּחִילַת מַטָּעֲתוֹ עֶשְׂרִים וְאַרְבַּע. וְחוּרְבָּנוֹ עֶשְׂרִים וְאַרְבַּע. אָמַר רְבִּי יוֹחָנָן בֵּית שַׁמַּאי מַחְמִרִין בְּחָרְבָּנוֹ יוֹתֵר מִמַּטָּעֲתוֹ. תְּחִילַת מַטָּעֲתוֹ שֵׁשׁ עֶשְׂרֵה וְחוּרְבָּנוֹ עֶשְׂרִים וְאַרְבַּע. וְכָל־הַדְּבָרִים בֵּית שַׁמַּאי מוֹסִיפִין שְׁלִישׁ. מָחוֹל הַכֶּרֶם עַל דַּעְתֵּיהּ דְּבֵית שַׁמַּאי שְׁמוֹנֶה עֶשְׂרֵה עַל דַּעְתֵּיהּ דְּבֵית הִלֵּל שְׁתֵּים עֶשְׂרֵה. וְהָתַנִּינָן מָחוֹל הַכֶּרֶם בֵּית

שַׁמַּאי אוֹמְרִים שֵׁשׁ עֶשְׂרֵה אַמָּה וּבֵית הִלֵּל אוֹמְרִים שְׁתֵּים עֶשְׂרֵה אַמָּה. אִית
דְּבָעֵי מֵימַר צֵא מֵהֶן אַרְבַּע אַמּוֹת לַעֲבוֹדָה נִמְצְאוּ שְׁתֵּים עֶשְׂרֵה עַל דַּעְתֵּיהּ
דְּבֵית שַׁמַּאי וּשְׁמוֹנֶה עַל דְּבֵית הִלֵּל.

Cahana said, they made it like the start of its planting. The House of
Shammai say, 24 at the start of planting, 24 at its destruction[13]. Rebbi
Johanan said, the House of Shammai are more restrictive in its destruction
than at the start of its planting. At the start of its planting 16, at its
destruction 24. In every case, the House of Shammai add one third[14]:
The circumference of a vineyard, according to the House of Shammai 18,
according to the House of Hillel 12[15]. But did we not state: "The
circumference of a vineyard, the House of Shammai say 16 cubits, the
House of Hillel say 12 cubits.[16]" Some want to say, deduct from this four
cubits for tending, there remain 12 cubits according to the House of
Shammai and 8 following the House of Hillel[17].

13   It is stated in Mishnah 4:9 that if
a vineyard consists of two rows distant
16 cubits, then it is not legally a
vineyard and a field may be sown in
between, 14 cubits wide for the entire
length of the rows of vines. In the
opinion of Cahana, that Mishnah
belongs only to the House of Hillel, and
by analogy we infer that the House of
Shammai require 24 cubits between the
two rows to permit sowing in between.
In the opinion of R. Johanan, Mishnah
4:9 is generally accepted, even by the
House of Shammai.

14   This third is taken from the top,
one third of 24, which is one half of 16.

15   This belongs to the statement of
R. Johanan that in all these
measurements, the measure of the
House of Shammai relates to that of the
House of Hillel as 3 to 2.

16   This *baraita* is not otherwise
preserved.

17   And again, $12 \div 8 = 3 \div 2$.
However, there is an inconsistency here
because the same argument applied to
the bald spot in a vineyard would lead
to $20 \div 12 = 5 \div 3$.

וַעֲבוֹדוֹת הַגֶּפֶן אֲדַעְתֵּיהּ דְּבֵית שַׁמַּאי שְׁמוֹנֶה אַמּוֹת וַאֲדַעְתֵּיהּ דְּבֵית הַלֵּל שֵׁשׁ
אַמּוֹת. וְהָתַנִּינָן לְפִיכָךְ הַזּוֹרֵעַ אַרְבַּע אַמּוֹת שֶׁבְּכֶרֶם בֵּית שַׁמַּי אוֹמְרִים קִידֵּשׁ
שׁוּרָה אַחַת וּבֵית הַלֵּל אוֹמְרִים קִידֵּשׁ (fol. 29b) שְׁתֵּי שׁוּרוֹת. נֵימַר בְּגִין בֵּית
הַלֵּל תַּנִּיתָהּ. וְהָתַנִּינָן אֵיזֶהוּ עָרִיס הַנּוֹטֵעַ שׁוּרָה שֶׁל חָמֵשׁ גְּפָנִים. שַׁנְיָיא הִיא
דְּאָמַר רִבִּי שִׁמְעוֹן בֶּן לָקִישׁ בֶּעָרִיס הַמְּעוּקָּם שָׁנוּ. עַל יְדֵי עֲקִימָה תַּרְתֵּיי
מִתְבַּלְּעָן.

But for tending a vineyard[18], according to the House of Shammai 8 cubits, according to the House of Hillel 6[19] cubits. But did we not state[20]: "Therefore, he who sows four cubits in a vineyard, the House of Shammai say that he sanctified one row, but the House of Hillel say that he sanctified two rows." Let us say that it[21] was stated because of the House of Hillel. But did we not state[22]: "What is a trellis? He who plants a row of five vines." There is a difference, since Rebbi Simeon ben Laqish said, this was taught about a curved trellis. By its curving, two are absorbed[23].

18   This discussion is independent of the previous paragraph, since an inconsistency was shown in the position of R. Joḥanan. Since the Mishnah does not define how much space is needed for tending a vineyard, this has to be established here.

19   This is the mss. text, but it is unacceptable since the following discussion clearly indicates that the reading is "4". The entire sentence is questionable since the contraction of על אדעתיה to דעתיה is Babylonian Aramaic.

20   Mishnah 4:5: "If somebody plants five vines in a row, the House of Shammai say it is a vineyard, the House

of Hillel say that there is no vineyard unless there are two rows. Therefore, he who sows *four cubits* in a vineyard, the House of Shammai say that he *sanctified* one row, but the House of Hillel say he *sanctified* two rows." Since the verse declares that sowing (grains or vegetables) in a vineyard *sanctifies* "the vineyard", the sown plants *sanctify* the nearest vineyard; for the House of Hillel this involves two rows. In any case, the House of Shammai is also mentioned in the Mishnah that puts the minimal distance of seeds from vines at slightly greater than 4 cubits.

21   "4 cubits."

22   Mishnah 6:1: "What is a trellis? If one plants a row of five vines near a fence 10 hand-breadths high or next to a ditch 10 hand-breadths deep and four wide, one gives it four cubits for tending. The House of Shammai say, one measures four cubits from the stem of the vines into the field, but the house of Hillel say, from the fence towards the field." The fact that the trellis makes a single row into a vineyard is needed only for the House of Hillel, since Mishnah 4:5 already had stated that five vines in a row are a vineyard for the House of Shammai.

23   Hence, for the House of Shammai the five vines would not form a vineyard were it not for the trellis; no conclusion can be drawn for the position of the House of Shammai on the measure of space for tending of a vineyard planted in a straight line.

(fol. 29a) **מֹשֶׁנָה ב**: וְאֵי זֶהוּ מָחוֹל הַכֶּרֶם בֵּין כֶּרֶם לַגָּדֵר. אִם אֵין שָׁם שְׁתֵּים עֶשְׂרֵה אַמָּה לֹא יָבִיא זֶרַע לְשָׁם. הָיוּ שָׁם שְׁתֵּים עֶשְׂרֵה אַמָּה נוֹתְנִים לָהּ עֲבוֹדָתוֹ וְזוֹרֵעַ אֶת הַמּוֹתָר.

Mishnah 2: What is the circumference of a vineyard? Between the vineyard and the fence. If less than 12 cubits are there, one should not introduce seeds there. If 12 cubits are there, one gives it[24] space for tending and sows the remaining area.

24   The vineyard. One leaves four cubits near the vines empty.

(fol. 29b)) **הֲלָכָה ב**: לֹא סוֹף דָּבָר גֵּדֶר אֶלָּא אֲפִילוּ עָשָׂה פַּסִּין אִם אֵין בֵּין פַּס לַחֲבֵירוֹ שְׁלֹשָׁה טְפָחִים נִידּוֹנִין כְּגָדֵר. אֲפִילוּ קָמָה וַאֲפִילוּ קַשִּׁין. וְאָתְיָא כַּיי דְּמַר רִבִּי חֲנִינָא אֵין הָאָסוּר נַעֲשָׂה מְחִיצָה לְהַצִּיל. סָבְרִין מֵימַר הָאָסוּר נַעֲשָׂה מְחִיצָה לֶיאָסֵר.

Halakhah 2: Not only a fence, but even if he puts up laths[25], if between one lath and the next there is less that three hand-breadths it is considered a fence[26]. Even standing grain and straw[27]? Or does it agree with what Rebbi Ḥanina said: Nothing forbidden may form a separation to save[28]? They are of the opinion that what is forbidden does form a separation to forbid.

25   The minimal width of a lath (as distinct from a pole) is given in Mishnah *Eruvin* 2:1.

26   Mishnah 4 explains that an opening less than three hand-breadths wide is still an effective barrier for goats. The Babli (e. g., *Sukkah* 7a, *Šabbat* 97a) considers openings of less than three hand-breadths as legally nonexisting. This theory is not found in the Yerushalmi.

27   Does a field on which the plants are higher than 10 hand-breadths act as a fence?

28   It is forbidden to sow grain in a vineyard, because this "sanctifies" the vineyard. Hence, grain of any kind cannot form a fence. One might think that, therefore, a vineyard surrounded by grain fields has no fence, and one may sow grain four cubits away from the vines. The rabbis infer from the statement of R. Ḥanina that standing grain ten hand-breadths high acts as a fence to forbid, i. e., the domain between vineyard and grain has the status of a bald spot around the vineyard and one needs 12 cubits minimum space to sow there.

(fol. 29a) **משנה ג:** רְבִּי יְהוּדָה אוֹמֵר אֵין זֶה אֶלָּא גֶדֶר הַכֶּרֶם וְאֵי זֶהוּ מָחוֹל הַכֶּרֶם בֵּין שְׁנֵי כְרָמִים. וְאֵי זֶהוּ גֶדֶר שֶׁהוּא גָבוֹהַּ עֲשָׂרָה טְפָחִים. וְחָרִיץ שֶׁהוּא עָמוֹק עֲשָׂרָה וְרָחָב אַרְבָּעָה.

Mishnah 3: Rebbi Jehudah says, that is only the fence of a vineyard[29]. What is the circumference of a vineyard? A vineyard between two vineyards. What is a fence[30]? If it is ten hand-breadths high, and a ditch is ten deep and four wide[31].

29   In his opinion, one may sow at a distance of four cubits from any vine between the vineyard and the fence.

30   From here to the end of the Mishnah the statement is generally accepted; this is no longer R. Jehudah's statement. The question is not what is a fence or a ditch materially but what legally counts as fence or ditch.

31   In the interpretation of Maimonides (*Kilaim* 7:14), "four hand-breadths wide" applies equally to the fence (presumably, a stone fence) and a ditch.

(fol. 29b) **הלכה ג**: עַל דַּעְתֵּיהּ דְּרִבִּי יְהוּדָה עָשָׂה כְּבְתוֹךְ הַכֶּרֶם. וְיוּסָר בְּשֵׁשׁ עֶשְׂרֵה. אָמַר רִבִּי יוֹנָה הָדָא דְתֵימַר כְּשֶׁאֵין הַכָּרְתִּים מְכוּוָּנִים. אֲבָל אִם הָיוּ הַכָּרְתִּים מְכוּוָּנִין אוֹסֵר בְּשֵׁשׁ עֶשְׂרֵה.

Halakhah 3: In the opinion of Rebbi Jehudah, it[32] is as in the interior of a vineyard. Then 16 should be forbidden! Rebbi Jonah said, it means that the trunks[33] are not aligned. But if the trunks are aligned, they forbid 16[34].

32   The status of the circumference of a vineyard.

33   In this Chapter, "trunk" is always spelled ברה. In the next Chapter, the spelling is always בורת, in the parallel Tosephta it is כוורת in the Vienna ms., כורת in the Erfurt ms. The Vienna reading is to be rejected, since כוורת (Arabic *kuwwara*) is a big basket, also used as beehive. Levy compares כורת "trunk" to קורה "log." But כָּרָתִי means leeks, not trunk. Hence, the vocalization כֶּרֶת is used here.

34   If the rows of the two vineyards are parallel, the space between them is a bald spot in one vineyard and 16 cubits are the minimum distance for sowing there. But if the two vineyards are planted so that the parallel rows of one vineyard are at a fixed non-zero angle to those of the other, then only 12 cubits of separation are needed.

עַד שֶׁיְּהֵא מוּקָף גֶּדֶר מֵאַרְבַּע רוּחוֹתָיו. מִן מַה דְּתַגִּינָן בֵּין שְׁנֵי כְרָמִים. הָדָא

אָמְרָה אֲפִילוּ מֵרוּחַ אַחַת. עַד שֶׁיְּהֵא מוּקָף גֶּדֶר כָּל־אוֹתוֹ הָרוּחַ. נִשְׁמְעִינָהּ מִן

הָדָא דְּאָמַר רִבִּי זְעִירָא רִבִּי יָסָא בְּשֵׁם רַב מַתָּנָה אֵין זָנָב לְכֶרֶם גָּדוֹל וְלֹא

מָחוֹל לְכֶרֶם קָטָן. אֵין זָנָב לְכֶרֶם גָּדוֹל. שֶׁאֵי אַתְּ זָקוּק לוֹ. וְלֹא מָחוֹל לְכֶרֶם

קָטָן. לוֹסַר חוּצָה לוֹ יוֹתֵר מִתּוֹכוֹ. תּוֹכוֹ שְׁמוֹנָה וְחוּצָה לוֹ שְׁתֵּים עֶשְׂרֵה. וְאֵי

זֶהוּ כֶרֶם קָטָן. שָׁלֹשׁ כְּנֶגֶד שָׁלֹשׁ. הָא שָׁלֹשׁ כְּנֶגֶד שָׁלֹשׁ כְּנֶגֶד שָׁלֹשׁ יֵשׁ לוֹ מָחוֹל.

אָמַר רִבִּי זְעִירָא הָדָא אָמְרָה עָשָׂה פַּסִּין כְּנֶגֶד שָׁלֹשׁ גְּפָנִים יֵשׁ לוֹ מָחוֹל.

Only if it is surrounded by a fence on all four sides[35]? From what we have stated: "Between two vineyards," that means even from one side only[36]. Only if the fence encloses all of that side[37]? Let us hear from the following that Rebbi Zeïra, Rebbi Yasa, said in the name of Rav Mattanah: There is no tail for a large vineyard and no circumference for a small vineyard[38]. There is no tail for a large vineyard because one does not need it. Neither a circumference for a small vineyard to forbid more outside than inside; inside eight[39] and outside twelve. What is a small vineyard? Three parallel three[40]. Hence, three parallel three parallel three, [the vineyard] has a circumference[41]. Rebbi Zeïra said, that means that if he made laths along three vines then [the vineyard] has a circumference[42].

35 Since מחול implies turning around in a full circle, does the rule of "circumference" apply only to a vineyard that is totally fenced in?

36 Otherwise, R. Jehudah would have to say "five vineyards," one in the middle and four around it.

37 Since we have established that the rule of מחול applies even if there is a fence only along one side, does this

fence have to be extended for the entire length of the vineyard?

38 A minimal vineyard is defined by the House of Hillel in Mishnah 4:6 as five vines, four of which form a rectangle and the fifth is on the prolongation of one of the edges of the rectangle. This fifth vine is the "tail" of that vineyard. Once all rows contain at least three vines, the "tail" no longer

has any function. A minimal vineyard which loses some vines is no longer a vineyard; it cannot have a "circumference".

39   In all cases, one may sow at a distance of 4 cubits from any vine. Hence, if two parallel rows in a vineyard are farther apart than 8 cubits, one may sow in the middle, unless he is in the situation of a bald spot or a circumference of a vineyard.

40   "Small" means one vine more than the minimal number.

41   Nine vines grown in three straight rows form a large vineyard.

42   Now one may answer the question asked at the start: Since three rows of three vines each form a large vineyard, if one makes a fence on one side of such a subvineyard of a larger vineyard the rules of circumference apply and he may not sow unless there is a distance of 12 cubits from the last vine to the fence. If the laths accompany only two vines one may sow at a distance of four cubits.

רִבִּי יוּדָן בָּעֵי עָשָׂה גֶדֶר לִפְנִים מִגֶּדֶר וְאָמַר אִם יֵשׁ שְׁלֹשָׁה טְפָחִים מוּתָּר לְהָבִיא זֶרַע לְשָׁם וְאִם לָאו אָסוּר לְהָבִיא זֶרַע לְשָׁם. רִבִּי יַעֲקֹב בַּר אִידִי בְּשֵׁם רִבִּי שִׁמְעוֹן בֶּן לָקִישׁ הָיָה שָׁם מָקוֹם שְׁתֵּים עֶשְׂרֵה אַמָּה נִיטַל הַמָּחוֹל. אָמַר רִבִּי חִזְקִיָּה וּבִלְבַד שְׁתֵּים עֶשְׂרֵה עַל שְׁתֵּים עֶשְׂרֵה. אָמַר רִבִּי מָנָא אֲפִילוּ מֵיצַר וְהוֹלֵךְ.

Rebbi Judan asked: What if he made a fence inside a fence? He said[43], if there are three hand-breadths one may sow there, otherwise one may not sow there. Rebbi Jacob bar Idi in the name of Rebbi Simeon ben Laqish: If there was a place of twelve cubits there, the circumference would be eliminated[44]. Rebbi Ḥizqiah said, only if it is twelve by twelve. Rebbi Mana said, even if it continuously narrows[45].

43   He answered his own question. If the outer fence, the one outside of which one sows other kinds, is 12 cubits away from any vine one may sow at a distance of 4 cubits from the vines.

44   That is, the requirement of "circumference" is satisfied and one may sow at a distance of 4 from the vines even where the distance to the fence is less that 12 cubits. The reading of the Rome ms. is בטל "disregarded" instead

גיטל **of**

45   It is not clear whether R. Mana disagrees with R. Ḥizqiah and accepts that one may sow in a circumference at a distance of 4 cubits if at one spot at least the distance to the fence was 12 cubits, or if he adds to R. Ḥizqiah's statement that beyond a length of 12 cubits the strip forming the circumference may get narrower. Maimonides does not quote either of these opinions in his Code.

(fol. 29a) **משנה ד**: מְחִיצַת הַקָּנִים אִם אֵין שָׁם בֵּין קָנֶה לַחֲבֵירוֹ שְׁלֹשָׁה טְפָחִים כְּדֵי שֶׁיִּכָּנֵס הַגְּדִי הֲרֵי זוּ כִמְחִיצָה. וְגָדֵר שֶׁנִּפְרַץ עַד עֶשֶׂר אַמּוֹת הֲרֵי הוּא כְפֶתַח. יוֹתֵר מִיכֵּן כְּנֶגֶד הַפִּירְצָה אָסוּר. נִפְרְצוּ בוֹ פְּרָצוֹת הַרְבֵּה אִם הָעוֹמֵד מְרוּבָּה עַל הַפָּרוּץ מוּתָּר וְאִם הַפָּרוּץ מְרוּבָּה עַל הָעוֹמֵד כְּנֶגֶד הַפִּירְצָה אָסוּר.

Mishnah 4: If there are less than three hand-breadths of distance between the sticks of a partition fence made from sticks, so that a kid goat cannot enter, then that is a valid partition wall[46]. Also, if a wall was torn down up to a length of ten cubits, that acts as a gate. If more than that, it is forbidden along the torn-down part[47]. If it is torn down in many places, if what is standing is more than what is torn down, it is permitted, but if the torn-down part is more than the standing one, it is forbidden at the torn-down places.

46   In this case, one may plant the vineyard up to the partition fence and on the other side one may sow his field up to the partition fence. One speaks here of a partition fence rather than a stone wall because one does not plant vines too close to a stone wall since the roots of the vines would damage the foundations of such a wall.

47   At such a place, the outside field must be separated from the vines by a minimum of four cubits. The same rule applies to the situation described in the next sentence. [The same rules apply for carrying on the Sabbath; a fenced-in domain is private only if a) the torn-down parts do not exceed 10 cubits at any one place and b) the sum

of the lengths of the standing walls   the lengths of the breaches in the wall.]
overall must be more than the sum of

(fol. 29d) **הלכה ד**: עֲשָׂרָה פַּסִּין כְּנֶגֶד הַבְּנַיִין וְיֵשׁ בְּעוֹמֵד אַרְבָּעָה וְהָעוֹמֵד רַבָּה
עַל הַפָּרוּץ כְּנֶגֶד הָעוֹמֵד מוּתָּר כְּנֶגֶד הַפִּרְצָה אָסוּר. עָשָׂה פַּסִּין כְּנֶגֶד הַגְּפָנִים
וְאֵין בְּעוֹמֵד אַרְבָּעָה וְהַפָּרוּץ רַבָּה עַל הָעוֹמֵד. פְּשִׁיטָא כְּנֶגֶד הָעוֹמֵד מוּתָּר כְּנֶגֶד
הַפִּרְצָה אָסוּר.

Halakhah 4: Ten laths at the in-betweens[48] and what is standing is
four hand-breadths wide, and what is standing is more than what is torn
down: where it is standing it is permitted, where it is torn down it is
forbidden. If one made laths in front of the vines[49], and what is standing
is less than four hand-breadths, and what is torn down is more than what
is standing, it is obvious[50] that where it is standing it is permitted, where it
is torn down it is forbidden.

48   Here one speaks of the situation
described at the end of the Mishnah,
viz., a wall with many breaches. If a
standing segment of wall is less than
four hand-breadths long, it is not
regarded as a partner with the two
other standing pieces to its left and
right. The laths one discusses here are
not put into the torn-down parts but
close to them, either before the front
or behind the back part of the wall;
therefore, they cannot be considered
parts of the wall. Hence, one may
plant vines up to the wall and sow
produce on the other side only where
an actual wall provides the separation;
everywhere else the minimal distance
must be 4 cubits.

49   This shields the vines from
being seen through the holes in the
wall but the laths are separated from
the wall.
50   It is obvious that one is
forbidden to sow near the open spaces
but it is not obvious at all that one is
permitted to sow near the standing wall
since both for the Sabbath (*Eruvin* 1:9,
fol. 19c) and for making a Sukkah
(*Sukkah* 1:1, fol. 52a) a piece of wall is
disregarded if it is not at least four
hand-breadths wide. The statement
then also contradicts the assertion of
the next paragraph, that the rules of
kilaim and Sabbath are identical. One
has to assume that, originally, instead
of ואין one read ויש

רִבִּי שִׁמְעוֹן בֶּן לָקִישׁ בְּשֵׁם רִבִּי יוּדָה בֶּן חֲנִינָה נָעַץ אַרְבָּעָה קָנִים בְּאַרְבָּעָה זָוִיּוֹת
שֶׁבְּכֶרֶם וְקָשַׁר גָּמֵי מִלְמַעְלָה מַצִּיל מְשׁוּם פֵּיאָה. אָמַר רִבִּי יוֹחָנָן[51] כִּמְחִיצַת
שַׁבָּת כֵּן מְחִיצַת כִּלְאַיִם. אָמַר רִבִּי יוֹחָנָן מַעֲשֶׂה שֶׁהָלַךְ רִבִּי יְהוֹשֻׁעַ בֶּן קָרְחָה
אֶצֶל רִבִּי יוֹחָנָן בֶּן נוּרִי לְנַגְנִינַר הֶרְאוּ הֶרְאוּ שָׂדֶה אַחַת. וּבֵית חֲבֵירָתָה הָיְתָה קָרְאַת.
וְהָיוּ שָׁם פְּרָצוֹת יוֹתֵר מֵעֶשֶׂר וְהָיָה נוֹטֵל אָעִין וְסוֹתֵם. דּוּקַרְנִין וְסוֹתֵם עַד
שֶׁמִּיעֵטָן פָּחוֹת מֵעֶשֶׂר. אָמַר כְּזֶה כֵּן מְחִיצַת שַׁבָּת. אָמַר רִבִּי זְעִירָא מוֹדֶה רִבִּי
שִׁמְעוֹן בֶּן לָקִישׁ לְעִנְיַן שַׁבָּת שֶׁאֵין הַפֵּיאָה[52] מַצֶּלֶת יוֹתֵר מֵעֶשֶׂר. אָמַר רִבִּי חַגַּי
מַתְנִיתָא אָמְרָה כֵּן מַקִּיפִין שְׁלֹשָׁה חֲבָלִים זֶה לְמַעְלָה מִזֶּה וְזֶה לְמַעְלָה מִזֶּה.
אִם אָמַר אַתְּ שֶׁהַפֵּיאָה מַצֶּלֶת יוֹתֵר מֵעֶשֶׂר דַּיּוֹ חֶבֶל אֶחָד.

[53]Rebbi Simeon ben Laqish in the name of Rebbi Judah ben Ḥaninah[54]:
If one put in four poles at the four corners of a vineyard and connected
them with a bast string on top[55], this saves as a symbolic fence[56]. Rebbi
Joḥanan said, the rules of separation walls for the Sabbath are the rules
for *kilaim*[57]. Rebbi Joḥanan said, it happened that Rebbi Joshua ben
Qorḥah went to Rebbi Joḥanan ben Nuri at Nagnigar[58]; he showed him a
field called *bet ḥaverata* whose wall had parts torn down more than ten[59]
wide. He took wood to insert, forked poles[60] to insert, until he reduced to
less than ten. He said, just like that is a dividing wall for the Sabbath.
Rebbi Zeïra said, Rebbi Simeon ben Laqish agrees that on the Sabbath, a
symbolic fence does not save more than ten[61]. Rebbi Ḥaggai said, the
Mishnah says so: "One surrounds it with three ropes, one above the
other[62]." If you say that the string saves, one rope would be sufficient[63].

51   In the Venice print: ר' יונה, but in
the two parallels in *Eruvin* and *Sukkah*
ר' יוחנן Since the statement is
bracketed by statements of R. Simeon
ben Laqish and R. Joḥanan, the reading
ר' יונה would be an anachronism. The

Babli in *Eruvin* 11a reports the
statement in the name of R. Simeon ben
Laqish. It cannot belong to an Amora
two generations younger.

52   Reading of the Rome ms. and
the Venice parallels in *Eruvin* and

Sukkah. Venice print here: שהפיאה.

53   This paragraph and the following ones are found also in *Eruvin* 1:9 (fol. 19c), *Sukkah* 1:1 (fol. 52a).

54   A Galilean Amora of the first generation.

55   The rope of bast connects one pole to the other, all around the vineyard. In the Babli (*Eruvin* 11a/b), the expression is זמורה, "shoot of a vine." The "string" used here may be a natural product; it does not have to be manufactured.

56   Cf. Chapter 1, Note 159.

57   The rules for Sabbath, the definition of walls that enclose a domain to make it private, are discussed in detail in tractate *Eruvin*, Chapters 1 and 2. In Babli *Eruvin* 11a/b, the statement of R. Simeon ben Laqish in the name of R. Judah ben Haninah explicitly excludes the expedient of the bast rope for the Sabbath, but R. Johanan excludes it also for *kilaim*. R. Simeon ben Laqish is reported there to accept for himself the statement attributed here to R. Johanan, that the rules for Sabbath and *kilaim* are identical, whereas R. Johanan rejects this in general. The position of the Babli is that R. Simeon ben Laqish only reports the opinion of R. Judah ben Haninah without accepting it himself, and that R.

Johanan prohibits the use of a rope for openings wider than 10 cubits. The Yerushalmi accepts R. Simeon ben Laqish's statement as describing his own position.

58   A place in lower Galilee; the name is spelled נגנגר, נגינר and, in the Babli, גגינר. The report in the Babli is quite different, but the essence is the same, *viz.,* that both for Sabbath and *kilaim* an opening may not be wider than 10 cubits, in the opinion of R. Johanan even with פיאה.

59   Ten cubits, making the wall invalid as separation.

60   Greek δίκραvov "pitchfork". The "woods" were planks put on the ground and connected to the wall; the poles were stuck into the ground. They were forked so that on each side a rope could be attached forming פיאה to the next pole. Cf. Latin *furcilla*; its use in vineyards is described by Varro I.8. This explanation from Musaphia is accepted by most Semitic linguists. [Symmachus uses δίκραvα to translate כילפות "hatchets" (*Ps.* 74:6).]

H. L. Fleischer derives the word from Semitic דקר "to pierce". Arabic دُقْرَان "trellis made for vines" might be an Aramaic loanword (S. Fränkel) or have a common root دقر "to bolt a door with a piece of wood" with دُقْر "bolt, lock", دَقْرَرَة "arid plain between mountains", دَقْر

"prosperous garden".

61   A string strung from one pole to the next creates the impression of a gate and a gate cannot be wider than 10 cubits.

62   Mishnah *Eruvin* 1:9: If a caravan camps in the desert during the Sabbath, in order to create a space where one is permitted to carry, one puts bags at the corners of the domain and connects them with three parallel rows of ropes so that no two ropes are more than 3 hand-breadths distant from each other. If the diameters of the three ropes add another hand-breadth, the upper rim of this symbolic wall is 10 hand-breadths above ground, one has created a valid separation, and the enclosed space is a private domain. (This speaks against Maimonides's interpretation of Mishnah 3 in this Chapter.) For *kilaim*, a wall made in this way by three ropes strung one above the other is accepted in Tosephta *Kilaim* 4:3.

63   The caravan clearly wants more space for animals and people than 10 by 10 cubits; if they park some camel loads at the four corners of their camp, they need a surrounding wall, not a surrounding gate. If it is possible to symbolize a wall with one rope, why does one need three?

רִבִּי יוֹנָה אָמַר רִבִּי יֹאשִׁיָה 64 בָּעֵי הָדָא פֵּיאָה מַה אַתְּ אָמְרָת מִלְּמַעֲלָן מִן הַצַּד. אִין תֵּימַר מִלְּמַעֲלָן הָא כָּל־שֶׁכֵּן מִן הַצַּד. אִין תֵּימַר מִן הַצַּד הָא לְמַעֲלָן לֹא. אִין תֵּימַר מִלְּמַעֲלָן יָאוּת אָמַר רִבִּי חַגַּי אִין תֵּימַר מִן הַצַּד 65 לֹא אָמַר רִבִּי חַגַּי כְּלוּם. מַה נַפְשָׁךְ אִם מִלְּמַעֲלָן הֲרֵי מִלְּמַעֲלָן. אוֹ מִן הַצַּד הֲרֵי מִן הַצַּד. רַבָּנִין דְּקֵיסָרִין בְּשֵׁם רִבִּי יִרְמְיָה תִּיפְתָּר בַּעֲשׂוּיִין כְּמִין דּוּקְרָן.

Rebbi Jonah said: Rebbi Hoshaia asked, what do you say about that symbolic fence, on top or at the sides[66]? If you say on top, so much more on the sides[67]. If you say on the sides, then not on the top. If you say on the top, Rebbi Ḥaggai said it correctly[68]. If you say from the sides, Rebbi Ḥaggai did not say anything[69]. What do you want to say[70], if on top, it must be on top. Or from the sides, it is on the sides. The rabbis of Caesarea in the name of Rebbi Jeremiah: Explain it if they were strung on forked poles[71].

64   In both parallels: רבי הושׁיא

65   This is the text of the Rome ms. and of the Venice parallels in *Eruvin* and *Sukkah*. The Venice text here is defective: אין חימר מלמעלן לא אמר ר' חגי בלום.

66   If four poles are put up at the four sides of the vineyard, does the string have to go from top to top, to create the impression of a gate, or is it strung at half height between the poles, to give the impression of a wall?

67   At least for *kilaim*, a wall is more of a separation than a gate.

68   Since the Mishnah in *Eruvin* does not require the lowest rope to be within three hand-breadths of the ground, it is clear that even if the rows are strung high one needs three ropes and not just one.

69   If the rope must be low, the case of פיאה is different from that of the Mishnah.

70   A technical term, indicating that the desired result can be obtained from both hypotheses. The inference here is that R. Haggai is correct in both cases, since the Mishnah is formulated to apply to both of them.

71   If the poles have separate hooks so that each side has a complete arrangement of poles and rope, then even R. Zeïra will admit that the rope forms a valid enclosure for the Sabbath. In this case, by necessity the rope is on top only. In this, the Yerushalmi parallels the final explanation of the Babli, *Eruvin* 11b, rejecting symbolic walls but accepting symbolic gates.

רבּי זְעִירָא רבִּי אָבוּדָמָא דְּחֵיפָה בְּשֵׁם רבִּי שְׁמְעוֹן בֶּן לָקִישׁ לְגוּבָהּ אֲפִילוּ עַד מֵאָה אַמָּה. אָמַר רבִּי יוּדָן הָדָא דְּאַתְּ אָמַר לְעִנְיַן כִּלְאַיִם אֲבָל לְעִנְיַן שַׁבָּת לֹא תְהֵא פֵּיאָה גְּדוֹלָה מִן הַקּוֹרָה. אָמַר רבִּי יוֹסֵי הִיא כִלְאַיִם הִיא שַׁבָּת. עַל דַּעְתֵּיהּ דְּרִבִּי יוֹסֵי מַה בֵּין קוֹרָה וּמַה בֵּין פֵּיאָה. פֵּיאָה אֵינָהּ מַצֶּלֶת מֵרוּחַ אַחַת. עַד שֶׁתְּהֵא מְגוּפֶּפֶת מֵאַרְבַּע רוּחוֹתֶיהָ. קוֹרָה מַצֶּלֶת מֵרוּחַ אַחַת. וְאִיתָא כָּהֲדָא דָּאָמַר רבִּי זְעִירָא בְּשֵׁם רַב הַמְנוּנָא הַפֵּיאָה אֵינָהּ מַצֶּלֶת עַד שֶׁתְּהֵא מְגוּפֶּפֶת מֵאַרְבַּע רוּחוֹתֶיהָ.

Rebbi Zeïra, Rebbi Eudaimon of Haifa, in the name of Rebbi Simeon ben Laqish: In height even one hundred cubits[72]. Rebbi Judan said, that is, for *kilaim*, but as regards the Sabbath, a symbolic fence should not be better than a beam[73]. Rebbi Yose said, it is the same for *kilaim* and

Sabbath. According to Rebbi Yose, what is the difference between a beam and a symbolic fence? A symbolic fence does not save from one side unless it is used to close all four sides; a beam saves in one direction. This may be compared to what Rebbi Zeïra said in the name of Rav Hamnuna: A symbolic fence does not save unless it seals all four sides[74].

72   If a rope is drawn from the top of one pole to the next, there are no height limitations (except, naturally, than it cannot be lower than 10 handbreadths.)

73   If the inhabitants of a dead-end street want to turn that dead-end street into a private domain in which one may carry on the Sabbath, they have to put in a visible border either in the form of a beam at the entrance of the dead-end street, going from the wall of one house to the wall of the opposite house, or they may put up a symbolic doorpost. Mishnah *Eruvin* 1:1 declares that the beam cannot be higher than 20 cubits to be valid.

74   The problem is not discussed in the Babli.

אָמַר רִבִּי בָּא בַּר מָמָל טְטְרַפֶּלִיוֹת שֶׁבִּכְרָמִים אָסוּר לְטַלְטֵל תַּחְתֵּיהֶן. שֶׁהֵן סוֹף תִּקְרָה וְאֵין סוֹף תִּקְרָה מַצִּיל מִשּׁוּם פֵּיאָה. אָמַר רִבִּי פִּינְחָס אָתָא עוּבְדָא קוֹמֵי רִבִּי יִרְמְיָה בְּאַרְבָּעָה עֲמוּדִין וַעֲלֵיהֶן אַרְבָּעָה פִּיסְטַלִיוֹת וְהִתִּיר לְטַלְטֵל תַּחְתֵּיהֶן מִשּׁוּם פֵּיאָה.

Rebbi Abba bar Mamal said, it is forbidden to carry under the four-gated[75] [bowers] in vineyards since they form the end of the roof and the end of a roof cannot save as symbolic fence. Rebbi Phineas said, a case came before Rebbi Jeremiah of four pillars and on them four beams[76]; he permitted to carry under them because of a symbolic fence.[77]

75   Greek τετράπυλον, τό, "archway entered from four sides." Bowers erected at the crossing of two paths, with only the posts and the connecting beams built, and the roof formed by plants climbing on the poles. Rebbi Abba bar Mamal considers these beams as קורה under which one may not carry

in a dead-end street. The vineyard in question is not enclosed by a wall, or it is enclosed but too large (larger than 5000 square cubits) to be considered a courtyard for the rules of Sabbath; hence, one may carry under the roof of the bower but not outside.

76   Greek ἐπιστύλιον, τό "architrave." (In *Eruvin*, the spelling is מצטליות with emphatic *s*.)

77   He disagrees with R. Abba bar Mamal.

רְבִּי בּוּן וְרַבָּנִין בָּעִין קוֹמֵי רְבִּי זְעִירָא פֵּיאָה מַהוּ שֶׁתַּצִּיל בְּסוּכָּה. אָמַר לוֹן פֵּיאָה מַצֶּלֶת בְּסוּכָּה. סוֹף סְכָךְ מַהוּ שֶׁיַּצִּיל בְּסוּכָּה. אָמַר לוֹן אֵין סוֹף סְכָךְ מַצִּיל בְּסוּכָּה. מַה בֵּין זֶה לְזֶה. זֶה נַעֲשָׂה לְכָךְ וְזֶה אֵינוֹ נַעֲשָׂה לְכָךְ. אָמַר רְבִּי אַבָּהוּ כָּל אִילֵּין מִילַיָּא לְעִנְיַן מַשָּׂא וּמַתָּן הָא לְהוֹרוֹת אָסוּר לְהוֹרוֹת. מָה אִם סוּכָּה קַלָּה אַתְּ אָמַר אָסוּר. שַׁבָּת הַחֲמוּרָה לֹא כָּל־שֶׁכֵּן.

Rebbi Abun and the rabbis asked before Rebbi Zeïra, does a symbolic fence save in a *sukkah*[78]? He said to them, a symbolic fence saves in a *sukkah*. Does the end of the roofing save in a *sukkah*[79]? He said to them, the end of the roofing does not save in a *sukkah*. What is the difference between them? One is made for the purpose, the other one is not made for the purpose. Rebbi Abbahu said, all these things[80] are for discussion's sake, but as far as teaching, it is forbidden to teach it. If this is forbidden for the minor commandment of *sukkah*, so much more for the strict commandment of Sabbath!

78   The hut one must build to live in on the festival of Tabernacles. The main requirement for such a hut is that the roofing must be plant material. The walls can be made of any material. The question is whether a virtual wall is permitted. (The Babli does not consider this problem but states that two full walls and part of a third must be actual walls.)

79   Since the roofing must have some support, the four corner posts of the *sukkah* must have some connection on which the roofing may rest. Can these connections be considered as *peah*, following R. Jeremiah in the preceding case?

80   The rulings of R. Zeïra. Build

ing a *sukkah* is a positive commandment but neglecting it is not punishable

in court. But desecrating the Sabbath is
a capital crime.

רְבִּי בּוּן בַּר חִייָה בָּעֵי קוֹמֵי רְבִּי זְעִירָא. מָאן תַּנָּא פֵּיאָה מַצֶּלֶת לֹא רְבִּי יוֹחָנָן
בֶּן נוּרִי. אָמַר לֵיהּ אַדְהִי תַּנָּא.

Rebbi Abun bar Ḥiyya asked before Rebbi Zeïra: Is not the Tanna,
according to whom a symbolic fence saves, Rebbi Joḥanan ben Nuri? He
said to him, that is the Tanna[81].

81   Hence, in regard to the Sabbath this is the opinion of a minority of one,
which cannot be operational practice.

נִמְצֵאת אוֹמֵר לְעִנְיַן כִּלְאַיִם כָּל־הַפָּחוֹת מִשְּׁלֹשָׁה כְּסָתוּם. מִשְּׁלֹשָׁה וְעַד אַרְבָּעָה
אִם הָעוֹמֵד רָבָה עַל הַפָּרוּץ מוּתָּר. וְאִם הַפָּרוּץ רָבָה עַל הָעוֹמֵד אָסוּר. מֵאַרְבַּע
וְעַד עֶשֶׂר אִם עוֹמֵד מְרוּבָּה עַל הַפָּרוּץ מוּתָּר. וְאִם פָּרוּץ מְרוּבָּה עַל הָעוֹמֵד
כְּנֶגֶד הָעוֹמֵד מוּתָּר. כְּנֶגֶד הַפָּרוּץ אָסוּר. יוֹתֵר מֵעֶשֶׂר אַף עַל פִּי שֶׁהָעוֹמֵד רָבָה
עַל הַפָּרוּץ כְּנֶגֶד הָעוֹמֵד מוּתָּר. כְּנֶגֶד הַפָּרוּץ אָסוּר. לְעִנְיַן שַׁבָּת כָּל־הַפָּחוֹת
מִשְּׁלֹשָׁה כְּסָתוּם. מִשְּׁלֹשָׁה וְעַד אַרְבָּעָה מֵאַרְבָּעָה וְעַד עֶשֶׂר אִם הָעוֹמֵד רָבָה עַל
הַפָּרוּץ מוּתָּר. וְאִם הַפָּרוּץ רָבָה עַל הָעוֹמֵד אָסוּר. יֵתֵר מֵעֶשֶׂר אַף עַל פִּי
שֶׁעוֹמֵד רָבָה עַל הַפָּרוּץ אָסוּר. רְבִּי חֲנַנְיָה רְבִּי יוּדָה בַּר פָּזִי בְשֵׁם רְבִּי יוֹחָנָן לֵית
כָּאן מִשְּׁלֹשָׁה וְעַד אַרְבָּעָה. יֵשׁ כָּאן פִּירְצָה שְׁלֹשָׁה אֵין כָּאן מְקוֹם אַרְבָּעָה.
מָתִיב רְבִּי מָנָא וְהָתַנִּינָן מַקִּיפִין בְּקָנִים וְקָנֶה יֵשׁ לוֹ מָקוֹם. אָמַר לֵיהּ לֹא
תִתִיבְנִי פָּחוֹת מִשְּׁלֹשָׁה שֶׁכָּל־הַפָּחוֹת מִשְּׁלֹשָׁה כְּסָתוּם הוּא. רְבִּי יוֹסֵי בֵּי רְבִּי
בּוּן בְּשֵׁם רַב מִכָּל־מָקוֹם מִכֵּיוָן שֶׁהָעוֹמֵד רָבָה עַל הַפָּרוּץ מוּתָּר.

"[82]It turns out that concerning *kilaim* everything less than three
hand-breadths is considered closed[83]. From three to four, if what is
standing is more than what is torn down it is permitted, but if what is torn
down is more than what is standing, it is forbidden. From four hand-
breadths[84] to ten cubits, if what is standing is more than what is torn

down, it is permitted; but if what is torn down is more than what is standing it is permitted where it is standing[85], forbidden where it is torn down. Concerning the Sabbath, everything less than three hand-breadths is considered closed. From three to four, and from four hand-breadths to ten cubits, it is permitted if what is standing is more than what is torn down, but forbidden if what is torn down is more than what is standing. More than ten, it is forbidden even though what is standing is more than what is torn down." Rebbi Ḥananiah, Rebbi Judah bar Pazi, in the name of Rebbi Joḥanan: There is no "from three to four.[86]" There is a hole of three and no place of four! Rebbi Mana objected: Did we not state: "One surrounds with reeds," does a reed form a place[87]? He said to him, do not object to me from a breach less than three hand-breadths, since anything less than three is considered closed! Rebbi Yose ben Rebbi Abun in the name of Rav: In any case, since what is standing is more than what is torn down, it is permitted[88].

82   This paragraph is also in *Eruvin* 1:8, fol. 19b/c. The *baraita* is similar to Tosephta *Kilaim* 4:6 quoted also in Babli *Eruvin* 16a. The main difference between Yerushalmi and Babli-Tosephta is that in the latter source, each breach has to be smaller than the surrounding wall whereas in the Yerushalmi only the total length of standing wall has to be larger than the total length of the missing parts.

83   An opening of less than three hand-breadths in a wall is disregarded.

84   The context and all corroborating evidence show that instead of

ארבע (fem.) one has to read ארבעה (masc.), referring to hand-breadths, not cubits. In computing the total length of the torn-down parts, breaches smaller than three hand-breadths in width are disregarded.

85   The Babli notes that not only are breaches up to three hand-breadths long disregarded as holes, but also standing pieces of wall up to three hand-breadths wide are disregarded as walls. This is the background of the discussion later in this paragraph.

86   R. Joḥanan wants to eliminate the middle part of the *baraita*, the one

dealing with breaches of between three and four hand-breadths, in case that the standing walls also are in pieces less than four hand-breadths wide. While a hole wider than three hand-breadths is considered a breach, a wall narrower than four hand-breadths is not a wall. In that case, there are only holes and no wall at all; the entire wall should be considered as non-existent! He requires in this case that any sown field should be at least four cubits distant from the vineyard.

87   Mishnah *Eruvin* 1:9. Since the reeds are counted and no reed is even

one hand-breadth wide, any piece of wall should be considered a wall. The answer is that as long as no two reeds are three hand-breadths distant from each other, the entire dividing fence is considered a solid wall.

88   This explicitly rejects the text of Babli/Tosephta, that no single hole may be wider than both adjacent pieces of standing wall; the wall is valid as long as the combined length of standing wall (of at least 4 hand-breadths length) is larger than the combined length of the breaches.

משנה ה: הַנּוֹטֵעַ שׁוּרָה שֶׁל חָמֵשׁ גְּפָנִים בֵּית שַׁמַּאי אוֹמְרִים כֶּרֶם. (fol. 29a)
וּבֵית הִלֵּל אוֹמְרִים אֵינוֹ כֶּרֶם עַד שֶׁיְּהוּ שְׁתֵּי שׁוּרוֹת. לְפִיכָךְ הַזּוֹרֵעַ אַרְבַּע אַמּוֹת
שֶׁבְּכֶרֶם בֵּית שַׁמַּאי אוֹמְרִים קִידֵּשׁ שׁוּרָה אַחַת וּבֵית הִלֵּל אוֹמְרִים שְׁתֵּי שׁוּרוֹת.

Mishnah 5: If somebody plants one row of five vines, the House of Shammai say that this is a vineyard[89]. But the House of Hillel say, [a planting] is not a vineyard unless it has two rows[90]. Therefore, if somebody sows within four cubits of a vineyard, the House of Shammai say that he sanctifies one row, but the House of Hillel say, two rows[91].

89   Less than 5 vines are single vines and one has to leave only 6 hand-breadths of free space around them. But a vineyard needs 4 free cubits on all four sides. In addition, while *kilaim*

is forbidden to be sown near a vine, only for a vineyard both vines and seeds become sanctified and forbidden for any use; for single vines the usufruct is not forbidden.

90   It will be clear from Mishnah 6 that the House of Hillel also put the minimal number of vines in a vineyard at 5 but require them to be planted in two rows.

91   The extent of what becomes forbidden to use is detailed in the Halakhah.

הלכה ח: וְהוּא שֶׁזָּרַע כְּנֶגֶד הָאֶמְצָעִי. זָרַע כְּנֶגֶד הָאֶמְצָעִי עַל דַּעְתֵּיהּ (fol. 29c) דְּבֵית שַׁמַּאי אוֹסֵר אֶת כָּל־הַשּׁוּרָה[91]. עַל דַּעְתֵּיהּ דְּבֵית הִלֵּל אוֹסֵר שָׁלֹשׁ כְּנֶגֶד שָׁלֹשׁ. זָרַע כְּנֶגֶד הַבֵּינַיִן שֶׁבְּאֶמְצָעִי. עַל דַּעְתִּין דְּבֵית שַׁמַּאי אוֹסֵר שְׁתַּיִם מִכָּאן וּשְׁתַּיִם מִכָּאן. חֲמִישִׁית אֵי זוֹהִי נֶאֱמָר. אִם הָיוּ זְרָעִין קְרוֹבִין לְאַחַת מֵהֶן הֲרֵי אֵלּוּ אֲסוּרוֹת. וְאִם לָאו הֲרֵי אֵלּוּ מוּתָּרוֹת. עַל דַּעְתֵּיהּ דְּבֵית הִלֵּל אָסוּר אַרְבַּע כְּנֶגֶד שְׁתַּיִם. זָרַע כְּנֶגֶד קֶרֶן הַזָּוִית. עַל דַּעְתֵּיהּ דְּבֵית שַׁמַּאי אֵי זוֹ שׁוּרָה אֲסוּרָה זוֹ זוֹ. עַל דַּעְתֵּיהּ דְּבֵית הִלֵּל אָסוּר שְׁתַּיִם כְּנֶגֶד שְׁתַּיִם וְאַחַת יוֹצֵא זָנָב מִכָּאן וְאַחַת יוֹצֵא זָנָב מִכָּאן. זָרַע כְּנֶגֶד הַבֵּינַיִן שֶׁבְּקֶרֶן הַזָּוִית. עַל דַּעְתֵּיהּ דְּבֵית שַׁמַּאי אוֹסֵר אֶת כָּל־הַשּׁוּרָה. עַל דַּעְתֵּיהּ דְּבֵית הִלֵּל אוֹסֵר שְׁתַּיִם כְּנֶגֶד שְׁתַּיִם וְאַחַת יוֹצֵא זָנָב מִכָּן. שִׁישִׁית אֵי זוֹ הִיא. שְׁלִישִׁית שֶׁבְּרִאשׁוֹנָה שְׁנִיָּה שֶׁבִּשְׁלִישִׁית.

Halakhah 5: That is, if sown in the middle[93]. If he sowed in front of a middle vine, in the opinion of the House of Shammai he makes the entire row forbidden[94]. In the opinion of the House of Hillel, he forbids three parallel three[95]. If he sowed in front of an interval in the middle, in the opinion of the House of Shammai, he forbids two on each side. What is said about the fifth? If the seeds were close to one vine, those are forbidden; if not, they are permitted[96]. In the opinion of the House of Hillel, four parallel two are forbidden[97]. If he sowed opposite the corner, which row is forbidden in the opinion of the House of Shammai? Both of them[98]! In the opinion of the House of Hillel, two parallel two and one forming a tail on each side are forbidden[99]. If one sowed in an interval at the corner[100], in the opinion of the House of Shammai he makes the entire row forbidden. In the opinion of the House of Hillel, two parallel two and one forming a tail are forbidden. What is the sixth? The third in the first row, the second in the third row.

92	Reading of Rome ms. and R. Simson. Venice: שדה.

93	This explains what is forbidden if somebody sowed too close to a vineyard. The situation is simple unless one sows at a corner of the vineyard. In the entire discussion, the seeds are sown outside the vineyard but less than 4 cubits distant from the next vine.

94	Not the entire row in a large vineyard, but the nearest row that forms a vineyard, which is 5 vines in one row. In this case, the vine in front of which the seed was sown becomes sanctified and with it two vines on each side in the front row.

95	The House of Hillel define a minimal vineyard as five vines planted in two rows. So in the first row, the vine in front of which the *kilaim* was sown, and one vine on each side are sanctified. In the second row, the vine behind the middle one in the first row certainly is forbidden, as well as one vine adjacent to it. But since there is no way of deciding between left and right in this case, both are forbidden.

96	If the seed in the middle were a mathematical point, we would have a problem. But in reality, if the perimeter of the growing plant is closer to one adjacent vine than to the other, the fifth is added at the closer side. If the growing plant is right in the middle, six vines become forbidden, three on each side.

97	In the next Mishnah, the House of Hillel state that a minimal vineyard consists of five vines in two rows, forming a rectangle and a "tail." In the interpretation of Maimonides, based on Gaonic sources, the "tail" is formed by a fifth vine forming an isosceles triangle with two of the other vines, together giving the vertices of a pentagon. In the interpretation of R. Simson, the minimal vineyard consists of two rows, three vines in one and two in the other, where two vines in each row are the vertices of a rectangle. According to Maimonides, both in his Commentary and his Code, the configuration of R. Simson is explicitly excluded in the next Mishnah. However, the Halakhah here seems to support R. Simson; I fail to see how the rest of the Halakhah can be interpreted by Maimonides. According to R. Simson, three vines in the first row and two in the second become sanctified; since we cannot intrinsically distinguish here between left and right, we have to choose four vines in the first row in the case where according to the House of Shammai one would have to choose six.

98   Since the seed is supposed to be exactly on the extension of the diagonal pointing to the corner, both edges coming together at the corner are equal candidates, and one has the corner vine and four others on each edge, for a total of nine that become sanctified.

99   The vines that become sanctified are the corner vine, two adjacent ones on each of the edges, and the vine next to the corner one on the diagonal. Then in any way one looks at the configuration, one has three vines in the first and two in the second rows, and four vines form a rectangle ("two parallel two.") The total number of forbidden vines is six. (It has to be noted that, since the vines in a vineyard are planted in orderly rows, a "tail" in the sense of Maimonides is impossible here, but not a "tail" in the sense of R. Simson.)

100   He sows between the corner vine and one of the adjacent vines. According to the House of Shammai there is no problem; he sanctifies the first five vines defined by the corner and the adjacent vine. According to the House of Hillel there is a problem, whether to take three vines in that row and two in the next, or to consider the seed to be placed between two rows, in which case we have to take three vines in the other edge starting from the corner, and the first two vines in the next row parallel to that edge, for a total of six vines. Another possible configuration, chosen in the next sentence, is to take three vines in the row in front of which the seed is sown, and perpendicular to it one vine in the outer and two in the next row perpendicular to it. Again, four vines form the rectangle at the corner and the other vines form minimal vineyards both in the direction of the edge in front of which was sown, and perpendicular to it.

(fol. 29a) **משנה ו**: הַנּוֹטֵעַ שְׁתַּיִם כְּנֶגֶד שְׁתַּיִם וְאַחַת יוֹצֵא זָנָב הֲרֵי זֶה כֶּרֶם. שְׁתַּיִם כְּנֶגֶד שְׁתַּיִם וְאַחַת בֵּינְתַיִּים. אוֹ שְׁתַּיִם כְּנֶגֶד שְׁתַּיִם וְאַחַת בָּאֶמְצַע אֵינוֹ כֶּרֶם עַד שֶׁיְּהוּ שְׁתַּיִם כְּנֶגֶד שְׁתַּיִם וְאַחַת יוֹצֵא זָנָב.

Mishnah 6: If somebody plants two parallel two and one which protrudes as tail[101], that is a vineyard. Two parallel two and one between them[102], or two parallel two and one in the middle[103], are not a vineyard, but two parallel two and one which protrudes as tail are.

101   As explained in the preceding Halakhah, four vines are planted in a rectangle and the fifth is in a straight line with two of these, on the extension of one of the edges of the rectangle, following the interpretation of R. Simson.

102   Four vines forming a rectangle with the fifth at the center of the rectangle.

103   The fifth is at the midpoint of one of the sides of the rectangle. Maimonides switches the interpretations of the last two cases.

(fol. 29c) **הלכה ו**:   רִבִּי חִייָה בַּר בָּא בְשֵׁם רִבִּי חִייָה בַּר יוֹסֵף אֶרֶץ כְּנַעַן לִגְבוּלוֹתֶיהָ. גְּבוּלוֹת שֶׁבָּדוּ לָהֶם הַכְּנַעֲנִים. רִבִּי אִימִּי בְּעִי וּלְמֵידִין מִן הַכְּנַעֲנִים.

Halakhah 6: Rebbi Ḥiyya bar Abba in the name of Rebbi Ḥiyya bar Joseph: (*Num.* 34:2) "The land of Canaan according to its domains." Domains that the Canaanites invented[104]. Rebbi Immi asked, does one learn from the Canaanites[105]?

104   The queer shape of a vineyard, consisting of 3 + 2 vines, does not originate from abstract reasoning but is a definition inherited from the Canaanites. The inference is drawn from the verse using the rare feminine form גבולה "domain" instead of the usual masculine גבול "border", even

though the description is not of the land but of its borders.

105   There are many verses in the Pentateuch warning the Jewish people not to learn from the Canaanites. The derivation is alluded to in Babli *Šabbat* 85a.

שְׁמוּאֵל אָמַר בְּמוֹדֵד לִכְּסָן. רִבִּי יוֹסֵי בַּר זְמִינָא בְשֵׁם רִבִּי יוֹחָנָן אַתְּ רוֹאֶה כִּילוּ אַחַת נְטוּעָה כָּאן.

Samuel said, one measures along the oblique line[106]. Rebbi Yose bar Zemina in the name of Rebbi Johanan: You consider it as if one were planted there[107].

106   Greek λοξός, -ή, -όν "slanting, crosswise, oblique."

107   Since we have a vineyard, one may not plant within four cubits of it. According to Samuel, the form of the vineyard is that of a trapezoid with two right angles, and one may not sow in a larger trapezoid. According to R.

Johanan, the shape of the vineyard is that of the smallest rectangle containing the trapezoid formed by the vines; i. e., one imagines that a vine be planted in the second row parallel to the fifth vine forming the tail. Then the forbidden domain is that of a larger rectangle.

רִבִּי יוֹנָה בָּעֵי נָטַע שְׁתַּיִם כְּנֶגֶד שְׁתַּיִם וְאַחַת יוֹצֵא זָנָב שְׁתַּיִם כְּנֶגֶד שְׁתַּיִם וְאַחַת יוֹצֵא זָנָב. אַתְּ רוֹאֶה כִּילוּ אַחֶרֶת נְטוּעָה כָאן וְאַחֶרֶת נְטוּעָה כָאן. נָטַע שָׁלֹשׁ כְּנֶגֶד שָׁלֹשׁ וְאַחַת מְכוּוֶנֶת נֶגֶד הָאֶמְצָעִי. אַתְּ רוֹאֶה כִּילוּ אַחֶרֶת נְטוּעָה כָאן לַעֲשׂוֹתוֹ כֶּרֶם גָּדוֹל. לֹא כֵאן אַתְּ אָמַר אֵין זָנָב לְכֶרֶם גָּדוֹל. בְּשָׁעָה שֶׁהוּא גָדוֹל. מַהוּ לִיתֵּן זָנָב לְכֶרֶם קָטָן וְלַעֲשׂוֹתוֹ גָדוֹל.

Rebbi Jonah asked: If somebody planted two parallel two and one which protrudes as tail, and another two parallel two and one which protrudes as tail, you consider it as if an additional one was planted here and another one there[108]. If one planted three parallel three and one added on the middle line, do you consider that an additional one was planted on either side to make it a large vineyard[109]? Did we not say that a large vineyard has no tail[110]? That is if it is large; the question is to admit the tail for a small one to make it large!

108   We have two rows, the first one with 6 vines, the second one with 4 (places 3 and 6 empty.) Then, according to R. Johanan, the entire

vineyard is considered as if there were 6 and 6 vines.

109   Here there are three rows; the first two have vines in places 1, 2, 3,

but the third has only one in place 2. If the first number indicates the row, the second the place in the row, the vines are labelled (1,1), (1,2), (1,3), (2,1), (2,2), (2,3), (3,2). In the first two rows, there are four corner vines. If one of them is not counted, there are four minimal vineyards that can be chosen from the first two rows. In addition, there are two minimal vineyards involving row three, either [(1,1), (2,1), (1,2), (2,2), (3,2)] or [(1,3), (2,3), (1,2), (2,2), (3,2)]. If we add the two virtual vines (3,1), (3,3) in row three, we have three rows of three vines, and that is a large vineyard to which the rules of bald spot and surroundings apply, rather than the 4-cubit rule; see Halakhah 4:3, 5:1.

110   If there are at least three rows with three vines each, the tail is not needed; it has no influence on the rules. In this opinion, the question does not even arise and one does not add the theoretical vines. The answer is that the statement applies only to a vineyard that was planted as a large vineyard, not to our question here. The final answer is given only in Halakhah 5:1.

(fol. 29a) **משנה ז**: הַנּוֹטֵעַ שׁוּרָה אַחַת בְּתוֹךְ שֶׁלּוֹ וְשׁוּרָה אַחַת בְּתוֹךְ שֶׁל חֲבֵירוֹ וְדֶרֶךְ הַיָּחִיד וְדֶרֶךְ הָרַבִּים בָּאֶמְצַע וְגֶדֶר שֶׁהוּא נָמוּךְ מֵעֲשָׂרָה[111] טְפָחִים הֲרֵי אִילוּ מִצְטָרְפִין. גָּבוֹהַּ מֵעֲשָׂרָה טְפָחִים אֵינָן מִצְטָרְפוֹת. רִבִּי יְהוּדָה אוֹמֵר אִם עֲרָסָן מִלְּמַעֲלָן הֲרֵי אִילוּ מִצְטָרְפוֹת.

Mishnah 7: If somebody plants one row on his own property and another row is on his neighbor's property[112], and a private or a public road[113] or a fence lower than ten hand-breadths are between them, they are counted together; if it is higher than ten hand-breadths, they are not counted together. Rebbi Jehudah says, if he lined them up on a common trellis, they are counted together[114].

111   Reading of the Rome and the Mishnah mss. Leyden: עשרה.

112   The two rows have two different owners but if they are less than

eight cubits apart and not separated by a wall at least ten hand-breadths high, they look like one vineyard and are treated as such. No sowing is permitted within four cubits of any vine.

113 A public access path less than 8 cubits wide; cf. *Peah* Chapter 2, Note 4.

114 Even over the wall. In *Peah* 2:3, even the rest of the Sages agree that a wall does not separate for *peah* if the crowns of the trees are intermeshed over the wall. However, *peah* is determined by the crowns of the trees which are the places of the fruits, but *kilaim* by the stems that control the growth of the trees. This is the interpretation of all old commentators except Maimonides who translates "if he intermeshed them on top"; cf. Chapter Six, Note 1.

(fol. 29c) **הלכה ז**: רִבִּי אֲחָי בָּעֵי לֵית הָדָא פְּלִיגָא עַל רִבִּי שִׁמְעוֹן דְּרִבִּי שִׁמְעוֹן אוֹמֵר אֵין אָדָם מַקְדִּישׁ דָּבָר שֶׁאֵינוֹ שֶׁלּוֹ. תַּמָּן אֵין אָדָם מַקְדִּישׁ דָּבָר שֶׁאֵינוֹ שֶׁלּוֹ. בְּרַם הָכָא שֶׁלּוֹ וְשֶׁל חֲבֵירוֹ מִצְטָרְפִין לֶאֱסוֹר אֶת הָאֶמְצָעִי. רִבִּי מָנָא לֹא אָמַר כֵּן אֶלָּא לֹא כֵן אָמַר רִבִּי שְׁמוּאֵל בְּשֵׁם רִבִּי זְעִירָא רִבִּי שִׁמְעוֹן כְּדַעְתֵּיהּ כְּמָה דְּרִבִּי שִׁמְעוֹן אָמַר אֵין אָדָם מַקְדִּישׁ דָּבָר שֶׁאֵינוֹ שֶׁלּוֹ כֵּן הוּא אָמַר אֵין אָדָם חוֹבֵשׁ דָּבָר שֶׁאֵינוֹ שֶׁלּוֹ. תַּמָּן אֵין אָדָם מַקְדִּישׁ דָּבָר שֶׁאֵינוֹ שֶׁלּוֹ. בְּרַם הָכָא שֶׁלּוֹ וְשֶׁל חֲבֵירוֹ מִצְטָרְפִין לֶאֱסוֹר אֶת הָאֶמְצָעִי.

Halakhah 7: Rebbi Aḥai said, does this not disagree with Rebbi Simeon, for Rebbi Simeon said, nobody can sanctify property that is not his own[115]? There, he said that nobody can sanctify property that is not his own, but here, his and his neighbor's property are counted together to forbid the ground in the middle[116]. Rebbi Mana did not say so, but did not Rebbi Samuel say in the name of Rebbi Zeïra: Rebbi Simeon follows his own opinion; just as Rebbi Simeon said that nobody can sanctify property that is not his own, so he said that nobody can jail property that is not his own[117], but here, his and his neighbor's property are counted together to forbid the ground in the middle.

115   R. Simeon's statement is in Mishnah 7:4: "Somebody who draws his vine over another person's grain sanctifies the latter and has to pay for it. R. Simeon and R. Yose say, nobody can sanctify property that is not his own." Cf. also Halakhah 2:7.

116   Since both rows were planted legally, they together forbid anything to be sown between them.

117   I. e., make it forbidden to be used. The original meaning of "jailing" is given in Halakhah 2:7; here it is taken in a wider sense. The implication is that if somebody planted vines illegally, encroaching on his neighbor's estate, the neighbor could sow as much as he wanted on his side of the ground between the vines and his border.

משנה ח: (fol. 29a) הַנּוֹטֵעַ שְׁתֵּי שׁוּרוֹת אִם אֵין בֵּינֵיהֶן שְׁמוֹנֶה אַמּוֹת לֹא יָבִיא זֶרַע לְשָׁם. הָיוּ שָׁלֹשׁ וְאִם אֵין בֵּין שׁוּרָה לַחֲבֵירְתָּהּ שֵׁשׁ עֶשְׂרֵה אַמָּה לֹא יָבִיא זֶרַע לְשָׁם. רִבִּי לִיעֶזֶר אוֹמֵר מִשּׁוּם חֲנַנְיָה בֶּן חֲכִינַאי אֲפִילוּ חָרְבָה הָאֶמְצָעִית וְאֵין בֵּין שׁוּרָה לַחֲבֵירְתָּהּ שֵׁשׁ עֶשְׂרֵה אַמָּה לֹא יָבִיא זֶרַע לְשָׁם. שֶׁאִילוּ מִתְּחִילָה נְטָעָהּ הָיָה מוּתָּר בִּשְׁמוֹנֶה אַמּוֹת.

Mishnah 8: If somebody plants two rows, he should not sow there unless there are eight cubits between them[118]. If there were three rows, he should not sow there unless there are sixteen cubits between one row and the next[119]. Rebbi Eliezer[120] said in the name of Ḥananiah ben Ḥakhinai[121]: He should not sow there unless there are sixteen cubits between one row and the next, even if the middle row dried up. But if he planted new [vines][122], it would be permitted with eight cubits.

118   Rows of vines less than 8 cubits apart are considered vineyard-forming, and one has to separate seeds from vines by a minimum of four cubits. Hence, between two rows one may not

sow unless there is a distance of more than 8 cubits.

119   The opinion of the anonymous Sages is that a large vineyard (at least three rows of three vines each) needs 8

cubits distance from each row; see
Halakhah 4:1.

120   This should be R. Eliezer ben
Jacob II, one of the last students of R.
Aqiba. His name is spelled out in full
in most Mishnah mss. and in the Rome
ms. R. Eliezer (ben Hyrcanus) was a
teacher of Rebbi Aqiba.

121   In most sources, he is given the
title Rebbi. He was among the early
students of R. Aqiba, almost one
generation older than R. Eliezer ben
Jacob II.

122   Then there would be only two
rows and the vineyard never would be
"large."

הלכה ח: אָמַר רִבִּי זְעִירָא שְׁמוֹנֶה חוּץ מִמְּקוֹם כָּרָתִּין. כְּמָה דְתֵימַר ((fol. 29c
שְׁמוֹנֶה חוּץ מִמְּקוֹם כָּרָתִּין. וְדִכְוָנָתַהּ אַרְבַּע חוּץ מִמְּקוֹם כָּרָתִּין

Halakhah 8: Rebbi Zeïra said, eight except for the space of the
trunks[123]. Just as you say, eight except for the space of the trunks, so also
four except for the space of the trunks[124].

123   If one has 16 cubits distance
between two rows in a vineyard, it still
is not enough since one needs 8 cubits
of fallow land on each side, not
counting the vines. This discussion is
referred to in Halakhah 5:5.

124   If there are only two rows and
one may sow with eight cubits distance,
one still has to have four cubits of
empty space on each side, not counting
the space of the vines.

אָמַר רִבִּי לְעָזָר הֶחֱמִירוּ תוֹכוֹ יוֹתֵר מֵחוּצָה לוֹ. אָמַר רִבִּי זְעִירָא עַד דַּאֲנָא תַמָּן
קִיְימַנְתָּהּ תוֹכוֹ שְׁמוֹנֶה חוּצָה לָהּ שֵׁשׁ עֶשְׂרֵה. אָמַר רִבִּי לְעָזָר מֵאַרְבַּע אַמּוֹת וְעַד
שְׁמוֹנֶה אָסוּר וּמְקַדֵּשׁ. מִשְּׁמוֹנֶה וְעַד שֵׁשׁ עֶשְׂרֵה אָסוּר וְאֵינוֹ מְקַדֵּשׁ.

Rebbi Eleazar said, they were more restrictive inside than outside[125].
Rebbi Zeïra said, when I was still there[126], I explained it that inside eight
[are required], outside sixteen: From four cubits to eight, it is forbidden
and sanctifies, from eight to sixteen it is forbidden but does not sanctify.

125   Except for the case of a distant
wall ("the circumference of the vine-

yard"), outside one never has to be
farther away than four cubits.

126   In Babylonia. He explains the statement of R. Eleazar, not that "outside" means outside of the vineyard (where in the most restrictive case one only needs 12 cubits) but "inside" is the empty ground that is only eight cubits wide, where any sowing will sanctify both crop and vines, so that no use whatsoever will be permitted, but for a strip wider than 8 and less than 16, when there is no vineyard but only single rows and, hence, the planting does not create an "inside" of any vineyard, anything sown at a distance greater than 6 hand-breadths from any vine is still forbidden but it will not become impossible to use it.

רִבִּי יוֹסֵי בְּשֵׁם רִבִּי יוֹחָנָן אַתְיָא דְּרִבִּי לִיעֶזֶר בֶּן יַעֲקֹב כְּבֵית שַׁמַּאי. כְּמָה דְבֵית שַׁמַּאי אֲמְרוּ שׁוּרָה אַחַת כֶּרֶם. כֵּן רִבִּי לִיעֶזֶר בֶּן יַעֲקֹב אָמַר שׁוּרָה אַחַת כֶּרֶם. מַה נַפְשָׁךְ כֶּרֶם גָּדוֹל הוּא אָסוּר בִּשְׁמוֹנֶה. כֶּרֶם קָטָן הוּא אָסוּר בִּשְׁמוֹנֶה. רִבִּי יוּדָן לֹא אָמַר כֵּן אֶלָּא שְׁמוֹנֶה אַמּוֹת אָסוּר. שְׁמוֹנֶה אַמּוֹת וְכָל־שֶׁהוּא מוּתָּר. אִית דְּבָעֵי מֵימַר שֶׁאִילוּ מִתְּחִילָּה נָטְעוֹ מַטַּע שֵׁשׁ עֶשְׂרֵה עַל שֵׁשׁ עֶשְׂרֵה הָיָה מוּתָּר בִּשְׁמוֹנֶה אַמּוֹת. רִבִּי יְהוּדָה בֶן פָּזִי בְּשֵׁם רִבִּי יוֹחָנָן אַתְיָא דְּרִבִּי לִיעֶזֶר בֶּן יַעֲקֹב כְּבֵית שַׁמַּאי. כְּמָה דְבֵית שַׁמַּאי מַחְמִירִין בָּהּ בְּחוּרְבָּנוֹ יוֹתֵר מִמַּטָּעָתוֹ כֵּן רִבִּי לִיעֶזֶר בֶּן יַעֲקֹב מַחְמִיר בְּחוּרְבָּנוֹ יוֹתֵר מִמַּטָּעָתוֹ.

Rebbi Yose in the name of Rebbi Joḥanan: It turns out that the statement of Rebbi Eliezer ben Jacob[127] is like that of the House of Shammai. Just as the House of Shammai say that one row constitutes a vineyard, so Rebbi Eliezer ben Jacob says that one row constitutes a vineyard[128]. What do you want to say? A large vineyard is forbidden by eight, a small vineyard is forbidden by eight[129]! Rebbi Judan did not say so but taught that eight cubits is forbidden, eight cubits plus any length[130] is permitted. Some want to state: "But if someone newly planted sixteen by sixteen[131], it would be permitted with eight cubits." Rebbi Jehudah ben Pazi in the name of Rebbi Joḥanan: It turns out that the statement of Rebbi Eliezer ben Jacob is like that of the House of Shammai. Just as the House of Shammai are more restrictive when it is dried up than when it is planted, so Rebbi Eliezer ben Jacob is more restrictive when it is dried up than when it is planted.

127 The one that in the Mishnah is attributed to "R. Eliezer."

128 The implication is that the opinion of R. Eliezer ben Jacob cannot possibly be the actual practice.

129 Since plants sanctify a vineyard only up to a distance of four cubits, how does one ever come to forbid sixteen?

130 The added width is defined in the Tosephta (*Kilaim* 4:9) either as one hand-breadth, or $5/6$ of a hand-breadth; see the discussion of the sources in *Tosefta Ki-fšuṭah*, p. 642. In the first opinion, that there is no difference between the widths admitted in large or small vineyards, any planting in which the vines are up to (but not including) eight cubits apart is a vineyard and protected by the laws of a vineyard. In the second opinion, exactly eight cubits still form a large vineyard (possibly not a small one), and only distances of more than eight turn the vines into single trees that have only six hand-breadths as protected area around them.

131 This is an extraordinary restriction. It implies that R. Eliezer ben Jacob considers vines as vineyard-forming if between any two vines the distance is up to sixteen cubits, not, as supposed in our version of the Mishnah, that the distance between vines in a row is up to eight cubits, only that between rows it is sixteen cubits! The question now arises whether this is a legitimate interpretation of the position of the House of Shammai. R. Joḥanan answers that R. Eliezer ben Jacob may well agree that vines farther than eight cubits apart are not vineyard-forming, only he holds that once it was a vineyard, it does not lose its properties automatically when it dries up unless the vines are actually removed.

(fol. 29a) **משנה ט:** הַנּוֹטֵעַ אֶת כַּרְמוֹ שֵׁשׁ עֶשְׂרֵה עַל שֵׁשׁ עֶשְׂרֵה אַמָּה מוּתָּר לְהָבִיא זֶרַע לְשָׁם. אָמַר רִבִּי יְהוּדָה מַעֲשֶׂה בְּצַלְמוֹן בְּאֶחָד שֶׁנָּטַע אֶת כַּרְמוֹ שֵׁשׁ עֶשְׂרֵה עַל שֵׁשׁ עֶשְׂרֵה אַמָּה הָיָה הוֹפֵךְ שְׂעַר שְׁתֵּי שׁוּרוֹת לְצַד אֶחָד וְזוֹרֵעַ אֶת

הַנִּיר וּבַשָּׁנָה הָאַחֶרֶת הָיָה הוֹפֵךְ אֶת הַשַּׂעַר לִמְקוֹם הַזֶּרַע וְזָרַע אֶת הַבּוּר וּבָא
מַעֲשֶׂה לִפְנֵי חֲכָמִים וְהִתִּירוּ. רִבִּי שִׁמְעוֹן וְרִבִּי מֵאִיר אוֹמְרִים אַף הַנּוֹטֵעַ אֶת
כַּרְמוֹ עַל שְׁמוֹנֶה אַמּוֹת מוּתָּר.

Mishnah 9: If somebody plants his vineyard sixteen by sixteen cubits, he may bring seeds there[132]. Rebbi Jehudah said, it happened that somebody in Ṣalmon[133] planted his vineyard sixteen by sixteen cubits. He turned the growth of two rows towards one another and sowed the ploughed area[134]. The next year, he turned the growth to the side that had been sown and sowed what was fallow. This came before the Sages and they permitted it. Rebbi Simeon and Rebbi Meïr say that this is permitted even for someone who plants his vineyard spaced eight cubits[135].

132 If between any two vines there is a 16 cubits space, the vines are isolated and one may sow everywhere except in the six hand-breadths close to any vine.

133 An unidentified place in the Land of Israel.

134 He worked in a two-year cycle, one year planting and one year letting lie fallow. Each of his rows bordered one strip that was sown and one that lay fallow. He did not want even the leaves of his vines to grow over the grains or vegetables he planted, so each year after trimming he trained them to grow over the fallow field.

135 Vines spaced eight cubits or more apart (according to R. Meïr, 40 hand-breadths) are not vineyard-forming.

(fol. 29c) **הלכה ט**: רִבִּי יוֹנָה בְּשֵׁם רַב מוּתָּר הַזֶּרַע וְאָסוּר לִזְרוֹעַ. רִבִּי יוֹסֵי
בְּשֵׁם רַב הִלְכְתָא מוּתָּר לִזְרוֹעַ. רַב חִייָא בַּר אַשִׁי בְּשֵׁם רַב הֲלָכָה כְּרִבִּי מֵאִיר
וְרִבִּי שִׁמְעוֹן. מַה מוּתָּר הַזֶּרַע וּמוּתָּר לִזְרוֹעַ. אוֹ מוּתָּר הַזֶּרַע וְאָסוּר לִזְרוֹעַ. מִן
מַה דְּאָמַר רִבִּי בָּא מָשַׁח לִי רַב חִייָא בַּר אַשִׁי כַּרְמִי מַטַּע שְׁמוֹנֶה עַל שְׁמוֹנֶה
הָדָא אֲמָרָה מוּתָּר הַזֶּרַע וּמוּתָּר לִזְרוֹעַ. רַב הוּנָא זָרַע כַּרְמֵיהּ כָּרָתִין. וְאֵינוּ
אָסוּר מִשּׁוּם כִּלְאַיִם. מְאַרְבְּבִין הַוְיָין וְאֵין עֲבוֹדָה לְגֶפֶן יְחִידִית אֶלָּא כְּרִבִּי

יִשְׁמָעֵאל. דְּרִבִּי יִשְׁמָעֵאל אָמַר אֵין עֲבוֹדָה לְגֶפֶן יְחִידִית דִּבְרֵי חֲכָמִים. רִבִּי
יַעֲקֹב בַּר אִידִי בְּשֵׁם רִבִּי יְהוֹשֻׁעַ בֶּן לֵוִי הֲלָכָה כְּדִבְרֵי מִי שֶׁהוּא מֵיקֵל בְּחוּצָה
לָאָרֶץ. אָמַר רִבִּי יַעֲקֹב בַּר אָחָא וְתַנֵּי תַמָּן הֲלָכָה כְּדִבְרֵי מִי שֶׁהוּא מֵיקֵל
בְּחוּצָה לָאָרֶץ.

Halakhah 9: Rebbi Jonah in the name of Rav: The seed is permitted
but one is forbidden to sow[135]. Rebbi Yose in the name of Rav: The
practice is that one is permitted to sow. Rav Hiyya bar Ashi in the name
of Rav: Practice follows Rebbi Meïr and Rebbi Simeon. Does it mean
that the seed is permitted and one is permitted to sow, or that the seed is
permitted but one is forbidden to sow[136]? Since Rebbi Abba said: Rav
Hiyya bar Ashi measured the layout of my vineyard eight by eight[137];
that means that the seed is permitted and one is permitted to sow. Rav
Huna sowed leeks in his vineyard[138]. Is that not forbidden because of
kilaim? They were mixed up[139] and a single vine needs no place to tend
it, following the words of Rebbi Ismael; as Rebbi Ismael said, the words of
the Sages are that a single vine needs no place to tend it. Rebbi Jacob bar
Idi in the name of Rebbi Joshua ben Levi: Practice outside the Land
follows the lenient opinion. Rebbi Jacob bar Aha said, there[140] they
stated: Practice outside the Land follows the lenient opinion.

135   The entire discussion is about
the statement of Rebbis Meïr and
Simeon which presents practice as was
explained in the preceding Halakhot.
The problem is, what did they permit?
Is it only that the produce is not
sanctified once the distance between
two vines is greater than eight cubits,
or would they tell the vintner to sow in
such a vineyard were he to ask them

about it?

136   Since we have two conflicting
statements, both in the name of Rav.

137   He means that Rav Hiyya bar
Ashi, companion of Rav in the latter's
Academy, provided him with a layout
for his vineyard so that he could sow
grain between the vines. There is no
more compelling evidence than the
action of a respected authority.

138   That vineyard must have been one in which not every vine was planted eight cubits from its nearest neighbor.

139   The vines were planted, or spontaneously growing, in an irregular pattern and nowhere in the vineyard was it possible to identify even a minimal vineyard (3 + 2 vines, 4 forming a rectangle) as required by the House of Hillel. Mishnah 5:1 shows that in such a case, there is an opinion that the planting represents a collection of vines, not a vineyard, and that each vine needs only 6 hand-breadths of empty space around it. Since Rav Huna lived in Babylonia, he had the right to follow the lenient ruling.

140   In Babylonia. The "Land" everywhere is the Land of Israel.

משנה א (fol. 29c): כֶּרֶם שֶׁחָרֵב אִם יֵשׁ בּוֹ לְלַקֵּט עֶשֶׂר גְּפָנִים לְבֵית סְאָה וּנְטוּעוֹת כְּהִלְכָתָן הֲרֵי זֶה נִקְרָא כֶּרֶם. כֶּרֶם דַּל שֶׁהוּא נָטוּעַ עִרְבּוּבְיָא. אִם יֵשׁ בּוֹ לְכַוֵּין שְׁתַּיִם כְּנֶגֶד שָׁלֹשׁ הֲרֵי זֶה כֶּרֶם. וְאִם לָאו אֵינוֹ כֶּרֶם. רִבִּי מֵאִיר אוֹמֵר הוֹאִיל וְהוּא נִרְאֶה כְתַבְנִית כְּרָמִים הֲרֵי זֶה כֶּרֶם.

Mishnah 1: A dried-up vineyard, if it contains ten producing vines per *bet seah* and they are planted regularly[1], is called vineyard. A poor vineyard, one that is planted irregularly, if in it one can ascertain three parallel to two[2] is a vineyard, otherwise it is not a vineyard. Rebbi Meïr said, since it has the appearance of vineyards, it is a vineyard.

1   If the surviving vines are equally spaced in one direction.

2   If somewhere in the vineyard one can identify a minimal vineyard following the House of Hillel.

הלכה א (fol. 29d)): אָמַר רִבִּי יוֹחָנָן הִיא קָרַחַת הַכֶּרֶם הִיא כֶּרֶם שֶׁחָרֵב. קָרַחַת הַכֶּרֶם מַקְרִיחִין אוֹתוֹ מֵאֶמְצָעִי. כֶּרֶם שֶׁחָרֵב מַקְרִיחִין אוֹתוֹ מִכָּל־צְדָדָיו.

Halakhah 1: Rebbi Joḥanan said: A bald spot in a vineyard is like a[3] vineyard that dried up. One clears the ground of a bald spot in a vineyard in its interior, one clears the ground of a dried-up vineyard on all sides.

3   Not that it is the same thing but that the same rules apply, and one may sow only at a distance of 16 cubits from the nearest vine. Clearing the ground means tearing out the dead vines.

רבִּי זְעִירָא מְחַוֵי לַחֲבֵרַיָּא. תִּשַׁע שׁוּרִין מִן שׁוּבַע שׁוּבַע. נְסַב שׁוּרָא פָּרָא שׁוּרָא

לִשְׁתֵי שׁוּרָא פָּרָא שׁוּרָא לְעֶרֶב. נִשְׁתַּיְּירוּ שָׁם עֶשְׂרִים גְּפָנִים. נְסַב תַּרְתֵּיי מִיכָּן

וְתַרְתֵּיי מִיכָּן חֲדָא מִיכָּא וַחֲדָא מִיכָּא. נִשְׁתַּיְּירוּ שָׁם עֲשֵׂר [4] גְּפָנִים. הָדָא דְתַגִּינָן

עֶשֵׂר גְּפָנִים לְבֵית סְאָה נִמְצְאוּ שְׁתַּיִם שְׁתַּיִם כְּנֶגֶד שְׁתַּיִם אַחַת יוֹצֵא זָנָב. שְׁתַּיִם כְּנֶגֶד

שְׁתַּיִם וְאַחַת יוֹצֵא זָנָב. שְׁתַּיִם כְּנֶגֶד שְׁתַּיִם וְאַחַת יוֹצֵא זָנָב. שְׁתַּיִם כְּנֶגֶד שְׁתַּיִם

וְאַחַת יוֹצֵא זָנָב.

Rebbi Zeïra showed to the colleagues: Nine rows of seven each[5]. Take away one next[6] to another for the warp and one next to another for the woof. There remain 20 vines. Take away two from each side in one direction, one from each side in the other direction[7]. There remain 10 vines. That is what we have stated: "Ten vines per *bet seah*". It turns out that there are four times two parallel two and one protrudes as tail[8].

4   Reading of Rome ms. and R. Simson. The reading of the Leyden ms. and Venice print, עשׂרים, is impossible since 20 – 10 = 10.

5   He explains the Mishnah by an example. We have a vineyard whose vines are planted 8 cubits apart from one another. This follows from the discussion later (Notes 17,18), but it is understood that one wants to construct a vineyard in which the 16-cubit rules forbid one to sow with a minimum number (10) of vines standing. Hence, the vines must be spaced as far apart as possible and still form a vineyard. In modern language, we make a model of that vineyard by drawing an (x,y)-coordinate system in the plane and indicating the vines by the points with integer coordinates, where in each row ("woof") $x = 1, 2, \ldots, 7$, and the rows are numbered by ("warp") $y = 1, 2, \ldots$, 9. In all, we have 63 vines. Now, we cross out alternate rows and columns, i. e., we cross out all points with coordinates $x = 2, 4, 6$ and $y = 2, 4, 6, 8$. There remain 5 y-coordinates (1,3,5,7,9) for each of the remaining 4 x-coordinates (1,3,5,7). Hence, there remain $5 \times 4 = 20$ vines.

6   Greek παρά.

7   On the long sides, one removes the two vines at the corners and the two adjacent ones, leaving only those in positions (1,5) and (7,5). On the short sides, one removes one additional vine each, leaving those in positions (5,1) and (5,9). That means that for $x =$

1, one has only $y = 5$, for $x = 3$, $y = 3,5,7$, for $x = 5$, $y = 1,3,5,7,9$, for $x = 7$, $y = 5$; the total of standing vines is $1 + 3 + 5 + 1 = 10$.

fig. 5-1

8　From any angle one looks at it, one can always find a minimal vineyard contained in the standing pattern. For example, the standing vines {(1,5) (3,5) (5,5) (3,7) (5,7)} form such a vineyard, as do {(1,5) (3,5) (5,5) (3,3) (5,3)} or {(5,9) (5,7) (5,5) (3,7) (3,5)} or {(5,1) (5,3) (5,5) (3,3) (3,5)} or even {(1,5) (3,7) (5,9) (3,5) (5,7)}. In all, one may identify 8 minimal vineyards. Hence, from all angles, the pattern describes a valid vineyard. (One certainly cannot simply create one large vineyard, three times three vines plus one additional, since the maximum area covered by such a vineyard is only 1532 square cubits.)

אַתְּ רוֹאֶה כִּילוּ אֲחֶרֶת נְטוּעָה כָאן. כִּילוּ אֲחֶרֶת נְטוּעָה כָאן. כִּילוּ אֲחֶרֶת נְטוּעָה כָאן. לִיטַּע כָאן אֵין אַתְּ יָכוֹל שֶׁהוּא זָנָב וְאֵין זָנָב לְזָנָב. לִיטַּע כָאן אֵין אַתְּ יָכוֹל שֶׁהוּא זָנָב וְאֵין זָנָב לְזָנָב. לִיטַּע כָאן אֵין אַתְּ יָכוֹל שֶׁהוּא זָנָב וְאֵין זָנָב לְזָנָב. הָדָא אָמְרָה שֶׁאֵין זָנָב לְכֶרֶם גָּדוֹל. הָדָא פְּשִׁיטָא שְׁאֵילָתֵיהּ דְּרִבִּי יוֹסֵי בָּר זְמִינָא בְּשֵׁם רִבִּי יוֹחָנָן אַתְּ רוֹאֶה כִּילוּ אֲחֶרֶת נְטוּעָה כָאן.

One assumes that[9] another [vine] was planted there, for all four sides[10]. One cannot actually plant on any of the four sides because it would form a tail and there is no tail for a tail. This implies that there is no tail for a large vineyard, which gives a simple answer to the question of Rebbi Yose ben Zabida in the name of Rebbi Joḥanan: one considers as if another [vine] was planted there[11].

9　כילו is a contracted form of בְּאִילוּ.

10　Since R. Zeïra explains the Mishnah according to R. Joḥanan, one has to follow the latter's opinion in Halakhah 4:6 that the area covered by a minimal vineyard is not the trapezoid defined by the segments containing, respectively, two and three vines, but the smallest rectangle containing the trapezoid, adding an imaginary third vine in the second row. In our case, one cannot actually have these vines added, because that would immediately generate three rows of three vines each, which define a large vineyard for which the rule of tail does not apply. Then the question arises of how to compute the area of the remaining vineyard. This will be dealt with in the next paragraph where it is shown that one cannot have exactly a *bet seah*

(2500 square cubits) as required by the Mishnah unless one reduces the distances between the vines.

11   In Halakhah 4:6, R. Yose bar Zemina in the name of R. Johanan had a statement, about which R. Jonah asked whether minimal vineyards can be combined to form a large vineyard. The answer given here is that one does not add the imaginary vines to form a theoretical large vineyard.

נִמְצְאוּ שְׁשִׁים וְאַרְבַּע עַל אַרְבָּעִים וּשְׁמוֹנֶה. נָסַב תַּרְתֵּי מִכָּא וִיהַב לוֹן הָכָא נִמְצְאוּ אַרְבָּעִים וּשְׁמוֹנֶה עַל אַרְבָּעִים וּשְׁמוֹנֶה. חַד בֵּינַיי עֲקַר חַד בֵּינַיי וְהָב חַד קָרַח שֵׁשׁ עֶשְׂרֵה עַל שֵׁשׁ עֶשְׂרֵה עֲבוֹדָתוֹ בִּשְׁמוֹנֶה אַמּוֹת. מַה אַתְּ עֲבַד לָהּ הוּא וַעֲבוֹדָתוֹ לְתוֹךְ בֵּית סְאָה. אוֹ חוּץ לַעֲבוֹדָתוֹ. אֵין תַּעֲבְדִינָהּ הוּא וַעֲבוֹדָתוֹ בְּתוֹךְ בֵּית סְאָה אַשְׁכַּח חָסֵר תְּלַת מֵאָוָן וְאַרְבָּעִין וּתְמָנְיָא. וְאֵין תַּעֲבְדִינָהּ חוּץ לַעֲבוֹדָתוֹ. אַשְׁכַּח יְתֵר מֵאַרְבַּע מֵאָוָן וְחַמְשִׁין וְתַרְתֵּיי. אֵין תֵּימַר כְּמִי[12] פְּלָגוֹת בִּיחִידִיּוֹת הֵן אֵין תֵּימַר בְּרוֹצֵף לֹא תַנִּינָן אֶלָּא עֶשֶׂר גְּפָנִים לְבֵית סְאָה. הֲוֵי לֹא מָצֵי תַנִּייָהּ.

It turns out to be 64 by 48[13]. Take two from here and put them there, that turns out to be 48 by 48[14]. Take out one in between, one in between, and make a bald spot 16 by 16 that can be tended by eight cubits[15]. How do you treat it[16]? Itself and the area to tend it within a *bet seah*, or without the area to tend it? If you take it with the area to tend it within the *bet seah*, then 348 are missing[17]. If you take it without the area to tend it, there is an excess of 452[18]. You might say, they are separated as single ones[19]. You might say, they are closer together[20]: we have stated only "10 per *bet seah*;" you could not state that.

12   The last three words are the reading of the Rome ms. Venice: במי.

13   One has to take the stems of the vines included in the eight cubits distance from one to the next, otherwise one could sow a row of vegetables between the rows of vines. Then the row of originally nine vines has a total length of 64 cubits and that of seven vines one of 48 cubits (Note 5). Since 64 × 48 = 3072, the area is 572 square cubits larger than the 2500 square cubits of a *bet seah*. Since we have removed the corners, we have to remove some of the area; the problem is to do it in a uniform way to end up with 2500 square cubits. [According to Samuel in Halakhah 4:6, the kite-shaped quadrilateral defined by the extremal vines in R. Zeïra's design has an area of only 1536 square cubits. Hence, Samuel's opinion may be disregarded.]

14   If, for example, one moves the vine at position (5,1) to (1,3), (7,3) to (1,7), and completes the rectangle, one has an area that falls 196 square cubits short of the required 2500.

15   The distance between two vines now is 16 cubits since every second vine was removed. Even according to him who in the preceding Mishnah treated a dried-up vineyard more severely than a newly planted one, one could think of removing two squares of 16 by 16 in the interior of the vineyard. But that would leave one with 3072 - 2×256 = 2560 square cubits, an area that is still too large.

16   Before continuing to compute, we have to settle the question whether the *bet seah* is the area defined by the standing vines or whether it includes the strip of 4 cubits all around the vineyard for tending the vineyard.

17   This number is difficult to explain. All commentators change the numerical value to agree with their computation. All we can do is understand the problem. The basis of the argument is the computation underlying the next sentence. There it is established that the area of the vineyard in R. Zeïra's example is cross-shaped (fig. 2), formed from the rectangle of sides 64 and 48 by excising corner squares of area 16×16, of area 2048 square cubits.

```
      x  o  x
   x  o  o  o  x
   o  o  o  o  o
      x  o  x
```

fig. 5-2

The strip of width 4 around it, not counting the corners, has area (64+48) ×2×4 = 896 square cubits. Of these four are concave corners that are counted twice, hence, one has to remove 4 times 16, for a total area of 832 square cubits. It is questionable whether one has to fill out the 90° circular sectors around the virtual vines but one has to add two 90° circular sectors of radius 4 at the two vines on the border of the vineyard. Hence, the total area in question here is $A = 2048 + 832 + 8\pi = 2880 + 8\pi$. Even if one uses the approximation $\pi \cong 3$, $A = 2500 + 404$ and not $A = 2500 + 348$ as asserted. It is impossible to account for the missing 56 square cubits.

On the other hand, the number 452 in the next sentence is certainly correct and both mss. have 348 here; emendation is impossible. All we can do is discover a possible way of computing the area, keeping in mind that in computations of this kind one suppresses fractions at the end. It seems that here the boundary strip is only three cubits wide except near where real vines are standing. Let h be the width of the boundary strip. Then the computation of the area of the boundary strip is done in five steps.

1. Since the perimeter of the figure is 224 (all measures in cubits), the strip along the sides except for the convex corners is $A_1 = 224h - 4h^2$ since the convex corners are counted twice in the first term.

2. On the top and bottom edges in fig. 2 are two real vines, both of which have to be enclosed in a circular domain of radius 4. Let

$$q = (16 - h^2)^{1/2}$$

and

$$\alpha = \arctan h/q.$$

Then the center angle of the sector outside the strip is

$$\varphi = \pi - 2\alpha;$$

the area to be added is

$$A_2 = 32\varphi - 2hq.$$

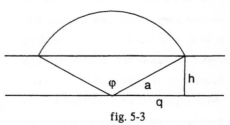

fig. 5-3

3. At the two vines in position (5,1) and (5,5), one adds two semicircles of radius 4 minus two isosceles right triangles of sides h, for

$$A_3 = 32\pi - 2h^2.$$

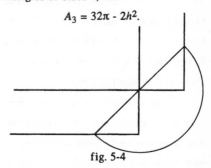

fig. 5-4

4. At the four concave corners with real vines, one has to add quarter disks

and subtract the parts covered by the strip wide h. The half-angle of the sector outside the strip is $\beta = \pi/4 - \alpha$. This yields

$$A_4 = 128\beta - 64\sin \alpha \, (\cos \alpha - \sin \alpha).$$

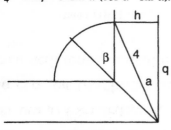

fig. 5-5

5. Finally, at the six convex corners occupied by virtual vines, one adds quarter discs of radius h, or $A_5 = 3\pi h^2$. The total area is the sum of these five. The entire computation is within the level of difficulty of Euclid's *Data*. The next problem is the determination of π. Mishnaiot *Eruvin* 3:1, *Ahilut* 12:6 state that $\pi = 3$. Maimonides writes that they adopted this raw approximation since in the opinion of Aristotle, the straight and the curved are original opposites and it is impossible to express curved quantities precisely in terms of linear measures. (In the framework of Archimedean mathematics, the falsity of this assertion was shown only in the Seventeenth Century by John Wallis.) Since we tend to disregard fractions in Talmudic computations, it seems reasonable to take $\pi = 3$. We do not

have access to the table of chords used by the Talmudists to compute the contribution of A_4 unless we want to take Ptolemy's table (Ptolemäus, *Handbuch der Astronomie*, transl. K. Manitius, ed. O. Neugebauer. Leipzig 1963, pp. 37-40). This means all our computations here are only an approximate reconstruction. If we take modern values for the trigonometric functions in step 4 the total area is 800 for $h = 2.94$. (For $h = 3$, the deviation of the modern value from Ptolemy's is negligible, about 0.001, much less than the precision of our computation.) It is reasonable to assume that in talmudic approximation, this means $h = 3$. [Better values of π known from Antiquity, $3^1/_8$ or $3^1/_7$, yield smaller values of h which have no reasonable explanation.]

18   According to R. Joḥanan, we have to add to the standing vines the ones that complete the minimal vines, i. e., the vines at positions $(1,3)$, $(1,7)$, $(3,1)$, $(3,9)$, $(7,3)$, $(7,7)$. This means that from the original 64×48, at each corner we excise a square of edge length 16. The remaining area is 3072 - 4×16×16 = 3072 - 1024 = 2048 = 2500 - 452 cubits.

19   Since the scheme of R. Zeïra does not work out to produce 10 vines on exactly 2500 square cubits, we have

to conclude that the 10 vines are isolated in the field. Then, each vine has 250 square cubits around it, which means that it is situated in the center of a square of edge $\sqrt{250}$ = 15.81 cubits. This length is also the distance of two vines (or better, the distance of the centers of any two vines) from one another, and this is just below the 16 cubits that would diqualify the field from being a "vineyard".

20   Than 15.811 cubits.

הַכּוֹרֶת מְכוּוָּן וְהַנּוֹף אֵינוֹ מְכוּוָּן הֲרֵי זֶה כֶּרֶם. הַנּוֹף מְכוּוָּן וְהַכּוֹרֶת אֵינוֹ מְכוּוָּן אֵינוֹ כֶּרֶם. הָיוּ דַקּוֹת וְאֵינָן מְכוּוָּנוֹת הֶעָבוֹת וַהֲרֵי הֵן מְכוּוָּנוֹת הֲרֵי זֶה כֶּרֶם. כֵּיצַד הוּא יוֹדֵעַ אִם מְכוּוָּנוֹת הֵן. מֵבִיא חוּט וּמוֹתֵחַ. אִית תַּנָּיֵי תַנֵּי מִבִּפְנִים וְאִית תַּנָּיֵי תַנֵּי מִבַּחוּץ. אָמַר רִבִּי יוֹנָה מָאן דְּאָמַר מִבִּפְנִים בְּתוֹךְ טֶפַח. מָאן דְּאָמַר מִבַּחוּץ צָרִיךְ שֶׁיְּהֵא נוֹגֵעַ בָּהֶן. שׁוּרָה הַחִיצוֹנָה שֶׁאֵינָהּ מְכוּוֶּנֶת כְּנֶגֶד הַכְּרָתִּין. נוֹתְנִין לָהּ עֲבוֹדָתָהּ וְזוֹרֵעַ אֶת הַמּוֹתָר. אָמַר רִבִּי יוֹסֵי שֶׁאִם הָיוּ זוֹרְעִין בְּתוֹךְ שִׁשָּׁה הַכֹּל אָסוּר. חוּץ לְשִׁשָּׁה הַגְּפָנִים מוּתָּרוֹת וְהַכֶּרֶם אָסוּר.

"[21]The trunk is aligned but the top is not aligned, that is a vineyard. The top is aligned but the trunk is not aligned, that is not a vineyard. If they were thin, but when they grow thick they will be aligned, that is a vineyard. How does one know that they are aligned? One brings a rope and stretches it." Some Tannaïm state: "From within[22]." But some Tannaïm state: "From without." Rebbi Jonah said, he who says "from within," within a hand-breadth, but he who says "from without" requires that it touches. "If the outer row is not aligned in its trunks, one reserves for it the space to tend it[23] and one may sow the rest." Rebbi Yose says, if one sows within six hand-breadths all is forbidden; outside of six hand-breadths single vines are permitted but a vineyard is forbidden[24].

21   Tosephta *Kilaim* 3:4; the text is almost identical with the one given here, including the queer use of the singular in the first two statements that make sense only if applied to at least three vines. The later statement, commented on by R. Yose, is from a source other than the Tosephta.

22 This Tanna requires that the centers of the trunks be aligned. That obviously is not directly measurable; hence, one has to measure from the outside and determine that the centers are within one hand-breadth of the streched rope. The second version, that one puts the rope along the outsides of the vines, is that of the Tosephta.

23 Since the vines in this case do not form a vineyard and do not belong to the vineyard, they are treated as single vines and have only six hand-breadths reserved for tending. The language of the Tosephta is: "If one [vine] deviates to the inside and one to the outside (i. e., the straight segments connecting the vines form a zig-zag line), that is not a vineyard."

24 Since a vineyard needs four cubits for tending.

וְאֵיזֶהוּ כֶּרֶם דַּל. אָמַר רִבִּי יוֹנָה דַּל בִּגְפָנִים וְעָשִׁיר בַּעֲבוֹדוֹת.

What means "a poor vineyard?[25]" Rebbi Jonah said, it is poor in vines but rich in tending areas.

25 The one mentioned in the Mishnah. It needs a large tending area since the imaginary vines also belong to the tending area.

(fol. 29c) **משנה ב:** כֶּרֶם שֶׁהוּא נָטוּעַ עַל פָּחוֹת מֵאַרְבַּע אַמּוֹת. רִבִּי שִׁמְעוֹן אוֹמֵר אֵינוֹ כֶרֶם. וַחֲכָמִים אוֹמְרִים כֶּרֶם. וְרוֹאִין אֶת הָאֶמְצָעִיּוֹת כִּילוּ אֵינָן.

Mishnah 2: A vineyard that is planted less that four cubits apart[26], Rebbi Simeon says that it is no vineyard. But the Sages say that it is a vineyard and one disregards the ones in the middle as if nonexistent[27].

26 This violates standard agricultural practice.

27 If every second vine is disregarded the remaining vines still are less than eight cubits apart and, hence, still form a vineyard. The argument of the Sages (made explicit in Babli *Baba Batra* 102b) is that vines planted too close to one another will not bear the best or the most fruit; hence, the

vintner might plant too many vines at the start and then, when it becomes clear which vines grow best, he will take out the rest and use as wood and replant the best ones as a regular vineyard. Rebbi Simeon is of the opinion that a vineyard is planted for its yield, so he waits until the vineyard is thinned before he imposes the restrictions of a vineyard. (In the Babli, R. Simeon is interpreted to mean that nobody plants a vineyard with the intention of thinning.) The Sages think that planting for a vineyard makes a vineyard from the start.

It is not quite clear what the minimum distance is; cf. Chapter 4, Note 2. The cubit of 52.6 cm would give 210.4 cm as minimal distance of two vines. R. A. H. Naëh defines the hand-breadth as 8.5 cm, which implies that 4 cubits of five hand-breadths each are 170 cm. Modern viticulture works with distances of 135 to 150 cm; one is best off by adopting the minimal interpretation of cubits.

(fol. 29d) **הלכה ב:** אָמַר לָהֶן רִבִּי שִׁמְעוֹן אוֹתָם שֶׁאַתֶּם אוֹמְרִים רוֹאִין אֶת הָאֶמְצָעִיּוֹת כִּילוּ אֵינָן. הֲרֵי הֵן עִיקָרוֹ שֶׁל כֶּרֶם. אָמַר רִבִּי חֲנַנְיָה הָדָא אֲמָרָה כְּשֶׁהָיוּ שֵׁשׁ כְּנֶגֶד שֵׁשׁ. אֲבָל אִם הָיוּ חָמֵשׁ כְּנֶגֶד חָמֵשׁ. כָּל־עַמָּא מוֹדֵיי שֶׁהֵן רוֹאִין אֶת הָאֶמְצָעִיּוֹת כִּילוּ אֵינָן. אָמַר רִבִּי מָנָא הָדָא דְתֵימַר כְּשֶׁהָיוּ חָמֵשׁ כְּנֶגֶד חָמֵשׁ. אֲבָל אִם הָיוּ שֵׁשׁ כְּנֶגֶד שֵׁשׁ אִילוּ אַתְּ רוֹאֶה אֶת הָאֶמְצָעִים כִּילוּ אֵינָן אִילוּ אִילוּ. מַהוּ הָדָא דְתַנִּינָן רוֹאִין אֶת הָאֶמְצָעִיּוֹת כִּילוּ אֵינָן. אָמַר רִבִּי הוּנָא שֶׁמּוּתָּר לְהַדְלוֹתָן עַל זַרְעוֹ[28]. אָמַר רִבִּי מָנָא הָדָא מְסַיְיעָא לְהַהִיא דְּאָמַר רִבִּי יוֹסֵי אִם הָיוּ זְרָעִים בְּתוֹךְ שִׁשָּׁה הַכֹּל אָסוּר. חוּץ לְשִׁשָּׁה גְּפָנִים מוּתָּרוֹת וְהַכֶּרֶם אָסוּר.

Halakhah 2: Rebbi Simeon said to them: Those about which you say that one disregards the ones in the middle as if nonexistent, are the essence of the vineyard! Rebbi Hananiah[29] said, that applies in the case where there are six parallel six. But if there are five parallel five, everybody agrees that one disregards the ones in the middle as if nonexistent. Rebbi Mana said, that means if there are five parallel five. But if there are six parallel six, if you disregard the ones in the middle as if

nonexistent, these are like those! What does that mean which we have
stated: One disregards the ones in the middle as if nonexistent? Rebbi
Huna said, that one is permitted to draw them[30] over his seeds. Rebbi
Mana said, that supports what Rebbi Yose had said, that if one sows within
six hand-breadths all is forbidden, outside of six hand-breadths single vines
are permitted[31] and a vineyard is forbidden

28   Reading of the Rome ms.
Venice and Leyden: על גבי גפנים.

29   R. Ḥananiah and R. Mana
disagree about the meaning of the last
statement of R. Simeon. According to
R. Ḥananiah, in the case of two rows of
five vines each, if one disregards any
vines numbered 2 and 4 in their rows,
one retains two rows of three vines
each forming a legal vineyard. But if
one has two rows of 6 each, one
eliminates either the even or the odd
numbered vines; the ones eliminated
would also form a vineyard and that is
unacceptable in the opinion of R.
Simeon. R. Mana has essentially the
same argument, only he says that the
disagreement concerns the first case,
when one would have a vineyard in

case one eliminates vines 2 and 4, but
not if one eliminates 1, 3, 5. However,
in the case of 6 or more vines, one
always retains a valid vineyard (and
the vines considered nonexistent do not
give the possibility of sowing there
since the distance from vine to
remaining vines is less than 8 cubits.)

30   If the domain at the border of
the vineyard is sown with other
produce, the shoots of the vines
destined to be taken out can be drawn
on a trellis that goes sideways over the
produce, since the vines will be
eliminated before they bear fruit.

31   In this interpretation, "single
vines" are those planted too close and
destined to be removed, even if
initially planted in a vineyard pattern.

שִׁמְעוֹן בַּר בָּא בְשֵׁם רבִּי יוֹחָנָן. כְּשֵׁם שֶׁהֵן חֲלוּקִין כָּאן כָּךְ חֲלוּקִין בִּשְׁכוּנַת
קְבָרוֹת. אָמַר רבִּי יוֹנָה וְלֹא דַמְיָא תַּמָּן מְרוּנְּחִין וּרְצָפָן יֵשׁ לָהֶן שְׁכוּנַת קְבָרוֹת.
רְצוּפָן וְרִיוְּחָן אֵין עֲלֵיהֶן שְׁכוּנַת קְבָרוֹת. בְּרַם הָכָא מְרוּנְּחִין וּרְצָפָן בְּמַחְלוֹקֶת.
רְצוּפִין וְרִיוְּחָן דִּבְרֵי הַכֹּל. בְּרַם הָכָא מַה פְּלִיגִין בְּשֶׁבָּא וּמְצָאָן רְצוּפִין. רבִּי
שִׁמְעוֹן אוֹמֵר אוֹמֵר אֲנִי גַּל נָפַל עֲלֵיהֶן וּרְצָפָן. וְרַבָּנָן אָמַר מְרוּנְּחִין הֵן וּרְצָפָן.

Simeon bar Abba in the name of Rebbi Johanan[32]: Just as they disagree here, they disagree about a graveyard[33]. Rebbi Jonah said, one cannot compare these. There, if graves were spaced apart and one moved them together, they would form a graveyard[34]. When they were close together and one spaces them apart, that does not make a graveyard[35]. But here, if they were spaced apart and one moved them closer, that is the disagreement[36]. If they were close and one moved them apart, everybody would agree[37]. But here[38], what is their disagreement? When one found them close together. Rebbi Simeon said, a landslide fell on them and compressed them[39]. But the Sages say, were they spaced apart and somebody brought them close together[40]?

32   This discussion is referred to in Babli *Baba Batra* 102b. A parallel to the text here is found in Yerushalmi *Nazir* 9:3, fol. 57b. The text there is slightly different from the text here. Since the Rome ms. here supports the text from *Nazir*, and the last sentences here show that both times the paragraphs are a confluence from texts from both sources, it is appropriate to give the full text of the paragraph there:

תמן תנינן כרם שהוא נטוע על פחות מ' אמות ר'
שמעון אומר אינו כרם. וחכמים אומרים כרם.
ורואין את האמצעיות כאילו אינן. שמעון בר בא
בשם ר' יוחנן כשם שהן חלוקין כאן כך הן חולקין
בשכונת קברות. א"ר יונה ולא דמייא תמן יש
עליהן שכונת קברות. ברם הכא אין עליה שכונת
קברות. א"ר יוסי ולא דמייא תמן מרווחין ורצפן
במחלוקת. רצופין וריווחן דברי הכל. ברם הכא

מהו פליגין. בשבא ומצאן רצופין ר"ש אומר גל
נפל עליהן ורצפן. ורבנן אמרי מרווחין היו ורצפן.
"There, we have stated: 'A vineyard which is planted less that four cubits apart, Rebbi Simeon says it is no vineyard. But the Sages say it is a vineyard and one disregards the ones in the middle as if nonexistent.' Simeon bar Abba in the name of Rebbi Johanan: Just as they disagree here, they disagree about a graveyard. Rebbi Jonah said, one cannot compare these. *There, they form a graveyard, here, they do not form a graveyard. Rebbi Yose said, one cannot compare these. There, if they were spaced apart and one moved them closer together, that is the disagreement. If they were close and one moved them apart, everybody would agree. But here,*

what is their disagreement? When one found them close together. Rebbi Simeon said, a landslide fell on them and compressed them. But the Sages say, were they spaced apart and somebody brought them close together?"

33   This refers to Mishnah *Nazir* 9:3: "If somebody stumbles upon a grave (on his property; he did not know that the grave was there), he removes it and its surroundings (the earth that absorbed the decomposed flesh of the deceased, for reburial.) If he found two, he takes them and their surroundings. If he found three and between any two graves is a distance from 4 to 8 cubits, space for the bier and its carriers, that is a graveyard (and cannot be disturbed) and one has to check another adjacent 20 cubits."
In a *baraita*, quoted only in Babli *Bava Batra* 102a, but presupposed in the Yerushalmi, there is a discussion about a group of several graves that are found closer than 4 cubits together. The Sages think that these indicate haphazard burials which do not constitute a graveyard, but R. Simeon holds that one disregards alternate graves and the rest form a graveyard that may not be disturbed. The Babli explains the obvious switch of opinions between R. Simeon and the Sages in that R. Simeon holds that nobody plants

vines for thinning, but that in graveyard there sometimes are emergency burials when one cannot observe all necessary distances, whereas the Sages hold that one plants a vineyard with the idea of selecting the best vines, but in a graveyard one never violates common decency by piling grave upon grave.

34   While it is forbidden to do so, if it is done, then according to everybody the sanctity of a graveyard will not be impaired.

35   This sentence, missing in *Nazir* and the Rome ms., is difficult to accept, since one always may make a new graveyard. What is meant is that the reburial does not retroactively make the burial place a graveyard. In a graveyard, the soil cannot be used for anything but burial. In a row of single graves, any soil that does not belong to the immediate surroundings of the graves may be used for any private purpose.

36   While this is not mentioned in the Mishnah, it is assumed that the Sages expect the new plantings to be thinned and R. Simeon does not.

37   This will create a vineyard.

38   "Here" is the Mishnah in *Nazir*. This shows that the text in *Nazir* is the original one.

39   Hence, they formed a graveyard

whose sanctity cannot be lost.

40   This is a most unlikely scenario and can be disregarded. The setting of the Mishnah is the Land of Israel where every grave is expected to be Jewish.

(fol. 29c) **משנה ג:** חָרִיץ שֶׁהוּא עוֹבֵר בְּכֶרֶם עָמוֹק עֲשָׂרָה וְרוֹחַב אַרְבָּעָה. רָבִּי לִיעֶזֶר בֶּן יַעֲקֹב אוֹמֵר אִם הָיָה מְפֻלָּשׁ מֵרֹאשׁ הַכֶּרֶם וְעַד סוֹפוֹ הֲרֵי זֶה נִרְאֶה כְּבֵין שְׁנֵי כְרָמִים זוֹרְעִין בְּתוֹכוֹ וְאִם לָאו הֲרֵי הוּא כְּגָת. הַגַּת שֶׁבְּכֶרֶם עֲמוּקָה עֲשָׂרָה וּרְחָבָה אַרְבָּעָה זוֹרְעִין בְּתוֹכָהּ דִּבְרֵי רִבִּי לִיעֶזֶר. וַחֲכָמִים אוֹסְרִין. שׁוֹמֵרָה שֶׁבְּכֶרֶם גָּבוֹהַּ עֲשָׂרָה וּרְחָבָה אַרְבָּעָה זוֹרְעִין בְּתוֹכָהּ וְאִם הָיָה שֵׂעָר כּוֹתֵשׁ אָסוּר.

Mishnah 3: A ditch that crosses a vineyard, ten hand-breadths deep and four wide. Rebbi Eliezer ben Jacob said, if it is open from one side of the vineyard to the opposite side it appears to be between two vineyards; one sows in it. Otherwise, it is like a vat[41]. If a vat in the vineyard is ten deep and four wide, one sows in it, the words of Rebbi Eliezer; but the Sages forbid it[42]. On a watchman's mound in a vineyard that is ten hand-breadths high and four wide one may sow; but if hair was pressing down[43], it is forbidden.

41   In Biblical Hebrew, גת denotes the winepress. In Mishnaic Hebrew, it may denote a winepress, the time of wine making, and the big vat into which the grape juice flows from the press, as well as any vat of similar size. Here, גת denotes the depression in which grapes are temporarily stored before being transported to the winepress.

42   As a matter of principle, a vertical distance of 10 hand-breadths creates a separate domain. If the domain is at least 4 hand-breadths wide, it can stand on its own (Mishnah *Eruvin* 7:2-5.) The Sages forbid planting if the separate low domain is "jailed" by the surrounding vines. In

the case of an elevated mound, they
consider it "jailed" only if branches of
vines reach the top of the mound (R.
David ben Zimra on Maimonides,

Kilaim 7:20).

43   If vine leaves touch the ground
on the hill; cf. Mishnah and Halakhah
Peah 2:3.

(fol. 29d) **הלכה ג:** עַד שֶׁיְּהֵא מְבָרֵיק כְּדֵי הוּא וַעֲבוֹדָתוֹ מִן מַה דְתַגֵּי מוֹדִין
חֲכָמִים לְרִבִּי לִיעֶזֶר בֶּן יַעֲקֹב בְּחָרִיץ מְבָרִיץ כְּדֵי הוּא וַעֲבוֹדָתוֹ. הֲוֵי כֵן רִבִּי
לִיעֶזֶר בֶּן יַעֲקֹב סָבַר מֵימַר אֲפִילוּ אֵינוֹ מְבָרֵיק כְּדֵי הוּא וַעֲבוֹדָתוֹ. מַה פְּלִיגִין
כְּשֶׁהָיוּ שְׁתֵּי שׁוּרוֹת מִיכָּן וּשְׁתֵּי שׁוּרוֹת מִיכָּאן. אֲבָל אִם הָיְתָה שׁוּרָה אַחַת מִיכָּן
וְשׁוּרָה אַחַת מִיכָּן מִכֵּיוָן שֶׁהוּא מַגִּיעַ כְּנֶגֶד שָׁלֹשׁ גְּפָנִים בָּטֵל הַכֶּרֶם.

Halakhah 3: Unless it separates[44] it and the area needed to tend it[45],
since we have stated: "The Sages agree with Rebbi Eliezer ben Jacob in
the case of a ditch that separates it and the area needed to tend it." Hence,
Rebbi Eliezer thinks that even if it does not separate it from the area
needed to tend it. When do they disagree? If there are two rows on each
side[46]. But if there was only one row on either side, once it reaches three
vines there no longer is a vineyard[47].

44   Reading מבריק as equivalent of
Biblical and Babylonian מפרק "dis-
assembles."

45   The Sages require either six
hand-breadths or four cubits free of
growth on either side of the ditch, to
separate the vines and their working
spaces from other growth.

46   Then on each side, there is a
vineyard. But if the ditch separates

two single rows, none of which is a
vineyard on its own, even the Sages
will agree that the ditch deep 10 is
enough to separate them.

47   If the two (parallel) rows did
form a vineyard, if afterwards the
ditch is dug and separates six vines,
three in each row, they no longer form
a vineyard.

תַּגֵּי פָחוֹת מִיכֵּן אָסוּר. דְלָכֵן מַה אֲנָן אָמְרִין עֲשָׂרָה אָסוּר תִּשְׁעָה לֹא כָל־שֶׁכֵּן.
אֶלָּא מַהוּ פָחוֹת מִיכֵּן לְרוֹחַב דְלָכֵן מַה אֲנָן אָמְרִין יַעֲשֶׂה כְסָתוּם וּתְהֵא מוּתָּר.

וְיַעֲשֶׂה כְּסָתוּם וִיהֵא מוּתָּר. לֹא כֵן תַּנֵּי שָׁרָשֵׁי פֵּיאָה נִכְנָסִין לְתוֹךְ אַרְבַּע אַמּוֹת
שֶׁבְּכֶרֶם. לְמַטָּה מִשְׁלוֹשָׁה טְפָחִים הֲרֵי אֵלּוּ מוּתָּרִין. שַׁנְיָיא הִיא שֶׁאֲוֵיר הַכֶּרֶם
מַקִּיף. אָמַר לָהֶן רבִּי לִיעֶזֶר בֶּן יַעֲקֹב אֵין אַתֶּם מוֹדִין לִי שֶׁעָמוֹק כְּגָבוֹהַּ אֶלָּא
שֶׁאֲוֵיר הַכֶּרֶם מַקִּיף. מִסְתַּבְּרָא (fol. 30a) רבִּי לִיעֶזֶר מוֹדֶה לְרבִּי לִיעֶזֶר בֶּן
יַעֲקֹב. רבִּי לִיעֶזֶר בֶּן יַעֲקֹב לֹא יוֹדֵי לְרבִּי לִיעֶזֶר. רבִּי לִיעֶזֶר יוֹדֵי לְרבִּי לִיעֶזֶר
בֶּן יַעֲקֹב שֶׁעָמוֹק כְּגָבוֹהַּ. רבִּי לִיעֶזֶר בֶּן יַעֲקֹב לֹא יוֹדֵי לְרבִּי לִיעֶזֶר שֶׁאֲוֵיר
הַכֶּרֶם מַקִּיף.

It was stated[48]: "Less than that is forbidden." Without it, would we not
have said that ten is forbidden, so much more nine? But what does it
mean that "less is forbidden?" Would we not say that it becomes as if
closed and would be permitted? It should become as if closed and be
permitted; was it not stated[49]: "Roots crossing a symbolic fence and
entering within four cubits of a vineyard are permitted if they are deeper
than three hand-breadths?" There is a difference, because the air[50] of the
vineyard surrounds[51]. Rebbi Eliezer ben Jacob said to them: Do you not
agree that depth is like height[52]? Only that the air of the vineyard
surrounds. It is reasonable to think that Rebbi Eliezer agrees with Rebbi
Eliezer ben Jacob but Rebbi Eliezer ben Jacob does not agree with Rebbi
Eliezer. Rebbi Eliezer agrees with Rebbi Eliezer ben Jacob that depth is
like height. Rebbi Eliezer ben Jacob does not agree with Rebbi Eliezer
because the air of the vineyard surrounds.

48   In a *baraita* stating the position
of the Sages as opposed to R. Eliezer
ben Jacob.

49   Tosephta *Kilaim* 4:11. The
passage already was quoted in Halakhah 1:8, cf. Chapter 1, Note 159.

50   Greek ἀήρ.

51   The Tosephta deals with plants
outside the vineyard whose roots
penetrate the area reserved for tending
the vineyard. Here we are dealing
with a ditch inside the vineyard where
the rules are stricter.

52   Why do the Sages agree that the

mound may be sown but the ditch may not? R. Eliezer ben Jacob will forbid sowing on the mound unless it extends from one side of the vineyard to the other. He also disagrees with R. Eliezer (ben Hyrkanos) because the vat does not divide the entire vineyard.

רְבִּי חִיָּיא בְּשֵׁם רְבִּי יוֹחָנָן צָרִיךְ שֶׁיְּהֵא שָׁם חָלָל ארבע[53]. אָמַר רְבִּי שְׁמוּאֵל בַּר רַב יִצְחָק הָדָא דְתֵימַר בַּעֲגוּלָה אֲבָל בִּמְרוּבַּעַת אֵינוֹ צָרִיךְ שֶׁיְּהֵא שָׁם חָלָל אַרְבָּעָה. רְבִּי חֲלַפְתָּא בֶּן שָׁאוּל אָמַר צָרִיךְ שֶׁיְּהֵא שָׁם שְׁלֹשָׁה טְפָחִים עָפָר מִלְמַעֲלָן. אָמַר רְבִּי יוֹסֵי הָדָא דְתֵימַר בַּעֲגוּלָה אֲבָל בִּמְרוּבַּעַת אֵינוֹ צָרִיךְ שֶׁיְּהֵא שָׁם שְׁלֹשָׁה טְפָחִים עָפָר מִלְמַעֲלָה.

Rebbi Ḥiyya in the name of Rebbi Joḥanan: It is necessary that there be an empty space of four hand-breadths. Rebbi Samuel bar Rav Isaac said, that is, if it is round[54]. But if it is square, it does not need an empty space of four hand-breadths. Rebbi Ḥalaphta ben Shaul said[55], it needs three hand-breadths of dirt on top. Rebbi Yose said, that is, if it is round. But if it is square, it does not need three hand-breadths of dirt on top.

53   It is clear from the context that one must read אַרְבָּעָה This is the reading of Maimonides (*Kilaim* 7:22) but not that of the two manuscripts.

54   As Maimonides explains, given the direction of the rows of vines, a round mound has the required size only at its diameter, but the lengths of the parallel chords go to zero and there is no separation at the circumference. For the same reason, a circular mound needs a dirt wall around the seeds.

55   The Rome ms. reads: "R. Ḥalaphta ben Shaul stated. . ." Since the author belongs to the generation between Tannaïm and Amoraïm, both readings are acceptable.

(fol. 29c) **משנה ד**: גֶּפֶן שֶׁהִיא נְטוּעָה בְנַת אוֹ בְנֶקַע נוֹתְנִין לָהּ עֲבוֹדָתָהּ וְזוֹרֵעַ אֶת הַמּוֹתָר. רִבִּי יוֹסֵי אָמַר אִם שָׁם אַרְבַּע אַמּוֹת לֹא יָבִיא זֶרַע לְשָׁם. וְהַבַּיִת שֶׁבְּכֶרֶם זוֹרְעִין אוֹתוֹ.

Mishnah 4: For a vine planted in a depression or in a cleft one allows the area needed for tending it and one sows the rest. Rebbi Yose said, if there are less than four cubits one should not bring seeds there[56]. A house in a vineyard may be sown[57].

56   Any area that does not contain a square of four by four cubits is not considered a separate domain; it would remain part of the vineyard.

57   A place surrounded by four walls and having a dirt floor. The walls separate between anything growing inside and the vines outside; no minimal distance has to be kept between vines and walls.

(fol. 30a) **הלכה ד**: מִשְׁלֹשָׁה וְעַד אַרְבָּעָה הִיא מַתְנִיתָא פָּחוֹת מִשְּׁלֹשָׁה כְּסָתוּם. מִשְּׁלֹשָׁה וְעַד אַרְבָּעָה מַשְׁלִים. אַרְבָּעָה זֶרַע מִיָּד.

Halakhah 4: The Mishnah deals with the case from three to four [hand-breadths]. With less than three it is closed; from three to four one has to complete, four one may sow immediately[58].

58   The depression or cleft has to be at least three hand-breadths wide, otherwise one may easily step over it and it can be disregarded. If the width w is between three and four hand-breadths, one has to leave on either side an empty strip $(4-w)/2$ hand-breadths wide. If the cleft is four wide, one may sow in it up to the wall; the six hand-breadths used to tend the seeds are only needed as lengthwise separation between the vine and the seeds (R. Simson).

רִבִּי אָבִין בְּשֵׁם שְׁמוּאֵל וּבְבָתֵּי כְלָאִים הֶחְבָּאוּ. שֶׁמַּחְבִּיאִים בּוֹ אֶת הַכִּלְאָיִם.

Rebbi Abin in the name of Samuel (*Is.* 42:22): "They were hidden in jail houses," where one hides from *kilaim*[59].

59   This refers to the last sentence of the Mishnah, that a house protects from *kilaim*. The Talmud identifies the roots כלא "to restrain, keep back" (Arabic كلأ) and כלא (Arabic كلى)

"double". (R. Simson reads: "R. Samuel in the name of R. Abin"; but then it would have to read: R. Samuel R. Abbahu.)

משנה ח: הַנּוֹטֵעַ יָרֶק בְּכֶרֶם אוֹ הַמְקַיֵּם הֲרֵי זֶה מְקַדֵּשׁ אַרְבָּעִים וְחָמֵשׁ גְּפָנִים. אֵימָתַי בִּזְמַן שֶׁהֵן נְטוּעוֹת אַרְבַּע עַל אַרְבַּע אוֹ חָמֵשׁ עַל חָמֵשׁ. הָיוּ נְטוּעוֹת עַל שֵׁשׁ שֵׁשׁ אוֹ עַל שֶׁבַע שֶׁבַע הֲרֵי זֶה מְקַדֵּשׁ (fol. 29d) שֵׁשׁ עֶשְׂרֵה אַמָּה לְכָל־רוּחַ עֲגוּלוֹת וְלֹא מְרוּבָּעוֹת.

Mishnah 5: He who plants vegetables in a vineyard or who lets them grow[60] sanctifies 45 vines. When is this? In case they are planted four four or five five apart. If they were planted six six or seven seven apart, he sanctifies sixteen cubits in every direction, circular but not square[61].

60   If the edible vegetable grew from wind-borne seeds.

61   The language of this Mishnah is so involved because of the special rule for a vineyard planted in spaces of five cubits. In general, vegetables can be planted in a vineyard only in a bald spot; according to Mishnah 4:1 that means at a distance of 16 cubits from the next vine. The rule of the Mishnah for vines planted more than 5 cubits apart is just that: In the interior of the circle of radius 16 and centered at the vegetable there may not be any vine.

The application of that principle to vines planted 4 apart leads to 45 sanctified vines. One assumes that the vegetable is sown closely around a vine. One takes the stem of that vine as center of a Cartesian coordinate system and takes the x-axis in the direction of the rows of vines, the y-axis perpendicular. The unit of measurement is the cubit. Points with coordinates $(4m,4n)$ with integer m, n represent vines. According to Pythagoras, the distance from the origin is <16 if and only if $m^2+n^2 < 16$. This means that for $m = 0, \pm1, \pm2, n = 0, \pm1, \pm2, \pm3$, and for $m = \pm3$, $n = 0, \pm1, \pm2$.

In all, there are $5 \cdot 7 + 2 \cdot 5 = 45$ admissible couples (m,n). This is explained in the Halakhah. There the language is that all acceptable couples are $m, n = 0, \pm 1, \pm 2, \pm 3$ except for couples $(\pm 3, \pm 3)$. The case of vines planted 5 apart is not treated; one has to assume that one excludes the vines at points $(5m, 5n)$ for $m^2 + n^2 < 25$ because vineyards planted 5 apart look similar to those planted 4 apart. (For an opposing opinion in the Tosephta cf. *Tosefta ki-fšuṭah* p. 629.)

(fol. 30a) **הלכה ה**: רִבִּי יוֹסֵי בֶּן חֲנִינָא אָמַר וְהוּא שֶׁזָּרַע כְּנֶגֶד הָאֶמְצָעִית. רִבִּי אָבִין בְּשֵׁם שְׁמוּאֵל וְהוּא שֶׁתְּהֵא הָאֶמְצָעִי עֲגוּלָה יֶרֶק. הֵיךְ עֲבִידָא. שׁוּבָע שׁוּרִין מִן שׁוּבָע שׁוּרִין. צֵא מֵהֶן אַרְבַּע גְּפָנִים לְאַרְבַּע זְוִיוֹת הַכֶּרֶם נִשְׁתַּיְּירוּ שָׁם אַרְבָּעִים וְחָמֵשׁ גְּפָנִים. הָדָא הוּא דְתַנִּינָן הֲרֵי הוּא מְקַדֵּשׁ אַרְבָּעִים וְחָמֵשׁ גְּפָנִים.

Halakhah 5: Rebbi Yose ben Ḥanina said, only if he sowed near the middle vine. Rebbi Abin in the name of Samuel: Only if the middle vine is surrounded by vegetables. How is it computed? Seven rows by seven rows. Subtract from them four vines at the four corners; there are 45 vines remaining. That is what we stated: "He sanctifies 45 vines"[62].

62   All this was explained in Note 61. There are 49 couples (m,n) for $|m|$, $|n| \leq 3$. The inadmissible ones are plants with coordinates $(\pm 3, \pm 3)$ at the corners of a 56 by 56 square.

אֵימָתַי בִּזְמַן שֶׁהֵן נְטוּעוֹת אַרְבַּע עַל אַרְבַּע אוֹ חָמֵשׁ עַל חָמֵשׁ. הָדָא מְסַייְעָא לְרִבִּי זְעִירָא דְּרִבִּי לְעָזָר אָמַר שְׁמוֹנָה חוּץ מִמְּקוֹם כָּרְתּוֹן. הָיוּ נְטוּעוֹת שֵׁשׁ עַל שֵׁשׁ אוֹ שֶׁבַע עַל שֶׁבַע הָדָא מְסַייְעָא לְרִבִּי לְעָזָר דְּרִבִּי לְעָזָר אָמַר מֵאַרְבַּע אַמּוֹת וְעַד שְׁמוֹנָה אָסוּר וּמְקַדֵּשׁ. מִשְּׁמוֹנָה וְעַד שֵׁשׁ עֶשְׂרֵה אָסוּר וְאֵינוֹ מְקַדֵּשׁ.

"When is this? In case they are planted four four or five five apart." This supports Rebbi Zeïra, since Rebbi Eleazar[63] said: Eight except for the place of the trunks. "If they were planted six six or seven seven apart", that supports Rebbi Eleazar, since Rebbi Eleazar[64] said: From four cubits to eight, it is forbidden and "sanctifies", from eight to sixteen it is forbidden but does not "sanctify".

63   This has to be "R. Zeïra", cf. Chapter 4, Note 122. If the trunks were counted in the distances, the four vines at distance 16 from the center on the axes would also be forbidden, for a total of 49, not 45.

64   In Chapter 4, Halakhah 8 (Note 125), this also is a statement of R. Zeïra. The argument here is that "eight eight" is not mentioned, which implies that vegetables in a vineyard planted eight cubits apart do not "sanctify".

(fol. 29d) **משנה ו**: הָרוֹאֶה יֶרֶק בַּכֶּרֶם וְאָמַר כְּשֶׁאַגִּיעַ לוֹ אֲלַקְטֶנּוּ מוּתָּר. כְּשֶׁאֶחֱזוֹר אֲלַקְטֶנּוּ. אִם הוֹסִיף בְּמָאתַיִם אָסוּר.

Mishnah 6: If somebody sees a vegetable in his vineyard and says, when I get to it I shall remove it, that is permitted; when I return I shall remove it, if in the meantime it increased by one twohundredth it is forbidden.

(fol. 30a) **הלכה ו**: רִבִּי יוֹסֵי בַּר חֲנִינָא אָמַר בְּפוֹעֵל שָׁנוּ.

Halakhah 6: Rebbi Yose ben Ḥanina said, they taught about the worker[65].

65   "Somebody" mentioned in the Mishnah is not the owner, whose negligence would sanctify vines and vegetable and not just make the vegetable forbidden. It cannot be a

stranger whose actions cannot influence the status of the farmer's goods. Hence, it must refer to the farm hand who works in the vineyard for the proprietor.

בַּעַל הַבַּיִת שָׁהוּא עָסוּק בִּמְלַאכְתּוֹ עָשׂוּ אוֹתוֹ כְּפוֹעֵל. בַּעַל הַבַּיִת שָׁקִייֵם יְרָקוֹת
שָׂדֶה בְּכֶרֶם אֲסוּרִין בֵּין לוֹ בֵּין לְאַחֵר. פּוֹעֵל שָׁקִייֵם יְרָקוֹת שָׂדֶה בְּכֶרֶם אָסוּר
לוֹ וּמוּתָּר לְכָל־אָדָם. וְקַשְׁיָא אִם אָסוּר לוֹ יְהֵא אָסוּר לְכָל־אָדָם. אִם מוּתָּר
לְכָל־אָדָם יְהֵא מוּתָּר לוֹ. אֶלָּא כְּרִבִּי שִׁמְעוֹן דְּאָמַר אֵין אָדָם מַקְדִּישׁ דָּבָר
שָׁאֵינוֹ שֶׁלּוֹ. אַף עַל גַּב דְּרִבִּי שִׁמְעוֹן אָמַר אֵין אָדָם מַקְדִּישׁ דָּבָר שָׁאֵינוֹ שֶׁלּוֹ.
מוֹדֶה הוּא הָכָא שֶׁאָסוּר לוֹ (בְּעָלֶה קָטָן אֶחָד)[66] [בְּלִקְטָן אַחֵר][67] אֲבָל אִם לִיקֵּט
הוּא אָסוּר בֵּין לוֹ בֵּין לְכָל־אָדָם.

They gave the owner occupied with his work the status of a farmhand[68]. If the owner kept field vegetables [growing] in his vineyard, they
are forbidden to him and to others. If a farmhand kept field vegetables
[growing] in the vineyard, they are forbidden to him but are permitted to
everybody else. This is difficult. If they are forbidden to him, they should
be forbidden to everybody. If they are permitted to everybody else, they
should be permitted to him. It must follow Rebbi Simeon who says that
nobody may sanctify anything that is not his own property. Even though
Rebbi Simeon says that nobody may sanctify anything that is not his own
property, he agrees here that it is forbidden to him if another person
harvested it[69]; but if he himself harvested, it is forbidden to him and to
everybody else.

---

66   Reading of the Venice print and
the Leyden ms. Rome ms: בלקט

67   Reading of R. David ben Zimra,
R. Simson, and R. Isaac ben Malchi-
ṣedeq Simponti. As B. Ratner has
pointed out, it seems that the entire
sentence was missing in the ms. before
R. Joseph Karo (כסף משנה on Maimonides, *Kilaim* 5:9).

68   While the rules for the vintner
are more strict that those for his
employees, that only applies if he is not
occupied tending his vineyard.

69   This is a fine for his laziness. If
he did not remove the vegetable when
he should have but returned later, the
strict rule of the Mishnah applies.

וְאִם הוֹסִיף בְּמָאתַיִם אָסוּר. דְּבֵי רִבִּי יַנַּאי מְשַׁעֲרִין בְּהָדֵין יַרְבּוּזָה. כֵּיצַד הוּא
בּוֹדֵק. רַב בִּיבִי בְשֵׁם רִבִּי חֲנִינָה לוֹקֵט אֶחָד וּמֵנִיחַ אֶחָד מַה שֶׁזֶה פּוֹחֵת זֶה
מוֹסִיף.

"If it increased by one twohundredth it is forbidden." Those of the
house of Rebbi Yannai estimate by purslain. How does one check? Rav
Vivian in the name of Rebbi Ḥaninah: He takes one out and leaves one in
[the ground]; what the first one is less, the other did increase.

(fol. 29d) **מִשְׁנָה ז:** הָיָה עוֹבֵר בְּכֶרֶם וְנָפְלוּ מִמֶּנּוּ זְרָעִים אוֹ שֶׁיָּצְאוּ עִם הַזְּבָלִים
אוֹ עִם הַמַּיִם. הַזּוֹרֵעַ וְסִיעֲרַתוֹ הָרוּחַ לְאַחֲרָיו מוּתָּר. סִיעֲרַתּוֹ הָרוּחַ לְפָנָיו. רִבִּי
עֲקִיבָה אוֹמֵר אִם עֲשָׂבִים יוּפָךְ. וְאִם אָבִיב יִנָּפֵץ. וְאִם הֵבִיאָה דָּגָן יִדָּלֵק.

Mishnah 7: If somebody was passing through a vineyard and
accidentally dropped some seeds, or that seeds were brought there by
manure or water, or someone sowed and the wind carried the seeds
behind him, all this is permitted[70]. If the wind carried the seeds before
him, Rebbi Aqiba says, if they produce greenery it should be plowed
under, if they are green stalks, they should be broken, if they produced
grain it must be burned[71].

70   Unintentional contamination has   clear the ground. If he is derelict in
no effect on the status of the vines.   his duties, the growth will be sancti-
71   Since the seeds fall on ground to   fied.
be worked on in the future, he has to

(fol. 30a) **הֲלָכָה ז:** אָמַר רִבִּי לֶעְזָר מַתְנִיתִין בְּעוֹמֵד בְּשָׂדֶה לָבָן וְסִיעֲרַתּוֹ הָרוּחַ
לִשְׂדֵה כֶרֶם. רִבִּי זְעִירָא בָּעֵי מַה אִיתְאַמְּרַת בְּעוֹמֵד אוֹ אֲפִילוּ עוֹמֵד. אֵין תֵּימַר
בְּלָבָן הָא בִשְׂדֵה כֶרֶם לֹא. אֵין תֵּימַר אֲפִילוּ עוֹמֵד הִיא הָדָא הִיא הָדָא.

נִישְׁמְעִינָהּ מִן הָדָא רִבִּי שִׁמְעוֹן בֶּן יוּדָא אוֹמֵר מִשּׁוּם רִבִּי שִׁמְעוֹן הַזּוֹרֵעַ

וְסִיעֲרָתוּ הָרוּחַ לַאֲחוֹרָיו מוּתָּר מִפְּנֵי שֶׁהוּא אוֹנֶס. מַה נָן קַיָּימִין אִי בְּעוֹמֵד

בִּשְׂדֵה כֶרֶם עוֹבֵד עֲבוֹדָה וְאַתְּ אָמַר מוּתָּר. אֶלָּא כִּי נָן קַיָּימִין בְּעוֹמֵד בִּשְׂדֵה

לָבָן וְסִיעֲרָתוּ הָרוּחַ לִשְׂדֵה כֶרֶם.

Halakhah 7: Rebbi Eleazar said, our Mishnah speaks of one standing in
a grain field while the wind carried the seeds into a vineyard. Rebbi Zeïra
inquired[72]: Was [the Mishnah] speaking about one standing in [a grain
field] or even one standing [in a vineyard]? If you say in a grain
field, then not in a vineyard. If you say even one standing [in a vineyard] there
is no difference. Let us hear from the following[73]: "Rebbi Simeon ben
Jehudah said in the name of Rebbi Simeon: If one was sowing and the
wind carried the seeds behind him, this is permitted, since it happened by
accident." What are we dealing with? If he stands in the vineyard he is
tending it, and you say it is permitted? But we must deal with the case of
one standing in a grain field and the wind carried the seeds into a
vineyard.

72   R. Zeïra shows that the statement of R. Eleazar about the part of
the Mishnah dealing with windswept
seeds is a logical necessity.

73   Tosephta *Kilaim* 3:12.   the
arguments of R. Zeïra and R. Eleazar
are accepted by Maimonides, *Kilaim*
5:17.

רִבִּי זְעִירָא רִבִּי שִׁמְעוֹן בֶּן לָקִישׁ בְּשֵׁם רִבִּי הוֹשַׁעְיָא. אִם עֲשָׂבִים יוֹפָךְ הַכֹּל

מוּתָּר. אִם אָבִיב יִנָּפֵץ הַקַּשִּׁין מוּתָּרִין וְהַדָּגָן אָסוּר. אִם הֵבִיאָה דָגָן תִּדָּלֵק

הַכֹּל אָסוּר. רִבִּי יוֹחָנָן אָמַר הַכֹּל אָסוּר. מַהוּ הָדָא דְּתַנִּינָן אִם עֲשָׂבִים יוֹפָךְ אִם

אָבִיב יִנָּפֵץ אִם הֵבִיאָה דָגָן תִּדָּלֵק. כְּהָהִיא דְּתַנִּינָן תַּמָּן הָעָרְלָה וּכְלְאֵי הַכֶּרֶם

אֶת שֶׁדַּרְכּוֹ לִשָּׂרֵף יִשָּׂרֵף אֶת שֶׁדַּרְכּוֹ לִיקָּבֵר יִקָּבֵר.

Rebbi Zeïra, Rebbi Simeon ben Laqish in the name of Rebbi Hoshaia:
"If they produce greenery it should be plowed under:" all is permitted. "If

they are green stalks, they should be broken:" the straw is permitted but the grains are forbidden. "If they produced grain it must be burned:" all is forbidden. Rebbi Joḥanan said, all is forbidden. What does our statement mean, "if they produce greenery it should be plowed under, if they are green stalks, they should be broken, if they produced grain it must be burned"? It parallels what we have stated there[74]: "*Orlah* and *kilaim* of a vineyard. Anything that usually is buried should be buried. Anything that usually is burned should be burned."

74   Mishnah *Temurah* 7:5. There, Rashi in the Babli explains that "what usually is buried" is fluids, "what usually is burned" is produce. This cannot be the position of R. Joḥanan here. Maimonides in his Commentary explains the Mishnah following R. Hoshaia, whose position is easily squared with the Mishnah in *Temurah*, but in his Code (*loc. cit.*) he follows R. Joḥanan since it is the position of the Babli that in a disagreement between R. Joḥanan and R. Simeon ben Laqish, practice almost always follows R. Joḥanan. (For *orlah* cf. Note 94).

רְבִּי יַעֲקֹב בַּר אִידִי בְּשֵׁם רְבִּי שִׁמְעוֹן בֶּן לָקִישׁ פְּעָמִים שֶׁהַקַּשִׁין מוּתָּרִין וְהַדָּגָן אָסוּר. פְּעָמִים שֶׁהַקַּשִׁין אֲסוּרִין וְהַדָּגָן מוּתָּר. הֵיךְ עֲבִידָא זָרַע בְּהֶיתֵּר וְסִיכֵּךְ עַל גַּבָּיו הַקַּשִׁין מוּתָּרִין וְהַדָּגָן אָסוּר. זָרַע בְּאִיסוּר וְהֶעֱבִיר אֶת הַסְּכָךְ הַקַּשִׁין אֲסוּרִין וְהַדָּגָן מוּתָּר. רְבִּי זְעִירָא בָּעֵי נִיחָה הַקַּשִׁין מוּתָּרִין וְהַדָּגָן אָסוּר. הַקַּשִׁין אֲסוּרִין וְהַדָּגָן מוּתָּר גָּדֵל מִתּוֹךְ אִיסוּר וְאַתְּ אֲמַר מוּתָּרִים. רְבִּי זְעִירָא כְּדַעְתֵּיהּ. דְּאָמַר רְבִּי זְעִירָא בְּשֵׁם רְבִּי יוֹנָתָן בָּצֵל שֶׁל כִּלְאֵי הַכֶּרֶם שֶׁעֲקָרוֹ וּשְׁתָלוֹ אֲפִילוּ מוֹסִיף כַּמָּה אָסוּר שֶׁאֵין גִּידוּלֵי אִיסוּר מַעֲלִין אֶת הָאִיסוּר.

Rebbi Jacob bar Idi in the name of Rebbi Simeon ben Laqish: Sometimes, the straw is permitted but the grain is forbidden, and sometimes the straw is forbidden and the grain is permitted. How is that? If his sowing was permitted but later he trained the leaves of a vine over it, the straw is permitted but the grain is forbidden If he sowed where it was forbidden and then removed the overhanging growth, the straw is forbidden but the grain is permitted[75]. Rebbi Zeïra inquired: It is understandable that the straw would be permitted but the grain forbidden. If the straw should be forbidden and the grain permitted, it grew while forbidden and you say is is permitted? Rebbi Zeïra follows his own opinion, as Rebbi Zeira said in the name of Rebbi Jonathan: An onion from *kilaim* in a vineyard that he removed from the soil and planted anew is forbidden even if it increases manifold, since growth of what is forbidden can never justify forbidden produce[76].

75   It is assumed that the grain developed only after the *kilaim* were removed. Then the grain is permitted. Similarly, in the first case it is assumed that the vines were drawn over the grain only after the stalks reached their full height, then the stalks grew while permitted and are permitted.

76   Since the onion is a root bulb, the root determines the growth of the plant. Since the root is forbidden, its

growth will always be forbidden, even if the greens grow only after the *kilaim* were removed. "Justify" here means that there is enough of permitted produce (60, 100, or 200 times the amount of other produce, as the case may be) so that the prohibited produce should be considered negligible. It is asserted here that growth from a forbidden root is never permitted.

(fol. 29d) **משנה ח**: הַמְקַיֵּים קוֹצִים בַּכֶּרֶם רְבִּי לִיעֶזֶר אוֹמֵר קִידֵּשׁ. וַחֲכָמִים אוֹמְרִים לֹא קִידֵּשׁ אֶלָּא דָבָר שֶׁכָּמוֹהוּ מְקַיְּימִים. הָאִירוֹס וְהַקִּיסּוֹס וְשׁוֹשַׁנַּת הַמֶּלֶךְ וְכָל־מִין זְרָעִים אֵינָן[77] כִּלְאַיִם בַּכֶּרֶם. הַקַּנְבַּס רְבִּי טַרְפוֹן אוֹמֵר אֵינוֹ כִּלְאַיִם. וַחֲכָמִים אוֹמְרִים כִּלְאָיִם. וְהַקִּינָרַס כִּלְאַיִם בַּכֶּרֶם.

Mishnah 8: If somebody keeps thistles growing in a vineyard, Rebbi Eliezer says he sanctified, but the Sages say only produce apt to be stored sanctifies. Iris[78], ivy[79], king's lily, and all kinds of seed-plants[80] are not *kilaim* in a vineyard. Hemp[81], Rebbi Tarphon says it is not *kilaim* but the Sages say it is *kilaim*. Artichokes[82] are *kilaim* in a vineyard.

77 Reading of all sources, including the Rome ms., except the Leyden ms. and the Venice print.

78 Greek ἶϱις, -ιδος, ἠ, "iris, orris root"; the root was used to produce an ointment.

79 Greek κισσός. One would not expect a plant holy to Osiris and Bacchus in a Jewish vineyard, but its leaves were sometimes used as spice (and possibly in medicine) and the name might also be applied to related

kinds of angelica of which both roots and berries were used. |Cf. κίσσινον, τό, name of a plaster (E. G.)|

80 Producing inedible seeds. The Babli (*Menaḥot* 15b) declares them to be *kilaim* by rabbinic decree.

81 Greek κάνναβις, Latin *cannabis*.

82 Greek κινάϱα, Modern Greek plural κινάϱας (H. L. Fleischer). Since artichoke is an edible thistle, it has to be mentioned as *kilaim*.

חלכה ח: אָמַר רִבִּי אַבָּהוּ טַעֲמָא דְּרִבִּי לִיעֶזֶר שָׁכֵּן מְקוֹמוֹת מְקַיְימִין (fol. 30a)
אוֹתָן לִגְמֵלִים בַּעֲרָבְיָא.

Halakhah 8: Rabbi Abbahu said, the reason of Rebbi Eliezer is that at some places in Arabia one lets them grow for camels[83].

83 See Chapter 1, Note 15.

הָאִירוֹס אָרְסִיה. הַקִּיסוֹס קְסוֹסָא. וְשׁוֹשַׁנַת הַמֶּלֶךְ קְרִינוֹן[84].

ἶϱός is אירוסיה κισσός is קסוסא. King's lily is κϱίνον.

84 Reading of R. Isaac Simponti. In the Leyden and Rome mss., קרינטון, possibly Greek κήϱινθος "bee-bread". As noted by the gloss in the Krotoszyn edition, κϱίνον, τό, "white lily, *Lilium candidum*" is used in Sirach (39:14) for

Hebrew שושנה, in the Syriac translation שושנת מלכא. In Herodotus, κϱίνον means "Egyptian bean" (*Nelubium speciosum*), cf. Chapter 1, Note 45. Maimonides translates שושנת המלך by Arabic שקאק אלנעמאן "anemone".

הַקָּנִים וְהָאֲגִין וְהַוֶּרֶד וְהָאָטָדִין מִין אִילָן וְאֵינָן כִּלְאַיִם בַּכֶּרֶם. הַשִּׁיפָה

וְהַחִיטוֹן[85] וְהַגְּמִי וּשְׁאָר כָּל־הַגְּדֵלִים בָּאֵפֶר מִין דְּשָׁאִים וְאֵינָן כִּלְאַיִם בַּכֶּרֶם.

וְהָתַנֵּי רִבִּי הוֹשַׁעְיָה אֵילוּ הֵן מִינֵי דְשָׁאִים הַקִּינָרַס וְהַחֲלְמָה וְהַדְּמוּעַ וְהָאָטָד.

תַּמָּן לִבְרָכָה וְכָאן לְכִלְאַיִם. אָמַר רִבִּי יוֹסֵי הָדָא אֲמְרָה אֶתְרוֹג אַף עַל פִּי שֶׁאַתְּ

אוֹמֵר עָלָיו בּוֹרֵא פְּרִי הָעֵץ אַתְּ אוֹמֵר עַל הַתְּמוּרָז שֶׁלוֹ בּוֹרֵא מִינֵי דְשָׁאִים.

"[86]Reeds, spiny bushes[87], roses, and way-thorn are trees and not *kilaim* in a vineyard. Reed-mace[88], rush[89], and bulrush, and all other plants growing in ashes are kinds of grasses and not *kilaim* in a vineyard[90]." But did Rebbi Hoshaiah not state[91]: "The following are the kinds of grasses: artichoke, *ḥalimah*, *demua*, and lycium." There for benedictions, here for *kilaim*. Rebbi Yose said[92], this means that while one says the benediction "Creator of the fruit of the tree" for an *etrog*, one says the benediction "Creator of kinds of grasses" for its *tmrz*[93].

85   Reading of Rome ms. Venice: החיטין.

86   Tosephta *Kilaim* 3:15. The next sentence is 3:14 there. The names of the plants appear in great variations, cf. תוספתא כפשוטה pp. 631-635.

87   In the Tosepha mss. החגין, Arabic حاج، حيج "spiny bush".

88   In the Tosephta and Mishnah *Makhširin* 5:5 חשיפה, in Mishnah *Kelim* 9:8 שיפה. A kind of reed, in the opinion of I. Löw *Typha angustata*. Rashi in Babli *Sukkah* 20a translates *paille* "straw".

89   The Gaonic commentary to Mishnah *Kelim* (9:8) defines this as equivalent of Arabic اسل "reeds used to

make lances"; the corresponding Arabic verb means "to pierce".

90   In the opinion of Maimonides (*Kilaim* 5:19), these are not *kilaim* because they are grasses. In the opinion of R. Abraham ben David they are not *kilaim* because they are not collected as staples, but there are kinds of grasses subject to the laws of *kilaim*. The difference seems to be that Maimonides reads here and in the Mishnah ואינן but R. Abraham ben David reads אינן There is no doubt that trees cannot be *kilaim* in a vineyard since they are not sown.

91   *Berakhot* 6:1; see there Notes 111-114 for the determination of the

plants mentioned.

92   His statement belongs to *Berakhot* 6:1; one has to wonder why it was not placed there after the statement of R. Hoshaiah. R. Yose refers to the statement in *Berakhot* of R. Joshua that the appropriate benediction for edible young palm shoots is "Creator of kinds of grasses" (*loc. cit.* Note 110). On this R. Yose notes that the same argument might apply to the soft sprouting parts of citrus that have just formed after the flower has fallen off.

93   The word is a *hapax* unless the ז is deleted. There are two possible translations of חמור: 1. "A new shoot growing straight up like a date palm"; 2. "A bud looking like a date", as in Mishnah *Ma'serot* 4:6. The second definition is preferred by R. Eliahu Fulda and all later commentators; both definitions are consistent with the parallel passage in *Berakhot*. The second meaning might be expressed in the Arabic root ثمر "to bear fruit".

הַצֶּלֶף בֵּית שַׁמַּאי אוֹמְרִים כִּלְאַיִם בַּכֶּרֶם וְאֵינוֹ כִּלְאַיִם בִּזְרָעִים. בֵּית הִלֵּל אוֹמְרִים אֵינוֹ כִּלְאַיִם לֹא בְכֶרֶם וְלֹא בִזְרָעִים. הַכֹּל מוֹדִין שֶׁהוּא חַיָּב בְּעָרְלָה. תָּנֵי רִבִּי חִינְנָא בַּר פַּפָּא אֶת שֶׁהוּא עוֹלֶה מִגִּזְעוֹ מִין אִילָן מִשָּׁרָשָׁיו מִין יֶרֶק. הֲתִיבוּן הֲרֵי הַכְּרוּב הֲרֵי הוּא עוֹלֶה מִגִּזְעוֹ. כָּאן בְּוַדַּאי כָּאן בְּסָפֵק.

The caper bush[94]. The House of Shammai say, it is *kilaim* in a vineyard[95] but not with grains. The House of Hillel say, it is never *kilaim*, neither in a vineyard nor with grains. Both agree that it is subject to *orlah*. Rebbi Ḥinena bar Papa[96] stated: Any plant that branches out from its stem is a tree; from its roots it is a vegetable. They objected: But cabbage forms its leaves from its stem! Here[97] when it is sure, there when it is doubtful.

94   A shortened version, not mentioning grains, is in Tosephta *Kilaim* 3:17 and Babli *Berakhot* 36a. The main place of the paragraph is *Ma'serot* 4:6, in a discussion of the caper bush.

95   The House of Shammai are unsure whether capers are trees or vegetables and therefore apply the stringency of vegetables for *kilaim* and those of fruit trees for *orlah*, ao that its fruit is forbidden the first three years

after planting (*Lev.* 19:23).

96   He is R. Ḥanina bar Pappai. His statement appears in another version (another redaction) in *Baba Batra* 5:5: "R. Ḥama bar 'Uqba in the name of R. Yose. Anything that grows from both root and stem is a root (a vegetable); from its stem but not from its root it is a tree." In that formulation, cabbage presents no problem since there is no piece of stem free of leaves.

97   The caper bush. Since for cabbage, the lower end of the stem is the lower end of the leaves, it is questionable whether the lowest leaves come from stem or root.

איזהו עריס פרק ששי

משנה א: אֵי זֶהוּ עָרִיס הַנּוֹטֵע שׁוּרָה שֶׁל חָמֵשׁ גְּפָנִים בְּצַד הַגָּדֵר שֶׁהוּא גָבוֹהַ עֲשָׂרָה טְפָחִים אוֹ בְּצַד חָרִיץ שֶׁהוּא עָמוֹק עֲשָׂרָה וְרָחָב אַרְבָּעָה נוֹתְנִין לוֹ עֲבוֹדָתוֹ אַרְבַּע אַמּוֹת. בֵּית שַׁמַּאי אוֹמְרִים מוֹדְדִין אַרְבַּע אַמּוֹת מֵעִיקַּר גְּפָנִים וְלַשָּׂדֶה. וּבֵית הִלֵּל אוֹמְרִין מִן הַגָּדֵר וְלַשָּׂדֶה. אָמַר רְבִּי יוֹחָנָן בֶּן נוּרִי טוֹעִין כָּל־הָאוֹמְרִין כָּךְ. אֶלָּא אִם יֵשׁ אַרְבַּע אַמּוֹת מֵעִיקַּר גְּפָנִים וְלַגָּדֵר נוֹתְנִין לוֹ עֲבוֹדָתוֹ וְזוֹרֵעַ אֶת הַמּוֹתָר. וְכַמָּה הִיא עֲבוֹדַת הַגֶּפֶן שִׁשָּׁה טְפָחִים לְכָל־רוּחַ. וְרִבִּי עֲקִיבָה אוֹמֵר שְׁלֹשָׁה.

Mishnah 1: What is a trellis[1]? If somebody plants a row of five vines along a fence ten hand-breadths high or a ditch ten hand-breadths deep and four wide, one gives it four cubits working space. The House of Shammai say one measures four cubits between the stems of the vines and the field. The House of Hillel say, between fence and field[2]. Rebbi Johanan ben Nuri said, anybody who affirms this is in error; if there are four cubits between the stems of the vines and the fence one gives it its working space and he may sow the rest. What is the working space of a vine[3]? Six hand-breadths in every direction; Rabbi Aqiba says three.

1   This is the interpretation of most commentaries, from Hebrew ערש "crib", Arabic عَرِيش "trellis, crib". R. Abraham ben David in his commentary to *Idiut* 2:4 explains that five vines in a row form a vineyard for the House of Hillel only if the vines are growing on a trellis near a fence, not if the fence is used as a trellis. This is the only possible explanation in *Idiut*, but in his Commentary on this Mishnah, Maimonides explains that vines lean on or upon the (stone) fence. He gives the same interpretation in his Code (*Kilaim*

8:2) but then has to come to the conclusion (*loc. cit.* 8:3) that the four cubits to be measured from the fence are on the side pointing away from the vines. R. Abraham ben David protests against this interpretation which "never entered the mind of any commentator." Maimonides's interpretation is difficult to accept, the tortured justifications of R. David ben Zimra and R. Joseph Caro in their commentaries on the Code notwithstanding, since the vines according to the Mishnah can be up to three cubits distant from the fence.

2   For them, the trellis (or plant-ation) is not quite a vineyard; it is irrelevant where in the strip near the fence the vines are planted.

3   A single vine. For R. Ismael, five vines in a row are never a vineyard; they are a collection of single vines; the restrictions of the Mishnah apply only because the trellis is too close to the fence. But as soon as the vines are a full four cubits distant from the fence, the vines are treated as isolated. For R. Aqiba, the working space must have a diameter of six hand-breadths.

(fol. 30b) **הלכה א**: וְקַשְׁיָא עַל דַּעְתֵּיהּ דְּבֵית שַׁמַּאי בְּלֹא כָךְ אֵינוֹ אָסוּר מִשּׁוּם כֶּרֶם. רִבִּי שִׁמְעוֹן בֶּן לָקִישׁ אָמַר בְּעָרִיס הַמְעוּקָם שָׁנוּ. אִם בְּעָרִיס הַמְעוּקָם שָׁנוּ בְּלֹא גֶדֶר אֵינוֹ אָסוּר מִשּׁוּם כֶּרֶם. רִבִּי יוֹנָה בָּעֵי מַהוּ לִיזְרֹע בֵּנְתַּיִם. בִּמְכֻוָּנוֹת הֵן וְאַתְּ אָמַר אָסוּר לִיזְרֹע בֵּנְתַּיִם. מַהוּ לִיזְרֹע בֵּין הַגְּפָנִים כְּמָה דְתֵימַר גַּבֵּי מוּקְשֶׁה אָסוּר לִיזְרֹע בֵּין הַגּוּמוֹת. אוּף הָכָא אָסוּר לִיזְרֹע בֵּין הַגְּפָנִים.

It is difficult. Is it not forbidden anyhow for the House of Shammai as a vineyard[4]? Rebbi Simeon ben Laqish said, this was taught about a curved trellis[5]. In that case, it would not be forbidden as a vineyard without a fence. Rebbi Jonah inquired[6]: May one sow in between? Is it in a straight line, that you say it is forbidden to sow in between? May one sow between the vines? As you say in the case of a row of gourds that it is forbidden to sow in between the pits, so here also it is forbidden to sow in between the vines.

4   Five vines in a row constitute a vineyard for the House of Shammai, Mishnah 4:5.

5   According to R. Simson, the trellis is in a straight line but the vines are planted alternatingly on both sides of the trellis; they are not in a straight line. According to R. Isaac Simponti, the trellis is built as arc of circle, to provide wider spacing for the branches of the vines exposed to the sun.

6   The interpretation of this paragraph and the next follows R. Iehiel Michel Halevi Epstein in his notes published as *Mēkhal Hammayîm*, Wilna 1928. The question is addressed to the House of Hillel in the interpretation of R. Simeon ben Laqish. For them, two parts of the definition of a vineyard are missing; there is only one row and the vines are not planted in a straight line. The Mishnah declares a trellis in front of a fence to have a status similar to a vineyard but it is not clear whether the rules of a vineyard are valid without change. Since in Mishnah 7, the space required to separate two trellises is only half the space required to separate two vineyards, it is clear that the rules of vineyards cannot be applied without change to trellises.

We have to assume that also along the trellis the vines are planted at least four cubits apart. Since the vines are planted in a zig-zag pattern, between two vines in the same row the distance is almost eight cubits. Rebbi Jonah now asks, according to R. Simeon ben Laqish does the forbidden area cover the union of circular disks of radius 4 centered at the vines or is the entire convex hull of that domain (the smallest convex set containing the disks) forbidden? In the first case, between the vines the minimal distance from the trellis is less than 4 cubits; this is "in between". The answer is that only in the case of vines planted in a straight line can one say that the interior of the parallel figure to the trellis in distance 4 is forbidden; here it seems that not even the entire parallel figure to the zig-zag line connecting the vines is forbidden but only the union of the five circular disks.

The second question then asks whether maybe not even the entire disks are forbidden but only the union of five polygons, each centered at a vine. Let v denote the center of a vine, a the point at distance 4 from v on the perpendicular from v to the fence, a' the reflection of a in v. On both sides of the line $a'va$ draw parallels in distance 1. They intersect the parallels to the zig-zag line through a and a' at $b, b'; c, c'$. The polygon attached to v is

then *abb'a'c'ca*. The forbidden area
around *a* now is 8, not $16\pi > 50$, and
even on the zig-zag line there is an
interval of almost 2 cubits that might
be sown. The answer is negative, with
reference to Halakhah 3:7.

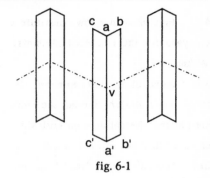

fig. 6-1

רִבִּי יוֹחָנָן אָמַר בֶּעָרִיס מְכוּוָּן שָׁנוּ. אִם בֶּעָרִיס הַמְכוּוָּן שָׁנוּ בְּלֹא גֶדֶר אֵינוֹ
אָסוּר מִשּׁוּם כָּרֶם. נֵימַר בְּגִין בֵּית הֶלֵּל תַּנִּיתָהּ. אָמַר רִבִּי חֲנַנְיָה מִסְתַּבְּרָא
מוֹדֶה רִבִּי שִׁמְעוֹן בֶּן לָקִישׁ לְרִבִּי יוֹחָנָן בֶּעָרִיס הַמְכוּוָּן שָׁנוּ בְּגִין בֵּית הֶלֵּל.
וּמוֹדֶה רִבִּי יוֹחָנָן לְרִבִּי שִׁמְעוֹן בֶּעָרִיס הַמְעוּקָם שָׁנוּ בְּגִין רִבִּי יוֹחָנָן בֶּן נוּרִי
דְּרִבִּי יוֹחָנָן בֶּן נוּרִי אָמַר טוֹעִין כָּל־הָאוֹמְרִים כֵּן. אֵין תֵּימַר בֶּעָרִיס הַמְכוּוָּן
שָׁנוּ מַה אִית בָּהּ טוֹעִין. בֵּין כְּמַאן דְּאָמַר מֵעִיקַּר הַגְּפָנִים מוֹשְׁחִין בֵּין כְּמַאן
דְּאָמַר מֵעִיקַּר הַגֶּדֶר מוֹשְׁחִין. מַה בֵּינֵיהוֹן. אָמַר רִבִּי יוֹנָה[7] תִּיפְתָּר שֶׁהָיוּ
הַכְּרָתִּין נְתוּנִין מִקְצָתוֹ בְּתוֹךְ אַרְבַּע אַמּוֹת וּמִקְצָתוֹ חוּץ לְאַרְבַּע אַמּוֹת. מָאן
דְּאָמַר מֵעִיקַּר הַגְּפָנִים מוֹשְׁחִין נִיחָא. מָאן דְּאָמַר מֵעִיקַּר הַגֶּדֶר מוֹשְׁחִין מָקוֹם
שֶׁהֶחוּט כָּלֶה אָסוּר וְהַשְּׁאָר מוּתָּר. הָיוּ שָׁם שְׁתֵּי אַמּוֹת מָאן דְּאָמַר מֵעִיקַּר
הַגְּפָנִים מוֹשְׁחִין אֵינוֹ אָסוּר אֶלָּא שְׁתֵּי אַמּוֹת. מָאן דְּאָמַר מֵעִיקַּר הַגֶּדֶר מוֹשְׁחִין
אָסוּר עַד שְׁתֵּי אַמּוֹת אַחֵר.

Rebbi Joḥanan said, the Mishnah was taught about a straight trellis. In
that case, would it not be forbidden as a vineyard without a fence[8]? Let
us say, it was stated because of the House of Hillel[9]. Rebbi Ḥananiah said,
it is reasonable to assume that Rebbi Simeon ben Laqish agrees with
Rebbi Joḥanan that it was taught about a straight trellis because of the
House of Hillel, and Rebbi Joḥanan agrees with Rebbi Simeon [ben
Laqish] that it was taught about a curved trellis because of Rebbi Joḥanan
ben Nuri, since Rebbi Joḥanan ben Nuri said that anybody who affirms

this is in error. If you say it was taught about a straight trellis, what can be in error[10]? What is the difference between him who says one measures from the roots of the vines and him who says one measures from the bottom of the fence? Rebbi Yose said, explain it if the stems were partially inside four cubits and partially outside of four cubits[11]. For him who says one measures from the roots of the vine, all is in order. For him who says one measures from the bottom of the fence, where the string drawn from the fence ends it is forbidden, the rest is permitted. If there were two cubits[12], only two cubits are forbidden for him who says one measures from the roots of the vines, but for him who says one measures from the bottom of the fence, another two cubits are forbidden.

7   Reading of both mss. and the Venice print. This reading is impossible since "R. Hanina" here is R. Hanania, the fifth generation Amora and colleague of R. Mana, R. Jonah's son. R. Hanina cannot possibly be the first generation Amora, a generation before Rebbis Johanan and Simeon ben Laqish. Therefore, one has to read 'ר יוֹסֵה .

8   For the House of Shammai.

9   In the opinion of R. Johanan, the presence of a trellis has no legal consequences for the House of Shammai; else he would have stated that for the House of Hillel a straight row on a trellis, for the House of Shammai even a curved trellis, would form a vineyard.

10   This rhetorical question is difficult to accept, since for R. Johanan ben Nuri only one cubit around a vine has to be left empty, but for the House of Shammai four cubits along the trellis are required. The question seems to be that in a normal case, if the trellis is parallel to the fence at a distance of three cubits there is no difference since one may not sow between the trellis and the fence (R. Yose in Mishnah 5:4) and the next cubit away from the fence is forbidden according to both Houses and R. Johanan ben Nuri. If the fence is a stone fence belonging in part to a neighbor, three cubits distance is the legal minimum (Mishnah *Baba Batra* 2:1).

11   The trellis is straight but not parallel to the fence; at one end one cubit from the trellis is more than

three cubits from the fence. If one measures from the vines, everything on this side of the fence is forbidden up to a distance of four cubits from the trellis; there is no difference between the House of Shammai and R. Johanan ben Nuri. But if one measures from the fence and the last vines are 4-ε cubits from the fence, then the House of Hillel forbid only a strip four cubits wide from the fence and R. Johanan ben Nuri will forbid up to 5-ε cubits from the fence.

12 This is a different situation and refers to the disagreement between the Houses of Shammai and Hillel, but not to R. Johanan ben Nuri. Here the trellis is only two cubits from the fence; the fence must be the sole

property of the vintner. According to Maimonides (loc. cit.), the House of Shammai will forbid only strips of two cubits each on both sides of the trellis but the House of Hillel will forbid an additional two cubits on the other side of the fence. According to R. Abraham ben David, the explanation of Maimonides defies all logic since a fence separates in all respects. R. Abraham explains that for the House of Shammai, a strip of width 2 is forbidden on each side of the vines. If the vines are d cubits wide, the total width of the forbidden strip is $4+d$. But for the House of Hillel, the width is only 4, less than the width required by the House of Shammai.

אָמַר רַבִּי יוֹחָנָן רַבִּי יוֹסֵי וְרַבִּי יִשְׁמָעֵאל וְרַבִּי יוֹחָנָן בֶּן נוּרִי שְׁלָשְׁתָּן אָמְרוּ דָבָר אֶחָד. רַבִּי יִשְׁמָעֵאל דְּתַגִּינָן עַל גַּנָּה קְטַנָּה שֶׁהִיא מוּקֶּפֶת עָרִיס אִם יֵשׁ בּוֹ מְלֹא בוֹצֵר סַלּוֹ מִיכָּן וּמְלוֹא בוֹצֵר סַלּוֹ מִיכָּן תִּיזָּרַע וְאִם לָאו לֹא תִזָּרַע. אָמַר רַבִּי יוֹנָה אַמָּה בוֹצֵר וְאַמָּה סַלּוֹ אַמָּה בוֹצֵר וְאַמָּה סַלּוֹ. הֲווֹן בָּעֵי מֵימַר מָאן דְּאָמַר מֵעִיקַּר גְּפָנִים מוֹשְׁחִין נִיחָא מָאן דְּאָמַר מֵעִיקַּר הַגָּדֵר מוֹשְׁחִין אֵין אוֹתָן הַכָּרְתִּין מְמַעֲטִין אַרְבַּע. תִּיפְתַּר שֶׁהָיוּ חֲבוּקִין לַכּוֹתֶל. לֹא אַרְבַּע אִינֶן כְּלוּם הִילְכוֹת עָרִיס בְּחָמֵשׁ. אָמַר רַבִּי חֲנַנְיָה תִּיפְתַּר שֶׁהָיוּ שְׁתַּיִם גְּפָנִים נְתוּנוֹת בְּקֶרֶן זָוִית אַחַת שֶׁאָם יִמְתְּחֵם הֵן נִרְאִין כְּאַרְבַּע בֵּינַיִין. רַבִּי יוֹסֵי דְּתַגִּינָן רַבִּי יוֹסֵי אוֹמֵר אִם אֵין שָׁם אַרְבַּע אַמּוֹת לֹא יָבִיא זֶרַע לְשָׁם. מָאן דְּאָמַר מֵעִיקַּר גְּפָנִים מוֹשְׁחִין נִיחָא מָאן דְּאָמַר מֵעִיקַּר הַגָּדֵר מוֹשְׁחִין אֵין אוֹתוֹ הַכּוֹרֶת מְמַעֵט אַרְבַּע. תִּיפְתַּר שֶׁהָיָה חָבוּק לַכּוֹתֶל. וְהֵכֵן רַבִּי יוֹחָנָן בֶּן נוּרִי דְּהָכָא. מִסְתַּבְּרָא רַבִּי

יוֹסֵי וְרִבִּי יִשְׁמָעֵאל יוֹדוּן לְרִבִּי יוֹחָנָן בֶּן נוּרִי. וְרִבִּי יוֹחָנָן בֶּן נוּרִי לֹא יוֹדֵי לְרִבִּי
יוֹסֵי וְרִבִּי יִשְׁמָעֵאל. רִבִּי יוֹסֵי יוֹדֵי לְרִבִּי יִשְׁמָעֵאל וְרִבִּי יִשְׁמָעֵאל לֹא יוֹדֵי לְרִבִּי
יוֹסֵי.

Rebbi Joḥanan said, Rebbi Yose, Rebbi Ismael and Rebbi Joḥanan ben Nuri, all three said the same thing.

Rebbi Ismael, as we have stated[13]: "About a small garden surrounded by a trellis, if there is room for the vintner and his basket on each side one may sow there, if not, it may not be sown." Rebbi Jonah said, the vintner requires one cubit, his basket one cubit on each side. They wanted to say, for him who says one measures from the roots of the vine, all is in order. For him who says one measures from the bottom of the fence, do the stems not diminish the measure of four cubits[14]? Explain it if they were clinging to the wall. But are there not only four and the rules of the trellis start with five? Rebbi Ḥananiah said, explain it that two vines are planted at a corner; if one stretches a rope one sees four intervals[15].

Rebbi Yose, as we have stated[16]: "If there are less than four cubits one should not bring seeds there." For him who says one measures from the roots of the vine, all is in order. For him who says one measures from the bottom of the fence, does the stem not decrease the measure of four cubits? Explain it if it was clinging to the wall. And similarly Rebbi Joḥanan ben Nuri here.

It is reasonable to assume that Rebbi Yose and Rebbi Ismael will agree with Rebbi Joḥanan ben Nuri, but Rebbi Joḥanan ben Nuri will not agree with Rebbi Yose and Rebbi Ismael[17]. Rebbi Yose will agree with Rebbi Ismael but Rebbi Ismael will not agree with Rebbi Yose.

13   Mishnah Idiut 2:4, of the statements about accepted practices coll-   ected when Rabban Gamliel was deposed and R. Eleazar ben Azariah

was installed as patriarch. The garden is a small plot, on each side a vine is planted and their branches are trained over a trellis. For a situation comparable to the one here one has to assume that plot and trellis are enclosed by a fence ten hand-breadths high.

14   If one measures two cubits from each side of the stem of thickness t the distance of the end of the forbidden domain from the fence will be $4+t > 4$ and R. Ismael cannot agree with R. Johanan ben Nuri that as soon as the distance is > 4 there are only isolated vines.

15   There are two possible interpretations of this statement. The traditional one is that there is a single vine on each side and an additional one planted at one corner for a total of six. But in that case, there are five intervals; in addition, the comparison between the opinions of R. Jose and R. Ismael would not work! R. Hananiah

must insist that the rules of trellis do not depend on the number of vines but on the number of spaces between them. In a linear order, for four spaces one needs five vines. But in a circular arrangement, four vines define four intervals. I prefer to read the statement as: "*Any* two vines form a corner, for a total of four intervals."

16   Mishnah 5:4.

17   R. Johanan ben Nuri might not agree that vines not planted in a straight line, even if strung on a trellis, ever need four cubits. But R. Yose and R. Ismael must agree that in the case of the Mishnah, the first four cubits are forbidden. R. Yose has to agree with R. Ismael since he requires four cubits even if the vines do not form a regular pattern, but we have no statement of R. Ismael if the stems of the vines do not form a square or at least a parallelogram.

רִבִּי יְהוּדָה בְּשֵׁם רַב הֲלָכָה כְּרִבִּי עֲקִיבָה. רִבִּי יַעֲקֹב בַּר אִידִי בְּשֵׁם רִבִּי יְהוֹשֻׁעַ בֶּן לֵוִי הֲלָכָה כְּדִבְרֵי מִי שֶׁהוּא מֵיקֵל בְּחוּצָה לָאָרֶץ. אָמַר רִבִּי יַעֲקֹב בַּר אָחָא וְתַנֵּי תַמָּן הֲלָכָה כְּדִבְרֵי מִי שֶׁהוּא מֵיקֵל בְּחוּצָה לָאָרֶץ.

Rebbi Jehudah[18] in the name of Rav: Practice follows Rebbi Aqiba. Rebbi Jacob bar Idi in the name of Rebbi Joshua ben Levi: Practice outside the Land follows him who is lenient. Rebbi Jacob bar Aha said, there they stated: Practice outside the Land follows him who is lenient.

18   This must be Rav Jehudah. The
following statement of R. Jacob bar Idi,
taken from the end of Chapter 4,
restricts the opinion of Rav to vineyards outside the Holy Land. The Babli
(*Qiddušin* 39a) disagrees and holds that

kilaim is forbidden only in the Holy
Land; elsewhere only sowing grain
directly under a vine is forbidden by
rabbinic decree since in the Holy Land
this would sanctify.

(fol. 30a) **משנה ב**: עָרִיס שֶׁהוּא יוֹצֵא מִן הַמַּדְרֵגָה. רבִּי לִיעֶזֶר בֶּן יַעֲקֹב אוֹמֵר
אִם עוֹמֵד בָּאָרֶץ (fol. 30b) וּבוֹצֵר אֶת כּוּלוֹ הֲרֵי זֶה אוֹסֵר אַרְבַּע אַמּוֹת בַּשָּׂדֶה
וְאִם לָאו אֵינוֹ אוֹסֵר אֶלָּא כְנֶגְדּוֹ. רבִּי לְעֶזֶר אוֹמֵר אַף הַנּוֹטֵעַ אַחַת בָּאָרֶץ
וְאַחַת בַּמַּדְרֵגָה אִם גָּבוֹהַּ עֲשָׂרָה טְפָחִים אֵינָהּ מִצְטָרֶפֶת עִמָּהּ וְאִם לָאו הֲרֵי זוֹ
מִצְטָרֶפֶת עִמָּהּ.

Mishnah 2: A trellis coming from a terrace. Rebbi Eliezer ben Jacob
says, if someone standing on the ground can harvest all [vines] then it
forbids four cubits in the field; otherwise it only forbids around it[19].
Rebbi Eliezer says[20], also if one plants one row on the ground and one on
a terrace, if the latter is ten cubits higher they do not combine; otherwise,
they do combine.

19   The rules of the trellis apply
only if the harvest can be conducted in
one plane; otherwise, the different
parts planted on different levels are
considered separate and its vines will
have the status of isolated ones unless
on each level there is a full trellis.

20   In the opinion of R. David ben
Zimra, the name should be deleted and

the statement taken as anonymous
Mishnah, since, in the discussion in the
second paragraph of the Halakhah, the
second statement is accepted as
practice while the first one is rejected.
A vineyard needs at least two rows; if
the rows are ten hand-breadths apart
in elevation no vineyard is formed.

הלכה ב: רִבִּי שְׁמוּאֵל בַּר נַחְמָן רִבִּי יוֹנָתָן בְּשֵׁם רִבִּי לִיעֶזֶר הַגּוֹמֵם אֶת כַּרְמוֹ

פָּחוֹת מִטֶּפַח חַיָּיב בְּעָרְלָה מִפְּנֵי מַרְאִית הָעַיִן דִּבְרֵי חֲכָמִים[21] עַד שֶׁיְגוֹם מֵעִם

הָאָרֶץ. רִבִּי שְׁמוּאֵל בַּר נַחְמָן בְּשֵׁם רִבִּי יוֹנָתָן בְּשֵׁם רִבִּי לִיעֶזֶר בֶּן יַעֲקֹב הָעוֹשֶׂה

כְּרִי מִן הַלֶּקֶט וּמִן הַשִּׁכְחָה וּמִן הַפִּיאָה חַיָּיב בִּתְרוּמָה גְדוֹלָה מִפְּנֵי מַרְאִית הָעַיִן.

רִבִּי שְׁמוּאֵל בַּר נַחְמָן בְּשֵׁם רִבִּי יוֹנָתָן וְרִבִּי לִיעֶזֶר בֶּן יַעֲקֹב מִשֵׁם בֵּית שַׁמַּאי

הַמֵּת מְטַמֵּא אַרְבַּע אַמּוֹת בִּרְשׁוּת הָרַבִּים מִפְּנֵי כְבוֹדוֹ. רִבִּי מָנָא אָמַר הָדָא

(fol. 30c) אַחֲרַיְיָתָא מְשׁוּם בֵּית שַׁמַּאי. רִבִּי יוֹסֵי בֵּי רִבִּי בּוּן אָמַר כּוּלְּהוֹן מְשׁוּם

בֵּית שַׁמַּאי. אָמַר רִבִּי יוֹנָה אוּף הָדָא דְתַנִּינָן מִפְּנֵי מַרְאִית הָעַיִן. דְּלֹא כֵן מַה

בֵּין הָעוֹמֵד בָּאָרֶץ מַה בֵּין הָעוֹמֵד בַּמַּדְרֵגָה.

Halakhah 2: Rebbi Samuel bar Naḥman, Rebbi Jonathan, in the name of Rebbi Eliezer[22]: He who prunes his vineyard down to less than a hand-breadth subjects it to *orlah* because of the bad appearance[23]. The Sages say, only if he prunes down to the ground. Rebbi Samuel bar Naḥman in the name of Rebbi Jonathan, in the name of Rebbi Eliezer ben Jacob: He who forms a heap from gleanings, forgotten sheaves, and *peah*, is subject to the Great Heave[24] because of the bad appearance. Rebbi Samuel bar Naḥman in the name of Rebbi Jonathan, Rebbi Eliezer ben Jacob in the name of the House of Shammai: A corpse in the public domain induces impurity four cubits around it, to sustain its dignity[25]. Rebbi Mana said, this last statement is in the name of the House of Shammai; Rebbi Yose ben Rebbi Abun said, all are in the name of the House of Shammai[26]. Rebbi Jonah said, also that which we stated here[27] is because of the bad appearance. If it were not so, what would be the difference whether one stands on the ground or on the terrace?

---

21   Reading of the Rome ms. here and all sources in the parallel *Ševi'it* 1:9, fol. 33c.

22   This is R. Eliezer ben Jacob, as

in the next statement, the parallel in *Ševi'it*, and the corresponding text in Babli *Soṭah* 43b. The traditions of the Babli are in the name of R. Joḥanan,

not R. Jonathan, and are not identical
with the statements here.

23   The person who sees vine
stumps less than a hand-breadth high
might think of them as new growth
whose yield is forbidden as *orlah* the
first three years after planting (cf.
Chapter 5, Note 93). The Sages apply
orlah only if all growth above ground
is cut off, and not as a matter of bad
impressions. The Babli deals with a
minimal vineyard of dwarf vines that
never grow a hand-breadth tall and
declares them to be permanent *orlah*.

24   This is the regular heave, called
"great" in contrast to the heave of the
tithe (cf. *Peah* Chapter 1, Note 127).
The Babli requires full tithing once a
heap is formed on the field from
exempt gifts to the poor (but the
townspeople know the poor who have
no land).

25   A person standing over a corpse
is forming a "tent" by his body and
becomes impure (*Num.* 19). The House
of Shammai extend this impurity by
rabbinic decree to anybody within four
cubits of the corpse, so that only those
occupied with the burial will come
near the corpse.

26   None of the statements in this
paragraph are practice to be followed.

27   The statement of R. Eliezer ben
Jacob in the Mishnah. If vines growing
on two different levels did form a
vineyard or a trellis in any Biblical
sense, the rabbis could not make the
definition dependent on whether all
grapes can be harvested from the
lower level. The other statements of R.
Eliezer ben Jacob in this paragraph
were introduced as background for R.
Jonah's statement.

גְּבוֹהָה. מַה גְּבוֹהָה שׁוּרָה גְּבוֹהָה מַדְרֵגָה. אֵין תֵּימַר גְּבוֹהָה שׁוּרָה שׁוֹפֵעַ
הַמַּדְרֵגָה כִּלְמַטָּן. אֵין תֵּימַר גְּבוֹהָה הַמַּדְרֵגָה שִׁיפּוּעַ הַשּׁוּרָה מִלְּמַעֲלָן. וְהָתַנֵּי
שְׁתֵּי שׁוּרוֹת בַּמַּדְרֵגָה. אִית לָךְ מֵימַר גְּבוֹהָה שׁוּרָה. לֹא גְּבוֹהָה מַדְרֵגָה. אָמַר
רִבִּי מָנָא כָּל־אוֹתָן עֲשָׂרָה טְפָחִים שֶׁבַּמַּדְרֵגָה עָשׂוּ אוֹתָם מָקוֹם בִּפְנֵי עַצְמוֹ.

"Higher[28]." Is the row higher or is the terrace higher? If you say that
the row is higher, the declivity of the terrace is counted as "below". If you
say the terrace is higher, the declivity of the row is counted as "above".
But did we not state: "Two rows on a terrace?[29]" Can you say that the
row is higher? No, the terrace has to be higher. Rebbi Mana said, they
declared the entire ten hand-breadths of the terrace a domain by itself[30].

28   Here starts the discussion of the second sentence of the Mishnah, of a row which is "higher than 10 hand-breadths" than the other row. In the entire discussion, "higher" means "higher than 10 hand-breadths". The question is whether the terrace wall has to be 10 hand-breadths high or whether it might be less if only the vines appear on the surface at an elevation "higher than 10 hand-breadths".

29   This must be from an otherwise unknown *baraita*, stating that one row below and two above do not form a "large vineyard" (cf. Halakhah 4:6) but a small vineyard on the top and an isolated row at the bottom. Since the two upper rows may be at slightly different heights but are counted together, their position cannot be the deciding factor.

30   R. Mana rejects the entire discussion and declares the (vertical) declivity to be a separate domain, not counted either way, so anything sown there is not impacted by anything planted below or above.

תַּמָּן תַּנִּינָן הַזּוֹרֵק אַרְבַּע אַמּוֹת בַּכּוֹתֶל לְמַעְלָה מֵעֲשָׂרָה טְפָחִים כְּזוֹרֵק בָּאֲוִיר
וּלְמַטָּה מֵעֲשָׂרָה טְפָחִים כְּזוֹרֵק בָּאָרֶץ. רַב חִסְדָּא אָמַר בְּמוֹדֵד לָכֶסֶן. וְאֵין
סוֹפָהּ לֵירֵד. רִבִּי חִיָּיא בְשֵׁם רִבִּי יוֹחָנָן תִּיפְתָּר שֶׁהָיְתָה דְּבֵילָה שְׁמֵינָה וְהִיא
נִיטוֹחָה. רִבִּי חַגַּי בָּעֵי קוֹמֵי רִבִּי יוֹסֵי לֵית הָדָא אֲמָרָה שִׁיפּוּעַ הַמַּדְרֵגָה כִּלְמַטָּן.
אָמַר לֵיהּ תַּמָּן זְרָעִין נֶהֱנִין מִן הַמַּדְרֵיגָה בְּרַם הָכָא דֶּרֶךְ בְּנֵי אָדָם לִהְיוֹת שָׁפִין
בָּהּ וְהִיא נוֹפָלֶת. אִילּוּ אָמַר כְּשֶׁהָיָה שָׁם חוֹר וְהִיא נֶהֱנָה מִן הַחוֹר כְּשֵׁם
שֶׁהַזְּרָעִין נֶהֱנִין מִן הַמַּדְרֵיגָה יָאוּת.

We have stated there[31]: "If somebody throws from four cubits [distance] to a wall, if [the projectile hits] higher than ten hand-breadths, he is like one throwing into the air, if lower than ten hand-breadths, he is like one throwing onto the ground." Rav Ḥisda said, if it extends slanting[32]. But will it not finally descend? Rebbi Ḥiyya in the name of Rebbi Joḥanan, explain it that it was a soft fig cake and it stuck[33]. Rebbi Ḥaggai asked before Rebbi Yose, does this not imply that the declivity of a terrace belongs to the level below[34]? He said to him, there the vegetables profit from the terrace but here people rub it and it falls down. If it would say, if there is a hole [in the wall] and it profits from the hole just as vegetables profit from the terrace, you would be justified.

31   Mishnah *Šabbat* 11:4. It is forbidden to transport anything in the public domain on the Sabbath a distance of more than four cubits. "Transporting" in the legal sense includes taking up, moving, and depositing. If one of these elements is missing, no offense occured. "Public domain" in this context extends only to ten hand-breadths above ground. Anything higher is free space to which the prohibition of transporting does not extend. Hence, if something was taken up from the public domain, thrown, and came to rest in free space, it is as if it was thrown and never came to rest; no offense occured. But if it came to rest within ten hand-breadths of the ground, the Sabbath was desecrated.

32   Taking מדד not as Biblical Hebrew "to measure", but from Arabic ﻣـﺪّ "to extend, to rise". R. Ḥisda's problem is that nothing can stop on a vertical wall. The same answer is given by R. Ḥisda's student and son-in-law Rava in Babli *Šabbat* 5b, the material there being sheets of paper or parchment. In the Yerushalmi, the discussion here is reproduced in *Šabbat* 11:3 (fol. 14a).

33   The same answer is given by R. Joḥanan himself in Babli *Šabbat* 7b, 100 a.

34   R. Ḥaggai assumes that the reason one insists on a separation of 10 hand-breadths is the same for the rules of the Sabbath and of *kilaim*. In that case, the Mishnah seems to extend the reach of any "bottom" upwards to 10 hand-breadths. He is answered that plants may grow on a slanted wall but anything sticking to the lower part of any wall bordering the public domain will be rubbed off; the fig cake cannot be considered to be at rest at such a place. The Babli (*Šabbat* 100a) disagrees with R. Yose and points out that even if a Tannaitic statement such as suggested by him did exist, it would not prove anything since R. Meïr [Yerushalmi *Šabbat* 11:3 (fol. 13a), *Eruvin* 10:8 (fol. 26b); Babli *Šabbat* 7b, 100 a, *Eruvin* 11b, 33b, 101b, *Yoma* 11b] considers any depression a separate domain excluded from "free space".

שְׁתֵּי גִינּוֹת זוֹ עַל גַּבֵּי זוֹ הַתַּחְתּוֹנָה עֲשׂוּיָה כֶּרֶם וְהָעֶלְיוֹנָה אֵינָהּ עֲשׂוּיָה כֶּרֶם.
זוֹרֵעַ אֶת הָעֶלְיוֹנָה עַד שֶׁהוּא מַגִּיעַ עַד לָאֲוֵיר עֲשָׂרָה. רִבִּי בּוּן בַּר חִיָּיא בְּעָיָא
קוֹמֵי רִבִּי זְעִירָא לֵית הָדָא אֶמְרָה שִׁיפּוּעַ הַמַּדְרֵגָה כִלְמַטָּן. אָמַר לֵיהּ מִשּׁוּם
זְרָעִין נוֹטִין לַאֲוֵיר הַכֶּרֶם. הָעֶלְיוֹנָה עֲשׂוּיָה כֶּרֶם וְהַתַּחְתּוֹנָה אֵינָהּ עֲשׂוּיָה כֶּרֶם
זוֹרֵעַ אֶת הַתַּחְתּוֹנָה וְאֶת הַמַּדְרֵגָה עַד שֶׁמַּגִּיעַ לְעִיקַר הַגְּפָנִים. אָמַר רִבִּי יוֹסֵי
לֵית כָּאן לְעִיקַר הַגְּפָנִים אֶלָּא לְמַטָּה מִשְּׁלֹשָׁה. כְּהָדָא דְּתַנֵּי שָׁרְשֵׁי פֵּיאָה
הַנִּכְנָסִין לְתוֹךְ אַרְבַּע אַמּוֹת שֶׁבְּכֶרֶם. לְמַטָּה מִשְּׁלוֹשָׁה טְפָחִים הֲרֵי אֵלּוּ מוּתָּרִין.

"Two gardens, one above the other, the lower one is made into a vineyard, the upper one is not made into a vineyard. One may sow the upper one until one reaches the airspace of ten[35]." Rebbi Abun bar Ḥiyya asked before Rebbi Zeïra, does this not imply that the declivity of a terrace belongs to the below? He said to him, because plants will bend into the airspace of the vineyard[36]. "If the upper one is made into a vineyard but the lower one is not made into a vineyard, one may sow the lower one and the declivity until one reaches the roots of the vines." Rebbi Yose said, one does not have here "the roots of the vines[37]" but "below three [hand-breadths]," following that which was stated: "roots of madder that enter within four cubits of a vineyard are permitted below three hand-breadths."

35   Tosephta *Kilaim* 3:9, in a slightly different text. Instead of "the airspace of ten", the Tosephta has: "the stems of the lower one." The text is missing in the Vienna ms.; the language is probably influenced by the second sentence. The version in the Yerushalmi permits sowing on the declivity above 10 hand-breadths from the bottom. The question of R. Abun bar

Ḥiyya refers to these lower 10 hand-breadths.

36   This part of the statement does not prove anything; since we speak about sowing on an incline, the growing plants will bend over the vines.

37   The depth of the "roots of the vines" would be different for different strains of grapes. R. Yose insists that

the three-hand-breadths rule proclaimed in Halakhah 1:8 (Notes 158 ff.)

and quoted by him is valid for all
plants, even vines.

(fol. 30b) **משנה ג:** הַמַּדְלֶה אֶת הַגֶּפֶן עַל מִקְצָת אפיפיירות לֹא יָבִיא זֶרַע אֶל
תַּחַת הַמּוֹתָר וְאִם הֵבִיא לֹא קִידֵּשׁ. וְאִם הוֹלֵךְ הֶחָדָשׁ אָסוּר. וְכֵן הַמַּדְלֶה עַל
מִקְצָת אִילָן סְרָק.

משנה ד: הַמַּדְלֶה אֶת הַגֶּפֶן עַל מִקְצָת אִילָן מַאֲכָל מוּתָּר לְהָבִיא זֶרַע אֶל
תַּחַת הַמּוֹתָר. וְאִם הוֹלֵךְ הֶחָדָשׁ יַחֲזִירֶנּוּ.

משנה ה: מַעֲשֶׂה שֶׁהָלַךְ רִבִּי יְהוֹשֻׁעַ אֵצֶל רִבִּי יִשְׁמָעֵאל מִכְּפַר עֲזִיז הִרְאָהוּ
גֶּפֶן שֶׁהוּא מוּדְלָה עַל מִקְצָת תְּאֵינָה. אָמַר לוֹ מַה אֲנִי לְהָבִיא זֶרַע תַּחַת הַמּוֹתָר
אָמַר לוֹ מוּתָּר. וְהֶעֱלֵהוּ מִשָּׁם לְבֵית מִגִינַיָּיא וְהִרְאָהוּ גֶּפֶן שֶׁהוּא מוּדְלָה עַל
מִקְצָת הַקּוֹרָה וְסַדָּן שֶׁל שִׁקְמָה וּבוֹ קוֹרוֹת הַרְבָּה אָמַר לוֹ תַּחַת הַקּוֹרָה הַזוֹ
אָסוּר וְהַשְׁאָר מוּתָּר.

Mishnah 3: If somebody trains a vine over part of a *papyrus*[38], he should not sow under the rest, but if he did, it does not become sanctified[39]. If the new growth expands it becomes forbidden. The same applies to one who trains over parts of a futile tree[40].

Mishnah 4: If somebody trains a vine over part of a fruit tree he may sow under the rest. If new grows expands, he must move it[41].

Mishnah 5: It happened that Rebbi Joshua visited Rebbi Ismael from Kefar Aziz[42]. He showed him a vine trained over parts of a fig tree and asked, may I sow under the rest? He told him, it is permitted. He took him from there to the armory and showed him a vine trained over part of a beam and a sycamore stump on which were many beams. He said to him, under that one beam it is forbidden, the rest is permitted.

38 Definition of the Gaonic commentary to *Kelim* 17.3. Some sources here and in *Kelim* have אפסיריו, a medieval commentator writes הפיפיריות. The latter reading, seeing in the prothetic א the definite article ה, is supported by the Halakhah which uses פיפור, פיפור and the similar reading of most commentaries in *Kelim*. Most moderns see in the word a form of Greek πάπυρος (but this fits better with Tosephta *Kelim b. m.* 5:15, כלי פפיר "paper vessels".) According to the Geonim, one takes rope from papyrus leaves (according to Maimonides, the reeds themselves) and puts them crosswise into a frame in order to form a platform that will be supported by posts. Sources confirming the use of papyrus rope in Antiquity are adduced by Loew in Krauss's Dictionary, *s. v.* פיפור.

[In view of the formal parallelism between "part of a *papyrus*" and "part of a futile tree", "part of a fig tree", one might also take *papyrus* as a living plant, rather than a rope or mat of papyrus fibers.

Papyrus antiquorum, mostly perennial grassy plants cultivated throughout the ancient world, had multiple commercial uses: e. g., *Cyperus esculentus* with edible, oil-rich bulbs (*Bulbuli Trasi, Dulcinia*), *Cyperus officinalis*, used medically, *Cyperus textilis*, used in basket-weaving and paper manufacture. A papyrus plant growing near a vine would therefore also make sense in a discussion of *kilaim*. (E. G.)]

39 It is clear from the last sentence in the Mishnah that one speaks here of a single vine, not a vineyard or a trellis of five vines. Therefore, only a minimal distance has to be kept from the stem of the vine. Since the vine will expand, and the area below the part of the papyrus not covered by the branches and leaves of the vine is certainly more than a cubit away from the stem and can be used for other crops. However, if either the sown plants or the vine expand so that now parts of the plants are directly under the vine, the plants become forbidden. A prudent farmer, therefore, will not even start sowing close to the vine.

40 In modern Hebrew, the term means "non-fruit-bearing tree" and סרק (2) has the general connotation of "useless, abortive". [סרק (1) means "to comb".] The word may be derived from the root that appears as Arabic סרק, Assyrian שרק, "to rob" (as in Saracen), a tree which robs the farmer of his labor if he would tend it. It is clear from the next Mishnah that a tree bearing cheap fruit is also אילן סרק

Because it does not bear high quality fruit, it has the same status as a rope or a beam.

41   He must move the vine to reestablish the required separation.

42   This is the reading of the Leyden ms. and the texts dependent on it. All other Mishnah texts have: "Rebbi Joshua visited Rebbi Ismael at Kefar Aziz", לכפר instead of מכפר. In that case, the host is R. Ismael (ben Elisha), the student of R. Joshua, who should have known his teacher's opinion. It therefore seems likely that the Yerushalmi version is superior and the host is a minor figure mentioned only here. The paragraph establishes the previous Mishnah as R. Joshua's.

(fol. 30c) **הלכה ג**: חִזְקִיָה אָמַר מִשְּׁלֹשָׁה וְעַד אַרְבָּעָה הִיא מַתְנִיתָא פָּחוֹת מִשְּׁלֹשָׁה כְּסָתוּם וְעַד אַרְבָּעָה מַשְׁלִים אַרְבָּעָה נַחַת הוּא לָהּ. עַד הֵיכָן. רִבִּי יַעֲקֹב בַּר אִידִי בְּשֵׁם רִבִּי שִׁמְעוֹן בֶּן לָקִישׁ עַד אַרְבַּע אַמּוֹת. רִבִּי אָחָא רִבִּי חִינָנָא בְּשֵׁם רִבִּי שִׁמְעוֹן בֶּן לָקִישׁ עַד שֵׁשׁ אַמּוֹת. אָמַר רִבִּי מָנָא אֲזֵלִית לְקֵיסָרִין וּשְׁמָעִית רִבִּי הוֹשַׁעְיָה בַּר שַׁמַּי בְּשֵׁם רִבִּי יִצְחָק בֶּן לָעְזָר אִם הָיוּ שְׁתֵּי פִיפְרוֹת מוּתָּר. אָמַר רִבִּי חִינָנָא וְתַגֵּי וּפַלִּיג אִם הָיָה דַרְכּוֹ לִפְסוֹעַ אָסוּר. וְתַגֵּי כֵן רִבִּי שִׁמְעוֹן בֶּן לָעְזָר אוֹמֵר אִם הָיָה דַרְכּוֹ לִפְסוֹעַ בֵּין פִיפוֹר לְפִיפוֹר כְּפִיפוֹר אֶחָד הוּא.

Halakhah 3: Ḥizqiah said, the Mishnah speaks about distances from three to four hand-breadths[43]. Less than three is close up, up to four one has to complete, four is easy for it. How far[44]? Rebbi Jacob bar Idi in the name of Rebbi Simeon ben Laqish, up to four cubits. Rebbi Aḥa, Rebbi Ḥinena in the name of Rebbi Simeon ben Laqish, up to six cubits. Rebbi Mana said: I went to Caesarea and heard Rebbi Hoshiah bar Shammai in the name of Rebbi Isaac ben Eleazar: If there were two papyri, it is permitted[45]. Rebbi Ḥinena said, a statement disagrees: If he usually oversteps, it is forbidden. It was stated thus: Rebbi Simeon ben Eleazar says, if he usually oversteps between lattices, it is treated as a single lattice.

43   In all respects, a distance of up to three hand-breadths is neglected, cf. Mishnah 4:4, *Eruvin* 1:9, *Sukkah* 1:9. Hence, sowing within three hand-breadths of a vine certainly sanctifies. If the distance is more than three but less than four, one tells the farmer to complete the four hand-breadths. More than four, while still forbidden, does not sanctify and even if the vine leaves grow they do not interfere as long as the distance is more than three hand-breadths.

44   How much does one have to separate from the place shaded by the vine leaves that it should not be forbidden to sow there? R. Jacob bar Idi applies the rules of a trellis to the vine trained over a lattice.   It is difficult to find a reason for the second opinion given in the name of R. Simeon ben Laqish and probably difficult to find a papyrus mat wide enough that away from the vine there should still be six unoccupied cubits. {It seems, therefore, that R. Simeon ben Laqish takes פיפיור as name of the plant; cf. Note 38.}

45   If two papyrus mats (or ropes, or plants) are laid out parallel over poles and a vine is trained over one of them, the other one is not affected. The opposing opinion states that if the vintner in the ordinary care of the vineyard usually steps from under one mat to under the other, they are considered as one and subject to the 4 cubits/6 cubits rule.

(fol. 30b) **מִשְׁנָה ו:** אֵי זֶהוּ אִילַן סְרָק כָּל־שֶׁאֵינוֹ עוֹשֶׂה פֵּירוֹת. רִבִּי מֵאִיר אוֹמֵר הַכֹּל אִילַן סְרָק חוּץ מִן הַזַּיִת וּמִן הַתְּאֵינָה. רִבִּי יוֹסֵי אוֹמֵר כֹּל שֶׁאֵין כָּמוֹהוּ נוֹטְעִין שָׂדוֹת שְׁלֵימוֹת הֲרֵי זֶה אִילַן סְרָק.

Mishnah 6: What is a futile tree? One which does not bear fruit. Rebbi Meïr says, every tree is futile except olive and fig trees. Rebbi Yose says, a futile tree is one of which one does not plant entire orchards.

(fol. 30c) **הֲלָכָה ד:** מַה בֵּין אִילַן סְרָק מַה בֵּין אִילַן מַאֲכָל. אָדָם מְבַטֵּל אִילַן סְרָק עַל גַּבֵּי נַפְנוֹ וְאֵין אָדָם מְבַטֵּל אִילַן מַאֲכָל עַל גַּבֵּי נַפְנוֹ.

Halakhah 4: What is the difference between a futile and a fruit tree?

A person will disregard a futile tree relative to his vine but nobody will disregard a fruit tree relative to his vine[46].

46   The "futile" tree will not be considered as more than the support of the vine and will not receive attention for its own sake.

תַּמָּן תַּנִּינָן כָּל־חֲמָתוֹת צְרוּרוֹת טְהוֹרוֹת חוּץ מִשֶּׁל עֲרָבִיִּים. רִבִּי מֵאִיר אוֹמֵר צְרוּר הַשָּׁעָה טְהוֹרוֹת צְרוּר עוֹלָם טְמֵאוֹת. רִבִּי יוֹסֵי אוֹמֵר כָּל־חֲמָתוֹת צְרוּרוֹת טְהוֹרוֹת. אִית תַּנָּיֵי תַּנֵּי מְחַלַּף. רִבִּי יַעֲקֹב בַּר אָחָא בְּשֵׁם רִבִּי יָסָא כְּמַתְנִיתִין. אָמַר רִבִּי יוּדָן סִימָנָא דְכֵלִים כִּלְאִים דְּלֹכֵן מַה בֵּין צְרוּר עוֹלָם מַה בֵּין צְרוּר שָׁעָה. דְּבֵי רִבִּי יַנַּאי אָמְרֵי צְרוּר עוֹלָם צָרִיךְ חִיתּוּךְ צְרוּר שָׁעָה אֵינוֹ צָרִיךְ חִיתּוּךְ.

There[47], we have stated: "All tied-up water skins are pure except those of Arabs. Rebbi Meïr says, temporarily tied ones are pure, permanently tied ones are impure. Rebbi Yose says, all tied ones are pure." Some Tannaïm state it inverted[48]. Rebbi Jacob bar Aḥa in the name of Rebbi Yasa: Like our Mishnah. Rebbi Yudan said, the indicator of *Kelim* is *Kilaim*[49], for if it were not so, what would be the difference between permanent and temporary tie? In the House of Rebbi Yannai they said: A permanent tie must be cut, a temporary tie does not have to be cut[50].

47   Mishnah *Kelim* 26:4. The only things that may be impure are living humans, dead humans and animals, vessels and garments, food and drink, and houses. Tractate *Kelim* deals with the impurity of vessels and textiles. In that tractate, "pure" means that the vessel in question cannot possibly become impure; "impure" means that it may become impure if exposed to impurity.

If a vessel is used as a container, it can become impure as long as it can be used as container. If an impure vessel springs a leak large enough to make it unusable for its primary purpose, it becomes pure. Animal hides used as containers for water or wine are obtained by skinning slaughtered lambs or sheep. The skin then is open at the neck, the tail, and the four feet. If the feet and tail end are sown tight, there is no doubt that a permanent container was formed which may become impure. If the feet are only tied with rope, they also can become untied; the vessel so created is temporary and cannot become impure. The anonymous Tanna states that Arabs never sow their skins; they have developed a technique to tie the skins with rope to create permanent vessels. R. Meïr extends the rule to all skins whose knots are not supposed to be opened. R. Yose notes that any knot can be untied without damaging the skin; hence, no knot is permanent.

48   They switch the statements attached to the names of R. Meïr and R. Yose. This invites comparison with the Mishnah here.

49   In *Kilaim*, a "futile" tree is turned into a prop for the vine and loses its character of tree by the vintner's intention as stated in the preceding paragraph; so likewise the

knots with which the skin is tied are temporary or permanent according to the intention of the owner. If we do not change the names in *Kelim*, the arguments of R. Meïr become consistent; the Mishnah *Kelim* should not be changed.

50   The House of Yannai disagree with R. Yasa: The difference between temporary and permanent knots is not one of intent but of fact. A temporary knot is one that may be untied by hand, even if it is intended to be permanent. A permanent knot is one that cannot be untied with one's fingers; it is so tight that it can be removed only by cutting the rope. In that case, a tool was needed to create the openings; this action is as if one used a drill to make a hole in a pot, which destroys the vessel and makes it pure. As a consequence, the permanently tied skin is a vessel and can become impure; there are parallel arguments in *Kelim* and *Kilaim*.

(fol. 30b) **מִשְׁנָה ז:** פִּיסְקֵי עָרִיס שְׁמוֹנֶה אַמּוֹת וְעוֹד. וְכָל־מִידוֹת שֶׁאָמְרוּ חֲכָמִים בַּכֶּרֶם אֵין בָּהֶן וְעוֹד חוּץ מִפִּיסְקֵי עָרִיס. אֵילוּ הֵן פִּיסְקֵי עָרִיס שֶׁחָרַב מֵאֶמְצַע וְנִשְׁתַּיְירוּ בּוֹ חָמֵשׁ גְּפָנִים מִכָּן וְחָמֵשׁ גְּפָנִים מִכָּן אִם יֵשׁ שָׁם

שְׁמוֹנֶה אַמּוֹת לֹא יָבִיא זֶרַע לְשָׁם. שְׁמוֹנֶה אַמּוֹת וְעוֹד נוֹתְנִין לוֹ עֲבוֹדָתוֹ וְזוֹרֵעַ
אֶת הַמּוֹתָר.

Mishnah 7: An interrupted trellis is more than eight cubits. No linear measurement stated by the Sages requires "more than" except an interrupted trellis. What is an interrupted trellis? A trellis [whose vines are] dried up in its middle, but there remained five vines on each side[51]. If between them are eight cubits, one should not sow there. If there are more than eight cubits, one gives each side its working space[52] and he may sow the rest.

51 One vine in the middle died. The original large trellis is now split into two small legal trellises.	52 The usual six hand-breadths around the trellises in each direction.

(fol. 30c) **הלכה ח**: לֵית הָדָא פְּלִיגָא עַל רִבִּי זְעִירָא. דְּרִבִּי זְעִירָא אָמַר שְׁמוֹנֶה חוּץ מִמְּקוֹם כָּרְתִּין. פָּתַר לָהּ שְׁמוֹנֶה אַמּוֹת וְכָל־שֶׁהוּא. וְלָמָּה לֹא תַנִיתָהּ וְלֹא תִיסְבּוֹר כְּהַהִיא דְּאָמַר רִבִּי יוֹחָנָן כָּל־מִידוֹת שֶׁאָמְרוּ חֲכָמִים וְעוֹד טֶפַח וְהֶן רִיבָה צִיבְחַר לְפוּם כֵּן לֹא תַנִיתָהּ.

Halakhah 5: Does this not disagree with Rebbi Zeïra since Rebbi Zeïra said[53], eight except for the place of the trunks? Explain that as eight cubits and a little more[54]. And why has this not been stated? Are you not concurring with Rebbi Joḥanan that in all linear measurements stated by the Sages, "more than" means [more by] a hand-breadth[55]? But what he added is little, therefore it was not stated.

53 Halakhah 4:8, speaking of the parallel rules for vineyards. 54 Less than a hand-breadth. As explained here, the minimal length of which formal congnizance is taken is a	hand-breadth, one sixth of a cubit; smaller distances are not enumerated in the Mishnah. If the Mishnah (*Eruvin* 1:3, *Ahilut* 12:6) states that the circumference of a circle of diameter 1

is 3 it means that $3 \leq \pi \leq {}^{19}/_6$ ($3 \leq \pi \leq {}^{16}/_5$).

55   The Tosephta (*Kilaim* 4:9) explains: כמה הוא ועוד אחד מששה טפחים באמה "How much is 'more than'? One of six hand-breadths per cubit." The correct interpretation has been given by R. S. Lieberman: In Tosephta *Kelim, Baba Meẓia'* 6:13, R. Meïr declares the cubits used in a vineyard to be cubits of five hand-breadths (cf. Chapter 5, Note 27). The Tosephta here redefines the hand-breadth to be added as one *new hand-breadth*, when 6 *new hand-breadths* are 5 common hand-breadths or one vine cubit. According to the Tosephta, "more than" means at least $^5/_6$ of a common cubit. This Tosephta text is in the manuscript and the *editio princeps*. R. Isaac Simponti, R. Simson and R. Abraham ben David read "one sixth of a cubit", leaving open the possibility that hand-breadth and cubit are the standard ones. Maimonides has another reading, "$^1/_{60}$ cubit", supported by *Caphtor Waperaḥ* and R. Bezalel Ashkenazi. However, as R. Abraham ben David points out, such a text would contradict the Yerushalmi here; the length added by R. Zeïra is certainly more than a tenth of a hand-breadth.

רְבִּי יוֹנָה בָּעֵי לָמָה לִי נָן אָמְרִין כָּל־מִידּוֹת שֶׁאָמְרוּ חֲכָמִים אֵין בָּהֶן וְעוֹד חוּץ מִפִּיסְקֵי עָרִיס. וְהָתַנִּינָן עֲשֶׂרֶת קַבִּין יְרוּשַׁלְמִיִּים שֶׁהֵן שִׁשָּׁה עֶשְׂרוֹנִין וְעֹדוּיָין. תַּמָּן לְמִידּוֹת וְכָאן לְאַמּוֹת. וְהָתַנִּינָן אָמַר רִבִּי יוֹסֵי בֶּן מְשׁוּלָם אוֹמֵר וְעוֹד קַב לְמֵאָה סְאָה שְׁתוּת לִמְדַּמֵּעַ. תַּמָּן לְמִידּוֹת וְכָאן לְאַמּוֹת. וְהָתַנִּינָן אָמַר רִבִּי יוּדָה בֶּן בָּבָא הַגִּינָה וְהַקַּרְפֵּף שֶׁהִיא שִׁבְעִים וְשִׁיֵרַיִם עַל שִׁבְעִים וְשִׁיֵרַיִם. שְׁמוּאֵל אָמַר בִּשְׁנֵי שְׁלִישֵׁי אַמָּה שָׁנוּ.

Rebbi Jonah asked: Why do we say: "No linear measurements stated by the Sages require 'more' except an interrupted trellis?" Did we not state[56]: "Ten Jerusalem *qab* which equal six *esronim* and excess"? There about volumes, here about linear measures. But did we not state[57]: "Rebbi Yose ben Meshullam said, 'more' is a *qab* per one hundred seah, a sixth of the amount that causes *dema*'"? There about volumes, here about linear measures. But did we not state[58]: "Rebbi Jehudah ben Baba said, the garden and the corral which are seventy and a remainder by seventy and a remainder"? Samuel said, they taught two thirds of a cubit[59].

56   Mishnah *Menaḥot* 7:2: "The flour sacrifice of a *Nazir* came in two parts, loaves and flatbreads, but no paste (from flour and oil). It turns out that these are 10 Jerusalem *qab* which equal six *esronim* and excess." Mishnah 7:1 had stated that the three kinds of bread for a thanksgiving sacrifice came from 10 *esronim* which were 15 Jerusalem *qab*. Hence, the breads of the *Nazir* are $6\frac{2}{3}$ *esronim*. The "excess" (in the Hebrew, an otherwise nonexisting plural of "more") is $\frac{2}{3}$ *issaron*. We use the expression "more" in a domain other than vineyards.

57   Mishnah *Terumot* 4:7:   "R. Eliezer says, heave can be lifted by one in 101. Rebbi Joshua says, by one in more than 100; that 'more' has no measure. Rebbi Yose ben Meshullam said, 'more' is a *qab* per one hundred seah, a sixth of the amount that causes *demaʿ*". *Demaʿ*, the mixture of profane food and heave, was discussed in *Demay*, Chapter 4, Note 27.   If the amount of heave is small, it is possible to remove an amount equal to the heave and transfer the holiness to that food; the remainder of the food then returns to profane status. R. Eliezer states that in this respect "small" means at most 1 in 100 (1 part heave in 101 overall). R. Joshua requires that the amount be at most 1 in $99+\varepsilon$; $\varepsilon>0$ being arbitrarily small. R. Yose ben Meshullam requires that the amount of heave be at most 1 in $99.166\overline{6}$; if the amount of heave is one *seah*, the amount of profane grain has to be 99 *seah* plus one sixth of the amount causing the trouble, i. e., $99^1/_6$ *seah*. [In Babli *Eruvin* 83a, "and more" is defined as one twentyfourth of the volume of an egg.]

58   Mishnah *Eruvin* 2:5:   "Additionally, R. Jehudah ben Baba said, one may carry (on the Sabbath) in a garden or a corral which measure seventy and a remainder by seventy and a remainder and are enclosed by a fence ten hand-breadths high on condition that they contain a watchman's place." On the Sabbath, one may carry his utensils in his house and in any enclosed space containing a human dwelling. Enclosed spaces no part of which is used as a human dwelling, such as vegetable plots and corrals, are accepted as private domain only if their surface area is not more that 5000 square cubits, the surface area of the enclosed space of the tabernacle (cf. *Peah* Chapter 2, Note 31). Since $\sqrt{5000}$ = 70.71068, R. Jehudah ben Baba's remainder is 0.71068 cubits, a linear measure.

59   Samuel notes that for non-mathematicians the domain is limited

to 70 cubits 4 hand-breadths square, 70.66̄6 cubits square. The excess over 70 is a genuine remainder, less than one cubit, but it is not a "more" which by definition can be at most one hand-breadth, the smallest unit of length accepted in these tractates of the Mishnah.

וְלָא שַׁנְיָא בֵּין שֶׁבָּנָה גֶדֶר וְאַחַר כָּךְ נָטַע אַחַת עֶשְׂרֵה גְפָנִים בֵּין שֶׁנָּטַע אַחַת עֶשְׂרֵה גְפָנִים וְאַחַר כָּךְ בָּנָה גֶדֶר וְאַחַר כָּךְ נִפְסְקָה הָאֶמְצָעִית יֵשׁ כָּאן עָרִיס וְיֵשׁ כָּאן פִּיסְקֵי עָרִיס. חָרֵב הַגֶדֶר אֵין כָּאן עָרִיס וְלֹא פִּיסְקֵי עָרִיס. רַבִּי אֶבְדּוּמֵי אֲחוּנָה דְּרַבִּי יוֹסֵי בָּעֵי חָזַר וּבְנָייָה אַתְּ אָמַר חָזַר עָרִיס לִמְקוֹמוֹ וְדִכְוָתָהּ חָזְרוּ פִּיסְקֵי עָרִיס לִמְקוֹמָן.

There is no difference whether one built a fence and then planted eleven vines or he planted eleven vines and then built a fence[60]. If the middle vine is destroyed we have trellis and interrupted trellis[61]. If the fence is destroyed, there is no trellis and no interrupted trellis. Rebbi Eudaimon, brother of Rebbi Yose, inquired: If he then rebuilt the fence, since the trellis was reconstituted, do you say that the interrupted trellis also was reconstituted[62]?

60   Cf. Note 1 for a discussion of the role of the fence.

61   There now are two legal trellises that form one interrupted trellis.

62   Since growing other crops in a vineyard is a potential transgression of a biblical prohibition, in doubt one has to take the more severe position. The absence of an answer therefore implies a positive answer.

רַבִּי יוֹסֵי בְּשֵׁם רַבִּי יוֹחָנָן מַעֲשֶׂה שֶׁשָּׂרַף רַבִּי יוֹחָנָן בֶּן נוּרִי בְּנַגְנֵיגָר. מַה שָׂרַף פִּיסְקֵי עָרִיס שָׂרַף. רַבִּי חִייָא בְּשֵׁם רַבִּי יוֹחָנָן מַעֲשֶׂה שֶׁשָּׂרַף רַבִּי יוֹחָנָן בֶּן נוּרִי בְּנַגְנֵיגָר. מַה שָׂרַף בֵּין עָרִיס לַגֶדֶר שָׂרַף. אָמַר רַבִּי יוֹסֵי קַשִׁייָתָהּ קוֹמֵי רַבִּי יַעֲקֹב בַּר אָחָא נִיחָא פִּיסְקֵי עָרִיס שָׂרַף דִּבְרֵי חֲכָמִים חֲלוּקִין עָלָיו. בֵּין עָרִיס לַגֶדֶר שָׂרַף דִּבְרֵי חֲכָמִים חֲלוּקִין עָלָיו. וְלָא שְׁמִיעַ דְּאָמַר רַבִּי יַעֲקֹב בַּר אָחָא

אִיתְפַּלְגוּן רִבִּי יוֹחָנָן וְרִבִּי שִׁמְעוֹן בֶּן לָקִישׁ עָרִיס עַצְמוֹ מַהוּ רִבִּי יוֹחָנָן אָמַר
אָסוּר וּמְקַדֵּשׁ. רִבִּי שִׁמְעוֹן בֶּן לָקִישׁ אָמַר אָסוּר וְאֵינוֹ מְקַדֵּשׁ.

Rebbi Yose in the name of Rebbi Johanan: Once Rebbi Johanan ben Nuri burned in Nagnegar[63]. What did he burn? He burned an interrupted trellis[64]. Rebbi Ḥiyya in the name of Rebbi Johanan: Once Rebbi Johanan ben Nuri burned in Nagnegar. What did he burn? He burned between the trellis and the fence. Rebbi Yose said, I pointed out a difficulty before Rebbi Jacob bar Aḥa: It is understandable, if he burned an interrupted trellis then the words of the Sages disagree with his[65]. But if he burned between the trellis and the fence, are there words of the Sages which disagree with his? He had not heard what Rebbi Jacob bar Aḥa said: Rebbi Johanan and Rebbi Simeon ben Laqish disagree about the trellis itself: Rebbi Johanan said, it is forbidden and sanctifies. Rebbi Simeon ben Laqish said, it is forbidden but does not sanctify[66].

63   Cf. Chapter 4, Note 58.
64   He considered the growth illegal and sanctified; therefore, he destroyed it by burning. Since this is recorded as a memorable event, it cannot be accepted as common practice; one does not make a statement every time an accepted law has been executed.
65   The majority follows Mishnah 7:3 that the prohibition of an interrupted trellis is rabbinical, not biblical. A crop growing there does not sanctify and should not be burned.
66   According to R. Johanan, five vines on a trellis form a vineyard in the biblical sense; according to R. Simeon ben Laqish there is never a vineyard in the biblical sense unless it contains at least two parallel rows.

וְהוּא שֶׁיְּהֵא בְּקֶרֶן זָוִית אַרְבָּעָה טְפָחִים כְּדֵי מָקוֹם.

All this applies if in the corner there are four hand-breadths of empty space[67].

67   The Mishnah is valid only if between any vine and any fence there are at least four hand-breadths of empty space; otherwise, six hand-breadths are forbidden around every vine, cf. Mishnah 5:4.

(fol. 30b) **משנה ח:** עָרִיס שֶׁהוּא יוֹצֵא מִן הַכּוֹתֶל מִתּוֹךְ קֶרֶן וְכָלָה. נוֹתְנִין לוֹ עֲבוֹדָתוֹ וְזוֹרֵעַ אֶת הַמּוֹתָר. רַבִּי יוֹסֵה אָמַר אִם אֵין שָׁם אַרְבַּע אַמּוֹת לֹא יָבִיא זֶרַע לְשָׁם. הַקָּנִים הַיּוֹצְאִין מִן הֶעָרִיס חָס עֲלֵיהֶן לְפָסְקָן כְּנֶגְדָּן מוּתָּר. עֲשָׂאָן כְּדֵי שֶׁיְּהַלֵּךְ בָּהֶן הֶחָדָשׁ אָסוּר.

Mishnah 8: A trellis which starts from a wall in a corner and ends there[68], one gives it its working space and he may sow the rest. Rebbi Yose said, if there are less than four cubits one should not bring seeds there[69]. Sticks that stand out from the trellis, if he worries whether to remove them[70], then under them it is permitted, but if he made them so that the new growth can expand on them, it is forbidden.

68   According to Maimonides, the trellis itself is built parallel to the walls, forming an angle. According to R. Simson (and apparently R. Abraham ben David), the five vines are in a straight line from one wall to the other, forming the base of a right triangle of which parts of the two walls form the legs. Then six hand-breadths from the base in the triangle are forbidden, the remainder may be sown even if the altitude of the triangle is less than four cubits.

69   Cf. Mishnah 5:4, Note 56.

70   The trellis has irregular cross beams. If he would like to cut them to one size but for some reason (e. g., not to touch a shaky trellis) does not do it, the excess width does not interfere with sowing. But if he intends to use the beams to support extending branches and leaves then they are part of the trellis and forbidden.

(fol. 30c) **הלכה ו**: תַּנִּינָן הָכָא רִבִּי יוֹסֵי וְתַנִּינָתָהּ תַּמָּן. אִילּוּ תַנִּינָתָהּ הָכָא וְלֹא

תַנִּינָתָהּ תַּמָּן הֲוֵינָן אֲמָרִין הָכָא עַל יְדֵי שֶׁהִיא הִלְכַת עָרִיס אַתְּ אָמַר אָסוּר תַּמָּן

עַל יְדֵי שֶׁאֵינוּ הִלְכַת עָרִיס אַתְּ אָמַר מוּתָּר. הֲוֵי צוּרְכָה מַתְנֵי תַּמָּן. אוֹ אִילּוּ

תַנִּינָתָהּ תַּמָּן וְלֹא תַנִּיתָהּ הָכָא הֲוֵינָן אֲמָרִין תַּמָּן עַל יְדֵי שֶׁהוּא מְגוּפָף מֵאַרְבַּע

רוּחוֹתָיו אַתְּ אָמַר אָסוּר הָכָא עַל יְדֵי שֶׁאֵינוּ מְגוּפָף מֵאַרְבַּע רוּחוֹית אַתְּ אָמַר

מוּתָּר. הֲוֵי צוּרְכָה מַתְנִיָּא הָכָא וְצוּרְכָה מַתְנִיָּא תַּמָּן.

Halakhah 6: We stated here the opinion of Rebbi Yose and stated it there[71]. If we had stated it here but not there, we would have said he says it is forbidden here because of the laws of the trellis, but there where one does not deal with the laws of the trellis he would say it is permitted. Hence, it is necessary to state it there. Or if we had stated it there but not here, we would have said there he says it is forbidden because it is enclosed on all four sides, but here where it is not enclosed on all four sides he would say it is permitted. Hence, it is necessary to state it both here and there.

71 Mishnah 5:4. True duplicate statements are not admitted in the Mishnah (except in collections of stated historical character, e. g., Tractate Idiut.) Therefore, if a duplicate statement does occur, one has to find reasons to explain the necessity of the duplication.

(fol. 30b) **משנה ט**: הַפֶּרַח הַיּוֹצֵא מִן הֶעָרִיס רוֹאִין אוֹתוֹ כִּילוּ מְטוּטֶלֶת תְּלוּיָה

בּוֹ כְּנֶגְדּוֹ אָסוּר. וְכֵן בְּדָלִית. הַמּוֹתֵחַ זְמוֹרָה מֵאִילָן לְאִילָן תַּחְתֶּיהָ אָסוּר.

סִיפְּקָהּ בְּחֶבֶל אוֹ בְּגָמֵי תַּחַת הַסִּיפּוּק מוּתָּר. עֲשָׂאוֹ כְּדֵי שֶׁיְהַלֵּךְ עָלָיו הֶחָדָשׁ

אָסוּר.

Mishnah 9: One looks at a blossom that comes out from the trellis as if a plumb-line were hanging down from it; under it it is forbidden[72]. The same holds for a branch[73]. Under a shoot of vine drawn from one tree to another, it is forbidden[74]. If he binds them together with a rope or bast, under the binding it is permitted[75]. But if he did that to accomodate future growth, it is forbidden.

72   Any growth expanding over the sides of the trellis extends the area under which nothing can be sown (plus its six hand-breadths of working space).

73   A branch of a single vine. The forbidden space is the interior of the parallel figure in distance 6 of the orthogonal projection of the entire vine into the ground.

74   Naturally plus six hand-breadths

on each side.

75   The vine is not long enough to reach from one tree to the next; the vintner tied a rope around the end of the shoot and the tree. Then the rope is not a vine and not subject to the laws of *kilaim*. But if the rope was drawn to support future growth of the vine or other shoots that will appear in the growing season, it becomes subject to the laws of vines.

(fol. 30c) **הלכה ז:** תַּמָּן אָמַר אַתְּ רוֹאֶה כִּילוּ שְׁפוּד שֶׁל מַתֶּכֶת תָּחוּב בּוֹ. שִׁמְעוֹן בַּר בָּא בְּשֵׁם רִבִּי יוֹחָנָן עַד מָקוֹם שֶׁהוּא נִקְמָן.

רִבִּי חָמָא בַּר עוּקְבָּא בְּשֵׁם רִבִּי יוֹסֵי בֶּן חֲנִינָא תַּחַת הָאֶשְׁכּוֹלוֹת אָסוּר וּמְקַדֵּשׁ תַּחַת הֶעָלִין לֹא. אָמַר רִבִּי יוֹסֵי אֲפִילוּ תַּחַת הֶעָלִין אָסוּר וּמְקַדֵּשׁ.

Halakhah 7: There[76] one says, one considers as if a metal spit was stuck there. Simeon bar Abba in the name of Rebbi Joḥanan: As far as was intended[77].

Rebbi Ḥama bar Uqba[78] in the name of Rebbi Yose ben Ḥanina: Under the grapes it is forbidden and sanctifies but not under the leaves. Rebbi Yose said, even under the leaves it is forbidden and sanctifies[79].

81   In Babylonia.

82   The translation is tentative. Medieval authors do not comment on

this sentence. R. Eliahu Fulda and almost everybody else identify נקמן with נקמז "shrunk". R. Eliahu Wilna explains as "bent". These explanations have no basis and make little sense. I am taking קמן in the sense of Arabic "to intend". Then this paragraph belongs to the preceding Halakhah: Under an irregular trellis, the width is forbidden as far as the vintner intended to let the vines grow. At the end of this space, it is as if a metal spit subtended the bars; the wood sticking out farther is not counted.

83   Galilean Amora of the third generation. He quotes R. Simeon ben Laqish and is reported as teacher of R. Yasa (Assi).

84   Vine leaves are also a commercial crop.

המבריך פרק שביעי

(fol. 30d) **משנה א**: הַמַּבְרִיךְ אֶת הַגֶּפֶן בָּאָרֶץ אִם אֵין עָפָר עַל גַּבָּהּ שְׁלֹשָׁה טְפָחִים לֹא יָבִיא זֶרַע עָלֶיהָ אֲפִילוּ הִבְרִיכָהּ בִּדְלַעַת אוֹ בְסִילוֹן. הִבְרִיכָהּ בְּסֶלַע אַף עַל פִּי שֶׁאֵין עָפָר עַל גַּבָּהּ אֶלָּא שָׁלֹשׁ אֶצְבָּעוֹת מוּתָּר לְהָבִיא זֶרַע עָלֶיהָ. הָאַרְכּוּבָה שֶׁבְּגֶפֶן אֵין מוֹדְדִין אֶלָּא מֵעִיקַר הַשֵּׁנִי.

Mishnah 1: If one sinks[1] a vine into the ground he should not bring seeds over it unless there are three hand-breadths of earth above it, even if he sank it in a gourd[2] or in a pipe[3]. If he sank it in a rock[4] it is permitted to bring seeds there even if it is covered only by three fingers'[5] depth of earth. For a knee-shaped vine one measures only from the second stem[6].

1 He takes a branch of a vine, bends it down into a ditch, covers the ditch with earth, and lets it come out again. Then the branch will grow roots in the earth and one has a new vine.

2 A dried-up gourd used as ditch.

3 A wooden or clay pipe.

4 It cannot really be a rock but must be ground hard as rock.

5 A finger is one fourth of a hand-breadth.

6 If a vine is bent back while growing and enters the ground again in a kind of natural sinking, the six hand-breadths for its working space are measured only from the point where it reappears above ground. (R. Simson explains: "a grafted vine" but this does not fit either language or context.)

הלכה א: לֹא יָבִיא זֶרַע עָלֶיהָ הָא מִן הַצַּד מוּתָּר. מַה נָן קַיְימִין אִי מִשּׁוּם זְרָעִים בְּאִילָן לָמָּה לִי גֶּפֶן אֲפִילוּ שְׁאָר כָּל־הָאִילָן. אִי מִשּׁוּם עֲבוֹדָה נִיתְנוּ שִׁשָּׁה. אֶלָּא כְּרַבִּי עֲקִיבָה דְּרִבִּי עֲקִיבָה אָמַר שְׁלֹשָׁה. אִי כְּרַבִּי עֲקִיבָה אֲפִילוּ מִן

הַצַּד נִיתְּנוּ שְׁלֹשָׁה. רִבִּי יִרְמְיָה בְּשֵׁם רִבִּי חִייָא בַּר אַבָּא מִשֵׁם זְרָעִים עַל גַּבֵּי הַגֶּפֶן.

Halakhah 1: "He should not bring seeds over it," therefore it is permitted on the side[7]. What are we dealing with? If it is because of seeds in a tree, why are we dealing with a vine and not any tree? If it is because of working space, they should mention six[8]. It might follow Rebbi Aqiba since Rebbi Aqiba says three. If it were following Rebbi Aqiba, it should mention three on the side. Rebbi Jeremiah in the name of Rebbi Ḥiyya bar Abba: It is because of seeds on top of a vine[9].

<table>
<tr>
<td>

7   In the Babli, *Baba Batra* 19b, this is stated as a *baraita*.

8   The Mishnah should state that six hand-breadths on each side of the buried shoot are forbidden as working

</td>
<td>

space, or at least three handbreadths following Rebbi Aqiba (Mishnah 6:1).

9   This confirms the original statement that the only forbidden space is on top of the buried shoot.

</td>
</tr>
</table>

תַּמָּן תַּנִּינָן מַרְחִיקִין אֶת הַזְּרָעִים וְאֶת הַמַּחֲרֵישָׁה וְאֶת מֵי רַגְלַיִם מִן הַכּוֹתֶל שְׁלֹשָׁה טְפָחִים. רִבִּי יִרְמְיָה אָמַר רִבִּי חָמָא בַּר עוּקְבָּא מַקְשֵׁי תַּמָּן אַתְּ אָמַר אֵין הַשָּׁרָשִׁים מְהַלְּכִין מִן הַצַּד. וְהָכָא אַתְּ אָמַר הַשָּׁרָשִׁים מְהַלְּכִין מִן הַצַּד. אָמַר רִבִּי יוֹסֵי כָּאן וְכָאן אֵין הַשָּׁרָשִׁים מְהַלְּכִין מִן הַצַּד. אֶלָּא שֶׁהֵן עוֹשִׂין עָפָר תְּחוּחַ וְהֵן מַלְקִין אַרְעִיתוֹ שֶׁל כּוֹתֶל. תֵּדַע לָךְ שֶׁהוּא כֵן דְּתַנִּינָן תַּמָּן מֵי רַגְלַיִם. וּמֵי רַגְלַיִם מְהַלְּכִין מִן הַצַּד. הָתִיב רִבִּי יוֹסֵי בֵּי רִבִּי בּוּן וְקָתַנִּינָן מַחֲרֵישָׁה. אִית לָךְ מֵימַר מַחֲרֵישָׁה מְהַלֶּכֶת מִן הַצַּד.

There[10], we have stated: "One keeps seeds, the plough, and urine three hand-breadths away from a wall." Rebbi Jeremiah said that Rebbi Ḥama bar Uqba raised a question: There[11], you say that the roots do not expand sideways and here you say, the roots do expand sideways! Rebbi Yose said, in both cases the roots do not expand sideways but they create soft earth and undermine the base of the wall[12]. You can see that because we also stated "urine". Does urine expand sideways? Rebbi Yose the son of Rebbi Abun explained, did we not also state "the plough"? Does the plough expand sideways?

10   Mishnah *Baba Batra* 2:1. The adobe wall is either common property of the landlord and his neighbor or totally the neighbor's; the landlord is required to take all necessary precautions to avoid damage to his fellow man's property.

11   "There" means *Kilaim* and "here" refers to *Baba Batra*. It is possible that this paragraph is copied here from a Tiberian version of *Baba Batra* that has not come down to us. In the transmitted Caesarean version of *Baba Batra* (2:1, fol. 13b), the statement of R. Yose refers to the prohibition of storing salt or quick lime near somebody else's wall. R. Simson reads "here" for "there" but it is not clear whether this is a genuine reading or an adaptation for the purposes of his commentary.

The argument is that crop plants are allowed to be grown near a buried vine; their roots are not supposed to expand over the buried shoot, but since they are not allowed to be grown near a wall, one expects their roots to expand sideways and damage the wall.

12   In Babli *Baba Batra* 19b, the printed editions quote the statement of R. Yose as "R. Ḥaga in the name of R. Yose." This version is impossible since R. Ḥaga (Ḥaggai) was older than R. Yose and a greater authority in his lifetime. One has to prefer the reading of all mss. (*Diqduqe Soferim Baba Bathra* p. מה) "R. Ḥana". In that case, "R. Yose" would probably be R. Yasa (Assi).

אֲפִילוּ הִבְרִיכָהּ בִּדְלַעַת אוֹ בְסִילוֹן. הָדָא דְתֵימָא בְּסִילוֹן שֶׁל חֶרֶס אֲבָל בְּסִילוֹן שֶׁל אֲבָר אֵינוֹ צָרִיךְ עַד שֶׁיְּהֵא שָׁם שְׁלֹשָׁה טְפָחִים עָפָר מִלְּמַעְלָן.

"Even if he sank it in a gourd or in a pipe." That means, in a clay pipe; but in a lead pipe it does not need three hand-breadths of earth on top.

הִבְרִיכָהּ בְּסֶלַע הָדָא דְתֵימָא בְּהָדֵין צַלְמָא אֲבָל בְּהָדֵין רְכִיכָא מִתְפַּתְּפֵת הוּא.

"If he sank it in a rock." That means, in hard [earth], but in soft [earth] it cleaves[13] it.

13   R. Simson reads מתפחחת "it [the root] can develop".

וְהַאי כְּשֶׁאֵין הָרִאשׁוֹן נִרְאֵית אֲבָל אִם הָיָה הָרִאשׁוֹן נִרְאֶה נוֹתֵן שִׁשָּׁה טְפָחִים
לְכָאן וְשִׁשָּׁה טְפָחִים לְכָאן.   תֵּדַע לָךְ שֶׁהוּא כֵן דְּתַנִינָן דְּבַתְרָהּ הַמַּבְרִיךְ שְׁלֹשָׁה
גְּפָנִים וְעִיקְּרֵיהֶן נִרְאִין וְתַגֵּי עֲלָהּ בַּמֶּה דְּבָרִים אֲמוּרִים לְעִנְיַין הַכָּרֶם אֲבָל
לְעִנְיַין עֲבוֹדָה נוֹתֵן שִׁשָּׁה טְפָחִים לְכָאן וְשִׁשָּׁה טְפָחִים לְכָאן.

That is[14] only if the first stem is not visible, but if the first stem is visible one allows six hand-breadths from either stem. You can see that because we also stated afterwards[15]: "If one sinks three vines and their stems are visible," and we have stated on this: When has this been said? For a vineyard[16]. But concerning the working space one allows six hand-breadths for either one.

14   Here starts the discussion of the last part of the Mishnah, regarding the knee-shaped vine.

15   Mishnah 7:2.

16   Regarding the conditions under which three vines can be extended to form a legal vineyard. If they are too close to or too far from one another, each one of the six vines so created is given its own working space.

משנה ב: הַמַּבְרִיךְ שְׁלֹשָׁה גְּפָנִים וְעִיקְּרֵיהֶן נִרְאִין. רַבִּי לָעֶזֶר בִּירַבִּי צָדוֹק אוֹמֵר
אִם יֵשׁ שָׁם בֵּינֵיהֶן מֵאַרְבַּע אַמּוֹת וְעַד שְׁמוֹנֶה הֲרֵי אֵלּוּ מִצְטָרְפוֹת וְאִם לָאו
אֵינָן מִצְטָרְפוֹת.   גֶּפֶן שֶׁיָּבְשָׁה אֲסוּרָה וְאֵינָהּ מְקַדֶּשֶׁת. רַבִּי מֵאִיר אוֹמֵר אַף גֶּפֶן
צֶמֶר[17] אָסוּר וְאֵינוֹ מְקַדֵּשׁ. רַבִּי אֶלְעָזָר בַּר רַבִּי צָדוֹק אוֹמֵר מִשְּׁמוֹ אַף עַל גַּבֵּי
הַגֶּפֶן אָסוּר וְאֵינוֹ מְקַדֵּשׁ.

If one sinks three vines and their stems are visible, Rebbi Eleazar bar Rebbi Zadoq says if there are between them from four to eight cubits, they go together; otherwise, they do not go together[18]. A dried-up vine is forbidden but does not sanctify[19]. Rebbi Meïr says, cotton also is forbidden but does not sanctify. Rebbi Eleazar bar Rebbi Zadoq says in his name[20], even on top of the vine it is forbidden[21] but does not sanctify.

17   Reading of the Genizah fragment and R. Eliahu Fulda. The other texts have צמר גפן, the Babylonian term for cotton. Since the plant is called "vine" it must be a potentially perennial plant from the family of Malvaceas, cotton, a linden-tree grown for its bast, or jute from a kind of *Corchorus*.

18   If one has three vines in a row and sinks a shoot from each one to get another row of three vines, if the distance between the rows and between the vines in one row is between four and eight cubits then one has a legal vineyard since five of the six vines would be enough (Halakhah 4:6). If the distances are too small, one has six single vines.

19   If one sows within six handbreadths from a dead vine it does not sanctify.

20   In R. Meïr's name. This attribution is missing in the Genizah ms., probably correctly; cf. Note 23.

21   The meaning of this sentence will be clarified in the Halakhah.

הלכה ב: אָמַר רִבִּי לֶעְזָר הֲלָכָה[22] דְּרִבִּי מֵאִיר הִיא.

Halakhah 2: Rebbi Eleazar said, the Mishnah is Rebbi Meïr's[23].

22   This word is missing in the Rome ms.

23   The Halakhah discusses only the second part of the Mishnah, listing the plants near which it is forbidden to sow but which do not sanctify. Since part of the Mishnah is attributed to R. Meïr, all of it belongs to R. Meïr. The statement makes more sense if the Mishnah follows the reading of the Genizah text, Note 20.

נִיחָא בְּסִיתְוָא אֲבָל בְּקַיְיטָא. אִית אֲתָרִין דְּמַתָּרָן טַרְפֵּיהוֹן אֲפִילוּ בְּקַיְיטָא.

One understands in winter[24], but in summer? There are places where they lose their leaves even in summer.

24   This refers to the statement that it is forbidden to sow next to a dead vine. The only reason for such a rule is bad appearance, that passers-by will not notice that the vine is dead and will think that the farmer sows forbidden seeds. One understands that this is a concern in late fall and early winter, after the old leaves have been shed and the new ones did not grow yet, but in summer when the leaves cover the ripening grapes there should be no problem. The answer is that there is a problem with varieties whose grapes ripen in June and will have lost their leaves by mid-July.

רִבִּי שְׁמוּאֵל בְּשֶׁם רִבִּי זְעִירָא עַל גַּבֵּי זְמוֹרָה הִיא מַתְנִיתָא. רִבִּי בּוּן בַּר חִייָא בְּשֶׁם רִבִּי שְׁמוּאֵל בַּר רַב יִצְחָק לַאֲוֵיר עֲשָׂרָה הִיא מַתְנִיתָא. אָמַר רִבִּי יוֹסֵי הֲוֵינָן סָבְרִין כֶּרֶם יֶשׁ לוֹ אֲוֵיר גֶּפֶן יְחִידִית אֵין לָהּ אֲוֵיר. מִן מַה דְּאָמַר רִבִּי בּוּן בַּר חִייָא בְּשֶׁם רִבִּי שְׁמוּאֵל בַּר רַב יִצְחָק לַאֲוֵיר עֲשָׂרָה הִיא מַתְנִיתָא. הָדָא אָמְרָה אֲפִילוּ גֶּפֶן יְחִידִית יֶשׁ לָהּ אֲוֵיר.

Rebbi Samuel in the name of Rebbi Zeïra: The Mishnah speaks of the space above the shoot[25]. Rebbi Abun bar Ḥiyya in the name of Rebbi Samuel bar Rav Isaac: The Mishnah speaks about the air space of ten[26]. Rebbi Yose said, we were of the opinion that a vineyard has air space; a single vine has no air space. Since Rebbi Abun bar Ḥiyya said in the name of Rebbi Samuel bar Rav Isaac: The Mishnah speaks about the air space of ten, that means that even a single vine has air space.

25   This refers to the last sentence in the Mishnah, "even on top of the vine it is forbidden but does not sanctify." Rebbi Zeïra refers this to the shoot of vine sunk under less than three hand-breadths of earth.

26   If the vines are on a terraced hill and the next terrace is at least ten hand-breadths higher, the wall of the terrace terminates the working space (for vineyard or single vine); planting inside six hand-breadths or four cubits, as the case may be, is forbidden but does not sanctify if the vertical distance is at least ten hand-breadths. {R. Simson thinks that one speaks about plants in flower pots hanging over the vines; Maimonides might agree with this interpretation.}

משנה ג: אֵלוּ אֲסוּרִין וְלֹא מְקַדְּשִׁין מוֹתָר חָרְבַּן הַכֶּרֶם מוֹתָר מָחוֹל הַכֶּרֶם מוֹתָר פִּיסְקֵי עָרִיס מוֹתָר אַפִּיפִירוֹת. אֲבָל תַּחַת גֶּפֶן וַעֲבוֹדַת הַגֶּפֶן וְאַרְבַּע אַמּוֹת שֶׁבְּכֶרֶם הֲרֵי אֵילוּ מְקַדְּשִׁין.

Mishnah 3: The following are forbidden but do not sanctify: The excess of a dried-up vineyard[27], the excess of the circumference of a vineyard[28], the excess of an interrupted trellis[29], and the excess of a papyrus[30]. But under a vine, the working space of a vine, and the four cubits of a vineyard do sanctify.

27   By Mishnah 4:1, if a vineyard dried up in the middle, a space of 16 cubits square cannot be sown. But only four cubits on each side are needed for working the vineyard. If the dried-up space contains a square of sides 16-ε, the inner (8-ε)-by-(8-ε) space cannot be worked on as a rabbinic, rather than a biblical prohibition. Working that inner space is forbidden but a transgression does not sanctify either growth or vineyard.

28   By Mishnah 4:2, 12 cubits have to be left empty between a vineyard whose outer rows have died and the fence. Again, if there are 12-ε cubits, of these only four are biblical, the remaining 8-ε have rabbinic status only.

29   Since the constituent parts of an interrupted trellis do not form vineyards by themselves, of the eight cubits between the inner vines only one cubit on each side (six hand-breadths) will sanctify, the remaining six cubits represent rabbinic prohibition.

30   If vines that do not form a vineyard are drawn over papyrus, only the space under any part of any vine is biblically forbidden; the rest is a rabbinic prohibition (Halakhah 6:3).

הלכה ג: מוֹתָר מָחוֹל הַכֶּרֶם אַרְבַּע אַמּוֹת מוֹתָר חָרְבַּן הַכֶּרֶם אַרְבַּע אַמּוֹת מוֹתָר פִּיסְקֵי עָרִיס שִׁשָּׁה טְפָחִים מוֹתָר הַפִּיפְיָירוֹת שִׁשָּׁה טְפָחִים.

Halakhah 3: The excess of the circumference of a vineyard is four cubits[31], the excess of a dried-up vineyard is four cubits, the excess of an interrupted trellis is six hand-breadths, and the excess of papyrus is six hand-breadths.

31   The language is elliptic: The
excess of the circumference of a
vineyard is defined as excess of the
distance over and above 4 cubits, as

explained in the Notes to the Mishnah.
The other statements have a
corresponding interpretation.

בֵּינְתַּיִם מַהוּ. רִבִּי יוֹחָנָן אָמַר אָסוּר וּמְקַדֵּשׁ. רִבִּי שִׁמְעוֹן בֶּן לָקִישׁ אָמַר אָסוּר
וְאֵינוּ מְקַדֵּשׁ. מַה נַפְשֶׁךְ כֶּרֶם גָּדוֹל הוּא לָמָּה לִי חָרְבָּנוּ אֲפִילוּ מַטָּעָתוֹ. כֶּרֶם
קָטָן הוּא אֵין לוֹ מָחוֹל. אֶלָּא כִּי נָן קַיָּמִין בְּכֶרֶם גָּדוֹל שֶׁנְּטָעוֹ עַל מַטַּע כֶּרֶם
קָטָן. אָמַר רִבִּי זְעִירָא הָדָא אָמְרָה כֶּרֶם גָּדוֹל שֶׁנְּטָעוֹ שְׁמוֹנָה עַל שְׁמוֹנָה אֵין לוֹ
מָחוֹל. אִין תֵּימַר מַטַּע שֵׁשׁ עֶשְׂרֵה עַל שֵׁשׁ עֶשְׂרֵה תּוֹכוֹ אָסוּר וּמְקַדֵּשׁ חוּצָה לוֹ
לֹא כָּל־שֶׁכֵּן.

What is the status of the intermediate spaces[32]? Rebbi Joḥanan said,
they are forbidden and sanctify. Rebbi Simeon ben Laqish said, they are
forbidden and do not sanctify. What can you say[33]? If it is a large
vineyard, what about its dry spot, even where it is planted[34]! If it is a
small vineyard, it has no circumference[35]. But we must deal with a large
vineyard planted in the manner of a small one[36]. Rebbi Zeïra said, this
implies that a large vineyard planted eight by eight has no
circumference[37]. If you say that the inside is forbidden and sanctifies if it
is planted 16 by 16, the outside not so much more[38]?

32   This refers to Mishnaiot 4:8-9,
that if a vineyard is planted in such a
way that the distance from one vine to
the next in both directions is more than
eight but less than 16 cubits, one may
not sow there. This situation really
should have been dealt with in our
Mishnah since in that configuration
there are points distant more than four
cubits from any vine. Since it is not

mentioned in our Mishnah, R. Joḥanan
concludes that sowing there must
sanctify. [The explanation of this
paragraph follows an idea of R. Eliahu
Wilna who, however, feels compelled
to rewrite the text.]

33   Here follows the argument of R.
Joḥanan against R. Simeon ben Laqish.

34   Since for R. Simeon ben Laqish
any spot distant more than eight but

less than 16 cubits is forbidden but does not sanctify, why does the Mishnah speak about a dry spot?

35   Chapter 4, Note 37. The Mishnah cannot speak about a "small" vineyard.

36   The distances from one vine to the other and between two rows of vines are at least four but definitely less than eight cubits. In that case, the objections do not apply.

37   Since the Mishnah declares that outside of eight it does not sanctify; dried-up vines cannot make the situation worse.

38   This is R. Simeon ben Laqish's argument against all the preceding. If inside it sanctifies up to 16 cubits there would be no reason to require only 12 on the outside.

אָמַר רְבִּי יוֹסֵי אֵין לוֹקִין אֶלָּא עַל עִיקַר הַכֶּרֶם.

Rebbi Yose said, one whips only for the main vineyard[39].

39   Even though the Mishnah establishes the cases in which the new growth sanctifies, the biblical commandment that can be enforced by the criminal court only refers to grain sown in a vineyard.

משנה ד: הַמְסַכֵּךְ אֶת גַּפְנוֹ עַל גַּבֵּי תְבוּאָתוֹ שֶׁל חֲבֵירוֹ הֲרֵי זֶה קִידֵּשׁ וְחַיָּיב בְּאַחֲרָיוּתוֹ. רְבִּי יוֹסֵי וְרְבִּי שִׁמְעוֹן אוֹמְרִים אֵין אָדָם מַקְדִּישׁ דָּבָר שֶׁאֵינוֹ שֶׁלּוֹ.

משנה ה: אָמַר רְבִּי יוֹסֵי מַעֲשֶׂה בְּאֶחָד שֶׁזָּרַע אֶת כַּרְמוֹ בַּשְּׁבִיעִית וּבָא מַעֲשֶׂה לִפְנֵי רְבִּי עֲקִיבָה וְאָמַר אֵין אָדָם מַקְדִּישׁ דָּבָר שֶׁאֵינוֹ שֶׁלּוֹ.

Mishnah 4: If somebody draws his vine over somebody else's grain it sanctifies and he is responsible for its alienation[40]. Rebbi Yose and Rebbi Simeon say, nobody can sanctify anything that is not his.

Mishnah 5: Rebbi Yose said, it happened that someone sowed in his vineyard in the Sabbatical year[41]. When this came before Rebbi Aqiba, he said nobody can sanctify anything that is not his.

40   The neighbor's grain has to be
burned but the neighbor has a claim
enforceable in court against the of-
fender. This position of the anonymous
Tanna is accepted as practice in Babli
Menahot 15b.

41   While the farmer remains the
owner of the land in the Sabbatical

year, the yield of that year is common
property of all people. That means
that while the vines remain private
property (except for the grapes
hanging on them), the grain never was
the private property of the person
sowing it.

הלכה ד: כְּתִיב לֹא תִזְרַע כַּרְמְךָ כִּלְאַיִם אֵין לִי אֶלָּא כַּרְמְךָ כֶּרֶם אַחֵר מְנַיִין
תַּלְמוּד לוֹמַר כִּלְאַיִם לֹא כֶרֶם וְלֹא כִלְאַיִם.[42] אָמַר רִבִּי לֶעָזָר דְּרִבִּי מֵאִיר הִיא.
דְּרִבִּי מֵאִיר אָמַר אֵין לְגוֹי קִנְיָין בְּאֶרֶץ יִשְׂרָאֵל לְפוֹטְרוֹ מִן הַמַּעְשְׂרוֹת. אָמַר
רִבִּי יוֹחָנָן דִּבְרֵי הַכֹּל הִיא תִּיפְתָּר בְּגוֹי שֶׁזָּרַע כַּרְמוֹ כִלְאַיִם וּלְקָחוֹ מִמֶּנּוּ יִשְׂרָאֵל.

Halakhah 4: It is written (*Deut.* 22:9): "Do not sow *kilaim* in your
vineyard." This refers to your own vineyard. From where about another
person's vineyard? The verse says, *kilaim*, no vineyard and no *kilaim*.[43]
Rebbi Eleazar said, this is Rebbi Meïr's, for Rebbi Meïr said that a Gentile
cannot acquire real estate in the Land of Israel to free it from tithes[44].
Rebbi Johanan said, it is the opinion of everybody, explain it by a Gentile
who sowed his vineyard *kilaim* and a Jew bought it from him[45].

42   Reading of the Rome ms. and
one ms. quoted by R. Solomon Adani in
his Mishnah commentary. Venice: כרם
ולא כלאים
43   The argument is slightly more
clear in the version of *Sifry Deut.* 230
on the verse: "Do not sow *kilaim* in
your vineyard, lest the fulness of the
seed you are sowing be sanctified
together with the yield of the vineyard." The *Sifry* reads: "I understand

not only a fruit-bearing vineyard, from
where a vineyard that is not fruit-
bearing? The verse says 'the vineyard',
any vineyard. I understand not only
your own vineyard, from where other
persons' vineyard? The verse says 'do
not sow *kilaim*', in any way." R. S.
Adani argues that in contrast to *Lev.*
19:19, where the direct object precedes
the predicate, in *Deut. 22:9* the
predicate precedes the direct object

and this is always taken as indicating that the prohibition stated at the beginning of the verse covers all situations the verse refers to. Hence, the operative word is not כרמך "your vineyard" but the last word of the sentence, הכרם "any vineyard."

44   Since the Mishnah makes no difference whether the neighbor is Jewish or Gentile, its author must hold that the laws of the Land are not abrogated by Gentile ownership.

45   Even in the scenario envisaged by R. Eleazar, one cannot infer anything since the Gentile is not required to follow the obligations which in Jewish opinion are a lien on the Land. They are only activated in case a Jew buys the real estate from the Gentile; then the neighbor is a Jew and nobody holds that the obligations are not in force.

רִבִּי יוֹנָה וְרִבִּי יוֹסָה תְּרַוֵּיהוֹן אָמְרִין דְּרִבִּי מֵאִיר הִיא. הַמְּעֻבָּד אִית תַּנָּיֵי תַגֵּי בֵּין שֶׁלּוֹ (fol. 31a) בֵּין שֶׁל אֲחֵרִים אָסוּר. אִית תַּנָּיֵי תַגֵּי שֶׁלּוֹ אָסוּר שֶׁל אֲחֵרִים מוּתָּר. הֲווֹן בָּעֲיֵי מֵימַר מָאן דְּאָמַר בֵּין שֶׁלּוֹ בֵּין שֶׁל אֲחֵרִים אָסוּר רִבִּי מֵאִיר וְרִבִּי יוּדָה. מָאן דְּאָמַר שֶׁלּוֹ אָסוּר שֶׁל אֲחֵרִים מוּתָּר רִבִּי יוֹסֵה וְרִבִּי שִׁמְעוֹן. רִבִּי יוֹסָה בְשֵׁם רִבִּי לָא דִּבְרֵי הַכֹּל הִיא. כַּמָה דְתֵימַר תַּמָּן דָּבָר שֶׁיֵּשׁ בּוֹ רוּחַ חַיִּים אַף עַל פִּי שֶׁאֵינוֹ נֶאֱסָר לְהֶדְיוֹט נֶאֱסָר לַגְּבוֹהַּ וְדִכְוָותָהּ דָּבָר שֶׁאֵינוֹ שֶׁלָּךְ אַף עַל פִּי שֶׁאֵינוֹ נֶאֱסָר לְהֶדְיוֹט נֶאֱסָר לַגְּבוֹהַּ.

Rebbi Jonah and Rebbi Yose, both of them say that it is Rebbi Meïr's[46]. [An animal] which was worshipped: Some Tannaïm state that it is forbidden[47] whether it is his own or somebody else's; some Tannaïm state that his own is forbidden, somebody else's is permitted. They wanted to say, the opinion that it is forbidden whether it is his own or somebody else's is Rebbi Meïr's and Rebbi Jehudah's; the opinion that his own is forbidden, somebody else's is permitted, is Rebbi Yose's and Rebbi Simeon's. Rebbi Yose in the name of Rebbi La: It is everybody's opinion. Just as you say there that a living thing is forbidden for Heaven even though it is permitted for the private person, so anything that is not yours may be forbidden for Heaven even though it is permitted for the private person[48].

46 The anonymous Tanna of the Mishnah cannot be either R. Yose or R. Simeon; anonymous statements of the Mishnah are attributed to R. Meïr unless an argument can be given to the contrary.

47 An animal used for idolatrous practices is unfit as a sacrifice (Mishnah *Temurah* 6:1). The Mishnah states that such an animal is forbidden as a

sacrifice but its meat may be eaten by private persons since usufruct of living things cannot become forbidden.

48 Since R. Yose and R. Simeon do not disagree with Mishnah *Temurah* 6:1 that an animal used for idolatrous purposes (or for sodomy) is forbidden as sacrifice under all circumstances. The argument about sacrifices is irrelevant for the rules of *kilaim*.

רְבִּי שִׁמְעוֹן בֶּן לָקִישׁ אָמַר קְנָסֵיהּ דְּרְבִּי מֵאִיר וַעֲבַד עוּבְדָּא דִּכְוָתֵיהּ מִן הָדָא. הַמְסַכֵּךְ אֶת גַּפְנוֹ עַל גַּבֵּי תְּבוּאָתוֹ שֶׁל חֲבֵירוֹ. וְכִי מַה עָשָׂה מַעֲשֶׂה. אֶלָּא כְּשֶׁהוֹסִיף לְפִי דַּעַת הוּא מוֹסִיף. חַד בַּר נַשׁ חֲוֵי סִלְעֵיהּ לְרְבִּי לָעָזָר אָמַר לֵיהּ טָבָא הִיא וְיִפְסָלַת. אֲתָא עוּבְדָּא קוֹמֵי רְבִּי שִׁמְעוֹן בֶּן לָקִישׁ וּקְנָסֵיהּ מִן הָדָא. הַמַּרְאֶה דִּינָר לְשׁוּלְחָנִי וְנִמְצָא רַע חַיָּיב לְשַׁלֵּם מִפְּנֵי שֶׁהוּא נוֹשֵׂא שָׂכָר. וְרְבִּי לָעָזָר נוֹשֵׂא שָׂכָר. רְבִּי יַעֲקֹב בַּר אָחָא בְּשֵׁם רְבִּי אֲבוּנָא הַמַּחֲזִיק בּוֹ כְּנוֹשֵׂא שָׂכָר. רְבִּי יוֹסֵי בֵּי רְבִּי אָבוּן לֹא אָמַר כֵּן אֶלָּא רְבִּי לָעָזָר אָמַר קְנָסָהּ דְּרַבָּנִין. וְרְבִּי שִׁמְעוֹן בֶּן לָקִישׁ אָמַר קְנָסָהּ דְּרְבִּי מֵאִיר. כָּךְ אֲתָא עוּבְדָּא שָׁאַל רְבִּי שִׁמְעוֹן בֶּן לָקִישׁ לְרְבִּי לָעָזָר קְנָסָא דְּמָאן. אֲמַר לֵיהּ דְּרַבָּנִין. אֲמַר לֵיהּ פּוּק שְׁלֵם.

Rebbi Simeon ben Laqish said, this is a fine imposed by Rebbi Meïr[49]. Did he act on that, "if somebody draws his vine over somebody else's grain . . ."? But what did that person do? When it grows, it grows according to his intention[50]. One person showed his tetradrachma to Rebbi Eleazar who told him that it was good[51]. It turned out to be worthless. This case came before Rebbi Simeon ben Laqish who fined him according to the following: If somebody shows a denar to the money-changer and it turns out to be bad, [the money-changer] has to pay because he takes a fee[52]. Does Rebbi Eleazar take a fee? Rebbi Jacob bar

Aḥa in the name of Rebbi Abuna: One who takes it into his hand has the status of one who takes a fee[53]. Rebbi Yose ben Rebbi Abun does not say so, but Rebbi Eleazar says that this fine is imposed by the rabbis; Rebbi Simeon ben Laqish says the fine is imposed by Rebbi Meïr. When the case came before Rebbi Simeon ben Laqish, he asked Rebbi Eleazar, who imposed this fine? He [Rebbi Eleazar] said, the rabbis. He [Rebbi Simeon ben Laqish] answered him, go and pay[54].

50   The anonymous Tanna does not dispute that in principle nobody can sanctify anything that does not belong to him, parallel to the position of R. Yose in the preceding paragraph. The order to destroy the growth under the vine is purely rabbinical and intended to punish the mischievous vintner. In contrast to the Babli which always accepts R. Meïr's decrees of fines, the Yerushalmi will accept only a fine imposed by a majority of the Synhedrion.

51   What could be the reason to impose the fine? When a person draws a vine over somebody else's grain, both the vine and the grain are permitted and legitimate. Since later he does not do anything further, of what could he be guilty? The answer is that the grain will continue to grow and that increase under the vine is a necessary consequence of the earlier action and covered by the responsibility for the prior action. In the language of the

Babli, nobody can claim missing intent by stating that he wanted only to cut off his victim's head, not to kill him. The Babli (*Baba Qama* 100b) extends the liability to the case when a stone fence between a vineyard and a grain field developed a hole and the owner after being apprised of the problem did nothing to repair it.

52   In the Babli, *Baba Qama* 100a, R. Simeon ben Laqish showed the coin to R. Eleazar and told him that he would hold him responsible if he gave the wrong appraisal.

53   A similar statement appears in the Babli (*Baba Qama* 59b). There, a distinction is made between a professional money-changer and an amateur, no mention of a difference between giving an opinion for a fee or for free. Some authors (Meïri and R. Asher ben Yeḥiel *ad loc.*) want to read the ruling of the Yerushalmi into the text of the Babli but their arguments are thoroughly refuted by R. Salomo

ben Adrat, *ad loc.*

54   It seems that this argument is an echo of the rule that a single judge who is shown to be in error has to pay the money he erroneously took from one party if he actually handled the money himself (*Giṭṭin* 5:4, fol. 47a). The argument is not accepted.

55   R. Simeon ben Laqish required R. Eleazar to pay not because the law was that he had to pay, but because R. Eleazar thought the law was that he had to pay. It follows that the Yerushalmi rejects the decrees of R. Meïr not supported by a majority of Sages.

In a similar case in the Babli (*Baba Qama* 99b), R. Ḥiyya paid up not because he had to, but because, in his opinion, a rabbinic authority is held to higher moral standards.

אָמַר רִבִּי יוֹחָנָן הַכֹּל מוֹדִין בָּעֲנָבִים שֶׁהֵן אֲסוּרוֹת. אָמַר לֵיהּ רִבִּי לְעָזָר הָאוֹסֵר אֵינוֹ נֶאֱסָר וְשֶׁאֵינוֹ אוֹסֵר נֶאֱסָר. מַה פְּלִיגִין בְּמֵסַכֵּךְ אֶת גַּפְנוֹ עַל גַּבֵּי תְבוּאָתוֹ שֶׁל חֲבֵירוֹ. אֲבָל הַמְסַכֵּךְ אֶת גַּפְנוֹ שֶׁל חֲבֵירוֹ עַל גַּבֵּי תְבוּאָתוֹ כָּל־עַמָּא מוֹדִין שֶׁהָאוֹסֵר נֶאֱסָר. הַמְסַכֵּךְ גַּפְנוֹ שֶׁל חֲבֵירוֹ עַל גַּבֵּי תְבוּאָתוֹ שֶׁל חֲבֵירוֹ. נִישְׁמְעִינָהּ מִן הָדָא. אָמַר רִבִּי יוֹסֵי מַעֲשֶׂה בְּאֶחָד שֶׁזָּרַע אֶת כַּרְמוֹ בַשְּׁבִיעִית וּבָא מַעֲשֶׂה לִפְנֵי רִבִּי עֲקִיבָה וְאָמַר אֵין אָדָם מַקְדִּישׁ דָּבָר שֶׁאֵינוֹ שֶׁלּוֹ. הֲרֵי אֵין הַגֶּפֶן שֶׁלּוֹ וְאֵין הַתְּבוּאָה שֶׁלּוֹ וְאִיתְתָבַת.

Rebbi Joḥanan said, everybody agrees that the grapes will be forbidden[55]. Rebbi Eleazar said to him, what makes forbidden is not forbidden and what is not forbidden will be forbidden[56]? They disagree if somebody draws his vine over somebody else's grain. But if somebody draws a neighbor's vine over his own grain, everybody agrees that what makes forbidden is forbidden[57]. If somebody draws a neighbor's vine over his neighbor's grain we can understand from the following: "Rebbi Yose said, it happened that someone sowed in his vineyard in the Sabbatical year[41]. When this came before Rebbi Aqiba, he said nobody can sanctify anything that is not his." This was given as answer[58]!

55   They belong to the offending party.

56   If the vine is drawn in a state in which it does not expand any further, only the growth of the grain under it makes the configuration forbidden, as stated earlier. Since the active grain is not forbidden, how can the passive grapes be forbidden?

57   The grain of the guilty party.

58   The anonymous first Tanna will hold also in the case under discussion that vines and grain have to be burned and the guilty party charged for all expenses and loss; Rebbis Yose and Simeon hold that nothing has happened.

(fol. 30d) **משנה ו**: הָאַנָּס שֶׁזָּרַע אֶת הַכֶּרֶם וְיָצָא מִלְּפָנָיו קוֹצְרִין אֲפִילוּ בְּמוֹעֵד. עַד כַּמָּה הוּא נוֹתֵן לְפוֹעֲלִין עַד שְׁלִישׁ. יוֹתֵר מִיכֵּן קוֹצֵר וְהוֹלֵךְ אֲפִילוּ לְאַחַר הַמּוֹעֵד. מֵאֵימָתַי נִקְרָא אַנָּס מִשֶּׁיִּשְׁקַע.

משנה ז: הָרוּחַ שֶׁעִילְעֲלָה אֶת הַגְּפָנִים עַל גַּבֵּי תְבוּאָה יִגְדּוֹר מִיַּד וְאִם אֵירְעוֹ אוֹנֶס מוּתָּר. תְּבוּאָה שֶׁהִיא נוֹטָה תַּחַת הַגֶּפֶן וְכֵן בְּיָרֶק מַחֲזִיר וְאֵינוֹ מְקַדֵּשׁ. מֵאֵימָתַי תְּבוּאָה מִתְקַדֶּשֶׁת מִשֶּׁתַּשְׁלִישׁ. וַעֲנָבִים מִשֶּׁיֵּעָשׂוּ כְּפוֹל הַלָּבָן. תְּבוּאָה שֶׁיָּבְשָׁה כָל־צָרְכָּהּ וַעֲנָבִים שֶׁבִּישְׁלוּ כָל־צָרְכָן אֵינָן מִתְקַדְּשׁוֹת.

Mishnah 6: The rapist[59] who sowed in a vineyard and it was taken from him[60], one cuts it even during a holiday[61]. How much does he have to give to the workers? Up to one third[62]. More than that he cuts normally, even after the holiday. When is the property called the rapist's? From the moment it is sunk[63].

Mishnah 7: [64]If a storm broke vines over grain, one should fix it immediately, but in an emergency it is permitted. Grain leaning under vines, and also vegetables, one turns back and it does not sanctify[65]. When does grain start to sanctify? When it is a third grown[66], and grapes once they have grown to the size of white beans. Completely dry grain and grapes completely ripe do not become sanctified.

59   A robber who terrorizes the farmer and illegally uses his land.

60   Law enforcement returned the use of the land to its owners.

61   The intermediate days of Passover or Tabernacles, when agricultural work is permitted only if its omission would cause great harm. In our case, one has to prevent the grain from growing in its owner's possession to avoid sanctifying the vineyard.

62   Since usually agricultural work cannot be done on the intermediate days of a holiday, the workers will know that the farmer is in a bind and raise their wage demands. The Halakhah will discuss what is meant by "a third" for the computation of the upper limit of wages the farmer must be ready to pay. If the workers overcharge, he may do without them and cut the grain after the holiday for regular wages.

63   If the name of the original owners disappears; if local people start referring to the property by the name of the person in possession who now becomes the owner (explanation of R. Simson). If the owner runs away for fear of the rapist (explanation of Maimonides).

64   The Mishnah mss. in the Maimonides tradition read יגרוד "shave them off" instead of יגדור "fence them off". The hurricane did not completely break the vines; now parts of the still living vine lie over grain.

65   As long as the roots are outside of the working space of a vine, if the plants turn towards the vine one has to turn them away. Only roots of plants can sanctify.

66   This may not be the intended meaning, cf. the Halakhah.

(fol. 31a) **הלכה ה**: רִבִּי בָּא בַּר יַעֲקֹב בְּשֵׁם רִבִּי יוֹחָנָן כֵּינִי מַתְנִיתָא מוּתָּר לְקוֹצְרוֹ אֲפִילוּ בְּמוֹעֵד.

Halakhah 5: Rebbi Abba bar Jacob in the name of Rebbi Johanan: So is the Mishnah: One may harvest it even on a holiday[67].

67   One should not think that the Mishnah prescribes that the illegal grain must be harvested on a holiday if the field reverts to its rightful owner on a holiday. All that is stated is that one may harvest it because it looks badly (if the workers are not too expensive) even though nobody can sanctify anything that is not his and harvesting on the intermediate days of a holiday is forbidden (cf. *Tosaphot Sukkah* 30b).

עַד כַּמָּה הוּא נוֹתֵן [לְפוֹעֲלִין]68 עַד שְׁלִישׁ. רַב חוּנָא וְרַב שֵׁשֶׁת חַד אָמַר שְׁלִישׁ לְשָׂכָר69 וְחַד אָמַר שְׁלִישׁ לְדָמִים.

"How much does he have to give to the workers? Up to one third." Rav Ḥuna and Rav Sheshet: One of them says, a third of the wages, the other says, a third of the value[70].

68   Text of the Mishnah. In the Yerushalmi mss.: לבעלין.

69   In Babli *Baba Qama* 9a, Rav Huna prescribes that for meritorious deeds one never should pay more than one third over the going rate.

(Maimonides follows the opinion of Rav Huna who has precedence over Rav Sheshet in matters of ritual).

70   The value of the crop endangered by the rapist's action.

מֵאֵימָתַי נִקְרָא אַנָּס מִשֶּׁיְּשֻׁקַע. אָמַר רִבִּי אָחָא נִשְׁתַּקְעוּ הַבְּעָלִים וְלֹא נִתְיָיְאֲשׁוּ הַבְּעָלִים אִיסּוּרוֹ דְּבַר תּוֹרָה. נִתְייָאֲשׁוּ הַבְּעָלִים וְלֹא נִשְׁתַּקְעוּ הַבְּעָלִים אִיסּוּרָן מִדִּבְרֵיהֶן. וְיֵשׁ קַרְקַע נִגְזָל. אָמַר רִבִּי לָא אַף עַל פִּי שָׁאֵין קַרְקַע נִגְזָל יֵשׁ יֵיאוּשׁ לְקַרְקַע.

"When is the property called the rapist's? From the moment it is sunk[63]." Rebbi Aḥa said: If the owners were forgotten but did not give up hope, the prohibition of the field is biblical[71]. If the owners did give up hope but they were not forgotten, the prohibition of the field is rabbinic. But can real estate be robbed[72]? Rebbi La said, even though real estate cannot be robbed, one can give up hope on real estate.

71   Since the Mishnah declares the property to be the rapist's once the names of the original owners have been forgotten, he sows on his own and sanctifies the crop. But if the names of the original owners are still known, even if these have given up hope to

recover the field through legal action, the rapist is not the owner and should not be able to sanctify anything that is not his. In that case, the prohibition has the status of a rabbinic fine.

74   Since real estate is documented, it always should be recoverable once

law enforcement has been re-established, cf. *Peah* Chapter 2, Note 132. In the opinion of the Babli, one may never legally give up hope on real estate, cf. *Tosaphot Sukkah* 30b. In Babylonia one never witnessed the prolonged abrogation of property rights by Jewish owners as in Palestine after the war of Bar Kokhba.

וּכְבֶן עַזַּאי יִסְפּוֹר. אַשְׁכָּח תַּנֵּי רִבִּי עֲקִיבָה אָמַר יַחֲזִיר. בֶּן עַזַּאי יִסְפּוֹר.

Following Ben Azai, one should shave them off. One found it stated: Rebbi Aqiba said, one should return them, Ben Azai said, one should shave them off[73].

73   This belongs to the second Mishnah, the case when a storm broke branches which now are spread over grain. R. Aqiba says one should adjust the broken branches and fasten them to the vine; Ben Azai said, one should cut them off.

אֵימָתַי מִתְקַדֶּשֶׁת מִשֶּׁתַּשְׁלִישׁ. אִית תַּנָּיֵי תַּנֵּי מִשֶּׁתַּשְׁרִישׁ. מָאן דְּאָמַר מִשֶּׁתַּשְׁלִישׁ מְסַייֵעָא לְרִבִּי יוֹחָנָן. מָאן דְּאָמַר מִשֶּׁתַּשְׁרִישׁ מְסַייֵעָא לְרִבִּי הוֹשַׁעְיָא.

"When does grain start to sanctify? When it is a third grown." Some Tannaïm state: When it grew roots. He who says when it is a third grown supports Rebbi Johanan. He who says when it grew roots supports Rebbi Hoshaia[74].

74   This refers to Chapter 5, Halakhah 7 (Note 74). The names must be switched because in 5:7 it is R. Johanan who asserts that all becomes sanctified once full roots are grown. While there is no manuscript evidence for this, it must have been the reading of Maimonides (*Kilaim* 5:13) who follows R. Johanan and formulates "when it grew roots".

וַעֲנָבִים מִשֶּׁיֵּעָשׂוּ כְּפוֹל הַלָּבָן. אָמַר רִבִּי חֲנַנְיָה בְּרֵיהּ דְּרִבִּי הִלֵּל דִּכְתִיב וּתְבוּאַת הַכָּרֶם. כֵּינֵי מַתְנִיתָא אֵינָן מִתְקַדְּשׁוֹת.

"And grapes once they have grown to the size of white beans." Rebbi Ḥananiah the son of Rebbi Hillel said, because it is written (*Deut.* 22:9): "And the produce of the vineyard[75]." So is the Mishnah: "They do not become sanctified"[76].

75　　The verse defines what is sanctified. Since it is called "produce", some kind of produce must be visible.

76　　This refers to the last sentence in the Mishnah, "completely dry grain and grapes completely ripe do not become sanctified." The Mishnah is formulated in the passive: completely dry produce cannot itself become sanctified because it no longer grows but produce still growing in its vicinity can become sanctified by its presence (R. S. Adani.)

(fol. 30d) **משנה ח:** אוֹמֵר זֶה וְזֶה אֲסוּרִין וְאֵינָן מְקַדְּשִׁין. הַמַּעֲבִיר עָצִיץ נָקוּב בַּכֶּרֶם אִם הוֹסִיף בְּמָאתַיִם אָסוּר.

Mishnah 8: A flower pot with a hole sanctifies in a vineyard[77], but one without a hole does not sanctify. Rebbi Simeon says, both are forbidden but neither one sanctifies[78]. If a flower pot with a hole is temporarily put in a vineyard, if it grew by one twohundreth it is forbidden[79].

77　　(Mishnah 8 in the separate Mishnah). A flower pot with a hole is part of the earth, Mishnah *Demay* 5:10.

78　　The Halakhah will explain that R. Simeon does not recognize any difference between flower pots with or without holes, except that he treats food grown in a pot with a hole like food grown on a field with respect to the laws of ritual impurities.

79　　Cf. Mishnah 5:6.

(fol. 31a) **הלכה ו:** תַּנֵּי אֵין בֵּין עָצִיץ נָקוּב לְעָצִיץ שֶׁאֵינוֹ נָקוּב אֶלָּא הַכְשֵׁר זְרָעִים בִּלְבָד. כְּרִבִּי שִׁמְעוֹן בְּרַם כְּרַבָּנִין אִית חוֹרָנִין. עָצִיץ נָקוּב מְקַדֵּשׁ בַּכֶּרֶם

וְשֶׁאֵינוֹ נָקוּב אֵינוֹ מְקַדֵּשׁ. הַתּוֹלֵשׁ מֵעָצִיץ נָקוּב חַיָּיב מִשֶּׁאֵינוֹ נָקוּב פָּטוּר.

עָצִיץ נָקוּב אֵינוֹ מַכְשִׁיר אֶת הַזְּרָעִים וְשֶׁאֵינוֹ נָקוּב מַכְשִׁיר אֶת הַזְּרָעִים. רִבִּי

יוֹסֵי אָמַר לָהּ סְתָם. רִבִּי חֲנִינָא מָטֵי בָהּ בְּשֵׁם רִבִּי שְׁמוּאֵל בַּר רַב יִצְחָק

הַתּוֹרָה רִיבָּת מִטָּהֳרַת זְרָעִים. וְכִי יִפּוֹל מִנִּבְלָתָם עַל כָּל־זֶרַע זֵרוּעַ אֲשֶׁר יִזָּרֵעַ

טָהוֹר הוּא.

Halakhah 6: It was stated: "The only difference between a flower pot without a hole and one with a hole regards preparation for impurity." That is for Rebbi Simeon[80], but for the rabbis there are others: A flower pot with a hole sanctifies in a vineyard, one without a hole does not. He who plucks from a flower pot with a hole is guilty, from one without a hole he is free from punishment[81]. A flower pot with a hole cannot prepare plants, one without a hole prepares[82]. Rebbi Yose referred to it as anonymous statement, Rebbi Ḥanina quoted it in the name of Rebbi Samuel bar Rav Isaac: The Torah extended the purity of growing plants (*Lev.* 11:37): "If any of their cadavers falls on any sown seed apt to be sown, it is pure[83]."

80 In the Babli, *Šabbat* 95a/b, this is a statement explicitly attributed to R. Simeon.

81 Mishnah *Šabbat* 10:7. Harvesting on the Sabbath is a criminal offense but one cannot harvest plants that do not grow on the earth. Plucking a plant from a pot without a hole is forbidden but cannot be cause for criminal prosecution. The Mishnah states that R. Simeon excludes prosecution in both cases.

82 Food can become impure only after the harvest and only after having been wetted, cf. *Demay* Chapter 2,

Note 141. A plant in a pot with hole is a plant in the earth and nothing can make it prepared for impurity at this stage. A plant in a pot without hole is already harvested since it can be plucked on the Sabbath without fear of prosecution; if it is watered, it becomes subject to possible impurity.

83 This explains why R. Simeon agrees with the rabbis that a flower pot with hole is immune from impurity and is not comparable to a pot with hole: The verse insists that anything sown in any way acceptable in agriculture is pure.

תַּנֵּי עָצִיץ שֶׁאֵינוֹ נָקוּב מַעְשְׂרוֹתָיו כַּהֲלָכָה וּתְרוּמָתוֹ אֵינָהּ מְדַמַּעַת וְאֵין חַיָּבִין
עָלֶיהָ חוֹמֶשׁ. רִבִּי יוֹסֵי בָּעֵי מַהוּ לוֹמַר עַל פִּתּוֹ הַמּוֹצִיא לֶחֶם מִן הָאָרֶץ. רִבִּי
יוֹנָה בָּעֵי כֵּן דְּלַעַת כְּתָלוּשׁ הוּא לְסַכֵּךְ בָּהּ. רִבִּי יוּדָה בַּר פָּזִי בָּעֵי נָטַע חָמֵשׁ
גֻּפְנִים בַּחֲמִשָּׁה עֲצִיצִין שֶׁאֵינָן נְקוּבִין וַעֲשָׂעָן שְׁתַּיִם כְּנֶגֶד שְׁתַּיִם וְאַחַת יוֹצֵא זָנָב
אַתְּ אָמַר כֶּרֶם הוּא. הוֹפְכוֹ וְיֵשׁ כֶּרֶם מִטַּלְטֵל.

It was stated: "The tithes from a flower pot without hole are of
practice[84], its heave does not create *dema'* and one does not owe a fifth
for it." Rebbi Yose asked: May one say "He Who created bread from the
earth" for it[85]? Rebbi Jonah asked: Is a gourd considered plucked that
one may use it as the cover [of a *sukkah*][86]? Rebbi Judah bar Pazi asked:
If somebody planted five vines in five pots without holes and arranged
them two parallel two and one as tail, can you say this is a vineyard? He
may rearrange, does there exist a movable vineyard[87]?

84   Rabbinic practice, not biblical
commandment. If symbolic heave from
such a pot is mixed with profane food,
it does not create *dema'* (cf. *Demay*
Chap. 4, Note 27) and if it is eaten in
error by a non-Cohen, only 100%, not
125%, has to be returned (*Lev.* 22:14).

85   What is the appropriate
benediction for bread made from flour
from grain not grown "on the earth"?

86   A hut for the feast of Tabernacles has to be covered by material

"not subject to impurity and grown
from the earth" (Mishnah *Sukkah* 1:4).
As noted in the preceding paragraph,
the majority opinion is that plants
growing in a pot without a hole are
subject to impurity; the question can be
asked only according to R. Simeon.

87   Since the vines can be re-
arranged, they cannot be considered a
vineyard. This is the only question that
is answered.

שְׁמוּאֵל אָמַר בְּמַעֲבִיר תַּחַת כָּל־גֶּפֶן וַגֶּפֶן. אָמַר רִבִּי יוֹחָנָן לַאֲוֵיר עֲשָׂרָה הִיא
מַתְנִיתָא.

Samuel said, put under any vine. Rebbi Joḥanan said, the Mishnah deals
within ten [hand-breadths][88].

88   This starts the discussion of the
last sentence in the Mishnah, about a
flower pot temporarily put into a
vineyard. Samuel said there is a
potential for sanctification only if the
flower pot is directly under a vine. If

the pot is moved from one vine to the
other but all the time is under one of
them, there is sanctification if the
plants in the pot grew by one half of
one percent.

הֶעֱבִיר חֲמִשָּׁה עֲצִיצִין שֶׁאֵינָן נְקוּבִין תַּחַת גֶּפֶן אַחַת פְּלוּגְתָא דְּרִבִּי לָעָזָר וְרִבִּי
יוֹחָנָן. הָאוֹסֵר אֵינוֹ נֶאֱסָר וְשֶׁאֵינוֹ אוֹסֵר נֶאֱסָר. אֲבָל אִם הֶעֱבִיר עָצִיץ אֶחָד
תַּחַת חָמֵשׁ גְּפָנִים כָּל־עֵמָּא מוֹדֵיי שֶׁהָאוֹסֵר נֶאֱסָר.

If one put five flower pots without holes under one vine, one has the
disagreement between Rebbi Eleazar and Rebbi Joḥanan[89]: what makes
forbidden is not forbidden and what is not forbidden will be forbidden?
But if a single pot was placed temporarily under five different vines,
everybody agrees that what makes forbidden will be forbidden[88].

89   Halakhah 4, Notes 56 ff. The
argument is not as simple as represented here: If the plants in the
aggregate of five pots increase by 0.5%
then at least in one pot the increase
must be $\geq 0.5\%$. That pot will certainly

be forbidden. The only question is
whether the five are considered as a
unit or not. In the latter case, the
grapes will be forbidden but part of
the grain will be permitted, still a
paradoxical situation.

כלאי הכרם פרק שמיני

(fol. 31a) **משנה א**: כִּלְאֵי הַכֶּרֶם אֲסוּרִין מִלְּזְרוֹעַ וּמִלְּקַיֵּים וַאֲסוּרִין בַּהֲנָאָה. כִּלְאֵי זְרָעִים אֲסוּרִין מִלְּזְרוֹעַ וּמִלְּקַיֵּים וּמוּתָּרִין בַּאֲכִילָה וְכָל־שֶׁכֵּן בַּהֲנָאָה. כִּלְאֵי בְגָדִים מוּתָּרִין בְּכָל־דָּבָר וְאֵינָן אֲסוּרִין אֶלָּא מִלְּלְבּוֹשׁ. כִּלְאֵי בְהֵמָה מוּתָּרִין לְגַדֵּל וּלְקַיֵּים וְאֵינָן אֲסוּרִין אֶלָּא מִלְּהַרְבִּיעַ. כִּלְאֵי בְהֵמָה אֲסוּרִין זֶה עִם זֶה.

Mishnah 1: *Kilaim* in a vineyard are forbidden to be sown or kept and are forbidden for any use. *Kilaim* of grains are forbidden to be sown or kept but are permitted for eating and certainly for use. *Kilaim* of textiles are permitted for everything; they are only forbidden to be worn. *Kilaim* of animals may be raised and kept; they are only forbidden to be mated. *Kilaim* of animals are forbidden [to be mated] with one another[1].

1   Since a mule is part horse and part donkey, mating of two mules implies double mating of parts of horse with parts of donkey and is forbidden for human intervention.

(fol. 31b) **הלכה א**: כִּלְאֵי הַכֶּרֶם אֲסוּרִין כו'. כְּתִיב לֹא תִזְרַע כַּרְמְךָ כִּלְאָיִם. אֵין לִי אֶלָּא הַזּוֹרֵעַ מְקַיֵּים מְנַיִין תַּלְמוּד לוֹמַר וְכֶרֶם וְלֹא כִלְאָיִם. מַה כְּרַבִּי עֲקִיבָה דְּרַבִּי עֲקִיבָה אוֹמֵר הַמְקַיֵּים עוֹבֵר בְּלֹא תַעֲשֶׂה. אָמַר רִבִּי יוֹסֵי דִּבְרֵי הַכֹּל הִיא הַכֹּל מוֹדִים בָּאָסוּר שֶׁהוּא אָסוּר בְּשֶׁלֹּא קַיֵּים עַל יְדֵי מַעֲשֶׂה אֲבָל אִם קַיֵּים עַל יְדֵי מַעֲשֶׂה לוֹקֶה. כְּהָדָא דְּתַנֵּי הַמְחַפֶּה בְּכִלְאַיִם לוֹקֶה.

Halakhah 1: "*Kilaim* in a vineyard are forbidden," etc. It is written (*Deut.* 22:9): "Do not sow *kilaim* in your vineyard." Not only sowing, how about keeping? The verse says, vineyard and no *kilaim*[2]. Does this follow Rebbi Aqiba, for Rebbi Aqiba said that he who keeps [*kilaim*] transgresses a prohibition[3]? Rebbi Yose said, it is the word of everybody. Everybody agrees that what is forbidden is forbidden if he did not preserve through an action, but if he preserved through an action he is whipped, as it is stated: He who covers *kilaim* is whipped.

2   Cf. Chapter 7, Note 44. The parallel to this argument is in *Sifra Qedošim* 2(18) [Babli *Mo'ed Qaṭan* 2b, *Avodah Zarah* 64a, *Makkot* 21b]: (*Lev.* 19:19): "'Your field you should sow no *kilaim*.' Not only sowing, how about keeping? The verse says, no *kilaim*, I told you only because of *kilaim*." This argument covers grains, vegetables, and vines. However, the same verse also mentions *kilaim* of animals and textiles in similar language and these may be kept in the opinion of the Mishnah. It follows that a derivation based on the verse *Lev.* 19:19 has to be rejected and only an argument parallel to that in Chapter 7 is acceptable.

3   "Prohibition" usually refers to a criminal offense. "Forbidden" refers to a moral obligation. Since the statement of R. Aqiba in Tosephta *Kilaim* 1:15 deals with *kilaim* of seeds (grains and vegetables), he cannot imply that passively keeping *kilaim* is prosecutable as a criminal offense. However, in the Babli (*Mo'ed Qaṭan* 2b, *Avodah Zarah* 64a), R. Aqiba is quoted in a *baraita* to the effect that keeping *kilaim* is a criminal offense. This forces Rashi and the other commentators to conclude that "keeping" here means "fencing in" or a similar activity. (Rashi to *Mo'ed Qaṭan* 2 is lost; the commentary is in *Avodah Zarah*.) The Yerushalmi has no such difficulty.

מְנַיִין שֶׁהוּא אָסוּר בַּהֲנָייָה נֶאֱמַר כָּאן פֶּן תִּקְדָּשׁ וְנֶאֱמַר לְהַלָּן פֶּן תּוּקְדָּשׁ בּוֹ מַה פֶּן הָאָמוּר לְהַלָּן אָסוּר בַּהֲנָייָה אַף פֶּן שֶׁנֶּאֱמַר כָּאן אָסוּר בַּהֲנָייָה. וְאִית דְּבָעֵי מֵימַר נֶאֱמַר כָּאן פֶּן תִּקְדַּשׁ וְנֶאֱמַר לְהַלָּן וְלֹא יִהְיֶה קָדֵשׁ מִבְּנֵי יִשְׂרָאֵל. מַה קָדֵשׁ הָאָמוּר לְהַלָּן אָסוּר בַּהֲנָייָה אַף כָּאן אָסוּר בַּהֲנָייָה. אָמַר רִבִּי הוּנָא בִּיאָתוֹ אֲסוּרָה בַּהֲנָייָה. אִית דְּבָעֵי נִישְׁמְעִינָהּ מִן הָדָא דְּאָמַר רִבִּי חֲנִינָא פֶּן תִּקְדַּשׁ פֶּן תּוּקַד אֵשׁ.

From where that it is forbidden for any use? It is said here (*Deut.* 22:9) "lest you sanctify it" and it is said elsewhere (lest it become sanctified by it)[4]. Since "lest" there means it is forbidden for any use, "lest" here means it is forbidden for all use. Some want to say, it is said here "lest you sanctify it" and it is said at another place "there shall be no *qadeš* among the Israelites." Since *qdš* there means forbidden for any use, so *qdš* here must mean forbidden for any use. Rebbi Huna said, his sex act is forbidden for all use[5]. Some want to understand it from the following, as Rebbi Ḥanina said, "lest you sanctify it", lest fire should be kindled[6]."

4   There is no such verse in the entire Hebrew Bible. It is the consensus of the commentators that it should read מן תנקש (*Deut.* 12:30) "lest you be caught", speaking of idolatrous objects that must be destroyed and every use of which is explicitly forbidden. One applies the principle that words in the Pentateuch have one invariable meaning; if that meaning is spelled out at one place, it can be transferred to any other occurrence of the same word.

5   The *qadeš* is the Semitic male temple prostitute. In the Talmudim, the notion which had become obsolete at that time was extended to all sexual relations of persons who could not legally marry one another, such as the relation between a slave and a free woman, or of a free Jew and a slave girl or a Gentile. Since the woman could not hope to be married, she could have no gain from the sex act; any pleasure she might have is strictly forbidden.

6   The same argument is in Babli *Qidduşin* 56b, *Ḥulin* 115a in the name of Ḥizqiah. No Tannaitic source proposes to change the text from תקדש to תקד אש.

כְּתִיב לֹא תִזְרַע כַּרְמְךָ כִּלְאָיִם. מְלַמֵּד שָׁאֵינוֹ חַיָּיב עַד שֶׁיִּזְרַע שְׁנֵי מִינִין בַּכֶּרֶם דִּבְרֵי רִבִּי יֹאשִׁיָּה רִבִּי יוֹנָתָן אָמַר אֲפִילוּ מִין אֶחָד. עַל דַּעְתּוֹ דְּרִבִּי יוֹנָתָן כְּתִיב שָׂדְךָ לֹא תִזְרַע כִּלְאַיִם לְאֵי זֶה דָבָר נֶאֱמַר לֹא תִזְרַע כַּרְמְךָ כִּלְאָיִם. חֲבֵרַיָּיא אָמְרִין לְהַחֲמִיר עָלָיו אֲפִילוּ מִין אֶחָד. עַל דַּעְתֵּיהּ דְּרִבִּי יֹאשִׁיָּה שָׂדְךָ לֹא תִזְרַע

כִּלְאַיִם לְאֵי זֶה דָּבָר נֶאֱמַר לֹא תִזְרַע כַּרְמְךָ כִּלְאָיִם. חֲבֵרַיָּיא אָמְרִין לְהַתְרָיָיה
שֶׁאִם הִתְרוּ בּוֹ מִשּׁוּם שָׂדְךָ לוֹקֶה. מִשּׁוּם כֶּרֶם לוֹקֶה. אָמַר רִבִּי בּוּן בַּר חִייָא
לִיתֵּן לוֹ שִׁיעוּר אַחֶרֶת מִן שִׁשָּׁה טְפָחִים. וְכָן אַרְבַּע אַמּוֹת. מַה נָן קַייָמִין אִם
בְּשֶׁעֲשָׂה גֶדֶר מִבִּפְנִים בָּטֵל הַכֶּרֶם. אִם בְּשֶׁעֲשָׂה גֶדֶר מִבַּחוּץ זֶהוּ הַמָּחוֹל. אֶלָּא
כֵּן[7] נָן קַייָמִין בְּשָׂדֶה שֶׁהָיָה שָׁם שְׂדֵה תְבוּאָה וְהִקְרִיחַ לְתוֹכָהּ אַרְבַּע אַמּוֹת.
וְאַתְיָא כִּדְאָמַר רִבִּי חֲנִינָה אֵין הָאוֹסֵר נַעֲשֶׂה מְחִיצָה לְהַצִּיל. סָבְרִין מֵימַר
אוֹסֵר נַעֲשֶׂה מְחִיצָה לֶיאָסֵר. עַל דַּעְתֵּיהּ דְּרִבִּי יוֹנָתָן כְּתִיב שָׂדְךָ לֹא תִזְרַע
כִּלְאַיִם לְאֵי זֶה דָּבָר נֶאֱמַר לֹא תִזְרַע כַּרְמְךָ כִּלְאָיִם. כְּהִיא דְּאָמַר רִבִּי הֵילָא הֵן
דְּאַתְּ אָמַר לֹא אֱמָרָה לְמָה אַתְּ אָמַר. אוֹ כְּהִיא דְּאָמַר רִבִּי זְעִירָא לֹא תִזְרַע
כַּרְמְךָ כִּלְאַיִם עִיקַר כַּרְמְךָ כִּלְאַיִם לֹא תִזְרַע.

It is written (*Deut.* 22:9): "Do not sow *kilaim* in your vineyard." This teaches us that one is not guilty unless he sows two kinds in the vineyard, the words of Rebbi Josia[8]. Rebbi Jonathan said, even one kind. In the opinion of Rebbi Jonathan it is written (*Lev.* 19:19) "in your field do not sow *kilaim*", why does it say "do not sow *kilaim* in your vineyard"? The colleagues say, to make it sinful even with one kind. In the opinion of Rebbi Josia, "in your field do not sow *kilaim*"; why does it say "do not sow *kilaim* in your vineyard"? The colleagues say, as a warning. If he was warned about "your field", he is whipped, if he was warned about "your vineyard", he is whipped[9]. Rebbi Abun bar Ḥiyya said, to give another measure besides six hand-breadths; here it is four cubits[10]. What are we talking about[11]? If he made a fence on the inside, the vineyard is abolished. If he made a fence on the outside, that is the circumference. But we deal with a field that was a grain field and he cleared four cubits in its midst. This agrees with what Rebbi Ḥanina said, nothing forbidden may form a separation to save. They were of the opinion that what is forbidden does form a separation to prohibit[12]. In the opinion of Rebbi Jonathan it is written (*Lev.* 19:19): "In your field do not sow *kilaim*", why does it say: "Do not sow *kilaim* in your vineyard"[13]? For that which Rebbi Hila said, if you would say [the Torah] did not say it, what would you say[14]? Or following what Rebbi Zeïra said, "do not sow your vineyard *kilaim*," creating your vineyard do not sow *kilaim*[15].

7   Reading of the Rome ms. Venice: אינן כי.

8   The Hebrew text לא תזרע כרמך כלאים is somewhat ambiguous. One may translate "do not sow *kilaim* in your vineyard" or "do not sow your vineyard as *kilaim*." R. Josia chooses the first possibility, R. Jonathan the second. There is no question that the verse of *Deut.* contains the rule of sanctification that does not apply to the situation of the verse in *Lev.*; the question is why the second verse does not refer to the first.

9   In talmudic legal theory, a verdict of guilty cannot be pronounced unless criminal intent was shown by the testimony of two witnesses. The standard way of proving intent is the testimony that the perpetrator was warned not to commit such and such an act because it is forbidden in the Torah and that therefore he committed the act in the knowledge of its illegality. The prohibition must be specified. In our case, since sowing something in a vineyard turns the vineyard into a field, either of the verses may be used.

This almost impossible standard of proof is needed only in order to convict somebody under biblical law which knows only flogging and the death penalty; it does not have to be strictly adhered to for convictions under police powers for which the punishment is jailtime.

10   Conviction for sowing *kilaim* in an enclosed field (and single vines considered as fields) is possible only if a minimal distance of six hand-breadths was not observed; cf. Halakhah 1:9. Four cubits is the minimum distance for an enclosed vineyard. The existence of two different verses is a precondition to the establishment of two different legal standards.

11   One tries to clarify the statement of R. Abun bar Ḥiyya. If the field is not enclosed, no minimum separation is required but only clear geometric shapes. If the field is enclosed either the enclosure passes through the vineyard, in which case there is no legal vineyard, or it encloses the vineyard, in which case the more stringent rules of the circumference apply (Mishnah 4:1).

The only possibility is that the field itself is the enclosure, that a spot was cleared inside the field containing a four-by-four square, to be used for planting an illegal vineyard.

12   This is explained in Chapter Four, Note 28.

13   According to R. Abun bar Ḥiyya, why does R. Jonathan use the verse to declare that somebody can be convicted of a biblical crime by sowing one foreign kind in a vineyard since the verses are needed to establish two different standards? This question is not a repetition of the one asked at the start of this paragraph.

14   Since the verse is needed first for the more stringent standard and then for the problem of sanctification, it is impossible to think that it should not have been written.

15   He takes the verse literally, "do not sow your vineyard as *kilaim*", not, as we would think, that "do not sow" refers to a preexisting vineyard which usually is planted, not sown. The only transgression that can be punished by biblical standards, i. e., whipping, is creating a vineyard as *kilaim*, sowing while the planted vines take root.

רְבִּי יוּדָן קַפּוֹדָקְיָא בָּעָא קוֹמֵי רְבִּי יוֹסֵי תַּמָּן אַתְּ אָמַר אֵין זַרְעֵי אִילָן קְרוּיִין זְרָעִים. וְהָכָא אַתְּ אָמַר זַרְעֵי אִילָן קְרוּיִין זְרָעִים. אָמַר לֵיהּ תַּמָּן מִיעֵט הַכָּתוּב אֶת שֶׁאֵין דֶּרֶךְ בְּנֵי אָדָם לִהְיוֹת קְרוּיִין זְרָעִים. בְּרַם הָכָא רִיבָּה הַכָּתוּב עַל כָּל־זֶרַע זֵרוּעַ אֲשֶׁר יִזָּרֵעַ.

Rebbi Yudan from Kappadokia asked before Rebbi Yose: There they say that tree seeds are called seeds but here you say that tree seeds are not called seeds. He said to him: There the verse excluded them since usually people do not call them "seeds," but here the verse added (*Lev.* 11:37) "any sown seed that may be sown."[16]

16   The text is from Tractate *Peah*, Halakhah 1:4, and is explained there in Notes 252-253. "There" is here, Tractate *Kilaim*, "here" is in *Peah*. No tree seeds form *kilaim* with grain and vegetables except grape seeds.

אָמַר רְבִּי יוֹחָנָן בְּשֵׁם רְבִּי יַנַּאי הַמְחַפֶּה בְּכִלְאַיִם לוֹקֶה. אָמַר לֵיהּ רְבִּי יוֹחָנָן וְלָאו מַתְנִיתָא הִיא כִּלְאַיִם הִיא כִּלְאַיִם בַּכֶּרֶם אֵיךְ אֶפְשָׁר כִּלְאַיִם עַל יְדֵי חֲרִישָׁה לֹא

בְּמַחֲפָּה. וַהֲוָה רִבִּי יַנַּיי מְקַלֵּס לֵיהּ הַזָּלִים זָהָב מִכִּיס וגו'. בְּנִי אַל יָלוֹזוּ
מֵעֵינֶיךָ חֵן לְחָכָם וְיֶחְכַּם עוֹד יִשְׁמַע חָכָם וְיוֹסִיף לֶקַח. אָמַר לֵיהּ רִבִּי שִׁמְעוֹן בֶּן
לָקִישׁ בָּתַר כָּל־אִילֵין קִילוּסַיָא יָכִיל אֲנָא פָּתַר לָהּ כְּרִבִּי עֲקִיבָה דְּרִבִּי עֲקִיבָה
אוֹמֵר הַמְקַיֵּים עוֹבֵר בְּלֹא תַעֲשֶׂה. כְּלוּם אָמַר רִבִּי עֲקִיבָה אֶלָּא לַעֲבוֹר שְׁמָא
לִלְקוֹת. וְהָכָא לִלְקוֹת אֲנַן קַיְימִין. וְעוֹד מִן הָדָא דְּתַנִּינָן שְׁבִיעִית אִית לָהּ
מֵימַר שְׁבִיעִית דְּרִבִּי עֲקִיבָה. פָּתַר לָהּ שְׁבִיעִית דְּרִבִּי לֶעָזָר דְּרִבִּי לֶעָזָר אָמַר
לוֹקִין עַל יְדֵי חֲרִישָׁה בַשְּׁבִיעִית. רִבִּי יוֹחָנָן אָמַר אֵין לוֹקִין עַל יְדֵי חֲרִישָׁה
בַשְּׁבִיעִית. מַה טַעַם דְּרִבִּי לֶעָזָר וְשָׁבְתָה הָאָרֶץ שַׁבָּת לַיי' כְּלָל. שָׂדְךָ לֹא תִזְרַע
וְכַרְמְךָ לֹא תִזְמוֹר פְּרָט. הַזֶּרַע וְהַזֶּמֶר בִּכְלָל הָיוּ וְלָמָּה יָצְאוּ לְהַקִּישׁ אֲלֵיהֶן
וְלוֹמַר לָךְ מַה זֶרַע וְזֶמֶר מְיוּחָד שֶׁהֵן עֲבוֹדָה בָאָרֶץ וּבְאִילָן אַף כָּל־דָּבָר שֶׁהוּא
עֲבוֹדָה בָאָרֶץ וּבְאִילָן. מַה עֲבַד לָהּ רִבִּי יוֹחָנָן. שְׁנֵי דְבָרִים הֵן וּשְׁנֵי דְבָרִים
יָצְאוּ מִן הַכְּלָל חוֹלְקִין. וְלֵית לֵיהּ לְרִבִּי אֶלְעָזָר חוֹלְקִין. אִית לֵיהּ לַחֲלוֹק אֵינָן
חוֹלְקִין הָא לְלַמֵּד מְלַמְּדִין. וְלֵית לֵיהּ לְרִבִּי יוֹחָנָן מְלַמְּדִין. שַׁנְיָיא הִיא שֶׁהַכְּלָל
בַּעֲשֵׂה וּפְרָט בְּלֹא תַעֲשֶׂה אֵין עֲשֵׂה מְלַמֵּד עַל לֹא תַעֲשֶׂה וְאֵין לֹא תַעֲשֶׂה מְלַמֵּד
עַל עֲשֵׂה.

Rebbi Johanan said in the name of Rebbi Yannai: He who covers *kilaim* is whipped. Rebbi Johanan said to him: Is that not a Mishnah? "*Kilaim* in a vineyard." How are *kilaim* possible by ploughing[17]? It must be by covering! Rebbi Yannai praised him (*Is.* 46:6:) "Those who pour out gold from the wallet, etc." (*Prov.* 3:21) "My son, they should not be removed from your eyes," (*Prov.* 9:9) "give to the wise that he shall become wiser," let the wise listen[18] "that he increase in knowledge." Rebbi Simeon ben Laqish said, after all these praises I can explain it following Rebbi Aqiba since Rebbi Aqiba said that he who keeps [*kilaim*] transgresses a prohibition. Rebbi Aqiba said only that he transgresses, did he say to whip? Here we are dealing with whipping. Further, from what we have stated "Sabbatical year[19]." Can you say that the Sabbatical year follows Rebbi Aqiba? Explain the Sabbatical year following Rebbi Eleazar, as Rebbi Eleazar said, one whips because of ploughing in the Sabbatical. Rebbi Johanan said, one does not whip because of ploughing in the Sabbatical. What is the reason of Rebbi Eleazar? (*Lev.* 25:2) "The Land should keep a Sabbath for the Eternal," a general statement. (*Lev.* 25:4) "Your field you should not sow, your vineyard you should not prune," detail. Sowing and trimming were in the general statement, why were they detailed? To trap with them and to tell you that just as sowing and pruning are particular as agricultural work on the earth or on a tree, so everything that is agricultural work on the earth or on a tree [is forbidden][20]. How does Rebbi Johanan deal with this? They are two things and two things that are specified from a general notion divide[21]. Does Rebbi Eleazar not hold that they divide? He holds that they do not divide but instruct. Does Rebbi Johanan not hold that they instruct? It is different here because the general statement is a positive commandment and the details are prohibitions; no positive commandment implies anything for a prohibition and no prohibition implies anything for a positive commandment.

17   Since a standard vineyard is planted with four cubits between vines and rows, there is no space for a plough which needs four cubits on each side. Hence, anything sown has to be sown on the unploughed earth and then covered; the verse calls covering seeds with earth "sowing".

18   In the verse: "inform the just".

19   According to R. Eleazar, everybody agrees that ploughing in the Sabbatical year is a criminal offense, while according to R. Johanan everybody agrees that ploughing in the Sabbatical year is not a criminal offense. There is no way to single out R. Aqiba's opinion.

20   The Babylonian version of this argument is in Babli *Mo'ed Qatan* 3a, a tannaïtic version in *Sifra Behar* 1. A comparison with the Babli should use only manuscripts or early editions; the

current versions have been corrupted by editors, cf. *Diqduqe Sopherim ad loc.* The relevant verses are *Lev.* 25:2-5: "(2) Speak to the Children of Israel and tell them, when you shall come to the Land which I am giving you, the Land shall rest for a Sabbath of the Eternal. (3) Six years you shall sow your field, six years you shall prune your vineyard and eat its yield. (4) But in the Seventh year, the Land shall have a Sabbath of rest; do not sow your field, do not prune your vineyard. (5) Your harvest's aftergrowth you shall not harvest, the grapes of your wild growth you shall not gather, a year of rest shall be for the Land." One's first impulse would be to consider verses (4) and (5) as a unit, following the rule known as כלל ופרט וכלל (the seventh rule of R. Ismael, *Sifra* introduction) that details flanked by general statements have to be taken as examples, rather than for themselves, and that all activities forbidden are those described by the intersection of the intensional definitions of the examples. This interpretation led the later editors of the Babli astray. The problem is that verse 4 by itself seems to have the structure בלל ופרט, a general statement followed by a particular one, which would imply that the particular statement is to be taken literally;

nothing is covered by the general statement that is not covered by the particular one. This forces the Babli to conclude that even R. Eleazar agrees with the principle [anonymous in the Yerushalmi, attributed to R. Ilaï (Hila, La) in the Babli] that a positive general statement and a negative particular one cannot form a unit. [The inverse statement, that a negative general statement and a positive particular one must be considered as unrelated, is an anonymous remark in Babli *Yebamot* 7a.]

If the first and the second parts of verse 4 have no direct connection, the question arises (in the formulation of *Sifra Behar*) whether one could think that all work is forbidden in the Seventh Year, including building roads and repairing aqueducts. The second part of the verse describes what is really forbidden. The second rule invoked here by R. Eleazar is *heqqēš* "trapping", meaning that a rule exemplified by different cases applies to all cases subsumed under the intersection of the intensional definitions of the examples. Everybody agrees that a rule exemplified by three different examples only applies to these three and nothing else, and a rule exemplified by one example applies to everything similar unless restricted, e.

g., by the use of a definite article. A
rule exemplified by two examples is
problematic; some think these are
examples only if they appear at
different places and some hold that for
illustration of a general rule the
examples must appear in the same
verse. This is the basis of the
following disagreement between R.
Eleazar and R. Joḥanan. (For the
meaning of all these rules, cf. H.
Guggenheimer, *Logical Problems in
Jewish Tradition*, in: Ph. Longworth,
ed., *Confrontations with Judaism*,
London 1966.)

21   The examples are separate; they
cannot be used in *heqqēš*.

עַל דַּעְתֵּיהּ דְּרִבִּי יוֹחָנָן נִיחָא מוּתָּר לַחְפּוֹר בּוֹ בּוֹרוֹת שִׁיחִין וּמְעָרוֹת. עַל דַּעְתֵּיהּ
דְּרִבִּי לָעָזָר מָהוּ לַחְפּוֹר בּוֹ בּוֹרוֹת שִׁיחִין וּמְעָרוֹת. כְּשֵׁם שֶׁאֵין מְלַמְּדִין לְעִנְיַן
אִיסּוּר כָּךְ לְעִנְיַן הֶיתֵּר לֹא יְלַמְּדוּ.

According to R. Joḥanan it is obvious that one is permitted to dig in it[22]
cisterns, ditches, and caves. According to R. Eleazar, may one dig in it
cisterns, ditches, and caves? If the verses have no implication for
prohibition they cannot have implications for permission[23].

22   The Sabbatical year. If ploughing is permitted, digging certainly is.

23   The question is asked the wrong
way: If R. Joḥanan asserts that two
examples together do not prove anything, they cannot prove that something
is permitted. On the other hand, R.
Eleazar (following *Sifra Behar*) only
prohibits work on the field and in the
vineyard, certainly not digging ditches.

אָמַר רִבִּי בָּא קַרְתִּיגְנָיָיא טַעַם דְּרִבִּי יוֹחָנָן שֵׁשׁ שָׁנִים תִּזְרַע שָׂדְךָ לֹא בַּשְּׁבִיעִית
וְשֵׁשׁ שָׁנִים תִּזְמוֹר כַּרְמֶךָ לֹא בַּשְּׁבִיעִית. כָּל־לֹא תַעֲשֶׂה שֶׁהוּא בָּא מִכֹּחַ עֲשֵׂה
עֲשֵׂה הוּא וְעוֹבֵר בַּעֲשֵׂה. רִבִּי יִרְמְיָה אָמַר עוֹבֵר בַּעֲשֵׂה. רִבִּי יוֹסָה אָמַר אֲפִילוּ
עֲשֵׂה אֵין בּוֹ לְיֵידָה מִילָה כְּתִיב וְשָׁבְתָה הָאָרֶץ שַׁבָּת לַיְיָ. לְעִנְיָן לֹא תַעֲשֶׂה
שַׁבָּה.

Rebbi Abba from Carthage said, the reason of Rebbi Joḥanan is (*Lev.*
25:3): "Six years you shall sow your field", not in the Seventh, "six years

you shall prune your vineyard," not in the Seventh. Every prohibition
derived from a positive commandment is a positive commandment; he
transgresses a positive commandment[24]. Rebbi Jeremiah said, he
transgresses a positive commandment. Rebbi Yasa said, there is not even
a positive commandment! Why is it written (*Lev.* 25:2): "the Land shall
rest for a Sabbath of the Eternal?" For the prohibitions in it[25].

24   In the opinion of R. Abba from
Carthage, R. Johanan only asserted that
ploughing is not overstepping a formal
prohibition. For him, ploughing is still
forbidden but the prohibition is not one
of criminal law since it is formulated in

a positive way.

25   He (R. Assi) sticks with the
prior explanation that two simultaneous
examples do not imply *heqqeš*; "the
prohibitions in it" are the two prohibitions spelled out in the verse.

יָכוֹל יְהוּ לוֹקִין עַל הַתּוֹסָפוֹת שֶׁבּוֹ. רִבִּי יוֹחָנָן פָּתַר מַתְנִיתָא יָכוֹל יְהוּ לוֹקִין עַל
חֲרִישָׁה בַּשְּׁבִיעִית. רִבִּי לָעֲזָר פָּתַר מַתְנִיתָא יָכוֹל יְהוּ לוֹקִין עַל אִיסּוּר שְׁנֵי
פְּרָקִים הָרִאשׁוֹנִים. אִית תַּנָּיֵי תַּנֵּי שֵׁשׁ שָׁנִים תִּזְרַע שָׂדֶךָ וְשֵׁשׁ שָׁנִים תִּזְמוֹר
כַּרְמֶךָ. אִית תַּנָּיֵי תַּנֵּי שָׂדֶךָ לֹא תִזְרָע וְכַרְמְךָ לֹא תִזְמוֹר. מָאן דְּאָמַר שֵׁשׁ שָׁנִים
תִּזְרַע שָׂדֶךָ וְשֵׁשׁ שָׁנִים תִּזְמוֹר כַּרְמֶךָ מְסַייְעָא לְרִבִּי יוֹחָנָן. מָאן דְּאָמַר שָׂדֶךָ לֹא
תִזְרַע וְכַרְמְךָ לֹא תִזְמוֹר מְסַייְעָא לְרִבִּי לָעֲזָר.

"I could think one would whip because of the additions.[26]" Rebbi
Johanan explains the *baraita*, I could think that one would whip because
of ploughing in the Sabbatical. Rebbi Eleazar explains the *baraita*, I could
think that one would whip because of the prohibition of the first two
terms[27]. Some Tannaïm state (*Lev.* 25:3): "Six years you shall sow your
field, six years you shall prune your vineyard." Some Tannaïm state (*Lev.*
25:4) "Your field you should not sow, your vineyard you should not
prune." He who states: "Six years you shall sow your field, six years you
shall prune your vineyard," supports Rebbi Johanan. He who states: "Your

field you should not sow, your vineyard you should not prune," supports Rebbi Eleazar[28].

26 This is a quote from a *baraita*; a similar one, also quoted in two separate pieces, is in Babli *Mo'ed Qaṭan* 3b. A *baraita* starting with "I could think that . . ." always ends with showing that it is not so. The "additions" are prohibitions not explicitly stated in the Pentateuch.

27 The prohibition to work after the harvest of the year preceding the Sabbatical, two different terms, one for fields and one for orchards (*Ševiʿit* 1:1,2:1). These regulations have purely

rabbinical character; the Biblical prohibition extends only to a short time before New Year's Day. R. Eleazar will agree that even transgression of the latter prohibition is not punishable in court but the expression "two terms" is inappropriate since it refers to rabbinical extensions.

28 The implications of these verses for the positions of the authors have been explained in the previous paragraphs.

מַתְנִיתָא פְּלִיגָא עַל רִבִּי לָעְזָר הִשָּׁמֶר לֹא תַעֲשֶׂה. וּכְתִיב שָׁם תַּעֲלֶה שָׁם תַּעֲשֶׂה. בְּגִין דִּכְתִיב הָא אִילוּ לֹא כְתִיב עֲשֵׂה הוּא. שֶׁלֹּא תֹאמַר כְּמָה דְתֵימָא גַּבֵּי שַׁבָּת חָפַר חָרַץ נָעַץ אֵינוֹ חַיָּיב אֶלָּא אַחַת. וְדִכְוָותָהּ שָׁחַט זָרַק וְהֶעֱלָה לֹא יְהֵא חַיָּיב אֶלָּא אַחַת. לְפוּם כֵּן צָרִיךְ מֵימַר חַיָּיב עַל כָּל־אַחַת וְאַחַת.

A *baraita* disagrees with Rebbi Eleazar[29]. "'Guard yourself' means a prohibition. And it is written: There you should present, there you should perform." Because that is written, otherwise I would have said it is a positive commandment[30]. But that you should not say as you say regarding the Sabbath that if somebody dug a hole, made a ditch, and dug to put in a pole, he is guilty only of one offense, so similarly, if somebody slaughtered, sprinkled the blood, and presented he should be guilty only of one offense[31]. Therefore, it is necessary to say that he is guilty for each action separately.

29 The *baraita* is preserved in *Sifry Deut.* 70-71, on the verses (*Deut.* 12-13): "*Guard yourself* not to present your burnt offerings at every place you see. Only at the place which the Eternal will choose from one of your tribes, there *you should present* your burnt offerings and there *you should perform* all that I am commanding you." The first verse contains a prohibition, the second a positive commandment and because of this difference, the verses cannot be taken together in the way R. Eleazar interpreted a similar situation regarding the Sabbatical year. Hence, R. Eleazar seems to contradict tannaïtic attitudes. Since in our sources R. Eleazar's interpretation of the verses *Lev.* 25:2-5 is found in *Sifra*, one may take this as an indication that *Sifra* was unknown to the compilers of the Yerushalmi, and that *Sifra* is a Babylonian compilation of tannaïtic material as is traditionally asserted.

30 Verses 13-14 show that sacrificing outside the precincts of the Tabernacle or the Temple is a criminal offense (v. 13) and a disregard of a positive injunction (v. 14). The two verses are parallel, not logically consecutive as R. Eleazar would require.

31 An argument is given that R. Eleazar could justify the different treatment of an apparently similar situation.

The Sabbath prohibitions are classified under 39 categories of "main works". An action similar to one of the main works is called a derivative. For example, ploughing as a preparation for sowing and digging a hole for the planting of a tree are main work and derivative respectively. If somebody performed both a main work and one of its derivatives in error, he has to bring one sacrifice of atonement. But if he transgressed prohibitions belonging to two distinct categories, he has to bring two sacrifices. In the case of sacrifices outside the Temple, presenting the sacrifice on the altar is really the last action; it is preceded first by the slaughter of the sacrificial animal and second by the sprinkling of its blood on the walls of the altar. These actions are classified as "performing". Since the order of the actions is inverted, first "presenting" then "acting", it follows that they are distinct and that slaughter and sprinkling are not legally derivatives of presenting. (In the *Sifry*, the interpretation is that the prohibition covers only those actions that are simultaneously a criminal offense and a disregard of a positive injunction.)

רִבִּי זְעִירָא רַב חִיָּיא בַּר אַשִׁי בְּשֵׁם כְּהָנָא הַנּוֹטֵעַ בַּשַּׁבָּת חַיָּיב מִשּׁוּם זוֹרֵעַ. רִבִּי זְעִירָא אָמַר הַזוֹמֵר כְּנוֹטֵעַ. נָטַע וְזָמַר בַּשַּׁבָּת עַל דַּעְתֵּיהּ דַּכְהָנָא חַיָּיב שְׁתַּיִם. עַל דַּעְתֵּיהּ דְּרִבִּי זְעִירָא אֵינוֹ (fol. 31b) חַיָּיב אֶלָּא אַחַת. כְּלוּם אָמַר רִבִּי זְעִירָא אֶלָּא הַזוֹמֵר כְּנוֹטֵעַ שֵׁמָּא הַנּוֹטֵעַ כְּזוֹמֵר. הַכֹּל הָיָה בִּכְלָל זְרִיעָה יָצְאַת זְמִירָה לְהַחֲמִיר עַל עַצְמָהּ. מִפְּנֵי שֶׁיָּצְאַת זְמִירָה לְהַחֲמִיר עַל עַצְמָהּ אַתְּ פּוֹטְרוֹ מִשּׁוּם[32] זוֹרֵעַ הֲוֵי לֹא שַׁנְיָא בֵּין עַל דַּעְתֵּיהּ דַּכְהָנָא בֵּין עַל דַּעְתֵּיהּ דְּרִבִּי זְעִירָא חַיָּיב שְׁתַּיִם.

Rebbi Zeïra, Rav Ḥiyya bar Ashi in the name of Cahana[33]: He who is planting on the Sabbath is guilty because of sowing[34]. Rebbi Zeïra said, he who prunes is like one who plants. If he planted and pruned on the Sabbath, according to Cahana he is guilty on two counts, according to Rebbi Zeïra only on one count. Did not Rebbi Zeïra say the pruner is like the planter, did he say the planter is like the pruner[35]? All was included in the notion of sowing; pruning was singled out for particular stringency[36]. Because pruning was singled out for particular stringency you want to exempt it because of sowing? There is no difference, both according to Cahana and according to Rebbi Zeïra he is guilty on two counts.

32   Reading of the mss. Venice print: שמו.

33   Since Rav Ḥiyya bar Ashi was among the older students of Rav, Cahana mentioned here cannot be the one who went to study under R. Joḥanan but must be an older Sage (Cahana I) who already was a recognized authority when Rav returned from Galilee to Babylonia.

34   Sowing is the category, planting a derivative.

35   Pruning is a subcategory of sowing concerning the Sabbath just as planting is, but planting is not like pruning for the Sabbatical year since planting belongs to sowing.

36   Following the argument made for the Sabbath, it would not have been necessary to have pruning singled out in the laws of the Sabbatical. Since it is obvious that for the Sabbatical, pruning is a separate offense, pruning can be a subcategory of sowing for the Sabbath only as a stringency, not a leniency.

(fol. 31a) **משנה ב:** בְּהֵמָה עִם בְּהֵמָה וְחַיָּה עִם חַיָּה בְּהֵמָה עִם חַיָּה וְחַיָּה עִם בְּהֵמָה טְמֵאָה עִם טְמֵאָה וּטְהוֹרָה עִם טְהוֹרָה טְמֵאָה עִם טְהוֹרָה וּטְהוֹרָה עִם טְמֵאָה אֲסוּרִין לַחֲרוֹשׁ וְלִמְשׁוֹךְ וּלְהַנְהִיג.

Mishnah 2: Domestic animal with [different] domestic animal and wild with [different] wild animal, domesticated with wild and wild with domesticated animal, unclean with [different] unclean and clean with [different] clean animal, unclean with clean and clean with unclean animal, all these are [combinations] forbidden for ploughing, drawing, and leading[37].

37   The source of this Mishnah is *Deut.* 22:10: "Do not plough with an ox and a donkey together." It is forbidden to take animals of two different species under a common yoke either for work (ploughing or drawing a cart) or to lead them. The Mishnah mss. of the Maimonides tradition start with: "When was this said", referring to the end of the previous Mishnah that "Kilaim of animals may be raised and kept; they are only forbidden to be mated"; this is only for "domestic animal with domestic animal, wild with wild animal, domesticated with wild and wild with domesticated animal, unclean with unclean and clean with clean animal." For Maimonides, the prohibition of ploughing, etc., refers only to combinations of unclean (i. e. animals that may not be eaten) and clean (animals that may be eaten) animals. The text of the Halakhah gives some support for such a reading since it starts with a discussion of mating different species.

(fol. 31c) **הלכה ב:** בְּהֵמָה עִם בְּהֵמָה כו'. יָכוֹל לֹא יְהֵא מַעֲמִיד זְכָרִים אֵצֶל הַנְּקֵבוֹת וּנְקֵבוֹת אֵצֶל הַזְּכָרִים תַּלְמוּד לוֹמַר בְּהֶמְתְּךָ לֹא תַרְבִּיעַ. אֵין אַתְּ אָסוּר אֶלָּא מִלְהַרְבִּיעַ אֲבָל מַעֲמִיד אַתְּ זְכָרִים אֵצֶל נְקֵבוֹת וּנְקֵבוֹת אֵצֶל זְכָרִים. וְכִי מַה עָשָׂה מַעֲשֶׂה לֹא כְּשֶׁהִטִּיל וּלְפִי דַעְתּוֹ הוּא מַטִּיל.

Halakhah 2: "Domestic animal with domestic animal, etc." I might think one cannot put a male next to a female nor a female next to a male; the verse says (*Lev.* 19:19) "do not cause your domestic animals to copulate". You are only forbidden to cause to copulate but you may put a male next to a female or a female next to a male. But what did he actually do[38]? When it ejaculates it does so by itself.

38   In order to commit a crime, the perpetrator has to perform a forbidden action. But if the male animal acts by itself, is not put on the female by a human, nothing has been perpetrated. (Explanation by R. Eliahu Fulda, following the Babli *Baba Meẓi'a* 91a. R. Moses Margalit and R. Eliahu Wilna explain: What is the crime committed by a person who causes animals to copulate by bringing the male bodily onto the female? The answer is that while ejaculation by the male is an automatic reaction, it fulfills the expectations of the human and therefore is induced by the human's action.)

אִיסִי בֶּן עֲקַבְיָה אוֹמֵר אָסוּר לִרְכֹּב עַל גַּבֵּי פִרְדָּה מִקַּל וָחוֹמֶר. וּמַה אִם בִּבְגָדִים שֶׁאַתְּ מוּתָּר לִלְבּוֹשׁ זֶה עַל זֶה אַתְּ אָסוּר בְּתַעֲרוּבָתָן. בְּהֵמָה שֶׁאַתְּ אָסוּר לְהַנְהִיג בָּהּ בְּזוֹ עִם זוֹ לֹא כָל־שֶׁכֵּן אַתְּ אָסוּר לִרְכּוֹב עָלֶיהָ. וְהָא כְּתִיב וַיִּרְכְּבוּ אִישׁ עַל פִּרְדּוֹ וַיָּנֻסוּ. אֵין לְמֵדִין מִן הַמַּלְכוּת. וְהָא כְּתִיב וְהִרְכַּבְתֶּם אֶת שְׁלֹמֹה בְנִי עַל הַפִּרְדָּה אֲשֶׁר לִי. בְּרִיָּה מִשֵּׁשֶׁת יְמֵי בְרֵאשִׁית הָיְתָה.

[39]Issi ben Aqabia[40] says: It is forbidden to ride on a mule by an argument of analogy. If garments which you may wear one upon the other are forbidden in mixture[41], you are certainly forbidden to ride on [a mixture of] animals you may not lead together. But is it not written (*2Sam.* 13:29): "Each one rode on his mule and they fled"? One does not learn from a king's family[42]. But is it not written (*1K.* 1:33): "Let my son Solomon ride on my she-mule"? That was a creature from Creation[43].

39   Tosephta *Kilaim* 5:6. The Tosephta rejects Issi's argument since it is written about David that he did all that was right in the eyes of the Eternal (*1K.* 15:5).

40   A Tanna of the last generation, student of R. Eleazar ben Shamua and R. Yose, who appears also as Issi ben

Gur Arieh, Issi ben Jehudah, Issi ben
Gamliel, Joseph the Babylonian, Joseph
from Hutsal, and maybe Rav Assi.

41   It might be permitted to wear a
woolen coat over a linen garment but it
is forbidden to wear any garment
containing both wool and linen; cf.

Chapter Nine, end of Halakhah 7.

42   They will not listen to religious
authority.

43   A wild animal, spontaneous
offspring of a wild horse and a wild
ass.

רְבִּי חָמָא בַּר עוּקְבָּא בְשֶׁם רְבִּי יוֹסֵי בֵּי רְבִּי חֲנִינָה אָמַר הַמַּנְהִיג קוֹלוֹ בְכִלְאַיִם
לוֹקֶה. וְתַנֵּי כֵן הַנְּהִיגָהּ הַמְשִׁיכָהּ קָרָא לָהּ וּבָאָת אַחֲרָיו נִתְחַיֵּיב בָּהּ לְשַׁלֵּם
כְּשׁוֹאֵל. וְהָתַנֵּי שְׁמוּאֵל הָיְתָה עוֹמֶדֶת חוּץ לִתְחוּם וְקָרָא לָהּ וּבָאָת אַחֲרָיו הֲרֵי
זֶה פָטוּר. תַּמָּן לְדַעְתָּהּ הִיא מְהַלָּכֶת. בְּרַם הָכָא עַל כָּרְחָהּ הִיא מְהַלֶּכֶת. וְהָתַנֵּי
טִיפַּח כְּנֶגֶד עֵינוֹ וְסִימֵּייהּ כְּנֶגֶד אָזְנוֹ וְחֵרְשָׁהּ לֹא יָצָא לְחֵירוּת. אָמַר רְבִּי לִיעֶזֶר
בֵּי רְבִּי יוֹסֵי קוֹמֵי רְבִּי יוֹסֵי שַׁנְיָיא הִיא שֶׁהוּא יָכוֹל לִבְרוֹחַ. תֵּדַע לָךְ שֶׁהוּא כֵן
דְּתַנֵּי תְּפָשׂ בּוֹ הֲרֵי זֶה חַיָּיב.

Rebbi Ḥama bar Uqba[44] said in the name of Rebbi Yose ben Rebbi
Ḥanina, he who leads *kilaim* by voice will be whipped[45]. We have stated
so: "If he led it, if he made it draw, if he called it and it came, he is
responsible to pay like a borrower.[46]" But did not Samuel state: "If it was
standing outside the Sabbath domain, he called it and it came after him, he
is free.[47]" There it comes of its own volition, here it is forced to walk[48]
But did we not state: "If he clapped before his [a slave's] eye and blinded
it, before his [a slave's] ear and made it deaf, he [the slave] does not attain
freedom.[49]" Rebbi Eliezer ben Rebbi Yose said before Rebbi Yose, there
is a difference because he [the slave] could have fled. Know that it is so
because we have stated: "If he grabbed him he is guilty."

44   A student of R. Yose ben Ḥanina
and teacher of Rebbis Jeremiah, Jonah,
Yose.

45   In the Babli, *Baba Meẓi'a* 90b,
this is a disagreement between R.
Joḥanan and R. Simeon ben Laqish.

The argument there is only whether speaking is considered an action, not as in the Yerushalmi that the yoking together of two animals of different species prepares the transgression.

46   If a person takes an animal which is not his in any of the ways indicated, he becomes responsible for all damages incurred as if he had borrowed the animal, until he formally returns it to its owner. In the Babli (*Qiddušin* 22b) and the Tosephta (*Qiddušin* 1:7), a parallel statement is given referring to acquisition of movables. In talmudic theory, payment alone does not transfer property; the property bought must be acquired by actually taking possession of at least some of it. If somebody bought a herd of cattle and then called one of them and it came, he has acquired the herd.

47   If his cattle was standing outside the domain he could walk in on the Sabbath (2000 cubits from the edge of his town) and he called it back, he has not infringed on the laws of the Sabbath since he did not actually step outside his domain. Hence, calling cannot be the same as actually leading.

48   Since leading two animals of different species is forbidden only if they are somehow bound together, which restricts the freedom of each animal to walk according to its own volition and makes the human the overpowering influence. The Babli (*Baba Meẕi'a* 90b) seems to reject this argument by noting that if somebody bound two animals together and then another person came and drove them, or if somebody muzzled the mouth of an ox far away from grain and another person then led it to thresh grain, only the second person is guilty in either case. This rule is accepted in Yerushalmi *Terumot* 9:4 (fol. 46d); it is considered irrelevant as argument here.

49   A slave gains his freedom if he is severely injured by his master (*Ex.* 21:26-27). If the master hits the slave on his body, the slave goes free; near the body only if the slave could not move away. Similarly, for *kilaim* the rancher is responsible only if he restricts the freedom of movement of his animals.

The parallel discussion is in Babli *Qiddušin* 24b.

(fol. 31a) **מֵשׁנָה ג:** הַמַּנְהִיג סוֹפֵג אֶת הָאַרְבָּעִים וְהַיּוֹשֵׁב בַּקָּרוֹן סוֹפֵג אֶת

הָאַרְבָּעִים. רבִּי מֵאִיר פּוֹטֵר. וְהַשְּׁלִישִׁית שֶׁהִיא קְשׁוּרָה לִרְצוּעוֹתֵיהֶן אֲסוּרָה.

Mishnah 3: The driver absorbs the forty[50] and the one sitting in the
cart absorbs the forty. Rebbi Meïr frees him from prosecution[51]. A third
animal tied to their harness is forbidden[52].

50　　This Mishnah deals with a cart
(Greek κάρρον, τό, "car, cart"; cf.
κάρρος, ὁ, Latin *carrus, carrum*, "two-
wheeled cart") drawn by two animals
of different species. "Absorbing the
forty" means being punished by 39
lashes.

51　　This reading is supported by
Sifry Deut. 231, Babli *Baba Meẓi'a* 8b,
against the opinion of Samuel who
exchanges the positions of R. Meïr and
the rabbis.

52　　If a cart is drawn by two animals of the same species and a third
animal is tied not to the cart but to the
harness of the other two, it is forbidden but not criminally prosecutable.
{According to Maimonides, a *qarōn* is
not a cart but a train of two carts, from
Arabic קרן "to bind two things
together". If one sits in the first of two
carts one is criminally liable; if a third
cart is added at the end one is
forbidden to sit there.}

(fol. 31c) **הֲלָכָה ג:** הַיּוֹשֵׁב בְּקָרוֹן רַבָּנִין אָמְרִין מִשְׁקָל הוּא וְרבִּי מֵאִיר אוֹמֵר
אֵינוֹ מִשְׁקָל.

Halakhah 3[53]: He who sits in a cart, the rabbis say he is a weight,
Rebbi Meïr says, he is no weight[54].

53　　In the Venice print and Leyden
ms, this is still part of Halakhah 2.

54　　The rabbis assert that the ani-

mals have to work harder because of
the passenger.

בָּרִאשׁוֹנָה לֹא הָיוּ אֶלָּא שְׁתַּיִם דִּכְתִיב וַיַּרְכֵּב אוֹתוֹ בְּמִרְכֶּבֶת הַמִּשְׁנֶה אֲשֶׁר לוֹ.
עָמַד פַּרְעֹה וְעָשָׂה שָׁלֹשׁ דִּכְתִיב וְשָׁלִשִׁים עַל כּוּלוֹ. עָמְדָה מַלְכוּת הָרְשָׁעָה וְעָשָׂה
אוֹתָן אַרְבָּעָה.

Originally there were only two as it is written (*Gen.* 41:43): "He made him ride in his two-horse carriage." Pharao came and made them three, as it is written (*Ex.* 14:7): "three-horse over everything." The evil kingdom[55] arose and made it four.

55   A standard name for the Roman government.

(fol. 31a) **משנה ד**: אֵין קוֹשְׁרִין אֶת הַסּוּס לֹא בְּצִדְדֵי הַקָּרוֹן וְלֹא לְאַחַר הַקָּרוֹן. וְלֹא אֶת הַלּוֹבְדְּקֶס לַגְּמַלִּים. רִבִּי יְהוּדָה אוֹמֵר כָּל־הַנּוֹלָדִים מִן הַסּוּס אַף עַל פִּי שֶׁאֲבִיהֶן חֲמוֹר מוּתָּרִין זֶה עִם זֶה. וְכֵן הַנּוֹלָדִים מִן הַחֲמוֹר אַף עַל פִּי שֶׁאֲבִיהֶן סוּס מוּתָּרִין זֶה עִם זֶה אֲבָל הַנּוֹלָדִים מִן הַסּוּס עִם הַנּוֹלָדִים מִן הַחֲמוֹר אֲסוּרִין זֶה עִם זֶה.

Mishnah 4: One does not tie a horse to the sides or the back of a cart, or a Libyan donkey to camels. Rebbi Jehudah says, all animals born from a horse are permitted one with the other even if their father was a donkey, all animals born from a donkey are permitted one with the other even if their father was a horse, but those born from a horse are forbidden with those from a donkey.

(fol. 31c) **הלכה ד**: אֵין קוֹשְׁרִין אֶת הַסּוּס לֹא לְצִדְדֵי הַקָּרוֹן וְלֹא לְאַחַר הַקָּרוֹן. תַּנֵּי רִבִּי מֵאִיר פּוֹטֵר. אִם הָיָה מְסַיְּיעוֹ בֵּין בְּמַעֲלָה בֵּין בִּירִידָה הַכֹּל מוֹדִין שֶׁהוּא אָסוּר. אָמַר רִבִּי יוֹחָנָן מִפְּנֵי שֶׁזֶּה נוֹשֵׂא עֲצֵלוּתוֹ שֶׁל זֶה וְזֶה נוֹשֵׂא עֲצֵלוּתוֹ שֶׁל זֶה. רַב אָמַר מִפְּנֵי שֶׁנִּשּׂוּאִין אֶת הַחֶבֶל שֶׁבֵּינְתַּיִם.

Halakhah 4[56]: "One does not tie a horse to the sides or the back of a cart." It is stated[57]: Rebbi Meïr frees from prosecution. If it supported, whether in ascent or in descent, everybody agrees that it is forbidden.

Rebbi Joḥanan said, because either one carries the laziness of the other[58]. Rav says, because the rope is carried between them.

56　In the Venice text, Halakhah 3.

57　In both *Sifry Deut.* 231, Tosephta *Kilaim* 5:4, it is stated that R. Meïr permits it; in his opinion it is not a non-prosecutable misdemeanor but is unquestionably permitted. The reason is stated in *Sifry*: Since it says, "do not plough with ox and donkey *together*", any use that is not together is permitted.

58　Since the ox before the cart and the horse tied to the cart do not walk with the same speed, they both influence the movement of the cart and are "together". In antiquity, horses were used for riding and drawing chariots but never civilian carts.

רִבִּי יִרְמְיָה בָּעֵי קְשָׁרָן בִּשְׂעָרָן. מַה נָן קַייָמִין אִם בְּשֶׁקְּשָׁרוֹ בִּשְׂעָרוֹ כָּךְ אָנוּ אוֹמְרִים אָסוּר לְהַרְכִּיב בְּהֵמָה עַל גַּבֵּי חֲבִירָתָהּ אִם בְּשֶׁקְּשָׁרוֹ הַחֶבֶל בִּשְׂעָרוֹ נֹאמַר מִפְּנֵי שֶׁהֵן נוֹשְׂאִין אֶת הַחֶבֶל שֶׁבֵּינְתַּיִם. רִבִּי יוֹנָה אָמַר אִיתְפַּלְגִין רַב וְרִבִּי יוֹחָנָן רִבִּי יוֹחָנָן אָמַר מִפְּנֵי שֶׁזֶּה נוֹשֵׂא עַצְלוּתוֹ שֶׁל זֶה וְזֶה נוֹשֵׂא עַצְלוּתוֹ שֶׁל זֶה. רַב אָמַר מִפְּנֵי שֶׁהֵן נוֹשְׂאִין אֶת הַחֶבֶל שֶׁבֵּינְתַּיִם. מַה נְפַק מִן בֵּינֵיהוֹן קְשָׁרוֹ בִּשְׂעָרוֹ בֵּין עַל דַּעְתֵּיהּ דְּרַב בֵּין עַל דַּעְתֵּיהּ דְּרִבִּי יוֹחָנָן פָּטוּר.

Rebbi Jeremiah asked: If he bound them by their hair[59]? Where do we hold? In case he bound them together by their hair[60], should we say that it is forbidden to let one animal ride on another? If he tied them by a rope, we say because they carry the rope between them. Rebbi Jonah said, Rav and Rebbi Joḥanan disagree, Rebbi Joḥanan said, because either one carries the laziness of the other. Rav says, because they carry the rope between them. What is the difference? Both according to Rav as also according to Rebbi Joḥanan, if he bound them by their hair[61] he is not punishable!

59　Is this permitted or forbidden? The question is not formulated clearly.

60　In this case, they cannot draw anything.

61   If no rope is used, the argument of Rav does not apply. Since the animals will not be able to draw if the cart is attached to their hair, the argument of R. Johanan does not apply.

וְלֹא הַלִּיבְדְקֵס. אִית תַּנָּיֵי תַּנֵּי נִיבְרֹקוֹס. מָאן דְּאָמַר הַלִּיבְדְקֵס עַל[62] שֵׁם לִיבּוּיֵ עַל שֵׁם לוּבִים וְכוּשִׁים בְּמִצְעָדָיו. מָאן דְּאָמַר נִיבְרֹקוֹס אבהטם מַהוּ אבהטם חֲמָר סָלָק. רִבִּי יוֹנָה רַב הוֹשַׁעְיָה בָּעֵי גֵּרִים הַבָּאִים מִלִּיבּוֹיֵ מַהוּ לְהַמְתִּין לָהֶן שְׁלֹשָׁה דוֹרוֹת. אָמַר רִבִּי יוֹנָה בּוֹצְרָיְיָה מִן מַה דַּאֲנַן חָמֵי הָהֵן פּוֹלָא מִצְרָיֵי כַּד רָטִיב אִינּוּן צְוָוחִין לֵיהּ לוּבִּי כַּד הוּא נְגִיב אִינּוּן צְוָוחִין לֵיהּ פּוֹל מִצְרָיֵי. הָדָא אֲמָרָה גֵּר מְלוּבֵּי צָרִיךְ לְהַמְתִּין שְׁלֹשָׁה דוֹרוֹת. הָדָא אֲמָרָה הִיא לוּב הִיא מִצְרָיִם.

[63]"And not a Libyan[64] donkey." Some Tannaïm state: "Not a *nybrqvs*[65]." He who says *libdēqēs* on the name of Lybian and (*Dan.* 11:43) "Lybians and Nubians in His train." He who says *nybrqvs 'bhṭs*[66], What is *'bhṭs*? A mounting donkey. Rebbi Jonah: Rav Hoshaia[67] asked: Do proselytes from Libya have to wait three generations[68]? Rebbi Jonah from Bostra[69] said, from what we see that they call a green Egyptian bean Libyan[70] but a dry one Egyptian, that means a proselyte from Libya has to wait three generations, it means that Libya is identical with Egypt.

62   Reading of the Rome ms. The word is missing in the Leyden ms. and Venice print.

63   A parallel text is in *Šabbat* 5:1. A very detailed study of the first six sentences here and in *Šabbat* was done by J. N. Epstein, מבוא לנוסח המשנה 2, Jerusalem 1964, pp. 97-99, where all variant readings of the names here, in *Šabbat*, and *Gen. rabba* are collected and commented on. The vocalization of ליבדקס is from the Kaufmann ms. of the Mishnah.

64   Perhaps the ending דקס refers to Latin *equus* "horse", "Libyan animal of the horse family" (E. G.).

65   An unexplained word that was unknown even to the rabbis of the Yerushalmi. The Arukh reads ניבדקוס, explainable by a change of liquids, *l* - *n*. Perhaps also a composite of *equus*, "Nubian animal of the horse family" (E.

G.).

66   The parallel in *Šabbat* reads אמבטס ἀμβάτης, poetic for ἀναβάτης "stallion". J. N. Epstein points out that because of the nasal pronunciation of מ in Galilean speech, an *m* can easily be inserted or disappear, so that אמבטס and אב(ה)טס are really one and the same and the text in *Kilaim* is not necessarily a corruption of the text in *Šabbat*.

67   Amora of the third generation, Babylonian student of Rav Jehudah and Rav Huna, who went to Galilee with his brother and became prominent in the academies of the successors of R. Johanan. The two brothers earned their livelihood as shoemakers; their main customers were prostitutes who used to swear by the lives of these holy rabbis who never even looked at them.

68   *Deut.* 23:8-9 prescribes that an Egyptian proselyte and his direct offspring may not marry anyone born to Jewish parents. {The discussion is purely theoretical since one holds that the political upheavals already from the time of Sanherib did displace all peoples originally mentioned in the Pentateuch, Mishnah *Yadayim* 4:4; cf. *Šulḥan 'Arukh Even Ha'ezer* 4:10.}

69   Amora of the fifth generation, mentioned in connection with R. Mana and Rebbi Huna.

70   A bean is لوبيا *lubia* in Arabic and Farsi; according to N. Brüll, the name is originally Coptic.

רִבִּי יִצְחָק בַּר נַחְמָן בְּשֵׁם רִבִּי הוֹשַׁעְיָה הֲלָכָה כְּדִבְרֵי הַתַּלְמִיד. דִּבְרֵי חֲכָמִים כָּל־מִין פִּרְדּוֹת אֶחָד.

Rebbi Isaac bar Naḥman in the name of Rebbi Hoshaiah: Practice follows the student[71]. The words of the Sages are that all kinds of mules are the same.

71   The "student" here is Rebbi Jehudah. It is implied that the opinion of the "Sages", that all kinds of mules are the same and may be mated with one another, is the opinion of R. Jehudah's teacher R. Aqiba. The ruling is also reported in the Babli (*Ketubot* 111b). In the generally accepted opinion of Maimonides, based on the Babli but which can be supported by the position of the "Sages" here, R. Jehudah is restrictive: Only mules of the same kind of mother can be mated, not different kinds of mules nor mules with the pure species of their mother (*Kilaim* 9:6-7). R. Jehudah holds that among animals the father counts; the Sages take the opposite position.

וְאֵילּוּ הֵן הַסִּימָנִין. אָמַר רִבִּי יוֹנָה כָּל־שֶׁאָזְנָיו קְטַנּוֹת אמּוֹ סוּסָה וְאָבִיו חֲמוֹר.
גְּדוֹלוֹת אמּוֹ חֲמוֹרָה וְאָבִיו סוּס. רִבִּי מָנָא מְפַקֵּד לְאִילֵּין דְּרִבִּי יוֹדָן נְשִׂיאָה אִין
בְּעִיתוּן מִיזְבּוֹן מוּלְוֹון אַתּוּן זְבַנִּין לוֹ אָזְנֵיהוֹן דְּקִיקִין שֶׁאמּוֹ סוּסָה וְאָבִיו חֲמוֹר.

These[72] are its signs: Rebbi Jonah says, if it has small ears, its mother is
a horse and its father a donkey; if it has large ears its mother is a donkey
and its father a horse. Rebbi Mana ordered those of the patriarch's estate:
If you want to buy a mule, you should buy one with small ears whose
mother is a horse and whose father is a donkey.

72   An almost identical text is in   have a practical criterion of how to
Berakhot 8:6, Notes 120 ff. Since   distinguish between the two kinds of
practice follows R. Jehudah, one has to   mule that cannot be mated.

הַלּוֹבֶן מִן הָאִישׁ שֶׁמִּמֶּנּוּ מוֹחַ וַעֲצָמוֹת וְהַגִּידִים. וְהָאוֹדֶם מִן הָאִשָּׁה שֶׁמִּמֶּנָּה
הָעוֹר וְהַבָּשָׂר וְהַדָּם. וְהָרוּחַ וְהַנֶּפֶשׁ וְהַנְּשָׁמָה מִשֶּׁל הַקָּדוֹשׁ בָּרוּךְ הוּא. וּשְׁלָשְׁתָּן
שׁוּתָּפִין בּוֹ.

The white is from the male, from him are brain, bones, and sinews.
The red is from the female, from her are skin, flesh, and blood. But
breath, life force, and soul are from the Holy One, may He be praised; all
three are partners in him[73].

73   "Him" is the child. A much   with animals, the paragraph is some-
more detailed explanation of the   what out of place since animals are
talmudic theory of heredity is in Babli   said not to have נשמה "soul" but only
Niddah 31a. Since the text here deals   נפש "the animal force of life."

רִבִּי בָּא רַב יְהוּדָה בְּשֵׁם רַב מוֹדִים חֲכָמִים לְרִבִּי יְהוּדָה בְּסוּס בֶּן סוּס בֶּן חֲמוֹר
עִם חֲמוֹר בֶּן חֲמוֹר בֶּן סוּס. רִבִּי חַגַּי רִבִּי זְעִירָא בְּשֵׁם רִבִּי אִיסָּת בְּנֵי עִזִּים בְּנֵי
רְחֵלִים אֲסוּרִין זֶה אִם אִם זֶה. דְּלָא כֵן מָה אֲנַן[74] אָמְרִין עֵז בֶּן עֵז בֶּן רָחֵל עִם רָחֵל
בֶּן רָחֵל בֶּן עֵז.

Rebbi Abba, Rav Jehudah in the name of Rav: The Sages agree with Rebbi Jehudah in the case of a horse from a horse from a donkey with a donkey from a donkey from a horse[75]. Rebbi Ḥaggai, Rebbi Zeïra in the name of Rebbi Issy[76]: descendants of she-goats and ewes are forbidden one with the other. If it were not so, why do we say "a goat from a goat from a ewe with a ewe from a ewe from a goat."

74   Reading of the Rome ms.
Venice: ‏ולא כן נן‎ .
75   The Sages hold that any two
animals half horse and half donkey can
be mated, but not an animal ⅔ horse

with an animal ⅔ donkey.
76   The otherwise unknown ‏איסח‎
must be ‏איסי‎ (Issy, Assi, Yasa), one of
the known teachers of R. Zeïra.

(fol. 31a) ‏משנה ח‎: הַפְּרוֹטִיּוֹת אֲסוּרוֹת וְהָרַמָּךְ מוּתָּר. וְאַדְנֵי הַשָּׂדֶה חַיָּה. רְבִּי יוֹסֵי אוֹמֵר מְטַמְּאוֹת בְּאוֹהֶל כְּאָדָם. הַקּוּפָּד וְחוּלְדַּת הַסְּנָאִין חַיָּה. חוּלְדַּת הַסְּנָאִין רְבִּי יוֹסֵי אוֹמֵר בֵּית שַׁמַּאי אוֹמֵר מְטַמֵּא בְּמַשָּׂא בִּכְזַיִת בְּמַשָּׂא וְכַעֲדָשָׁה בְּמַגָּע.

Mishnah 5: *Perotiot*[77] are forbidden and wild horses[78] are permitted. A great ape[79] is a wild animal; Rebbi Yose says they cause impurity in a tent like a human[80]. The hedgehog[81] and a squirrel mole[82] are wild animals. About the squirrel mole, Rebbi Yose says that the House of Shammai say it defiles in the amount of the volume of an olive in carrying, but in the volume of a lentil by touch.

77   All commentaries depending on
gaonic sources declare these to be
mules about which it is unknown
whether their mother was a horse or a
donkey and whose ears do not allow to

determine the species of their mother.
This implies that the opinion of R.
Jehudah in the preceding Mishnah is
accepted here as opinion of the
anonymous majority and, therefore,

practice to be followed. This would make superfluous the statement of R. Isaac bar Naḥman in the preceding Halakhah. Now in Arabic, פָּרַט فَرَط is "a horse which outruns all others" (from the root فرط "to surpass"). It might be that the entire sentence speaks of horses and that thoroughbreds are considered a separate species created by what today would be called genetic engineering, while wild horses are the same as a standard domesticated horse. (Cf. also Medieval Latin *paraveredus, parifredus* "horse" (E. G.).)

77   Definition of Maimonides.

79   Maimonides explains by Arabic נסנאס, نَسْنَاس "a fabled animal having only one foot," in accordance with the Halakhah here, but in his Commentary to Mishnah *Yadayim* 1:5 he notes that an ape (قرد) in Egypt is called נסנאס (in modern Farsi, it means Orang Utan). Rebbi Yose holds in *Yadaim* 1:5 that a great ape is not a human but the Sages there disagree.

80   Only human corpses cause

impurity in a tent, cf. Chapter 2, Note 180.

81   Biblical קֻפָּד. The Arabic quoted by Maimonides, קנפד, means either "rat" or "hedgehog."

82   חולדה, the Biblical חֹלֶד, means "mole" (*Ḥagigah* 1:5, fol. 80c). In *Lev.* 11:29, the mole is classified with the "crawling things". The problem is with the qualifier סנאי (or סניי), which the older commentaries derive from סנה "small bush, tree producing fruit every second year", but it is difficult to see a mole living in a bush. Maimonides describes the animal as "a kind of fox looking like a mole". If this animal is classified as "wild animal", its carcass or parts of it will make impure if touched or carried (even without touching) but only if there is at least the volume of an average olive; if it is classified as a "crawling thing" it does not make impure by being carried, but by touch it makes impure already by the volume of a small lentil.

הלכה ה: הַפְּרוֹטוֹת אֲסוּרוֹת וְהָרַמָּךְ מוּתָּר. רִבִּי אִימִּי בְּשֵׁם רִבִּי לְעָזָר (fol. 31c) רַמְכָא דְּלָא כַלִּיוָס. כְּמָה דְּתֵימַר בְּנֵי הָרַמָּכִים.

Halakhah 5: "*Perotiot* are forbidden and wild horses are permitted." Rebbi Ammi in the name of Rebbi Eleazar: *Ramak* is without χαλινός "bit". As one says (*Est.* 8:10): "the sons of wild horses"[83].

83 While in Arabic, רמך (rimāk, armāk) is a mare, R. Ammi insists that in the verse the masculine ending is appropriate and the horses used by the Persian imperial mail were born to domesticated mares but sired by wild (unbridled) horses.

אַבְנֵי הַשָּׂדֶה חַיָּה. יִיסֵי עֶרְקִי בַּר נַשׁ דְטוּר הוּא וְהוּא חַיי מִן טִיבּוּרְיֵיהּ אִיפְסַק טִיבּוּרְיֵיהּ לָא חַיי. רִבִּי חָמָא בַּר עוּקְבָּא בְּשֵׁם רִבִּי יוֹסֵי בֶּן חֲנִינָה טַעֲמָא דְּרִבִּי יוֹסֵי וְכָל־אֲשֶׁר יִגַּע עַל פְּנֵי הַשָּׂדֶה בְּגָדֵל עַל פְּנֵי הַשָּׂדֶה.

"'Field Stones'[84] is an animal." Yassi from Arke: It is a mountain man and lives from its navel. If its umbilical cord is cut, it cannot live. Rebbi Ḥama bar Uqba in the name of Rebbi Yose ben Ḥanina: The reason of Rebbi Yose (Num. 19:16): "All that touches [a slain person] on the surface of the field", when it grows on the field.

84 Reading of the Venice print; the Leyden ms. has two dots over the ב. But also in Sifra Šemini 4|6|5 it is stated on Lev. 11:27: "'All that walks on its soles' that is the monkey, 'all that walks' includes hedgehog and squirrel mole, field stones and seals." אבני השדה for אדני השדה refers to Job 5:23: "Your covenant is with 'field stones'."

הַיָּרוֹרוֹת וְהַנַּעֲמִית הֲרֵי הֵן כְּעוֹף לְכָל־דָּבָר. וְהַנָּחָשׁ הֲרֵי הוּא כְחַיָּה.

Yaror[85] and ostrich are like birds in all respects. The snake is like a wild animal.

85 In Tosephta Kilaim 5:8 ירורין. From the context, the name must refer to a walking bird, with a voice resembling that of a jackal. The word was used for birds both in Symmachos and the Peshitto, cf. R. S. Lieberman, תוספתא כפשוטה זרעים (New York 1956) p. 652. The determinations here refer to the rules of defilement by dead animals. The rule for the snake is given in Lev. 11:42 which states that "all that walk on their bellies and all that walk on four legs" follow the same rules.

רְבִּי חִיָּיה בְּשֵׁם רִבִּי יוֹחָנָן שִׁשָּׁה סְפֵיקוֹת הֵן. הַצְּלָף בְּאִילָן כְּבֵית שַׁמַּאי. כְּלֵי
חֶרֶס כִּכְלֵי נֶתֶר כְּבֵית שַׁמַּאי. חוּלְדַּת הַסְּנָאִים בִּשְׁרָצִים כְּבֵית שַׁמַּאי. פּוּל
הַמִּצְרִי בְּזְרָעִים. וְאַנְדְּרוֹגִינוֹס בָּאָדָם. כּוֹי בְּחַיָּה דִּבְרֵי הַכֹּל. רִבִּי חָמָא בַּר
עוּקְבָּא אָמַר וְאַמָּה טְרִיקְסִין. מַהוּ וְאַמָּה טְרִיקְסִין רִבִּי יוֹנָה בּוֹצְרָיָיה אָמַר
טְרִיקְסוֹן מַה מִבִּפְנִים מַה מִבַּחוּץ. אָמַר רִבִּי יוֹסֵי מִן מַה דִּכְתִיב וְאַרְבָּעִים אַמָּה
הָיָה הַבַּיִת הוּא הַהֵיכָל לִפְנֵי הָדָא אֲמָרָה מִבִּפְנִים. אָמַר לֵיהּ רִבִּי מָנָא וְהָכְתִיב
וַיַּעַשׂ אֶת בֵּית קָדְשֵׁי הַקֳּדָשִׁים עֶשְׂרִים אַמָּה אוֹרֶךְ וְעֶשֶׂר רוֹחַב. הָדָא אֲמָרָה
מִבַּחוּץ.

Rebbi Ḥiyya in the name of Rebbi Joḥanan: There are six unresolved doubts. The caper-bush among trees following the House of Shammai[86], clay vessels like potash vessels following the House of Shammai[87], the squirrel mole among the crawling things following the House of Shammai[88]; the Egyptian bean among seed-vegetables[89], the hermaphrodite among humans[90], the *koi* among wild animals according to everybody[91-]. Rebbi Ḥama bar Uqba said, also the *triqsin* cubit[92]. What is the *triqsin* cubit? Rebbi Jonah from Bostra said, confusion[93], "what is inside-outside?" Rebbi Yose said, since it is written (*1K.* 6:17) "forty cubits was the House, that is the inner Temple," it means it is counted inside[94]. Rebbi Mana said to him, but it is written (*2Chr.* 3:8) "He made the holiest of holies twenty cubits long and ten wide,[95]" that means it is counted outside.

---

86   In Halakhah 5:6, the House of Shammai make the caper-bush subject to the restrictions both of vegetables and of trees (Note 92).

87   Tosephta *Kelim Baba Qama* 2:1: "Vessels made of potash, the House of Shammai say they may become impure from the inside and their airspace like clay vessels and from the outside like metal vessels." Clay vessels cannot become impure if an impurity touches their outside, cf. *Berakhot* Chapter Eight, Note 51.

88   In the Mishnah here.

89   Halakhah 3:2.

90   Whether he is treated as a male

or a female. This is detailed in Tosephta *Bikkurim* 2.

91　　Tosephta *Bikkurim* 2:1. *Ḥulin* 80a: "*Koi* is the wild goat; some people say it comes from a male goat and a female deer. Rebbi Yose said, *koi* is a separate species and the Sages were unable to decide whether it follows the rules of domesticated animals or those of wild animals." The difference between domesticated and wild *kasher* animals is explained in Chapter 1, Note 104.

92　　The space in the Temple between the holy and the holiest of holies parts. The problem is whether it is part of the Temple hall or of the holiest of holies.

93　　Jastrow's explanation is Greek τάραξιν, accusative of τάραξις "confusion". [Maimonides (Commentary to *Middot* 4:7) declares the word to be the name of the dividing wall in the first Temple.] A Gaonic commentary to *Yoma* explains טרקסין by an Arabic word בראסתג of unknown meaning. *Arukh* and Rashi declare טרקסין (spelling of Mishnah *Middot* 4:7) to be a Greek word and "inside-outside" its meaning. Compare Latin *intro*, adv. "inside" and *extra*, adv. "outside" for composite *inTREXtra* (E. G.).

94　　Since no provision is made for the wall, the wall is not part of the main part of the main room of the Temple but must be under the rules of the holiest of holies.

95　　That verse is badly misquoted: ויעש את בית קדשי הקדשים ארכו על פני רחב הבית אמות עשרים ורחבו אמות עשרים. It makes no difference for the objection.

(fol. 31b) **משנה ו**: שׁוֹר בַּר מִין בְּהֵמָה רִבִּי יוֹסֵי אוֹמֵר מִין חַיָּה. כֶּלֶב מִין חַיָּה רִבִּי מֵאִיר אוֹמֵר מִין בְּהֵמָה. הַחֲזִיר מִין בְּהֵמָה. הָעָרוֹד מִין חַיָּה. הַפִּיל וְהַקּוֹף מִין חַיָּה. וְהָאָדָם מוּתָּר עִם כֻּלָּן לַחֲרוֹשׁ וְלִמְשׁוֹךְ.

Mishnah 6: The bison is a domesticated animal; Rebbi Yose says a wild animal[96]. The dog is a wild animal; Rebbi Meïr says a domesticated animal. The pig is a domesticated animal, the wild donkey a wild animal.

Elephant and monkey are wild animals. A human is permitted to plough and draw with all of them.

96 For the Sages one is permitted to mate bison and cattle and to plough	with an ox and a bison yoked together; for R. Yose it is forbidden.

(fol. 31c) **הלכה ו:** שׁוֹר בַּר מִין בְּהֵמָה. רַבָּנִין אָמְרֵי מִיכָּא הֲוָה וְעָרק לְתַמָּן. רִבִּי יוֹסֵי אוֹמֵר עִיקָּרֵיהּ מִן תַּמָּן הֲוָה. הָא שׁוֹר אִם שׁוֹר בַּר אֵינָן כִּלְאַיִם דְּלֹא כְרִבִּי יוֹסֵה דְּרִבִּי יוֹסֵה אוֹמֵר כִּלְאַיִם. וְאִילֵין דִּמְתַרְגְּמִין וְתוֹרֵי בַּר וְרֵאמְנִין כְּרִבִּי יוֹסֵה.

Halakhah 6: "The bison is a domesticated animal." The rabbis say it was from here and escaped there[97]. Rebbi Yose says, its roots were from there. Hence an ox and a bison are not *kilaim*, not following Rebbi Yose, since Rebbi Yose says it is *kilaim*. But those who translate "wild oxen and antelopes" follow Rebbi Yose[98].

97 "Here" is agricultural society, "there" is the wild. The rabbis consider bison as cattle that became wild.	98 Targum Pseudo-Jonathan translates ודישן ותאו in the list of wild animals of *Deut.* 14:5 as וְרִימְנִין וְתוֹרֵי בַּר.

רִבִּי בָּא בְשֵׁם רִבִּי שְׁמוּאֵל אַוָּז עִם אַוָּז מִדְבָּר כִּלְאַיִם זֶה בְזֶה. אַוָּז עִם אַוָּז הַיָּם תַּנֵּה רִבִּי יוּדָה בֶּן פָּזִי דְּבַר דְּלָיָה וְלָא יָדְעִין מָאן תַּנֵּה. קַל וָחוֹמֶר מַה אִם בְּשָׁעָה שֶׁשְּׁנֵיהֶן בַּיַּבָּשָׁה אַתְּ אָמַר אָסוּר בְּשָׁעָה שֶׁאֶחָד בַּיַּבָּשָׁה וְאֶחָד בַּיָּם לֹא כָל־שֶׁכֵּן.

Rebbi Abba in the name of Rebbi Samuel: Goose and desert goose are *kilaim* one with the other. About goose and sea goose, Rebbi Judah ben Pazi stated in the name of Bar Dalaiah and we do not know what he stated. It is a conclusion *a minori ad majus*: If you say they are forbidden when both of them are on dry land, so much more if one is on dry land and one at sea.

וְאָדָם מוּתָּר בְּכוּלָן (fol. 31d) לַחֲרוֹשׁ וְלִמְשׁוֹךְ. כְּתִיב לֹא תַחֲרוֹשׁ בְּשׁוֹר וּבַחֲמוֹר
יַחְדָּיו. בְּשׁוֹר וּבַחֲמוֹר אֵין אַתְּ חוֹרֵשׁ אֲבָל חוֹרֵשׁ אַתְּ בְּשׁוֹר עִם אָדָם בַּחֲמוֹר עִם
אָדָם.

"A person is permitted to plough and draw with all of them." It is written (*Deut.* 22:10): "Do not plough with an ox and a donkey together." (*Sifri Deut.* 231) You may not plough with an ox and a donkey but you may plough with an ox and a human, a donkey with a human.

אינו אסור פרק תשיעי

(fol. 31d) **משנה א**: אֵינוֹ אָסוּר מִשׁוּם כִּלְאַיִם אֶלָּא צֶמֶר וּפִשְׁתִּים. וְאֵינוֹ מִטַּמֵּא בִּנְגָעִים אֶלָּא צֶמֶר וּפִשְׁתִּים. אֵין הַכֹּהֲנִים לוֹבְשִׁין לְשַׁמֵּשׁ בַּמִּקְדָּשׁ אֶלָּא צֶמֶר וּפִשְׁתִּים. צֶמֶר גְּמַלִּים וְצֶמֶר רְחֵלִים שֶׁטְּרָפָן זֶה בָזֶה אִם רוֹב מִן הַגְּמַלִּים מוּתָּר. אִם רוֹב מִן הָרְחֵלִים אָסוּר. מֶחֱצָה לְמֶחֱצָה אָסוּר. וְכֵן הַקַּנַּבֹּס וְהַפִּשְׁתָּן שֶׁטְּרָפָן זֶה בָזֶה.

Mishnah 1: Only wool and linen are forbidden as *kilaim*[1]. Only wool and linen can become impure by mold disease[2]. Only wool and linen are worn by priests for their service in the temple[3]. If one mixed camel wool and sheep wool, if most is camel wool it is permitted, if most is sheep wool it is forbidden, half and half is forbidden[4]. The same applies if hemp[5] and linen are mixed.

1   This chapter deals with *šaʻaṭnēz* (*Lev.* 19:19, *Deut.* 22:11) defined as mixing of linen and wool.
2   *Lev.* 13:47-59. Wool and linen are the only textiles mentioned there but leather is under the same rules.
3   The materials decribed in *Ex.* 28:5 are interpreted to be gold, wool died dark blue, purple, crimson, and fine linen. Gold was used only for the garments of the High Priest.
4   Since the prohibition is biblical, in case of doubt the prohibition prevails.
5   Latin *cannabis*, also *cannabum;* Greek κάνναβις, κάνναβος.

הלכה א: אֵינוֹ אָסוּר מִשׁוּם כִּלְאַיִם כו'. כְּתִיב לֹא תִלְבַּשׁ שַׁעַטְנֵז צֶמֶר וּפִשְׁתִּים יַחְדָּיו. הָיִיתִי אוֹמֵר אֵינוֹ אָסוּר אֶלָּא מִלְּבוֹשׁ תַּלְמוּד לוֹמַר לֹא יַעֲלֶה עָלֶיךָ. אִי לֹא יַעֲלֶה עָלֶיךָ הָיִיתִי אוֹמֵר לֹא[6] יַפְשִׁיל אֶת הַקּוּפָה לַאֲחוֹרָיו תַּלְמוּד לוֹמַר

לֹא תִלְבַּשׁ מַה מַלְבּוּשׁ מְיוּחָד דָּבָר שֶׁהוּא מְחַנֶּה אֶת הַגּוּף אַף אֵין לִי אֶלָּא דָּבָר
שֶׁהוּא מְחַנֶּה אֶת הַגּוּף. לְאֵי זֶה דָּבָר נָאֱמַר לֹא יַעֲלֶה עָלֶיךָ. רִבִּי נִיחָא בַּר סַבָּה
רִבִּי יוֹחָנָן בְּשֵׁם רִבִּי זְעִירָא שֶׁאִם הָיָה גָּדוֹל קְצָתוֹ יֵשׁ בּוֹ כִּלְאַיִם וּמוּנַח
בָּאָרֶץ וּמִקְצָתוֹ אֵין בּוֹ לֹא יְכַסֶּה בּוֹ מִצַּד הַשֵּׁנִי. הָיִיתִי אוֹמֵר אֲפִילוּ פִּשְׁתָּן שֶׁל
יָם אֲפִילוּ קַנַּבְּס תַּלְמוּד לוֹמַר צֶמֶר וּפִשְׁתִּים מַה צֶּמֶר שֶׁאֵין לוֹ שֵׁם לְוַויי אַף
כָּל־דָּבָר שֶׁאֵין לוֹ שֵׁם לְוַויי. מְנַיִין שֶׁאֵין לוֹ שֵׁם לְוַויי אָמַר רִבִּי יְהוֹשֻׁעַ בֶּן לֵוִי
כְּתִיב וּמֵישַׁע מֶלֶךְ מוֹאָב הָיָה נוֹקֵד. מַהוּ נוֹקֵד רוֹעֶה. וְהֵשִׁיב לְמֶלֶךְ יִשְׂרָאֵל
מֵאָה אֶלֶף כָּרִים וּמֵאָה אֶלֶף אֵילִים צָמֶר. אֵין לָךְ קָרוּי צֶמֶר אֶלָּא צֶמֶר אֵלִים
בִּלְבַד.

Halakhah 1: "Only [wool and linen] are forbidden as *kilaim*". It is written (*Deut.* 22:11): "Do not wear *ša'aṭnez*, wool and linen together."[7] I would say one is only forbidden to wear it; the verse says (*Lev.* 19:19): "It shall not come on you." If it shall not come on you I would say one may not carry a chest on his back[8]; the verse says "do not wear." Since a garment is specifically useful to the body, [included are] only things useful to the body. Why was it said that "it shall not come on you?" Rebbi Niḥa bar Sava[9], Rebbi Johanan in the name of Rebbi Zeïra, if there was a large piece of cloth, in a part of which was *kilaim* and that part was lying on the ground, one cannot cover himself with the other part. I would say, it includes even sea flax[10], even hemp; the verse says "wool and linen"; just as wool cannot have an epithet so nothing else can have an epithet. From where that [wool] has no epithet? Rebbi Joshua ben Levi said, it is written (*2K.* 3:4) "Mesha', the king of Moab, was a *nôqēd*;" what is a *nôqēd*? A shepherd! "He delivered to the king of Israel 100'000 lambs and 100'000 wool rams." Only ram's wool is called "wool"[11].

6   Reading of the Rome and all *Sifry* mss. Venice: לך.

7   In *Sifry Deut.* 232, the text is somewhat more complete: "I would say

one is only forbidden to wear it; from where do we know that one may not cover oneself with it (in a blanket)?"

8 A peddler's chest full of textiles to peddle to Gentiles.

9 A Galilean Amora of the fifth generation, student of R. Jonah. Since R. Zeïra was R. Johanan's student, it is clear that the second name in the list must be "R. Jonah". In the Babylonian tradition, this is a Tannaïtic statement (Tosephta *Kilaim* 5:13).

10 Shell silk, also called "byssus", from threads, excreted by shells under water, which harden when exposed to air, used already in antiquity.

11 All others carry the name of the animal from which they come as an epithet.

אֵין מְטַמֵּא בִּנְגָעִים אֶלָּא צֶמֶר וּפִשְׁתִּים. דִּכְתִיב בְּבֶגֶד צֶמֶר אוֹ בְּבֶגֶד פִּשְׁתִּים. יָכוֹל יְהוּ מְטַמְּאִין בֵּין צְבוּעִין בֵּין שָׁאֵינָן צְבוּעִין תַּלְמוּד לוֹמַר בֶּגֶד צֶמֶר אוֹ בֶגֶד פִּשְׁתִּים. מַה פִּשְׁתִּים כִּבְרִיָּיתָהּ אַף צֶמֶר כִּבְרִיָּיתוֹ. אוֹצִיא אֶת הַצָּבוּעַ בִּידֵי אָדָם וְלֹא אוֹצִיא אֶת הַצָּבוּעַ בִּידֵי שָׁמַיִם תַּלְמוּד לוֹמַר לַפִּשְׁתִּים וְלַצָּמֶר מַה פִּשְׁתִּים לְבָנָה אַף צֶמֶר לָבָן.

"Only wool and linen can become impure by mold disease," for it is written (*Lev.* 13:47) "on woolen cloth or on linen cloth." I could think they can become impure whether dyed or natural; the verse says "woolen cloth or linen cloth." Just as linen is in its natural state so wool must also be in its natural state[12]. I might exclude what was dyed by humans but not what was dyed by nature; the verse says (*Lev.* 13:48): "For *the* linen and for *the* wool[13]", just as linen is white so wool has to be white.

12 *Sifra Paršat Nega'im* 13(3-4). It seems that the name of פשתים was used only for undyed linen cloth; dyed cloth had other names.

13 The implied definite article restricts this to what is certainly called linen and woolen cloth, not ארגמן, תכלת, תולעת שני, etc. The Babli (*Bekhorot* 17a) quotes a *baraita* using the same verse to exclude wool from *kilaim* of sheep and goats.

תַּנִּינָן תְּרֵין כְּלָלִין וְלָא דָּמְיָן דֵּין לְדֵין. תַּנִּינָן אֵין אָסוּר מְשׁוּם כִּלְאַיִם אֶלָּא
צֶמֶר וּפִשְׁתִּים בֵּין צְבוּעִין בֵּין לְבָנִין. תַּנִּינָן אֵין מְטַמֵּא בִּנְגָעִים אֶלָּא צֶמֶר
וּפִשְׁתִּים וּבִלְבַד לְבָנִים. רִבִּי יוֹנָה בּוֹצְרָיָיה בָּעָא קוֹמֵי רִבִּי מָנָא תַּמָּן אַתְּ אָמַר
בֵּין צְבוּעִין בֵּין לְבָנִים וְהָכָא אַתְּ אָמַר וּבִלְבַד לְבָנִים. אָמַר לֵיהּ שַׁנְיָיא הִיא
שֶׁשָּׁנָה עָלָיו הַכָּתוּב צֶמֶר צֶמֶר שְׁנֵי פְעָמִים מָה פִּשְׁתִּים כִּבְרִיָּיתָהּ אַף צֶמֶר
כִּבְרִיָּיתוֹ.

We have stated two rules and they do not resemble one another. We
have stated: Only wool and linen are forbidden as *kilaim*, whether dyed
or white. We have stated: Only wool and linen can become impure by
mold disease, but only white. Rebbi Jonah from Bostra asked before
Rebbi Mana: There, you say "whether dyed or white", but here you say
"but only white"? He said to him, there is a difference because the verse
repeated twice "wool, wool"; just as linen is in its natural state so also wool
must be in its natural state.

אָמַר רִבִּי זְעִירָא כְּתִיב כְּתוֹנֶת בַּד קוֹדֶשׁ יִלְבָּשׁ בַּד שֶׁהִיא עוֹלֶה יְחִידִי. וַהֲרֵי
צֶמֶר עוֹלֶה יְחִידִי. פֵּירֵשׁ בְּקַבָּלָה וְלֹא יַעֲלֶה עֲלֵיהֶם צֶמֶר בְּשָׁרְתָם בְּשַׁעֲרֵי
הַפְּנִימִית וּבֵיתָה. הָא מִבַּחוּץ מוּתָּר לַעֲלוֹת עֲלֵיהֶם. מִנַּיִן שֶׁהֵן מוּתָּרִין בְּכִלְאַיִם
שֶׁנֶּאֱמַר וְאֶת הַמִּצְנֶפֶת שֵׁשׁ וְאֶת פַּאֲרֵי הַמִּגְבָּעוֹת שֵׁשׁ וְאֶת מִכְנְסֵי הַבַּד שֵׁשׁ מָשְׁזָר
וְאֶת הָאַבְנֵט שֵׁשׁ מָשְׁזָר תְּכֵלֶת וְאַרְגָּמָן וְתוֹלַעַת שָׁנִי. וּכְתִיב פַּאֲרֵי פִשְׁתִּים יִהְיוּ
עַל רֹאשָׁם וּמִכְנְסֵי פִשְׁתִּים יִהְיוּ עַל מָתְנֵיהֶם אַל יַחְגְּרוּ בַּיָּזַע. אַתְּ דְּרַשׁ שֵׁשׁ
מְשֵׁשׁ שֵׁשׁ מִפַּאֲרֵי פַּאֲרֵי מִפַּאֲרֵי. (fol. 32a) מַה שְּׁנִי תוֹלַעַת דָּבָר שֶׁיֵּשׁ בּוֹ רוּחַ
חַיִּים אַף כָּל־דָּבָר שֶׁיֵּשׁ בּוֹ רוּחַ חַיִּים. מַה צֶּמֶר שֶׁאֵין לוֹ שֵׁם לְוַיי אוֹף פִּשְׁתִּים
שֶׁאֵין לָהּ שֵׁם לְוַיי.

[14]Rebbi Zeïra said: It is written (*Lev.* 16:4) "He shall wear a garment of
holy *bad*," growing singly[15]. But wool also grows in single strands[16]. It is
explained in tradition (*Ez.* 44:17): "There should be no wool on them
when they officiate inside the inner doors[17]." Therefore, on the outside

wool may be on them. From where that they may wear *kilaim*? As it says (*Ex.* 39:28): "The cap of byssus, the hat-turbans of byssus, the cloth trousers of spun byssus, and the belt of spun byssus, blue, purple, and crimson[18]." And it is written (*Ez.* 44:18): "Linen turbans shall be on their heads, linen trousers shall be on their hips, they shall not belt with sweat." You infer "byssus" from "byssus", "byssus" from "turbans", "turbans" from "turbans".[19] Just as crimson is made from a living being, so the rest is made from a living being[20]. Just as wool cannot have an epithet so linen cannot have an epithet.

14 This refers to the priestly garments mentioned in the Mishnah. A parallel is in Babli *Yoma* 71b.

15 Since בד can mean (1) single strand, connected with Hebrew בדד, Arabic ﺪ "to separate", or (2) linen cloth. It is not explicit in the text that the garments of the High priest for the service of the Day of Atonement have to be of white linen. The meaning (2) of בד is established in this paragraph. In *Sifra Aḥare* 1(3) בד is taken to mean "double cloth".

16 Nothing here proves that בד means linen cloth, not woolen cloth; this shows that the modern acceptation of בד "cloth (of any kind)" was current in the times of the Yerushalmi.

17 In order to make the point clear, the verse is slightly misquoted, "inner doors" instead of "the gates of the inner courtyard". Since the courtyard re-

served for the priests had no gates, the sentence is taken as referring to the *ṭriqsin* cubit (Chapter 8, Note 93).

18 One has to prove that "blue, purple, and crimson" mentioned in the description of the priestly garments and the gobelins of the Tabernacle always refers to blue, purple, and crimson wool.

19 This proves that שש means "linen cloth". שש is defined by its use as material for the priests' turbans, which are described as made of linen by Ezechiel. [The Babli (Note 14) interprets שש to mean "spun six-fold"; this is not known to the Yerushalmi.]

20 Since the red color of crimson is made from insects [*Sifra Meẓora'* (14)], so the material of the series in which crimson appears should be of animal origin. [In Hebrew, the terms חיים and רוח חיים only apply to animals, never to

plants.) Therefore, it should be some kind of wool. The next sentence then refers back to the discussion that only sheep's wool and linen do not need a qualifier in their descriptions.

רבִּי יוֹנָה עוּלָּא בַּר יִשְׁמָעֵאל בְּשֵׁם רבִּי לָעְזָר צֶמֶר וּפִשְׁתִּים שֶׁטְּרָפָן אָסוּר. כֵּיצַד הוּא עוֹשֶׂה מֵבִיא לִיטְרָא וְעוֹד צֶמֶר גְּמָלִים וּמְבַטְּלָן. אַבָּא בַּר רַב הוּנָא בְּשֵׁם רבִּי יִרְמְיָה צֶמֶר וּפִשְׁתִּים שֶׁטְּרָפָן בְּטָלָן. רַב אָמַר אָסוּר בְּתַעֲרוּבְתָּן. מַה מַפְלִיג. מַה דְּאָמַר רַב בְּשֶׁעֲשָׂאוֹ בֶּגֶד בִּפְנֵי עַצְמוֹ מַה דְּאָמַר רבִּי יִרְמְיָה בְּהַהוּא דְּבָעֵי מְעָרְבָתֵּהּ עִם חוֹרָן.

Rebbi Jonah, Ulla bar Ismael in the name of Rebbi Eleazar: Blended wool and flax are forbidden. What can one do? One adds more than a pound of camel's hair and makes it insignificant[21]. Abba bar Rav Huna in the name of Rebbi Jeremiah[22]: Blended wool and flax are neutral. Rav said, they are forbidden in mixture. Do they disagree? Rav speaks about the case when he made the material itself into a garment, Rebbi Jeremiah speaks about the case where he wants to mix it with other things.

21   It is a general principle in Jewish law that one may not neutralize a prohibited substance by mixing it with a large quantity of permitted material. R. Eleazar notes that the Mishnah here decrees a remarkable exception in that wool and flax blended before spinning can be made acceptable by using for every pound of *kilaim* somewhat more than a pound of neutral material. This does not apply to woolen or linen threads which together in one garment always constitute *kilaim*.

22   He is Rav Jeremiah in the Babli. Since R. Jeremiah already was an authority in Babylonia before the title "Rav" was introduced, the title "Rebbi" is more correct.

רבִּי הִלֵּל בֵּי רבִּי וַלֶּס הָיָה לוֹ בֶּגֶד בִּשְׁלֹשִׁים רִיבּוֹא דֵּינָר (וְיתְוֵיהּ לְרבִּי)[23] וּמָצָא בּוֹ כִלְאַיִם וּשְׂרָפוּ. רבִּי מָנָא הָיָה לוֹ בֶּגֶד בִּשְׁלֹשִׁים רִיבּוֹא דֵּינָר וִיהָבֵיהּ לְרבִּי חִיָּיה בַּר אָדָא אָמַר לֵיהּ זְבָנִית לְמִית וַהֲוָה עֲלוֹי עַד דְּהוּא מְכָרֵהּ. אָמַר רבִּי

חַגַּי רִבִּי שְׁמוּאֵל בַּר יִצְחָק מַייתֵי מָאנָא מִבֵּי קַצָרָא וּמַייתַב עָלָיו עֲשָׂרָה חוּטִין מְפַשְׁפְּשִׁין לֵיהּ. אָמַר רִבִּי חַגַּי רִבִּי שְׁמוּאֵל בַּר רַב יִצְחָק הֲוָה מְפַקֵּד נּוּ בֵּייתֵיהּ דְּלָא מוֹקְמָה נְבַל דְּעִמֶּר מֵיקַמֵּיהּ נְבַל דְּכִיתָּן בְּגִין פִּיפָה.

Rebbi Hillel ben Rebbi Vales[24] had a garment worth 30'000 denar, (he gave it to Rebbi who) found *kilaim* in it and burnt it. Rebbi Mana had a garment worth 30'000 denar[25]. He gave it to Rebbi Hiyya bar Ada and told him that he had bought it for the dead. He kept it until he was wrapped in it[26]. Rebbi Haggai said, Rebbi Samuel bar Isaac brought a garment from the cleaner; there were on it ten threads and he rubbed them off[27]. Rebbi Haggai said, Rebbi Samuel bar Isaac commanded his house not to put a bale of wool next to a bale of flax because of the fibers[28].

23   Missing in the Rome ms.

24   Cf. Chapter 1, note 30. Probably Rebbi (Jehudah Nesia) suspected the garment to contain the very expensive Egyptian byssus, used to make transparent garments. The denars here are the worthless money of the military anarchy.

25   Shrouds for the dead may contain *kilaim*, cf. Mishnah 4 and Halakhah 4.

Reading of the Rome ms: רִבִּי מָנָא הָיַה לוֹ בֶגֶד בִּשְׁלֹשִׁים רִיבּוֹא דֵינָר וּמָצָא בוֹ כְּלְאַיִם וִיהָבֵיהּ לְרִבִּי חִייָה בַּר אָדָא אָמַר לֵיהּ זְבָנִית לְמִיתָה וְקִייֵם עֲלוֹי עַד קָרְחָייָה. "Rebbi Mana had a garment worth

30'000 denar in which he found *kilaim*. He gave it to Rebbi Hiyya bar Ada and told him that he had bought it for the dead. He kept it until it got threadbare (probably to sit on it)."

26   When he had died.

27   The threads might be *kilaim*. Even though they were only clinging to the garment, were not sown on or otherwise permanently affixed and never could be legal *kilaim*, he insisted of removing all potential *kilaim*.

28   The fibers that might be blown from one bale to the next. Latin *fibra, ae,* "fiber, filament", but also cf. Note 153.

מִשְׁנָה ב: הַשִּׁירָיִין וְהַכַּלָךְ אֵין בָּהֶן מִשּׁוּם כִּלְאַיִם אֲבָל אֲסוּרִין מִפְּנֵי(fol. 31d)
מַרְאִית הָעַיִן. הַכָּרִים וְהַכְּסָתוֹת אֵין בָּהֶן מִשּׁוּם כִּלְאַיִם וּבִלְבַד שֶׁלֹּא יְהֵא בְשָׂרוֹ
נוֹגֵעַ בָּהֶן. אֵין עֲרַאי לְכִלְאַיִם. לֹא יִלְבַּשׁ כִּלְאַיִם עַל גַּבֵּי עֲשָׂרָה אֲפִילוּ לִגְנוֹב
אֶת הַמֶּכֶס.

Mishnah 2: Raw silk and *kalak* silk are not subject to *kilaim* but are forbidden because of the bad impression[29]. Mattresses and pillows are not subject to *kilaim* but one's skin should not touch them. There is no provisional *kilaim*[30]. One may not wear *kilaim* over ten other garments[31], not even to trick the customs.

29 Since raw silk looks like flax and *kalak* silk (cf. Note 33) like wool.	the *kilaim* garment as such and derives no bodily comfort from it. Since
30 One may not wear *kilaim* even temporarily as explained in the next sentence.	customs officials are dishonest and charge more than the legal amounts, one does not have to be honest with
31 In this case one does not need	them, cf. *Demay* 2:3.

הֲלָכָה ב: הַשִּׁירָיִין וְהַכַּלָךְ. הַשִּׁירָיִין מֶטַקְסָה. וְהַכַּלָךְ אַגְבִּין קֵיסָרָיֵי. (fol. 32a)
אָמַר רַבָּן שִׁמְעוֹן בֶּן גַּמְלִיאֵל חִיזַרְתִּי עַל כָּל־מַפְרְשֵׁי הַיָּם וְאָמְרוּ כַּלְכָּא שְׁמוֹ.

Halakhah 2: "Raw silk and silk noil". Raw silk is μέταξα[32]. *Kalak* silk is imperial *'gbyn*[33]. Rabban Simeon ben Gamliel said, I went around among all sea-faring men and they told me that it was called *kalka*.

32 Greek "raw silk", early Latin form *mataxa*. The Babli, *Šabbat* 20b translates כלך by either μέταξα or שירא פרנדא, i. e. *sera* "silk" (Syriac, Aramaic), פֶּרַנד (*parand*, Arabic *firind*) "silk" (Persian, Arabic). Also compare *sera* with Latin *sericum* "Chinese stuff, silk."	R. Simson and R. Isaac Simponti read אצבין In *Šabbat*, Maimonides explains כלך by "silk"; the expression there is usually taken to mean "silk noil". Rabban Simeon ben Gamliel explains that the current trade name in the Eastern Mediterranean was *kalka*, cf. Greek κάλχη, ἤ "murex, purple dye".
33 The Rome ms. here has אכבין the mss. in Mishnah *Šabbat* 2:1 have אנבין	The reading אגבין is possibly a

contraction from ארגון "purple"; the determination of כלך as "imperial purple" parallels κάλχη. The Yerushalmi seems to define כלך as purple silk (E. G.).

אֲבָל אֲסוּרִין מִפְּנֵי מַרְאִית הָעַיִן. רַב אָמַר כָּל־שֶׁהוּא אָסוּר מִפְּנֵי מַרְאִית הָעַיִן אֲפִילוּ בְּחַדְרֵי חֲדָרִים אָסוּר. מַתְנִיתָה פְּלִיגָא עַל רַב פְּשִׁתָּן שֶׁצְּבָעָהּ בְּחֶרֶס לֹא יַעֲשֶׂה מִמֶּנָּה אִימְרָה מְפוֹרְסָמָה. בְּכָרִים וּכְסָתוֹת מוּתָּר. מַתְנִיתָה פְּלִיגָא עַל רַב נִתְפַּזְּרוּ מָעוֹתָיו לִפְנֵי עֲבוֹדָה זָרָה לֹא יְהֵא שׁוֹחֶה וּמְלַקֵּט שֶׁלֹּא יְהֵא כְּמִשְׁתַּחֲוֶה לַעֲבוֹדָה זָרָה וְאִם הָיָה מָקוֹם צָנוּעַ מוּתָּר. מַתְנִיתָה פְּלִיגָא עַל רַב פַּרְצוּפוֹת שֶׁהֵן מַטִּילִין מַיִם בִּכְרַכִּים לֹא יְהֵא נוֹתֵן פִּיו עַל פִּיו שֶׁלֹּא יְהֵא כִּמְנַשֵּׁק לַעֲבוֹדָה זָרָה. וְאִם הָיָה מָקוֹם צָנוּעַ מוּתָּר. מַתְנִיתָה פְּלִיגָא עַל רַב אֵין שׁוֹחֲטִין בְּגוּמָא אֲבָל עוֹשֶׂה הוּא גוּמָא בְּתוֹךְ בֵּיתוֹ בִּשְׁבִיל שֶׁיִּכָּנֵס הַדָּם בְּתוֹכוֹ וּבַשׁוּק לֹא יַעֲשֶׂה כֵן שֶׁלֹּא יְחַקֶּה אֶת הַמִּינִין. מַתְנִיתָה פְּלִיגָא עַל רַב הִגִּיעַ לֶחָצֵר הַחִיצוֹנָה שׁוֹטְחָן בַּחַמָּה אֲבָל לֹא כְּנֶגֶד הָעָם. מַתְנִיתָה פְּלִיגָא עַל רַב בִּיב שֶׁהוּא קָמוּר אַרְבַּע אַמּוֹת בִּרְשׁוּת הָרַבִּים אֵין שׁוֹפְכִין לְתוֹכוֹ מַיִם בַּשַׁבָּת. וְתַנֵּי עָלָהּ אִם הָיְתָה מְזַחִילָה מוּתָּר עוֹנַת גְּשָׁמִים מוּתָּר צִינּוֹרוֹת מְקַלְּחִין אֲסוּרִין. תַּנֵּי בַּר קַפָּרָא אִם הָיָה מָקוֹם צָנוּעַ מוּתָּר. אִילֵּין פְּלִיגִין דְּרַב וְלֵית לְהוֹן קִיּוּם.

"But they are forbidden because of the bad impression." Rav said that everything forbidden because of a bad impression is forbidden even in the most private room[34]. A *baraita* contradicts Rav: "One should not make a visible fringe of linen dyed with soot, but for mattresses and pillows it is permitted.[35]" A *baraita* contradicts Rav: "If one's coins were strewn before an idol he should not bow down to collect them lest he look as if he was prostrating himself before the idol. But if it occurred at a hidden place it is permitted.[36]" A *baraita* contradicts Rav: "In a fortified place one should not put his face on gargoyles in the form of faces lest he look as if he was kissing an idol. But if it occurred at a hidden place it is permitted." A Mishnah contradicts Rav: "One does not slaughter into a pit in the ground but he may dig a pit in his house so that the blood may be collected there. In public, he should not do it so as not to imitate the sectarians.[37"] A *baraita* contradicts Rav: "Once he arrived at the outermost courtyard he may spread them out in the sun but not where it is generally visible.[38"] A *baraita* contradicts Rav: "One does not pour water on the Sabbath into a sewage pipe covered the length of four cubits.[39"] We have stated on this: If water was flowing in it it is permitted, in the winter it is permitted. If aquaeduct pipes spout it is forbidden. Bar Qappara stated that if it occurred at a hidden place it is permitted[40]. All these statements contradict Rav and he cannot explain them.

34   In Babli *Šabbat* 64b, 146b, *Beẓah* 9a, *Avodah Zarah* 12a this is accepted practice while it is rejected in the Yerushalmi, cf. *Roš Šabbat* 22:9.

35   Since linen usually is bleached, not dyed, this will look like wool. Nevertheless, such decorations are permitted in the bedroom and only forbidden where others may see them and suspect the owner of wearing *kilaim*.

36   This and the following *baraita* are found also in Tosephta *Avodah Zarah* 6:4,6 and Babli *Avodah Zarah* 12a. Instead of "if it occurred at a hidden place it is permitted", these Babylonian sources read: "If it cannot be seen it is permitted." This is reinterpreted in the Babli to mean: "If he can arrange it so that he will not be

seen bowing down to (or kissing) the idol, it is permitted," for example by collecting the coins kneeling with his back to the idol. Such a reinterpretation is impossible in the Yerushalmi's version.

37   *Ḥulin* 2:9, Babli 41a. It is not known to which sect the Mishnah refers. The Babli does not count the Mishnah as contradicting Rav.

38   Babli *Šabbat* 146b, speaking of a man whose clothes got wet on the Sabbath who might be suspected of having washed them that day. In the version of the Babli, Rebbi Eliezer and Rebbi Simeon prohibit spreading out any clothes at all.

39   A similar text in Mishnah *Eruvin* 8:10, a *baraita* permitting to pour the water in wintertime Babli

Eruvin 88b; a parallel text *Eruvin* 8:10 (fol. 25b). The situation referred to is a sewage pipe leading away from a courtyard. The water poured out in the courtyard will run into the pipe and flow away into the public domain. While no Sabbath prohibition has been violated by pouring out water in one's own private courtyard, the water flowing in the pipe will give the impression that it was poured into the public domain, a desecration of the Sabbath. The rabbinic prohibition of pouring water does not apply if either the pipe is covered all the way or if the pipe was carrying water before anything was poured out into the courtyard.

40   Against the opinion of Rav. This statement is not in the Babli.

בַּכָּרִים וּבַכְּסָתוֹת מוּתָּר. הָדָא דְתֵימַר בְּרֵיקָן אֲבָל בְּמָלֵא אָסוּר בְּנָתוּן עַל גַּבֵּי מַסְטְוָוה אֲבָל בְּנָתוּן עַל גַּבֵּי הַמִּיטָה אֲפִילוּ רֵיקָן אָסוּר.

"It is permitted for mattresses and pillows."[41]   That means if they are empty but if stuffed they are forbidden. When they are put on a stone bench, but on a bed they are forbidden even empty.

41   Quote from the *baraita* in the preceding paragraph. The reasons are explained in the last paragraph of this Halakhah.

הֲרֵי שֶׁהָיָה מְהַלֵּךְ בַּשּׁוּק וְנִמְצָא לָבוּשׁ כִּלְאַיִם תְּרֵין אֲמוֹרָאִין חַד אָמַר אָסוּר וְחָרָנָה אָמַר מוּתָּר מָאן דְּאָמַר אָסוּר דְּבַר תּוֹרָה וּמָאן דְּאָמַר מוּתָּר כְּהַהִיא דְּאָמַר רְבִּי זְעִירָא גָּדוֹל כְּבוֹד הָרַבִּים שֶׁהוּא דוֹחֶה אֶת הַמִּצְוָה בְּלֹא תַעֲשֶׂה שָׁעָה אֲחַת.

If somebody was walking in public and discovered that he was wearing *kilaim*. Two Amoraïm, one said he is forbidden[42], the other one said he is permitted. The one who said he is forbidden, because it is a word of the Torah. The one who said he is permitted follows what R. Zeïra said: The dignity of the public is important enough to temporarily override a prohibition[43].

42   He has to strip off the garment
immediately.

43   In the Babli, *Berakhot* 19b,
Megillah 3b this statement is anon-

ymous, possibly tannaïtic, and un-
opposed. In the Babylonian version, the
reason is self-esteem (כבוד הבריות)
rather than the dignity of the public.

תַּנֵּי אֵין מְדַקְדְּקִין בְּמֵת וְלֹא בְּכִלְאַיִם בְּבֵית הַמִּדְרָשׁ. רַבִּי יוֹסֵי הֲוָה יָתִיב מַתְנֵי
וַהֲוָה תַמָּן מֵתָא. מָן דְּנָפַק לֵיהּ לֹא אָמַר לֵיהּ כְּלוּם. וּמָן דְּיָתִיב לֵיהּ לֹא אָמַר
לֵיהּ כְּלוּם. רַבִּי אִימִּי הֲוָה יָתִיב מַתְנֵי אָמַר חַד לְחַבְרֵיהּ אַתְּ לְבוּשׁ כִּלְאַיִם.
אָמַר לֵיהּ רַבִּי אִימִּי שְׁלַח מָאנָךְ וִיהַב לֵיהּ.

It was stated: One does not investigate for a dead person[25] nor in the
house of study[44]. Rebbi Yose was sitting and teaching where a dead body
was present. He did not say anything either to those who left or to those
who remained sitting[45]. Rebbi Immi was sitting and teaching when one
said to his neighbor: you are wearing *kilaim*. Rebbi Immi told him: strip
yourself of your garment and give it to him.

44   A place of public assembly.

45   Cf. *Berakhot* Halakhah 3:1
(Notes 68,69). The story is inserted
here to emphasize the statement of R.
Zeïra, that in the house of study one

tolerates not only temporary
transgression of the law of *kilaim* but
also of the prohibition of defilement of
Cohanim.

תַּנֵּי אֵין עֲרַאי לְכִלְאַיִם בְּבֵית הַמִּקְדָּשׁ. וְהָא תַּנֵּי כֹּהֵן שֶׁיָּצָא לְדַבֵּר עִם חֲבֵירוֹ
אִם הִפְלִיגוֹ טָעוּן טְבִילָה אִם לְשָׁעָה טָעוּן קִידּוּשׁ יָדַיִם וְרַגְלַיִם. כָּאן בְּבִגְדֵי זָהָב
כָּאן בְּבִגְדֵי לָבָן.

It was stated: There is no provisional *kilaim* in the Temple[46]. But did
we not state[47]: A Cohen who stepped outside to talk with somebody, if it
was for any length of time he needs immersion, if it was for a moment he
needs to wash hands and feet[48]? One for the golden garments, the other
for the linen garments.

46   Since the belt of the Cohen was *kilaim,* he was not permitted to wear priestly garb outside the Temple precinct even for a second. In the Babli, *Tamid* 27b, there is a dispute whether the belt of a simple priest was *kilaim.*

47   Tosephta *Kippurim* 1:16, formulated only for the High Priest. A parallel in Babli *Zebaḥim* 20b is formulated for a common priest: "If he stepped outside the wall of the courtyard, if it was for any length of time . . ." It is explained that he stepped outside to relieve himself. Since the lavatory for priests was subterranean (Mishnah *Tamid* 1:1), not

holy and not profane, the prohibition of *kilaim* does not apply there.

48   If the Cohen is forbidden to leave the Temple precinct in his priestly garment, how could the case of the *baraita* ever arise? The answer is that this was possible only for the High Priest on the Day of Atonement when he wore linen garments; he might not leave the precinct if he wore his "golden" garments that were all *kilaim* except for his hat. It is reported in Mishnah *Yoma* that sometimes the High Priest spoke to the king (or a visiting foreign king) during the few breaks he had on the day of Atonement.

לֹא יַעֲלֶה עָלֶיךָ מוּתָּר לְהַצִּיעוֹ תַּחְתֶּיךָ אֲבָל אָמְרוּ חֲכָמִים לֹא יַעֲשֶׂה כֵן שֶׁלֹּא תְהֵא נִימָא אַחַת עוֹלָה עַל בְּשָׂרוֹ.

(*Lev.* 19:19) "[*Kilaim* cloth] shall not come upon you." You are permitted to spread it out under you but the Sages said one should not do it lest one thread should be over his flesh[49].

49   *Sifra Qedošim Pereq* 4(18), Babli *Beẓah* 14b. The Babli is much more restrictive and decrees that one

may not sit on a *kilaim* carpet even if the latter is covered by ten layers of unobjectionable material.

(fol. 31d) **משנה ג**: מִטְפְּחוֹת הַיָּדַיִם מִטְפְּחוֹת הַסְּפָרִים מִטְפְּחוֹת הַסַּפָּג אֵין בָּהֶן מִשּׁוּם כִּלְאַיִם. רִבִּי לְעָזָר אוֹסֵר. וּמִטְפְּחוֹת הַסַּפָּרִים אֲסוּרוֹת מִשּׁוּם כִּלְאַיִם.

Mishnah 3: Hand towels, scroll wraps[50], towels of the bath attendant[51] are not subject to *kilaim*. Rebbi Eliezer forbids. Barber's towels are forbidden for *kilaim*[52].

50   The covers of Torah scrolls. Wrappers of other book scrolls are not subject to *kilaim* even for R. Eliezer.

51   The סָפָּג is the bath attendant

using the סְפוֹג, Greek σπόγγος "sponge".

52   These are put on the client's shoulders and breast, they are "on him".

(fol. 32a) **הלכה ג:** מִטְפָּחוֹת הַיָּדַיִם כו'. תַּמָּן תַּנִּינָן שָׁלֹשׁ מִטְפָּחוֹת הֵן שֶׁל יָדַיִם טְמֵאָה מִדְרָס וְשֶׁל סְפָרִים טְמֵאָה מֵת שֶׁל תַּכְרִיךְ נִבְלֵי בְנֵי לֵוִי טְהוֹרָה מִכְּלוּם. רִבִּי לָא בְשֵׁם רִבִּי יוֹחָנָן מִפְּנֵי שֶׁהוּא נוֹתְנָהּ עַל הַכֶּסֶת וְיָשֵׁן עָלֶיהָ. רַב אָמַר מִפְּנֵי שֶׁהוּא נוֹתְנָהּ תַּחַת אֲצִילֵי יָדָיו.

Halakhah 3: "Hand towels, etc." There[53], we have stated: "There are three kinds of towels. Hand towels may become impure by load; scroll wraps may become impure by the dead; the wrappings of the Levites' harps[54] are always pure." Rebbi La in the name of Rebbi Joḥanan, because one may put them on the pillow and sleep on them. Rav said, because he puts them under his upper arms[55].

53   Mishnah *Kelim* 24:12. The entire chapter deals with classification of the types of impurity of כלים, i. e., vessels, tools, and garments. Vessels can only acquire original impurity if they are made to be sat on; they become actually impure if a person with gonorrhea sits on them, if they carry his "load". In all other cases, vessels can only acquire derivative impurity; this is exemplified by a vessel standing in the same tent with a corpse.

Hence, "impure by the dead" in these Mishnaiot simply means "may acquire derivative impurity." Vessels or textiles that are only used to serve other vessels, not humans directly, cannot become impure (Mishnah *Kelim* 16:7). Cf. also *Demay*, Chapter 2, Note 136, and above Chapter 2, Note 180.

54   The mss. of the Maimonides tradition read "wrappings (of the dead) and covers of Levites' harps."

55   A reason has to be found why

hand towels are considered manufactured for the purpose that either one should sit or lie on them or exert pressure ("load") on them, for only this can make them susceptible to the impurity of "load".

רַב אָמַר אָסוּר וַהֲלָכָה כְדִבְרֵי הָאוֹסֵר. וְלָמָּה לֹא אָמַר כְרִבִּי אֱלִיעֶזֶר. אִית תַּנָּיֵי תַּנֵּי מָחְלָף.

Rav said they[56] are forbidden and practice follows him who forbids. Why does he not say one follows Rebbi Eliezer. There are Tannaïm who switch their statements[57].

56   The three kinds mentioned as not under the laws of *kilaim*.

57   In Tosephta *Kilaim* 5:17, R. Meïr presents the text of the Mishnah, R. Jehudah switches the names and says that the Sages forbid. In a dispute between R. Meïr and R. Jehudah, practice as a rule follows R. Jehudah.

רִבִּי יוֹחָנָן יְהַב מַפָּה עַל מָנוֹי וְאֵינוּ אָסוּר מִשּׁוּם כִּלְאַיִם דְּלָא יְנָבְלוּן מָאנוֹי. אָמַר רִבִּי זְרִיקָן יְהִיבוֹ לְרִבִּי אֲבוּנָא בֵּיעֲתָא בְמַפָּה דְּאִית בָּהּ כִּלְאַיִם וְהוּא לֹא מְקַבֵּל עַל שֶׁלֹּא יִתְכַּוְּנוּ בָה בַחַמָּה מִפְּנֵי הַחַמָּה וּבִגְשָׁמִים מִפְּנֵי הַגְּשָׁמִים.

Rebbi Johanan put a cloth on his garment. Is that not forbidden because of *kilaim*? [He did it] so that his garments should not wear out[58]. Rebbi Zeriqan said, they gave Rebbi Avina an egg on a towel containing *kilaim*, but he did not accept it because of[59] "they[60] should not intend to use them as protection from the sun in summer and from the rains in winter."

58   He never wore them as garment.

59   Mishnah 5; he did not want to use *kilaim* to protect his hands from the heat of the egg.

60   Sellers of *kilaim* garments.

מִטְפְּחוֹת סְפָרִים. רִבִּי שְׁמוּאֵל בַּר נַחְמָן בְּשֵׁם רִבִּי יוֹנָתָן מִפְּנֵי שֶׁהוּא עוֹשֶׂה אוֹתָן כְּמִין תִּיק וְנוֹתֵן סֵפֶר תּוֹרָתוֹ עָלֶיהָ. רִבִּי בָּא רִבִּי חִיָּיא בַּר יוֹסֵף בְּשֵׁם רַב

מִפְּנֵי שֶׁהוּא מְחַמֵּם בָּהּ יָדָיו. אָמַר רִבִּי בּוּן בַּר חִייָה לְרִבִּי בָּא בְּלֹא כָךְ אֵינוּ

אָסוּר מִשּׁוּם כִּלְאָיִם. אָמַר לֵיהּ לֹא רַב הוּא וְרַב אָמַר אָסוּר וַהֲלָכָה כְדִבְרֵי

הָאוֹסֵר. אָמַר רִבִּי יוֹנָה לְרִבִּי בָּא וְלָמָּה לֹא אָמַר לֵיהּ מָלֵא מְסַלְּקָתָהּ אִלּוּ אָמַר

לֵיהּ בְּלֹא כָךְ אֵינָהּ אֲסוּרָה בַּהֲנָיָיה. מַה הֲוָה לֵיהּ מֵימוֹר לֵיהּ.

"Scroll wraps." Rebbi Samuel bar Naḥman in the name of Rebbi

Jonathan: Because he makes them into a kind of container[61] and puts his

Torah scroll on them. Rebbi Abba Rebbi Ḥiyya bar Joseph in the name of

Rav: Because he uses it to warm his hands[62]. Rebbi Abun bar Ḥiyya said

to Rebbi Abba: Without that would it not be forbidden because of

kilaim? He said to him, is not Rav the author? And Rav said they are

forbidden and practice follows him who forbids[63]. Rebbi Jonah said to

Rebbi Abba, and why did you not say to him that he removes it full[64]. If

he had said to him, would it not be forbidden for usufruct, what could you

have said to him?

---

61   Greek θήκη. R. Jonathan
follows the text of our Mishnah that
scroll wraps are not subject to *kilaim*.
However, the reason is not that they
are only to serve other vessels (cf. Note
51) because in that case there would
not have been any need to specify them
in the Mishnah.

62   In Babli *Beẓah* 14b, this reason
is given for the requirement that
curtains may not contain *kilaim*.

63   Rav gives the reason why he
rules following R. Eliezer in the
Mishnah.

64   The Torah scroll is put into its
ark or chest wrapped in its wrapper.
Since the wrapper is dedicated to a
holy object, it should become forbidden for all profane use and the
reason given by Rav could not possibly
apply. The prohibition of the use of
ancillaries to holy objects is explicit in
a Babylonian *baraita* (Babli *Megillah*
26b); R. Abba points out that adoption
of that Babylonian standard would
invalidate Rav's reason to apply the
standard of *kilaim* to wrappers of
Torah scrolls.

מִטְפָּחוֹת הַסַּפָּג פְּעָמִים שֶׁהוּא רוֹאֶה אֶת רַבּוֹ וּמִתְעַטֵּף בּוֹ. רְבִּי אַבָּהוּ בְּשֵׁם רְבִּי
יוֹחָנָן בַּלְנְרֵי נָשִׁים אֲסוּרִין מִשּׁוּם כְּלְאַיִם. הִיא בַּלְנְרֵי נָשִׁים הִיא בַּלְנְרֵי אֲנָשִׁים.
מַהוּ בַּלְנְרֵי אֲנָשִׁים רַבָּנִין דְּקֵיסָרִין אָמְרֵי אנטיטיה. מִטְפָּחוֹת הַסַּפָּג הָדָא
דְּתֵימַר בְּמִתְכַּוֵּין לְשֵׁם מַלְבּוּשׁ אֲבָל אִם אֵינוּ מִתְכַּוֵּין לְשֵׁם מַלְבּוּשׁ לֹא בְּדָא.

"Towels of the bath attendant," sometimes seeing his teacher he wraps himself in them[65]. Rebbi Abbahu in the name of Rebbi Johanan: women's bath towels[66] are not subject to *kilaim*. Women's bath towels are the same as men's bath towels. What are men's bath towels? The rabbis of Caesarea say, אנטיטיה[67]. Towels of the bath attendant, that means if he intends them as clothing, but if he does not intend them as clothing, not about that[68].

---

65 Hence, we follow Rav in his ruling that *kilaim* is forbidden for bath towels.

66 R. Johanan's statement is a Tosephta (*Kilaim* 5:16); there the term is בלארי Latin *balnearia, ium*, n. "bathing utensils." The Tosephta adds that these are not subject to *kilaim* only if they are pieces of cloth, not sewn.

67 In *Mo'ed Qatan* 3:2 (fol. 82a) the reading is אנטיניא. One might derive the word from Syrian Arabic نطا نطا "to be wet"; the meaning would be wet towels. Another possible derivation is from Latin *natatorius* (adj.) "belonging to a swimmer" (E. G.).

68 The prohibition of *kilaim* does not apply. Since the reason for following Rav here applies only to men, even Rav has to agree that women's towels may contain *kilaim*.

(fol. 31d) **מִשְׁנָה ד**: תַּכְרִיכֵי הַמֵּת וּמַרְדַּעַת שֶׁל חֲמוֹר אֵין בָּהֶן מִשּׁוּם כְּלְאַיִם. לֹא
יִתֵּן אֶת הַמַּרְדַּעַת עַל כְּתֵיפוֹ אֲפִילוּ לְהוֹצִיא עָלֶיהָ אֶת הַזֶּבֶל.

Mishnah 4: Shrouds of the dead and the pack-saddle of the donkey do not fall under *kilaim*. One should never carry a pack-saddle on his shoulder even to transport garbage.

(fol. 32a) **הלכה ד**: תַּכְרִיכֵי הַמֵּת כו'. כְּתִיב בַּמֵּתִים חָפְשִׁי כֵּיוָן שָׁאָדָם מֵת
נַעֲשָׂה חָפְשִׁי מִן הַמִּצְוֹת.

"Shrouds of the dead, etc." It is written (*Ps.* 88:6): "Among the dead is freedom." When a person dies he becomes free from the Commandments.

רְבִּי צִוָּה שְׁלשָׁה דְבָרִים בִּשְׁעַת פְּטִירָתוֹ מִן הָעוֹלָם. אַל תָּזוּז אַלְמָנָתִי מִבֵּיתִי.
וְאַל תִּסְפְּדוּנִי בָּעֲיָירוֹת. וּמִי שֶׁנִּיטְפַּל בִּי בְחַיַּי יִטַּפֵּל בִּי בְמוֹתִי. אַל תָּזוּז
אַלְמָנָתִי מִבֵּיתִי. וְלָאו מַתְנִיתָא הִיא אַלְמָנָה שֶׁאָמְרָה אֵי אֶפְשִׁי לָזוּז מִבֵּית בַּעֲלִי.
אָמַר רִבִּי דְרוֹסָאי[69] דְּלָא יֵימְרוֹן לָהּ בֵּיתָה דִנְשִׂיאוּתָה הוּא מְשׁוּעֲבָד הוּא
לִנְשִׂיאוּתָה. אָמַר רִבִּי לְעָזָר בַּר יוֹסֵה כְּהָדָא דְתַנֵּי דָּרָה בַבָּתִּים כְּשֵׁם שֶׁהָיְתָה
דָּרָה בָּהֶן וּבַעֲלָהּ נָתוּן בִּמְדִינַת הַיָּם. וּמִשְׁתַּמֶּשֶׁת בִּכְלֵי כֶסֶף וּבִכְלֵי זָהָב כְּשֵׁם
שֶׁהָיְתָה מִשְׁתַּמֶּשֶׁת וּבַעֲלָהּ נָתוּן בִּמְדִינַת הַיָּם. וְנִיזוֹנֶת כְּשֵׁם שֶׁהָיְתָה נִיזוֹנֶת
וּבַעֲלָהּ נָתוּן (fol. 32b) בִּמְדִינַת הַיָּם. וְאַל תִּסְפְּדוּנִי בָּעֲיָירוֹת מִפְּנֵי הַמַּחֲלוֹקֶת.
וּמִי שֶׁנִּיטְפַּל בִּי בְחַיַּי יִטַּפֵּל בִּי בְמוֹתִי. אָמַר רִבִּי חֲנַנְיָה דְצִיפּוֹרִין כְּגוֹן יוֹסֵי
אֶפְרָתִי וְיוֹסֵף חֶפָנִים. רִבִּי חִזְקִיָּה מוֹסִיף אַל תַּרְבּוּ עָלַי תַּכְרִיכִין. וּתְהֵא אֲרוֹנִי
נְקוּבָה בָּאָרֶץ. מִילְּתָא אָמְרִין בְּסַדִּין אֶחָד נִקְבַּר רְבִּי. דְּרְבִּי אָמַר לָא כְּמָה דְבַר
אִינָשׁ אָזַל הוּא אָתֵי. וְרַבָּנִין אָמְרִין כְּמָה דְבַר נָשׁ אָזַל הוּא אָתֵי. תַּנֵּי בְּשֵׁם רִבִּי
נָתָן כְּסוּת הַיּוֹרֶדֶת עִם אָדָם לִשְׁאוֹל הִיא בָאָה עִמּוֹ מַה טַעֲמָא תִּתְהַפֵּךְ כְּחוֹמֶר
חוֹתָם וְיִתְיַצְּבוּ כְּמוֹ לְבוּשׁ. אַנְטוֹלִינוֹס שָׁאַל לְרִבִּי מַהוּ תִּתְהַפֵּךְ כְּחוֹמֶר חוֹתָם
אָמַר לֵיהּ מִי שֶׁהוּא מֵבִיא אֶת הַדּוֹר הוּא מַלְבִּישׁוֹ.

Rebbi commanded three things on his death-bed[70]: My widow should not move from my house; do not eulogize me in small towns; and he who served me during my lifetime should serve me in my death. "My widow should not move from my house," is that not a Mishnah? "The widow who said, I cannot possibly move from my husband's house . . .[71]" Rebbi Dositheos[69] said, that they should not say, this is the house of the patriarchate and must serve the patriarchate[72]. Rebbi Eleazar bar Yose said, as we have stated[73]: "She lives in the houses just as she lived while her husband was overseas, she uses silver and golden vessels just as she used to while her husband was overseas, she is fed just as she was fed while her husband was overseas." "Do not eulogize me in small towns" because of the quarrels[74]. "He who served me during my lifetime should serve me in my death;" Rebbi Ḥananiah from Sepphoris said, for example Yose Ephrati and Joseph from Haifa. Rebbi Ḥizqiah added, do not use many shrouds on me and let my coffin have holes at the bottom[75]. These words say that Rebbi was buried in a single shroud since Rebbi said, not as a man left, he will come[76]. But the rabbis say, just as a man left, he will come. It was stated in the name of Rebbi Nathan[77]: The garment that went with a person to the grave will come back with him. What is the reason? (*Job* 38:14) "The seal[78] turns itself around like clay, they appear in dress." Antoninus[79] asked Rebbi, what is the meaning of "The seal turns itself around like clay?" He said to him, He Who brings the generation clothes it[80].

69   In the parallel in *Ketubot* 12:3 (fol. 35a), ר' דוסא . In the parallel *Gen. rabba* 100(3), ר' דוסתאי , Dositheos. The text in *Gen. rabba* seems to be the original text from which the one here is an abbreviation.

70   In addition to the two Yerushalmi sources mentioned in the previous Note, there is a Babylonian source *Ketubot* 103. Since the Mishnah mentions shrouds, there follows a lengthy insertion about burials.

71   Mishnah *Ketubot* 12:3: "If a widow said, I cannot possibly move from my husband's house, the heirs may

not say, go to your father's house and we shall support you there, but they support her and give her an apartment corresponding to her standard of living." The Mishnah does not require that the widow keep the identical apartment she occupied during her marriage, only an equivalent one. In the tradition of the Babli, Rebbi's widow was not the mother of his children, his heirs.

72   In the opinion of *Gen. rabba*, the argument would have been valid if the house of the patriarch had been built with public money. But since Rebbi

built his house with his own money, his successor could not occupy this house.

73   The Babylonian version is in Babli *Ketubot* 103a and, in shortened form, in Tosephta *Ketubot* 11:5: The woman whose husband died lives in the houses she lived in during her husband's lifetime, uses slaves and handmaidens, silver and gold vessels she used during her husband's lifetime, for so he writes to her (in the marriage document): You shall live in my house and be supported by my property as long as you are a widow in my house.

74   That there should not be competition among places which were not really able to provide decent eulogizers. The Babli (*loc. cit.* 103b) explains that in small villages the crowds are too small to give the honor due.

75   (Cf. *Šulḥan 'arûkh Yôrē Dē'ā* ⁋362.) In *Gen. rabba*, the explanation is that the body should decompose rapidly. It is talmudic doctrine that the soul suffers during decomposition of the body and, except for those sinners whose place is in hell, the suffering stops when only the bones are left (Babli *Berakhot* 18b).

76   At Resurrection.

77   The quote in *Yalquṭ Sim'oni Job* 924 reads: R. Jonathan.

78   The "seal" of a person are the characteristics differentiating him from all others: voice, looks, and thinking [*Sanhedrin* Yerushalmi 3:13 (fol. 22b), Babli 38a].

79   A Roman emperor of the Severan dynasty who reputedly was a crypto-Jew. Since all emperors of that dynasty adopted the name of Antoninus together with that of Augustus, speculations about the identity of this Antoninus are rather futile.

80   God will not only create the flesh as described in Ezechiel's vision of the dry bones but the clothing with it, as He did for Adam. An echo of this discussion is in Babli *Sanhedrin* 90b, bottom.

רִבִּי יוֹחָנָן מְפַקֵּד מַלְבְּשׁוּנִי בִּירִירִיקָא לָא חִיוּוְרֵי וְלָא אוּכְמִין. אִין קָמִית בֵּינֵי
צַדִּיקַיָּא לָא נִבְהָת. אִין קָמִית בֵּינֵי רְשִׁיעַיָּא לָא נִבְהָת. רִבִּי יֹאשַׁיָּא מְפַקֵּד
אַלְבְּשׁוּנִי חִיוּוְרֵי חֲפִיתִין. אָמְרִין לֵיהּ וּמַה אַתְּ טָב מִן רַבָּךְ. אָמַר לָן וּמַה אֲנָא
בְהִית בְּעָבְדָּאי. רבי יִרְמְיָה מְפַקֵּד אַלְבְּשׁוּנִי חִיוּוְרִין חֲפִיתִין אַלְבְּשׁוּנִי בְּנָרְסַיי
יְהָבוּן מִסָּנַי בְּרַגְלַי וְחוּטְרָא בְיָדַיי וִיהַבוּנִי עַל סִיטְרָא אִין אֲתֵי מְשִׁיחָא אֲנָא
מְעַתַּד.

Rebbi Joḥanan[81] commanded: Dress me in beige[82], not white and not black. If I rise among the just I shall not be ashamed, if I rise among the wicked I shall not be ashamed. Rebbi Joshia commanded: Dress me in clean white. They said to him, in what are you better than your teacher? He said to them, why should I be ashamed of my deeds? Rebbi Jeremiah commanded: Dress me in clean white, dress me in my socks[83], put my shoes on my feet and a walking stick in my hand, lay me on my side, when the Messiah comes I shall be ready.

81   In the parallel Babli Šabbat 114a, R. Yannai. The reading here is confirmed by the second sentence, since R. Joshia was a student of R. Joḥanan.

82   In the parallel Ketubot 12:3 (fol. 35a), בורידיקא. This cannot mean "pink" since "rose colored" in the Yerushalmi is ורדינון, Greek ῥόδινος. Since יריר means pus, ידידיקא is taken to mean "pus colored".

83   The word נרס is not in the dictionaries. The Rome ms. has here לא לבשון לי דרסי "do not dress me in worn-out (shoes)" but Gen. rabba 100(3) has אלכשוני דרדסאי "dress me in my socks," which may be the best reading. If נרס is a genuine word, it should be Arabic מרסה مَرَسَة "cord, rope".

The messianic idea of bodily resurrection with the dead fully clothed and equipped is not part of actual Jewish burial customs. [But a strange echo of these discussions appears in Heine's poem about a dying veteran of Napoleon's failed Russian campaign, who wants to be buried in his native France, wearing his military decorations, gun in hand, sword by his side. He plans to rise from his grave fully armed, ready to protect his Emperor, who at the time was widely regarded as a messianic figure:

Das Ehrenkreuz am rothen Band
Sollst du aufs Herz mir legen;
Die Flinte gieb mir in die Hand,
Und gürt mir um den Degen.

. . . .

Dann steig' ich gewaffnet hervor aus dem Grab,

Den Kaiser, den Kaiser zu schützen!
(H. Heine, Romanzen, *Die Grenadiere*). (E. G.)]

צִיפּוֹרָיָא אָמְרִין מָאן דַּאֲמַר לָן רִבִּי דְּמָה אֲנַן קָטְלִין לֵיהּ. אָדִּיק לוֹן בַּר קַפָּרָא
רֵישֵׁי מְכַסֵּי מָאנוֹי מְבַזְּעִין וַאֲמַר לוֹן יְצוּקִים וְאֶרְאֶלִים תְּפוּסִין בַּלּוּחוֹת הַבְּרִית
וְגָבְרָה יָדָן שֶׁל אֶרְאֶלִים וְחָטְפוּ אֶת הַלּוּחוֹת. אָמְרִין לֵיהּ דְּמָה רִבִּי. אֲמַר לוֹן
אַתּוּן אֲמַרְתּוֹן וְקָרְעוּן וַאֲזַל קָלָא דְּקָרְעוּן לְגוֹפָפְתָּא מַהֲלָךְ תְּלָתָא מִילִין.

The[84] people from Sepphoris said: We shall kill anybody who tells us
that Rebbi died. Bar Qappara associated with them, his head covered and
his garments torn. He said to them: Earthlings and angels held the
Tablets of the Covenant; the angels were stronger and they took away the
Tablets. They said to him: Rebbi died. He said to them: You said it.
They tore their clothes and the sound of the tearing was heard at Goffta[85]
at a distance of three *mil.*

84   Parallels *Ketubot* Yerushalmi   85   An unidentified place which
12:3 (fol. 35a), Babli 104a.   had a synagogue (*Nazir* 7:1).

רִבִּי נַחְמָן בְּשֵׁם רִבִּי מָנָא מַעֲשֶׂה נִיסִּין נַעֲשׂוּ בְּאוֹתוֹ הַיּוֹם. עֶרֶב שַׁבָּת הָיְתָה
וְנִתְכַּנְּסוּ כָּל־הָעֲיָירוֹת לְהַסְפִּידוֹ וְאַשִׁירוֹנֵיהּ תְּמַנֵּי עֶשְׂרֵה כְּנִישָׁן וְאַחְתּוֹנֵיהּ לְבֵית
שָׁרַיי וְתָלָה לוֹן יוֹמָא עַד שֶׁהָיָה כַּל־אֶחָד וְאֶחָד מַגִּיעַ לְבֵיתוֹ וּמְמַלֵּא לוֹ חָבִית שֶׁל
מַיִם וּמַדְלִיק לוֹ אֶת הַנֵּר. כֵּיוָן שֶׁשָּׁקְעָה הַחַמָּה קָרָא הַגֶּבֶר שָׁרוֹן מְצִיקִין.
אָמְרִין דִּילְמָא דְחַלְּלִינַן שַׁבָּתָא. יֶצְתָה בַּת קוֹל וְאָמְרָה לָהֶן כָּל־מִי שֶׁלֹּא נִתְעַצֵּל
בְּהֶסְפֵּידוֹ שֶׁל רִבִּי יְהֵא מְבוּשָׂר מֵחַיֵּי הָעוֹלָם הַבָּא חוּץ מִן קַצְרָא. כֵּיוָן דְּשָׁמַע כֵּן
סָלַק לֵיהּ לְאִיגְרָא וּטְלַק גַּרְמֵיהּ וּמִית. נְפָקַת בַּת קָלָא וְאָמְרָה וַאֲפִילוּ קַצְרָא.

Rebbi Naḥman in the name of Rebbi Mana: Miracles happened that
day. It was Sabbath eve and all the surrounding towns came together to
eulogize him. They made him [Rebbi] rest in eighteen synagogues until
they brought him to his resting place but the day extended for them until
each one had time to get to his house, fill an amphora of water, and light
the candles. When the sun set, the rooster crowed[86]. They were anxious
and said, maybe we did desecrate the Sabbath? There came a voice and

said to them, every one who was not lazy for the eulogies of Rebbi shall
be announced for the life of the Future World, except the fuller[87]. When
the latter heard this, he ascended the roof, threw himself down, and died.
There came a voice and said, including the fuller.

86   To announce the following   87   In the Babli it is explained that
morning. This clause is missing in the   during Rebbi's stay in Sepphoris, the
Rome ms. In the parallel in the Babli,   fuller appeared every day in his court
only the last two sentences of this   but on the day Rebbi died, the fuller
paragraph appear.   was absent for some reason.

רִבִּי הֲוָה יָתִיב לֵיהּ בְּצִיפּוֹרִין שְׁבַע עֶשְׂרֵה שְׁנִין וְקָרָא עַל גַּרְמֵיהּ וַיְחִי יַעֲקֹב
בְּאֶרֶץ מִצְרַיִם שְׁבַע עֶשְׂרֵה שָׁנָה. וַיְחִי יְהוּדָה בְּצִיפּוֹרִין שְׁבַע עֶשְׂרֵה שָׁנָה. וּמִין
גּוֹבְעִין[88] עֲבַד תְּלַת עֶשְׂרֵה שְׁנִין חֲשַׁשׁ בְּשִׁנּוֹי. אָמַר רִבִּי יוֹסֵי בֵּי רִבִּי בּוֹן
כָּל־אוֹתָן שְׁלֹשׁ עֶשְׂרֵה שָׁנָה לֹא מֵתָה חַיָּה בְּאֶרֶץ יִשְׂרָאֵל וְלֹא הִפִּילָה עוּבָּרָה
בְּאֶרֶץ יִשְׂרָאֵל. וְלָמָּה חָשׁ שְׁנּוֹי. חַד זְמָן עֲבַר חָמָא חַד עִיגַל מִנְכַּס גָּעָה וְאָמְרָה
לֵיהּ רִבִּי שֵׁיזְבִי אֲמַר לֵיהּ לְכָךְ נוֹצָרְתָּ. וּבְסוֹף אֵיךְ אִינְשְׁמַת. חֲמָתוֹן קְטָלִין חַד
קַן דְּעַכְבָּרִין אֲמַר אַרְפּוּנוֹן וְרַחֲמָיו עַל כָּל־מַעֲשָׂיו כְּתִיב.

Rebbi dwelt in Sepphoris seventeen years and applied to himself (*Gen.*
47:28): "Jacob lived in Egypt seventeen years," Jehudah lived in Sepphoris
seventeen years. Of these he suffered from toothache for thirteen years.
{Rebbi Yose ben Rebbi Abun said, all these thirteen years no woman
lying-in died in the Land of Israel and no pregnant woman had a
miscarriage in the Land of Israel.} Why did he have a toothache[91]? Once
he saw a calf to be slaughtered when it bellowed and said to him, Rebbi,
save me! He said to it, for that you were created. At the end, how was he
healed? He saw them killing a burrow of rats. He said to them, let them
live, it is written (*Ps.* 145:9) "His mercy extends to all His creatures."

רבִּי הֲוָה עָנְוָן סַגִּין וְהֲוָה אָמַר כָּל־מַה דְּיֵימֵי לִי בַּר נַשָׁא אֲנָא עֲבִיד חוּץ מִמַּה
שֶׁעָשׂוּ זִקְנֵי בְּתֵירָא לִזְקֵנֵי דְשָׁרוֹן גַּרְמוֹן מִנְשִׂיאוּתֵיהּ וּמְנוֹנֵיהּ. אִין סְלִיק רַב
הוּנָא רֵישׁ גָּלוּתָא לְהָכָא אֲנָא מוֹתִיב לֵיהּ לְעֵיל מִנַּיי דְּהוּא מִן יְהוּדָה וַאֲנָא
מִבִּנְיָמִין דְּהוּא מִן דְּכְרַיָּא וַאֲנָא מִן נְקוּבְתָּא. חַד זְמַן אָעַל רִבִּי חִיָּיה רוּבָא
לְגַבֵּיהּ אָמַר לֵיהּ הָא רַב הוּנָא לְבָר נִתְכַּרְכְּמוּ פָּנָיו שֶׁל רִבִּי. אָמַר לֵיהּ אֲרוֹנוֹ
בָא. אָמַר לֵיהּ פּוּק וְחָמֵי מָאן בָּעֵי לָךְ לְבָר. וּנְפַק וְלָא אַשְׁכַּח בַּר נַשׁ וְיָדַע
דְּהוּא כָּעֵיס עֲלוֹי. עֲבַד דְּלָא עֲלִיל עֲלֵיהּ תַּלְתִּין יוֹמִין. אָמַר רִבִּי יוֹסֵי בַּר בּוֹן
כָּל־אִינּוּן תַּלְתּוֹיֵי יוֹמַיָּא יְלִיף רַב מִנֵּיהּ כְּלָלֵי דְאוֹרַיְיתָא. לְסוֹף תְּלַת עֲשַׂרְתֵּי
שְׁנַיָּא וּתְלַתְתּוֹי יוֹמַיָּא אָעַל אֵלְיָהוּ לְגַבֵּיהּ בִּדְמוּת רִבִּי חִיָּיה רוּבָה. אָמַר לֵיהּ
מַה מָּרִי עָבִיד. אָמַר לֵיהּ חַד שִׁינַּיי מְעִיקָה לִי. אָמַר לֵיהּ חֲמֵי לָהּ לִי וְחָמֵי לָהּ
לֵיהּ וִיהַב אֶצְבְּעָתֵיהּ עֲלָהּ וְאִינְּשִׁמַתּ. לְמָחָר אָעַל רִבִּי חִיָּיה רוּבָה לְגַבֵּיהּ אָמַר
לֵיהּ מַה עֲבַד רִבִּי הַאי שִׁינָּךְ מַה הִיא עֲבִידָא. אָמַר לֵיהּ מִן הַהִיא שַׁעֲתָא דְּיַהַב
אֶצְבְּעָתָךְ עֲלָהּ אִינְּשִׁימָת. בְּאוֹתָהּ שָׁעָה אָמַר אִי לָכֶם חַיּוֹת שֶׁבְּאֶרֶץ יִשְׂרָאֵל אִי
לָכֶם עוּבָּרוֹת שֶׁבְּאֶרֶץ יִשְׂרָאֵל. אָמַר לֵיהּ אֲנָא לָא הֲוֵינָא מִן הַהִיא שַׁעֲתָא נְהִיג
בֵּיהּ בִּיקָר. כַּד הֲוָה עֲלִיל לְבֵית וַעְדָּא הֲוָה אָמַר יִכְנֵס רִבִּי חִיָּיא רוּבָא לְפָנִים.
אָמַר לוֹ רִבִּי יִשְׁמָעֵאל בֵּי רִבִּי יוֹסֵי לְפָנִים מִמֶּנִּי. אָמַר לוֹ חַס וְשָׁלוֹם אֶלָּא רִבִּי
חִיָּיא רוּבָה לְפָנִים וְרִבִּי יִשְׁמָעֵאל בֵּי רִבִּי יוֹסֵי לְפָנֵי לְפָנִים. רִבִּי הֲוָה מַתְנֵי
שְׁבָחֵיהּ דְּרִבִּי חִיָּיא רוּבָה קוֹמֵי רִבִּי יִשְׁמָעֵאל בֵּי רִבִּי יוֹסֵי. חַד זְמַן חָמֵי גּוֹ בְּנֵי
וְלָא אִיתְכְּנַע מִן קוֹמוֹי. אָמַר לֵיהּ אֲהֵנּוּ דְּאַתְּ מַתְנֵי שְׁבָחֵיהּ. אָמַר לֵיהּ מַה עֲבַד
לָךְ. אָמַר לֵיהּ חָמִתֵּיהּ גּוֹ בְּנֵי וְלָא אִיתְכְּנַע מִן קוֹמוֹי. אָמַר לֵיהּ לָמָּה עֲבַדְתְּ כֵּן.
אָמַר לֵיהּ כְּמוֹ יָבֹא עָלַי יִיתֵיי[89] עָלַי דְּאִין סְחִית לָא יָדְעִית בְּהַהִיא שַׁעֲתָא
אַשְׁגָּרִית עֵינַיי בְּכָל־סֵפֶר תִּילִים אַגָּדָה. מִן הַהִיא שַׁעֲתָא מָסַר לֵיהּ שְׁנֵי
תַלְמִידִין דִּיהַלְכוּן עִמֵּיהּ בְּגִין סָכוּתָא[90] .

Rebbi[92] was very meek and said, all a man might ask from me I am
ready to do, except what the elders of Bathyra did for my ancestor: they
divested themselves of their presidency and appointed him[93]. If Rav
Huna, the Head of the Diaspora, would come here I would let him sit
higher than myself since he is from the tribe of Judah and I am from

Benjamin, he is from the male line and I am from the female. Once, the elder Rebbi Ḥiyya visited him and said, Rav Huna is outside. The face of Rebbi became saffron-colored. He [R. Ḥiyya] said to him, his coffin arrived. He [Rebbi] said to him, go outside and look who wants you there. He stepped outside and did not find anybody; he understood that he [Rebbi] was angry with him[94]. He did not visit him again for thirty days. {Rebbi Yose bar Abun said, in those thirty days did Rav learn from him [R. Ḥiyya] the principles of Torah[95].} At the end of thirteen years and thirty days[96], Elijah visited him [Rebbi] in the likeness of the older Rebbi Ḥiyya. He said to him, how does my lord feel? He said to him, one tooth hurts me. He said to him, show it to me. He showed it to him, he put his finger on it and it was healed. The next day, the older Rebbi Ḥiyya came to him and asked him, how does Rebbi feel, what is with that tooth? He said to him, from the moment that you put your finger on it, it was healed. At that moment, he said, woe on you, lying-in women of the Land of Israel, woe on you, pregnant women of the Land of Israel! He [R. Ḥiyya] said to him, that was not me. From that moment on, he [Rebbi] treated him with honor.

When he [Rebbi] went to the assembly hall, he said, may the older Rebbi Ḥiyya come inside. Rebbi Ismael ben Rebbi Yose asked, closer than me? He said, beware! The older Rebbi Ḥiyya inside, and Rebbi Ismael ben Rebbi Yose innermost. Rebbi used to state the praises of the older Rebbi Ḥiyya before Rebbi Ismael ben Rebbi Yose. Once, he [R. Ismael ben R. Yose] saw him [R. Ḥiyya] in the bathhouse and he did not show him reverence. He [R. Ismael ben R. Yose] said to him [Rebbi], is that the one of whom you state praises? He said, what did he do to you? He said, I saw him in the bathhouse and he did not show me reverence. He [Rebbi] said to him [R. Ḥiyya], why did you do that? He said to him, so much should come over me if I realized that I was washing myself, at that time my eyes were occupied with the allegorical interpretation of the entire book of Psalms. From that moment on, he [Rebbi] appointed two students to accompany him [R. Ḥiyya] to watch out for him.

88   In the parallel *Ketubot* 12:3 (fol. 35a) גּוּבְיהֶן This word has been translated. The word used here ("their hills") is probably a misspelling explained as writing from the spoken word.

89   Reading of the Rome ms. Venice: ייעול.

90   Reading of the Leyden ms. סכותא is Onqelos's translation of Hebrew צופים (*Num.* 23:14). The printed editions have here and in *Ketubot* סכנתא "danger". In the parallel [*Gen. rabba* 33(3)], the students are appointed to go with him to the אשונא so he should not stay too long and endanger himself. אשונא is shown by L. Ginzburg (Notes to Kohut's *Arukh*, p. 436) to be Syriac אשחונא "*calidarium*, sauna"; Lieberman (הירושלמי כפשוטו ע' יא) translates סכותא by *unctuarium*.

91   Parallel in Babli *Baba Meẓi'a* 85a. There, the calf ran to hide itself in Rebbi's garment but did not talk to Rebbi. In the parallel *Gen. rabba* 33(3), the calf is said to have been bellowing "as if to say, save me!"

92   *Gen. rabba* 33(3).

93   The ancestor is Hillel, *Pesaḥim*

6:1, Babli 66a; Babli *Baba Meẓi'a* 85a. The family of Hillel traces its origins to a woman of Davidic origin. The Heads of the Diaspora are the descendants of King Joiachin.

94   In the Babli, *Mo'ed Qaṭan* 16b, the reason for R. Ḥiyya's disgrace is that he disregarded Rebbi's injunction not to teach Torah in a public place (market or street). As noted in the next paragraph, R. Ḥiyya (and his sons) spent most of their time in outreach programs to the unlearned.

95   In *Gen. rabba*, it is added that he taught Rav all the rules in which Babylonian tradition differs from the Galilean, things he could not teach in Rebbi's academy. In Yerushalmi sources, Rav is always called "son of R. Ḥiyya's sister." In Babylonian sources, Rav is called "son of R. Ḥiyya's half-brother and half-sister." In *Mo'ed Qaṭan* it is added that R. Ḥiyya taught not only Rav but also R. Abba bar Ḥana, nephew from a full brother.

96   In *Gen. rabba*: At the end of these thirty days (when R. Ḥiyya could appear again before Rebbi following the rules of temporary bans).

רִבִּי יוֹסֵי צָם תְּמָנֵיי יוֹמִין לְמֵיחְמֵי רִבִּי חִייָה רוֹבָה וּלְסוֹפָא חָמָא וְרַגְזוּן יְדֵיה
וּכְהוּ עֵינֵיי. וְאִין תֵּימַר דַּהֲוָא רִבִּי יוֹסָה בַּר נָשׁ זְעֵיר. חַד גְּרְדַּיי אֲתָא לְגַבֵּי רִבִּי
יוֹחָנָן אֲמַר לֵיה חָמִית בְּחֵילְמִי דִרְקִיעַ נְפַל וְחַד מִתַּלְמִידָךְ סְמַךְ לֵיה. אֲמַר לֵיה
וְחַכִּים אַתְּ לֵיה. אֲמַר לֵיה אִין אֲנָא חָמֵי לֵיה אֲנָא חַכַּם לֵיה. עֲבַר כָּל־תַּלְמִידוֹי
קוֹמוֹי וְחַכִּים לְרִבִּי יוֹסָה. רִבִּי שִׁמְעוֹן בֶּן לָקִישׁ צָם תְּלַת מָאוָן צוֹמִין לְמֵיחְמֵי
רִבִּי חִייָה רוֹבָה וְלָא חֲמָתֵיה. וּבְסוֹפָא שָׁרָא מִצְטַעֵר אֲמַר מַה הֲוָה לְעֵי
בְּאוֹרַיְתָא סַגִּין מִינַּיי. אָמְרוּ לֵיה רִיבֵּץ תּוֹרָה בְּיִשְׂרָאֵל יוֹתֵר מִמָּךְ וְלֹא עוֹד
אֶלָּא דַהֲוָה גְּלִי. אֲמַר לוֹן וְלָא הֲוֵינָא גְּלִי. אֲמְרִין לֵיה אַתְּ הֲוֵיתָה גְּלִי מֵילַף
וְהוּא הֲוָה גְּלִי מַלְפָא.

Rebbi Assi[97] fasted eighty days to see the old Rebbi Ḥiyya. In the end,
he saw him, his hands trembled and his eyes were dimmed[98]. If you say
that Rebbi Assi was an insignificant person, one weaver came to Rebbi
Joḥanan and said, I saw the sky falling but one of your students supported
it. He asked him, could you recognize him? He said, if I would see him, I
would recognize him. He made all his students pass before him [the
weaver], and he recognized Rebbi Assi. Rebbi Simeon ben Laqish fasted
three hundred fasts to see the old Rebbi Ḥiyya but did not see him. In the
end, he stopped feeling bad and said, maybe he did study Torah more than
I did. They said to him, he spread Torah more than you did[99] and in
addition he went into exile. He said to them, did I not also go into exile?
They said to him, you went into exile to study, he went into exile to
teach[100].

97   Since he is a student of R.
Joḥanan, he must be the Amora usually
called Yasa, Assi in the Babli.

98   In the parallel *Ketubot* 12:3 (fol.
35a), "he saw one of his court, and a
Cohen was lying next to him."

99   In the Babli, *Baba Meẓi'a* 85b, R.
Simeon ben Laqish was not able to find
the cave in which R. Ḥiyya was buried;
there it is explicit that "they" who
argue with him are heavenly voices.

100   He was a Babylonian, emigrat-

ing from rich Babylonia to poor
Galilee. He reorganized elementary

education in Galilee (*Baba Mezi'a* 85b).

כַּד דְּמָךְ רַב הוּנָא רֵיש גָּלוּתָא אַסְקוּנֵיהּ לְהָכָא. אֲמְרֵי אָן אֲנָן יְהָבִין לֵיהּ. אֲמְרִין נֵיתִינֵיהּ גַּבֵּי רִבִּי חִיָּיה רוֹבָה דְּהוּא מִן דִּידְהוּ. אֲמְרִין מָאן בְּעֵי מֵיהַב לֵיהּ. (fol. 32c) אָמַר רִבִּי חַגַּיי אֲנָא עֲלִיל יְהַב לֵיהּ. אֲמְרוּ לֵיהּ עִילְּתָא אַתְּ בָּעֵי דְּאַתְּ גְּבַר סָב וְאַתְּ בָּעֵי מֵיעוֹל מֵיתַב לָךְ תַּמָּן. אֲמַר לוֹן יְהָבוּן מְשִׁיחָתָא בְּרַגְלַיי וְאֵין עֲנִיַית אַתּוּן גְּרֵשִׁין. אָעַל וְאַשְׁכַּח תְּלַת דָּנִין יְהוּדָה בְּנִי אַחֲרֵיךְ וְאֵין עוֹד. חִזְקִיָּה בְּנִי אַחֲרֵיךְ וְאֵין עוֹד. אַחֲרֵיךְ יוֹסֵף בֶּן יִשְׂרָאֵל וְאֵין עוֹד. תָּלָה עֵינוֹי מִסְתַּכְּלָה אִיתְאֲמַר לֵיהּ אַפֵּיךְ אַפֵּיךְ שְׁמַע קָלֵיהּ דְּרִבִּי חִיָּיה רַבָּא אֲמַר לְרַב יְהוּדָה בְּרֵיהּ נְפִיש לְרַב חוּנָה יְתִיב לֵיהּ וְלָא קְבִיל עֲלוֹי מָתִיב לֵיהּ אֲמְרִין כְּמָה דְּלָא קְבִיל עֲלוֹי מָתִיב לֵיהּ כֵּן זַרְעִיתֵיהּ לָא פְּסִיקָא לְעוֹלָם. וְיָצָא מִשָּׁם וְהָיָה בֶּן שְׁמוֹנִים שָׁנָה וְנִכְפְּלוּ לוֹ שָׁנָיו.

When Rav Huna, the Head of the Diaspora[101], died they brought him here. They said, where shall we put him? They said, let us put him next to Rebbi Ḥiyya the elder for he is one of them[102]. They said, who might want to bring him there? Rebbi Ḥaggai said, I shall go up to put him there. They said to him, you are looking for a pretext, for you are an old man and you want to go to rest there yourself. He said to them, put some string on my feet and when I shall be weak[103] you pull. He went in and found the three arguing. "Jehudah my son, after you, and no more. Ḥizqiah my son, after you, and no more. Joseph ben Israel, after you, and no more.[104]" He [R. Ḥaggai] lifted his eyes to look, it was said to him turn around, turn around. He heard the voice of Rebbi Ḥiyya the elder who said to his son Rav[105] Jehudah, make space for Rav Ḥuna that he may rest there. But [Rav Ḥuna] did not accept this. They said, since he did not accept that one made space for him, so his descendants will never end. He [R. Ḥaggai] exited from there and his years were doubled[106].

101   He obviously cannot be identical with the Rav Huna in the story of Rebbi. The Babylonian traditions about the Heads of the Diaspora are quite confusing. In the Babli, *Mo'ed Qatan* 25a, the story is told only about "Rav Huna" without a title, but in all versions of *Seder Olam zuta*, the person whose coffin (i. e., the ossuary) was buried next to Rebbi Hiyya is Rav Huna, Head of the Diaspora. In one of the versions, this Rav Huna has a great-great-grandfather Rav Huna. In R. Sherira Gaon's letter (ed. Neubauer, p. 30), the second Rav Huna buried in Israel is called "from the family of the heads of the Diaspora"; he died in 608 Sel. = 296 C. E.

102   R. Hiyya was related to the Davidic dynasty.

103   In the parallel *Ketubot* 12:3 (fol. 35a), עמיח "if I become blind", cf. Arabic עמי "to be blind".

104   This implies that R. Hiyya had been buried in the burial cave of Joseph, near Sichem. They seem to imply that there is no place for Rav Huna there.

105   The sons of R. Hiyya, Jehudah and Hizqiah, while leaders of their generation, usually are mentioned without title. In the Babli, *Eruvin* 103b, *Zevahim* 19a, many mss. give Jehudah the title "Rebbi".

106   In the version of the Babli, R. Haggai (Hagga) ran into a wall of fire and left the ossuary of R. Huna standing at the entrance to the cave.

כְּתִיב וּנְשָׂאתַנִי מִמִּצְרַיִם וּקְבַרְתַּנִי בִּקְבוּרָתָם. יַעֲקֹב כָּל־הֶן דְּהוּא מָה הוּא מְנַכֵּי. רִבִּי לֶעָזָר אָמַר דְּבָרִים בְּגֵב. רִבִּי חֲנִינָא אָמַר דְּבָרִים בְּגֵב. רִבִּי יְהוֹשֻׁעַ בֶּן לֵוִי אָמַר דְּבָרִים בְּגֵב. מַהוּ דְּבָרִים בְּגֵב. רִבִּי שִׁמְעוֹן בֶּן לָקִישׁ אָמַר אֶתְהַלֵּךְ לִפְנֵי יי בְּאֶרֶץ הַחַיִּים. וַהֲלֹא אֵין אַרְצוֹת הַחַיִּים אֶלָּא צוֹר וַחֲבֵרוֹתֶיהָ וְקֵיסָרִין וַחֲבֵרוֹתֶיהָ תַּמָּן זוֹלָא תַּמָּן שׂוֹבְעָא. רִבִּי שִׁמְעוֹן בֶּן לָקִישׁ בְּשֵׁם בַּר קַפָּרָא אֶרֶץ שֶׁמֵּיתֶיהָ חַיִּין תְּחִילָה לִימוֹת הַמָּשִׁיחַ. וּמָה טַעַם נוֹתֵן נְשָׁמָה לְעָם עָלֶיהָ. אֶלָּא מֵעַתָּה רַבּוֹתֵינוּ שֶׁבַּגּוֹלָה הִפְסִידוּ. אָמַר רִבִּי סִימַי מַחְלִיד הַקָּדוֹשׁ בָּרוּךְ הוּא לִפְנֵיהֶן אֶת הָאָרֶץ וְהֵן מִתְגַּלְגְּלִין כְּנוֹדוֹת וְכֵינָן שֶׁהֵן מַגִּיעִין לְאֶרֶץ יִשְׂרָאֵל נַפְשָׁן חוֹזָרוֹת עֲלֵיהֶן. וּמָה טַעַם וְהִנַּחְתִּי אֶתְכֶם עַל אַדְמַת יִשְׂרָאֵל וְנָתַתִּי רוּחִי בָּכֶם וִחְיִיתֶם.

[107]It is written (*Gen.* 47:30): "You shall carry me from Egypt and bury me in their burial place." What would Jacob lose at any place he would be? Rebbi Eleazar gave an inner reason, Rebbi Ḥanina gave an inner reason, Rebbi Joshua ben Levi gave an inner reason[108]. What is the inner reason? Rebbi Simeon ben Laqish said, (*Ps.* 116:9) "I will walk before the Eternal in the Land of Life." But the lands of life are only Tyre and its surroundings and Caesarea (maritima) and its surroundings[109]; there is cheap (food), there is satiety. Rebbi Simeon ben Laqish in the name of Bar Qappara, the Land whose dead will live again in the days of the Messiah. What is the reason? (*Is.* 42:9) "He gives soul to the people on it." That would mean that our teachers in the diaspora would lose out! Rebbi Simai said, the Holy One, praised be He, makes the earth erode before them and they roll like wine barrels[110]. When they arrive at the Land of Israel their souls return to them. What is the reason? (*Ez.* 37:12) "I shall deposit you on the territory of Israel[111]," (v. 14) "give My spirit into you, and you will live."

107   There are many parallel treatments of the topic of this paragraph. Uncharacteristically, the different sources of the Yerushalmi tradition all have their own formulation; they borrow the idea but not the language: *Gen. rabba* 96(7), *Tanḥuma Wayeḥi* 3, *Tanḥuma Buber Wayeḥi* 6, *Pesiqta rabbati* 1, fol. 2b. Only *Ketubot* 12:3 (fol. 35b) has the same language as here. Babylonian sources *Ketubot* 111a, *Yoma* 71a.

108   Note that the chronological or-der is inverted. In most other sources, the argument of R. Simeon ben Laqish is attributed to R. Eleazar.

109   These are not part of the Land of Israel, at least not in the geography of the Second Commonwealth. Hence, the verse cannot apply to this world but must apply to the Future World which in the Yerushalmi is identified with the Days of the Messiah.

110   In *Gen. rabba*: "He makes cavities in which they move".

111   In the verse: "I shall bring you

to the territory of Israel." The return   by two verses.
of the body precedes the return of life

רְבִּי בְּרֶכְיָה שָׁאַל לְרִבִּי חָלְבּוֹ. רִבִּי חֶלְבּוֹ שָׁאַל לְרִבִּי אִמִּי. רְבִּי אִימִי שָׁאַל
לְרִבִּי אֶלְעָזָר. רְבִּי לֶעָזָר שָׁאַל לְרִבִּי חֲנִינָה וְאִית דְּאָמְרִין רְבִּי חֲנִינָה שָׁאַל לְרִבִּי
יְהוֹשֻׁעַ בֶּן לֵוִי. אֲפִילוּ כְגוֹן יָרָבְעָם בֶּן נְבָט וַחֲבֵירָיו. אָמַר לֵיהּ גָּפְרִית וָמֶלַח
שְׂרֵיפָה כָל־אַרְצָהּ. אָמַר רִבִּי בְּרֶכְיָה מַה הֵן שָׁאַל לָהֶן וְהֵן שָׁאַל לָהֶן לֹא שְׁמָעִינָן
מִינָהּ כְּלוּם. מַיי כְדוֹן. כֵּיוָן שֶׁנִּשְׂרְפָה אֶרֶץ יִשְׂרָאֵל נַעֲשָׂה בָהֶן מִדַּת הַדִּין. תַּנֵּי
בְשֵׁם רִבִּי יְהוּדָה שֶׁבַע שָׁנִים עָשַׂת אֶרֶץ יִשְׂרָאֵל נִשְׂרָפָה הָדָא הוּא דִכְתִיב וְהִגְבִּיר
בְּרִית לָרַבִּים שָׁבוּעַ אֶחָד. כּוּתִים שֶׁבָּהּ מַה הָיוּ עוֹשִׂין מַטְלִיּוֹת מַטְלִיּוֹת וְחָיְתָה
נִשְׂרֶפֶת.

Rebbi Berekhiah asked Rebbi Ḥelbo. Rebbi Ḥelbo asked Rebbi Immi.
Rebbi Immi asked Rebbi Eleazar. Rebbi Eleazar asked Rebbi Ḥanina,
some say Rebbi Ḥanina asked Rebbi Joshua ben Levi: Even those like
Jeroboam ben Nabat and his kind? He said to him, (*Deut.* 29:22) "Sulphur
and salt, conflagration throughout the country." Rebbi Berekhiah said, one
asked the other and we understand nothing from it. What does it mean?
Since the Land of Israel was burned, judgment was executed on it[112]. We
have stated in the name of Rebbi Jehudah[113]: Seven years was the Land
of Israel burned; that is what is written (*Dan.* 9:27) "The Covenant
overtook the public for one week." What did the Samaritans in it do[114]?
Pieces, pieces and it was burned.

112   Once judgment is executed, the
sinner is free from his sin. This
opinion, spelled out in detail in *Pesiqta
rabbati* (cf. Note 105), contradicts
Mishnah *Sanhedrin* 10:2 which excludes
three kings (Jeroboam, Ahab, Manasseh) from the Future World; it is in line

with the Babli's conclusion in the name
of "those looking for hints", *Sanhedrin*
104b-105a.
113   In the Babli, *Yoma* 54a (*Seder
Olam* 27), this statement is attributed to
R. Yose. In the old Yerushalmi source,
Ekhah rabbati, *Petiḥah* (towards the

end), the name is R. Jehudah. In
Pesiqta deRav Cahana (Buber) p. 114a,
it is R. Simeon bar Iohai.

114   Since the Samaritans were
settled in Samaria by the Assyrian
kings and were there when the Jews
returned from Babylonia, they must
somehow have survived in the meantime. The answer is shortened here

[and *Ketubot* 12:3 (fol. 35b)] to
incomprehensibility. The full text is
preserved in *Ekhah rabbati* and *Pesiqta
deRav Cahana*: זורעין אותה מטליות מטליות
זורעין כאן והיא נשרפת זורעין כאן והיא נשרפת.
"They sow it pieces by pieces. They
were sowing here and it was burned,
they were sowing there and it was
burned."

כְּתִיב וְאַתָּה פַּשְׁחוּר וְכֹל יוֹשְׁבֵי בֵיתֶךָ תֵּלְכוּ בַשֶּׁבִי. וּבָבֶל תָּבֹא וְשָׁם תָּמוּת וְשָׁם

תִּקָּבֵר. רִבִּי אַבָּא בַּר זְמִינָא אָמַר רִבִּי חֶלְבּוֹ וְרִבִּי חָמָא בַּר חֲנִינָא. חַד אָמַר מֵת

שָׁם וְנִקְבַּר שָׁם יֵשׁ בְּיָדוֹ שְׁתַּיִם. מֵת שָׁם וְנִקְבַּר כָּאן יֵשׁ בְּיָדוֹ אַחַת. וְחָרָנָה אָמַר

קְבוּרָה שֶׁבְּכָאן מְכַפֶּרֶת עַל מִיתָה שֶׁלָּהֶן.

It is written[113] (*Jer.* 20:6-7): "But you, Pashhur, and all inhabitants of

your house will go into captivity. You will come to Babylon, die there,

and be buried there[116]." Rebbi Abba bar Zemina said, Rebbi Helbo and

Rebbi Hama bar Hanina. One of them said, if somebody dies there and is

buried there, he has two [detriments] in hand. If he dies there and is

buried here, he has one [detriment] in hand. The other one said, burial

here atones for death there.

115   *Ketubot* 12:3 (fol. 35b), also
Pesiqta rabbati 1. In the second source,
the first opinion is explicitly attributed
to R. Helbo, the second to R. Hama bar
Hanina. The topic begun here is taken
up again in the last paragraph of this
Halakhah; it is interrupted only to

accomodate a homily of R. Hama bar
Hanina.
116   Since the passage is a curse
upon Pashhur, dying in Babylon and
being buried there are two separate
curses.

רִבִּי יוֹנָה בְּשֵׁם רִבִּי חָמָא בַּר חֲנִינָה רִיגְלוֹי דְּבַר נַשָׁא עֲרָבָתֵיהּ לְמִיקְמָתֵיהּ
כָּל־הֶן דְּהוּא מִתְבָּעֵי. כְּתִיב מִי יְפַתֶּה אֶת אַחְאָב וְיַעַל וְיִפֹּל בְּרָמוֹת גִּלְעָד.
וְיָמוֹת בְּבֵיתוֹ וְלֹא תַמָּן. אֱלִיחוֹרֶף וַאֲחִיָּה תְּרֵין אִיסְקְרִיטוֹרֵיי[117] דִּשְׁלֹמֹה. חָמָא
מַלְאַךְ מוֹתָא מִסְתַּכֵּל בּוֹן וַחֲרִיק בְּשִׁינּוֹי. אֲמַר מִילָּה וִיהָבוֹן בְּחַלָּלָא. אֲזַל
וּנְסַבְהוֹן מִן תַּמָּן אֲתָא קָאִים לֵיהּ גָּחִיךְ לְקָבְלֵיהּ אֲמַר לֵיהּ הַהִיא שַׁעֲתָא הֲוֵיתָא
אִיחְרוֹק בְּשִׁינָּיִיךְ וּכְדוֹן אַתְּ גָּחִיךְ לָן. אֲמַר לֵיהּ אֲמַר לִי[118] רַחֲמָנָא דְּיִנְסַב
לֶאֱלִיחוֹרֶף וַאֲחִיָּה מִן חֲלָלָה וְאָמְרִית מִי יְהִיב לִי אִילֵּין לְהֶן דְּאִישְׁתַּלְּחִית
מִינְסִיבִינִין[119] וְיהַב בְּלִיבָּךְ לְמֶיעֲבַד כֵּן בְּגִין דְּנַעֲבִיד שְׁלִיחוּתִי. אֲזַל וְאִיטְפַל בּוֹן
מִן תַּמָּן.[120] תְּרֵי בְּרוֹיי דְּרִבִּי דְּרַאוּבֵן בַּר אִיסְטְרוֹבִילוֹס תַּלְמִידוֹי דְּרִבִּי. חָמָא
מַלְאָכָא דְּמוֹתָא מִסְתַּכֵּל בּוֹן וַחֲרִיק בְּשִׁינּוֹי וַאֲמַר נִיגְלִינוֹן לִדְרוֹמָא שֶׁמָּא
הַגָּלוּת מְכַפֶּרֶת. אֲזַל וְנַסְתּוּן מִתַּמָּן.

Rebbi Jonah in the name of Rebbi Hama bar Hanina: A human's feet
guarantee to put him where he is wanted[121]. It is written (*1K*. 22:20)
"Who will seduce Ahab that he should go and fall in Ramot Gilead?"
Might he not die in his house rather than there? Elihoref and Ahiah were
two of Solomon's secretaries[122]. He [Solomon] saw the Angel of Death
looking at them and grinding his teeth. He said a word and put them into
space[123]. He [the Angel of Death] went and took them from there, then
he came laughing before him [Solomon]. He said to him, just before you
were grinding your teeth and now you are laughing at us? He said to him,
the Merciful told me to take Elihoref and Ahiah from space and I was
wondering who would put them there where I was sent to take them; He
put it into your mind to do so that I could complete my mission. I went
and dealt with them there. The two sons of Rebbi Reuben ben
Strobilos[124] were students of Rebbi. He [Rebbi] saw the Angel of Death
looking at them and grinding his teeth and said, let us exile them to the
South, maybe the exile atones[125]. He [the angel of death] went and took
them from there.

117   Reading in *Ketubot*. The reading here is איסקבטידיי.

118   Reading in *Ketubot* and Rome ms. The two words are missing in the Venice text.

119   Reading in *Ketubot*. The reading here is מיתבינין.

120   Reading in *Ketubot* and Rome ms. Venice: זמן תמן.

121   A parallel in Babli *Sukkah* 53a quotes the statement in the name of R. Johanan.

122   Eliḥoref and Aḥiah the sons of Shisha were *Soferim* (*1K.* 4:4). In rabbinic Hebrew, סופר means "scribe"; late Latin *secretarius*.

123   In the parallel in the Babli, Solomon sends them to the mythical city of Luz whose inhabitants never die, but the Angel of Death takes them at the entrance gate.

124   A Tanna of the fourth generation, reputed to speak Latin like a Roman. Late Hellenistic Greek στροβιλᾶς, ᾶ, ὁ "dealer in pine cones" but, since pine cones were used in pagan worship, it might be better to derive the name from Greek ἀστραβηλάτης, ου, ὁ "muleteer".

125   The doctrine that exile atones is found in Babli *Berakhot* 56a, *Sanhedrin* 37b. It is based on the biblical law of exile for the homicide.

עוּלָּא נְחוּתָא הֲוָה. אִידְמָךְ תַּמָּן שָׁרֵי בָּכִי. אָמְרִין לֵיהּ מַה אַתְּ בָּכִי אֲנָן מַסְקִין לָךְ לְאַרְעָא דְּיִשְׂרָאֵל. אָמַר לוֹן וּמַה הֲנָיָה לִי. אֲנָא מוֹבַד מַרְגָּלִיתִי גּוּ אַרְעָא מְסָאַבְתָא. לֹא דוֹמֶה הַפּוֹלֵטָה בְּחֵיק אִמּוֹ לַפּוֹלֵטָה בְּחֵיק נָכְרִיָּה. רִבִּי מֵאִיר הֲוָה אִידְמִיךְ לֵיהּ בְּאַסְיָא. אָמַר אֵימוֹרִין לִבְנֵי אַרְעָא דְּיִשְׂרָאֵל הָא מְשִׁיחְכוֹן דִּידְכוֹן. אֲפִילוּ כֵן אֲמַר לוֹן יְהַבוּן עַרְסִי עַל גֵּיף יַמָּא דִּכְתִיב כִּי הוּא עַל יַמִּים יְסָדָהּ וְעַל נְהָרוֹת יְכוֹנְנֶיהָ.

Ulla was an emigrant. He was dying there and started to cry. They said to him, why are you crying? We shall bring you to the Land of Israel. He said to them, how does this help me? I am losing my pearl in an impure land. One cannot compare one who expires in the bosom of his mother to one who expires in the bosom of a strange woman[126]. Rebbi Meïr was dying in Assos. He said, tell the people of the Land of Israel, there is your Messiah[127]. With all that, he said to put his bier on the seacape[128] since it is written (*Ps.* 24:2): "For He founded it on seas, based it on rivers."

126 Ulla seems to hold that dying outside the Land of Israel is detrimental only for an inhabitant of the Land.

127 It is not clear what the sentence means. The consensus of the commentators is that he sent there so a delegation should come and return the bones of the most famous teacher of his time to the Land, and that his burial on the sea shore was only a temporary measure.

128 Since Assos (Behramkoi) is on a high cliff, he probably wanted to be buried in a place from which the sea could be seen. גיף is the same as Syriac כיף "rock." The verse given as the reason leads to the digression about the seas and lakes of the Land of Israel.

שִׁבְעָה יַמִּים סוֹבְבִין אֶת אֶרֶץ יִשְׂרָאֵל. יַמָּא רַבָּא יַמָּא דְטִיבֶּרְיָא יַמָּא דְסַמְכוֹ יַמָּא דְמִילְחָא יַמָּא דְחוֹלָתָא יַמָּא דְשַׁלְיִית יַמָּא דְאַפַּמְיָא. וְהָא אִיכָּא יַמָּא דְחָמְץ דִּיְקְלֵיטִיָנוּס הֲקֵנָה נְהוֹרוֹת וַעֲשָׂאוֹ. כְּתִיב הַנִּשְׁקָפָה עַל פְּנֵי הַיְשִׁימוֹן. אָמַר רבִּי חִיָּיא בְּרְיָא כָּל־מִי שֶׁהוּא עוֹלֶה לְהַר יְשִׁימוֹן וּמָצָא כְּמִין כְּבָרָה בְּיַם טִיבֶּרְיָא זוֹ הִיא בּוֹרָהּ שֶׁל מִרְיָם. (fol. 32d) אָמַר רבִּי יוֹחָנָן שַׁעֲרוּנָהּ רַבָּנִין וְהָא הִיא מְכוּוָּנָא כָּל־קֳבֵיל תַּרְעָא מְצִיעָיָא דִכְנִישְׁתָּא עַתִּיקְתָּא דְסרונגין.

"Seven seas surround the Land of Israel[129]: The ocean, lake Tiberias, lake *Samkho*, the salt sea, lake Ḥolata, lake Sheliat, lake Apamea." But does there not also exist the lake of Ḥomṣ? Diocletian dammed up rivers and created it. It is written (*Num.* 21:20): "Looking down on the desert." Rebbi Ḥiyya from Biria[130] said, if one ascends the desert mountain one finds the likeness of a sieve in lake Tiberias, that is the well of Miryam[131]. Rebbi Joḥanan said, the rabbis estimated it and it is assessed opposite the middle gate of the old synagogue of *Sarongin*[132].

129 The list is not only in the parallel in *Ketubot* but also in Babli *Baba Batra* 74b, *Midrash Psalms* 24, and, as a secondary source, *Yalqut*

Psalms 24. The latter source and the Munich, Rome and Hamburg mss. of *Baba Batra* have "lake Paneas" (Banias) instead of "lake of Apamea". The pool of the Jordan source at Banias is in the Land of Israel, Apamea is in Northern Syria (but Ḥoms is also in Syria). The ocean is the Mediterranean, Lake Tiberias is Lake Genezareth, the salt sea is the Dead Sea. Lake Ḥuleh in Greek sources is lake Samokhonites. What is missing in the list is Birket Ram on the Golan heights and possibly a pool at Ḥamat Gader, mentioned in Babli *Šabbat* 109a. Since lake Samkho is lake Ḥuleh, ימא דחולתא "the lake of the dunes" cannot be Lake Ḥuleh but might have been a swamp in the plain between Haifa and Acco since in *Yalquṭ* it is called "the lake of Acco".

130 An otherwise unknown Amora.

131 The well accompanying the tribes of Israel during their forty years in the desert (*Seder Olam*, Chap. 5). The version באֹרה in the Rome ms., instead of בּוֹרה, is an intrusion of Babylonian traditions. The parallel in Babli *Šabbat* 35a identifies the mountain as Mount Carmel. As noted by the editor of *Kaftor waPeraḥ* (p. קלט), this is an intrusion from the preceding mention of Mt. Carmel (cf. Yerushalmi *Berakhot* p. 54) since the Munich ms. of the Babli identifies the sea as Lake Tiberias. The original name of the mountain in the Babylonian tradition is lost.

The place of Balaam's vision must have been near the Dead Sea, not Lake Tiberias.

132 In *Ketubot*, יסרוטגין. The place is unidentified.

רבִּי בַּרְקִירְיָא וְרבִּי לְעָזָר הַוֹּו מְטַיְילִין בְּאִיסְטְרִין רָאוּ אֲרוֹנוֹת שֶׁהָיוּ בָּאִין מֵחוּצָה לָאָרֶץ לָאָרֶץ. אָמַר רבִּי בַּרְקִירְיָא לְרבִּי לְעָזָר מַה הוֹעִילוּ אֵילוּ. אֲנִי קוֹרֵא עֲלֵיהֶם וְנַחֲלָתִי שַׂמְתֶּם לְתוֹעֵבָה בְּחַיֵּיכֶם. וַתָּבוֹאוּ וַתְּטַמְּאוּ אֶת אַרְצִי בְּמוֹתַתְכֶם. אָמַר לֵיהּ כֵּיוָן שֶׁהֵן מַגִּיעִין לְאָרֶץ יִשְׂרָאֵל הֵן נוֹטְלִין גּוּשׁ עָפָר וּמַנִּיחִין עַל אֲרוֹנָן. דִּכְתִיב וְכִפֶּר אַדְמָתוֹ עַמּוֹ.

Rebbi Bar Qiria[133] and Rebbi Eleazar were talking a walk on the road when they saw coffins being brought into the Land from abroad. Rebbi Bar Qiria said to Rebbi Eleazar: What good is that going to do them? I am reading for them (*Jer.* 2:7) "My inheritance your considered an abomination[134]" during your lifetime, "you came and made My Land impure[135]" in your death. He said to him, when they arrive in the Land, one takes a lump of earth and puts it on the coffin, as it is written (*Deut.* 32:43) "His earth atones for His people.[136]"

133   An otherwise unknown Amora. The name tradition of this paragraph is thoroughly unsatisfactory. In *Gen. rabba* 97 as well as *Tanḥuma Wayeḥi* it is Rebbi (R. Jehuda II Nesia) and R. Eleazar. In *Pesiqta rabbati* 1 it is (a likewise unknown) R. Beroqia and R. Eleazar.

134   Since you did not live in the Land.

135   By the impurity of the dead.

136   Therefore, one puts earth from the Holy Land into or on a coffin even for burial outside the Land. *Yalquṭ Psalms* 116 directly connects *Deut.* 32:43 with the earlier statement that even Jeroboam and people like him have a part in the Future World.

(fol. 31d) **משנה ה:** מוֹכְרֵי כְסוּת מוֹכְרִין כְּדַרְכָּן וּבִלְבַד שֶׁלֹּא יִתְכַּוְּנוּ בַחַמָּה מִפְּנֵי הַחַמָּה וּבִגְשָׁמִים מִפְּנֵי הַגְּשָׁמִים. וְהַצְּנוּעִין מַפְשִׁילִין לַאֲחוֹרֵיהֶן בְּמַקֵּל.

Mishnah 5: Sellers of clothing sell in the professional way[137], but they should not intend in summer because of the sun and in winter because of the rains. But the religious ones[138] let them hang over their shoulder on a stick.

משנה ו: תּוֹפְרֵי כְסוּת תּוֹפְרִין כְּדַרְכָּן וּבִלְבַד שֶׁלֹּא יִתְכַּוְּנוּ בַחַמָּה מִפְּנֵי הַחַמָּה וּבִגְשָׁמִים מִפְּנֵי הַגְּשָׁמִים. וְהַצְּנוּעִין תּוֹפְרִין בָּאָרֶץ.

Mishnah 6: Taylors sew in the professional way, but they should not intend in summer because of the sun and in winter because of the rains. But the religious ones sew on the ground.

משנה ז: הַבּרְסִים וְהַבָּרְדְסִין וְהַדַּלְמַטִיקִיּוֹן וּמִנְעֲלוֹת הַפִּינוֹן לֹא יִלְבְּשֵׁם עַד שֶׁיִּבְדּוֹק. רַבִּי יוֹסֵי אוֹמֵר אַף הַבָּאִים מֵחוֹף הַיָּם וּמִמְּדִינַת הַיָּם אֵינָן צְרִיכִין בְּדִיקָה מִפְּנֵי שֶׁחֶזְקָתָן בְּקַנַּבָס. וּמִנְעַל שֶׁל זֶרֶד אֵין בּוֹ מִשּׁוּם כִּלְאַיִם.

Mishnah 7: *Birsīm*[139], *Burdesīm*[140], and Dalmatian garb as well as *pinon*[141] shoes one should not wear unless one checks them. Rebbi Yose says, those coming from the sea shore in maritime countries do not have to be checked because usually they are made from hemp. Padded[142] shoes have no problem with *kilaim*.

137   They may put *kilaim* cloth over their arms to present it to Gentile buyers. They may not use that cloth to shield themselves from the sun.

138   For this meaning of צנוע cf. *Demay* Halakhah 6:8.

139   In the Leyden ms. הבדסים, the Rome ms. היכרסין, the Cambridge ms. of the Yerushalmi Mishnah הבידסין, some Genizah fragments הבירדסין. In *Sifry Deut.* 234 the readings are בורסים in most sources, but also בירסין, בידטרין, in Tosephta *Kelim Baba batra* 5:11 בורסין. *Arukh* reads בדס. Since the word itself was no longer understood by the Amoraïm, the explanation is given in the Halakhah.

140   Reading of most Mishnah mss.; the only variant is הברדיסין. In *Sifry* בורדסים, ברדסין, בירדסין, כרדסין, בררסין In *Tosephta* ברחסין

141   Mishnah readings פונון, פיבון and Rome ms. פיטין. The common explanation is from Greek πῖλος, ὁ, "felt (as lining of helmets, shoes, etc.); felt cloth", but felt is commonly called לבד in Mishnah and Tosephta; the Halakhah defines these "shoes" as socks.

142   The Mishnah mss. of the Maimonides tradition, the Rome ms., and the Leyden text in the Halakhah, all read זרב, this has been taken as the basis of the translation.

הלכה ח: הַבּוּרְסִין בְּרְיָה. הַבְּרְדְּסִין דֵּילְמָא. הַדַּלְמַטִיקוֹן קוֹלָבִין[143] (fol. 32d) וּמַעְפּוֹרִין וּמִנְעֲלוֹת הַפִּינוֹן דַּרְדְּסִין.

Bursīn are *birri*[144]. *Burdesīn* are *delma*[145]. Dalmatian garb are short sleeved tunics and overcoats. *Pinon* shoes are socks[146].

143   Reading of the Rome ms., supported by the other occurrences of this word. Leyden and Venice: קובלין. Cf. Greek κολόβιον "short sleeved

tunic".

144   Latin *birrus, i, m.*, also *birrum, i, n.* raincoat of silk or wool, mentioned in *Ed. Diocl;* garments in the style of

the Gallic tribe of the Burri. In *Sifry* (*loc. cit.* 137) the garments are described as "not rectangular"; the Gallic tribes wore trousers and jackets, rather than togas.

145   The Rome ms. has דלמא but this is the Rome scribe's usual style for the rhetorical דֵיל'מָא. The dictionaries explain the word from from Byzantine δουλαμά "loose garment, wrapping garment"; this would fit the context but

H. L. Fleischer has shown that δουλαμά is derived from Turkish *dolamak*, "to wrap around", cf. Turk. *dolman* "fur-trimmed military jacket"; the dictionary explanation looks like an anachronism. R. Isaac Simponti reads הולמא.

146   Maimonides, while declaring his ignorance as to the meaning of these words, declares all four pieces of garment to be woolen *calze* "stockings".

רְבִּי יוֹסֵי אוֹמֵר אַף הַבָּאִין מֵחוֹף הַיָּם וּמִמְּדִינַת הַיָּם. מַה חוֹף הַיָּם וּמִמְּדִינַת הַיָּם אוֹ מֵחוֹף הַיָּם שֶׁמִּמְּדִינַת הַיָּם. מִן מַה דְתַנֵּי כְּגוֹן צוֹר וַחֲבֵרוֹתֶיהָ וְקֵיסָרִין וַחֲבֵרוֹתֶיהָ. הָדָא אָמְרָה מֵחוֹף הַיָּם שֶׁמִּמְּדִינַת הַיָּם.

"Rebbi Yose says, those coming from the sea shore in maritime countries." Does this mean "from the sea shore and from overseas countries" or "from the seashore of maritime countries"? Since it was stated: For example, Tyre and its surroundings, Caesarea (maritima) and its surroundings, it means "from the seashore of maritime countries".

אֵינָן צְרִיכִין בְּדִיקָה. הָדָא דְתֵימַר בָּרִאשׁוֹנָה שֶׁלֹּא הָיְתָה הַפִּשְׁתָּן מְצוּיָה בְּכָל־מָקוֹם. אֲבָל עַכְשָׁיו שֶׁהַפִּשְׁתָּן מְצוּיָה בְּכָל־מָקוֹם צְרִיכִין בְּדִיקָה.

"They do not have to be checked." That means in earlier times when flax was not found everywhere. But today, when flax is found everywhere, they need to be checked.

מִנְעַל שֶׁל זֶרֶב. אִית אַתְרִין דְּגָרְבִין עִימֵּיהּ מִן גּוֹ[147] כְּהָדָא דְרִבִּי זְעִירָא מְפַקֵּד לְרִבִּי אַבָּא בַּר זְמִינָא[148] וְיֹאמַר לְבַר רִאשׁוֹן דְּלָא יְחוֹט לֵיהּ מְסָאנֵיהּ בְּכִיתָּן אֶלָּא בִּרְצוּעָה. מוֹדֵי רִבִּי זְעִירָא בְּאָהֵן דְּאָסַר פִּיסְקֵי דַּעֲמַר עַל דְּכִיתָּן דְּהוּא שָׁרֵי. דְּהוּא שָׁנַץ גַּרְמֵיהּ דְּהִיא נַחְתָּא לָהּ.

"Padded shoes". There are places where they are padded from the outside[149]. As Rebbi Zeïra said to Rebbi Abba bar Zemina to tell Bar Rishon[150] not to sew his shoes with flax but with [leather] strips. Rebbi Zeïra agrees that if one bound a woolen belt over a linen garment that would be permitted, for if he makes himself thin, it will fall down.

147 Reading of the Rome ms: גב.
This is a Babylonism.
148 Reading of the Rome ms.
Venice: זבינא "the seller", otherwise
unknown.

149 So that it should be clear that
the shoes are not wholly made of
leather.
150 Probably the shoemaker's father
was called בכור, Primus, or Protos.

בָּעִין קוֹמֵי רבִּי לָא. מַהוּ מֵיחוֹט מְסָאנֵיהּ דְּכִיתָּן. אֲמַר לוֹן בְּגִין דְּרבִּי זְעִירָא. דְּרבִּי זְעִירָא אָמַר אָסוּר. מוֹדֶה רבִּי אִילָא בָּהֶן דְּיִלְבַּשׁ דַּרְדְּסִין דַּעֲמַר עַל גַּבֵּי דְּכִיתָּן דְּהוּא אָסוּר. דְּלָא שָׁלַח עִילֵּיי לָא שָׁלַח עַרְעֵיי. אָבוֹי דְּרב סַפְרָא שְׁאַל לְרבִּי זְעִירָא מַהוּ מִיתַּן פְּרִיטִין גּוֹ גוֹלְתָה וּמִקְטְרִינוֹן בְּחוּט דְּכִתָּן. מַהוּ מִיתַּן פְּרִיטִין גּוֹ סַדִּינֵיהּ וּמִקְטְרִינוֹן בְּחוּט דַּעֲמַר. אָמַר לֵיהּ חָכַם רבִּי לְרב הוּנָא. דְּרב הוּנָא אָמַר אָסוּר. רבִּי אֲבִינָא אָמַר אָסוּר. שְׁמוּאֵל אָמַר מוּתָּר. רבִּי יַעֲקֹב בַּר אָחָא בְּשֵׁם רבִּי יַסָא אָמַר מוּתָּר.

They asked before Rebbi Illaï: May one sew one's shoes with flax? He said to them, because of Rebbi Zeïra, for Rebbi Zeïra said it is forbidden. Rebbi Illaï will agree that it is forbidden to wear woolen socks over linen socks since he cannot take off the inner ones unless he first takes off the outer ones. The father of Rav Safra asked Rebbi Zeïra: May one put coins in a woolen bag and tie it with a linen thread, or put coins on a linen cloth and tie it with a woolen thread? He said to him, does the rabbi not know Rav Huna? For Rav Huna said, it is forbidden. Rebbi Avina said, it is forbidden. Samuel said, it is permitted. Rebbi Jacob bar Ada in the name of Rebbi Yasa said, it is permitted.

(fol. 31d) **משנה ח:** אֵין אָסוּר מְשׁוּם כִּלְאַיִם אֶלָּא טָווּי וְאָרִיג שֶׁנֶּאֱמַר לֹא תִלְבַּשׁ שַׁעַטְנֵז דָּבָר שֶׁהוּא שׁוּעַ טָווּי וְנוּז. רַבִּי שִׁמְעוֹן בֶּן אֶלְעָזָר אוֹמֵר נָלוֹז וּמֵלִיז אֶת אָבִיו שֶׁבַּשָּׁמַיִם עָלָיו.

Mishnah 8: Only spun and woven cloth is forbidden because of *kilaim* since it is said (*Deut.* 22:11): "Do not wear *ša'aṭnez*", anything carded, spun, or woven[151]. Rabbi Simeon ben Eleazar said, he has turned aside and turned his Father in Heaven against him[152].

משנה ט: הַלְּבָדִין אֲסוּרִין מִפְּנֵי שֶׁהֵן שׁוּעִין. פִּיף שֶׁל צֶמֶר בְּשֶׁל פִּשְׁתָּן אָסוּר מִפְּנֵי שֶׁהֵן חוֹזְרִין כָּאָרִיג. רַבִּי יוֹסֵי אוֹמֵר מְשִׁיחוֹת שֶׁל אָרִיג אֲסוּרוֹת מִפְּנֵי שֶׁהוּא מוֹלֵל עַד שֶׁהוּא קוֹשֵׁר. לֹא יִקְשׁוֹר סֶרֶט שֶׁל צֶמֶר בְּשֶׁל פִּשְׁתָּן לַחֲגוֹר בּוֹ אֶת מָתְנָיו אַף עַל פִּי שֶׁהָרְצוּעָה בָּאֶמְצַע.

Mishnah 9: Felt is forbidden because it is carded. A woolen border[153] on a linen garment is forbidden because it goes around like the woven part. Rabbi Yose says, woven ropes are forbidden because he stitches them before he ties them[154]. One should not bind a strip of wool on one of linen to gird his hips even if a leather belt is in between[155].

151   The word שעטנז of unknown etymology is taken as an abbreviation and split into three: שע ט נז. Maimonides declares נוז "to weave" as Armenian. The Halakhah will show that the conjunction ו has to be understood as "or", not as "and".

152   This homily takes נז as shorthand for נלוז

153   This meaning of פיף is attested to by all Gaonic sources and the commentaries dependent on them; cf. Note 28. Musaphia's derivation from the Greek (derived from R. Simson's interpretation of פיף as "fringes") ἐφυφή "woof" and accepted by the dictionaries makes no sense, as recognized by I. Löw.

154   One may not make a belt out of two strips, one of wool and one of linen, even if they are not permanently sewn together since one will loosely stitch them together so that they should not separate when worn. About stitching see Mishnah 10.

155   One may not permanently sew wool on one side and linen on the other side of a leather belt since the stitches,

even when made of a neutral material together.
like cotton, will bind wool and linen

(fol. 32d) **הלכה ה**: נִיתְנֵי שעז וְלָא נִיתְנֵי טָוִי. אִילּוּ תַּנִּינָן שעז וְלָא תַּנִּינָן טָוִי
הֲוֵינָן אֲמְרִין הָא טָוּוּי מוּתָּר. מַתְנִיתָא לֹא אֲמְרָה כֵן. אֶלָא אֵין אָסוּר מִשׁוּם
כִּלְאַיִם אֶלָּא טָוּוּי וְאָרִיג. נִיתְנֵי שעט וְלָא נִיתְנֵי נוז. אִילּוּ תַּנִּינָן שעט וְלָא
תַּנִּינָן נוז הֲוֵינָן אֲמְרִין הָא לָנוֹז מוּתָּר. מַתְנִיתָא לֹא אָמַר כֵן. אֶלָּא פִּיף שֶׁל
צֶמֶר בְּשֶׁל פִּשְׁתָּן אָסוּר מִפְּנֵי שֶׁהֵן חוֹזְרִין כְּאָרִיג. נִיתְנֵי טנז וְלָא נִיתְנֵי שע.
אִילּוּ תַּנִּינָן טנז וְלָא תַּנִּינָן שע הֲוֵינָן אֲמְרִין הָא שֹׁעַ מוּתָּר. מַתְנִיתָא לֹא אֲמְרָה
כֵן. אֶלָּא הַלְּבָדִין אֲסוּרִין מִפְּנֵי שֶׁהֵן שׁוּעִין.

Halakhah 5: It[156] could have stated שעז and not טוי. If it had stated
שעז but not טוי we would have said that spinning is permitted. But the
Mishnah does not say so, but "only spun and woven cloth is forbidden
because of *kilaim*." It could have stated שעט and not נוז. If it had stated
שעט but not נוז we would have said that weaving is permitted. But the
Mishnah does not say so, but "a woolen border on a linen garment is
forbidden because it goes around like the woven part." It could have
stated טנז and not שע. If it had stated טנז but not שע we would have said
that carding is permitted. But the Mishnah does not say so, but "felt is
forbidden because it is carded."

156   Instead of "it", i. e., the Torah, whether some three-letter combination
one might translate "He", God as Giver would do. Since it does not, one
of the Torah. concludes that the word is shorthand,
   The five letter root שעטנז is cf. Note 151.
declared non-Semitic. One investigates

מְשִׁיחוֹת שֶׁל אַרְגָּמָן אֲסוּרוֹת. אִית תַּנֵּיי תַּגֵּי מוּתָּרוֹת. מָאן דְּאָמַר אֲסוּרוֹת כְּגוֹן
אִילֵּין טַרְסִיָּיה דְּהוּא מַכְפַּת בֵּיהּ. מָאן דְּאָמַר מוּתָּרוֹת דְּהוּא שָׁנַץ גַּרְמֵיהּ וְהִיא
נַחְתָּא לָהּ.

Ropes of purple wool are forbidden[157]. Some Tannaïm state, they are permitted. He who says they are forbidden, for example those of embroiderers who tie them on[158]. He who says they are permitted, for if he makes himself thin, it will fall down.

(fol. 31d) **מֹשׁנה י**: אוֹתוֹת הַגֹּרְדִים וְאוֹתוֹת הַכּוֹבְסִין אֲסוּרוֹת מֹשׁוּם כִּלְאָיִם. הַתּוֹכֵף תְּכִיפָה אַחַת אֵינָהּ חִיבּוּר וְאֵין בָּהּ מֹשׁוּם כִּלְאָיִם וְהַשּׁוֹמְטָהּ בַּשַּׁבָּת פָּטוּר. עָשָׂה שְׁנֵי רָאשִׁיןָ בְּצַד אֶחָד חִיבּוּר וְיֵשׁ בָּהּ מֹשׁוּם כִּלְאָיִם וְהַשּׁוֹמְטָהּ בַּשַּׁבָּת חַיָּיב. רַבִּי יְהוּדָה אוֹמֵר עַד שֶׁתְּשַׁלֵּשׁ. וְהַשַּׂק וְהַקּוּפָה מִצְטָרְפִין לְכִלְאָיִם.

Mishnah 10: Tags of weavers and washermen[159] are forbidden because of *kilaim*. If one stiches one pin-stitch there is no connection, it does not fall under *kilaim*, and if he removes it on the Sabbath he is not prosecutable[160]. If the two ends appear on the same side it is a connection, it falls under *kilaim*, and if he removes it on the Sabbath he is guilty. Rebbi Jehudah says, only if there are three pin-stitches. A sack or a chest bring together for *kilaim*[161].

161   One may not carry a sack or a chest containing both woolen and linen clothing. All *Sifry* mss. (*Deut.* 232) as well as the Mishnah and Maimonides mss. in the family of Rabbi Qafeḥ read מצרפין instead of מצטרפין, but there can be no doubt that in the language of the Mishnah, the *t*-passive מצטרפין has the meaning of active מצרפין. The *Sifry*, in the understanding of Maimonides, reads: "'Together' in any way, this forces you to state that sack and chest bring together."

(fol. 32d) **הלכה ז**: רִבִּי חֲנִינָה אָמַר עַד יְחוֹת כָּל־סִיטְרָא. אָמַר רִבִּי יַנַּאי אָמְרוּ לוֹ לְרִבִּי חֲנִינָא צֵא וּקְרָא. וְהָתַנִּינָן עָשָׂה שְׁנֵי רָאשֶׁיהָ לְצַד אֶחָד. מֵעַתָּה עַד יְחוֹת וְיִסּוֹק. וְהָתַנֵּי רִבִּי יְהוּדָה אוֹמֵר עַד שֶׁיְּשַׁלֵּשׁ. מֵעַתָּה עַד יְחוֹת וְיִסּוֹק וְיחוֹת אֶלָּא הָכֵין וְהָכֵין.

Halakhah 7: Rebbi Ḥanina said, not until it comes down an entire side[162]. Rebbi Yannai said, they said to Rebbi Ḥanina, get out and read! Did we not state, "if the two ends appear on the same side?" That means, only if it goes down and up. And did we not state, "Rebbi Jehudah says, only if there are three needle-stitches." That means [the thread] goes down, up, and down. But so and so[163].

162   For him, woolen and linen cloth create *kilaim* only if a full seam was sown. This clearly contradicts the Mishnah which requires only two or three needle-stitches. The Halakhah does not decide whether one follows the anonymous Tanna or R. Jehudah. [This paragraph and the next are also in *Šabbat* 7 (fol. 10c)].

163   Either one follows the rabbis of R. Jehudah; in no case does one need more than three stitches.

חוּט שֶׁהַשְׁחִילוֹ לַמַּחַט אֲפִילוּ קָשׁוּר מִכָּן וּמִכָּן אֵינוֹ חִיבּוּר לַבֶּגֶד. הַחוּט חִיבּוּר לַבֶּגֶד וְאֵינוֹ חִיבּוּר לַמַּחַט. רִבִּי יוֹנָה וְרִבִּי יוֹסֵה תְּרֵיהוֹן אָמְרִין בְּקָשׁוּר מִכָּן וּמִכָּן. מִילֵּיהוֹן דְּרַבָּנָן פְּלִיגִין דְּאָמַר רִבִּי בָּא רִבִּי יִרְמְיָה בְּשֵׁם רַב. הַמַּמְתִּיחַ צְדָדִיו בַּשַּׁבָּת חַיָּיב מִשּׁוּם תּוֹפֵר. וְיֵּימַר מִשּׁוּם תּוֹפֵר וּמִשּׁוּם קוֹשֵׁר.

A thread drawn through by means of a needle, even it if has a knot on each side, is no connection for cloth[164]. The thread is a connection for cloth but not for the needle. Rebbi Jonah and Rebbi Yose both say, only if it is knotted on both sides. The words of the rabbis disagree since Rebbi Abba, Rebbi Jeremiah[165] said in the name of Rav: He who straightens out the sides on the Sabbath[166] is guilty because of sewing[167]. He should have said "because of sewing and making knots."

164   If one stitch has been made and now the needle is sticking in the cloth, this does not count since the needle will eventually be removed. In order to create *kilaim*, the thread alone must cross the cloth two times, for one regular stitch. The next sentence is the justification for the rule.

165   Rav Jeremiah in the Babli.

166   According to Maimonides (*Šabbat* 10:9), it is the regular procedure in sewing a garment that when a seam is sewn the two sides are stretched to be equal before the thread

is knotted. According to Rashi in Babli *Šabbat* 95a, it refers to a garment ready to wear or already worn, of which a seam became loose. The explanation of Maimonides is the only one compatible with the Yerushalmi.

167   The parallel in Babli *Šabbat* 95a simply says, "is guilty" without stating the reason. Then the argument of the Yerushalmi is impossible. The Babli supports R. Jonah and R. Yose in the name of R. Johanan, that a double stitch is counted as permanent connection only if knotted at both ends.

אָמַר רִבִּי סִימוֹן טַעֲמָא דְרִבִּי יוֹסֵי עַל יְדֵי שְׁלִישִׁי מְלַאכְתּוֹ מִתְקַיֶּימֶת. מַה רִבִּי יוּדָה כְּרִבִּי אֱלִיעֶזֶר. דְּתַנִּינָן תַּמָּן רִבִּי לִיעֶזֶר אוֹמֶר הָאוֹרֵג שְׁלֹשָׁה חוּטִין בַּתְּחִילָּה וְאֶחָד עַל הָאָרִיג חַייָב. אָמַר רִבִּי עוּלָּא. טַעֲמָא דְרִבִּי לִיעֶזֶר תַּמָּן עַל יְדֵי שְׁלִישִׁי מְלַאכְתּוֹ מִתְקַייֶמֶת. בְּרַם הָכָא פָּחוֹת מִכֵּן מִסְתַּתֵּר הוּא.

Rebbi Simon said, the reason of Rebbi Yose[168] is that by the third his work becomes permanent. Does Rebbi Jehudah hold with Rebbi Eliezer? As we have stated there[169], "Rebbi Eliezer says that he who weaves three threads at the start or one thread on a piece of weaving already begun is guilty." Rebbi Ulla said, the reason of Rebbi Eliezer is that by the third his work becomes permanent. But here, might less than that be undone[170]?

168   It seems that this should be "R. Jehudah".   Maybe the manuscript before the scribes simply had ר״י

169   Šabbat Mishnah 13:1. The parallel in Halakhah 13:1 is all in the name of R. Ulla and has the names of R. Eliezer and R. Jehudah switched. Maybe "R. Simon" here is an intrusion from the next paragraph.

170   If the weaver made three passes with his shuttle, he can leave his work

for the next day without fear that it will unravel by itself. That does not mean that in the case of the Mishnah R. Eliezer requires three needle-stitches; maybe two needle-stitches only, and R. Eliezer may disagree with R. Jehudah about sewing. The question cannot be asked in the Babli since two stitches knotted at both ends are at least as good as three unsecured ones.

רִבִּי סִימוֹן בְּשֵׁם רִבִּי יְהוֹשֻׁעַ בֶּן לֵוִי. לֹא שָׁנוּ אֶלָּא שַׂק. הָא סַל לֹא. אַשְׁכַּח תַּנֵּי הַסַּל וְהַשַּׂק וְהַקּוּפָה. מִצְטָרְפִין בְּכִלְאַיִם. אוֹהָלִים אֵין בָּהֶן מִשׁוּם כִּלְאַיִם.

Rebbi Simon in the name of Rebbi Joshua ben Levi: They stated only "sack". Hence not a basket. It was found stated: The basket, the sack, and the chest bring together for *kilaim*. Tents have nothing to do with *kilaim*[171].

171   Tent cloth may contain linen and wool; linen and woolen garments

stored in the same tent do not produce *kilaim*.

רִבִּי יִרְמְיָה בָּעֵי. הוּא וּבְנוֹ מַהוּ שֶׁיִּצְטָרְפוּ בְּכִלְאַיִם. הֵיךְ עֲבִידָא. הוּא לְבִישׁ מָאנִין דַּעֲמַר. וּבְרֵיהּ לְבִישׁ מָאנִין דְּכִיתָּן. נְסַב פִּיסְקֵי דְּעֲמַר וְעָגְלָהּ עַל תְּרַוַּויְהוֹן. אָמַר רִבִּי יוֹסֵי וְהֶן נוֹ נָשׁוּךְ. רִבִּי חַגַּיי בָּעֵי. הוּא עַצְמוֹ מַהוּ שֶׁיִּצְטָרֵף בְּכִלְאַיִם. הֵיךְ עֲבִידָא. הוּא לְבוּשׁ דַּרְדְּסִין דַּעֲמַר בְּחָדָא רִיגְלַיְיָא. וְדַרְדְּסִין דְּכִיתָּן בְּחָדָא רִיגְלַיְיָא. אָמַר רִבִּי יוֹסֵי וְהֶן נוֹ נָשׁוּךְ. לָא צוֹרְכָא וְלֹא הָיוּ בְּרָאשֵׁי פְצָעִיּוֹת יְהַב סִיפְלָנֵי דְּמַרְטוּט דַּעֲמַר עַל חָדָא וְסִיפְלָנֵי דְּמַרְטוּט דְּכִיתָּן עַל חָדָא. אָמַר רִבִּי יוֹסֵי וְהֶן נוֹ נָשׁוּךְ. אֵין לָךְ אָסוּר אֶלָּא נָשׁוּךְ בִּלְבַד.

Rebbi Jeremiah asked, can he and his son combine for *kilaim*? How
may this be? He wears woolen clothes but his son wears linen clothes.
He takes a woolen belt and winds it around both of them. Rebbi Yose
said, where is it bitten[172]? Rebbi Ḥaggai asked, can he himself bring
together for *kilaim*? How may this be? He wears a woolen sock on one
foot and a linen one on the other foot. Rebbi Yose said, where is it
bitten? No, it is needed if he had the ends of wounds, put a plaster[173] of a
woolen patch on one end and a linen patch on the other end. Rebbi Yose
said, where is it bitten? Nothing is forbidden unless there is biting.

---

172   "Biting" means a direct connection, that one piece of cloth is inside
the other or a thread is physically in
both. Mere touching means nothing. גו
is a contraction of ניהו "he, it".

173   Latin *splenium*, Greek
σπλήνιον. The word usually appears
as אָסְפְּלָנִית in both Galilean and
Babylonian texts.

Introduction to Tractate Ševi'it

The Tractate deals with the rules of the Sabbatical year, based on *Ex.* 23:10-11, *Lev.* 25:1-7, and *Deut.* 15:1-11. The first two groups of verses concern the agricultural aspects of the Sabbatical year, which are discussed in the first nine chapters of the Tractate. The last group of verses, on the remission of debts in the Sabbatical year, is the subject of the last chapter. In *Leviticus*, the institution of the Sabbatical year is tied to that of the Jubilee year, in which all prior sales of agricultural land were annulled. Since the Jubilee was tied to the land distribution under Joshua, it disappeared with the deportation of the Northern tribes and was never re-instituted in the Second Commonwealth. As a consequence, the Jubilee is not treated in this Tractate (except for a short notice in Chapter 10). The few aspects of the Jubilee of importance for the Second Commonwealth are treated in Mishnah *'Arakhin.*

A few topics of general interest are treated in the text. Since the borders of the Jewish State of the Second Commonwealth were not those of the First, the domain of applicability of the laws of the Land is a major topic of Chapter Six. The description of the border exists not only in the Talmud Yerushalmi but also in two versions of the Tosephta and a mosaic floor in the Beth Shean valley. The sources are parallel in general; the implications of the small variations of the text for the study of Jewish history in the Eastern Roman empire have been examined by Samuel Klein.

A connected topic, taken up several times in the Tractate, is the status of the biblical agricultural laws during and after the Second Commonwealth. A common theme of all chapters of the treatise is the statement that the observation of the rules of the Sabbatical is rabbinical convention as long as the Jubilee cannot be observed.

Chapters 1 and 2 deal with the preparation for the Sabbatical, Chapters 3 to 5 with agricultural work permitted or prohibited during the Sabbatical. Chapter 6 is devoted to the domain of applicability of the rules as indicated above. Chapters 7-9 deal with Sabbatical produce, its sanctity, and the restrictions imposed on its use. Chapter 10 finally deals with the remission of debts and the non-remission of mortgages.

For the interpretation, the main guides are Maimonides and R. Simson of Sens. Of the Eighteenth Century commentators, the most useful is R. Eliahu Fulda; the least useful are R. Moses Margalit (פני משה), R. Eliahu Wilna and, from the twentieth century, R. H. Kanievski all of whom tend to emend away the difficult portions. Similarly, the preliminary translation and explanation by Allan J. Avery-Peck (Chicago 1991) heavily depends on the emended Wilna text. The manuscript evidence, while meager, definitely excludes most emendations. Of modern commentaries, that by R. Saul Lieberman (*Tosefta ki-fshutah*, New York, 1955) and R. Y. Qafeḥ's commented edition of Maimonides's Commentary are most useful. Other sources are quoted by name when used.

עד אימתי פרק ראשון

מִשְׁנָה א: עַד אֵימָתַי חוֹרְשִׁין בִּשְׂדֵה הָאִילָן עֶרֶב שְׁבִיעִית בֵּית שַׁמַּאי אוֹמְרִים כָּל־זְמָן שֶׁהוּא יָפֶה לַפֶּרִי. וּבֵית הֶלֵּל אוֹמְרִים עַד הָעֲצֶרֶת. וּקְרוֹבִים דִּבְרֵי אֵלּוּ לִהְיוֹת כְּדִבְרֵי אֵלּוּ.

Mishnah 1: Until when may one plough an orchard in the year preceding the Sabbatical? The House of Shammai say, as long as it helps the fruits, the House of Hillel say, until Pentecost. Their words do not differ by much.

הֲלָכָה א: עַד אֵימָתַי חוֹרְשִׁין כו'. כְּתִיב שֵׁשֶׁת יָמִים תַּעֲשֶׂה מַעֲשֶׂיךָ וּבַיּוֹם הַשְּׁבִיעִי תִּשְׁבּוֹת. וּכְתִיב בֶּחָרִישׁ וּבַקָּצִיר תִּשְׁבּוֹת. מַה אֲנָן קַיָּימִין אִם לְעִנְיַן שַׁבָּת בְּרֵאשִׁית וַהֲלֹא כְּבָר נֶאֱמַר שֵׁשֶׁת יָמִים תַּעֲבֹד וְעָשִׂיתָ כָּל־מְלַאכְתֶּךָ. וְאִם לְעִנְיַן שַׁבְּתוֹת שָׁנִים וַהֲלֹא כְּבָר נֶאֱמַר שֵׁשׁ שָׁנִים תִּזְרַע שָׂדֶךָ וְשֵׁשׁ שָׁנִים תִּזְמוֹר כַּרְמֶךָ. אֶלָּא אִם אֵינוֹ עִנְיָן לְשַׁבָּת בְּרֵאשִׁית וְלֹא לְעִנְיַן שַׁבְּתוֹת שָׁנִים תְּנֵיהוּ עִנְיָין בְּאִיסּוּר שְׁנֵי הַפְּרָקִים הָרִאשׁוֹנִים. בֶּחָרִישׁ וּבַקָּצִיר תִּשְׁבּוֹת בֶּחָרִישׁ שֶׁקְּצִירוֹ אָסוּר וְאֵי זֶה זֶה חָרִישׁ שֶׁל עֶרֶב שְׁבִיעִית שֶׁהוּא נִכְנָס לַשְּׁבִיעִית. וּבַקָּצִיר שֶׁחֲרִישׁוֹ אָסוּר וְאֵי זֶה זֶה קָצִיר שֶׁל שְׁבִיעִית שֶׁהוּא יוֹצֵא לְמוֹצָאֵי שְׁבִיעִית.

Halakhah 1: "Until when may one plough, etc." It is written[1] (*Ex.* 23:12): "Six days you shall do your work but on the Seventh Day you shall rest." And it is written (*Ex.* 34:21): "You shall rest from ploughing and harvesting.[2]" Where do we hold? If one speaks about the Sabbath of Creation[3], was it not already said (*Ex.* 20:9): "Six days you shall labor and do all your work?" If one speaks about Sabbatical years, was it not already said (*Lev.* 25:3): "Six years you shall sow your field and six years you shall prune your vineyard?" If it cannot refer to the Sabbath of Creation nor to Sabbatical years, let it refer to the prohibition of the first two terms[4]. "You shall rest from ploughing and harvesting," from ploughing when harvesting is forbidden; what is this? This is ploughing in the year preceding the Sabbatical in preparation of the Sabbatical. And from harvesting when ploughing is forbidden, what is this? That is the harvest of Sabbatical growth after the Sabbatical.

1   Shortened versions of this discussion are in the Babli, *Roš Haššanah* 9b, *Makkot* 8b. In both places, the argument is attributed to the school of R. Aqiba. In *Mekhilta deR. Simeon bar Iohai* to 34:22, it is attributed to R. Jehudah. Practice noted in the next paragraph follows the school of R. Ismael as explained in Mishnah 5.

2   The argument is somewhat elliptic. *Ex.* 23:12 reads: "Six days you shall do your work but on the Seventh Day you shall cease, so that your donkey and your ox may rest and the son of your bondsmaid and the stranger may recuperate." *Ex.* 34:21: "Six days you shall work; on the Seventh day you shall rest, from ploughing and harvesting you shall rest." It would seem more natural to quote the second verse *in toto*; this is the approach of the commentaries which emend the first quote away but such an approach is impossible since our text clearly quotes two different verses. The explanation is in the *Mekhiltot* (*deR. Ismael, Massekhta dekhaspa*, p. 331; *deR. Simeon bar Iohai, Mishpatim*, p. 217): It says in the Ten Commandments, that "six days you shall labor and do *all* your work." Hence, one could think that the Sabbath has to be kept only if *all* work is permitted on weekdays. This would exclude the Sabbath days of the Sabbatical year since most agricultural work is forbidden in the Sabbatical. Hence, the verse *Ex.* 23:12 is necessary to include the Sabbath days of the Sabbatical years; this only makes sure that *Ex.* 34:21 is redundant as far as both Sabbath day and Sabbatical year are concerned.

3   The Sabbath day.

4   The "two terms" are the two
periods during which agricultural work

has to cease before the onset of the
Sabbatical year, one for orchards and
one for fields.

וְאִם כֵּן לָמָּה נֶאֱמַר חוֹרְשִׁין עַד רֹאשׁ הַשָּׁנָה. רִבִּי קְרוּסְפִּי בְּשֵׁם רִבִּי יוֹחָנָן רַבָּן
גַּמְלִיאֵל וּבֵית דִּינוֹ הִתִּירוּ בְאִיסּוּר שְׁנֵי פְרָקִים הָרִאשׁוֹנִים. רִבִּי יוֹחָנָן בָּעֵי לֹא
כֵן תַּנִּינָן אֵין בֵּית דִּין יָכוֹל לְבַטֵּל דִּבְרֵי בֵית דִּין חֲבֵירוֹ עַד שֶׁיְהֵא גָדוֹל מִמֶּנּוּ
בְחָכְמָה וּבְמִנְיָן. רִבִּי קְרוּסְפִּי בְּשֵׁם רִבִּי יוֹחָנָן שֶׁאִם בִּקְשׁוּ לַחֲרוֹשׁ יַחֲרוֹשׁוּ.
וְיַעַקְרוּ אוֹתָן מִן הַמִּשְׁנָה. רִבִּי קְרוּסְפִּי בְּשֵׁם רִבִּי יוֹחָנָן שֶׁאִם בִּקְשׁוּ לַחֲזוֹר
יַחֲזוֹרוּ.

If it is so, why was it said: One ploughs until the New Year[5]? Rebbi
Crispus in the name of Rebbi Johanan: Rabban Gamliel and his court
abolished the prohibition of the first two terms. Rebbi Johanan asked:
Did we not state: No court may annul the words of another court unless
it is greater in wisdom and numbers[6]? Rebbi Crispus in the name of
Rebbi Johanan: If they wanted to plough, they may plough[7]. Then it
should have been eliminated from the Mishnah! Rebbi Crispus in the
name of Rebbi Johanan: If they wanted to re-establish it, they may do so.

5   From some *baraita*. The
statement of R. Johanan is a Tosephta
(*Ševi'it* 1:1). In the Babli (*Mo'ed qatan*
3b) the statement is attributed to R.
Joshua ben Levi; in neither Talmud is it
presented as a tannaïtic statement.

6   Mishnah *Idiut* 1:5. Rabban
Gamliel and his court are inferior to
the Men of the Great Assembly both in
stature and in numbers.

7   Since the institution of the

Sabbatical year is interwoven with that
of the Jubilee year and the Jubilee is
possible only if the Twelve Tribes are
living on their ancestral lands, the
Sabbatical in the times of the Second
Commonwealth is not a biblical but a
rabbinic institution. It is a general rule
in dealing with institutions of the Men
of the Great Assembly that one is
restrictive in interpretation while the
Temple exists and lenient when the

Temple does not exist. Since one hopes that the Temple will be re-established, the rules have to be stated in the Mishnah for future generations (Interpretation of Rav Ashi in Babli *Mo'ed Qatan* 4a).

הָתִיב רִבִּי יוֹנָה הֲרֵי פָּרָשַׁת מִילוּאִין הֲרֵי פָּרָשַׁת דּוֹר הַמַּבּוּל הֲרֵי אֵינָן עֲתִידִין לַחֲזוֹר מֵעַתָּה יַעַקְרוּ אוֹתָן מִן הַמִּשְׁנָה. אֶלָּא כְּדֵי לְהוֹדִיעָךְ. וְכָא כְּדֵי לְהוֹדִיעָךְ. אָמַר רִבִּי מָנָא כַּיי דְתַנִּינָן תַּמָּן שֶׁאִם יֹאמַר אָדָם כָּךְ אֲנִי מְקוּבָּל יֹאמְרוּ לוֹ כְּדִבְרֵי רִבִּי אִישׁ פְּלוֹנִי שָׁמַעְתָּ. וְכֵן שֶׁאִם יֹאמַר אָדָם שָׁמַעְתִּי שֶׁאָסוּר לַחֲרוֹשׁ עַד רֹאשׁ הַשָּׁנָה יֹאמַר לוֹ בְּאִיסּוּר שְׁנֵי הַפְּרָקִים הָרִאשׁוֹנִים שָׁמַעְתָּ.

Rebbi Jonah objected: There is the chapter on the induction and the chapter on the generation of the deluge which will have no future use[8]. Should they have been eliminated from what is studied? They are there to inform you. So here also to inform you. Rebbi Mana said, as we stated there[9]: "If a person says, so is my tradition, one will say to him, you heard the opinion of Rebbi X." And so, if somebody should say, I heard that it is forbidden to plough until the New Year, they will say to him, you heard the prohibition of the first two terms.

8   The induction of Aaron and his sons into the priesthood is described twice in the Torah, once as commandment (*Ex.* 29) and once in its execution (*Lev.* 8-9). The rules given there have no future application since the priesthood of the descendants of Aaron is permanent. Similarly, since God has sworn that there will be no more global deluge (*Gen.* 9:11), the story of the deluge has no future applications.

9   Mishnah *Idiut* 1:6, explaining why the Mishnah also transmits opinions which are rejected in practice. The information about rejected opinions is necessary for the future.

רִבִּי אָחָא בְּשֵׁם רִבִּי יוֹנָתָן בְּשָׁעָה שֶׁאָסְרוּ לַמִּקְרָא סָמְכוּ וּבְשָׁעָה שֶׁהִתִּירוּ לַמִּקְרָא סָמְכוּ. בְּשָׁעָה שֶׁאָסְרוּ לַמִּקְרָא סָמְכוּ בֶּחָרִישׁ וּבַקָּצִיר תִּשְׁבּוֹת בֶּחָרִישׁ

שֶׁקְּצִירוֹ אָסוּר וְאֵי זֶה זֶה זֶה חָרִישׁ שֶׁל עֶרֶב שְׁבִיעִית שֶׁהוּא נִכְנָס לַשְּׁבִיעִית.
וּבְקָצִיר שֶׁחָרִישׁוֹ אָסוּר וְאֵי זֶה זֶה זֶה קְצִיר שֶׁל שְׁבִיעִית שֶׁהוּא יוֹצֵא לְמוֹצָאֵי
שְׁבִיעִית. וּבְשָׁעָה שֶׁהִתִּירוּ לַמִּקְרָא סָמְכוּ. שֵׁשֶׁת יָמִים תַּעֲבוֹד וְעָשִׂיתָ
כָּל־מְלַאכְתֶּךָ מַה עֶרֶב שַׁבָּת בְּרֵאשִׁית אַתְּ מוּתָּר לַעֲשׂוֹת מְלָאכָה עַד שֶׁתִּשְׁקַע
הַחַמָּה אַף עֶרֶב שַׁבָּתוֹת שָׁנִים אַתְּ מוּתָּר לַעֲשׂוֹת מְלָאכָה עַד שֶׁתִּשְׁקַע הַחַמָּה.

Rebbi Aḥa in the name of Rebbi Joḥanan: When they forbade it, they
were inspired by Scripture[10], and when they permitted it, they were
inspired by Scripture. When they forbade it, they were inspired by
Scripture, (*Lev.* 25:3): "You shall rest from ploughing and harvesting,"
from ploughing when harvesting is forbidden; what is this? This is
ploughing in the year preceding the Sabbatical in preparation of the
Sabbatical. And from harvesting when ploughing is forbidden, what is
this? That is the harvest of Sabbatical growth after the Sabbatical. When
they permitted it, they were inspired by Scripture, (*Ex.* 20:9): "Six days you
shall labor and do all your work," just as on the eve of the Sabbath of
Creation[3] one may do work until sundown, also before the start of the
Sabbatical year one may work until sundown[11].

10   It is not claimed that the rules
of the Sabbatical year in the Second
Commonwealth are biblical, only that
they are inspired by the interpretation
of biblical verses.

11   Sundown of the eve of New
Year's Day.

The Babli (*Mo'ed qaṭan* 3b-4a) has

another interpretation, based on R.
Ismael's opinion in Mishnah 1:5. It
cannot accept the interpretation here
since in the theory of the Babli one is
obliged by biblical decree to start Sabbath and holidays some time before
sundown (*Yoma* 82b, *Roš Haššanah* 9a).

וְלָמָּה עַד הָעֲצֶרֶת עַד כָּאן הוּא יָפֶה לַפְּרִי מִכָּן וְאֵילָךְ הוּא מְנַבֵּל פֵּירוֹתָיו. וְהָא
תַּנִּינָן אֶחָד אִילָן סְרָק וְאֶחָד אִילָן מַאֲכָל עַד כָּאן הוּא מְעַבֶּה אֶת הַכּוּרֶת מִכָּן

וְהֵילַךְ הוּא מַתִּישׁ אֶת כּוֹחוֹ. (fol. 33b) וְיַחֲרוֹשׁ מִתּוֹךְ שֶׁהוּא יוֹדֵעַ שֶׁהוּא מַתִּישׁ

כּוֹחוֹ שֶׁל אִילָן אַף הוּא אֵינוֹ מִתְכַּוֵּין לַעֲבוֹדַת הָאָרֶץ.

Why until Pentecost? Until then it is good for the fruits, from there on
he degrades his fruits. But did we not state: Both for a useless tree[12] and
a fruit tree, until then[13] it fortifies the stem, from there on it weakens its
force. Let him plough! Because he knows that he will weaken the tree,
he does not intend to work the ground.

12   For the definition of "useless   ploughing makes sense only as
tree", cf. *Kilaim* Chapter 6, Note 40.   preparation for the next season, the
13   Pentecost. After that time, any   Sabbatical.

וְלָמָּה לֹא תַנִּיתָהּ מִקּוּלֵי בֵית שַׁמַּאי וּמֵחוּמְרֵי בֵית הִלֵּל. פְּעָמִים שֶׁאֵין הַגְּשָׁמִים

מְצוּיִין וְאֵין הַלֵּיחָה מְצוּיָה וְהוּא עָתִיד לַחֲרוֹשׁ קוֹדֶם לָעֲצֶרֶת כְּדִבְרֵי בֵית שַׁמַּאי.

בֵית הִלֵּל אוֹמְרִים עַד הָעֲצֶרֶת.

Why did we not state this with the leniencies of the House of Shammai
and the stringencies of the House of Hillel? Sometimes there is no rain
and no moisture and he would plough only before Pentecost following the
House of Shammai[14]. The House of Hillel say, until Pentecost.

14   Ploughing in a time of draught   case, the House of Shammai is more
robs the ground of moisture. In that   restrictive than the House of Hillel.

(fol. 33a) **מִשְׁנָה ב:** אֵי זֶהוּ שְׂדֵה הָאִילָן כָּל־שְׁלֹשָׁה אִילָנוֹת לְבֵית סְאָה אִם

רְאוּיִין לַעֲשׂוֹת כִּכַּר דְּבֵילָה שֶׁל שִׁשִּׁים מָנֶה בָּאִיטַלְקִי חוֹרְשִׁין כָּל־בֵּית סְאָה

בִּשְׁבִילָן. פָּחוֹת מִכֵּן אֵין חוֹרְשִׁין לָהֶן אֶלָּא מְלֹא הָאוֹרֶה וְסַלּוֹ חוּצָה לוֹ.

Mishnah 2: What is an orchard? Any three trees on a *bet seah*[15]; if they may produce a fig cake in the weight of a talent of 60 Italic minas[16] one ploughs the entire *bet seah* because of them. If it is less, one ploughs for them only to accomodate the harvester and his basket beside him.

15   2500 square cubits, cf. *Kilaim* Chapter 1, Note 195.

16   Since an Italic denar weighed $1/_{96}$ of a Roman pound, or 3.59 g, 60 minas or 6000 denar are approximately 21.5 kg. Maimonides estimates this as 62.48 *rotl*. He declares (*Terumot* 4:10) a *rotl* to be a Roman pound (the common apothecary's weight in the Middle Ages); in Roman measures, 60 minas are 62.5 Roman pounds.

הלכה ב: רַב יְהוּדָה בְשֵׁם שְׁמוּאֵל רִבִּי אַבָּהוּ בְשֵׁם רִבִּי יוֹחָנָן הַקוֹנֶה שְׁלשָׁה אִילָנוֹת בְּתוֹךְ שֶׁל חֲבֵירוֹ רְחוֹקִים מַטָּע עֶשֶׂר לְבֵית סְאָה קְרוּבִין כְּדֵי שֶׁיְּהֵא הַבָּקָר עוֹבֵר בְּכֵלָיו. קָנָה קַרְקַע שֶׁתַּחְתֵּיהֶן קַרְקַע שֶׁבֵּינֵיהֶן שָׁחוּצָה לָהֶן מְלֹא הָאוֹרֶה וְסַלּוֹ. רַב אָמַר בַּעֲשׂוּיִין צוֹבֶר. וּשְׁמוּאֵל אָמַר בַּעֲשׂוּיָה שׁוּרָה. אָמַר רִבִּי יוֹסֵי תַּמָּן אִיתְאַמָּרַת וְכָא לָא אִיתְאַמָּרַת. אָמַר רִבִּי יוֹנָה אֲפִילוּ הָכָא אִיתְאַמָּרַת בִּקְרוֹבִים. אָמַר לֵיהּ רִבִּי מָנָא וְאִם בִּקְרוֹבִין וְהָא תַנִּינָן כְּדֵי שֶׁיִּהְיֶה הַבָּקָר עוֹבֵר בְּכֵלָיו. אִיתָא חֲמֵי בְּשָׁעָה שֶׁהַבָּקָר עוֹבֵר בְּכֵלָיו הַשָּׁרָשִׁין מְהַלְּכִין מִן הַצַּד וּבְשָׁעָה שֶׁאֵין הַבָּקָר עוֹבֵר בְּכֵלָיו אֵין הַשָּׁרָשִׁין מְהַלְּכִין מִן הַצַּד.

Halakhah 2: Rav Jehudah in the name of Samuel, Rebbi Abbahu in the name of Rebbi Johanan[17]: If somebody buys three trees on another person's property, spaced so that ten trees could be planted in a *bet seah*[18] and that the ox and its harness could pass between them[19], then he acquired the ground under them, the ground between them, and outside the space for the harvester and his basket. Rav said, if they form a group[20]. Samuel says, also if they are in a straight line. Rebbi Yose said, this refers to there but not to here[21]. Rebbi Jonah said, it refers even to here, if they are close[22].   Rebbi Mana said to him, did we not state "that the ox and its harness could pass between them"? Come and see, if the ox and its harness can pass between them, the roots can expand laterally, but if the ox and its harness cannot pass between them, the roots cannot expand laterally.

17   A very shortened version of this statement is in *Baba Batra* 5:5 (fol. 15a), a parallel is in Babli *Baba Batra* 82b-83a, where the allowable distances are determined in a lengthy discussion. Probably the statement in (Caesarean) Yerushalmi *Baba Batra* is the original one; the extended (Tiberian) version here must be the result of a derivation parallel to the arguments of the Babli. The rules established in *Baba Batra* deal with transactions without special stipulations; the parties in a sale are free to specify exactly what is sold and what is not sold but if the details are not mentioned in the contract of sale then the rules given here are valid by default.

18   This is the minimum of trees in a *bet seah* that constitutes an orchard. If the trees are planted in a regular pattern, each tree is the center of a square of 250 square cubits. Hence, the distance of two trees is $250^{1/2} = 15.811$ cubits. (In the Babli, the distance is required to be "less than 16 cubits.")

19   This is defined as "working space" of 4 cubits in *Kilaim*, Halakhah 5:3. In all cases, the stems of the trees are not included in the measurements, cf. *Kilaim*, Halakhah 4:8.

20   If the trees form a triangle. The correct version is in a Genizah fragment, בעשויין ציבה, referring to צובה "tripod". The Venice text has the word in *Eruvin* 5:2, in a rule concerning three villages close one to another, where Rav requires them to be built "like a tripod" and Samuel allows them to be aligned.

21   The minimal and maximal distances apply to civil contracts, not to the laws of the Sabbatical.

22   Fruit trees planted less than four cubits apart cannot grow; they are planted either in a tree nursery to be transferred later to genuine agricultural use or they are grown for their wood and will be cut down. In no case is ploughing the field for them justified.

רִבִּי לִיעֶזֶר שָׁאַל מִזּוֹ לְזוֹ שֵׁשׁ עֶשְׂרֵה וּלְצַד עֶשְׂרִין וְחָמֵשׁ. רִבִּי שְׁמוּאֵל בַּר רַב

יִצְחָק בָּעֵי הָיוּ נְתוּנִין בְּצַד הַגָּדֵר חוֹרְשִׁין כָּל־בֵּית סְאָה בִּשְׁבִילָן. אָמַר רִבִּי יוֹסֵי

אִין בָּעֵי נִיתֶּן לָהֶם בֵּית אַרְבַּעְתָּם²³ סְאָה. סְאָה מִכָּן וְסְאָה מִכָּן סְאָה מִכָּן

וְסְאָה מִכָּן. רִבִּי יִרְמְיָה בָּעֵי הָיְתָה גֶּפֶן אַחַת מוּדְלָה עַל גַּבֵּי שְׁתֵּי סָאִין אַתְּ

חוֹרֵשׁ קַרְקַע שֶׁתַּחְתֶּיהָ וְקַרְקַע שֶׁחוּצָה לוֹ מְלֹא הָאוֹרֶה וְסַלּוֹ חוּצָה לוֹ.

Rebbi Eliezer asked, from one to the other sixteen and on the sides twenty five[24]? Rebbi Samuel ben Rav Isaac asked: If they were next to a fence, does one plough the entire *bet seah* because of them[25]? Rebbi Yose said, if you want that, we should give them their four *bate seah*, two *bate seah* here, two *bate seah*[26] there. Rebbi Jeremiah asked, if there was one vine drawn over two *seah*, do you plough the ground under it and outside it for the harvester and his basket[27]?

23   Reading of a Genizah fragment. In the other mss: ארבעים

24   If the three trees are planted in a straight line (following Samuel), almost 16 cubits apart (Note 18), is it necessary to assume that the trees are exactly in the middle of the field and that in the perpendicular direction there are 25 cubits on both sides? One has to assume that the question also is whether there have to be 9 cubits between any extremal tree and the border of the field. It seems that instead of "R. Eliezer" one should read "R. Eleazar", but there is no ms. evidence to back this up.

25   A question in opposition to R.

Eliezer's. If the three trees are close to a fence, if one may plough a field even if the trees are not in the center, may one then plough both sides of the fence to a distance of 50 cubits if the fields on opposite sides belong to the same owner?

26   If it is possible to plough a *bet seah* because of a row of trees somewhere on it, one would be able to define a cross-shaped area to be ploughed, four partially overlapping *bate seah*. If the distance between two trees is *a*, one has two fields 50 wide and 50 long on each side of the trees and two fields 50 wide and 25-*a* long on each side straddling the line on

which the trees are planted. One has to assume that in each direction there is a *bet seah*, a 50-by-50 field, but the four fields have a considerable area in common so that the total area is < 4 *bate seah*. This interpretation is necessary because even the two lateral fields must have in common the strip carrying the trees and be wide (8 + width of the stems); it agrees with the very careful formulation of the sentence that lead those copyists astray who understood what they were copying. The argument shows that the question must be answered in the negative.

27   In this case, one ploughs much more that a *bet seah* but there is no reason to see in this situation a contradiction to our Mishnah.

בְּאִיסוּר שְׁנֵי פְרָקִים הָרִאשׁוֹנִים אֵלּוּ מִלְמַעְלָן חוֹרְשִׁין בּוֹ מִלְמַטָּן. וְאֵלּוּ מִלְמַטָּן חוֹרְשִׁין בּוֹ מִלְמַעְלָן. נִיחָא אֵלּוּ מִלְמַעְלָן חוֹרְשִׁין בּוֹ מִלְמַטָּן וְלֹא מִלְמַטָּן חוֹרְשִׁין בּוֹ מִלְמַעְלָן. נִישְׁמָעִינָה מִן הָדָא מַרְחִיקִין אֶת הָאִילָן מִן הַבּוֹר עֶשְׂרִים וְחָמֵשׁ אַמּוֹת. וְתַנֵּי עֲלֵיהּ בֵּין מִלְמַעְלָן בֵּין מִלְמַטָּן. אוֹ נֵימַר בֵּין שֶׁהָאִילָן לְמַעְלָן וְהַבּוֹר לְמַטָּן בֵּין שֶׁהָאִילָן וְהַבּוֹר מִלְמַטָּן. וְהָתַנֵּי אִילָן מִלְמַעְלָן וְהַבּוֹר מִלְמַטָּן אִילָן מִלְמַטָּן וְהַבּוֹר מִלְמַעְלָן נִיחָא. אִילָן מִלְמַעְלָן וְהַבּוֹר מִלְמַטָּן אִילָן מִלְמַטָּן וְהַבּוֹר מִלְמַעְלָן וְדֶרֶךְ הַשָּׁרָשִׁים לַעֲלוֹת מִלְמַעְלָן. אָמַר רְבִּי חֲנִינָא לֹא מִפְּנֵי הַשָּׁרָשִׁם אֶלָּא שֶׁהֵן עוֹשִׂין עָפָר תּוֹחֵחַ וְהֵן מַלְקִין אַרְעִיתוֹ שֶׁל בּוֹר. אֲתָא עוֹבְדָא קוֹמֵי רְבִּי יָסָא בֵּי רְבִּי בּוּן אָמַר יְחִידִי הוּא וְלֹא סָמְכִין עָלָיו. וְתַנֵּי עֲלָהּ רְבִּי שִׁמְעוֹן אוֹמֵר כְּשֵׁם שֶׁאָמְרוּ מִלְמַעְלָן כָּךְ אָמְרוּ מִלְמַטָּן.

Regarding the prohibition of the first two terms, those above plough downwards and those below plough upwards[28]. It seems reasonable that those above plough downwards but not that those below plough upwards. Let us hear from the following[29]: "One removes a tree 25 cubits from a cistern." We have stated on that: Both higher and lower. Or let us say both if the tree is higher and the cistern lower or if tree and cistern are on the same level. In this sense, we stated[30]: "Whether the tree is higher and the cistern lower or the tree lower and the cistern higher"; is that reasonable? If the tree is higher and the cistern lower[31]; but the tree lower and the cistern higher, do roots climb? Rebbi Ḥanina said not because of the roots [climbing], but they loosen the earth and damage the bottom of the cistern[32]. A case came before Rebbi Yose ben Abun[33]; he said that is a single opinion and we do not rely on it, for we have stated on this: "Rebbi Simeon says, just as they said higher so they said lower.[34]"

28   Following R. Eliezer, one ploughs 25 cubits on both sides of a row of trees, even if the trees are planted on a slope. The problem is that one may plough the entire field because the roots of the trees have the entire field to expand in, but we do not expect the roots to expand upwards as much as they expand downwards.

29   Mishnah *Baba Batra* 2:11. The chapter deals with the obligation of every citizen to avoid damaging his neighbor's property. If a tree is planted too close to a cistern, the roots might penetrate the wall of the cistern. The full Mishnah reads: "One removes a tree 25 cubits from a cistern, and a sycomore tree fifty cubits, both higher or on the same level." In some Mishnah mss. one reads "both higher and lower", cf. *Diqduqe Soferim Baba Batra* p. כו Note ב.

30   This *baraita* is quoted in Babli *Baba Batra* 25b as current practice.

31   This is understandable.

32   In the Babli, this reason is given by R. Ḥaga (Ḥaggai).

33   About a tree planted near a cistern; he rejects the argument of R. Ḥanina and decides following R. Yose.

34   Tosephta *Baba Batra* 1:12. The opponent of R. Simeon is R. Yose (ben Ḥalaphta) who insists that agricultural land is meant for agricultural use and the owner of the cistern should not have built it too close to the border of his domain. In general, R. Yose is a higher authority than R. Simeon. In the Babli, R. Yose's opinion is not mentioned; practice follows R. Simeon. In Yerushalmi *Baba Batra*, Halakhah 2:11/12, no position is taken between R. Yose and the rabbis.

(fol. 33a) **משנה ג**: אֶחָד אִילַן סְרָק וְאֶחָד אִילַן מַאֲכָל רוֹאִין אוֹתָן כְּאִילּוּ הֵן תְּאֵנִים אִם רְאוּיִין לַעֲשׂוֹת כִּכָּר דְּבֵילָה שֶׁל שִׁשִּׁים מָנֶה בְּאִיטַלְקִי חוֹרְשִׁין כָּל־בֵּית סְאָה בִּשְׁבִילָן. פָּחוֹת מִכֵּן אֵין חוֹרְשִׁין לָהֶן אֶלָּא צוֹרְכָן.

Mishnah 3: Any useless[12] or fruit trees are considered as if they were fig trees[35]. If they would produce a fig cake in the weight of a talent of 60 Italic minas[16] one ploughs the entire *bet seah* because of them. If less, one ploughs for them only as necessary[36].

35 A fig tree of the size of the tree in question.	36 Space for the harvester and his basket.

(fol. 33b) **הלכה ג**: אֶחָד אִילַן סְרָק כו'. וְלָמָּה אָמְרוּ תְּאֵנִים עַל יְדֵי שֶׁפֵּירוֹתֵיהֶן גַּסִּין וְהֵן עוֹשׂוֹת הַרְבֵּה. הֲרֵי אָתְרוֹג פֵּירוֹתָיו גַּסִּין וְאֵינוֹ עוֹשֶׂה הַרְבֵּה. הֲרֵי זֵיתִין עוֹשִׂין הַרְבֵּה וְאֵין פֵּירוֹתֵיהֶן גַּסִּין. וְאֵלּוּ עוֹשׂוֹת הַרְבֵּה וּפֵירוֹתֵיהֶן גַּסִּין. אָמַר רִבִּי חִיָּיא בַּר אָדָא כָּל־אִילָנַיָּא עֲבְדִין שָׁנָה פָּרָא שָׁנָה וְהָדָא תְאֵינְתָא עֲבְדָא כָּל־שָׁנָה.

Halakhah 3: "Any useless tree, etc." Why did they mention fig trees? Because their fruits are large and they produce many. The Etrog tree[37] has large fruits but it produces few of them. Olive trees produce much but its fruits are not large. But these produce much and its fruits are large. Rebbi Ḥiyya bar Ada said, all trees produce one year less[38] than another year but the fig tree produces every year.

37 *Citrus medica.*	38 Latin *parum*, cf. Demay p. 521.

מֶשׁנָה ד: הָיָה אֶחָד עוֹשֶׂה כִּכַּר דְּבֵילָה וּשְׁנַיִם אֵין עוֹשִׂין אוֹ שְׁנַיִם (fol. 33a)
עוֹשִׂין וְאֶחָד אֵינוֹ עוֹשֶׂה אֵין חוֹרְשִׁין לָהֶן אֶלָּא צוֹרְכָּן. עַד שֶׁיְּהוּ שְׁלֹשָׁה
וּמִשְּׁלֹשָׁה וְעַד תִּשְׁעָה. הָיוּ עֲשָׂרָה וּמֵעֲשָׂרָה וּלְמַעְלָה בֵּין עוֹשִׂין בֵּין שֶׁאֵינָן עוֹשִׂין
חוֹרְשִׁין כָּל־בֵּית סְאָה בִּשְׁבִילָן שֶׁנֶּאֱמַר בֶּחָרִישׁ וּבַקָּצִיר תִּשְׁבּוֹת.

Mishnah 4: If one tree yields a "fig cake" but two do not, or two do
and one does not, one only ploughs for them as necessary, unless there are
three, and so from three to nine[39]. If there are ten or more than ten one
ploughs the entire *bet seah* because of them, whether they produce or not,
since it is said (*Ex.* 34:21): : "You shall rest from ploughing and
harvesting.[40]"

39 The tree must yield at least 20 minas in weight, its share in the 60 minas expected from three trees. The Halakhah will explain the meaning of	"from three to nine". 40 Without good reason, one may not plough.

הֲלָכָה ד: הָיָה אֶחָד עוֹשֶׂה כו'. רְבִּי בִּיבִי בְּשֵׁם רְבִּי חֲנִינָה וּבִלְבַד שֶׁלֹּא (fol. 33b)
יִפְחוֹת מֵחֶשְׁבּוֹן מְשׁוּלָשִׁים. זְעִירָא בַּר חִינָנָא אָמַר וּבִלְבַד שֶׁלֹּא יִפְחוֹת מֵחֶשְׁבּוֹן
מְתוּשָׁעִים.

Halakhah 4: "If one tree yields, etc." Rebbi Vivian in the name of
Rebbi Ḥanina: Only he should not diminish from the computation of
triads. Zeïra bar Ḥinena said, only he should not diminish from the
computation of nonads[41].

41 According to the first opinion, it must be possible to split the trees into groups of trees, each of which	produces a talent. According to the second opinion, all nine trees together have to produce three talents.

הָיוּ אַרְבָּעָה וְהַבָּקָר עוֹבֵר בְּכֵלָיו. שְׁנַיִם וְאֵין הַבָּקָר עוֹבֵר בְּכֵלָיו מְכִינָן שֶׁאֵין הַבָּקָר עוֹבֵר בְּכֵלָיו אַתְּ רוֹאֶה אוֹתָן כְּאִילוּ חֲמִשָׁה. הָיוּ חֲמִשָׁה. תִּפְלוּגְתָּא דְּרִבִּי שִׁמְעוֹן וְרַבָּנִין דְּתַנִּינָן תַּמָּן כֶּרֶם שֶׁהוּא נָטוּעַ עַל פָּחוֹת מֵאַרְבַּע אַמּוֹת. רִבִּי שִׁמְעוֹן אוֹמֵר אֵינוֹ כֶּרֶם. וַחֲכָמִים אוֹמְרִים כֶּרֶם. וְרוֹאִין אֶת הָאֶמְצָעִיּוֹת כְּאִלּוּ אֵינָן.

If there were four and the ox may pass between them with its harness and two where the ox cannot pass with its harness, you consider it as if there were five. If there are five, we have the disagreement of Rebbi Simeon and the rabbis, as we have stated there[42]: "A vineyard planted less that four cubits apart, Rebbi Simeon says that it is no vineyard. But the Sages say that it is a vineyard and one disregards the ones in the middle as if nonexistent."

42 Mishnah *Kilaim* 5:2, cf. there, Note 27. Here also, the ox and its harness need four cubits. The rabbis disregard the additional trees and only require one group yielding a talent. R. Simeon forbids ploughing unless one group produces a talent and the remaining three trees (of which two are planted too close together) produce ⅔ of a talent.

וְחוֹרְשִׁין כָּל־בֵּית סְאָה בִּשְׁבִילָן שֶׁנֶּאֱמַר בֶּחָרִישׁ וּבַקָּצִיר תִּשְׁבּוֹת. לָא אַתְיָא דְּלָא עַל רֵישָׁא אֵין חוֹרְשִׁין לָהֶן אֶלָּא צוֹרְכָן שֶׁנֶּאֱמַר בֶּחָרִישׁ וּבַקָּצִיר תִּשְׁבּוֹת.

"One ploughs the entire *bet seah* because of them since it is said (*Ex.* 34:21): 'You shall rest from ploughing and harvesting.'" That refers only to the first part, "one ploughs for them only as necessary because it is said 'you shall rest from ploughing and harvesting.'".

מָשׁנָה ה: אֵין צָרִיךְ לוֹמַר חָרִישׁ וְקָצִיר שֶׁל שְׁבִיעִית אֶלָּא חָרִישׁ שֶׁל(fol. 33a)
עֶרֶב שְׁבִיעִית שֶׁנִּכְנָס לַשְּׁבִיעִית. וְקָצִיר שֶׁל שְׁבִיעִית שֶׁהוּא יוֹצֵא לְמוֹצָאֵי
שְׁבִיעִית. רְבִּי יִשְׁמָעֵאל אוֹמֵר מַה חָרִישׁ רְשׁוּת אַף קָצִיר רְשׁוּת יָצָא קְצִיר
הָעוֹמֶר.

Mishnah 5: One does not have to mention ploughing and harvesting of the Sabbatical, but it refers to ploughing in the year preceding the Sabbatical in preparation of the Sabbatical, and harvesting of Sabbatical growth after the Sabbatical. Rebbi Ismael says, just as ploughing is voluntary so harvesting is voluntary; this excludes the harvest of the *'omer*[43].

43   This belongs to the discussion of the verse (Ex. 34:21): : "You shall rest from ploughing and harvesting," as given in Halakhah 1, Notes 1-4. The only addition is the statement of R. Ismael, that the verse refers to the Sabbath day, on which all ploughing is forbidden; this has no definite date assigned to it. For him, while the verse is formulated as a prohibition, it implies the commandment to cut the sheaf of barley "on the day after the day of rest" following Passover (*Lev.* 23:15), even if that day should be a Sabbath (the 16th of Nissan for Pharisees, the 22nd of Nissan for the author of the book of Jubilees.) Cf. *Mekhilta deR. Simeon bar Iohai* to *Ex.* 34:22.

הלכה ה: אֵין צָרִיךְ לוֹמַר כו'. רְבִּי יִשְׁמָעֵאל כְּדַעְתֵּיהּ דְּרְבִּי יִשְׁמָעֵאל(fol. 33b)
אָמַר אֵין הָעוֹמֶר בָּא מִסּוּרְיָּה יָצָא קְצִיר הָעוֹמֶר שֶׁיְּהֵא מִצְוָה.

Halakhah 5: "One does not have to mention, etc." Rebbi Ismael is consistent since Rebbi Ismael said the *'omer* may not come from Syria; the harvesting of the *'omer* is different, it is a commandment[44].

44   The main place of this argument is in *Šeqalim* 4:1. For the definition of Syria cf. *Peah* Chapter 7, Note 119. Since R. Ismael holds that the barley of

the 'omer is intrinsically holy, he holds that the cutting of the barley is an action of the Temple and paid for by the yearly Temple tax, hence relative to the Sabbath it has the status of a sacrifice and must be performed on the Sabbath if necessary. For him, the prohibition of ploughing before the Sabbatical has no scriptural base.

(fol. 33a) **משנה ו**: שְׁלשָׁה אִילָנוֹת שֶׁל שְׁלשָׁה אֲנָשִׁים הֲרֵי אֵלּוּ מִצְטָרְפִין וְחוֹרְשִׁין כָּל־בֵּית סְאָה בִּשְׁבִילָן. וְכַמָּה יְהֵא בֵּינֵיהֶן רַבָּן שִׁמְעוֹן בֶּן גַּמְלִיאֵל אוֹמֵר כְּדֵי שֶׁיְּהֵא הַבָּקָר עוֹבֵר בְּכֵלָיו.

Mishnah 6: Three trees belonging to three different owners are counted together and one may plough the entire *bet seah* for them. How much space must be between them? Rabban Simeon ben Gamliel says, so that the ox and its harness can pass[42].

(fol. 33b) **הלכה ו**: שְׁלשָׁה אִילָנוֹת כו'. תַּנֵּי רִבִּי חִייָא אִילָנוֹת שֶׁל אָדָם אֶחָד וְקַרְקַע שֶׁל אָדָם אֶחָד מִצְטָרְפִין וְחוֹרְשִׁין כָּל־בֵּית סְאָה בִּשְׁבִילָן. אָמַר רִבִּי יוֹסֵה אַף אֲנָן תַּנִּינָן דְּרַבָּא שְׁלשָׁה אִילָנוֹת שֶׁל שְׁלשָׁה אֲנָשִׁים הֲרֵי אֵלּוּ מִצְטָרְפִין וְחוֹרְשִׁין כָּל־בֵּית סְאָה עַד רֹאשׁ הַשָּׁנָה.

Halakhah 6: "Three trees, etc." Rebbi Ḥiyya stated: Trees belonging to one owner and ground belonging to a second owner are counted together and one may plough the entire *bet seah* for them. Rebbi Yose said, we have stated more: Three trees belonging to three different owners are counted together and one may plough the entire *bet seah* until the New Year[45].

45   The clearest formulation is in
Tosephta *Ševi'it* 1:1: "Three trees
belonging to three different owners
and the field belonging to a forth.

Even though the field's owner plough
for his own needs, the field is permitted [to be ploughed]."

(fol. 33a) **משנה ז:** עֶשֶׂר נְטִיעוֹת מְפוּזָּרוֹת לְתוֹךְ בֵּית סְאָה חוֹרְשִׁין כָּל־בֵּית סְאָה
בִּשְׁבִילָן עַד רֹאשׁ הַשָּׁנָה. הָיוּ עֲשׂוּיוֹת שׁוּרָה וּמוּקָּפוֹת עֲטָרָה אֵין חוֹרְשִׁין לָהֶן
אֶלָּא צוֹרְכָן.

Mishnah 7: Ten saplings[46] distributed on a *bet seah*, one ploughs the
entire *bet seah* for them until the new year. If they formed a row or
were surrounded by a grate[47] one ploughs only what is necessary for
them.

46   Ten saplings have the same
status as three fully grown trees. As R.
Simson points out, all these rules
became moot with the elimination of
the first two periods.

47   This is the interpretation of R.

Simson, based on the similar meaning
of עטרה in Mishnah *Ahilut* 14:1, *Middot*
3:8. Maimonides explains "planted in
an arc of circle", but the expression
מוקף in Mishnaic Hebrew only means
"surrounded by".

(fol. 33b) **הלכה ז:** עֶשֶׂר נְטִיעוֹת כו'. רִבִּי זְעִירָא רִבִּי לָא רִבִּי יָסָא בְּשֵׁם רִבִּי
יוֹחָנָן עֲרָבָה הֲלָכָה לְמֹשֶׁה מִסִּינַי וּדְלָא כְאַבָּא שָׁאוּל דְּאַבָּא שָׁאוּל אָמַר עֲרָבָה
דְּבַר תּוֹרָה. וְעֲרְבֵי נַחַל שְׁתַּיִם. חַד עֲרָבָה לְלוּלָב וַעֲרָבָה לְמִקְדָּשׁ. רִבִּי בָּא רִבִּי
חִיָּיא בְּשֵׁם רִבִּי יוֹחָנָן עֲרָבָה וְנִיסּוּךְ הַמַּיִם הֲלָכָה לְמֹשֶׁה מִסִּינַי וּדְלָא כְרִבִּי
עֲקִיבָה דְּרִבִּי עֲקִיבָה אָמַר נִיסּוּךְ הַמַּיִם דְּבַר תּוֹרָה. בְּשֵׁינִי וְנִסְכֵּיהֶם. בְּשִׁישִׁי
וּנְסָכֶיהָ. בְּשְׁבִיעִי כְּמִשְׁפָּטָם. מֵ״ם יוֹ״ד מֵ״ם מַיִם. רִבִּי חִיָּיא בַּר אַבָּא בְּעָא
קוֹמֵי רִבִּי יוֹחָנָן לָמָּה הֵן חוֹרְשִׁין בִּזְקֵינוֹת. אָמַר לֵיהּ בְּשָׁעָה שֶׁנִּיתְּנָה
הֲלָכָה נִיתְּנָה שֶׁאִם בִּקְשׁוּ לַחֲרוֹשׁ יַחֲרוֹשׁוּ.

Halakhah 7: "Ten saplings, etc." Rebbi Zeïra, Rebbi La, Rebbi Yasa in the name of Rebbi Johanan[48]: The "willow" is practice going back to Moses on Mount Sinai. This is against Abba Shaul, since Abba Shaul said the willow is a word of the Torah (*Lev.* 23:40): "Brook willows," two[49]. One willow for the *lulab*[50], the other willow for the Temple. Rebbi Abba, Rebbi Hiyya in the name of Rebbi Johanan, willow and pouring of water are practice going back to Moses on Mount Sinai. This is against Rebbi Aqiba, since Rebbi Aqiba said the pouring of water is a word of the Torah[51]. On the second day, (*Num.* 29:19) "and their libations." On the sixth day, (*Num.* 29:31) "and its libations." On the seventh day, (*Num.* 29:33) "and its rules." מ י מ spells "water"[52]. Rebbi Hiyya bar Abba asked before Rebbi Johanan, why does one now plough because of old trees? He said to him, when the practice was established it was given so that when they desired to plough they might plough[7].

---

48   This paragraph (from *Sukkah* 4:1, fol. 54b) is an introduction to the next one which will mention the ten saplings. It deals with the laws of the feast of Tabernacles when in addition to the ceremonies prescribed by the Torah the altar was adorned by long willow twigs and water was poured as libation on the altar, against the opposition of the Sadducees.

49   Babli *Sukkah* 34a. In the Babli, it is not implied that taking the willows in the Temple is a separate biblical commandment. (In the opinion of I. Löw, ערבה denotes not the willow but the Euphrates poplar but in Arabic ערב means "willow".)

50   The three kinds of branches taken together on Tabernacles, *Lev.* 23:40.

51   Babli *Zebahim* 110b. There, the derivation of R. Aqiba parallels the argument of Abba Shaul here, that (*Num.* 29:31) "and its libations" implies two libations, one of wine and one of water.

52   In *Sifry Num.* 150, the argument is given in the name of R. Jehudah ben Batyra. In *Num.* 29:17-34, the sacrifices for the intermediate days of Taber

nacles are given in identical language after the mention of the number of animals required. The only deviations from the identical patterns are ונסכיהם, ונסכיה instead of ונסכה and כמשפטם instead of במשפט. The additional letters are taken to form the word for

"water." Rabbenu Hillel notes in his commentary that ונסכיהם has two letters in excess over ונסכה so that the word to be formed would be מיים, in the time of the Yerushalmi the standard spelling of מים.

רִבִּי בָּא בַּר זַבְדִּי בְּשֵׁם רִבִּי חוֹנְיָה דְּבֵית חַוְרָן עֲרָבָה וְנִיסּוּךְ הַמַּיִם וְעֶשֶׂר נְטִיעוֹת מִיסוֹד הַנְּבִיאִים הָרִאשׁוֹנִים הֵם. מַה וּפְלִיג. רִבִּי יוֹסֵי בֵּי רִבִּי בּוּן בְּשֵׁם לֵוִי כָּךְ הָיְתָה הֲלָכָה בְּיָדָם וּשְׁכָחוּהָ וְעָמְדוּ הַשְּׁנִיִּים וְהִסְכִּימוּ עַל דַּעַת הָרִאשׁוֹנִים. לְלַמְּדָךְ שֶׁכָּל־דָּבָר שֶׁבֵּית דִּין נוֹתְנִין נַפְשָׁם עָלָיו סוֹף לְהִתְקַיֵּים בְּיָדָם כְּמָה שֶׁנֶּאֱמַר לְמֹשֶׁה בְּסִינַי. וְאַתְיָיא כַּיי דָּמַר רִבִּי מָנָא כִּי לֹא דָבָר רֵק הוּא מִכֶּם. וְאִם רֵק הוּא מִכֶּם לָמָּה שֶׁאֵין אַתֶּם יְגִיעִין בּוֹ. כִּי הִיא חַיֵּיכֶם. אֵימָתַי הִיא חַיֵּיכֶם בְּשָׁעָה שֶׁאַתֶּם יְגֵעִין בּוֹ.

Rebbi Abba bar Zabdi in the name of Rebbi Onias from Hauran[53]: Willow, water libation, and ten saplings are institutions of the early prophets[54]. Do they disagree[55]? Rebbi Yose ben Rebbi Abun in the name of Levi: That was the current practice; they forgot it, but the later ones got up and agreed to the opinion of the earlier ones to teach you that everything the Court insists on will come to be in the end just as Moses was told on Sinai; as Rebbi Mana said (*Deut.* 32:47): "For it is not an empty word, from you," if it is empty it is from you because you do not exert yourself about it. "Because it is your life," when is it your life? At the time that you exert yourself!

53 In the parallel, Babli *Sukkah* 44a, he is called Neḥoniah from the valley of Bet Ḥoron; the name in the

Yerushalmi is correct since he was a first generation Amora from the Golan heights and an authority on the

halakhic boundaries of the Land of
Israel in that region.

54   Samuel and David.

55   Do they assert that these rules

were never promulgated by Moses?
The rest of the paragraph is also in
Peah 1:1, Notes 74-75.

רִבִּי יוֹחָנָן אָמַר לְרִבִּי חִיָּה בַּר וָא בַּבְלַיָּיא תְּרֵין מִילִין סַלְּקוּן בְּיֶדְכוּן
מִפְשׁוּטִיתָא דְּתַעֲנִיתָא וַעֲרָבְתָא דְיוֹמָא שְׁבִיעָיָא. וְרַבָּנִין דְּקֵיסָרִין אֱמְרִין אַף
הָדָא מִקְזְתָא.

Rebbi Johanan said to Rebbi Hiyya bar Abba: Babylonian, two things
came from you, prostrating oneself on fast days[56] and the willow of the
seventh day[57]. The rabbis of Caesarea say, and the moving[58].

56   On fast days, the silent prayer
after the *Amidah* was said lying on the
floor (*Avoda zarah* 4:1, fol. 43d). In the
parallel in *Avodah zarah* it is added
that in prostrating oneself outside the
Temple one may not have one's face
downward but must turn it sideways.
From the Yerushalmi it seems that the
Sephardic custom to prostrate oneself
only on Yom Kippur is the original one;
the Ashkenazic custom which permits
prostrating also on New Year's Day is
secondary.

57   On the seventh day of Tabernacles, one uses willow twigs in the
prayers for winter rains. In Babli
Sukkah 44a, R. Johanan states that this
is a Babylonian custom, instituted by

the prophets of the exile, in
remembrance of the procession in the
Temple around the altar surrounded by
willow twigs.

58   According to J. Levy, the word
is derived from קזז "to push aside, to
move". The commentaries take the
word to be derived from מקיז "to
bleed". Bleeding was no Babylonian
medical specialty and Levy's interpretation is supported by the text in *Sukkah*
which adds that in computing the
calendar one may move New Year's
Day to protect the ceremony of the
willow (which is impossible on a
Sabbath) in preference to enabling the
blowing of the *shofar* on New Year's
day.

תַּנֵּי נְטִיעָה מֵעֵין עֶשֶׂר וּזְקֵינָה מֵעֵין שָׁלֹשׁ. אָתָא חֲמֵי נְטִיעָה שֶׁהִיא נִרְאֵית
כִּזְקֵינָה אַתְּ נוֹתֵן לָהּ כִּזְקֵינָה וְאַתְּ אָמַר נְטִיעָה מֵעֵין עֶשֶׂר. אָמַר רִבִּי חוּנָה מַהוּ
מֵעֵין עֶשֶׂר שֶׁאֵין נְטִיעָה מֵעֵין שָׁלֹשׁ. שֶׁלֹּא תֹאמַר שָׁלֹשׁ נְטִיעוֹת שֶׁהֵן עוֹשׂוֹת
כְּעֶשֶׂר שֶׁאֵינָן עוֹשׂוֹת. וְדִכְוָותָהּ שָׁלֹשׁ זְקֵינוֹת שֶׁהֵן עוֹשׂוֹת כְּעֶשֶׂר שֶׁאֵינָן עוֹשׂוֹת
לְפוּם כֵּן צָרִיךְ מֵימַר נְטִיעָה מֵעֵין עֶשֶׂר.

It was stated[59]: "A sapling by the rule of ten and an old tree by the rule of three." Come and see, a sapling appearing like an old tree[60] you consider as an old tree; and you say a sapling by the rule of ten? Rebbi Ḥuna said, what means "by the rule of ten"? That a sapling does not follow the rule of three[61]. That you should not say, three producing saplings are like ten non-producing ones[62] and, similarly, three producing old ones[63] are like ten non-producing ones. Therefore, it is necessary to say: "A sapling by the rule of ten."

59   Tosephta *Ševi'it* 1:2: "An old tree appearing like a sapling is a sapling, a sapling appearing like an old tree is an old tree. What is the difference between a sapling and an old tree? An old tree until Pentecost, a sapling until the New Year. An old tree by the rule of three, a sapling by the rule of ten." An old tree looking like a sapling is one which was cut down and now new growth rises from the stump. The rule of three is one requiring a talent of yield, the rule of ten requires ten saplings on a *bet seah* but no yield at all.

60   A sapling yielding a third of a

talent of fruit.

61   The next sentence explains what is meant.

62   That one may plough the *bet seah* until New Year's Day following the rule of saplings.

63   These "old ones" are the saplings producing adult yield; one should not say that since the entire *bet seah* may be ploughed because of these three, one applies to them the leniencies of old trees (3 trees per *bet seah*) and saplings (ploughing until New Year's day.) Explanation of this paragraph follows R. Eliahu Fulda and R. Saul Lieberman.

שָׂדֶה קָנִים נִידּוֹנוֹת כִּשְׂדֶה תְבוּאָה. רִבִּי אַבָּהוּ בְשֵׁם רִבִּי יוֹסֵה בַּר חֲנִינָה בְסָאתִים שָׁנוּ.

"A field of reeds is judged[64] like a field of grain[65]." Rebbi Abbahu in the name of Rebbi Yose ben Ḥanina: This was taught about dispersed ones[66].

64   Probably one should read נידונית instead of נידונות

65   In Tosephta 1:2: "A field of reeds is judged like saplings." For reeds grown as commercial crops, cf. *Demay* Chapter 6, Notes 100-101. R. Abbahu has to explain the difference between the *baraita* quoted in the text and the Tosephta by restricting the *baraita* to a very special case. Fields of grain can be ploughed only until Passover (Mishnah 2:1).

66   The translation (and the vocalization of סאתים) are offered tentatively. The classical commentators read סָאתַיִם "two seah" which they take unidiomatically to mean "two *batte seah*" and give widely divergent interpretations, none of which is convincing. R. S. Lieberman recognized that סאתים must describe some special kind of reeds used commercially; R. Abbahu recognizes that in general reeds follow the rules of the Tosephta. Lieberman tentatively suggests to derive the word from Syriac סתא, סאתא "vine, stem, branch" (Payne-Smith p. 2754). I am suggesting, equally tentatively, to derive the word from Arabic שת, שתא "to be dispersed, strewn about", meaning that the reeds in question do not grow tightly packed.

לֵית הָדָא פְלִינָא עַל שְׁמוּאֵל (fol. 33c) דִּשְׁמוּאֵל אָמַר בַּעֲשׂוּיִין שׁוּרָה. תַּמָּן עַל יְדֵי שֶׁהֵן מְפוּזָרוֹת בְּתוֹךְ בֵּית סָאָה אַתְּ רוֹאֶה אוֹתָהּ כְּאִילוּ מְלֵיאָה בְּרַם הָכָא כּוּלָן נְתוּנִים בְּמָקוֹם אֶחָד.

Does this not contradict Samuel, since Samuel said, even when they form a line[67]. There, since they are dispersed in a *bet seah* you consider it as if it were full, but here they are all at one place.

67   In Halakhah 2 (Note 20), Samuel declares that three trees free the entire *bet seah* if they are planted in a straight line. In Mishnah 7, ten saplings in a straight line do not free the entire *bet seah* but only four cubits around them. It was shown in Halakhah 2 that the rule of Samuel applies only if the trees are planted in the middle of the field and one has half a *bet seah* on each side. It is now asserted that Mishnah 7 presupposes that the saplings are not planted in a regular pattern.

(fol. 33a) **משנה ח**: הַנְּטִיעוֹת וְהַדִּילוּעִין מִצְטָרְפִין לְתוֹךְ בֵּית סְאָה. רַבָּן שִׁמְעוֹן בֶּן גַּמְלִיאֵל אוֹמֵר עֲשָׂרָה דִּילוּעִין לְתוֹךְ בֵּית סְאָה חוֹרְשִׁין כָּל־בֵּית סְאָה עַד רֹאשׁ הַשָּׁנָה.

Mishnah 8: Saplings and gourds go together in a *bet seah*. Rabban Gamliel says, if there are ten gourds in a *bet seah*, one ploughs the entire *bet seah* until New Year's Day.

(fol. 33c) **הלכה ח**: הַנְּטִיעוֹת וְהַדִּילוּעִין כו'. וְהֵן שֶׁיְּהוּ נְטִיעוֹת רָבוֹת עַל דִּילוּעִין. רִבִּי חֲנַנְיָה בְּרֵיהּ דְּרִבִּי הֶלֵּל בָּעֵי לֹא מִסְתַּבְּרָא בִּדְלַעַת יְוָנִית. הָתִיב רִבִּי מָנָא וְהָתַגֵּי שְׁלֹשָׁה קִישׁוּאִין וּשְׁלֹשָׁה דִּילוּעִין וְאַרְבַּע נְטִיעוֹת מִצְטָרְפִין וְחוֹרְשִׁין כָּל־בֵּית סְאָה בִּשְׁבִילָן. לָא אַתְיָא דְּלָא עַל סֵיפָא רַבָּן שִׁמְעוֹן בֶּן גַּמְלִיאֵל אוֹמֵר עֲשָׂרָה דִּילוּעִין לְבֵית סְאָה חוֹרְשִׁין כָּל־בֵּית סְאָה עַד רֹאשׁ הַשָּׁנָה עָלֶיהָ. רִבִּי חֲנַנְיָה בְּרֵיהּ דְּרִבִּי הֶלֵּל בָּעֵי לֹא מִסְתַּבְּרָא בִּדְלַעַת יְוָנִית.

Halakhah 8: "Saplings and gourds, etc." That is only if there are more saplings than gourds[68]. Rebbi Ḥananiah ben Rebbi Hillel[69] asked, is that not reasonable only for Greek gourd? Rebbi Mana objected, did we not state[70]: "Three green melons, three gourds, and four saplings go together

and one ploughs the entire *bet seah* because of them." It fits only for the
last sentence: Rabban Gamliel says, if there are ten gourds in a *bet seah*,
one ploughs the entire *bet seah* until New Year's Day. Rebbi Ḥananiah
ben Rebbi Hillel asked, is that not reasonable only for Greek gourd[71]?

68   For the anonymous Tanna,
against Rabban Gamliel.
69   Galilean Amora of the fifth
generation, a student of R. Mana's
father R. Jonah.
70   A similar statement in Tosephta
Ševi'it 1:2. For "green melon" (in modern Hebrew: "zucchini") and "Greek

gourd", cf. *Kilaim* 1:2 (Notes 38,59).
Greek gourd is described as needing
the most space among all gourd
varieties.
71   For other varieties, Rabban
Gamliel will not disagree with the
anonymous Tanna.

(fol. 33a) **משנה ט**: עַד אֵימָתַי נִקְרְאוּ נְטִיעוֹת רִבִּי לֶעְזָר בֶּן עֲזַרְיָה אוֹמֵר עַד
שֶׁיָּחוֹלוּ. רִבִּי יְהוֹשֻעַ אוֹמֵר שֶׁבַע שָׁנִים. רִבִּי עֲקִיבָה אוֹמֵר בְּאִילָן נְטִיעָה כִשְׁמָהּ.
אִילָן שֶׁנִּגְמַם וְהוֹצִיא חֲלִיפִין מִטֶּפַח וּלְמַטָּן כִּנְטִיעָה מִטֶּפַח וּלְמַעֲלָן כְּאִילָן דִּבְרֵי
רִבִּי שִׁמְעוֹן.

Mishnah 9: How long are they called saplings? Rebbi Eleazar ben
Azariah said, until they become profane. Rebbi Joshua said, seven years.
Rebbi Aqiba said, tree saplings when they are called so. A tree which was
cut down and grows anew, if it was cut lower than one hand-breadth it is
like a sapling, higher than a hand-breadth it is a tree, the words of Rebbi
Simeon.

(fol. 33c) **הלכה ט**: עַד אֵימָתַי נִקְרְאוּ נְטִיעוֹת כו'. מַהוּ עַד שֶׁיָּחוֹלוּ עַד שֶׁיִּפָּדוּ
אוֹ עַד שֶׁיֵּעָשׂוּ חוּלִין מֵאֵילֵיהֶן. רִבִּי אַבָּא בַּר יַעֲקֹב בְּשֵׁם רִבִּי יוֹחָנָן כֵּינִי

מַתְנִיתָא עַד שֶׁיֵּעָשׂוּ חוּלִין מֵאֲלֵיהֶן. אָמַר רִבִּי יוּדָן מַתְנִיתָא מְסַייְעָא לְרִבִּי
יְהוֹשֻׁעַ אָמַר רִבִּי[72] אַף שֶׁאָמְרוּ בְּנוֹת חָמֵשׁ בְּנוֹת שֵׁשׁ בְּנוֹת שֶׁבַע אֶלָּא בִּגְפָנִים
בְּנוֹת חָמֵשׁ. בִּתְאֵינִים בְּנוֹת שֵׁשׁ. בְּזֵיתִים בְּנוֹת שֶׁבַע. וְאֲנָן חָמֵי מַרְבִּיתָא
דִתְאֵינְתָא אַתְיָא בְּפֵירֵי.[73] אָמַר רִבִּי יוּדָן כִּרְבִּי[74] טְרִיפָן לְעוּבְיָהּ.

Halakhah 9: "How long are they called saplings[75], etc." What means
"until they become profane"? Until they are redeemed[76] or until they
become profane by themselves. Rebbi Abba bar Jacob in the name of
Rebbi Joḥanan: The Mishnah means "until they become profane by
themselves[77]." Rebbi Yudan said, a *baraita* supports Rebbi Joshua:
"[78]Rebbi says, when they said five, six, or seven years old, for vines five
years old, for figs six years old, for olives seven years old." But do we not
see the growth of the fig tree come with fruits? Rebbi Yudan said,
according to Rebbi we throw it on its width[79].

72   Reading of the parallel, *Orlah*
1:3 (fol. 61a), here: ואתיא כרבי יהושע
כדתני רבי יושע אומר.

73   Reading of the parallel in *Orlah*,
instead of בפורי here.

74   Reading of the parallel in *Orlah*.
Venice: כד טריפן "when they are torn".

75   This is important both for the
Sabbatical year and *orlah* since around
trees one may plough until the New
Year but elsewhere only until 30 days
before the New Year, and years for
orlah are also counted from the New
Year.

76   A fruit tree is *orlah* for three

years, must be redeemed in the fourth,
and becomes fully profane in its fifth
year; cf. *Lev.* 19:24.

77   Only in this way can the
definition be consistent.

78   In Tosephta 1:2, R. Joshua says
"five, six, and seven years", and Rebbi
explains "five for vines, etc." In that
version, the comment of R. Yudan
would be superfluous. Hence, the text
here is from an independent *baraita*.

79   In growing olive trees, the
thickness of the stem counts, not the
bearing of fruit.

רְבִּי שִׁמְעוֹן וְרִבִּי לִיעֶזֶר בֶּן יַעֲקֹב שְׁנֵיהֶן אָמְרוּ דָּבָר אֶחָד דְּאָמַר רְבִּי שְׁמוּאֵל בַּר
נַחְמָן רִבִּי יוֹנָתָן בְּשֵׁם רְבִּי לִיעֶזֶר בֶּן יַעֲקֹב הַגּוֹמֵם אֶת כַּרְמוֹ פָּחוֹת מִטֶּפַח חַיָּיב
בְּעָרְלָה מִפְּנֵי מַרְאִית הָעַיִן דִּבְרֵי חֲכָמִים עַד שֶׁיְּגוֹם מֵעם הָאָרֶץ.

Rebbi Simeon and Rebbi Eliezer ben Jacob said the same thing since
Rebbi Samuel bar Naḥman, Rebbi Jonathan, said in the name of Rebbi
Eliezer ben Jacob[80]: He who prunes his vineyard down to less than a
hand-breadth is subject to the rules of *orlah* because of the bad
appearance. The Sages say, only if he prunes down to the ground.

80   *Kilaim* 6:2, Note 23. Since R.
Eliezer ben Jacob states that a trunk
sticking out from the ground less than
a hand-breadth is forbidden as *orlah*
only by rabbinic decree, it follows that
R. Simeon in the Mishnah also treats
the prohibition of ploughing before the
Sabbatical year as rabbinic. Otherwise,
he and R. Eliezer ben Jacob would not
say the same thing.

(fol. 33c) **משנה א:** עַד אֵימָתַי חוֹרְשִׁין שְׂדֵה הַלָּבָן עֶרֶב שְׁבִיעִית מִשֶּׁתִּיכְלֶה הַלֵּיחָה כָּל־זְמָן שֶׁבְּנֵי אָדָם חוֹרְשִׁין לִיטַע מִקְשָׁאוֹת וּמִדְלָעוֹת. אָמַר רְבִּי שִׁמְעוֹן נָתַתָּ תוֹרַת כָּל־אֶחָד וְאֶחָד בְּיָדוֹ. אֶלָּא בִשְׂדֵה הַלָּבָן עַד הַפֶּסַח וּבְשְׂדֵה הָאִילָן עַד הָעֲצֶרֶת.

Mishnah 1: Until when may one plough a shadeless[1] field in the year preceding the Sabbatical? After the humidity stops[2], as long as people plough to plant melon and gourd fields. Rebbi Simeon said, you put the instruction for every individual in his own hand! But a shadeless field until Passover, a field with trees until Pentecost[3].

1   "White field", bright in the sunshine.

2   After the surface of the unirrigated field becomes dry after the spring rains. An irrigated field may be ploughed until the New Year, as explained in Mishnah 2. The reading משתיכלה is that of the Yerushalmi Mishnah (ed. Low) and of the Leyden ms.; the Babylonian Mishnah, Rome ms., and a Genizah fragment of the Yerushalmi read עד שתיכלה "until it stops". Since the operative sentence is the following, "as long as people plough to plant melon and gourd fields", the difference is purely stylistic.

3   The opinion of the House of Hillel in Mishnah 1:1.

הלכה א: עַד אֵימָתַי חוֹרְשִׁין כו'. מָאן תַּנָּא לְחָה רְבִּי מֵאִיר הִיא. וְרְבִּי מֵאִיר כְּבֵית שַׁמַּאי וְרְבִּי שִׁמְעוֹן כְּבֵית הַלֵּל. וְכֵן אֲתִינָן מַתְנִיתָא רְבִּי מֵאִיר כְּבֵית שַׁמַּאי וְרְבִּי שִׁמְעוֹן כְּבֵית הַלֵּל. אֶלָּא רְבִּי מֵאִיר כְּמִשְׁנָה רִאשׁוֹנָה. וְרְבִּי שִׁמְעוֹן

כְּמִשְׁנָה אַחֲרוֹנָה. וְכֵן אֲתִינָן מַתְנִיתָא רבִּי מֵאִיר כְּמִשְׁנָה הָרִאשׁוֹנָה וְרבִּי שִׁמְעוֹן
כְּמִשְׁנָה אַחֲרוֹנָה. אֶלָּא רבִּי מֵאִיר שְׁנָיָיה מַחֲלוֹקֶת וְרבִּי שִׁמְעוֹן שְׁנָיָיה כְּדִבְרֵי
הַכֹּל. הֲוֵי מָאן תַּנָּא עַד אֵימָתַי חוֹרְשִׁין שְׂדֵה הַלָּבָן עֶרֶב שְׁבִיעִית רבִּי מֵאִיר.
בְּרַם כְּרבִּי שִׁמְעוֹן דִּבְרֵי הַכֹּל עַד הָעַצֶּרֶת.

Halakhah 1: "Until when may one plough," etc. Who is the Tanna who considers humidity? He is Rebbi Meïr[4]. Then Rebbi Meïr follows the House of Shammai and Rebbi Simeon the House of Hillel. Could we conclude that in our Mishnah Rebbi Meïr follows the House of Shammai and Rebbi Simeon the House of Hillel[5]? It must be that Rebbi Meïr follows the first Mishnah and Rebbi Simeon the later Mishnah[6]. Could we conclude that in our Mishnah Rebbi Meïr follows the first Mishnah and Rebbi Simeon the later Mishnah[7]? But for Rebbi Meïr it is taught as a disagreement[8] and for Rebbi Simeon it is the opinion of everybody. Hence, the author of "until when may one plough a shadeless field in the year preceding the Sabbatical" is Rebbi Meïr, but following Rebbi Simeon everybody agrees to "until Pentecost."

4   An anonymous Mishnah is supposed to be R. Meïr's unless proven to have a different author. The Mishnah makes ploughing dependent on the state of the field; in Mishnah 1:1 the House of Shammai permit ploughing according to the individual circumstances of every orchard.

5   Since practice has to follow the House of Hillel, R. Meïr's opinion is to be superseded by that of R. Simeon. The Yerushalmi holds that R. Simeon is

a higher authority than R. Meïr if R. Meïr is mentioned by name (cf. below, Halakhah 8:7); cf. also *Demay* Chapter 5, Notes 117-120.

6   The previous answer is unsatisfactory. If Rebbi wanted to indicate that practice does not follow R. Meïr, he would not formulate his as the anonymous (operative) opinion. Hence, while practice follows R. Simeon, we have to assume that practice will follow R. Meïr if the two periods

before the Sabbatical year, abolished by Rabban Gamliel, will be re-instituted.

7   There would be an internal inconsistency in the Mishnah; the two authors would then talk about two different subjects and the formulation as a disagreement would be wrong.

8   There is a disagreement in the interpretation of the House of Hillel

for shadeless fields if it rains after Passover, when the House of Hillel will permit continued ploughing, while for R. Simeon the stated limits are absolute. In this interpretation, the opinion of the House of Shammai is disregarded, and the later statement "following R. Simeon everybody agrees to 'until Pentecost'" is shorthand for the entire statement of R. Simeon in the Mishnah.

לֹא סוֹף דָּבָר בְּשֶׁיֵּשׁ בּוֹ מִקְשָׁה וּמוֹדְלָה אֶלָּא אֲפִילוּ מֵאַחַר שֶׁבְּנֵי אָדָם עֲתִידִין לִיטַע בַּמִּקְשָׁיוֹת וּבַמְדְלָעוֹת מוּתָּר.

Not only a field planted with melons and gourds but even when people intend to plant melons and gourds in the future it is permitted[9].

9   This text is redundant with the Mishnah text given here (and in the Leyden ms. as well as the Munich ms. of the Babli.) It refers to the Mishnah text in most of the remaining mss: "as

long as people plough to plant *in* melon and gourd fields." Then it is stated that the field does not have to be a melon or gourd field at the time of ploughing.

(fol. 33d) אָמַר רִבִּי שִׁמְעוֹן נָתַתָּ תּוֹרַת כָּל־אֶחָד וְאֶחָד בְּיָדוֹ. זֶה אוֹמֵר כָּלָה לֵחָה שֶׁלִּי וְזֶה אוֹמֵר לֹא כָלָה לֵחָה שֶׁלִּי. אֶלָּא בִּשְׂדֵה הַלָּבָן עַד הַפֶּסַח וּבִשְׂדֵה הָאִילָן עַד הָעֲצֶרֶת.

"Rebbi Simeon said, you put the instruction for every individual in his own hand!" One will say, the moisture of my field is gone; the other one will say, the moisture of my field is not yet gone. "But a shadeless field until Passover, a field with trees until Pentecost."

מַה בֵּין שְׂדֵה הַלָּבָן לִשְׂדֵה הָאִילָן. שְׂדֵה הַלָּבָן עַל יְדֵי שֶׁהִיא עָתִיד לְזוֹרְעָהּ
בַּתְּחִילָה צָרִיךְ שֶׁתְּהֵא הַלֵּחָה קַיֶּמֶת אֲבָל שְׂדֵה הָאִילָן עַל יְדֵי שֶׁהִיא נְטוּעָה
מִכְּבָר אֵינוֹ צָרִיךְ שֶׁתְּהֵא הַלֵּחָה קַיֶּמֶת.

What explains the difference[10] between a shadeless field and an orchard? Since a shadeless field will be newly sown it needs existing superficial moisture but an orchard which already is planted does not need superficial moisture.

10   The difference in rules applying to the different kinds of fields.

(fol. 33c) **משנה ב:** מְזַבְּלִין וּמְעַדְּרִין בְּמִקְשָׁאוֹת וּבְמִדְלָאוֹת עַד רֹאשׁ הַשָּׁנָה. וְכֵן
בְּבֵית הַשַּׁלְחִין. מְיַבְּלִין[11] וּמְפָרְקִים וּמְאַבְּקִין וּמְעַשְּׁנִין עַד רֹאשׁ הַשָּׁנָה. רִבִּי
שִׁמְעוֹן אוֹמֵר אַף נוֹטֵל הוּא אֶת הֶעָלֶה מִן הָאֶשְׁכּוֹל בַּשְּׁבִיעִית.

Mishnah 2: One fertilizes and hoes in melon and gourd fields until the New Year; the same applies to irrigated fields. One trims, removes[12], dusts, and smokes until the New Year. Rebbi Simeon said, one may even remove a leaf from a bunch in the Sabbatical year.

11   Reading of most Mishnah mss., the Yerushalmi from the Genizah and the Rome ms.; Leyden ms. and Munich ms. of the Babli: מזבלים. However, in the Halakhah the Leyden ms. also has מיבלים (as a correction.)

12   The leaves, as explained in the Halakhah. According to Maimonides, R. Simeon permits this particular activity also in the Sabbatical year. However, it seems that R. Simeon permits only the removal of leaves from bunches of grapes if otherwise the grapes would rot; see the Halakhah.

(fol. 33d) **הלכה ב:** מְזַבְּלִין וּמְעַדְּרִין בְּמִקְשָׁאוֹת כו'. מַהוּ לַחֲרוֹשׁ לָהֶם. תַּנֵּי

כָּל־זְמָן שֶׁאַתְּ מוּתָּר לַחֲרוֹשׁ אַתְּ מוּתָּר לְזַבֵּל וּלְעַדֵּר אִם אֵין אַתְּ מוּתָּר לַחֲרוֹשׁ

אֵין אַתְּ מוּתָּר לֹא לְזַבֵּל וְלֹא לְעַדֵּר. אָמַר רִבִּי יוֹסָה וּמַתְנִיתָא אֲמָרָה כֵן

מְזַבְּלִין וּמְעַדְּרִין בְּמִקְשָׁיוֹת וּבְמִדְלָאוֹת עַד רֹאשׁ הַשָּׁנָה וְכֵן בְּבֵית הַשַּׁלְחִין. וְתַנֵּי

עָלָהּ חוֹרְשִׁין בֵּית הַשַּׁלְחִין עַד רֹאשׁ הַשָּׁנָה. רִבִּי אוֹמֵר עַד לִפְנֵי רֹאשׁ הַשָּׁנָה

שְׁלֹשָׁה יָמִים כְּדֵי שֶׁיִּזְרַע וְיַשְׁרֵשׁ וְיִטַּע וְיַשְׁרֵשׁ. וְאִלּוּ עוֹשֶׂה שָׁרָשִׁים לִשְׁלֹשָׁה

יָמִים. רִבִּי אוֹמֵר עַד לִפְנֵי רֹאשׁ הַשָּׁנָה שְׁלֹשָׁה חֳדָשִׁים כְּדֵי שֶׁיִּזְרַע אוֹרֶז וְיַשְׁרִישׁ

וְיִטַּע אוֹרֶז וְיַשְׁרִישׁ.

Halakhah 2: "One gives manure and one hoes in melon fields", etc. May one plough for these[13]? It was stated: "As long as one may plough one may fertilize and hoe; if one may not plough then one may neither fertilize nor hoe." Rebbi Yose said, the Mishnah implies this: "One fertilizes and hoes in melon and gourd fields until the New Year; the same applies to irrigated fields," and we have stated on this[14]: "One ploughs irrigated fields until the New Year; Rebbi says until three days before the New Year so that one may sow and it starts to form roots, or one plants and it starts to form roots." If it would grow roots in three days! "Rebbi says, until three months before the New Year so that one may sow rice, have it form roots, transplant it and have the roots take hold.[15]"

13 Plough the manure under; otherwise the fertilizer would not be effective.

14 Tosephta 1:12: "One ploughs an irrigated field and irrigates them [the plants growing there] 30 days before the New Year. Rebbi says, until [Vienna ms. thirty days] [Erfurt ms. and printed text: three days] before the New Year, so that one may sow and it starts to form roots, or one plants and it starts to form roots." The first hand of the Leyden ms. has only the quote of the Mishnah and the reformulated statement of Rebbi. R. S. Lieberman (*Tosefta ki-fshutah Zeraïm* p. 494)

wants to prove from this that the
reading "three days" is found only in
the corrector's text, but this is
contradicted by the majority of the
Tosephta sources. The "30 days"

reading in the Tosephta is unsub-
stantiated.
15   Since rice usually is trans-
planted, this corrected version makes
more sense.

מְיַבְּלִין מַעֲבִירִין אֶת הַיִּבוֹלֶת. מְפָרְקִין בְּעָלִין. מְאַבְּקִין עוֹשֶׂה לָהּ אָבָק.
מְעַשְּׁנִין מַתְנִינָן לָהּ תַּנֵּי מְכַוְּנִין מְצַדְּדִין מְכַוְּנִין לָהּ מְצַדְּדִין. חֲבֵרַיָּיא אָמְרֵי
עוֹשֶׂה לָהּ דִּיקְרָן. רִבִּי יוֹסָה אוֹמֵר תּוֹלֶה לָהּ אָבֶן.

One trims to remove outgrowths[16]. One removes leaves. One dusts,
puts dust over it. One smokes, one makes smoke under it. It was stated[17]:
"One straightens them, one makes them grow sidewise." One straightens
for it. One makes it grow sidewise: The colleagues say, one makes a
forked support for it; Rebbi Yose says, one weighs it down by a stone.

16   The technical terms used in the
Mishnah are explained. All the terms
refer to trees, not to sown plants.
17   A Tosephta (1:11) also uses the
term מצדדין. It seems that מכוונין refers
to training fruit trees on an espalier.
The translation of מצדדין as "make it
grow sidewise" is adequate only for the
explanation of R. Yose, that one weighs

the branches down so they cannot grow
upwards. In the interpretation of the
colleagues, one supports branches
growing sideways by putting forked
supports (cf. *Kilaim* Chapter 4, Note
60) under branches heavy with fruit.
The disagreement shows that the
expression was no longer in use in
Amoraic times.

תַּנֵּי מְווַתְּרִין וּמְשַׁמְּטִין כֵּינִי מַתְנִיתָא מְווַתְּרִין בַּגְּפָנִים וּמְשַׁמְּטִין בַּקָּנִים. מָקוֹם
שֶׁנָּהֲגוּ לְווַתֵּר וּלְשַׁמֵּט קוֹדֶם לְחָג מְווַתְּרִין וּמְשַׁמְּטִין קוֹדֶם לְחָג. לְאַחַר הֶחָג
מְווַתְּרִין וּמְשַׁמְּטִין לְאַחַר הֶחָג. רִבִּי שִׁמְעוֹן אוֹמֵר וּבִלְבַד מִן הַבִּקְעָה וּלְמַעֲלָה.

It was stated[18]: "One strings and spreads." So is the *baraita*: One
strings vines and spreads them on the poles. "At a place where one

usually[19] strings and spreads before Sukkot one strings and spreads before Sukkot; after Sukkot, one strings and spreads after Sukkot. Rebbi Simeon says, only higher than the notch[20]."

18   Tosephta 1:7. Since the text deals with the care of trees, it is impossible to derive the verbs from Rabbinic Hebrew וחר "to be indulgent, forgo one's rights" , שמט "to loosen, cause release" or Biblical Hebrew שמט "to renounce". One has to derive the first term from Arabic וחר (Hebrew יחר) "to string, stretch, draw tight" (the branches of the vine on the espaliers) which somehow may be connected with יחר "to increase, make more bountiful" (also found in Accadic). The verb שמט in classical Arabic means "to spread out the foliage (of a tree)". There is an Arabic technical term מסמט "vine prop" fitting the context. [R. S. Lieberman (*Tosefta ki-fshutah* p. 490) wants to explain (from rabbinic Hebrew) that one slips the vines off the supporting poles. The derivation from the Arabic technical term seems preferable.]

19   In non-Sabbatical years. Any work belonging to the produce of the sixth year is permitted if it is customary.

20   It is difficult to see what kind of stringing or propping up could be done lower than the first notch from which the stem branches out.

רִבִּי יִרְמְיָה בְּשֵׁם רִבִּי הוֹשַׁעְיָא רִבִּי יַעֲקֹב בַּר אָחָא רִבִּי יוֹסֵי בַּר חֲנִינָא בְּשֵׁם רִבִּי חָמָא אֲבוֹי דְּרִבִּי הוֹשַׁעְיָה נוֹטֵל אֶת הַקָּבוּצִין עִמָּהּ.   רִבִּי שִׁמְעוֹן אוֹמֵר אַף נוֹטֵל הוּא אֶת הֶעָלִין מִן הָאֶשְׁכּוֹל בַּשְּׁבִיעִית.   מָחְלְפָה שִׁיטָתֵיהּ דְּרִבִּי שִׁמְעוֹן תַּנִּינָן תַּמָּן מְמָרְסִין אֶת הָאוֹרֶז בַּשְּׁבִיעִית דִּבְרֵי רִבִּי שִׁמְעוֹן אֲבָל לֹא מְכַסְּחִין.   וְכָא הוּא אָמַר אָכֵין.   שַׁנְיָיא הִיא הָכָא שֶׁהוּא כְּמַצִּיל מִן הַדְּלֵיקָה.

Rebbi Jeremiah in the name of Rebbi Hoshaia, Rebbi Jacob bar Aḥa, Rebbi Yose bar Ḥanina in the name of Rebbi Ḥama, father of Rebbi Hoshaia: He takes all accumulations with it[21]. "Rebbi Simeon said, one may even remove a leaf from a bunch in the Sabbatical year." The position of Rebbi Simeon is inverted: We have stated there (Mishnah

2:10): "One may tear off[22] rice in the Sabbatical year; the words of Rebbi Simeon are that one may not trim[23]." And here, he says so? There is a difference here, he is like one who saves from a fire[24].

21   This refers to the statement of R. Simeon in the Mishnah, quoted in the next sentence. When one removes leaves to expose the grape bunches, he may also remove anything needed to be removed, even other bunches, and is not guilty of harvesting for his own use in the Sabbatical year.

22   This follows R. Y. Qafeḥ in his translation of Maimonides's Mishnah Commentary; he notes that Maimonides's Arabic expression מרס may mean (1) "to macerate in water" and (2) "to tear off in irregular fashion, mutilate"; in the dictionaries (2) is given as translation of מרש. All halakhic commentaries (R. Simson, R. Isaac Simponti, and the commentators to Maimonides's *Šemiṭṭah weYovel* 1:15) give the root the meaning "to water"; this does not fit the sense of Rabbinic ממרס which elsewhere means either (1) "to stir" or (2) "to crush, quash". Arabic and Hebrew meanings (2) may be supported by Accadic *marašu* "to get into bad shape".

23   In his translation of Maimonides's Mishnah Commentary, Alḥarizi translates כסח as "to hoe".

24   He is only permitted to remove the leaves if otherwise the bunches would be ruined, not as regular tending.

(fol. 33c) **משנה ג**: מְסַקְּלִין עַד רֹאשׁ הַשָּׁנָה. מְקָרְסְמִין מְזָרְדִין וּמְפַסְּלִין עַד רֹאשׁ הַשָּׁנָה. רִבִּי יְהוֹשֻׁעַ אוֹמֵר כְּזֵירוּדָהּ וּכְפִיסוּלָהּ שֶׁל חֲמִישִׁית כֵּן שֶׁל שִׁשִּׁית. רִבִּי שִׁמְעוֹן אוֹמֵר כָּל זְמָן שֶׁאֲנִי רַשַּׁאי בַּעֲבוֹדַת הָאִילָן אֲנִי רַשַּׁאי בְּפִיסּוּלוֹ.

Mishnah 3: One may remove stones[25] until the New Year. One cuts[26], prunes, and shapes until the New Year. Rebbi Joshua says, like the pruning and shaping of the fifth year[27], so is that of the sixth. Rebbi Simeon says, any time that I may work the tree I may shape it.

25   From his field.

26   Really "nibbles", in an unsyst-
ematic way. "Pruning" means eliminating unwanted new shoots, "shaping"

means eliminating dead wood.

27   When there are no time limits
on any agricultutal work.

(fol. 33d) **חלכה ג:** מְסַקְּלִין עַד רֹאשׁ הַשָּׁנָה כו'. תַּמָּן תַּנִּינָן הַמְּסַקֵּל נוֹטֵל אֶת
הָעֶלְיוֹנוֹת וּמֵנִיחַ אֶת הַנּוֹגְעוֹת בָּאָרֶץ. וְכָא אַתְּ אָמַר הָכֵין. אָמַר רבִּי יוֹנָה כָּאן
בְּתָלוּשׁ כָּאן בִּמְחוּבָּר.

Halakhah 3: "One may remove stones until the New Year", etc. There,
we have stated[28]: "He who removes stones takes the upper ones and
leaves those lying on the ground." And here you say so? Rebbi Jonah
said, there when they are loose, here when they are connected to the
ground.

28   Mishnah 3:7, dealing with work
permitted during the Sabbatical year.
If one may remove stones during the
Sabbatical year, there seems to be no

reason why removing the stones should
be restricted to the time before the
New Year.

אָמַר רבִּי יוֹסֵי הֲוֵינָן סָבְרִין מֵימַר דְּרבִּי שִׁמְעוֹן כְּרבִּי יְהוֹשֻׁעַ בְּקִירְסוֹם דְּאִינּוּן
תְּרֵין תַּנָּאִין מְסַקְּלִין עַד רֹאשׁ הַשָּׁנָה מְקַרְסְמִין מְזָרְדִין וּמְפַסְּלִין עַד רֹאשׁ הַשָּׁנָה
כְּרַבָּנָן. רבִּי יְהוֹשֻׁעַ אוֹמֵר כְּזֵירוּדָה וּכְפִיסּוּלָה שֶׁל חֲמִישִׁית כֵּן שֶׁל שִׁשִּׁית. הֲוֵי
תְּלָתָה תַנָּאִין אִינּוּן. מְסַקְּלִין עַד רֹאשׁ הַשָּׁנָה מְקַרְסְמִין מְזָרְדִין וּמְפַסְּלִין עַד
רֹאשׁ הַשָּׁנָה כְּרַבָּנָן. רבִּי יְהוֹשֻׁעַ אוֹמֵר כְּזֵירוּדָה וּכְפִיסּוּלָה שֶׁל חֲמִישִׁית כֵּן שֶׁל
שִׁשִּׁית אֲפִילוּ יוֹתֵר מִכֵּן. רבִּי שִׁמְעוֹן אוֹמֵר כָּל־זְמָן שֶׁאֲנִי רַשַּׁאי בַּעֲבוֹדַת הָאִילָן
אֲנִי רַשַּׁאי בְּפִיסּוּלוֹ עַד הָעֲצֶרֶת.

Rebbi Yose said, we were of the opinion to say that Rebbi Simeon holds
with Rebbi Joshua in cutting, that there are two tannaïtic positions: "One
may remove stones until the New Year, one cuts, prunes, and shapes until

the New Year" following the rabbis. "Rebbi Joshua says, like the pruning
and shaping of the fifth year, so is that of the sixth." But there are three
Tannaïm. "One may remove stones until the New Year, one cuts, prunes,
and shapes until the New Year" following the rabbis. "Rebbi Joshua says,
like the pruning and shaping of the fifth year, so is that of the sixth," even
after that. "Rebbi Simeon says, any time that I may work the tree I may
shape it," until Pentecost.

(fol. 33c) **משנה ד:** מְזַהֲמִין אֶת הַנְּטִיעוֹת וְכוֹרְכִין אוֹתָן וְקוֹטְמִין אוֹתָן וְעוֹשִׂין
לָהֶן בָּתִּים וּמַשְׁקִין אוֹתָן עַד רֹאשׁ הַשָּׁנָה. רִבִּי לָעְזָר בֵּי רִבִּי צָדוֹק אוֹמֵר אַף
מַשְׁקֶה הוּא אֶת הַנּוֹף בַּשְּׁבִיעִית אֲבָל לֹא אֶת הָעִיקָר.

Mishnah 4: One dirties[29] saplings, ties them[30], clips them, builds them
shelter, and waters them until the New Year. Rebbi Eleazar ben Rebbi
Zadoq says, one may water the leaves in the Sabbatical year but not the
stem.

29   One treats saplings with evil
smelling chemicals if necessary
(according to Maimonides, with a
mixture of meat sauce and vinegar, to
keep worms and insects away.) The

notion of "sapling" was defined in
Halakhah 1:9.
30   One ties the branches to the
stem.

(fol. 33d) **הלכה ד:** מְזַהֲמִין אֶת הַנְּטִיעוֹת כו'. מַתְנִיתָא דְּרִבִּי בְּרָם כְּרַבָּנִין
מְזַהֲמִין מִתַּלְּעִין בַּשְּׁבִיעִית אֲבָל לֹא בַּמּוֹעֵד. כָּאן וְכָאן אֵין מְנַזְּמִין אֲבָל נוֹטֵל
הוּא אֶת הָרוֹאֶה.

Halakhah 4: "One dirties saplings" etc. The Mishnah follows Rebbi, but according to the rabbis one dirties, one removes worms in the Sabbatical year but not on [the intermediate days of] holidays[31]. In neither case does one cup[32] but one may remove what one sees[33].

31   When all non-urgent agricultural work is forbidden, as detailed in Tractate *Mo'ed Qaṭan*.

32   This *baraita* is quoted in Babli *Avodah Zarah* 50b by R. Abba bar Jeremiah. Rashi explains there that "cupping" means cutting branches so as to create new notches from which multiple branches will sprout. The corresponding Arabic word is גזם "to

cut". A somewhat parallel version in the Tosephta (1:11), referring only to the Sabbatical year, has מגמזים by metathesis.

33   "Removing worms" means drilling into a tree to remove worms from inside the tree. This one may not do on a holiday but worms or moths visible from the outside may be removed.

רִבִּי יוֹסָה אָמַר רִבִּי אָבוּנָא בָּעֵי מַה בֵּין הַמְזַהֵם לָעוֹשֶׂה לָהּ בַּיִת. הַמְזַהֵם אֵינוֹ אֶלָּא כְּמוֹשִׁיב שׁוֹמֵר בַּיִת עוֹשֶׂה לָהּ צֵל וְהִיא גְדֵילָה מַחֲמָתָן.

Rebbi Yose said that Rebbi Abuna asked: What is the difference between dirtying and making a shelter[34]? Dirtying is like appointing a watchman, a shelter creates shadow [for the plant] and it grows because of that.

34   Why do the rabbis permit dirtying during the Sabbatical year but not building a shelter. Dirtying is a

prophylactic against damage but building a greenhouse around a plant helps in promoting growth.

תַּמָּן תַּנִּינָן הַמְבַקֵּעַ בַּזַּיִת לֹא יַחְפֶּה בֶּעָפָר אֲבָל מְכַסֶּה הוּא בָּאֲבָנִים וּבַקַּשׁ. רִבִּי יוֹנָה אָמַר רִבִּי אָבוּנָא בָּעֵי מַה בֵּין קַשִּׁין וּמַה בֵּין עָפָר. קַשִּׁין אֵינוֹ אֶלָּא כְּמוֹשִׁיב שׁוֹמֵר עָפָר עוֹשֶׂה לָהּ טִינָא וְהִיא גְדֵילָה מַחֲמָתוֹ.

There (Mishnah 4:5), we have stated: "He who breaks off [branches] from an olive tree should not cover with dust but he may cover with stones or straw." Rebbi Jonah said that Rebbi Abuna asked: What is the difference between straw and dust? Straw may only be compared to appointing a watchman, dust creates clay and [the plant] grows because of that.

תַּנֵּי רִבִּי יוֹסֵי בֶּן כּוֹפָר אָמַר מְשׁוּם רִבִּי לָעֶזֶר בֶּן שַׁמּוּעַ בֵּית שַׁמַּאי אוֹמְרִים מַשְׁקֶה עַל הַנּוֹף וְיוֹרֵד עַל הָעִיקָר וּבֵית הֶלֵּל אוֹמְרִים מַשְׁקֶה בֵּין עַל הַנּוֹף בֵּין עַל הָעִיקָר. דְּבֵית רִבִּי יַנַּאי מַשְׁקֶה בְּסַלָּא אָמַר רִבִּי יִצְחָק בַּר טְבֶלַיי מַשְׁקֶה בְּסַלָּא. אָמַר רִבִּי חִייָא בַּר בָּא רִבִּי יוּדָן בַּר גּוּרְייָא מַשְׁקֶה בְּסַלָּא וְעָדַר וְכִי מִתְכַּוֵּין לַעֲבוֹד הָאָרֶץ. בְּיוֹמֵי דְּרִבִּי חִייָא בַּר בָּא הֲווֹן מַשְׁקִין דִּיקְלַייָא בִּכְנִישְׁתָא חַדְתָא וְחָרְוָתָה.

It was stated[35]: "Rebbi Yose ben Kippar said in the name of Rebbi Eleazar ben Shammua' that the House of Shammai say, one waters the leaves and it trickles down to the root, but the House of Hillel say, one waters both on the leaves and on the root." In the House of Rebbi Yannai one watered with a basket[36]. Rebbi Isaac ben Tevele said, one waters with a basket. Rebbi Ḥiyya bar Abba: Rebbi Yudan bar Guria[37] watered with a basket and hoed. Did he intend to work the land? In the days of Rebbi Ḥiyya bar Abba they watered date palms with new brooms and dried branches.

35 Tosephta 1:5. There, the tradition is in the name of R. Eliezer, and the House of Hillel argue that either watering is permitted or it is forbidden; there can be no partial permission. Since R. Yose ben Kippar, Tanna of the fifth generation, was a student of R. Eleazar ben Shammua', the text here is the better one.

36 In order not to water in a

professional way.

37   An Amora mentioned only here,
in a disapproving way. He loosened
the earth around the stem so the water
should reach the root. It is objected

that this is professional tending of the
tree. If it is necessary to loosen the
earth around the stem, it should be
done in a non-professional way, using a
hard broom or dried branches.

(fol. 33c) **משנה ה**: סָכִין אֶת הַפַּגִּין וּמְנַקְּבִין אוֹתָן עַד רֹאשׁ הַשָּׁנָה. פַּגֵּי עֶרֶב
שְׁבִיעִית שֶׁנִּכְנְסוּ לַשְּׁבִיעִית וְשֶׁל שְׁבִיעִית שֶׁיָּצְאוּ לְמוֹצָאֵי שְׁבִיעִית לֹא סָכִין וְלֹא
מְנַקְּבִין אוֹתָן. רִבִּי יְהוּדָה אוֹמֵר מָקוֹם שֶׁנַּהֲגוּ לָסוּךְ אֵין סָכִין מִפְּנֵי שֶׁהִיא
עֲבוֹדָה מָקוֹם שֶׁלֹּא נָהֲגוּ לָסוּךְ סָכִין. רִבִּי שִׁמְעוֹן מַתִּיר בְּאִילָן מִפְּנֵי שֶׁהוּא
רַשָּׁאי בַּעֲבוֹדַת הָאִילָן.

Mishnah 5: One rubs unripe figs and pricks them until the New
Year[38]. One may not rub or prick unripe figs entering the Sabbatical
year, or those of the Sabbatical year leaving it. Rebbi Jehudah says, at a
place where people usually rub them, one may not rub them because that
is agricultural work, but in a place where one does not usually rub, he
may do so. Rebbi Simeon permits it for a tree since one may work a
tree[39].

38   Commentary of Maimonides:
"At some places here figs do not ripen
unless one takes a toothpick, rubs it
with oil, and uses it to prick each
single fruit." If a fig is still unripe
shortly before New Year's day, chances
are it would not ripen without human
intervention. In Babli *Avodah Zarah*

50b, the Mishnah is quoted in the form:
"One rubs unripe figs [with oil], pricks
and *fattens* them until the New Year".
All rubbing is done with olive oil.

39   Since R. Simeon in Mishnah 2
forbade all work on a tree after
Pentecost, his statement here can apply
only to a tree full of unripe figs at the

end of the Sabbatical year when one
may work on these fruits since they

never were edible in the Sabbatical
year.

(fol. 33d) **הלכה ח**: סָכִין אֶת הַפַּגִּין כו'. אֲנָן תַּנֵּינָן סָכִין אֶת הַפַּגִּין תַּנֵּיי דְּבֵי

רִבִּי וְאֵילוּ הֵן פַּגֵּי עֶרֶב שְׁבִיעִית שֶׁנִּכְנְסוּ לַשְׁבִיעִית. רִבִּי לֶעָזָר כְּמַתְנִיתִין רִבִּי

יוֹחָנָן כְּהָדָה דְּתַנֵּיי דְּבֵית רִבִּי. עַל דַּעְתֵּיהּ דְּרִבִּי לֶעָזָר לֹא בָא רִבִּי יוּדָה אֶלָּא

לְהָקֵל. עַל דַּעְתֵּיהּ דְּרִבִּי יוֹחָנָן לֹא בָא רִבִּי יוּדָה אֶלָּא לְהַחֲמִיר.

Halakhah 4: "One rubs unripe figs," etc. We have stated: "One rubs
unripe figs." In the House of Rebbi they stated[40]: "These are the unripe
figs from the year before the Sabbatical which enter the Sabbatical."
Rebbi Eleazar follows our Mishnah. Rebbi Johanan follows those who
stated in the House of Rebbi. In the opinion of Rebbi Eleazar, Rebbi
Jehudah comes only to make things easy[41]. In the opinion of Rebbi
Johanan, Rebbi Jehudah comes only to make things harder.

40　　　Tosephta 1:8. This Tosephta
cannot be the source of the Yerushalmi
since it does not mention the opinion of
the anonymous Tanna. The Tosephta
makes clear that, in its opinion, nobody
permits treating the unripe figs in the
year following the Sabbatical.

41　　　Since the anonymous Tanna
permits only until the New Year, R.

Jehudah permits where the anonymous
Tanna forbids. Since in the Tosephta,
the first Tanna is not mentioned but R.
Jehudah is mentioned by name, it
follows that for the Tosephta the unnamed majority will allow unrestricted
oiling of unripe figs left over from the
preceding year's harvest.

(fol. 33c) **משנה ו**: אֵין נוֹטְעִין וְאֵין מַבְרִיכִין וְאֵין מַרְכִּיבִין עֶרֶב שְׁבִיעִית פָּחוֹת

מִשְׁלֹשִׁים יוֹם לִפְנֵי רֹאשׁ הַשָּׁנָה וְאִם נָטַע אוֹ הִבְרִיךְ אוֹ הִרְכִּיב יַעֲקוֹר. רִבִּי

יְהוּדָה אוֹמֵר כָּל־הַרְכָּבָה שֶׁאֵינָהּ קוֹלֶטֶת לִשְׁלֹשָׁה יָמִים שׁוּב אֵינָה קוֹלֶטֶת. רְבִּי יוֹסֵי וְרִבִּי שִׁמְעוֹן אוֹמֵר לִשְׁתֵּי שַׁבָּתוֹת.

Mishnah 6: One does not plant, sink[42], or graft in the year preceding a Sabbatical year later than thirty days before the New Year; if he planted, sank, or grafted he has to uproot it. Rebbi Jehudah said, any graft that does not take hold within three days will never take hold[43]; Rebbi Yose and Rebbi Simeon say, within two weeks.

42   This was defined in Mishnah *Kilaim* 7:1, Note 1.

43   According to Rashi, in the opinion of the Babli (*Roš Haššanah* 10b) Rebbis Jehudah, Yose, and Simon are restrictive and require that the graft take hold thirty days before the New Year.   According to Rabbenu Tam, it is permitted to plant up to three days (or two weeks) before New Year's day.   Which opinion is supported by the Yerushalmi depends on the interpretation of the sources discussed above, Note 12.

(fol. 33d) **הלכה ו**: אֵין נוֹטְעִין וְאֵין מַרְכִּיבִין כו'. רִבִּי לְעָזָר בְּשֵׁם רִבִּי יוֹסֵי בַּר זִימְרָא מַתְנִיתָא בִּסְתָם הָא דָבָר בָּרִיא שֶׁחָרַשׁ מוּתָּר.

Halakhah 6: "One does not plant . . . or graft", etc. Rebbi Eleazar in the name of Rebbi Yose bar Zimra: Our Mishnah [deals with the] unadvertised [case][44], but if it is clear [e. g. when] he ploughed, it is permitted.

44   The prohibition of the Mishnah is not biblical but rabbinic, because people could think the planting, etc. was done during the Sabbatical year. If   it is made clear to everybody that the ground was prepared before New Year's day, one may plant until the New Year.

אֵין נוֹטְעִין וְאֵין מַבְרִיכִין וְאֵין מַרְכִּיבִין עֶרֶב שְׁבִיעִית פָּחוֹת מִשְׁלֹשִׁים יוֹם לִפְנֵי רֹאשׁ הַשָּׁנָה וְאִם נָטַע אוֹ הִבְרִיךְ אוֹ הִרְכִּיב יַעֲקוֹר. לֹא עָקַר פֵּירוֹתָיו מַה הֵן.

רְבִּי בָּא רְבִּי לָא הֲווֹן יָתְבִין בְּצוֹר אֶתָא עוּבְדָא קוֹמֵיהוֹן הוֹרֵי רְבִּי לָא יִשְׁפְכוּ
פֵּירוֹתָיו. אָמַר רְבִּי בָּא אֲנִי לֹא נִמְנֵיתִי עִמְּהֶן בַּעֲלִיָּה. אָמְרִין נֵצֵא לְחוּץ נִלְמַד
נֶפְקוּן וְשָׁמְעוּן רְבִּי יוֹנָה רְבִּי יִצְחָק בַּר טְבֶלַיי בְּשֵׁם רְבִּי לֶעָזָר אֵין מְחַדְּשִׁין עַל
הַגְּזֵירָה. רְבִּי יוֹסֵי רְבִּי יִצְחָק בַּר טְבֶלַיי בְּשֵׁם רְבִּי לֶעָזָר אֵין מוֹסִיפִין עַל
הַגְּזֵירָה.

"One does not plant, sink, or graft in the year preceding a Sabbatical year later than thirty days before the New Year; if he planted, sank, or grafted he has to uproot it." If one did not uproot, what is with its yield[45]? Rebbi Abba and Rebbi La were sitting in Tyre when a case came before them. Rebbi La taught that the fruits should be thrown away. Rebbi Abba said, I was not counted with them on the upper floor[46]. They said, let us go out and study. They went out and heard Rebbi Jonah, Rebbi Isaac bar Tevele in the name of Rebbi Eleazar: One does not make a new restriction. Rebbi Yose, Rebbi Isaac bar Tevele in the name of Rebbi Eleazar: One does not add to a restriction[47].

45   Since a newly planted or grafted tree is forbidden for three years as *orlah*, the question is the status of a forbidden tree after three years. A parallel to this text is in *Ma'aser Šeni* 1:1 (fol. 52c).

46   Most cases in which the Mishnah reports on the circumstances in which a rabbinic restriction was decreed, it is said that the Sages assembled on the upper floor (e. g., *Šabbat* 1:2). Rebbi Abba wants to say that he was no party to the tannaïtic deliberations in the matter; he objects to R. La's statement that the fruits produced by a tree planted in the Sabbatical are permanently forbidden.

47   Since the Mishnah does not state that the fruits are permanently forbidden, no Amora has the power to decree that they should be forbidden.

It seems that in the text, גזירה "restriction" should be replaced by הלכה "practice". This is the reading of the Rome ms. here in both instances, and of the Venice text in *Ma'aser Šeni* in the

learned in the Babli. This increases the
importance of the testimony of the
Rome ms. in these cases; the scribe of
that ms. was, in the words of R. S.
Lieberman, בור ועם הארץ "uncivilized
and uneducated".

נָטְעוֹ וּמֵת בְּנוֹ מַהוּ שֶׁיְּהֵא מוּתָּר לְקַיְּימוֹ. תַּנֶּה רְבִּי יַעֲקֹב בַּר אַבַּיֵי דְּבַר דְּלָיָה
נָטְעוֹ וּמֵת בְּנוֹ אָסוּר לְקַיְּימוֹ. וְאַתְיָא כְּמָאן דְּאָמַר מִפְּנֵי הֶחָשָׁד אֲבָל מִפְּנֵי
הַבִּינְיָין אַב בְּנוֹ בּוֹנֶה.

If he planted and died, may his son keep it? Rebbi Jacob bar Abbai
stated from Bar Delaiah: If he planted and died, his son may not keep it.
This follows the one who says because of the suspicion[44], but because of
the building of the father, his son may build[48].

48   This phrase is close to being
unintelligible. The translation here
follows R. Moses Margalit who explains
that if the reason is not because of
what other people could think but is a
fine imposed on the perpetrator, there
would be no reason to fine the heir. R.
Eliahu Fulda and some others want to
correct בונה, מניין into בונה, בניין ; this
has no support in the sources. As B.

Ratner notes, it seems that the entire
clause was missing in the Yerushalmi
before R. David ben Zimra
(Maimonides, *Šemiṭṭah weYovel* 2:11)
who writes: "'The heir may not keep it';
the Yerushalmi notes that this is
obviously because of the suspicion."
The Rome ms. has אֲבָל מִפְּנֵי הַבִּינְיָין אַף אֲנִי
בּוֹנֶה "but because of building, I also can
build," worse than the Venice text.

תַּנֵּי הַנּוֹטֵעַ הַמַּבְרִיךְ הַמַּרְכִּיב שְׁלֹשִׁים יוֹם לִפְנֵי רֹאשׁ הַשָּׁנָה עָלְתָה לוֹ שָׁנָה
תְמִימָה וּמוּתָּר לְקַיְּימוֹ בַּשְּׁבִיעִית פָּחוֹת מִשְּׁלֹשִׁים יוֹם לִפְנֵי רֹאשׁ הַשָּׁנָה לֹא
עָלְתָה לוֹ שָׁנָה תְמִימָה וְאָסוּר לְקַיְּימוֹ בַּשְּׁבִיעִית. אֲבָל אָמְרוּ פֵּירוֹת נְטִיעָה זוֹ

אֲסוּרִין עַד חֲמִשָּׁה עָשָׂר בִּשְׁבָט. מַה טַעַם רִבִּי יָסָא בְּשֵׁם רִבִּי יוֹחָנָן וּבַשָּׁנָה. מַה
אַתְּ שְׁמַע מִינָהּ אָמַר רִבִּי זְעִירָא שָׁלֹשׁ שָׁנִים יִהְיֶה לָכֶם עֲרֵלִים לֹא יֵאָכֵל.
וּבַשָּׁנָה.

It was stated[49]: "If somebody planted, sank, or grafted 30 days before
the New Year, it counts for him as a full year[50] and he is permitted to
keep it in the Sabbatical year. Less than 30 days before the New Year, it
does not count for him as a full year and he is not permitted to keep it in
the Sabbatical year. Truly, they said[51], the fruits from this planting are
forbidden until the fifteenth of Shevaṭ.[52]" What is the reason? Rebbi
Yasa in the name of Rebbi Joḥanan (*Lev.* 19:24): "And in the year." How
do you understand this? Rebbi Zeïra said (*Lev.* 19:23): "Three years they
shall be uncircumcised for you, and in the [fourth] year.[53]"

49   Tosephta 2:3, Babli *Roš Haš-*
šanah 9b, *Masekhet Semaḥot* end of
Chap. 2. A parallel of this and the
following paragraph is in *Roš Hašša-*
nah 1:2 (fol. 57a).

50   For the prohibition of *orlah* the
first three years and the obligation to
redeem the fruits in the fourth year,
Lev. 19:23-24. This is spelled out in the
Tosephta–Babli version. Mishnah *Roš*
Haššanah declares the first of Tishre
to be the start of a new year for
saplings, i. e., for the rules of *orlah*.

51   This clause, which makes the
statement unchangeable practice, is not
in the Tosephta–Babli version.
52   The New Year for tithes from
trees, Mishnah *Roš Haššanah* 1:2.
53   The fourth year may be, or must
be, included in the three years of *orlah*.
This applies only to the special case
considered here (interpretation of Maimonides) or in all cases (R. Zeraḥiah
Halevi, R. Nissim Gerondi). The text in
Roš Haššanah 1:2 mentions the fourth
year explicitly.

אָמַר רִבִּי בָּא בַּר מָמָל קוֹמֵי רִבִּי זְעִירָא נִרְאִין הַדְּבָרִים כְּשֶׁנְּטָעוּ לִפְנֵי רֹאשׁ
הַשָּׁנָה שְׁלֹשִׁים יוֹם הָא אִם לֹא נִטְּעוּ שְׁלֹשִׁים יוֹם לִפְנֵי רֹאשׁ הַשָּׁנָה. אִיתָא חֲמֵי

שָׁנָה שְׁלֵימָה עֶלְתָה לוֹ וְאַתְּ אָמַר הָכֵין. אָמַר לֵיהּ וְאִין כֵּנִי וַאֲפִילוּ נְטָעוּ
שְׁלֹשִׁים יוֹם לִפְנֵי (fol. 34a) רֹאשׁ הַשָּׁנָה יְהֵא אָסוּר עַד שְׁלֹשִׁים יוֹם לִפְנֵי רֹאשׁ
הַשָּׁנָה. מַיי כְדוֹן. אָמַר רִבִּי מָנָא מִכֵּיוָן שֶׁעוֹמֵד בְּתוֹךְ שְׁנָתוֹ שֶׁל אִילָן מַשְׁלִים
שְׁנָתוֹ.

Rebbi Abba bar Mamal said before Rebbi Zeïra: It is understandable if
they were planted thirty days before the New Year[54]. But if they were
not planted thirty days before the New Year? Come and see: A full year
is counted for him, and you say so[55]? He said to him: If it is so, even if
they were planted thirty days before the New Year, should it not be
forbidden until thirty days before the New Year[56]? What about it? Rebbi
Mana said, since it stands in the middle of its year[57], it has to finish its
year.

54   The question is about the mixing
of the rules of the Sabbatical with
those of *orlah*. Either the 15th of
Shevaṭ (cf. Note 52) should not apply to
trees planted less than 30 days before
New Year's day or one should not have
to wait more than one year, to the
following New Year's Day, to count
year 2 of the sapling planted less than
30 days before the end of the current
year..

55   Even though the second year of
the tree starts on Tishre 1, one has to
wait another $4^1/_2$ months to use its
fruit.

56   If the 15th of Shevaṭ is not a
universal date, should not any fruit be
forbidden for three full years, counted
individually?

57   Since "middle of the year" excludes the last 30 days, one will have
to wait until the fourth New Year to
use the fruit since the years have to be
completed; then one does not have to
wait for the 15th of Shevaṭ (interpretation of Maimonides). According
to Maimonides, if a sapling was planted
earlier than 44 days before New Year's
Day (14 days for the roots to take hold
and 30 days to grow) one does not have
to wait for the 15th of Shevaṭ but may
use the fruit on New Year's Day
(*Ma'aser Šeni* 9:9).

(fol. 33c) **משנה ז:** הָאוֹרֶז וְהַדּוֹחָן וְהַפְּרָגִין וְהַשּׁוּמְשְׁמִין שֶׁהִשְׁרִישׁוּ לִפְנֵי רֹאשׁ
הַשָּׁנָה מִתְעַשְּׂרִין לְשֶׁעָבָר וּמוּתָּרִין בַּשְּׁבִיעִית. וְאִם לָאו אֲסוּרִין בַּשְּׁבִיעִית
וּמִתְעַשְּׂרִין לַשָּׁנָה הַבָּאָה.

Mishnah 7: Rice, millet, poppies, and sesame that took root before the
New Year are tithed for the past year and are permitted in the Sabbatical
year[58]. Otherwise they are forbidden in the Sabbatical[59] and tithed for the
coming year[60].

58 They may be treated as private property of the farmer and be harvested during the Sabbatical year. If tithes are given for this crop from another place, it must be from produce	of the preceding year. 59 Forbidden to be harvested and stored as seeds but permitted to be taken by everybody. 60 In a year not Sabbatical.

(fol. 34a) **הלכה ז:** הָאוֹרֶז וְהַדּוֹחָן כו'. בְּפֵירוֹת הִילְכוּ אַחַר שְׁלִישׁ וּבְאוֹרֶז אַחַר
הַשְׁרָשָׁה וּבְיָרֶק בִּשְׁעַת לְקִיטָתוֹ עִישּׂוּרוֹ. מְנַיִין שֶׁהִילְכוּ בְּפֵירוֹת אַחַר הַשְּׁלִישׁ.
מִגָּרְנְךָ וּמִיְּקְבֶךָ מִגָּרְנְךָ וְלֹא כָל־גָּרְנְךָ מִיְּקְבֶךָ וְלֹא כָל־יְקָבֶךָ. מֵעַתָּה אֲפִילוּ
פָחוֹת מִשְּׁלִישׁ. אָמַר רִבִּי זְעִירָא כְּתִיב עַשֵּׂר תְּעַשֵּׂר אֶת כָּל־תְּבוּאַת זַרְעֶךָ דָּבָר
שֶׁהוּא נִזְרַע וּמַצְמִיחַ יָצָא פָחוֹת מִשְּׁלִישׁ שֶׁאֵינוֹ נִזְרַע וּמַצְמִיחַ. מֵעַתָּה שְׁלִישׁ
הָרִאשׁוֹן לְשֶׁעָבָר וּשְׁלִישׁ הַשֵּׁנִי לָבוֹא. אָמַר רִבִּי יוֹחָנָן מֵחַג הַסּוּכּוֹת מַה חַג
הַסּוּכּוֹת לָבוֹא וְאַתְּ מְהַלֵּךְ בּוֹ לְשֶׁעָבָר וְאֵילוּ הוֹאִיל וְזֶה לָבָא אַתְּ מְהַלֵּךְ בָּהֶן
לְשֶׁעָבָר.

Halakhah 7: "Rice, millet," etc. For produce[61] they went after its
being a third [ripe], for rice after roots taking hold, and for vegetables the
collection is the time of its tithing. From where that they could go[62] after
its being a third [ripe] for produce? (*Deut.* 16:16) "From your threshing-
floor and from your wine-press." "From your threshing-floor", not all
your threshing-floor, "from your wine-press", not all your wine-press[63].

Then also if it is less than a third [ripe]? Rebbi Zeïra said, it is written (*Deut.* 14:22): "Tithe! You should tithe all produce of your seed," something which may be sown and will sprout; this excludes produce less than a third [ripe] which when sown will not sprout[64]. Then one should tithe the first third for the past and the other two thirds for the future![65] Rebbi Joḥanan said, from the holiday of Tabernacles[66]. Just as Tabernacles belongs to the next year but you celebrate it for the past, so this one is for the future and you celebrate it for the past.

61   Any agricultural produce not under the following two categories. The argument does not refer to the Sabbatical year but to tithes. The details are given in *Ma'serot* Chapter 1. The argument is based on (Deut. 14:22): "Tithe! You should tithe all produce of your seed which comes out of your field *year by year*." This implies that all produce must be tithed in the year of its growth. It is not necessary that tithes be given separately from each harvested batch, but it is necessary that only this year's produce be used to fulfill the obligations pertaining to any of this year's growth. Since produce is described as coming out of the field, it is the growth rather than the harvest which is the determining factor.

62   Since the verse only gives the outline of the obligation, it is up to the religious authorities to spell out the

details. For this, the verse has to give them authority.

63   In talmudic interpretation, the prefix מ means "part of". Here it is taken to subject to tithes produce not really ready for the threshing-floor or the wine-press. The *Sifry* (*Deut.* 140) has a different approach of interpretation, see below Note 76. The rule for the Sabbatical is treated in *Sifra Behar* (9): R. Jonathan says, from where that if produce is one-third ripe before the New Year you may bring it into storage in the Sabbatical year, the verse says (Lev. 25:3): "[Six years you shall sow your field] and harvest its harvest," if it is one-third ripe.

64   This proves that "one-third ripe" does not mean one-third of the growing period but one-third of the ripening time of the fully formed fruit or grain (cf. *Peah* Chapter 4, Note 86).

65   Since the effects of the growing periods are indistinguishable in the ripe fruit, tithing could never be accomplished.

66   (Deut. 16:16) "Make for yourself a festival of Tabernacles when you gather from your threshing-floor and from your wine-press." Since Tabernacles is 15 days after the New Year, it clearly belongs to the next year but celebrates the harvest of the preceding year. Therefore, one can harvest this year and tithe it as growth of the preceding year. This argument also appears in the name of R. Joḥanan in the Babli, *Roš Haššanah* 12b; the rabbinic character there is made clear by R. Zeïra and Rav Assi.

נאמר אַף בְּאוֹרֶז וּבְדוֹחָן וּבְפְרָגִין וּבְשׁוּמְשְׁמִין כֵּן. רִבִּי חוּנָא בַּר חִייָא אָמַר
שְׁאֵי אֶפְשָׁר לַעֲמוֹד עָלָיו. מְתִיבִין לְחוּנָא בַּר חִייָא וְהָתַנֵּי צוֹבֵר אֶת גּוֹרְנוֹ לְתוֹכוֹ
וְנִמְצָא מְעַשֵּׂר מִזַּרְעוֹ עַל יַרְקוֹ וּמִיַּרְקוֹ עַל זַרְעוֹ. אָמַר רִבִּי יוֹסֵה קַיְימָא חוּנָא
בַּר חִייָא[67] רִבִּי יוֹנָה חוּנָא בַּר חִייָא בְּשֵׁם שְׁמוּאֵל כְּתִיב עַשֵּׂר תְּעַשֵּׂר אֶת
כָּל־תְּבוּאַת זַרְעֶךָ מְעַשֵּׂר אַתְּ מְעַשֵּׂר אֶחָד בְּשָׁנָה אַחַת וְאֵין אַתְּ מְעַשֵּׂר שְׁנֵי
מַעְשְׂרוֹת בְּשָׁנָה אַחַת. הָתֵיבוֹן הֲרֵי פּוֹל הַמִּצְרִי הֲרֵי הוּא שְׁנֵי מַעְשְׂרוֹת בְּשָׁנָה
אַחַת. דְּתַנֵּי צוֹבֵר אֶת גָּרְנוֹ לְתוֹכוֹ וְנִמְצָא מְעַשֵּׂר מִזַּרְעוֹ עַל יַרְקוֹ וּמִיַּרְקוֹ עַל
זַרְעוֹ. אָמַר רִבִּי זְעִירָא כְּתִיב שֵׁשׁ שָׁנִים תִּזְרַע שָׂדֶךָ וְאָסַפְתָּ שִׁשָּׁה זְרָעִין וְשִׁשָּׁה
אֲסִיפִין לֹא שִׁשָּׁה זְרָעִין וְשֶׁבַע אֲסִיפִין. אָמַר רִבִּי יוֹנָה בְּשִׁיתָא לֵי נָן יָכְלִין
קַיְימִין אֶלָּא בְשִׁבְעָה אֶלָּא כֵּינֵי בְּשִׁשָּׁה זְרָעִין וְשֶׁבַע אֲסִיפִין לֹא שִׁשָּׁה זְרָעִין
וַחֲמִשָּׁה אֲסִיפִין. הָתֵיבוֹן הֲרֵי פּוֹל הַמִּצְרִי שֶׁהֲרֵי שִׁשָּׁה זְרָעִים וַחֲמִשָּׁה אֲסִיפִין.
דְּתַנֵּי צוֹבֵר אֶת גּוֹרְנוֹ לְתוֹכוֹ וְנִמְצָא מְעַשֵּׂר מִזַּרְעוֹ עַל יַרְקוֹ וּמִיַּרְקוֹ עַל זַרְעוֹ.

One might say, this similarly applies to rice, millet, poppy seeds, and sesame[68]! Rebbi Ḥuna bar Ḥiyya[69] said, there it is impossible to recognize. They objected to Ḥuna bar Ḥiyya, was it not stated: He collects it together with his threshing, it turns out that he tithes from his seeds for his vegetable and from his vegetable for his fruits[70]? Rebbi Yose said, Ḥuna bar Ḥiyya confirmed it; Rebbi Jonah, Ḥuna bar Ḥiyya in the name of Samuel[71]: It is written (*Deut.* 14:22): "Tithe! You should tithe all produce of your seed," you give one tithe in one year but not two tithes in one year[72]. They objected, does not Egyptian bean require two tithes in one year[73]? Was it not stated: He collects it together with his threshing, it turns out that he tithes from his seeds for his vegetable and from his vegetable for his fruits? Rebbi Zeïra said, it is written (*Lev.* 25:3): "Six years you shall sow your field and harvest." Six sowings and six harvests, not six sowings and seven harvests[74]. Rebbi Jonah said, we cannot hold with six but instead hold with seven; so it is: Six sowings and seven harvests, not six sowings and five harvests. They objected, does not Egyptian bean have six sowings and five harvests[75]? As it was stated: He collects it together with his threshing, it turns out that he tithes from his seeds for his vegetable and from his vegetable for his fruits.

67 Reading of the Rome ms. Venice and Leyden: חמא No Rav or Rebbi Huna bar Hama is known from the Talmudim.

68 There seems to be no reason why the kinds enumerated in the Mishnah should be treated differently from produce in general. R. Huna bar Hiyya explains that the principle of "one-third ripe" is not practical for these kinds. This answer would be impossible if prohibitions of the Sabbatical year were biblical since then in a questionable case one could not be more lenient than in a certain one. A biblical justification is given in

the next paragraph, but see the last paragraph in Chapter 9. There is no problem with the rules of tithing since biblical law requires tithing only of דגן יצהר ותירוש "grain, olive oil, and wine". All quotes of biblical verses in this Halakhah have to be taken as establishing guidelines for rabbinic decrees, not as giving hard biblical rules (R. Abraham ben David, Commentary to *Sifra, Behar Pereq* 1.)

69 One of the original members of the Yeshivah of Rav in Babylonia. In the Babli, his title always is "Rav". It is not impossible that he exercised rabbinic functions before the title of

"Rav" was introduced; then either he should have no title or the title of "Rebbi". He became rich as a tax farmer; for this he was shunned by some of his colleagues and could not attain the status of a major figure in either of the Talmudim.

70 This refers to the next Mishnah, that according to some opinions, Egyptian beans (cf. *Kilaim* Chapter 1, Note 45) follow the rules of rice. Now beans can be planted either as produce for their beans or as vegetable for their pods. The obligations of a field of beans therefore are determined by the intentions of the farmer. If the farmer changes his mind during the growing season then, as it is stated in Tosephta 2:5, R. Simeon from Shezur, whose opinion is reported in Mishnah 8, is of the opinion that now produce and vegetable are inseparably mixed in the ripe bean pod and that after "threshing", separating the beans from their pods, beans and pods have to be mixed for the purpose of taking common heave. The *baraita* quoted here explains the same in different wording; for the full text see Note 84. The objection here already implies the ruling given in Halakhah 8 that practice follows R. Simeon from Shezur. [In the Babli, *Roš Haššanah*

13b, a *baraita* is quoted closer to the Tosephta.}

71 R. Yose and R. Jonah disagree about who is the first author of the following statement.

72 Cf. Note 61. The argument is about the last part of the verse which was not quoted, *year by year.*

73 One for produce and one as vegetable.

74 R. Zeïra reinforces the attack against R. Huna bar Hiyya; in the case of R. Simeon from Shezur, only tithing in common may permit six harvests for the purpose of tithing; otherwise one would have to admit seven. Rebbi Jonah supports R. Huna bar Hiyya and notes that one must admit "seven" harvests (which for two harvests every year adds up to 12 harvests in six years.) The *Sifra* (*Behar* 7-8) has a different (Babylonian?) approach to the verses quoted: "From where that you may store in the Sabbatical year rice, millet, poppy seeds, and sesame that took root before the New Year? The verse says (*Lev.* 25:3): 'you should harvest its yield', even in the Sabbatical. I could think [this applies] even if they did not take root, the verse says (Lev. 25:3): 'six years you shall sow your field and harvest.' Six sowings and six harvests, not six

sowings and seven harvests."
75   If the planting is late, there may
be no harvest in either year. Hence,
any number of harvests are possible,

and the entire argument started by R.
Zeïra is moot. The reason of R. Huna
bar Ḥiyya remains unproven and
uncontradicted.

מְנַיִין שֶׁהִילְכוּ בְיָרֶק בִּשְׁעַת לְקִיטָתוֹ עִישׂוּרוֹ. מִגָּרְנְךָ וּמִיָּקְבָךְ מַה גּוֹרֶן וְיֶקֶב שֶׁהֵן
חַיִין מִמֵּי הַשָּׁנָה שֶׁעָבְרָה אַתְּ מְהַלֵּךְ בָּהֶן לְשֶׁעָבָר. וְאִילּוּ הוֹאִיל וְהֵן חַיִין מִמֵּי
הַשָּׁנָה הַבָּאָה אַתְּ מְהַלֵּךְ בָּהֶן לָבֹא. הֲתִיבוֹן הֲרֵי פוֹל הַמִּצְרִי זְרָעוֹ לְזֶרַע מִתְעַשֵּׂר
לְשֶׁעָבָר זְרָעוֹ לְיֶרֶק מִתְעַשֵּׂר לָבֹא. וּקְסָמָה בְּיָדֵיהּ זְרָעוֹ לְזֶרַע הוּא חָיָה מִמֵּי
הַשָּׁנָה שֶׁעָבְרָה זְרָעוֹ לְיֶרֶק הוּא חָיָה מִמֵּי הַשָּׁנָה הַבָּאָה.

On which basis did they rule that for vegetables their collection is the
time of tithing? (*Deut.* 16:16) "From your threshing-floor and from your
wine-press." Threshing-floor and wine-press are sustained by the waters of
the preceding year, you go for them after the past. These live from the
waters of the coming year, you go for them to the future[76]. They
objected, but Egyptian beans, if one sowed them for the beans, are tithed
for the past, but if he sowed for vegetable, they are tithed for the future.
Does it hold a charm [to know that] if one sowed them for the beans, they
drink from the past year, but if he sowed them as vegetable, they drink
from the future year?[77]

76   In the Babli (*Roš Haššanah* 14a)
and in *Sifry Deut.* 140, this argument is
given in the name of the Tanna R. Yose
the Galilean. According to R. Aqiba
(in *Sifry*) vegetables are grown by
irrigation; they do not depend on the
seasons and, therefore, must be tithed
independent from the agricultural year

at harvest time.
77   The reason given above is
rejected and, except for grain one-third
ripe, all time limits given are rabbinic
in character.

The expression וקסמה ביהיה is
inspired by *Num.* 22:7.

(fol. 33c) **משנה ח**: רְבִּי שִׁמְעוֹן שְׁזוּרִי אוֹמֵר פּוֹל הַמִּצְרִי שֶׁזְרָעוֹ לְזֶרַע בַּתְּחִילָה

כְּיוֹצֵא בָהֶן. רְבִּי שִׁמְעוֹן אוֹמֵר אֲפוּנִין הַגַּמְלוֹנִים כְּיוֹצֵא בָהֶן. רְבִּי לְעָזָר אוֹמֵר

אֲפוּנִים הַגַּמְלוֹנִים שֶׁתִּירְמְלוּ לִפְנֵי רֹאשׁ הַשָּׁנָה.

Mishnah 8: Rebbi Simeon from Shezur says, Egyptian bean which one
sowed originally for its beans has the same rules[70]. Rebbi Simeon says,
large peas have the same rules. Rebbi Eleazar says, [only] large peas when
they formed pods before the New Year.

(fol. 34a) **הלכה ח**: מַהוּ תִּירְמְלוּ עָבְדוֹן קַנְקוּלִין.

What means חרמילו? They produced pockets[78].

78   R. S. Lieberman (*Tosefta ki-*
fshutah p. 502) explains as Greek

καλύκιον, "small calyx, pod, seed
pouch", with an exchange of liquids *n-l*.

רְבִּי בָּא בַּר זַבְדָּא בְשֵׁם רְבִּי שִׁמְעוֹן בֶּן לָקִישׁ הֲלָכָה כְרְבִּי שִׁמְעוֹן הַשְּׁזוּרִי. אָמַר

רְבִּי יוֹסָה הוֹרֵי רְבִּי לְעָזָר לְרְבִּי שִׁיבְתַי דְצָדוֹקֵי כְהָדָא דְרְבִּי שִׁמְעוֹן שְׁזוּרִי.

Rebbi Abba bar Zavda in the name of Rebbi Simeon ben Laqish:
Practice follows Rebbi Simeon from Shezur. Rebbi Yosa said, Rebbi
Eleazar instructed Rebbi Sabbatai Zadoq's[79], following Rebbi Simeon from
Shezur.

79   An Amora of the second
generation, usually associated with R.
Eleazar. He is the only Amora whose

patronymic is given in Greek form (A
B's instead of the usual A son of B.)

תַּנֵּי שֵׁשׁ מִידוֹת אָמְרוּ חֲכָמִים בְּפוֹל הַמִּצְרִי זְרָעוֹ לְזֶרַע מִתְעַשֵּׂר לְשָׁעָבַר זְרָעוֹ

לְיֶרֶק מִתְעַשֵּׂר לָבָא. זְרָעוֹ לְזֶרַע וְיֶרֶק אוֹ שֶׁזְּרָעוֹ לְזֶרַע וְחִישֵׁב עָלָיו לְיֶרֶק מְעַשֵּׂר

מִזַּרְעוֹ עַל יַרְקוֹ וּמִיַּרְקוֹ עַל זַרְעוֹ. בְּשֶׁהֵבִיא שְׁלִישׁ לִפְנֵי רֹאשׁ הַשָּׁנָה אֲבָל אִם

הֵבִיא שְׁלִישׁ אַחַר רֹאשׁ הַשָּׁנָה זְרָעוֹ מִתְעַשֵּׂר לְשָׁעָבַר וְיַרְקוֹ מִתְעַשֵּׂר בְּשָׁעַת

לְקִיטָתוֹ עִישּׂוּרוֹ. בְּשֶׁלָּקַט מִמֶּנּוּ לִפְנֵי רֹאשׁ הַשָּׁנָה אֲבָל אִם לָקַט מִמֶּנּוּ לְאַחַר

רֹאשׁ הַשָּׁנָה בֵּין זַרְעוֹ בֵּין יַרְקוֹ מִתְעַשֵּׂר לָבָא.

It was stated: The Sages enumerated six cases for Egyptian bean. If
one sowed it for seeds it is tithed for the past[80]; if he sowed it as vegetable
it is tithed for the future. If he sowed it for both seeds and vegetable, or
if he sowed for seeds and then wanted it as vegetable, one may tithe from
its seed on vegetable and from vegetable on seeds, on condition that it
was one-third ripe before the New Year. But if it was only ripe one-third
after the New Year, its seed is tithed for the past and its vegetable is
tithed at the moment of its being plucked if it was collected before the
New Year[81]. But if some of it was collected after the New Year, both
seed and vegetable are tithed for the future.

80   In that case the beans are left
on the field until the pods are hard and
no longer usable as vegetable. In that
case, beans fall under the rules of
produce. If the green pods are sold as
vegetable, it must be tithed at the

moment of harvest. "Tithed for the
past" means "tithed as part of last
year's harvest."
81   The Tosephta (2:7) has a similar
rule for dill and coriander.

זְרָעוֹ לְזֶרַע וְחִישֵּׁב עָלָיו לְיֶרֶק בָּאִין מַחֲשָׁבָה. זְרָעוֹ לְיֶרֶק וְחִישֵּׁב עָלָיו לְזֶרַע
לְעוֹלָם אֵין מַחֲשֶׁבֶת זֶרַע חָלָה עָלָיו אֶלָּא אִם כֵּן מָנַע מִמֶּנּוּ שָׁלֹשׁ מוֹרְבִיּוֹת.
בְּשֶׁהֵבִיא שְׁלִישׁ לִפְנֵי רֹאשׁ הַשָּׁנָה אֲבָל אִם הֵבִיא שְׁלִישׁ אַחַר רֹאשׁ הַשָּׁנָה אֲפִילוּ
לֹא מָנַע מִמֶּנּוּ שָׁלֹשׁ מוֹרְבִיּוֹת. זְרָעוֹ לְזֶרַע וְעָשָׂה כּוּלוֹ קְצָצִין גְּמוּרִין לִפְנֵי רֹאשׁ
הַשָּׁנָה זַרְעוֹ מִתְעַשֵּׂר לְשֶׁעָבַר יַרְקוֹ מִתְעַשֵּׂר בְּשָׁעַת לְקִיטָתוֹ עִישּׂוּרוֹ. מִקְצָתוֹ
עָשָׂה קְצָצִין גְּמוּרִין וּמִקְצָתוֹ לֹא עָשָׂה הָדָא הִיא צוֹבֵר גּוֹרְנוֹ לְתוֹכוֹ וְנִמְצָא
מְעַשֵּׂר מִזַּרְעוֹ עַל יַרְקוֹ וּמִיַּרְקוֹ עַל זַרְעוֹ. תַּנָּא רִבִּי אָבוּדַמָא דְּחֵיפָה וַאֲפִילוּ לֹא
עָשָׂה כּוּלוֹ קְצָצִין גְּמוּרִין לִפְנֵי רֹאשׁ הַשָּׁנָה זַרְעוֹ מִתְעַשֵּׂר לְשֶׁעָבַר יַרְקוֹ מִתְעַשֵּׂר

בִּשְׁעַת לְקִיטָתוֹ עִישׂוּרוֹ. אָמַר רִבִּי יוֹסֵי וְהוּא שֶׁהֵבִיא שְׁלִישׁ לְמַחֲשָׁבֶת זֶרַע אֲבָל
אִם הֵבִיא שְׁלִישׁ לְמַחֲשֶׁבֶת יָרָק אֵיפְשָׁר לוֹמַר זַרְעוֹ מִתְעַשֵּׂר לְשֶׁעָבַר. יָרָקוֹ
מִתְעַשֵּׂר בִּשְׁעַת לְקִיטָתוֹ עִישׂוּרוֹ וְאַתְּ אָמַר צוֹבֵר אֶת גּוֹרְנוֹ לְתוֹכוֹ וְנִמְצָא מְעַשֵּׂר
מִזַּרְעוֹ עַל יַרְקוֹ וּמִיַּרְקוֹ עַל זַרְעוֹ.

If he sowed it for seeds and then thought about it for vegetable, it
follows his thought[82]. If he sowed it as vegetable, the thought of seeds
cannot take hold on it unless he withheld three *morbiot*[83]. That is, if it
was one-third ripe before the New Year, but if it was not one-third ripe
before the New Year, even if he did not withhold three *morbiot*. If he
sowed for seeds and all [plants] formed complete pods before the New
Year, its seeds are tithed for the past year, its greens are tithed at the time
of their harvest. If some [plants] had formed complete pods but some did
not, that is the case of[84]: "He collects it together with his threshing, it
turns out that he tithes from his seeds for his vegetable and from his
vegetable for his fruits". Rebbi Eudaimon from Haifa stated: Even if not
all [plants] formed complete pods before the New Year, its seeds are tithed
for the past year, its greens are tithed at the time of their harvest. Rebbi
Yose said, that is if it was one-third ripe for the intention of seeds. But if
it was one-third ripe for the intention of vegetables, it is impossible to say
that its seeds are tithed for the past year and its greens are tithed at the
time of their harvest, since you say that "he collects it together with his
threshing; it turns out that he tithes from his seeds for his vegetable and
from his vegetable for his seeds[85]".

82   Maimonides (*Ma'aser Šeni* 1:10)
reads באין אחר מחשבתו ; this is the basis
of the translation.

83   Tosephta 2:4 is practically
identical with Mishnah 9, except that in
the case of *ba'al* fields, the Tosephta

states that for the field to qualify as seed field, one must withhold two (or three) מריעות, instead of עונות in the Mishnah. The Tosephta is partially quoted in *Ma'serot* 4:5 (fol. 51b), where the reading is מודייות [two] *modii*.

R. Abraham ben David (*Ma'aser Šeni* 1:10) deduces from the Mishnah that מוריות, מריעות are instances of irrigation; R. S. Lieberman reads the words as derived from מרביעות "fertilizations," but it might be better to take the word from מרויות "waterings". בעל fields of produce other than grains, while not irrigated permanently, are watered occasionally (Mishnah 9).

Maimonides, followed by the commentators of his Code and J. Levy, translates מורביות (or מרביות in the Rome ms.) as "trimmings"; that meaning is found in the Babli (*Sukkah* 45a, *Tamid* 29a). R. Abraham ben David wonders why Maimonides in his Code follows an unclear Tosephta instead of a clear Mishnah.

84   Cf. Note 70.

85   In the Babli, *Roš Haššanah* 13b, this is accepted since Samuel decrees that "all goes by the time the fruit is ripe".

זָרְעוֹ לְזֶרַע לִפְנֵי רֹאשׁ הַשָּׁנָה שְׁבִיעִית וְנִכְנְסָה בֵּין זַרְעוֹ בֵּין יַרְקוֹ מוּתָּר. זָרְעוֹ לְיָרָק לִפְנֵי רֹאשׁ הַשָּׁנָה הַשְּׁבִיעִית וְנִכְנְסָה שְׁבִיעִית בֵּין זַרְעוֹ בֵּין יַרְקוֹ אָסוּר. זָרְעוֹ לְזֶרַע וּלְיָרָק לִפְנֵי רֹאשׁ הַשָּׁנָה הַשְּׁבִיעִית וְנִכְנְסָה שְׁבִיעִית פְּשִׁיטָא זַרְעוֹ מוּתָּר יַרְקוֹ מַהוּ. תַּנֵּי רִבִּי חִיָּיה אָסוּר תַּנֵּי רִבִּי חֲלַפְתָּא בֶּן שָׁאוּל מוּתָּר. מָאן דְּאָמַר מוּתָּר דְּבַר תּוֹרָה מָאן דְּאָמַר אָסוּר מִפְּנֵי מַרְאִית הָעַיִן. רִבִּי סִימוֹן בַּר זַבְדָּא בָּעָא קוֹמֵי רִבִּי יוֹסֵי וַאֲפִילוּ לְהַאֲכִיל אֶת בְּהֶמְתּוֹ יְהֵא אָסוּר מִפְּנֵי מַרְאִית הָעַיִן. אָמַר לֵיהּ לֹא יִתֵּן לֹא לִבְנוֹ וְלֹא לִשְׁלוּחוֹ וְלֹא יְהֵא לוֹקֵט עַל אוֹמָן. אָמַר רִבִּי יוֹסָה בֵּי רִבִּי בּוּן אִם נֶעֶקְרָה הַגּוּמָא מוּתָּר וַאֲפִילוּ כְּמָאן דְּאָמַר אָסוּר הָיָה לוֹקֵט וְנִמְצָא בְּתוֹכוֹ יֶרֶק מוּתָּר. כְּהָדָא בַּר נַשׁ עָאַל טָעוּן עֶשֶׂר מֵיסָרִין דְּלוֹבֵי מַעֲשֵׂר לְרִבִּי יִרְמְיָה. אָמַר לֵיהּ לֹא תֵיעֲבֵד כֵּן לֹא תְלַקֵּט אֶלָּא צוֹרְכָה דְלִפְצָה.

If one sowed it for seeds before the Sabbatical New Year[86], then in the Sabbatical year both seeds and vegetables are permitted. If one sowed it as vegetable before the Sabbatical New Year, then in the Sabbatical year both seeds and vegetables are forbidden. If one sowed it both for seeds and vegetable before the Sabbatical New Year, then in the Sabbatical year clearly seeds are permitted. What is the status of vegetables? Rebbi Ḥiyya stated "forbidden", Rebbi Ḥalaphta ben Shaul stated "permitted". He who says "permitted" follows the word of the Torah. He who says "forbidden", because of the bad impression[87]. Rebbi Simeon bar Zevida asked before Rebbi Yose: Then it should be forbidden even to use it to feed one's animals, because of the bad impression[88]. He said to him, one should not give to his son or to his agent, nor should he harvest in a row. Rebbi Yose ben Rebbi Abun said, if a hole was torn out it is permitted[89]. Even according to him who says it is forbidden, if he harvested and found vegetable in it[90], it is permitted. Similarly, when a man came carrying ten bundles of Lybian [beans][91] as tithe to Rebbi Jeremiah, he said that this should not be done; do not harvest more than what is needed for the pan[92].

86   Assuming that the roots are well formed before the New Year. As vegetable all is forbidden since both tithes and the Sabbatical status are determined by the time of the harvest.

87   Since the goal of the planting is purely in the mind of the farmer, other people will suspect that he planted for vegetables and now illegally takes the growth of the Sabbatical year for himself.

88   Cf. *Kilaim* 9:2, Notes 32 ff. The questioner follows Rav in his opinion that any prohibition because of a bad impression is absolute. The answer is that reasonable behavior will prevent gossip. The rest of the paragraph defines reasonable behavior.

89   This is unprofessional harvesting and certainly permitted in the Sabbatical year.

90   A few pods that still can be eaten as vegetable. If the harvest is for the white beans, most pods will be

inedible and the few green ones will
not cause gossip.

91   See *Kilaim*, Note 67; green

Egyptian beans are called Lybian.

92   A Greek word, cf. *Peah*, pp. 239,
335.

זָרְעוּ לִפְנֵי ראשׁ הַשָּׁנָה הַשְּׁמִינִית וְנִכְנְסָה שְׁמִינִית בֵּין זַרְעוּ בֵּין יַרְקוּ אָסוּר.
זָרְעוּ לְיָרָק לִפְנֵי ראשׁ הַשָּׁנָה הַשְּׁמִינִית וְנִכְנְסָה שְׁמִינִית בֵּין זַרְעוּ בֵּין יַרְקוּ
מוּתָּר. זָרְעוּ לְזֶרַע וּלְיָרָק לִפְנֵי ראשׁ הַשָּׁנָה הַשְּׁמִינִית וְנִכְנְסָה שְׁמִינִית זַרְעוּ
אָסוּר וְיַרְקוּ מוּתָּר.

If one sowed it [for seeds][93] before the New Year of the eighth year,
then in the eighth year both seeds and vegetables are forbidden. If one
sowed it as vegetable before the New Year of the eighth year, then in the
eighth year both seeds and vegetables are permitted. If one sowed it both
for seeds and vegetable before the New Year of the eighth year, then in
the eighth year seeds are forbidden and the vegetable is permitted.

93   Missing in the mss. and the print
but clearly necessary by the context.
Here again, "forbidden" means "forbidden to be treated as private
property and to be stored as seeds";

"permitted" means "permitted to be
treated as private property and to be
stored as seeds." The reasons are the
same as for the Sabbatical year and do
not have to be spelled out.

(fol. 33c) **מִשְׁנָה ט**: בְּצָלִים הַסָּרִיסִים וּפוֹל הַמִּצְרִי שֶׁמָּנַע מֵהֶן מַיִם שְׁלֹשִׁים יוֹם
לִפְנֵי ראשׁ הַשָּׁנָה מִתְעַשְּׂרִין לְשֶׁעָבַר וּמוּתָּרִין בַּשְּׁבִיעִית וְאִם לָאו אֲסוּרִין
בַּשְּׁבִיעִית וּמִתְעַשְּׂרִין לְשָׁנָה הַבָּאָה. וְשֶׁל בַּעַל שֶׁמָּנַע מֵהֶן מַיִם שְׁתֵּי עוֹנוֹת דִּבְרֵי
רִבִּי מֵאִיר וַחֲכָמִים אוֹמְרִים שָׁלשׁ.

Mishnah 9: Sterile onions and Egyptian beans from which water was withheld thirty days before the New Year are tithed for the past [year] and may be kept in the Sabbatical year[58]; otherwise they are forbidden in the Sabbatical year[59] and are tithed for the coming year. For those from a *ba'al* field[94], if one withheld water for two periods[83], the words of Rebbi Meïr, but the Sages say three.

94   An unirrigated field that must be watered by hand if used for vegetables.   The term seems to be taken from pagan neighbors since Ba'al is the Semitic rain god, equivalent of the Greek Zeus. The Tosephta (Note 83) makes it explicit that the first rule speaks of fields irrigated by a permanent installation.

(fol. 34a) **חלכח ט**׃ מַהוּ בְּצָלִים הַסָּרִיסִין אִילֵין בּוֹצְלַיָּא כּוּפְרַיָּא דְּלָא עָבְדִין זֶרַע.

Halakhah 9: What are sterile onions? Those rural onions which do not form seeds.

אָמַר רְבִּי מָנָא מִכֵּיוָן שֶׁמָּנַע מֶהֶן מַיִם שְׁלֹשִׁים יוֹם לִפְנֵי רֹאשׁ הַשָּׁנָה נַעֲשׂוּ כְּבַעַל.

Rebbi Mana said, since he withheld water for thirty days before New Year's Day, they are as on a *ba'al* [field].

רְבִּי יוֹנָה בָּעֵי לְמַפְרֵיעוֹ הוּא נַעֲשָׂה זֶרַע זַרְעוֹ מִיכָּן לָבָא. מַה נָּפַק מִבֵּינֵיהוֹן לָקַט בְּתוֹךְ שְׁלֹשִׁים וּלְאַחַר שְׁלֹשִׁים. אִין תֵּימַר לְמַפְרֵיעוֹ הוּא נַעֲשָׂה זֶרַע מְעַשֵּׂר מִזֶּה עַל זֶה אִין תֵּימַר מִיכָּן וְלָבָא אֵינוֹ מְעַשֵּׂר מִזֶּה עַל זֶה.

Rebbi Jonah asked: Do they become seed-plants retroactively [or are] they seed-plants for the future? What would be the difference? If he took some within the thirty days and some afterwards, if you say that they become seed-plants retroactively, he tithes from one for the other; if you say, only in the future, he may not tithe from one for the other.

(fol. 33c) ‏מִשְׁנָה י:‏ ‏הַדִּילוּעִין שֶׁקִּיְּימָן לְזֶרַע אִם הוּקְשׁוּ לִפְנֵי רֹאשׁ הַשָּׁנָה וְנִפְסְלוּ‏
‏מֵאוֹכֶל מוּתָּר לְקַיְּימוֹ בַּשְּׁבִיעִית וְאִם לָאו אָסוּר לְקַיְּימוֹ בַּשְּׁבִיעִית.‏ ‏הַתִּימָרוֹת‏
‏שֶׁלָּהֶן אֲסוּרוֹת בַּשְּׁבִיעִית.‏ ‏מַרְבְּצִין בְּעָפָר לָבָן דִּבְרֵי רִבִּי שִׁמְעוֹן רִבִּי אֱלִיעֶזֶר בֶּן‏
‏יַעֲקֹב אוֹסֵר.‏ ‏מְמָרְסִים בָּאוֹרֶז בַּשְּׁבִיעִית דִּבְרֵי רִבִּי שִׁמְעוֹן אֲבָל לֹא מְכַסְּחִין.‏

Mishnah 10: If gourds kept for seeds became hard before the New
Year and unusable as food, one may keep them in the Sabbatical year;
otherwise, it is forbidden to keep them in the Sabbatical year[93]. Their
buds are forbidden in the Sabbatical year. One may sprinkle with water
on white dust[95], the words of Rebbi Simeon; Rebbi Eliezer ben Jacob
forbids it. One may tear off[22] rice in the Sabbatical year; the words of
Rebbi Simeon are that one may not trim[23].

95   Technical term for earth in an
orchard whose trees are standing suf-
ficiently apart (not more than 10 trees
per *bet seah*.)

(fol. 34a) ‏הלכה י:‏ ‏לָמָּה לִי הָקְשׁוּ אֲפִילוּ לֹא הוּקְשׁוּ.‏ ‏מִכֵּיוָן שֶׁהוּקְשׁוּ נַעֲשׂוּ‏
‏כִּשְׁאָר זֵירְעוֹנֵי גִינָה שֶׁאֵין נֶאֱכָלִין.‏

Halakhah 10: Why do I need that they became hard? Even if they did
not become hard! If they became hard they fall under the rules of kitchen
seed plants that are not eaten[96].

96   Non-food is not subject to the
rules of the Sabbatical year. For
"kitchen seed plants" cf. *Kilaim* Chapter 2, Note 22 and Mishnah 2.

(fol. ‏כֵּיצַד הוּא בּוֹדֵק.‏ ‏רִבִּי יוֹסֵי בֶּן חֲנִינָה אוֹמֵר עוֹקְצוֹ אִם נִתְאָחֶה אָסוּר וְאִם‏
34b) ‏לָאו מוּתָּר.‏

How does one check[97]? He pricks it; if it heals, it is forbidden,
otherwise it is permitted.

97   Whether the gourd has hardened.

רִבִּי יוֹנָה בּוֹצְרַיָּא אָמַר קרמולין פְּטוּרִין מִן הַמַּעֲשֵׂר. הָדָא דְתֵימַר עַד שֶׁלֹּא
עָשָׂה דִילוּעִין אֲבָל אִם עָשׂוּ דִילוּעִין כְּיֶרֶק הֵן.

Rebbi Jonah from Bostra said: *qarmals*[98] are free from tithes. That is, as long as they did not form gourds; but when they formed gourds they are like vegetables.

98   This plant has not been identified; the explanations of the dictionaries are based on misprints in the traditional Tosephta texts, as pointed out by R. S. Lieberman.. Tosephta 4:19 states that one may import saplings and *qarmal* into Israel during the Sabbatical. In the Erfurt ms. of the Tosephta, the reading is קרומנין. In Arabic, קרמל is "an insignificant spineless tree".

הוֹרֵי[99] רִבִּי יוֹסֵי בְּאִילֵּין עָלֵי קוֹלָקַסַּיי שֶׁאָסוּר לִגְמוֹת בָּהֶן מַיִם מִפְּנֵי שֶׁהַצְּבָאִין
אוֹכְלִין אוֹתָן.

Rebbi Yose taught that it is forbidden to sip water from colocasia[100] leaves because they are food for deer[101].

99   Reading of the text in *Nedarim* 7:1 (fol. 40b) and of a Genizah fragment here. Venice: מאן הורו כן.
100   *Colocasia antiquorum,* a tropical plant with edible roots.
101   Since it says (*Lev.* 25:6): "For your domestic animals and the wild animals in your Land shall all its yield serve as food", Sabbatical growth that is animal fodder is forbidden for any other use. One may not use the leaves as cups.

מַרְבְּצִין בְּעָפָר לָבָן דִּבְרֵי רִבִּי שִׁמְעוֹן רִבִּי אֱלִיעֶזֶר בֶּן יַעֲקֹב אוֹסֵר. אַתְיָא דְרִבִּי
שִׁמְעוֹן כְּרַבָּנָן וּדְרִבִּי אֱלִיעֶזֶר בֶּן יַעֲקֹב בְּשִׁיטָתֵיהּ דְּתַנִּינָן תַּמָּן מוֹשְׁכִין אֶת הַמַּיִם
מֵאִילָן לְאִילָן וּבִלְבַד שֶׁלֹּא יַשְׁקוּ אֶת כָּל־הַשָּׂדֶה כּוּלָהּ. רִבִּי מָנָא אָמַר לָהּ סְתָם

רִבִּי אָבִין בְּשֵׁם שְׁמוּאֵל בִּסְתָם חוֹלְקִין. מָה נָן קַיָּמִין אִם בִּמְרוּנָחִין דִּבְרֵי הַכֹּל
אָסוּר אִם בִּרְצוּפִין דִּבְרֵי הַכֹּל מוּתָּר. אֶלָּא כֵּינָן קַיָּמִין בִּנְטוּעִין מַטַּע עֶשֶׂר
לְבֵית סְאָה. רִבִּי לִיעֶזֶר בֶּן יַעֲקֹב עֲבַד לוֹן כִּמְרוּנָחִין וְרַבָּנִין עֲבְדִין לוֹן כִּרְצוּפִין.
הָא רַבָּנִין אָמְרִין בִּמְרוּנָחִין אָסוּר לְהַשְׁקוֹת מַהוּ לְהַמְשִׁיךָ. נֵילַף הָדָא דְרַבָּנִין
מִן דְּרִבִּי לִיעֶזֶר בֶּן יַעֲקֹב כְּמָה דְּרִבִּי לִיעֶזֶר בֶּן יַעֲקֹב אָמַר בִּמְרוּנָחִין אָסוּר
לְהַשְׁקוֹת וּמוּתָּר לְהַמְשִׁיךָ כֵּן רַבָּנַן אָמְרִין מוּתָּר לְהַמְשִׁיךָ וְאָסוּר לְהַשְׁקוֹת. לֹא
כֵן סָבְרִינָן מֵימַר בִּמְרוּנָחִין דִּבְרֵי הַכֹּל אָסוּר וְהֵן עָפָר לָבָן לֹא בִּמְרוּנָחִין הוּא
אֶלָּא כָּאן בַּשְּׁבִיעִית כָּאן בְּמוֹעֵד.

"One may sprinkle with water on white dust, the words of Rebbi
Simeon; Rebbi Eliezer ben Jacob forbids it." Rebbi Simeon follows the
rabbis and Rebbi Eliezer ben Jacob is consistent, as we have stated
there[102]: "One may continue [to draw] water from tree to tree on
condition not to water the entire field." Rebbi Mana said it anonymously,
Rebbi Abin in the name of Samuel: They disagree anonymously[103].
Where are we holding? If they are widely spaced, it is forbidden
according to everybody, if they are tightly planted, it is permitted
according to everybody. But we deal with the case that they are planted
ten to a *bet seah*[104]. Rebbi Eliezer ben Jacob makes them widely spaced,
the rabbis make them tightly planted. So the rabbis said, if they are
widely spaced, it is forbidden to irrigate[105]. May one continue? Let us
learn the opinion of the rabbis from that of Rebbi Eliezer ben Jacob. Just
as Rebbi Eliezer ben Jacob says, it is forbidden to irrigate but permitted to
continue, so the rabbis say it is permitted to continue but forbidden to
irrigate. Did we not think that according to everybody if they are widely
spaced, it is forbidden; but is white dust not when they are widely
spaced[95]? But here it is the Sabbatical, there the holiday[106].

102   Mishnah *Mo'ed Qatan* 1:3, in the name of R. Eliezer ben Jacob. During the intermediate days of a holiday, only agricultural work necessary to avoid losses is permitted. R. Eliezer ben Jacob does not permit to water a field but, if necessary, he allows one to water the depression around a tree and then to make a shallow channel from one tree to the next, on condition that the water be confined to trees and channels and not cover the entire field.

103   Since the Mishnah is in the name of R. Eliezer ben Jacob, not anonymous, it follows that the rabbis, whose opinion is ignored in the Mishnah, must disagree. From here to the end of the Chapter, the text is found also in *Mo'ed Qatan* 1:3 (fol. 80c).

104   Cf. Mishnah *Kilaim* 5:1. Everywhere, ten trees planted on a *bet seah* are a model orchard. "Widely spaced" means less than ten to a *bet seah*, "tightly planted" more than ten.

105   Irrigate the entire field at the same time.

106   R. Eliezer ben Jacob may agree with the rabbis about the rules of a widely spaced orchard on a holiday and still disagree in matters of the Sabbatical year.

מַה בֵּין שְׁבִיעִית וּמַה בֵּין מוֹעֵד. שְׁבִיעִית עַל יְדֵי שֶׁהוּא מוּתָּר בִּמְלָאכָה הִתִּירוּ בֵּין דָּבָר שֶׁהוּא טוֹרַח בֵּין דָּבָר שֶׁאֵינוֹ טוֹרַח. מוֹעֵד עַל יְדֵי שֶׁהוּא אָסוּר בִּמְלָאכָה לֹא הִתִּירוּ אֶלָּא דָּבָר שֶׁהוּא אָבַד וּבִלְבַד דָּבָר שֶׁאֵינוֹ טוֹרַח. וְאִית דְּבָעֵי נִישְׁמְעִינָהּ מִן הָדָא שְׁבִיעִית עַל יְדֵי שֶׁזְּמַנָּהּ מְרוּבָּה הִתִּירוּ מוֹעֵד עַל יְדֵי שֶׁזְּמַנּוֹ קָצוּר אָסוּר. וְאוֹתָן שִׁבְעַת יָמִים אֲחֵרוֹת לֹא מִיסְתַּבְּרָא מֵעַבְדִּינָן כְּשִׁבְעַת יְמֵי הָרֶגֶל וְיִהְיוּ אֲסוּרִין. אַשְׁכָּח תַּנֵּי מַרְבִּצִין בְּעָפָר לָבָן בַּשְּׁבִיעִית אֲבָל לֹא בְּמוֹעֵד דִּבְרֵי רִבִּי שִׁמְעוֹן רִבִּי אֱלִיעֶזֶר בֶּן יַעֲקֹב אוֹסֵר.

What is the difference between Sabbatical and holiday? In the Sabbatical year, because work is permitted they permitted work needing effort as well was work not needing much effort. On a holiday, because work is forbidden[107] they only permitted work to prevent loss and only if it does not need much effort. Some want to understand it from this: During the Sabbatical year, which lasts for a long time, they permitted;

during holiday, which is a short time, they forbade. But would it not be reasonable to make these other seven days[108] equal to the seven days of the holiday, and should they not be forbidden? It was found stated: "One may sprinkle with water on white dust during the Sabbatical year but not during the holiday, the words of Rebbi Simeon; Rebbi Eliezer ben Jacob forbids it.[109]"

107 All unnecessary work is forbidden during the intermediate days of a 7 or 8 day holiday. The work permitted is work needed for the enjoyment of the holiday and work to prevent a possible loss. [In addition, public works are permitted if this will save taxpayers' money.]

108 Probably, one should read שבעת ימים אחרונות "the last seven days [of the Sabbatical year]" but there is no manuscript evidence for this.

109 There is no exception made for the last seven days. It follows that the first explanation is correct but the second one is not. In *Mo'ed Qaṭan*, the quote reads only: "One may sprinkle with water on white dust during the Sabbatical year but not during the holiday."

(fol. 34b) **משנה א:** מֵאֵימָתַי מוֹצִיאִין זְבָלִים לָאַשְׁפָּתוֹת מִשֶּׁיִּפְסְקוּ עוֹבְדֵי עֲבוֹדָה דְּבְרֵי רִבִּי מֵאִיר. רִבִּי יְהוּדָה אוֹמֵר מְשֶׁיָּבַשׁ הַמָּתוֹק. רִבִּי יוֹסֵי אוֹמֵר מְשֶׁיְּקָשֵׁר. עַד כַּמָּה מְזַבְּלִים עַד שָׁלֹשׁ אַשְׁפָּתוֹת לְבֵית סְאָה שֶׁל עֶשֶׂר מַשְׁפְּלוֹת וְשֶׁל לֶתֶךְ לֶתֶךְ. מוֹסִיפִין עַל הַמַּשְׁפְּלוֹת וְאֵין מוֹסִיפִין עַל הָאַשְׁפָּתוֹת רִבִּי שִׁמְעוֹן אוֹמֵר אַף עַל הָאַשְׁפָּתוֹת.

Mishnah 1: When may one bring out manure to form dungheaps? From the moment the agricultural workers[1] stop, the words of Rebbi Meïr. Rebbi Jehudah says, when the colocynth[2] dried up. Rebbi Yose says, when it forms its fruit[3]. How much manure may one use? Up to three dungheaps for a *bet seah*, each one containing ten boxes of a *letekh*[4] each. One may add boxes but not dungheaps; Rebbi Simeon says, also dungheaps.

1 Some Mishnah mss. of the Maimonides tradition have: עובדי עבירה "the sinners". The meaning of both versions is the same: One may make dungheaps on his field only after those who work their fields in the regular manner have stopped doing so, when it is too late to fertilize for this year's crop. One may not spread out the manure on the field but it should be stored in heaps of 150 *seah*.

2 Definition of the Halakhah. Colocynth (*citrullus colocynthis*, in Pliny *cucumis colocynthis*) is a gourd used as laxative; [מתוק "sweet" is a euphemism.]

3 Interpretation of Maimonides. An exact translation would be "when it forms nodes." The colocynth, a relative of the cucumber, has no thickened

parts except the fruit developing from the female flower.

4   15 *seah*. A *bet seah* is 2500 square cubits, cf. *Peah* p. 89.

(fol. 34c) **הלכה א**: מֵאֵימָתַי מוֹצִיאִין כו'. עַד שֶׁלֹּא פָסְקוּ עוֹבְדֵי עֲבוֹדָה מַהוּ שֶׁיִּהְיֶה מוּתָּר לַעֲשׂוֹת אַשְׁפָּה עַל פֶּתַח חֲצֵירוֹ. סִילָנִי שָׁאַל לְרִבִּי חִייָא בַּר בָּא וְאָסַר לֵיהּ. רִבִּי חֲנִינָא אָמַר שָׁרָא לֵיהּ וַהֲווֹן אָמְרִין דּוּ נָסַב מַעֲשֵׂר וְהוֹרֵי עַל גַּרְמֵיהּ לָצֵאת לְחוּץ לָאָרֶץ דְּלָא לְמֵיסַב מַעֲשֵׂר. מֵעַתָּה אֲפִילוּ מִשֶּׁפָּסְקוּ עוֹבְדֵי עֲבוֹדָה יְהֵא אָסוּר מִפְּנֵי מַרְאִית הָעַיִן שֶׁלֹּא יְהוּ אוֹמְרִים לְתוֹךְ שָׂדֶה בֵית הַשַּׁלְחִין שֶׁלּוֹ הוּא מוֹצִיא. יוֹדְעִין הֵן בְּנֵי עִירוֹ אִם יֶשׁ לוֹ בֵּית הַשַּׁלְחִין אִם אֵין לוֹ. אָמַר רִבִּי יוֹסֵי הָדָא אָמְרָה לֹא חָשׁוּ לְעוֹבְרִין וּלְשָׁבִין מִפְּנֵי מַרְאִית הָעַיִן.

Halakhah 1: "When may one bring out," etc. Is it permitted to assemble a dungheap at the door of one's courtyard before the agricultural workers stop? Silanus asked Rebbi Ḥiyya bar Abba and he forbade it to him. Rebbi Ḥanina[5] said, he permitted it, and they were gossipping about him that he was taking the tithe[6]. He instructed himself to leave the Land, so that he could not take the tithe. Then should it be forbidden even after the agricultural workers did stop because of the bad impression, that they would not say, he brings it out to his irrigated field? The people of one's town know whether he has an irrigated field or not. Rebbi Yose said, this means that they did not worry about a bad impression on passers-by[7].

5   He is the fifth generation Amora R. Ḥananiah, not the first generation Amora R. Ḥanina. There is no need to amend the text for reasons of chronology.

6   R. Ḥiyya bar Abba was a Cohen and Silanus, a rich land owner, used to give him his tithes. The people gossipped that R. Ḥiyya was bending the law to please his benefactor. R. Ḥiyya, a Babylonian, returned to Babylonia the following year, in order not to profit from the yield that his ruling produced. We know from the

Babylonian Talmud that R. Ḥiyya bar Abba sometimes argued inperson with Baby-lonian Sages.

7   This is in line with the position of the Yerushalmi in *Kilaim*, Chapter 9, Notes 32 ff.

בְּאִיסוּר שְׁנֵי פְרָקִים מַהוּ שֶׁיְּהֵא מוּתָּר לַעֲשׂוֹת כְּסֵדֶר הַזֶּה. נִישְׁמְעִינָהּ מִן הָדָא מוֹכְרִין וּמוֹצִיאִין זְבָלִים עִם הָעוֹשִׂין שְׁבִיעִית עַד רֹאשׁ הַשָּׁנָה. עִם הַגּוֹי וְעִם הַכּוּתִי אֲפִילוּ בַּשְּׁבִיעִית וּבִלְבַד שֶׁלֹּא יִפְרוֹק אֶת הַמַּשְׁפְּלוֹת. לֹא אָמַר אֶלָּא שֶׁלֹּא יִפְרֵיק אֶת הַמַּשְׁפְּלוֹת. הָא לָצֵאת מוֹצִיא הָדָא אֲמְרָה שֶׁהוּא מוּתָּר. וְאִין תֵּימַר שֶׁהוּא אָסוּר יְהֵא אָסוּר מִלְהוֹצִיא.

May one do that during the prohibition of the first two terms[8]? Let us hear from the following[9]: "One may sell and transport manure with those who work during the Sabbatical year until the New Year, with a Gentile and a Samaritan even during the Sabbatical year on condition that he not unload the boxes." It said only, "on condition that he not unload the boxes," hence he is permitted to transport. That means it is permitted[10]. If you say it is forbidden, he should be forbidden to transport.

8   Chapter 1, Note 4.

9   A different text is in Tosephta 1:4: "One sells and transports manure from a Jew suspected of violating the Sabbatical before the Sabbatical year; from a Gentile or a Samaritan it is permitted even during the Sabbatical. How long may one fertilize? Anytime one may plough one may fertilize."

Since the agricultural Sabbatical is certainly rabbinic, if there is no Jubilee year and no Temple the Samaritans are not bound by its rules. The language of the Tosephta binds the prohibition of fertilizing to that of ploughing; when the two terms were abolished for ploughing they automatically were abolished for fertilizing.

10   Since the condition that one may not unload is stipulated only for working with a Gentile during the Sabbatical but does not apply to working with a Jew suspected of violating the rules of the Sabbatical. Then certainly he is permitted to transport and unload for himself.

מִשֶּׁיָּבֵשׁ הַמָּתוֹק. פְּקוּעָה. אָמַר רִבִּי מָנָא הָהֵן פְּקוּעָה דְּבִקְעָתָה.

"When the colocynth dried up." *Citrullus colocynthis.* Rebbi Mana said, that means the colocynth of the open field[11].

11   Not the colocynth of a watered garden plot which may grow throughout the entire year.

מִשֶּׁיְּקַשֵּׁר. מִשֶּׁיַּעֲשֶׂה קְשָׁרִים קְשָׁרִים. אָמַר רִבִּי חֲנַנְיָה מִכֵּיוָן שֶׁנִּתְקַשֵּׁר בּוֹ קֶשֶׁר הָעֶלְיוֹן מִיַּד הוּא יָבֵשׁ. וְתַנֵּי עֲלָהּ קְרוֹבִין דִּבְרֵיהֶן לִהְיוֹת שָׁוִין.

"When it forms its fruit." When it forms many fruits. Rebbi Ḥananiah said, when its uppermost fruit is fully formed, it immediately dries up. About this we have stated: Their statements[12] are close to each other.

12   Rebbis Jehudah and Yose.

אָמַר רִבִּי יִרְמְיָה בְּפוֹחֵת מִן הַמַּשְׁפֵּלוֹת הָא שְׁתַּיִם מוּתָּר. רִבִּי יוֹסֵי בָּעֵי. אִם בְּפָחוֹת מִן הַמַּשְׁפֵּלוֹת הָא שְׁתַּיִם אָסוּר. אֶלָּא כִּי נָן קַיָּימִין בְּעוֹשֶׂה יוֹתֵר מִן כַּשִּׁיעוּר כְּהָדָה דְּתַנֵּי אֵין מוֹסִיפִין לֹא עַל הַמַּשְׁפֵּלוֹת וְלֹא עַל הָאַשְׁפָּתוֹת דִּבְרֵי רִבִּי מֵאִיר. וַחֲכָמִים אוֹמְרִים מוֹסִיפִין עַל הַמַּשְׁפֵּלוֹת וְאֵין מוֹסִיפִין עַל הָאַשְׁפָּתוֹת. וּמוֹסִיפִין עַל הַמַּשְׁפֵּלוֹת לֹא כַּשִּׁיעוּר. וְדִכְוָתָהּ מוֹצִיאִין עַל הָאַשְׁפָּתוֹת אֲפִילוּ כַשִּׁיעוּר.

Rebbi Jeremiah said, if he uses fewer boxes; hence, two are permitted[13]. Rebbi Yose questioned, if he uses fewer boxes, then two should be forbidden[14]. But where do we hold? If he exceeds the measure[15], as we have stated[16]: "Rebbi Meïr says, one may not add boxes or dungheaps, but the Sages say, one may add boxes but not dungheaps." If one adds boxes, are they not of full measure[17]? Similarly, one brings out to the dungheap even full measures[18].

13   Since the Mishnah discusses the number of dungheaps and their size and then discusses whether one may add to the numbers stated, but does not discuss whether one may make smaller dungheaps, it follows that one may not make dungheaps of smaller size because that would look like fertilizing one's field. It seems that the Mishnah insists only on a minimal size, not on a minimal number of dungheaps.

14   A possible interpretation of the Mishnah is that one may not start dungheaps on the field (for next year's use) unless the total amount is 30 *letekh*, 450 *seah*. Then making only two standard sized dungheaps would be forbidden.

15   If he uses boxes holding more than 10 *letekh* each.

16   Tosephta 2:14. The opinion of the Sages is there attributed to R. Jehudah; R. Simeon permits more, but not fewer, dungheaps.

17   Since a dungheap may contain more than 150 *seah*, one may make two dungheaps only on condition that together they contain at least 450 *seah*.

18   This refers to the next Mishnah where it is stated that one may gradually build up one's dungheap after the agricultural season. Even though the Mishnah speaks of "a little", it may be as much as a full single basket at one time and still people will not think that he is going to fertilize his field in the Sabbatical year.

(fol. 34b) **משנה ב:** עוֹשֶׂה אָדָם אֶת שָׂדֵהוּ שָׁלֹשׁ שָׁלֹשׁ אַשְׁפָּתוֹת לְבֵית סְאָה יוֹתֵר מִכֵּן אָסוּר דִּבְרֵי רִבִּי שִׁמְעוֹן וַחֲכָמִים אוֹמְרִים עַד שֶׁיַּעֲמִיק שְׁלֹשָׁה אוֹ עַד שֶׁיַּגְבִּיהַּ שְׁלֹשָׁה. עוֹשֶׂה אָדָם אֶת זִבְלוֹ אוֹצָר רִבִּי מֵאִיר אוֹמֵר עַד שֶׁיַּעֲמִיק שְׁלֹשָׁה אוֹ עַד שֶׁיַּגְבִּיהַּ שְׁלֹשָׁה. הָיָה לוֹ דָבָר מוּעָט מוֹסִיף עָלָיו וְהוֹלֵךְ רִבִּי אֶלְעָזָר בֶּן עֲזַרְיָה אוֹמֵר עַד שֶׁיַּעֲמִיקוּ אוֹ עַד שֶׁיַּגְבִּיהַּ שְׁלֹשָׁה אוֹ עַד שֶׁיִּתֵּן עַל הַסֶּלַע.

Mishnah 2: A person may fill his entire field with dungheaps, three each per *bet seah*; more is forbidden[20], the words of Rebbi Simeon. But

the Sages say[21], only if he raises or lowers it by three [hand-breadths][22].
A person may store his entire manure together[22]; Rebbi Meïr says only if
he raises or lowers it by three [hand-breadths]. If he had little[18], he may
continuously add to it; Rebbi Eleazar ben Azariah says only if he raises or
lowers it by three [hand-breadths] or puts it on a rock.

20 The manuscript tradition here is
thoroughly unsatisfactory. The text is
that of the Leyden ms. In the Rome
ms., some Mishnah mss., and the
standard printed Mishnah the text
reads יתר מכן מחציב דברי ר' שמעון "more
than that he chisels, the words of R.
Simeon"; that text makes no sense at all.
Most Mishnah mss. read simply יתר מכן
דברי ר' שמעון ; one Genizah fragment
reads ויתיר, which seems to be the
reading underlying the Yerushalmi
Halakhah and the commentaries of
Maimonides, R. Simson of Sens and R.
Isaac Simponti: "even more, the words
of R. Simeon." This is the only text
compatible with the opinion of R.
Simeon as given in the Tosephta (Note

16).

21 In all Mishnah mss. except the
Leyden ms. (and that of R. S. Cirillo),
the reading is אוסרין "(the Sages) forbid
it." This is also the Leyden text in the
Halakhah.

22 One may not put more than
three dungheaps on one field, even one
much larger than a *bet seah*, unless it is
shown that the intent is for dungheaps,
not for a fraudulent fertilizing of the
field by making as many dungheaps as
possible that automatically will fertilize the soil beneath. The dungheaps
are only permitted if the soil beneath
them is visibly higher or lower than the
surrounding field.

22 In one large heap.

הלכה ב: וְלָמָּה תַּנִּיתָהּ תְּרֵיין זִימְנִין. אָמַר רִבִּי יִרְמְיָה כָּאן בְּפוֹחֵת מִן (fol. 34c)
הַמַּשְׁפֵּלוֹת. בְּרַם הָכָא בְּעוֹשֶׂה בִּכְשִׁיעוּר. וְתַנֵּי כֵן עַל דְּרָבִּי שִׁמְעוֹן וּבִלְבַד שֶׁלֹּא
יִפְחוֹת לָאַשְׁפָּה מִשָּׁלֹשׁ מַשְׁפֵּלוֹת.

Halakhah 2: Why is this stated twice[23]? Rebbi Jeremiah said, there if
he used fewer boxes, but here if he makes it according to the measure.

We have stated thus about Rebbi Simeon: "On condition that he use no less than three boxes per dungheap.[24]"

23   Since R. Jeremiah inferred from the preceding Mishnah that the Sages will not permit more than three dungheaps, why does this have to be stated here explicitly? The answer is that the Sages will not permit any dungheap of less than 150 *seah*; the Mishnah is needed to give the background of R. Simeon's statement.

24   Even R. Simeon will not permit any dungheap to contain less than 45 *seah*.

וַחֲכָמִים אוֹסְרִין בְּעוֹשֶׂה יוֹתֵר מִכְּשִׁעוּר. אֲבָל בִּכְשִׁעוּר בִּשְׁלֹשָׁה מְקוֹמוֹת מוּתָּר בְּמָקוֹם אֶחָד לֹא כָּל־שֶׁכֵּן.

"But the Sages forbid.[25]" When he brings more than the measure. But if the full measure is permitted in three places, so much more in one place.

25   Quote from the correct Mishnah, cf. Note 21. The Sages will permit 450 *seah* of manure directly on one field (of at least one *bet seah* surface area) in one, two, or three places.

פָּתַר לָהּ תְּרֵין פִּתְרִין. בְּשֶׁהָיָה לוֹ דָבָר מוּעָט בְּתוֹךְ שָׂדֵהוּ בִּשְׁבִיעִית הֲרֵי זֶה מוֹסִיף עָלָיו וְהוֹלֵךְ. מִשֶּׁפָּסְקוּ עוֹבְדֵי עֲבוֹדָה רִבִּי לַעְזָר בֶּן עֲזַרְיָה אוֹסֵר. מַה טַעְמָא דְּרִבִּי לִיעֶזֶר בֶּן עֲזַרְיָה. שֶׁמָּא יִמָּצֵא לוֹ זֶבֶל וְנִמְצָא מְזַבֵּל אֶת אוֹתוֹ הַמָּקוֹם. פָּתַר לָהּ פָּתַר חוֹרָן כְּשֶׁהָיָה לוֹ דָבָר מוּעָט בְּתוֹךְ בֵּיתוֹ עֶרֶב שְׁבִיעִית וְהוּא מְבַקֵּשׁ לְהוֹצִיאוֹ לְתוֹךְ שָׂדֵהוּ בִּשְׁבִיעִית הֲרֵי זֶה מוֹסִיף עָלָיו וְהוֹלֵךְ. מִשֶּׁפָּסְקוּ עוֹבְדֵי עֲבוֹדָה רִבִּי לַעְזָר בֶּן עֲזַרְיָה אוֹסֵר. מַה טַעְמָא דְּרִבִּי לַעְזָר בֶּן עֲזַרְיָה. שֶׁמָּא לֹא יִמָּצֵא לוֹ זֶבֶל וְנִמְצָא מְזַבֵּל אֶת אוֹתוֹ הַמָּקוֹם. וְלֹא כְבָר הוּא מְזוּבָּל מֵעֶרֶב שְׁבִיעִית. רִבִּי בָּא רִבִּי יִרְמְיָה רִבִּי בּוּן בַּר חִייָה בְּשֵׁם רִבִּי בָּא בַּר מָמָל. מִפְּנֵי מַרְאִית הָעַיִן עַד שֶׁיּוֹצִיא עֶשֶׂר מַשְׁפְּלוֹת כְּאַחַת. וְלֵית לְרַבָּנִין מִפְּנֵי מַרְאִית הָעַיִן. אָמַר רִבִּי אִידִי דְּחוּטְרָא סַלּוֹ וּמַגְרֵיפוֹ מוֹכִיחִין עָלָיו שֶׁהוּא עוֹשֶׂה אַשְׁפָּה.

26One may give two explanations: If he had little [manure] on his field27, he may continuously add to it after the agricultural workers stopped; Rebbi Eleazar ben Azariah forbids it. What is the reason of Rebbi Eleazar ben Azariah? Maybe there will be manure and it will turn out that he fertilizes that place28. One may give another explanation: If he had little [manure] in his house before the Sabbatical year and he wants to transport it to his field during the Sabbatical, he may continuously add to it after the agricultural workers stopped; Rebbi Eleazar ben Azariah forbids it. What is the reason of Rebbi Eleazar ben Azariah? Maybe there will be no more manure and it will turn out that he fertilizes that place. Has it not been fertilized before the Sabbatical year29? Rebbi Abba, Rebbi Jeremiah, Rebbi Abun bar Ḥiyya in the name of Rebbi Abba bar Mamal: Because of the bad impression [it is forbidden] unless he transports ten boxes together30. Do the rabbis not care for a bad impression? Rebbi Idi said his stick, his basket, and his shovel prove that he intends to make a dungheap.

26   This paragraph and the next with major variations are also in *Mo'ed Qaṭan* 1:2 (fol. 83a). The paragraphs refer to the last part of the Mishnah (indicated in *Mo'ed Qaṭan* but not here), the disagreement between the Sages and R. Eleazar ben Azariah.

27   In *Mo'ed Qaṭan*: If he had little [manure] in his house before the Sabbatical year and he wants to transport it to his field during the Sabbatical, he may continuously add to it after the agricultural workers stopped; Rebbi Eleazar ben Azariah forbids it. What is the reason of Rebbi Eleazar ben Azariah? Maybe there will be no more manure and it will turn out that he fertilizes that place. [This is identical with the second scenario both here and in *Mo'ed Qaṭan*. The only difference in both explanations is that in the first case, R. Eleazar ben Azariah is said to accept the opinion of R. Yose (Mishnah *Baba Meẓi'a* 5:8) who

forbids short sales of manure because manure always is in short supply.]

28   If the manure is added in small portions, the soil under the dungheap will be thoroughly fertilized next year when the manure is spread out over the entire field.

29   This objection assumes that the dungheap was started before the Sabbatical year.

30   R. Eleazar ben Azariah forbids adding small increments only because people could think he was going to fertilize his field.

רבי יוֹסֵי בֵּי רבִּי בּוּן אָמַר אִילֵין שְׁמוּעָתָא דְּהָכָא דְּתַנִּינָן. רבִּי לֶעֶזָר בֶּן עֲזַרְיָה אָמַר אֵין עוֹשִׂין אֶת הָאַמָּה בַּתְּחִילָּה בְּמוֹעֵד וּבַשְּׁבִיעִית. אָמַר רבִּי זְעִירָא מִפְנֵי שֶׁהוּא מַכְשִׁיר אֶת צְדָדֶיהַ לַזְרִיעָה. רבִּי יִרְמְיָה רבִּי בּוּן בַּר חִיָּיה בְּשֵׁם רבִּי בָּא בַּר מָמָל מִפְנֵי מַרְאִית הָעַיִן. הֲווֹן בָּעֵי מֵימַר מָאן דְּאָמַר תַּמָּן מִפְנֵי מַרְאִית הָעַיִן וְהָכָא מִפְנֵי מַרְאִית הָעַיִן. מָאן דְּאָמַר מִפְנֵי שֶׁהוּא מַכְשִׁיר אֶת צְדָדֶיהַ לַזְרִיעָה הָכָא מִי אִית לָךְ לְמֵימַר. לֵית לָךְ אֶלָּא כְּהָדָא שֶׁמָּא לֹא יִמְצָא לוֹ זֶבֶל וְנִמְצָא מְזַבֵּל אֶת אוֹתוֹ מָקוֹם. מַה נָפַק מִבֵּינֵיהוֹן. חָפַר לַעֲשׂוֹת אַמָּה שֶׁל בְּנְיַן. הֲווֹן בָּעֵי מֵימַר מָאן דְּאָמַר תַּמָּן מִפְנֵי מַרְאִית הָעַיִן וְהָכָא מִפְנֵי מַרְאִית הָעַיִן. וּמָאן דְּאָמַר תַּמָּן מִפְנֵי שֶׁהוּא מַכְשִׁיר צְדָדֶיהַ לַזְרִיעָה הֲרֵי אֵינוֹ מַכְשִׁיר צְדָדֶיהּ לַזְרִיעָה. הַכֹּל מוֹדִין שֶׁאִם הָיָה לוֹ שָׁם סִיד אוֹ צְרוֹרוֹת אוֹ אֲבָנִים אוֹ גִיפְסוֹס מוּתָּר.

Rebbi Yose ben Rebbi Abun applied these traditions from here, as we have stated[31]: "Rebbi Eleazar ben Azariah said, one does not build a new water canal during the intermediate days of holidays or during the Sabbatical year." Rebbi Zeïra said, because he would prepare its banks to be sown[32]. Rebbi Jeremiah, Rebbi Abun bar Ḥiyya in the name of Rebbi Abba bar Mamal: Because of the bad impression. They wanted to say, the one who says there "because of the bad impression" says here[33] "because of the bad impression"; the one who says "because he would prepare its banks to be sown", what can he say here? The only answer would be "maybe there will be no more manure and it will turn out that he fertilizes that place.[34]" What would be the difference between them[35]? If he dug to build a water canal for a building. They wanted to say, the one who says there "because of the bad impression" will say in this case "because of the bad impression," but the one who says there "because he would prepare its banks to be sown," here its banks will not be prepared to be sown. Everybody agrees that if he built there with lime, pebbles, stones, or cement[36] it would be permitted.

31   Mishnah *Mo'ed Qaṭan* 1:2. Nonessential agricultural work is forbidden during the intermediate days of a holiday; construction work is permitted. The Sages consider building a new water canal as construction and permitted; the question is the rationale of the prohibition by R. Eleazar ben Azariah.

32   This reason would be valid both for the holidays and the Sabbatical year.

33   In the previous paragraph.

34   The second explanation offered in the previous paragraph is valid since it extends to the case of *Mo'ed Qaṭan*; the first explanation has to be rejected.

35   Is there a practical difference where the ruling would allow one to choose between the two arguments proffered for the position of R. Eleazar ben Azariah?

36   Greek γύψος. If the banks of a water canal are of stone or mortar, it is obviously not an agricultural construction.

(fol. 34b) **משנה ג:** הַמְדַיֵּר אֶת שָׂדֵהוּ עוֹשֶׂה סַהַר לְבֵית סָאתַיִם עוֹקֵר שָׁלֹשׁ רוּחוֹת וּמְשַׁיֵּר אֶת הָאֶמְצָעִיּוֹת נִמְצָא מְדַיֵּר בֵּית אַרְבַּעַת סְאִין. רִבִּי שִׁמְעוֹן בֶּן גַּמְלִיאֵל אוֹמֵר בֵּית שְׁמוֹנַת סְאִין. הָיְתָה כָּל־שָׂדֵהוּ בֵּית אַרְבַּעַת סְאִין מְשַׁיֵּר מִמֶּנּוּ מִקְצָת מִפְּנֵי מַרְאִית הָעַיִן. וּמוֹצִיא מִן הַסַּהַר וְנוֹתֵן לְתוֹךְ שָׂדֵהוּ כְּדֶרֶךְ הַמְזַבְּלִין.

Mishnah 3: He who wants his field to be fertilized[37] makes a corral enclosing two *bet seah*. He may remove the walls in three directions and leave the middle one; then he may fertilize four *bet seah*[38]; Rabban Simeon ben Gamliel says eight *bet seah*[39]. If his entire field was only four *bet seah*, he leaves out part of it because of the bad impression[40]. He may take [manure] out from the corral and put it on his field the way professionals do it[41].

37   He lets his animals stay in a temporary corral on the field to collect their dung on the field.

38   If the corral has the form of a rectangle, he removes three walls and puts them on the other side of the remaining wall.

39   Repeating the operation three times, covering a rectangle homothetic to the first one by a factor of two.

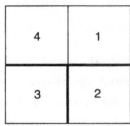

fig. 3-1

40   That people would not say that he intends to fertilize his field in the Sabbatical year.

41   Making three dungheaps per *bet seah*.

(fol. 34c) **הלכה ג**: תַּמָּן תַּנִּינָן שָׂדֶה שֶׁנִּתְקַוְוצָה תִּזָּרַע לְמוֹצָאֵי שְׁבִיעִית. נִיטַיְיבָה אוֹ שֶׁנִּדַּיְּירָה לֹא תִזָּרַע לְמוֹצָאֵי שְׁבִיעִית. אָמַר רִבִּי יוֹנָה כֵּינִי מַתְנִיתָא הָרוֹצֶה לְהַעֲמִיד צֹאן בְּתוֹךְ שָׂדֵהוּ עוֹשֶׂה סַהַר בֵּית סָאתַיִם.

Halakhah 3: There[42], we have stated: "A field cleared of thistles may be sown after the Sabbatical year. If it was improved or manured, it may not be sown after the Sabbatical year." Rebbi Jonah said, so is the Mishnah: He who wants to put his flock on his field makes a corral enclosing two *bet seah*.

42   Mishnah 4:2. That Mishnah seems to forbid what the present Mishnah permits. The current Mishnah is re-interpreted to mean that the owner intends to legally use his field in the Sabbatical year instead of abandoning it.

בְּכֹל עוֹשִׂין סִיחָרִין בְּמַחֲצָלוֹת. וּבְקַשׁ וּבָאֲבָנִים. אֲפִילוּ שְׁלֹשָׁה חֲבָלִים זֶה לְמַעֲלָה מִזֶּה.

With everything one makes [walls of] corrals, with bast mats, straw, or stones, or even three ropes one above the other[43].

43   Tosephta 2:19: "With everything one makes [walls of] corrals, with stones, bast mats, straw, sticks, stalks, or even three ropes one above the other on condition that between one rope and the next there be less that three hand-breadths where a kid goat could pass through," cf. Mishnah *'Eruvin* 1:9; *Kilaim* 4:4, Note 61.

וּבִלְבַד שֶׁלֹּא יְהָא בֵּין סַהַר לְסַהַר כִּמְלוֹא סַהַר. אוֹתוֹ הַמָּקוֹם חוֹלֵב בּוֹ. גּוֹזֵז בּוֹ וּמוֹלִיךְ וּמֵבִיא אֶת הַצֹּאן דֶּרֶךְ עָלֶיהָ.

On condition[44] that between one corral and the next there be less than a full corral. In that place he milks, shears, and through it leads his flock in and out.

44   This does not refer to our Mishnah which requires that consecutive corrals be adjacent but to a text similar to Tosephta Chapter 2: "15. He who wants his field to be manured makes a corral enclosing two *bet seah*. If it is filled, he removes the corral, makes dungheaps on his field in the way people treat dung, and makes a new corral. . . 16. He removes [the walls] from the old corral and uses them for the new one, on condition that between one corral and the next be less than eight *bet seah*, the words of R. Dositheos ben Rebbi Jehudah; Rebbi Yose ben Kipper said in the name of R. Eliezer, two *bet seah*. In these two *bet seah* he milks . . ." It is clear that the Tosephta is not the source of the Yerushalmi.

תַּנֵּי רִבִּי שִׁמְעוֹן בֶּן לְעָזָר אוֹמֵר אִם רָצָה תּוֹקֵעַ אֶת הַיָּתֵד בָּאָרֶץ וְעוֹשֶׂה סְחָרִין
אַרְבָּעָה בְּאַרְבַּע רוּחוֹתֶיהָ שֶׁל שְׁמוֹנַת סְאִין.

It was stated[45]: "Rebbi Simeon ben Eleazar says, if he wishes he sticks a
peg into the ground and makes four corrals in the four cardinal directions
for a total of eight *bet seah*."

45   A similar statement appears in   to make several corrals at the same
Tosephta 2:15. In fig. 3-1, the position   time, Rabban Simeon ben Gamliel only
of the peg is indicated by a small   one after the other.
circle. R. Simeon ben Eleazar permits

אֵין מְדַיְּירִין לֹא בְשַׁבָּתוֹת וְלֹא בְיָמִים טוֹבִים וְלֹא בְחוּלוֹ שֶׁל מוֹעֵד אֲפִילוּ
בְטוֹבָה וְאֵינוֹ רַשַּׁאי לְהוֹשִׁיב שׁוֹמֵר וְלֹא לְנָעֵר אֶת הַצֹּאן וְאִם בָּאוּ מֵאֲלֵיהֶן אֵין
מְסַיְּיעִין אוֹתָן.   וְאִם הָיוּ עוֹשִׂין עִמּוֹ בְשַׁבָּתוֹת וּבְיָמִים טוֹבִים הוּא רַשַּׁאי
לְהוֹשִׁיב שׁוֹמֵר וּלְנָעֵר אֶת הַצֹּאן.   וְאִם בָּאוּ מֵאֲלֵיהֶן מְסַיְּיעִין אוֹתָן.   תַּנֵּי רַבָּן
שִׁמְעוֹן בֶּן גַּמְלִיאֵל אוֹמֵר בַּשַּׁבָּת מְדַיְּירִין בְּטוֹבָה.   וּבְיוֹם טוֹב בִּמְזוֹנוֹת.   וּבְחוּלוֹ
שֶׁל מוֹעֵד אֲפִילוּ בְשָׂכָר.

"[45]One does not fertilize on the Sabbath[46], on holidays, or on the
intermediate days of holidays, even if only for goodwill[47]. One is not
permitted to put a watchman there, nor to have the flock relieve
themselves[48], and if they came by themselves one may not help them.
But if they were working with him over the Sabbaths and holidays[49], he is
permitted to put a watchman there, to have the flock relieve themselves,
and if they came by themselves he may help them." It was stated:
"Rabban Simeon ben Gamliel says, on the Sabbath [workers] fertilize for
goodwill, on the holidays for meals, and on the intermediate days of
holidays even for wages."

45   A similar text appears in To-sephta 2:20 and, restricted to the inter-mediate days of a holiday, in Babli *Mo'ed Qaṭan* 12a. The statement of Rabban Simeon ben Gamliel is ascribed to Rebbi in Tosephta and Babli. The Yerushalmi source, which separates the statement of Rabban Simeon ben Gamliel from the other text, clearly indicates that the latter disagrees with the entire prior statement.

46   From the following it becomes clear that one speaks of Gentile workers, or neighbors, who come to lead the Jewish owner's flock on the Sabbath. Even though leading the flock is not prohibited on the Sabbath, one may not charge a Gentile to do it.

47   The Gentile neighbor does it only so the Jew will do him a favor sometime in the future.

48   One leads the animals around to speed up their evacuations.

49   If the Gentile is hired by the month or for longer periods, one may indicate to him to care for the flock in his usual way on the Sabbath and the holidays.

תַּנֵּי הַשּׂוֹכֵר אֶת הַצֹּאן אָסוּר לְנָעֲרָהּ. מַהוּ לְנָעֲרָהּ מוֹלִיכָהּ מִמָּקוֹם לְמָקוֹם. הָדָא אֲמְרָה בְּשֶׁשְׂכָרָהּ לִזְמַן מוּעָט. אֲבָל בְּשֶׁשְׂכָרָהּ לִזְמַן מְרוּבָּה מוּתָּר. אוֹתוֹ הַיּוֹם הָאַחֲרוֹן אָסוּר.

[50]It was stated[51]: "He who rents a flock may not help them to relieve themselves[48]." What means to help them to relieve themselves? He moves the animals from place to place. That is, if he rented them for a short time. But if he rented it for a longer period it is permitted; only the last day is forbidden.

50   Here starts Halakhah 4 in the Venice text.

51   The *baraita* belongs to *Baba Meẓi'a*, probably an excerpt from a list of conditions in a standard rental contract. The topic is not mentioned in *Baba Meẓi'a;* probably it was not usual to rent flocks, in contrast to the wide-spread custom of renting cattle. The renter may not deprive the owner of manure.

רִבִּי חוֹנָה בְּשֵׁם רַב נַחְמָן בַּר יַעֲקֹב הָהֵן דַּאֲזַל לֵיהּ לְצוֹרְכָא וְלָא מִתְעֲנֵי יִיזֵיל מִן
אֲתַר לְאֲתַר וְהוּא מִתְעֲנֵי. רִבִּי חוֹנָא בְּשֵׁם מַר עוּקְבָּן חַפְרִיתָה עִיקָר טָב לִמְעִיהּ.

Rebbi Ḥuna in the name of Rab Naḥman bar Jacob: He who goes to
do his needs and cannot relieve himself should walk around and he will be
able to relieve himself[52]. Rebbi Ḥuna in the name of Mar Uqba:
Ḥafrita[53] root is good for the intestines.

52   Since the previous paragraph
dealt with evacuations of animals, one
discusses here the human aspect. In the
Babli, *Šabbat* 62a, Rav Ḥisda recom-
mends gymnastics.

53   An unidentified plant. Elsewhere, חפירה is a grass or grain. But

the plant here must have a root used
for medicinal purposes. The best
hypothesis is H. L. Fleischer's, to
explain the name by metathesis from
חרף "to be spicy, hot", as in Arabic חרף
hurf "*Lepidium sativum L.*, common
garden pepper cress."

רִבִּי חִייָא בַּר בָּא שָׁאַל עַד שֶׁלֹּא פֶּסְקוּ עוֹבְדֵי עֲבוֹדָה מַהוּ שֶׁיְּהֵא מוּתָּר לְהוֹצִיא
מִן הַסַּהַר וְלִיתֵּן לְתוֹךְ שָׂדֵהוּ כְּדֶרֶךְ הַמְזַבְּלִין.

Rebbi Ḥiyya bar Abba asked: Before the agricultural workers stopped,
may one be permitted to take from the corral and put on his field in the
way people treat dung[54]?

54   Since the Mishnah does not
mention agricultural workers in this
connection. Maimonides (*Šemiṭṭah*

weYovel 2:6) answers the question in
the affirmative.

(fol. 34b) **משנה ד:** לֹא יִפְתַּח אָדָם מַחְצֵב בִּתְחִילָּה לְתוֹךְ שָׂדֵהוּ עַד שֶׁיְּהוּ שָׁם
שָׁלֹשׁ מוֹרְבִּיוֹת שֶׁהֵן שָׁלֹשׁ עַל שָׁלֹשׁ עַל רוּם שָׁלֹשׁ שִׁיעוּרִין עֶשְׂרִים וְשֶׁבַע אֲבָנִים.

Mishnah 4: Nobody should start a quarry inside his field[55] unless there were three heaps of three by three standard stones[56], 27 stones in all.

משנה ה: גֶּדֶר שֶׁיֵּשׁ בּוֹ עֶשֶׂר אֲבָנִים שֶׁל מַשּׂוֹי שְׁנַיִם שְׁנַיִם הֲרֵי אֵלּוּ יִנָּטֵלוּ. שִׁעוּר גֶּדֶר עֲשָׂרָה טְפָחִים פָּחוֹת מִכֵּן מַחְצֵב וְגוֹמְמוֹ עַד פָּחוֹת מִן הָאָרֶץ טֶפַח.

Mishnah 5: A stone wall containing ten stones, each a load for two carriers, may be taken away. The measure of a stone wall is ten hand-breadths. Less than that is a quarry; he may cut it down to a distance of less than a hand-breadth from the soil.

55   If he has a rock inside his field and wants to quarry it to level it so its place can be covered with earth and used for agriculture the next year, he should not do it in the Sabbatical year unless he started to quarry in the preceding year. A heap consists of three rows of three stones each.

56   The Halakhah will explain that a standard building stone is four hand-breadths wide.

הלכה ה: (fol. 34c) הֵיךְ עֲבִידָא תְּלָתָא זִימְנִין מִן תֵּשַׁע תִּשְׁעָה זִימְנִין מִן תְּלָת עֶשְׂרִין וְשֶׁבַע.

Halakhah 5: How is this? Three times nine, nine times three, 27.

תַּנֵּי מַחְצֵב שֶׁבֵּינוֹ לְבֵין חֲבֵירוֹ וּפָתַח בּוֹ חֲבֵירוֹ בְּהֶתֵּיר מוּתָּר. וְאִם הָיְתָה רֵיקָה אָסוּר.

It was stated: If there was a quarry between him and his neighbor and the neighbor had started to quarry it when it was permitted, this is permitted. But if it was empty of stones[57] it is forbidden.

57   If the neighbor already had flattened his part of the rock and cleaned out his part, there is no pre-existing quarry.

תַּמָּן תַּנִינָן הַזִּיז מֵבִיא אֶת הַטּוּמְאָה בְּכָל־שֶׁהוּא הַגִּזְרָה הַגּוֹבְלִית בְּפוֹתֵחַ טֶפַח.

אָמַר רִבִּי חִייָה בַּר בָּא הָדָא אֲמָרָה זֶה שֶׁהוּא מְקַבֵּל נִדְבָּךְ מֵחֲבֵירוֹ צָרִיךְ לַעֲשׂוֹת

לוֹ אַרְבָּעָה טְפָחִים כְּדֵי (fol. 34d) מָקוֹם. אָמַר רִבִּי יוֹסֵי מַתְנִיתָא אֲמָרָה כֵן

וּבְמָה אָמְרוּ הַזִּיז מֵבִיא אֶת הַטּוּמְאָה בְּכָל־שֶׁהוּא בְּזִיז שֶׁהוּא גָבוֹהַּ מִן הַפֶּתַח

שְׁלֹשָׁה נִדְבָּכִין שֶׁהֵן שְׁנֵים עָשָׂר טֶפַח. וְלָמָּה תַנִינָן נִדְבָּכִין לְמִדַּת הַדִּין.

There[58], we have stated: "Any moulding[59] brings impurity, the frieze[60] [and] the Giblean frieze[61] [only] when they are open one hand-breadth." Rebbi Ḥiyya sayd, that means that anybody who receives a row of building stones from another person must prepare for it a space of four hand-breadths[62]. Rebbi Yose said, the Mishnah says so: "When did they say that any moulding brings impurity? For a moulding higher than the door by three rows of stones which is twelve hand-breadths." Why did they state "rows of stones?" For the legal standard[63].

---

58   Mishnah *Ahilut* 14:1. Tractate *Ahilut* deals with the impurity brought on anything in a "tent" by a corpse in that tent (*Num.* 19). Any person or vessel under one roof with the corpse becomes impure; cf. *Kilaim* Chapter 6, Note 25.

59   A moulding is defined as a frieze along the outer wall of a house which is u-shaped downwards. The outer rim of the frieze points downward; its prolongation is considered a virtual wall closing off the house; anything between this virtual wall and the house itself is considered as part of the "tent".

60   The "frieze" is u-shaped upwards; the bottom of the frieze contributes to the "tent" only if it is substantial, if it extends at least one hand-breadth outside the wall of the house.

61   In the style of the city of Byblos, Hebrew גבל, Arabic جبيل. The Tosephta *Ahilut* defines this as a frieze u-shaped upwards at its ends and flat in the middle; this definition is accepted by the Gaonic commentary to *Ahilut*.

62   The proof is from the part of the Mishnah quoted by R. Yose. The 12 hand-breadths mentioned are a maximum height; friezes higher than 12

hand-breadths above the door (according to Maimonides, above the doorstep) are disregarded.

63   For the rules of impurity, the mention of the rows of stones is superfluous.

רִבִּי חִיָּה בַּר בָּא שָׁאַל אִילֵין שִׁיעוּרַיָּא כְּאִינּוּן שִׁיעוּרַיָּא. רִבִּי חִזְקִיָּה רִבִּי64
יַעֲקֹב בַּר אָחָא בְּשֵׁם רִבִּי יוֹסֵי בֶּן חֲנִינָא אִילֵין שִׁיעוּרַיָּא כְּאִינּוּן שִׁיעוּרַיָּא. הָכָא
אַתְּ אָמַר שִׁיעוּר גֶּדֶר עֲשָׂרָה טְפָחִים פָּחוֹת מִכֵּן מַחְצֵב וְכָא אַתְּ אָמַר הָכֵין. מַה
נָן קַיָּימִין אִם כְּשֶׁהָיוּ שְׁנֵי נִדְבָּכִין נִיתְּנָן שְׁמוֹנָה טְפָחִים. אִם כְּשֶׁהָיוּ שְׁלֹשָׁה
נִיתְנִי שְׁנֵים עָשָׂר טְפָחִים. אָמַר רִבִּי יוֹסֵי צֵא חֲצִי טֶפַח לְסִיתּוּת מִכֵּן וַחֲצִי טֶפַח
לְסִיתּוּת מִכָּאן וְכֵן לְחַבְרֵיהּ נִמְצָא שְׁלֹשָׁה שֶׁל נִדְבָּכִין שֶׁל עֲשָׂרָה טְפָחִים. פָּחוֹת
מִיכֵּן אֵינוֹ לֹא גֶּדֶר וְלֹא מַחְצֵב.

Rebbi Ḥiyya bar Abba asked, are these standards like those standards[65]? Rebbi Ḥizqiah, Rebbi Jacob bar Aḥa in the name of Rebbi Yose ben Ḥanina: These standards are like those standards. Here you say "the measure of a stone wall is ten hand-breadths, less than that is a quarry;" and there you say so? Where do we stand? If there were two rows of stones, one should state "eight hand-breadths"; if there were three one should state "twelve hand-breadths!" Rebbi Yose said, deduct half a hand-breadth for hewing top and bottom and so for the next row, one finds three rows of ten hand-breadths[66]. Less than that is neither a stone wall nor a quarry[67].

64   Reading of the Rome ms. Venice: בר
65   May the commercial standard of stones indicated in *Ahilut* 14:1 be applied to *Ševi'it*?

66   The height of four hand-breadths is required in a standard contract only for unhewn stones.
67   Unless the conditions of Mishnah 3 are satisfied.

(fol. 34b) **מִשְׁנָה ו**: בְּמֶה דְבָרִים אֲמוּרִים מִתּוֹךְ שֶׁלּוֹ אֲבָל מִתּוֹךְ שֶׁל חֲבֵירוֹ מַה שֶׁהוּא רוֹצֶה יִטּוֹל. בְּמֶה דְבָרִים אֲמוּרִים בִּזְמָן שֶׁלֹּא הִתְחִיל בּוֹ מֵעֶרֶב שְׁבִיעִית. אֲבָל אִם הִתְחִיל בּוֹ מֵעֶרֶב שְׁבִיעִית מַה שֶׁהוּא רוֹצֶה יִטּוֹל.

Mishnah 6: That is, from his own[68]. But from another person's, he may take what he wants. That is, if he did not start it[69] before the Sabbatical year. But if he started it before the Sabbatical year, he may take what he wants.

68 In the Mishnah codices, this is part of Mishnah 5 and refers to it. Stones are not abandoned in the Sabbatical, and one must pay for the	stones he takes from another's property. 69 Dismantling the stone wall.

(fol. 34d) **הֲלָכָה ו**: תַּנֵּי אָמַר רִבִּי יוּדָה בְּמֶה דְבָרִים אֲמוּרִים בִּזְמָן שֶׁלֹּא נִתְכַּוֵּון לְתִיקּוּן שָׂדֵהוּ. אֲבָל אִם נִתְכַּוֵּון לְתִיקּוּן שָׂדֵהוּ אֲפִילוּ יוֹתֵר מִיכֵּן מוּתָּר. אָמַר רַבָּן שִׁמְעוֹן בֶּן גַּמְלִיאֵל בְּמֶה דְבָרִים אֲמוּרִים בִּזְמָן שֶׁלֹּא נִתְכַּוֵּון לְתִיקּוּן שָׂדֵהוּ. אֲבָל אִם נִתְכַּוֵּון לְתִיקּוּן שָׂדֵהוּ אֲפִילוּ פָּחוֹת מִיכֵּן אָסוּר. אָמַר רִבִּי בִּיבִי הֹרֵי רִבִּי יָסָא כְּדוֹן תַּנְיָא לְקוּלָה.

Halakhah 6: We have stated[70]: "Rebbi Jehudah said that is if he did not intend to improve his field; but if he intended to improve his field even more is permitted. Rabban Simeon ben Gamliel said, that is if he did not intend to improve his field; but if he intended to improve his field even less is forbidden." Rebbi Vivian said, Rebbi Assi taught following the Tanna who is lenient.

70 Tosephta 3:1-2: "Rebbi Jehudah said that is if he intended to improve his field; but if he did not intend to improve his field even more is per-	mitted. Rabban Simeon ben Gamliel said, that is if he did not intend to improve his field; but if he intended to improve his field anything is for

bidden." From Maimonides's Code (*Ševi'it weYovel* 2:8) it seems that he read in the Yerushalmi as in the Tosephta; R. Isaac Simponti quotes the Yerushalmi as in the Tosephta. From the silence of all Medieval commentators one may conclude that they all read the text of the Tosephta in the Yerushalmi. In the early Sixteenth Century, R. Joseph Caro had the text of the Yerushalmi as given here, as can be seen from his commentary to Maimonides (*loc. cit.*) Cf. *Tosefta ki-fshtutah* p. 512.

(fol. 34b) **משנה ז**: אֲבָנִים שֶׁזִּיְעַזְעָתָן הַמַּחֲרֵישָׁה אוֹ שֶׁהָיוּ מְכוּסוֹת וְנִתְגַּלּוּ אִם יֵשׁ בָּהֶן שְׁתַּיִם שֶׁל מַשּׂוֹי שְׁנַיִם שְׁנַיִם הֲרֵי אֵלּוּ יִנָּטְלוּ. וְהַמְסַקֵּל אֶת שָׂדֵהוּ נוֹטֵל אֶת הָעֶלְיוֹנוֹת וּמַנִּיחַ אֶת הַנּוֹגְעוֹת בָּאָרֶץ. וְכֵן גַּרְגֵּר שֶׁל צְרוֹרוֹת אוֹ גַל שֶׁל אֲבָנִים נוֹטֵל אֶת הָעֶלְיוֹנוֹת וּמַנִּיחַ אֶת הַנּוֹגְעוֹת בָּאָרֶץ אִם יֵשׁ הַתַּחְתּוֹן סֶלַע אוֹ קַשׁ הֲרֵי אֵלּוּ יִנָּטְלוּ.

Mishnah 7: Stones which the plough displaced or which were hidden and became uncovered may be taken if among them there are two which are a load for two carriers[71]. He who clears his field from stones takes the upper ones[72] and leaves those which touch the soil. And so from a round heap[73] of pebbles or a stone heap, he takes the upper ones and leaves those which touch the soil; if beneath them is rock or straw they may be taken.

71   The size of the stones indicates that he is not engaged in agricultural work.

72   Since they do not touch the ground, taking them is not working the soil.

73   This is the dictionaries's guess of a secondary meaning of גרגיר "kernel." The better reading is that of the Maimonides tradition of the Mishnah and the Kaufmann ms.: גרגש "lump". The rule refers to lumps of stones on

agricultural soil, but if the pebbles lie
either on bare rock or are separated
from the soil by a layer of straw they
may be taken.

(fol. 34d) **הלכה ז**:   לֹא סוֹף דָּבָר בְּשֶׁיְּעַזְעֲתָן הַמַּחֲרֵישָׁה אֶלָּא אֲפִילוּ מַחֲרֵישָׁה
עֲתִידָה לְזַעְזְעָן.   אָמַר רִבִּי יוֹסֵי מַתְנִיתָה אָמְרָה כֵן.   אִם יֵשׁ בְּכָל אַחַת וְאַחַת שֶׁל
מַשּׂוֹי שְׁנַיִם שְׁנַיִם הֲרֵי אֵלּוּ יִנָּטְלוּ.

Halakhah 7:   Not only if the plough displaced them, but even if the
plough might displace them in the future.   Rebbi Yose said, a *baraita* says
so[74]: "They may be taken if among all of them there are two which are a
two-person load".

74   Probably the reference is to
some text similar to Tosephta 3:4
"Sitting stones which the plough dis-
places may be taken if among them
there are two which are a load for two
carriers".   Sitting stones have not yet
been moved.   The expression "all of
them" is difficult to understand.

רִבִּי יַעֲקֹב בַּר בּוּן בְּשֵׁם רִבִּי שִׁמְעוֹן בֶּן לָקִישׁ.   זֹאת אוֹמֶרֶת שֶׁאָסוּר לְלַקֵּט
צְרוֹרוֹת מִתּוֹךְ שָׂדֶה חֲבֵירוֹ דִּי מְנַכֵּשׁ וְיַהֵב עִיסְבֵּיהּ עֲלֵיהוֹן.   הָדָא דְתֵימָא
בִּבְקְעָה אֲבָל בֶּהָרִים וּבִטְרָשִׁים מוּתָּר וְטִיבוּ חָשֵׁב לֵיהּ.

[75]Rebbi Jacob bar Abun in the name of Rebbi Simeon ben Laqish: This
means[76] that it is forbidden to collect pebbles from another person's field,
for if he weeds, he will put his grasses there.   That is, in an agricultural
area, but on mountains and rocks it is permitted and he will think of it as
a kindness.

75   In the Venice print, here starts
Halakhah 8.
76   Since the stones have not been
taken in the course of the regular
tending of the field.

(fol. 34b) **משנה ח:** אֵין בּוֹנִין מַדְרֵיגוֹת עַל פִּי גֵיאָיוֹת עֶרֶב שְׁבִיעִית מִשֶּׁפֶּסְקוּ גְשָׁמִים מִפְּנֵי שֶׁהוּא מְתַקְּנוֹ לַשְּׁבִיעִית. אֲבָל בּוֹנֶה הוּא בַּשְּׁבִיעִית מִשֶּׁפֶּסְקוּ גְשָׁמִים מִפְּנֵי שֶׁהוּא מַתְקִינָן לְמוֹצָאֵי שְׁבִיעִית. וְלֹא יִסְמוֹךְ בֶּעָפָר אֲבָל עוֹשֵׂהוּ חַיִיץ. כָּל־אֶבֶן שֶׁהוּא יָכוֹל לִפְשׁוֹט אֶת יָדָיו וְלִיטְלָהּ הֲרֵי זוֹ תִינָּטֵל.

Mishnah 8: One does not build steps[77] out of ravines[78] before the Sabbatical year after the rains stopped because that is preparation for the Sabbatical. But he may build during the Sabbatical year after the rains stopped because that is preparation for the year after the Sabbatical. One should not fill with earth but he may use it for a divider. Any stone may be taken if he can stretch out his hand and take it[79].

[77] This is the standard meaning of the word; Maimonides explains it by Arabic דרג "staircase". The explanation given by the classical commentaries is that hewn stairs down the ravine make it easier to draw water for manual irrigation. It seems to me that a better interpretation would be: "One does not build terraces out of ravines." There is nothing in the Halakhah that would contradict this interpretation. If the Mishnah permits building terraces during the dry season of the Sabbatical year, it makes sense that one may not fill the terraces with earth since that clearly would be agricultural work. If one speaks of stairs, it is difficult to see why one would want to fill up with earth what will be washed away by next winter's rains.

[78] Translation of Maimonides, Arabic אונדק.

[79] Without a tool.

(fol. 34d) **הלכה ח:** רִבִּי קְרִיסְפָּא בְשֵׁם רִבִּי יוֹחָנָן. חֲנַנְיָה בֶּן גַּמְלִיאֵל בְּאִיסוּר שְׁנֵי פְרָקִים הִיא מַתְנִיתָא. תַּנֵּי רִבִּי יוּדָה וְרִבִּי נְחֶמְיָה אוֹסְרִין. לֹא בְאִיסּוּר שְׁנֵי פְרָקִים וְכָא בְּאִיסּוּר שְׁנֵי פְרָקִים. רִבִּי שַׁמַּאי בָּעֵי אִם בְּאִיסּוּר שְׁנֵי פְרָקִים כְּהָדָא תַּנִּינָן לַחֲרוֹשׁ מוּתָּר וְלִבְנוֹת אָסוּר. אֶלָּא בְּהֶיתֵּר שְׁנֵי פְרָקִים. אִם בְּהֶיתֵּר שְׁנֵי פְרָקִים כְּהָדָא תַּנִּינָן אֲבָל בּוֹנֶה הוּא בַּשְּׁבִיעִית מִשֶּׁפֶּסְקוּ גְשָׁמִים

מִפְּנֵי שֶׁהוּא מַתְקִינָן לְמוֹצָאֵי שְׁבִיעִית. אָמַר רְבִי מָנָא יֵאוּת. אָמַר רְבִי שַׁמַּאי
הָדָא קַדְמִיתָא לַחֲרוֹשׁ מוּתָּר מִפְּנֵי שֶׁהוּא מַתְקִינָן לְמוֹצָאֵי שְׁבִיעִית. לִבְנוֹת
אָסוּר מִפְּנֵי שֶׁהוּא מַתְקִינָן לַשְּׁבִיעִית. מַתְנִיתָא לֹא אָמַר כֵּן אֶלָּא אֲבָל בּוֹנֶה
הוּא בַּשְּׁבִיעִית מִשֶּׁפָּסְקוּ גְשָׁמִים מִפְּנֵי שֶׁהוּא מַתְקִינָן לְמוֹצָאֵי שְׁבִיעִית.

Halakhah 8: Rebbi Crispus in the name of Rebbi Johanan, Hananiah ben Gamliel[80]: The Mishnah refers to the prohibition of the two terms[81]. It was stated: "Rebbi Jehudah and Rebbi Nehemiah forbid it[82]." Does this not refer to the prohibition of the two terms, so here also about the prohibition of the two terms. Rebbi Shammai inquired: If this is about the prohibition of the two terms, did we state that one is permitted to plough[83] but forbidden to build? So it must refer to the permission of the two terms. If it refers to the permission of the two terms, we have stated: "But he may build during the Sabbatical year after the rains stopped because that is preparation for the year after the Sabbatical." Rebbi Mana said, is Rebbi Shammai correct? In the first case, one is permitted to plough because that prepares for the year after the Sabbatical[84]. It is forbidden to build since that prepares for the Sabbatical. The Mishnah does not say so, "but he may build during the Sabbatical year after the rains stopped because that is preparation for the year after the Sabbatical.[85]"

80　　He might be R. Hananiah ben Gamliel, oldest son of Rabban Gamliel, brother of Rabban Simeon ben Gamliel, Tanna of the fourth generation. In that case, it would be difficult to disagree with his determination, since he would have heard from his father that with the two terms he also abolished the prohibition of building.

81　　Cf. Chapter 1, Note 5. Since the prohibition was lifted, the Mishnah would no longer be operative.

82　　This fragment of a *baraita* contradicts Tosephta 3:4: "Rebbi

Nehemiah says one builds steps out of ravines in the year before the Sabbatical and fills them with earth during the Sabbatical down to the ravine." If there is a text by R. Nehemiah that forbids building, that text would refer to the prohibition of the two terms and the Tosephta to the permission.

83   After the rains stopped, some time before Passover, it is possible to plough until Pentecost at least, but it would be forbidden to build. This does not make sense since ploughing is a direct agricultural activity but building is only an indirect one.

84   It is good practice to plough a field with large furrows before letting it lay fallow.

85   Hence R. Crispus in the name of Rebbi Johanan is justified and practice should follow R. Nehemiah in the Tosephta.

לֹא יִסְכֹּךְ בֶּעָפָר אֲבָל עוֹשֵׂהוּ חַיִיץ. מַהוּ חַיִיץ. חָיִיץ לֵיהּ כְּמָה דְתֵימַר וְהוּא בּוֹנֶה חַיִיץ.

"He should not cover it[86] with earth but he may use it for a divider." What is a divider? It divides, as it is said (Ez. 13:10): "He is building a dividing wall."

86   This reading in the Mishnah, יסכך, is only in the Leyden ms. The Arukh and the Tosafists' tradition read יסבוך "scramble". Some late mss. have יסכור "dam up".

משנה ט: אַבְנֵי כָתֵף בָּאוֹת מִכָּל־מָקוֹם. וְהַקַּבְּלָן מְבִיאָן מִכָּל־מָקוֹם. וְאֵילוּ הֵן אַבְנֵי כָתֵף כָּל־שֶׁאֵינָהּ יְכוֹלָה לִינָּטֵל בְּאַחַת יַד דִּבְרֵי רִבִּי מֵאִיר. רִבִּי יוֹסֵי אוֹמֵר אַבְנֵי כָתֵף כִּשְׁמָן כָּל־שֶׁהֵן נִיטָּלוֹת שָׁלֹשׁ אוֹ שְׁתַּיִם עַל הַכָּתֵף.

Mishnah 9: Shoulder stones come from anywhere[87]. The contractor[88] may bring them from anywhere. These are shoulder stones: Any which cannot be taken up with one hand, the words of Rebbi Meïr. Rebbi Yose says shoulder stones are what their name indicates; all that can be carried on the shoulder by three's or two's.

87   Used for building, not for agriculture.

88   According to Maimonides, a person who contracts for the upkeep of fields. According to R. Simson of Sens, a building contractor. According to R. Isaac Simponti, a contractor for building materials. The interpretations of RR. Simson and Isaac are preferable since all people in the contractor's town know that he does not collect the stones to clean out a field.

(fol. 34d) **הלכה ט:**   אַבְנֵי כָתֵף בָּאוֹת מִכָּל־מָקוֹם אֲפִילוּ מִתּוֹךְ שֶׁלּוֹ וְהַקּוּבְּלָן מֵבִיא מִכָּל־מָקוֹם אֲפִילוּ פָּחוֹת מֵאַבְנֵי כָתֵף.

Halakhah 9: "Shoulder stones come from anywhere," even from his own [property] and "the contractor may bring from anywhere," even smaller than shoulder stones.

(fol. 34b) **משנה י:** הַבּוֹנֶה גָדֵר בֵּינוֹ וּבֵין רְשׁוּת הָרַבִּים מוּתָּר לְהַעֲמִיק עַד הַסֶּלַע. מַה יַעֲשֶׂה בֶּעָפָר צוֹבְרוֹ בִּרְשׁוּת הָרַבִּים וּמַתְקִינוֹ דִּבְרֵי רִבִּי יְהוֹשֻׁעַ. רִבִּי עֲקִיבָה אוֹמֵר כְּדֶרֶךְ שֶׁאֵין מְקַלְקְלִין בִּרְשׁוּת הָרַבִּים כָּךְ לֹא יְתַקֵּן. מַה יַעֲשֶׂה בֶּעָפָר צוֹבְרוֹ בְּתוֹךְ שָׂדֵהוּ כְּדֶרֶךְ הַמְזַבְּלִין וְכֵן הַחוֹפֵר בּוֹר וְשִׁיחַ וּמְעָרָה.

Mishnah 10: Somebody building a fence between his property and the public domain may dig down to the bedrock. What should he do with the soil? He makes heaps in the public domain and then uses it to improve [the public domain], the words of Rebbi Joshua. Rebbi Aqiba says, just as one may not damage the public domain, so one may not improve it.

What should he do with the soil? He makes heaps on his own property in the way of those who manure[89]. The same rule applies to somebody digging a cistern, a ditch, or a cave.

89   Three heaps of 150 *seah* each per *bet seah*.

(fol. 34d) **הלכה י:**   רְבִּי חִייָה בְשֵׁם רְבִּי יוֹחָנָן לֹא שָׁנוּ אֶלָּא בֵּינוֹ לְבֵין רְשׁוּת הָרַבִּים. הָא בֵּינוֹ לְבֵין חֲבֵירוֹ אָסוּר בַּשְּׁבִיעִית. אֲבָל בְּמוֹעֵד אֲפִילוּ בֵּינוֹ לְבֵין רְשׁוּת הָרַבִּים אָסוּר. בְּפִירְצָה שֶׁהִיא סָגָה אֶת הֶעָפָר אֲבָל בְּפִירְצָה שֶׁאֵינָהּ סָגָה אֶת הֶעָפָר מוּתָּר לְגוֹדְרָהּ בַּשְּׁבִיעִית. וְתַנֵּי כֵן כָּל־פִּירְצָה שֶׁהִיא סָגָה בֶּעָפָר אָסוּר לְגוֹדְרָהּ בַּשְּׁבִיעִית. וְשֶׁאֵינָהּ סָגָה אֶת הֶעָפָר מוּתָּר לְגוֹדְרָהּ בַּשְּׁבִיעִית. וְשֶׁאֵינָהּ מַכְשֶׁלֶת אֶת הָרַבִּים אֲבָל אִם הָיְתָה מַכְשֶׁלֶת אֶת הָרַבִּים אַף עַל פִּי שֶׁהִיא[90] סָגָה אֶת הֶעָפָר מוּתָּר לְגוֹדְרָהּ בַּשְּׁבִיעִית.

Halakhah 10: Rebbi Ḥiyya in the name of Rebbi Joḥanan: They stated only "between his property and the public domain"; hence, between his own and his neighbor's properties [building] is forbidden in the Sabbatical year. But on the intermediate days of a holiday, even between his property and the public domain it is forbidden. [91]About a breach that fences soil; but a breach that does not fence soil[92] may be repaired in the Sabbatical year. We have stated so: "Any breach that fences soil one is forbidden to repair in the Sabbatical year; any breach that does not fence soil one may repair in the Sabbatical year." That is, if it does not endanger the public, but if it endangers the public one may repair even if it does fence soil[93].

90   Reading of the parallel in *Mo'ed Qaṭan* 1:4. Here: שאינה.

91   From here to the end of the paragraph, the text is also in *Mo'ed Qaṭan* 1:4 (fol. 80c).

92   If the wall between two private

properties does not divide agricultural soil but stony ground or a road, it may be repaired in the Sabbatical year because this is not agricultural work.

93 While in general one does not sow too close to a public road, if a solid stone fence separates the field from the road, all land inside may be used for crops and repairing the fence is an agricultural activity unless the breach in the wall constitutes a danger for those on the public road.

כְּתִיב וְשָׂם דֶּרֶךְ אַרְאֶנּוּ בְּיֵשַׁע אֱלֹהִים. שַׁנְיָיא הִיא הָכָא שֶׁהוּא תִּיקוּן וְסוֹפוֹ קִילְקוּל. דְּאָמַר רבִּי שִׁמְעוֹן בֶּן לָקִישׁ שָׁאוּל לֹא זָכָה לַמְּלוּכָה אֶלָּא עַל יְדֵי שֶׁהָיָה זְקֵינוֹ מַדְלִיק נֵר לָרַבִּים נִקְרָא שְׁמוֹ נֵר. כָּתוּב אֶחָד אוֹמֵר וְנֵר הוֹלִיד אֶת קִישׁ. וְכָתוּב אֶחָד אוֹמֵר קִישׁ בֶּן אֲבִיאֵל. וַהֲלֹא אֲבִיאֵל הָיָה שְׁמוֹ אֶלָּא עַל יְדֵי שֶׁהָיָה זְקֵינוֹ מַדְלִיק נֵר לָרַבִּים נִקְרָא שְׁמוֹ נֵר.

It is written (*Ps.* 50:23): "To him who makes a road I shall show the help of God.[94]" There is a difference here, because this is an improvement which becomes a defect[95]. Since Rebbi Simeon ben Laqish said, Saul merited the kingship only because his grandfather lit lights for the public; for that he was called "Ner". One verse (*1Chr.* 8:33) says "Ner begot Qish." Another verse (*1S.* 9:1) says "Qish the son of Abi'el." Was not his name Abi'el? But his name became Ner because his grandfather lit lights for the public.

94 This refers to the opinion of R. Aqiba that a private person may not make improvements in the public domain. The verse is explained in *Lev. rabba* 9(2), *Tanḥuma Teẓawweh* 9, to refer to those who install lighting on public roads at their own expense. Hence, improving the public domain is a meritorious deed. The text which proves this, from "Since R. Simeon . . . " to the end of the paragraph, is a slightly shortened version of the Midrash text.

95 Filling potholes with earth alone is only a temporary expedient that will lead to larger potholes the next rainy season.

רְבִּי אָבוּן בָּעֵי עַד שֶׁלֹּא פֶּסְקוּ עוֹבְדֵי עֲבוֹדָה מַהוּ לִצְבּוֹר עָפָר בְּתוֹךְ שָׂדֵהוּ כְדֶרֶךְ הַמְזַבְּלִין.

Rebbi Abun asked: Before the agricultural workers stop, may one make heaps on his own property in the way of those who spread manure[96]?

96 Since "in the way of those who spread manure" implies that the work is done only after the end of the agricultural season, does this condition carry over to the case here where it makes no direct sense? Maimonides does not take up the problem.

(fol. 34d) **משנה א**: בָּרִאשׁוֹנָה הָיוּ אוֹמְרִים מְלַקֵּט אָדָם עֵצִים וַאֲבָנִים וַעֲשָׂבִים מִתּוֹךְ שֶׁלּוֹ כְּדֶרֶךְ שֶׁהוּא מְלַקֵּט מִתּוֹךְ שֶׁל חֲבֵירוֹ אֶת הַגַּס הַגַּס. וּמִשֶּׁרָבוּ עוֹבְרֵי עֲבֵירָה הִתְקִינוּ שֶׁיְּהֵא זֶה מְלַקֵּט מִתּוֹךְ שֶׁל זֶה וְזֶה מְלַקֵּט מִתּוֹךְ שֶׁל זֶה שֶׁלֹּא בְטוֹבָה וְאֵין צוֹרֶךְ לוֹמַר שֶׁיִּקְצֹץ לָהֶן מְזוֹנוֹת.

Mishnah 1: In earlier times they said a person may collect wood, stones, and grasses on his own property in the way he may collect on somebody else's property, but only large pieces[1]. But after transgressors became numerous[2] they decreed that everybody only collect from somebody else's without reciprocity[3] and it goes without saying that he does not have to allot him food[4].

1 Since agricultural land is accessible to everybody in the Sabbatical year, one may collect not only food but also weeds, etc. But it is forbidden to weed and to improve one's property in the Sabbatical; therefore, the owner only is permitted to remove large pieces from his field, not small weeds and small stones whose removal requires the most effort.

2 They said that they were taking large pieces when in effect they were weeding and clearing their fields from stones.

3 He arranges to clear a friend's field and the friend will clear his.

4 The last clause is unnecessary. If a person removing weeds and pebbles from another person's field cannot expect that the other person will do the same for him, he cannot expect the other person to feed him while he is cleaning his field.

(fol.35) **הלכה א:** בָּרִאשׁוֹנָה הָיוּ אוֹמְרִים כו'. אָמַר רִבִּי יוֹנָה הָכֵין צוֹרְכָא

מִיתְנֵי בָּרִאשׁוֹנָה הָיוּ אוֹמְרִים מְלַקֵּט אָדָם עֵצִים וַעֲשָׂבִים מִתּוֹךְ שֶׁלּוֹ אֶת הַגַּס

הַגַּס כְּדֶרֶךְ שֶׁהוּא מְלַקֵּט לְשֶׁל חֲבֵירוֹ בֵּין דַּקִּים בֵּין גַּסִּים. נֶחְשְׁדוּ לִהְיוֹת מְלַקְּטִין

וְהֵן אוֹמֵר בַּגַּסִּים לִיקַּטְנוּ. הִתְקִינוּ שֶׁיְּהֵא זֶה מְלַקֵּט מִתּוֹךְ שֶׁל זֶה וְזֶה מְלַקֵּט

מִתּוֹךְ שֶׁל זֶה שֶׁלֹּא בְטוֹבָה. נֶחְשְׁדוּ לִהְיוֹת מְלַקְּטִין בְּטוֹבָה וְהֵן אוֹמֵר שֶׁלֹּא

בְטוֹבָה לִיקַּטְנוּ. הִתְקִינוּ שֶׁיְּהוּ מְבִיאִין מִן הַקָּרוֹב וּמִן הַמָּצוּי.

Halakhah 1: "In earlier times they said," etc. Rebbi Jonah said, the Mishnah has to be stated as follows[5]: In earlier times they said, a person may collect wood, stones, and grasses on his own property, but only large pieces, in the way he may collect on somebody else's property both large and small pieces. When they suspected that people were collecting but were saying, we took only large pieces, they decreed that everybody only collect from somebody else's property without reciprocity. When they suspected that people were collecting in reciprocity but saying, we collected without reciprocity, they decreed that one may collect only from close by and from what is in ample supply[6].

5   A much shortened version of this is in Tosephta 3:8.

6   The commentators, from R. Eliahu Fulda to R. Saul Lieberman,

translate המצוי by "ownerless property", but this acceptation is not supported by any parallels.

אָמַר רִבִּי זְעִירָא רִאשׁוֹנָה רִאשׁוֹנָה מִתְקַיְּימִין.

Rebbi Zeïra said, first and first are supported[7].

7   Of the three restrictions indicated by R. Jonah and the Tosephta, only the first two, that one may not collect from one's own other than

coarse matter and that one may not collect in reciprocity, are valid. The third one, not mentioned in the Mishnah, is not practice.

הָיְתָה בְהֶמְתּוֹ שָׁם בְּהֶמְתּוֹ מוֹכַחַת עָלָיו. הָיְתָה כִּירָתוֹ שָׁם כִּירָתוֹ מוֹכַחַת עָלָיו.
לִיקֵּט בְּנִסִּין מַהוּ שֶׁיַּחֲזִיר וִילַקֵּט מִן הַנַּסִּים שֶׁבְּדַקִּים. אִם אָמַר אַתְּ כֵּן אַף הוּא
מְלַקֵּט אֶת כָּל־שָׂדֵהוּ בַּשְּׁבִיעִית.

If his animal was there, his animal is proof for him[8]. If his cooking
stove was there, his cooking stove proves for him[9]. If he collected the
coarse pieces, may he come back and collect the coarsest of the smaller
ones? If you say so, he will collect his entire field.

8   He collects weeds as animal   fragment has כורתו "his basket" instead
fodder, not to weed his field.   of כירתו "his cooking stove"; this might
9   He collects fallen wood as fuel, be the better reading.
not to clean his field. A Genizah

הָיְתָה שָׂדֵהוּ מְלֵיאָה נַסִּין תַּרְתֵּין מַתְנָיִין חָדָא אָמַר שָׁרֵי וְחָדָא אָמְרָה אָסוּר.
הַמְסַקֵּל שָׂדֵהוּ נוֹטֵל אֶת הָעֶלְיוֹנוֹת וּמַנִּיחַ אֶת הַנּוֹגְעוֹת בָּאָרֶץ הָדָא אָמְרָה שָׁרֵי.
אֵי זֶהוּ הַמֵּידַל אַחַת אוֹ שְׁתַּיִם הָדָא אָמְרָה אָסוּר.

If his field was full of coarse pieces[10], there are two Mishnaiot; one said,
it is permitted, one said, it is forbidden. (Mishnah 3:7) "He who clears his
field from stones takes the upper ones and leaves those which touch the
ground[11];" that means it is permitted. (Mishnah 4:4) "Who is the one who
thins out? He takes one or two;[12]" that means it is forbidden.

10   If he takes all the coarse pieces,   12   The Mishnah deals with a
his field is weeded and cleaned.   person pruning olive trees. One may
11   There is no limit on the number   thin but one may not clean out. The
of stones he may remove; even if his   one who thins cuts one or two
entire property is covered with stones   branches; more is cleaning. This Mish-
he may remove them. Since the   nah stipulates that one may not clean
Mishnah here does not indicate any   his olive tree completely; by analogy
limit on what one may take, there is no   one may not clean out his field.
limit.

אַף בְּמוֹעֵד כֵּן. אַשְׁכַּח תַּנָּא תַּנֵּי מְלַקֵּט אָדָם עֵצִים וַעֲשָׂבִים מִתּוֹךְ שֶׁלוֹ אֶת הַגַּס
הַגַּס כְּדֶרֶךְ שֶׁהוּא מְלַקֵּט מִתּוֹךְ שֶׁל חֲבֵירוֹ בֵּין דַּקִּין בֵּין נַסִּין. בַּשְּׁבִיעִית אֲבָל
לֹא בְּמוֹעֵד. אַף בָּאֲבָנִים כֵּן. אַשְׁכַּח תַּנֵּי אַף בָּאֲבָנִים. הַלֵּב יוֹדֵעַ אִם לְעַקֵּל אִם
לַעֲקַלְקָלוֹת. רִבִּי יוֹסָה בְּשֵׁם מְנַחֵם רִבִּי עֲקִיבָה עֲבַד כְּשִׁיטָתֵיהּ. חָמָא חַד
אִיזְמַר כַּרְמָא. אֲמַר לֵיהּ וְלֵית אָסוּר. אֲמַר לֵיהּ לְעַקְלִין אֲנָא בָּעֵי הַלֵּב יוֹדֵעַ
אִם לְעַקֵּל אִם לַעֲקַלְקָלוֹת.

Is it the same on the intermediate days of a holiday? A Tanna was
found who stated: "A person may collect wood, stones, and grasses on his
own property, but only large pieces, in the way he may collect on
somebody else's property both large and small pieces, in a Sabbatical year
but not during he intermediate days of a holiday." Is it the same for
stones[13]? It was found stated "including stones". "The heart knows
whether it is straight or crooked.[14]" Rebbi Yosah in the name of
Menaḥem: Rebbi Aqiba followed his own rule. He saw a person pruning
his vineyard. He said to him, is that not forbidden? He said to him, I
need it to make basket weave. The heart knows whether it is for basket
weave or for crookedness.

13   Since stones were mentioned in
the preceding *baraita*, the question
seems to be out of place. One has to
assume that the *baraita* before the
editors of the Yerushalmi did not
mention stones. Tosephta 3:8 in all
sources has "olives" instead of "wood,
stones, and grasses"; this must be an old
corruption.

14   Tosephta 3:8. R. S. Lieberman
notes that the saying, traced to R.
Aqiba in the next sentences, is an
untranslatable pun on עקל (noun)
"basket weave" and עקל (verb) "to
straighten what is curved". As a hint,
both meanings are used in the
translation, one here and one at the end
of the paragraph.

(fol. 34d) **משנה ב**: שָׂדֶה שֶׁנִּתְקַוְוצָה תִּיזָּרע לְמוֹצָאֵי שְׁבִיעִית. שֶׁנִּטַיְּיבָה אוֹ שֶׁנִּדַּיְירָה לֹא תִיזָרע לְמוֹצָאֵי שְׁבִיעִית. שָׂדֶה שֶׁנִּטַיְּיבָה. בֵּית שַׁמַּאי אוֹמְרִים אֵין אוֹכְלִין פֵּירוֹתֶיהָ בַּשְּׁבִיעִית. וּבֵית הֶלֵּל אוֹמְרִים אוֹכְלִין. בֵּית שַׁמַּאי אוֹמְרִים אֵין אוֹכְלִין פֵּירוֹת שְׁבִיעִית בְּטוֹבָה. וּבֵית הֶלֵּל אוֹמְרִים בְּטוֹבָה וּשֶׁלֹא בְּטוֹבָה. רִבִּי יְהוּדָה אוֹמֵר חִילוּף הַדְּבָרִים זֶה מִקּוּלֵּי בֵית שַׁמַּאי וּמֵחוּמְרֵי בֵית הֶלֵּל.

Mishnah 2: A field that had been cleared of thistles may be sown at the end of the Sabbatical year. [A field] improved or fertilized should not be sown at the end of the Sabbatical year. A field that was improved, the House of Shammai say one does not eat its produce in the Sabbatical year, but the House of Hillel say one does. The House of Shammai say one does not eat Sabbatical produce in reciprocity[3], but the House of Hillel say in reciprocity and without reciprocity. Rebbi Jehudah says it the other way around; this is one of the leniencies of the House of Shammai and stringencies of the House of Hillel[15].

15   This is the position of the anonymous Tanna of Tosephta 3:10 who reports that Shammai himself wanted to forbid eating in reciprocity but only a later Court really forbade it.

(fol. 35a) **הלכה ב**: שָׂדֶה שֶׁנִּיקַוְוצָה כו'. תַּמָּן אֲמְרִין בְּשֶׁנִּיטְּלוּ קוֹצֶיהָ. וְרַבָּנִין דְּהָכָא אֲמְרִין מִשֶּׁחָרַשׁ. עַל דַּעְתְּיהוּ דְּרַבָּנִין דְּהָכָא אִי זֶהוּ הַטִּייּוּב כָּל־הָעָם חוֹרְשִׁין פַּעַם אַחַת וְהוּא חוֹרֵשׁ שְׁנֵי פְעָמִים. וְכָא כֵן. אָמַר רִבִּי יוֹסֵי בֵּי רִבִּי בּוּן תַּמָּן אֵין הַמַּלְכוּת אוֹנֶסֶת. בְּרַם הָכָא הַמַּלְכוּת אוֹנֶסֶת.

Halakhah 2: "A field that had been cleared of thistles", etc. There[16] they say, when its thistles were removed, but the rabbis here say, when they were ploughed under[17]. What is improvement in the opinion of the rabbis here? Everybody ploughs once and he ploughs twice[18]. How can that be? Rebbi Yose ben Rebbi Abun said, there the government does not oppress, but here the government oppresses[19].

16   In Babylonia, in the Persian empire.

17   This implies that ploughing one's field in the Sabbatical year is permitted, against all principles stated in Mishnaiot 1:1, 2:1.

18   In Tosephta 3:10, "if everybody ploughs five and he ploughs six", meaning he ploughs narrower furrows to turn the earth over more thoroughly.

19   Start of an extensive description of the oppression by the Roman government and its legal consequences.

בָּרִאשׁוֹנָה כְּשֶׁהָיְתָה הַמַּלְכוּת אוֹנֶסֶת. הוֹרֵי רְבִּי יַנַּאי שֶׁיְּהוּ חוֹרְשִׁים חֲרִישָׁה רִאשׁוֹנָה. חַד מְשׁוּמָּד הֲוָה אִיעֲבַר[20] חֲמָתוֹן רַמִייָן[21] קוּבְעֲתָה. אֲמַר לוֹן הַסְטוּ שָׁרָא לְכוֹן מִירְדִי. שָׁרָא לְכוֹן רַמִייָן קוּבְעֲתָה.

When the government was oppressing the first time[22] Rebbi Yannai instructed to plough a single ploughing. An apostate was passing by, he saw them putting up the harrow. He said to them, hey you[23]! Is it permitted for you to plough? Is it permitted for you to put up the harrow?

20   Reading of the parallel in *Sanhedrin* 3:6, fol. 21b, where this and the following paragraphs are found. Venice: אני עבר.

21   Reading of the parallel in *Sanhedrin*; Venice רמיין.

22   One has to assume that under the Severan dynasty, Jewish farmers did not have to deliver provisions (*annona*) to the army during the Sabbatical year. R. Yannai can be dated to the early military anarchy in the third Century. In the Babli (*Sanhedrin* 26a) it is stated that R. Yannai proclaimed: Go and sow in the Sabbatical year because of the *annona*.

23   Latin *heus tu*; cf. Levy's dictionary, vol. 4, p. 241; E. and H. Guggenheimer, *Notes on the Talmudic Vocabulary* 12-15, לשוננו 39 (1975), pp. 62-69.

אָמַר רְבִּי יַעֲקֹב בַּר זַבְדִּי קוֹמֵי רְבִּי אַבָּהוּ לֹא כֵן אָמַר רְבִּי זְעִירָא וְרְבִּי יוֹחָנָן
בְּשֵׁם רְבִּי יַנַּאי רְבִּי יִרְמְיָה רְבִּי יוֹחָנָן בְּשֵׁם רְבִּי שִׁמְעוֹן בֶּן יוֹצָדָק נִמְנוּ בַּעֲלִיַּית
בֵּית לְבְזֶה בְּלוֹד. עַל כָּל־הַתּוֹרָה מְנַיִין אִם יֹאמַר גּוֹי לְיִשְׂרָאֵל לַעֲבוֹר עַל אַחַת
מִכָּל־מִצְוֹת הָאֲמוּרוֹת בַּתּוֹרָה חוּץ מֵעֲבוֹדָה זָרָה וְגִילּוּי עֲרָיוֹת וּשְׁפִיכוּת דָּמִים
יַעֲבוֹר וְלֹא יְהָרֵג. הָדָא דְתֵימָא בֵּינוֹ לְבֵין עַצְמוֹ. אֲבָל בְּרַבִּים אֲפִילוּ מִצְוָה
קַלָּה לֹא יִשְׁמַע לוֹ. כְּגוֹן לוּלְיָינוּס וּפַפּוֹס אָחִיו שֶׁנָּתְנוּ לָהֶן מַיִם בִּכְלִי זְכוּכִית
צְבוּעָה וְלֹא קִיבְּלוּ מֵהֶן. אָמַר לֹא מִתְכַּוֵּון מְשַׁמַּדְתְכוֹן וְלָא אִתְכַּוֵּון אֶלָּא מִיגְבֵּי
אַרְנוֹנִין. כַּמָּה הֵן רַבִּים. רַבָּנִין דְּקֵיסָרִין אֱמְרִין עֲשָׂרָה דִכְתִיב וְנִקְדַּשְׁתִּי בְּתוֹךְ
בְּנֵי יִשְׂרָאֵל.

Rebbi Jacob bar Zabdi said before Rebbi Abbahu: Did not Rebbi Zeïra and Rebbi Johanan in the name of Rebbi Yannai, Rebbi Jeremiah, Rebbi Johanan in the name of Rebbi Simeon ben Yozadaq, say that they voted on the upper floor of the Libzah house[24] in Lydda: About all the Torah, if a Gentile tells a Jew to transgress any commandment of the Torah except those concerning idolatry, incest and adultery, and murder he should transgress and not be killed. That is in private, but in public he should not follow him even for the slightest commandment, as exemplified by Julianus and his brother Pappos whom they gave water in a colored glass[25] and they did not accept.

He said, they do not intend to lead you to apostasy, they only want to collect *annona*.

What means "in public"? The rabbis of Caesarea say ten, as it is written[26] (*Lev.* 22:32): "I shall be sanctified in the midst of the Children of Israel."

24   In the Babli, *Sanhedrin* 74a, this is called the Nitzah house.

25   Julianus and Pappos were famous martyrs from the time of

Trajan. It is not clear which commandment they were ordered to transgress. (A change of consonant from J
to L also occurs in Italian *Luglio*
("month of July") from Latin *Julius*.

26   In the Babli, *Sanhedrin* 74b, it is
noted that the verse in itself does not
prove anything but that one has to
compare the wording "I shall be

sanctified in *the midst* of the Children
of Israel," with *Num.* 16:21 "separate
yourselves from *the midst* of this
congregation", where Qoraḥ and his
adherents were 10. The main inference
from the verse is that the public has to
be Jewish; a single Jew with many
Gentiles is not in public.

רבּי אֲבוּנָא זְעֵירָא חַמְנוּנֵיה פָּרֵי חוֹרֵי חַמְרָא בְּשׁוּבְתָּא. רבּי יוֹנָה וְרבּי יוֹסֵה
הוֹרוֹן מֵפֵּי לְאַרְסְקִינוּס בְּשׁוּבְתָּא. אָמַר רבּי מָנָא קְשִׁיתָה קוֹמֵי רבּי יוֹנָה אַבָּא
לֹא כֵן אָמַר רבּי זְעֵירָא רבּי יוֹחָנָן בְּשֵׁם רבּי יַנַּאי רבּי יִרְמְיָה רבּי יוֹחָנָן בְּשֵׁם
רבּי שִׁמְעוֹן בֶּן יוֹצָדָק נִמְנוּ בַּעֲלִיַת בֵּית לִבְזָה בְּלוֹד. עַל כָּל־הַתּוֹרָה מְנַיִין אִם
יֹאמַר גּוֹי לְיִשְׂרָאֵל לַעֲבוֹר עַל אַחַת מִכָּל־מִצְוֹת הָאֲמוּרוֹת בַּתּוֹרָה חוּץ מִן
הָעֲבוֹדָה זָרָה וְגִילּוּי עֲרָיוֹת וּשְׁפִיכוּת דָּמִים יַעֲבוֹר וְלֹא יֵיהָרֵג. הָדָא דְתֵימָא
בֵּינוֹ לְבֵין עַצְמוֹ. אֲבָל בְּרַבִּים אֲפִילוּ מִצְוָה קַלָּה לֹא יִשְׁמַע לוֹ. כְּגוֹן לוּלְיָינוּס
וּפַפּוֹס אָחִיו שֶׁנָּתְנוּ לָהֶן מַיִם בִּכְלִי זְכוּכִית צְבוּעָה וְלֹא קִיבְּלוּ מֵהֶן. אָמַר לֹא
אִתְכַּוֵּון מְשַׁמַּדְתוֹן אֶלָּא מֵיכוֹל פִּיתָּה חֲמִימָא. כַּמָּה הֵן רַבִּים. רַבָּנִין דְּקֵיסָרִין
אָמְרִין עֲשָׂרָה דִכְתִיב וְנִקְדַּשְׁתִּי בְּתוֹךְ בְּנֵי יִשְׂרָאֵל.

They saw the young Rebbi Abuna[27] collecting donkey's dung on the
Sabbath. Rebbi Jonah and Rebbi Yose permitted baking for Ursicinus[28]
on the Sabbath. Rebbi Mana said, I asked before my father Rebbi Jonah,
did not Rebbi Zeïra and Rebbi Joḥanan in the name of Rebbi Yannai,
Rebbi Jeremiah, Rebbi Joḥanan in the name of Rebbi Simeon ben
Yoẓadaq, say that they voted on the upper floor of the Libzah house in
Lydda: About all the Torah, if a Gentile tells a Jew to transgress any
commandment of the Torah except those concerning idolatry, incest and

adultery, and murder he should transgress and not be killed. That is in
private, but in public he should not follow him even for the slightest
commandment, as exemplified by Julianus and his brother Pappos whom
they gave water in a colored glass and they did not accept. He said, he
does not intend to lead you to apostasy, he only wants to eat warm bread.
What means "in public"? The rabbis of Caesarea say ten, as it is written
(*Lev.* 22:32): "I shall be sanctified in the midst of the Children of Israel."

27   Nothing is known about him and
about the circumstances under which
he was forced to collect dung.

28   Legate in Syria (351-354) of the
emperor Gallus. At that time, the
Roman government already was
Christian and, while they did not yet
try to convert the Jews by force, they
certainly welcomed an opportunity to
force the Jews to break their law. The
argument of the rabbis implies that
martyrdom is required only if the
Gentile wants to force his religion on
the Jew, not if he wants to force him to
transgress the laws of the Torah. The
Babli (*Sanhedrin* 74b) comes to the
same conclusion in the case of fire
worshippers who take fire for their
temple where everybody comes to
warm themselves.

רְבִּי אֲבוּנָא בָּעָא קוֹמֵי רְבִּי אִימִי גּוֹיִם מַהוּ שֶׁיְהוּ מְצוּוִין עַל קִידּוּשׁ הַשֵּׁם. אָמַר
לֵיהּ וְנִקְדַּשְׁתִּי בְּתוֹךְ בְּנֵי יִשְׂרָאֵל. יִשְׂרָאֵל מְצוּוִין עַל קִידּוּשׁ הַשֵּׁם וְאֵין הַגּוֹיִם
מְצוּוִין עַל קִידּוּשׁ הַשֵּׁם. רְבִּי נָסָא בְּשֵׁם רְבִּי לֶעְזָר שָׁמַע לָהּ מִן הָדָא. לְדָבָר
הַזֶּה יִסְלַח יי לְעַבְדֶּךָ וגו'. יִשְׂרָאֵל מְצוּוִין עַל קִידּוּשׁ הַשֵּׁם וְאֵין הַגּוֹיִם מְצוּוִין
עַל קִידּוּשׁ הַשֵּׁם.

Rebbi Abuna asked before Rebbi Ammi: Are Gentiles required to
sanctify the Name[29]? He said to him (*Lev.* 22:32): "I shall be sanctified in
the midst of the Children of Israel." Israel are required to sanctify the
Name; the Gentiles are not required to sanctify the Name. Rebbi Nasa in
the name of Rebbi Lazar understood it from the following (*2K.* 5:18):

"May the Eternal forgive His servant for this[30], etc." Israel are required to
sanctify the Name; the Gentiles are not required to sanctify the Name.

29   "To sanctify the Name" means to
suffer martyrdom for one's faith (under
the conditions spelled out before.)

30   Elisha permitted Naaman to
accompany his king to a pagan temple

and to bow down there; for a Jew that
would be unthinkable. Same argument
in Babli *Sanhedrin* 74b, in the name of
the school of Rav.

רבִּי אַבָּא בַּר זְמִינָא הֲוָה מְחַיַיט גַּבֵּי חַד אֲרַמָּאי בְּרוֹמִי. אַיְיתֵי לֵיהּ בְּשַׂר
דִּנְבֵלָה אֲמַר לֵיהּ אֱכוֹל. אֲמַר לֵיהּ לֵינָא אָכִיל. אֲמַר לֵיהּ אֱכוֹל דִּילְכֵן אֲנָא
קָטִילְנָא לָךְ. אֲמַר לֵיהּ אִין בָּעִית מִיקְטַל קְטוֹל דַּאֲנָא לֵינָא מֵיכַל בְּשַׂר דִּנְבֵלָה.
אֲמַר לֵיהּ מָהֵן מוֹדַע לָךְ דְּאִילּוּ אֲכָלְתְּ הֲוֵינָא קָטִיל לָךְ. (fol. 35b) אוֹ יְהוּדַיי
יְהוּדַאי אוֹ אֲרַמָּאי אֲרַמָּאי. אֲמַר רבִּי מָנָא אִילּוּ הֲוָה רבִּי אַבָּא בַּר זְמִינָא
שָׁמַע מִילֵּיהוֹן דְּרַבָּנִין מֵיכַל הֲוָה.

Rebbi Abba bar Zemina was working as a tailor in Rome at the place
of an Aramean[31]. He[32] brought him[33] meat of a carcass and told him[33] to
eat. He[33] said to him, I will not eat. He said to him[33] eat! Otherwise I
shall kill you. He[33] said to him, if you have to kill, kill, for I shall not eat
meat of a carcass. He said to him[33], certainly you should know that I
would have killed you, had you eaten. Either one is a Jewish Jew or an
Aramean Aramean. Rebbi Mana said, if Rebbi Abba bar Zemina had
understood the words of the rabbis, he would have eaten[34].

31   An Aramaic speaking Gentile.
32   The Gentile.
33   R. Abba bar Zemina.
34   Since R. Abba then would have

been killed, it follows that the statement from the Libzah house must be
modified according to circumstances.

טִייְבָה וּמֵת בְּנוֹ מַהוּ שֶׁיְהֵא מוּתָּר לְזוֹרֵעַ. רְבִּי יַעֲקֹב בַּר אָחָא רְבִּי אִימִי בְּשֵׁם רְבִּי יוֹסֵה בֵּי רְבִּי חֲנִינָה טִייְבָה וּמֵת בְּנוֹ מוּתָּר לְזוֹרְעָה. טִייְבָה וּמְכָרָהּ אָסוּר לְזוֹרְעָה. עָבַר וּזְרָעָהּ מוּתָּר שֶׁלֹּא גָזְרוּ אֶלָּא עַל הַגֶּדֶר שֶׁהוּא יָכוֹל לַעֲמוֹד בּוֹ.

If somebody improved [his field] and died, may his son sow? Rebbi Jacob bar Aḥa, Rebbi Immi in the name of Rebbi Yose ben Rebbi Ḥanina: If somebody improved [his field] and died, his son may sow; if he improved [his field] and sold it, it is forbidden to be sown. If [the buyer] transgressed and sowed, it is permitted since they did decide only on a fence[35] that one may live with.

35 The "fence" around the Law which is the basis of all rabbinic decrees, Mishnah *Avot* 1:1. In many cases, it would be impossible for the buyer to verify that the field had been improved during the Sabbatical year. The expression גזרו instead of גדרו is Babylonian spelling; in a series of parallel Tosephtot (3:13) the language is שלא גדרו אלא גדר שיכול לעמוד.

טִייֵב בְּזְמַן זֶה מַהוּ. רְבִּי יִרְמְיָה סָבַר מֵימַר שָׁרֵי. אָמַר רְבִּי יוֹסֵה וְלֹא שְׁמִיעַ רְבִּי יִרְמְיָה שֶׁהוּא לוֹקֶה. לֹא שְׁמִיעַ שֶׁהוּא פָּסוּל מִן הָעֵידוּת. חָזַר וְאָמַר אֵין דְּהוּא שְׁמִיעַ אֶלָּא כְּאֵינָשׁ דְּשָׁמַע מִילָה וּמַקְשֵׁי עֲלָהּ. אָמַר רְבִּי חִזְקִיָּה אִתְתָּבַת קוֹמֵי רְבִּי יִרְמְיָה דְּאָמַר וְכִי אֵין זֶה בֵּית דִּין עָמַד וּבִיטֵל. חֵילֵיהּ דְּרִבִּי יִרְמְיָה מִן הָדָא. בַּת יִשְׂרָאֵל שֶׁבָּאת לְהַדְלִיק מִן הַכֹּהֶנֶת טוֹבֶלֶת אֶת הַפְּתִילָה שֶׁמֶן שְׂרֵיפָה וּמַדְלֶקֶת. רְבִּי חוּנָה בְּשֵׁם דְּבֵית רְבִּי יַנַּאי שְׁעַת מִשְׁלַחַת זְאֵבִים הָיְתָה וְלֹא עָמַד בֵּית דִּין וּבִיטֵל. כְּמָה דְתֵימַר תַּמָּן לֹא עָמַד בֵּית דִּין וּבִיטֵל וְכָא לֹא עָמַד בֵּית דִּין וּבִיטֵל.

What are the rules if somebody improved today? Rebbi Jeremiah wanted to say, it is permitted. Rebbi Yose said, did Rebbi Jeremiah not hear that he would be whipped? Did he not hear that he would be unacceptable for testimony[36]? He turned around and said, certainly he had heard! But he is like someone who hears a statement and questiones it. Rebbi Ḥizqiah said, it was objected before Rebbi Jeremiah, there seems not to have been a court which disestablished[37]! The force of Rebbi Jeremiah is from the following[38]: "An Israel woman who comes to a priestly woman[39] to get fire dips the wick into oil to burn and lights." Rebbi Ḥuna in the name of the house of Rebbi Yannai: It was a time of wolf packs[40]; there was no court which disestablished[41]. As you say there, there was no court which disestablished, so here there was no court which disestablished[42]!

36   Both whipping and the exclusion from being a witness are rabbinic decrees since only activities mentioned in the verse are biblical prohibitions.

37   A rabbinic decree passed by a competent court can only be lifted by a court of higher standing. Since the rabbinic restrictions of the Sabbatical year go back to the Men of the Great Assembly, the minimum standing such a court would have to have is that of Rabban Gamliel who disestablished the prohibition of the first two terms (Halakhah 1:1). No court of later times has that standing.

38   *Terumot* 11:10. "Oil to burn" is olive oil of the heave that became impure and can no longer be consumed. It is the Cohen's property and must be burned either for heat or for light. By rabbinic decree, the burning also must

be for the benefit of the Cohen or his family. The *baraita* permits some use of the oil by non-Cohanim.

39   The wife or unmarried daughter of a Cohen.

40   A time of emergency when people tried to be out on the street as little as possible.

41   The short-cut described was never endorsed by a court but was tolerated by the rabbis of the time. Since the *baraita* is an unconditional statement, it follows that a rabbinic decree that fell into general disuse because of special circumstances remains in disuse even in normal times; no court is needed to lift the decree. In this case, the power of the people is greater than the power of the court.

42   No court was needed once permission was given to work for the Roman government.

וְדִכְוָתָהּ מֵאֵימָתַי אָדָם זָכָה בְּפֵירוֹתָיו בַּשְּׁבִיעִית. רִבִּי יִרְמְיָה סָבַר מֵימַר
מִשֶּׁיִּתְּנֵם בְּתוֹךְ כֵּלָיו. רִבִּי יוֹסֵי סָבַר מֵימַר אֲפִילוּ נְתָנָם לְתוֹךְ כֵּלָיו לֹא זָכָה הָכֵן
הוּא סָבַר דְּאִינּוּן דִּידֵיהּ. וְלֵית אִינּוּן דִּידֵיהּ. כְּהָדָא רִבִּי טַרְפוֹן יָרַד לֶאֱכוֹל
קְצִיעוֹת מִתּוֹךְ שֶׁלּוֹ שֶׁלֹּא בְטוֹבָה כְּבֵית שַׁמַּאי. חֲמוּנֵיהּ סַנְטֵירַיָּיא וְשׁוּרוֹן
חַבְטוֹן עֲלוֹי. כַּד חָמָא גַרְמֵיהּ בְּסַכָּנָה. אָמַר לוֹן בְּחַיֵּיכוֹן אֲמָרִין גּוֹ בֵיתֵיהּ
דְּטַרְפוֹן עַתְדִין לֵיהּ תַּכְרִיכִין. כַּד שְׁמְעוֹן כֵּן אִישְׁתַּטְחוֹן עַל אַפֵּיהוֹן אָמְרִין לֵיהּ
רִבִּי שְׁרֵי לוֹן. אָמַר לוֹן יֵיתֵי עָלַי עַל כָּל־חוֹטֶר וְחוֹטֶר דַּהֲוָה נְחִית עָלַי. הֲוֵינָא
שָׁרֵי לְכוֹן עַל קַדְמַיָּא. בְּאִילֵּין תַּרְתֵּי מִילַּיָּא נְהַג רִבִּי טַרְפוֹן כְּבֵית שַׁמַּאי וּסְכֵין.
בְּהָדָא וּבְקִרְיַת שְׁמַע. רִבִּי אַבָּהוּ בְשֵׁם רִבִּי חֲנִינָה בֶּן גַּמְלִיאֵל כָּל־יָמָיו שֶׁל רִבִּי
טַרְפוֹן הָיָה מִתְעַנֶּה עַל הַדָּבָר הַזֶּה וְאוֹמֵר אִי לִי שֶׁנִּתְכַּבַּדְתִּי בְּכִתְרָהּ שֶׁל תּוֹרָה.

A similar case: When does a man acquire Sabbatical fruit? Rebbi
Jeremiah wanted to say, when he puts them in his vessels. Rebbi Yose
wanted to say, even if he puts them into his vessels he did not acquire
them; he thinks that they are his but they are not his[43]. Compare the
following[44]: Rebbi Tarphon went to eat single figs from somebody's
property without reciprocity, following the House of Shammai. The
watchmen[45] saw him and started whipping him. When he saw himself in
danger, he said to them, by your lives, tell in Tarphon's house to have his
burial shrouds ready. When they heard this, they prostrated themselves
before him and said, Rebbi, forgive us. He said to them, so and so should
come upon me if I did not forgive you beforehand every stick that was
coming down on me. In these two instances did Rebbi Tarphon follow the
House of Shammai and endangered himself, in the case here and in the
recitation of Shema'[46]. Rebbi Abbahu in the name of Rebbi Ḥanina ben
Gamliel: All his life did Rebbi Tarphon repent about this happening and
said, woe to me that I used the Crown of the Torah[47].

43   If the fruits had a human owner, they would become property of the person who takes them. If somebody steals fruit from a farmer, once the fruit is in his vessel he is the owner but owes the farmer the value of the fruit he took. However, Sabbatical fruit are God's property; even after they have been harvested they retain the holiness of the Sabbatical. They may be eaten but not used for industrial purposes.

Hence, they cannnot be acquired as property.

44   Different versions of the story are in *Massekhet Kallah;* Babli *Nedarim* 62a.

45   Jastrow takes the word as *saf'el* of נטר "to guard". (In Arabic, the word means "cymbal".)

46   Berakhot, Mishnah 1:7.

47   Mishnah *Avot* 1:13: "He who uses the Crown disappears."

(fol. 34d) **משנה ג:** חוֹכְרִים נִירִין מִן הַגּוֹיִם בַּשְּׁבִיעִית אֲבָל לֹא מִיִּשְׂרָאֵל. וּמְחַזְּקִין יְדֵי גּוֹיִם בַּשְּׁבִיעִית. אֲבָל לֹא עַל יְדֵי יִשְׂרָאֵל. וְשׁוֹאֲלִין בִּשְׁלוֹמָן מִפְּנֵי דַרְכֵי שָׁלוֹם.

Mishnah 3: One rents ploughed fields[48] from Gentiles in the Sabbatical year but not from Jews. One encourages[49] Gentiles in the Sabbatical year but not Jews. One greets them for communal peace.

48   Fields ploughed after the harvest, to sow them after the end of the Sabbatical year.

49   A Gentile working his field in the Sabbatical year may be praised for his work, but not a Jew in the same situation.

(fol. 35b) **הלכה ג:** חוֹכְרִין נִירִין כו'. רִבִּי חִיָּיה רִבִּי אִימִּי חַד אָמַר חֲרוֹשׁ בָּהּ טָבוּת וַאֲנָא נִיסַּב לָהּ מִינָךְ בָּתַר שְׁמִיטָתָא. וְחָרָנָא אָמַר אַיַּשַּׁר. מָאן דְּאָמַר בָּהּ טָבָאוּת וַאֲנָא נֵסַב לָהּ מִינָךְ בָּתַר שְׁמִיטָתָא. מַהוּ שׁוֹאֲלִין בִּשְׁלוֹמָן אַיַּשַּׁר. מָאן דְּאָמַר אַיַּשַּׁר מַהוּ שׁוֹאֲלִין בִּשְׁלוֹמָן בְּשָׁלוֹם יִשְׂרָאֵל שָׁלוֹם עֲלֵכֶם.

Halakhah 3: "One rents ploughed fields," etc. Rebbi Ḥiyya, Rebbi Ammi[50]. One said: "Plough it well; then I will rent it after the Sabbatical." The other one said: "May you succeed.[51]" For him who says plough it well, then I will rent it after the Sabbatical, what means "one greets them"? "May you succeed." For him who says may you succeed, what means "one greets them"? Jewish greeting, "Peace upon you."

50   This does not refer to the quote from the Mishnah but discusses the meaning of the second sentence, one supports Gentiles. The entire Halakhah is also in *Avodah Zarah* 4:10 (fol. 44b); the parallel in Babli *Giṭṭin* 62a recognizes only the second opinion.

51   Short for אישר חילך "may your effort be lucky."

דְּלְמָא רְבִּי חִינְנָא בַּר[52] פַּפָא וְרְבִּי שְׁמוּאֵל בַּר נַחְמָן. עָבְרוּן עַל חַד מֵחוֹרְשֵׁי שְׁבִיעִית. אָמַר לֵיהּ רְבִּי שְׁמוּאֵל בַּר נַחְמָן אַיַּשַׁר. אָמַר לֵיהּ רְבִּי חִינְנָא בַּר פַּפָא לֹא כֵן אִילְפָן רְבִּי וְלֹא אָמְרוּ הָעוֹבְרִים מִכָּאן שֶׁאָסוּר לוֹמַר לְחוֹרְשֵׁי שְׁבִיעִית אַיַּשַׁר. אָמַר לֵיהּ לִקְרוֹת אַתָּה יוֹדֵעַ. לְדְרוֹשׁ אֵי אַתָּה יוֹדֵעַ. וְלֹא אָמְרוּ הָעוֹבְרִים אֵלּוּ אוּמּוֹת הָעוֹלָם שֶׁהֵן עוֹבְרִין מִן הָעוֹלָם וְלֹא אָמְרוּ לְיִשְׂרָאֵל בִּרְכַּת יי' עֲלֵיכֶם מַה יִשְׂרָאֵל אוֹמְרִין לָהֶם בֵּרַכְנוּ אֶתְכֶם בְּשֵׁם יי'. לֹא דַייְכֶם כָּל־הַבְּרָכוֹת הַבָּאוֹת לָעוֹלָם בִּשְׁבִילֵינוּ וְאֵין אַתֶּם אוֹמְרִים לָנוּ בּוֹאוּ וּטְלוּ לָכֶם מִן הַבְּרָכוֹת הַלָּלוּ אֶלָּא שֶׁאַתֶּם מְנַלְגְּלִין עָלֵינוּ פִיסִים וְזֵימִיּוֹת גּוּלְגּוֹלִיּוֹת וְאַרְנוֹנִיּוֹת.

Explanation: Rebbi Ḥinena bar Pappa[53] and Rebbi Samuel bar Naḥman passed by one of the ploughmen[54] in the Sabbatical. Rebbi Samuel bar Naḥman said to him, may you succeed. Rebbi Ḥinena bar Pappa said to him, did not Rebbi teach us (*Ps.* 129:8): "The passers-by did not say," this implies that it is forbidden to say "may you succeed" to one who ploughs in the Sabbatical. He told him, you know how to read but you do not know how to make a homily. "The passers-by did not say," refers to the nations of the world who pass out of the world[55], they did not say to Israel "the blessing of the Eternal is on you." What does Israel say to them, "we bless you in the Name of the Eternal." All blessings that come into the world because of us[56] are not enough for you, you do not say, come and take from these blessing for yourselves, but you roll over us pro-rated contributions and fines[57], head taxes and *annonae*[22].

52 The word is missing in the Venice print.

53 It seems that he is the R. Ḥinena who usually is quoted without patronymic.

54 A Jew.

55 In contrast to Israel, these nations have only a limited life span.

56 The material blessing given by God because the Jews keep the laws of the Torah. [Cf. H. Guggenheimer, *The Scholar's Haggadah* (Northvale 1995), pp. 205-208.]

57 Greek ζημία, ῆ.

הוֹרֵי רִבִּי אִמִּי לִרְדוֹת עִמּוֹ אָסוּר.[58]

Rebbi Ammi taught that one may not take out together with him.

58 The last word is only in the parallel in *Avodah Zarah* fol. 44b. The sentence has no place here but refers to Mishnah *Avodah Zarah* 4:10: "One does not make dough or form breads with a baker who works in impurity but one may bring bread with him to the retail store." On this, R. Ammi notes that a Jew following the rules of purity may not take pitta breads out of the oven together with someone who does not follow these rules.

(fol. 34d) **משנה ד:** הַמֵּידַל בַּזֵּיתִים בֵּית שַׁמַּאי אוֹמְרִים יָגוֹם. וּבֵית הִלֵּל אוֹמְרִים יְשָׁרֵשׁ. וּמוֹדִים בְּמַחֲלִיק עַד שֶׁיָּגוֹם. וְאֵי זֶהוּ הַמֵּידַל אֶחָד אוֹ שְׁנַיִם.

הַמַּחֲלִיק שְׁלֹשָׁה זֶה בְּצַד זֶה. בְּמַה דְּבָרִים אֲמוּרִים מִתּוֹךְ שָׁלוֹ. אֲבָל מִתּוֹךְ שֶׁל
חֲבֵירוֹ אַף הַמַּחֲלִיק יְשָׁרֵשׁ.

Mishnah 4: If somebody thins out olive trees[59], the House of Shammai
say he should cut them off, the House of Hillel say he may take out the
roots, but they agree that one who levels may only cut off. What is
thinning? One or two. Levelling are three adjacent to one another.
When has this been said? On his own property. But from another's
property, even one who flattens may take out the roots.

---

59   He takes out entire trees to give
the remaining ones more space to grow.
The House of Shammai require him to
cut the stems near the ground but to
leave the roots in because removing the
roots is intensive agricultural work.

(fol. 35b) **הלכה ד**: הַמֵּידַל בַּזֵּיתִים כו'. מַהוּ הַמֵּידַל נוֹטֵל אֶחָד וּמֵנִיחַ שְׁנַיִם.
אוֹ נוֹטֵל שְׁנַיִם וּמֵנִיחַ אֶחָד. תַּנֵּי דְבֵית רִבִּי נוֹטֵל אֶחָד וּמֵנִיחַ שְׁנַיִם. וְהָא תַּנִּינָן
הַמַּחֲלִק בִּגְפָנִים שְׁלֹשָׁה זֶה בְּצַד זֶה. הָא מֵידַל נוֹטֵל שְׁנַיִם וּמֵנִיחַ אֶחָד. אָמַר
רִבִּי יוֹנָה מַתְנִיתָא בְּמֵידַל מִכְּבָר בַּתְּחִילָּה. וּמַה דְּתַנֵּיי דְבֵית רִבִּי בְּמֵידַל מִכְּבָר.

Halakhah 4: "If somebody thins out olive trees," etc. What is
thinning? He removes one and leaves two, or removes two and leaves
one. It was stated by the House of Rebbi: He removes one and leaves
two. But did we not state: If somebody levels among vines, three
adjacent to one another. Therefore, thinning must mean that one removes
two and leaves one. Rebbi Jonah said, the *baraita* when he thins out the
first time, and what was stated by the House of Rebbi when he already
had thinned.

אֵין מַצִּיתִין אֶת הָאוֹר בְּאִישׁוּת קָנִים מִפְּנֵי שֶׁהִיא עֲבוֹדָה. רַבָּן שִׁמְעוֹן בֶּן[60]
גַּמְלִיאֵל מַתִּיר. וְכֵן הָיָה רַבָּן שִׁמְעוֹן בֶּן גַּמְלִיאֵל אוֹמֵר נוֹטְעִין אִילָן סְרָק
בַּשְּׁבִיעִית. וְאֵין מְלַמְּדִין אֶת הַפָּרָה לַחֲרוֹשׁ אֶלָּא בְּחוֹלוֹת. רַבָּן שִׁמְעוֹן בֶּן
גַּמְלִיאֵל אוֹמֵר אֲפִילוּ בְּתוֹךְ שָׂדֶה חֲבֵירוֹ מוּתָּר. וּבִלְבַד שֶׁלֹּא יִסְמוֹךְ אֶת הַמַּעֲנָה.

"[61]One does not start a fire in reed thickets[62] because that is [agricultural] work. Rabban Simeon ben Gamliel permits it. Similarly, Rabban Simeon ben Gamliel said, one may plant a useless tree[63] in the Sabbatical year. One teaches a cow to plough only in dunes; Rabban Simeon ben Gamliel says, it is permitted also in somebody else's field on condition that one not make parallel furrows.[64]"

60 Word missing in Venice print.	62 In the Tosephta: בחישת
61 A similar text in Tosephta 3:14.	63 Cf. Chapter 1, Note 12.
There, it reads" One does not harvest	64 It should not look like pro-
reeds from a thicket.	fessional work.

תַּנֵּי אַבָּא שָׁאוּל אוֹמֵר מְבַדִּין בְּחֲרָשִׁין וְגוֹמֵם הָאָרֶץ וּבִלְבַד שֶׁלֹא יָקוּץ בְּקַרְדוֹם. אֵין בּוֹדְקִין אֶת הַזְּרָעִים בָּאֲדָמָה בֶּעָצִיץ אֲבָל בּוֹדְקִין אוֹתוֹ בִּגְלָלִים בֶּעָצִיץ. וְשׁוֹרִין אוֹתָן בַּשְּׁבִיעִית לְמוֹצָאֵי שְׁבִיעִית וּמְקַיְּימִין אֶת הָאֲלוֹי בְּרֹאשׁ הַגַּג וְלֹא מַשְׁקִין אוֹתָן. אֵין תּוֹלִין תּוֹבִין בַּתְּאֵינִים. כֵּיצַד הוּא עוֹשֶׂה מַייְתֵי יִחוּר דִּתְאֵינָה שָׁטַר וְתָלֵ֫: בָּהּ וְאָמַר לָהּ הָדָא עֲבְדָה וְאַתּ לֵית אַתּ עֲבְדָה. וְלֹא כֵן תַּנֵּי אִילָן שֶׁהוּא מְנַבֵּל פֵּירוֹתָיו סוֹקְרִין אוֹתוֹ בְּסִיקְרָא וּמַטְעוֹנִין אוֹתוֹ אֲבָנִים וּמְבַהֲתִין לֵיהּ דְּיַעֲבוֹד. אָמְרִי תַמָּן דְּלָא יַתִּיר[65] פֵּירוֹתָיו. בְּרַם הָדָא דְּיַעֲבִיד לְכַתְּחִילָה.

It was stated[66]: "Abba Shaul says one clears groves by cutting near the ground on condition that one should not fell with an axe. One does not try out seeds in soil in a flower pot but one tries them out in dung in a flower pot; one puts them in water in the Sabbatical year for the year after the Sabbatical[67]. One keeps aloe on the roof but does not water it. One[68] does not put wild figs onto fig trees." What does one do? One brings a branch of a wild fig, hangs it onto it, and tells it: That one produced and you did not produce! Did we not state[69]: "If a tree sheds its fruits, one colors it red with vermilion, loads it with stones, and frightens it into producing." They said, there that it should not loosen its fruits, here that it should start to produce.

65   Reading of the parallel in *Ma-'aser Šeni* 5:1; the text here reads יחן.

66   Tosephta 3:20; the first sentence only.

67   The seeds may be caused to sprout in the water for planting in the next year.

68   Tosephta 1:9. תובא is Syriac "wild fig tree"; cf. I. Löw, *Die Flora der Juden* I, p. 233.

69   *Ma'aser Šeni* 5:1 (fol. 52d); Babli *Šabbat* 67a, Hulin 77b.

אֵין מַרְכִּיבִין דְּקָלִים מִפְּנֵי שֶׁהִיא עֲבוֹדָה. שֶׁלֹּא תֹאמַר הוֹאִיל וְחָזָא רוֹבָה שָׁרֵי לְפוּם כֵּן צָרִיךְ מֵימַר אָסוּר.

One does not graft date palms because that is [agricultural] work[70]. That you should not say because it could bear it is permitted; therefore it is necessary to say that it is forbidden.

70   One cannot graft date palms. The paragraph refers to the technique of putting bunches of male flowers into the crown of a female tree to insure fertilization by the wind. One could think that this is permitted because a similar technique was approved in the preceding paragraph for fig trees (which, however, have both male and female flowers) and because without help the date palm might still produce some fruit. This "grafting" is forbidden in the Sabbatical because it is the standard agricultural technique.

מִשְּׁלֹשָׁה וְעַד תִּשְׁעָה הִיא מַתְנִיתָא.

The Mishnah speaks about three to nine[71].

71   "Levelling" in the Mishnah is permitted (under the restrictions given there) if one removes not more than nine trees.

(fol. 34d) **משנה ה:** הַמַּבְקִיעַ בַּזֵּיתִים לֹא יְחַפֵּהוּ בֶּעָפָר. אֲבָל מְכַסֵּהוּ בָּאֲבָנִים אוֹ בְקַשׁ. הַקּוֹצֵץ קוֹרַת שִׁקְמָה לֹא יְחַפֵּהוּ בֶּעָפָר. אֲבָל מְכַסֵּהוּ בָּאֲבָנִים אוֹ בְקַשׁ. אֵין קוֹצְצִין בְּתוּלַת שִׁקְמָה בַּשְּׁבִיעִית. מִפְּנֵי שֶׁהִיא עֲבוֹדָה. רִבִּי יְהוּדָה אוֹמֵר כְּדַרְכָּהּ אָסוּר. אֶלָּא אוֹ מַגְבִּיעַ עֲשָׂרָה טְפָחִים אוֹ גוֹמֵם מֵעַם הָאָרֶץ.

Mishnah 5: If somebody cuts down an olive tree, he should not cover [the stump] with dust but cover it with stones or straw. If somebody cuts down a sycamore trunk[71], he should not cover [the stump] with dust but cover it with stones or straw. One does not cut a virgin sycamore in the Sabbatical year because that is [agricultural] work. Rebbi Jehudah says, in a normal way it is forbidden but he [may] cut higher than ten hand-breadths or cut it down level with the ground.

71   Sycamores regenerate; it is possible to cut the same plant many times.
In order to obtain larger logs it is necessary to first cut down the first
("virgin") growth.

(fol. 35b) **הלכה ה:** הַמַּבְקִיעַ בַּזַּיִת כו'. תַּנֵּי הַקּוֹצֵץ בַּקָּנִים רִבִּי יוּדָה אוֹמֵר מָקוֹם שֶׁנָּהֲגוּ לִקוֹץ יִתּוֹק. לְתוֹק יָקוֹץ. וּמַגְבִּיהַּ טֶפַח וְקוֹצֵץ. הַקּוֹצֵץ בַּקּוֹרוֹת לֹא יְהֵא מַחֲלִיק וּמַדְרִיג מַדְרִיג וּמַחְבִּיק. אֶלָּא מִתְכַּוֵּין שֶׁתְּהֵא קִיצָּן שָׁוָה. תַּנֵּי רַבָּן שִׁמְעוֹן בֶּן גַּמְלִיאֵל אוֹמֵר מָקוֹם שֶׁנָּהֲגוּ לְהַחֲלִיק יַדְרִיג. לִדְרוֹג יַחֲלִיק וְגוֹמֵם עַם הָאָרֶץ. וּבִלְבַד שֶׁלֹּא יִקוֹץ בְּקוֹרְדוֹם.

"If somebody cuts down an olive tree," etc. It was stated[72]: "If somebody cuts reeds, Rebbi Jehudah says at a place where one is used to cut, he should tear out; at a place where one is used to tear out, he should cut. In any case, he should cut higher than a hand-breadth[73]. If somebody cuts down for logs, he should not plane and cut in steps, cut in steps to create joints, but he should try to cut them straight[74]." It was stated[75]: "Rabban Simeon ben Gamliel said, at a place where one usually planes, he should cut in steps, in steps he should plane and cut down at the ground[73], but he should not cut with an axe."

72   Tosephta 3:19, in the name of Rabban Simeon ben Gamliel instead of R. Jehudah. For reeds as a commercial crop, cf. *Demay* Chapter 6, Note 100.

73   To cut unprofessionally.

74   He should not treat the logs in public as objects of trade. Since one may cut wood in the Sabbatical year as fuel, the act of cutting in itself does not create a bad appearance.

75   Tosephta 3:19, in the name of Abba Shaul, restrics to cutting in tree groves.

(fol. 34d) **מִשְׁנָה ו**: הַמְזַגֵּב בַּגְּפָנִים (fol. 35a) וְהַקּוֹצֵץ בַּקָּנִים רִבִּי יוֹסֵי הַגָּלִילִי אוֹמֵר יַרְחִיק טֶפַח וְרִבִּי עֲקִיבָה אוֹמֵר קוֹצֵץ כְּדַרְכּוֹ בְּקֶרְדּוֹם בְּמַגָּל וּבִמְגֵירָה וּבְכָל־מַה שֶׁיִּרְצֶה. אִילָן שֶׁנִּפְשַׁח קוֹשְׁרִין אוֹתוֹ בַּשְּׁבִיעִית. לֹא שֶׁיַּעֲלֶה אֶלָּא שֶׁלֹּא יוֹסִיף.

Mishnah 6: If somebody cuts shoots of vines[76] or cuts reeds, Rebbi Yose the Galilean says he leaves a hand-breadth but Rebbi Aqiba says he cuts as he is used to, with an axe, a sickle, or a saw, or anything he wants. In the Sabbatical year one may bind a tree that was split, not to heal it but to stop [the split] from widening.

76   Cutting of the green new shoots that look like tails. This is not counted as forbidden trimming as long as no wood is taken.

(fol. 35b) **הֲלָכָה ו**: רִבִּי יוֹסֵי הַגָּלִילִי כְּבֵית שַׁמַּאי. וְרִבִּי עֲקִיבָה כְּבֵית הִלֵּל. וְכֵן אֲתִינָן מַתְנֵי רִבִּי יוֹסֵי הַגָּלִילִי כְּבֵית שַׁמַּאי וְרִבִּי עֲקִיבָה כְּבֵית הִלֵּל. אֶלָּא רִבִּי יוֹסֵי הַגָּלִילִי חָשׁ לַעֲבוֹדַת הָאָרֶץ.

Halakhah 6[77]: Rebbi Yose the Galilean follows the House of Shammai, Rebbi Aqiba follows the House of Hillel[78]. Can we come to state that Rebbi Yose the Galilean follows the House of Shammai, Rebbi Aqiba follows the House of Hillel[79]? But Rebbi Yose the Galilean worries about agricultural work[80].

77   In the Venice print, this is still part of Halakhah 5.

78   We have no statements of the Houses of Shammai and Hillel on this point, but in Mishnah 4 the House of Shammai was more restrictive than the House of Hillel as far as cutting for wood is concerned.

79   Since R. Yose the Galilean was a student of Rabban Yoḥanan ben Zakkai at Yabneh, when the House of Shammai already was no longer a dominant force in Jewish thought, the hypothesis seems to be illogical.

80   Cutting is too close to biblically prohibited trimming.

(fol. 35a) **מִשְׁנָה ז:** מֵאֵימָתַי אוֹכְלִין פֵּירוֹת הָאִילָן בַּשְּׁבִיעִית. הַפַּגִּים מִשֶּׁהִזְרִיחוּ אוֹכֵל בָּהֶן פִּיתוֹ בַּשָּׂדֶה. בִּיחִילוּ כוֹנֵס לְתוֹךְ בֵּיתוֹ. וְכֵן כַּיּוֹצֵא בָּהֶן בִּשְׁאָר שְׁנֵי שָׁבוּעַ חַיָּיבִין בְּמַעְשְׂרוֹת. הַבּוֹסֶר מִשֶּׁהֵבִיא מַיִם אוֹכֵל בָּהֶן פִּיתוֹ בַּשָּׂדֶה הִבְאִישׁ כּוֹנֵס לְתוֹךְ בֵּיתוֹ וְכֵן כַּיּוֹצֵא בּוֹ בִּשְׁאָר שְׁנֵי שָׁבוּעַ חַיָּיבִין בְּמַעְשְׂרוֹת.

Mishnah 7: When does one start to eat tree fruits in the Sabbatical year? Unripe figs when they started to be radiant[81] one eats with his bread in the field; when they became large one takes them into his house and in this state in other years of the Sabbatical cycle they must be tithed[82]. Unripe grapes when they contain fluid one eats them with his bread on the field; when their skin became transparent one takes them into his house and in this state in other years of the Sabbatical cycle they must be tithed.

81   When their skin becomes food acting as a laxative.
smooth enough to reflect sunlight. 82   In this state, they are potential
These unripe figs might be eaten as commercial product.

(fol. 35b) **הלכה ז**: הַמְזַגֵּב בַּגְּפָנִים כו'. מַהוּ בִּיחִילוּ רִבִּי חִיָּיא בַּר בָּא אָמַר
חַיָּיתָה כְּמַה דְּתֵימַר וְגַם נַפְשָׁם בָּחֲלָה בִי.

Halakhah 7[83]: "If somebody cuts shoots of vines," etc. What means
בּיחילו? Rebbi Ḥiyya bar Abba said, if it comes alive, as you say (*Zach.*
11:8): "And their souls were too much for me[84]."

83   In the Venice print, Halakhah 6. etymology given here [and in *Ma'serot*
The quote from Mishnah 6 is induced 1:2 (fol. 48d)] by R. Ḥiyya bar Abba.
by this error in numeration. {From the Arabic بخل "to be stingy" one
84   This incomprehensible Biblical might translate in the Mishnah "If they
verse is also quoted in Babli *Niddah* are barely ripe".}
47a by Rabba bar bar Ḥana for the

כְּתִיב וְלִבְהֶמְתְּךָ וְלַחַיָּה אֲשֶׁר בְּאַרְצֶךָ תִּהְיֶה כָל־תְּבוּאָתָהּ לֶאֱכֹל. רִבִּי חִיָּיא בַּר
בָּא אָמַר שְׁתֵּי תְּבוּאוֹת אַחַת מִן הַבַּיִת וְאַחַת מִן הַשָּׂדֶה וּכְתִיב מִן הַשָּׂדֶה תֹּאכְלוּ
אֶת תְּבוּאָתָהּ.

It is written (*Lev.* 25:7): "For your domestic animals and the wild
animals of your Land shall all its yield be food." Rebbi Ḥiyya bar Abba
said, two kinds of yield, one from the house and one from the field, and it
is written (*Lev.* 25:12): "From the field you shall eat its yield.[85]"

85   This explains why the Mishnah following paragraph, the edible
has to give two terms for each kind of produce of the Sabbatical year may be
produce. As will be explained in the used only as unaltered food to be eaten.

רִבִּי יוֹסֵה בֶּן חֲנִינָא בָּעֵי פַּגִּין מַהוּ לַעֲשׂוֹת מֵהֶן מָלוּגְמָא שֶׁהוּא אוֹכֵל בָּהֶן פִּיתּוֹ בַּשָּׂדֶה יְהֵא אָסוּר. אוֹ מֵאַחַר שֶׁהוּא מַכְנִיסָן לַבַּיִת יְהֵא מוּתָּר.

86 Rebbi Yose ben Ḥanina asked: May one make a plaster (emollient)[86] of unripe figs? After he can eat his bread with them in the field it will be forbidden. Or since he may bring them into his house it might be permitted[87].

86   Greek μάλαγμα, cf. *Berakhot* p. 385. Once growth of the Sabbatical year is food, it cannot be used for anything else as stated in Mishnah 8:1.

87   Since unripe figs are not food in the usual sense; it might be permitted to treat unripe figs like, e. g., mint leaves, and use them for medical purposes.

תַּמָּן תַּנִּינָן הַפַּגִּין וְהַבּוֹסֶר רִבִּי עֲקִיבָה אוֹמֵר מִטַּמֵּא טוּמְאַת אוֹכְלִין. רִבִּי יוֹחָנָן בֶּן נוּרִי אוֹמֵר מִשֶּׁיָּבוֹאוּ לְעוֹנַת הַמַּעְשְׂרוֹת. תַּנֵּי כָאן מִיַּד וְלֵית כָּאן מִיַּד. רִבִּי חֲנַנְיָה בְּשֵׁם רִבִּי שִׁמְעוֹן בֶּן לָקִישׁ בְּפַגֵּי תְאֵינִים הִיא מַתְנִיתָא הָא בִּשְׁאָר כָּל־הַפַּגִּין אֵינָן (fol. 35c) מִטַּמְּאִין טוּמְאַת אוֹכְלִין עַד שֶׁיָּבוֹאוּ לְעוֹנַת הַמַּעְשְׂרוֹת. אָמַר רִבִּי יוֹסֵה מַתְנִיתִין אֶמְרָה כֵן הַפַּגִּין מִשֶּׁיַּזְרִיחוּ אוֹכֵל בָּהֶן פִּיתּוֹ בַּשָּׂדֶה. רִבִּי פְּדָת בְּשֵׁם רִבִּי יוֹחָנָן הַכֹּל מוֹדִין בַּשְּׁבִיעִית. הַכֹּל מוֹדִין חֲבֵרַיָּיא אָמְרִין שֶׁאֵינָן מִטַּמְּאִין טוּמְאַת אוֹכְלִין.

There, we have stated (Mishnah *'Uqeẓin* 3:6): "Unripe figs and grapes, Rebbi Aqiba said they may become impure by the impurity of food; Rebbi Johanan ben Nuri said only after they come to the period of tithing[88]." We have stated here "immediately" but is it "not immediately"[89]? Rebbi Hananiah in the name of Rebbi Simeon ben Laqish: The Mishnah speaks only about unripe figs, but unripe fruit of any other kind may not become impure by the impurity of food until it reaches the period of tithing.

Rebbi Yose said, our Mishnah implies this: "Unripe figs[90] when they
started to be radiant one eats them with his bread in the field." Rebbi
Pedat[91] in the name of Rebbi Joḥanan: Everybody agrees about the
Sabbatical year. "Everybody agrees," the colleagues said that the figs do
not become impure by the impurity of food[92].

88   Earlier, they are considered as
pieces of wood that cannot become
impure.

89   R. Aqiba assumes that anything
edible under circumstances of need is
food; does he hold this as a general
principle or only in this special case?

90   גס without qualifier means only
"unripe fig." Since the Mishnah gives

no qualifier, it can apply only to figs.

91   Son of the Amora R. Eleazar
(ben Pedat).

92   Even R. Aqiba will agree that
unripe figs and grapes in the Sabbatical
year are not yet food since legal
restrictions prevent their being used as
food except by the worker on the field.

הַקּוּר כְּעֵץ לְכָל־דָּבָר אֶלָּא שֶׁהוּא נִלְקָח בְּכֶסֶף מַעֲשֵׂר וְכַפּוֹנִיּוֹת לְאוֹכְלִין
נִפְטָרוֹת מִן הַמַּעְשְׂרוֹת. דָּרַשׁ רְבִּי יוּדָה בַּר פָּזִי בְּבֵית מִדְרָשׁ הַקּוּר אֵין קְדוּשַׁת
שְׁבִיעִית חָלָה עָלָיו. וְרְבִּי יוֹסֵה מְפַקֵּדִין עַל שׁוֹאֲלַיָּא וְאָמְרִין לוֹן מִן לְכוֹן מֵימַר
כֵּן. וַהֲווֹן אָמְרִין הוּא אָמַר לוֹן רְבִּי יוֹסֵה מַתְנִיתָא פְּלִיגָא עַל רְבִּי יוּדָה בֶּן פָּזִי
וּמְסַיְּיעָה לָן דְּתַנֵּי הַפַּגִּין שֶׁל שְׁבִיעִית אֵין שׁוֹלְקִין אוֹתָן וּבִמְסוּיָּיפוֹת מוּתָּר מִפְּנֵי
שֶׁהִיא מְלַאכְתָּן.

"[93]The palm pith[94] is wood in every respect except that it may be
bought with tithe money[95]. Palm spathe[96] used as food is free from
tithes." Rebbi Judah ben Pazi explained in the study house: Palm pith is
not subject to the holiness of the Sabbatical year[97]. But Rebbi Yose
commanded about those who were asking[98]; they said that it was said
from his part. He made them say that Rebbi Yose told them, a *baraita*

disagrees with Rebbi Judah ben Pazi and supports us, as it was stated[99]: "One may not cook unripe figs of the Sabbatical year but it is permitted for the late ones because that is their treatment."

93 Mishnah 'Uqezin 3:7. The paragraph is a follow-up to the Mishnah 'Uqezin quoted earlier.

94 The new growth on top of the date palm in the spring which may be eaten as a vegetable as long as it is soft. If not removed, it becomes wood.

95 Money from the Second Tithe that, in the times of the Temple, must be used for food in Jerusalem.

96 Explanation of the Gaonic commentary to Tahorot and Maimonides. Arukh and Rashi explain: Dates which never ripen. I. Löw: The male flower of the date palm. (The Arabic word used by the Gaonim and Maimonides, טֶלַע, means mainly "spathe" in classical Arabic, but also "palm frond" (meaning chosen by Al-Ḥarizi), and "pollen"; as טֶלַע the latter is the only meaning in Iraqi dialect. It does not seem reasonable to replace "pollen" by "male flower.")

97 Since it is a kind of wood, it may be used otherwise than as food.

98 They were checking with him whether the statement of R. Judah ben Pazi was true. He had them reveal the source of their statement.

99 Tosephta 3:21, and there the language is: "One may not split (?) unripe figs of the Sabbatical year but it is permitted for the late ones because that is their treatment; it is permitted for palm pith and palm spathe." Late figs do not ripen on the tree; if one wants to use them as food one makes them into preserves. Similarly, palm pith and palm spathe are food only if cooked. Since everybody will agree that late figs are food, one also has to agree that palm pith and spathe are food under the rules of the Sabbatical. The argument is valid only if one assumes that R. Yose was quoting the entire Tosephta or an equivalent text. (The commentators of the Tosephta replace "split" by "cook" on the basis of the Yerushalmi but this reading has no support in the Tosephta mss.)

מֵאֵימָתַי אוֹכְלִין פֵּירוֹת כו'.   קוֹר וכְפָנִיּוֹת הֲרֵי הֵן כְּעֵץ וְכֵן אָנוּ אוֹמְרִים וְעֵץ
אָסוּר לְשׁוֹלְקוֹ אֶלָּא מִשּׁוּם דִּקְדוּשַׁת שְׁבִיעִית חָלָה עָלָיו לְפוּם כֵּן צָרִיךְ מֵימַר
אָסוּר.

[100]"When does one start to eat fruits", etc. Since we say that palm pith
and spathe are like wood, is wood forbidden to be cooked? But because
the holiness of the Sabbatical falls on them one has to say that it is
forbidden[101].

100   Here, in the middle of R. Yose's
argument, starts Halakhah 7 in the
Venice print. The quote from the
Mishnah has to be disregarded.

101   Because of the Tosephta quoted
in Note 99, the commentators want to
change "forbidden" into "permitted"
without any manuscript evidence.

However, since this paragraph still
belongs to R. Yose's argument against
R. Jehudah ben Pazi, "forbidden" here
is appropriate since it implies that even
for palm pith and spathe, once they
have been taken from the tree any use
conflicting with the holiness of the
Sabbatical is forbidden.

הלכה ח: הַבּוֹסֶר מִשֶּׁהֵבִיא מַיִם כו'.   גַּבֵּי בּוֹסֶר מַה אִית לָךְ אָמַר.   אָמַר רִבִּי
אָבוּן שֶׁכֵּן דֶּרֶךְ הַקְּיִהוֹת אוֹכְלוֹת אוֹתוֹ.

"Unripe grapes when they contain fluid", etc. What argument can you
give for unripe grapes? Rebbi Abun said, because at that stage usually the
owls eat it[102].

102   By Lev. 25:7, food for wild
animals is legal food in the Sabbatical

year; cf. Mishnah 8:1.

(fol. 35a) **משנה ח:** זֵיתִים שֶׁהִכְנִיסוּ רְבִיעִית לִסְאָה פּוֹצֵעַ וְאוֹכֵל בַּשָּׂדֶה. הִכְנִיסוּ

חֲצִי לוֹג כּוֹתֵשׁ וְסָךְ בַּשָּׂדֶה. הִכְנִיסוּ שְׁלִישׁ כּוֹתֵשׁ בַּשָּׂדֶה וְכוֹנֵס לְתוֹךְ בֵּיתוֹ. וְכֵן

כַּיּוֹצֵא בָהֶן בִּשְׁאָר שְׁנֵי שָׁבוּעַ חַיָּבִין בְּמַעְשְׂרוֹת. וּשְׁאָר כָּל־פֵּירוֹת הָאִילָן כְּעוֹנָתָן

לְמַעְשְׂרוֹת כָּךְ עוֹנָתָן לַשְּׁבִיעִית.

Mishnah 8: Olives containing a quarter *log* [of oil] per *seah* one may
break open and eat in the field. When they contain half a *log*, one may
pound them and [use the oil to] anoint oneself in the field. When they
contain a third, one may pound them on the field and bring them to the
house; in a similar circumstance in the other years of the Sabbatical cycle
they are subject to tithes. For all other tree fruits, as their time for
tithes[103] so is their time for the Sabbatical year.

103   Given in *Ma'serot* Chapter 1.

(fol. 35c) **הלכה ט:** זֵיתִים שֶׁהִכְנִיסוּ רְבִיעִית לִסְאָה כו'. מַהוּ שְׁלִישׁ לוֹג.

מַתְנִיתָא שֶׁהֵן עוֹשִׂין שְׁלֹשֶׁת לוּגִּין לִסְאָה.

Halakhah 9: "Olives containing a quarter *log* per *seah*," etc. What is
"a third"? Of a *log*. The Mishnah for those which produce three *log* per
seah[104].

104   A quarter *log* therefore simply   average. For the definition of *log* and
means that the olives already contain   *seah*, cf. *Berakhot* Chapter 3, Note 164.
$1/12$ of the oil a ripe olive yields on the

כְּתִיב כִּי יוֹבֵל הִיא קוֹדֶשׁ תִּהְיֶה לָכֶם וְגוֹמֶר. מַה הִיא קוֹדֶשׁ אַף תְּבוּאָתָהּ קוֹדֶשׁ.

It is written (*Lev.* 25:12): "Because it is *yovel*, holy should it be for you,
etc." Just as [the year] is holy, so its yield is holy[105].

105   The full verse reads: "Because it is *yovel*, holy should it be for you; from the field you should eat its yield." The yield of Sabbatical and Jubilee years has to be treated as holy and may not be used for industrial purposes. On the other hand, as explained in Note 85, lenient rules are valid for eating in the field.

רבּי יוֹסֵה בֶּן חֲנִינָה מְנַשֵׁק לְכִיפְתָא דְּעַכּוֹ וְאָמַר עַד כֹּה הִיא אַרְעָא דְיִשְׂרָאֵל. רבּי זְעִירָא עָבַר יוֹרְדְּנָא בְּמָנוֹי. רבּי חִייָא בַּר אַבָּא מִתְעַגֵּל בַּהֲדָה אִילוֹסִיס דְּטִיבֶּרְיָא. רבּי חִייָה רוֹבָה מַתְקַל כִּיפֵי. רבּי חֲנַנְיָה מַתְקַל גּוּשַׁייָא לְקַייֵם מַה שֶׁנֶּאֱמַר כִּי רָצוּ עֲבָדֶיךָ אֶת אֲבָנֶיהָ וְאֶת עֲפָרָהּ יְחֹנֵנוּ.

Rebbi Yose ben Ḥanina[106] kissed the cliffs of Acco and said, up to here is the Land of Israel. Rebbi Zeïra crossed the Jordan in his clothing[107]. Rebbi Ḥiyya bar Abba rolled himself in the step[108] of Tiberias. The elder Rebbi Ḥiyya weighed rocks. Rebbi Ḥananiah weighed earth lumps to fulfill what was said (Ps. 102:19): "For Your servants desired its stones and they loved its dust."

106   The parallels are in Babli *Ketubot* 112a.
107   According to the Babli he did not find a ferry when he came to Israel from Babylonia, only a rope stretched over the ford; he walked along the rope in his garments to enter the Land as quickly as possible.
108   Cf. Greek ἔλευσις, -εως, ἡ, "coming, arrival".

מִשְׁנָה ט: מֵאֵימָתַי אֵין קוֹצְצִין אֶת הָאִילָן בַּשְּׁבִיעִית בֵּית שַׁמַּאי (fol. 35a) אוֹמְרִים כָּל־הָאִילָן מִשֶּׁיּוֹצִיא. וּבֵית הֵלֵּל אוֹמְרִים הֶחָרוּבִים מִשֶּׁיְּשַׁלְשְׁלוּ וְהַגְּפָנִים מִשֶּׁיַּגְרִיעוּ וְהַזֵּיתִים מִשֶּׁיָּנִיצוּ וּשְׁאָר כָּל־הָאִילָן מִשֶּׁיּוֹצִיא. וְכָל־הָאִילָן

כֵּיוָן שֶׁבָּא לְעוֹנַת הַמַּעְשְׂרוֹת מוּתָּר לְקוֹצְצוֹ. וְכַמָּה יְהֵא בַּזַּיִת וְלֹא יְקוֹצֶנּוּ רוֹבַע. רַבָּן שִׁמְעוֹן בֶּן גַּמְלִיאֵל אוֹמֵר הַכֹּל לְפִי הַזַּיִת.

Mishnah 9: When may one not cut down a tree in the Sabbatical year[109]? The House of Shammai say, every tree when it starts[110]. But the House of Hillel say, carob trees when they form clusters, vines when they produce fluid[111], olive trees when they have flower buds, all other trees when they start. Any tree may be cut down[112] once it[s fruit] has reached the stage of tithes. How much should be on an olive tree so one should not cut it down? A quarter [*qab*]. Rabban Simeon ben Gamliel says, all according to the olive tree[113].

109 One may not cut down a fruit tree as long as it is valuable (*Deut.* 20:19). This is discussed at the end of this Mishnah. In the Sabbatical year, when the fruit is public property, one may not cut down a tree once it has started to bear fruit until all fruit has been harvested from it.

110 According to Maimonides, when its fruit has started to develop;

according to Rashi (*Pesaḥim* 52b/53a) when it started to grow new leaves. "Forming chains" refers to developing clusters of pods containing seeds.

111 Cf. Arabic جرع "to drink".

112 After the fruits have been harvested from the tree.

113 If the value of the olive wood is greater than the value of the olive harvest from the tree.

(fol. 35c) **הלכה י:** מֵאֵימָתַי אֵין קוֹצְצִין כו'. תַּנָּא רִבִּי חִינְנָא בַּר פַּפָּא חֲרוּבִין שֶׁלְּשׁוּלָן הוּא חֲנָטָן. גְּפָנִים מִשֶּׁיַּגְרִיעוּ. אָמַר רִבִּי יוֹנָה מִשֶּׁיְּזַלְחוּ[114] מַיִם. כְּמָה דְּאַתְּ אָמַר כִּי יִגְרַע נִטְפֵי מָיִם יָזוּקּוּ מָטָר לְאֵידוֹ. זֵיתִים מִשֶּׁיָּנֵיצוּ. אָמַר רִבִּי יוֹנָה מִשֶּׁהַכְנִיסוּ רוֹבַע. מַה רוֹבַע נֵץ אוֹ רוֹבַע זֵיתִים. אָמַר רִבִּי יוֹנָה לְאֵי דוּ נֵץ שֶׁהוּא עוֹשֶׂה רוֹבַע זֵיתִים.

"When may one not cut down", etc. Rebbi Ḥinena bar Pappa stated, for carob trees their forming clusters means their sprouting. "Vines when they produce fluid," Rebbi Jonah said when they flow with water, as you say (*Job* 36:27): "He draws the waterdrops that distill rain from their mist." "Olive trees when they have flower buds", Rebbi Jonah said, when they bring a quarter [*qab*]. A quarter [*qab*] of flower buds or a quarter [*qab*] of olives? Rebbi Jonah said, that means, flower buds which will yield a quarter [*qab*] of olives.

114   Reading of a Genizah fragment.   *hapax* of undetermined meaning.
Leyden ms. and Venice print: משיזהלו, a

אָמַר רִבִּי יוֹנָה כִּי יִשַּׁל זֵיתֶיךָ. חַד לִתְלַת מֵאָה וְאַרְבָּעִין קָיֵים בָּהּ. אָמַר רִבִּי יוֹנָה כִּי עֵץ נָשָׂא פִרְיוֹ מַגִּיד שֶׁלֹּא נָשָׂא פִרְיוֹ בָּעוֹלָם הַזֶּה. וּתְאֵינָה וַגֶּפֶן נָתְנוּ חֵילָם מַגִּיד שֶׁלֹּא נָתְנוּ חֵילָם בָּעוֹלָם הַזֶּה.

Rebbi Jonah[115] said (*Deut.* 28:40): "Your olives will fall off," one in 340 were kept[116] Rebbi Jonah said (*Joel* 2:22): "For the tree will bear its fruit" means that the tree is not bearing its fruit in this world[117], "and fig tree and vine will give their strength" means that they are not giving their strength in this world.

115   Since R. Jonah was mentioned in the preceding paragraph, his homilies are appended here.
116   The numerical value of ישל is 340.
117   "This world" in the Yerushalmi means the world before the coming of the Messiah. The implication is that in the days of the Messiah produce will be so abundant that the rabbinic rules governing the details of tithing and Sabbatical will have to be changed.

אָמַר רִבִּי יוֹנָה בְּשֵׁם רִבִּי חָמָא בַּר חֲנִינָא הַמֵּת בְּשֶׁבַע שְׁנֵי גוֹג אֵין לוֹ חֵלֶק לֶעָתִיד לָבוֹא סִימָנָא דְּאָכַל פְּרְטַגְּמִיָּא אֲכִיל מַשְׁתּוּתָא. שָׁמַע רִבִּי יוֹסֵי וְאָמַר וְיֵאוּת עַד כְּדוֹן אִית תּוֹתְבָה לְעָלְמָא דְּאָתֵי. רִבִּי יוֹנָה בְּשֵׁם רִבִּי חִייָה בַּר אֲשֵׁי

עֲתִידִין הֵן חֲבֵירִין לְהִתְנַגֵּעַ מִבָּתֵּי כְנֵסִיּוֹת לְבָתֵּי מִדְרָשׁוֹת מַה טַעֲמָא יֵלְכוּ מֵחַיִל אֶל חָיִל יֵרָאֶה אֶל אֱלֹהִים בְּצִיּוֹן עַד יֵרָאֶה אֶל אֱלֹהִים אֶל אֱלֹהִים בְּצִיּוֹן.[118]

Rebbi Jonah said in the name of Rebbi Ḥama bar Ḥanina: He who dies in the seven years of Gog[119] has no part in the Future World. Its sign is, he who ate at the preliminary wedding feast[120] shall eat at the wedding feast. Rebbi Yose heard this and said, is that true? So far there is repentance for the Future World[121]! Rebbi Jonah in the name of Rebbi Ḥiyya bar Ashi[122]: In the future, fellows will exert themselves from synagogues to houses of study. What is the reason? (*Ps.* 84:8) "They will go from strength to strength, he will see the Power, God, in Zion," until he will see the Power, God, in Zion[123].

118 The last five words are only in the Leyden ms.

119 Described in *Ez.* Chapters 38-39. In the opinion of the preacher here, the days of Gog are immediately followed by the coming of the Messiah and the resurrection of the dead. According to this opinion, one who dies immediately before the resurrection has no part in it, otherwise he would not have died.

120 Cf. *Demay* p. 484.

121 Everybody has his chance at the Future World.

122 He is Rav Ḥiyya bar Ashi. In the Babli, *Berakhot* 64a, his statement is quoted as originating with Rav.

123 This Zion is the Heavenly Zion, place of the resurrection, since in this world, God cannot be seen. This leads to the next paragraph on those who have part in the resurrection.

רַבָּנִין דְּקֵיסָרִין אָמְרִין קְטַנֵּי גוֹיִם וְחַיָּילוֹתָיו שֶׁל נְבוּכַדְנֶצֶר לֹא חַיִּין וְלֹא נְדוֹנִין וַעֲלֵיהֶן הוּא אוֹמֵר וְיָשְׁנוּ שְׁנַת עוֹלָם וְלֹא יָקִיצוּ. מֵאֵימָתַי קְטַנֵּי יִשְׂרָאֵל חַיִּין רִבִּי חִיָּיא רוֹבָה וְרִבִּי שִׁמְעוֹן בְּרִבִּי חַד אָמַר מִשֶּׁיִּוָּלְדוּ. וְחַד אָמַר מִשֶּׁיְּדַבְּרוּ. מָאן דְּאָמַר מִשֶּׁיִּוָּלְדוּ יָבוֹאוּ וְיַגִּידוּ צִדְקָתוֹ לְעַם נוֹלָד כִּי עָשָׂה. וּמָאן דְּאָמַר מִשֶּׁיְּדַבְּרוּ זֶרַע יַעַבְדֶנּוּ יְסוּפַּר לַיָי לַדּוֹר. תַּנֵּי בְּשֵׁם רִבִּי מֵאִיר מִשֶּׁהוּא יוֹדֵעַ

לַעֲנוֹת אָמֵן בְּבֵית הַכְּנֶסֶת מַה טַעֲמָא פִּתְחוּ שְׁעָרִים וְיָבוֹא גּוֹי צַדִּיק שׁוֹמֵר

אֱמוּנִים. תַּמָּן אָמְרִין מִשֶׁיִּמּוֹלוּ נָשָׂאתִי אֵימֶיךָ אָפוּנָה. וְרַבָּנִין דְּהָכָא אָמְרִין

מִשֶׁיִּוָּלְדוּ וּלְצִיּוֹן יֵאָמַר אִישׁ אִישׁ יֻלַּד בָּהּ וְהוּא יְכוֹנְנֶיהָ עֶלְיוֹן. רִבִּי לָעֶזֶר אָמַר

אֲפִילוּ נְפָלִים מַה טַעֲמָא וּנְצוּרֵי יִשְׂרָאֵל לְהָשִׁיב. וּנְצִירֵי יִשְׂרָאֵל לְהָשִׁיב.

The rabbis of Caesarea say, Gentile minors[124] and the armies of
Nebucadnezzar will not live and will not be judged; about them it says
(*Jer.* 51:39,57): "They will sleep an eternal sleep and never wake up."
From when do Jewish minors live? The elder Rebbi Ḥiyya and Rebbi
Simeon ben Rebbi, one said from when they are born, the other said from
when they talk[125]. He who says from when they are born (*Ps.* 22:32):
"they shall come and tell His justice to the born people He made." He
who says from when they talk (*Ps.* 22:31): "Seed will worship Him, it will
by told to the Master by the generation." It was stated in the name of
Rebbi Meïr: From the time [the child] knows to answer Amen in the
synagogue. What is the reason? (*Is.* 26:2) "Open the gates, let the just
people come who keep trust[126]." There they say, from when they are
circumcised (*Ps.* 88:16): "I carried your fear, I cease[127]" But the rabbis
from here say, from when they are born (*Ps.* 87:5): "He will say to
Zion[128], everybody [who] was born [is] in it." Rebbi Eleazar says, even the
still-born, what is the reason? (*Is.* 49:6) "The watched ones of Israel to
return", the created ones of Israel to return[129].

---

124   In the Babli, *Sanhedrin* 110b,
this is restricted to minor children of
evil Gentiles. Cf. *Berakhot* Chapter
Nine, Notes 71 ff.

125   Also in the Babli, *Sanhedrin*
110b.

126   In the Babli, *Sanhedrin* 110b and
Sabbath 119b, it is explained that those
who keep trust are those who respond
Amen, "trustworthy".

127   For the translation, cf. Arabic

نى "to cease". Once the baby carries
the fear of the Eternal, being circumcised, even if it ceases to exist it has
part of the salvation expressed in the
Psalm.

128   The Heavenly Zion.

29   "The watched ones" נצורי is *qere*
(read), "the created ones" נצירי *ketib*
(written).

בנות שוח פרק חמישי

(fol. 35c) **משנה א:** בְּנוֹת שׁוּחַ שְׁבִיעִית שֶׁלָּהֶן שְׁנִיָּה שֶׁהֵן עוֹשׂוֹת לְשָׁלֹשׁ שָׁנִים.
רְבִּי יְהוּדָה אוֹמֵר הַפֵּרְסָאוֹת שְׁבִיעִית שֶׁלָּהֶן מוֹצָאֵי שְׁבִיעִית שֶׁהֵן עוֹשׂוֹת לִשְׁתֵּי
שָׁנִים אָמְרוּ לוֹ לֹא אָמְרוּ אֶלָּא בְּנוֹת שׁוּחַ.

Mishnah 1: The Sabbatical of white figs[1] is the second year[2] since they produce after three years. Rebbi Jehudah says, the Sabbatical of Persian figs is the year after the Sabbatical since they need two years to produce. One said to him, they mentioned only white figs.

1   Cf. *Demay* Chapter 1, Note 5.
2   The second year of the new Sabbatical cycle. Maimonides (*Ševi'it* 4:16) notes that it is possible that the fruits are edible and subject to the laws of tithes already at the end of the first year of the cycle. The trees mentioned here carry both ripened fruit and flowers at the same time.

(fol. 36d) **הלכה א:** בְּנוֹת שׁוּחַ כו'. מַהוּ בְּנוֹת שׁוּחַ פֵּיטֵירִיָה. מַה בְּכָל־שָׁנָה
וְשָׁנָה הֵן עוֹשׂוֹת אוֹ אַחַת לְשָׁלֹשׁ שָׁנִים. בְּכָל־שָׁנָה וְשָׁנָה הֵן עוֹשׂוֹת אֶלָּא שֶׁאֵין
פֵּירוֹתֵיהָ מִנַּמְרִין אֶלָּא לְאַחַר שָׁלֹשׁ שָׁנִים. כֵּיצַד הוּא יוֹדֵעַ. רְבִּי יוֹנָה אָמַר
מִשֶּׁיְּקַשֵּׁר עָלָיו חוּט. תַּנֵּי שְׁמוּאֵל תּוֹחֵב בָּהֶן קִיסְמִין.

Halakhah 1: "White figs", etc. What are white figs? Stonies[3]. Do they bear every year or only once in three years? They bear every year but their fruits ripen only after three years. How does one know? Rebbi Jonah said, from when he binds a string around them[4]. Samuel stated, one sticks a splint into them.

3   Greek adj. πετραῖος, α, ον,   4   Presumably a different kind of
Latin petraeus, a, um, "stony, of stone".   string every year.

תַּנֵּי רַבָּן שִׁמְעוֹן בֶּן גַּמְלִיאֵל אוֹמֵר שֶׁחָנַט קוֹדֶם חֲמִשָּׁה עָשָׂר בִּשְׁבָט
מִתְעַשֵּׂר לְשֶׁעָבַר. לְאַחַר חֲמִשָּׁה עָשָׂר בִּשְׁבָט מִתְעַשֵּׂר לָבֹא. תַּנֵּי אָמַר רבי
נְחֶמְיָה בְּמֶה דְּבָרִים אֲמוּרִים בְּאִילָן שֶׁהוּא עוֹשֶׂה שְׁתֵּי גְרָנוֹת בַּשָּׁנָה. אֲבָל
בְּאִילָן שֶׁהוּא עוֹשֶׂה גוֹרֶן אֶחָד בַּשָּׁנָה כְּגוֹן זֵיתִים וּתְמָרִים וְחָרוּבִין אַף עַל פִּי
שֶׁחֶנְטוּ קוֹדֶם לַזְּמָן הַזֶּה הֲרֵי הֵן כִּלְעָתִיד לָבוֹא. אָמַר רִבִּי יוֹחָנָן נָהֲגוּ בְחָרוּבִין
כְּרִבִּי נְחֶמְיָה. מוֹתִיב רִבִּי שִׁמְעוֹן קוֹמֵי רִבִּי יוֹחָנָן וְהָא תַּנִּינָן בְּנוֹת שׁוּחַ שְׁבִיעִית
שֶׁלָּהֶן שְׁנִיָּיה שֶׁהֵן עוֹשׂוֹת לְשָׁלֹשׁ שָׁנִים. עַל דַּעְתָּךְ מַה שֶּׁעָשׂוּ בַּשְּׁבִיעִית יְהוּ
שְׁבִיעִית וְהוּא מְקַבֵּל מִינֵיהּ. אָמַר רִבִּי בּוּן בַּר כַּהֲנָא וְתַמְיָּא אֲנָא אֵיךְ הֲוָה
מוֹתִיב רִבִּי שִׁמְעוֹן קוֹמֵי רִבִּי יוֹחָנָן וְהוּא מְקַבֵּל מִינֵיהּ. וְיתִיבִינֵיהּ אֲנָא אָמַר
חָרוּבִין וְאַתְּ אָמַר בְּנוֹת שׁוּחַ. אֲנָא אָמַר מִנְהָג וְאַתְּ אָמַר הֲלָכָה. אֲנָא אָמַר רִבִּי
נְחֶמְיָה וְאַתְּ אָמַר רַבָּנִין. אֶלָּא הִיא חָרוּבִין הִיא בְּנוֹת שׁוּחַ. הִיא מִנְהָג הִיא
הֲלָכָה. הִיא רִבִּי נְחֶמְיָה הִיא רַבָּנִין.

It was stated[5]: "Rabban Simeon ben Gamliel says, a tree that buds
before the fifteenth of *Ševaṭ*[6] is tithed for the past [year]; after the
fifteenth of *Ševaṭ* it is tithed for the coming [year]." It was stated: "Rebbi
Nehemiah said, when has this been said? For a tree producing two
threshing floors[7] a year. But trees making only one threshing floor per
year, such as olive trees, date palms and carob trees, even if they budded
before this day, belong to the future." Rebbi Johanan said, people use to
follow Rebbi Nehemiah for carobs. Rebbi Simeon objected before Rebbi
Johanan: Did we not state that "the Sabbatical of white figs is the second
year since they produce after three years"? According to you, those
ripened in the Sabbatical year should be Sabbatical! He accepted that[8].
Rebbi Abun bar Cahana[9] said, I wonder how Rebbi Simeon ben Laqish

could bring this objection before Rebbi Joḥanan and he accepted it. Could
he not object: I am speaking about carobs and you about white figs, I am
speaking about custom and you about practice[10], I am speaking about
Rebbi Neḥemiah and you about the rabbis[11]! It follows that the rules are
equal for carobs and white figs, custom and practice, Rebbi Neḥemiah and
the rabbis[12].

5   In the Babylonian sources (*Roš
Haššanah* 15b, *Tosephta Ševi'it* 4:20),
the statement is anonymous, repre-
senting the opinion of the majority of
Sages.

6   New Year's Day for trees (Mishnah *Roš Haššanah* 1:1), cf. Chapter 2,
Note 52.

7   Fruits of trees are not threshed;
"threshing floor" means here "harvest
of all the fruits of a tree at one time",
to exclude figs and similar fruits that
ripen and are harvested over a long
period of time. The Babylonian
sources use בריכה "brood (of pigeons)"
for the same meaning.

8   In the opinion of the Babli, if R.
Joḥanan did not find an answer to the
objection it does not imply that he

accepted its inference as practice to be
followed, in disagreement with the
Yerushalmi.

9   In the Babli, R. Abba Cohen; in
other places of the Yerushalmi, R.
Abba bar Cohen.

10   Practice is the generally accepted ruling of the rabbis; custom is what
the people do, without explicit rabbinic
endorsement.

11   Of the anonymous Mishnah
which, according to R. Joḥanan, should
always guide practice.

12   Hence, the Babylonian text
which omits the mention of Rabban
Simeon ben Gamliel is justified; the
statement is generally accepted and R.
Neḥemiah explains it but does not
disagree.

תַּמָּן אָמְרִין אִילָן שֶׁחָנַט קוֹדֶם רֹאשׁ הַשָּׁנָה שֶׁלְעוֹלָם מִתְעַשֵּׂר לְשֶׁעָבַר לְאַחַר
רֹאשׁ הַשָּׁנָה שֶׁלְעוֹלָם מִתְעַשֵּׂר לְבָא. הָתִיב רִבִּי יוּדָן בַּר פְּדָיָא קוֹמֵי רִבִּי יוֹנָה
הֲרֵי חָרוּבִין הֲרֵי הֵן חוֹנְטִין קוֹדֶם רֹאשׁ הַשָּׁנָה שֶׁל עוֹלָם וְהֵן מִתְעַשְּׂרִין לְבָא.
וְלָא שְׁמִיעַ דְּאָמַר רִבִּי חִינָּנָא בַּר פָּפָא חָרוּבִין שֶׁלְשׁוּלָן הוּא חַנְטוֹ.

There[13], they say: A tree which buds before the New Year's Day of the World[14] is tithed for the past; after the New Year's Day of the World it is tithed for the future. Rebbi Yudan bar Pedaiah objected before Rebbi Jonah: But carob trees form buds before New Year's Day and are tithed for the future! He had not heard what Rebbi Ḥinena bar Pappos said, for carob trees the forming of clusters[15] is [counted as] their forming buds.

13   In Babylonia. This opinion is not mentioned in the Babylonian Talmud.

14   The First of Tishre, usually called simply "New Year's Day".

15   The clustering of carob pods is visible.

אָמַר רִבִּי יַסָּא הֵבִיא שְׁלִישׁ קוֹדֶם רֹאשׁ הַשָּׁנָה שֶׁל עוֹלָם מִתְעַשֵּׂר לְשֶׁעָבַר לְאַחַר רֹאשׁ הַשָּׁנָה שֶׁל עוֹלָם מִתְעַשֵּׂר לָבֹא. הָתִיב רִבִּי זְעִירָא קוֹמֵי רִבִּי יַסָּא פְּעָמִים שֶׁהַשָּׁנִים מַעֲפִילוֹת וּתְמָרִים מַטִּילוֹת שְׂאוֹר לְאַחַר רֹאשׁ הַשָּׁנָה שֶׁל עוֹלָם וְהֵן מִתְעַשְּׂרוֹת לְשֶׁעָבַר. אָמַר רִבִּי זְעִירָא לֹא מִן דַּעְתֵּיהּ הֲוָה רִבִּי יַסָּא אָמַר הָדָא מִילְתָא אֶלָּא מִן הָדָא דְּרִבִּי יוֹחָנָן דְּרִבִּי שִׁמְעוֹן בֶּן לָקִישׁ. רִבִּי יַעֲקֹב בָּר אָחָא בְּשֵׁם שְׁמוּאֵל בַּר אַבָּא הֵבִיא שְׁלִישׁ קוֹדֶם לַחֲמִשָּׁה עָשָׂר בִּשְׁבָט מִתְעַשֵּׂר לְשֶׁעָבַר. לְאַחַר חֲמִשָּׁה עָשָׂר בִּשְׁבָט מִתְעַשֵּׂר לָבֹא. אָמַר רִבִּי זְעִירָא וְיֵאוּת הֲרֵי אֶתְרוֹג עֲקָרְתָּהּ חֲנָטוֹ לֹא עֲקָרְתָּהּ שְׁנָתוֹ וְכָאן עֲקָרְתָּהּ שְׁנָתוֹ לֹא עֲקָרְתָּהּ חֲנָטוֹ.

Rebbi Assi said, if it was one-third ripe before the New Year's Day of the World it is tithed for the past, after the New Year's Day of the World it is tithed for the future. Rebbi Zeïra objected before Rebbi Assi: Some years are late[16] and dates start to have sap after the New Year's Day of the World but they are tithed for the past! Rebbi Zeïra said, Rebbi Assi did not say this on his own but following Rebbi Joḥanan, Rebbi Simeon ben Laqish[17]. Rebbi Jacob bar Aḥa in the name of Samuel bar Abba: "If it was one-third ripe before the Fifteenth of Ševaṭ it is tithed for the past, after the Fifteenth of *Ševat* for the future[18]." Rebbi Zeïra said, that is correct; for an *etrog,* did one not eliminate its budding but not its year[19]; but here did one eliminate its year but not its budding?

16   That means, New Year's Day is early in the solar year.

17   Since R. Joḥanan, following the objection of R. Simeon ben Laqish, decided that practice had to follow R. Neḥemiah and tithing for trees with only one harvest did not depend on the Fifteenth of *Ševat.* Hence, it must depend on the First of Tishre, following the teachers from "there".

18   This is identical with the opin-ion of the Sages there, except that the New Year of trees substitutes for the New Year of the World.

19   Mishnah *Bikkurim* 2:4 states the opinion of Rabban Gamliel (which is practice to be followed) that an *etrog* (*citrus medica*) is not like a tree fruit in that it is tithed in the year it is harvested, not the year it is formed. Hence, all other tree fruits have to be tithed in the year of their formation.

רִבִּי בּוּן בַּר חִיָּיא בָּעָא קוֹמֵי רִבִּי זְעִירָא מַעֲתָּה שְׁלִיש הָרִאשׁוֹן לְשֶׁעָבַר וּשְׁלִיש הַשֵּׁנִי לָבָא. אָמַר לֵיהּ שְׁלִיש הָרִאשׁוֹן קָשֶׁה לָבוֹא מִכֵּיוָן שֶׁהוּא בָּא מִיַּד הוּא גָדֵל. אָמַר רִבִּי בָּא בְּאָרִיס אוּמָּן יְלִיף לָהּ רִבִּי זְעִירָא. שְׁמוּאֵל אָמַר שִׁיתִּין יוֹמִין שִׁיתָה עָלֵיי שִׁיתָא יוֹמִין שִׁיתִין עָלֵיי. תַּנֵּי רַבָּן שִׁמְעוֹן בֶּן גַּמְלִיאֵל אוֹמֵר מֵהוֹצָאַת עָלִין וְעַד הַפַּגִּין חֲמִשִּׁים יוֹם מִן הַפַּגִּין וְעַד הַשִּׁיתִין הַנּוֹבְלוֹת חֲמִשִּׁים יוֹם מִן הַשִּׁיתִין הַנּוֹבְלוֹת וְעַד הַתְּאֵינִים חֲמִשִּׁים. רִבִּי אוֹמֵר כּוּלְהֶן אַרְבָּעִים אַרְבָּעִים יוֹם. לָקַט תְּאֵינָה וְאֵינוֹ יוֹדֵעַ אֵימָתַי חָנְטָה אָמַר רִבִּי יוֹנָה מוֹנֶה מֵאָה יוֹמִין לְמַפְרֵעַ אִם חָל לְתוֹכָן חֲמִשָּׁה עָשָׂר בִּשְׁבָט וְהוּא יוֹדֵעַ אֵימָתַי חָנְטָה.

Rebbi Abun bar Ḥiyya asked before Rebbi Zeïra: Does this mean, the first third for the past, the second third for the future[20]? He said to him, the first third is slow in coming; afterwards it grows rapidly. Rebbi Abba said, Rebbi Zeïra learned that from a competent sharecropper. Samuel said, sixty days for six leaves, six days for sixty leaves. It was stated[21]:

"Rabban Simeon ben Gamliel said, from the appearance of leaves to the bud fifty days, from the bud to the wind-fall[22] fifty days, from wind-fall to figs fifty days. Rebbi says, all of them by forty days." If somebody harvested figs and does not know when their buds were formed, Rebbi Jonah said he counts a hundred days backwards; if the Fifteenth of Ševat falls in this period he knows when they budded.

20   Should one-third of the tithes be counted for the past year and two thirds for the coming one? The question would arise if a farmer tithes all his yield from one source, not each batch singly. The answer is that growth of the first third of the time

between flowering and ripening of the fruit does not count since the volume produced is negligible.

21   Tosephta 4:20.

22   שיתין are שחיתין, "waste figs" which cannot ripen and fall off before they get heavy.

אָמְרוּ לוֹ וַהֲרֵי עִמָּךְ בְּטִיבֶּרְיָא וְהֵן עוֹשׂוֹת לְשָׁנָה אַחַת. אָמַר לָהֶן וַהֲרֵי עִמָּכֶם בְּצִיפּוֹרִין וְהֵן עוֹשׂוֹת לִשְׁתֵּי שָׁנִים.

They[23] said to him, but they are with you in Tiberias and they produce in one year. He said to them, but there they are with you in Sepphoris[24] and they need two years!

23   This refers to the dispute in the Mishnah between R. Jehudah and the Sages regarding Persian figs.

24   Sepphoris is on a cool mountain top, Tiberias in a hot depression below sea level.

(fol. 35c) **משנה ב:** הַטּוֹמֵן אֶת הַלּוּף בַּשְּׁבִיעִית רְבִּי מֵאִיר אוֹמֵר לֹא יִפְחוֹת
מִסְּאתַיִם עַד גּוֹבַהּ שְׁלֹשָׁה טְפָחִים וְטֶפַח עָפָר עַל גַּבָּיו. וַחֲכָמִים אוֹמְרִים לֹא
יִפְחוֹת מֵאַרְבַּעַת קַבִּין עַד גּוֹבַהּ טֶפַח וְטֶפַח עָפָר עַל גַּבָּיו וְטוֹמְנוֹ בִּמְקוֹם דְּרִיסַת
הָאָדָם.

Mishnah 2: If somebody stores arum[25] in the Sabbatical year, Rebbi
Meïr says it should not be less than two *seah*[26] and [in a hole] three
hand-breadths deep, with a hand-breadth of earth on top. But the Sages
say, it should not be less than four *qab*, one hand-breadth deep, with a
hand-breadth of earth on top, and should be stored where people step on
it[27].

25   See Mishnah *Peah* 6:9. "Storing"
is done in a hole in the ground covered
with earth. Since arum is planted, not
sown, one has to store it in a way that

is clearly different from planting.
26   12 *qab*, cf. *Berakhot* Chapter 3,
Note 164.
27   So nothing will grow there.

(fol. 36d) **הלכה ב:** הַטּוֹמֵן אֶת הַלּוּף. עַד כְּדוֹן לוּף בְּצָלִים. אָמַר רְבִּי יוֹנָה הִיא
לוּף הִיא בְּצָלִים. אָמַר רְבִּי יוֹסֵה מִסְתַּבְּרָא בִּבְצָלִים אֲפִילוּ פָּחוֹת מִכֵּן מוּתָּר
דְּאֵינָן שָׁפִין.

Halakhah 2: "If somebody stores arum". This takes care of arum.
Onions? Rebbi Jonah said, arum and onions follow the same rules[28].
Rebbi Yose said, it is reasonable that a lesser quantity be permitted for
onions for they are smoothed[29].

28   The commentators from
Maimonides to Lieberman, except
Arukh and R. Isaac Simponti, take this
sentence to mean that arum is onion.
This does violence to the style of the
Yerushalmi, cf. the text at Note 12.

(Hebrew לוּף denotes a different plant
than Arabic لوف "dishcloth gourd".)
29   The roots are removed before
storage. There is no danger that the
stored onions could grow out of the
earth.

(fol. 35c) **משנה ג:** לוּף שֶׁעָבְרָה עָלָיו שְׁבִיעִית רִבִּי לִיעֶזֶר אוֹמֵר אִם לָקְטוּ הָעֲנִיִּים אֶת עָלָיו לָקְטוּ וְאִם לָאו יַעֲשֶׂה חֶשְׁבּוֹן עִם הָעֲנִיִּים. רִבִּי יְהוֹשֻׁעַ אוֹמֵר אִם לָקְטוּ הָעֲנִיִּים אֶת עָלָיו לָקְטוּ וְאִם לָאו אֵין לָעֲנִיִּים עִמּוֹ חֶשְׁבּוֹן.

Mishnah 3: Arum after the Sabbatical. Rebbi Eliezer says, if the poor collected the leaves, they collected; otherwise, he should settle with the poor. Rebbi Joshua says, if the poor collected the leaves, they collected; otherwise, the poor have nothing to settle with him[30].

30   This Mishnah is explained in the first paragraph of the Halakhah.

(fol. 36d) **הלכה ג:** לוּף שֶׁעָבְרָה עָלָיו שְׁבִיעִית כו'. רִבִּי אַבָּהוּ בְּשֵׁם רִבִּי יוֹחָנָן אַתְיָא דְּרִבִּי יוּדָה כְּרִבִּי לְעֶזֶר וּדְרִבִּי יוֹסֵי כְּרִבִּי יְהוֹשֻׁעַ. דְּתַנִּינָן תַּמָּן הָעֲנִיִּים אוֹכְלִין אַחַר הַבִּיעוּר אֲבָל לֹא עֲשִׁירִים דִּבְרֵי רִבִּי יוּדָה. רִבִּי יוֹסֶה אוֹמֵר אֶחָד עֲנִיִּים וְאֶחָד עֲשִׁירִים אוֹכְלִין אַחַר הַבִּיעוּר.

Halakhah 3: "Arum after the Sabbatical", etc. Rebbi Abbahu in the name of Rebbi Johanan: It turns out that Rebbi Jehudah follows Rebbi Eliezer and Rebbi Yose follows Rebbi Joshua. As we have stated there[31]: "Poor persons eat after the removal but not rich ones, the words of Rebbi Jehudah[32]. Rebbi Yose says poor and rich persons may eat after the removal.[33]"

31   Mishnah 9:8. *Lev.* 25:6-7 reads: "The Sabbatical of the Land shall be food for you, for you, your male and female slaves, your employees and the non-citizens who dwell with you. All its yield shall be eaten by your domesticated animals as well as the wild animals of your land." As

explained in Mishnah 7:1, this is taken to mean that people may eat Sabbatical produce only as long as wild animals can find that particular produce on the fields. When nothing more is left for the wild animals, the produce may no longer be stored; all produce harvested and stored has to be distributed for immediate consumption; this is called *removal*.

32   Since R. Jehudah's father, R. Illaï, was one of the few known students of R. Eliezer, it is reasonable to assume that R. Eliezer's opinion here underlies the later statement of R. Jehudah. It will be stated in Mishnah 7:1 that only the leaves of arum are subject to removal; the roots are hidden from the wild animals and not subject to removal. Since the poor have the right to harvest the leaves (as vegetables) after the time of removal, any leaves remaining after the Sabbat-

ical are the property of the poor. If the leaves grow again in the following rainy season, the farmer who harvests the leaves as vegetable during that year has to compute the share of the poor and separate it from his harvest.

33   Since everybody may take the leaves after the time of removal, the poor have no claim to anything the next year. Cf. also Chapter 9, Note 116. One has to assume that the Mishnah deals with minute amounts since there would be no removal if considerable amounts were available on the fields.

רְבִּי אַמִּי בָּעָא קוֹמֵי רְבִּי יוֹחָנָן מַתְנִיתָא עַד שֶׁלֹּא גָזְרוּ עַל הַסְּפִיחִין. אָמַר לֵיהּ וְכִי בַּעֲלִיָּיה הָיִית. סָבַר רְבִּי אִימִּי מֵימַר אִיסּוּר סְפִיחִין תּוֹרָה.

Rebbi Ammi asked before Rebbi Joḥanan: Does our Mishnah go back to the time before they decreed about spontaneous growth[34]? He said to him, where you there on the upper floor[35]? Rebbi Ammi inferred that the prohibition of spontaneous growth is from the Torah[36].

34   *Lev.* 25:5 reads: "The spontaneous growth of your grain you should not harvest . . ." On this, *Sifra Behar* 1(3) comments: From here the Sages found support to forbid spontaneous growth in the Sabbatical. The verse forbids only commercial harvest of grain. R. Ammi notes that the leaves of

Arum whose roots were in the earth long before the Sabbatical must have the status of spontaneous growth of vegetable.

35   In all cases where details of the enactment of rabbinical prohibitions have come down to us, the vote was taken on the upper floor of some

house. R. Joḥanan notes that no record
of such a vote is available.

36   The different positions in this

matter will be described in Chapter
Nine.

אָמַר רִבִּי יִרְמְיָה בְּעָלֵי לוּף שׁוֹטֶה הִיא מַתְנִיתָא. אַייתִי רַב הוֹשַׁעְיָה מַתְנֵי דְּבַר
קַפָּרָא מִן דְּרוֹמָא וְתַנֵּי עָלֵי לוּף וְעָלֵי בְצָלִים. אִית לָךְ מֵימַר עָלֵי בְצָלִים
הַשּׁוֹטִין. מִילְתֵיהּ דְּרִבִּי יִרְמְיָה אָמְרָה דָּבָר שֶׁיֵּשׁ לוֹ בִיעוּר שֶׁנִּמְצָא בְּתוֹךְ דָּבָר
שֶׁאֵין לוֹ בִיעוּר יֵשׁ לוֹ בִיעוּר. מַה עָבַד לָהּ רִבִּי יִרְמְיָה פָּתַר לָהּ בְּשֶׁשִּׁיקֵף בְּעָלִין.

Rebbi Jeremiah said, the Mishnah deals with the leaves of false arum[37].
Rav Hoshaiah brought a *baraita* of Bar Qappara from the South and
stated[38]: "The leaves of arum or of onions." Can you speak of leaves of
false onions? The word of Rebbi Jeremiah implies that anything subject
to removal found inside something not subject to removal is subject to
removal[39]. How does Rebbi Jeremiah deal with this? He explains it if he
trampled on the leaves[40].

37   A plant looking like arum but
without a bulb. Its leaves are pure
vegetable (if they are young and not
bitter, Mishnah *Uqeẓin* 3:4).

38   Bar Qappara's version of the
Mishnah supports R. Jonah, that arum
and onion follow the same rules. False
onions do not exist.

39   R. Jeremiah does not want to
apply the rules of the Mishnah to
genuine arum; he must be of the
opinion that the entire arum plant is
subject to removal since its leaves,

being sold as leaf vegetables, are
subject to removal. This would
contradict the statement of the Mishnah which explicitly excludes the roots
and speaks only of the leaves.

40   Since no non-bulbous plant has
leaves like onions, he must explain that
the onion leaves in the *baraita* of Bar
Qappara had been trampled down
before the start of the Sabbatical and,
therefore, do not grow any longer from
the bulb.

רבִּי יוֹסֵה פָּתַר לָהּ מַתְנִיתָא לִפְנֵי רֹאשׁ הַשָּׁנָה שְׁבִיעִית. נָטְעוּ לִפְנֵי רֹאשׁ הַשָּׁנָה
שְׁבִיעִית עָשָׂה בֵצִים לִפְנֵי שְׁבִיעִית וְדִיכְּנוֹ בַּשְּׁבִיעִית עֲקָרוֹ בְּמוֹצָאֵי שְׁבִיעִית. אִין
תֵּימַר דִּיכּוּן כְּעִיקָר כּוֹלוֹ לָעֲנִיִּים. אִין תֵּימַר אֵין דִּיכּוּן כְּעִיקָר אֵין כּוֹלוֹ לָעֲנִיִּים.
מִסְפֵּק יַעֲשֶׂה חֶשְׁבּוֹן עִם הָעֲנִיִּים.

Rebbi Yose explains the Mishnah before the New Year of the
Sabbatical: If one planted before the New Year of the Sabbatical, it
formed a bulb before the Sabbatical; he pressed [the leaves] down during
the Sabbatical and tore them out after the Sabbatical. If you say that
pressing down is like tearing out[41], everything is for the poor. If you say
that pressing down is not like tearing out, not everything is for the poor.
Because of this doubt, he should settle with the poor.

41 Since breaking petioles of the leaves in bending them will stop the growth. R. Yose explains only the	position of R. Eliezer. It is implied that R. Joshua is sure that pressing down is not like tearing out.

רבִּי חִזְקִיָּה פָּתַר מַתְנִיתָא עֶרֶב רֹאשׁ הַשָּׁנָה שְׁבִיעִית. נָטַע עֶרֶב רֹאשׁ הַשָּׁנָה
שְׁבִיעִית וְעָשָׂה בֵיצָה בִּתְחִילַּת שְׁבִיעִית וְדִיכְּנוֹ בַּשְּׁבִיעִית וַעֲקָרוֹ בְּסוֹף שְׁבִיעִית.
אִין תֵּימַר דִּיכּוּן כְּעִיקּוּר כּוֹלוֹ לְבַעַל הַבַּיִת. אִין תֵּימַר אֵין דִּיכּוּן כְּעִיקּוּר אֵין
כּוֹלוֹ לְבַעַל הַבַּיִת לְפִיכָךְ אֵין לָעֲנִיִּים עִמּוֹ חֶשְׁבּוֹן.

Rebbi Ḥizqiah explains the Mishnah as referring to the eve of New
Year's Day of the Sabbatical. If he planted on the eve of New Year's Day
of the Sabbatical, it grew a bulb at the start of the Sabbatical; then he
pressed [the leaves] down during the Sabbatical and tore them out after
the Sabbatical. If you say that pressing down is like tearing out,
everything belongs to the farmer[42]. If you say that pressing down is not
like tearing out, not everything belongs to the farmer[43]; therefore, the
poor have no settlement with the farmer.

42   Since there will be no more growth, the farmer is under no obligation.

43   That means, nothing is for the farmer; the poor take all without computation, even that which grew in the sixth year of the Sabbatical cycle.

עָשָׂה בָאָרֶץ שָׁלֹשׁ שָׁנִים נוֹתֵן לָעֲנִיִּים רוֹבַע. שְׁתֵּי שָׁנִים (fol. 36a) נוֹתֵן לָעֲנִיִּים שְׁלִישׁ שָׁנָה אַחַת נוֹתֵן לָעֲנִיִּים מֶחֱצָה. רִבִּי יוֹסֵה פָּתַר מַתְנִיתָא לִפְנֵי רֹאשׁ הַשָּׁנָה שְׁבִיעִית. רִבִּי חִזְקִיָּה פָּתַר מַתְנִיתָא עֶרֶב רֹאשׁ הַשָּׁנָה שְׁבִיעִית.

"If it was in the ground three years, he gives one quarter to the poor. Two years, he gives one half to the poor.[44]" Rebbi Yose explains the *baraita* before New Year's Day of the Sabbatical, Rebbi Ḥizqiah explains the Mishnah [as dealing with] the eve of New Year's Day of the Sabbatical.

44   Tosephta 4:3, explaining the position of R. Eliezer. He assumes that the growth rate is constant from year to year. Hence, the poor's part in a plant that started growing at the beginning of the Sabbatical and grew n full years after the Sabbatical is $1/_{n+1}$.

(fol. 35c) **מִשְׁנָה ד:** לוּף שֶׁל עֶרֶב שְׁבִיעִית שֶׁנִּכְנַס לַשְּׁבִיעִית. וְכֵן בְּצָלִים הַקַּיְצוֹנִים וְכֵן פּוּאָה שֶׁל עִידִית בֵּית שַׁמַּאי אוֹמְרִים עוֹקְרִין אוֹתָן בְּמַאֲרוּפוֹת שֶׁל עֵץ. וּבֵית הִלֵּל אוֹמְרִים בְּקַרְדּוּמוֹת שֶׁל מַתֶּכֶת. וּמוֹדִין בְּפוּאָה שֶׁל צְלָעוֹת שֶׁעוֹקְרִין אוֹתָן בְּקַרְדּוּמוֹת שֶׁל מַתֶּכֶת.

Arum of the year before the Sabbatical entering the Sabbatical[45], as well as summer onions and madder growing on choice land[46], the House of Shammai say, one takes them out with wooden shovels but the House of Hillel say with iron spades. They agree that one takes out madder growing on slopes with iron spades.

45   Since it stopped growing during the dry season, it is legitimate to harvest it commercially even during the Sabbatical. The House of Shammai require that in the Sabbatical the harvest not be done in a professional way.

46   Maimonides explains "madder of best quality", but this does not fit the usual meaning of עידית. Also, in the next sentence, the problem is not the quality of madder but the difficulty of access to the land.

(fol. 37a) **הלכה ד**: לוּף שֶׁל עֶרֶב שְׁבִיעִית כו'. רִבִּי בּוּן בַּר חִיָּיה בְּעָא קוֹמֵי רִבִּי זְעִירָא אַף בִּשְׁאָר שְׁנֵי שָׁבוּעַ כֵּן. וְהָא תַנֵּי הָיְתָה שְׁנִייָה נִכְנֶסֶת לַשְּׁלִישִׁית אֵינוּ מְרַכְּנוֹ וְאֵינוּ מוֹנֵעַ מִמֶּנּוּ מַיִם בִּשְׁבִיל שֶׁיְּהֵא מַעֲשֵׂר שֵׁנִי.[47] הָיְתָה שְׁלִישִׁית נִכְנֶסֶת לָרְבִיעִית מְרַכְּנוֹ וּמוֹנֵעַ מִמֶּנּוּ מַיִם בִּשְׁבִיל שֶׁיְּהֵא מַעֲשֵׂר עָנִי. הָדָא אָמְרָה שְׁרִכּוּן כְּעִיקּוּר. רִבִּי יוֹסֵי בְּשֵׁם רִבִּי לָא תִּיפְתָּר שֶׁעֲקָרָן עַד שֶׁלֹא צִימְחוּ.

"Arum of the year before the Sabbatical" etc. Rebbi Abun bar Ḥiyya asked before Rebbi Zeïra: Is it not so also in the other years of the cycle[48] since we have stated[49]: "If it was the second year entering the third, he may not bend it or withhold water from it so it should be Second Tithe[50]; if it was the third year entering the fourth, he may bend it and withhold water from it so it should be tithe of the poor"? This implies that bending down is like tearing out![51] Rebbi Yose in the name of Rebbi La: Explain that he tore them out before they started to grow.

47   The last word is only in the Rome ms.

48   The argument seems to refer not to our Mishnah here but to the explanations of Rebbis Yose and Hoshaiah of the difference between R. Eliezer and

R. Joshua in Mishnah 3, cf. Note 41.

49   Tosephta 2:10.

50   If it does not grow any more after New Year's Day, the Second Tithe is all the farmer's and the poor have no claim whatsoever. Years 3 and 6 are

years of the tithe of the poor; in these years the farmer has no part in the second tithe.

51   This contradicts the prior statement that the question is unsettled.

52   He did not only bend the plants down but lifted them a little bit to separate the roots from the ground. In that case, the plants will certainly grow no longer and there is no room for any doubt.

בְּצָלִים הַקַּיְצוֹנִים קַיְטִינָאֵי. מוֹדִין בְּפוּאָה שֶׁל צִילָעוֹת פֵּיטְרָא. וְתַנֵּי עֲלָהּ
מָקוֹם שֶׁנָּהֲגוּ לַחֲרוֹשׁ יַחֲרוֹשׁ לְנַכֵּשׁ יְנַכֵּשׁ.

"Summer onions", summer ones[53]. "They agree that one takes out madder growing on rocky slopes[54]. We have stated on that[55]: "At a place where one is used to plough, he may plough, to harrow, he may harrow[56]."

53   The Aramaic trade name for the kind described in Hebrew in the Mishnah.

54   Greek πέτρα "rock".

55   A similar statement is in Tosephta 5:23: "On does not tear out spontaneous growth of the Sabbatical with his hand but one ploughs as usual, as animals graze as usual."

56   Under a regime of crop rotation, ploughing under the remains of the previous crop is only a preliminary step; it is not yet ploughing for a new crop and not under the prohibition of the Sabbatical. If it is a usual procedure, no bad impression will be created.

(fol. 35c) **משנה ה:** מֵאֵימָתַי מוּתָּר אָדָם לִיקַּח לוּף בְּמוֹצָאֵי שְׁבִיעִית רִבִּי יְהוּדָה
אוֹמֵר מִיַּד. וַחֲכָמִים אוֹמְרִים מִשֶּׁיִּרְבֶּה הֶחָדָשׁ.

Mishnah 5: When may a person buy arum after the end of the Sabbatical? Rebbi Jehudah says, immediately. But the Sages say, after the new [crop] is dominant.

(fol. 37a) **הלכה ח**: מֵאֵימָתַי מוּתָּר אָדָם לִיקַח לוּף כו'. מַה טַעֲמָא דְּרְבִּי יוּדָה גָּזְרוּ עַל הַלּוּף וְלֹא גָזְרוּ עַל הַיֶּרֶק מֵעַתָּה אֲפִילוּ בַּשְּׁבִיעִית יְהֵא מוּתָּר. בְּטָמוּן אֲנָן קַייָמִין שֶׁלֹּא יֵלֵךְ וְיָבִיא מִן הָאָסוּר וְיֹאמַר מִן הַטָּמוּן הֵבֵאתִי.

Halakhah 5: "When may a person buy" etc. What is the reason of Rebbi Jehudah? They made a decree regarding arum but not regarding vegetables[57]. Then it should be permitted even during the Sabbatical! We deal with what was stored, that one should not go and bring from the forbidden crop and say, I brought from storage[58].

57 Mishnah 4 requires that arum be harvested during the Sabbatical with indequate tools. This rabbinic decree does not extend to vegetables. Therefore one may assume that vegetables offered for sale during the Sabbatical or immediately after its end are grown during the Sabbatical but one may assume that arum offered for sale is from the stored produce of the sixth year.

58 This is the reason for the Sages who require that one wait until there is a new crop.

תַּנֵּי אָמַר רְבִּי יוּדָה מַעֲשֶׂה שֶׁהָיִינוּ בְעֵין כּוּשִׁין וְאָכַלְנוּ לוּף עַל פִּי רְבִּי טַרְפוֹן בְּמוֹצָאֵי הַחַג שֶׁל מוֹצָאֵי שְׁבִיעִית. אָמַר לוֹ רְבִּי יוֹסֵה עִמָּךְ הָיִיתִי וְלֹא הָיָה אֶלָּא מוֹצָאֵי הַפֶּסַח.

It was stated[59]: "Rebbi Jehudah said, it happened that we were at Ein Kushin[60] and ate arum at the end of the holiday at the end of the Sabbatical[61] following instructions by Rebbi Tarphon. Rebbi Yose told him, I was with you but it was only the end of Passover."

59 Tosephta 4:4, with slightly different wording.

60 A place which according to the Yerushalmi [Avodah Zarah 5:4 (fol. 44d)] is near Kefar Shalem and according to the Babli (Avodah Zarah 31a) near Birat Sareqa (fortification of the Saracens). None of these places has been convincingly identified.

61 The 23rd of Tishre, soon after

the end of the Sabbatical. An in-   must represent practice.
struction given by a major authority

מ**שנה ו:** אֵילוּ כֵלִים שֶׁאֵין הָאוּמָּן רַשַּׁאי לְמוֹכְרָן בַּשְּׁבִיעִית מַחֲרִישָׁה (fol. 35c)
וְכָל־כֵּלֶיהָ הָעוֹל וְהַמִּזְרָה וְהַדֶּקֶר. אֲבָל מוֹכֵר הוּא מַגַּל יַד וּמַגַּל קָצִיר וַעֲגָלָה
וְכָל־כֵּלֶיהָ. זֶה הַכְּלָל כָּל־שֶׁמְּלַאכְתּוֹ מְיוּחֶדֶת לַעֲבוֹדָתוֹ אָסוּר לְאִיסּוּר וּלְהֶיתֵר
מוּתָּר.

Mishnah 6: These are the implements which the professional may not
sell during the Sabbatical: A plough and all its implements, a yoke, a
winnowing fork and an axe. But he may sell a hand sickle, a grain sickle,
a carriage and all its implements. This is the principle: Everything that is
used only for its work[62] is forbidden; [if it is usable] for both forbidden
and permitted [work] it is permitted.

62   In most Mishnah mss: לעבירה "for sinful activity".

הלכה ו: אֵילוּ כֵלִים כו'. אָמַר רִבִּי יוֹנָה כֵּינִי מַתְנִיתָא אֵילוּ כֵלִים (fol. 37a)
שֶׁאֵין הָאוּמָּן רַשַּׁאי לְמוֹכְרָן בַּשְּׁבִיעִית לֶחָשׁוּד עַל הַשְּׁבִיעִית. סְתָמָן מַהוּ מִן מַה
דְּתַנֵּי לְאִיסּוּר וּלְהֶיתֵר מוּתָּר הָדָא אָמְרָה סְתָמָן מוּתָּר.

Halakhah 6: "These are the implements", etc. Rebbi Jonah said: So is
the Mishnah[63]: "These are the implements which the professional may not
sell during the Sabbatical to a person suspected of violating the Sabbatical." If one does not know[64], what is the rule? Since it was stated "[if
it is usable] for both forbidden and permitted [work] it is permitted", that
means that it is permitted if one does not know.

63   The interpretation of the Mish-   extent of religious observation of the
nah given in his time.   prospective buyer.

64   The seller does not know the

משנה ז: הַמּוֹכֵר מוֹכֵר חָמֵשׁ כַּדֵּי שֶׁמֶן וַחֲמֵשׁ עֶשְׂרֵה כַּדֵּי יַיִן שֶׁכֵּן דַּרְכּוֹ (fol. 35c)
לְהָבִיא מִן הַהֶבְקֵר אִם הֵבִיא יוֹתֵר מִיכֵּן מוּתָּר. וּמוֹכֵר לַגּוֹיִם בָּאָרֶץ וּלְיִשְׂרָאֵל
בְּחוּצָה לָאָרֶץ.

Mishnah 7: The seller[65] may sell five oil amphoras and fifteen wine
amphoras because so much one brings from ownerless property[66]. If he
brought more than that amount, it is permitted. He may sell to Gentiles
in the Land and to Jews outside of the Land.

65   This text is only found in the   this should be the text here also.
Leyden ms. and the Venice print. All   66   Since all produce in the Sab-
other sources have הַיּוֹצֵר "the potter".   batical is ownerless, this is what one
The quote in the Halakhah shows that   usually collects under Sabbatical rules.

הלכה ז: הַיּוֹצֵר מוֹכֵר. וְחָשׁ לוֹמַר שֶׁמָּא הֶחֱלִיף. אָמַר רִבִּי יוֹנָה נִכָּרוֹת (fol. 37a)
הֵן. אֵלּוּ שֶׁל יַיִן וְאֵלּוּ שֶׁל שֶׁמֶן. אָמַר רִבִּי עוּלָּא אַדְרָא דְּאִילֵּין חֲכִימָא וְאַדְרָא
דְּאִילֵּין חֲכִימָא.

Halakhah 7: "The potter may sell". Should we not worry and say,
maybe he will switch? Rebbi Jonah said, one recognizes, these are for
wine and those for oil. Rebbi Ulla said, the material of these is known and
the material of those is known[68].

67   According to R. Jonah, the   material. In the translation, ארדא
amphoras are distinguished by their   "material, earth" is read for אדרא "skin",
shapes, according to R. Ulla by their   following R. E. D. Lapp.

מוֹכֵר לַגּוֹיִם בָּאָרֶץ וַאֲפִילוּ יוֹתֵר מִכֵּן וּלְיִשְׂרָאֵל בְּחוּצָה לָאָרֶץ אֲפִילוּ מִן הַקָּנוּי בָּאָרֶץ.

"He may sell to Gentiles in the Land" even a larger quantity "and to Jews outside of the Land" even for what was bought in the Land.

(fol. 35c) **משנה ח:** בֵּית שַׁמַּאי אוֹמְרִים לֹא יִמְכּוֹר לוֹ פָּרָה חוֹרֶשֶׁת בַּשְּׁבִיעִית וּבֵית הַלֵּל מַתִּירִין מִפְּנֵי שֶׁהוּא יָכוֹל לְשׁוֹחֲטָהּ. וּמוֹכֵר לוֹ פֵּירוֹת אֲפִילוּ בִשְׁעַת הַזֶּרַע וּמַשְׁאִיל לוֹ סְאָתוֹ אַף עַל פִּי שֶׁהוּא יוֹדֵעַ שֶׁיֵּשׁ לוֹ פּוֹעֲלִין וּפוֹרֵט לוֹ מָעוֹת אַף עַל פִּי (fol. 35d) שֶׁהוּא יוֹדֵעַ שֶׁיֵּשׁ לוֹ פּוֹעֲלִין. וְכוּלָּן בְּפֵירוּשׁ אֲסוּרָה.

Mishnah 8: The House of Shammai say, one may not sell to him[68] a ploughing cow during the Sabbatical but the House of Hillel permit it because he might slaughter it. One may sell him produce even during the sowing season and lend him one's measuring device even though one knows that he has workers, and one may exchange coins for him even though one knows that he has workers. In all cases it is forbidden if specified.

68   The person known to flout the laws of the Sabbatical.

(fol. 37a) **הלכה ח:** בֵּית שַׁמַּאי אוֹמְרִים כו'. תַּנֵּי הַמּוֹכֵר שׁוֹר לַחֲבֵירוֹ וְנִמְצָא נוֹגְחָן רַב אָמַר מֶקַח טָעוּת הוּא וּשְׁמוּאֵל אָמַר יָכִיל הוּא מֵימַר לֵיהּ לִשְׁחִיטָה מְכַרְתִּיו לָךְ. מַה אֲנָן קַיָּימִין אִם בְּשֶׁמְּכָרוֹ לְאָרִיס דִּבְרֵי הַכֹּל לַחֲרִישָׁה מָכַר. אִם בְּשֶׁמְּכָרוֹ לְטַבָּח דִּבְרֵי הַכֹּל לִשְׁחִיטָה מָכַר. אֶלָּא כִּי נָן קַיָּימִין בְּשֶׁמְּכָרוֹ לְסִירְסוּר. רַב אָמַר מֶקַח טָעוּת הוּא. שְׁמוּאֵל אָמַר יָכוֹל הוּא מֵימַר לִשְׁחִיטָה מְכַרְתִּיו לָךְ. מַחְלְפָה שִׁיטָתֵיהּ דְּרַב מַחְלְפָה שִׁיטָתֵיהּ דִּשְׁמוּאֵל. דְּאִיתְפַּלְּגוּן

מְכָרָהּ לוֹ בְּיוֹבֵל עַצְמוֹ רַב אָמַר קָנָה וְיוֹצֵא מִיָּדוֹ בַּיוֹבֵל שְׁמוּאֵל אָמַר לֹא קָנָה. מַחְלְפָה שִׁיטָתֵיהּ דְּרַב תַּמָּן הוּא אָמַר קָנָה וְכָא הוּא אָמַר לֹא קָנָה. תַּמָּן יוֹבֵל מְפוּרְסָם הוּא בְּרַם הָכָא מֶקַח טָעוּת הוּא. מַחְלְפָה שִׁיטָתֵיהּ דִּשְׁמוּאֵל תַּמָּן הוּא אָמַר לֹא קָנָה וְכָא אָמַר קָנָה. לְאֵי זֶה דָבָר מְכָרָהּ לוֹ לֹא לִזְרִיעָה. בְּרַם הָכָא יָכוֹל הוּא מֵימַר לֵיהּ לִשְׁחִיטָה מָכַרְתִּיו לָךְ.

Halakhah 8: "The House of Shammai say", etc. It was stated[69]: If somebody sells an ox and it turns out be a goring one, Rav said it is an erroneous transaction[70] but Samuel says, he can tell him: I sold it to you for slaughtering. What are we talking about? If he sold it to a sharecropper, he sold it for ploughing. If he sold it to a butcher, he sold it for slaughter. But we are considering that he sold it to a broker[71]. Rav said it is an erroneous transaction but Samuel says, he can tell him I sold it to you for slaughtering. The reasoning of Rav is inverted, the reasoning of Samuel is inverted. For they disagreed[72]: If he sold it[73] during the Jubilee year itself, Rav said he acquired it and it leaves his hand in the Jubilee year; Samuel says he did not acquire. The reasoning of Rav is inverted: there he said he acquired and here he said he did not acquire. There the Jubilee is public knowledge[74] but here there is an erroneous transaction. The reasoning of Samuel is inverted: there he said he did not acquire and here he said he acquired. For what purpose did he sell it to him if not for sowing[75]? But here he can tell him I sold it to you for slaughtering.

69   The expression usually is reserved for Tannaitic statements; this Amoraic statement is found in Babli *Baba Qama* 46a, *Baba Batra* 92a. The statement is identical but the interpretation is radically different: Samuel is interpreted to hold that probabilities are not admitted in suits about monetary claims while Rav will admit probabilistic arguments in civil suits.

70   The buyer may return what he bought for a full refund.

71   The Babli notes that usually an ox trained for ploughing is much more valuable than one sold for slaughter and we are forced to conclude that we are dealing with the unlikely case that the two prices are about equal and one cannot determine the use of the ox by the price paid. This argument is discussed in the next paragraph.

72   Babli *Arakhin* 29b. The argument is purely theoretical since the institution of the Jubilee, in which all agricultural land reverts to the family who received it under Joshua, was not

(and could not have been) revived during the Second Commonwealth.

73   A field. Since the Jubilee is also a Sabbatical, the buyer could never have any benefit from his buy.

74   Nobody can claim ignorance of the basic rules of the Jubilee; hence, the transaction was entered upon in the full knowledge of its futility. But in the case of the ox, the buyer has no advance knowledge of its dangerous behavior.

75   It is stated in *Lev.* 25:15 that fields are sold for future harvests. Therefore, a transaction that cannot lead to a harvest is illegal.

רַב כְּבֵית שַׁמַּאי. וּשְׁמוּאֵל כְּבֵית הֵלֵל. רַב כְּבֵית שַׁמַּאי. וּשְׁמוּאֵל כְּבֵית הֵלֵל. רַב כְּבֵית שַׁמַּאי וַאֲפִילוּ יִסְבּוֹר כְּבֵית הֵלֵל לֵית אוֹרְחָא מַשְׁהָתָה תַּלְתִּין יוֹמִין וְיַתִּין תְּלָתְתֵי יוֹמַיָּא לֹא מֶקַח טָעוּת הוּא. וּשְׁמוּאֵל כְּבֵית הֵלֵל וַאֲפִילוּ יִסְבּוֹר כְּבֵית שַׁמַּאי לֵית אוֹרְחָא דְּבַר נָשָׁא מֵיכוֹס תּוֹרָא רַדְּיָיא.

Does Rav follow the House of Shammai and Samuel the House of Hillel? Rav follows the House of Shammai and Samuel the House of Hillel. Rav follows the House of Shammai, but even if he would follow the thinking of the House of Hillel, people do not usually keep[76] for thirty days. If he keeps it for thirty days would it not be an erroneous transaction[77]? Samuel follows the House of Hillel, but even if he would follow the thinking of the House of Shammai, people do not usually slaughter ploughing cattle[78].

76 Cattle bought for slaughter.	matter of monetary claim and in suits
77 Even for Samuel.	over money it is incumbent on the
78 In the case of the Mishnah, he	claimant to prove his claim; he cannot
would agree with the House of Sham-	have recourse to an argument about
mai that a cow bought explicitly for	probabilities. For Rav and Samuel the
ploughing is not to be slaughtered. But	case of the goring ox has no parallel in
in the case of the goring ox it is a	the Mishnah here.

רִבִּי אָחָא רִבִּי תַּנְחוּם בַּר חִייָא בְּשֵׁם רִבִּי יוֹחָנָן הִשְׁאִיל לוֹ סְאָתוֹ וּבָא וּמְצָאוֹ
מוֹדֵד בָּהּ אֵינוֹ זָקוּק לוֹ כָּל־שֶׁכֵּן בְּמַשְׂכִּירָהּ לוֹ.

Rebbi Aha, Rebbi Tanhum bar Hiyya in the name of Rebbi Johanan: If
somebody lent his measuring cup and found him using it[79], he does not
have to say anything; much less if he rented it out.

79 The lender found the borrower	Sabbatical crop, in violation of the
using his measuring vessel for a	rules.

(fol. 35d) **משנה ט:** מַשְׁאֶלֶת אִשָּׁה לַחֲבֶירְתָהּ הַחֲשׁוּדָה עַל הַשְּׁבִיעִית נָפָה וּכְבָרָה
וְרֵיחַיִם וְתַנּוּר אֲבָל לֹא תָבוֹר וְלֹא תִטְחוֹן עִמָּהּ. אֵשֶׁת חָבֵר מַשְׁאֶלֶת לְאֵשֶׁת עַם
הָאָרֶץ נָפָה וּכְבָרָה וּבוֹרֶרֶת וְטוֹחֶנֶת וּמְרַקֶּדֶת עִמָּהּ אֲבָל מִשֶּׁתַּטִּיל אֶת הַמַּיִם לֹא
תִגַּע אֶצְלָהּ שֶׁאֵין מְחַזְּקִין יְדֵי עוֹבְרֵי עֲבֵירָה. וְכוּלָּם לֹא אָמְרוּ אֶלָּא מִפְּנֵי דַרְכֵי
שָׁלוֹם. וּמַחֲזִיקִים יְדֵי גּוֹיִם בַּשְּׁבִיעִית אֲבָל לֹא יְדֵי יִשְׂרָאֵל. וְשׁוֹאֲלִין בִּשְׁלוֹמָן
מִפְּנֵי דַרְכֵי הַשָּׁלוֹם.

Mishnah 9: A woman may lend to her neighbor whom she suspects in
matters of the Sabbatical a coarse sieve[80], a fine sieve, grindstones and an
oven[81] but she should neither cull nor grind with her. The wife of a

fellow may lend to the wife of a vulgar[82] a coarse sieve and a fine sieve, she may cull, grind and sift with her, but she may not touch hers once water has been put in[83] because one does not support transgressors[84]. All this has only been said for communal peace. One[85] encourages Gentiles in the Sabbatical year but not Jews. One greets them for communal peace.

80   According to Maimonides, נפה is a sieve for flour and כברה ("braided from twigs") is a sieve for seeds, but the Halakhah shows that נפה is coarse and כברה fine (the Arabic כְּרְבִּיל given by Maimonides for כברה denotes a fine sieve). The root verbs are כבר "to sift" and נוף "to move to and fro". [Cf. also Latin corbis "basket", corbula "little basket" (E. G.).]

81   A movable clay stove. One must assume that the stove is impure since the vulgar will certainly make it impure by using it (R. Simson).

82   The definition of "vulgar" and "fellow" are given in the Introduction to Tractate Demay. The vulgar may be assumed to be impure and to impart impurity to prepared food.

83   Food becomes susceptible to impurity by contact with water, cf. Demay, Chapter 2, Note 141

84   Since one may not cause ḥallah to be impure if one can help it, but the ḥallah of a vulgar is always impure and may not be eaten.

85   This is repeated from Mishnah 4:3 (Note 49). The entire Mishnah and Halakhah is repeated in Giṭṭin, 5:9.

הלכה ט: רְבִּי זְעִירָא בָּעָא קוֹמֵי רְבִּי מָנָא מַתְנִיתָא בִּסְתָם הָא (fol. 37a) בִּמְפוֹרָשׁ לֹא. אָמַר לֵיהּ וּסְתָמוֹ לָאו כְּפֵירוּשׁוֹ הוּא אֲנִי אוֹמֵר נָפָה לִסְפּוֹר בּוֹ מָעוֹת. כְּבָרָה לִכְבּוֹר בּוֹ חוֹל. רֵיחַיִים לִטְחוֹן בּוֹ סַמְמָנִים. תַּנּוּר לִטְמוֹן בּוֹ אוּנִּין שֶׁל פִּשְׁתָּן.

Halakhah 9: Rebbi Zeïra asked before Rebbi Mana: Does our Mishnah deal with the implicit case[86], rather than the explicit? He said to him, is the implicit case not explicit[87]? I can say a coarse sieve to count coins, a sieve to sift sand, grindstones to grind spices, a stove to put in flax bundles.

86   If the borrower does not specify
for which purpose she needs the
implements.

87   For what may sieve, grindstones,
and oven be used if not to prepare
food. Since the borrower must be
assumed to transgress the laws of the
Sabbatical, does one not give his
implements in the knowlcdge that they
will be used for sinful activity?

רִבִּי פִּינְחָס בָּעֵי בְּמַה קָנְסוּ. בְּמָקוֹם שֶׁזּוֹרְעִין וְאוֹכְלִין אוֹ בְּמָקוֹם שֶׁזּוֹרְעִין וְלֹא
אוֹכְלִין. מַה נְפַק מִבֵּינֵיהוֹן. רָאוּ אוֹתוֹ לוֹקֵחַ מִן הַסִּירְקִי אִי תֵּימַר בְּמָקוֹם
שֶׁזּוֹרְעִין וְאוֹכְלִין רָאוּ אוֹתוֹ לוֹקֵחַ מִן הַסִּירְקִי אָסוּר. אֵין תֵּימַר בְּמָקוֹם
שֶׁזּוֹרְעִין וְאֵין אוֹכְלִין רָאוּ אוֹתוֹ לוֹקֵחַ מִן הַסִּירְקִי מוּתָּר.

Rebbi Phineas asked: For what did they impose a fine[88]? At a place
where they sow and eat[89] or at a place where they sow but do not eat?
What is the difference? If one saw him buying from Saracens[90]. If you
say at a place where they sow and eat, if one saw him buying from
Saracens it is forbidden; if you say at a place where they sow but do not
eat, if one saw him buying from Saracens it is permitted.

88   That one may not sift or grind
with the borrower.

89   The farmers transgress in raising cash crops in the Sabbatical but
they themselves would not eat commercial Sabbatical produce. [Most commentators explain that "eating" refers
to the time when wild animals would
no longer find any food on the fields,
when the consumption of stored
Sabbatical yield, in a way stolen from
the wild animals, is forbidden. But
then the mention of sowing would be
meaningless.]

90   Saracen traders do not bring
their merchandise long distance so that
their produce might be imported and
permitted.

רִבִּי יוֹסֵי בַּר חֲנִינָה בָּעֵי עַל כָּל־פִּירְקָא אִיתְאַמְרַת אוֹ עַל הָדָא הִילְכְתָא
אִיתְאַמְרַת. רַבָּנִין דְּקֵיסָרִין בְּשֵׁם רִבִּי יוּדָה בַּר טִיטוֹס מִן מַה דְּלָא תַּנִּינָן בְּגִיטִין
אֶלָּא הָדָא הִילְכְתָא הָדָה אֶמְרָה עַל הָדָא הִילְכְתָא אִיתְאַמְרַת.

Rebbi Yose bar Ḥanina asked: Has this[91] been said for all of this chapter or only for this Mishnah? The rabbis of Caesarea in the name of Rebbi Judah bar Titus: From the fact that we state only this Mishnah in *Giṭṭin*[85] it follows that it was said only for this Mishnah.

91   That collaboration with the   sake of communal peace.
unobservant is permitted only for the

תַּמָּן תַּנִּינָן נַחְתּוֹם שֶׁהוּא עוֹשֶׂה בְּטוּמְאָה לֹא לָשִׁין וְלֹא עוֹרְכִין עִמּוֹ. וְתַנֵּי עֲלָהּ לֹא בוֹרְרִין וְלֹא טוֹחֲנִין וְלֹא מַרְקִידִין עִמּוֹ. וְהָכָא הוּא אָמַר הָכֵן. אָמַר רְבִּי לָא כָּאן לְחוּלִּין כָּאן לִתְרוּמָה. אִית לָךְ מֵימַר נַחְתּוֹם בִּתְרוּמָה. חַבְרַיָּיא אָמְרֵי כָּאן בְּלוֹתֵת כָּאן בְּשֶׁאֵינוֹ לוֹתֵת. מַתְנִיתָא מְסַיְּיעָא לַחֲבֵרַיָּא אֲבָל מִשֶּׁתַּטִּיל אֶת הַמַּיִם לֹא תִגַּע אֶצְלָהּ שֶׁאֵין מְחַזְּקִין יְדֵי עוֹבְרֵי עֲבֵירָה. וְכוּלָּם לֹא אָמְרוּ אֶלָּא מִפְּנֵי דַרְכֵי שָׁלוֹם.

There[92], we have stated: One[93] does not knead or form bread with a baker working in impurity. And it was stated additionally: One should neither cull nor grind nor sift with him. And here, it says so[94]? Rebbi La said, Here for profane [bread], there for heave. Can you say heave at a baker's[95]? The colleagues[96] say, one if he washes[97], there if he does not wash. The Mishnah supports the colleagues: "But she may not touch hers once water has been put in because one does not support transgressors. All this has only been said for communal peace."

92   An extended form of this   with the wife of a vulgar.
baraita is in Babli *Avodah Zarah* 55b.   95   Heave is given to the Cohen
93   A fellow as long as it was   who is responsible to keep it in purity
possible to prepare food in ritual   and may not hand it over to a baker.
purity.   96   R. Ḥanaiah and R. Oshaia the
94   To perform the same actions   colleagues of the rabbis.

97   If the baker washes the grain   the flour is prepared for impurity.
before grinding to eliminate impurities,

וְכוּלָן לֹא אָמְרוּ אֶלָּא מִפְּנֵי דַּרְכֵי שָׁלוֹם. רִבִּי חִייָה וְרִבִּי אִימִּי חַד אָמַר חֲרוֹשׁ
לָהּ טָבָאוּת וַאֲנָא וְסַב לָהּ מִינָךְ בָּתָר שְׁמִיטְּתָא. וְחָרְנָא אָמַר אַיַשֵּׁר. מָן דְּאָמַר
טָבָאוּת מַה שׁוֹאֲלִין בִּשְׁלוֹמָן אַיַשֵּׁר. מָאן דְּאָמַר אַיַשֵּׁר מַהוּ שׁוֹאֲלִין בִּשְׁלוֹמָן
יִשְׂרָאֵל שָׁלוֹם עֲלֵכֶם.

"All this has only been said for communal peace.[98]"   Rebbi Ḥiyya,
Rebbi Ammi. One said: "Plough it well then I will rent it from you after
the Sabbatical." The other one said: "May you succed" For him who says
plough it well, what means "one greets them"? "May you succed." For
him who says may you succed, what means "one greets them"? Jewish
greeting, "Peace upon you."

98   From here to the end of the   some spelling variations) with that in
chapter the text is identical (except for   Chapter 4, Halakhah 3.

דְּלְמָא רִבִּי חִינְנָא בַּר פַּפָּא וְרִבִּי שְׁמוּאֵל בַּר נַחְמָנִי עָבְרוּן עַל חַד מֵחוֹרְשֵׁי
שְׁבִיעִית. אָמַר לֵיהּ שְׁמוּאֵל בַּר נַחְמָן אַיַשֵּׁר. אָמַר לֵיהּ רִבִּי חִינְנָא בַּר פַּפָּא לֹא
כֵן אוּלְפָן רִבִּי וְלֹא אָמְרוּ הָעוֹבְרִים בִּרְכַּת יי עֲלֵיכֶם. שֶׁאָסוּר לוֹמַר לְחוֹרְשֵׁי
שְׁבִיעִית אַיַשֵּׁר. אָמַר לֵיהּ לִקְרוֹת אַתָּה יוֹדֵעַ. לִדְרוֹשׁ אֵין אַתָּה יוֹדֵעַ. וְלֹא
אָמְרוּ הָעוֹבְרִים אֵלּוּ אוּמּוֹת הָעוֹלָם שֶׁעוֹבְרִין מִן הָעוֹלָם. וְלֹא אָמְרוּ לְיִשְׂרָאֵל
בִּרְכַּת יי עֲלֵיכֶם. מַה יִשְׂרָאֵל אוֹמְרִין לָהֶם בֵּרַכְנוּ אֶתְכֶם בְּשֵׁם יי. לֹא דַיֵּיכֶם
שֶׁכָּל-הַבְּרָכוֹת הַבָּאוֹת לָעוֹלָם בִּזְכוּתֵינוּ וְאֵין אַתֶּם אוֹמְרִים בּוֹאוּ וּטְלוּ לָכֶם מִן
הַבְּרָכוֹת הָאֵילוּ. וְלֹא עוֹד אֶלָּא שֶׁאַתֶּם מְנַלְגְּלִין עָלֵינוּ פִּיסִים וְזִימִיּוֹת
גּוּלְגּוֹלִיּוֹת וְאַרְנוֹנִיּוֹת.

Explanation: Rebbi Ḥinena bar Pappa and Rebbi Samuel bar Naḥman
passed by one of the ploughmen in the Sabbatical. Rebbi Samuel bar

Naḥman said to him, may you succed. Rebbi Ḥinena bar Pappa said to him, did not Rebbi teach us (*Ps.* 129:8): "The passers-by did not say, the blessing of the Eternal be on you," that it is forbidden to say "may you succeed" to one who ploughs in the Sabbatical. He told him, you know to read but you do not know to make a homily. "The passers-by did not say," these are the nations of the world who pass out of the world, they did not say to Israel "the blessing of the Eternal is on you." What does Israel say to them, "we bless you in the Name of the Eternal." All blessings that come into the world because of us are not enough for you, you do not say, come and take from these blessings for yourselves, but you roll over us pro-rated contributions and fines, head taxes and *annonae*.

שלש ארצות פרק ששי

משנה א: שָׁלשׁ אֲרָצוֹת לַשְּׁבִיעִית כָּל־שֶׁהֶחֱזִיקוּ עוֹלֵי בָבֶל מִן גְּזִיב וְעַד (fol. 36b) אֶרֶץ יִשְׂרָאֵל לֹא נֶאֱכָל וְלֹא נֶעֱבָד. כָּל־שֶׁהֶחֱזִיקוּ עוֹלֵי מִצְרַיִם מִגְּזִיב וְעַד הַנָּהָר וְעַד אֲמָנוֹס נֶאֱכָל אֲבָל לֹא נֶעֱבָד. מִן הַנָּהָר וּמֵאֲמָנָה וְלִפְנִים נֶאֱכָל נֶעֱבָד.

Mishnah 1: There are three territories regarding the Sabbatical. Every place held by the immigrants from Babylonia from Akhzib[1] inside the Land of Israel cannot be eaten from[2] or worked. Every place held by the immigrants from Egypt between Akhzib and Euphrates and Amanus[3] can be eaten from but not worked. From Euphrates or Amanus to their side they can be eaten from and worked.

1   A *tell* between Nahariah and the Tyrian Ladder.

2   There are three essentially different interpretations of this expression. It is stated in the Torah (*Lev.'* 25:6): "The Sabbatical yield shall be food for you." Therefore, it is a positive obligation to eat Sabbatical fruits; they may not be used for industrial purposes or intentionally wasted (Mishnah 8:2). In the opinion of R. Isaac ibn Ghiat produce grown by a Jew in violation of the Sabbatical is forbidden for all Jews. In the opinion of R. Simson, the Mishnah refers to the time when no produce is left on the fields for the wild animals; then no Sabbatical produce harvested earlier may be kept or eaten. This is a biblical commandment based on *Lev.* 25:7 and explained in Mishnah 9:2.

In the opinion of Maimonides in his Code (*Šemiṭṭah weYovel* 4:26), in the later versions of his Mishnah Commentary (see the edition of R. Y. Qafeḥ), and explained at length in a responsum (ed. Blau #128, *Peër Hador* #15) the Mishnah refers to the rabbinic prohibition to buy in the Holy Land during the Sabbatical any produce that has to be sown and tended since we are concerned that a ready market for this produce will tempt people to work their fields. Only wild growing vegetables and fruits of trees may be bought. Clearly, any produce collected by one's family from abandoned fields may be eaten (and stored as long as there are fruits left for the wild animals on the field.) The commentary follows the interpretation of Maimonides.

3   The Southernmost chain of the Taurus mountains between Turkey and Syria. Jewish tradition (the Yerushalmi Targumim, Babli *Gittin* 8a) identifies Mount Hor (*Num.* 34:7) with Taurus Amanus. The Euphrates as border of the Holy Land is mentioned in *Deut.* 1:7. Amanus and Euphrates are the borders of promise, not the actual borders. The rules given in this sentence apply only to the territory North of Akhzib described in the book of Joshua as part of the tribal distribution. The rest of the territory is "Syria" (cf. *Peah*, Chapter 7, Note 119).

חלכה א: כְּתִיב אֵלֶּה הַחֻקִּים וְהַמִּשְׁפָּטִים אֲשֶׁר תִּשְׁמְרוּן לַעֲשׂוֹת בָּאָרֶץ. בָּאָרֶץ אַתָּה חַיָּבִין לַעֲשׂוֹת. וְאֵי אַתֶּם חַיָּבִים לַעֲשׂוֹת בְּחוּצָה לָאָרֶץ. אַדַּיִין אָנוּ אוֹמְרִים מִצְוֹת שֶׁהֵן תְּלוּיוֹת בָּאָרֶץ אֵינָן נוֹהֲגוֹת אֶלָּא בָּאָרֶץ. יָכוֹל אֲפִילוּ מִצְוֹת שֶׁאֵינָן תְּלוּיוֹת בָּאָרֶץ לֹא יְהוּ נוֹהֲגוֹת אֶלָּא בָּאָרֶץ. תַּלְמוּד לוֹמַר הִשָּׁמְרוּ לָכֶם פֶּן יִפְתֶּה לְבַבְכֶם וְחָרָה אַף יי בָּכֶם וגו'. וְשַׂמְתֶּם אֶת דְּבָרַי אֵלֶּה עַל לְבַבְכֶם וגו'. אֲפִילוּ גוֹלִים. וְשַׂמְתֶּם אֶת דְּבָרַי אֵלֶּה עַל לְבַבְכֶם וְעַל נַפְשְׁכֶם. מַה אִית לָךְ כְּגוֹן תְּפִילִין וְתַלְמוּד תּוֹרָה. מַה תְּפִילִין וְתַלְמוּד תּוֹרָה שֶׁאֵינָן תְּלוּיִין בָּאָרֶץ נוֹהֲגִין בֵּין בָּאָרֶץ בֵּין בְּחוּצָה לָאָרֶץ. אַף כָּל־דָּבָר שֶׁאֵינוֹ תָלוּי בָּאָרֶץ יְהֵא נוֹהֵג בָּאָרֶץ וּבְחוּצָה לָאָרֶץ.

Halakhah 1: It is written (*Deut.* 12:1): "These are the statutes and the rules of law which you will be required to follow in the Land." In the Land you are required to follow them but not outside the Land. Still we say obligations depending on the Land apply only in the Land, but we might think that obligations not depending on the Land also should apply only in the Land. The verse says (*Deut*. 11:16-18) "Guard yourselves, lest your heart be seduced . . . And the Eternal's rage be inflamed against you, etc. Put these words on your hearts, etc." Even if you are exiled. (*Deut*. 11:18) "Put these words on your hearts and your persons." You have to say, for example *tefillin* and the study of Torah. Just as *tefillin* and the study of Torah do not depend on the Land and apply both in the Land and outside the Land, so everything not depending on the Land applies both in the Land and outside the Land[4].

4   The argument goes as follows: *Deut*. 11:16 is a general exhortation against idolatry, a sin not connected with agriculture in the Land. V. 17 then declares that the punishment for idolatry will be exile from the Land. Verses 18,19, which now must be talking about the obligations of a Jew in exile, contain the obligations of *tefillin* and the study of Torah. Therefore, it is impossible that no obligations at all should be imposed on Jews in exile. It is reasonable to assume that the restriction of

obligations to the Land extends only to obligations connected with agriculture in the Land.

A different argument is in *Sifri Deut*. 59 and Babli *Qiddušin* 37a: Verse *Deut*. 12:1 ends: "all the days you are living on the soil." "Soil" is everywhere on earth; it is not restricted to the Land. The details of the argument there for distinguishing between obligations of the Land and others is best understood as depending on the argument here.

מֵעַתָּה מִשֶּׁנָּלוּ יְהוּ פְּטוּרִין. כְּתִיב וַיַּעֲשׂוּ כָל־הַקָּהָל הַבָּאִים מֵהַשְּׁבִי הַסּוּכּוֹת וַיֵּשְׁבוּ בַסּוּכּוֹת. כִּי לֹא עָשׂוּ מִימֵי יְהוֹשֻׁעַ בֶּן נוּן. וְלָמָּה יְהוֹשֻׁעַ רַבִּי הִלֵּל בְּרֵיהּ דִּשְׁמוּאֵל בַּר נַחְמָן פָּגַם הַכָּתוּב כְּבוֹד צַדִּיק בַּקֶּבֶר מִפְּנֵי כְּבוֹד צַדִּיק בְּשַׁעְתּוֹ הֶקִישׁ בִּיאָתָן בִּימֵי עֶזְרָא לְבִיאָתָן בִּימֵי יְהוֹשֻׁעַ. מַה בִּיאָתָן בִּימֵי יְהוֹשֻׁעַ פְּטוּרִין הָיוּ וְנִתְחַיְּיבוּ. אַף בִּיאָתָן בִּימֵי עֶזְרָא פְּטוּרִין הָיוּ וְנִתְחַיְּיבוּ. מִמָּה נִתְחַיְּיבוּ.

רִבִּי יוֹסֵי בַּר חֲנִינָה אָמַר מִדְּבַר תּוֹרָה נִתְחַיְּיבוּ הָדָא הוּא דִּכְתִיב וְהֱבִיאֲךָ ¹¹
אֱלֹהֶיךָ אֶל הָאָרֶץ אֲשֶׁר יָרְשׁוּ אֲבוֹתֶיךָ וִירִשְׁתָּהּ. הֶקִּישׁ יְרוּשָׁתְךָ לִירוּשַׁת
אֲבוֹתֶיךָ. מַה יְרוּשַׁת אֲבוֹתֶיךָ מִדְּבַר תּוֹרָה. אַף יְרוּשָׁתְךָ מִדְּבַר תּוֹרָה. וְהֱטִיבְךָ
וְהִרְבְּךָ מֵאֲבוֹתֶיךָ. אֲבוֹתֶיךָ פְּטוּרִין הָיוּ וְנִתְחַיְּיבוּ וְאַתֶּם פְּטוּרִין הָיִיתֶם
וְנִתְחַיַּיבְתֶּם. אֲבוֹתֶיךָ לֹא הָיָה עֲלֵיהֶם עוֹל מַלְכוּת. וְאַתֶּם אַף עַל פִּי שֶׁיֵּשׁ
עֲלֵיכֶם עוֹל מַלְכוּת. אֲבוֹתֵיכֶם לֹא נִתְחַיְּיבוּ אֶלָּא לְאַחַר אַרְבַּע עֶשְׂרֵה שָׁנָה שֶׁבַע
שֶׁכִּיבְּשׁוּ וְשֶׁבַע שֶׁחִלְּקוּ. אֲבָל אַתֶּם כֵּיוָן שֶׁנִּיכְנַסְתֶּם נִתְחַיַּיבְתֶּם. אֲבוֹתֶיךָ לֹא
נִתְחַיְּיבוּ עַד שָׁעָה שֶׁקָּנוּ כּוּלָּהּ. אֲבָל אַתֶּם רִאשׁוֹן רִאשׁוֹן קוֹנֶה וּמִתְחַיֵּיב.

If it is so, they should have been freed once they were exiled[5]. It is written (*Neh.* 8:17): "All the congregation coming from captivity made *Sukkot* and sat in tabernacles . . . something nobody had done since the days of Joshua bin Nun.[6]" Why Joshua? Rebbi Hillel, the son of Samuel ben Naḥmani[7]: The verse damaged the reputation of the just person in his grave for the reputation of the just person in his time; it compares their coming in the days of Ezra to the coming in the days of Joshua. As at the coming in the days of Joshua they had been free and became obligated, also at the coming in the days of Ezra they had been free and became obligated. How did they become obligated? Rebbi Yose ben Ḥanina said, they became obligated by the words of the Torah; that is what is written (*Deut.* 30:5): "The Eternal, your God, will bring you to the Land that your fathers had inherited and you will inherit it." Just as the inheritance of your fathers was by the words of the Torah, so your inheritance is by the words of the Torah. "He will be good to you and give increase to you more than to your forefathers[8]." Your fathers had been free and became obligated, also you had been free and became obligated. On your fathers was no yoke of government[9], but you even though there is on you the yoke of government. Your fathers did become obligated only after 14 years, seven they conquered and seven they distributed[10], but you became obligated immediately when you entered. Your fathers did become obligated only after they had acquired all, you become obligated for every single piece at the moment you acquire it.

5   This sentence, taken out of context, is the basis of the first part of Spinoza's Politico-Theological Treatise.

6   The wording has not been corrected following the masoretic text.

7   Son of R. Samuel ben Naḥmani; no halakhic statements of his are recorded.

8   In this homily, "increase" is interpreted as increase in obligations, not increase in benefits.

9   מלכות in both Talmudim means "Gentile government."

10   The universally accepted computation that from the crossing of the Jordan to the assembly at Shilo there passed 14 years is given in *Seder Olam*, Chap. 11 (in the author's edition, Northvale NJ 1998, pp. 116-119.)

אָמַר רִבִּי לָעְזָר מֵאֵילֵיהֶן קִיבְּלוּ עֲלֵיהֶן אֶת הַמַּעְשְׂרוֹת. מַה טַעַם וּבְכָל־זֹאת אֲנַחְנוּ כּוֹרְתִים אֲמָנָה וְכוֹתְבִים וְעַל הֶחָתוּם שָׂרֵינוּ לְוִיֵּנוּ וְכֹהֲנֵינוּ. מַה מְקַיֵּים רִבִּי לָעְזָר בְּכוֹרוֹת בְּקָרֵינוּ וְצֹאנֵינוּ. מִכֵּיוָן שֶׁקִּיבְּלוּ עֲלֵיהֶן דְּבָרִים שֶׁלֹּא הָיוּ חַייָבִין עֲלֵיהֶן. אֲפִילוּ דְּבָרִים שֶׁהָיוּ חַייָבִין עֲלֵיהֶן הֶעֱלָה עֲלֵיהֶן כְּאִילוּ מֵאֵילֵיהֶן קִיבְּלוּ עֲלֵיהֶן.

Rebbi Eleazar said, they accepted the tithes voluntarily. What is the reason? (*Neh.* 10:1) "In view of all this, we execute a contract and write, signed by our princes, Levites, and priests.[11]" How does Rebbi Eleazar uphold (10:37): "The first-born of our cattle and flock[12]"? Since they accepted upon themselves matters they were not obligated for, even matters they were obligated for are credited to them as if they were accepted voluntarily[13].

11   Neh. 10 contains the contract
between the people and God in which
they accept the Biblical obligations
connected with Land and Temple. If
the obligations were Biblical, no contract would have been needed.

12   Even though *Ex.* 13:11 explicitly
connects the sanctity of the first–born
to the conquest of the Land, it is
generally accepted that the obligation
does not depend on the Land.

13   The Babli (*Qiddušin* 31a, *Baba*

Qama 38a, 87a, *Avodah Zarah* 3a) holds
that the person who is obligated receives greater reward than the person
who is not obligated. This opinion,
quoted in the name of R. Ḥanina and
undisputed in the Babli, clearly is not
accepted in the Yerushalmi and is
never quoted there. One must assume
that the statement was the opinion of
R. Ḥanina when he was still in
Babylonia.

מַה מְקַיֵּים רְבִּי יוֹסֵי בַּר חֲנִינָא וּבְכָל־זֹאת. מִכֵּיוָן שֶׁקִּיבְּלוּ עֲלֵיהֶן בְּסֵבֶר פָּנִים
יָפוֹת הֶעֱלָה עֲלֵיהֶן הַכָּתוּב כְּאִילוּ מֵאֵילֵיהֶן קִיבְּלוּ עֲלֵיהֶן. מַה מְקַיֵּים רְבִּי לְעָזָר
מֵאֲבוֹתֶיךָ. פָּתַר לָהּ לְעָתִיד לָבוֹא. דְּאָמַר רְבִּי חֶלְבּוֹ שִׁמְעוֹן בַּר בָּא בְשֵׁם רְבִּי
יוֹחָנָן אֲבוֹתֶיךָ יָרְשׁוּ אֶרֶץ שֶׁל שִׁבְעַת עַמְמִים. וְאַתֶּם עֲתִידִין לִירַשׁ אֶרֶץ שֶׁל עֶשֶׂר
עַמְמִים. תִּלָתֵי חוֹרָנַיָּיתָא אִילֵין אִינּוּן אֶת הַקֵּינִי וְאֶת הַקְּנִיזִּי וְאֶת הַקַּדְמוֹנִי.
רְבִּי יוּדָה אָמַר עֲרָבִיָּא שַׁלְמַיָּא נַבְטַיָּא. רְבִּי שִׁמְעוֹן אוֹמֵר אַסְיָא וְאִסְפַּמְיָא
וְדַמְשָׂק. רְבִּי לִיעֶזֶר בֶּן יַעֲקֹב אוֹמֵר אַסְיָא וְקָרְתִּגְנִי וְתוֹרְקִי. רְבִּי אוֹמֵר אֱדוֹם
וּמוֹאָב וְרֵאשִׁית בְּנֵי עַמּוֹן. מֵאֲבוֹתֶיךָ. אֲבוֹתֶיךָ אַף עַל פִּי שֶׁנִּגְאֲלוּ חָזְרוּ
וְנִשְׁתַּעְבָּדוּ. אֲבָל אַתֶּם מִשֶּׁאַתֶּם נִגְאָלִין עוֹד אֵין אַתֶּם מִשְׁתַּעְבָּדִין. מַה טַעַם
שַׁאֲלוּ נָא וּרְאוּ אִם יֹלֵד זָכָר. כְּשֵׁם שֶׁאֵין הַזָּכָר יוֹלֵד כָּךְ אַתֶּם מִשֶּׁאַתֶּם נִגְאָלִין
עוֹד אֵין אַתֶּם מִשְׁתַּעְבָּדִין.

How does Rebbi Yose bar Ḥanina explain "In view of all this"? Since
they accepted [the obligations] with good grace, the verse credits it to
them as if they had accepted it voluntarily[13]. How does Rebbi Eleazar
explain "more than your forefathers?" He explains it for the future since
Rebbi Ḥelbo, Simeon bar Abba said in the name of Rebbi Johanan: Your

forefathers inherited the land of seven peoples[14], but you will in the future inherit the land of ten peoples. The three others are *(Gen.* 15:19) "the Qenites, the Qenizites and the Qadmonites.[15]" Rebbi Jehudah said, [these are] Arabia, Salmaia[16] and Nabataea. Rebbi Simeon says, Asia, Spain, and Damascus[17]. Rebbi Eliezer ben Jacob says, Asia, Cartagena, and Thrace[18]. Rebbi says, Edom, Moab, and the best of Ammon[19]. "More than your forefathers": Your forefathers, even though they were redeemed, were later subjugated again. But you when you are redeemed will not be subjugated again. What is the reason? *(Jer.* 30:6) "Inquire and see whether a male gives birth." Just as a male cannot give birth so you, after you are redeemed, will not be subjugated again[20].

14   *Deut.* 7:1: The Hittites, Girgashites, Emorites, Canaanites, Perizites, Ḥiwwites, Yebusites.

15   These three, promised to Abraham, are never mentioned by Moses. The list, with minor deviations, also appears in *Gen. rabba* 44(27) and Babli *Baba Batra* 56a.

16   A people living in the desert between Syria and Mesopotamia [Pliny *Hist. Nat.* vi, 26, 30.] These identifications are given in the Midrash in the name of Rebbi, in the Babli in the name of R. Meïr.

17   The same list in *Gen. rabba*; in the Babli the list contains Asia, Spain, and an unidentified region variously written ערדיסקיס, ערדסקס, ערסקיס, אדרסקא, עידסקיס.

18   In *Gen. rabba.* תרקי The last identification is a conjecture by A. Neubauer. The word cannot mean Turkey since in Talmudic times the Turk peoples were still living in the Altai mountains. This list is not in the Babli.

19   This is attributed to the rabbis in *Gen. rabba*, to R. Jehudah in the Babli.

20   The image of the male as symbol of the sterility of the days of the Messiah is found in Yerushalmi Midrashim [*Mekhilta deR. Ismael, Bešallaḥ* 1 (ed. Horovitz-Rabin p. 118), *Cant. rabba* 1(37)]. It is discussed at length in the author's *The Scholar's Haggadah* (Northvale NJ, 1995), pp. 314-316.

הַמְהַלֵּךְ מֵעַכּוֹ לְאַכְזִיב מִימִינוֹ לְמִזְרַח הַדֶּרֶךְ טְהוֹרָה מִשּׁוּם אֶרֶץ הָעַמִּים וְחַיֶּיבֶת בְּמַעְשְׂרוֹת וּבַשְּׁבִיעִית עַד שֶׁתִּיוָּדַע לָךְ שֶׁהִיא פְּטוּרָה. מִשְּׂמֹאלוֹ לְמַעֲרָב הַדֶּרֶךְ טְמֵיאָה מִשּׁוּם אֶרֶץ הָעַמִּים וּפְטוּרָה מִן הַמַּעְשְׂרוֹת וּמִן הַשְּׁבִיעִית עַד שֶׁתִּיוָּדַע לָךְ שֶׁהִיא חַיֶּיבֶת עַד שֶׁהוּא מַגִּיעַ לְאַכְזִיב. רַבִּי יִשְׁמָעֵאל בֵּי רַבִּי יוֹסֵי אָמַר מִשּׁוּם אָבִיו עַד לַבְלָב. עַכּוֹ עַצְמָהּ מַה הִיא. רַבִּי אָחָא בַּר יַעֲקֹב בְּשֵׁם רַבִּי אִימִּי. מִן תְּרֵין עוֹבְדוֹי דְרַבִּי אֲנָן יָלְפִין עַכּוֹ יֵשׁ בָּהּ אֶרֶץ יִשְׂרָאֵל וְיֵשׁ בָּהּ חוּצָה לָאָרֶץ. רַבִּי הֲוָה בְעַכּוֹ חֲמָתוּן אָכְלוּן פִּיתָּה נְקָייָא (fol. 36c) אָמַר לוֹן מַה אַתּוּן לָתִין. אָמְרוּ לֵיהּ תַּלְמִיד אֶחָד בָּא לְכָאן וְהוֹרָה לָנוּ עַל מֵי בֵּיצִים שֶׁהֵן כְּשֵׁרִין. סָבְרִין מֵימַר וַאֲנָן שָׁלְקִין בֵּיעִין וְלָתוּן בְּמֵיהֶן סָבְרִין מֵימַר מֵי שָׁלָק שֶׁל בֵּיצִים וְלֹא אָמַר אֶלָּא מֵי בֵּיצִים עַצְמָן. אָמַר רִבִּי יַעֲקֹב בַּר אִידִי מֵאוֹתָהּ שָׁעָה גָּזְרוּ שֶׁלֹּא יְהֵא תַלְמִיד מוֹרֶה הוֹרָייָא. רִבִּי חִייָה בְשֵׁם רִבִּי הוּנָא תַּלְמִיד שֶׁהוֹרָה אֲפִילוּ כַהֲלָכָה אֵין הוֹרָאָתוֹ הוֹרָייָה.

If[21] one walks from Acco to Akhzib, to one's right hand side and the East the road is pure regarding the land of Gentiles and is subject to tithes and the Sabbatical unless it was known to you to be exempt. To one's left and the West, the road is impure regarding the land of Gentiles and is free from tithes and the Sabbatical unless it was known to you to be obligated, until one arrives at Akhzib; Rebbi Ismael ben Rebbi Yose said in his father's name, as far as Lablab[22]. What is the status of Acco itself? Rebbi Aḥa bar Jacob in the name of Rebbi Immi: From two actions of Rebbi we learn that Acco is partly of the Land of Israel and partly outside the Land. Rebbi was in Acco when he saw them eating clean bread[23]; he asked them, how did you wash [the grains]? They said to him, a student came here and instructed us that egg water is in order. They thought, we will cook eggs and wash with the cooking water [because] they thought he was talking about cooking water of eggs when he spoke only of egg fluid[24]. Rebbi Jacob bar Idi said, at that moment they decreed that a student may not render decisions.   Rebbi Ḥiyya in the name of Rebbi Ḥuna: If a student gives instructions even according to practice, his instructions are no instructions.

21   Tosephta *Ahilut* 18:14, also quoted in Babli *Giṭṭin* 7b.

22   In the Tosephta לכלאבי (Ms. Vienna). The place is unidentified and the ל might be a preposition "to".

23   People he knew as "fellows" who ate their food in ritual purity. The bread was of the finest white flour, which proved that it was milled from washed grain and, therefore, was liable to impurity (cf. *Demay* Chapter 2, Note 141) and probably became impure in

handling.

24   The fluid contents of a raw egg do not prepare for impurity since only water (including water used for cooking), wine, olive oil and human body fluids can do so. The instruction given by the student was correct but was delivered in a misleading way. The entire story makes sense only if Acco is considered to be of the Land since any other land is impure in itself.

תַּנֵּי תַּלְמִיד שֶׁהוֹרָה הֲלָכָה לִפְנֵי רַבּוֹ חַיָּיב מִיתָה. תַּנֵּי בְשֵׁם רִבִּי לִיעֶזֶר לֹא מֵתוּ נָדָב וַאֲבִיהוּא אֶלָּא שֶׁהוֹרוּ בִּפְנֵי מֹשֶׁה רַבָּן. מַעֲשֶׂה בְּתַלְמִיד אֶחָד שֶׁהוֹרָה הֲלָכָה לִפְנֵי רִבִּי לִיעֶזֶר רַבּוֹ. אָמַר לְאִימָּא שָׁלוֹם אִשְׁתּוֹ אֵינוֹ יוֹצֵא שַׁבָּתוֹ. וְלֹא יָצָא שַׁבָּתוֹ עַד שֶׁמֵּת. אָמְרוּ לוֹ תַּלְמִידָיו רִבִּי נָבִיא אַתָּה. אָמַר לָהֶן לֹא נָבִיא אָנֹכִי וְלֹא בֶן נָבִיא אָנֹכִי אֶלָּא כָךְ אֲנִי מְקוּבָּל שֶׁכָּל־תַּלְמִיד הַמּוֹרֶה הֲלָכָה לִפְנֵי רַבּוֹ חַיָּיב מִיתָה. תַּנֵּי אָסוּר לְתַלְמִיד לְהוֹרוֹת הֲלָכָה בִּפְנֵי רַבּוֹ עַד שֶׁיְּהֵא רָחוֹק מִמֶּנּוּ שְׁנֵים עָשָׂר מִיל כְּמַחֲנֵה יִשְׂרָאֵל. וּמַה טַעַם וַיַּחֲנוּ עַל הַיַּרְדֵּן מִבֵּית הַיְשִׁימוֹת עַד אָבֵל הַשִּׁטִּים וְכַמָּה הֵן שְׁנֵים עָשָׂר מִיל. כְּהָדָא רִבִּי תַנְחוּם בַּר חִיָּיה הֲוָה בְחֶפָר וַהֲווֹן שָׁאֲלִין לֵיהּ וְהוּא מוֹרֶה שָׁאֲלִין לֵיהּ וְהוּא מוֹרֶה. אָמְרִין לֵיהּ וְלֹא כֵן אוּלְפָן רִבִּי שֶׁאָסוּר לְתַלְמִיד לְהוֹרוֹת הֲלָכָה לִפְנֵי רַבּוֹ עַד שֶׁיְּהֵא רָחוֹק מִמֶּנּוּ שְׁנֵים עָשָׂר מִיל כְּמַחֲנֵה יִשְׂרָאֵל. וְהָא רִבִּי מָנָא רַבָּךְ יְתִיב בְּצִיפּוֹרִין. אָמַר לוֹן יֵיתִי דְלָא יָדְעִית. מִן הַהוּא שַׁעֲתָּא לָא אוֹרֵי.

It was stated: A student who gave instructions about practice in front of his teacher has committed a deadly sin[25]. It was stated in the name of Rebbi Eliezer: Nadab and Abihu died only because they determined practice in the presence of their teacher Moses[26]. It happened that a student gave instructions about practice in front of his teacher Rebbi Eliezer. The latter said to his wife Imma Shalom[27]: That one will not live out his week. The week was not completed when he died. His students said to him: Rebbi, you are a prophet. He said to them (*Amos* 7:14) "I am neither a prophet nor the disciple of a prophet" but I have received a tradition that any student who gives instructions about practice in front of his teacher has committed a deadly sin. It was stated: A student is forbidden to give instructions about practice during the lifetime of his teacher unless he be at a distance of at least 12 *mil* from him, [the breadth of] the camp of Israel. What is the reason? (*Num.* 33:49) "They encamped along the Jordan from Bet Hayyešimot to Abel Haššiṭṭim"; how far is this? Twelve *mil*[28]. Like this: Rebbi Tanḥum ben Ḥiyya was in Ḥefer[29]; they asked him repeatedly and he gave instructions about practice. They said to him, did the rabbi not teach us that a student may not give instructions about practice during the lifetime of his teacher unless he be at a distance of at least 12 *mil* from him, [the breadth of] the camp of Israel; and your teacher Rebbi Mana sits at Sepphoris! He said to them, so it should come over me that I did not know! From that moment on he did no longer give instructions.

25   Babli *Berakhot* 31b, *Eruvin* 63a, Yerushalmi *Giṭṭin* 1:2. This insert takes up the theme of unauthorized ruling from the previous story. However, in the previous case it was assumed that the student was not ordained; he is

prohibited from giving instructions by a late rabbinic ordinance. In the present paragraph the student is ordained; nevertheless, he may not issue instructions at his teacher's place by a Biblical injunction. (The story of Rebbi at Acco is continued in the next paragraph.)

26   They died because they presented "a strange fire that was not commanded to them." Since they must have had some rationale for their actions, it follows that they acted on their own judgment, not consulting their teacher Moses. Since Moses was not with them at that moment, it also follows that "in front of his teacher" means "while his teacher is alive", in that case, in the encampment of the Israelites in the desert. Their argument is hinted at in Babli *Yoma* 53a.

27   The sister of Rabban Gamliel. The parallel is in Babli *Eruvin* 63a; there R. Eliezer speaks of a year, not a week.

28   In the Babli (*Eruvin* 55b, *Yoma* 75b) this is a determination of Rabba bar bar Ḥana. The text here shows that in the Babli the reading "3 parasangs" (12 *mil*) of the mss. is to be preferred over "3 parasangs square" of the Venice edition, against the opinion of R. Rabbinovicz (*Diqduqe Soferim Eruvin* p. 224, Note ב.)   A *mil* is 2000 cubits, cf. *Kilaim* Chapter 5, Note 25.

29   The Biblical Gat Ḥefer, possibly the village El-Mešad near Kafr Kanna, not far from Sepphoris.

רִבִּי הֲוָה בְּעַכּוֹ, חָמָא חַד בַּר נַשׁ סָלַק מִן כֵּיפְתָא וּלְעֵיל. אֲמַר לֵיהּ לֵית אַתְּ בְּרֵיהּ דְּפַלָן כַּהֲנָא לֹא הֲוָה אָבוּךְ כֹּהֵן. אֲמַר לֵיהּ עֵינָיו שֶׁל אַבָּא הָיוּ גְבוֹהוֹת וְנָשָׂא אִשָּׁה שֶׁאֵינָהּ הוֹגֶנֶת לוֹ וְחִילֵּל אֶת אוֹתוֹ הָאִישׁ.

Rebbi was in Acco when he saw a man going up over the rock. He said to him, "are you not the son of the Cohen X, was your father not a Cohen[30]?" He said to him, "the eyes of my father were high, but he married a woman unfit for him and profaned this man."

30   Since a Cohen may not defile himself willingly, in Rebbi's time a Cohen was forbidden to leave the Land (even though the impurity of the airspace of land outside the Holy Land is only a rabbinical ordinance). Since

Rebbi assumed that the man was a Cohen violating the prohibition, he spoke to him in Aramaic as to an uneducated vulgar. The man answered in learned Hebrew that his father had married a woman forbidden to him as a Cohen (a divorcee or a prostitute) and, therefore, he himself was no Cohen

and was permitted to be outside the Land. This story proves that parts of Acco were outside the Land.

It is standard Talmudic style that a person who has to deprecate himself refers to himself as 'this man"; cf. *Berakhot* Chapter 3, Notes 195-199.

תְּחוּמֵי אֶרֶץ יִשְׂרָאֵל כָּל־שֶׁהֶחֱזִיקוּ עוֹלֵי בָבֶל. פָּרָשַׁת דשקלין[31] חומות מגדל שיד. ושינא דרור ושורא דעכו וקציריא דגליל וכברתה ובית זניתה וקובעיא ומילתא דביר וביריי רבתא תפניסא וסנפתה מחרתה דיתייר וממציא דאבהתא וראש מי געתון וגעתון עצמה מי ספר ומרחשת ומגדל חרוב ואולם רבתה ונוקבתא דעיון ותוקרת ברכה רבה ובר סנגדא ותרנגולא עילאה דלמעלה מן קיסרין וטרכונא דמתחם לבוצרא ומלח דזרכאיי ונמרין ובית סכל וקנת ורפיח דחגרא ודרך הגדולה ההולכת למדבר חשבון ויבקא ונחלא דזרד ויגר שהדותא ורקם דגועה וגניא דאשקלון.

31   Reading of the Rome ms., word missing in Leyden ms. and Venice print but certainly original. The text in the Yerushalmi is largely unexplainable. The *baraita* exists in three more versions: The mosaic of the Synagogue of Reḥov [published by J. Sussman, *Tarbiz* 43(1974) 88-158, 45(1976) 213-257], *Sifry Deut.* #52, and Tosephta *Ševiït* 4:11. The last two sources have many incompatible variant readings, cf. the editions of Finkelstein and Lieberman.

S. Klein points out that Caesarea Maritima is mentioned under its pre-Herodian name of Straton's Tower, which shows the old roots of the *baraita.* But the differences between the sources may derive not only from scribal errors but, in particular in the detailed description of the border between Acco and Caesarea Philippi, from changes in the actual border of Jewish settlement from Mishnaic to Byzantine times.

Text from Reḥov.

תְּחוּמֵי אֶרֶץ יִשְׂרָאֵל מָקוֹם שֶׁהֶ[חֱזִיקוּ] עוֹלֵי בָּבֶל פּוֹרָשַׁת אַשְׁקְלוֹן וְחוֹמַת מִגְדַּל שָׁרוֹשַׁן דּוֹר
וְחוֹמַת עַכּוֹ וֹרֹאשׁ מֵי גֵיאַתוֹ וְגֵיאַתוֹ עַצְמָהּ וְכַבָּרַ[תָא וּבֵי]ח זְנִיתָה וְקַסְטְרָא דְגָלִילָא וְקוּבְּעַיָּא
דְאַיְיתָא וּמִמַּצִיָּיה דְיָרְבְּתָה וּמִלְתָה דְכוֹרַיִים וּסְחַרְתָּה דְיַתִּיר וְנַחֲלָה דִבְצָאל וּבֵית עַיִט וּבַרְשָׁתָה
וְאוּלֵי רַבְּתָה וְנִיקְבְּתָה דְעִיּוּן וּמֵיסַב סְפַנְחָה וּפְרָכָה דְבַר סַנְגּוֹרָה וְתַרְנְגוֹלָה עִילָּיָיה דְקֵיסָרְיוֹן וּבֵית
סַבָּל וּקְנָת וּרְקַם טְרָכוֹן זִמְרָה דִמְחָם לְכוֹצְרַה יַבֹּקָה וְחֶשְׁבּוֹן וְנַחֲלָה דְזֶרֶד אִיגַר סַהֲדוּתָא
נִימְרִין וּמְלָח רְזִיזָה רְקַם דְגֵיאָה וְגִנַּיְיה דְאַשְׁקְלוֹן וְדֶרֶךְ הַגְדוֹלָה הַהוֹלֶכֶת לַמִּדְבָּר.

The boundaries of the Land of Israel, the domain acquired by the returnees from Babylonia: The road-crossing of Ascalon, the wall of Straton's Tower[32], Dor, the wall of Acco, the head of the waters of Gaaton[33], Gaaton itself, Kabarata[34] and Bet Zenita[35], the *castrum* of Galilee[36], the waterholes of Aita[37], the best of Yorkata[40], the wall of Koraim[38], the corral of Yattir[39], the brook Beṣal[40], Bet Ayiṭ, Barshata[41], great Uleh[42], the water source of Iyun[43], the surroundings of Sepanḥah[44], the fortification of Bar Sangura, the upper cock of Caesarea[45], Bet Sabbal[46], Qanat, Reqam of Trachonitis[47], Zimra which borders on Bostra[48], Yabboq, Ḥesban, the brook Zered, Yegar Sahaduta[49], Nimrin[50], the salt flat of Raziza[40], Reqam of Geia[51], the gardens of Ascalon and the main road which leads to the desert.

32　Caesarea Maritima.

33　Nahr Mafšukh, flowing into the Sea at Nahariyya. Gaaton is Khirbet Ja'ṭun.

34　Khirbet Al-Kabari, 5 km SE of Akhzib.

35　Khirbet Zuënita, NE of Al-Kabari.

36　Khirbet Jelil, 13 km NE of Akhzib.

37　Kafr 'Aita, 30 km NE of Khirbet Jelil. For the translation of קובעייא see

Tosefta ki-fshutah, p. 535.

38 Khirbet al-Koriyya, 8 km NE of Kafr 'Aita.

39 Kafr Yatir, N. of al-Koriyya.

40 Unidentified.

41 Bir 'Asit, E. of Yatir.

42 The conjectures about this place are collected by Lieberman, p. 536. Sussmann reads: Huleh, but this does not fit the geography of the description which moves from about Nahariyya to Banias without enclaves or exclaves. The reading of the Yerushalmi, אולם רבחה, would lead to 'Almon on Nahr Khasimiyye.

43 Merj 'Ayyoun.

44 Unidentified, in Tosephta and *Sifri* ספנחא.

45 Cf. *Demay* Chapter 2, Note 74.

46 All other sources read בית סכל or בית סכות While it is true that the mosaic shows a dark stone at the right hand side bottom of the letter, it is not impossible that this designates כ; then this and the next two places are SW of Damascus.

47 קנת is Al-Qonut NW of the Hauran, רקם is Ar-Raqim near Damascus. (רקם "heap of stones".)

48 Cf. *Demay* Chapter 2, Note 8.

49 Biblical names from Transjordan; the Mishnaic tradition of identification of these places is lost.

50 If this Nimrin is the place mentioned in Yerushalmi *Ketubot* 2:8 (fol. 26d) it must be in Trachonitis (Jebel Druz) since the last place mentioned in that region is Bostra. Maybe it is Bet-Nimra (*Jos.* 13:27).

51 Petra. In the Targumim, רְקַם גִּיאָה is the translation of Qadeš Barnea'.

אַשְׁקְלוֹן עַצְמָהּ רִבִּי יַעֲקֹב בַּר אָחָא בְּשֵׁם רִבִּי זְעִירָא מִן מַה דְתַגֵּי גִּנַּיְיָא דְאַשְׁקְלוֹן הָדָא אָמְרָה אַשְׁקְלוֹן כִּלְחוּץ. רִבִּי סִימוֹן בְּשֵׁם חוּלְפַּיי. דְּבֵי רִבִּי יִשְׁמָעֵאל בֵּי רִבִּי יוֹסֵי וּבֶן הַקַּפָּר נִמְנוּ עַל אֲוֵיר אַשְׁקְלוֹן וְטִיהֲרוּהוּ. מִפִּי רִבִּי פִּינְחָס בֶּן יָאִיר שֶׁאָמַר שֶׁהָיוּ יוֹרְדִין לְסֵירְקֵי שֶׁל אַשְׁקְלוֹן וְלוֹקְחִין חִטִּין וְעוֹלִין לְעִירֵנוּ וְטוֹבְלִין וְאוֹכְלִין בִּתְרוּמָתֵינוּ. לְמָחָר נִמְנוּ עָלֶיהָ לְפוֹטְרָהּ מִן הַמַּעְשְׂרוֹת. מָשַׁךְ רִבִּי יִשְׁמָעֵאל בֵּי רִבִּי יוֹסֵי אֶת יָדָיו שֶׁהָיָה מִסְתַּנֵּךְ עַל בֶּן הַקַּפָּר. אָמַר לוֹ בְּנִי לָמָּה לֹא אָמַרְתָּ לִי מִפְּנֵי מַה מָשַׁכְתָּ אֶת יָדֶיךָ מִמֶּנִּי הָיִיתִי אוֹמֵר לָךְ אֶתְמוֹל אֲנִי הוּא שֶׁטִּימֵּאתִי אֲנִי הוּא שֶׁטִּיהַרְתִּי וְעַכְשָׁיו אֲנִי אוֹמֵר שֶׁמָּה נִתְכַּבְּשָׁה מִדְּבַר תּוֹרָה. וְהֵיאַךְ אֲנִי פּוֹטְרָהּ מִדְּבַר תּוֹרָה.

Ashqelon itself? Rebbi Jacob bar Aḥa in the name of Rebbi Zeïra: Since we have stated "the gardens of Ascalon" it follows that Ascalon is outside. Rebbi Simon in the name of Hilfai: The House of Rebbi Ismael ben Rebbi Yose and Ben Qappara voted on the airspace of Ascalon and declared it pure from the testimony of Rebbi Phineas ben Yaïr who said, we were descending to the Saracen [market] at Ascalon[52] where we bought wheat, returned to our town, immersed ourselves[53] and ate our heave. The next day they voted to free it from tithes[54]. Rebbi Ismael ben Rebbi Yose removed his hand that was leaning on Ben Qappara. He said to him, my son, why did you not say to me: why did you remove your hand? I would have told you that yesterday I was he who declared it impure[55], I am he who declared it pure. But now I am saying, maybe it was conquered within the meaning of the Torah, how can I free it from the meaning of the Torah[56]?

52   Since he was eating heave, he must have been a Cohen and forbidden to leave the Land.

53   Cf. Mishnah *Berakhot* 1:1.

54   This ruling would contradict the previous one and declare Ascalon outside the Land.

55   Not really he personally, but he is like one of the rabbis who decreed impurity on the airspace outside the Holy Land.

56   He must follow R. Yose bar Ḥanina and hold that the obligation of tithes in the Second Commonwealth was biblical.

אֵימָתַי הִיא טְמֵיאָה מְשׁוּם אֶרֶץ הָעַמִּים. אָמַר רְבִּי סִימוֹן מִשֶּׁתִּשְׁהֶא הַגְּזֵירָה אַרְבָּעִים יוֹם. אָמַר רְבִּי יִרְמְיָה וְלֹא בְּטָעוּת אָנוּ מַחֲזִיקָם אֶלָּא מִיַּד הִיא טְמֵיאָה מְשׁוּם אֶרֶץ הָעַמִּים. אָמַר רְבִּי מָנָא לֹא כֵן אָמַר רְבִּי יַעֲקֹב בַּר אָחָא בְּשֵׁם רְבִּי זְעִירָא מִן מַה דְּתַנֵּי גִּנַּייָא דְּאַשְׁקְלוֹן הָדָא אָמְרָה אַשְׁקְלוֹן כִּלְחוּץ. וְכִי

צוֹר אֵינוֹ אָסוּר לֵילֵךְ לְשָׁם וְהַקוֹנֶה שָׁם אֵינוֹ מִתְחַיֵּיב דְּלָא תִסְבּוֹר מֵימַר אַף
הָכָא כֵן לְפִיכָךְ נִמְנוּ עָלֶיהָ לְפוֹטְרָהּ מִן הַמַּעַשְׂרוֹת.

When is it impure because of territory of Gentiles[57]? Rebbi Simeon said, if the decision stands for forty days. Rebbi Jeremiah said, did we not hold it by error[58]? Certainly it is immediately impure because of territory of the Gentiles! Rebbi Mana said, did not Rebbi Jacob bar Aḥa say in the name of Rebbi Zeïra: Since we have stated "the gardens of Ascalon" it follows that Ascalon is outside. Is it not forbidden to go to Tyre[59] and is the one who buys there not obligated[60]? They voted to exempt it from tithes that you should not say the same in this case.

57   This refers to the rabbinic decree that Gentile settlements, even in the Land of Israel, are impure since Gentiles bury their still-born babies anywhere, even under dirt floors of houses or under dirt roads. Anybody walking through such a settlement might become impure by the impurity of the "tent" (cf. *Kilaim* Chapter 2, Note 180.)

58   Ascalon was erroneously held to be pure by R. Phineas ben Yaïr; the decree is not new.

59   In the time of Rebbi, when a Cohen was forbidden to leave the Land, he might not go to Tyre since this is far to the North of Akhzib. In the time of R. Mana this rule apparently was disregarded since it is reported (*Berakhot* 3:1, note 94) that R. Ḥiyya bar Abba, a Cohen, went to Tyre to see the emperor Diocletian.

60   Cf. *Demay* Chap. 1, Note 168.

רְבִּי סִימוֹן וְרְבִּי אַבָּהוּ הֲווֹן יְתִיבִין. אָמַר הָא כְתִיב וַיִּלְכּוֹד יְהוּדָה אֶת עַזָּה וְאֶת
גְּבוּלָהּ. לֵיתֵי עַזָּה. אֶת אַשְׁקְלוֹן אֶת גְּבוּלָהּ. לֵיתֵי אַשְׁקְלוֹן. מֵעַתָּה הָהֵן נַחַל
מִצְרָיִם. לֵיתֵי נַחַל מִצְרָיִם.

Rebbi Simon and Rebbi Abbahu were sitting. He said, is it not written (*Jud.* 1:18) "Jehudah conquered Gaza and its territory"? Include Gaza[61].

"Ascalon and its territory", include Ascalon. If it is so, what about the
brook of Egypt[62]? Include the brook of Egypt.

61   This refers to the question of
tithes due from the territory conquered
by the twelve tribes under Joshua even
if they could not hold onto their
conquests, as argued by R. Ismael ben
R. Yose. For this opinion, all that is
described in the Torah and the book of
Joshua is subject to tithes. The
commentators translate עזה ליתי by "this

is not Gaza", meaning that Gaza town is
not the Gaza mentioned in the verse.
But the Yerushalmi uses ליח only as "no;
not", never as "not being"; the latter is
always spelled out ליתי ; לא אית as
verbal form can be derived only from
אתי "to come", not from אית "to be".
62   Jos. 15:4. Num. 34.9, identified
by R. Saadia Gaon as Wadi el-'Arish.

אָמַר רִבִּי יְהוֹשֻׁעַ בֶּן לֵוִי כְּתִיב וַיִּבְרַח יִפְתָּח מִפְּנֵי אֶחָיו וַיֵּשֶׁב בְּאֶרֶץ טוֹב זוֹ
סוּסִיתָא. וְלָמָּה נִקְרָא שְׁמָהּ טוֹב שֶׁיִּפְטוֹר מִן הַמַּעְשְׂרוֹת. רִבִּי אִימִי בָּעֵי וְלֹא
מִמַּעֲלֵי מִסִּין הֵן. סָבַר רִבִּי אִימִי מַעֲלֵי מִסִּין כְּמִי שֶׁנִּתְכַּבְּשׁוּ. דְּאָמַר רִבִּי
שְׁמוּאֵל בַּר נַחְמָן שָׁלֹשׁ פרסטיגיות שָׁלַח יְהוֹשֻׁעַ לְאֶרֶץ יִשְׂרָאֵל עַד שֶׁלֹּא יִכָּנְסוּ
לָאָרֶץ מִי שֶׁהוּא רוֹצֶה לְהַפָּנוֹת יִפָּנֶּה. לְהַשְׁלִים יַשְׁלִים. לַעֲשׂוֹת מִלְחָמָה יַעֲשֶׂה.
גִּרְגָּשִׁי פִּינָּה וְהֶאֱמִין לוֹ לְהַקָּדוֹשׁ בָּרוּךְ הוּא וְהָלַךְ לוֹ לְאַפְרִיקֵי. עַד בּוֹאִי
וְלָקַחְתִּי אֶתְכֶם אֶל אֶרֶץ כְּאַרְצְכֶם. זוֹ אַפְרִיקֵי. גִּבְעוֹנִים הִשְׁלִימוּ וְכִי הִשְׁלִימוּ
יוֹשְׁבֵי גִבְעוֹן אֶת יִשְׂרָאֵל. שְׁלֹשִׁים וְאֶחָד מֶלֶךְ עָשׂוּ מִלְחָמָה וְנָפָלוּ.

Rebbi Joshua ben Levi said it is written (*Jud.* 11:3): "Jephtah fled
because of his brothers and dwelled in the land Good," that is Hippos.
Why is it called "Good", because it frees from tithes. [63Rebbi Immi asked:
Are these not of the taxpayers? Rebbi Immi is of the opinion that
taxpayers count as if they were conquered.] For Rebbi Samuel bar
Naḥman said, Joshua sent three orders[64] to the Land of Israel before they
entered the Land: Those who want to evacuate should evacuate, those
who want to make peace should make peace, those who want to go to

war should go to war. The Girgasites[65] evacuated, believed in the Holy
One, praised be He, and went to Africa[66]. (2K. 18:32, Is. 36:17) "Until I
come and take you to a land like your Land," that is Africa. The people
of Gibeon made peace, (Jos. 10:1) ". . . that the inhabitants of Gibeon had
made peace with Israel." Thirty-one kings went to war and fell.

63   The passage in brackets is from
Demay, Chapter 2 (at Note 97); it
refers to Kefar Ẓemaḥ, a place within
the municipality of Hippos with a
Jewish quarter, in contrast to Gentile
Hippos. It has no connection with the
theme of this paragraph other than the
mention of Hippos.

64   The word in the Yerushalmi
(both mss.) seems to be corrupt. In the
parallel Lev. rabba 17(6) the reading is
פרוזדוגמאות in the printed editions and
פרסטיגמאות in Arukh. Compare Greek

πρόσταγμα "command, edict".

65   Even though the Girgasites are
mentioned in Jos. 24:11 as having
fought against Israel, they are not
mentioned anywhere in the report on
the conquest.

66   The Roman province of Africa
on the Southern shore of the Mediterranean. In the Babli (Sanhedrin 94a),
the identification is quoted in the name
of Mar Zuṭra, a late Amora known for
his quotes of sermons of early
authorities.

מִפְּנֵי מָה לֹא גָזְרוּ עַל אוֹתָהּ הָרוּחַ שֶׁבְּגְרָרִיקוֹ. רַבִּי סִימוֹן בְּשֵׁם רַבִּי יְהוֹשֻׁעַ בֶּן
לֵוִי מִפְּנֵי שֶׁנִּיוֶיהָ רַע. עַד הֵיכָן. רַבִּי חָנִין בְּשֵׁם רַבִּי שְׁמוּאֵל בַּר רַב יִצְחָק עַד
נַחַל מִצְרַיִם. וַהֲרֵי עַזָּה נִיוֶיהָ יָפָה. פִּישְׁפְּשָׁה אָמַר קוֹמֵי רַבִּי יוֹסֵי שָׁאֵלִית לְרַבִּי
אָחָא וְשָׁרָא.

Why did they make no decree about the direction of Gerar[67]? Rebbi
Simon in the name of Rebbi Joshua ben Levi: Because its oases are poor.
How far? Rebbi Ḥanin in the name of Rebbi Samuel ben Rabbi Isaac: Up
to the brook of Egypt[62]. But is not the oasis of Gaza a good one?
Pishpesha[68] said before Rebbi Yose: I asked Rebbi Aḥa and he permitted.

67   The desert part of the Negev.
This is part of the Biblical Holy Land
that was not settled by the returnees
from Babylon but which is so sparsely
inhabited and infrequently visited that
no decree was deemed necessary.

68   Name of an otherwise unknown
person (or a nickname "inquirer into
details") who must have been a Cohen
since he was worried about the impurity of Gentile territory.

רִבִּי זְעִירָא אֲזַל לְחַמְּתָא דִפְחָל וַהֲוָה חָמֵי גַרְמֵיהּ יְהִיב לְבַר (מִן) מִדִיקְלַיָּא
דְּבָבֶל שָׁלַח שָׁאַל לְרִבִּי חִיָּיא בַּר וָא שָׁאַל רִבִּי חִיָּיא בַּר וָא לִתְרֵין בְּנוֹי דְּרִבִּי
אֶבְיָתָר דְּדָמָא אָמְרִין לֵיהּ נְהִיגִין כֹּהֲנַיָּא מָטֵיי עַד תַּמָּן. כָּהֲנַיָּא שְׁאָלוּן לְרִבִּי
יוֹחָנָן הָהֵן חוּטָא דְנָוֶה. אָמַר לוֹן רִבִּי יוֹחָנָן בְּשֵׁם רִבִּי חוּנְיָא דִבְרַת חַוְרָן.
נְהִיגִין כֹּהֲנַיָּא מָטֵיי עַד דְּרֵיי וְהָהֵן חוּטָא דְבָצְרַיָּיא עַד דְּפַרְדֵיסָא.

Rebbi Zeïra went to the hot springs of Pella[69] and found himself
outside of the "Babylonian date palms". He sent to ask Rebbi Ḥiyya bar
Abba; Rebbi Ḥiyya bar Abba asked the two sons of Rebbi Eviatar from
Dama[70] who said to him, Cohanim are used to go there. The Cohanim
asked Rebbi Joḥanan about that strip around Naveh. Rebbi Joḥanan said
to them in the name of Rebbi Onias from Ḥauran: Cohanim are used to
go there up to Edrei, and in the region of Bostra[48] up to the orchard.

69   In Perea, South of Naveh. Since
this place is West of Bostra, there
should not have been any question that
it is within the Land of Israel. But
since a group of date palms was called
"Babylonian", there arose a question
whether their place followed the rules

of Babylonia.
70   Nothing is known about this
person. He is referred to by his place
(Dameh in the plane of Ḥattin) to
distinguish him from the (originally
Babylonian) R. Eviatar quoted elsewhere.

אָמַר רִבִּי אַבָּהוּ יֵשׁ עֲיָירוֹת שֶׁל כּוּתִים שֶׁנָּהֲגוּ בָהֶן הֵיתֵר מִימֵי יְהוֹשֻׁעַ בֶּן נוּן וְהֵן
מוּתָּרוֹת. רִבִּי יוֹסֵי בָּעֵי מֵעַתָּה לֹא יָחוּשׁוּ כֹּהֲנִים עַל חַלָּתָן. וַאֲנָן חָמֵיי רַבָּנִין

חֹשְׁשִׁין. אָמַר רבִּי יוּדָה בֶּן פָּזִי לָא בְגִין מִילְתָא דְּאַתְּ אֲמְרַת אֶלָא בְּגִין דְּלָא
חָלַטּתוּן מַלְכוּתָא בְּיָדָא.

Rebbi Abbahu said: There are Samaritan places permitted since the days of Joshua bin Nun and they remain permitted[71]. Rebbi Yose inquired: If that is so, Cohanim should not worry about their *ḥallah*. But we see that rabbis worry[72]! Rebbi Judah ben Pazi said, it is not because of what you said, but because it never was absolutely under government control[73].

71   The entire Land of Israel was permitted from the time of the conquest under Joshua. R. Abbahu notes that there were places held by the returnees from Babylonia that in his time were occupied by Samaritans. Since the territory acquired the status of holiness with their return, it cannot lose it again even if the place is occupied by people who cannot be trusted in matters of ritual purity and Cohanim may go there.

72   They do treat Samaritan *ḥallah* as impure.

73   The places were never included in the Persian province of Yehud nor consolidated into the Hasmonean kingdom.

רבִּי יָסָא שָׁמַע דְּאָתִית אִימֵּיהּ לְבָצְרָה. שָׁאַל לְרבִּי יוֹחָנָן מַהוּ לָצֵאת. אָמַר לֵיהּ
אִם מִפְּנֵי סַכָּנַת דְּרָכִים צֵא. אִם מִשּׁוּם כְּבוֹד אִמָּךְ אֵינִי יוֹדֵעַ. אָמַר רבִּי
שְׁמוּאֵל בַּר רב יִצְחָק עוֹד הִיא צְרִיכָה לְרבִּי יוֹחָנָן אַטְרָח עֲלוֹי וְאָמַר גָּמַרְתָּה
לָצֵאת תָּבוֹא בְשָׁלוֹם. שָׁמַע רבִּי לֶעָזָר וָמַר אֵין רְשׁוּת גְּדוֹלָה מִזּוּ.

[74]Rebbi Yasa heard that his mother had come to Bostra. He went and asked Rebbi Yohanan, may I leave? He said to him, if it is because of danger on the road, leave. If it is in order to honor father and mother, I do not know. Rebbi Samuel bar Rav Isaac said, Rebbi Yohanan still needs to answer. He importuned him, so he said: If you decided to go, return in peace. Rebbi Eleazar heard this and said: there is no greater permission than that.

74   This text is also in Berakhot 3:1   Qiddušin 31b.
(Notes 103 ff.); a parallel in Babli

רְבִּי שִׁמְעוֹן בֶּן לָקִישׁ שָׁאַל (fol. 36d) לְרְבִּי חֲנִינָה הַקּוֹנֶה בְּעַמּוֹן וּמוֹאָב מַהוּ.
אָמַר לֵיהּ אֲנִי לֹא שְׁמַעְתִּיהָ מֵרְבִּי חִיָּיה הַגָּדוֹל אֶלָּא מִפְּרָשַׁת אַשְׁקְלוֹן וּלְחוּץ.
וְקַשְׁיָא דְּהוּא שָׁאַל לֵיהּ הָדָא וָמַר לֵיהּ הָדָא. אֶלָּא בְּגִין דְּלֵית רְבִּי חֲנִינָה אָמַר
מִילָה דְּלֹא שָׁמַע מִן יוֹמוֹי וּבְגִין דְּלָא מְפִיקְתֵּיהּ רֵיקָן בְּגִין כֵּן שָׁאַל לֵיהּ הָדָא
וּמֵגִיב לֵיהּ חָדָא.

Rebbi Simeon ben Laqish asked Rebbi Haninah: What is the status of
one who buys in Ammon and Moab[75]? He said to him, I heard from the
great Rebbi Hiyya only "outside the crossroads of Ascalon." That is
difficult, he asked him this and he answered that[76]? But since Rebbi
Haninah never said anything he had not heard and because he did not
want to send him away emptyhanded, he [R. Simeon] asked him one topic
and he [R. Hanina] answered another.

75   What is the status for Sabbatical
and tithes? From the discussion in the
paragraph after the next it will be
clear that "Ammon and Moab" does not
refer to the Biblical states but to the

domain of the former tribes Reuben
and Gad in Transjordan.
76   He asked him about Northern
Transjordan and the answer was given
for Southern Cisjordan.

רְבִּי שִׁמְעוֹן בֶּן לָקִישׁ אֲזַל לִבְצָרָה אֲתוֹן לְגַבֵּיהּ. אֲמְרוּ לֵיהּ חָמֵי לָן בַּר נָשׁ דָּרִישׁ
דַּיָּין סֹפֵר חַזָּן עֲבִיד כָּל־צוּרְכָּנִין חָמָא חַד בַּבְלָיִי. אָמַר לֵיהּ חָמִית לָךְ חַד אָתָר
טָב אֲתָא לְגַבֵּיהּ רְבִּי יוֹחָנָן אָמַר לֵיהּ מִן בָּבֶל לְבָבֶל. אָמַר רְבִּי יַעֲקֹב בַּר אַבָּא
מִן דְּאָמַר רְבִּי יוֹחָנָן מִן בָּבֶל לְבָבֶל הָדָא אֲמְרָה הַקּוֹנֶה שָׁם אֵינוֹ מִתְחַיֵּיב. וְכִי
צוֹר אֵינוֹ אָסוּר לֵילֵךְ לְשָׁם וְהַקּוֹנֶה שָׁם אֵינוֹ מִתְחַיֵּיב. אַשְׁכָּח תַּנֵּי סִימֵן לְעַמּוֹן
וּמוֹאָב וּלְאֶרֶץ מִצְרַיִם שְׁתֵּי אֲרָצוֹת. אַחַת נֶאֱכֶלֶת וְנֶעֱבֶדֶת וְאַחַת נֶאֱכֶלֶת וְלֹא
נֶעֱבֶדֶת. סָבַר רְבִּי יוֹחָנָן מֵימַר אֶת בֶּצֶר בַּמִּדְבָּר. שָׁאַל לְרְבִּי שִׁמְעוֹן בֶּן לָקִישׁ
בֶּצֶר בְּצָרָה.

Rebbi Simeon ben Laqish went to Bostra; they came to him and said to him: Select for us a man as preacher, judge, scribe, reader; one who will do everything we need[77]. He selected a Babylonian and said to him, I have a good place for you. He went to Rebbi Johanan who said to him, from Babylonia to Babylonia[78]. Rebbi Jacob bar Abba said, since Rebbi Johanan said from Babylonia to Babylonia, that means one who buys there is not obligated. But is it not forbidden to go to Tyre[79], and if one buys there is he not obligated? It was found stated: A sign for Ammon, Moab, and the Land of Egypt: There are two regions[80]. From the first one eats and it may be worked[81], from the other one eats and it may not be worked. Rebbi Johanan wanted to refer to (*Deut.* 4:43): "Beṣer in the prairie[82]". He asked Rebbi Simeon ben Laqish: Is Beṣer Bostra?

77   Full job description of a paid practicing rabbi.

78   You came from Babylonia to be in the Holy Land; do not leave the Land. This ruling contradicts the one given to R. Assi.

79   Since Tyre is North of Akhzib, it is not in the Holy Land. Nevertheless, the rules of the Sabbatical are kept there.

80   Each country contains two regions. It is stated in Mishnah *Yadayim* 4:3 that a "new decree", enacted after the destruction of the Temple, requires Jewish farmers in these regions to give tithes of the poor. It is stated here that these obligations apply only to those parts of these countries which border on the Holy Land.

81   One eats under the rules of the holiness of the Sabbatical; one works (or may not work) the land in the Sabbatical.

82   One of the cities of refuge, in the territory of Reuben. If Bostra is Beṣer then it belonged to the Biblical land of Israel and to the land held by the returnees from Babylonia, and must be obligated for all duties upon the Land. This was R. Johanan's opinion when he told R. Assi (a Cohen) to go there to meet his mother. But then he asked R. Simeon ben Laqish, changed his mind and placed Bostra just outside

the borders of the Land. In the Babli (*Avodah Zarah* 58b), the identification is R. Simeon's and R. Johanan insists that these are different places. (Bostra is in the North, at the Eastern end of the Bashan highlands; Beṣer is in the South, in the low plain near the Dead Sea.)

רִבִּי יִצְחָק בַּר נַחְמָן וְרִבִּי שִׁמְעוֹן בֶּן לָקִישׁ שָׁאַל לְרִבִּי חֲנִינָה הַקּוֹנֶה מֵעַמּוֹן וּמוֹאָב מַהוּ. אָמַר [רִבִּי זְעִירָא]‏83 קְשִׁיתָהּ קוֹמֵי רִבִּי יָסָא לֵית עַמּוֹן וּמוֹאָב דְּמֹשֶׁה. אָמַר רִבִּי מָנָא קְשִׁיתָהּ קוֹמֵי רִבִּי חַגַּיי לֵית עַמּוֹן וּמוֹאָב דְּמֹשֶׁה. לֵית עַמּוֹן וּמוֹאָב דְּרִבִּי לֶעְזָר בֶּן עֲזַרְיָה. אָמַר רִבִּי יוֹסֵי בֵּי רִבִּי בּוּן כְּתִיב כִּי חֶשְׁבּוֹן עִיר סִיחוֹן מֶלֶךְ הָאֱמוֹרִי הִיא צְרִיכָה לְרִבִּי שִׁמְעוֹן טָהֲרָה מִיַּד סִיחוֹן וְעוֹג אוֹ לֹא טָהֲרָה. אִין תֵּימַר טָהֲרָה חַיֶּיבֶת. אִין תֵּימַר שֶׁלֹּא טָהֲרָה פְּטוּרָה. אָמַר רִבִּי תַנְחוּמָא הָחֵל רָשׁ לָרֶשֶׁת אֶת אַרְצוֹ עָשִׂיתִי אֶת אַרְצוֹ חוּלִין לְפָנֶיךָ.

Rebbi Isaac bar Naḥman: Did not Rebbi Simeon ben Laqish ask Rebbi Ḥaninah: What is the status of one who buys in Ammon and Moab[75]? Rebbi Zeïra said, I asked this question before Rebbi Assi: Are not Ammon and Moab from Moses? Rebbi Mana asked this question before Rebbi Ḥaggai: Are not Ammon and Moab from Moses? Ammon and Moab are not from Rebbi Eleazar ben Azariah[84]! Rebbi Yose ben Rebbi Abun said, it is written (*Num.* 22:26): "For Ḥešbon is the city of Siḥon, the king of the Amorites." Rebbi Simeon was not sure whether it was purified from the hand of Siḥon and Og or not. If you say it was purified it is obligated, if you say it was not purified it is free. Rebbi Tanḥuma said (*Deut.* 2:31): "Make profane for inheritance, to inherit his land." I made his land profane before you[85].

83   Reading of Rome ms. Venice text: א״ל (i. e., אמר ליה).

84   In Mishnah *Yadayim* 4 there is a list of decrees enacted on the day R. Eleazar ben Azariah was made head of the Synhedrion. On the authority of R.

Joshua it was decreed that "Ammon and Moab" (i. e., the domains of the former tribes Reuben and Gad) must give tithe of the poor in the Sabbatical. This implies that the land there is cultivated during the Sabbatical. Therefore, Transjordan cannot be part of the Holy Land where work is forbidden.

85 Even in the times of Moses and Joshua, Transjordan did not have the status of a Holy Land. The opposite conclusion is drawn from the same verses in Babli *Ḥulin* 60b.

רִבִּי חוּנָא בָּעֵי מִשְׁרֵי הָהֵן יַבְּלוֹנָה אָתָא לְגַבֵּי רִבִּי מָנָא אָמַר לֵיהּ הָא לָךְ חֲתוֹם וְלָא קְבִילֵי עִילָוֵי מִיחְתּוֹם לְמָחָר קָם עִימֵּיהּ רִבִּי חִייָא בַּר מַדְיָא. אָמַר לֵיהּ יָאוּת עֲבָדַת דְּלֹא הָתַמְתְּ. דְּרִבִּי יוֹנָה אָבוּךְ הֲוָה אָמַר אַנְטוֹנִינוּס יְהָבָהּ לְרִבִּי תְּרֵין אַלְפִין דַּשְׁנִין בַּאֲרִיסוּ. לְפִיכָךְ נֶאֱכָל אֲבָל לֹא נֶעֱבָד כְּסוּרְיָא וּפָטוּר מִן הַמַּעְשְׂרוֹת מִפְּנֵי שֶׁהִיא כִשְׂדוֹת גּוֹיִים.

Rebbi Ḥuna wanted to permit the Gebalitis[86]. He came to Rebbi Mana and said to him: This is for you to sign. He did not agree to sign. The next day, Rebbi Ḥiyya bar Madia[87] came to him and said, you did well that you did not sign, for your father, Rebbi Jonah, used to say that Antoninus[88] gave there to Rebbi two thousand[89] gifts for sharecropping. Therefore it may be eaten[2] but not worked like Syria and is free from tithes since one deals with Gentile fields.

86 For a discussion of the cases of substitution of י for ג see Y. F. Gumpertz, *Mivṭa'e Śefatenu* (Jerusalem 1953), pp. 51-86. Gebalitis was the name of the region of Petra.

87 Elsewhere, his name is R. Ḥiyya bar Maria; a student of rabbis Jonah and Yose.

88 Cf. *Kilaim* Chapter 9, Note 79.

89 This word is missing in the Rome ms. The text is elliptic; it seems that Rebbi received the income from two imperial properties in that region but never obtained title to the parcels. Since Gebalitis was not part of the Idumea absorbed into the Hasmonean state, the rules of the Holy Land certainly did not apply.

רַב הוּנָא אָמַר כֵּינִי מַתְנִיתָא מִגְּזִיב וְעַד הַנָּהָר מִגְּזִיב וְעַד אֲמָנָה. תַּנֵּי אֵי זוֹ הִיא הָאָרֶץ וְאֵי זוֹ הִיא חוּץ לָאָרֶץ. כָּל־שֶׁשּׁוֹפֵעַ מִטַּוְרוֹס אֲמָנֹס⁹⁰ וְלִפְנִים אֶרֶץ יִשְׂרָאֵל. מִטַּוְרוֹס אֲמָנֹס וּלְחוּץ חוּץ לָאָרֶץ. הַגֵּיסִין שֶׁבַּיָּם אַתְּ רוֹאֶה אוֹתָן כְּאִילוּ חוּט מָתוּחַ מִטַּוְרֵי אֲמָנָה עַד נַחַל מִצְרָיִם. מֵהַחוּט וְלִפְנִים אֶרֶץ יִשְׂרָאֵל. מֵהַחוּט וּלְחוּץ חוּץ לָאָרֶץ. רִבִּי יוּדָה אָמַר כָּל־שֶׁהוּא כְּנֶגֶד אֶרֶץ יִשְׂרָאֵל הֲרֵי הוּא כְּאֶרֶץ יִשְׂרָאֵל שֶׁנֶּאֱמַר וּגְבוּל יָם וְהָיָה לָכֶם הַיָּם הַגָּדוֹל וּגְבוּל. שֶׁבַּצְּדָדִין מֵהֶן אַתְּ רוֹאֶה אוֹתָן כְּאִילוּ חוּט מָתוּחַ מִקְּפַלָּרְיָא וְעַד אוֹקְיָנוֹס מֵחוּט וְלִפְנִים אֶרֶץ יִשְׂרָאֵל. מֵהַחוּט וּלְחוּץ חוּץ לָאָרֶץ.

Rav Huna said: So is the Mishnah: "Between Akhzib and Euphrates, between Akhzib and Amanus.[91]" It was stated[92]: What is the Land and what is outside the Land? From the slopes of Taurus Amanus inwards is the Land of Israel[3], from Taurus Amanus to the outside is outside the Land. About the islands in the sea, one looks at them as if a string were drawn from Taurus Amanus to the brook of Egypt; from the string to the inside is the Land of Israel, from the string to the outside is outside the Land. Rebbi Jehudah said, all that lies before the Land of Israel is like the Land of Israel since it is said (*Num.* 34:6): "The Eastern border shall be for you the Great Sea[93] as border." Assuming that a string were drawn from Cephalaria[94] to the Ocean, inside the string is the Land of Israel, outside is outside the Land.

90　Reading of the Rome ms. Venice: מטורי אמנה.

91　It is not "between Akhzib and (Taurus Amanus and Euphrates)"; one does not speak about the point at which the Euphrates breaks through the Taurus range.

92　Tosephta *Terumot* 2:12, *Ḥallah* 2:11, Yerushalmi *Ḥallah* 4:8, Babli *Giṭṭin* 8a.

93　The Mediterranean. The entire width of the sea is the border. The tradition of R. Jehudah is an old one; Josephus (*Antiquities* I.130) in his description of the list of peoples (*Gen.* 10) writes that the domain of the Canaanites did extend "to the Ocean". The commentators to Josephus take this as a reference to the Indian Ocean; the text here shows that the Ocean is, as always in Greek literature, the Atlantic Ocean (at the straits of Gibraltar).

According to R. Jehudah, Crete (and possibly Sicily) was first settled by Canaanite tribes and promised to Abraham.

94   Called by Pliny (*Hist. nat.* V (18) 21) *promunturium Syriae Antiochiae.*

אָמַר רִבִּי יוּסְטָא בַּר שׁוּנֶם כְּשֶׁיַּגִּיעוּ הַגָּלִיּוֹת לְטוּרֵי אֲמָנָה הֵן עֲתִידוֹת לוֹמַר שִׁירָה. מַה טַעַם תָּשׁוּרִי מֵרֹאשׁ אֲמָנָה.

Rebbi Justus bar Shunem said, when the people of the Diaspora arrive at Taurus Amanus[95] they will sing. What is the reason? (*Cant.* 4:8) "Sing from the top of Amanah".

95   In the times of the Messiah, when all of Israel will be gathered in the Land of Israel in its Biblical borders. The same text (slightly shortened) is in *Ḥallah* 4:8, Midrash *Šir rabba* 4(18).

(fol. 36b) **משנה ב**: עוֹשִׂין בְּתָלוּשׁ בְּסוּרְיָא אֲבָל לֹא בִמְחוּבָּר. דָּשִׁים וְזוֹרִים וְדוֹרְכִים וּמְעַמְּרִין אֲבָל לֹא קוֹצְרִים וְלֹא בוֹצְרִין וְלֹא מוֹסְקִין. כְּלָל אָמַר רִבִּי עֲקִיבָה כָּל־שֶׁכִּיּוֹצֵא בוֹ מוּתָּר בָּאָרֶץ עוֹשִׂין אוֹתוֹ בְסוּרְיָא.

Mishnah 2: One works in Syria what is plucked but not what is standing[96]. One threshes, winnows, treads, and makes sheaves, but one harvests neither grain, nor grapes or olives. Rebbi Aqiba stated a rule: Everything that is permitted in the Land of Israel one does in Syria.

96   A worker can hire himself out
to a Jew who is not observing the
Sabbatical if the produce is already
harvested. The rule of R. Aqiba means:

Everything that in the Land of Israel
the farmer may do for himself, a hired
hand may do in Syria for any employer.

(fol. 36d) **הלכה ב**: עוֹשִׂין בְּתָלוֹשׁ בְּסוּרְיָא כו'. אָמַר רִבִּי אַבָּהוּ שֶׁלֹּא יְהוּ הוֹלְכִין

וּמִשְׁתַּקְעִין שָׁם. בְּתָלוֹשׁ לָמָה הוּא מוּתָּר מִן גּוֹ דוּ חָמֵי רַוְוחָא קְרִיב לָא נְפִיק.

Halakhah 2: "One works in Syria what is plucked", etc. Rebbi Abbahu

said, so that they should not go and stay there permanently[97]. Then why

may he work what is plucked? Since he sees only small gain he will not

leave[98].

97   Since Syria was not conquered
by all of Israel, from the Torah all
work is permitted in Syria. The
prohibition of harvesting is purely
rabbinical, with the intention that Syria
should not have too much of an

economic advantage over the Land of
Israel.
98   The monetary advantage one
gets from agriculture when harvest is
forbidden is too small to induce people
to leave the Land.

רִבִּי יוֹסֵי בֵּי רִבִּי בּוּן בְּעָא קוֹמֵי רִבִּי מָנָא מַהוּ לִטְחוֹן עִם הַגּוֹי בָּאָרֶץ. אָמַר לֵיהּ

מַתְנִיתָא אָמַר שֶׁהוּא אָסוּר דְּתַנִּינָן עוֹשִׂין בְּתָלוֹשׁ בְּסוּרְיָא אֲבָל לֹא בִמְחוּבָּר

הָא בָאָרֶץ אֲפִילוּ בְתָלוֹשׁ יְהֵא אָסוּר.

Rebbi Yose ben Rebbi Abun asked before Rebbi Mana: May one mill

with a Gentile in the Land? He said to him, the Mishnah tells us that it is

forbidden, as it is stated: "One works in Syria what is plucked but not

what is standing;" therefore in the Land it should be forbidden even when

it was plucked.

מָקוֹם שֶׁהוּא נֶאֱכָל וְלֹא נֶעֱבָד. מַהוּ לְהַשְׂכִּיר בְּהֶמְתּוֹ שָׁם. רְבִּי לֵוִי עֲנַבְרָיָא
שָׁאַל לְרִבִּי יִצְחָק וּלְרִבִּי אִימִּי וְאָסְרוּן. רִבִּי הוֹשַׁעְיָה יְהַב לְעַמְמַיָּא פְּרִיטִין לֹא
דְהוּא אָסוּר אֶלָּא שֶׁלֹּא לְיַיחֵד בְּהֶמְתּוֹ עִם הַגּוֹי.

At a place where one may eat but not work, may one rent out one's
animals there[99]? Rebbi Levi from Sennabaris[100] asked Rebbis Isaac and
Immi and they forbade it. Rebbi Hoshaia gave money to the Gentiles[101],
not because it would have been forbidden but so as not to leave his
animal alone with a Gentile.

99   There is no obligation to give
one's animals rest during the Sabbatical
year, in contrast to the Sabbath day.
There is no doubt that renting out one's
animals is permitted under biblical law;
the only question is whether it is prohibited by rabbinic ordinance to avoid
helping sinners who disregard the
Sabbatical prohibitions.

100   He is mentioned only here. His
place, mentioned by Josephus (*Jewish
War* III ix 7) is at the Southern end of

Lake Genezareth.

101   He hired Gentiles to work with
their animals. He disagrees with
Rebbis Isaac and Immi: From the point
of view of Sabbatical law it would be
proper to rent out one's animals to
Gentiles who are not subject to the
Sabbatical but still one may not do this
since (Mishnah *Avodah Zarah* 2:1) "one
may not put an animal into a Gentile's
stable because they are suspected of
sodomy."

וּמַה אֲנַן קַייָמִין. אִם בְּפֵירוֹת שְׁשִׁית שֶׁנִּכְנְסוּ לַשְּׁבִיעִית אֲפִילוּ בָּאָרֶץ מוּתָּר.
אִם בְּפֵירוֹת שְׁבִיעִית שֶׁיֵּצְאוּ לְמוֹצָאֵי שְׁבִיעִית לַחֲרוֹשׁ מוּתָּר וְלִקְצוֹר אָסוּר.
אֶלָּא כִּי אֲנַן קַייָמִין בְּפֵירוֹת שְׁבִיעִית בַּשְּׁבִיעִית.

What are we dealing with[102]? If about produce of the sixth year held
over to the Sabbatical, even in the Land it is permitted[103]. If produce of
the Sabbatical is held over to the year after the Sabbatical, one is

permitted to plough but forbidden to harvest. But one deals with produce
of the Sabbatical[104] in the Sabbatical.

102   Here starts the discussion of the
Mishnah. Under which circumstances
are the activities described in the Mishnah permitted in Syria and forbidden in
the Land?

103   In this case, even commercial
harvesting is permitted in the Land.

104   Spontaneous growth which even
in the Land is forbidden only by
rabbinic decree.

רִבִּי חוּנָא אָזַל לְצוֹר וְאָסַר לוֹן הָדָא אַשְׁקְיָיתָא. שָׁמַע רִבִּי יוֹסֵי וְאָמַר וְיָאוּת
וְהָדָא לֹא בִמְחוּבָּר הִיא. וְהָא תַּנִּינָן מַשְׁקִין בֵּית הַשְּׁלָחִין בְּמוֹעֵד וּבַשְּׁבִיעִית.
אָמַר רִבִּי יוּדָן לְזְרָעִים שֶׁבּוֹ. רִבִּי מָנָא בָּעֵי מֵעַתָּה יְהֵא מוּתָּר לַחֲרוֹשׁ לָהֶן.

Rebbi Ḥuna went to Tyre and forbade them a kind of irrigation. Rebbi
Yose heard this and said, this is correct, is this not about [plants] connected
to the ground? But did we not state (Mishnah Mo'ed Qaṭan 1:1): "One
irrigates a field in intensive agriculture both during the intermediate days
of a holiday[105] and during the Sabbatical year?" Rebbi Yudan said, only
for the vegetables there[106]. Rebbi Mana said, then it should also be
permitted to plough for them[107]!

105   When normal agricultural work
is forbidden.

106   R. Ḥuna would have permitted
irrigation of plots planted with delicate
plants which would die if deprived of
water for any length of time. But the
"kind of irrigation" he forbade was one

to improve the soil.

107   To plough not for new seeds but
to loosen the earth for irrigation. This
is the opinion of R. Meïr in Mo'ed
Qaṭan 1:1; one is at a loss to understand
the position of the rabbis who forbid it.

(fol. 36b) **משנה ג:** בְּצָלִים שֶׁיָּרְדוּ עֲלֵיהֶן גְּשָׁמִים וְצִימְחוּ אִם הָיוּ הֶעָלִין שֶׁלָּהֶן שְׁחוֹרִים אֲסוּרִין. הוֹרִיקוּ הֲרֵי אִילוּ מוּתָּרִין. רִבִּי חֲנִינָא בֶּן אַנְטִיגְנָס אוֹמֵר אִם אֵינָן יְכוֹלִין לְהִיתָּלֵשׁ בֶּעָלִין שֶׁלָּהֶן אֲסוּרִין כְּנֶגֶד כֵּן מוֹצָאֵי שְׁבִיעִית מוּתָּרִין.

Mishnah 3: Onions[108] growing after it rained on them, if the leaves are black[109] they are forbidden, becoming green[110] they are permitted. Rebbi Ḥanina ben Antigonos[111] says, if they cannot be drawn out by their leaves they are forbidden; in the same case in the year after the Sabbatical they are permitted.

108 Onions planted in the sixth year on which rain descended after New Year's day of the Sabbatical.

109 Dark green. The dark color is taken as a sign that the onions ripened during the Sabbatical year; this makes the added part forbidden as after-growth.

110 Light green, color of the leaves of young onions.

111 Tanna of the third generation, specialist for the rules of the Temple.

(fol. 36d) **הלכה ג:** כֵּינֵי מַתְנִיתָא שְׁחוֹרִין אֲסוּרִין וִירוֹקִין מוּתָּרִין.

Halakhah 3: So is the Mishnah: Black are forbidden, green are permitted[112].

112 The expression הוֹרִיקוּ "becoming green" in the Mishnah is misleading. Young onions have light green leaves; as long as the leaves are light green the onions are permitted. (The Rome ms. reads here שְׁחוֹרִין מוּתָּרִין וִירוֹקִין אֲסוּרִין "black are permitted and green forbidden". Since the Halakhah does not discuss the statement, the Rome reading must be a scribal error.)

רִבִּי יוֹסֵי בְּשֵׁם רִבִּי יוֹחָנָן בָּצֵל שֶׁעֲקָרוֹ וּשְׁתָלוֹ מִכֵּיוָן שֶׁהִשְׁחִיר מִתְעַשֵּׂר לְפִי כוּלּוֹ.

רִבִּי חִייָה בְּשֵׁם רִבִּי יוֹחָנָן בָּצֵל שֶׁעֲקָרוֹ וּשְׁתָלוֹ מִכֵּיוָן שֶׁהִשְׁרִישׁ מִתְעַשֵּׂר לְפִי כוּלּוֹ.

וְלֹא שַׁנְייָא בֵּין שֶׁעֲקָרוֹ בַּשְּׁבִיעִית וּשְׁתָלוֹ לְמוֹצָאֵי שְׁבִיעִית בֵּין שֶׁעֲקָרוֹ בַּשְּׁבִיעִית.

Rebbi Yose in the name of Rebbi Joḥanan: An onion taken out of the ground and replanted once it darkened has to be tithed completely[113]. Rebbi Ḥiyya in the name of Rebbi Joḥanan: An onion taken out of the ground and replanted once it developed new roots has to be tithed completely. There is no difference whether it was taken out in the Sabbatical year and replanted in the year after or was taken out in the Sabbatical year.

113   As explained in the last sentence of this paragraph, one speaks of an onion growing in the Sabbatical and replanted in the following year. The Sabbatical produce is exempt from tithes but the growth of the following year is obligated. Since the new growth takes over, the entire onion plant is subject to tithes. The statement is quoted in the name of Rebbi Joḥanan in the Babli (*Nedarim* 59a) and rejected there.

רִבִּי זְעִירָא אָמַר מִכֵּיוָן שֶׁרָבָה עָלָיו הֶחָדָשׁ מוּתָּר. רִבִּי לָא רִבִּי אִימִּי תְּרַוֵּיהוֹן אֲמְרֵי אָסוּר. מַתְנִיתִין פְּלִינָא עַל רִבִּי לָא וְעַל רִבִּי אִימִּי. דְּתַנֵּי זֶה הַכְּלָל שֶׁהָיָה רִבִּי שִׁמְעוֹן אוֹמֵר מִשׁוּם רִבִּי יְהוֹשֻׁעַ כָּל־דָּבָר שֶׁיֵּשׁ לוֹ מַתִּירִין כְּגוֹן טֶבֶל וּמַעֲשֵׂר שֵׁנִי וְהֶקְדֵּשׁ וְחָדָשׁ לֹא נָתְנוּ לָהֶן חֲכָמִים שִׁעוּר אֶלָּא מִין בְּמִינוֹ בְּכָל־שֶׁהוּא וְשֶׁאֵינוֹ בְּמִינוֹ בְּנוֹתֵן טַעַם. וְכָל־דָּבָר שֶׁאֵין לוֹ מַתִּירִין כְּגוֹן תְּרוּמָה וְחַלָּה וְעָרְלָה וְכִלְאַיִם נָתְנוּ לָהֶן חֲכָמִים שִׁעוּר מִין בְּמִינוֹ וּשֶׁלֹּא בְמִינוֹ בְּנוֹתֵן טַעַם. הָתִיבוּן הֲרֵי שְׁבִיעִית הֲרֵי אֵין לָהּ מַתִּירִין וְלֹא נָתְנוּ לָהּ חֲכָמִים שִׁעוּר. אֲמַר לָהֶן לֹא אִם אֲמַרְתֶּם בַּשְּׁבִיעִית שֶׁאֵינָהּ אוֹסֶרֶת כָּל־שֶׁהוּא אֶלָּא בְּבִעוּר אֲבָל לַאֲכִילָה בְּנוֹתֵן טַעַם. מַה עָבְדִין לָהּ. רִבִּי הִילָא וְרִבִּי אִימִּי פְּתָרִין לָהּ בְּעֵירוּבִין אֲבָל בְּגִידּוּלִין חוֹמֶר הוּא בְגִידּוּלִין. דְּאָמַר רִבִּי זְעִירָא בְּשֵׁם רִבִּי יוֹנָתָן בָּצָל שֶׁל כִּלְאֵי הַכֶּרֶם שֶׁעֲקָרוֹ וּשְׁתָלוֹ אֲפִילוּ הוֹסִיף כַּמָּה אָסוּר שֶׁאֵין גִּידּוּלֵי אִיסוּר מַעֲלִין אֶת הָאוֹסֵר. מַתְנִיתָא פְּלִינָא עַל רִבִּי זְעִירָא דְּתַנִינַן גִּידּוּלֵי תְרוּמָה תְּרוּמָה וְגִידּוּלֵי גִידּוּלֵיהֶן חוּלִּין אֲבָל טֶבֶל וּמַעֲשֵׂר רִאשׁוֹן וּסְפִיחֵי שְׁבִיעִית וּתְרוּמַת מַעֲשֵׂר

וְהַמְּדוּמָע וְהַבִּיכּוּרִין גִּידוּלֵיהֶן חוּלִין. וְתַנֵּי עָלָהּ בְּמָה דְבָרִים אֲמוּרִים בְּדָבָר
שֶׁזַּרְעוֹ כָלָה. אֲבָל בְּדָבָר שֶׁאֵין שָׁאֵין זַרְעוֹ כָלָה גִּידוּלֵי כָלָה גִּידוּלִין אֲסוּרִין. מַה
עֲבַד לָהּ רִבִּי זְעִירָא. פָּתַר לָהּ בִּקְדוּשַׁת שְׁבִיעִית בְּבִיעוּר אֲבָל לְאָכִילָה כֵּיוָן
שֶׁרָבָה עָלָיו הֶחָדָשׁ מוּתָּר.

Rebbi Zeïra said, once the new growth is the majority it is
permitted[114]; Rebbi Hila and Rebbi Immi both say it is forbidden[115]. A
baraita disagrees with Rebbi Hila and Rebbi Immi, as it was stated[116]:
"This is the rule Rebbi Simeon proclaimed in the name of Rebbi Joshua:
For everything that may become permitted through some action, such as
ṭevel[117], Second Tithe[118], donations to the Temple[119], and new grain[120],
the Sages did not fix any limits, but a kind with its own is forbidden in the
minutest amount, a kind with a different kind if it can be tasted[121]. But
for everything that cannot become permitted through any action, such as
heave[122], *ḥallah,* and *orlah*[123], the Sages did fix as limit both a kind with
itself or with a different kind if it can be tasted. They objected[124]: but
there is the Sabbatical that admits no act to permit it and the Sages did not
fix a limit! He said to them, no. When you mention the Sabbatical, its
produce is forbidden in the minutest amount only after it must be
destroyed[125], but for food if it can be tasted." What do they do with it?
Rebbi Hila and Rebbi Immi explain it in mixtures, but as far as growing
plants are concerned, this is more severe since Rebbi Zeïra said in the
name of Rebbi Jonathan[126]: An onion of *kilaim* in a vineyard, taken out
of the ground and replanted, stays forbidden even if it grows enormously
because growth of something forbidden cannot neutralize the prohibition.
A Mishnah disagrees with Rebbi Zeïra as we have stated (*Terumot* 9:4): "A
growth from heave is heave but the growth from its growth is profane.

But the growth from *tevel*, First Tithe, aftergrowth of the Sabbatical, heave of the tithe, *dema'*, and First Fruits is profane." We have stated on this: "When is this true? If the seed disappears. But if the seed does not disappear even growth from growth is forbidden[127]." How does Rebbi Zeïra deal with this? He explains it that the sanctity of the Sabbatical applies when it must be destroyed, but for food once the new growth is the majority it is permitted.

114   If a plant was forbidden as aftergrowth of the Sabbatical, if it grew after the Sabbatical by more than 100% everything will be permitted.

115   In the Babli (*Nedarim* 57b), Rebbi Immi (Ammi) is quoted as having no answer.

116   Parallels in Babli *Nedarim* 58a, Yerushalmi *Nedarim* 6:8 (fol. 39d). The principle stated by R. Simeon is generally accepted.

117   Cf. *Peah* Chapter 1, Note 303. *Tevel* is forbidden but taking heave and tithes turns *tevel* into profane food.

118   Second tithe can be redeemed; the sanctity is transferred from the vegetables to the coins used for redemption (cf. Introduction to Tractate Demay, p. 348).

119   Not sacrifices but donations of valuables to the Temple. As long as these are the property of the Temple, any private use is larceny. Upon sale of the property by the Temple officials, the sold object is totally profane.

120   The grain crop of a year becomes permitted only upon presentation of the *'Omer* sacrifice on the 16th of Nisan (or, in the absence of a Temple, after the 16th of Nisan automatically). Therefore, early grain becomes permitted simply by waiting. [Summer grain that develops roots only after the 16th of Nisan is forbidden until the 16th of Nisan the following year. The climatic conditions in Israel do not permit the planting of summer wheat. Cf. *Orlah* 3:8, Philo *The Special Laws* II.125.]

121   In most cases, Babylonian authorities fixed the limit of something that can be tasted in foreign food at 1.667%.

122   Heave (and *Hallah* which is a kind of heave) must be eaten in purity by a Cohen or burned if impure. It can

never become profane food; cf. *Berakhot* Chapter 1, note 3.

123 Tree fruits during the first three years after planting are forbidden for all use (*Lev.* 19:23).

124 Even though התיבון is Galilean Aramaic, it takes the place of אמרו לו in the Babylonian version and is part of the *baraita*.

125 Cf. Mishnah 7:10 and Note 2. Since it is written (*Lev.* 25:7) "For your domestic animals and the wild animals on your Land shall be all its produce for food." One concludes from this that produce taken during the Sabbatical may be eaten by humans only as long as there is similar produce for the wild animals in the fields. If there is nothing left for the wild animals,

produce taken for humans must be destroyed.

126 In the Rome ms., this statement is in the name of a long and garbled list of tradents ending with R. Johanan. This name seems more likely since R. Zeïra often quotes R. Johanan and a similar statement in the Babli (*Nedarim* 57b) is also attributed to R. Johanan. The case discussed there is one of 'orlah, but both 'orlah and *kilaim* in a vineyard are forbidden for all usufruct and follow the same principles. "Enormously" is quantified in the Babli as "200 fold."

127 Neither Yerushalmi nor Babli (*Nedarim* 60a) give an example of a new plant growing from seeds that remain recognizable.

רְבִּי אַבָּהוּ עָל לְאַרְבֵּל וְאִיתְקַבֵּל גַּבֵּי אַבָּא בַּר בִּנְיָמִין אָתוּן וּשְׁאָלוּן לֵיהּ בְּאִילֵּין בְּצָלַיָּא וְהוֹרֵי לוֹן הָדָא דְרִבִּי זְעִירָא מִכֵּיוָן שֶׁרָבָה עָלָיו הֶחָדָשׁ מוּתָּר. חֲמָתוֹן סְמִיכִין עֲלוֹי אָמַר (fol. 37a) לוֹן אֲנִי לֹא אָמַרְתִּי אֶלָּא בְּמוּרְכָּנִין. אָמַר רִבִּי יוֹדָה בַּר פָּזִי אֲנָא יְדַע רֹאשָׁהּ וְסוֹפָהּ כַּד דְּשָׁמַע רִבִּי לָא וְרִבִּי אִימִי פְּלִיגִין שְׁרַע מִינֵּיהּ.

Rebbi Abbahu went up to Arbel[128] and was received by Abba bar Benjamin. They came and asked him about these onions; he taught them the statement of Rebbi Zeïra[129] "once the new growth is the majority it is permitted." He saw them relying on him; then he said to them: I was referring only to those that are bent down[130] Rebbi Jehudah bar Pazi said, I know beginning and end[131]; when he heard that Rebbi Hila and Rebbi Ammi disagreed, he shrank from it.

128   Even though R. Abbahu was from Caesarea Philippi (Banias), on his way to Arbel he had to pass through low lying Tiberias and then climb up to the plane of Ḥittim.

129   Since R. Abbahu was much older than R. Zeïra, one cannot translate "following R. Zeïra".

130   The unlikely case that the leaves of the onions arched down, rather than go straight up. This practically annulled his former ruling. [The Babli, *Nedarim* 58a, reads מדוכנים "broken ones".]

131   Of the story. He asserts that R. Abbahu formally rescinded his former ruling and did not simply restrict it to an improbable case.

(fol. 36b) **משנה ד**: מֵאֵימָתַי מוּתָּר אָדָם לִיקַח יֶרֶק בְּמוֹצָאֵי שְׁבִיעִית מִשֶּׁיֶּעֱשֶׂה כַּיּוֹצֵא בָהּ. עָשָׂה הַבַּכִּיר הִתִּיר הָאָפֵל. רִבִּי הִתִּיר לִיקַח יֶרֶק מוֹצָאֵי שְׁבִיעִית מִיַּד.

Mishnah 4: When may one buy vegetables in the year following the Sabbatical? After similar ones are ready. When the early ripe one is ready, the late is permitted. Rebbi permitted to buy vegetables immediately after the end of the Sabbatical[132].

132   For another version of the story, see *Peah* Chapter 7, Notes 80-81. The last sentence is also in Tosephta Ševiit 5:1.

(fol. 37a) **הלכה ד**: בָּרִאשׁוֹנָה הָיָה הַיֶּרֶק אָסוּר בִּסְפָרֵי אֶרֶץ יִשְׂרָאֵל הִתְקִינוּ שֶׁיְּהֵא הַיֶּרֶק מוּתָּר בִּסְפָרֵי אֶרֶץ יִשְׂרָאֵל. אַף עַל פִּי כֵן הָיָה אָסוּר לְהָבִיא יֶרֶק

מְחוֹץ לָאָרֶץ לָאָרֶץ. הִתְקִינוּ שֶׁיְּהֵא מוּתָּר לְהָבִיא יָרֶק מְחוֹץ לָאָרֶץ לָאָרֶץ. אַף
עַל פִּי כֵן הָיָה אָסוּר לִיקַח יָרֶק בְּמוֹצָאֵי שְׁבִיעִית מִיַּד. רִבִּי הִתִּיר לִיקַח יָרֶק
מוֹצָאֵי שְׁבִיעִית מִיַּד בַּר מִן קַפְלוֹטָא. מַה עֲבְדִיּוּן לֵיהּ צִיפּוֹרָיֵי אַלְבִּשׁוּנֵיהּ סַקָּא
וְקִיטְמָא. וְאַיְיתוֹנֵיהּ קוֹמֵי רִבִּי. אָמְרִין לֵיהּ מַה חָטָא דֵין מִן כָּל־יַרְקָא וְשָׁרָא
לֵיהּ הוֹן.

Halakhah 4: Originally, vegetable was forbidden at border settlements
of the Land of Israel. They decreed that vegetable should be permitted at
border settlements of the Land of Israel but it would still be forbidden to
import vegetables from outside into the Land. Then they decreed that it
was permitted to import vegetables from outside into the Land but it
would still be forbidden to buy vegetables immediately after the end of
the Sabbatical. Rebbi permitted to buy vegetables immediately after the
end of the Sabbatical except for leeks. What did the Sepphorians do?
They clothed one specimen in sack and ashes and brought it before Rebbi,
saying what sin did this one commit among all vegetables? He permitted
it to them[133].

133   It will be clear from the next
two paragraphs that the entire develop-
ment, from permitting vegetables at
border settlements to the general
permission (a) to import vegetables into
the Land of Israel, (b) to buy
vegetables immediately after New
Year's Day of the following year,
happened during Rebbi's presidency.

As long as the rules of impurity can be
kept strictly, one would forbid
importation at least of vegetables since
(a) some soil might cling to vegetables
transported with their roots (Babli
Nedarim 53b) and (b) the vegetables
will be moistened for the transport and,
therefore, be impure (cf. *Demay*,
Chapter 2, Notes 136-137).

עוּלָא בַּר יִשְׁמָעֵאל בְּשֵׁם רִבִּי חֲנִינָה. רִבִּי וְרִבִּי יוֹסֵי בַּר יְהוּדָה נַחְתּוּן לְעַכּוֹ.
וְאִיתְקַבְּלוּן גַּבֵּי רִבִּי מָנָא. אָמַר לָהֶן רִבִּי עָשָׂה לָנוּ לִפַס אֶחָד שֶׁל יָרֶק עֲבַד לֵיהּ

קוּפָּד. לְמָחָר אָמַר לֵיהּ עֲשֵׂה לָנוּ לְפַס אֶחָד שֶׁל יָרָק עֲבַד לֵיהּ תַּרְנְגוֹלְתָּא. אָמַר
רַבִּי נִיכָּר הוּא זֶה שֶׁהוּא מִפֶּתַח שֶׁל סָמָאֵל.[134]   אָמַר לֵיהּ רִבִּי יוֹסֵי בֵּי רִבִּי
יְהוּדָה אֲפִילוּ מִפֶּתַח שֶׁל סָמָאֵל אֵינוּ. וְלָמָּה עֲבַד כֵּן דּוּ תַלְמִיד מִן תַּלְמִידוֹי
דְּרִבִּי יוּדָה. דְּרִבִּי יוּדָה אָמַר הַיָּרָק אָסוּר בִּסְפָרֵי אֶרֶץ יִשְׂרָאֵל. כַּד אֲתָא לְגַבֵּהּ
תַּנֵּי לֵהּ עוּבְדָא. אָמַר לֵיהּ צָרִיךְ הֲוֵיתָה עֲבִיד כְּוָתִין.

Ulla bar Ismael in the name of Rebbi Ḥanina: Rebbi and Rebbi Yose
ben Rebbi Jehudah descended into Acco and were received by Rebbi
Mana[135]. Rebbi said to them, make us a dish[136] of vegetables; he made
him red meat. The next day, he said again make us a dish of vegetables;
he made him chicken. Rebbi said, this one is recognizable as coming from
the door of Samaël[137]. Rebbi Yose ben Rebbi Jehudah said to him, he is
not even coming from the door of Samaël. Why did he do this? Because
he is a student from the students of Rebbi Jehudah, and Rebbi Jehudah
said vegetables are forbidden in the border settlements of the Land of
Israel. When he met him, he told him the facts[138]. He said to him, you
should have acted following us[139].

134   Reading of the Rome ms.
Venice text: שמואל.

135   Since this R. Mana is a Tanna,
he precedes the Amora R. Mana I by at
least one generation. He is not mentioned again in the Talmudim. As
noted in Halakhah 1, Acco was a border town since the domain between the
Roman road leading North from Acco
and the sea was Gentile territory.

136   Cf. *Peah* p. 279.

137   The angel ruling over hell.

Rebbi took R. Mana's actions as
showing off his wealth.

138   Rebbi Mana confirmed that he
served meat only because he followed
the teachings of R. Jehudah of the
previous generation.

139   This implies that Rebbi's decree
permitting buying vegetables was not a
private ruling but an official pro-
nouncement by Rebbi's Academy acting
as a kind of Synhedrion.

תַּמָּן תַּנִּינָן מִן הַיֶּרֶק מוּתָּר בְּיַרְקוֹת הַשָּׂדֶה שֶׁהוּא שֵׁם לְוָי. וְתַנֵּי עָלָהּ הַנּוֹדֵר מִן
הַיֶּרֶק בַּשְּׁבִיעִית אָסוּר אַף בְּיַרְקוֹת הַשָּׂדֶה. תַּנֵּי רְבִּי קְרִיסְפָּא בְּשֵׁם רְבִּי חֲנַנְיָה
בֶּן גַּמְלִיאֵל וְאָמַר טַעְמָא. הָדָא דְתֵימַר עַד שֶׁלֹּא הִתִּיר רְבִּי לְהָבִיא יֶרֶק מִחוּץ
לָאָרֶץ לָאָרֶץ אֲבָל מִשֶּׁהִתִּיר רְבִּי לְהָבִיא יֶרֶק מִחוּץ לָאָרֶץ לָאָרֶץ. הִיא שְׁבִיעִית
הִיא שְׁאָר שְׁנֵי שָׁבוּעַ. רְבִּי יוֹסֵי בַּר חֲנִינָא אוֹמֵר עוּלְשִׁין חֲשׁוּבוֹת הֵן לְטַמֵּא
טוּמְאַת אוֹכְלִין בַּשְּׁבִיעִית. הָדָא דְתֵימַר עַד שֶׁלֹּא הִתִּיר רְבִּי. אֲבָל מִשֶּׁהִתִּיר
הִיא שְׁבִיעִית הִיא שְׁאָר שְׁנֵי שָׁבוּעַ.

There[140], we have stated: "From vegetables", he is permitted field vegetables because these have an additional name. We have stated on that: "He who makes a vow to abstain from vegetables in the Sabbatical is also forbidden field vegetables[141]." Rebbi Crispus stated the reason in the name of Rebbi Ḥananiah ben Gamliel[142]: That means, as long as Rebbi did not permit to import vegetables into the Land. But since Rebbi permitted to import vegetables into the Land there is no difference between the Sabbatical and the remaining years of the Sabbatical cycle. Rebbi Yose bar Ḥanina says, endives[143] are important enough to become impure as food in the Seventh year. That means, as long as Rebbi did not permit. But since he permitted, there is no difference between the Sabbatical and the remaining years of the Sabbatical cycle[144].

140 Mishnah *Nedarim* 6:13. "He who vows to abstain from vegetables ..." The paragraph is copied in *Nedarim* 6:13, fol. 39d; a parallel is in the Babli (*Nedarim* 53a-b).

141 According to the commentary to *Nedarim* from the school of Rashi, usually one means by "vegetables"

those grown in irrigated garden beds. But in the Sabbatical year, all garden beds also are abandoned to the poor and even well-to-do persons will use field vegetables. According to R. Nissim Gerondi, garden beds will not yield anything in the Sabbatical since nothing is planted and, usually, garden

beds are carefully harvested, so there
will be no spontaneous growth.

142   In the Babli (*Nedarim* 53b), R.
Ḥananiah ben Gamliel states that one
imports vegetables into the Land. This
refers to the aftermath of the war of
Bar Kokhba, about 60 years prior to
Rebbi's activity, and does not imply
official sanctioning.

143   One of the bitter herbs admis-

sible for Passover; the implication here
is that endives were not grown in
extensive agriculture but considered as
a weed. Hence, in regular years they
are not food and cannot become
impure.

144   Since garden vegetables are
available year round during the
Sabbatical.

הֲווֹן בְּעָיִין מֵימַר לָא פְּלוֹגִין.   אַשְׁכַּח תַּנֵּי רבִּי יוֹדָה אָמַר עַד גְּזִיב.   רבִּי שִׁמְעוֹן
אוֹמֵר עַד אֲמָנָה.

They wanted to say that there is no disagreement[145]. It was found
stated: Rebbi Judah said, up to Akhzib. Rebbi Simeon is saying, up to
Amanus.

145   The definition of the Land,
important for this Halakhah and the
next, was assumed to be given by the
Tosephta quoted in Halakhah 1
according to everybody. Here, it is
stated that R. Simeon disagrees and
does not restrict the laws of the Holy
Land to the territory settled by the

returnees from Babylonia. In the next
two Mishnaiot, Rebbi agrees with R.
Simeon. This seems to indicate that for
the Yerushalmi, practice should follow
the majority, R. Simeon and Rebbi. In
the Babli, only R. Jehudah's position is
ever mentioned and practice follows
him.

(fol. 36b) **משנה ה**: אֵין מוֹצִיאִין שֶׁמֶן שְׂרֵיפָה וּפֵירוֹת שְׁבִיעִית מֵהָאָרֶץ לְחוּצָה לָאָרֶץ. אָמַר רִבִּי שָׁמַעְתִּי בְּפֵירוּשׁ שֶׁמּוֹצִיאִין לְסוּרְיָה וְאֵין מוֹצִיאִין לְחוּצָה לָאָרֶץ.

Mishnah 5: One does not export oil to be burned[146] and produce of the Sabbatical from the Land to outside the Land. Rebbi said, I heard explicitly that one exports to Syria but not to outside the Land.

146   Olive oil given for heave that became impure and must be burned. It may be used as fuel but must still be treated as holy and cannot be contaminated with the impurity of Gentile soil. [In *Sifra Behar Pereq* 1(9), the statement of Rebbi is attributed to R. Simeon.]

(fol. 37a) **הלכה ה**: תַּנֵּי פֵּירוֹת הָאָרֶץ שֶׁיָּצְאוּ לְחוּץ לָאָרֶץ מִתְבַּעֲרִין בִּמְקוֹמָן דִּבְרֵי רִבִּי שִׁמְעוֹן. רִבִּי שִׁמְעוֹן בֶּן אֶלְעָזָר אוֹמֵר מְבִיאָן לָאָרֶץ וּמְבַעֲרָן דִּכְתִיב בְּאַרְצֶךָ תִּהְיֶה כָל־תְּבוּאָתָהּ לֶאֱכוֹל. אָמַר רִבִּי יַעֲקֹב בַּר אָחָא. הוֹרֵי רִבִּי אִמִּי כְהֵן תַּנְיָא קַמַּיָּא לְקוּלָּא. אָמַר רִבִּי הִילָא וּבִלְבַד שֶׁלֹּא יַעֲבִירֵם מִמָּקוֹם לְמָקוֹם.

Halakhah 5: It was stated: "Produce of the Land that was exported is removed at its place, the words of Rebbi Simeon. Rebbi Simeon ben Eleazar says, one returns it to the Land and removes it, as it is written (*Lev.* 25:7): 'In your Land shall all its produce be food.'"[147] Rebbi Jacob bar Aḥa said, Rebbi Immi taught following the first Tanna for leniency[148]. Rebbi Hila said, but he should not move it from place to place[149].

147   Tosephta 5:1. In the Tosephta, the opinion of R. Simeon is attributed to Rebbi, in the Babli (*Pesaḥim* 52b) it is anonymous. In the Land, the produce has to be removed (e. g., by being given away to the poor to be eaten) if nothing of its kind is left on the fields for wild animals.

148   In the Babli, this ruling is attributed to R. Abbahu.

149   When the time of removal comes, the produce should be destroyed

at its place since Sabbatical fruit must be eaten in the Land. According to Rashi in *Pesaḥim*, everybody will agree that the produce may be returned to the Land to be given to the local poor.

(fol. 36b) **משנה ו**: אֵין מְבִיאִין תְּרוּמָה מֵחוּצָה לָאָרֶץ לָאָרֶץ. אָמַר רבִּי שָׁמַעְתִּי בְּפֵירוּשׁ שֶׁמּוֹצִיאִין מִסוּרְיָה וְאֵין מְבִיאִין מֵחוּצָה לָאָרֶץ.

Mishnah 6: One does not bring heave from outside the Land into the Land. Rebbi said, I heard explicitly that one may bring from Syria but not from outside the Land[150].

150   Even though heave can be given outside the Land in a way that leaves it ritually pure, since heave is a duty on the Land its status should not be diminished by accepting outside heave into the Land. The only problem is Syria according to Rebbi Simeon and Rebbi; they declare heave of Syria to be genuine.

(fol. 37a) **הלכה ה**: תַּמָּן תַּנִּינָן אֲרִיסְטוֹן הֵבִיא בִיכּוּרִים מֵאַסְפַּמְיָא וְקִיבְּלוּ מִמֶּנּוּ. וְיָבִיא תְרוּמָה. אָמַר רבִּי הוֹשַׁעְיָה בִּיכּוּרִים בָּאַחֲרָיוּת בְּעָלִים. תְּרוּמָה אֵינָהּ בָּאַחֲרָיוּת בְּעָלִים. אִם אָמַר אַתְּ כֵּן אַף הֵן מְרַדְּפִין אַחֲרֵיהֶם לְשָׁם.

Halakhah 5: There[151], we have stated: "Ariston brought First Fruits[152] from Apamea and they received them from him." Why could he not bring heave? Rebbi Hoshaia said, First Fruits are the responsibility of the owners, heave is not the responsibility of the owners. If you would say so, they would run after it there.

151   Mishnah *Ḥallah* 4:12. There, the text is better, אממיא Apamea in Syria. In the Babli in particular, Apamea is usually given as איספמיא which occasionally means "Spain".

152   *Deut.* 26:1-11. The text makes it quite clear that the obligation of bringing First Fruits is discharged only upon delivery of the fruits in the Temple courtyard. Heave is given to the Cohen from the barn; the transport is at the Cohen's expense. If heave from Syria were acceptable, a Cohen might be tempted to leave the Land for Syria to collect heave from the Jews there.

כלל גדול פרק שביעי

(fol. 37a) **משנה א:** כְּלָל גָּדוֹל אָמְרוּ בַּשְּׁבִיעִית כָּל־שֶׁהוּא מַאֲכַל אָדָם וּמַאֲכַל בְּהֵמָה וּמִמִּין הַצּוֹבְעִים וְאֵינוֹ מִתְקַיֵּם בָּאָרֶץ יֵשׁ לוֹ שְׁבִיעִית וּלְדָמָיו שְׁבִיעִית. יֵשׁ לוֹ בִיעוּר וּלְדָמָיו בִיעוּר.

Mishnah 1: They established a comprehensive principle[1] for the Sabbatical: Everything that is food for humans or animals or material for dye and cannot be preserved in the ground[2] is subject to the Sabbatical and its proceeds are subject to the Sabbatical[3]; it is subject to removal and its proceeds are subject to removal[4].

1   A discussion of the notion "comprehensive principle" is in *Šabbat* 7:1 (Babli *Šabbat* 68a).

2   Roots that stay edible in the ground until after the Sabbatical are not subject to removal since they are always available to wild animals.

3   If Sabbatical produce is sold, its proceeds become Sabbatical and must be used to buy other produce that has

to be eaten in the Land under the rules of the Sabbatical.

4   If nothing of the kind for which the money was obtained is left on the fields for wild animals, the money must be spent for food that has to be distributed to the poor. In the unlikely case that there are no poor, the money has to be thrown into the Dead Sea.

(fol. 37b) **הלכה א:** צְבָעִין לְאָדָם מַהוּ שֶׁיְּהֵא עֲלֵיהֶן קְדוּשַׁת שְׁבִיעִית. נִישְׁמְעִינָהּ מִן הָדָא לָכֶם כָּל־שֶׁהוּא צוֹרֶךְ לָכֶם. וְתַגֵּי עֲלָהּ כְּגוֹן אֲכִילָה וּשְׁתִיָּה וְסִיכָה וּצְבִיעָה. יָצְאַת מְלוּגְמָא שֶׁאֵינָהּ אֶלָּא לְחוֹלִין. יָצְאַת אֲלֵינְתִּין שֶׁאֵינוֹ אֶלָּא לַתַּפִּילִין. רִבִּי יוֹנָה בְּעֵי וְלָמָּה יָצְאַת מְלוּגְמָא שֶׁאֵין עָלֶיהָ קְדוּשַׁת שְׁבִיעִית.

וְהָתַנֵּי דֵּין וְצָד וְזֶרַע אִיסְטִיס שֶׁזּוֹרְעִין אוֹתָן בְּמוֹצָאֵי שְׁבִיעִית קְדוּשַׁת שְׁבִיעִית

חָלָה עֲלֵיהֶם. מַיי כְדוֹן לָכֶם הַשָּׁוֶה לְכָלְכֶם. רִבִּי יוֹסֵי בְּשֵׁם רִבִּי לָא שָׁמַע מִן

הָדָא תִהְיֶה. אַף לְהַדְלָקַת הַנֵּר וְלִצְבּוֹעַ בּוֹ צֶבַע. וְלֹא נִמְצָא מְאַבֵּד אֶת אוֹכְלֵי

בְהֵמָה. תִּיפְתָּר בִּצְבוּעִין לְאָדָם. אָמַר רִבִּי מָנָא תִּיפְתָּר בְּאָכְלֵי בְהֵמָה לְאָדָם

וְלֵית אַתְּ שָׁמַע מִנֵּיהּ כְּלוּם.

Halakhah 1: Does the sanctity of the Sabbatical fall on dyes for humans[5]? Let us hear from the following (*Lev.* 25:6): "For you", all that is needed by you[6]. We have stated on that: For example eating, drinking, anointing, and coloring. This excludes wound dressing which is only for the sick. This excludes *olentia*[7] which are only for the malodorous. Rebbi Jonah asked: Why does one exclude wound dressing because the sanctity of the Sabbatical cannot fall on it? But did we not state[8]: "Sanctity of the Sabbatical falls on *din, ṣad*, and indigo seed that one sows after the end of the Sabbatical." What is that? "For you", for all of you equally. Rebbi Yose in the name of Rebbi Hila understood it from the following (*Lev.* 25:7)[9]: "Shall be", even to kindle the light and to dye. Does this not destroy animal feed? Rebbi Mana said, explain it if animal feed is used for human needs and you cannot infer anything from it[10].

5   Cosmetics.

6   "The Sabbath of the Land shall be for you (plural) to eat, for you (singular), your slave, and your hand-maiden, your hired hand and your (Gentile) resident who dwell with you." The first "for you" seems to be superfluous. Since the verse gives permission to a slave owner to eat Sabbatical produce, it follows that the rich may eat. The poor are given permission to eat in *Ex.* 23:11: "The Seventh Year you shall let lie fallow and abandon it so that the needy of your people may eat; the remainder the wild animals of the field shall eat." It is inferred that "for you" means all legitimate human needs that apply to all equally.

7   See *Berakhot*, pp. 87, 501. תפילין is derived from Arabic תַּפַּל "mal

odorous".

8   A related text is in Tosephta 5:7: "*Din, Bṣr*, and indigo usually are sown after the end of the Sabbatical." As R. S. Lieberman notes, the identity of the first two plants can no longer be established. The isatis plant is used as dye (indigo) but the seeds are good only for sowing.   Hence, seeds harvested in the Sabbatical retain their Sabbatical quality even after the end of the year. {For דן cf. Arabic דאן "to be of inferior quality", for צד Arabic צדא "rust".}

The argument goes as follows: It is stated in Mishnah 8:1 that animal feed may be used to make wound dressing; only Sabbatical human food may not be used. In itself, animal feed has the sanctity of the Sabbatical and cannot be used for industrial purposes. Then one cannot understand why dyestuff seeds retain their sanctity but wound dressing does not. The answer is that the next argument will show that human needs have precedence over animal needs but once the product is no longer available for all of mankind it cannot have sanctity attached.

9   *Sifra Behar Pereq* 1(10). "For your domestic animal and the beast in your Land shall be all its yield as feed." It is clear from the preceding verse that not *all* growth of the Sabbatical is for animals since humans were given prior permission to eat it. Therefore, the expression "shall be" is interpreted as: All that is not used for humans shall be animal feed.

10   For potential human food.

(fol. 37a) **משנה ב**: וְאֵי זֶה זֶה זֶה עָלֶה הַלּוּף הַשּׁוֹטֶה. הָרִנְדְּנָה הָעוּלְשִׁין וְהַכְּרֵשִׁין וְהָרְגִילָה וְנֵץ הֶחָלָב. וּמַאֲכַל בְּהֵמָה הַחוֹחִים וְהַדַּרְדָּרִים. וּמִמִּין הַצּוֹבְעִים סְפִיחֵי אַסְטִיס וְקוֹצָה יֵשׁ לָהֶן שְׁבִיעִית וְלִדְמֵיהֶן שְׁבִיעִית. יֵשׁ לָהֶן בִּיעוּר וְלִדְמֵיהֶן בִּיעוּר.

Mishnah 2: What are these? This is the leaf of wild arum[11], mint[12], endives[13], leeks[14], purslain[15] and *milk bud*[16]. Animal feed, thistles and thorns. Dyestuffs, the wild growth of isatis and safflower[17]. These are

subject to the Sabbatical and their proceeds are subject to the Sabbatical;
both they and their proceeds are subject to removal.

11   Cf. *Kilaim* 2:5, Note 69.

12   Definition of Maimonides and
Arukh (אלנענע). All sources except the
Leyden ms. read הדנדה.

13   Cf. *Kilaim* 1:2, Note 41.

14   Cf. *Kilaim* 1:2, Note 42.

15   Definition of Maimonides and
Arukh, Arabic רגלה.

16.   Definition of Maimonides in the
majority of mss.: "parsley". Some
Maimonides mss.: "Mahaleb." Arukh:
White flowers, some say a grass pro-

ducing wolf's milk. The Gaonic
commentary to *Uqezin*: Arabic חרשף
"artichoke; anything rough and hard".
Since artichokes for human food are
קינרס, the thistles referred to here are
animal feed.

17   Maimonides notes that "some
commentators explain קוצה as safflower;" he expresses no opinion.
Arukh defines as "madder", but madder
appears in Mishnah 4 as פואה under a
different legal category.

(fol. 37b) **הלכה ב:** צִבְעִין לִבְהֵמָה מַהוּ שֶׁיְּהֵא עֲלֵיהֶן קְדוּשַׁת שְׁבִיעִית.
נִישְׁמְעִינָהּ מִן הָדָא עִיקַר הַוֶּרֶד וְעִיקַר הָאַנָּה וְעִיקַר הָאוֹג אֵין בָּהֶן קְדוּשַׁת
שְׁבִיעִית. מִינֵי (כְּנִיסוֹת) מַהוּ שֶׁיְּהֵא עֲלֵיהֶן קְדוּשַׁת שְׁבִיעִית. נִישְׁמְעִינָהּ מִן הָדָא
הַיַּרְעֲנִין וְהַבּוֹרִית וְהָאָהָל יֵשׁ לָהֶן קְדוּשַׁת שְׁבִיעִית. בְּשָׂמִים מַהוּ שֶׁיְּהֵא עֲלֵיהֶן
קְדוּשַׁת שְׁבִיעִית. נִישְׁמְעִינָהּ מִן הָדָא הַפַּרְחָלָבָן וְהָאוֹרֶן[18] אֵין עֲלֵיהֶן קְדוּשַׁת
שְׁבִיעִית. חֲבֵרַיָּיא דְּרָבִּי שִׁמְעוֹן הוּא. דְּרָבִּי שִׁמְעוֹן אָמַר אֵין לְקְטָף שְׁבִיעִית
מִפְּנֵי שֶׁאֵינוֹ פְרִי. רָבִּי שְׁמוּאֵל בְּשֵׁם רָבִּי אַבָּהוּ תִּיפְּתָּר דִּבְרֵי הַכֹּל כְּהָדָא
נְסוֹרָתָה. מִינֵי אַדְלָקוֹת מַה אִית לָךְ כְּגוֹן הָהֶן פְּקוּעָה.

Halakhah 2: Does the sanctity of the Sabbatical fall on dyes for
animals? Let us hear from the following[19]: "Roots of rose, thornbush, and
sumac have no sanctity of the Sabbatical." Does the sanctity of the
Sabbatical fall on cleansing materials[20]? Let us hear from the following:
Asphodel[21], potash[22], and aloë fall under the sanctity of the Sabbatical.

Does the sanctity of the Sabbatical fall on perfumes? Let us hear from the following: *Parḥalabin*[23] and laurel trees have no sanctity of the Sabbatical. The colleagues: This is by Rebbi Simeon, since Rebbi Simeon said[24]: Balsamum has no sanctity of the Sabbatical since it is no fruit. Rebbi Samuel in the name of Rebbi Abbahu: Explain it according to everybody referring to jonquil[25]. What about fuel, for example oakum[26]?

18   Reading of the Rome ms. Leyden: אורז "rice".

19   In Tosephta 5:3, rose root is mentioned together with pine roots; in Tosephta 5:6, thornbush root is mentioned with carob tree root. The Tosephta agrees that these have no sanctity in the Sabbatical. Perhaps these roots were used as dye for animals (to designate the owner?). For sumac, cf. *Peah*, Chapter 1 Note 243.

20   Reading כְּבִיסוֹת "cleaning agents" instead of כניסות "entrances" with all commentators. Rome ms: סכוכות "glasses".

21   A plant used by Palestinian Bedouin to clean their hands [E. Hare-

ubeni, מצמחי הארץ, *Sinai* 4(1939) 622-624.]

22   Potash obtained by burning salty plants.

23   The identity of this plant has not been determined. In the Tosephta (5:6): הפרחבלין. It is possible to read in the Leyden ms. הפרח לבן which Kohut takes as "flower of the styrax (لبنى)". This fits the context but not the grammar, since it would have to be פרח הלָבָן.

24   Mishnah 7:9.

25   Persian and Arabic נסרין, a very aromatic flower.

26   The answer to this question, from the Tosephta, is given at the end of the Halakhah.

וְהָהֶן וֶרֶד תַּנֵּי בָּהּ תְּלַת מִילִין. עָלִין שֶׁלּוֹ יֵשׁ לָהֶן שְׁבִיעִית וְלִדְמֵיהֶן שְׁבִיעִית. יֵשׁ לָהֶן בִּיעוּר וְלִדְמֵיהֶן בִּיעוּר. פִּיקָה שֶׁלּוֹ יֵשׁ לָהּ שְׁבִיעִית וְלִדְמֵיהֶן שְׁבִיעִית. אֵין לוֹ בִּיעוּר וְלֹא לִדְמֶיהָ בִּיעוּר. עִיקָּר שֶׁלּוֹ אֵין לוֹ שְׁבִיעִית וְלֹא לְדָמָיו שְׁבִיעִית אֵין לוֹ בִּיעוּר וְלֹא לְדָמָיו בִּיעוּר. רִבִּי יִרְמְיָה בְּעָא קוֹמֵי רִבִּי אַבָּהוּ מַהוּ לִכְבּוֹשׁ מִן הָהֶן וֶרֶד. אָמַר לוֹ וְכִי יֵשׁ לוֹ מְלָאכָה אֶחֶרֶת. תַּנֵּי רִבִּי חִייָא אוֹכֶל אָדָם הוּא.

About roses, three things were stated: Their leaves are subject to the
Sabbatical and so are their proceeds; they are subject to removal and so
are their proceeds. Their spine[27] is subject to the Sabbatical and so are its
proceeds; it is not subject to removal, neither are its proceeds. Its root is
not subject to the Sabbatical nor are its proceeds; it is not subject to
removal, neither are its proceeds[28]. Rebbi Jeremiah asked before Rebbi
Abbahu: May one make preserves from roses[29]? He said to him, do they
have any other use? Rebbi Ḥiyya stated that it is human food.

27   Translation by Musaphia.   In general, Sabbatical produce may not
Usually, פיקה means "small globe". Rose   be cooked if it can be eaten raw. R.
wood may be used industrially and is   Abbahu notes that rose leaves cannot
subject to the Sabbatical. The plant is   be eaten raw. But as human food they
a perennial and need not be removed.   fall under the rules of the Sabbatical;
28   Tosephta 5:3.   this implies that it must be permitted to
29   In Mishnah 7:10, it is stated that make preserves from rose leaves.
rose leaves were preserved in olive oil.

הוֹרֵי רִבִּי מָנָא אוֹרֶסָטִין שָׁרֵי קִטְרָטוֹן שָׁרֵי מִירְסִנָטוֹן שָׁרֵי דרמינון שָׁרֵי
אִידְרוֹמִירוֹן אָסוּר דִיוֹמִילָן אָסוּר.

Rebbi Mana taught: *orosatin*[30] is permitted, *kitraton*[31] is permitted,
myrsinaton[32] is permitted, *drmynwn*[33] is permitted, *hydromyron*[34] is
forbidden, *diomelon*[35] is forbidden.

30   Probably *rosatum, i,* n. "rose   in medical use in his time.
wine", also "preserves of roses" (Api-   31   Latin *citratus, a, um,* adj.,
cius). The Leyden ms. has a second   "steeped in citrus oil" (Pliny). Compare
form אודורוסטין (in the Rome ms.   also *citreum* "citron"; *citrium* "a kind of
אודורודוסטין) which Musaphia has ex-   gourd."
plained as ὑδρορόσατον "rose water",   32   Cf. Latin *myrtites, ae,* m., from

Greek μυρτίτης οἶνος, "myrtle wine".

33   No reasonable explanation of
this word has been offered; Musaphia
conjectures Greek ῥοδόμυρον, ῥόδινον
μύρον "rose ointment." {Kohout thinks
of absinth, Farsi درنه *darmneh*. But the
word cannot mean a plant; it designates
food or drink made from the plant
whose name would be a composite like
(درنه رومى.)

34   The Venice print has אידרוטיירון
but the Leyden ms. אידרומירון as already
conjectured by most Hebrew lexicographers. Kohout notes that the closest
word is ὑδρόμηλον, τό "drink of water

and μηλόμηλι, honey flavored with
quinces". He conjectures that it should
be *ὑδρόμυρρον for "myrrh water" but
notes that this word is not found in the
dictionaries. {Cf. Greek ὑγρόμυρον
"liquid ointment" (E. G.)}

35   Reading of the Leyden ms. Cf.
perhaps Greek διὰ μελίτων "salve
made from honey." (E. G.)

The Venice print and Rome ms.
have דיומידן which the lexicographers
read with Musaphia as דימורון (Syriac
דימירו), Greek διὰ μόρων "medicine
from black mulberry juice and honey".

צִיפּוֹרָיֵי שָׁאֲלוּן לְרִבִּי אִימִי מַהוּ לְחַטֵּן בְּחוֹחִין.[36]   אָמַר לוֹ אַתּוּן אֲמָרִין בְּשֵׁם
רִבִּי חֲנִינָה אֲפִילוּ עֲלֵי קִינָרִיסָא[37] שָׁרֵי. אָמַר רִבִּי יֹאשָׁיָה לְעוֹבְדָּא וּסְמוֹךְ עָלַיי.
אָמַר רִבִּי יֹאשָׁיָה אֵין לָךְ מְיוּחָד לִבְהֵמָה אֶלָּא חָצִיר בִּלְבַד וּשְׁלָקָחוֹ לְחַטִּין בּוֹ
מוּתָּר לְחַטֵּן בּוֹ.

The Sepphoreans asked Rebbi Immi: May one keep moist with
thistles[38]? He said to them, you say in the name of Rebbi Ḥanina[39], even
leaves of artichokes[40] are permitted. Rebbi Yoshaia said, this is to act on,
you may rely on me. Rebbi Yoshaia said, the only food exclusively for
animals is green grass; if it was bought to moisturize one may use it to
keep moist.

36   Reading of Rome ms. Leyden:
חוטין "strings".

37   Reading of Rome ms. Leyden:
קורסייא "weaver's thread".

38   This is noted in Mishnah *Makhširin* 3:5; people used to collect grasses
to put on top of their grain heaps to

keep the latter from losing moisture. Since thistles are camel food, the question is about use of Sabbatical animal food for humans. In the Mishnah, and the Tosephta

corresponding to the quote in the next paragraph, the spelling is להטין.

39   In the Rome ms: R. Yose ben R. Hanina.

40   Edible thistles.

וְתַנֵּי חָצִיר וְכָל־שְׁאָר יְרָקוֹת שֶׁלְּקָחָן לַחַטּוֹן בָּהֶן מוּתָּר לַחַטּוֹן בָּהֶן. חִישֵׁב עֲלֵיהֶן לְאֵכָל אָדָם אָסוּר לַחַטּוֹן בָּהֶן. תַּנֵּי בַּר קַפָּרָא מוּתָּר לַחַטּוֹן בָּהֶן וְאָסוּר לָלוֹת41 מֵהֶן לָמָּה שֶׁיֵּשׁ עֲלֵיהֶן קְדוּשַׁת שְׁבִיעִית וְאוֹכְלֵי בְהֵמָה אֵין עֲלֵיהֶן קְדוּשַׁת שְׁבִיעִית דְּאַתְּ אָמַר עוֹשִׂין מֵהֶן מְלוּגְמָא לְאָדָם. אָמַר רִבִּי יוֹסֵי שְׁמָעִינָן שֶׁעוֹשִׂין מֵהֶן מְלוּגְמָא לְאָדָם וּשְׁמָעִינָן שֶׁמּוּתָּר לְסוֹחֲטָן וְלַעֲשׂוֹתָן מִן סַמְמָנִין לְאָדָם.

It was stated[42]: "Green grass and any other vegetables he took to moisturize may be used to moisturize. When he thought about them as human food it is forbidden to use them to moisturize." Bar Qappara stated: One may use them[43] to moisturize but he may not squeeze out from them because the holiness of the Sabbatical is on them. But there is no Sabbatical holiness on animal feed since you say one may use them to make wound dressing for humans. Rebbi Yose said, we understand that one may use them to make wound dressing for humans, and we understand that one may press them to prepare medication for humans.

41   Reading of Rome ms. Leyden: ללוות "to borrow".

42   Tosephta 5:16 following the Erfurt ms. The traditional text and the Vienna ms. have "permitted" and "forbidden" switched.

43   Vegetables collected or bought as human food. They cannot be squeezed for their moisture because this would destroy the plants so that they would no longer be food.

תַּמָּן תַּנִּינָן לוּלְבֵי זְרָדִים (וְשֶׁל עָרְלָה) וַעֲלֵי לוּף שׁוֹטֶה אֵין מְטַמְּאִין טוּמְאַת אוֹכְלִין עַד שֶׁיִּמְתְּקוּ לָמָּה שֶׁהֵן מָרִין. וְתוּרְמוֹסִין לָאו אִינּוּן מָרִין שַׁנְיָיא הִיא תוּרְמוֹסִין שֶׁעִיקָּרָן אוֹכָל אָדָם. לֹא צוֹרְכָא דְלֹא שְׁמָעִינָן שֶׁאֵין קְדוּשַׁת שְׁבִיעִית חָלָה עֲלֵיהֶן עַד שֶׁיִּמְתְּקוּ.

There, we have stated[44]: "Sprouts of new shoots, [of nasturtium,] and the leaves of wild arum cannot receive impurity of food until they become sweet." Why? Because they are bitter. But are lupines not also bitter[45]? It is different with lupines since they are human food from the start[46]. It is different for these[47]; we would not know that the sanctity of the Sabbatical would not fall on them unless they become sweet.

44   Mishnah *Uqeẓin* 3:4. The translation follows the text there: לוּלְבֵי זְרָדִים וְשֶׁל עָדָל וַעֲלֵי הַלּוּף הַשּׁוֹטֶה since the text enclosed in parenthesis, של ערלה "of *orlah*", makes no sense. *Orlah* is forbidden for any use, certainly for food. Soft new shoots (mainly of vines) can be used as food, but for most people they are simply pieces of wood. Hence, they do not have the status of food unless somebody takes them as such.

45   The question refers to a text close to Tosephta *Uqeẓin* 3:9: "Sprouts of new shoots of vines and carob trees cannot receive impurity of food until they become sweet. But arum, mustard, lupines, and all other foods that need to be cooked [before they can be eaten] can receive impurity of food whether they have become sweet or not." (cf. *Demay*, Chapter 2, Note 141.)

46   They are only cultivated as human food.

47   The kinds mentioned in Mishnah *Uqeẓin*.

לֹא כֵן אָמַר רִבִּי יוֹסֵי בֶּן חֲנִינָה עֳלָשִׁין חֲשׁוּבוֹת הֵן לְטַמֵּא טוּמְאַת אוֹכְלִין בַּשְּׁבִיעִית וְאִיתְּמַר טַעֲמָא הָדָא אֲמָרָה עַד שֶׁלֹּא הִתִּיר רִבִּי לְהָבִיא יֶרֶק מֵחוּצָה לָאָרֶץ לָאָרֶץ. אֲבָל מִשֶּׁהִתִּיר רִבִּי לְהָבִיא יֶרֶק מֵחוּץ לָאָרֶץ לָאָרֶץ הִיא שְׁבִיעִית הִיא שְׁאָר שְׁנֵי שָׁבוּעַ. וְכָא לֹא יְהוּ חֲשׁוּבוֹת עַד שֶׁיַּחְשׁב עֲלֵיהֶן. וּמָצִינוּ דָבָר

בַּתְּחִילָה קְדוּשַׁת שְׁבִיעִית חָלָה עָלָיו. וּבְסוֹף אֵין קְדוּשַׁת שְׁבִיעִית חָלָה עָלָיו. הָתִיבוּן הֲרֵי הַסִּיאָה וְהָאֵזוֹב וְהַקּוֹרְנִית שֶׁלְּקָטָן לְעֵצִים אֵין קְדוּשַׁת שְׁבִיעִית חָלָה עֲלֵיהֶן. חִישֵׁב עֲלֵיהֶן לְאוֹכְלִין קְדוּשַׁת שְׁבִיעִית חָלָה עֲלֵיהֶן. אָמַר רִבִּי חֲנַנְיָה שֶׁכֵּן אִם לְקָטָן מִתְּחִילָה לְאוֹכְלִין קְדוּשַׁת שְׁבִיעִית חָלָה עֲלֵיהֶן מִיַּד.

[48]Did not Rebbi Yose ben Ḥanina say: Endives are important enough in the Sabbatical to become susceptible to impurity of food?[49] The reason was spelled out: This is, before Rebbi permitted the importation of vegetables from outside the Land into the Land. But after Rebbi permitted the importation of vegetables from outside the Land into the Land, there is no difference between the Sabbatical and the other years of the sabbatical cycle. Then they should not be important unless somebody thinks about them! Do we find anything on which from the start the sanctity of the Sabbatical (falls) [does not fall] but in the end the sanctity of the Sabbatical (does not fall) [may fall] on them[50]? They objected: "The sanctity of the Sabbatical does not fall on calamint, hyssop[51], and thyme if one collected them as wood[52]. If he considered them as food, the sanctity of the Sabbatical falls on them." Rebbi Ḥananiah said, if he collected them first as food, the sanctity of the Sabbatical falls on them immediately[53].

48   Here starts the discussion of the examples given in the Mishnah. Why do these plants have to be singled out?

49   Chapter 5, Note 143.

50   All commentators switch the statements here (and in the following Tosephta) since it is clear that anything that is sanctified cannot lose its status as long as it is in existence. Both mss. have the text as it is given here but R. Simson quotes as his text וּמָצִינוּ דָּבָר בַּתְּחִילָה קְדוּשַׁת שְׁבִיעִית חָלָה עָלָיו. וּבְסוֹף אֵין קְדוּשַׁת שְׁבִיעִית חָלָה עָלָיו, this is the text translated in brackets.

51   Maimonides defines אזוב as صعتر ṣa'tar "wild thyme;" this seems to be the

acceptation in Yerushalmi and Tosephta. (In commercial usage today, *za'tar* is oregano.)

52   In Mishnah 8:1, the three kinds mentioned here are counted as weeds that become food only by the intention of the harvester.

53   While one would expect clear rules what is and what is not covered by the sanctity of the Sabbatical, so that belated switches between profane and holy should be excluded, it is enough that the possibility of such a clear-cut decision exists even if in this particular case it becomes only clear retroactively which possibility was chosen.

הַסִּיאָה צִתְּרָה. אֵיזוֹב אֵיזוֹבָא. קוֹרְנִית קוֹרְנִיתָא. מַהוּ חַלְבִּיצִין בֵּיעֵי נֵץ חָלָב.

Calamint is *ṣatra*, hyssop is *esoba*, thyme is *qornita*. What are *ḥalbiẓin*[54]? Eggs of milk bud[16].

54   These are mentioned in Mishnah 4. Maimonides declares the word to be unexplained. Arukh explains: "Egg shaped seeds developing like *ferula* (Italian, meaning 'gigantic fennel'). Some people say, eggs of milk buds and that is a white flower." In Syriac, the word means "Bethlehem star" (a flower). Arukh's note, "some people say", indicates that he had two Yerushalmi versions: the one before us from the Leyden ms./Venice print, and the reading of the Rome ms. in Halakhah 4: חלבנין , Arabic חַלְבּוּן "mercury" (*Mercurialis*, a plant); in Löw's opinion *Euphorbia tinctoria*, a close relative of mercury.

(fol. 37a) **משנה ג:** עוֹד כְּלָל אַחֵר אָמְרוּ כָּל-שֶׁהוּא מַאֲכַל אָדָם וּמַאֲכַל בְּהֵמָה וּמִמִּין הַצּוֹבְעִים וּמִתְקַיֵּם בָּאָרֶץ יֶשׁ לוֹ שְׁבִיעִית וּלְדָמָיו שְׁבִיעִית. אֵין לוֹ בִּיעוּר וְלֹא לְדָמָיו בִּיעוּר.

משנה ד: אֵי זֶה זֶה זֶה עִיקַּר הַלּוּף הַשּׁוֹטֶה וְעִיקַּר הָרַנְדָּנָה הָעַרְקַבְּלִין
וְהַחַלְבִּיצִין וְהַבּוּפָרְיָה. וּמִין הַצּוֹבְעִים הַפּוּאָה וְהַרִכְפָּא יֵשׁ לָהֶן שְׁבִיעִית
וְלִדְמֵיהֶן שְׁבִיעִית. אֵין לָהֶן בִּיעוּר וְלֹא לִדְמֵיהֶן בִּיעוּר.

משנה ה: רִבִּי מֵאִיר אוֹמֵר דְּמֵיהֶן מִתְבַּעְרִין עַד רֹאשׁ הַשָּׁנָה. אָמְרוּ לוֹ לָהֶן
אֵין בִּיעוּר קַל וָחוֹמֶר לִדְמֵיהֶן.

Mishnah 3: They established another principle for the Sabbatical: Everything that is[55] food for humans or animals or dyestuff and is preserved in the ground is subject to the Sabbatical; its proceeds are subject to the Sabbatical; it is not subject to removal[56] nor are its proceeds subject to removal.

Mishnah 4: What are these? These are the root of wild arum, the root of mint[12], ceterach[57], *ḥalbiẓin*[54], and wild nard[58]. Kinds of dyestuffs: madder and campeachy-wood[59]. These and their proceeds are subject to the Sabbatical; these and their proceeds are not subject to removal.

Mishnah 5: Rebbi Meïr says, their[60] proceeds have to be removed before New Year's Day. They said to him, they do not have to be removed, *a fortiori* their proceeds.

---

55   This is the reading of the Leyden ms., many of the best Mishnah mss., and R. Simson but not of Maimonides, the Mishnah mss. in the Maimonides tradition, and the Rome ms. These all read: Everything that is not . . .; cf. *The Mishnah with variant readings*, vol. Zeraïm II (Jerusalem 1975) p. 57, Note 14.

56   It cannot be subject to removal since there always remains something in the ground.

57   In all manuscript sources except the Leyden ms., the name is עקרבלין or עקרבנין. This corresponds to Arabic עֲקְרְבַּאן.

58   Latin *baccar, baccaris*, Greek βάκχαρις, an aromatic root also called *nardum rusticum* (Pliny), used against evil spells. Arukh: Arabic בנגר "beet". Maimonides: Meaning unclear.

59   *Reseda luteola*, definition of

Maimonides, Arabic בקם . Definition of
Arukh: Arabic שגרה מרים "Miriam's
tree", a tree, known to Arabic writers,

used for dye.

60   The plants mentioned in the
preceding Mishnah.

(fol. 37b) **הלכה ג**: אָמַר לָהֶן רִבִּי מֵאִיר מַחְמִיר אֲנִי בִּדָמִין מִן הָעִיקָר. שֶׁהַשֶּׁמֶן
שֶׁל שְׁבִיעִית מַדְלִיקִין בּוֹ מְכָרוֹ וְלָקַח בּוֹ שֶׁמֶן אֵין מַדְלִיקִין בּוֹ. רִבִּי אִימִּי בְּשֵׁם
רִבִּי יוֹחָנָן הֶחֱלִיף שֶׁמֶן בְּשֶׁמֶן שְׁנֵיהֶן אֲסוּרִין. כֵּיצַד הוּא עוֹשֶׂה רִבִּי חִזְקִיָּה בְּשֵׁם
רִבִּי יִרְמְיָה מַחֲלִיף שְׁנֵיהֶן שֶׁל חוּלִין. הֶחֱלִיף יַיִן בְּשֶׁמֶן כְּמָה דְאַתְּ אָמַר יַיִן אֵין
סָכִין אוֹתוֹ. וְדִכְוָותֵיהּ שֶׁמֶן אֵין מַדְלִיקִין. הֶחֱלִיף עָלִין בְּלוּלָבִין. כְּמָה דְתֵימַר
עָלִין יֵשׁ לָהֶן בִּיעוּר וְדִכְוָותֵיהּ לוּלָבִין יֵשׁ לָהֶן בִּיעוּר. הֶחֱלִיף אוֹכְלֵי אָדָם
בְּאוֹכְלֵי בְהֵמָה כְּמָה דְתֵימַר אוֹכְלֵי אָדָם אֵין עוֹשִׂין מֵהֶן מָלוּגְמָא וְדִכְוָותִין
אוֹכְלֵי בְהֵמָה אֵין עוֹשִׂין מֵהֶן מָלוּגְמָא. וְהָתַנִּינָן מוֹכְרִין אוֹכְלֵי אָדָם וְאוֹכְלֵי
בְהֵמָה לִיקַּח בָּהֶן אוֹכְלֵי אָדָם אֲבָל לֹא אוֹכְלֵי בְהֵמָה אוֹכְלֵי בְהֵמָה לִיקַּח בָּהֶן
אוֹכְלֵי בְהֵמָה וְכָל־שֶׁכֵּן אוֹכְלֵי אָדָם (לִיקַּח בָּהֶן אוֹכְלֵי בְהֵמָה).

Halakhah 3: "[61]Rebbi Meïr said to them: I am more restrictive with
the proceeds than with the main [produce]. For one may light with
Sabbatical oil but if one sold it and bought oil with it he may not light
with it." Rebbi Ammi in the name of Rebbi Johanan: If one exchanged
oil for oil, both of them are forbidden[62]. What can he do? Rebbi Ḥizqiah
in the name of Rebbi Jeremiah: He barters both for profane [oil]. If he
exchanged wine for oil; just as you say that he may not anoint with wine
so he may not light with oil. If he exchanged leaves for sprouts, just as
you say that leaves are subject to removal so sprouts are subject to
removal. If he exchanged human food for animal feed, just as one may
not make a wound dressing from human food so he may not make a
wound dressing from animal feed. We also have stated[63]: "One may sell
human food and animal feed to buy human food with the proceeds,

animal feed to buy animal feed and certainly human food (to buy animal feed)."

61   A parallel, speaking about other plants, is in Tosephta 5:3-4.

62   Since Sabbatical produce may be traded only as food, Sabbatical olive oil that was food, fuel, and ointment, after the sale is food only. Even if the money was used to buy profane (pre-Sabbatical) oil, the sanctity of the Sabbatical is transferred to the profane oil by the money, which may be used only for food. Therefore, in order to obtain fuel, the Sabbatical oil must be bartered, not sold, against profane oil. The following statements are applications of the same principle.

63   The text as it stands is difficult to accept. A similar text is in Tosephta 5:19. The Vienna ms. of the Tosephta reads: "One may sell human food and animal feed to buy human food with the proceeds; one does not sell animal feed to buy animal feed and human food; it is not necessary to mention that one does not sell human food to buy animal feed." The Erfurt ms. reads: "One may sell human food and animal feed to buy human food with the proceeds; one does not sell animal feed to buy animal feed and one does not sell human food to buy animal feed." The text of the Venice print of the Tosephta is very close to the Erfurt text. However, the Yerushalmi text cannot be emended following the Tosephta texts (which might represent a Babylonian tradition); there is no reason to believe that the Yerushalmi would forbid trading animal feed for animal feed and human food. The best option is to disregard the clause put in parentheses.

וְהָדָא קְנִיבְתָא דְיַרְקָא מַסְקִין לָהּ לְאִיגְרָא וְהִיא יָבְשָׁה מִן גַּרְמָהּ. רְבִּי יוֹחָנָן בְּשֵׁם רְבִּי שִׁמְעוֹן בֶּן יוֹצָדָק בְּיַיִן עַד הַפֶּסַח. (fol. 37c) בְּשֶׁמֶן עַד הָעֲצֶרֶת וּבִגְרוֹגְרוֹת עַד הַפּוּרִים. רְבִּי בֵּיבַי בְּשֵׁם רְבִּי חֲנִינָה וּבִתְמָרִין עַד הַחֲנוּכָּה.

The leaves removed from vegetables one puts on the roof and they dry up by themselves[64]. Rebbi Johanan in the name of Rebbi Simeon ben Yozadaq: Wine until Passover, oil until Pentecost, dried figs until Purim. Rebbi Bibi in the name of Rebbi Ḥanina: Dates until Ḥanukkah[65].

64   Wilted leaves and greenery of vegetables that would detract from the value of the vegetables are removed before the vegetables are sold or used. They also have to be removed at the end of the Sabbatical but they may be stored somewhere where they by themselves dry out (or rot) and are no longer human food.

65   The deadline after which Sabbatical produce must be eaten or destroyed after the end of the Sabbatical. The corresponding text in the Babli (*Pesaḥim* 53a) is formulated as a *baraita*: "One eats grapes until Passover, olives until Pentecost, dried figs until Ḥanukkah, dates until Purim. Rav Bibi: Rebbi Joḥanan switches two in the *baraita*". (Rebbi Joḥanan follows the text of the Yerushalmi for figs and dates.)

רבי יוֹחָנָן וַחֲבֵרוֹתֵיהּ הֲווֹן יָתְבִין מַקְשִׁיָן אָמַר יֵשׁ לָהֶן בִּיעוּר אוֹ אֵין לָהֶן בִּיעוּר. עֲבַר רבי יַנַּאי. אָמְרוּן הַאי[66] גַּבְרָא מִישְׁאֲלִינִית אָתוֹ שְׁאָלוּנֵיהּ אָמַר לָהֶן כָּל־דָּבָר שֶׁדַּרְכּוֹ לִישׁוֹר יֵשׁ לוֹ בִּיעוּר. וּשְׁאֵין דַּרְכּוֹ לִישׁוֹר אֵין לוֹ בִּיעוּר. וְאֵילֵי מֶהֶן דַּרְכּוֹ לִישׁוֹר וּמֶהֶן שֶׁאֵין דַּרְכּוֹ לִישׁוֹר וּשְׁרַע תַּנָּיָה מִינָהּ.

Rebbi Joḥanan and his colleagues were sitting and discussed the problem whether these are subject to removal or not[67]. Rebbi Yannai was passing by. They said, this is a man worth asking. They asked him and he said to them: Everything that normally falls from the tree is subject to removal, but what does not normally fall is free from removal. Which ones normally fall, or normally do not fall, the Tanna refrained from [stating].

66   Reading of the Rome ms. Leyden: אמר הא "he said, there is".

67   This refers to the second part of the Mishnah and Tosephta 5:3, giving examples of fruits and produce subject to the rules of Mishnah 3.

(fol. 37a) **מּשׁנה ו**: קְלִיפֵּי רִמּוֹן וְהַנֵּץ שָׁלוֹ קְלִיפֵּי אֱגוֹזִים וְהַגַּלְעִינִין. יֵשׁ לָהֶן

שְׁבִיעִית וְלִדְמֵיהֶן שְׁבִיעִית. הַצַּבָּע צוֹבֵעַ לְעַצְמוֹ לֹא יִצְבַּע בְּשָׂכָר. שָׁאֵין עוֹשִׂין

סְחוֹרָה בְּפֵירוֹת שְׁבִיעִית. וְלֹא בִּבְכוֹרוֹת וְלֹא בִּתְרוּמוֹת. וְלֹא בִּנְבֵילוֹת וְלֹא

בִּטְרֵיפוֹת וְלֹא בִּשְׁקָצִים וְלֹא בִּרְמָשִׂין. וְלֹא יְהֵא לוֹקֵחַ יַרְקוֹת שָׂדֶה וּמוֹכֵר

בַּשּׁוּק אֲבָל הוּא לוֹקֵט וּבְנוֹ מוֹכֵר עַל יָדוֹ. לָקַח לְעַצְמוֹ וְהוֹתִיר מוּתָּר לְמוֹכְרוֹ.

Mishnah 6: Pomegranate skins[68] and its peduncles, nut shells[68], and

pits are subject to the Sabbatical and so are their proceeds. The dyer dyes

for himself; he should not dye for payment[69] because one does not treat

the produce of the Sabbatical as merchandise, nor firstlings or heaves,

carcasses, torn animals, abominations[70], and crawling things[71]. One may

not buy vegetables to sell them on the market but he may collect and his

son sells for him. If he bought for himself and has leftovers, it is

permitted to sell them.

68 Tanning material and dyestuff.	year.
69 He may work for wages if he	70 E. g., seafood and reptiles.
has vegetable dyes from the preceding	71 Invertebrates.

(fol. 37c) **הלכה ד**: מַהוּ לִצְבּוֹעַ בְּטוֹבַת הֲנָייָה. מִן מַה דְתַנֵּי הַשַּׁלְשׁוּשִׁית

וְהַחַלְבִּיצִין הַתַּגָּר עוֹשֶׂה לְעַצְמוֹ הָדָא אֲמָרָה שֶׁאָסוּר לִצְבּוֹעַ בְּטוֹבַת הֲנָייָה.

Halakhah 4: May one dye for goodwill[72]? Since it was stated: "Milk

thistle[73] and *halbizin* the trader prepares for himself[74]", that means that it

is forbidden to dye for goodwill.

72 Not for money but for the	to the rules of the Sabbatical.
prospect of future business.	74 Since it does not say, "but not
73 According to I. Löw, *Crozo-*	for wages", this implies that all com-
phora tinctoria, a plant used to produce	mercial use is forbidden.
dye, mentioned Tosephta 5:5 as subject	

כְּתִיב טְמֵאִים הֵמָּה לָכֶם. מַה תַלְמוּד לוֹמַר וּטְמֵאִים יִהְיוּ לָכֶם. אֶלָּא אֶחָד אִיסוּר אֲכִילָה וְאֶחָד אִיסוּר הֲנָיָיה. כָּל־דָּבָר שֶׁאִיסוּרוֹ דְּבַר תּוֹרָה אָסוּר לַעֲשׂוֹת בּוֹ סְחוֹרָה. וְכָל־דָּבָר שֶׁאִיסוּרוֹ מִדִּבְרֵיהֶן מוּתָּר לַעֲשׂוֹת בּוֹ סְחוֹרָה. וַהֲרֵי חֲמוֹר. לִמְלַאכְתּוֹ הוּא גָדֵל. וַהֲרֵי גָמָל. לִמְלַאכְתּוֹ הוּא גָדֵל. רִבִּי יְהוֹשַׁעְיָה נָסַב וִיהַב בַּהֲדֵין מוּרייֵיס. רִבִּי חוּנָא נְסַב וִיהַב בַּהֲדֵין חִלְתּוּתָא.

It is written (*Lev.* 11:28): "They are impure for you". Why does it say (*Lev.* 11:35) "they shall be impure for you"? One is for the prohibition of eating, the other for the prohibition of usufruct[75]. Anything forbidden by the Torah is forbidden for trade but everything whose prohibition is rabbinical is permitted for trade. But is there not the donkey[76]? It is raised for work. Is there not the camel? It is raised for work. Rebbi Yehoshaiah traded in *muries*[77], Rebbi Huna traded in asafoetida[78].

75   The argument is also found in *Orlah* 3:1 (fol. 63d), *Pesahim* 2:1 (fol. 28c), *Baba Qama* 7:10 (fol. 6a), Babli *Pesahim* 21b, *Qiddušin* 56b, *Baba Qama* 41a, *Hulin* 114b. The formulation in the Babli is: R. Abbahu said, every place where it is stated "it should not be eaten, do not eat" implies both prohibition as food and of usufruct unless the Torah details the permission of usufruct as for cadavers (*Deut.* 14:21). One has to assume that "anything forbidden" mentioned here also means "anything forbidden as food."

76   Donkey meat is forbidden. The camel should have been mentioned first since it is mentioned explicitly as forbidden animal; donkey meat is forbidden by the general clause permitting only ruminants.

77   Brine possibly made with wine (cf. *Demay* Chapter 1, Note 156). The nature of the prohibition is discussed in *Terumot* 11:1 (fol. 47c); it is agreed that the prohibition is rabbinical.

78   It is not clear how and why asafoetida would be prohibited. The best explanation is that of *Pene Moshe* (Margalit) that medicines are neither food nor dyestuff and, hence, may be traded in the Sabbatical year.

תַּנֵּי לֹא יְהוּ חֲמִשָּׁה מְלַקְּטִין יֶרֶק וְאֶחָד מוֹכֵר אֲבָל מוֹכֵר הוּא שֶׁלּוֹ וְשֶׁל חֲבֵירוֹ. חֲמִשִּׁין אַחִים מְלַקְּטִין וְאֶחָד מוֹכֵר עַל יְדֵיהֶן. אָמַר רִבִּי יוֹסֵי בֵּי רִבִּי בּוּן וּבִלְבַד שֶׁלֹּא יַעֲשׂוּ פְלַטֵּיר. שֶׁלֹּא יְהֵא מַזְבִּין בְּהוּא אָתָר בְּכָל־שָׁנָה. וְאִית דְּבָעֵי מֵימַר דְּלֹא יְהֵא מַזְבִּין בְּכָל־שָׁעָה.

It was stated[79]: "There should not be five people collecting and one selling for them, but one may sell his own and that of a colleague. 50 brothers may collect and one sells for them." Rebbi Yose ben Rebbi Abun said, but only should they not have a store[80], [i. e.], that he should not sell at the same place all year round; some say that he should not sell at all hours.

<hr>

79   Tosephta 6:21-22. There, the text is: "If five people were collecting there should not be one selling for them, but one may sell his own and theirs. Five brothers may collect and one sells for them but they should not open a store." The reading "50" may be an error for "5", but the Yerushalmi

definitely does not permit a person to sell more than what he and one other person collects.
80   Greek πρατήρ, cf. *Demay*, Chapter 5, Note 75. The Rome ms. has here an addition: "What means 'that they not have a store'? That he should not sell . . . ."

<hr>

תַּנֵּי הַחֶנְוָנִי שֶׁהָיָה מְבַשֵּׁל יְרָקוֹת בַּשְּׁבִיעִית לֹא יְהֵא מְחַשֵּׁב שְׂכָרוֹ עַל דְּמֵי שְׁבִיעִית אֲבָל מְחַשֵּׁב הוּא עַל הַיַּיִן וְעַל הַשֶּׁמֶן וְעַל הָאַבְטָלָה. רִבִּי לָא מְפַקֵּד לְאִלּוּן חֲלָטַרְיָא לָא תַהֲווֹן מְחַשְּׁבִין אַגְרֵיכוֹן עַל מִישְׁחָא אֶלָּא עַל חִיטַּיָּא.

It was stated[81]: "The store owner[82] who was cooking vegetables during the Sabbatical should not compute his profit on the value of Sabbatical [produce] but rather compute it on wine, oil[83], and lost time." Rebbi La commanded the makers of fried food[84]: "Do not compute your gain on the oil but on the wheat."

81   Tosephta 6:22.

82   He sells raw and cooked food.

83   Presumably oil and wine are
from the preceding year.

84   They make חליטא, dough baked
swimming in oil. In this case, one has
to assume that the oil is Sabbatical but
the wheat is not.

(fol. 37a) **משנה ז**: לָקַח בְּכוֹר לְמִשְׁתֶּה בְּנוֹ אוֹ לְרֶגֶל וְלֹא צָרִיךְ לוֹ מוּתָּר לְמוֹכְרוֹ.
צָדֵי חַיָּה עוֹפוֹת וְדָגִים שֶׁנִּתְמַמּוּ לָהֶן מִינִין טְמֵאִין מוּתָּר לְמוֹכְרָן. רִבִּי יְהוּדָה
אוֹמֵר אַף מִשֶּׁנִּתְמַמֶּה לוֹ לְפִי דַרְכּוֹ לוֹקֵחַ וּמוֹכֵר. וּבִלְבַד שֶׁלֹּא יְהֵא אוּמְנָתוֹ בְּכָךְ.
וַחֲכָמִים אוֹסְרִין.

Mishnah 7: If somebody bought a first-born animal[85] for his son's
wedding or for a holiday and now does not need it, he may sell it.
Catchers of wild animals, birds, or fish who accidentally caught impure
species may sell them. Rebbi Jehudah says, even one who incidentally has
such an opportunity[86] may take and sell them on condition that this not
be his profession, but the Sages prohibit it.

85   A first-born calf or lamb becomes the property of the Cohen. If
the first-born develops a defect it may
be eaten by everybody (*Deut.* 15:21); it
may be sold by the Cohen to a layman.
But since the first-born is a sacrifice
from birth, it must be treated with
respect and cannot become an object of
trade. However, an occasional private
sale is permitted under special circumstances.

86   He is not a professional bird
catcher or fisherman. An impure
animal or fish crosses his way and he
has the opportunity to grab it with the
intent to sell it to Gentiles. For
professionals it is clear that they may
take impure species only if they
accidentally catch them in their nets.

הלכה ח: תַּמָּן תַּנִּינָן. אָמַר רִבִּי יְהוּדָה אֵימָתַי בִּזְמָן שָׁאֵין לוֹ אוּמָנוּת(fol. 37c)
אֶלָּא הוּא אֲבָל יֶשׁ לוֹ אוּמָנוּת שֶׁלֹּא הוּא הֲרֵי זֶה מוּתָּר. הֵיךְ עֲבִידָא. הָיָה יוֹשֵׁב
וּבָטֵל מִמְּלַאכְתּוֹ כָּל־שְׁנֵי שָׁבוּעַ כֵּיוָן שֶׁבָּאֵת שְׁבִיעִית הִתְחִיל מְפַשֵּׁיט יָדוֹ וְנוֹשֵׂא
וְנוֹתֵן בְּפֵירוֹת עֲבֵירָה אִם יֶשׁ עִמּוֹ מְלָאכָה אַחֶרֶת כָּשֵׁר וְאִם לָאו פָּסוּל. אֲבָל
אִם הָיָה יוֹשֵׁב וְעוֹסֵק בִּמְלַאכְתּוֹ כָּל־שְׁנֵי שָׁבוּעַ כֵּיוָן שֶׁבָּאֵת שְׁבִיעִית הִתְחִיל
מְפַשֵּׁיט יָדוֹ וְנוֹשֵׂא וְנוֹתֵן בְּפֵירוֹת עֲבֵירָה אַף עַל פִּי שָׁאֵין עִמּוֹ מְלָאכָה אַחֶרֶת
מוּתָּר. רִבִּי בָּא בַּר זַבְדָּא. רִבִּי אַבָּהוּ בְּשֵׁם רִבִּי לֶעְזָר. הֲלָכָה כְּרִבִּי יוּדָה
דְמַתְנִיתִין. אֶקְלַס רִבִּי בָּא בַּר זַבְדָּא דָּמַר שְׁמוּעָה בְּשֵׁם זְעֵיר מִינֵּיהּ. תַּנֵּי רִבִּי
יוּדָה לְחוּמְרָה. הֵיךְ עֲבִידָא הָיָה יוֹשֵׁב וְעוֹסֵק בִּמְלַאכְתּוֹ כָּל־שְׁנֵי שָׁבוּעוֹת.
וּבַשְּׁבִיעִית הִתְחִיל וּמְפַשֵּׁיט אֶת יָדוֹ לִישָׂא וְלִיתֵּן בְּפֵירוֹת עֲבֵירָה אִם יֶשׁ עִמּוֹ
מְלָאכָה אַחֶרֶת מוּתָּר וְאִם לָאו אָסוּר. (אֲבָל אִם הָיָה עוֹסֵק בִּמְלַאכְתּוֹ כָּל־שְׁנֵי
שָׁבוּעוֹת כֵּיוָן שֶׁבָּאֵת שְׁבִיעִית הִתְחִיל מְפַשֵּׁיט יָדוֹ וְנוֹשֵׂא וְנוֹתֵן בְּפֵירוֹת עֲבֵירָה.
אַף עַל פִּי שָׁאֵין עִמּוֹ מְלָאכָה אַחֶרֶת אָסוּר) לֹא בְדָא. רִבִּי בָּא בַּר זַבְדָּא. רִבִּי
אַבָּהוּ בְּשֵׁם רִבִּי לֶעְזָר. הֲלָכָה כְּרִבִּי יוּדָה מַתְנִיתִין. אֶקְלַס רִבִּי בָּא בַּר זַבְדָּא
דָּמַר שְׁמוּעָה בְּשֵׁם זְעֵיר מִינֵּיהּ. אוּף הָכָא כֵּן. אָמַר רִבִּי יוֹסֵי בֵּי רִבִּי בּוּן תַּמָּן
אֵין מַלְכוּת אוֹנֶסֶת. בְּרַם הָכָא הַמַּלְכוּת אוֹנֶסֶת.

Halakhah 5: There, we have stated[87]: "Rebbi Jehudah said, when is
that? If he has no other, different profession. But if he has another,
different profession it is permitted." How is this implemented? If he was
sitting idle all the years of the sabbatical cycle but when the Sabbatical
began he became active and traded in forbidden produce, if he has
another profession on the side he is acceptable, otherwise he is
unacceptable. But if he was working in his profession all the years of the
sabbatical cycle and when the Sabbatical began he became active and
traded in forbidden produce, even if he has no other profession on the side
he is permitted. Rebbi Abba bar Zavda, Rebbi Abbahu in the name of
Rebbi Eleazar: Practice follows Rebbi Jehudah of our Mishnah. Rebbi

Abba bar Zavda was publicly praised for presenting a tradition in the name of a younger person. It was stated[88]: Rebbi Jehudah is restrictive. How is this implemented? If he was working in his profession all the years of the sabbatical cycles but when the Sabbatical began he became active and traded in forbidden produce, if he has another profession on the side he is permitted, otherwise he is forbidden. (But if he was working in his profession all the years of the sabbatical cycles and when the Sabbatical began he became active and traded in forbidden produce, even if he has no other profession on the side he is forbidden.)[89] With this we are not concerned. Rebbi Abba bar Zavda, Rebbi Abbahu in the name of Rebbi Eleazar[90]: Practice follows Rebbi Jehudah of our Mishnah. Rebbi Abba bar Zavda was publicly praised for presenting a tradition in the name of a younger person. Here also should it be so[91]? Rebbi Yose ben Rebbi Abun said, there the government is not oppressive, here the government is oppressive.

87   Mishnah *Sanhedrin* 3:6. The Mishnah gives a list of people whose testimony cannot be trusted in court: Gamblers, usurers, organizers of animal fights, and traders in Sabbatical produce. R. Jehudah says, these are unacceptable as witnesses (since they will sin for monetary gain and, therefore, are open to bribery) only if they make their living from these activities, not if gambling, etc., is done only on the side. The entire discussion appears word by word in *Sanhedrin* 3:6,

fol. 21a-b.

88   In *Sanhedrin*, "R. Ḥiyya stated".

89   The text in parentheses is missing in *Sanhedrin* and in the quotes of this paragraph by Maimonides, R. Simson, and R. Isaac Simponti. It is dittography and should be disregarded.

90   Even though the Babli holds (in the name of the first generation R. Joshua ben Levi) that all statements of R. Jehudah in the Mishnah which start with אימתי are explanations of the anonymous text, not disagreements, and

are always practice to be followed (*Sanhedrin* 24b, *Erubin* 81b-82a); the Babli (*Sanhedrin* 26b) states explicitly in the name of R. Abbahu and R. Eleazar that practice follows R. Jehudah. One has to take that as an echo of the discussion in the Yerushalmi.

91   Do the restrictive rules of R. Jehudah effectively apply to dealers in Sabbatical produce? R. Yannai permitted growing crops in the Sabbatical (Halakha 4:2) because of the tax burden on farmers; the tannaitic rules cannot be enforced as long as the tax is collected whether there is a crop or not.

(fol. 37a) **משנה ח:** לוּלְבֵי זְרָדִים וְהֶחָרוּבִין יֵשׁ לָהֶן שְׁבִיעִית וְלִדְמֵיהֶן שְׁבִיעִית. יֵשׁ לָהֶן בִּיעוּר וְלִדְמֵיהֶן בִּיעוּר. לוּלְבֵי הָאֵלָה וְהַבּוֹטְנָא וְהָאֲטָדִים יֵשׁ לָהֶן שְׁבִיעִית וְלִדְמֵיהֶן שְׁבִיעִית. אֵין לָהֶן בִּיעוּר וְלֹא לִדְמֵיהֶן בִּיעוּר. אֲבָל לֶעָלִים יֵשׁ לָהֶן בִּיעוּר. מִפְּנֵי שֶׁהֵן נוֹשְׁרִין מֵאָבִיהֶן.

Mishnah 8: Bundles of new sprouts[44] and carobs are subject to the Sabbatical and so are their proceeds; they are subject to removal and so are their proceeds. Branches of terebinth, pistachio, and thornbushes are subject to the Sabbatical and so are their proceeds; they are not subject to removal nor are their proceeds[92]. But the leaves are subject to removal since they fall from their stems.

92   If nobody took them they would stay on the trees which are perennial. It follows that pine needles, if they could be used as food, would not be subject to removal.

(fol. 37c) **הלכה ו:** בָּרֹאשָׁא דְּפִירְקָא אַתְּ אָמַר אֵין אוֹכְלִין עַל הָעִיקָּר. וְכָא אַתְּ אָמַר אוֹכְלִין עַל הָעִיקָר. אָמַר רִבִּי פִּינְחָס תַּמָּן אֵין סוֹפוֹ לְהַקְשׁוֹת. בְּרַם הָכָא סוֹפוֹ לְהַקְשׁוֹת מִכֵּיוָן שֶׁהֶקְשׁוּ נַעֲשׂוּ כָאָבִיהֶן.

Halakhah 6: At the beginning of the chapter you said that one does not eat because of the roots[93] and here you say one does eat because of the roots? Rebbi Phineas said, there they will not ultimately harden; here they will ultimately harden; after they hardened they become part of the stem.

93   In Mishnah 2, arum, mint, etc., were made subject to removal even though their roots remain in the ground and will produce again the next year. Here the young shoots of vines and carobs are exempted from removal.

תַּנֵי וְכוּלָן שֶׁנִּכְנְסוּ מִשִּׁשִּׁית לַשְּׁבִיעִית שִׁשִּׁית. חוּץ מִן הֶעָדָל. מִפְּנֵי שֶׁהוּא כְיֶרֶק. רְבִּי אַבָּהוּ בְשֵׁם רְבִּי יוֹחָנָן לֵית כָּאן מִשִּׁשִּׁית לַשְּׁבִיעִית שִׁשִּׁית אֶלָא שְׁבִיעִית. וְהָתַנֵי הַסִּיאָה וְהָאֵזוֹב וְהַקּוֹרְנִית שֶׁהוֹבִילוּ לֶחָצֵר. אֲבָל אִם הָיְתָה שְׁנִייָה נִכְנֶסֶת לַשְּׁלִישִׁית שְׁלִישִׁית מִשִּׁשִּׁית לַשְּׁבִיעִית שִׁשִּׁית. הָכָא אַתְּ מָנֵי לַחוֹרֵיה. וְכָא אַתְּ מָנֵי לְקוֹמֵיה. אָמַר רְבִּי יוֹסֵי שְׁלִישִׁית וְשִׁשִּׁית אַף עַל פִּי שֶׁאֵין בָּהֶן מַעֲשֵׂר שֵׁנִי יֵשׁ בָּהֶן מַעְשְׂרוֹת שְׁבִיעִית אֵין בָּהּ מַעְשְׂרוֹת כָּל־עִיקָר. לֹא כֵן אָמַר רְבִּי אַבָּהוּ בְשֵׁם רְבִּי יוֹחָנָן לֵית כָּאן מִשִּׁשִּׁית לַשְּׁבִיעִית שִׁשִּׁית אֶלָא שְׁבִיעִית. תַּמָּן בִּרְשׁוּת הַבְּעָלִים בְּרַם הָכָא בִּרְשׁוּת הֶעָנִי הֵן. מוּטָב לוֹ[94] אֶחָד בְּוַדַּאי וְלֹא שְׁנַיִם בְּסָפֵק.

It was stated[95]: "And all those which remained from the sixth year into the Sabbatical belong to the sixth except for nasturtium which is like a vegetable[96]." Rebbi Abbahu in the name of Rebbi Johanan: There is no [rule that] "from the sixth year into the Sabbatical they belong to the sixth" but [they belong] to the Sabbatical. But did we not state: "Calamint, hyssop, and thyme he brought to the courtyard[97], (but) if it was from the second year into the third they belong to the third; from the sixth year into the Sabbatical they belong to the sixth?" Here, you count the past [year], there the coming! Rebbi Yose said, in the third and sixth years, even though there is no second tithe, there are tithes; in the Sabbatical there is no tithe whatsoever. But did not Rebbi Abbahu say in the name of Rebbi Joḥanan: There is no "from the sixth year into the Sabbatical they belong to the sixth" but they belong to the Sabbatical? There it is in the possession of the landowners, here it is in the possession of the poor[98]. He prefers one which is certain to two which are possible[99].

94 Reading of the Rome ms. Leyden: לֵית לִי "I do not have".

95 Tosephta 5:11 has a similar text. The *baraita* quoted here must have had a beginning similar to the Tosephta: "Branches of terebinth, pistachio, thornbushes, *and nasturtium* . . ."

96 The status of trees is determined by the time of blossoming, that of vegetables by the time of the harvest.

97 These plants grow as weeds in Galilee, but if they are collected as spices and stored they are subject to tithes (Mishnah *Ma'serot* 3:9).

98 Since in the Sabbatical everybody has the right to enter the fields and take the produce.

99 There is little to be taken by the poor in the Sabbatical since nothing is sown, but it is in the poor's hand to take. The tithe of the poor may be larger but it is in the farmer's hand to decide whom to give; a sparrow in the hand is better than a pigeon on the roof.

עָלִין שֶׁכְּבָשָׁן עִם לוּלְבִין אִית תַּנָּיֵי תַּנֵּי בֵּין אִילוּ וּבֵין אִילוּ יֵשׁ לָהֶן בִּיעוּר. וְאִית תַּנָּיֵי תַּנֵּי בֵּין אִילוּ וּבֵין אִילוּ אֵין לָהֶן בִּיעוּר. וְאִית תַּנָּיֵי תַּנֵּי עָלִין יֵשׁ לָהֶן בִּיעוּר לוּלְבִין אֵין לָהֶן בִּיעוּר. מָאן דְּאָמַר אֵין לָהֶן בִּיעוּר רִבִּי יְהוֹשֻׁעַ. מָאן דְּאָמַר יֵשׁ לָהֶן בִּיעוּר לוּלְבִין אֵין לָהֶן בִּיעוּר רַבָּן גַּמְלִיאֵל.

About leaves preserved with sprouts, some Tannaïm state: both of them are subject to removal. Some Tannaïm state: neither of them is subject to removal. Leaves are subject to removal, sprouts are not subject to removal. He who says [both] are not subject to removal is Rebbi Joshua; he who says [leaves] are subject to removal but sprouts are not subject to removal is Rabban Gamliel[100].

100   This refers to Mishnah 9:5: "If somebody preserves three kinds in one barrel, R. Eliezer says, one eats according to the first; R. Joshua says, according to the last; Rabban Gamliel says everything whose kind has disappeared from the field should be removed from the house. Rebbi Simeon says, all kinds of vegetables have the same status; one eats purslain until *sinariot* disappear from the Bet Neṭofa valley." R. Eliezer demands that all be removed if one of the kinds has to be removed. In our case, he requires that the sprouts be removed if the leaves have to be removed. R. Joshua requires that all kinds be removed together when the last has to be removed. Since sprouts do not have to be removed, nothing has to be removed. Rabban Gamliel thinks that the requirement of removal is on the produce, not on its taste. The taste of one absorbed by the other is irrelevant; therefore, each kind has to be removed in its time: Leaves have to be removed but not sprouts.

(fol. 37a) **משנה ט**: הָוֶרֶד וְהַכּוֹפֶר וְהַקְּטָף וְהַלּוֹטֶם. יֵשׁ לָהֶן שְׁבִיעִית וְלִדְמֵיהֶן שְׁבִיעִית. רַבִּי שִׁמְעוֹן אוֹמֵר אֵין לַקְּטָף שְׁבִיעִית מִפְּנֵי שֶׁאֵינוֹ פֶּרִי.

Mishnah 9: Roses, henna[101], balsamum, and chestnut are subject to the Sabbatical and so are their proceeds. Rebbi Simeon says, balsamum is not subject to the Sabbatical because it is not a fruit[102].

101   Definition of Maimonides. Arukh and Geonim: cloves.

102   But a sap. He implies that no sap falls under sabbatical prohibitions.

(fol. 37c) **הלכה ז**: רַבִּי פְּדָת[103] רַבִּי יוֹסָה בְּשֵׁם רַבִּי יוֹחָנָן אַתְיָא דְרַבִּי שִׁמְעוֹן כְּרַבִּי יְהוֹשֻׁעַ. דְּתַנִּינָן תַּמָּן אָמַר רַבִּי יְהוֹשֻׁעַ שָׁמַעְתִּי שֶׁהַמַּעֲמִיד בִּשְׂרַף הֶעָלִין וּבִשְׂרַף הָעִיקָרִין מוּתָּר בִּשְׂרַף הַפַּגִּין אָסוּר מִפְּנֵי שֶׁהוּא פְּרִי. אָמַר רַבִּי זְעִירָא לְרַבִּי פְּדָת כְּמָה דְתֵימָא תַּמָּן הֲלָכָה כְּרַבִּי יְהוֹשֻׁעַ. וְכָא אָמַר הֲלָכָה כְּרַבִּי שִׁמְעוֹן.

אָמַר רִבִּי יוֹנָה וְדַמְיָא הִיא כָּל־רַבָּה קְטָף בָּטֵל עַל גַּבֵּי שְׂרָפוֹ. אִילָן אֵינוֹ בָטֵל
עַל גַּבֵּי שְׂרָפוֹ. אוֹכְלֵי בְהֵמָה קְדוּשַׁת שְׁבִיעִית חָלָה עֲלֵיהֶן וְאֵין קְדוּשַׁת עָרְלָה
חָלָה עֲלֵיהֶן. אָמַר רִבִּי אָבִין אִית לָךְ חוֹרִי. רִבִּי יְהוֹשֻׁעַ אֲמָרָהּ שְׁמוּעָה. וְרִבִּי
שִׁמְעוֹן בְּשֵׁם גַּרְמֵיהּ אֲמָרָהּ לָמָה.

Halakhah 7: Rebbi Pedat, Rebbi Assi, in the name of Rebbi Johanan:
Rebbi Simeon follows that of Rebbi Joshua, as we have stated there[104]:
"Rebbi Joshua said, I heard that making curds[105] with the sap of leaves or
roots is permitted, with the sap of unripe fruits it is forbidden because that
is a fruit." Rebbi Zeïra said to Rebbi Pedat, since we say there that
practice follows Rebbi Joshua, would you have to say here that practice
follows Rebbi Simeon[106]? Rebbi Jonah said, are the situations similar? It
is the other way[107]: Balsamum is essentially sap, a tree is essentially in its
sap. The holiness of the Sabbatical falls on animal feed, but the holiness
of *orlah* never falls on it. Rebbi Abun said, there is another one: Rebbi
Joshua quoted it as a tradition, Rebbi Simeon said it in his own name[108].

103   Reading of the Rome ms. and
the parallel in *Orlah* 1:7 (fol. 61b) In
the Leyden ms. : ז' פדא.
104   Mishnah *Orlah*: 1:7; its topic is
the use of any part of an *orlah* plant
(cf. *Kilaim* Chapter 5, Note 93).
105   To make cheese with vegetable
rennet.
106   The opponent of R. Joshua in
Mishnah *Orlah* is R. Eliezer; therefore
practice has to follow R. Joshua. In the
parallel in the Babli, *Niddah* 8b, the
disagreement is explained that for R.
Eliezer sap has the status of fruit and

for the Sages who oppose R. Simeon in
the Mishnah here, sap of a tree which
produces no edible fruit has the status
of fruit, whereas for R. Joshua no sap
has the status of fruit. Therefore, the
Babli accepts the position of R. Pedat
which here is questioned. The verse
(*Lev.* 19:23) restricts the holiness of
orlah to fruits only.
107   כל רבה corresponds to Babylonian אדרבא.
108   Since he gives a reason, it is his
own argument and not one he was
taught by his teachers.

שְׂרָף פֵּירִי פַּגִּין פֵּירִי. וְאִין תֵּימַר שְׂרָף פֵּירִי עָשָׂה כֵן בִּתְרוּמָה אָסוּר.[109] וְאִין
תֵּימַר פַּגִּין פֵּירִי עָשָׂה כֵן בִּתְרוּמָה מוּתָּר.[110] לָמָּה שֶׁהַנָּיַת תְּרוּמָה מוּתֶּרֶת
וַהַנָּיַת עָרְלָה אֲסוּרָה.

Sap may be fruit, unripe fruits may be fruit[111]. If you say that sap has
the status of fruit, if he did it with heave it is forbidden[112]. If you say that
unripe fruits are fruit, if he did it with heave it is permitted[113]. Why?
Because usufruct of heave is permitted but usufruct of *orlah* is forbidden.

109   Reading of R. Simson from a ms.   tive use of a fruit is also forbidden.
Venice print and mss: מותר.   112   Cheese made with sap of heave
110   Reading of the parallel text in   is forbidden to anybody who is not a
Orlah.   Cohen since rennet, which turns milk
111   This refers to the statement of   into cheese, cannot be considered
R. Joshua in Mishnah *Orlah*. Is the   nonexistent even if it is only a minute
cheese forbidden because the sap of   part of the final volume.
unripe fruits is considered fruit or is   113   Since only fruit is subject to
sap not fruit but for *orlah* and deriva-   heave, the sap would be profane.

(fol. 37a) **משנה י:** וֶרֶד חָדָשׁ שֶׁכְּבָשׁוֹ בְּשֶׁמֶן יָשָׁן יַלְקֵט הַוֶּרֶד. (fol. 37b) וְיָשָׁן
בְּחָדָשׁ חַיָּב בְּבִיעוּר. חָרוּבִים חֲדָשִׁים שֶׁכְּבָשָׁן בְּיַיִן יָשָׁן וִישֵׁנִים בְּחָדָשׁ חַיָּבִין
בְּבִיעוּר. זֶה הַכְּלָל כָּל־שֶׁהוּא בְּנוֹתֵן טַעַם חַיָּב לְבָעֵר מִין בְּשֶׁאֵינוֹ מִינוֹ. וּמִין
בְּמִינוֹ כָּל־שֶׁהוּא. שְׁבִיעִית אוֹסֶרֶת כָּל־שֶׁהוּא בְּמִינוֹ וּשְׁלֹא בְמִינוֹ בְּנוֹתֵן טַעַם.

Mishnah 10: If new roses were preserved in old oil, the roses should
be taken out[114]. Old in new are subject to removal. New carobs
preserved in old wine and old ones in new are subject to removal[115]. This
is the principle: Anything that gives flavor to another kind is subject to

removal, in its own kind in the minutest amount[116]. The Sabbatical makes
forbidden in the minutest amount in its own kind, and by giving taste in
another kind.

114   If no rose leaves are left for the
wild animals, the preserved Sabbatical
leaves have to be given to the poor to
eat but the oil, pressed from non-
Sabbatical olives, may be retained by
the owner.   But if Sabbatical rose
leaves are preserved in post-Sabbatical
oil, everything has to be removed since
the older leaves, which should have
been removed, immediately give taste
to the oil. One cannot explain "old in
new" by "sixth year roses in Sabbatical
oil" since these never would be subject
to removal.

115   Since the carobs will quickly
leave their taste in the oil.   The
Tosephta (5:15) states identical rules
for carob pods and rose leaves; the
author of the Tosephta must hold that
the hard carob pods leave taste in the
oil only if they are steeped in it a very
long time.

116   Since the taste of forbidden and
permitted food cannot be distinguished
if they are of the same kind, a minute
admixture of forbidden food makes
permitted food of the same kind also
forbidden.

(fol. 37c) **הלכה ח**: הָכָא אַתְּ אָמַר יְלָקֵט הַוֶּרֶד. וְכָא אַתְּ אָמַר חַיָּיב בְּבִיעוּר.
רְבִּי אַבָּהוּ בְשֵׁם רְבִּי יוֹחָנָן תְּרֵין תַּנָּיִין אִינּוּן. אָמַר רְבִּי זְעִירָא יָכִיל אֲנָא פָתַר
לְהוֹן טוּרְדֵּי בִּתְרֵי תְּנַיֵּי וֶרֶד חָדָשׁ שֶׁכְּבָשׁוֹ בְשֶׁמֶן יָשָׁן. וֶרֶד שֶׁל שְׁבִיעִית שֶׁכְּבָשׁוֹ
בְשֶׁמֶן שֶׁל שִׁשִׁית וְיָשָׁן בְּחָדָשׁ וֶרֶד שְׁבִיעִית שֶׁכְּבָשׁוֹ שֶׁל שְׁמִינִית.

Halakhah 8: In the first case, you say "the roses should be taken out",
in the second case "all is subject to removal"? Rebbi Abbahu in the name
of Rebbi Joḥanan: This is from two [different] Tannaïm. Rebbi Yose said,
I can explain those roses by two conditions: "If new roses are preserved in
old oil", Sabbatical roses preserved in oil of the sixth year; "old in new",
Sabbatical roses preserved in eighth year's [oil].

כלל גדול אמרו פרק שמיני

(fol. 37d) **משנה א:** כְּלָל גָּדוֹל אָמְרוּ בַּשְּׁבִיעִית כָּל־הַמְיוּחָד לְאוֹכֶל אָדָם אֵין עוֹשִׂין מִמֶּנּוּ מְלוּגְמָא לְאָדָם וְאֵין צוֹרֶךְ לוֹמַר לִבְהֵמָה. וְכָל־שֶׁאֵינוּ מְיוּחָד לְאוֹכֶל אָדָם עוֹשִׂין מִמֶּנּוּ מְלוּגְמָא לְאָדָם אֲבָל לֹא לִבְהֵמָה. וְכָל־שֶׁאֵינוּ מְיוּחָד לֹא לְאוֹכֶל אָדָם וְלֹא לְאוֹכֶל בְּהֵמָה חִשֵּׁב עָלָיו אוֹכֶל אָדָם וְאוֹכֶל בְּהֵמָה נוֹתְנִין עָלָיו חוּמְרֵי אָדָם וְחוּמְרֵי בְהֵמָה. חִשֵּׁב עָלָיו לְעֵצִים הֲרֵי הוּא כְעֵצִים כְּגוֹן הַסִּיאָה וְהָאֵזוֹב וְהַקּוּרְנִית.

Mishnah 1: They established a comprehensive principle for the Sabbatical: Nothing that is exclusively food for humans may be used for a wound dressing[1] for humans or, it goes without saying, for animals. Anything that is not exclusively food for humans may be used for a wound dressing for humans but not for animals. Anything that is not exclusively food, for humans or for animals, if intended as food for humans or animals one puts on it all restrictions regarding humans or animals; if intended as wood then it is wood. Examples are calamint, hyssop[2], and thyme.

1   Or any other medical use except medicines that are ingested.

2   Cf. Chapter 7, Note 51. These plants grow as weeds.

הלכה א: כְּלָל גָּדוֹל אָמְרוּ בַּשְּׁבִיעִית כו'. רִבִּי בּוּן בַּר חִייָה בָּעָא קוֹמֵי רִבִּי זְעִירָא אוֹכְלֵי אָדָם וְאוֹכְלֵי בְהֵמָה הָיוּ בַּפָּרָשָׁה. מַה חָמִית מֵימַר אוֹכְלֵי אָדָם אֵין עוֹשִׂין מֵהֶן מָלוּגְמָא וְאוֹכְלֵי בְהֵמָה עוֹשִׂין מֵהֶן מָלוּגְמָא. אָמַר לֵיהּ וְהָיְתָה

שַׁבַּת הָאָרֶץ לָכֶם לְאָכְלָה מִיעוּט. מִיעֵט אוכְלֵי אָדָם אֵין עוֹשִׂין מֵהֶן מָלוּגְמָא. וּמִיעֵט אוּכְלֵי בְהֵמָה. אָמַר רבִּי בּוּן בַּר חִייָה כָּל־מִדְרָשׁ שֶׁאַתְּ דּוֹרֵשׁ וְשׁוּבֵר מִדְרָשׁ רִאשׁוֹן אֵין זֶה מִדְרָשׁ. רבִּי יוֹסֵי לֹא אָמַר כֵּן אֶלָּא וְהָיְתָה שַׁבַּת הָאָרֶץ לָכֶם לְאָכְלָה מִיעֵט. לְךָ וּלְעַבְדְּךָ וְלַאֲמָתֶךָ מִיעוּט אַחַר מִיעוּט. לְרַבּוֹא אוּכְלֵי אָדָם שֶׁאֵין עוֹשִׂין מָלוּגְמָא. וְרִבָּה אוּכְלֵי בְהֵמָה. כַּיי דָמַר רבִּי בּוּן בַּר חִייָה כָּל־מִדְרָשׁ שֶׁאַתְּ דּוֹרֵשׁ וְשׁוּבֵר מִדְרָשׁ רִאשׁוֹן אֵין זֶה מִדְרָשׁ. אָמַר רבִּי מַתַּנְיָיה כְּשֶׁמִיעַטְתָּה אוּכְלֵי אָדָם מִיעַטְתָּה וּכְרִיבִּיתָה אוּכְלֵי בְהֵמָה רִיבִּיתָה.

Halakhah 1: "They established a comprehensive principle for the Sabbatical," etc. Rebbi Abun bar Ḥiyya asked before Rebbi Zeïra: Human and animal food is mentioned in the paragraph[3]. What reason do you have to say that from human food one cannot make a wound dressing but from animal feed one may make a wound dressing? He said to him (*Lev.* 25:6): "The Land's Sabbath shall be for you as food", an exclusion. It excludes human food that cannot be made into wound dressing. It also excludes animal feed! Rebbi Abun bar Ḥiyya said, any interpretation you give which contradicts the prior interpretation is not valid[5]. Rebbi Yose did not say so, but (*Lev.* 25:6): "The Land's Sabbath shall be for you as food", an exclusion, "for you, your slave, and your handmaid", an exclusion after an exclusion, to add that human food cannot be made into wound dressing[4]. He added animal feed! As Rebbi Abun bar Ḥiyya said, any interpretation you give which contradicts the prior interpretation is not valid[5]. Rebbi Mattaniah said, when you did exclude, you excluded from human food; when you included, you included animal feed[6].

3   Lev. 25:6-7: "The Land's Sabbath shall be for you (*pl.*) as food, for you (*sing.*), your slave, and your handmaid, your hired hand and your sojourner who are dwelling with you. Also for your (*sing.*) domestic animals,

as well as the wild animals in your land, shall all its yield be food."

4   Here we find an essential difference between the exegesis of Babli and Yerushalmi. In the Babli, a double restriction always means an addition, no restriction at all. For the Yerushalmi, any exclusion remains an exclusion; one adds exclusions that otherwise would not be thought of. The verse really contains more exclusions and inclusions: "The Land's Sabbath shall be for you (*pl.*)", not for the Gentile (Tosephta 5:21) but for all your needs (Mishnah 8:2), "as food", not for industrial use and not for sacrifices [*Sifra Behar* 1(10)]. "For you (*sing.*), your slave, and your handmaid," seems to be an addition since this allows rich people to eat Sabbatical produce [*Sifra Behar* 1(10)], even though it is written (*Ex.* 23:11): "Abandon the yield of the Sabbatical, so it may be eaten by the destitute of your people . . ." The verse here permits slaveholders, i. e., people of means, to eat Sabbatical produce. According to *Mekhilta Mišpaṭim* 20, still only poor people may eat Sabbatical produce under the obligation of removal. It follows that "you, your slave, and your handmaid," is stated on condition that there be food for the wild animals, and can be considered a restriction. "Your hired hand and your sojourner who are dwelling with you" are Gentile employees hired for a period of time ("dwelling with you"), not hourly workers. They are exempt from the ban to give Sabbatical fruit to Gentiles. "Also for your domestic animals, as well as the wild animals in your land, shall all its yield be food," domestic animals can be fed stored food in the stable only as long as they could find it in the fields by themselves.

The argument in the Halakhah seems to be the following: Since Sabbatical produce is "for you", one could think that this (1) only excludes the Gentile, but a Jew may use Sabbatical produce for anything he needs. It is specified "for you, your slave, and your handmaid," which (2) excludes use of Sabbatical produce for any but human use. Wound dressings (as well as emetics) are used for human needs. If there were only one exclusion, I would include medical uses. But since there are two, one has to give an expansive interpretation of the exclusion; the only uses permitted are those needed equally by master and slave, the healthy and the sick. Therefore, medical (non-food) uses are forbidden, washing and heating is permitted. This argument is diametrically opposed to any Babylonian argument which treats two consecutive exclusions as inclusion.

5　R. Bun bar Ḥiyya refutes the arguments of R. Zeïra and R. Yose: Since "for you, your slave, and your handmaid," is a necessary addition, as explained above, to permit the rich person to eat, it cannot be treated as an exclusion. The explanations are in-

valid.

6　It is enough to have one exclusion mentioned for humans; since there is no similar exclusion for animals, which have the right to Sabbatical produce whether owned by a Jew or not, it is reasonable to have a restrictive tradition for human food but not for animal feed.

אוֹכְלֵי בְהֵמָה מַהוּ לַעֲשׂוֹת מֵהֶן צְבוּעִין לָאָדָם. מָה אִם אוֹכְלֵי אָדָם שֶׁאֵין עוֹשִׂין מֵהֶן מָלוּגְמָא לְאָדָם עוֹשִׂין מֵהֶן צְבוּעִין לָאָדָם אוֹכְלֵי בְהֵמָה שֶׁעוֹשִׂין מֵהֶן מָלוּגְמָא לְאָדָם לֹא כָּל־שֶׁכֵּן שֶׁעוֹשִׂין מֵהֶן צְבָעִין לָאָדָם. מִינֵי מָלוּגְמִיּוֹת מַהוּ לַעֲשׂוֹת מֵהֶן צְבָעִין לָאָדָם. מָה אִם אוֹכְלֵי אָדָם שֶׁאֵין עוֹשִׂין מֵהֶן מָלוּגְמָא לְאָדָם עוֹשִׂין מֵהֶן צְבָעִין לְאָדָם מִינֵי מָלוּגְמִיּוֹת שֶׁעוֹשִׂין מֵהֶן מָלוּגְמָא לְאָדָם לֹא כָּל־שֶׁכֵּן שֶׁתִּעֲשֶׂה מֵהֶן צְבָעִין לְאָדָם. לֹא צוּרְכָא דְלֹא אוֹכְלֵי אָדָם מַהוּ לַעֲשׂוֹת מֵהֶן צְבָעִין לִבְהֵמָה. כְּמָה דְאַתְּ אָמַר בְּאוֹכְלֵי אָדָם. שֶׁאֵין עוֹשִׂין מֵהֶן מָלוּגְמָא לְאָדָם עוֹשִׂין מֵהֶן צְבָעִין לְאָדָם וְדִכְוָתָהּ אוֹכְלֵי בְהֵמָה שֶׁאֵין עוֹשִׂין מֵהֶן מָלוּגְמָא לִבְהֵמָה נַעֲשָׂה צְבָעִין לִבְהֵמָה. אָמַר רִבִּי יוֹסֵי מִפְּנֵי מָה אוֹכְלֵי אָדָם עוֹשִׂין מֵהֶן צְבָעִין לְאָדָם שֶׁכֵּן צִיבְעֵי אָדָם יֵשׁ לָהֶן קְדוּשָׁה וְעָשָׂה מֵאוֹכְלֵי בְהֵמָה צְבָעִין לִבְהֵמָה וּצְבָעִין לִבְהֵמָה אֵין לָהֶן קְדוּשָׁה.

May one make dyes[7] for humans from animal feed? Since one may make dyes for humans from human food even though one may not use human food for a wound dressing, one certainly may make dyes for humans from animal feed since one may use animal feed for a wound dressing. May one make dyes for humans from materials for wound dressings? Since one may make dyes for humans from human food even

though one may not use human food for a wound dressing, one certainly
may make dyes for humans from wound dressing materials since one may
use wound dressing materials for a wound dressing. The only question[8] is:
May one make animal dyes[9] from human food? Just as you say for
human food that one may use it to make human dyes even though one
may not use it for wound dressing, similarly animal feed, though one may
not use it for animal wound dressing, should be usable for animal dyes.
Rebbi Yose said, why may one make dyes from human food? Because
human dyes have holiness[10]. Should one be able to make animal dyes
from animal feed when animal dyes have no holiness[11]?

7 Cosmetics. They fill a need equal for all humans.	10 Since they fill a genuine human need, they fall under all restrictions of the use of Sabbatical produce and cannot be exported or sold to Gentiles.
8 The previous argument about wound dressing materials was trivial.	
9 Probably to paint owner's marks on animals.	11 The answer to the question is negative.

נִיחָא חוּמְרֵי אָדָם וְחוּמְרֵי בְהֵמָה. שֶׁאָסוּר לְשׁוֹלְקָן. תַּנֵּי הַמּוֹכֵר מוֹכֵר לְאוֹכְלִין
וְהַלּוֹקֵחַ לוֹקֵחַ לְעֵצִים לֹא הַכֹּל מִמֶּנּוּ. הַמּוֹכֵר מוֹכֵר לְאוֹכְלִין וְהַלּוֹקֵחַ לוֹקֵחַ
לְאוֹכְלִין וְחִישֵׁב עֲלֵיהֶן לְעֵצִים לֹא הַכֹּל מִמֶּנּוּ. הַמּוֹכֵר מוֹכֵר לְעֵצִים וְהַלּוֹקֵחַ
לְאוֹכְלִין וְחִישֵׁב עֲלֵיהֶן לְעֵצִים. מַה נָן קַייָמִין אִם כְּשֶׁנָּתַן לוֹ מָעוֹת וְאַחַר כָּךְ
מָשַׁךְ דְּמֵי עֵצִים נָתַן לוֹ. אִם בְּשֶׁמָּשַׁךְ וְאַחַר כָּךְ נָתַן לוֹ מָעוֹת דְּמֵי אוֹכְלִין נָתַן
לוֹ. אֶלָּא כִּי (fol. 38a) נָן קַייָמִין בְּשֶׁנָּתַן לוֹ מָעוֹת וְאַחַר כָּךְ מָשַׁךְ תַּפְלוּגְתָּא דְּרִבִּי
יוֹחָנָן וְרִבִּי שִׁמְעוֹן בֶּן לָקִישׁ. עַל דַּעְתֵּיהּ דְּרִבִּי יוֹחָנָן דּוּ אָמַר אֵין הַמָּעוֹת קוֹנִין
דְּבַר תּוֹרָה דְּמֵי אוֹכְלִין נָתַן לוֹ. עַל דַּעְתֵּיהּ דְּרִבִּי שִׁמְעוֹן בֶּן לָקִישׁ הַמָּעוֹת קוֹנִין
דְּבַר תּוֹרָה דְּמֵי עֵצִים נָתַן לוֹ. הַמּוֹכֵר מוֹכֵר לְעֵצִים וְהַלּוֹקֵחַ לוֹקֵחַ לְאוֹכְלִין.

We understand "one puts on it all restrictions regarding humans and animals" that it is forbidden to boil them to a pulp[12]. We have stated: If the seller sells as food and the buyer buys as wood, the latter is not determining. If the seller sells as food and the buyer buys as food and then thinks of them as wood, the latter is not determining. If the seller sells as wood[13] and the buyer buys as food and then thinks of them as wood? Where do we hold? If he gave him the money and afterwards took it up, he paid for wood[14]. If he took it up and afterwards gave him the money, he paid for food. We must hold that he gave him the money and afterwards took it up; this is the disagreement between Rebbi Joḥanan and Rebbi Simeon ben Laqish[15]. According to Rebbi Joḥanan, who said that [transfer of] money does not mean acquisition by Torah law, he paid for food. According to Rebbi Simeon ben Laqish who said that [transfer of] money does mean acquisition by Torah law, he paid for wood.

12   Here starts the discussion of the third part of the Mishnah about produce used both as food (human or animal) or as wood.

13   While wood usually costs less than food, the seller has an interest in selling as wood since then the proceeds are not under Sabbatical restrictions and can be used for any purpose (R. H. Kanievski).

14   It is agreed that by rabbinic practice, handing over the money does not transfer property rights to the buyer; only taking possession (either actual or symbolic) can do that.

However, the *baraita* states that the opinion of the seller counts. Since the seller is not a party to the buyer's taking possession, his opinion can be determining only if he is the owner at the moment of payment.

15   According to one opinion, since לוקח "to take" also means "to buy", rabbinic practice simply follows the biblical decree. In this case, ownership is vested in the seller until the buyer actually takes possession. The other opinion notes that Abraham bought the field of Makhpela by paying money; it follows that the Torah recognizes pay-

ment as effecting transfer of ownership. According to this opinion,
rabbinic practice was introduced to cut
down on fraudulent transactions, so
that the seller could not sell nonexisting goods and later claim that they
did exist at the time of payment but
before delivery were destroyed in a
fire.

The position ascribed here (and in
Yerushalmi *Erubin* 7:11, fol. 24d) to R.
Johanan is that of R. Simeon ben Laqish
in the Babli (*Baba Meẓia'* 46b-47a,
Erubin 81b) and vice-versa. However,

the Talmud of Caesarea (Yerushalmi
Baba Meẓia' 4:2, fol. 9d) states that R.
Johanan asked (and followed) R.
Yannai's opinion in the matter and the
latter stated that payment transfers
property rights by Torah law and that
rabbinic practice was only instituted to
cut down on fraud. Since practice
almost always follows R. Johanan
against R. Simeon ben Laqish, Tiberian
practice followed the opinion of R.
Johanan in the text here, Babylonian
and Caesarean that of R. Simeon ben
Laqish.

הָיָה זֶה מַעֲמִיד וְזֶה מַעֲמִיד יֵיבָא16 כְּהָדָא אִם הַמּוֹכֵר תּוֹבֵעַ לְלוֹקֵחַ יַעֲשׂוּ כְדִבְרֵי
הַלּוֹקֵחַ. וְאִם הַלּוֹקֵחַ תּוֹבֵעַ לְמוֹכֵר יַעֲשׂוּ כְדִבְרֵי הַמּוֹכֵר. וְכָא כֵן.

If each one keeps to his word, it should be treated as follows[17]: "If the
seller sues the buyer one follows the buyer, if the buyer sues the seller,
one follows the seller." And here [one follows] the same [rule].

16   Reading of Rome ms. and פני
משה. Leyden and Venice: ריבה "added".
17   Tosephta *Qiddušin* 2:9. "One
says for 100, the other says for 200.
Each went to his own house and then
they sued one another. If the seller sues
the buyer one follows the buyer, if the
buyer sues the seller, one follows the
seller." This cryptic text was explained
by Maimonides (*Hilkhot Mekhirah*
20:1): "If somebody wants to buy from

another person and the seller says I
will sell for 200, the buyer says I shall
buy only for 100. They separate
without a deal and when they come
together again, the buyer takes the
article without saying anything. If the
seller sues the buyer after he handed
over the article, the latter has to pay
only 100. If the buyer came and took
the article, he has to give 200."

(fol. 37d) **משנה ב:** שְׁבִיעִית נִיתְּנָה לַאֲכִילָה וְלִשְׁתִּיָּיה וּלְסִיכָה לוֹכַל דָּבָר שֶׁדַּרְכּוֹ לוֹכַל וְלָסוּךְ דָּבָר שֶׁדַּרְכּוֹ לָסוּךְ וְלֹא יָסוּךְ יַיִן וְחוֹמֶץ אֲבָל סָךְ אֶת הַשֶּׁמֶן. וְכֵן בִּתְרוּמָה וּמַעֲשֵׂר שֵׁנִי. קַל מֵהֶן שְׁבִיעִית שֶׁנִּיתְּנָה לְהַדְלָקַת הַנֵּר.

Mishna 2: Sabbatical produce is to be used for food, drink, and anointing; to eat everything commonly eaten, to anoint with what commonly is used for anointing. One should not anoint with wine or vinegar, but with olive oil. The same rules apply for heave and second tithe[18], except that the Sabbatical admits the additional leniency that its [oil] may be used for lighting[19].

18 First heave of which the heave of the tithe has been taken is totally profane in the hand of the Levite.	Cohen's family. If the oil becomes impure it must be destroyed by burning; impure heave is used as fuel and for that reason is called "oil for burning". Hence, "heave" in this Mishnah means "pure heave".
19 Pure heave of olive oil must be used for a Cohen's family's food or for anointing on a pure member of a	

(fol. 38a) **הלכה ב:** כֵּיצַד לוֹכַל דָּבָר שֶׁדַּרְכּוֹ לוֹכַל אֵין מְחַייְבִין אוֹתוֹ לוֹכַל לֹא פַת שֶׁעִיפְּשָׁה וְלֹא קְנוּבַת יָרֵק וְלֹא תַּבְשִׁיל שֶׁנִּתְקַלְקֵל צוּרָתוֹ. וְכֵן הוּא שֶׁבִּיקֵשׁ לוֹכַל תַּרְדִּין חַיִּין אוֹ לַכּוֹס חִיטִּין חַיּוֹת אֵין שׁוֹמְעִין לוֹ. כֵּיצַד לִשְׁתּוֹת דָּבָר שֶׁדַּרְכּוֹ לִשְׁתּוֹת. אֵין מְחַייְבִין אוֹתוֹ לִשְׁתּוֹת אֲנִיגָרוֹן וְלֹא אִיקְסִיגָרוֹן וְלֹא יַיִן וּשְׁמָרִים. הַחוֹשֵׁשׁ בְּשִׁינָּיו לֹא יְהֵא מְגַמֵּא חוֹמֶץ וּפוֹלֵט אֲבָל מְגַמֵּא הוּא וּמַבְלִיעַ וּמִטַבֵּל כָּל־צָרְכּוֹ וְאֵינוֹ חוֹשֵׁשׁ. הַחוֹשֵׁשׁ גְּרוֹנוֹ לֹא יְעַרְעֶנּוּ בְּשֶׁמֶן אֲבָל נוֹתֵן הוּא שֶׁמֶן הַרְבֵּה לְתוֹךְ אֲנִיגָרוֹן וְגוֹמֵא.

Halakhah 2: What means "to eat everything commonly eaten"? "One does not oblige anybody to eat mouldy bread, or discarded leaves of vegetables, or spoiled food[20]." On the other hand, if somebody wants to eat raw beets[21] or chew raw wheat kernels one does not listen to him.

What means "to drink everything one commonly drinks"[22]? "[23]One does not oblige anybody to drink oily fish sauce[24], or sour fish sauce[25], or wine with yeast. He who has a toothache should not sip vinegar and spit out but he may sip and swallow. He may dip his food in as much [vinegar] as he wants without second thoughts[26]. He who has a throat ache should not gargle with oil but he may load fish sauce with oil and sip it."

20   Tosephta 6:2, in different order of items.

21   Definition of the Gaonim, Arukh, and Maimonides. In modern Hebrew: spinach.

22   This clause is in only a few Mishnah mss. It is in Tosephta 6:1.

23   Tosephta 6:3, in different order.

24   I. Löw defines as ἐλαιόγαρον, "olive oil with fish sauce" with change

of the liquids *n* - *l*, which fits the spelling better than οἰνόγαρον ("fish in wine sauce") given by earlier authors.

25   Greek ὀξύγαρον "fish sauce with vinegar". The Tosephta reads סניגרין both here and in *Terumot* 9:10'

26   Even if healthy people would not eat their food with as much vinegar.

לֹא יָסוּךְ יַיִן וְחוֹמֶץ אֲבָל סָךְ הוּא אֶת הַשֶּׁמֶן. הַחוֹשֵׁשׁ אֶת רֹאשׁוֹ אוֹ שֶׁעָלוּ בוֹ חֲטָטִין סָךְ שֶׁמֶן אֲבָל לֹא יָסוּךְ יַיִן וְחוֹמֶץ. אֵין מְפַטְמִין שֶׁמֶן שֶׁל שְׁבִיעִית אֲבָל לוֹקֵחַ הוּא שֶׁמֶן עָרֵב שְׁבִיעִית וְאֵינוֹ חוֹשֵׁשׁ. רִבִּי אִימִּי סָבַר מֵימַר אֲפִילוּ מִן הֶחָשׁוּד. אָמַר לֵיהּ רִבִּי יוֹסֵי לֹא אָמְרוּ אֶלָּא בְּשֶׁאֵינוֹ יוֹדֵעַ אִם חָשׁוּד אִם אֵינוֹ חָשׁוּד. הָא דָּבָר בָּרִיא שֶׁהוּא חָשׁוּד אָסוּר.

"One should not anoint with wine or vinegar, but with olive oil."[27] "If somebody has a headache or he has a scab, he may rub with oil but not with wine or vinegar."[28] One does not use Sabbatical oil as base for perfumes but one may buy sweet oil[29] before the Sabbatical without worry[30]. Rebbi Ammi thought, even from one who is suspect[31]. Rebbi Assi[32] told him, they said that only if one does not know whether he is suspect or not. But if it is clear that he is suspect, it is forbidden.

27 Quote from the Mishnah.

28 Tosephta 6:4: "If somebody has a headache or a scab, he may rub with oil but not with wine or vinegar since oil is commonly used for rubbing but wine and oil are not."

29 Perfumed oil, cf. *Berakhot* 8:5, Note 109.

30 It does not need a rabbinic endorsement that it was prepared with non-Sabbatical oil since it is denatured and cannot become edible again.

31 A person suspected of illegal trading with Sabbatical produce.

32 Reading יוסה for יוסי for chronological reasons.

מַהוּ לְפַטֵּם יַיִן שֶׁל שְׁבִיעִית. נִישְׁמְעִינָהּ מִן הָדָא קַל מֵהֶן שְׁבִיעִית שֶׁנִּיתְּנָה לְהַדְלָקַת הַנֵּר. הָדָא אֲמָרָה שֶׁהוּא מוּתָּר. וְהָתַנֵּי אָסוּר. אָמַר רִבִּי אֶלְעָזָר דְּרִבִּי יְהוּדָה הִיא. דְּרִבִּי יְהוּדָה מַתִּיר מִפְּנֵי שֶׁהוּא מַשְׁבִּיחוֹ.

May one spice Sabbatical wine? Let us hear from the following: "The Sabbatical admits the additional leniency that its [oil] may be used for lighting"; that means it is permitted[33]. But did we not state[34] that it is forbidden? Rebbi Eleazar said, it is Rebbi Jehudah's, since Rebbi Jehudah permits it because it enhances its value[35].

33 Mishnah *Ma'aśer Šeni* 2:1: "One may not use second tithe oil as base for perfume, one may not buy perfumed oil with second tithe money, but one may spice [second tithe] wine." Since the rules of the Sabbatical are declared to be more lenient that those of heave and second tithe, what is permitted for second tithe *a fortiori* is permitted for the Sabbatical.

34 In some *baraita* not otherwise preserved.

35 Mishnah *Terumot* 11:1: "One does not cook wine of heave because this reduces its volume. Rebbi Jehudah permits it because it improves it." If one may thicken wine by boiling (while it then loses its alcohol), one also may make spice wine from heave and, *a fortiori*, from Sabbatical wine.

קַל מֵהֶן שְׁבִיעִית שֶׁנִּיתְּנָה לְהַדְלָקַת הַנֵּר. וּתְרוּמָה לֹא נִיתְּנָה לְהַדְלָקַת הַנֵּר. תְּרוּמָה טְמֵיאָה נִיתְּנָה לְהַדְלָקַת הַנֵּר. שְׁבִיעִית אֲפִילוּ טְהוֹרָה נִיתְּנָה לְהַדְלָקַת

הַנֵּר. רִבִּי חִזְקִיָּה עַל מִסְחֵי יְהַב צְלוֹחִיתָא לְזוֹסִימִי אוֹרְיָרָא.[36] אָמַר לֵיהּ אַעֵיל

לָהּ לִי[37] לָאֲשׁוּנָא. אָמַר לֵיהּ לֵית אָסוּר. אָתָא שָׁאַל לְרִבִּי יִרְמְיָה. אָמַר לֵיהּ

אָתָא וְאָמַר לֵיהּ לְמַדְתָּנוּ וְתַנֵּי כֵן אֵין סָכִין שֶׁמֶן שֶׁל שְׁבִיעִית בַּמֶּרְחָץ אֲבָל סָךְ

הוּא מִבְּחוּץ וְנִכְנַס.

"The Sabbatical admits the additional leniency that its [oil] may be used
for lighting"; that means it is permitted" May heave not be used for
lighting? Impure heave may be used for lighting; even pure Sabbatical oil
may be used for lighting. Rebbi Ḥizqiah went to the bath. He gave a
flask to Zosimos the bath attendant; he said to him: bring that to the
inner room[38] for me. He said to him, is that not forbidden? He went to
ask Rebbi Jeremiah. He said to him[39], he came and said to him, you
yourself taught us, and we stated so: One does not rub in Sabbatical oil in
the bath house but he may rub it in outside and enter.

36   Reading of the Rome ms.,
Orearius for *olearius*, a form found also
in Yerushalmi *Baba Batra* 4:1 (fol. 14c),
Mishnah *Ṭahorot* 7:7. Leyden and
Venice: אודייתא "fire wood".
37   Reading of Rome ms. Leyden
and Venice: אעלליה לי , to be read as
אעל ליה לי .
38   The heated inner room where
everybody is naked and no holy things

are permitted; cf. *Berakhot* pp. 185-186.
39   Either this is dittography (as
assumed by most commentators) or it
means "he" (the messenger urgently
dispatched by R. Ḥizqiah) "reported to
him" (R. Ḥizqiah) that R. Jeremiah
came and said that R. Ḥizqiah himself
had taught ... (פמי משה). This explanation is too ingenious to be correct.

וְלֹא שֶׁמֶן שְׂרֵיפָה לֹא בְּבָתֵּי כְנֵסִיּוֹת וְלֹא בְּבָתֵּי מִדְרָשׁוֹת מִפְּנֵי בִּזָּיוֹן קֳדָשִׁים.

And oil for burning neither in synagogues nor in houses of study
because of degradation of sacred things[40].

40 R. Simson's text reads: "Impure heave cannot be used for lighting in synagogues and houses of study." This sentence cannot mean that impure heave can never be used for lighting in synagogues and houses of study since Mishnah *Terumot* 11:10 states explicitly that impure heave is used to illuminate synagogues and houses of study *with* *permission by a Cohen.* The statement must mean that such use represents degradation of holy things if done without explicit permission by a Cohen. The sentence cannot belong to the previous paragraph dealing with anointing since one never may anoint himself in a holy place.

(fol. 37d) **משנה ג:** אֵין מוֹכְרִין פֵּירוֹת שְׁבִיעִית לֹא בְמִדָּה וְלֹא בְמִשְׁקָל וְלֹא בְמִנְיָן וְלֹא תְאֵינִים בְּמִנְיָן וְלֹא יָרָק בְּמִשְׁקָל. בֵּית שַׁמַּאי אוֹמֵר אַף לֹא אֲגוּדוֹת. וּבֵית הִלֵּל אוֹמְרִים אֶת שֶׁדַּרְכּוֹ לֶאֱגוֹד אוֹתוֹ בַּבַּיִת אוֹגְדִין אוֹתוֹ בַּשּׁוּק כְּגוֹן הַכְּרֵישִׁין וְנֵץ הֶחָלָב.

Mishnah 3: Sabbatical produce should not be sold[41] by measure, weight, or count. Figs may not be sold by count nor vegetables by weight[42]. The House of Shammai say, not [vegetables] in bundles. But the House of Hillel say, anything usually stored in bundles in the house may be bundled on the market; for example leeks and milk bud[43].

41 Some produce collected in the Sabbatical may be routinely sold since it is collected from the wild, not from cultivated fields; Mishnah 9:1. Other produce may be sold if a surplus has been collected.

42 These are examples illustrating the preceding sentence.

43 Chapter 7, Note 16.

(fol. 38a) **הלכה ג:** לָמָּה כְּדֵי שֶׁיִּמָּכְרוּ בְזוֹל. וְיִשָּׁקְלוּ בְלִיטְרָא וְיִמָּכְרוּ בְזוֹל. אִם אָמַר אַתְּ כֵּן אַף הוּא אֵינוֹ נוֹהֵג בָּהֶן בִּקְדוּשָׁה.

Halakhah 3: Why? So it should be sold cheaply. Why could it not be cheaply sold by the pound[44]? If you say so, he will not treat it as holy.

44   Vegetables usually sold by the   wholesale and therefore cheaper.
ounce, when sold by the pound are

תַּנֵּי פֵירוֹת חוּץ לָאָרֶץ שֶׁנִּכְנְסוּ לָאָרֶץ. לֹא יְהוּ נִמְכָּרִין לֹא בְמִידָה וְלֹא בְמִשְׁקָל

וּבְמִנְיָן אֶלָּא כְפֵירוֹת הָאָרֶץ וְאִם הָיוּ נִיכָּרִין מוּתָּר. אָמַר רִבִּי יוֹסֵי בֵּי רִבִּי בּוּן

אִילֵּין כְּגוֹן[45] אִילֵּין קוֹרדְקִיא דְּסָלְקִין וּמִזְדַּבְּנִין מִן סוּסִיתָא לְטִיבֶּרְיָא.

It was stated[46]: "Produce from outside the Land that entered the Land should not be sold by measure, weight, or count, but only like produce of the Land." It they are recognizable, it is permitted. Rebbi Yose ben Rebbi Abun said, for example *qwrdqy'*[47] brought up from Hippos and sold to Tiberias.

45   Reading of the Rome ms. The   47   This fruit has not been
word is missing in the Leyden ms. and   identified. One possibility is to derive
Venice print.   the word from Persian گردکان *gardekān*
46   Tosephta 4:18: "*Sabbatical*   "walnut". The language is unclear since
Produce from outside the Land that   produce brought from high-lying Hip-
entered the Land should not be sold by   pos to low-lying Tiberias is brought
measure, weight, or count, but *it is* like down, not up, unless one denotes all
produce of the Land." That text does   import into the Holy Land as "bringing
not permit trade of recognizable   up".
imports.

רִבִּי חִזְקִיָּה בְּשֵׁם רִבִּי אַבָּא בַּר מֶמָל זֶה שֶׁהוּא מוֹדֵד בִּכְפִישָׁה וְנִסְתַּיְּימָה לוֹ

שָׁנַיִם וּשְׁלֹשָׁה פְעָמִים. אָסוּר לָמוּד בָּהּ. אָמַר רִבִּי הוֹשַׁעְיָה אָסוּר מֵימַר עֲבַד

עֲצִבְּעָךְ.

Rebbi Ḥizqiah in the name of Rebbi Abba bar Mamal: If somebody measures with a box in which he made a sign two or three times, he may no longer use it for measuring[48]. Rebbi Hoshaiah said, it is forbidden to say, give me your finger's length.

48   Even though the box was not created for measuring, when he made signs that indicate certain volumes, even if not those desired now, the box now has the status of a measuring device and is forbidden. Similarly, it is assumed that everybody knows the length of his own index finger; measuring by the length of his finger is like measuring by a measuring rod.

טַבָּח כֹּהֵן שֶׁנִּתְמַנֶּה לוֹ בְּכוֹר מַהוּ מְקַטְּעָתָהּ קוּפָּדִין וּמְזַבְּנַתָּהּ גְּוָא שׁוּקָא. רבִּי יִרְמְיָה סָבַר מֵימַר שָׁרֵי מִן הָדָא אֶת שֶׁדַּרְכּוֹ לֵיאָגֵד בַּבַּיִת אוֹגְדִין אוֹתוֹ בַּשּׁוּק. אָמַר רבִּי מָנָא כָּל־נַּרְמָא הִיא אָמְרָה דְהוּא אָסוּר שֶׁלֹּא יְהֵא כְעוֹשֶׂה סְחוֹרָה בְּגוּפוֹ.

If a butcher who is a Cohen gets hold of a first-born[49], may he cut it up into roasts and sell it on the market? Rebbi Jeremiah wanted to say it is permitted, analogous to "anything usually stored in bundles in the house may be bundled on the market[50]". Rebbi Mana said, that statement itself implies that it is forbidden, that he should not treat its body as merchandise.

49   A first-born calf, lamb, or kid goat is a sacrifice by its birth and must be given to a Cohen. If it develops a defect that invalidates it as a sacrifice, it is the Cohen's profane property (*Deut.* 15:21-22). However, it may not be treated with disrespect. The details are given in Tractate *Bekhorot*.

50   If the first-born is slaughtered for home use, in the absence of refrigeration it is either cut into large pieces for festive meals or into smaller pieces to be smoked or pickled; neither of them is the kind of cut one does for the market.

(fol. 37d) **מֹשְׁנָה ד:** הָאוֹמֵר לַפּוֹעֵל הֵילָךְ אִיסּוּר זֶה וְלַקֵּט לִי יֶרֶק הַיּוֹם שְׂכָרוֹ מוּתָּר. לַקֵּט לִי בּוֹ יֶרֶק הַיּוֹם שְׂכָרוֹ אָסוּר. לָקַח מִן הַנַּחְתּוֹם כִּכָּר בְּפוֹנְדִיוֹן כְּשֶׁאֶלְקוֹט יַרְקוֹת שָׂדֶה אָבִיא לָךְ מוּתָּר. לָקַח מִמֶּנּוּ סְתָם לֹא יְשַׁלֵּם מִדְּמֵי שְׁבִיעִית שֶׁאֵין פּוֹרְעִין חוֹב מִדְּמֵי שְׁבִיעִית.

Mishnah 4: Is somebody says to a day-laborer: "Here you have an *as*[51] and collect vegetables for me today", these wages are permitted. "For its value collect vegetables for me today", these wages are forbidden. If somebody bought from the baker a loaf in the value of a *dupondius*[52] [and says], when I collect vegetables from the field I shall bring to you, that is permitted. If he took from him silently he should not pay with the proceeds of Sabbatical [produce] since one may not pay a debt with proceeds of the Sabbatical.

51   A quarter of a drachma. If the laborer is hired for some wages and only afterwards given the task to collect vegetables from Sabbatical growth, his wages are profane and he may spend them in any way he wants. But if the wages are given for the explicit purpose of collecting Sabbatical growth, the wages become Sabbatical and may be used only to buy Sabbatical produce. The Babli (*Avodah Zarah* 62b) does not accept this fine distinction but declares all limitations imposed on payment for the explicit purpose of working during the Sabbatical as fines. Cf. also Notes 94,95.

52   Half a drachma. It is permitted to exchange Sabbatical produce for other produce. But if food was bought on credit one may not pay with Sabbatical produce or its proceeds.

(fol. 38a) **הֲלָכָה ד:** מַה בֵּין הָאוֹמֵר לַקֵּט לִי מַה בֵּין הָאוֹמֵר לַקֵּט לִי בּוֹ. רִבִּי יוֹסֵי בְּשֵׁם רִבִּי יוֹסֵי בֶּן חֲנִינָה מֵהֵילָכוֹת שֶׁל עִימְעוּם הִיא. תַּמָּן תַּנִּינָן לֹא יֹאמַר אָדָם לַחֲבֵירוֹ הַעַל הַפֵּירוֹת הָאֵלֶּה לִירוּשָׁלַם לְחַלֵּק. אֶלָּא אוֹמֵר לוֹ הַעֲלֵם שֶׁנֹּאכְלֵם וְנִשְׁתֵּם בִּירוּשָׁלַם. מַה בֵּין הָאוֹמֵר לְחַלֵּק מַה בֵּין הָאוֹמֵר הַעֲלֵם

שֶׁנֹּאכַל וְנִשְׁתֶּה בִּירוּשָׁלֵם. רִבִּי זְעִירָא בְשֵׁם רִבִּי יוֹנָתָן מֵהִילְכוֹת שֶׁל עִימְעוּם
הוּא. תַּמָּן תַּנִּינָן שׁוֹאֵל אָדָם מֵחֲבֵירוֹ כַּדֵּי יַיִן וְכַדֵּי שֶׁמֶן. וּבִלְבַד שֶׁלֹּא יֹאמַר לוֹ
הַלְוֵינִי. מַה בֵּין הָאוֹמֵר הַלְוֵנִי מַה בֵּין הָאוֹמֵר הַשְׁאִילֵנִי. אָמַר רִבִּי זְעִירָא בְשֵׁם
רִבִּי יוֹנָתָן מֵהִילְכוֹת שֶׁל עִימְעוּם הִיא.

What[53] is the difference between him who says "collect for me" and him who says "for its value collect for me"? Rebbi Yose in the name of Rebbi Yose ben Ḥanina, this is one of the practices of obfuscation[54]. There, we have stated[55]: "One should not say to another person, bring these fruits to Jerusalem to distribute, but he should say: bring them that we should eat and drink them there." What is the difference between him who says "to distribute" and him who says "bring them that we should eat and drink them in Jerusalem?" Rebbi Zeïra in the name of Rebbi Jonathan, this is one of the practices of obfuscation. There, we have stated[56]: "A person may borrow from another pitchers of wine or oil but he should not say: lend me." What is the difference between him who says "let me borrow" and him who says "lend me"? Rebbi Zeïra in the name of Rebbi Jonathan, this is one of the practices of obfuscation.

53 This paragraph and the next appear (with minor changes in the order of subjects) in *Ma'aser Šeni* 3:1 (fol. 54a), *Šabbat* 1:6 (fol. 3c), *Avodah Zarah* 2:9 (fol. 41d). In the Babli (*Avodah Zarah* 62a/b), all prohibitions are explained as fines.

54 Compare Arabic עמעם, Hebrew גמגם "to mutter, to stutter". While the reason was explained in Note 51, the difference in practice is purely

semantic and one should not permit an action whose intent is to circumvent the law. The answer is that as a practical necessity, the rabbis found a way to legitimize popular behavior by obscuring the strict interpretation of the law.

55 Mishnah *Ma'aser Šeni* 3:1. It is forbidden to pay one's debt with Second Tithe. Therefore one has to formulate a transportation contract in

such a way as to give to the transporter a claim to part of the food before the start of the contract.

56   Mishnah *Šabbat* 23:1. It is forbidden to make commercial transactions on the Sabbath. Exchanges between neighbors are permitted but any mention of monetary values is forbidden. [There is no Yerushalmi extant for the last four chapters of *Šabbat*. In the Babli (*Šabbat* 148a) this is not one of the obscure practices; the mention of monetary values is forbidden as rabbinic ordinance to avoid any temptation to write things down. It seems that the Babli considers even monetary transactions between neighbors as friendly exchanges, permitted under biblical law.]

פִּיתָּן רִבִּי יַעֲקֹב בַּר אָחָא בְּשֵׁם רִבִּי יוֹנָתָן עוֹד הִיא מֵהִילְכוֹת שֶׁל עִימְעוּם. אָמַר רִבִּי יוֹסֵי קַשִּׁייָתָהּ קוֹמֵי רִבִּי יַעֲקֹב בַּר אָחָא. מַהוּ מֵהִלְכוֹת שֶׁל עִמְעוּם הוּא כָּךְ אֲנִי אוֹמֵר בְּמָקוֹם שֶׁאֵין פַּת יִשְׂרָאֵל מְצוּיָה בְּדִין הוּא שֶׁתְּהֵא פַּת גּוֹי מוּתֶּרֶת וְעִימְעַמוּ עָלֶיהָ וְאֲסָרוּהָ. אָמַר רִבִּי מָנָא וְיֵשׁ עִימְעוּם לְאִיסּוּר. וּפַת לֹא כְתַבְשִׁילֵי גוֹים הִיא. כָּךְ אָנוּ אוֹמְרִים בְּמָקוֹם שֶׁתַּבְשִׁילֵי יִשְׂרָאֵל אֵינָן מְצוּיִּין שָׁם בְּדִין הוּא שֶׁיְּהוּ תַבְשִׁילֵי גוֹיִם מוּתָּרִין וְעִימְעַמוּ עָלֵיהֶן וְאֲסָרוּם. אֶלָּא כֵן הָיָה בְּמָקוֹם שֶׁאֵין פַּת יִשְׂרָאֵל מְצוּיָה בְּדִין הוּא שֶׁתְּהֵא פַּת גּוֹיִם אֲסוּרָה וְעִימְעַמוּ עָלֶיהָ וְהִתִּירוּהָ מִפְּנֵי חַיֵּי נֶפֶשׁ. רַבָּנִין דְּקֵיסָרִין בְּשֵׁם רִבִּי יַעֲקֹב בַּר אָחָא כִּדְבָרֵי מִי שֶׁהוּא מַתִּיר וּבִלְבַד מִן הַפְלָטֵר. וְלָא עָבְדִין כֵּן.

Their[57] bread. Rebbi Jacob bar Aḥa in the name of Rebbi Jonathan: This also belongs to the practices of obfuscation. Rebbi Yose said, I objected before Rebbi Jacob bar Aḥa: Why should it belong to the practices of obfuscation? I say that at a place where no Jewish bread is available it is logical that Gentile bread should be permitted, but they[59] obfuscated the matter and forbade it. Rebbi Mana said: Does there exist obfuscation for prohibition[58]? Is bread not like Gentile cooking? So we say: At a place where no Jewish cooking is to be found it is logical that

Gentile cooking should be permitted, but they obfuscated the matter and forbade it[60]. But so it was: At a place where no Jewish bread is available it is logical that Gentile bread should be forbidden, but they obfuscated the matter and permitted it as a necessity of life. The rabbis of Caesarea in the name of Rebbi Jacob bar Aḥa [hold] with the one who permits, but only from a store[61]. But one does not follow this[62].

57   Gentile bread. Anything cooked or baked by a Gentile is forbidden, according to the Yerushalmi (*Šabbat* 1:6, fol. 3c) as one of the "eighteen decrees" enacted at the start of the first revolt against the Romans to separate Jews from Gentiles; according to the Babli (*Avodah Zarah* 35b) it is an older rabbinic prohibition enacted to cut down on intermarriage. In biblical law, food prepared by Gentiles according to Jewish dietary laws is permitted (*Deut.* 2:6,28).

58   There do exist prohibitions whose origin is most unclear, such as the prohibition of Gentile cheese made with vegetable rennet. But the technical term "obfuscation" is only used in connection with practices the rabbis had to condone and permit.

59   According to the Mishnah (*Avodah Zarah* 2:9), Rebbi and his court

permitted Gentile bread.

60   According to the Babli (*loc. cit.*), in this case Gentile cooking is certainly forbidden because of the dangers of intermarriage.

61   The Babli (*loc. cit.*) agrees that this was the original meaning of Rebbi's ruling, but the people interpreted it to permit any Gentile bread, as implied here by the next sentence.

62   The Babli accepts the original statement of the Yerushalmi that Gentile bread is permitted only in the absence of a store selling bread baked by Jews. ("Baked by Jews" in the Babli means that the oven was lit by a Jew; all other work may be done by Gentiles.) A statement attributed to R. Joḥanan in the Babli even forbids all Gentile bread in town and allows it only for consumption in the fields.

רבּי שׁמְעוֹן בֶּן לָקִישׁ אָמַר בְּמַרְאֶה לוֹ אֶת הַקּוֹלֵחַ שֶׁאֵינוֹ אֶלָּא כְּנוֹתֵן לוֹ שְׂכַר
רַגְלוֹ. רִבִּי יוֹחָנָן אָמַר אֲפִילוּ לֹא הֶרְאֶה לוֹ כְּמִי שֶׁהֶרְאֶה לוֹ. מַתְנִיתָא פְּלִיגָא
עַל רִבִּי שִׁמְעוֹן בֶּן לָקִישׁ. דְּתַנֵּי הַשּׂוֹכֵר אֶת הַפּוֹעֵל לְהָבִיא יַיִן לְחוֹלֶה אוֹ תַפּוּחַ
לְחוֹלֶה אִם הֵבִיא חַיָּיב לִיתֶּן לוֹ וְאִם לָאו אֵינוֹ חַיָּיב לִיתֶּן לוֹ. אֲבָל אִם אָמַר לוֹ
יַיִן לְחוֹלֶה מִמָּקוֹם פְּלוֹנִי תַּפּוּחַ לְחוֹלֶה מִמָּקוֹם פְּלוֹנִי בֵּין שֶׁהֵבִיא בֵּין שֶׁלֹּא
הֵבִיא חַיָּיב לִיתֶּן לוֹ שְׂכַר רַגְלָיו הוּא נוֹתֵן לוֹ. מַה עֲבִיד לָהּ רבּי שׁמְעוֹן בֶּן לָקִישׁ
פָּתַר לָהּ בְּמַרְאֶה לוֹ. מַתְנִיתָא פְּלִיגָא עַל רִבִּי יוֹחָנָן. דְּתַנֵּי לֹא יֹאמַר אָדָם
לַחֲבֵירוֹ הָא לָךְ דֵּינָר זֶה וַהֲבֵא לִי לֶקֶט הַיּוֹם. הֲבֵא לִי פֵּיאָה הַיּוֹם אֶלָּא אוֹמֵר
לוֹ בְּלֶקֶט שֶׁתָּבִיא לִי הַיּוֹם בְּפֵיאָה שֶׁתָּבִיא לִי הַיּוֹם. וְכֵן אַתְּ מוֹצֵא בְּבֶן לֵוִי.
וַהֲרֵי לֹא הֶרְאֶה לוֹ וְאַתְּ אָמַר כְּמִי שֶׁהֶרְאֶה לוֹ. מַה עֲבַד לָהּ רבּי יוֹחָנָן קַל
הֵקִילוּ בַּשְּׁבִיעִית שֶׁהִיא מִדְּרַבָּנָן.

Rebbi Simeon ben Laqish said, if he shows him the stump[63]; then he
pays him only the wages of his feet[64]. Rebbi Johanan said, even if he did
not show it to him it is as if he had. A *baraita* disagrees with Rebbi
Simeon ben Laqish, as it was stated[65]: "If somebody hires a worker to
bring wine for a sick person, or an apple for a sick person, if he delivered
it, he must pay, otherwise he does not have to pay. But if he said to him,
wine for a sick person from place X, or an apple for a sick person from
place X, he has to pay him whether he delivered or not because he pays
him the wages of his feet." What does Rebbi Simeon ben Laqish do with
this? He explains that he showed him. A *baraita* disagrees with Rebbi
Johanan, as it was stated: "Nobody should say to his neighbor[66], here you
have a denar and bring me gleanings today, bring me *peah* today. But he
may say to him, for gleanings you will bring today, for *peah* you will
bring today. The same rules apply to a Levite." Here, he did not show
him; is it considered as if he showed him? What does Rebbi Johanan do

with this? They were particularly lenient with the Sabbatical because it is rabbinical[67].

<table>
<tr>
<td>

63   This means, if he indicates the places where the worker should go and collect. Most commentators delete the word but it is confirmed by both mss.

64   Since the contract was only for the transport, the wages are not Sabbatical.

65   This *baraita* is also quoted *Avodah Zarah* 5:1 (fol. 44c). In the first case, it is a contract for delivery, in the second case a contract for work. Since the expression used by R. Simeon ben Laqish, "wages of his feet", are used in the *baraita* regarding an unrestricted contract for work, the restrictive use of

</td>
<td>

R. Simeon ben Laqish seems to be unjustified.

66   The rich person says to the poor one that he is willing to pay for the gleanings the poor will collect. Since gleanings and *peah* become the unrestricted property of the poor, the transaction is legitimate if the poor man is paid for delivery of the produce; it is illegitimate if the poor man is hired to collect as agent for the rich person. The same rules apply for a Levite and First Tithe.

67   Cf. Chapter 1, Note 7.

</td>
</tr>
</table>

לָקַח מִן הַנַּחְתּוֹם כִּכָּר בְּפוֹנְדְיוֹן כְּשֶׁאֶלְקוֹט יַרְקוֹת שָׂדֶה אָבִיא לָךְ מוּתָּר. תַּנֵּי רִבִּי יוּדָה וְרִבִּי נְחֶמְיָה אוֹסְרִין. מַה נָן קַיָּימִין כְּהַהוּא דְּאָמַר הַב לִי וּבָרִי לִי אֲנָא יְהַב לָךְ רִבִּי יוּדָה וְרִבִּי נְחֶמְיָה אוֹסְרִין שֶׁאֵין יַרְקוֹת שָׂדֶה מְצוּיִין. וַחֲכָמִים מַתִּירִין מִפְּנֵי שֶׁיַּרְקוֹת שָׂדֶה מְצוּיִין.

"If somebody bought from the baker a loaf in the value of a *dupondius* [and says], when I collect vegetables from the field I shall bring to you, that is permitted.[68]" It was stated: "Rebbi Jehudah and Rebbi Nehemiah forbid it[69]." What are we talking about? About one who says, give it to me and it is clear to me [where to find it], I shall bring it to you; Rebbi Jehudah and Rebbi Nehemiah forbid it because vegetables on the field are rare; but the Sages permit it because vegetables on the field are abundant.

68   Quote from the Mishnah.

69   Tosephta 6:21. The discussion here is fragmentary; the full text is in *Ma'aser Šeni* 3:1 (fol. 54a): If the baker says, here it is, bring me later, this is forbidden according to everybody (since one may not pay a debt with Sabbatical produce). If the buyer says, give it to me and I shall give to you (what I already have collected), that is permitted according to everybody. But if the buyer says, give it to me and I know where to find, that is the disagreement between Rebbis Judah and Nehemiah and the Sages, as described here.

(fol. 37d) **משנה ה:** אֵין נוֹתְנִין לֹא לְבַיָּיר וְלֹא לְבַלָּן וְלֹא לְסַפָּר וְלֹא לְסַפָּן. אֲבָל נוֹתֵן הוּא לְבַיָּיר לִשְׁתּוֹת. וּלְכוּלָּן הוּא נוֹתֵן מַתָּנוֹת חִינָּם.

One gives neither to the water drawer, nor to the bath attendant, nor to the barber, nor to the ship owner[70], but one may give to drink to the water drawer. And to all of these one may give free gifts.

70   As explained in Mishnah 2, Sabbatical produce has to be consumed and may not be given in payment. But it may be given to drink (or to eat). It may be given for goodwill (according to the House of Hillel in Mishnah 4:2).

(fol. 38a) **הלכה ה:** תַּנֵּי רְבִּי יוֹסֵי אוֹמֵר אַף לֹא לַמַּבַּיָּיר. מַחְלְפָה שִׁיטָתֵיהּ דְּרְבִּי יוֹסֵי. תַּמָּן הוּא אוֹמֵר אֵין לוֹקְחִין הֵימֶנּוּ מַיִם וּמֶלַח. וְהָכָא הוּא אָמַר הָכֵן. אָמַר רְבִּי יוֹסֵי מַה פְּלִיגִין (fol. 38b) בְּשֶׁתַּשְׁמְשׁוֹ אֲבָל בִּשְׁתִייָה אוּף רְבִּי יוֹסֵי מוֹדֵי הֲוֵי. מָאן תַּנָּא אֲבָל נוֹתֵן הוּא לְבַיָּיר לִשְׁתּוֹת רְבִּי יוֹסֵי. אָמַר רְבִּי יוֹסֵי דְּבְרֵי הַכֹּל הִיא כָּאן לְאָדָם וְכָאן לִבְהֵמָה.

Halakhah 5: It was stated[71]: "Rebbi Yose says, not even to the water drawer." The opinions of Rebbi Yose are contradictory. There, he says[72]: "One does not use them to buy water and salt," and here he says so[73]?

Rebbi Yose[74] said, they disagree for general usage[75], but for drinking even Rebbi Yose would agree. Who is the Tanna of "but one may give to drink to the water drawer"? Rebbi Yose! Rebbi Yose[74] said, it is the opinion of everybody; one statement refers to humans, the other to animals[76].

71   In some *baraita* it was stated that R. Yose forbids to give drinks made from Sabbatical fruits to the water drawer. Since this seems to contradict Mishnah 2, one has to investigate what this statement means.

72   Tosephta 6:25: "One may not use Sabbatical produce to buy water and salt; *Rebbi Yose says, one may use Sabbatical produce to buy water and salt.*"

73   In the Tosephta, he permits

using proceeds of Sabbatical fruits to buy water and salt which in themselves are not food, and here he seems to forbid using even drinks made from Sabbatical fruits as drinks!

74   The Amora.

75   For anything but nourishment.

76   The *baraita* fragment quoted at the start refers to giving Sabbatical drinks to animals. This use would not be sanctioned by Mishnah 2.

תַּנֵּי מַעֲיָין שֶׁל בְּנֵי הָעִיר הֵן וַאֲחֵרִים קוֹדְמִין הֵן לַאֲחֵרִים. אֲחֵרִים וּבְהֶמְתָּן אֲחֵרִים קוֹדְמִין לִבְהֶמְתָּן. כְּבִיסָתָן וְחַיֵּי אֲחֵרִים כְּבִיסָתָן קוֹדֶמֶת לְחַיֵּי אֲחֵרִים. אָמַר רִבִּי יוֹחָנָן מָאן תַּנָּא כְּבִיסָה חַיֵּי נֶפֶשׁ רִבִּי יוֹסֵי. דְּתַנֵּי אֵין נוֹתְנִין מֵהֶן לֹא לְמִשְׁרָה וְלֹא לִכְבִיסָה. וְרִבִּי יוֹסֵי מַתִּיר לִכְבִיסָה. מִחְלְפָה שִׁיטָתֵיהּ דְּרִבִּי יוֹסֵי. תַּמָּן הוּא אוֹמֵר אֵין רְחִיצָה חַיֵּי נֶפֶשׁ. וְכָא הוּא אָמַר הַכְּבִיסָה חַיֵּי נֶפֶשׁ. אָמַר רִבִּי מָנָא אָדָם מְגַלְגֵּל בִּרְחִיצָה וְאֵין אָדָם מְגַלְגֵּל בִּכְבִיסָה.

It was stated[77]: "A water source belonging to the townspeople, between them and outsiders, they have precedence over outsiders. Between outsiders and their animals, the outsiders have precedence. Their washing[78] and the lives of outsiders, their washing has precedence over the lives of outsiders." Rebbi Johanan said, who is the Tanna who said that washing is a necessity for survival? Rebbi Yose! As it was stated: "One may use it neither for steeping nor for washing. But Rebbi Yose permits it for washing.[79]" The opinions of Rebbi Yose are contradictory. There[80] he says, washing oneself is not a necessity of life. And here, he says washing one's garments is a necessity of life. Rebbi Mana said, a person might put off washing himself but nobody puts off washing his clothes[81].

77   Babli *Nedarim* 80b, a text close to the one given here, a different text Tosephta *Baba Mezi'a* 11:33-36. In the Tosephta, R. Yose declares that the animals of the town have precedence over the lives of outsiders. Therefore, the argument given here does not apply to R. Yose's opinion in the Tosephta; the latter represents neither of the two Talmudim. A text close to the paragraph given here is in *Nedarim* 11:1 (fol. 42c). The paragraph is inserted here because it deals with seemingly contradictory opinions of the Tanna R.

Yose.

78   Washing their clothes, not themselves.

79   A similar text is in Babli *Sukkah* 40a, *Moëd Qaṭan* 101b, where however steeping and washing clothes are treated equally.

80   Mishnah *Nedarim* 11:1. Rebbi Yose does not consider a vow to stop washing himself a vow of deprivation.

81   In the Babli, Samuel states that sickness caused by a dirty body can be healed but dirty clothing induces insanity which is incurable.

יְהוּדָה אִישׁ חוּצִי עֲבַד טְמִיר בִּמְעָרְתָא תְּלָתָא יוֹמִין בְּעֵי לְמֵיקַם עַל הָדֵין טַעֲמָא מְנַיָּין שְׁחַיֵּי הָעִיר הַזֹּאת קוֹדְמִין לְחַיֵּי עִיר אַחֶרֶת. אָתָא לְגַבֵּי רִבִּי יוֹסֵי בַּר חֲלַפְתָּא אָמַר לֵיהּ הֵן הֲוֵיתָה. אָמַר לֵיהּ עֲבָדִית טְמִיר בִּמְעָרְתָא תְּלָתָא יוֹמִין בְּעֵי לְמֵיקַם עַל הָדֵין טַעֲמָא מְנַיָּין שְׁחַיֵּי הָעִיר הַזֹּאת קוֹדְמִין לְחַיֵּי עִיר אַחֶרֶת. קָרָא לְרִבִּי אֲבִירוֹדִימָס בְּרֵיהּ. אָמַר לֵיהּ אַגִּיב הָהֶן טַעֲמָא מְנַיָּין שְׁחַיֵּי הָעִיר הַזֹּאת קוֹדְמִין לְחַיֵּי עִיר אַחֶרֶת. אָמַר לֵיהּ תִּהְיֶינָה הֶעָרִים הָאֵלֶּה תִּחְיֶינָה עִיר וָעִיר וְאַחַר כָּךְ וּמִגְרְשֵׁיהָ סְבִיבוֹתֵיהָ. אָמַר לֵיהּ מָאן גָּרַם לָךְ דְּלָא פָלְתָה עִם חֲבֵירָךְ.

Jehudah from Ḥuṣī[82] hid himself in a cave for three days because he wanted to find the reason why the necessities of life of one's town have precedence over the necessities of life of another town. He came to Rabbi Yose bar Ḥalaphta who asked him, where have you been? He said, I was hiding in a cave for three days because I wanted to find the reason why the necessities of life of one's town have precedence over the necessities of life of another town. He called his son Rebbi Vardimos and said to him, answer, what is the reason why the necessities of life of one's town have precedence over the necessities of life of another town. He said to him (*Num.* 35:15): "These [six] cities shall be", each town shall live[83], and only afterwards their surroundings around them[84]. He [R. Yose] said to him [Jehudah from Ḥuṣī], what did cause you [this embarassment]? That you did not search with your companions!

82   An otherwise unknown personage from tannaïtic times. Neither the tradition of his name nor that of his place are certain.

83   It seems that this is based on identifying ה and ח which not only where pronounced identically but also written almost identically, with the left leg of ה touching the roof slightly towards the middle, the left leg of ח being at the extreme left end and going up slightly over the roof. Since היה indicates permanency, one might also explain the argument that the first duty of the city government is to insure the continued survival of its inhabitants.

84   The surroundings are mentioned in slightly different formulations *Num.* 35:2,3. In the Babli, *Nedarim* 81a, verse 3 "their surroundings [of the Levitic town] shall be for its animals and its life-necessities" is explained (following R. Yose) "for its animals and clothes-washing."

מִשְׁנָה ו: תְּאֵינִים שֶׁל שְׁבִיעִית אֵין קוֹצִין אוֹתָן בְּמוּקְצֶה אֲבָל קוֹצֶה(fol. 37d)
הוּא בַּחַרְבָּה. וְאֵין דּוֹרְכִין עֲנָבִים בַּגַּת אֲבָל דּוֹרֵךְ הוּא בַּעֲרִיבָה. וְאֵין עוֹשִׂין
זֵיתִים בַּבַּד וּבְקוֹטְבִי אֲבָל כּוֹתֵשׁ וּמַכְנִיס לְבוֹדִידָא. רבי שִׁמְעוֹן אוֹמֵר אַף טָחוּן
הוּא בְּבֵית הַבַּד וּמַכְנִיס לְבוֹדִידָא.

Mishnah 6: One does not cut Sabbatical figs with the fig-knife but he may cut with a dagger[85]. One does not tread grapes in the wine press but he may tread in a trough. One does not work olives in the oil press and with a roller[86] but he pounds them and puts them into a hand press. Rebbi Simeon says, one may grind them in the oil press house and put them into the hand press.

85   The reason for the Mishnah, as explained in the Halakhah, is that one may not process the harvest in a professional way.

86   Explanation of Arukh and Gaonim. (Arukh has a second explanation: "some say" it means a basket. Maimonides explains as "small oil press", בודידה as "very small oil press".)

הלכה ו: (fol. 38b) כְּתִיב וְאֶת סְפִיחַ קְצִירְךָ לֹא תִקְצוֹר. הָא קְצִירָה כְּנֶגֶד
הַקּוֹצְרִים לֹא. אָמַר רבי לָא אִם אֵינוּ עִנְיָין לִסְפִּיחֵי אִיסּוּר תְּנֵיהוּ עִנְיָין
לִסְפִיחֵי הֶיתֵר. אָמַר רבי מָנָא לְכָךְ נִצְרְכָה כְּשֶׁעָלוּ מֵאֲלֵיהֶן שָׁמָּה לֹא תֹאמַר
הוֹאִיל וְעָלוּ מֵאֲלֵיהֶן יְהוּ מוּתָּרִין לְפוּם כֵּן צָרִיךְ מֵימַר אָסוּר. אֶת סְפִיחַ קְצִירְךָ
לֹא תִקְצוֹר וְאֶת עִנְּבֵי נְזִירֶךָ לֹא תִבְצוֹר. מִן הַשָּׁמוּר בָּאָרֶץ אֵין אַתְּ בּוֹצֵר
בּוֹצֵר אַתְּ מִן הַמּוּבְקָר. לֹא תִבְצוֹר כְּדֶרֶךְ הַבּוֹצְרִין מִכָּן אָמְרוּ תְּאֵינִים שֶׁל
שְׁבִיעִית אֵין קוֹצִין אוֹתָן בְּמוּקְצֶה אֲבָל קוֹצֶה הוּא בַּחַרְבָּה. וְאֵין דּוֹרְכִין עֲנָבִים
בַּגַּת אֲבָל דּוֹרֵךְ הוּא בַּעֲרִיבָה. וְאֵין עוֹשִׂין זֵיתִים בַּבַּד וּבְקוֹטְבִי וְרַבּוֹתֵינוּ
הִתִּירוּ לַעֲשׂוֹת בְּקוֹטְבִי.

Halakhah 6: It is written[87] (*Lev.* 25:5) "The aftergrowth of your harvest you should not reap." That means, not in the way of reapers[88].

Rebbi La said, if it cannot refer to forbidden aftergrowth[89], take it to refer to permitted aftergrowth. Rebbi Mana said, it is needed for itself when it grew by itself[90]. You should not say that since it grew by itself it is permitted; therefore it was necessary to say that it is forbidden. "The aftergrowth of your harvest you should not reap and the grapes of your wild growth you should not process into wine.[91]" You may not harvest grapes from what is being watched over on the land, but you may gather grapes from what is abandoned. "You should not process into wine," not in the way of vintners. From here, they said that "one does not cut Sabbatical figs with the fig-knife but he may cut with a dagger. One does not tread grapes in the wine press but he may tread in a trough. One does not work olives in the oil press and with a roller." Our teachers permitted to use a roller[92].

87   *Sifra Behar Pereq* 1(3), in slightly different wording.

88   As Maimonides explains, since Sabbatical produce is for everybody to eat, the verse cannot mean that one may not reap grain or gather grapes at all. Therefore, it must mean that professional harvesting in all its aspects is forbidden.

89   Since aftergrowth is forbidden only by rabbinic ordinance, the verse cannot refer to forbidden aftergrowth.

90   One should not say that the prohibition of professional harvesting applies only to aftergrowth on a field

that was planted for the same crop the previous year. If the plants appear at other places, which really is spontaneous growth, they still fall under the same rule.

91   Not only collecting the grapes but the entire processing of the harvest, ending with the production of wine.

92   Since this is used only for small quantities of grapes in the other years of the Sabbatical cycle. The Tosephta (6:27) spells out that "our teachers" are Rabban Gamliel (III, the son of Rebbi) and his academy.

רְבִּי יוֹחָנָן הוֹרֵי לְאִילֵין דְּרְבִּי יַנַּאי לִטְחוֹן בְּרֵיחַיִם כְּרְבִּי שִׁמְעוֹן וְלַעֲשׂוֹת בְּקוֹטְבִּי כְּרַבָּנָן. רְבִּי יוֹחָנָן הוֹרֵי לְאִילֵין דְּבֵית רְבִּי יַנַּאי שֶׁלֹּא יְהוּ נוֹטְלִין שְׂכַר בַּדֵּיהֶן יַיִן אֶלָּא מָעוֹת כְּרְבִּי יוּדָה וּכְרְבִּי נְחֶמְיָה הוֹרֵי לוֹן.

Rebbi Joḥanan taught those of [the House of] Rebbi Yannai to grind in a mill following Rebbi Simeon, and to work with a roller, following the rabbis. Rebbi Joḥanan taught those of the House of Rebbi Yannai not to take the rent of their oil presses in wine[93] but in money; he taught them following Rebbi Jehudah and Rebbi Neḥemiah.

93 Most commentators emend "in wine" to "in olive oil" since wine is not made in an oil press. However, the manuscript evidence forbids the emen-dation. What R. Joḥanan stated was that for processing Sabbatical produce, no Sabbatical produce at all should be accepted as payment; cf. Note 69.

תַּגֵּי הַחֲמָרִין וְהַכַּתָּפִין כָּל־הָעוֹשׂוֹת שְׁבִיעִית שְׂכָרָן שְׁבִיעִית. אָמַר רְבִּי זְעִירָא בְּפֵירוֹת הֶיתֵּר הִיא מַתְנִיתִין. מַהוּ שְׂכָרָן שְׁבִיעִית שֶׁיְּהוּ נוֹטְלִין מִמַּה שֶׁיְּהוּ עוֹשִׂין שְׂכָרָן שְׁבִיעִית. וִיהֵא דְּהוֹרֵי רְבִּי יוֹחָנָן לְאִילֵין דְּרְבִּי יַנַּאי שֶׁלֹּא יְהוּ נוֹטְלִין שְׂכַר בַּדֵּיהֶן יַיִן אֶלָּא מָעוֹת. כְּרְבִּי יוּדָה וּכְרְבִּי נְחֶמְיָה הוֹרֵי לוֹן. רְבִּי הִילָא בִּמְכַתְּפֵי פֵּירוֹת עֲבֵירָה הִיא מַתְנִיתָא. וּמָה הִיא שְׂכָרָן שְׁבִיעִית. כַּיי דָּמַר רְבִּי אַבָּהוּ רְבִּי יוֹחָנָן יַיִן נֶסֶךְ קָנָס קְנָסוּהוּ וָכָא קָנָס קְנָסוּהוּ.

It was stated[94]: "The wages of donkey drivers, carriers, and all those working with Sabbatical produce are Sabbatical." Rebbi Zeïra said, this *baraita* deals with permitted produce. What is the meaning of "the wages are Sabbatical"? That they may take their wages in the form of Sabbatical produce. Then it must be that, when Rebbi Joḥanan taught those of [the House of] Rebbi Yannai not to take the wages of their oil presses in wine but in money, he taught them following Rebbi Jehudah and Rebbi Neḥemiah[95]. Rebbi Hila[96]: the *baraita* deals with those who carry

forbidden produce[97]. What is the meaning of "the wages are Sabbatical"?
As Rebbi Abbahu, Rebbi Johanan said, they fined him with wine of
libations[98]; here also, they fined him.

94   Tosephta 6:26; there camel
drivers are mentioned instead of "all
those working". The quote in the Babli
(*Avodah Zarah* 62a) mentions only
donkey drivers.

95   The *baraita* is taken as the
position of the rabbis opposing Rebbis
Jehudah and Nehemiah (Note 69). This
position is rejected in the Babli (*loc.
cit.*) since the text does not include "all
those working with produce". It is held
that poorly paid workers may be paid
in kind following the rules of Mishnah
5 but not highly paid donkey drivers,
following Rebbi Abbahu.

96   He is R. La.

97   Produce from guarded fields or
harvested in a professional way.

98   This refers to Mishnah *Avodah
Zarah* 5:1 which states that the wages
of a Jewish worker earned by a contract which specifies work for wine
used, or to be used, for idolatrous
libations is forbidden for all usufruct.
R. Abbahu (*Avodah Zarah* Halakhah
5:1) notes that no principle of law
requires that the wages be forbidden; it
is a rabbinic ordinance imposed to
avoid situations in which pagan wine
might be sold to Jews, and the same
situation applies here.

(fol. 37d) **משנה ז:** אֵין מְבַשְּׁלִין יָרָק שֶׁל שְׁבִיעִית בְּשֶׁמֶן שֶׁל תְּרוּמָה שֶׁלֹּא יְבִיאֶנּוּ
לִידֵי פְסוּל. רִבִּי שִׁמְעוֹן מַתִּיר וְהָאַחֲרוֹן אַחֲרוֹן נִתְפָּשׂ בַּשְּׁבִיעִית וְהַפֵּירִי לְעַצְמוֹ
אָסוּר.

Mishnah 7: One may not cook Sabbatical vegetables in heave oil
because it should not be made unusable[99]. Rebbi Simeon permits it.
Always the last substitute is caught and the fruit remains forbidden[100].

99 Sabbatical produce has a status of holiness. However, in contrast to sacrifices, Sabbatical produce cannot be redeemed and does not have to be kept in purity. The rabbis note that Sabbatical produce cooked in heave oil will become inedible if impure and this should not happen. The sentence "because it should not be made unusable" means "one should not use it in a way by which it might become unusable."

100 The rules of this Mishnah are deduced in *Sifra Behar Pereq* 3(3) because the verse equates the rules of the Jubilee year with those of the Sabbatical: "(*Lev.* 25:12) 'Because a Jubilee it is, holy it should be for you'; just as holy things absorb their redemption money (any sanctified object other than a valid sacrifice can be redeemed and the sanctity transferred to the money), also the Sabbatical produce absorbs its money. Then just as holy things become profane, Sabbatical produce should become profane. But the verse says *it is* (in a permanent state), it remains in its holiness." The details of the transfer to the last redeemed property are given in the Halakhah. The argument of *Sifra* is reproduced in Babli *Sukkah* 40b, *Qiddušin* 58a; there the permanent state is implied by 'Because a Jubilee it is, holy *it should be* for you' (in the Babli, scriptural use of the verb היה is always taken to imply permanence.)

(fol. 38b) **הלכה ז:** תַּמָּן תַּנִּינָן וּבְכוּלָּן הַכֹּהֲנִים רַשָּׁאִין לְשַׁנּוֹת בַּאֲכִילָתָן וּלְאוֹכְלָן צְלוּיִין שְׁלוּקִין וּמְבוּשָׁלִים וְלִיתֵּן לְתוֹכָן תַּבְלֵי חוּלִין וְתַבְלֵי תְרוּמָה דִּבְרֵי רִבִּי שִׁמְעוֹן. רִבִּי מֵאִיר אוֹמֵר לֹא יִתֵּן לְתוֹכָן שֶׁלֹּא יָבִיא אֶת הַתְּרוּמָה לִידֵי פְסוּל. אַתְיָא דִיחִידָיָיה דְהָכָא כִּסְתָמָה דְתַמָּן (וְדִיחִידָיָיה דְהָכָא כִּסְתָמָה דְתַמָּן). אֶלָּא דִּסְתָמָה דְהָכָא רִבִּי מֵאִיר דְתַמָּן. רִבִּי מֵאִיר וְרִבִּי שִׁמְעוֹן הֲלָכָה כְרִבִּי שִׁמְעוֹן. אָמַר רִבִּי יוֹסָה אֶשְׁתָּאֲלִית לְאִילֵּין דְּבֵית רִבִּי יַנַּאי אָמְרִין נְהִיגִין הֲוֵינָן מְבַשְׁלִין עַל יַד עַל יַד וְאוֹכְלִין. מַיי כְדוֹן. הֲלָכָה כְרִבִּי מֵאִיר דְּתַמָּן הִיא רַבָּנִין דְהָכָא.

Halakhah 7: There[101], we have stated: "The Cohanim are permitted in all cases to change the preparation of the food, to eat it broiled, cooked a long time,[102] or plain; to add profane and heave spices, the words of Rebbi

Simeon. Rebbi Meïr says, he should not add [heave spices], to cause heave to become unusable[103]." It turns out that the anonymous statement here becomes the minority opinion there. Is the anonymous statement here the minority opinion there[104]? But the anonymous statement here is the opinion of Rebbi Meïr there and between Rebbi Meïr and Rebbi Simeon, practice follows Rebbi Simeon[105]. Rebbi Assi said, I asked those of the House of Rebbi Yannai and they said, we used to cook small portions and eat[106]. How is that[107]? Practice follows Rebbi Meïr there for his is the anonymous opinion here.

101   Mishnah *Zebaḥim* 10:7, speaking of the way Cohanim ate sacrificial meat in the Temple.

102   Since sacrifices had to be eaten in one or at most two days, one could have thought that a way of cooking usually reserved for vegetable preserves was forbidden.

103   Since the Cohanim might not be able to consume all sacrificial meat in time, the remainder would have to be burned, including the spices from heave.

104   The first clause of Mishnah *Zebaḥim*, speaking of the different kinds of preparation of meat, is in fact anonymous. But the part about spices, which we are interested in, is R. Simeon's.

105   Therefore, R. Simeon's opinion should count as an anonymous one. This is a decision of R. Joḥanan (*Terumot* 3:1, fol. 42a). In the Babli (*Erubin* 46b), the question of precedence between Rebbis Simeon and Meïr is declared to be undecidable. [Cf. also *Demay*, Chapter 5, Note 120, *Terumot* Chapter 3, Note 25.]

106   R. Meïr might agree with the practice to use heave spices in small dishes that will be eaten immediately since then the danger to the heave is minimized. The precaution to cook only small portions would be unnecessary for R. Simeon. This proves that R. Yannai did not follow R. Simeon and his practical decision should be followed.

107   How could this be justified?

הָאַחֲרוֹן אַחֲרוֹן נִתְפָּשׂ בַּשְּׁבִיעִית וְהַפֵּירִי לְעַצְמוֹ אָסוּר הָא כֵּיצַד לָקַח בְּפֵירוֹת
שְׁבִיעִית בָּשָׂר אֵילוּ וְאֵילוּ מִתְבָּעֲרִין בַּשְּׁבִיעִית. לָקַח בְּבָשָׂר דָּגִים יָצָא בָשָׂר
נִתְפְּשׂוּ דָגִים. לָקַח בְּדָגִים שֶׁמֶן יָצְאוּ דָגִים וְנִכְנָס שֶׁמֶן הָאַחֲרוֹן אַחֲרוֹן נִתְפָּשׂ
בַּשְּׁבִיעִית וְהַפֵּירִי לְעַצְמוֹ אָסוּר.

"Always the last substitute is caught and the fruit remains forbidden".
How is this? If[108] he took meat in exchange for Sabbatical fruits, both are
subject to removal in the Sabbatical. If he exchanged the meat for fish,
the meat is released and the fish are obligated. If he exchanged fish for
oil, the fish are released and the oil enters [into the obligation.] Always
the last substitute is obligated and the fruit remains forbidden.

108   *Sifra Behar Pereq* 3(3), Babli *Sukkah* 40b.

בָּעֵי מִינֵיהּ מֵרבִּי יוֹחָנָן שְׁבִיעִית מַהוּ שֶׁתֵּצֵא דֶּרֶךְ חִילוּל. אָמַר לָהוּ וְלָמָּה לֹא.
אָמַר רִבִּי לָעֶזָר אֵין שְׁבִיעִית יוֹצֵא דֶּרֶךְ חִילוּל אֶלָּא דֶּרֶךְ מְכִירָה. מַתְנִיתָא
מְסַייְעָא לְדֵין וּמַתְנִיתָא מְסַייְעָא לְדֵין. מַתְנִיתָא מְסַייְעָא לְרִבִּי יוֹחָנָן כָּל־מִי
שֶׁיֶּשׁ לוֹ מָעוֹת מִדְּמֵי שְׁבִיעִית וְהוּא רוֹצֶה לְחַלְּלָן עַל עִיסָתוֹ מְחַלְּלוֹ. מַתְנִיתָא
מְסַייְעָא לְרִבִּי לָעֶזָר. מִי שֶׁיֶּשׁ לוֹ סֶלַע מִדְּמֵי שְׁבִיעִית וְהוּא רוֹצֶה לִיקַּח לוֹ חָלוּק
הוֹלֵךְ אֵצֶל הַחֶנְוָנִי הָרָגִיל אֶצְלוֹ וְאָמַר תֶּן לִי בְזוֹ פֵּירוֹת וְהוּא נוֹתֵן לוֹ וְהוּא
אוֹמֵר לוֹ הֲרֵי פֵּירוֹת הָאֵלּוּ נְתוּנִים לָךְ בְּמַתָּנָה וְהַחֶנְוָנִי אוֹמֵר לוֹ הֲרֵי סֶלַע זוֹ
נְתוּנָה לָךְ בְּמַתָּנָה וְחוֹזֵר וְלוֹקֵחַ לוֹ חָלוּק.

They asked Rebbi Johanan: May Sabbatical produce become freed by
redemption[109]? He said to them, why not? Rebbi Eleazar said, Sabbatical
produce cannot become freed by redemption, only by sale. A *baraita*
supports one, a *baraita* supports the other. A *baraita* supports Rebbi
Johanan: "Anybody who has money that is Sabbatical and he wants to
redeem it by his dough may redeeem it." A *baraita*[110] supports Rebbi

Eleazar: "If somebody has a tetradrachma of Sabbatical money and he wants to buy a garment goes to the grocer he usually deals with and says to him, give me fruits for this. He gives them to him. Then he says, these fruits are given to you as a gift and the grocer says, this tetradrachma is given to you as a gift. Then he goes and buys himself a garment."

109 Since the Mishnah and the Tosephta speak only about substitution, the question remains whether Sabbatical produce can be redeemed the way Temple property (other than valid sacrifices) can be, by offering money or money's worth with the explicit intent of transferring sanctity.

A lengthy discussion of this topic is in Babli *Sukkah* 40b-41a, where it is asserted that R. Joḥanan also permits redemption only for substitutions, not for Sabbatical produce itself. This can be read also into the Yerushalmi since the latter deals only with Sabbatical money, not with Sabbatical produce.

110 Tosephta 6:25, in a shortened version. Babli *Sukkah* 41a, a version close to the one quoted here.

רִבִּי יוֹחָנָן שָׁתֵי חַמְרָא וְיָהַב פְּרִיטוֹי. עַד כְּדוֹן רִבִּי יוֹחָנָן דְּהוּא מִתְיְיהֵימָן הָא שְׁאָר כָּל־אָדָם דְּלָא מִתְיְיהֵמְנִין. רִבִּי יַעֲקֹב בַּר אָחָא בְּשֵׁם רִבִּי אֲבִינָא מֶחֲוֵי לֵה כְּחֲדָא וּנְסִיב כְּחֲדָא. רִבִּי חִזְקָיָה הֲוָה אֲמַר לֵיהּ הַב לִי קוֹמוֹי מִן גַּוּ דּוּ אֲמַר לֵיהּ הַב לִי קוֹמוֹי כְּמָאן דְּלָא יְהִיב לֵיהּ מִדְּמֵי שְׁבִיעִית.

Rebbi Joḥanan drank wine and then gave money[111]. That goes for Rebbi Joḥanan who is trustworthy; what about other people who are not so trustworthy[112]? Rebbi Jacob bar Aḥa in the name of Rebbi Avina: He shows him with one [hand] and takes with the other [hand]. Rebbi Ḥizqiah used to say, "give me for this before you[113]". Since he said, give me that before you, he is one who does not give Sabbatical money.

111 Since one may not pay one's debts with Sabbatical money, the money paid afterwards was in liquidation of a debt and cannot be Sabbat

ical even if the wine was Sabbatical. Then the question of redemption does not even arise.

112   If the seller wants the money before he hands over the merchandise. The answer is that even the untrustworthy buyer will get credit if he shows that he has money in his hand to cover the debt incurred. Then he can take up the buy and acquire it by lifting it up, incur a debt by this act, and then hand over the money to liquidate the debt, not to acquire the produce.

113   This is essentially the same device as that used by R. Jacob bar Aḥa: The buyer puts up the money required but does not hand it over.

(fol. 37d) **משנה ח:** אֵין לוֹקְחִין עֲבָדִים וְקַרְקָעוֹת וּבְהֵמָה טְמֵאָה מִדְּמֵי שְׁבִיעִית. אִם לָקַח יֹאכַל כְּנֶגְדָן. אֵין מְבִיאִין קִינֵּי זָבִין וְקִינֵּי זָבוֹת קִינֵּי יוֹלְדוֹת מִדְּמֵי שְׁבִיעִית וְאִם לָקַח יֹאכַל כְּנֶגְדָן. אֵין סָכִין כֵּלִים בְּשֶׁמֶן שֶׁל שְׁבִיעִית וְאִם סָךְ יֹאכַל כְּנֶגְדָן.

Mishnah 8: One does not buy slaves, real estate, and unclean animals from Sabbatical money[114]. If he bought them, he has to eat their worth[115]. One does not bring nests[116] for men with gonorrhea, women with discharges, or women who had given birth from Sabbatical money. If he bought them, he has to eat their worth. One does not rub vessels with Sabbatical oil[117]. If he did, he has to eat its worth.

114   One may only buy food or things necessary to prepare food.

115   He has to set aside an amount equal to the sum spent on illegitimate expenses and use it for food items.

116   "Nest" is a technical term for a couple of pigeons or turtle doves, prescribed as sacrifice for these cases in *Lev.* 12:8, 15:14, 15:29. There are other situations when "nests" are required (*Lev.* 5:7, 14:22) but they are infrequent.

117   This is industrial use even if it is necessary to turn the vessel into a finished product ready to be used in cooking or baking.

(fol. 38b) **הלכה ח**: אָמַר רִבִּי יוֹסֵי זֹאת אוֹמֶרֶת שֶׁאָסוּר לִיקַח לוֹ אִשָׁה מִדְּמֵי
שְׁבִיעִית. הֲלָכָה מַה בֵּין הַקּוֹנֶה אִשָׁה מַה בֵּין הַקּוֹנֶה שִׁפְחָה.

Halakhah 8: Rebbi Yose said, this means that it is forbidden to acquire
a wife with Sabbatical money. In practice, what is the difference between
one who acquires a wife and one who acquires a slave girl[118]?

118 A wife must first be acquired
by a monetary gift before she can be
married to the groom (cf. *Peah*,
Chapter 6, Note 46, *Demay* Chapter 1,
Note 185). Since the biblical term אם
יקח איש אשה "if a man takes a wife"
means in the rabbinic vocabulary "if a
man acquires a wife", it is inferred
(Mishnah *Qiddušin* Chapter 1) that the
rules of acquiring in general can be
derived from the rules of acquiring a
wife. The fact that the money (or
money's worth) is given to the bride in
the case of marriage but to a third
party, the seller, in the case of
acquisition of slaves and real estate,
does not make any difference here
since the transfer of bride money is
only valid if it would be valid in any
other act of acquisition.

תַּנֵּי שֶׁמֶן שֶׁל שְׁבִיעִית אֵין חוֹסְמִין בּוֹ תַּנּוּר וְכִירַיִים וְלֹא סָכִין בּוֹ מִנְעָלִים
וְסַנְדָּלִים וְלֹא יָסוּךְ אָדָם אֶת רַגְלוֹ וְהוּא בְתוֹךְ מִנְעָלוֹ וְהוּא בְתוֹךְ סַנְדָּלוֹ. אֲבָל
סָךְ הוּא אֶת רַגְלוֹ וְנוֹתְנָהּ לְתוֹךְ מִנְעָלוֹ וּלְתוֹךְ סַנְדָּלוֹ. סָךְ שֶׁמֶן וּמִתְעַגֵּל עַל גַּבֵּי
קַטַבְּלְיָא וְאֵינוֹ חוֹשֵׁשׁ. לֹא יִתְּנֶנָּה לֹא עַל גַּבֵּי טַבְלָה שֶׁל שַׁיִּשׁ לְהִתְעַגֵּל בָּהּ.
רַבָּן שִׁמְעוֹן בֶּן גַּמְלִיאֵל מַתִּיר.

It was stated[119]: One may not use Sabbatical oil to caulk[120] an oven or
a hearth[121]; one does not use it to rub on shoes and sandals. Nobody
should anoint his foot in a shoe or sandal but he may anoint his foot and
step into his shoe or his sandal. One may anoint himself and roll on a
tarpaulin[122] without worry. One should not put it on a marble slab[123] to
roll himself in it, but Rabban Gamliel permits it[124].

119   Tosephta 6:9-12, in different order.

120   This is the usual definition given by the dictionaries. One also might translate "to finish (to make the vessel workable)", from the meaning of חסם in Arabic.

121   An oven is a clay vessel in the shape of a frustrum of a cone. The fire is at the bottom, the food to be baked hangs in the opening or clings to the sides. A hearth is a portable (usually double) fire place also made from clay.

122   Cf. Greek κατάβλημα, τó, "anything let down; tarpaulin; curtain, outer wrapper, etc." (E. G.). The Gaonic commentary to *Kelim* 16:4 translates the word by Arabic נטע "leather mat used as tablecloth or gaming board, in former times also during executions."

123   Latin *tabula* "slab, table," cf. *Peah* Chapter 7, Note 61. Here some oil is lost by necessity. Rabban Gamliel permits gymnastics as legitimate exercise.

(fol. 37d) **משנה ט:** עוֹר שֶׁסָכוֹ בְּשֶׁמֶן שֶׁל שְׁבִיעִית. רְבִּי לִיעֶזֶר אוֹמֵר יִדָּלֵק. וַחֲכָמִים אוֹמְרִים יֹאכַל כְּנֶגְדָן. אָמְרוּ לִפְנֵי רְבִּי עֲקִיבָה הָיָה רִבִּי לִיעֶזֶר עוֹר שֶׁסָכוֹ בְּשֶׁמֶן שֶׁל שְׁבִיעִית יִדָּלֵק. אָמַר לָהֶן שְׁתוּקוּ לֹא אוֹמַר לָכֶם מַה רְבִּי לִיעֶזֶר אָמַר בּוֹ.

Mishnah 9: Leather oiled with Sabbatical oil, Rebbi Eliezer said, should be burned, but the Sages say, one has to eat its worth. They said before Rebbi Aqiba: Rebbi Eliezer used to say that leather oiled with Sabbatical oil should be burned. He said to them: be silent! I shall not tell you what Rebbi Eliezer said about this.

(fol. 38b) **הלכה ט:** עוֹר שֶׁסָכוֹ בְּשֶׁמֶן מַה אָמַר בּוֹ רְבִּי לִיעֶזֶר. אָמַר רְבִּי יוֹסֵי עַצְמוֹתָיו שֶׁל אוֹתוֹ הָאִישׁ יִשָּׂרְפוּ. רִבִּי חִזְקִיָּה בְּשֵׁם רִבִּי אָחָא מוּתָּר.

Halakhah 9: What does Rebbi Eliezer say about him who oiled leather? Rebbi Yose said, that man's bones should be burned. Rebbi Ḥizqiah in the name of Rebbi Aḥa: It is permitted[124].

124   According to R. Yose, using Sabbatical oil to oil leather is an unforgivable sin. According to R. Ḥizqiah, it is completely permitted and one does not even set money aside in the value of the oil used. [Maimonides accepts the opinion of R. Ḥizqiah, probably because R. Ḥizqiah precedes R. Yose in time but his opinion is quoted last for emphasis.] R. Aqiba did not want to communicate R. Eliezer's opinions because they were too lenient.

(fol. 37d) **משנה י**: וְעוֹד אָמְרוּ לְפָנָיו אוֹמֵר הָיָה רְבִּי לִיעֶזֶר הָאוֹכֵל פַּת כּוּתִי כְּאוֹכֵל בְּשַׂר חֲזִיר. אָמַר לָהֶן שְׁתוֹקוּ לֹא אוֹמֵר לָכֶם מַה רְבִּי לִיעֶזֶר אָמַר בּוֹ.

Mishnah 10: They also said before him: Rebbi Eliezer used to say that one who eats Samaritan bread is like one who eats pork. He said to them: be silent! I shall not tell you what Rebbi Eliezer said about this.

(fol. 38b) **הלכה י**: וְעוֹד אָמְרוּ לְפָנָיו. אָמַר רְבִּי יוֹסֵי זֹאת אוֹמֶרֶת שֶׁאָסוּר לְחָבֵר[125] לִיקַח בִּתּוֹ שֶׁל עַם הָאָרֶץ. רְבִּי חִזְקִיָּה בְּשֵׁם רְבִּי אָחָא מַתִּיר הָיָה רְבִּי לִיעֶזֶר חֲמֵיצָן שֶׁל כּוּתִים לְאַחַר הַפֶּסַח מִיַּד.

Halakhah 10: "They also said before him." Rebbi Yose said, this implies that a fellow is forbidden to marry the daughter of a vulgar[126]. Rebbi Ḥizqiah in the name of Rebbi Aḥa: Rebbi Eliezer used to permit the leavened matter of a Samaritan immediately after Passover[127].

125   The word appears in both mss. but is missing in the prints.

126   For the definition of these terms, see the Introduction to Tractate

Demay. Rebbi Yose's argument is that as the Samaritans, who accept the written Torah but not the oral tradition, while trying to comply with the laws of the Torah will unwittingly transgress many of them, so also the children of the uneducated will not be able to have a kosher household even if they want to. This argument uses the Babylonian definition of "vulgar"!

127   Since the Samaritans reject the oral law, they will completely eliminate their leavened matter before Passover, rather than sell it to a Gentile. Therefore, after Passover they will have no forbidden leavened matter they would not eat but could try to sell to a Jew.

(fol. 37d) **משנה יא:** מֶרְחָץ שֶׁהוּסְקָה בְּתֶבֶן וּבְקַשׁ שֶׁל שְׁבִיעִית מוּתָּר לִרְחוֹץ בָּהּ. אִם מִתְחַשֵּׁב הוּא הֲרֵי זֶה לֹא יִרְחוֹץ.

Mishnah 11: One may bathe in a bathhouse heated with Sabbatical straw and chaff. If somebody considers himself an important person, he should not bathe there[128].

128   Materials unfit as food may be burned without hesitation. But one is afraid that for an important person, the bath attendants will burn fragrant wood or even edibles which cannot legally be burned.

(fol. 38b) **הלכה יא:** הָדָא דְּתֵימָא בְּאִילֵּין דֵּמוֹסִיָּיא בְּרַם בְּאִילֵּין פְּרִיבָטָה אָסוּר.

Halakhah 11: This means, in public baths[129], but in private ones[130] it is forbidden.

129   Greek δημόσιος, α, ov "belonging to the public or the state" [e. g., βαλανεῖα, "baths"]. Even though straw is animal fodder and as such sanctified in the Sabbatical, the utility of public use overrides the potential abuse of

Sabbatical matter.   (baths)".

130   Latin *privata* (*balnea*), "private

אָם מִתְחַשֵּׁב הוּא הֲרֵי זֶה לֹא יִרְחַץ. וְאָם הָיָה אָדָם שֶׁל צוּרָה הֲרֵי זֶה לֹא

יִרְחוֹץ. כְּהָדָא רְבִּי יְהוֹשֻׁעַ בֶּן לֵוִי אֲזַל מִן לוֹד לְבֵית גֻּבְרִין בְּגִין מִיסְחֵי.

"If somebody considers himself an important person, he should not

bathe there". If somebody is an important person, he should not bathe[131].

For example, Rebbi Joshua ben Levi went from Lod to Bet Gubrin[132] to

bathe.

131   This is a case where a show of   132   He was not known in Bet Gubrin
modesty is inappropriate.   which is a day's walk South of Lod.

רְבִּי שִׁמְעוֹן בֶּן לָקִישׁ הֲוָה בְּבוֹצְרָה. חֲמְתוֹן מְזַלְּפִין לְהָדָא אַפְרוֹדִיטִי אָמַר לוֹן

לֵית (fol. 38c) אֲסִיר. אָתָא שָׁאַל לְרְבִּי יוֹחָנָן. אָמַר לֵיהּ רִבִּי יוֹחָנָן בְּשֵׁם רִבִּי

שִׁמְעוֹן בֶּן יוֹצָדָק אֵין דָּבָר שֶׁל רַבִּים אָסוּר.

Rebbi Simeon ben Laqish was in Bostra. He saw them sprinkling at

that Aphrodite[132]. He said to them, is that not forbidden? He went to ask

Rebbi Joḥanan. Rebbi Joḥanan told him in the name of Rebbi Simeon ben

Yoẓadaq: Nothing public is forbidden.

132   This paragraph serves as back-   even if dedicated to Aphrodite is not
ground for the permission to burn   forbidden to Jews. Even if a fountain
potential animal fodder in a public   in the form of a statue of Aphrodite
bath. It also deals with public baths in   was in the hot room, if used to provide
general; in that respect it belongs to   water for sprinkling it was an
Mishnah *Avodah Zarah* 3:4 which states   implement and not an object of pagan
that a bath, built with public money,   worship.

(fol. 38c) **משנה א:** הַפֵּיגָם וְהָרִיבוּזִין הַשּׁוּטִין וְהַחֲלוֹגְלוֹגוֹת כּוּסְבָּר שֶׁבֶּהָרִים
וְכַרְפַּסְ¹ שֶׁבַּנְּהָרוֹת וְנַרְגֵּר (שֶׁבַּנְּהָרוֹת)² שֶׁל אֶפָר פְּטוּרִין מִן הַמַּעְשְׂרוֹת וְנִלְקָחִין
מִכָּל־אָדָם בַּשְּׁבִיעִית שֶׁאֵין כִּיוֹצֵא בָהֶן נִשְׁמָר. רִבִּי יְהוּדָה אוֹמֵר סְפִיחֵי חַרְדָּל
מוּתָּרִין שֶׁלֹא נֶחְשְׁדוּ עֲלֵיהֶן עוֹבְרֵי עֲבֵירָה. רִבִּי שִׁמְעוֹן אוֹמֵר כָּל־הַסְּפִיחִין
מוּתָּרִין חוּץ מִסְּפִיחֵי כְרוּב שֶׁאֵין כִּיוֹצֵא בָהֶן בְּיַרְקוֹת שָׂדֶה וַחֲכָמִים אוֹמְרִים
כָּל־הַסְּפִיחִין אֲסוּרִין.

Mishnah 1: Rue[3], wild amaranth[4], purslain[5], mountain coriander, river celery[6], and wild rocket[7] are free from tithes and can be bought from everybody during the Sabbatical since no similar plants are guarded[8]. Rebbi Jehudah says, spontaneous growth of mustard is permitted because the unobservant are not suspected in this respect[9]. Rebbi Simeon says, all spontaneous growth is permitted except that of cabbage since nothing similar grows wild on the fields. But the Sages say, all spontaneous growth is forbidden[10].

1   Reading of the Rome ms. and all Mishnah mss. Leyden and Venice: כוסבר, a dittography.

2   Reading of the Leyden ms. and Venice print only, by dittography.

3   Cf. *Kilaim* Mishnah 1:8.

4   In most Mishnah mss., ירבוז. This is also the name of the plant in Arabic.

(Rashi in Babli *Sukkah* 39b translates by French *oseille* "sorrel". The Talmud text accepted by Rashi reads השיטין instead of השוטין. Rashi defines this as "asparagus")

5   Cf. *Peah* Chapter 8, Note 64.

6   The Halakhah will define this as parsley.

7　　In Arabic also גרגר

8　　Since money paid for Sabbatical produce becomes holy as Sabbatical money which may be spent only on food, one may not buy Sabbatical produce from people who are not trustworthy in this respect. But weeds and other wild plants that usually are not planted commercially are not subject to either tithes or the sanctity of the Sabbatical; payment for these plants does not acquire Sabbatical holiness.

9　　To sell mustard seed from cultivated plants during the Sabbatical.

10　　Spontaneous growth on cultivated fields may not be harvested commercially (*Lev.* 25:5). R. Simeon permits buying it from anybody unless it is clear that it comes from a cultivated field; the Sages treat spontaneous growth as regular produce. [The Babli, *Pesaḥim* 51b, quotes a version in which R. Simeon forbids all spontaneous growth except cabbage; this cannot be squared with the tradition of the Yerushalmi; cf. N. Sacks, ed., *The Mishnah with Variant Readings, Order Zeraïm II*, Jerusalem 1975, p. עט, Note 13.]

הלכה א: הַפִּיגָם וְהָרִיבוֹזִין וכו'. אָמַר רבי חַגַּיי סִירוּגִין וַחֲלוּגְלוֹגוֹת וּמִי גָדוֹל בְּחָכְמָה וּבְשָׁנִים אַצְרַכְתְּ לַחֲבֵרַיָּיא אֲמָרִין נֵיסּוֹק וְנִשְׁאַל לְאִילֵּין דְּבְבֵית רבי סַלְקוּן מִישְׁאוֹל וְיָצָאת שִׁפְחָה מִשָּׁל בֵּית רבי וְאָמְרָה לָהֶן הַכְנִיסוּ לְשְׁנַיִם אֲמָרִין יֵיעוֹל פְּלָן קֶדְמַאי יֵיעוֹל פְּלָן קֶדְמַאי שׁוֹרוֹן עָלְלִין קְטָעִין קְטָעִין. אָמְרָה לָהֶן מִפְנֵי מַה אַתֶּם נִכְנָסִין סִירוּגִין סִירוּגִין. חַד רבי הֲוָה טְעִין פַּרְפָּחוֹנַיָּא בְגוֹלְתֵיהּ וְנָפְלוּן מִינֵּיהּ. אָמְרָה לֵיהּ רבי רבי נִתְפַּזְּרוּ חֲלוּגְלוֹגוֹתֶיךָ.

Halakhah 1: "Rue, wild amaranth," etc. Rebbi Ḥaggai said[11], the colleagues did not know what סירוגין, חלגלוגות means and "who is superior, in wisdom or in years." They said, let us go and ask somebody from the house of Rebbi[12]. They went to ask; a servant girl from the house of Rebbi came out and told them: enter in pairs. Each one said, that one should enter before me. As a result, they entered is separate groups. She said to them, why do you enter intermittently? One rabbi was carrying purslain in his overcoat; it fell from him. She said to him: Rabbi, rabbi, your purslain is dispersed.

11   The same text is in *Megillah* 2:2 (fol. 73a); similar ones in Babli *Roš Haššanah* 26b, *Megillah* 18a. The word חלגלוגות is from the Mishnah here, סירוגין is in Mishnah *Megillah* 2:1. The last question, whether precedence belongs to one superior in wisdom or in age, refers to Mishnah *Sanhedrin* 4:2, that in criminal cases the senior judges must be heard last in a discussion so as not to influence the other judges.

12   As the story shows, Rebbi required all members of his household, including his slaves, to speak pure Hebrew. Note that the rabbis speak Aramaic among themselves but the slave girl speaks pure Hebrew.

מַהוּ כַּרְפַּס שֶׁבַּנְּהָרוֹת. רִבִּי יוֹסֵי בַּר חֲנִינָה אָמַר פֵּיטְרוֹסֵילִינוֹן.

What is "river celery"? Rebbi Yose bar Ḥanina said, πετροσέλινον "parsley".

וְלָמָּה לֹא תַנִּינָן הַסִּיאָה וְהָאֵזוֹב וְהַקּוֹרְנִית עִמְּהוֹן שֶׁלֹּא תֹאמַר אֵילוּ נִשְׁמָרִין בֶּחָצֵר וְחַיָּיבִין. וְאֵילוּ נִשְׁמָרִין בֶּחָצֵר וּפְטוּרִין. אֶלָּא אֵילוּ וְאֵילוּ אִם הָיוּ נִשְׁמָרִין בֶּחָצֵר חַיָּיבִין. אֵילוּ נִשְׁמָרִין בְּגִינָה וְחַיָּיבִין.[13] וְאֵילוּ נִשְׁמָרִין בְּגִינָה וּפְטוּרִין. אֶלָּא אֵילוּ וְאֵילוּ אִם נִשְׁמָרִין בְּגִינָה פְטוּרִין. וְלָמָּה לֹא תַנִּינָן אֶלָּא אֵילֵין הוּא שֶׁלֹּא תֹאמַר הוֹאִיל וְרוֹב הַמִּינִין הַלָּלוּ נִזְרָעִין וּבָאִין מִן הָאָסוּר יְהוּ אֲסוּרִין לְפוּם כֵּן צָרִיךְ מֵימַר מוּתָּרִין.

Why did we not state "calamint, hyssop, and thyme" with them[14]? That you should not say, these if guarded in the courtyard are obligated, those if guarded in the courtyard are free. But these and those if guarded in the courtyard are obligated; these if guarded in the garden plot are obligated, those if they are guarded in the garden plot are free[15]. But these and those if guarded in the garden plot are free! Why did we state only these? That you should not say that since most of these kinds come from forbidden growth they all should be forbidden; therefore it is necessary to say they are permitted[16].

13   Word missing in the Venice print.

14   Mishnah 8:1 declares these kinds as wood, not subject to the rules of the Sabbatical, if collected as wood. Mishnah *Ma'serot* 3:9 declares them as free from tithes unless grown specifically in a courtyard. This implies that in a garden plot they are exempt.

15   Since the Mishnah seems to connect exemption from tithes with exemption from the rules of the Sab-

batical, one should not ask why rue, etc., are exempt in the courtyard while calamint, etc., are subject to tithes and Sabbatical, since in Mishnah 8:1 calamint, etc., raised in a garden plot as food are also subject to tithes and Sabbatical. But the exemption of rue, etc., is general and unconditional.

16   The exemption stated in the Mishnah extends to commercially grown crops of the kinds enumerated.

מַהוּ שֶׁיְּהוּ אֲסוּרִין מְשׁוּם סְפִיחִין נִשְׁמְעִינָהּ מִן הָדָא. רַבִּי יְהוּדָה אוֹמֵר סְפִיחֵי חַרְדָּל מוּתָּרִין שֶׁלֹּא נֶחְשְׁדוּ עֲלֵיהֶן עוֹבְרֵי עֲבֵירָה. לֹא אָמְרוּ אֶלָּא שֶׁלֹּא נֶחְשְׁדוּ עֲלֵיהֶן עוֹבְרֵי עֲבֵירָה וְאֵלּוּ הוֹאִיל וְלֹא נֶחְשְׁדוּ עֲלֵיהֶן עוֹבְרֵי עֲבֵירָה יְהוּ מוּתָּרִין.

Are these[17] forbidden as spontaneous growth? Let us hear from the following: "Rebbi Jehudah says, spontaneous growth of mustard is permitted because the unobservant are not suspected concerning it." They said only "because the unobservant are not suspected concerning it." These, because the unobservant are not suspected concerning them, will be permitted.

17   The plants enumerated in the Mishnah. Since the plants mentioned in the first part of the Mishnah are exempt according to everybody, their status cannot be worse than that of

mustard. Since R. Jehudah does not apply the decree about spontaneous growth to mustard, nobody can apply it to the plants enumerated.

עַד כְּדוֹן יַרְקוֹ זַרְעוֹ אֵיפְשַׁר מֵימַר זַרְעוֹ מוּתָּר יַרְקוֹ לֹא כָּל־שֶׁכֵּן.

So far its greens; its seeds[18]? Is it impossible to say that if its seeds are permitted, its greens not so much more?

18   Probably one has to read: "So far its seeds, what about its greens?" However, there is no manuscript evidence for this. The question is about mustard that is collected, in general, only for its seeds. It should be obvious that R. Jehudah will permit Sabbatical mustard plants as vegetable without any restriction. Since the final decision will go against R. Jehudah, the problem does not have to be discussed in detail.

רבִּי שִׁמְעוֹן בֶּן לָקִישׁ הָיָה בְחִיקוֹק חֲמָתוֹן מְגַלְגְּלִין בְּהָדֵין חַרְדְּלָא נְפַל מִינֵיהּ וְהוּא לָא נְסַב לֵיהּ. אֲמַר מָאן דְּמַייְתֵי לִי חַרְדְּלָא אֲנָא מוֹרֵי כְרבִּי יוּדָה.[19] אֲמַר רבִּי בָּא בַר זַבְדָּא הוֹרֵי רבִּי חוֹנְיָא דְמִין חַוְרָן בְּבֵית חַוְרָן כְּהָדָה דְרבִּי יוּדָה. עָאל רבִּי יוֹחָנָן וְדָרַשׁ כְּרַבָּנִין דְהָכָא וּכְרַבָּנִין דְּתַמָּן.

Rebbi Simeon ben Laqish was in Ḥiqoq[20]. He saw them dealing with mustard plants. One of these fell down and he [a townsman] did not take it up[21]. He [R. Simeon] said, if somebody will bring a mustard plant to me I shall rule following Rebbi Jehudah. Rebbi Abba bar Zavda said, Rebbi Onias from Hauran ruled in Bet Hauran following Rebbi Jehudah. Rebbi Johanan rose and publicly proclaimed following the rabbis here and there[22].

19   Reading of Rome ms., as conjectured by all commentators. Venice and Leyden: R. Jonah.

20   This place has not be identified.

21   He considered it a kind of weed; therefore he was ruling following R. Jehudah.

22   It seems that a sentence is missing here, preserved in *Beẓah* 1:1 (fol. 60a): "Rebbi Ḥanina ruled for the Sepphorites following R. Jehudah in matters of mustard and egg." As an answer, R. Johanan ruled in Sepphoris against R. Ḥanina in both matters (but,

because of R. Ḥanina's seniority, his ruling was not followed.) The case of the egg is treated in the next two paragraphs whose source is *Beẓah* 1:1.

רְבִּי אַבָּא בַּר זְמִינָא בְּשֵׁם רְבִּי יַצְחָק מִן קוֹמוֹי אִילֵין תַּרְתֵּיי מִילַיָּיא נְחַת לֵיהּ רְבִּי יוֹחָנָן מִצִּיפּוֹרִין לִטְבֵּירִיָּא. אָמַר מָה אֲתִיתוֹן לִי הָדֵין דַּיָּינָא סַבָּא דְּאִי אֲנָא שָׁרֵי וְהוּא אָסַר אֲנָא אָסַר וְהוּא שָׁרֵי. אָמַר רְבִּי זְרָא אֲתָא עוֹבְדָּא קוֹמֵי רְבִּי יָסָא וּבְעָא מֵיעֲבַד כְּרְבִּי יוֹחָנָן כַּד שָׁמַע דְּרַב וְרְבִּי חֲנִינָא מִתְפַּלְגִין שָׁרַע מִינֵּיהּ. דְּאִיתְפַּלְגִין שְׁיָרֵי פְתִילָה שְׁיָרֵי מְדוּרָה שְׁיָרֵי (fol. 38d) שֶׁמֶן שֶׁכָּבוּ בְּשַׁבָּת מַהוּ לְהַדְלִיק בְּיוֹם טוֹב. רַב וְרְבִּי חֲנִינָא תְּרֵיהוֹן אָמְרִין אָסוּר. וְרְבִּי יוֹחָנָן אָמַר מוּתָּר. אָמַר רְבִּי יוּדָן קוֹמֵי רְבִּי מָנָא מִפְכָּה לָהּ גַּבֵּי בֵּיצָה אָמַר לֵיהּ מִן מָה דַּאֲנַן חָמֵיי רַבָּנִין מְדַמֵּיי לָהּ הָדָא אָמַר הִיא הָדָא הִיא הָדָא.

Rebbi Abba Bar Zemina in the name of Rebbi Isaac: Because of these two things did R. Joḥanan descend from Sepphoris to Tiberias. He said, you brought this old judge who forbids what I permit and permits what I forbid[23]! Rebbi Abba said, there came a case before Rebbi Assi and he wanted to act following Rebbi Joḥanan but when he heard that Rav and Rebbi Ḥanina disagreed he refrained. Because they disagree: May the remainders of a wick, a fire, or oil that burned out on the Sabbath be lit on the holiday[24]? Rav and Rebbi Ḥanina both say it is forbidden, but Rebbi Joḥanan says, it is permitted. Rebbi Judan said before Rebbi Mana, is it the reverse regarding an egg[25]? He said to him, since the rabbis compare it, it means that the cases are identical[26].

23   The historicity of this remark is questionable since R. Joḥanan was R. Ḥanina's student in Sepphoris (at least in matters of Aggadah.) It is reasonable to accept the fact that R.

Joḥanan went to Tiberias because there he could be Chief Rabbi.

24   If the holiday falls on a Sunday. It is forbidden to light fire on the Sabbath; therefore, the unburned oil or

wood from a fire that was burning at the beginning of the Sabbath but later burned out or was extinguished by the wind are no longer usable during that Sabbath. For the Sabbath, it is a requirement that (*Ex.* 16:5) "they have to prepare what they are going to bring (to use)". Therefore, on the Sabbath one may use only what was usable before the Sabbath. This rule, if transferred to the holidays, implies that the wood and oil, not being usable a minute before the start of the holiday, cannot become usable on the holiday. If the rule is not transferred to apply to holidays, the fuel becomes permitted at the end of the Sabbath as if it were a weekday.

25   Mishnah *Beẓah* 1:1: "An egg laid on the holiday, the House of

Shammai say, it may be eaten, the House of Hillel say, it may not be eaten." According to the Yerushalmi, in the opinion of the house of Shammai the egg is prepared since the hen itself is potential food before the holiday and an egg inside a slaughtered hen is permitted food. According to the House of Hillel, the egg becomes something new by being laid and the new egg was not usable before the holiday.

26   At least for the House of Hillel. Tosephta *Yom Ṭob* 1:3: "An egg laid on the Sabbath may be eaten on the holiday. Rebbi Jehudah said in the name of Rebbi Eliezer, the dispute is the same;" in the Yerushalmi (*Beẓah* 1:1): "this is the dispute of the House of Shammai."

מִשּׁוּם אַרְבָּעָה זְקֵנִים אָמְרוּ כָּל־הַנֶּאֱכָל עירוּבוֹ בָּרִאשׁוֹן הֲרֵי הוּא כִּבְנֵי עִירוֹ בַּשֵּׁינִי. רַב הוּנָא בְּשֵׁם רַב הֲלָכָה כְּאַרְבָּעָה זְקֵנִים. רַב חִסְדָּא בְּעֵי מַחְלְפָא שִׁיטָתֵיהּ דְּרַב. תַּמָּן הוּא עֲבַד לָהּ שְׁתֵּי קְדוּשׁוֹת. וָכָא הוּא עֲבַד לָהּ קְדוּשָׁה אַחַת. דְּאִיתְפַּלְגִין שְׁיֵרֵי פְתִילָה שְׁיֵרֵי מְדוּרָה שְׁיֵרֵי שֶׁמֶן שֶׁכָּבוּ בְשַׁבָּת מַהוּ לְהַדְלִיק בְּיוֹם טוֹב. רַב וְרַבִּי חֲנִינָא תְּרֵיהוֹן אֲמְרִין אָסוּר. וְרַבִּי יוֹחָנָן אָמַר מוּתָּר. אָמַר רְבִּי מָנָא קוֹמֵי רְבִּי יוּדָן מַה אַפְכָה לָהּ פְּתִילָה גַּבֵּי בֵּיצָה אָמַר לֵיהּ מִן מָה דַּאֲנָן חָמֵיי רַבָּנִין מְדַמּוֹי לָהּ הָדָא אָמַר הִיא הָדָא הִיא הָדָא.

They said in the name of four elders: If somebody's *eruv* was eaten on the first [day] he is like the people of his town on the second [day][27]. Rav

Huna in the name of Rav: Practice follows the four elders[28]. Rav Ḥisda asked: The arguments of Rav seem to be inverted. There, he makes it two sanctities, but here he makes it one sanctity[29]. Because they disagree: May the remainders of a wick, a fire, or oil that burned out on the Sabbath be lit on the holiday? Rav and Rebbi Ḥanina both say it is forbidden, but Rebbi Joḥanan says it is permitted. Rebbi Mana said before Rebbi Judan, are the rules different for a wick and an egg? He said to him, since the rabbis compare it, it means that the cases are identical[30].

27   The parallels are *Beẓah* 1:1(fol. 60a), *Erubin* 3:9(fol. 21b), Babli *Erubin* 38b. In Tosefta *Erubin* 4:2, the statement is attributed to R. Meïr, in the Babli to Rabban Simeon ben Gamliel, R. Ismael ben R. Joḥanan ben Beroqa, R. Eleazar ben R. Simeon, and R. Yose ben R. Jehudah. The notion of *eruv* was explained in *Peah*, Chapter 8, Note 56.

28   In the Babli, Rav states that his ruling is based on the theory that any two consecutive holy days represent two distinct sanctities and, therefore, an *eruv* valid for one day has no influence on the other. This is the opinion of R. Eliezer in Mishnah *Eruvin* 3:8.

29   "There" is *Eruvin*. "Here" is *Beẓah*, dealing with leftover fuel from fires that burned out on the Sabbath. This shows that the original place of

this piece is *Beẓah*. Since the holiday is a new sanctity and one may light fires on the holiday, it is difficult to see how Rav could forbid using the fuel on the second day. The Babli (*loc. cit.* Note 27) notes that Rav Ḥisda asked the question only after Rav Huna's death so that the latter had no opportunity to explain himself.

30   The Babli gives several tentative explanations of Rav's position. The one consistent with the Yerushalmi is that only weekdays can prepare for holidays (cf. Note 24) but the Sabbath cannot prepare for a holiday. Since the reason for Rav's ruling in the case of fuel is not based on the number of sanctities involved, there is no inconsistency in his decisions. It is difficult to understand why the Yerushalmi has no answer to R. Ḥisda's question.

שֶׁאֵין כְּיוֹצֵא בָהֶן בְּיַרְקוֹת הַשָּׂדֶה. וּמִפְּנֵי שֶׁאֵין כְּיוֹצֵא בָהֶן בְּיַרְקוֹת הַשָּׂדֶה יְהוּ
אֲסוּרִין. רְבִּי חָמָא בַּר עוּקְבָּא בְּשֵׁם רִבִּי יוֹסֵי בַּר חֲנִינָא מִפְּנֵי שֶׁדַּרְכָּן לְגַדֵּל
אִמָּהוֹת. וּמִפְּנֵי שֶׁדַּרְכָּן לְגַדֵּל אִמָּהוֹת יְהוּ אֲסוּרִין. אָמַר רִבִּי שְׁמוּאֵל בַּר רַב
יִצְחָק כָּל־הַיֶּרֶק אַתְּ יָכוֹל לַעֲמוֹד עָלָיו אִם חָדָשׁ הוּא אִם יָשָׁן הוּא בְּרַם הָכָא
שֶׁלֹּא יֵלֵךְ וְיָבִיא מִן הָאִיסּוּר וְיֹאמַר מִן הָאִמָּהוֹת הֲבֵאתִי.

"Since nothing similar is growing wild on the fields." And since nothing
similar is growing wild on the fields should they be forbidden[31]? Rebbi
Ḥama bar Uqba in the name of Rebbi Yose bar Ḥanina said, because they
usually grow layers. And because they usually grow layers should they be
forbidden? Rebbi Samuel bar Rebbi Isaac said, for all other vegetables
one can recognize whether they are new or old but here one should not
go and bring from what is forbidden and say I brought from the layers[32].

31   There seems to be no reason   plant and not spontaneous growth, so it
why R. Simeon should forbid cabbage.   is not subject to the rules restricting
32   This is growth from the original   the use of spontaneous growth.

אֵין מְחַייְבִין אוֹתוֹ לַעֲקוֹר אֶת הַלּוּף בַּשְּׁבִיעִית. אֲבָל מַנִּיחוֹ כְּמוֹת שֶׁהוּא אִם
צִימַּח מוֹצָאֵי שְׁבִיעִית מוּתָּר. אֵין מְחַייְבִין אוֹתוֹ לְשָׁרֵשׁ הַקִּינָרִיס בַּשְּׁבִיעִית.
אֲבָל מְשַׁקֵּף בְּעָלִים אִם צָמְחוּ מוֹצָאֵי שְׁבִיעִית מוּתָּר. וְלֹא נִמְצָא מְאַבֵּד אוֹכְלֵי
בְהֵמָה. מֵאֵילֵיהֶן הֵן אֲבוּדִין.

"One does not oblige him to uproot arum in the Sabbatical but he
leaves it in place and if it sprouted after the end of the Sabbatical it is
permitted. One does not oblige him to uproot artichokes in the Sabbatical
but he knocks off its leaves and if it sprouted after the end of the
Sabbatical it is permitted."[33]   Does he not waste animal food?
Automatically they are lost[34].

33   Tosephta 2:11-12. The Tosephta starts: "Any vegetables irrigated before New Year's Day may be kept during the Sabbatical. If they were thin, one may not keep them because of the bad impression. One does not oblige . . . " Arum and artichokes survive several years. For artichokes one has to knock off enough leaves to ruin them as produce for the current year.

34   The removed artichoke leaves can be given to cattle; if they are left lying to rot and no animal comes to eat them, it is not the owner's problem.

רִבִּי שִׁמְעוֹן בֶּן יוֹחַי הֲוָה עֲבַר בִּשְׁמִיטְתָא וְחָמָא חַד מְלַקֵּט שְׁבִיעִית. אֲמַר לֵיהּ וְלֵית אָסוּר וְלָאו סְפִיחִין אִינּוּן. אֲמַר לֵיהּ וְלָא אַתְּ הוּא מַתִּירָן. אֲמַר לֵיהּ וְאֵין חֲבִירַיי חֲלוּקִין עָלַי. קָרָא עָלָיו וּפוֹרֵץ גָּדֵר יִשְׁכֶנּוּ נָחָשׁ וְכֵן הֲוַת לֵיהּ.

Rebbi Simeon ben Iohai was travelling in the Sabbatical when he saw somebody collecting Sabbatical [produce][35]. He said to him, is this not forbidden, is that not spontaneous growth? He said to him, are not you the one who permits it? He said to him, are not my colleagues disagreeing with me? He read for him (*Eccl.* 10:8): "He who tears down a fence[36] will be bitten by a snake." That is what happened to him.

35   This is explained in *Berakhot* 1:2, Note 130. Parallels are in Midrash *Gen. rabba* 79(6), *Eccl. rabbati* 10(11).

36   "Making a fence" is the usual metaphor for a rabbinic prohibition.

Even if the Sabbatical is to be observed as biblical commandment, spontaneous growth is forbidden only by rabbinical decree.

רִבִּי שִׁמְעוֹן בֶּן יוֹחַי עֲבַד טְמִיר בִּמְעַרְתָּא תְּלַת עֲשַׂר שְׁנִין בִּמְעָרַת חָרוּבִין. (דתרומה)[37] עַד שֶׁהֶעֱלָה גוּפוֹ חֲלוּדָה לְסוֹף תְּלַת עֲשַׂר שְׁנִין. אֲמַר לֵינָה נְפַק חָמֵי מַה קָלָא עָלְמָא נְפַק וְיָתִיב לֵיהּ עַל פּוּמָא דִמְעַרְתָּא חָמָא חַד צַייָד צָיֵיד צִיפּוֹרִין פְּרַס מְצוּדָתֵיהּ שְׁמַע בְּרַת קָלָא אָמְרָה דִימוֹס וְאִישְׁתֵּיזָבַת. אֲמַר צִיפּוֹר מִבַּלְעֲדֵי שְׁמַיָּא לָא יִבְדָּא. וְכָל־שֶׁכֵּן בַּר נַשָׁא. כַּד חָמָא דִשְׁדְכָן מִילַיָּא אֲמַר

נִיחוֹת נִיחֲמוּ בַּהֲדֵין דֵּימוֹסִין דְּטִיבֶּרְיָא אָמַר צְרִיכִין אֲנָן לַעֲשׂוֹת תַּקָּנָה כְּמוֹ
שֶׁעָשׂוּ אֲבוֹתֵינוּ הָרִאשׁוֹנִים וַיִּחַן אֶת פְּנֵי הָעִיר. שֶׁהָיוּ עוֹשִׂין אִיטְלִיסִין וּמוֹכְרִין
בַּשּׁוּק. אָמַר נִידְכֵי טִיבֶּרְיָא וַהֲוָה נָסֵב תּוּרְמוֹסִין וּמְקַצֵּץ וּמְקַלֵּיק וְכָל־הֶן דַּהֲוָה
מִיתָא הֲוָה טַיֵּיף וְסָלַק לֵיהּ מִן לְעֵיל. חֲמָתֵיהּ חַד כּוּתִי אָמַר לֵינָה אֲזַל מַפְלֵי
בְּהוֹן סַבָּא דִיוּדָאֵי נְסַב חַד מִית אֲזַל וְאַטְמְרֵיהּ הֶן דְּדָכִי. אֲתָא לְגַבֵּי רִבִּי
שִׁמְעוֹן בֶּן יוֹחַי אָמַר לֵיהּ לָא דְכִית אֲתַר פְּלָן. אִיתָא וַאֲנָא מַפִּיק לָךְ מִתַּמָּן.
צָפָה רִבִּי שִׁמְעוֹן בֶּן יוֹחַי בְּרוּחַ הַקּוֹדֶשׁ שֶׁנְּתָנוֹ שָׁם. וְאָמַר גּוֹזֵר אֲנִי עַל הָעֶלְיוֹנִים
שֶׁיֵּרְדוּ וְעַל הַתַּחְתּוֹנִים שֶׁיַּעֲלוּ וְכֵן הֲוָת לֵיהּ. מִי עָבַר קוֹמֵי מוּגְדָּלָא שְׁמַע קָלֵיהּ
דְּסָפְרָא אֲמַר הָא בַּר יוֹחַי מַדְכֵּי טִיבֶּרְיָא. אֲמַר לֵיהּ יָבוֹא עָלַי אִם לֹא שְׁמַעְתִּי
שֶׁטִּיבֶּרְיָא עֲתִידָה לִיטָהֵר. אֲפִילוּ כֵן לָא הֵימְנִין הָיִיתָ מִיַּד נַעֲשָׂה גַּל שֶׁל עֲצָמוֹת.

[37]Rebbi Simeon ben Iohai was hidden in a cave for thirteen years, in a
carob cave, until his body was covered with rust. At the end of thirteen
years he said, should I not go out and see what voice is in the world? He
went and sat at the entrance to the cave. He saw a catcher out to catch
birds spreading out his net. He heard a heavenly voice saying "acquitted",
and [the bird] was saved. He said, no bird will be adjudicated without
Heaven, so much less a human. When he saw that words of intercession
were given, he said, let us go down and warm ourselves in the public
baths of Tiberias. He said, we need to do something like our forefathers
(*Gen.* 33:18): "He graced the entrance to the city," they were putting up
duty free shops and selling at wholesale prices. He said, let us purify
Tiberias. He took lupines, cut them up and threw them down in irregular
fashion. Where there was a corpse it was floating and came to the
surface. A Samaritan saw him and said, should I not make fun of this old
Jew? He took a corpse, went, and buried it at a purified place. He came
to Rebbi Simeon bar Iohai and said to him, did you not purify place X?

Come, and I shall take out [a corpse] from there! Rebbi Simeon bar Iohai saw by the Holy Spirit that he had put it there. He said, I decree that the upper ones shall go down and the lower ones come up. So it happenend to him. When he passed by Magdala, he heard the voice of the scribe who said, so bar Iohai purifies Tiberias? He said, it should come upon me if I did not hear that Tiberias once will be purified. Even so, you did not believe me! Immediately he turned into a bone heap.

37   The parallels are in Midrash *Gen. rabba* 79(6), *Eccl. rabbati* 10(11), Babli *Šabbat* 33b-34a. The text here is deficient in several places; the text of the Babli is clearly derivative. The best text is that of *Gen. rabba* on the verse *(Gen.* 33:18): "He graced the entrance to the city," which is explained as "they were putting up duty free shops and selling at wholesale prices." Since the verse is given here also as a reason (in a shortened and rather incomprehensible connection), it is best to give the entire text from *Gen. rabba*, which is explicit where the text here is cryptic:

"R. Simeon ben Iohai *and his son R. Eleazar* were hidden in a cave for thirteen years during the time of persecution [after the war of Bar Kokhba]. They ate dry carobs until their bodies were covered with rust. At the end of thirteen years he went and sat at the entrance to the cave. He saw a catcher out to catch birds. When he heard a heavenly voice saying *dimissus* [acquitted], it escaped, *when he heard* spicula *[arrows], it was caught.* He said, no bird will be caught without Heaven, much less a human. He went out and saw that words of intercession were given *and the decree had been rescinded.* They came and bathed in the hot waters of Tiberias. His son said to him, all this benefit we had from Tiberias and we do not cleanse it from the slain? He said, we need to do something good as our forefathers did when they were putting up duty free shops [ἀτελής] and selling at wholesale prices. What did he do? He took lupines, cut them up and threw *the pieces* down in irregular fashion. Everywhere there was a slain body, it was floating *and they removed it. Everywhere there was no impurity, the*

lupines remained unmoved. *He put up
signs indicating which places were pure
and which impure until he had cleansed
it completely.* A *vulgar* Samaritan saw
him and said, should I not make a fool
of this old Jew? He took a corpse
(*some people say from the cooper's
market, some say from the sack-
maker's*), went, and buried it where the
ground was purified. The next
morning, he came to them and said, did
you say that bar Yoḥai purified Tiberias? Come and see this corpse! R.
Simeon bar Ioḥai saw by the Holy Spirit
that he had put it there. He said, I
decree that the upper one shall go
down [die] and the lower one come up
[live]. So it happenend to him. He [R.
Simeon bar Ioḥai] went up to spend the
Sabbath in his house. When he passed
by Magdala *of the dyers*, he heard the

voice of *Nikai* the scribe who said, *did
you not say* bar Ioḥai purified Tiberias?
They found a corpse! He said, It should
come upon me if I *did not have traditions in the number of the hairs on my
head* that Tiberias is pure, *except
places X and Y. Were you not in the
meeting when we declared it pure? You
broke down the fence of the Sages;
about you it was said* (*Eccl.* 10:8): '*He
who tears down a fence will be bitten by
a snake*'! Immediately he turned into a
bone heap."

When Herod Antipas built Tiberias
on the site of the Biblical Raqqat, he
destroyed a cemetery (Josephus, *Antiquities*, XVIII. 2. 3) so that no priest or
anybody keeping the laws of purity
could visit there. Thereiore, up to the
time of R. Simeon ben Ioḥai Tiberias
was only a place of the vulgar.

(fol. 38c) **משנה ב:** שָׁלֹש אֲרָצוֹת לַבִּיעוּר יְהוּדָה וְעֵבֶר הַיַּרְדֵּן וְגָלִיל. וְשָׁלֹש שָׁלֹש
אֲרָצוֹת לְכָל־אַחַת וְאַחַת. גָּלִיל הָעֶלְיוֹן וְגָלִיל הַתַּחְתּוֹן וְהָעֵמֶק. מִכְּפַר חֲנַנְיָה
וּלְמַעֲלָן כָּל־שֶׁאֵינָהּ מְגַדֵּל שִׁיקְמִין גָּלִיל הָעֶלְיוֹן. וּמִכְּפַר חֲנַנְיָה וּלְמַטָּן כָּל־שֶׁהוּא
מְגַדֵּל שִׁיקְמִין גָּלִיל הַתַּחְתּוֹן. וּתְחוּם טְבֶרְיָא וְהָעֵמֶק. וּבִיהוּדָה הָהָר הַשְּׁפֵלָה
וְהַנֶּגֶב וּשְׁפֵילַת לוֹד כִּשְׁפֵילַת הַדָּרוֹם וְהָהָר שֶׁלָּהּ כְּהַר הַמֶּלֶךְ. מִבֵּית חוֹרוֹן וְעַד
הַיָּם מְדִינָה אַחַת.

Mishnah 2: There are three regions for removals[38], Judea, Transjordan[39], and Galilee. Each of them has three subregions: Upper Galilee, Lower Galilee, and the Valley. From Kefar Ḥananiah[40] upwards, everywhere no sycamores can grow, is Upper Galilee. From Kefar Ḥananiah downwards, everwhere sycamores do grow, is Lower Galilee. And the district of Tiberias and the Valley[41]. In Jehudah the hills, the lowland, and the Southland. The lowlands of Lydda are like the Southern lowlands[42], its hills are like King's Mountain[43]. From Bet Ḥoron to the Sea is one domain[44].

38 The time when Sabbatical produce stored in one's house must be removed (by being eaten or distributed to the poor) after nothing of the same kind is left on the fields for wildlife, is determined separately for each of the nine regions settled by Jews in the Holy Land. According to the Tosephta Chap. 8, the distribution is a communal action directed by the court and can be a drawn-out affair with nobody getting more than food for three meals at one time. However, it is stated in Halakhah 5 that in Amoraic times the obligation of removal was circumvented by formal abandonment of the produce.

39 In the Pentateuch, עבר הירדן can mean either the West or the East bank of the Jordan. According to Maimonides, in this Mishnah "the side of the Jordan" denotes the region between Bet Ḥoron and the Sea. The Halakhah contradicts this determination; also it would call "side of the Jordan" only the parts of Southern Ephraim between the Jordan and the watershed. The Halakhah defines עבר הירדן as the Transjordan parts of Jewish Palestine, not included in Jehudah and Galilee; cf. Halakhah 6:1.

40 The center of the pottery industry in Galilee. Its location has not been convincingly determined.

41 The Jordan valley South of the Sea of Galilee. The Jezreël valley is counted as part of Lower Galilee.

42 The entire lowland from Antipatris North of Lydda to the South has the same status even though it is not one domain.

43 Cf. Demay Chapter 5, Note 115, and Note 63 below.

44 The Halakhah will define this as an additional domain.

חלכה ב: וְלִבְהֶמְתְּךָ וְלַחַיָּה אֲשֶׁר בְּאַרְצֶךָ כו'. כָּל־זְמָן שֶׁחַיָּה אוֹכֶלֶת מִן(.fol 38d) הַשָּׂדֶה הַבְּהֵמָה אוֹכֶלֶת מִן הַבַּיִת. כָּלָה לַחַיָּה מִן הַשָּׂדֶה כָּלָה לִבְהֶמְתְּךָ מִן הַבַּיִת.

Halakhah 2: (*Lev.* 25:7): "For your domesticated animals and the wildlife in your land,[45] etc." Any time a wild animal finds food on the field, your domesticated animal can eat from the house. If it is finished for wildlife on the field, it is finished for the domesticated animal from the house.

45   ". . . shall all its yield be food." The verse is interpreted to mean that wildlife and domesticated animals have equal rights to Sabbatical produce. [*Sifra Behar Pereq* 1(8); Babli *Pesaḥim* 52b, *Ta'anit* 6b.]

רִבִּי חָמָא בַּר עוּקְבָּא בְּשֵׁם רִבִּי יוֹסֵי בַּר חֲנִינָא שִׁיעֲרוּ לוֹמַר אֵין הַחַיָּה שֶׁבְּהַר גְּדֵילָה בָּעֵמֶק וְלֹא גְּדֵילָה חַיָּה שֶׁבְּעֵמֶק בָּהַר. דִּיקְלֵיטִיָּאנוּס אָעִיק לִבְנֵי פַּנְיָיס. אָמְרִין לֵיהּ אֲנָן אָזְלִון. אָמַר לֵיהּ סוֹפִיסְטָה לָא אָזְלוּן לוֹן וְאִין אָזְלִין חָזְרוּן לוֹן. וְאִי בָּעִית מִיבְדְּקָא אַייְתֵי טַבְיָין וְשַׁלְחוֹן לְאַרְעָא דִרְחִיקָא וּבְסוֹף אִינּוּן חָזְרִין לְאַתְּרֵיהוֹן. עֲבַד כֵּן אַייְתֵי טַבְיָין וְחָפֵי קַרְנָתְהוּ בִּכְסַף וְשַׁלְחוֹן לְאַפְרִיקִי וּבְסוֹף תְּלָת עֶשְׂרֵה שְׁנִין חָזְרוּ לְאַתְּרֵיהוֹן.

Rebbi Ḥama bar Uqba in the name of Rebbi Yose bar Ḥanina: They were of the opinion that mountain wildlife does not develop in the valley, nor does valley wildlife develop on the mountains[46]. Diocletian oppressed the people of Paneias[47]; they told him: we are leaving. A Sophist[48] told him, they will not go, and if they go they will return. If you want to check, bring deer and send them to a distant land; in the end they will return to their places. He did so, brought deer, covered their antlers with silver, and sent them to Africa. At the end of thirteen years they returned to their places[49].

46   If wild animals migrate one could eat at one place until all produce anywhere in the country is used up.

47   Caesarea Philippi, at the Jordan source (today Banias).

48   Greek σοφιστής "Sophist, ex-

pert"

49   The story is impossible since deer grow new antlers every year. ("13 years" in the Leyden, "30 years" in the Venice texts.)

תָּנֵי רַבָּן שִׁמְעוֹן בֶּן גַּמְלִיאֵל אוֹמֵר סִימָן לֶהָרִים מֵילִין. לָעֲמָקִים תְּמָרִים לַנְחָלִים קָנִים. לַשְּׁפֵילָה שִׁיקְמִים. וְאַף עַל פִּי שֶׁאֵין רְאָיָה לַדָּבָר זֵכֶר לַדָּבָר וְאֶת הָאֲרָזִים נָתַן כַּשִּׁיקְמִים אֲשֶׁר בַּשְּׁפֵלָה לָרוֹב. אִית דְּבָעֵי מֵימַר לְמִידַת הַדִּין אִיתְּמַר וְאִית דְּבָעֵי מֵימַר לְעֶגְלָה עֲרוּפָה אִיתְּמַר.

It was stated[50]: "Rabban Simeon ben Gamliel says, a sign for mountains are ash trees[51], for valleys dates, for brooks reeds, for the lowland sycamores. Even if it is no proof, there is a sign (*1K.* 10:27, *2Chr.* 1:19, 9:27)): 'Cedars he [Solomon] gave as many as sycamores in the lowland.'" Some people want to say it was said[52] as a legal term, others say it refers to the calf whose neck is to be broken.

50   Tosephta 7:11. The text is quoted Babli *Pesaḥim* 53a.

51   Greek μελία (Musaphia). Rashi and R. Ḥananel in *Pesaḥim* define as "gall-oak." Lieberman defines as "pine"; in Arabic מילא is "a leafy tree".

52   The sign for brooks, which is not needed for the laws of the Sabbatical. The sign is needed either to

standardize legal terms (that a contract for sale of a brook which has no reeds is invalid unless their absence is noted in the contract) or as definition of the "abandoned brook" at which an unsolved murder case must be atoned for (*Deut.* 21). The Babli takes the entire Tosephta as defining legal terms.

אֵי זֶהוּ עֵמֶק בַּגָּלִיל כְּגוֹן בִּקְעַת גִּינוֹסַר וַחֲבֵירוֹתֶיהָ וְכֵן כַּיּוֹצֵא בָּהֶן. אֵי זֶהוּ הַר שֶׁבִּיהוּדָה זֶה הַר הַמֶּלֶךְ. וּשְׁפֵלָתוֹ זוּ שְׁפֵלַת דָּרוֹם. וְעֵמֶק שֶׁלּוֹ מֵעֵין גֶּדִי וְעַד

יְרִיחוֹ. אֵי זֶהוּ הַר שֶׁבְּעֵבֶר הַיַּרְדֵּן. תַּנֵּי רִבִּי שִׁמְעוֹן בֶּן אֶלְעָזָר אוֹמֵר כְּגוֹן הָרֵי
מַכְוָר וּגְדוֹר וְכֵן כְּיוֹצֵא בָּהֶן וּשְׁפֵלָתוֹ חֶשְׁבּוֹן וְכָל־עָרֶיהָ אֲשֶׁר בַּמִּישׁוֹר דִּיבוֹן
וּבָמוֹת בַּעַל וּבֵית בַּעַל מְעוֹן וְכֵן כְּיוֹצֵא בָּהֶן. וְעֵמֶק שְׁלוֹ בֵּית הָרָן וּבֵית נִמְרָה
וְכֵן כְּיוֹצֵא בָּהֶן. וּבָעֵמֶק בֵּית הָרָן וּבֵית נִמְרָה וְסוּכּוֹת וְצָפוֹן יֶתֶר מַמְלְכַת סִיחוֹן
מֶלֶךְ הָאֱמוֹרִי אֲשֶׁר מָלַךְ בְּחֶשְׁבּוֹן. בֵּית הָרִים בֵּית רָמָתָא בֵּית נִמְרָה בֵּית נִמְרִין.
סוּכּוֹת תַּרְעָלָה צָפוֹן עַמָּתוֹ.

"[53]What is the Valley in Galilee? For example, the valley of Genezareth[54] and its companions," and all similar ones. What is the Mountain in Judea? King's Mountain[43]. Its Lowlands are the Southern lowlands. Its Valley from En Gedi to Jericho. What is the Mountain in Transjordan? It was stated: "Rebbi Simeon ben Eleazar said, for example Mount Machaerus and Gadara and all similar ones. Its Lowlands, (*Jos.* 13:17) 'Ḥesbon and all its towns in the plain, Dibon, Bamot Ba'al, and Ba'al Me'on' and all similar ones. Its Valley (*Jos.* 13:27) 'Bet Haran[55], Bet Nimra, Sukkot, and Ṣaphon, the remainder of the kingdom of Siḥon' the Emorite king who ruled in Ḥesbon." Bet Harim is Bet Ramata, Bet Nimra Bet Nimrin[56], Sukkot Tar'ala[57], Ṣaphon Amato[58].

---

53 All Tosephta texts are from 6:11, a rather badly preserved text. It may be assumed that all sentences starting with "what is" and the answers given come from a *baraita*.

54 Not the Jordan valley but the side valley pointing towards Safed. Similarly, all deep side valleys of the Jordan valley are "Valley".

55 In Scripture, "Bet Haram", possibly Tell Bet Haran, S. E. of Jericho.

56 Today Nimreïn.

57 Eusebius and St. Jerome put Tarala due East of Bet Shean on the East bank of the Jordan.

58 Mentioned by Josephus (*Antiquities* XIII v 10), today Amatheh.

שְׁפֵלָה שֶׁבָּהָר כְּהָר וְשֶׁבַּשְׁפֵלָה כִּשְׁפֵלָה. מִן מָה דְּתַגֵּי הַר וְהָרוּ עֵמֶק וְעִמְקוּ שָׁפֵל וּשְׁפֵלָתוֹ הָדָא אָמְרָה שְׁפֵלָה שֶׁבָּהָר כְּהָר וְהַר שֶׁבַּשְׁפֵלָה כִּשְׁפֵלָה. אָמַר רִבִּי יוֹסֵי מַתְנִיתִין אָמַר כֵּן וְהָהָר שֶׁלָּהּ כְּהַר הַמֶּלֶךְ.

Is a depression in the mountains like the mountains, a hill in the lowlands like the lowlands? Since we stated[59]: "Mountain and its mountain, Valley and its valley, Lowland and its lowlands," that means that a depression in the mountains is like the mountains, a hill in the lowlands is like the lowlands. Rebbi Yose said, our Mishnah says so: "its hills are like King's Mountain."

59 Tosephta 7:10: "Why were Mountain, Lowlands, and Valley mentioned? Because one does not eat on the mountain because of what is in the valley, and not in the valley because of what is on the mountain, but Mountain and its mountain, Valley and its valley, Lowland and its lowlands."

מִבֵּית חוֹרוֹן וְעַד הַיָּם מְדִינָה אַחַת פָּרָא כּוֹרִין. אָמַר רִבִּי יוֹחָנָן עוֹד הִיא יֶשׁ בָּהּ הַר וּשְׁפֵלָה וְעֵמֶק. מִבֵּית חוֹרוֹן וְעַד אֶמָּאוּס הַר מֵאֶמָּאוּס וְעַד לוֹד שְׁפֵלָה מִלּוֹד וְעַד הַיָּם עֵמֶק. נִיתְּנוּ אַרְבַּע מְעוּרְבּוֹת הֵן.

"From Bet Ḥoron to the Sea is one domain." Without regions[60]? Rebbi Joḥanan said, still there is Mountain, Lowland, and Valley. From Bet Ḥoron to Emmaus it is Mountain, from Emmaus to Lydda Lowland, from Lydda to the Sea Valley. Then there should be four stated[61]? They are adjacent.

60 A word unrecognized by the dictionaries, Arabic كورة *kurah* "region, country".
61 If there are four domains, four should have been stated. The answer is that the region between Bet Ḥoron and the sea is adjacent to Judea (i. e., it is part of Biblical Ephraim but Maccabean Judea.)

תַּנֵּי אֵין בְּסוּרְיָה שָׁלֹשׁ אֲרָצוֹת.

It was stated[62]: "There are not three regions in Syria."

<table>
<tr><td>62   Tosephta 7:10: "In Syria, no three regions were declared but one eats from the first produce until the very last has disappeared." Since the</td><td>obligation of the Sabbatical in Syria was never biblical, one follows the most lenient interpretation.</td></tr>
</table>

(fol. 38c) **משנה ג**: וְלָמָּה אָמְרוּ שָׁלֹשׁ אֲרָצוֹת שֶׁיְּהוּ אוֹכְלִין בְּכָל־אַחַת וְאַחַת עַד שֶׁיְּכְלֶה הָאַחֲרוֹן שֶׁבָּהּ. רִבִּי שִׁמְעוֹן אוֹמֵר לֹא אָמְרוּ שָׁלֹשׁ אֲרָצוֹת אֶלָּא בִיהוּדָה וּשְׁאָר כָּל־הָאֲרָצוֹת כְּהַר הַמֶּלֶךְ. וְכָל־הָאֲרָצוֹת כְּאַחַת לַזֵּיתִים וְלַתְּמָרִים.

Mishnah 3: Why did they mention three regions? That in each one may eat until the last produce has vanished. Rebbi Simeon says, they mentioned three regions only for Judea; all other regions follow King's Mountain[63]. All regions are one for olives and dates.

<table>
<tr><td>63   In Tosephta 7:10: "Rebbi Simeon says, they mentioned three regions only for Judea; all other regions continue to eat their produce until it vanishes from Bet El and the periphery of Caesarion." Since King's Mountain is described as the hill region representing Judea, it</td><td>cannot be the region between Bet El and Caesarion (Caesarea Philippi) as maintained by R. S. Klein and R. S. Lieberman. The farthest reach of King's Mountain is the region extending N. of Jerusalem to the Northern border of Hasmonean Judea.</td></tr>
</table>

(fol. 38d) **הלכה ג**: אִיתָא חָמֵי אִילֵּין עֲמָק שֶׁבִּיהוּדָה אֵינוֹ אוֹכֵל עַד הַר יְהוּדָה וְעֵמָק שֶׁבַּגָּלִיל אוֹכֵל עַד הַר יְהוּדָה.

Halakhah 3: Come and see: Those in the valley of Judea cannot eat based on the mountains of Judea but in the valleys of Galilee they eat based on the mountains of Judea[64]!

64   The opinion of R. Simeon is paradoxical since he permits every-   where outside Judea to eat fruits still available at Bet El!

כָּל־הָאֲרָצוֹת כְּאַחַת לַזֵּיתִים וְלַתְּמָרִים. תַּנֵּי אַף לֶחָרוּבִין. תַּנֵּי אוֹכְלִין עַל הַתְּמָרִים עַד שֶׁיִּכְלוּ מִירִיחוֹ וְעַל הַזֵּיתִים עַד שֶׁיִּכְלוּ מִמֶּרוֹן וּמִגּוּשׁ חָלָב.

"All regions are one for olives and dates." It was stated[65]: "Also for carobs." It was stated: "One eats dates until they disappear from Jericho[66], one eats olives until they disappear from Meron and Giscala[67]."

65   In Tosephta 7:17: "Rebbi Simeon ben Eleazar says, [all trees are] like carob trees; one eats from them until the winter rains (when there are no fruits left on the trees)."

66   In Tosephta 7:17: "Until the last ones disappear from Zoar."

67   In Tosephta 7:17: "Until the last ones disappear from Tekoa; R. Eliezer ben Jacob says, also at Giscala." It is generally agreed that the best olive region in Palestine is the central upper Galilee, between Meron and Giscala. Tekoa is recognized as the best origin in Judea, but still much inferior to Galilee (Mishnah *Menaḥot* 9:3).

מַתְנִיתִין דְּרִבִּי שִׁמְעוֹן. כְּתִיב מִן הַשָּׂדֶה תֹּאכְלוּ אֶת תְּבוּאָתָהּ. כָּל־זְמָן שֶׁאַתְּ אוֹכֵל מִן הַשָּׂדֶה אַתְּ אוֹכֵל מֵהַבַּיִת. כָּלָה מִן הַשָּׂדֶה כָּלָה מִן הַבַּיִת. (fol. 39a) מַה טַעֲמָא דְּרִבִּי שִׁמְעוֹן. אַתְּ הוּא שֶׁגָּרַמְתָּ לָךְ שֶׁלֹּא לוֹכַל.

Our Mishnah follows Rebbi Simeon[68]. It is written[69] (*Lev.* 25:12): "From the field you should eat its yield." Any time you find food on the field, you can eat from the house. If it is finished on the field, it is finished in the house. What is the reason of Rebbi Simeon? You caused yourself not to eat[70].

68   It seems that this refers to the next Mishnah, that one may no longer eat of any kind if all remaining produce is on guarded fields not abandoned to the public and guarded against intrusion of wildlife.

69   *Sifra Behar Pereq* 3(4). This derivation is accepted by everybody.

71   Since you did not obey the injunction to abandon your crop to the public and to wildlife, you cannot use that crop as an excuse to continue eating Sabbatical produce.

(fol. 38c) **משנה ד**: אוֹכְלִין עַל הַמּוּבְקָר אֲבָל לֹא עַל הַשָּׁמוּר. רַבִּי יוֹסֵי אוֹמֵר אַף עַל הַשָּׁמוּר. אוֹכְלִין עַל הַטּפָחִין וְעַל הַדִּיפְרָא אֲבָל לֹא עַל הַסְּתָוָנִיּוֹת. רַבִּי יְהוּדָה מַתִּיר כָּל־זְמַן שֶׁבִּיכְּרוּ עַד שֶׁיִּכְלֶה הַקַּיִץ.

Mishnah 4: One eats based on what is abandoned but not on what is guarded[72]. Rebbi Yose says, also on what is guarded. One eats because of swollen fruit[73] and because of a second crop[74], but not on winter growth[75]. Rebbi Jehudah permits it on condition that they brought first fruits before the end of the summer.

72   According to Maimonides, in his Commentary and in his Code, "guarded" is only what develops in a walled-in area. If it is not walled in, even if there is a watchman it is not considered "guarded".

73   Reading of R. Nathan Ab Hayyešibah, טיפוחין. Because these are undesirable, they are left on the tree or the field for a long time; cf. Note 76. Following Maimonides, טפיחין are fruits or grain that for some reason either do not ripen or ripen extremely slowly; therefore they are on the tree or in the earth for most of the year because nobody takes them. [The explanation of Arukh, in the name of his brother, that טפיחים are kernels collected by birds nesting in a טפיח, a clay or wooden container, is accepted by the commentators from R. Simson to R. S. Lieberman, but is extremely unlikely.]

74   Greek δίφορος, ον (adj.)
"bearing fruit twice a year (E. G.). This
produce never has to be removed.

75   Fruits or produce ripening only
in the winter following the Sabbatical.

(fol. 39a) **הלכה ד:** מַתְנִיתִין דְּרִבִּי יוֹסֵי דְּתַנֵּי אֵין אוֹכְלִין עַל הַסְּפִיחִין שֶׁבְּעַכּוֹ.
רִבִּי יוֹסֵי אָמַר אוֹכְלִין עַל הַסְּפִיחִין שֶׁבְּעַכּוֹ. אָמַר רִבִּי יוֹסֵי הֲוֵינָן סָבְרִין מֵימַר
מַפְלִיגִין רִבִּי יוֹסֵי וְרַבָּנִין בְּסִיתְוָנִיּוֹת הָא בְּדִפָּרִין לֹא. אַשְׁכָּח תַּנֵּי רִבִּי יוּדָה
מַתִּיר בְּדִפָּרִים וְהֵם שֶׁבִּיכְּרוּ עַד שֶׁלֹּא יִכְלֶה הַקַּיִץ.

Halakhah 4: Our Mishnah is Rebbi Yose's since is is stated: "One does
not eat because of swollen fruits in Acco. Rebbi Yose says, one eats
because of swollen fruits in Acco[76]." Rebbi Yose[77] said, we were of the
opinion that Rebbi Yose and the rabbis disagree about winter fruits,
therefore not about double yields. It was found stated: Rebbi Jehudah
permits second crop on condition [the tree] produce first fruits[78] before
the end of summer.

76   Tosephta 7:15; there the reading
is הרפיחין ("the swollen ones") in the
Vienna and הרחיפין (Arabic رخف רחף "to
be soft") in the Erfurth mss. (printed
edd. הסספיחין). The ms. Tosephta
readings probably are no corruptions
since they support R. Nathan's reading

and explanation. It is difficult to
understand what role Acco plays in the
discussion unless it stands for all
border regions.

77   The Amora.

78   Of the second crop.

(fol. 38c) **משנה ה:** הַכּוֹבֵשׁ שְׁלֹשָׁה כְבָשִׁים בְּחָבִית אַחַת. רִבִּי אֱלִיעֶזֶר אוֹמֵר
אוֹכְלִין עַל הָרִאשׁוֹן. וְרִבִּי יְהוֹשֻׁעַ אוֹמֵר אַף עַל הָאַחֲרוֹן. רַבָּן גַּמְלִיאֵל אוֹמֵר

כָּל־שֶׁכָּלָה מִינוֹ מִן הַשָּׂדֶה יְבָעֵר מִינוֹ מִן הַבָּיִת. רְבִּי שִׁמְעוֹן אוֹמֵר כָּל־יֶרֶק אַחַת

לְבִיעוּר. אוֹכְלִין בִּרְגִילָה עַד שֶׁיִּכְלוּ סִנְדִּיוֹת מִבִּקְעַת בֵּית נְטוֹפָה.

Mishnah 5: He who preserves three kinds[79] in one barrel, Rebbi Eliezer says one eats because of the first kind[80], but Rebbi Joshua says, even because of the last. Rabban Gamliel says, anything whose kind has disappeared from the fields must be removed from the house[81]. Rebbi Simeon says, all vegetables are one kind for removal; one eats purslain until there are no more *sindiot*[82] in the Bet Neṭofa valley.

79 Three different kinds of Sabbatical produce are preserved by pickling or cooking, and all three kinds are subject to removal.

80 Only as long as all three kinds may be kept. According to R. Joshua, one may keep all three as long as one of them may be kept.

81 In most Mishnah mss., מן החבית "from the barrel". But the reading of the Leyden ms. and Venice print is supported by מלאכת שלמה as the correct text. Also, most Mishnah mss. add: "and

practice follows him."

82 Maimonides declares not to be able to determine this kind of vegetable. The mss. in the Maimonides tradition read סנריות, explained by Arukh as "artichokes" (which, however, in talmudic sources is קינרא.) R. Abraham ben David reads סנדיות in *Sifra Behar Pereq* 3, but gives no explanation. The Munich ms. of the Babli has הנידיות which Levy reads as הנדיות "vetch". Cf. Arabic סָנְדִּיָאן "holm oak, *ilex*".

(fol. 39a) **הלכה ה**: מַה טַעֲמָא דְּרִבִּי לִיעֶזֶר הָרִאשׁוֹן נוֹתֵן טַעַם בָּאַחֲרוֹן. מַה טַעַם דְּרִבִּי יְהוֹשֻׁעַ הָאַחֲרוֹן נוֹתֵן טַעַם בָּרִאשׁוֹן. וְקַשְׁיָא עַל דְּרִבִּי יְהוֹשֻׁעַ אֵין הָרִאשׁוֹן נוֹתֵן טַעַם בָּאַחֲרוֹן. רַבָּן גַּמְלִיאֵל אוֹמֵר כָּל־שֶׁכָּלָה מִינוֹ מִן הַשָּׂדֶה יְבָעֵר מִינוֹ מִן הַבָּיִת. תַּנֵּי וַהֲלָכָה כִדְבָרָיו.

Halakhah 5: What is the reason of Rebbi Eliezer? The first kind gives taste to the last. What is the reason of Rebbi Joshua? The last kind gives taste to the first. It is difficult for Rebbi Joshua, does not the first kind gives taste to the last? "Rabban Gamliel says, anything whose kind has disappeared from the fields must be removed from the house."[83] It was stated: Practice follows his words[84].

83 Rebbis Eliezer and Joshua consider taste an essential element for Sabbatical removal, R. Eliezer for restriction and R. Joshua for leniency. But Rabban Gamliel considers taste irrelevant; as long as the different kinds are recognizable, each one has its own time for removal.

84 This confirms that the Galilean version of the Mishnah did not have this clause.

חִזְקִיָּה אָמַר מִכֵּיוָן שֶׁהִתְחִיל בָּאוֹצָר כִּמְבוֹעָר הוּא. אָתָא עוּבְדָּא קוֹמֵי רבִּי יָסָא וְהוֹרֵי כְחִזְקִיָּה לָא דַאֲנָא סְבַר כְּוָתֵיהּ אֶלָּא מִן מַה דַאֲנָן חָמְיָן רַבָּנִין עָבְדִין עוּבְדָּא כְּוָתֵיהּ. רבִּי יִצְחָק בַּר רְדִיפָה הֲוָה לֵיהּ עוּבְדָּא אָתָא שָׁאַל לְרבִּי יִרְמְיָה. אָמַר לֵיהּ מַה אַרְיָוָתָא קָמָךְ וְאַתְּ שָׁאַל לְתַעֲלַיָּא. אָתָא שָׁאַל לְרבִּי יֹאשִׁיָה. אָמַר לֵיהּ חָמֵי לָךְ תְּלָתָא רְחִמִין וְאַבְקְרָה קוֹמֵיהוֹן. קַפּוֹדָקָאֵי דְצִיפּוֹרִין שָׁאֲלוּן לְרבִּי אִימִּי בְּגִין דְּלֵית לְאִילֵּין עַמָּא רְחֵם וְלָא שָׁאַל שְׁלֵם אֵיךְ צוּרְכָּא מֵיעֲבַד. אֲמַר לוֹן כַּד תֶּחֱמוּן רַגְלָא צְלִילָא תַּהֲוֵין מַפְקִין לָהּ לְשׁוּקָא וּמַבְקְרִין לָהּ וְחָזְרִין וְזַכְיָין בָּהּ.

Hizqiah said, once he started with his storage it is as if removed[85]. A case came before Rebbi Assi and he instructed following Hizqiah, not that I am agreeing with him but since we see that the rabbis do act following him. Rebbi Isaac bar Redifah[86] had a case, he came before Rebbi Jeremiah who said to him, there are lions before you, why do you ask foxes? He went and asked Rebbi Joshia who said to him, look for three people who love you and declare it abandoned before them. The Kappadokians[87] of Sepphoris asked Rebbi Ammi: Since we have nobody who loves us or even greets us, what should we do? He said to them, when you see that [the market is] clear from steps, bring it out to the market, declare it abandoned, and acquire it again.

85   It is forbidden to eat one's Sabbatical produce after the time of removal.   It is permitted to eat Sabbatical produce after the removal (Mishnah 8) if it is not one's property. Ḥizqiah, of the first generation of Amoraïm, notes that if Sabbatical produce is removed from storage, it might be considered removed and the owners then can acquire property rights again and continue eating the produce. The teachers of the following generations do agree that the economic situation of the times required a device by which to avoid the consequences of removal but they are opposed to the informality of Ḥizqiah's approach and require a formal declaration of abandonment. They therefore counsel to abandon the property in such a way that no other person has the opportunity to take the produce before its previous owners could repossess it. Cf. *Tosafot Pesaḥim* 52b, *s. v.* מתבערין.

86   A student of Rebbi Ammi, who must have known of R. Ammi's hesitation in the matter. The question must have arisen after R. Ammi's death.

87   The Rome ms. has קפודאי "the amiss-takers"; this might be the better reading.

רבּי חַגַּי מַפְלֵג לָהּ צְלוּחִיּין צְלוּחִיּין. רבּי אֶלְעָזָר מַפְלֵג לָהּ צְלוּחִיּין צְלוּחִיּין. רבּי חִזְקִיָּה סָלַק גַּבֵּי רבּי יִרְמְיָה אָמַר לֵיהּ זָכִיתִי בְּהֶן אוֹצָרָה. אָמַר לֵיהּ צוֹר לִי אִילֵּין פְּרִיטַיָּיא גַּבֵּיךְ אָמַר לֵיהּ הֲרֵי מְקוֹמָן מוּשְׂכָּר לִי. אָמַר לֵיהּ לֹא כֵן אַפְקְתָּהּ חֲזֹר וְזָכִיתָה בָּהּ.

Rebbi Ḥaggai distributed it pitcher by pitcher. Rebbi Eleazar distributed it pitcher by pitcher[88]. Rebbi Ḥizqiah came to Rebbi Jeremiah and said to him, let me acquire that storage. He said to him, bind these coins together; then he said to him, for these the place is rented to me. He said to him, did you not take it out? Go back and acquire it[89]!

88   These two rabbis did not want to avail themselves of the subterfuge to avoid distributing their Sabbatical wine.

89   R. Ḥizqiah asked R. Jeremiah to help him legally to keep the Sabbatical produce he had in his barn. R. Jeremiah took some coins, gave them to R. Ḥizqiah and told him to acquire them by tying them together, as rental payment of the barn. Then he told him, since he had already declared the produce as abandoned property, he could take it back without actually removing it since it was now stored in R. Jeremiah's domain. It may be assumed that at the end of the transaction, R. Jeremiah got his coins back. (Explanation combined from the commentaries of R. Eliahu Fulda and R. J. I. Kanievski.)

(fol. 38c) **מֹשְׁנָה ו:** הַמְלַקֵּט עֲשָׂבִים לַחִים עַד שֶׁיָּבֵשׁ הַמָּתוֹק. וְהַמְנֻבָּב בְּיָבֵשׁ עַד שֶׁתֵּרֵד רְבִיעָה שְׁנִיָּה. עֲלֵי קָנִים וַעֲלֵי גְפָנִים עַד שֶׁיַּישָׁרוּ מֵאֲבִיהֶן. וְהַמְנֻבָּב יָבֵשׁ עַד שֶׁתֵּרֵד רְבִיעָה שְׁנִיָּה. וְרִבִּי עֲקִיבָה אוֹמֵר בְּכוּלָּם עַד שֶׁתֵּרֵד רְבִיעָה שְׁנִיָּה.

Mishnah 6: One may pluck green grasses until the colocynth[90] dries up, and collect dry ones until the second rainfall[91], leaves of reeds and vines until they fall off from their stems, and collect dry ones until the second rainfall. But Rebbi Aqiba says, all until the second rainfall.

90   Cf. Mishnah 3:1.   91   Cf. *Peah* Mishnah 8:1, Note 3.

(fol. 39a) **הֲלָכָה ו:** רִבִּי אָבִין בְּשֵׁם רִבִּי יוֹחָנָן לֵית כָּאן עֲלֵי קָנִים אֶלָּא עֲלֵי גְפָנִים. עֲלֵי קָנִים אֵין לָהֶן בִּיעוּר. וְתַנֵּי כֵן עֲלֵי קָנִים וַעֲלֵי הָאוֹג וַעֲלֵי חָרוּבִין אֵין לָהֶן בִּיעוּר מִפְּנֵי שֶׁאֵין מִינָן כָּלָה.

Halakhah 6: Rebbi Abin in the name of Rebbi Joḥanan: One does not have here leaves of reeds, only leaves of vines. Leaves of reeds do not have to be removed. We have stated thus[92]: Leaves of reeds, sumac, and carob tree have no removal because their kinds never disappear.

92   A different formulation is in Tosephta 5:6: "The stems of carob tree, thistles, sumac, laurel, and rice are not subject to removal, neither is money received for them." It is necessary to state this since reeds, sumac, and carob are subject to *peah*.

(fol. 38c) **משנה ז**: כְּיוֹצֵא בוֹ הַמַּשְׂכִּיר בַּיִת לַחֲבֵירוֹ עַד הַגְּשָׁמִים עַד שֶׁתֵּרֵד רְבִיעָה שְׁנִייָה. הַמּוֹדֵר הֲנָייָה מֵחֲבֵירוֹ עַד הַגְּשָׁמִים עַד שֶׁתֵּרֵד רְבִיעָה שְׁנִייָה. עַד אֵימָתַי נִכְנָסִין עֲנִייִם לְפַרְדֵיסוֹת עַד שֶׁתֵּרֵד רְבִיעָה שְׁנִייָה. עַד אֵימָתַי נֶהֱנִין וְשׂוֹרְפִין בַּתֶּבֶן וּבַקַּשׁ שֶׁל שְׁבִיעִית עַד שֶׁתֵּרֵד רְבִיעָה שְׁנִייָה.

Mishnah 7: Similarly, if one rents out a house until the rains, that is until the second rainfall. If somebody makes a vow not to have any profit from another person until the rains, that is until the second rainfall[93]. Until when may the poor enter orchards? Until the second rainfall. Until when may one use and burn Sabbatical straw and chaff? Until the second rainfall.

93   This sentence is also in Mishnah *Nedarim* 8:5; there Rabban Simeon ben Gamliel disagrees and lets the vow expire not at the actual onset of the rains but at the expected time of the second rainfall, the 23rd of Marḥeshwan.

(fol. 39a) **הלכה ז**: רִבִּי זְעִירָא בָּעֵי אָמַר עַד הַגֶּשֶׁם עַד שֶׁיֵּרֵד גֶּשֶׁם אֶחָד.

Halakhah 7: Rebbi Zeïra investigated: If somebody said "until the rain", until the first rain[94]?

94   In Babli *Nedarim* 62b, R. Zeira
declares that, while there is disagreement about the meaning of "until
the rains", "until the rain" in a vow
means until the expected time of the
first rainfall, the 7th of Marḥeshwan.

This paragraph and the next are also in
Nedarim 8:6 (fol. 41a). There, the
language is: Rebbi Zeïra investigated:
If somebody said "until the rain", is he
forbidden until the rain comes down a
second time?

תַּמָּן תַּנִּינָן הָאוֹמֵר הֲרֵי עָלַי עֵצִים לֹא יִפְחוֹת מִשְּׁנֵי גְּזִירִן. אָמַר רבי יוֹסֵי בֵּי
רִבִּי בּוּן אָמַר רבי בָּא בַר מָמָל בָּעֵי אָמַר הֲרֵי עָלַי עֵץ מֵבִיא גִיזֶר אֶחָד. אָמַר
רבִּי לִיעֶזֶר מַתְנִיתָא אָמַר כֵּן שֶׁזֶּה קָרְבָּן בִּפְנֵי עַצְמוֹ וְזֶה קָרְבָּן בִּפְנֵי עַצְמוֹ.
דְּתַנִּינָן שְׁנַיִם בְּיָדָן שְׁנֵי גְזִירֵי עֵצִים.

There[95], we have stated: "If somebody says, I am taking upon me [to
offer] logs, he should not bring less than two." Rebbi Yose ben Rebbi
Abun said, Rebbi Abba bar Mamal asked: If he said, I am taking upon me
[to offer] a log, does he bring one log? Rebbi Eleazar[96] said, a Mishnah
says that each one is a separate sacrifice, as we have stated[97]: "Two,
holding in their hands two wooden logs."

95   Mishnah *Šeqalim* 6:8, *Menaḥot*
13:2. The paragraph is also in *Šeqalim*
6:6 (fol. 50b). It seems that the
argument is inserted here because
"rain" means second rainfall, and "logs"
means at least two logs.

96   While all mss. have "Eliezer"
both here and in *Šeqalim*, the name
must be Eleazar since there is no
known Galilean Amora called Eliezer.

97   Mishnah *Yoma* 2:5, noting that
the daily afternoon sacrifice was
brought to the altar by 11 Cohanim, 9

for the parts of the sheep and two
holding the logs for burning. Each
Cohen is reponsible for a separate
sacrifice since it is written (*Lev.* 1:8):
"The sons of Aaron, the Cohanim,
should put the pieces, the head and the
innards, on the logs that are burning on
the altar." However, for the morning
sacrifice, it says (*Lev.* 6:5): "The Cohen
should burn logs on [the altar] every
morning;" this indicates that in the
morning two logs together form one
obligation. Without that difference

between morning and afternoon service there never would have been a

question whether one log alone could be a sacrifice.

תָּנֵי רִבִּי יוֹסֵי אוֹמֵר כָּל־דָּבָר שֶׁהוּא תָלוּי בִּרְבִיעָה עַד שֶׁתֵּרֵד רְבִיעָה שְׁנִיָּיה וּשְׁאֵינוֹ תָלוּי בִּרְבִיעָה עַד שֶׁיַּגִּיעַ זְמַנָּהּ שֶׁל רְבִיעָה. תַּנֵי רַבָּן שִׁמְעוֹן בֶּן גַּמְלִיאֵל אוֹמֵר שִׁבְעַת יָמִים שֶׁיֶּרְדוּ בָּהֶן גְּשָׁמִים וְלֹא פָסְקוּ יֵשׁ בָּהֶן כְּדֵי רְבִיעָה שְׁנִיָּיה. תָּנֵי רִבִּי חִייָא בְשֵׁם רַבָּן שִׁמְעוֹן בֶּן גַּמְלִיאֵל וְלָמָּה נִקְרָא שְׁמָהּ רְבִיעָה שֶׁהִיא רוֹבַעַת אֶת הָאָרֶץ.

It was stated[98]: Rebbi Yose says, everything that depends on fertility[99] extends until the second rainfall, if it is not dependent on fertility, until the expected time of the second rainfall. It was stated[100]: Rabban Simeon ben Gamliel says, if rains came for seven uninterrupted days, they include the second rainfall. Rebbi Ḥiyya stated in the name of Rabban Simeon ben Gamliel[101]: Why is it called רביעה? Because it fertilizes the land.

98   In Tosephta Ta'aniot 1:4, the language is the opposite: "Rebbi Yose says, everything that depends on fertility extends until the expected time of the second rainfall, if it is not dependent on fertility, until the second rainfall." This version seems to be corrupted.

99   In matters of agriculture, only the rain counts. If the rains are mentioned only as a sign, as in a vow, they are mentioned according to the expected schedule.

100   Tosephta Ševi'it 7:19, Ta'aniot 1:4. This is also quoted in Babli Ta'anit 6b.

101   In the Babli, Ta'anit 6b, this is an Amoraic statement of R. Abbahu.

אָמַר רִבִּי חֲנִינָה מִכֵּינָן שֶׁתִּסְרַח מַה שֶּׁבְּשָׂדֶה הוּתַּר מַה שֶּׁבַּבַּיִת. תַּנֵי רִבִּי הוֹשַׁעְיָה אֲפִילוּ אַחַר שָׁלֹשׁ שָׁנִים אָסוּר עַד שֶׁיִּסְרַח.

Rebbi Ḥanina said, when [produce] on the field starts to rot, that in the house is permitted[102]. Rebbi Hoshaia stated: Even after three years it is forbidden until it starts to rot[103].

102   Here starts the discussion of Sabbatical straw and chaff. The reading of our Mishnah, "Until when may one use and burn Sabbatical straw and chaff," is only found in the Leyden ms. of the Yerushalmi; in all other ms. sources the reading is "From when may one start to use and burn . . ." It seems that there were two competing versions; one "until when may one use Sabbatical straw and chaff", until the second rains, and a second one, מאימתי "from when may one start to use and burn Sabbatical straw and chaff." The first version deals with straw as fodder; this is permitted only as long as straw

is fodder for wildlife. The second version deals with straw as industrial raw material; this is permitted only after straw is no longer fodder for wildlife (cf. R. Asher ben Yeḥiel on the Mishnah). The discussion here refers to the second version, not the Mishnah text. (See the discussion in *The Mishnah with Variant Readings*, Jerusalem 1975, vol. ii, p. 86, Note 63.)

103   R. Hoshaia disagrees with the Mishnah (second version) and rules out the use of rain periods as criterion; he requires that Sabbatical straw on the field be decayed before any industrial use is permitted.

תֶּבֶן שֶׁל שְׁבִיעִית אֵין שׁוֹרִין אוֹתוֹ בְּטִיט. שָׁרְיָנוֹ[104] בְּטִיט בָּטֵיל וְהוּא שֶׁגְּבָלוֹ. תֶּבֶן שֶׁל שְׁבִיעִית אֵין נוֹתְנִין אוֹתוֹ בְּכָר. נְתָנוֹ בְכָר בָּטֵיל וְהוּא שֶׁיָּשַׁן עָלָיו.

One does not steep Sabbatical straw in mud. If one steeped it in mud it would lose its character, on condition that he kneaded it[105]. One does not fill a pillow with Sabbatical straw. If he put it in a pillow it would lose its character, on condition that he slept on it.

104   Reading of the Rome ms. and R. Eliahu Fulda.   Leyden and Venice:

שדייו "he threw it".
105   Professional use by builders.

תֶּבֶן שֶׁל שְׁבִיעִית מַהוּ שֶׁיְּהֵא אָסוּר מִשּׁוּם סְפִיחוֹן. רִבִּי לֵוִי צֶנַבְרָיָה שָׁאַל לְרִבִּי
בָּא בַּר זַבְדָּא וְשָׁרָא. אָמַר רִבִּי זְעִירָא וַאֲנָא דְלָא סָמְכִית עֲלַי אִשְׁתְּאֵלֵת
לְאִילֵּין דְּבֵית בַּרְסָנָא וְאָמְרִין נָהֲגִין הֲוֵינָא כְּנַשִׁין תֶּבֶן מִן עֵרוּבָא שְׁמִיטְתָא.
וְכַד מְחַסְּרִין מַייְתֵי מִן שׁוּרַיָּא. אָמַר רִבִּי יִרְמְיָה מַתְנִיתָא אָמַר שֶׁהוּא מוּתָּר.
דְּתַנֵּי הַצַּבָּעִין וְהַפַּטָּמִין לוֹקְחִין מוּרְסָן מִכֵּל מָקוֹם וְאֵינָן חוֹשְׁשִׁין. רִבִּי יִרְמְיָה
סָבַר מֵימוֹר אֲפִילוּ מִן הֶחָשׁוּד. אָמַר לֵיהּ רִבִּי יוֹסֵי לֹא אָמְרוּ אֶלָּא כְּשֶׁאֵינוּ
יוֹדֵעַ אִם חָשׁוּד הוּא. אִם אֵינוֹ חָשׁוּד הָא דָבָר בָּרִיא שֶׁהוּא חָשׁוּד אָסוּר. אָמַר
רִבִּי שַׁמַּאי מַתְנִיתָא אָמַר שֶׁהוּא אָסוּר. דְּתַנִּינָן תַּמָּן וּבַשְּׁבִיעִית וּבְכִלְאֵי הַכֶּרֶם
וְהֶקְדֵּשׁ אִם יֵשׁ בַּזֶּרַע וּבָעֵץ כְּדֵי לִיתֵּן טַעַם.

Is Sabbatical straw forbidden as aftergrowth? Rebbi Levi from
Sennabaris asked Rebbi Abba bar Zavda and he permitted it. Rebbi Zeïra
said, since I did not want to rely on myself[106] I asked those from Beit
Barsana[107] and they said, we used to collect straw before the start of the
Sabbatical and when we are running out, we bring it from the walls[108].
Rebbi Jeremiah said, a *baraita* states that it is permitted, as it was
stated[109]: "Dyers and cattle feeders may buy coarse bran from everywhere without worry." Rebbi Jeremiah wanted to say, even from one
who is suspect. Rebbi Yose said to him, they said that only if he does not
know whether he is suspect[110]. Only if he might not be suspect; therefore
if it is clear that he is suspect, it is forbidden. Rebbi Shammai said, a
Mishnah says that it is forbidden, as we have stated there[111]: "In matters
of Sabbatical, *kilaim* in a vineyard, or dedicated things, if there is enough
in both seed and wood to give taste."

106　In the Rome ms. "on him", i. e., R. Babylonian, did not want to decide in
Abba bar Zavda. It is also possible matters of Galilean agriculture.
that the reading of the text is correct 107　The location of this place is
and that R. Zeïra, as a native unknown.

108 It is not clear whether this means from grain growing on a stone wall, not on the ground, and exempt from the laws of the Sabbatical, or from close to the wall, from grain not harvested and not subject to the Sabbatical. In any case, the people rejected the permission given by R. Abba bar Zavda.

109 Tosephta 5:8. Coarse bran is animal feed, not human food.

110 If one might buy grain-based animal feed from everybody, it would prove that there is no rabbinic decree against using grain by-products as animal feed; straw from spontaneous growth would be permitted. But if it is forbidden to buy from people reputed to deal in Sabbatical produce then the Tosephta only proves that most people dealing in Sabbatical produce concentrate on more expensive human

food; it has no implication for our question of spontaneous growth.

111 Mishnah *Terumot* 10:5: "Fenugreek that fell into a cistern, regarding heave or Second Tithe if the seeds give taste, regarding Sabbatical, *kilaim* in a vineyard, or dedicated things, if there is enough in both seed and wood to give taste." If heave or Second Tithe fenugreek fell into a cistern, it induces the holiness of heave or Second Tithe in the water if the seeds in themselves impart the taste of fenugreek to the water. But if the fenugreek was Sabbatical, "sanctified" *kilaim*, or Temple property, it induces the holiness already if the seeds together with the branches impart the taste. That means that for the Sabbatical, the holiness of the produce (e. g., grain) extends to the wood (e. g., straw).

לֹא נִמְצָא מְאַבֵּד אוֹכְלֵי בְהֵמָה. תִּיפְתָּר בְּאוֹכְלֵי בְהֵמָה לָאָדָם. אָמַר רִבִּי מָנָא תִּיפְתָּר בְּקְדוּשַׁת שְׁבִיעִית בְּבִיעוּר וְלֵית אַתְּ שְׁמַע מִינָהּ כְּלוּם.

Does one not destroy animal feed[112]? Explain it that animal feed is used for humans. Rebbi Mana said, explain it about the sanctity by removal of the Sabbatical[113], and it does not imply anything.

112 This refers to the statement at the beginning of the Halakhah, that after the second rains one may use

Sabbatical straw as building material. The answer is that for human use (e. g., medicinal concoctions), animal fodder may be denatured.

113 Straw taken before the second rains is Sabbatical, taken after the second rains it is profane.

(fol. 38c) **משנה ח**: מִי שֶׁהָיוּ לוֹ פֵּירוֹת שְׁבִיעִית וְהִגִּיעָה שְׁעַת הַבִּיעוּר מְחַלְּקָן מָזוֹן שָׁלֹשׁ סְעוּדוֹת לְכָל־אֶחָד וְאֶחָד וְהָעֲנִיִּים אוֹכְלִין אַחַר הַבִּיעוּר אֲבָל לֹא עֲשִׁירִים דִּבְרֵי רִבִּי יְהוּדָה. רִבִּי יוֹסֵי אוֹמֵר אֶחָד עֲנִיִּים וְאֶחָד עֲשִׁירִים אוֹכְלִין אַחַר הַבִּיעוּר.

Mishnah 8: If somebody had Sabbatical produce when the time of removal came, he distributes food for three meals[114] to everybody. The poor may eat[115] after removal but not rich persons, the words of Rebbi Jehudah. Rebbi Yose says, both poor and rich persons may eat[116] after removal.

114 Enough food for one Sabbath.
115 Sabbatical produce.
116 In the autograph Mishnah of

Maimonides and many mss. of the Maimonides tradition: "may *not* eat".

(fol. 39a) **הלכה ח**: מַה טַעֲמָא דְּרִבִּי יוּדָה וְאָכְלוּ אֶבְיוֹנֵי עַמֶּךָ וְיִתְרָם. מַה טַעֲמָא דְּרִבִּי יוֹסֵי וְאָכְלוּ אֶבְיוֹנֵי עַמֶּךָ וְיִתְרָם. תַּנֵּי רִבִּי שִׁמְעוֹן אוֹמֵר עֲשִׁירִין אוֹכְלִין מִן הָאוֹצָר אַחַר הַבִּיעוּר. מַה טַעֲמָא דְּרִבִּי שִׁמְעוֹן וְאָכְלוּ אֶבְיוֹנֵי עַמֶּךָ עַד יִתְרָם.

Halakhah 8: What is the reason of Rebbi Jehudah: (*Ex.* 23:11) "The destitute of your people should eat including the remainder[117]." What is the reason of Rebbi Yose: (*Ex.* 23:11) "The destitute of your people should eat with the remainder." It was stated[118]: Rebbi Simeon says, rich persons may eat from storage. What is the reason of Rebbi Simeon: (*Ex.* 23:11) "The destitute of your people should eat, and the remainder[119]."

117   "The Seventh year you must let rest and abandon it, so the destitute of your people may eat, the wildlife on the fields should eat the remainder."

118   Tosephta 8:2.

119   The "remainder" are the people who are not poor.

משנה ט: מִי שֶׁהָיוּ לוֹ פֵּירוֹת שְׁבִיעִית שֶׁנָּפְלוּ לוֹ לִירוּשָׁה אוֹ שֶׁנִּיתְּנוּ לוֹ (fol. 38c)
מַתָּנָה. רִבִּי לִיעֶזֶר אוֹמֵר יִינָּתְנוּ לְאוֹכְלֵיהֶן. וַחֲכָמִים אוֹמְרִים אֵין הַחוֹטֵא
נִשְׂכָּר אֶלָּא יִמָּכְרוּ לְאוֹכְלֵיהֶן וּדְמֵיהֶן יִתְחַלְּקוּ לְכָל־אָדָם. הָאוֹכֵל מֵעִיסַּת
שְׁבִיעִית עַד שֶׁלֹּא הוּרְמָה חַלָּתָהּ חַיָּיב מִיתָה.

Mishnah 9: If somebody had Sabbatical produce which fell to him as inheritance or was given to him as a gift, Rebbi Eliezer says it should be given to those who eat it. But the Sages say, a sinner should not be rewarded, but it should be sold to those who eat it and the payment distributed to anybody[120]. He who eats from Sabbatical dough of which *hallah* was not taken commits a deadly sin[121].

120   This Mishnah will be explained in the Halakhah.

121   Since Sabbatical produce is exempt from heave and tithes, one could think that dough made from Sabbatical grain was exempt from

hallah which has to be eaten under the rules of heave. Therefore, it is necessary to spell out that Sabbatical dough is not exempt from *hallah*. (For the obligation of *hallah*, cf. *Berakhot*, Chapter 8, Note 55).

(fol. 39a) **הלכה ט**: רְבִּי שִׁמְעוֹן בֶּן לָקִישׁ אָמַר בְּפֵירוֹת עֲבֵירָה הִיא מַתְנִיתִין. וְהָתַנֵּי הַמּוֹצִיא פֵּירוֹת עֲבֵירָה אָסוּר לִיגַּע בָּהֶן. שַׁנְיָיא הִיא מְצִיאָה שַׁנְיָיא הִיא שֶׁנָּפְלוּ לוֹ עַל כָּרְחוֹ.

Halakhah 9: Rebbi Simeon ben Laqish said, the Mishnah deals with unlawful produce. But was it not stated: He who finds unlawful produce may not touch it. There is a difference between a find and something that fell to him automatically[122].

122   In this interpretation, R. Eliezer seems to hold that produce harvested unlawfully, i. e., from fields or orchards not abandoned to the public, is forbidden only to the person who harvests it or who actively acquired it, but not to any passive recipient.

רְבִּי יוֹחָנָן אָמַר בְּפֵירוֹת הֶתֵר הִיא מַתְנִיתִין. כְּהָדָא תַּנִּינָן רְבִּי לִיעֶזֶר אוֹמֵר יִנָּתְנוּ לָאוֹכֵל. רְבִּי לִיעֶזֶר דְּהוּא שַׁמּוּתִי. דְּתַנִּינָן אוֹכְלִין פֵּירוֹת שְׁבִיעִית בְּטוֹבָה וּשֶׁלֹּא בְטוֹבָה כְּדִבְרֵי בֵית שַׁמַּאי. כְּהָדָא רַבָּנִין מְתִיבִין לֵיהּ שֶׁאֵין הַחוֹטֵא נִשְׂכָּר. בְּשִׁיטָתוֹ הֱשִׁיבוּהוּ בְּשִׁיטָתָךְ שֶׁאַתְּ אוֹמֵר יִנָּתְנוּ לָאוֹכְלֵיהֶן שֶׁאֵין הַחוֹטֵא נִשְׂכָּר.

Rebbi Johanan said, the Mishnah deals with permitted produce. For that we stated: Rebbi Eliezer said, it should be given to those who eat it[123]. Since Rebbi Eliezer is a Shammaiite, did we state: One does eat Sabbatical produce in reciprocity and without reciprocity, following the House of Shammai[124]? For that, the rabbis answer him that the sinner should not be rewarded[125]? They answered him according to his argument: Against your argument, when you say that it should be given to those who eat it, a sinner should not be rewarded[126].

123　The recipient of the inheritance or gift, and his family.

124　But Mishnah 4:2 states that the House of Shammai forbid to eat Sabbatical produce in reciprocity, if goodwill is extended to the giver. Since the giver of the gift can expect goodwill from the recipient, R. Eliezer would be expected to forbid accepting a gift of Sabbatical produce.

125　Since they follow the House of Hillel, they permit the use of Sabbatical produce to create goodwill. It is incomprehensible how they could label the recipient of a gift a sinner.

126　The rabbis hold that the recipient of an inheritance or gift may treat the produce as his own Sabbatical produce without restrictions. They only point out that R. Eliezer should have forbidden the produce to its recipient.

אָמַר רִבִּי בִּיבִי הוֹרֵי רִבִּי יָסָא בְּאִילֵּין קוֹנדסיא שֶׁיֵּלְכוּ מָעוֹתֵיהֶן לְיַם הַמֶּלַח. רִבִּי מָנָא שָׁאַל לְרִבִּי חִזְקִיָּה מַהוּ מֵייכְלָא כְּפוֹנִייָן לְאַשְׁקְלוֹן אָמַר לֵיהּ אָסוּר. רִבִּי חִזְקִיָּה הֲוָה קָאִים בְּשׁוּקָא דְּקֵיסָרִין חָמָא חַד טְעִין עֲלָל מִן אִיסּוּרָא הֲפַךְ אַפּוֹי דְלָא מֵיחְמִינֵיהּ. תַּנֵּי פְּרַק כָּל־כָּךְ לָמָּה כְּדֵי שֶׁיַּעֲשֶׂה מְקוֹמוֹ הוֹכִיחַ. שָׁמַע רִבִּי יַעֲקֹב בַּר אָחָא וְאָמַר אִמָּהּ דְּהֵן יֵלְדַת בַּר.

Rebbi Vivian said, Rebbi Assi instructed regarding *qwndsy'*[127] that their proceeds should be thrown into the Dead Sea. Rebbi Mana asked Rebbi Hizqiah, may one eat *kafan*-dates of Ascalon? He said, it is forbidden[128]. Rebbi Hizqiah stood in the market place of Caesarea when he saw a person carrying forbidden produce. He turned away his face in order not to see him and stated: take down! Why all that? That his place should be one of rebuke. Rebbi Jacob bar Aha heard and said, the mother of this one gave birth to a son[129]!

127　Most commentators and dictionaries read קינרסי "artichokes". Since artichokes usually are not abandoned to the public, they are forbidden. R.

Assi's ruling shows that practice follows R. Simeon ben Laqish in the interpretation of the Mishnah.

128　Since Ascalon itself is not in the

Land (Halakhah 6:1), this must be the trade name of a fruit not usually abandoned to the public in the

Sabbatical.

129　R. Ḥizqiah did all that was expected of him.

רִבִּי יְהוֹשֻׁעַ בֶּן לֵוִי הֲוָה מְפַקֵּד לְתַלְמִידֵיהּ לֹא תֵיזְבּוּן לִי יָרָק אֶלָּא מִן גִּינָתָא דְסִיסְרָא. קָם עִמֵּיהּ זָכוּר לַטוֹב אָמַר לֵיהּ אֵיזִיל אֵימָא לְרַבָּךְ לֵית הָדָא גִּינָתָא דְסִיסְרָא דִיהוּדָיי הֲוָת וּקְטָלֵהּ וּנְסָבָהּ מִינֵיהּ אִין בְּעֵיתָהּ מַחְמְרָא עַל נַפְשָׁךְ אִישְׁתְּוֵי לְחַבְרָךְ.

Rebbi Joshua ben Levi commanded his student: Do not buy me vegetables except from Sisera's garden[130]. He, may he be remembered for the good, stood nearby and said to him: Go tell your teacher that this is not Sisera's garden; it did belong to a Jew but he killed him and took it away from him. If you want to be restrictive for yourself, be made equal to your friend[131].

130　This paragraph is from *Demay* 2:1, Notes 56 - 58.

131　The better reading is in *Demay*: אישתרי "permit it".

חַד בַּר נָשׁ הֲוָה חָשִׁיד עַל שְׁמִיטְתָא אֲמַר לְאִיתְּתֵיהּ אַפְקִין חַלָּתָה. אֲמְרָה לֵיהּ הַהוּא גַבְרָא חָשִׁיד עַל שְׁמִיטְתָא וְאַתְּ אֲמַר אַפְקוּן חַלָּה. אֲמַר לָהּ חַלָּה מִדְּבַר תּוֹרָה שְׁבִיעִית מִדְּרַבָּן גַּמְלִיאֵל וַחֲבֵירָיו.

A man was suspected of [trading in] Sabbatical [produce][132]. He said to his wife, take *ḥallah*. She said to him, that man is suspected of Sabbatical [trading], and you say, take *ḥallah*? He said to her, *ḥallah* is [an obligation] from the Torah[133], the Sabbatical is from Rabban Gamliel and his colleagues.

132　This paragraph shows that "suspected of Sabbatical trading" really means "known to be a Sabbatical pected of Sabbatical trading" really trader."

133   In the Babli (*Ketubot* 25a) the   a rabbinic obligation as long as not all
prevailing opinion is that *ḥallah* is only   Jews live in the Land.

(fol. 39b) **משנה א:** הַשְּׁבִיעִית מְשַׁמֶּטֶת אֶת הַמִּלְוֶה בִּשְׁטָר וְשֶׁלֹּא בִשְׁטָר. הַקָּפַת הֶחָנוּת אֵינָהּ מְשַׁמֶּטֶת. אִם עֲשָׂאָהּ מִלְוֶה הֲרֵי זוֹ מְשַׁמֶּטֶת. רְבִּי יְהוּדָה אוֹמֵר הָרִאשׁוֹן הָרִאשׁוֹן מְשַׁמֵּיט. שְׂכַר שָׂכִיר אֵינוֹ מְשַׁמֵּט וְאִם עֲשָׂאוֹ מִלְוֶה הֲרֵי זוֹ מְשַׁמֵּיט. רְבִּי יוֹסֵי אוֹמֵר כָּל־מְלָאכָה שֶׁהִיא פוֹסֶקֶת בַּשְּׁבִיעִית מְשַׁמֶּטֶת אֵינָהּ פוֹסֶקֶת בַּשְּׁבִיעִית אֵינָהּ מְשַׁמֶּטֶת.

Mishnah 1: The Sabbatical remits any loan[1], with or without a document[2]. Store credit is not remitted; if it is transformed into a loan it is remitted. Rebbi Jehudah says, any preceding one is remitted[3]. Wages of a hired hand are not remitted; if they are transformed into a loan they are remitted; Rebbi Yose says, for any work that stops in the Sabbatical they are remitted; if it does not stop they are not remitted[4].

1   The end of the Sabbatical year.

2   In Talmudic tradition, there are three kinds of loan by document. If there is no surety given in the document, the status of the loan is the same as that of a loan given in front of two witnesses, without a written document. The standard loan contract establishes a lien by the creditor on all real estate the borrower may have. (Some tannaitic authorities hold that the absence of such a lien from a document is an error of the scribe; the existence of a lien may always be assumed.) Since the lien (known as "alienation of property") is not specified, the lender can foreclose on such a loan only by lengthy court proceedings. If the loan is documented and given as a mortgage on a specific parcel of real estate, in the theory of the Yerushalmi it is a loan on a pledge and not remitted, as stated in Mishnah 2.

3 R. Jehudah holds that any new credit given by a store to a customer automatically transforms any previous credit into a loan.

4 It is to be discussed whether the work has to stop *because of* the Sabbatical or only *during* the Sabbatical. The hired hand cannot be a day-worker because the wages of a person hired for the day must be paid that same day.

ה*לכה א*: הַשְּׁבִיעִית מְשַׁמֶּטֶת כו'. נִיחָא שֶׁלֹּא בִשְׁטָר. בִּשְׁטָר וְיַעֲשֶׂה כְמִלְוָה עַל הַמַּשְׁכּוֹן וְלֹא יְהֵא מְשַׁמֵּט. אָמַר רִבִּי יוֹחָנָן תִּיפְתָּר בִּשְׁטָר שֶׁאֵין בּוֹ אַחֲרָיוּת נְכָסִים וּכְרִבִּי מֵאִיר. אָתָא עוֹבְדָא קוֹמֵי רִבִּי יוֹחָנָן בִּשְׁטָר שֶׁאֵין בּוֹ אַחֲרָיוּת נְכָסִים וְהוֹרֵי מְשַׁמְּטָא מִפְּנֵי שֶׁאָנוּ לְמֵידִין מִן הַהֲלָכָה אָנוּ עוֹשִׂין אוֹתוֹ.

Halakhah 1: "The Sabbatical remits any loan, etc." [5]We can understand if it is without a document. With a document it should be treated similar to a loan on a pledge[6] and not be remitted. Rebbi Joḥanan said, explain it for a document from which alienation of property is missing, following Rebbi Meïr[7]. A case came before Rebbi Joḥanan of a document without alienation of property and he instructed that it was remitted. Because we are interpreting the Mishnah, should we act on this[8]?

5 In the Babli, *Giṭṭin* 37a, Rav and Samuel explain the Mishnah that "with a document" means a document with the alienation clause, "without a document" means either a document without the alienation clause or an oral loan. R. Joḥanan and R. Simeon ben Laqish explain "with a document" as a loan with a document without the alienation clause, and "without a document" as a loan executed before witnesses but without any written document, but a loan on a correct document, with the alienation clause, is always like a loan on a pledge and never remitted. The opinion of Rav and Samuel is accepted as practice in the Babli; the reports there on the positions of Rav and R. Joḥanan are not totally in accordance with the Yerushalmi.

6 A loan on a pledge is not

remitted in the Sabbatical, as stated in Mishnah 2.

7   He states in Mishnah *Baba Meẓi'a* 1:6 that a document without an alienation clause cannot be foreclosed in court.

8   Since we reject R. Meïr's opinion and hold that the court will force the borrower to pay for every loan proven by a valid document, and will even allow the lender to foreclose real estate if the borrower does not pay, we cannot consider the Mishnah here practice to be followed. The same argument is quoted in the Babli, *Giṭṭin* 37a, referring to a case brought by R. Assi before R. Joḥanan.

אָמַר רִבִּי יִרְמְיָה בְּשָׁאֵין לוֹ קַרְקַע הָא יֵשׁ לוֹ קַרְקַע אֵינוֹ מְשַׁמֵּט. אָמַר רִבִּי יוֹסֵי
אֲפִילוּ יֵשׁ לוֹ קַרְקַע מְשַׁמֵּט. אַתְיָא דְּרִבִּי יוֹסֵי כְרַב. דְּאָמַר רִבִּי בָּא בְשֵׁם רַב
יִיחַד לוֹ קַרְקַע מְשַׁמֵּט. לֹא אָמְרוּ אֶלָּא יִיחַד לוֹ הָא לֹא יִיחַד אֵינוֹ מְשַׁמֵּט.

Rebbi Jeremiah said, it is only if he has no real estate[9]. Hence, if he has real estate it is not remitted. Rebbi Yose said, even if he has real estate it is remitted[10]. Rebbi Yose parallels Rav, since Rebbi Abba said in the name of Rav if he singled out real estate it is remitted[11]. They said only "if he singled out"; therefore, if he did not single out it is not remitted.

9   Since the alienation of property clause refers only to real estate, such a clause in a contract with a landless borrower is devoid of meaning and without legal consequences.

10   He takes the Mishnah to apply to all borrowings (except mortgaging a well-defined piece of real estate), following Samuel and Rav in the Babli; cf. Note 5.

11   While this text appears in both mss., in this and the next sentences the expressions "singled out" and "did not single out" must be switched: "Rebbi Yose parallels Rav, since Rebbi Abba said in the name of Rav if he did not single out real estate it is remitted. They said only 'if he did not single out'; therefore, if he singled out it is not remitted." Everybody agrees that a mortgage written on a well-defined piece of real estate is no longer a debt owed by the borrower but a lien on the land.

The statement ascribed to Rav here parallels a *baraita* in Babli *Giṭṭin* 37a and in content, but not in the formulation, a Tosephta (8:6, speaking about a document of *hypotheke*, mortgage, cf. Note 22). [The treatment of mortgages in Yerushalmi and Babli cannot be directly compared since the Babli admits irrevocable mortgages for which the lender obtains the right to all yield of the land for a fixed period, usually 20 years, after which the parcel reverts to the original owner without repayment of the capital. In the Yerushalmi, all mortgages are redeemable.]

הַמְשַׁעְבֵּד שָׂדֶה לְאִשְׁתּוֹ וְהָלַךְ וּמְכָרָהּ אִם רָצָה לִגְבּוֹת מִמֶּנּוּ גוֹבָה[12] מִשְׁאָר נְכָסִים גּוֹבָה. אָמַר רְבִּי הִילָא הוֹרֵי רְבִּי לָעֶזֶר כָּהֵן תַּנְיָיא. חֲבִירַיָּיא בְּעַיִין לֹא תִגְבֶּה אֶלָּא מִנְּכָסִים מְשׁוּעְבָּדִין. אָמַר לוֹן רְבִּי יוֹסֵי בְּנֵי חוֹרִין לְפָנֶיהָ וְאַתְּ אֲמַרְתְּ מְשׁוּעְבָּדִין. מַתְנִיתָא בְּשֶׁלֹּא אָמַר לָהּ לֹא יְהֵא לָךְ פֵּירָעוֹן אֶלָּא מִזֶּה. אֲבָל אִם אָמַר לָהּ לֹא יְהֵא לָךְ פֵּירָעוֹן אֶלָּא מִזֶּה אֵינָהּ גּוֹבָה אֶלָּא מִמֶּנָּה.

"If somebody established a lien on a field for his wife but then went and sold it, if she wishes she collects from this field or she collects from any other property.[13]" Rebbi Hila said, Rebbi Eleazar instructed following this *baraita*. The colleagues asked: Should she not collect only from the properties that are under the lien? Rebbi Yose said to them, there are unencumbered properties[14] and you say, those under the lien? The *baraita* [applies] if he did not say[15] you shall be paid only from this. But when he said, you shall be paid only from this, she may collect only from this[16].

12   Reading of the Rome ms., missing in the Leyden ms. The word makes the text much clearer but it might be an intrusion of Babylonian style.

13   The lien is part of the marriage contract and covers the payments due the wife in case of dissolution of the marriage either by divorce or by the husband's death. A parallel *baraita* in the Babli (*Giṭṭin* 41a) gives the option both to the wife and to any lienholder,

both of whom have the choice of either going after unincumbered property of the husband or debtor or to choose the more complicated procedure of foreclosing the property from the buyer, letting the buyer then sue the seller to recover his damages. In the Babli, Rabban Simeon ben Gamliel declares the original sale invalid if the lienholder is the wife since women cannot be expected to be willing to go through lengthy and complicated court proceedings.

14   Which the wife can take with a minimum of legal steps.

15   In all these statements, "to say" means "to write into the appropriate document."

16   The piece of real estate on which she holds the lien.

הַמְשַׁעְבֵּד שָׂדֶה לַחֲבֵירוֹ וְהָלַךְ וּמְכָרָהּ. רְבִּי אָחָא אָמַר מְכוּרָה לְשָׁעָה. רְבִּי יוֹסֵי אָמַר אֵינָהּ מְכוּרָה לְשָׁעָה. חֵיילֵיהּ דְּרִבִּי יוֹסֵי מִן הָדָא שׁוֹר מָצוּי הוּא לְהַבְרִיחוֹ. שָׂדֶה אֵינוֹ מָצוּי לְהַבְרִיחָהּ. הַגַּע עַצְמָךְ שֶׁהָיְתָה מְכוּרָה לְבַעַל זְרוֹעַ. אָמַר רִבִּי יוּדָן אָבוֹי דְּרִבִּי מַתַּנְיָה מְצוּיִין הֵן בַּעֲלֵי זְרוֹעַ לִיפּוֹל.

If somebody established a lien for another person on his field and then went and sold it; Rebbi Aha said, it is temporarily sold[17]. Rebbi Yose said, even temporarily it is not sold[18]. The strength of Rebbi Yose is from the following: He may induce his ox to flee; he cannot induce his field to flee[19]. Think about it, if [the field] was sold to a violent person[20]! Rebbi Yudan, the father of Rebbi Mattaniah, said: Violent persons are apt to fall[21].

17   In the time between the sale and the lienholder's foreclosure, the buyer is the rightful owner in all respects. This is the unquestioned position of the Babli.

18   Since the sale does not break the lien, the sale is invalid as far as the lienholder is concerned. The lienholder has only to enforce his rights vis-à-vis the debtor but does not have to sue the buyer of the land.

19   This refers to the rule, not otherwise quoted in the Yerushalmi, and brought as a statement of fifth-

generation Amora Rava (Rav Abba bar Joseph bar Ḥama) in the Babli (*Baba Qama* 11b, *Baba Batra* 44b), that a mortgage on cattle is not valid, since the disposition of animals is outside the control of the lienholder. This implies that a valid lien puts the mortgaged property at the disposal of the lien-holder.

20 The lienholder might be afraid of the consequences if he brings the buyer into court.

21 Even if the lien is temporarily unenforceable, nobody will give up his claim because of this.

תַּנֵּי הַכּוֹתֵב שָׂדֶה אֲפוֹתֵיקֵי לְאִשָּׁה בִּכְתוּבָתָהּ וּלְבַעַל חוֹב בְּחוֹבוֹ מְכָרָהּ הֲרֵי זוֹ מְכוּרָה וְהַלּוֹקֵחַ יָחוּשׁ לְעַצְמוֹ. מַתְנִיתָא בְּשֶׁאָמַר לָהּ יְהֵא לָךְ פֵּירָעוֹן מִזּוֹ. מַה פְּלִיגִין בְּשֶׁאָמַר לָהּ לֹא יְהֵא לָךְ פֵּירָעוֹן אֶלָּא מִזּוֹ.

It was stated: "If somebody mortgages[22] a field to a woman for her *ketubah*[23] or a creditor for his claim and then sells it, that is sold and the buyer should beware for himself.[24]" This *baraita* if he said to her: you should be paid from this. They disagree if he says, you should only be paid from this[25].

22 Greek ὑποθήκη "mortgage".

23 Cf. *Peah* Chapter 3, Note 155.

24 This *baraita* seems to support R. Aḥa only. In *Yebamot* 7:1 (fol. 8a), Rabban Simeon ben Gamliel disagrees and decrees that in the case of a *ketubah* the sale is void since we cannot require a woman to sue a third party for her rights.

25 In this case, R. Yose declares the sale invalid, which does not contradict the *baraita*.

רַב אָמַר פִּגְּמָה וְלֹא זָקְפָה זָקְפָה אַף עַל פִּי שֶׁלֹּא פִגְּמָה. תַּנֵּי רִבִּי חִייָא עַד שֶׁתִּפְגּוֹם וְתִזְקוֹף.

Rav said, if she compromised [her *ketubah*], even if she did not extend credit, if she extended credit even though she did not compromise. Rebbi Ḥiyya stated: Unless she would compromise it and extend credit[26].

26   This refers to Tosephta 8:4: "A woman's *ketubah*, if she compromised it and extended credit, is subject to remission. If she compromised it but did not extend credit, if she extended credit but did not compromise, it is not subject to remission." "Compromised" means that she obtained partial payment of the *ketubah* and now cannot use the original *ketubah* document for the remaining claim but must produce a new document from the husband (for a divorcee) or the heirs (for a widow) for the remainder. "Extending credit" means that she does not insist on immediate payment but on payment terms as if it were the repayment of a loan. The Tosephta text follows Rebbi Hiyya; Rav makes the *ketubah* subject to remission in the Sabbatical even if only one of the conditions is met. (In the Babli, Gittin 18a, the position of R. Hiyya is ascribed to Rav and that of Rav to Samuel.)

וּמִפְּנֵי שֶׁהוּא מַקִּיף לוֹ פַּעַם שְׁנִיָּה נַעֲשֵׂית רִאשׁוֹנָה מִלְוָה. אָמַר רִבִּי לְעָזָר דְּרִבִּי יוּדָה הִיא וְרָאוּי לְתוֹבְעוֹ בְּרֹאשׁ הַשָּׁנָה. רִבִּי בָּא בְּשֵׁם רִבִּי זְעִירָא בְּמָמוֹן שֶׁהוּא רָאוּי לְהַאֲמִינוֹ. וּמִכֵּיוָן שֶׁהוּא רָאוּי לְתוֹבְעוֹ כְּמִי שֶׁהוּא רָאוּי לִיתֶּן לוֹ מָעוֹת. וְכָאן הוֹאִיל וְרָאוּי לִיתֶּן לוֹ מָעוֹת וְלֹא נָתַן נַעֲשֵׂית רִאשׁוֹנָה מִלְוָה.

Because he extends him credit a second time, is the first turned into a loan?[27]   Rebbi Eleazar said, this follows Rebbi Jehudah[28].   But can he require payment on New Year's Day[29]?   Rebbi Abba in the name of Rebbi Zeïra: About money for which he can believe him[30].   And since he could ask him for payment, he should be able to give him money.   And here, because he should have been able to give him money and he did not give, the first [debt] is turned into a loan[31].

27   This refers to the Mishnah, where R. Jehudah declares that the exemption of store credit from the laws of the Sabbatical only covers the last credit extended.

28   This statement seems to be obvious since R. Jehudah only restricts the exemption of store credit. But the reference here is to Mishnah 2, where it is stated that store debt incurred on

New Year's Day may be subject to remission. While this Mishnah is anonymous, it is stated here (and in Halakhah 2) that it also is R. Jehudah's and refers to a customer who took food from the store on both days of the New Year. For R. Jehudah this implies that the debt incurred the first day is subject to remission (at the end of the Sabbatical year.)

29 Since handling money is forbidden on a holiday, payment cannot be asked for.

30 The prior argument is rejected.

If the customer is creditworthy, extending credit is tantamount to asking for payment and extending credit is permitted on the holiday.

31 The storekeeper is implicitly asking for payment by providing the food; cf. Note 36. Hence, non-payment automatically turns the credit into a loan and the farmer has a great incentive to ask for his money during the Sabbatical. The same argument applies to the butcher mentioned in Mishnah 2.

רבִּי יוֹחָנָן אָמַר בְּגִין חֲרִישָׁה. רבִּי שִׁמְעוֹן בֶּן לָקִישׁ אָמַר בְּגִין בִּנְיָן. עַל דַּעְתֵּיהּ דְּרבִּי יוֹחָנָן כָּל־מְלָאכָה שֶׁהִיא פּוֹסֶקֶת בַּשְּׁבִיעִית. עַל דַּעְתֵּיהּ דְּרבִּי שִׁמְעוֹן בֶּן לָקִישׁ כָּל־מְלָאכָה שֶׁהִיא פּוֹסֶקֶת מֵאֵילֶיהָ. מַה רבִּי יוֹסֵי כְּרבִּי יוּדָה דְּרבִּי יוֹסֵי אוֹמֵר כָּל־מְלָאכָה שֶׁהִיא פּוֹסֶקֶת בַּשְּׁבִיעִית מְשַׁמֶּטֶת וְשֶׁאֵינָהּ פּוֹסֶקֶת בַּשְּׁבִיעִית אֵינָהּ מְשַׁמֶּטֶת. וְלֹא רבִּי יוֹסֵי כְּרבִּי יוּדָה אַף עַל גַּו דְּרבִּי יוּדָה אָמַר אֵין דֶּרֶךְ הַשּׁוּלְחָנִי לִהְיוֹת נוֹתֵן אִיסָר עַד שֶׁיִּטּוֹל דֵּינָר מוֹדֶה הוּא בְּשָׂכָר שָׂכִיר שֶׁאֵינוֹ אֶלָּא בְּסוֹף.

[32]Rebbi Johanan says, for ploughing. Rebbi Simeon ben Laqish said, for building. In the opinion of Rebbi Johanan, any work that stops because of the Sabbatical. In the opinion of Rebbi Simeon ben Laqish, any work that stops in any way. Does Rebbi Yose hold with Rebbi Jehudah[33]; does not Rebbi Yose say, for any work that stops in the Sabbatical they are remitted, if it does not stop they are not remitted? But Rebbi Yose does not hold with Rebbi Jehudah[34]; while "Rebbi Jehudah says that it is not the

way of a banker to give an *as* unless he has received a *denar*," he agrees
that the wages of the hired man are due only at the end[35].

32   This refers to the last sentence
in the Mishnah, where R. Yose declares
that wages for an unfinished job are
remitted if not paid during the
Sabbatical. R. Joḥanan holds that this
applies only if the Sabbatical is the
cause of the interruption; R. Simeon
ben Laqish disagrees.

33   Does R. Yose hold that payment
for work done is turned into a loan the
moment the work is finished and was
not paid? This would parallel the
opinion of R. Jehudah about store
credit.

34   This probably should read: R.
Jehudah does not hold with R. Yose.
The statement of R. Jehudah is in
Mishnah *Šebu'ot* 7:5, that a banker
never can be believed if he claims to
have given change before he received
the large coin.

35   The payment is due only during
the Sabbatical and not subject to
remission since only debts incurred
before the Sabbatical must be remitted.
The argument about store credit is not
appropriate here.

משנה ב: הַשּׁוֹחֵט אֶת הַפָּרָה וְחִילְקָהּ בְּרֹאשׁ הַשָּׁנָה אִם הָיָה הַחוֹדֶשׁ מְעוּבָּר
מְשַׁמֵּיט וְאִם לָאו אֵינוֹ מְשַׁמֵּיט. הָאוֹנֵס וְהַמְפַתֶּה וְהַמּוֹצִיא שֵׁם רַע וְכָל־מַעֲשֵׂה
בֵית דִּין אֵינָן מַשְׁמִיטִין. הַמַּלְוֶה עַל הַמַּשְׁכּוֹן וְהַמּוֹסֵר שְׁטָרוֹתָיו לְבֵית דִּין אֵין
מַשְׁמִיטִין.

Mishnah 2: If somebody slaughters a cow and divides it up on New
Year's Day[36], if the month was long it is subject to remission[37], otherwise
it is not subject to remission. The rapist, the seducer, the calumniator[38],
and all court documents are not subject to remission. If somebody gives
loans on pledge[39], or deposits his documents[40] with the court, they are not
subject to remission.

36 The butcher gives away meat both days of the New Year of the Sabbatical. It is forbidden to transact business on the holiday; therefore, the Mishnah avoids speaking about selling meat; the meat is distributed on the holiday, billed later by estimate.

37 If the month of Elul was 30 days, the first day of the New Year really was the 30th of Elul, the second day the first of Tishre. The debt incurred on the first day enters the Sabbatical and is subject to remission; the debt of the second day is contracted during the Sabbatical and not subject to remission.

38 These are all fines, and fines are never remitted. The fine for the rapist is spelled out in *Deut.* 22:29, the one for the seducer *Ex.* 22:16, the one for the calumniator who accuses his bride of adultery between the preliminary and actual marriages, *Deut.* 22:19.

39 The pledge is in the hand of the lender; the loan is not a claim on another person but the borrower must come and redeem his pledge.

40 The obligation of remission of debt is one on real persons only.

הלכה ב: רְבִּי אוֹמֵר נִיסָן לֹא נִתְעַבֵּר מִיָּמָיו וְהָא תַּנִּינָן אִם בָּא חוֹדֶשׁ בִּזְמַנּוֹ. אִם בָּא לֹא בָּא. רַב אָמַר תִּשְׁרֵי לֹא נִתְעַבֵּר מִיָּמָיו וְהָא תַּנִּינָן אִם הָיָה חוֹדֶשׁ מְעוּבָּר. אִם הָיָה לֹא הָיָה.

Halakhah 2: [41]Rebbi says, Nisan never was lengthened[42]. But did we not state[43]: "If the New Moon appeared in time"? If it would appear, it did not appear. Rav said, Tishre was never lengthened[44]. But did we not state[45]: "If the month was long"? If it would be, it never was.

41 This paragraph and the three following ones are from *Roš Haššanah* 3:1 (fol. 58c). They are included here only because the two days of the New Year are mentioned in the Mishnah.

42 This means that the *start* of Nisan (and Tishre) was never delayed when the New Moon was declared only after it had been observed. In these two months, messengers were sent to proclaim the exact dates of the holidays (*Roš Haššanah* 1:5). [For the details of the Tannaitic calendar, see the author's *Seder Olam* (Northvale, NJ,

1998), p. 268 - 269.]

43 Mishnah *Šeqalim* 4:5: Incense was prepared in one batch for an entire year, starting with the first of Nisan. Then it is stated that on the first of Nisan, "if the New Moon appeared in time, incense was taken from the new batch; otherwise, it was taken from the incense prepared the previous year." This Mishnah implies that the month of Adar preceding Nisan could have either 29 or 30 days. Rebbi implies that this Mishnah is purely hypothetical.

44 Babli *Roš Haššanah* 19b, also in the name of Rav, stating a tradition going back to the days of Ezra. The same statement is also in Yerushalmi *Šeqalim* 10:2 (fol. 39b), *Sanhedrin* 1:2 (fol. 18d).

45 In the Mishnah here.

וּכְשֶׁקִּידְּשׁוּ אֶת הַשָּׁנָה בְּאוּשָׁה בַּיּוֹם הָרִאשׁוֹן עָמַד רְבִּי יִשְׁמָעֵאל בְּנוֹ שֶׁל רְבִּי יוֹחָנָן בֶּן בְּרוֹקָה אָמַר כְּדִבְרֵי רִבִּי יוֹחָנָן בֶּן נוּרִי. אָמַר רַבָּן שִׁמְעוֹן בֶּן גַּמְלִיאֵל לֹא הָיִינוּ נוֹהֲגִין כֵּן בְּיַבְנֶה. בַּיּוֹם הַשֵּׁנִי עָבַר רִבִּי חֲנַנְיָה בְּנוֹ שֶׁל רְבִּי יוֹסֵי הַגְּלִילִי. אָמַר כְּדִבְרֵי רִבִּי עֲקִיבָה. (fol. 39c) אָמַר רַבָּן שִׁמְעוֹן בֶּן גַּמְלִיאֵל כֵּן הָיִינוּ נוֹהֲגִין בְּיַבְנֶה. וְהָתַנֵּי קִידְּשׁוּהוּ בָּרִאשׁוֹן וּבַשֵּׁנִי. רִבִּי זְעִירָא בְּשֵׁם רַב חִסְדָּא אוֹתָהּ שָׁנָה נִתְקַלְקְלָה מַה בֵּין הָרִאשׁוֹן וּמַה בֵּין הַשֵּׁנִי. רִבִּי בּוּן בְּשֵׁם רַב שָׁנָה רִאשׁוֹנָה וְשָׁנָה שְׁנִיָּיה. וְהָתַנֵּי יוֹם רִאשׁוֹן יוֹם הַשֵּׁנִי.

[46]"When they sanctified the year at Usha[47], on the first day Rebbi Ismael, the son of Rebbi Johanan ben Baroqa led[48] and recited following the opinion of Rebbi Johanan ben Nuri. Rabban Simeon ben Gamliel said, we did not follow this at Jabneh. On the second day, Rebbi Hananiah, the son of Rebbi Yose the Galilean led and recited following the opinion of Rebbi Aqiba. Rabban Simeon ben Gamliel said, this we did follow at Jabneh." But does this not mean that they sanctified it on the first and the second day[49]? Rebbi Zeïra in the name of Rav Hisda: That year was disorganized[50]. What is "the first, the second"[51]? Rebbi Abun in the name of Rav: The first year, the second year[52]! But was it not stated: the first day, the second day?

46　　Tosephta *Roš Haššanah* 3:11, also quoted in Yerushalmi *Roš Haš-šanah* 4:6 (59c), *Nedarim* 6:13 (40a), *Sanhedrin* 1:2 (18d); Babli *Roš Haš-šanah* 32a; *Sifra Emor Parašah* 11(5).

47　　When the Synhedrion was re-constituted under a Roman emperor in the later second century. Any recollec-tion that Rabban Simeon could have had of the Synhedrion at Jabneh must have been from his childhood.

48　　He was the reader for the *musaph* prayer on New Year's Day which consists of nine benedictions. The three first and the three last ones are those of everyday prayers; there are three additional ones proclaiming God's Kingdom, מַלְכִיּוֹת, His remem-bering all living creatures, זִכְרוֹנוֹת, and the *shofar* blowing connected with the theophany on Mount Sinai, שׁוֹפָרוֹת, each one followed by blowing the *shofar*. R. Ismael ben R. Joḥanan ben Beroqa takes *malkhiyot* together with the third benediction, "sanctification of the Name", and has as fourth benediction the usual holiday benediction, without *shofar* blowing. R. Aqiba takes the holiday benediction as part of *mal-khiyot*; this is the rule followed today as established by Rabban Simeon ben Gamliel in the Tosephta.

49　　The story contradicts the assertion by Rav that Elul was never 30 days because, if it is clear that Elul is only 29 days one observed only one day for the New Year at the place of the Synhedrion.

50　　Something happened that made the Synhedrion unsure which day was the right one; in that case, the story must date to the beginning of Rabban Simeon's presidency when his authority was not yet established. This is confirmed by the fact that Rabban Simeon could not instruct the other rabbis on which rule to follow.

51　　Reading with the text in *Roš Haššanah*: מֶהוּ הָרִאשׁוֹן וּמֶהוּ הַשֵּׁנִי .

52　　Rav insists that his tradition is correct and that the two prayers were said in two different years. It is pointed out that this contradicts the language of the Tosephta; the problem remains unresolved.

קִדְשׁוּהוּ קוֹדֶם לִזְמַנּוֹ אוֹ אַחַר עִיבּוּרוֹ יוֹם אֶחָד יָכוֹל יְהֵא מְעוּבָּר. תַּלְמוּד לוֹמַר אוֹתָם אַתֶּם אֵלָּא הֵם מוֹעֲדָי. לִפְנֵי זְמַנּוֹ אֵין אֵלָּא מוֹעֲדָי. לִפְנֵי זְמַנּוֹ עֶשְׂרִים וְתִשְׁעָה יוֹם לְאַחַר עִיבּוּרוֹ שְׁלֹשִׁים וּשְׁנַיִם יוֹם. וּמְנַיִין שֶׁמְּעַבְּרִין אֶת הַשָּׁנָה עַל

הַגְּלִיּוֹת שֶׁיָּצְאוּ וַעֲדַיִין לֹא הִגִּיעוּ תַּלְמוּד לוֹמַר בְּנֵי יִשְׂרָאֵל מוֹעֲדָי. עֲשֵׂה אֶת
הַמּוֹעֲדוֹת שֶׁיַּעֲשׂוּ אוֹתָן כָּל־יִשְׂרָאֵל. אָמַר רִבִּי שְׁמוּאֵל בַּר נַחְמָן. וְהֵן שֶׁהִגִּיעוּ
לִנְהַר פְּרָת.

If they sanctified it before its time or after its lengthening, should I
assume it was lengthened[53]? The verse says (*Lev.* 23:2) "them", you, "these
are My holidays.[54]" Before its time is not "My holidays." Before its time,
the 29th day, after its lengthening, the 32nd day. From where that one
intercalates the year because of the [men of the] diaspora that set out but
did not yet arrive[55]? The verse says (*Lev.* 23:2), "the Children of Israel,
my holidays". Make the holidays so they can be observed by all of Israel.
Rebbi Samuel bar Naḥman said, only if they had reached the river
Euphrates.

53   Since a month can only be
either 29 or 30 days, New Year's Day
can be only the 30th or the 31st of Elul.
If the Synhedrion did not proclaim New
Year's on the 30th of Elul, then the
31st is automatically sanctified;
whether it needs a proclamation is a
matter of controversy (Mishnah *Roš
Haššanah* 2:8).

54   This is explained in Babli *Roš
Haššanah* 25a and *Sifra Behar Parashah* 9(3). In *Lev.* 23:2 (Tell the
Children of Israel and say to them, the
holidays of the Eternal, you have to
proclaim *them* as holy assemblies, *these
are My holidays*), *Lev.* 22:4 (These are
the holidays of the Eternal, holy

assemblies; you have to declare *them* at
their times), and *Lev.* 22:37 (These are
the holidays of the Eternal; you have to
declare *them* as holy assemblies) the
word "them" is written defective אֹתָם so
that it could also be read as אַתֶּם "you".
This is taken to imply that no holiday
is sacred that is not proclaimed by the
Synhedrion. Since the Synhedrion is
human, it is error prone. The three
"them - you" are explained in the Babli
as "you, even if unintended, you, even
if intentionally wrong, you, even in
error." In the *Sifra*, the three cases are
"even if forced by an act of God, unintended, or in error." This interpretation is the basis of the Jewish

computed calendar which, being based on a constant mean synodal month and a base line outside the Land of Israel, is necessarily in error if compared with astronomical computations of the motions of the moon.

55   This argument does not belong to the discussion about one or two days of the New Year since the intercalary month always has to precede Passover. The intercalary month is a necessary

feature of any lunar–solar calendar. It is included here probably because it refers to the same verse and appears in *Sifra Behar Parashah* 9(1). Since both the Children of Israel and God's holidays are mentioned in *Lev.* 23:2, it is inferred that the holidays must be appropriate for all Children of Israel. (The rule itself, without Scriptural justification, is in Babli *Sanhedrin* 11a.)

רִבִּי יַעֲקֹב בַּר אָחָא רִבִּי אִימִּי בְּשֵׁם רִבִּי יוּדָה בַּר פָּזִי קִידְּשׁוּהוּ וְאַחַר כָּךְ נִמְצְאוּ הָעֵדִים זוֹמְמִין הֲרֵי זֶה מְקוּדָּשׁ. קָם רִבִּי יוֹסָה עִם רִבִּי יוּדָה בֶּן פָּזִי. אָמַר לֵיהּ אַתְּ שָׁמַעַת מִן אָבוּךְ הָדָא מִילְתָא אָמַר לֵיהּ כֵּן. רִבִּי אַבָּא אָמַר בְּשֵׁם רִבִּי יוֹחָנָן אֵין מְדַקְדְּקִין בְּעֵידֵי הַחוֹדֶשׁ.

Rebbi Jacob bar Aḥa, Rebbi Ammi, in the name of Rebbi Jehudah bar Pazi: If they sanctified it and afterwards the witnesses turned out to be perjured, it still is sanctified[56]. Rebbi Assi stayed with Rebbi Jehudah bar Pazi and asked him: Did you hear this from your father? He said, yes. Rebbi Abba said in the name of Rebbi Joḥanan: One does not cross-examine the witnesses of the New Moon.

56   The verses quoted in Note 54 imply that the holidays have to be declared. Since they are defined by the calendar months, it follows that the months have to be declared. Since the declaration is valid even if in error, it is not rescinded if an error is found. In any case, the error can not be of more

than one day. The rules given here are implied by Mishnah *Roš Haššanah* 2:9; they are not explicit in the Babli. The paragraph here is the source of Maimonides, *Qidduš Haḥodeš* 2:2 (not recognized by the commentators *ad loc.*)

אָמַר רִבִּי לְעָזָר דְּרִבִּי יוּדָה הִיא וְרָאוּי לְתוֹבְעוֹ בְּרֹאשׁ הַשָּׁנָה. רִבִּי בָּא בַּר מָמָל רַב[57] עַמְרָם רַב מַתָּנָה בְּשֵׁם רַב הַמַּלְוֶה אֶת חֲבֵירוֹ עַל מְנָת שֶׁלֹּא לְתוֹבְעוֹ שְׁבִיעִית מְשַׁמְּטָתוֹ. וְהָתַנֵּי הַשּׁוֹחֵט אֶת הַפָּרָה וְחִילְקָהּ בְּרֹאשׁ הַשָּׁנָה וְאָמַר רִבִּי לְעָזָר דְּרִבִּי יוּדָה הִיא וְרָאוּי הוּא לְתוֹבְעוֹ בְּרֹאשׁ הַשָּׁנָה. כַּיי דָּמַר רִבִּי בָּא בְשֵׁם רִבִּי זְעִירָא מִכֵּיוָן שֶׁהוּא רָאוּי לְתוֹבְעוֹ כְּמִי שֶׁהוּא רָאוּי לְהַאֲמִינוֹ. וּמִכֵּיוָן שֶׁהוּא רָאוּי לְהַאֲמִינוֹ כְּמִי שֶׁהוּא רָאוּי לִיתֵּן לוֹ מָעוֹת. וְכָאן הוֹאִיל וְהוּא רָאוּי לִיתֵּן לוֹ וְלֹא נָתַן נַעֲשֵׂית רִאשׁוֹנָה מִלְוָה.

Rebbi Eleazar said, this follows Rebbi Jehudah since he could ask him for payment on New Years's Day. Rebbi Abba bar Mamal, Rav Amram, Rav Mattanah in the name of Rav: If somebody makes a loan to another person stipulating that he will not press for repayment, the Sabbatical will remit it[58]. We did state: "If somebody slaughters a cow and divides it up on New Year's Day," and Rebbi Eleazar said, this follows Rebbi Jehudah[59]. But can he require payment on New Year's Day? As Rebbi Abba said in the name of Rebbi Zeïra: Since he could ask him for payment, he can believe him. And since he could believe him, he could pay him[60]. And here, because he could have given him but did not give, the first [debt] is turned into a loan[61].

57 From the parallel in *Makkot* 1:5 (fol. 31a); title missing here. Rav Amram was a Babylonian Amora, probably a student of Rav Sheshet and Rav Hisda.

58 One should assume that the loan is not remitted in the Sabbatical since it can never be claimed and the Sabbatical law applies only to loans that

can be claimed (*Deut.* 15:2).

59 Since it is assumed that payment cannot be claimed on New Year's Day since it cannot be given.

60 The case of the butcher cannot be used to support Rav's statement; in practice, Rav's statement is rejected.

61 This sentence does not belong here but to Mishnah 1, cf. Note 31.

רְבִּי יוֹסֵי בְּי רְבִּי בּוּן בְּשֵׁם רַב הַמַּלְוֶה אֶת חֲבֵירוֹ עַל מְנָת שֶׁלֹּא תַשְׁמְטֶנָּה
שְׁבִיעִית אֵין הַשְּׁבִיעִית מְשַׁמְטַתּוֹ. וְהָתַנִּינָן בֵּין נוֹתְנִין מִיכָּן וְעַד שְׁלֹשִׁים יוֹם בֵּין
נוֹתְנִין מִיכָּן וְעַד עֶשֶׂר שָׁנִים. וְיֵשׁ עֶשֶׂר שָׁנִים בְּלֹא שְׁמִיטָה. אָמַר רַב הוּנָא
אִתְפַּלְגוּן רַב נַחְמָן בֶּן יַעֲקֹב וְרַב שֵׁשֶׁת חַד אָמַר בְּמַלְוֶה עַל הַמַּשְׁכּוֹן. וְחָרְנָה
אָמַר בְּכוֹתֵב לוֹ פְּרוֹזְבּוֹל.

Rebbi Yose ben Rebbi Abun in the name of Rav: If somebody gives a
loan to a person on condition that the Sabbatical not remit it, the
Sabbatical does not remit[62], as we have stated[63]: "Whether he gives it
after thirty days or after ten years." Are there ten years without a
Sabbatical? Rav Huna said, Rav Naḥman bar Jacob and Rav Sheshet
disagreed. One of them said, if the loan was given on a pledge[64], but the
other said, if he writes him a *prozbol*[65].

62   In the Babli (*Makkot* 3b), Samuel is reported to have declared that the
Sabbatical will remit. In the end, a fine
distinction is made in the wording. If
the contract reads that the debtor will
not enforce the remission, that condition is valid. But if the contract
reads that the Sabbatical should have
no influence, that would mean
abrogating a Torah law and the
condition is invalid.

63   Mishnah *Makkot* 1:2, dealing

with witnesses who falsely testify that
a debtor has promised to pay within 30
days when in fact he is obligated to
pay after ten years, they are sentenced
to pay the present value of the debt
due in ten years.

64   As noted in the Mishnah. In the
Babli, this explanation is attributed to
the later Amora Rava.

65   Explained in the next Mishnah,
cf. Note 80.

תַּנֵּי שְׁלֹשִׁים יוֹם לֹא אֲיתֵיי. מַהוּ שְׁלֹשִׁים יוֹם לֹא אֲיתֵיי שְׁמוּאֵל אָמַר בְּמַלְוֶה
אֶת חֲבֵירוֹ סְתָם שֶׁאֵינוֹ רַשַּׁאי לְתוֹבְעוֹ עַד שְׁלֹשִׁים יוֹם. אָעַל רַב יְהוּדָה וְאָמַר
טַעֲמָא קֵרְבָה שְׁנַת הַשֶּׁבַע שְׁנַת הַשְּׁמִיטָה לֹא הִיא שְׁנַת הַשֶּׁבַע וְלֹא הִיא שְׁנַת

הַשְּׁמִיטָה. מַה תַּלְמוּד לוֹמַר קָרְבָה שְׁנַת הַשֶּׁבַע שְׁנַת הַשְּׁמִיטָה. שֶׁלֹא תֹאמַר

כָּל־שְׁלֹשִׁים יוֹם אֵינוֹ רַשַׁאי לְתוֹבְעוֹ. לְאַחַר שְׁלֹשִׁים יוֹם בְּהַשְׁמֵט יוֹם כְּסָפִים וְהוּא

לֹא יִגְבֵּינוֹ לְפוּם כֵּן צָרִיךְ מֵימַר קָרְבָה שְׁנַת הַשֶּׁבַע שְׁנַת הַשְּׁמִיטָה. לֹא כֵן אָמַר

רִבִּי בָּא בַּר מָמָל רַב[57] עַמְרָם רַב מַתָּנָה בְּשֵׁם רַב הַמַּלְוֶה אֶת חֲבֵירוֹ עַל מְנָת

שֶׁלֹּא לְתוֹבְעוֹ שְׁבִיעִית מְשַׁמְטָתוֹ. אַשְׁכַּח תַּנֵּי רִבִּי יִשְׁמָעֵאל קָרְבָה שְׁנַת הַשֶּׁבַע

שְׁנַת הַשְּׁמִיטָה. לֹא הִיא שְׁנַת הַשֶּׁבַע שְׁנַת הַשְּׁמִיטָה. וּמַה תַּלְמוּד לוֹמַר קָרְבָה

שְׁנַת הַשֶּׁבַע שְׁנַת הַשְּׁמִיטָה שֶׁלֹּא תֹאמַר כָּל־שֵׁשׁ שָׁנִים שָׂדֵהוּ לְפָנַי כַּרְמוֹ לְפָנַי

וּלְאַחַר שֵׁשׁ שָׁנִים בְּהַשְׁמֵט כְּסָפִים וְהוּא לֹא יִגְבֵּינוֹ לְפוּם כֵּן צָרִיךְ מֵימַר קָרְבָה

שְׁנַת הַשֶּׁבַע שְׁנַת הַשְּׁמִיטָה.

It was stated: "For thirty days he will not come." What means "for thirty days he will not come"? Samuel said, if somebody gives a loan to a person without specifying details, he has no right to ask for payment until after 30 days[66]. Rav Jehudah came and explained (*Deut.* 15:9): "The Sabbatical year, the remitting year, is close." Is not the Sabbatical year the remitting year? Why does the verse say: "The Sabbatical year, the remitting year, is close"? That you should not say, I am not permitted to ask for payment until after 30 days; after 30 days the debt will be remitted and I will not collect; therefore, it must say that "the Sabbatical year, the remitting year, is close."[67] Did not Rebbi Abba bar Mamal, Rav Amram, Rav Mattanah say in the name of Rav: If somebody makes a loan to another person stipulating that he will not press for repayment, the Sabbatical will remit it? It was found stated in the name of Rebbi Ismael (*Deut.* 15:9): "The Sabbatical year, the remitting year, is close." Is not the Sabbatical year the remitting year? Why does it have to say, "the Sabbatical year, the remitting year, is close"? That you should not say, all six years long his field is before me, his vineyard is before me, but after six years the debt is remitted and I cannot collect; therefore, it has to say "the Sabbatical year, the remitting year, is close.⁶⁸"

66   This is a statement of Tosephta *Baba Meẓi'a* 10:1, where however the rule is qualified so that it is superseded by local usage if such usage is determined. This means that for the Tosephta, the 30 day rule is rabbinic in character. In the Babli (*Makkot* 3b), the rule is quoted by Samuel as a Tannaitic statement and the biblical proof given here by R. Jehudah is attributed there to Rav Mattanah.

67   The entire verse reads: "Guard yourself, lest there be in your heart an unworthy thought saying, behold, the Sabbatical year, the remitting year, is close, and you will be badly disposed towards your needy brother and not give him; when he would appeal against you to the Eternal then sin will be in you." The verse is taken to deal with a case where the Sabbatical will remit without any possibility for the lender to recoup his loan. The only case found is that of an unsecured loan given less than 30 days before the date of remission when repayment cannot be claimed but the debt will be remitted.

68   The statement of R. Ismael gives a different explanation of the verse; therefore, the biblical character of the 30 day rule is not established and the Yerushalmi is in accordance with the Tosephta, against the Babli.

The argument in the *baraita* goes as follows: If one gives a loan during a regular year, even if it is not a mortgage the lender might recover his loan from the crop of the borrower. But in the Sabbatical, there is no commercial crop, and when the next crop grows, the debt already is remitted. Hence, the verse speaks of any loan given in the sixth year, and nothing can be implied about the 30 day rule. [In *Sifry Deut.* #117, R. Yose the Galilean points out that the expression "the Seventh year, the remitting year" is needed to show that the Seventh year is not the seventh year after a loan has been granted but the seventh calendar year.]

הָאוֹנֵס וְהַמְפַתֶּה וְהַמּוֹצִיא שֵׁם רַע. רַב יְהוּדָה אָמַר רַב דְּרִבִּי מֵאִיר הִיא דְּרִבִּי מֵאִיר אָמַר בְּמַלְוָה הַדָּבָר תָּלוּי.

"The rapist, the seducer, the calumniator[38]." Rav Jehudah said, Rav [said]: This follows Rebbi Meïr, since Rebbi Meïr said, it depends on the one extending credit[69].

69   Since the persons mentioned here have to pay only by order of a court, the question is why these cases have to be mentioned in the Mishnah separately and are not subsumed under the general notion of court judgments. The fines for the rapist and the seducer are spelled out in the Torah only for the נערה, a minor. The fines have to be paid to the father if at the time of judgment and payment the girl was a minor, to the woman if she was an adult at the time of judgment. The problem is, who receives the fine if she was minor at the time of judgment but an adult at the moment of payment. In *Ketubot* 4:2, R. Simeon says that the fines are paid as a consequence of a court document, the money goes to the woman, and the obligation is not remitted in the Sabbatical. The rabbis hold that the obligation is a civil one, a "loan", the payment goes to the creditor of the loan, *viz.*, the father, and is remitted in the Sabbatical. The position ascribed to R. Meïr in this Mishnah is that the status of the obligation is that of a loan which is not remitted in the Sabbatical. [R. Simson holds that the position of R. Meïr is that of the rabbis, that the claims to fines are not remitted in the Sabbatical but that any judgment for fines not collected before the Sabbatical is remitted. If that were true, the position here should be described as that of the rabbis.]

The main differences between loan and court decree is that in a forcible execution, loans are paid from the borrower's real estate of average quality but court judgments covering torts from the best quality.

וְכָל־מַעֲשֵׂה בֵית דִּין אֵילּוּ גִּזְרֵי דִינִין.

"And all court judgments," these are court decisions.[70]

70   Reading of the Rome ms: דיינין "of judges".

פְּשִׁיטָא דָא מִילְתָא מִלְוָה שֶׁהִיא נַעֲשֵׂית כַּפְרָנִית אֵינָהּ מְשַׁמֶּטֶת. כַּפְרָנִית שֶׁהִיא נַעֲשֵׂית מִלְוָה מְשַׁמֶּטֶת. רִבִּי יִרְמְיָה בָּעֵי אַף[71] לְמִידַת הַדִּין כֵּן לֹא צוֹרְכָה דְּלֹא[72] מִלְוָה שֶׁהִיא נַעֲשֵׂית כַּפְרָנִית[73] גּוֹבָה. [כַּפְרָנִית שֶׁהִיא נַעֲשֵׂית מִלְוָה[74] גּוֹבָה בְּבֵינוֹנִית.

This is obvious: A loan that is disputed[75] is not remitted. A loan that was disputed but is now a [confirmed] loan, is remitted[76]. Rebbi Jeremiah asked: Is this also true for judgments? It is not necessary to say that a loan that was disputed can be collected[77]. A disputed loan turned into a [confirmed] loan is collected from property of average quality[76].

71 Reading of the Rome ms. Leyden and Venice: אם

72 The last three words are only here, not in the parallel *Gittin* 5:1 (fol. 46c).

73 From the text in *Gittin*; here: מלוה

74 From the text in *Gittin*; missing in the text here.

75 The debtor claims he does not owe the lender. As long as the case is not settled in court, everything is suspended. The loan cannot be remitted in the Sabbatical because it cannot be collected. If judgment is given for the lender, the judgment is a court document which is not subject to remission.

76 If, after the court established the validity of the loan, the lender does not insist on immediate payment, the loan regains its original status.

77 After a court judgment on a disputed loan, the debt can be collected after the Sabbatical.

הַמַּלְוֶה עַל הַמַּשְׁכּוֹן שְׁמוּאֵל אָמַר אֲפִילוּ עַל הַמַּחַט. וַאֲשֶׁר יִהְיֶה לְךָ אֶת אָחִיךָ תַּשְׁמֵט יָדֶיךָ. פְּרָט לְמָה שֶׁיֵּשׁ לְאָחִיךָ תַּחַת יָדֶיךָ. וַאֲשֶׁר יִהְיֶה לְךָ אֶת אָחִיךָ תַּשְׁמֵט יָדֶיךָ וְלֹא הַמּוֹסֵר שְׁטָרוֹתָיו לְבֵית דִּין.

"If somebody makes a loan on a pledge", Samuel says, even on a needle[78]. (*Deut.* 15:3): "What you have on your brother you shall release;"

that excludes your brother's [property] in your hand. "What you have on your brother you shall release," which excludes one who hands over his documents to the court[79].

78   This parallels the statement of Samuel in Babli *Šebuot* 43b: "If somebody gave a loan of 1000 tetradrachmas and took as pledge the handle of a sickle, if he lost the handle he lost the 1000 tetradrachmas." The

Babli disagrees in practice and rules that the sum not remitted in the Sabbatical is equal to the value of the pledge.

79   The last two sentences are also in *Sifri Deut.* 113.

(fol. 39b) **משנה ג:** פְּרוֹזְבּוֹל אֵינוֹ מְשַׁמֵּט. זֶה אֶחָד מִן הַדְּבָרִים שֶׁהִתְקִין הִלֵּל הַזָּקֵן כְּשֶׁרָאָה שֶׁנִּמְנְעוּ הָעָם מִלְּהַלְווֹת זֶה אֶת זֶה וְעוֹבְרִין עַל מַה שֶּׁכָּתוּב בַּתּוֹרָה שֶׁנֶּאֱמַר הִשָּׁמֶר לְךָ פֶּן יִהְיֶה דָבָר בִּלְבָבְךָ בְלִיַּעַל לֵאמוֹר וגו'. הִתְקִין הִלֵּל פְּרוֹזְבּוֹל.

Mishnah 3: A *prozbol*[80] does not remit. This is one of the ordinances of Hillel the elder. When he saw that the people refrained from giving loans to one another and transgressed what is written in the Torah, as it is said (*Deut.* 15:9): "Guard yourself, lest there be in your heart an unworthy thought saying,[67] etc.", he instituted the *prozbol*.

80   A Greek legal term, προσβολή, "document recording the knocking down of a lot to a purchaser", cf. *Peah* Chapter 3, Note 120. By Mishnah 2, instruments of indebtedness delivered to the court for collection are not

subject to remission. Hillel substituted for actual delivery a document declaring the intent of the creditor to transfer his documents to the authority of the court without actually delivering them.

(fol. 39c) **הלכה ג:** מִיכָּן סָמְכוּ לִפְרוֹזְבּוֹל שֶׁהוּא מִן הַתּוֹרָה. וּפְרוֹזְבּוֹל דְּבַר תּוֹרָה. כְּשֶׁהִתְקִין הִלֵּל סָמְכוּהוּ לִדְבַר תּוֹרָה.

Halakhah 3: From here[81] they supported the notion that *prozbol* is from the Torah. But is *prozbol* from the Torah[82]? When Hillel instituted it, they supported it from words of the Torah.

81   The sentence just preceding the Mishnah, giving biblical support to the rule that instruments of indebtedness in the possession of the court are not subject to remission.

82   Since the documents are not delivered, *prozbol* cannot be biblical.

אָמַר רִבִּי חוּנָא קַשְׁיָיתָהּ קוֹמֵי רִבִּי יַעֲקֹב בַּר אָחָא כְּמָאן דְּאָמַר מַעְשְׂרוֹת [מִדִּבְרֵיהֶם נִיחָא שֶׁיִּתַּקֵן הִלֵּל פְּרוֹזְבּוֹל בְּרַם מָאן דְּאָמַר מַעְשְׂרוֹת][83] מִדְּבַר תּוֹרָה. וְהִלֵּל מַתְקִין עַל דְּבַר תּוֹרָה. אָמַר רִבִּי יוֹסֵי וְכִי מִשָּׁעָה שֶׁגָּלוּ יִשְׂרָאֵל לְבָבֶל לֹא נִפְטְרוּ מִן הַמִּצְוֹת הַתְּלוּיוֹת בָּאָרֶץ וְהַשְׁמֵט כְּסָפִים נוֹהֵג בֵּין בָּאָרֶץ בֵּין בְּחוּצָה לָאָרֶץ דְּבַר תּוֹרָה [מִשּׁוּם דְּחוֹבַת הַגּוּף הֵן].[83] חָזַר רִבִּי יוֹסֵי וְאָמַר וְזֶה דְּבַר הַשְׁמִיטָה שָׁמוֹט בְּשָׁעָה שֶׁהַשְׁמִיטָה נוֹהֶגֶת דְּבַר תּוֹרָה הַשְׁמֵט כְּסָפִים נוֹהֵג בֵּין בָּאָרֶץ בֵּין בְּחוּצָה לָאָרֶץ דְּבַר תּוֹרָה. וּבְשָׁעָה שֶׁהַשְׁמִיטָה נוֹהֶגֶת מִדִּבְרֵיהֶן הַשְׁמֵט כְּסָפִים נוֹהֶגֶת בֵּין בָּאָרֶץ בֵּין בְּחוּצָה לָאָרֶץ מִדִּבְרֵיהֶם. תַּמָּן אָמְרִין אֲפִילוּ כְּמָאן דְּאָמַר מַעְשְׂרוֹת דְּבַר תּוֹרָה מוֹדֶה בַשְּׁמִיטָה שֶׁהִיא מִדִּבְרֵיהֶן. דְּתַנֵּי וְזֶה דְּבַר הַשְּׁמִיטָה שָׁמוֹט. רִבִּי אוֹמֵר שְׁנֵי שְׁמִיטִין הַלָּלוּ שְׁמִיטָה וְיוֹבֵל. בְּשָׁעָה שֶׁהַיּוֹבֵל נוֹהֵג שְׁמִיטָה נוֹהֶגֶת דְּבַר תּוֹרָה. פָּסְקוּ יוֹבֵילוֹת שְׁמִיטָה נוֹהֶגֶת מִדִּבְרֵיהֶן. אֵימָתַי פָּסְקוּ יוֹבֵילוֹת [כָּל־][83] יוֹשְׁבֶיהָ. בִּזְמַן שֶׁיּוֹשְׁבֶיהָ עָלֶיהָ לֹא בִזְמַן שֶׁגָּלוּ מִתּוֹכָהּ. הָיוּ עָלֶיהָ אֲבָל הָיוּ מְעוּרְבָּבִין שֵׁבֶט יְהוּדָה בְּבִנְיָמִין וְשֵׁבֶט בְּנְיָמִין בִּיהוּדָה יָכוֹל יְהוּ הַיּוֹבְלוֹת נוֹהֲגִין. תַּלְמוּד לוֹמַר יוֹשְׁבֶיהָ לְכָל־יוֹשְׁבֶיהָ נִמְצֵאתָ אוֹמֵר כֵּיוָן שֶׁגָּלוּ שֵׁבֶט רְאוּבֵן וְגָד וַחֲצִי שֵׁבֶט הַמְּנַשֶּׁה בָּטְלוּ הַיּוֹבְלוֹת.

Rebbi Huna said, I asked before Rebbi Jacob ben Aḥa: Following him who says tithes [are from their words, it is understandable that Hillel instituted *prozbol*. But following him who says tithes] are from the Torah, does Hillel institute anything against the words of the Torah[84]? Rebbi Yose said, from the moment that Israel was exiled to Babylonia, did they not become free from all commandments connected with the Land, but the remission of debts applies both in the Land and outside the Land from the words of the Torah [because it is an obligation of the person[85]]? Rebbi Yose turned and said, (*Deut.* 15:2) "this is the word of the abandonment, remit" as long as abandonment[86] is followed as a word of the Torah, remission of debts applies both in the Land and outside the Land from the words of the Torah, but when abandonment is followed as their word, remission of debts applies both in the Land and outside the Land from their word. There[87], they say that even one who holds that tithes are from the Torah will hold that the Sabbatical is from their word. As we have stated (*Deut.* 15:2): "this is the word of the remission, remit!" Rebbi says, these two remissions are the Sabbatical and the Jubilee. As long as the Jubilee is operative, the Sabbatical is from words of the Torah. If the Jubilees are abolished, the Sabbatical is operative from their words. When were the Jubilees abolished? (*Lev.* 25:10) "[All its] inhabitants.[88]" In the time when its inhabitants lived on it, not when they went into exile. If they lived on it but intermingled, the tribe of Judah in Benjamin, and the tribe of Benjamin in Judah, I could think that the Jubilee is operative. The verse mentions its inhabitants, "All its inhabitants;" you find that when the tribes of Reuben, Gad, and half the tribe of Manasseh went into exile, the Jubilees were disestablished.

83   The clauses in brackets are from the Rome ms., missing in Leyden ms., Venice and modern prints.

84   The disagreement about tithes is between R. Yose ben R. Ḥanina and R. Eleazar in Halakhah 6:1 (Note 11). "Their words" are the rabbinic institutions.

85   While this may be the correct reason, the language is Babylonian rabbinic Hebrew; the insert probably is a gloss that found its way into the text. In *Sifry Deut.* 111, the reason given is not this logical argument but the verse (*Deut.* 15:2): "this is the word of the remission: every creditor remit what is in his hand, what he loaned to his fellow; he shall not press his fellow *because a remission was declared for the Eternal.*" Since God is Lord over the universe, remission is applicable everywhere in the universe.

86   Agricultural Sabbatical.

87   Babylonia. The Babli (*Giṭṭin* 36a) quotes only Rebbi's statement below. The commentators of the Babli assume that the majority of rabbis oppose Rebbi. There seems to be no basis for that assumption. The sketchy treatment of the subject in the Babli is explained by Meïri (*Magen Avot*, ed. Last, London 1909, Chap. 15.).

88   From here to the end of the Halakhah, the argument is also in Babli *Arakhin* 32b and *Sifra Behar Pereq* 2(3). The verse reads: "You shall sanctify the fiftieth year and call freedom for all its inhabitants, a Jubilee it shall be for you so that everybody return to his ancestral land, everybody return to his family." "Ancestral land" is the plot given to the family in the original distribution after the conquest. It follows that there can be no Jubilee if the distribution of land by Joshua is no longer known.

(fol. 39b) **משנה ד**: זֶהוּ גוּפוֹ שֶׁל פְּרוֹזְבּוֹל מוֹסֵר אֲנִי לָכֶם אִישׁ פְּלוֹנִי וּפְלוֹנִי הַדַּיָּנִים שֶׁבְּמָקוֹם פְּלוֹנִי שֶׁכָּל־חוֹב שֶׁיֵּשׁ לִי שֶׁאֶגְבֶּנּוּ כָּל־זְמַן שֶׁאֶרְצֶה וְהַדַּיָּנִים חוֹתְמִין לְמַטָּן אוֹ הָעֵדִים.

Mishnah 4: This is the essence[89] of *prozbol*: I declare before you, judges X and Y at place Z, that I shall collect any debt due me any time I wish. The judges sign at the bottom or the witnesses.

89   In addition, all legal formalism   incorporated into the *prozbol*.
that makes a document valid must be

הלכה ד: רִבִּי חִזְקִיָּה בְּשֵׁם רִבִּי יִרְמְיָה וַאֲפִילוּ נְתוּנִּין בְּרוֹמֵי. (fol. 39c)

Halakhah 4: Rebbi Ḥizqiah in the name of Rebbi Jeremiah: Even if
they are in Rome[90].

90   It is possible to write a *prozbol*   This implies that *prozbol* and the
on the names of judges at another   related documents do not have to be
place (who probably will never know   deposited with any court.
about the existence of this *prozbol*.)

רִבִּי בָּא בְשֵׁם רַבָּנִין דְּתַמָּן שְׁלֹשָׁה שֶׁדָּנוּ וּמֵת אֶחָד מֵהֶן חוֹתְמִין בִּשְׁנַיִם וְאָמַר אַף
עַל פִּי שֶׁחָתַמְנוּ בִשְׁנָיִם דָּנַנוּ בִשְׁלֹשָׁה. אָמַר רִבִּי חַגַּיי מַתְנִיתִין אָמַר כֵּן וְהַדַּייָנִים
חוֹתְמִין לְמַטָּה אוֹ הָעֵדִים. וּלְמֵידִין מִידַּת הַדִּין מִפְּרוֹזְבּוּל. (fol. 39d) אַשְׁכָּח תַּנֵּי
הוּא מִידַּת הַדִּין לָמַד מִפְּרוֹזְבּוּל.

Rebbi Abba in the name of the rabbis there[91]: If three sat in judgment
and one of them died, two sign and note: Even though we are two who
sign, we were three in judging. Rebbi Ḥaggai said, our Mishnah implies
this: "The judges sign at the bottom or the witnesses." Does one learn
court documents from *prozbol*? It was found stated: This about court
documents was learned from the rules of *prozbol*.

91   In the Babli (*Ketubot* 22a), this   Mishnah mentions only two judges and
is also a statement of Rebbi Abba (in   equates the signatures of judges and
Babylonian Aramaic). A court usually   witnesses. Since witnesses must always
is composed of three judges (Mishnah   be two, it follows that there is a
Sanhedrin 1:1); in the opinion of the   situation in which the signature of two
majority of authorities, a court of two   judges is valid even for those who
judges is incompetent. Now the   disallow a court of two judges.

אֵין לוֹ קַרְקַע וּלְחַיָּיבִין לוֹ קַרְקַע כּוֹתְבִין כּוֹתְבִין לוֹ פְּרוֹזְבּוֹל. הֵיךְ עֲבִידָא רְאוּבֵן חַיָּיב לְשִׁמְעוֹן וְלֵוִי חַיָּיב לִרְאוּבֵן. רְאוּבֵן אֵין לוֹ קַרְקַע וְלֵוִי יֶשׁ לוֹ קַרְקַע כּוֹתְבִין לְשִׁמְעוֹן עַל נְכָסָיו שֶׁל לֵוִי.

If he has no real estate but his debtors have real estate, one writes a *prozbol* for him[92]. How is that done? Ruben owes Simeon and Levi owes Ruben. Ruben has no real estate, Levi has real estate. One writes for Simeon on the properties of Levi.

92   It is stated in Mishnaiot 6 and *Peah* 3:8 that *prozbol* can be written only on the basis of real estate; the possession of one square inch is enough. In Tosephta *Ševi'it* 8:9 it is made clear that the *debtor* must have real estate (to give the *prozbol* a status similar to a mortgage which is not remitted.) In Tosephta 8:8, the anonymous majority holds that in a chain of debtors, only the creditor of a debtor with real estate may write a *prozbol* but Rabban Simeon ben Gamliel asserts that the real estate of one of the debtors is good for all. The Yerushalmi here and a similar Babli (*Giṭṭin* 37a) follow Rabban Simeon ben Gamliel without mentioning his name.

(fol. 39b) **מִשְׁנָה ה**: פְּרוֹזְבּוֹל הַמּוּקְדָּם כָּשֵׁר וְהַמְאוּחָר פָּסוּל. שְׁטָרֵי חוֹב הַמּוּקְדָּמִין פְּסוּלִין וְהַמְאוּחָרִין כְּשֵׁרִין. אֶחָד לֹוֶה מֵחֲמִשָּׁה כּוֹתְבִין פְּרוֹזְבּוֹל לְכָל־אֶחָד וְאֶחָד. חֲמִשָּׁה לֹוִין מִן אֶחָד אֵינוֹ כוֹתֵב אֶלָּא פְּרוֹזְבּוֹל אֶחָד לְכוּלָּן.

Mishnah 5: A predated *prozbol* is valid, postdated it is invalid. Predated documents of indebtedness are invalid, postdated they are valid. If one person borrows from five, one writes a *prozbol* for each single [creditor]. If five persons borrow from one, he writes only one *prozbol* for all of them.

(fol. 39d) **הלכה ח**: פְּרוֹזְבּוֹל הַמּוּקְדָּם כָּשֵׁר מִפְּנֵי שֶׁהוּא מוֹרַע כּוֹחוֹ. וְהַמְאוּחָר פָּסוּל מִפְּנֵי שֶׁמְּיַפֶּה כּוֹחוֹ. שְׁטָרֵי חוֹב הַמּוּקְדָּמִין פְּסוּלִין מִפְּנֵי שֶׁמְּיַפֶּה כֹּחָן. וְהַמְאוּחָרִין כְּשֵׁרִין מִפְּנֵי שֶׁהוּא מֵירַע כּוֹחָן.

Halakhah 4: "A predated *prozbol* is valid" because he diminishes its power, but "postdated it is invalid" because he increases its power[93]. "Predated documents of indebtedness are invalid" because he increases their power, but "postdated they are valid" because he diminishes their power[94].

93   Since a *prozbol* is a declaration that all documents in the hand of the creditor have to be considered as delivered to the court, predating the *prozbol* does not increase the number of documents covered, but postdating may increase their number. In the latter case, the testimony of the witnesses affixed to the document would be perjured.

94   As explained in Note 2, a document of indebtedness creates a lien on the real estate of the debtor. If the debtor sells any of his real estate after the document has been created, the lien is not removed. In case of nonpayment, the creditor can foreclose the parcel that was sold and let the buyer then try to recoup his money from the seller. Predating a document of indebtedness therefore might create a false claim to parcels sold before the document was executed; such a document must be invalid. But postdating the document might protect a buyer from the creditor; this is valid.

מִי מֵידַע שִׁמְעוֹן בַּר בָּא בְּשֵׁם רִבִּי יוֹחָנָן הַחֲתוּמִים בַּשְׁטָר. לֹא כֵן אָמַר רִבִּי שִׁמְעוֹן בֶּן לָקִישׁ עָשׂוּ דִּבְרֵי הַחֲתוּמִים כְּמִי שֶׁנֶּחְקְרָה עֵידוּתָן בְּבֵית דִּין. תַּמָּן אוֹתָן כְּשֶׁאָמְרוּ לֹא חָתַמְנוּ כָּל־עִיקָּר. בְּרַם הָכָא אָמְרֵי עַל זֶה חָתַמְנוּ וְלֹא חָתַמְנוּ עַל זֶה.

Who notifies[95]? Simeon bar Abba in the name of Rebbi Johanan: the signatories of the document. But did not Rebbi Simeon ben Laqish say, they treated the statement of the signatories of a document as if their testimony had been cross-examined by the court[96]? There[97], it is about those who would say: We did not sign at all. But here they say, on this we signed, on that we did not sign.

95 Who may inform that a *prozbol* or document is pre- or postdated? The Rome ms. reads מודע which might be the more correct form.

96 Since in Jewish law, a witness may not change his testimony without disqualifying himself, a witness to a document is not admitted to testify to the falsity of the document unless he admits to perjury. Hence, testimony that a *prozbol* was predated or a financial document postdated can never be given by any witness to the

document if genuinness of the signature of the witness is established from another source. [The statement of R. Simeon ben Laqish is discussed, in the same sense, in Babli *Ketubot* 18b, *Giṭṭin* 3a.]

97 The rule of R. Simeon ben Laqish only applies if the authenticity of the document is in question. But for the *prozbol* they could assert that they signed for the fact of the *prozbol* but not the date.

רִבִּי יוֹחָנָן אָמַר פְּסוּלִין מַמָּשׁ. רִבִּי שִׁמְעוֹן בֶּן לָקִישׁ אָמַר אֵינוֹ מוֹנֶה אֶלָּא מִשְׁעַת הַכְּתָב. וְהָתַנֵּי פְּרוֹזְבּוֹל בֵּין מוּקְדָּם בֵּין מְאוּחָר כָּשֵׁר וְאֵינוֹ מוֹנֶה אֶלָּא מִשְׁעַת הַכְּתָב. אִם אוֹמֵר אַתְּ כֵּן בִּשְׁטָרוֹת מַה בֵּין פְּרוֹזְבּוֹל מַה בֵּין שְׁטָר.

Rebbi Joḥanan said, they are really invalid[98]. Rebbi Simeon ben Laqish said, he only counts from the time of writing. But did we not state: "A *prozbol* is valid, whether predated or postdated, but it only counts from the time of writing"? If you assert this for financial documents, what is the difference between a *prozbol* and a financial document[99]?

98 Predated documents of indebtedness.

99 Since the Mishnah stated that the rules of *prozbol* and debt docu-

ments are opposites, it is impossible to accept R. Simeon ben Laqish's position

for debt documents and probably also the *baraita* quoted.

שְׁטָר שֶׁזְּמַנּוֹ כָּתוּב בְּשַׁבָּת אוֹ בַּעֲשָׂרָה בְּתִשְׁרֵי. רִבִּי יוּדָה מַכְשִׁיר וְרִבִּי יוֹסֵי פּוֹסֵל. אָמַר לוֹ רִבִּי יוּדָה מַעֲשֶׂה בָּא לְפָנֶיךָ בְּצִיפּוֹרִי וְהִכְשַׁרְתָּה. אָמַר לוֹ אֲנִי לֹא הִכְשַׁרְתִּי וְאִם הִכְשַׁרְתִּי הִכְשַׁרְתִּי. חָוֹון בָּעֵיי מֵימַר מָאן דְּאָמַר פָּסוּל מִשּׁוּם מְאוּחָר. וּמָאן דְּאָמַר כָּשֵׁר מִשּׁוּם מוּקְדָּם אֶלָּא מָאן דְּאָמַר פָּסוּל מִשּׁוּם זִיּוּף.

"A document dated on a Sabbath or on the Tenth of Tishrē, Rebbi Jehudah declares it valid and Rebbi Yose invalid. Rebbi Jehudah said to him, a case came before you in Sepphoris and you declared it valid. He said to him, I did not declare it valid, but if I did it, I did it.[100]" They wanted to say that he who holds it invalid [does so] because it[101] might be later, and he who holds it valid [does so] because it might be earlier[102]; but he who holds it invalid [does so] because it might be forged[103].

100   Tosephta *Makkot* 1:3, a slightly different version Babli *Baba Batra* 171a. The date normally is written by the day of the month; if one checks one may find that the date given fell on a Sabbath. In the case of the Day of Atonement, one must assume that the date is given in terms of a Gentile calendar.

101   The writing of the document, which makes the document predated. [The commentators all switch "later" and "earlier" in this statement, to adapt the language to that of the Mishnah. But the testimony of the two mss.

forbids this emendation.]

102   And the document would be postdated.

103   R. Yose also will agree that a document dated on a Sabbath or Day of Atonement, if genuine, probably is postdated and valid. He only states that the impossible date is *prima facie* evidence to declare the document forged, but he is open to proof that the document is genuine. This explains his equanimity when confronted with an apparent contradiction between his action and his formal statement. He will hold the document forged unless

presented with evidence to the
contrary. (The different interpretation
of the Babli does not explain R. Yose's

agreement with the statement of R.
Jehudah.)

(fol. 39b) **משנה ו**: אֵין כּוֹתְבִין פְּרוֹזְבוֹל אֶלָּא עַל הַקַּרְקַע אִם אֵין לוֹ מְזַכֶּה הוּא
בְּתוֹךְ שָׂדֵהוּ כָּל־שֶׁהוּא. הָיְתָה לוֹ שָׂדֶה מְמוּשְׁכֶּנֶת בָּעִיר כּוֹתְבִין עָלֶיהָ פְּרוֹזְבוֹל.
רְבִּי חוּצְפִּית אוֹמֵר כּוֹתְבִין לְאָדָם עַל נִכְסֵי אִשְׁתּוֹ. וְלִיתוֹמִין עַל נִכְסֵי
אָפִּיטְרוֹפִּין.

Mishnah 6: One writes *prozbol* only on the basis of real estate. If
he[104] has none, [the other party] gives him the right to a minute area of
their field. If he had a field mortgaged[105] in town, one writes a *prozbol*
on it. Rebbi Ḥuẓpit says, one writes for a man on his wife's properties[106]
and for orphans on those of the guardians[107].

104   It was shown in Note 92 that
one of his debtors must have real estate
for a creditor's *prozbol*.

105   Even if the loan is paid back in
instalments, that for a fixed number of
terms the creditor works the field and
takes all its yield, it remains the
property of the debtor.

106   Even if this is separate property,
not dowry which becomes the husband's property for the duration of the
marriage.

107   Greek ἐπίτροπος "guardian,
attorney". In the opinion of the Babli
(*Giṭṭin* 37a), documented claims of
minor orphans are always under the
supervision of the court, have the status
of court documents, and do not need
prozbol. The Babli is therefore obliged
to interpret the Mishnah as speaking of
debts incurred by the guardians for the
living expenses of the orphans. This
does not seem to be the position of the
Yerushalmi.

הלכה ו: רַב אָמַר וְהוּא שֶׁיְּהֵא קַרְקַע לְמַלְוֶה וּלְלֹוֶה. וְרִבִּי יוֹחָנָן אָמַר(fol. 39d)
לְמַלְוֶה אַף עַל פִּי שֶׁאֵין לְלֹוֶה לְלֹוֶה אַף עַל פִּי שֶׁאֵין לְמַלְוֶה. אֵין לוֹ קַרְקַע
וּלְחַיָּיבִין קַרְקַע כּוֹתְבִין לוֹ פְּרוֹזְבּוּל. רִבִּי בָּא בְשֵׁם רַב מִי שֶׁאֵין לוֹ אֶלָא קֶלַח
אֶחָד בְּתוֹךְ שָׂדֵהוּ כּוֹתְבִין לוֹ פְּרוֹזְבּוּל. וְהָתַנֵּי הַשּׁוּתָפִין וְהָאֲרִיסִין וְהָאֲפִּיטְרוֹפִּין
אֵין לָהֶן פְּרוֹזְבּוּל. אָמְרִין תַּמָּן כָּל־קֶלַח וְקֶלַח שֶׁל שׁוּתָפוּת הוּא בְּרַם הָכָא הוּא
שֶׁלוֹ.

Halakhah 6: Rav said, only if both lender and borrower have real
estate. But Rebbi Joḥanan says, if the creditor does but not the
borrower[108], or the borrower but not the lender[109]. If he has no real
estate but one who owes him[110] has real estate then one writes him a
prozbol. Rebbi Abba in the name of Rav: Even if he has only one stalk
in a field, one writes him a *prozbol*. But did we not state: Partners,
sharecroppers, and guardians[111] have no *prozbol*? They say, there each
single stalk is property of the partnership but here it is his.

108   Then the lender can give a
borrower a stalk in his field and write
the *prozbol*.

109   This is the original institution of
prozbol.

110   Only one of the many debtors

for whom the *prozbol* will be used, cf.
Note 92.

111   Neither of them is the sole
owner of the property administered by
him.

מָהוּ לִכְתּוֹב לָאֲפִּיטְרוֹפִּין עַל נִכְסֵי יְתוֹמִין נִישְׁמְעִינָהּ מִן הָדָא כּוֹתְבִין לְאִישׁ עַל
נִכְסֵי אִשְׁתּוֹ. מָהוּ לִכְתּוֹב לְאִשָּׁה עַל נִכְסֵי בַּעֲלָהּ נִישְׁמְעִינָהּ מִן הָדָא וְכֵן
לִיתוֹמִין עַל נִכְסֵי אֲפִּיטְרוֹפִּין.

May one write for a guardian based on the orphans' real estate? Let us
hear it from the following: "One writes for a husband on his wife's
properties[112]". May one write for a woman on her husband's prop

erties[113]? Let us hear it from the following: "And for orphans on those of the guardians".

112   The standard case that the husband administers his wife's separate property is parallel to the guardians administering the orphans' properties.

113   This must refer to a case where the wife gives up her right to be supported by her husband for the right to earn her own separate money. If the guardian administers the property of the landless orphans, then the Mishnah permits a *prozbol* purely on the basis of his being trustee for others as well as property owner for himself. Similarly, we should admit the possibility of *prozbol* simply by the marriage of the lender to a property owner.

(fol. 39b) **מִשְׁנָה ז:** כַּוֶּרֶת דְּבוֹרִים. רִבִּי אֱלִיעֶזֶר אוֹמֵר הֲרֵי הִיא כְקַרְקַע וְכוֹתְבִין עָלֶיהָ פְּרוֹזְבּוֹל וְאֵינָהּ מְקַבֶּלֶת טוּמְאָה בִמְקוֹמָהּ. וְהָרוֹדֶה מִמֶּנָּה בַּשַּׁבָּת חַיָּב. וַחֲכָמִים אוֹמְרִין אֵינָהּ כְקַרְקַע וְאֵין כּוֹתְבִין עָלֶיהָ פְּרוֹזְבּוֹל וּמְקַבֶּלֶת טוּמְאָה בִמְקוֹמָהּ. וְהָרוֹדֶה מִמֶּנָּה בַּשַּׁבָּת פָּטוּר. הַמַּחֲזִיר חוֹב בַּשְּׁבִיעִית אוֹמֵר לוֹ מְשַׁמֵּט אֲנִי. אִם אָמַר לוֹ אַף עַל פִּי כֵן יְקַבֵּל הֵימֶינּוּ שֶׁנֶּאֱמַר וְזֶה דְּבַר הַשְּׁמִיטָה.

Mishnah 7: A bee hive. Rebbi Eliezer says, it is like real estate: one may write a *prozbol* on it, it is not subject to impurity in its place[114], and somebody who takes honey from it on the Sabbath is guilty[115]. But the Sages say, it is not like real estate, one may not write a *prozbol* on it, it is subject to impurity in its place, and somebody who takes honey from it on the Sabbath is not sanctionable[116].

If somebody returns a debt in the Sabbatical, he [the lender] says to him: "I am remitting." If he [the borrower] says "anyway", he [the lender] should accept it, for it is said (*Deut.* 15:2): "This is the word of remission[117]".

114   No real estate and nothing permanently connected to the ground can become impure.

115   Removing food from the ground is the definition of harvesting.

116   While it is not permitted outright, there is no punishment for the action since no biblical Sabbath prohibition has been violated. The first part of the Mishnah is also in *Uqeẓin* 3:10.

117   Once the word "remission" has been uttered, duty has been fulfilled.

(fol. 39d) **הלכה ז**: רְבִּי אַבָּהוּ בְשֵׁם רְבִּי שִׁמְעוֹן בֶּן לָקִישׁ טַעֲמָא דְרְבִּי אֱלִיעֶזֶר וַיָּבֹא הָעָם אֶל הַיַּעַר וְהִנֵּה הֶלֶךְ דְּבָשׁ. מַה אַתְּ שְׁמַע מִינָהּ. אָמַר רְבִּי מָנָא חוֹרְשָׁא מַפִּיק דְּבָשׁ. וְאִילּוּ אָמַר וַיִּטְבּוֹל אוֹתָהּ בְּיַעֲרַת הַדְּבָשׁ יָאוּת. רְבִּי יוֹסֵי בֵּי רְבִּי בּוּן בְּשֵׁם רְבִּי שִׁמְעוֹן בֶּן לָקִישׁ אָמַר שְׁמְעָהּ יַתָּהּ כֵּן וַיִּטְבּוֹל אוֹתָהּ בְּיַעֲרַת הַדְּבָשׁ.

Halakhah 7: Rebbi Abbahu in the name of Rebbi Simeon ben Laqish: The reason of Rebbi Eliezer (*1S.* 14:26): "The people came to the forest and behold, there was a flow of honey." What do you understand from this? Rebbi Mana said, the thicket produced honey. If he had said from (*1S.* 14:27): "He dipped it into the forest of honey", it would have been better. Rebbi Yose ben Rebbi Abun said in the name of Rebbi Simeon ben Laqish: He really understood it from (*1S.* 14:27): "He dipped it into the forest of honey[118]."

118   Since both יער "forest, bush country" and יערה "honeycomb" are based on the root وعر, "to have a rough surface", the words are identified.

מַה נָן קַיָּימִין אִם בִּמְחוּבֶּרֶת לְקַרְקַע כָּל־עַמָּא מוֹדֵיי שֶׁהִיא כְּקַרְקַע אִם בִּנְתוּנָה
עַל גַּבֵּי שְׁתֵּי יְתֵידוֹת כָּל־עַמָּא מוֹדֵיי שֶׁאֵינָן כְּקַרְקַע אֶלָּא כִּי נָן קַיָּימִין בְּמוּנַחַת
עַל גַּבֵּי קַרְקַע. וְאַתְיָא כַּיי דָאמַר רִבִּי זְעִירָא בְּשֵׁם רִבִּי יִרְמְיָה כּוֹתְבִין פְּרוֹזְבּוֹל
עַל מְקוֹמוֹ שֶׁל תַּנּוּר וְעַל מְקוֹמָהּ שֶׁל כִּירָה. רִבִּי חִיָּיא בַּר אָדָא אָמַר אַף עַל
מְקוֹמוֹ שֶׁל נֵר.

Where do we hold[119]? If it is connected to the ground, everybody
agrees that it belongs to the ground. If it is on two bars, everybody agrees
that it is not like ground. But where we hold is if it rests on the
ground[120]. It compares to what Rebbi Zeïra said in the name of Rebbi
Jeremiah: One writes a *prozbol* on the space for an oven, also on the
space for a hearth[121]. Rebbi Ḥiyya bar Ada said, also on the space for a
lamp.

119 What is the disagreement between R. Eliezer and the Sages?
120 The beehive sits on the ground
but is not fastened to it.
121 Oven and hearth are movable
clay vessels that sit on the ground without being fastened. The Babli (*Giṭṭin*
37a) notes that the statement is needed
only if the ground on which the oven
sits is rented, not owned.

אַף בְּפַת כֵּן מַחְלוֹקֶת רִבִּי אֱלִיעֶזֶר וַחֲכָמִים. דְּבַשׁ גִּידּוּלֵי כַוֶּרֶת. פַּת אֵינוֹ
גִּידּוּלֵי תַנּוּר.

Is it also the same for the space for bread, is that the disagreement
between Rebbi Eliezer and the Sages? Honey is a product of the bee hive,
bread is not a product of the oven[122].

122 This refers to the statement that
for Rebbi Eliezer, taking honey from
the bee hive on the Sabbath is a
desecration of the Sabbath. It is
generally accepted that on the Sabbath
one may take bread from the oven if it
was fully baked before the Sabbath.
The question is, does Rebbi Eliezer

agree or does he disagree and for some reason his dissent was not considered in the rules of the Sabbath? He agrees that taking out the bread is not harvesting.

הַמַּחֲזִיר חוֹב בַּשְּׁבִיעִית וְאוֹמֵר לוֹ מְשַׁמֵּט אֲנִי רוּחַ חֲכָמִים נוֹחָה הֵימֶנּוּ. רַב הוּנָא אָמַר בְּשָׂפָה רָפָה. וְהַיָּמִין פְּשׁוּטָה לְקַבֵּל.

If somebody repays a debt in the Sabbatical even though he [the lender] says to him: "I am remitting," the Sages are pleased with him. Rav Huna said, he says it in a soft voice and his right hand is stretched out to receive.

(fol. 39b) **משנה ח**: כְּיוֹצֵא בּוֹ רוֹצֵחַ שֶׁגָּלָה לְעִיר מִקְלָט וְרָצוּ אַנְשֵׁי הָעִיר לְכַבְּדוֹ. יֹאמַר לָהֶן רוֹצֵחַ אֲנִי אָמְרוּ לוֹ אַף עַל פִּי כֵן יְקַבֵּל מֵהֶן שֶׁנֶּאֱמַר וְזֶה דְּבַר הָרוֹצֵחַ.

Mishnah 8: Similarly, a homicide exiled to a city of refuge whom the citizens of the town wanted to honor, should say to them: I am a homicide. If they tell him, anyway, he should accept it, for it is said (*Deut.* 19:4): "This is the word of a homicide."

(fol. 39d) **הלכה ח**: אָמַר רִבִּי יוֹסֵי הָדָא אָמְרָה בַּר נַשׁ דְּתַנֵּי חָדָא מֵיכְלָא וְהוּא אֲזַל לְאָתָר וְאִינּוּן מוֹקְרִין לֵיהּ בְּגִין תַּרְתֵּיי צָרִיךְ מֵימַר לוֹן אֲנָא חָדָא מֵיכְלָא אֲנָא חָכַם.

Halakhah 8: Rebbi Yose said, this means that if a person who knows one collection[123] goes to a place and they honor him for two, he has to tell them: "I know one collection."

123   He has memorized and under-   statements (usually in the feminine,
stands one collection of Tannatitic   מְכִילְתָא).

(fol. 39b) **משנה ט**: הַמַּחֲזִיר חוֹב בַּשְּׁבִיעִית רוּחַ חֲכָמִים נוֹחָה הֵימֶנּוּ. הַלֹוֶה מִן
הַגֵּר שֶׁנִּתְגַּיְּירוּ בָנָיו עִמּוֹ לֹא יַחֲזִיר לְבָנָיו וְאִם הֶחֱזִיר רוּחַ חֲכָמִים נוֹחָה הֵימֶנּוּ.
כָּל־הַמִּיטַלְטְלִין נִקְנִין בִּמְשִׁיכָה וְכָל־הַמְקַיֵּים אֶת דְּבָרוֹ רוּחַ חֲכָמִים נוֹחָה
הֵימֶנּוּ.

Mishnah 9: If somebody repays a debt in the Sabbatical, the Sages are
pleased with him. If somebody borrows from a convert whose sons
converted with him, he does not have to repay the sons but if he repaid,
the Sages are pleased with him[124]. Movables are acquired only by being
drawn close, but the Sages are pleased with everybody who keeps his
word[125].

124   This is the text in all Mishnah   Gerondi in his commentary to Alfassi
mss., whether Palestinian, Babylonian,   (*Qiddušin* #596): Since a convert is
or Maimonidean traditions. However,   like a newborn for Jewish law, the
the Babli (*Qiddušin* 17b/18a) quotes   children converting with him are not
the Mishnah in the form "the Sages are   legally his Jewish children and the law
displeased with him," and the text here,   will not force the debtor to pay after
"the Sages are pleased with him," is   the lender's death. However, the
given only as a *baraita*. The meaning   children are his own children and not
of the distinctions made in the Babli is   to pay the sons after their father's
not clear; therefore, Maimonides omits   death is reprehensible. If the convert
the rule in his Code. The only coherent   has children after his conversion, they
explanation of the Mishnah is that   are his Jewish children and all laws of
given by Rabbi Isaac in Tosaphot   inheritance apply. The only problem
(*Qiddušin* 18a, s. v. כאן) and R. Nissim

arises if his pregnant wife converted with him. The Babli notes that in such a case, the Sages are displeased with any repayment to the child born after conversion. The reason given by the commentators is that the child is Jewish by birth; if the laws of inheritance did apply one would conclude that the child is legally a relative of his father and his older siblings. But the fact is that a Gentile father never can have a legal relationship with his child by a Jewish mother. For example, if a Jewish man marries his late father's other wife, this relationship is incestuous and the marriage is non-existent; the woman can marry another man without a divorce. But if the child conceived as a Gentile would marry one of his late father's wives other than his mother, while the marriage is not tolerated it is valid and would need a formal divorce. The Yerushalmi does not consider this unlikely case. [The *Šulḥan Arukh, Ḥošen Mišpaṭ* §127(2) decides otherwise, following what is reported in the name of Rashi.]

125   The rules of acquisition are spelled out in Mishnah *Qiddušin* 1:5. The rule is that by rabbinic decree, transfer of movable property can be accomplished only by actual or symbolic possession. This means that if the buyer pays before he takes possession, the seller is legally free to return the money and sell the goods to a higher bidder. However, doing so is morally reprehensible and the tricked buyer may ask the court to declare (Mishnah *Baba Meẕi'a* 4:2): "He Who made the generation of the Deluge and the generation of the Tower of Babylon pay, He will make him pay who does not stand by his word."

(fol. 39d) **הלכה ט**: רִבִּי לֶעְזָר אָמַר וּבִלְבַד לְבָנָיו. רִבִּי יוֹסֵי בָּעֵי מַהוּ וּבִלְבַד לְבָנָיו. אִם יֶשׁ לוֹ בָנִים יַחֲזִיר לְבָנָיו. אִם אֵין לוֹ בָנִים יַחֲזִיר לִבְנוֹתָיו. שֶׁלֹּא תֹאמַר הוֹאִיל וְאֵין יְרוּשַׁת הַגֵּר דְּבַר תּוֹרָה יַחֲזִיר לְבָנָיו כְּיוֹצֵא בוֹ מִי שֶׁמֵּת סוֹף מִשְׁפַּחְתּוֹ וְאֵין לוֹ יוֹרֵשׁ אֶלָּא אִמוֹ לֹא יַחֲזִיר וְאִם הֶחֱזִיר רוּחַ חֲכָמִים נוֹחָה הֵימֶנּוּ.

Halakhah 9: Rebbi Eleazar said, only to his sons. Rebbi Yose asked, what means "only to his sons?" If he has sons, one should return it to his sons. If he has no sons, one should return it to his daughters. That you should not say, since the inheritance of the convert is not settled in the Torah[126], he should return it to the children. Similarly, if somebody died who was the last of his family and he has no heir[127] except his mother one does not have to repay, but if the debtor repaid the Sages are pleased with him.

126 The laws of inheritance in *Num.* 27:6-11 appoint the sons as heirs; daughters are to inherit only if there are no sons. [However, by rabbinic decree unmarried daughters may claim a dowry before the inheritance can be distributed.] In the absence of children, the father's family inherits in ascending and descending order; the mother's family never inherits.

127 No relative on his father's side can be found after diligent search.

הַגַּזְלָן שֶׁעָשָׂה תְשׁוּבָה וּבִיקֵשׁ לְהַחֲזִיר אֶת הַגְּזֵילָה הַמְּקַבֵּל הֵימֶנּוּ אֵין רוּחַ חֲכָמִים נוֹחָה הֵימֶנּוּ.

[128]The robber who repents and wants to return what he robbed, if somebody accepts it from him, the Sages are displeased with him.

128 Tosephta 8:11 and Babli *Baba Qama* 94d, speaking of "the robber or one who lends on interest." The Babli restricts the advice only to those robbers and lenders who have no income whatsoever except robbery and interest, and probably refers only to Rebbi's time.

רִבִּי חִיָּיה בְּשֵׁם רִבִּי יוֹחָנָן אָמַר הַנּוֹשֵׂא וְהַנּוֹתֵן בִּדְבָרִים דְּאַתְּ אָמַר אֵין רוּחַ חֲכָמִים נוֹחָה הֵימֶנּוּ. וְזִימְנִין דְּאַתְּ אָמַר אֵין מוֹסְרִין אוֹתוֹ אֶלָּא לְמִי שֶׁפָּרַע.

Rebbi Ḥiyya in the name of Rebbi Joḥanan: If somebody trades in promises[129], there you say the Sages are displeased with him. But sometimes you say only[130] that one gives him up to "Him who made pay[125]".

129   Nothing has been written, no money has yet changed hands, no act of acquisition has been performed. (The text here follows the Rome ms., the Leyden ms. and Venice print have מניין דאת אמר.) Parallels are in Tosephta *Baba Meẓi'a* 3:14 (quoted in Babli *Baba Meẓi'a* 49a, where Rav disagrees and holds that one is free to change his mind) and Yerushalmi *Baba Meẓi'a* 4:3,4 (fol. 9c-d).

130   "Only" must be a scribal error since the curse by the court is more of a punishment than the displeasure of the Sages. The case here applies when money has changed hands but no act of acquisition has taken place.

רִבִּי זְעִירָא רִבִּי אַבָּהוּ בְּשֵׁם רִבִּי יוֹחָנָן הַנּוֹתֵן עִירָבוֹן טַבַּעַת לַחֲבֵירוֹ וּבִיקֵשׁ לַחֲזוֹר בּוֹ חוֹזֵר בּוֹ. רִבִּי זְעִירָא בָּעָא קוֹמֵי רִבִּי אַבָּהוּ זָהוּב אָמַר לֵיהּ טַבַּעַת. מַה בֵּין זָהוּב וּמַה בֵּין טַבַּעַת. זָהוּב דַּרְכּוֹ לְהִשְׁתַּנּוֹת טַבַּעַת בְּעֵיינָהּ הִיא.

Rebbi Zeïra, Rebbi Abbahu in the name of Rebbi Joḥanan: He who gives a ring as surety and wants to get out of the deal, may get out of the deal[131]. Rebbi Zeïra asked before Rebbi Abbahu: A gold coin? He said to him, a ring. What is the difference between a gold coin and a ring? Gold coins are exchanged[132], a ring remains as it is.

131   Since the ring is a deposit, taking the ring is not an act of acquisition. The Babli (*Baba Meẓi'a* 48b) disagrees and considers taking a pledge as an act of acquisition.

132   If payment is made, the depositor can reclaim only a gold coin of the same value, not the identical piece.

רִבִּי יַעֲקֹב בַּר זַבְדִּי רִבִּי אַבָּהוּ בְּשֵׁם רִבִּי יוֹחָנָן אָמַר לִיתֵּן מַתָּנָה לַחֲבֵירוֹ וּבִיקֵשׁ לַחֲזוֹר בּוֹ חוֹזֵר בּוֹ. קָם רִבִּי יוֹסֵי עִם רִבִּי יַעֲקֹב בַּר זַבְדִּי אָמַר לֵיהּ הָהֵן לָאו צֶדֶק וְהֵין צֶדֶק אָמַר בְּשָׁעָה שֶׁאָמַר הֵין שֶׁל צֶדֶק הָיָה. רַב פְּלִיג דְּרַב אָמַר כַּד אֲנָא אָמַר לִבְנֵי בֵיתִי לִיתֵּן מַתָּנָה לְבַר נַשׁ לֵינָה חָזַר בִּי. מַתְנִיתָא פְּלִיגָא עַל רַב אֵימָתַי אָמְרוּ הַמִּטַלְטְלִין נִקְנִין בִּמְשִׁיכָה בִּרְשׁוּת הָרַבִּים אוֹ בְחָצֵר שֶׁאֵינָהּ שֶׁל שְׁנֵיהֶן בִּרְשׁוּת הַלּוֹקֵחַ כֵּיוָן שֶׁקִּיבֵּל עָלָיו בִּרְשׁוּת הַמּוֹכֵר לֹא קָנָה עַד שֶׁיַּגְבִּיהַּ אוֹ

עַד שֶׁיִּמְשׁוֹךְ וְיוֹצֵא אֶת כָּל מֶרְשׁוּת הַבְּעָלִים בִּרְשׁוּת זֶה שֶׁהָיוּ מוּפְקָדִים אֶצְלוֹ לֹא
קָנָה עַד שֶׁיְזִיכֵינוּ בָהֶן אוֹ עַד שֶׁיַשְׂכִּיר לוֹ אֶת מְקוֹמָן. מַה עָבַד לָהּ רַב כָּאן
כְּשֶׁהֶעֱמִידוֹ עִמּוֹ כָּאן כְּשֶׁלֹּא הֶעֱמִידוֹ עִמּוֹ. רַב פְּלִיג דְּרַב אָמַר כַּד אֲנָא אָמַר
לִבְנֵי בֵיתִי לִיתֵּן מַתָּנָה לְבַר נַשׁ לֵינָה חָזַר בִּי. תֵּדַע לָךְ חַד בַּר נַשׁ אַפְקֵיד עֵירָבוֹן
עַל מִילְחָה וְיָקְרָת. אָתָא לְנַבֵּי רַב אָמַר לֵיהּ אוֹ יִתֵּן לוֹ אֶת כָּל־עֵירָבוֹנוֹ אוֹ
יִמְסוֹר לוֹ לְמִי שֶׁפָּרַע. מְחִלְפָה שִׁיטָתֵיהּ דְּרַב. תַּמָּן הוּא אָמַר כַּד אֲנָא אָמַר
לִבְנֵי בֵיתִי לִיתֵּן מַתָּנָה לְבַר נַשׁ לֵינָה חָזַר בִּי. וְכָא הוּא אָמַר הָכֵין. תַּמָּן לְמִידַת
הַדִּין הוּא וּמַה דְּרַב נָהִיג לְמִידַת חֲסִידוּת.

Rebbi Jacob bar Zavdi, Rebbi Abbahu in the name of Rebbi Joḥanan:
If somebody wanted to change his mind after he had promised a gift to
another person, he may change his mind[133]. Rebbi Yose was with Rebbi
Jacob bar Zavdi; he said to him: Is that just no (*Lev.* 19:36) "and just
yes?[134]" He said, when he said it, it was a just yes. Rav disagrees since
Rav said, when I tell my family to give a gift to somebody, I never change
my mind[135]. A *baraita* disagrees with Rav: "[136]Where did they say that
movables are acquired by being drawn close? In the public domain or in a
courtyard which is not their joint property. In the domain of the buyer,
when the deal was accepted[137]; in the domain of the seller one never
acquires until either he lift it up or he draw and remove everything from
the prior owner's property. In the domain of a depositary he cannot
acquire unless he gave permission or rented their place out to him." What
does Rav do with this[138]? One is if he was standing with him[139], the other
if he was not standing with him.

Rav disagrees since Rav said, when I tell my family to give a gift to
somebody, I never change my mind. You should know because somebody
had given surety on salt[140]; it rose in price. He came before Rav who

said, either he should give corresponding to the surety[141] or he should be given up to "Him who made pay". The arguments of Rav are contradictory. There he says, when I tell my family to give a gift to somebody, I never change my mind and here he says so[142]? There it is for a legal rule; what Rav did himself was a measure of piety.

133   Also in *Ma'ser Šeni* 4:7 (fol. 55b), *Baba Meẓi'a* 4:2 (fol. 9c-d), Babli *Baba Meẓi'a* 49a. In the Babli, the statement is restricted to large gifts.

134   This cryptic statement is explained in *Sifra Qedošim Pereq* 8(7), Babli *Baba Meẓi'a* 49a: "Why does the verse mention 'a just *epha* and a just *hin*'? Is not a *hin* a part of an *epha*, how can one have correct measures for one and not the other? One takes biblical *hîn* as rabbinic *hēn* 'yes'. That your yes should be a yes and your no a no, the same in your mind and your mouth."

135   This is taken as a legal statement; at the end it will be accepted as a moral precept only.

136   Tosephta *Qiddušin* 1:8, *Baba Batra* 5:2; Yerushalmi *Qiddušin* 1:4 (fol. 60b), *Giṭṭin* 8:1 (fol. 49b); Babli *Baba Batra* 85a.

137   Things deposited on a persons's real estate are his property as soon as he has the right to them.

138   Why should he not change his mind since there was no acquisition and no money given?

139   In this provisional answer, it is only asserted that the promise of a gift to another person is binding. But the question remains, why should it be binding if there was no acquisition, which could only be effected by removing the gift from the donor's property?

140   In the Babli, *Baba Meẓi'a* 48b, the story is told of R. Ḥiyya bar Josef, who appeared before R. Joḥanan.

141   In the Babli, *loc. cit.*, Rav holds that a surety gives a claim for the value of the surety while R. Joḥanan holds that a surety establishes a claim for the entire lot in question. The version of the story here implies that Rav was the judge.

142   For his own gifts he establishes the rule that a gift is unchangeable, for commercial transactions he says that they are reversible, even if that would be morally wrong.

Indices

Index of Biographical Notes

Index of Biblical Quotations

Index of Greek and Latin Words

Index of Hebrew and Arabic Words

General Index